THE WOMEN'S CHRONOLOGY

CHRONOLOGY

A Year-by-Year Record,
from
Prehistory to the Present

JAMES TRAGER

A Henry Holt Reference Book

HENRY HOLT AND COMPANY / NEW YORK

A Henry Holt Reference Book
Henry Holt and Company, Inc.
Publishers since 1866
115 West 18th Street
New York, New York 10011

Henry Holt ® is a registered
trademark of Henry Holt and Company, Inc.

Copyright © 1994 by James Trager
All rights reserved.
Published in Canada by Fitzhenry & Whiteside Ltd.,
195 Allstate Parkway, Markham, Ontario L3R 4T8.

Library of Congress Cataloging-in-Publication Data
Trager, James.
The women's chronology : a year-by-year record from prehistory to
the present / James Trager. — 1st ed.
p.   cm. — (A Henry Holt reference book)
Includes index.
1. Women—History—Chronology.   2. Chronology, Historical.
I. Title   II. Series
HQ1122.T73   1994   93-41513
305.4'09—dc20   CIP

ISBN 0-8050-2975-3

Henry Holt books are available for special promotions
and premiums. For details contact:
Director, Special Markets.

First Edition—1994

DESIGNED BY LUCY ALBANESE

Printed in the United States of America
All first editions are printed on acid-free paper. ∞

1   3   5   7   9   10   8   6   4   2

Preface

It is men, not women, who have dominated most accounts of ages past. The women who so often were the guiding forces behind the men have traditionally received short shrift from historians, yet in many cases it has been women who made the key decisions that decided the fate not merely of their own families but of nations.

These chronicles aim in some small measure to correct a historical oversight and to provide a compact overview of women in history. Designed as a handy desk reference, *The Women's Chronology* relates events as they happened, giving precise dates and details wherever possible, to record landmarks in the rise of women through the years. It integrates all facets of women's role, how women have been treated, the developments that have most affected them, what women have achieved, what some of them have said, and what has been said about them.

Events affecting women unfold in a larger context of world history—plagues, wars, economic changes, and the developments in technology and medicine that have affected everyone, regardless of gender. While frequent references to these broader aspects of history appear in the pages that follow, a book with a wider focus, such as *The People's Chronology,* will provide fuller coverage of these aspects and may serve as a useful companion to this volume.

Entries in *The Women's Chronology* are grouped by category rather than organized vertically by nation or geographical area. The categories appear in a standard order, and each may include a variety of related subjects. To help the reader find information quickly and easily, graphic symbols in the margins flag the twenty-nine different categories. These omnibus categories include:

- political events—and the politically powerful women whose voices sometimes determined the course of history
- human rights—woman suffrage, the labor movement, female circumcision, sexual harassment, and family leave

- exploration—pioneers, frontierswomen, venturesome travelers, and today's cosmonauts and astronauts

- economics and business—women entrepreneurs, retailers, and executives

- technology—its effects on women, as well as the women who contributed to it

- science—astronomers, geneticists, and mathematicians

- health and medicine—physicians, nurses, midwives, and issues involving women's health and medical treatment

- religion—religious leaders, religious orders, and saints

- education—educators, schools, colleges, and sororities

- everyday life—society, women's clubs and associations, fashion, cosmetics, and labor-saving devices

- population—including issues of abortion and birth control

The more than 13,000 entries frequently contain references to prior or subsequent dates to help guide the reader; an extensive alphabetical index is also provided.

But while the book is all-embracing it is hardly all-inclusive: The teacher who inspired a student, the nurse who saved a life, the office secretary whose tact saved a business—the lives of women in these traditionally "female" positions generally go unsung. So do the lives of most who have entered fields once reserved exclusively for men. And since the names of so many devoted mothers, wives, aunts, sisters, and daughters have gone unrecorded, not even the most comprehensive book can begin to chronicle women's true—and enormous—contribution to world history.

Acknowledgments

Many women participated in producing this Chronology. None of them is responsible for the oversights inevitable in a work of this sort. Outstanding among the participants were Marie Ged; Shelia Murphy of Aurum Press, London; Doris Palca; Carol Shookhoff; Laura X of the Women's History Research Center Library at Berkeley, Calif.; my editor, Paula Kakalecik, at Henry Holt; and my good wife, Chie Nishio, whose photographs represent only a part of her contribution.

It is impossible to list all of the biographies and other works that were used as reference sources but the following books were especially helpful:

Bédé, Jean Albert, and William B. Edgerton, editors, *Columbia Dictionary of Modern European Literature,* 2nd edition. New York: Columbia University Press, 1980.

Crawford, Anne, Tony Hayter, Ann Hughes, Frank Prochaska, Pauline Stafford, and Elizabeth Vallance, *The Europa Biographical Dictionary of British Women.* London: Europa Publications, 1983.

Evory, Ann, Hal May, James G. Lesniak, Linda Metzger, Clare D. Kinsman, James M. Ethridge, Barbara Kopala, et al., *Contemporary Authors.* Detroit: Gale Research, 1964 ff.

Hine, Darlene Clark, editor, *Black Women in America: An Historical Encyclopedia.* Brooklyn, N.Y.: Carlson, 1993.

Hitchcock, H. Wiley, and Stanley Sadie, editors, *The New Grove Dictionary of American Music.* London: Macmillan, 1986.

Magnusson, Magnus, editor, *The Cambridge Biographical Dictionary.* Edinburgh: W. & R. Chambers, 1990.

Mintz, Steven, and Susan Kellogg, *Domestic Revolutions: A Social History of American Family Life.* New York: Free Press, 1988.

Papachristou, Judith, *Women Together: A History in Documents of the Women's Movement in the United States.* New York: Knopf, 1976.

Sadie, Stanley, editor, *The New Grove Dictionary of Music and Musicians.* London: Macmillan, 1980.

Sherr, Lynn, and Jurate Kazickas, *The American Woman's Gazetteer.* New York: Bantam, 1976.

Sicherman, Barbara, and Carol Hurd Green, editors, *Notable American Women: The Modern Period.* Cambridge: Harvard University Press, 1980.

Stibbs, Anne, editor, *A Woman's Place: Quotations about Women.* London: Bloomsbury Publishing, 1992.

Key to Symbols

✖	political events	🎭	theater, film
✊	human rights, social justice	🎼	music
✳	exploration, colonization	🏃	sports
＄	economics, finance, retailing	⏱	everyday life
⚡	energy	🍃	tobacco
✦	transportation	⊞	crime
⚙	technology	🏛	architecture
⚗	science	🌐	environment
⚕	medicine	🌾	agriculture
∞	religion	👤	food availability
🎓	education	🍎	nutrition
‖	communications, media	☂	consumer protection
✒	literature	✗	food and drink
🎨	art	👫	population
📷	photography		

The Women's
Chronology

Prehistory

3 million B.C.

An upright-walking australopithecine appears on the earth in the late Pliocene period and has thumb-opposed hands in place of forefeet, permitting her to use tools. (Cleveland Museum of Natural History archaeologist Donald Carl Johanson will find the half-complete fossil of a teenaged female at Hadar, Ethiopia, in A.D. 1974 and call her "Lucy.") Palaeontologists will later conjecture that, unlike a quadruped, which is sexually receptive to males only during limited periods of estrus, the erect ape-woman can conceive and bear children at any time of year. Her pelvic canal has narrowed as she has evolved, and natural selection has favored those individuals who bear premature infants small enough to emerge from these narrowed canals. Because such infants cannot stand on their feet immediately after birth and require longer postnatal care, female australopithecines become growingly dependent on males for food and protection while they nurse their babies.

1.75 million B.C.

Anthropoids use patterned tools (Oldowan choppers).

1 million B.C.

Australopithecines become extinct as the human species evolves. *Homo erectus erectus* is unique among primates in having a high proportion of meat relative to dietary plant foods, but like other primates is omnivorous, a scavenger who competes with hyenas and other scavengers while eluding meat-eating predators such as lions and leopards.

400,000 to 360,000 B.C.

Homo erectus hominid of the Middle Pleistocene period (Peking woman) may use fire to cook venison, which supplements a diet of berries, roots, nuts, acorns, legumes, and grains. By conserving his energies, the male of the species is able to track down swifter animals that lack his growing intelligence.

120,000 to 75,000 B.C.

Neanderthals of the Upper Pleistocene period have large front teeth, which can be used as tools. Less than half of surviving infants reach age 20, and nine out of 10 of these die before age 40.

75,000 B.C.

Neanderthals care for their sick and aged but engage in cannibalism when necessary.

Neanderthals can communicate by speech, setting them apart from other mammals.

50,000 B.C.

 Neanderthals may be on the west coast of the Western Hemisphere and may even have reached the continent 20,000 years earlier.

38,000 B.C. ———————————

Homo sapiens emerges from Neanderthals and, while physically less powerful, has a more prominent chin, a much larger brain volume, and superior intelligence. *Homo sapiens* will split into six major divisions, or stocks—Negroids, Mongoloids, Caucasoids, Australoids, Amerindians, and Polynesians, and some of these will have subdivisions (Caucasoids, for example, will include Alpine, Mediterranean, and Nordic stocks).

Their control of fire, their development of new, lightweight bone and horn tools, weapons, and fishhooks, and their superior intelligence permit people to obtain food more easily and to preserve it longer. Hunters provide early tribes with meat from bison and antelope, while other tribespeople fish and collect honey, fruits, and nuts.

Increased availability of food will lead to an increase in human populations.

33,000 B.C. ———————————

Homo sapiens becomes the dominant species on earth with no serious rivals.

25,000 B.C. ———————————

Homo sapiens uses small pits lined with hot embers or pebbles preheated in fires to cook food that may be covered with layers of leaves or wrapped in seaweed to prevent scorching.

10,000 B.C. ———————————

Goats are domesticated by Near Eastern hunter-gatherer tribespeople who have earlier domesticated the dog.

Homo sapiens increase in number to roughly 3 million.

8500 B.C. ———————————

Goat's milk becomes a food source in the Near East, where goats have been domesticated for the past 1,500 years (as determined by carbon 14 radioactivity decay studies on fossil evidence found at Asiab, Iran).

8000 B.C. ———————————

Europe's final postglacial climatic improvements begin. They will produce a movement of people to the north of the continent, where the settlers will eat fish caught in nets of hair, thongs, and twisted fiber, along with shellfish, goose, and honey.

Agriculture begins at the end of the Pleistocene era in the Near East. Women use digging sticks to plant the seeds of wild grasses. When the seeds are seen to produce crops of grain in the fall (or the following spring), people will be encouraged to give up their nomadic life of hunting and gathering, live in one place, raise families, and start communities. Settled agricultural communities will be the basis of civilization (*see* 7000 B.C.; population, below).

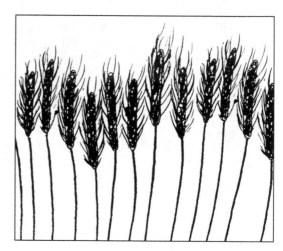

Women's invention of agriculture to replace hunting and gathering led to the start of civilization.

Earth's human population soars to 5.3 million, up from 3 million in 10,000 B.C., as agriculture provides a more reliable food source. Where it has taken 5,000 acres to support each member of a hunter-forager society, the same amount of land can feed 5,000 to 6,000 people in an agricultural society.

7700 B.C.

Ewe's milk becomes a food source and supplements goat's milk and mother's milk as lamb and mutton begin to play a large role in human diets in the Near East, where sheep are domesticated.

7200 B.C.

Sheep are domesticated in Greece (Argissa-Magula) (*see* 7700 B.C.).

Populations in the Middle East will increase in the next two millennia, and more permanent communities will be established by people who have lived until now in small groups that shifted camps every 3 or 4 months. Seed collecting and planting will become more important to the food supply.

7000 B.C.

Emmer wheat (*Triticum dicoccum*), domesticated from the wild *Triticum dicoccoides*, grows in the Kurdistan area lying between what will be southeastern Turkey and northwestern Iran (*see* 8000 B.C.). Barley (*Hordeum spolitaliceum*), millet (*Panicum miliaceum*), and certain legumes, including lentils, are cultivated in Thessaly, where the Greeks may also have domesticated dogs and pigs (based on evidence found in excavations at Argissa-Magula). (Domestication of swine has been delayed by the need of pigs for shade from the sun and by the fact that they cannot be milked, cannot digest grass, leaves, or straw, and must therefore be given food that people can eat—acorns, nuts, cooked grain, or meat scraps.)

6500 B.C.

The aurochs, ancestor of domestic cattle, will be domesticated in the next two centuries if it has not been domesticated earlier. The fierce beast will be the last major food animal to be tamed for use as a source of milk, meat, power, and leather.

6000 B.C.

Village farmers begin to replace food-gathering tribespeople in much of Greece (*see* 7000 B.C.).

Inhabitants of the Swiss lake regions have domesticated dogs and plow oxen.

Swiss lake dwellers (above) make bread of crushed cereal grains and keep dried apples and legumes (including peas) in the houses they build on stilts.

The first true pottery evolves, permitting new forms of cookery (although food has earlier been boiled in gourds, shells, and skin-lined pits into which hot stones were dropped).

4000 B.C.

Peoples of the Indus Valley raise wheat, barley, peas, sesame seeds, mangoes, and dates on irrigated fields, but the large fields of grain encourage a multiplication of insects, and the stores of dry grain bring an explosion in rodent populations. Asses, horses, buffalo, camels, and cattle are bred for meat and for use as draft animals. Bananas, lemons, limes, and oranges are cultivated, as are grapes for wine, which is also made from flowers.

The world's population reaches roughly 85 million.

3500 B.C.

The Sumerian society that marks the beginning of human civilization develops in the valleys of the Tigris and Euphrates rivers, where annual floods deposit fresh layers of fertile silt. Agricultural tribespeople settle in communities and evolve an administrative system governed by priests.

A written cuneiform alphabet developed by the Sumerians (above) facilitates communication.

The Sumerians (above) harness domestic animals to plows, drain marshlands, irrigate desert lands, and extend areas of permanent cultivation. By reducing slightly the number of people required to raise food, they permit a few people to become priests, artisans, scholars, and merchants.

Antiquity

3000 B.C.

Cotton fabric is woven in the Indus Valley (*see* 4000 B.C.).

Gilgamesh, written in Sumerian cuneiform, is the first known written legend.

Sumerian foods mentioned in *Gilgamesh* include caper buds, wild cucumbers, ripe figs, grapes, several edible leaves and stems, honey, meat seasoned with herbs, and bread—a kind of pancake made of barley flour mixed with sesame seed flour and onions.

The world's population reaches 100 million.

2640 B.C.

Silk manufacture is pioneered by the wife of the Chinese emperor Huang Ti.

1850 B.C.

The Petri Papyrus describes a tampon used by Egyptian women during their menstrual periods. The homemade device is made of shredded linen and the powder of crushed acacia branches, which will later be called gum arabic.

The Petri Papyrus (above) describes methods employed by Egyptians to avert pregnancy. They include coitus interruptus, coitus obstructus (in which ejaculated semen is forced into the bladder by depressing the base of the uterus), and a mixture of crocodile dung and honey which a woman is advised to insert in her vagina before intercourse (the sharp acidity of the dung acts as a spermicide).

1760 B.C.

Laws promulgated by the sixth Mesopotamian king Hammurabi provide that husbands may spare their adulterous wives from execution, but only the king may spare the wives' lovers; men wishing to divorce their wives must provide financial compensation; prisoners' wives may sleep with other men "if there is nothing to eat in the house"; and widows have use of their husbands' property for as long as they live (year approximate).

1680 B.C.

Leavened (raised) bread is invented in Egypt (time approximate).

1512 B.C.

Egypt's Thutmose I is deposed after a 13-year reign in which he has led successful expeditions as far as the Euphrates. His bastard son will reign until 1504 B.C. with his wife and half-sister, Hatshepsut, as Thutmose II.

1504 B.C.

Egypt's Thutmose II dies at a young age after successful military campaigns against the Nubians and Syrians. Hatshepsut rules as regent for her infant nephew Thutmose III and will assume the title of queen next year.

 Silk is woven by the Chinese, who also use potter's wheels.

 Aryan nomads from the Eurasian steppes push into the Indian subcontinent, bringing with them flocks of sheep and herds of cattle. They introduce a diet heavily dependent on dairy products, using *ghee* (clarified butter) rather than whole butter, which is too perishable for India's climate.

1485 B.C.

 Two monumental obelisks are erected at Karnak by the Egyptian queen Hatshepsut, whose daughter's

Hatshepsut ruled ancient Egypt with her husband and half-brother, Thutmose II, and erected obelisks. VATICAN LIBRARY

tutor, Senenmut, has built a magnificent temple on the west side of the Nile near Thebes and had its walls decorated with pictorial representations of an expedition to the land of Punt (whose queen is depicted as being very fat).

1483 B.C.

 Thutmose III comes of age and begins a 33-year reign in which Egypt will reach the height of her power, extending hegemony from below the fourth cataract of the Nile in the south to the Euphrates in the east. The title "pharaoh," or "Great House," will come into use under Thutmose III, who builds walls around his aunt Hatshepsut's obelisks at Karnak and tries to destroy all evidence of her existence.

1450 B.C.

 Mesopotamian men have absolute power over their wives, but are less brutal than Assyrian men, who may beat their wives and even cut off their noses or ears if they disobey. A Mesopotamian woman is subject first to the will of her father, then of her husband and father-in-law, and finally of her sons. A man may endow his wife with paternal powers in anticipation of his death, but a widow may neither sell nor give away any part of her inheritance, and if she exceeds her rights her sons are permitted to chase her naked from the house.

1374 B.C.

∞ Monotheism is introduced by the Egyptian king Amenhotep IV, who will be called Ikhnaton (Akhenaten or Akhnaton), meaning "Aten is satisfied." The pharaoh establishes a new cult that worships the sun god (or solar disk) Aten, and he opposes the priests of Amen, possibly due to the influence of his beautiful wife, Nefertiti (or Nefretete), who will bear six princesses.

1358 B.C.

 Egypt's Ikhnaton dies after a 17-year reign and is succeeded by his son-in-law, 9, who will rule until 1350 B.C. The new pharaoh, Tutankhamen, has accepted the sun worship faith of his wife and her father but will return to the religion of the priests of

Nefertiti bore the Egyptian king Amenhotep IV six princesses and may have made him a sun worshiper.

Amen and move Egypt's capital back to Thebes from the new city of Akhetaton.

1272 B.C.

✗ Egypt's Ramses II marries a daughter of the Hittite king and arranges a permanent peace with the Hittites. Princesses of royal lineage have been exchanged, often as infants, throughout the Middle East for well over a century to cement alliances between the courts of Babylon and Thebes.

1200 B.C.

✱ The Egyptians have learned to make fine linen from flax stalks, and their high priests wear only linen, which is used also to wrap embalmed bodies (*see* flax, 6000 B.C.).

1193 B.C.

✗ King Priam's city of Troy at the gateway to the Hellespont in Asia Minor falls to Greek forces under Agamemnon after a 10-year siege in the Trojan War (*see* Homer, 850 B.C.).

1150 B.C.

✗ Egyptian aristocrats enjoy leavened bread and drink some wine (but mostly beer) as they dine at tables and sit on chairs which they have developed, but in the bread stalls of village streets, only flat breads are commonly available.

990 B.C.

✗ Absalom, third (and favorite) son of Judea's King David, kills his half-brother David's eldest son, Amnon, in revenge for the rape of his full sister, Tamar. David banishes Absalom from Judea (date approximate).

961 B.C.

✗ Judea's King David dies and is succeeded by his son Solomon, who will reign until 922 B.C., making alliances with Egypt's ruling priests and with the Phoenician king Hiram of Tyre. Solomon is David's son by his second wife, Bathsheba (David murdered her first husband in order to marry her).

950 B.C.

✗ The household of Judea's King Solomon includes 700 wives and 300 concubines and consumes 10 oxen on an ordinary day, along with the meat of harts, gazelles, and hartebeests.

853 B.C.

✗ Ahab, king of Israel, joins with allies to defeat Assyrian forces at the Battle of Karkar. Ruling from his capital at Samaria, he has extended his alliances to the north by marrying Jezebel, the Phoenician princess whose father, Ethbaal, is king of Tyre and Sidon.

∞ Jezebel (above) has introduced Phoenician idol worship into Samaria, antagonizing the Jewish prophet Elijah.

850 B.C.

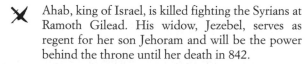

✕ Ahab, king of Israel, is killed fighting the Syrians at Ramoth Gilead. His widow, Jezebel, serves as regent for her son Jehoram and will be the power behind the throne until her death in 842.

🖋 The *Iliad* and the *Odyssey* are inscribed by the blind Greek poet Homer, so the historian Herodotus will write some four centuries hence, but the date may be as much as a century earlier, and while references to "the deathless laughter of the blessed gods" appear in both works, they may have been written by different people employing earlier lays handed down orally before articulation in the "winged words" of Homer.

The *Iliad* is an epic poem of Ilium (Troy) and its siege by the Greeks from 1194 to 1184 B.C., a poem mixing gods and mortals in its history of Priam, Helen, Paris, Menelaus, Hector, Achilles, Aphrodite, Agamemnon, and Odysseus (Ulysses); its conflict is based on a quarrel between Achilles and Agamemnon over the disposition of a beautiful slave girl taken as booty (military commanders are entitled to their pick of such women according to their rank), and Homer mentions that he shares his tent and bed with a captive girl.

The *Odyssey* is an epic poem about the wanderings of Odysseus (Ulysses), who is kept as a lover for nearly 8 years by the goddess Calypso while his wife, Penelope, home at Ithaca, is besieged by suitors and unwanted guests and his son, Telemachus, is growing to manhood, which, once attained, allows the young man to silence his mother. "Day-long she wove at the web but by night she would unravel what she had done" (XXIV, a reference to wife Penelope, who has vowed to accept no second husband until she has completed a winding-sheet for her aged father-in-law, a ruse she continues until she is betrayed after 3 years by one of her serving maids).

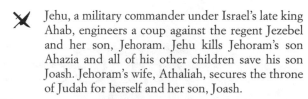

843 B.C.

✕ Jehu, a military commander under Israel's late king Ahab, engineers a coup against the regent Jezebel and her son, Jehoram. Jehu kills Jehoram's son Ahazia and all of his other children save his son Joash. Jehoram's wife, Athaliah, secures the throne of Judah for herself and her son, Joash.

∞ Athaliah (above) comes under attack from Judah's Jewish priests for supporting the worship of idols, notably Baal.

842 B.C.

✕ The usurper Jehu has Israel's regent, Jezebel, thrown from a window and crushes her to death beneath his chariot. He will reign until 815 B.C., founding a dynasty that will rule a weakened Israel that must pay tribute to the Assyrians.

837 B.C.

✕ Judah's priests overthrow Athaliah, put her to death, and make her son, Joash, king.

812 B.C.

✕ Assyria's Shamshiadad V, son of Shalmaneser, dies after a 12-year reign in which he has ended a revolt with Babylonian aid but has lost part of his empire. He is succeeded by his brother Adadnirari V, but the queen mother, Sammuramat (Semiramis), will rule for four years.

753 B.C.

✹ Rome is founded, according to legend, on a wooded Italian hilltop overlooking the Tiber. Its founders are the infant brothers Romulus and Remus, who are suckled by a "she-wolf" who may actually be the prostitute Acca Laurentia (the Latin word *lupa* for she-wolf can also mean prostitute), wife of Faustulus, whose death will be commemorated for many years in the February 15 fertility festival called the Lupercalia in which girls put love messages into urns and boys draw them out (the festival will give rise in later centuries to St. Valentine's Day).

7th Century B.C.

687 B.C. ────────────────────

✖ The Lydian king Candaules is killed by his bodyguard, Gyges—allegedly at the urging of his wife, who has wanted revenge upon Candaules for letting Gyges see her naked. She marries Gyges, who becomes Lydia's new king (year approximate).

680 B.C. ────────────────────

✖ Mesopotamia's queen mother Naqia (Zakutu) helps her youngest son, Esarhaddon, triumph in a dynastic feud with his brothers, who murdered Naqia's husband, Sennacherib, last year in revenge for his destruction of Babylon (year approximate).

✒ Greek lyric poet Arilochus, 25, writes (in Ionic dialect) of the object of his unrequited love, "Already the beauty of your skin is fading and sad old age is plowing his furrows in it."

624 B.C. ────────────────────

💲 Corinth's tyrant Periander invites the city-state's nobility to a party and has his soldiers strip the women of their gold jewelry and of gowns adorned with golden thread. The gold will finance Periander's government for decades to come.

621 B.C. ────────────────────

∞ The Book of Deuteronomy, compiled by Israelite scribes, is among the five books of Moses (Pentateuch, or Torah) containing what purports to be the dying testament of Moses to his people.

✖ The Law of Moses in Deuteronomy (above) imposes dietary restrictions, permitting meat only from any animal "that parts the hoof and has the hoof cloven in two, and chews the cud," but proscribing meat from camels, hares, and rock badgers as well as from pigs. Also proscribed as "unclean" are fish without fins and scales, certain birds, and anything "that dies of itself." And "You shall not boil a kid in its mother's milk" (*see Sharia,* A.D. 628; Maimonides, A.D. 1163).

610 B.C. ────────────────────

✒ The Greek poet Sappho flourishes on the island of Lesbos, where she has founded a boarding school for well-born young women, teaching them poetry, music, and social graces in preparation for marriage. As priestess of a feminine love cult, she celebrates the love of women for other women in poems that will survive in papyrus fragments and in quotations by later critics. The geographer Strabo will write some 600 years hence that "Sappho was something to be wondered at. Never within human memory has there been a woman to compare with her as a poet" (year approximate).

600 B.C. ────────────────────

‖ Greek men gather at *symposions* to discuss the affairs of the day while they eat, drink, and enjoy

The Greek poet Sappho on the island of Lesbos wrote in her verses of women's love for other women.

entertainments put on by beautiful young girls and boys. No free women are permitted to attend, but some men are accompanied by their "hired" women.

Girls of Sparta in the Greek Peloponnesus are trained in running, javelin- and discus-throwing, and wrestling in order that they may develop robust, healthy bodies and deliver strong, healthy babies.

Phoenicians develop the first true soap through a saponification process that involves boiling goat fat, water, and ash high in potassium carbonate; by allowing the liquid to evaporate, they wind up with a solid, waxy cake that can be used to bathe or to wash clothing (year approximate). The Greeks and other peoples still use alkali solutions, as people have for millennia, but will gradually adopt the Phoenician invention.

6th Century B.C.

534 B.C.

∞ Women in parts of Greece celebrate the annual festival of Dionysus, heretofore observed only by men. They go off in groups to mountainsides and forests outside of towns, drink wine, throw off all usual restraints, dance wildly, sing out praises to the god Bacchus (Dionysus), and capture rabbits and small deer, which they tear to shreds with their bare hands and eat raw. Dionysus is the only god believed to have been born of mortal woman (his mother was allegedly Semele, daughter of Cadmus, king of Thebes).

529 B.C.

✗ The Persian emperor Cyrus the Great dies, by some accounts in battle with the forces of Tomyris, widowed queen of the Massagetae, who has rejected his offers of marriage and threatened him with death should he cross her border.

509 B.C.

✗ Rome overthrows her Tarquin (Etruscan) king, becomes a republic, and begins her struggle to dominate Italy and the world. Legend will relate the uprising to the rape of Lucretia, beautiful and virtuous wife of the Roman general Lucius Tarquinius Collatinus, by Sextus Tarquinius, a son of the king Tarquinius Superbus. Lucretia tells her father and husband about the rape, makes them swear vengeance, and stabs herself to death. Her husband's cousin Lucius Junius Brutus agitates against the Tarquins, raises a people's army, and drives out the Tarquins.

The rape of Lucretia, wife of a Roman general, led to the expulsion of the Etruscans from Italy. LIBRARY OF CONGRESS

500 B.C.

👫 "In ancient times, people were few but wealthy and without strife," writes the Chinese philosopher Han Fei-tzu. "People at present think that five sons are not too many, and each son has five sons also and before the death of the grandfather there are already 25 descendants. Therefore people are more and wealth is less; they work hard and receive little. The life of a nation depends on having enough food, not upon the number of people."

5th Century B.C.

495 B.C.

The Chinese philosopher Kong Fuzi (Confucius) resigns as prime minister of Lu at age 56 when the ruler gives himself up to pleasure. In the next 12 years, Confucius will wander from state to state teaching precepts dealing with morals, the family system, and statecraft, with maxims that make up a utilitarian philosophy. A brief record of Confucian teachings will be embodied in the *Analects*, one of the Four Books of Chinese classics, and his Golden Rule will be honored (often in the breach) throughout the world: "What you do not like when done to yourself, do not do unto others." But Confucian philosophy will be used for millennia in Oriental countries to keep women subservient.

480 B.C.

The Battle of Salamis September 23 ends in victory for a Greek fleet of fewer than 400 vessels over a Persian fleet of more than 1,000, thus saving Athens from invasion. One of the few survivors on the Persian side is Artemesia, queen of Halicarnassus, who has advised against engaging the Greeks in a sea battle but, once the battle has begun, outwits her enemies. Furious that a woman has dared make war on them, the Greeks have offered a reward of 10,000 drachmas for her capture, but she fights them off ably. It will be said that the Persian king Xerxes, watching from a cliff, remarked, "My men have behaved like women and my women like men."

458 B.C.

Theater: The Oresteian trilogy by the Greek playwright Aeschylus includes the plays *Agamemnon*, *The Libation Bearers* (*Choephoroi*), and *The Eu-*

menides; its story of the blood feud in the house of Atreus will have a powerful influence on future writers and thinkers. Clytemnestra is murdered by her son Orestes for her murder of his father, Agamemnon, and although he has been urged to commit the act by the god Apollo, he is pursued by the Furies. Orestes flees to Athens, where the goddess Athena establishes the court of Areopagus, grants forgiveness to Orestes, and changes the name of the Furies to "the kindly ones."

445 B.C.

The Athenian statesman Pericles discards his wife and takes as his live-in mistress the courtesan Aspasia of Miletus, who runs a house of young *hetairai* (courtesans) but has captivated such men as Plato and Socrates not only with her beauty but also with her learned and witty conversation. Athens is scandalized by Pericles's action, but his eloquence will protect Aspasia and keep her by his side until his death in 429 B.C.

440 B.C.

Theater: *Antigone* by the Greek playwright Sophocles is a tragedy whose heroine defies Creon, king of Thebes, and buries a declared traitor, claiming authority higher than the king's. She is condemned to death and kills herself before Creon, who has changed his mind, can save her or his son (who has been betrothed to Antigone and who also commits suicide).

431 B.C.

Theater: *Medea* by the Greek playwright Euripides depicts the reactions of a wife discarded in favor of a younger rival. "They say we live a life free from danger in the house while they fight!" says the fiery barbarian princess. "What fools! I'd be ready to take my stand in battle three times rather than give birth just once." Daughter of Agamemnon, she destroys her rival and kills her own children by the faithless Jason. (Euripides uses the neuter word *oikourema* for woman—a thing for looking after the house; apart from bearing children, the Athenian woman's role is that of chief female domestic servant.)

429 B.C.

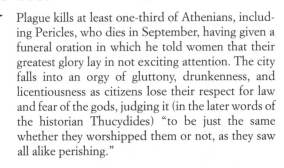 Plague kills at least one-third of Athenians, including Pericles, who dies in September, having given a funeral oration in which he told women that their greatest glory lay in not exciting attention. The city falls into an orgy of gluttony, drunkenness, and licentiousness as citizens lose their respect for law and fear of the gods, judging it (in the later words of the historian Thucydides) "to be just the same whether they worshipped them or not, as they saw all alike perishing."

Spared by the plague is the physician Hippocrates the Great (as distinguished from one previous and five future Greek physicians named Hippocrates). He is the first to say that no disease is entirely miraculous or adventitious in origin and that disease is not sent as punishment by the gods. "In the case of women," he writes, "it is my contention that when during intercourse the vagina is rubbed and the womb is disturbed, an irritation is set up in the womb which produces pleasure and heat in the rest of the body. . . . Once intercourse has begun, she experiences pleasure throughout the whole time, until the man ejaculates. If her desire for intercourse is excited, she emits before the man, and for the remainder of the time she does not feel pleasure to the same extent; but if she is not in a state of excitement, then her pleasure terminates along with that of the man." Hippocrates believes, however, that symptoms in women that have no medical cause are rooted in the uterus (*hystera*; the English words *hysteria* and *hysterical* will be based on the teachings of Hippocrates).

428 B.C.

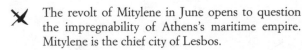 The revolt of Mitylene in June opens to question the impregnability of Athens's maritime empire. Mitylene is the chief city of Lesbos.

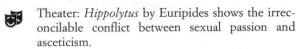 Theater: *Hippolytus* by Euripides shows the irreconcilable conflict between sexual passion and asceticism.

427 B.C.

Mitylene surrenders to Athens in July; the Athenians punish the city with cruel severity.

424 B.C.

Theater: *Oedipus Rex* (or *Oedipus Tyrannus*) by Sophocles (date approximate). Oedipus, king of Thebes, has left his native Corinth to escape fulfillment of a prophecy that he would kill his father and marry his mother, but Oedipus investigates the murder of his predecessor, Laius of Thebes, and discovers that he himself killed Laius, that Laius rather than the king of Corinth was his father, and that his wife, Jocasta, is also his mother. Jocasta kills herself, and Oedipus blinds himself (the tragedy will deeply affect future generations).

420 B.C.

Greek men decide, when a child is born, whether to keep it or not and may abandon it, especially if it is a girl. The infant is taken to a wild place and left, perhaps in a jar known as a *pithos*, where a passerby may take pity on it and adopt it (childless couples are sometimes alerted to the fact that a baby will be abandoned). A child may be abandoned because it is considered unhealthy (after being tested by rubbing it with wine, icy water, or urine) or—more usually—because the father does not want his small estate divided into too many parts. The practice has existed for more than a century and will continue for at least 2 centuries to come.

Theater: *The Suppliant Women* by Euripides.

419 B.C.

 Theater: *Andromache* by Euripides, whose new play is not performed at Athens: "The hearts of men sicken for love more than do the hearts of women, but honor curbs desire." " 'Tis woman's nature to bear her ills on lip and tongue with mournful pleasure."

415 B.C.

 Theater: *The Trojan Women* by Euripides is presented shortly after the massacre by Athenians of the male population of Melos, which has tried to remain neutral in the Peloponnesian War.

413 B.C.

 Theater: *Electra* by Euripides, who puts the legend of Orestes's revenge in modern dress and depicts the ancient matricide as a contemporary crime.

411 B.C.

 Theater: *Iphigenia in Tauris* by Euripides, whose heroine priestess of Artemis finds that the intended victims of human sacrifice are her brother Orestes and his friend; she outwits the barbarian king and organizes an escape. *Lysistrata* and *The Women at the Thesmophoria* (*Thesmophoriazusae*) by the Athenian playwright Aristophanes. The women in *Lysistrata* revolt against war by denying their sexual favors to their husbands. "You can't live with them, you can't live without them," he says, using an already old aphorism.

408 B.C.

 Theater: *Orestes* by Euripides, who continues the theme of his 413 B.C. tragedy *Electra*; *The Phoenician Women* by Euripides and other playwrights who have helped to complete the work. Euripides leaves Athens in dissatisfaction and travels to the court of Archelaus in Macedonia, where he will die in the winter of 407–406 B.C. at age 77, leaving incomplete his *Iphigenia at Aulis*.

 "The beauty of Helen was a pretext for the gods to send the Greeks against the Phrygians" (in the Trojan War), says Euripides in *Orestes* (above), "and to kill many men so as to purge the earth of an insolent abundance of people." Greek city-states have few resources and are not organized to support large numbers.

405 B.C.

 The Erectheum is completed in Ionian style on the Acropolis after 16 years of construction. The female figures that support its roof are called Caryatids because they are modeled after girls from the town of Caryae.

4th Century B.C.

380 B.C.

 Greek women are permitted no independent status in what is essentially a masculine society and may not enter into any transaction worth more than one *medimnos* of barley; they are not allowed to own property other than their own clothing and jewelry and their slaves (slaves make up fully one-third of the Athenian population of 300,000 and are vital to the economy of the city-state). Fathers select husbands for their daughters without consulting them. Peasant women of Attica help their husbands in

Greek women had no rights, married men their fathers chose, and carried their full share of responsibilities.

the fields. Inside the home, a woman has charge of baking the bread, making the clothes, running the household, and seeing to the education of her children.

337 B.C.

 Philip II of Macedon shocks his court by announcing that he will marry the Macedonian noblewoman Cleopatra, even though he already has a wife. His son Alexander is his designated heir, but his second son, Arrhidaeus, is an epileptic and Philip wants a third son to safeguard the succession.

 Greek girls of noble birth learn in *gynacaea* (where no men are permitted) how to spin, weave, cook, and manage their families' workshops and slaves. A few are taught to read and write. The most intellectually developed and artistically cultivated Athenian women are prostitutes (*hetairai*).

336 B.C.

 Philip II of Macedon is assassinated at Aeges during the wedding feast of his daughter. His son Alexander, 20, will carry out Philip's planned expedition against Persia.

335 B.C.

The Greek scholar Aristotle returns to Athens from Macedon and opens a *lyceum* in an elegant gymnasium dedicated to Apollo Lyceus, god of shepherds.

Aristotle (above) advises abortion for parents with too many children, and he writes in *Politics* that "... neglect of an effective birth control policy is a never failing source of poverty which, in turn, is the parent of revolution and crime." (Aristotle says a male fetus becomes human 40 days after conception, whereas a female fetus requires 90 days.) Disregarding his advice, the Greeks (and later the Romans) will encourage large families lest they have a dearth of recruits for their armies.

324 B.C.

Alexander the Great of Macedon, who has conquered the Persians, has 90 of his Graeco-Macedonian lieutenants marry daughters of the Median and Persian nobility in order to link the countries. Some 10,000 of his soldiers will also marry Persians. Alexander himself has married Roxana, daughter of the Scythian chief Oxartes, in Samarkand.

323 B.C.

Alexander the Great of Macedon dies at Babylon in the spring at age 32. His widow, Roxana, is expecting a child, and he has taken another wife, Satira, daughter of the late Persian king Darius III, before leaving Susa for Babylon.

316 B.C.

Macedonia's regent Polysperchon is defeated and overthrown by Cassander, 34, son of Alexander the Great's late general Antipater, who seizes Olympias, mother of the late Alexander the Great, has her stoned to death, and marries Thessaloniki, half-sister of Alexander, with whom he will rule until 297 B.C.

Eumenes and Antigonus, rivals to Cassander for control of Macedonia, meet in battle in Media, with Eumenes commanding a force of 36,700 foot soldiers, 6,050 cavalrymen, and 114 elephants against 22,000 foot soldiers, 900 horsemen, and 65 elephants for Antigonus. But cavalrymen sent out by Antigonus take advantage of cover provided by dust raised by the elephants and seize the baggage camp of Eumenes, whose cavalrymen desert. Antigonus offers to return the baggage camp and the wives he has captured if the enemy will desert and hand over Eumenes, who is put to death by his guard after a week's captivity.

315 B.C.

The Macedonian port city of Thessalonica is founded by Cassander, whose wife, Thessaloniki, was named by her father, Philip II of Macedon, to commemorate his victory (Niki) over Thessaly in 338 B.C.

310 B.C.

Cassander, who has imprisoned Roxana, widow of the late Alexander the Great, has her put to death along with her young son, Alexander IV.

3rd Century B.C.

285 B.C.

✗ Egypt's Ptolemy Soter abdicates at age 82 after a 38-year reign that has founded a dynasty which will rule until 30 B.C. He is succeeded by his son, 24, who will rule as Ptolemy II Philadelphus until 246 B.C., first with the daughter of Lysimachus as his wife and thereafter (from 276 B.C.) with his own sister as his wife.

270 B.C.

✗ The Persian king Xerxes (Ahasuerus), who is extending his realm from India to Ethiopia, gives a feast for all the men of Susa (year approximate; Persia had several kings named Xerxes, and it is not clear which one was the Ahasuerus mentioned in the Old Testament). His wife, Queen Vashti, daughter of the last Babylonian king, Belshazzar, gives a feast for the women in her chambers; when the king summons her to appear and display her beauty, she refuses. On the advice of an obscure official named Memuchan, who will later be known as Haman, Ahasuerus repudiates his queen lest other women follow her example of disobedience, she is promptly executed, and the kingdom is combed for a beautiful successor. The king chooses Esther, cousin and ward of the pious and learned Jew Mordecai, who has advised her to conceal her Jewish origin. Through her influence, Mordecai becomes an adviser to the king, and when he discovers a plot against the king's life by two of his chamberlains, he reports the conspiracy to Esther, who, in turn, conveys it to her husband in Mordecai's name. The traitors are hanged (*see* 269 B.C.).

269 B.C.

✗ Persia's Xerxes (Ahasuerus) appoints Haman prime minister (*see* 270 B.C.). Haman, who has confiscated the wealth of the kings of Judah and made himself one of Persia's richest men, persuades Xerxes to issue a royal decree requring that all the king's servants prostrate themselves before Haman. The Jew Mordecai refuses, and Haman vows revenge. Invested with absolute powers, he issues a sealed order that all Jews, including women and children, are to be massacred on the 13th of Adar (the last month of the year in the Hebrew calendar). Mordecai learns of the secret order, spreads news of the impending attack, and instructs Esther to reveal her Jewish identity and implore the king's mercy. Xerxes has not summoned her for the past month, and no one is permitted to approach him uninvited on pain of death, but she appears in his inner court, is welcomed, and asks that the king and Haman attend a banquet that she is preparing. At the banquet, she invites them to a second banquet to be held the following day. At this second banquet she accuses Haman of plotting to kill her people, the king orders that he be hanged on the gallows that Haman has had built for Mordecai, he then learns for the first time that his wife is Mordecai's cousin, and he installs Mordecai in Haman's place. Jews will celebrate the 14th of Adar as the Feast of Purim, reading the Book of Esther in synagogues everywhere.

250 B.C.

∞ Athenians worship the goddess Athena, whose influence will be dominant throughout this century in secular life as well—the warrior and supreme judge who is believed to have sprung full-blown from a wound in the forehead of her father, Zeus (who was intimidated by his wife, Metis, swallowed her when she was pregnant, developed a headache, and was then struck in the head by an axe). Thought to have invented practical intelligence, Athena is said to inspire potters, weavers, and other craftsmen and to guide pilots safely through shoals and currents.

bastard son of a prostitute by a merchant, Shihuang will prove himself a brilliant general.

Egypt's Ptolemy II dies at age 63 and is succeeded after a peaceful reign of 39 years by his son, 36, who will reign less peacefully until 221 B.C. as Ptolemy III. Ptolemy III invades Syria, seeking vengeance for the death of his murdered sister, Berenice (*see* 247 B.C.). He throws his armies against Seleucus II.

247 B.C.

 Berenice, daughter of Ptolemy II, is widowed by the death of the Syrian king Antiochus II, whose first wife, Laodice, he repudiated 7 years ago to marry Berenice. Ptolemy III rushes to his sister's aid, leaving Antioch the only Seleucid stronghold in Syria (*see* 246 B.C.).

246 B.C.

 Modern China has her beginnings in the Qin (Chin) dynasty founded by Qin Shihuang, 28. The

221 B.C.

 Egypt's Ptolemy III dies at age 61 after a 25-year reign. He is succeeded by his son, 23, who will rule with his sister-wife, Arsinoe III, until 203 B.C. as Ptolemy IV; court favorites will dominate the reign.

200 B.C.

 Theater: *Stichus* by Roman playwright Titus Maccius Plautus: "An unwilling woman given to a man in marriage is not his wife but an enemy."

2nd Century B.C.

186 B.C.

∞ Rome's Senate orders a ban on the Bacchanalian orgies that have turned the annual Feast of Dionysus into occasions of drunkenness, sexual promiscuity, and general debauchery (*see* 534 B.C.).

170 B.C.

🌐 The world's first paved streets are laid out in Rome. The new streets are passable in all weather and easier to keep clean, but they add to the din of traffic.

✗ Rome's first professional cooks appear in the form of commercial bakers, but most Roman households continue to grind their own flour and bake their own bread.

Prisoners taken by Rome's legions were sold into slavery, and women generally fetched much higher prices. FROM A PAINTING IN THE MUSEUM OF LUXEMBOURG

168 B.C.

⚔ The Battle of Pydna gives Roman forces a victory over the Macedonian king Perseus, who has succeeded Philip V. The Roman general Lucius Aemilius Paulus, 51, returns with Perseus in his triumphal procession.

✊ Macedonians captured by Paulus (above) are sold into slavery at Rome. Females fetch as much as 50 times the price of a male.

166 B.C.

🎭 Theater: *The Women of Andros* (*Andria*) by Roman playwright Terence (Publius Terentius Afer), 24, with flute music by his fellow slave Flaccus at the Megaleusian games in April. "Obsequiousness makes friends; truth breeds hate" (I, i).

165 B.C.

🎭 Theater: *The Mother-in-Law* (*Hecyra*) by Terence, who has adopted a play by Apollodorus.

161 B.C.

🎭 Theater: *The Eunuch* (*Eunuchus*) by Terence: "I know the nature of women;/ When you want to, they don't want to;/ And when you don't want to, they desire exceedingly" (IV, vii).

160 B.C.

 Theater: *Brothers* (*Adelphoe*) by Terence: "It is better to bind your children to you by a feeling of respect, and by gentleness, than by fear" (I, i). A Carthaginian who was brought to Rome as a slave for a senator, Terence will die next year.

146 B.C.

Carthage falls to Roman legions led by Scipio Aemilianus in 6 days and nights of house-to-house fighting after a long blockade. Some 900 Roman deserters torch the Temple of Aesculapius and choose death by fire rather than execution, Hasdrubal surrenders his garrison, his wife contemptuously throws herself and her children into the flames of the temple. The city's ashes are plowed under, its environs become the Roman province of Africa, and the Third Punic War is ended.

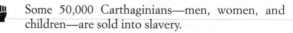 Some 50,000 Carthaginians—men, women, and children—are sold into slavery.

1st Century B.C.

62 B.C.

∞ Women in the household of the Roman general Julius Caesar hold ceremonies to celebrate the Earth Mother Bona Dea, sacrificing a sow in a room decorated with vine leaves and flowers. Vestal virgins play a prominent role in the rites, which are supervised by the magistrate's wife and attended only by women, who never speak the name of Bona Dea in a man's presence. The dissolute rake Clodius, who has designs on Caesar's second wife, Pompeia, disguises himself as a woman and tries to enter the house; discovered, he is charged with sacrilege and prosecuted by the lawyer Cicero, who destroys his alibi, but Clodius bribes the jurors and escapes punishment. Caesar divorces Pompeia, saying, "Caesar's wife must be above suspicion."

54 B.C.

✗ Julius Caesar's daughter, Julia, who has married Gnaeus Pompey, dies in childbirth; Pompey refuses to make another marriage alliance with Caesar, and the triumvirate that rules Rome begins to fall apart (*see* 48 B.C.).

48 B.C.

✗ Julius Caesar defeats Gnaeus Pompey June 29 at Pharsalus in southern Thessaly and becomes absolute ruler of Rome. Pompey flees to Egypt, where he is slain at Pelusium. Caesar arrives at Alexandria, learns of Pompey's murder, but remains to carry on a war in behalf of Egypt's dethroned queen, Cleopatra VII, 20. Her brother Ptolemy XII Philopator is killed, and a younger brother succeeds as co-ruler.

47 B.C.

✗ Cleopatra charms Julius Caesar into spending 3 months with her in Egypt.

46 B.C.

✗ Julius Caesar returns to Italy, quells a mutiny of the legions in Campania, crosses to Africa, and destroys a republican army of 14 legions under Scipio at Thapsus April 6. Most republican leaders are killed, Cato commits suicide. Caesar enters Rome triumphantly in late July with Cleopatra as his mistress, is made dictator for 10 years, and sails in November for Spain, where Pompey's sons hold out.

44 B.C.

✗ Julius Caesar is made dictator for life but is assassinated at the Senate March 15 by conspirators. His mistress, Cleopatra, returns to Egypt with her son, Caesarion, and arranges the murder of her brother (and former husband) Ptolemy XIII Philopater.

41 B.C.

✗ Egypt's Cleopatra meets Marc Antony, a Roman orator turned general, at Tarsus, and Antony, 42, succumbs to Cleopatra, now 28, just as Julius Caesar, at 51, succumbed 8 years ago. Antony had planned to punish Cleopatra but follows her to Egypt.

40 B.C.

✘ Marc Antony's wife, Fulvia, and his brother Lucius Antoninus make war against the faithless Antony but are defeated at Perusia (Perugsia). Fulvia dies, and Marc Antony is left free to remarry. He marries the sister of Octavian (Octavia). Octavian marries Scribonia, a kinswoman.

39 B.C.

✘ Octavian divorces his second wife, Scribonia, on the very day that she gives birth to his only child (a daughter, Julia) and marries Livia, previously the wife of Tiberius Claudius Nero, who has a son by that first marriage and soon gives birth to a second son, Nero Claudius Drusus.

36 B.C.

✘ Parthian forces defeat Marc Antony. He retreats to Armenia and openly marries his mistress, Cleopatra, despite his existing marriage to Octavia.

32 B.C.

✘ Octavian arouses fears in Rome that Egypt's Cleopatra will dominate the Empire. He publishes what he purports to be the will of Marc Antony, a will in which Antony bequeaths Rome's eastern possessions to Cleopatra. Marc Antony divorces Octavia, and her brother has the comitia annul Antony's imperium.

31 B.C.

✘ The Battle of Actium September 2 ends in a naval victory for Octavian, who becomes ruler of the entire Roman world. Cleopatra escapes to Egypt

Egypt's Cleopatra charmed Julius Caesar and Marc Antony but failed to find favor with Octavian. FROM A PAINTING BY J. L. GEROME

with 60 ships, followed by Antony, whose army then surrenders to Octavian.

30 B.C.

✘ Marc Antony commits suicide after hearing a false report that Cleopatra has killed herself. She dies August 29, applying an asp to her breast after failing to seduce Octavian upon his arrival at Alexandria. Cleopatra's son, Caesarion, is murdered and Egypt becomes a Roman province.

27 B.C.

✘ The Roman Empire that will rule most of the Western world until A.D. 476 is founded January 23 by Octavian, who 1 week earlier received the name Augustus Caesar from the Senate in gratitude for his achievements. Helped by the rich Roman merchant Mycenas and urged on by his third wife,

27 B.C.

Livia, Octavian makes himself emperor at age 35 with the title Imperator Caesar Octavianus, a title he will soon change to Augustus Caesar as he begins a 41-year reign.

25 B.C.

 Roman girls from rich families generally marry at age 13 or 14 (and sometimes as early as 12), but poorer girls, who cannot find husbands able to afford slaves to do household chores, marry in their late teens or early 20s; boys may marry as young as 14. Many marriages are arranged, but couples can dissolve a marriage simply by mutual consent.

18 B.C.

 The emperor Augustus uses his power as tribune to issue new regulations governing marriage that are designed to repopulate the country. His *Lex Julia adulterias coercindis* makes conjugal infidelity a public crime as well as a private offense: after a husband divorces a suspected wife he, or the woman's father, may prosecute her and her lover; if this is not done within 60 days, any accuser may bring the charge before a newly established jury court. Under certain circumstances the husband may even kill his wife's lover. Wives convicted of adultery are liable to banishment to a small island, and conniving husbands are also subject to penalties. Professional informers bring accusations that clog the new courts, but the law has little effect on real offenders, who find subterfuges (e.g., fictitious weddings) to evade the law, which in any case will never be consistently enforced. Another law bars celibates above a certain age, and widowers below a certain age who do not remarry, from receiving inheritances or legacies (except from close relations) and from attending the public games. Men with three or more children are offered quicker advancement in their public careers.

$ The property of rich Roman wives is separate from that of their husbands. Only the woman's dowry goes to her husband, and while a bride's father is duty-bound to provide a dowry it is not mandatory for legitimate marriage as it was in Athens and other, earlier, societies, where the dowry constituted the daughter's share of the family estate. In Rome, a daughter can expect a substantial share in her father's estate at his death, perhaps even equal to that of her brother. The dowry of a rich Roman's daughter is likely to be about 5 to 10 percent of her father's estate.

7 B.C.

∞ Mary, a Jewish carpenter's wife from Nazareth who professes to be a virgin, gives birth at Bethlehem, near Jerusalem, to a son whom she names Jesus. Mary's firstborn will be baptized at age 30 by her cousin John the Baptist after working as a carpenter and rabbi at Nazareth. (Year of the nativity determined by modern astronomers on the basis of a conjunction of the planets Saturn and Jupiter within the constellation Pisces, a conjunction that

Mary of Nazareth gave birth to a son at Bethlehem, near Jerusalem—a nativity that would prove momentous. FROM THE 1632 GERRIT VAN HONTHURST PAINTING *ADORATION OF THE VIRGIN*

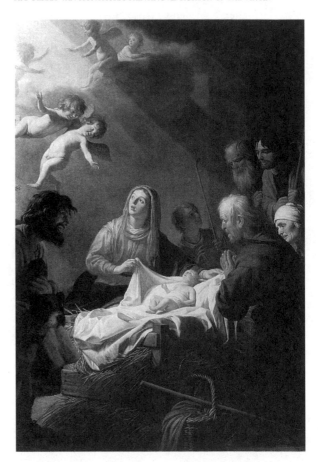

gives the appearance of a great new star and the ful-fillment of a prophecy by Jewish astrologers at Sip-par in Babylon, who have predicted the arrival of a long-awaited Messiah at some time when the two planets would meet. Some astronomers, however, will cite Chinese and Korean annals referring to a stellar flare-up, or nova, that blazed in the skies for 70 days in the spring of 5 B.C.)

The population of the world reaches roughly 250 million, up from 100 million in 3000 B.C. (*see* A.D. 1650).

2 B.C.

Poetry: *Ars Amandi,* or *Ars Amatoria,* by the Roman poet Ovid (Publius Ovidius Naso), 41, who has been educated for a career in law but has devoted himself instead to writing love poems. The emperor Augustus has expressed a desire to remake Roman morality in an older style, but Ovid, who has taken little interest in any of his three wives, preferring to pursue other women, says, "Let the past please oth-ers. I congratulate myself on being born into this age, whose ways are so congenial to my own." Voluptaries accept his concept of love as expressed in his textbook on ways to flirt, attract lovers, and consummate adultery; moralists blame it for many of the empire's social ills. "A woman is always buy-ing something" (I); "When the rose dies, the thorn is left behind" (II, cxvi); "Delay is a great procuress" (III); "What they love to yield/ They would often rather have stolen. Rough seduction/ Delights them, the boldness of rape/ Is a compliment."

1st Century A.D.

2

Lucius, son of the Roman emperor Augustus, dies suddenly at Massilia, and it is suspected that he has been poisoned on orders from the empress Livia and her son Tiberius, 43 (*see* 4).

4

Caius, son of the Roman emperor Augustus, dies at Lycia after sustaining a slight wound. As in the case of his brother Lucius 2 years ago, there are suspicions that he was poisoned by Livia and her son Tiberius.

8

Augustus exiles the poet Ovid, now 51, to the Roman outpost of Tomis (Constanza) on the Black Sea, in part for his elegiac poem instructing a man in the art of winning and keeping a mistress and instructing a woman on how to win and hold a lover (the poet may also have been implicated in a scandal, possibly involving the emperor's granddaughter Julia). Ovid destroys his new masterpiece at news of his banishment, but copies made by his friends will survive with such lines as "Love and dignity cannot share the same abode" (II).

14

The emperor Augustus dies September 14 at age 76 after a 41-year reign; the Senate declares him divine 3 days later, and his widow, Livia, whom he has named Augusta in his will, becomes priestess of his cult. She has overcome legal obstacles to dynastic succession by having her older son by her first marriage made the successor; now 55, he will reign until 37 as the emperor Tiberius.

15

Agrippina, a granddaughter of the late emperor Augustus, daughter of Julia and her husband Agrippa, goes on campaign with her husband, Germanicus, despite being pregnant, and gives birth in November on the banks of the Rhine to a daughter, who will be called Agrippina the Younger.

19

Germanicus returns to Syria and dies soon afterward, convinced that he has been poisoned. His widow, Agrippina, is sure that Tiberius has had him poisoned and begins a vendetta against the emperor.

23

Drusus, son of the emperor Tiberius, is poisoned by order of Lucius Aelius Sejanus, equestrian prefect of the Praetorian Guard, who has designs on the imperial throne. Livilla, Drusus's wife, has borne him twins and the succession has seemed secure, but Tiberius names Agrippina's children Nero and Drusus as heirs apparent.

29

Tiberius's mother, Livia, dies at age 82 (or 86), but the emperor refuses to carry out the terms of her will or permit her to be deified. Former wife of the late emperor Augustus (and, before him, of Tiberius Claudius Nero), she has been accused of trying to dominate the empire since Augustus's death 15 years ago.

Agrippina the Elder, widow of Germanicus, is arrested by order of the emperor Tiberius and exiled to Pandateria with her son, Nero (Tiberius will exile her second son, Drusus II, next year). She has opposed the growing power of Sejanus, who has come to dominate the emperor and hopes to supplant him, and Sejanus has raised the emperor's suspicions that Agrippina, who has been hostile to him for 10 years and exercises a strong influence over the legions, is conspiring to get rid of him and wants either to ensure the succession of one of her sons or to become empress through a second marriage to a senatorial usurper.

30

The Jewish rabbi Jesus of Nazareth, said by his followers to be the "son of God," is arrested April 6 on charges of blasphemy and subversion, tried by a Jewish council, and crucified April 30 at Jerusalem by order of the Roman authorities (*see* 7 B.C.). He is survived by his grieving mother, Mary, and followers who will be called apostles (*see* Paul, A.D. 53).

31

The emperor Tiberius receives a message from Antonia, widow of his brother Drusus, revealing the intrigues of Sejanus against Agrippina the Elder and her family. Sejanus is executed October 18 following a sentence of death passed by the Senate; his widow admits that he removed Tiberius's son Drusus by poison 8 years ago, but Tiberius is unable to set aside his distrust of Agrippina (who will die while on a hunger strike in exile) and her sons. Son Nero is placed in prison, where he starves himself to death, and son Drusus II, probably a mental defective, is incarcerated (he will be murdered in A.D. 33).

Tiberius considers Agrippina's third son, Gaius, too young to be dangerous, although he is kept a virtual prisoner at the imperial palace on Capri.

37

The emperor Tiberius dies March 16 at age 78 and is succeeded by his nephew Gaius Caesar, 25, youngest son of the late Agrippina and her husband, Germanicus. The new emperor, who is called Caligula because of the *caligae*, or soldiers' boots, he has worn, will rule with such excess as even to horrify his sister Agrippina the Younger, whom he exiles (she had her first sexual experience at age 12 with him, soon afterward began sleeping with her cousin, Aemilius Lepidus, and was married off by the emperor to Gnaeus Domitius Eanobarbus, an aristocrat who has deliberately run over and killed a boy on the Appian Way, gouged out the eye of a knight in the Roman Forum for giving him offense, generally engaged in drunken, adulterous debauchery, and is now having an incestuous relationship with his sister Lepida). Agrippina the Younger gives birth at the seaside town of Anteum (Anzio) on the east coast of the Tyrrhenian Sea to a boy, Domitius, who will be called Nero.

38

The emperor Caligula develops a passion for his depraved sister Drusilla and compels her to leave her husband and live with him as his wife, following the practice of Egyptian kings and their sisters. Drusilla dies after a short illness, and Caligula becomes totally unbalanced.

39

Two Vietnamese sisters, Trung Trac and Trung Nhi, lead the first revolt in Southeast Asia against Chinese domination. Trung Trac's husband has been killed by the Chinese, she has been raped, and the army of vassals that she and her sister raise includes one Phung Thi Chinh, who goes into battle when nine months pregnant and, after giving birth, stops only to strap her infant to her back before fighting her way clear (*see* A.D. 42).

The emperor Caligula banishes his sister Agrippina the Younger in December, accusing her of improper sexual relations with a Sicilian horse breeder. Having ordered others to commit suicide, he has Agrippina's cousin Aemilius Lepidus murdered and sends her son Nero (Lucius Domitius Nero Eanobarbus) to his father's sister, Domitia Lepida, who will raise the boy in squalid conditions.

40

✗ Gnaeus Domitius Eanobarbus, husband of Agrippina the Younger and father of her son Nero, dies of dropsy, and his brother Gaius makes off with what remains of the family fortune.

41

✗ The Roman emperor Caligula declares himself a god and is stabbed to death January 24 by two Praetorian tribunes (his wife and infant daughter are also murdered). His reckless extravagances have exhausted the treasury surplus left by Tiberius, and he has raised new funds by extortion and appropriation, confiscating the lands of provincials as well as of Romans. Caligula is succeeded by his uncle, Claudius, 50, who is believed (mistakenly) to be mentally deficient. The new emperor was married for the third time in A.D. 38 to his second cousin Valeria Messalina, now 16, daughter of Domitia Lepida and a granddaughter of Octavia, who bore him a daughter, Octavia, in A.D. 39 and now bears him a son, Tiberius Claudius Britannicus. Claudius recalls Caligula's sister Agrippina the Younger from exile (she is both Messalina's niece and her aunt by marriage). After visiting the palace, she calls on Domitia Lepida and finds her son Nero living in poverty. Her own property was appropriated by her brother Caligula when he banished her, but her sister-in-law Domitia, sister of Domitia Lepida, is married to the rich Roman Passienus Crispus. Agrippina persuades him to divorce Domitia and marry her, and when he dies shortly thereafter Agrippina the Younger inherits his wealth.

42

✗ Chinese troops put down the Vietnamese revolt begun in A.D. 39. The Trung sisters drown themselves in a river rather than allow themselves to be captured (*see* 248).

Julia Livilla, sole surviving sister of Agrippina the Younger, who was banished along with Agrippina and recalled by Claudius, is accused by the empress Messalina of having been intimate with the philosopher Lucius Annaeus Seneca. She is banished again.

48

✗ The Roman empress Messalina, now 23 and notorious for her promiscuity, takes advantage of her husband Claudius's absence from Rome to go through the formalities of a marriage ceremony with the consul-designate Gaius Silius, one of her many lovers. Claudius returns, is told of the incident, and has Gaius Silius put to death. Messalina tries to commit suicide and is helped to that end by an attendant officer. Claudius then marries his niece Agrippina the Younger, now 33, who allies herself with the freedman Narcissus and others, representing herself as a Roman matron whose only desire is to restore the reputation of the imperial family. Lollia Paulina, a rich woman who has been Agrippina's rival for the hand of Claudius, is banished on grounds that she consulted astrologers about the prospects of her marrying Claudius, and her properties are confiscated. Calpurnia, a woman whose beauty has caught Claudius's eye, is similarly banished.

Agrippina the Younger induces Claudius to adopt her son Nero, now 11, who is renamed Nero Claudius Augustus Germanicus and given precedence over Britannicus, Claudius's own son by the late Messalina. Determined to have the son by her previous marriage succeed to the throne instead of letting it go to Britannicus, Agrippina engineers a plot to have Claudius believe that his 11-year-old daughter Octavia's fiancé, the praetor Lucius Silanus, is guilty of incest with his sister Julia Calvina. Claudius breaks off Octavia's engagement.

49

✗ The Roman praetor Lucius Silanus commits suicide early in the year on the day that his former fiancée, Octavia, is betrothed to Agrippina's son Nero. Claudius recalls Seneca to Rome, names him praetor, and entrusts him with Nero's education.

50

 Cologne has its beginnings in the town of Colonia Agrippina built on the left bank of the Rhine at the site of Oppidum Ubiorum, chief town of the Ubii. The emperor Claudius fortifies the town at the request of his wife, Agrippina the Younger, who was born in the place. She rides at the head of Rome's legions against the warrior-queen Cartimandua.

53

 The Roman princess Octavia, now 16, is married to the heir apparent Nero, son of Agrippina the Younger and now, through Agrippina's marriage to Claudius, Octavia's step-brother. Agrippina suspects her sister-in-law Domitia Lepida of trying to regain control over Nero by flattering him and plying him with gifts; Domitia Lepida is sentenced to death following charges by Agrippina that she has engaged in witchcraft and has not properly controlled her slaves in Calabria.

 The apostle Paul travels to Greece on a journey that will take 3 years. "For man was not made from woman," he will say in his *Epistle to the Corinthians*, referring to the biblical story of the creation of woman from Adam's rib, "but woman from man. Neither was man created for woman, but woman for man." He uses the story of Eve's disobedience in the Garden of Eden as evidence of women's inherent weakness, and will scold them for adorning themselves, counseling modesty in the tradition of earlier Hebrew prophets. "It is good for a man not to touch a woman. Nevertheless, to avoid fornication, let every man have his own wife, and let every woman have her own husband. . . . I would that all men were even as I myself. . . . I say, therefore, to the unmarried and widows, it is good for them if they abide, even as I, but if they cannot contain, let them marry: for it is better to marry than to burn." Paul's successors will speak of the inconveniences and discomforts attending marital intercourse—the pangs of childbirth and the anxieties inherent in raising a family as compared with the advantages of chastity. Virginity, they will say, places one in closer relation to God. Christianity will adhere to Hebrew law forbidding a woman to enter a place of worship for 33 days after giving

Agrippina the Younger, degenerate mother of Nero, sought to rule the world. He had her assassinated. LIBRARY OF CONGRESS

birth to a son and for 66 days after the birth of a daughter.

54

 The Roman emperor Claudius dies October 13 at age 64 after eating poisoned mushrooms given him by the expert poisoner Locusta and, when that proves too slow, with poison administered to his throat on a feather by the physician Stertinius Xenophon (who says he wants Claudius to vomit in order to relieve his indigestion) as part of a plot inspired by the empress. She will seek to rule Rome through her son Nero, now 17, who inherits the throne in preference to Britannicus, Claudius's son by Messalina, and will reign as emperor until A.D. 68. Nero, whose jealousy has been encouraged by his mother, will have Britannicus poisoned next year.

💲 Agrippina the Younger (above) works with Seneca and with Roman statesmen who include Afranius Burrus to frame an economic program that includes imperial free trade, a better administration of the corn supply, recognition of the Senate's importance in a secure government, and measures for improving the general welfare, but courtiers led by Seneca and Burrus will soon oppose Agrippina (*see* A.D. 59).

58 ────────────────────

✕ Poppea Sabina, who has borne a son to her husband, Rufius Crispinus, becomes mistress to the emperor Nero's friend Marcus Salvius Otho. Crispinus is soon pushed aside and Poppea becomes Otho's wife, but she quickly catches the eye of the emperor Nero.

59 ────────────────────

✕ The scheming empress-mother Agrippina the Younger is assassinated on orders from her son, the emperor Nero, who has been influenced by his mistress, Poppea. Agrippina, who has sought to rule the world, has been so overtly affectionate toward Nero that there have been rumors of an incestuous relationship (*see* Suetonius, A.D. 122).

60 ────────────────────

✕ Roman troops under the command of the procurator in Britain flog Boadicea (or Boudicca), queen of the Iceni, whose Celtic king, Prasutagas, has died. They rape her two daughters. Boadicea vows revenge, and gathers support from other British tribes such as the Trinovantes (year approximate).

61 ────────────────────

✕ Boadicea, queen of the Iceni, finds that the occupying Roman general, Suetonius Paulinus, has moved off to suppress a Druid revolt in Anglesey. She gath-

ers an army that slaughters the garrison at the unwalled colony of Camulodunum (Colchester), moving on to Verulamium (St. Albans), and Londinium (London). Boadicea's forces destroy all three towns, kill 70,000 Romans, and force at least one Roman leader to flee for his life to Gaul. Q. Petilius Cerealis marches south from Lincoln with a detachment from his legion but is caught and annihilated before he can reach Londinium, only his cavalry escaping. Suetonius Paulinus finally returns and rallies the scattered Roman forces to suppress the insurgency. Boadicea and her Celtic warriors suffer a crushing defeat at the hands of javelin-throwing Roman troops; she takes poison rather than surrender.

62 ────────────────────

✕ The emperor Nero, now 25, divorces his wife, Octavia, places her under military surveillance in Campania, marries his mistress, Poppea, sends his dissolute friend Otho to a distant post, and then exiles Octavia to Pandateria, where he has her murdered June 9.

65 ────────────────────

✕ The emperor Nero kicks his pregnant wife, Poppea, and she dies from her injuries.

68 ────────────────────

✕ The emperor Nero is sentenced to death by the Roman Senate and commits suicide June 9 at age 30, ending the Julio-Claudian line that has ruled for 128 years. His successor, Galba, will rule for less than 6 months.

69 ────────────────────

✕ Eight Roman legions on the Rhine refuse allegiance to the emperor Galba, he is murdered January 15 by Marcus Salvius Otho, now 36, and the Senate recognizes Otho as emperor. Otho commits suicide in April after a defeat in the field, and Titus Flavius

Sabinus Vespasianus, 59, who takes over in December, will reign until A.D. 79 as the emperor Vespasian.

70

✗ Flavius Sabinus Vespasianus Titus, 31, older son of the emperor Vespasian, sacks Rome September 7 and gives part of Judea to Marcus Julius "Herod" Agrippa II, whose sister Berenice has become his mistress. Daughter of Herod Agrippa I, Berenice has had four husbands, including her uncle and brother, but she follows Titus on his return to Rome.

79

✗ The emperor Vespasian dies June 23 at age 69. His elder son, Titus, will reign until A.D. 81, and Titus's younger brother, Titus Flavius Domitianus, will reign until A.D. 96 as the emperor Domitian.

🌐 The volcano Vesuvius on the Bay of Naples erupts August 24, burying the cities of Herculaneum and Pompeii under tons of molten lava, mud, and ash.

90

∞ The emperor Domitian has Cornelia, chief priestess of the Vestal Virgins, buried alive following allegations that she has had an affair with a former magistrate. Other Vestal Virgins convicted of adultery are executed. Chosen by the emperor in his capacity as *pontifex maximus*, the guardians of the hearth-goddess Vesta are required to remain virginal on pain of death, and although Cornelia protests her innocence to the end, her pleas are unavailing.

93

✗ The Roman lawyer-historian Publius (or Gaius Cornelius) Tacitus, 38, returns from a 4-year sojourn in the north to work on his monograph *Germania*, in which he will write of the Germanic tribes that their battalions are composed of families and clans. "Close by them, too, are those who are dearest to them, so that they hear the shrieks of women, the cries of infants. They [the women] are to every man the most sacred witnesses of his bravery—they are the most generous applauders. The soldier brings his wounds to his mother and wife. . . . Tradition says that armies already wavering or giving way have been rallied by women who, with earnest entreaties and bosoms laid bare, have vividly represented the horrors of captivity. . . . They [the Germans] even believe that the sex has a certain sanctity and prescience, and they do not despise their counsels or make light of their answers. . . . They venerated Aurinia [as a divinity], and many other women, but not with servile flatteries or with sham deifications" (*see* A.D. 102).

96

✗ The emperor Domitian is stabbed to death by a freedman September 18 at age 44 after a 15-year reign. Domitian has taken one of his nieces as his mistress. The empress, Domitia, and officers of the court have conspired against him.

98

✗ The emperor Nerva, who has succeeded Domitian, dies January 25 at age 63 and is succeeded by his adopted son, who will reign until A.D. 117 as the emperor Trajan.

100

✗ Plotina, wife of the Roman emperor Trajan, is offered the title of Augusta but refuses. She is admired for her simplicity and virtue (but *see* A.D. 105).

2nd Century

102

Germanic forces engage the Roman legions at Aquae Sextiae, with women as well as men throwing themselves against the enemy. As the historian Plutarch, now 56, will write, "the fight had been no less fierce with the women than with the men themselves. . . . They charged with swords and axes, and fell upon their opponents uttering a hideous outcry. . . . When summoned to surrender, they killed their children, slaughtered one another, and hanged themselves to trees." Bodies of women in full armor are found among the fallen Marcomanni and Quadi.

105

Plotina accepts the title of Augusta that she refused 5 years ago as Rome wallows in corruption while her husband, the emperor Trajan, extends the frontiers of his realm through conquests in Dacia (Romania), Armenia, and Mesopotamia while pursuing public works projects at home.

Pliny the Younger, who heads Rome's drainage administration, writes to the aunt of his third wife, Calpurnia, "I do not doubt that it will be a source of great joy to you to know that [Calpurnia] has turned out to be worthy of her father, worthy of you, and worthy of her grandfather. Her shrewdness and frugality are of the highest order. She loves me—a sign of her purity. To these virtues is added an interest in literature, which she has taken up out of fondness for me. She has read, repeatedly reads, and even learns by heart my works. What anxiety

Rome's people, like Rome's rulers, indulged in licentious behavior; virtuous women were the exception.

she feels when I am about to speak in court! What joy when I have finished! She arranges for messengers to tell her of the approval and applause I win as well as the outcome of the case." (Year approximate; Calpurnia is still in her teens, Pliny in his 40s.) Women are not permitted to participate in Rome's political and court systems, so Calpurnia can share in her husband's public life only as a spectator. Few women are educated to the same level as their husbands.

emerging from the royal couch of her son Nero with his semen on her lips (*see* A.D. 59).

115

The Chinese astronomer, mathematician, poet, and historian Ban Zhao dies at age 70 following a difficult journey to visit her son, a provincial magistrate. Her writings include *Lessons for Women*, a book on morality.

116

The Roman lawyer and satirist Juvenal (Decimus Junius Juvenalis), 61, catalogues female faults in his sixth *Satire*, saying that a wife is a tyrant, the more so if her husband is fond or loving. Cruelty is natural to women; they torment their husbands, whip their housekeepers, and enjoy having slaves flogged almost to death. They are stupid enough to believe in astrology and addicted to religion. Their sexual lusts are disgusting, and they prefer slaves, actors, and gladiators.

117

The emperor Trajan dies of a stroke August 8 at age 63; his wife, Plotina, is with him at his death and asserts that he has adopted his second cousin, Publius Aelius Hadrianus, 41, who comes to power and will reign until 148 as the emperor Hadrian. Plotina hurries to Rome together with her mother, Matidia; Hadrian remains in Syria, sending an apologetic note to the Senate.

122

The emperor Hadrian dismisses his private secretary, Suetonius, after finding that the latter failed to observe court etiquette with regard to the emperor's wife, Julia, while Hadrian was visiting his troops in Britain. The author of the *Lives of Famous Men*, Suetonius is denied access to official archives but continues nevertheless to work on his *Lives of the Caesars*, in which he retails gossip about the late empress Agrippina the Younger having been seen

140

The Roman satirist Juvenal dies after a career in which he has attacked vice, poverty, and the extravagance of the ruling classes while revealing a special hatred for women.

147

The Chinese dowager empress, whose brother Liang Chi has brought her family to the height of its power, places the infant Huandi on the throne (*see* 168).

161

The Roman emperor Antoninus Pius dies March 7 and is succeeded by his son-in-law, Marcus Aurelius Antoninus, who married his cousin (and the emperor's daughter) Faustina the Younger in 145. Marcus Aurelius is a nephew of the wife of the late emperor Hadrian and, like her, is of Spanish descent. His adoptive brother, Lucius Varus, is co-emperor, but since he is a weak sensualist, the real power is in the hands of the stoic philospher Marcus Aurelius.

168

The Chinese emperor Huandi dies in January without an heir after a 21-year reign. His widow, the empress Dou, is named dowager, ennobles her father, Dou Wu, and sends 1,000 eunuchs to fetch a 12-year-old boy to Loyang as the new emperor; she tries to put her late husband's nine concubines to death but kills only one before the eunuchs stop her, and when the new emperor arrives, her father vows to kill the eunuchs. The new emperor, Lingti, supported by the eunuchs, wins a power struggle, the dowager empress is imprisoned, and her father dies by his own hand. Lingti will reign until his death in 189, but the power of the eunuchs has undermined the Han dynasty.

180

✖ The Roman emperor Marcus Aurelius dies at Vindobona (Vienna) March 17 and is succeeded by Commodus.

192

✖ The Roman emperor Commodus is murdered December 31, ending the Antonine line, which has held power since 138. The emperor's mistress, Marcia, his chamberlain, Eclectus, and the prefect of praetorians, Laetus, have found their names on the imperial execution list and have hired the wrestler Narcissus to strangle Commodus (*see* 193).

193

✖ The Roman Senate chooses a 67-year-old man to succeed the late Commodus, but the strict economical policies of Publius Helfius Pertinax win him few friends and he is murdered March 28 by members of the Praetorian Guard, who invade the imperial palace. Rome's richest senator, Didius Julianus, 61, then virtually buys the empire at auction for 300 million sesterces, but a 47-year-old Pannonian legate offers his troops on the Danube huge bonuses if they will leave immediately for Rome. He marches them 800 miles in 40 days, enters Rome June 1 in full battle dress, has Didius Julianus put to death in the palace baths, and will reign until 211 as the emperor Septimius Severus.

200

✖ The Japanese empress Jingu sends a vast fleet to invade Korea. The Koreans capitulate at sight of the huge multi-oared ships and offer tribute.

✊ Some 400,000 slaves perform the menial work of Rome, with middle-class citizens often owning eight, the rich from 500 to 1,000, an emperor as many as 20,000. Free urban workers enjoy 17 to 18 hours of leisure each day, with free admission to baths, sports events, and gladiatorial contests.

⚕ Roman medical students are prohibited from visiting brothels.

🌐 Rome is a city of about 1.5 million, its people housed mostly in 46,600 *insulae*, or apartment blocks, each three to eight stories high, flimsily made of wood, brick, or rubble, with shutters and hangings to deaden the nightly din of iron-rimmed cartwheels in the streets.

✖ The average Roman breakfasts on bean meal mash and unleavened breadcakes cooked on cinders and dipped in milk or honey. The midday meal, or *prandium,* often eaten standing up in a public place, consists generally of fruit, a sweetmeat, cheese, and watered wine. The evening meal, or *convivium*, may include meat, fish, broccoli, cereals, and a porridge of bread crumbs and onions fried in oil and seasoned with vinegar and chickpeas.

3rd Century

202

✗ Gaius Fulvius Plautianus, the African-born Roman commander-in-chief who is even more powerful than Sejanus was under Tiberius, persuades the emperor to let his daughter, Plautilla, marry Septimius Severus's son, who is known as Caracalla and rules as co-emperor. Septimius Severus's wife, Julia Domna, opposes the match.

∞ The Carthaginian theologian Tertullian (Quintus Septimius Florens Tertullianus), 42, a convert to Christianity, writes to his wife, "I thought it meet, my best beloved fellow servant in the Lord, even from this early period, to provide for the course you must pursue after my departure from the world, if I should be called before you." In *Ad Uxorem*, he instructs her not to remarry, comparing a second marriage to outright adultery. Widowhood is God's call to sexual abstinence, Tertullian maintains, and God much prefers that men and women practice celibacy. "It is better to marry only because it is worse to burn. It is still better neither to marry nor to burn."

211

✗ The African-born Roman emperor Septimius Severus dies in Britain February 4 at age 64 and is succeeded by his eldest son, Caracalla, whose 6-year reign will be dominated by his Syrian mother, Julia Domna.

217

✗ The Roman emperor Caracalla is assassinated at Antioch after instigating a false charge of treason against his father-in-law, Plautianus; his mother, Julia Domna, dies soon after, and it is said that she has starved herself to death for grief at the loss of her son. Julia Domna has patronized Rome's leading philosophers, jurists, scientists, artists, and scholars, including the physician Galen.

218

✗ The Roman emperor Macrinus is defeated June 8 near Antioch and put to death together with his son by supporters of Varius Avitus, 16, who has changed his name to Marcus Aurelius Antoninus and claims to be a son of the late emperor Caligula. Encouraged by Julia Maesa, daughter of a Syrian consul and a sister of the late Julia Domna, he worships the sun god and now calls himself Elagabalus (Heliogabalus). He rules with Julia Maesa as his adviser, and it is really she who directs the government as Elagabalus occupies himself with ritual ceremonies and debaucheries, appointing worthless favorites to high positions.

221

✗ The debauched Roman emperor Elagabalus is murdered by his troops June 27 at age 19 along with his mother, probably at the instigation of Julia

Maesa. He is succeeded by the 14-year-old son of Julia Mamaea, a daughter of Julia Maesa. The boy will reign as Alexander Severus until 235 with his mother and grandmother dominating his regime.

222

 Julia Maesa has her sister, Julia Soaemius, killed by the Praetorian Guards for flirting with the emperor Alexander Severus.

226

 Julia Maesa dies and her daughter, Julia Mamaea, gains further influence over the regime of the emperor Alexander Severus. In addition to the rank of Augusta, she acquires the title "Mother of Augustus and the camps and the Senate and the Fatherland" ("mater e Augusti et castorum et Senatus et patriae") and, jealous of any rival, will soon drive even her son's wife into exile.

235

 The Roman emperor Alexander Severus is overthrown and executed; his mutinous soldiers, led by a Thracian peasant, Gaius Julius Varus Maximinus, who has risen through the ranks to high command, murder the emperor's mother, Julia Mamaea, who is blamed, as regent, for the defeat of a Roman army by Persian forces 3 years ago. Her death ends the line of Julias who have had such influence on Roman affairs since the accession of Caracalla in 211. Maximinus is proclaimed emperor.

239

 The Japanese queen Himiko of Yamatai sends an envoy to Loyang; he returns with a gold seal signifying that the queen is an ally of China.

247

 Japan has civil war following the death of her queen, Himiko of Yamatai, who has gone to war against the ruler of a state in Kyushu. Her request for Chinese support has been rejected, and her brother has usurped her throne, defying the traditional female right of inheritance. Himiko's daughter Iyo is placed on the throne as priestess-queen to restore order.

248

 Vietnamese patriot Trieu Au raises an army of 1,000 to liberate her country from the Chinese (*see* A.D. 42). When her brother pleads with her to desist, she replies, "I want to rail against wind and tide, kill the whales in the ocean, sweep the whole country to save people from slavery, and I have no desire to take abuse." Prints will show her wearing golden armor, holding a sword in each hand, and riding an elephant, but her revolt will fail, and, like the Trung sisters in 42, she will take her own life.

249

 Cyprian, bishop of Carthage, writes a letter to a fellow church leader saying, "I have read . . . your letter . . . asking and desiring us to write again to you and say what we thought of those virgins who, after having once determined to continue in that condition and firmly to maintain their continency, have afterwards been found to have remained in the same bed side by side with men (of whom you say one is a deacon); and yet that the same virgins declare that they are chaste. . . . We must interfere at once with such as these, that they be separated while yet they can be separated in innocence, because by and by they will both become firmly joined by a guilty conscience. . . . And do not let any of them think to defend herself by saying that she may be examined and proven a virgin, for both the hands and the eyes of the midwives are often deceived, and even if she be found to be a virgin in that particular in which a woman may be so, yet she may have sinned in some other part of her body which may be corrupted and yet cannot be examined. Assuredly if they are lying together, the mere embracing, the very talking together, and the act of kissing, and the disgraceful and foul slumber of two persons lying together, how much of dishonor and crime does it confess!"

251 ───────────────────

∞ Agatha, a Sicilian Christian, rejects the love of the Roman consul, Quintilianus, who has her killed with great cruelty. The martyred Agatha will be the patron saint of Catania.

267 ───────────────────

✘ Palmyra's Prince Odenaethus, a staunch ally of Rome since his rebuff by Persia's Shapur I, is assassinated along with his eldest son and chosen successor, evidently on orders from the emperor Gallienus. His second wife, who has borne some younger princes, takes power as Septimia Zenobia and prepares to expand her desert realm to reach from the Nile to the Black Sea.

269 ───────────────────

✘ Palmyra's Septimia Zenobia conquers Egypt, giving her control of Rome's grain supply.

271 ───────────────────

✘ Palmyra's Septimia Zenobia declares independence from Rome; her son Vaballathus assumes the title Augustus, and she becomes Augusta.

272 ───────────────────

✘ The Roman emperor Aurelianus lays siege to Palmyra; his horsemen capture Septimia Zenobia and her young son Vaballathus on the banks of the Euphrates.

274 ───────────────────

✘ Septimia Zenobia of Palmyra is forced to parade in gold chains before the emperor's chariot in his triumphal procession at Rome, which includes 20

Septimia Zenobia of Palmyra dared to challenge Roman rule. The Romans responded by humiliating her. CULVER PICTURES, INC.

elephants and 200 tamed wild animals, but she rides in a golden chariot and slaves support the heavy chains. Aurelianus spares her life, and she marries a Roman senator, but she dies soon afterward.

300 ───────────────────

🖋 The *Kama Sutra*, or *Aphorisms on Love*, by the Indian sage Vatsayan Mallagana of Benares, is a Sanskrit guide of 1,250 verses on the various pleasures of sexual love (date approximate). Based on the Hindu religious philosophy that sexuality is basic to human life, it is written from a man's point of view, but its authors suggest that prospective brides read it before marriage.

4th Century

304

∞ Agnes, a 12-year-old Christian who has refused marriage and consecrated her virginity to God, is killed at Rome (year approximate). Hailed as a martyr, she will be honored as the patron saint of virgins.

307

∞ Catherine, a virgin of royal descent at Alexandria, makes public confession of Christian gospel at a sacrificial feast ordered by the emperor Maximinus. She is tortured on a spiked wheel (it will later be called a "catherine wheel") and beheaded; her remains are spirited to Mount Sinai.

321

∞ The emperor Constantine issues a proclamation July 3 making Sunday a day of rest throughout the Roman Empire. Jews continue to observe the Sabbath on Saturday.

326

✗ The emperor Constantine executes his older son, Flavius Julius Crispus, at Pola, possibly on charges of adultery; Constantine's second wife, Fausta, who is the mother of his three younger sons, is executed later in the year.

∞ Constantine's mother, Helena, claims to have discovered the Holy Cross and the Holy Sepulchre (Jesus's tomb) in Jerusalem. The Church of the Holy Sepulchre will be consecrated there in 335.

337

✗ The emperor Constantine dies May 22 at age 49. He is succeeded by three sons—Constantine II, Constans, and Constantius—born to his second wife, Fausta. Constantine II is soon killed in a battle with Constans, whose troops at Constantinople put to death all male relatives except two young nephews, Gallus and Julian. Constans and Constantius then divide the empire, the latter controlling the east with the addition of Thrace.

350

● The Chinese "mother of calligraphy," Wei Furen, dies after a career in which she has been honored in the *Book of One Hundred Beauties,* established the art of beautiful writing, and inspired the country's most prominent calligraphers.

375

✗ The emperor Valentinian, who has reigned since 364, moves into Illyrium to repel an invasion of the Quadi and Sermatians but becomes so enraged that he dies of a stroke November 17. His son Gratian, now 16, takes over the government at Trier, but ministers of the late emperor, wishing to retain the loyalty of the Illyrian army and fearing a usurper, proclaim Valentinian's 4-year-old son emperor Valentinian II with his mother, Justina, as regent. Gratian accepts the arrangement, but it is Justina who will rule the western empire.

379

✗ The emperor Gratian elevates the son of a successful general in Britain to the title of co-Augustus for the east January 19; Flavius Theodosius, 32, will reign until 395.

380

∞ The Roman widow Paula, 33, whose husband has just died leaving her with five children, gives up her affluent life to join a circle of well-born Christian women, headed by the widow Marcella, who have been meeting since 350 and living ascetic lives (wearing coarse, unwashed clothing, eating and sleeping no more than is absolutely necessary, avoiding social functions, remaining celibate, reading nothing but Scripture, and keeping to themselves except to visit Christian shrines and churches) (*see* 385).

383

✗ Roman legions in Britain proclaim a new emperor, Magnus Maximus, who seizes Gaul. The emperor Gratian is deserted by his troops and killed August 25 at Lugdunum at age 25, leaving a young widow, Laeta. Panonia and Africa maintain their allegiance to the emperor Valentinian II, now 12, whose mother, Justina, rules in his name. Theodosius makes no effort to avenge the death of Gratian but cedes Dacia and Macedonia to Valentinian.

384

∞ The Christian prophet Jerome writes a letter to Eustochium, daughter of the ascetic Paula (*see* 380). "I need not speak of the drawbacks of mar-

riage," he says, and then proceeds to enumerate them, listing pregnancy, the crying of infants, the anguish caused by a rival, household chores. He praises marriage, "but only because it gives me virgins. I gather the rose from the thorns, the gold from the earth, the pearl from the shell," and tells her specifically how to remain a virgin. To avoid all temptations she must avoid wine and eat only the smallest and simplest meals, because "the rumbling of our intestines . . . the emptiness of our stomach . . . [and] the inflammation of our lungs . . . [are] the only ways of protecting chastity." Do not visit the homes of the rich and look upon the ways of luxury, he advises, but rather read much, fast often, wear the meanest clothes, remain at home, and weep for your sins each night. But few Christians follow such advice.

385

∞ The Roman synod exiles the prophet Jerome, who departs for Egypt, Bethlehem, and Jerusalem, accompanied by the Christian ascetic Paula, who leaves her other children behind and takes only her oldest daughter, Eustochium, as a companion (*see* 384). Settling at Bethlehem, Paula supports the establishment of four communities—three female, one male—modeled after a monastery founded by another rich Roman widow, Melania the Elder. Eustochium, who will learn Hebrew, will head the female monasteries after her mother's death in 404 and will edit Jerome's translation of the Bible, which will become the Latin Vulgate.

387

✗ The Roman emperor Maximus invades Italy; Valentinian II and his mother, Justina, flee to Thessalonica, where Justina will die next year.

390

✊ Theodosius suppresses a rebellion at Thessalonica, massacring 7,000.

391

✘ Theodosius returns to Constantinople, leaving Italy and Illyria under the rule of Valentinian II.

395

✘ The Roman emperor Theodosius the Great dies at Milan January 17 at age 49 and his empire is split into eastern and western empires. His favorite niece, Serena, has married his master of troops, Stilicho, a man of Vandal ancestry who installs the emperor's son Arcadius, 17, as emperor at Constantinople and his brother Honorius, 10, on the throne at Milan. The boys' mother died in childbirth last year, leaving also a daughter, Galla Placidia, now 7, who was sent by her father to Rome, where she has been in the care of Serena.

398

✘ The Roman emperor Honorius, now 13, is married to Maria, daughter of the general Stilicho, whose wife, Serena, is well known for her scholarship.

∞ John, bishop of Constantinople, receives a delegation from clergymen who want to close the pagan temples at Gaza where worshipers are openly defying the law. The bishop works through a eunuch who has great power over the emperor Arcadius,

and within a week an imperial constitution is issued closing the temples, but the official appointed to execute the order is bribed to spare the principal temple of Marneum (*see* 400).

400

✘ Bishops from Gaza arrive at Constantinople to ask the eastern emperor, Arcadius, that he close the pagan temple at Marneum (*see* 398). Advised to approach the pious empress, Eudoxia, via her eunuch, they find her sympathetic. She presents their case to her husband, but Arcadius says the people of Gaza have a good record of paying their taxes promptly and refuses to create trouble there. The bishops, who include Mark, tell Eudoxia that if she can change the emperor's mind God will reward her by making the child that she is carrying a boy who will reign for many years. A boy, Theodosius, is born and proclaimed Augustus. Eudoxia advises the bishops to draw up a petition containing their requests, secure places outside the church door, and present the petition to the man who carries her son out of the church after his baptism. The man, who is part of the scheme, then puts the document in the child's hand and announces that the boy has given his approval. Arcadius is annoyed by the text of the petition but is too weak to refuse his assent; a new constitution in accord with the petition is drawn up in the name of the two Augusti.

5th Century

404

∞ John Chrysostom, 54, patriarch of Constantinople, is expelled from the city following his attacks on the extravagant lifestyle of the empress Eudoxia. He had himself baptized into Christianity at age 20 and was made bishop of Constantinople 6 years ago.

408

✕ The Roman emperor Honorius, now 23, has his father-in-law, Stilicho, murdered August 22 as Visigoths under Alaric lay siege to Rome, whose hungry citizens are fed by Laeta, widow of the late emperor Gratian.

The eastern emperor, Arcadius, whose eunuch general, Eutropius, has been unable to thwart barbarian invasions, dies at age 31 and is succeeded by his son of 7, who will reign until 450 as Theodosius II but will be dominated by his sister Pulcheria (see 414).

410

✕ Visigothic forces under Alaric lay siege to the imperial court at Ravenna, and then besiege Rome once again. Some Gothic slaves open that city's Silerian Gate August 24, the Visigoths plunder the city for 3 days, and they then move south, taking with them all the loot they can carry and also, as hostage, the emperor's sister, Galla Placidia, now 21. Alaric dies of fever in the fall. The court at Ravenna demands the return of Galla Placidia, her Christian captors

The "barbarians" who conquered Rome behaved little worse, and often with more morality, than did the Romans.

treat her with the courtesy appropriate to royalty, but while they appear prepared to bargain they keep raising their ransom demands.

412

✕ Atahualf, who succeeded to the leadership of the Visigoths upon the death of Alaric, wants to marry the Roman princess Galla Placidia and make her queen of the Visigoths. She appears to share this desire, but her brother, the Roman emperor Honorius, is appalled at the idea and has his chief general, Constantius, send a message again demanding that she be returned to her family.

414 ——————————————

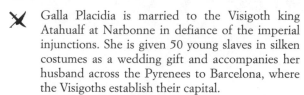 Galla Placidia is married to the Visigoth king Atahualf at Narbonne in defiance of the imperial injunctions. She is given 50 young slaves in silken costumes as a wedding gift and accompanies her husband across the Pyrenees to Barcelona, where the Visigoths establish their capital.

Pulcheria, 2 years older than her weak-willed brother Theodosius II, turns 15, takes over the regency, is proclaimed Augusta, and will virtually rule the eastern empire until she is ousted from favor by intrigue in 442 or 443 (*see* 450). Women and eunuchs play no official part in government but often wield the real power when immature or weak-minded men hold imperial titles; Pulcheria, although a Christian by birth, has been educated in pagan learning, speaks Greek and Latin fluently, and has taken a deep interest in medicine and natural science.

415 ——————————————

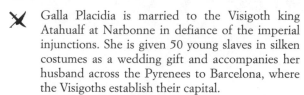 The Visigothic chief Atahualf is murdered by an attendant, expressing in his final words the wish that Galla Placidia be sent home to Ravenna. Now 27, the widow finds herself in the midst of alien people who no longer regard her as their queen. Atahualf's successor, Sigerice, crowns himself king and celebrates by forcing Galla Placidia and his other Roman prisoners to walk on foot for 12 miles in front of the horses that bear him in royal splendor. He is murdered a week later, and rule passes to another Gothic chieftain, Wallia, who agrees to send Galla Placidia back to Ravenna.

A mob incited by Alexandria's new bishop Cyril, 39, who has driven out the city's Jews, tears the Neoplatonic philosopher Hypatia, 45, from her chariot in March, strips her naked, scrapes her to death with oyster shells, and burns her body. Daughter of the mathematician Theon, Hypatia established a reputation as a mathematician in her own right while studying at Athens under Plutarch the Younger and his daughter Asclepegeneia. She has attracted scholars from throughout the Greek world to her lectures on geometry, algebra, and astronomy at the University of Alexandria, but her authority as a woman has run against the dogma of Christianity.

417 ——————————————

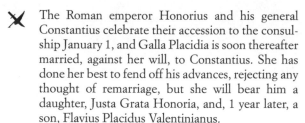 The Roman emperor Honorius and his general Constantius celebrate their accession to the consulship January 1, and Galla Placidia is soon thereafter married, against her will, to Constantius. She has done her best to fend off his advances, rejecting any thought of remarriage, but she will bear him a daughter, Justa Grata Honoria, and, 1 year later, a son, Flavius Placidus Valentinianus.

421 ——————————————

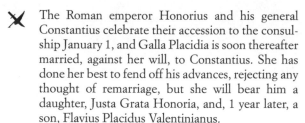 The Roman emperor Honorius makes his brother-in-law Constantius co-emperor, with his sister, Galla Placidia, as Augusta, or empress. Constantius III dies of pleurisy in September, and Galla Placidia, now 33, is told by Honorius to go back to Rome. Fearing for her safety and that of her two small children, she takes them instead to Constantinople, where her nephew rules as the Emperor Theodosius II.

423 ——————————————

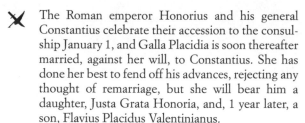 The Roman emperor Honorius dies at Ravenna August 15. His nephew at Constantinople, Theodosius II, dislikes and distrusts his aunt, Galla Placidia, but grudgingly grants her and her son, Valentinian, the imperial rank they enjoyed in the West.

424 ——————————————

The eastern emperor Theodosius II organizes an invasion fleet to seize the western empire. His aunt, Galla Placidia, goes along with her two children.

425

✗ Galla Placidia takes her 6-year-old son to the Imperial Forum at Rome and sees him hailed as the emperor Valentinian III October 3. By law, a Roman emperor must rule his own empire, and there can be no regent, but Galla Placidia, now 36, will effectively control the Western empire for the next decade. As a woman, she cannot enforce her will by taking command of what remains of the legions, but she will use her wiles to manipulate the various rival generals, shrewdly playing them off against the court officials as she plays off the great landowners against one another.

426

∞ *The City of God* (*De civitate Dei*) by the Christian philosopher Augustine, 72, declares that empires like Rome are merely temporal and that the only permanent community is the Church, visible and invisible: the city of God. Augustine has written that his mother had bruises from the regular beatings that she meekly suffered at the hands of his father, and that most other wives in the small North African town of Thagaste had similar bruises. He holds that original sin is attached to virgins and celibates along with everyone else; since parentage and new life come about only by means of a pleasurable sexual act, all flesh is inherently depraved and all mankind a "mass of perdition": "Marriage and fornication are not two evils, the second of which is worse, but marriage and continence are two goods, the second of which is better." While conceding that the sexual act is the "keenest of all pleasures," Augustine notes that "at the crisis of excitement it practically paralyzes all power of deliberate thought." The earlier in life that couples can refrain from sexual intercourse with each other, the better they will appear in God's eyes, he argues.

The purpose of marriage is procreation, says Augustine (above). Lust, even in marriage, is justified only when it has the single and immediate aim of begetting children, he says, and his view will dominate Church thinking for more than 15 centuries.

Marriage in Western Europe and the eastern empire has now come under clerical domination and is regarded as a holy act that cannot be dissolved by personal wish. It is a rare wedding that does not include an ecclesiastical benediction.

431

 The cult of the Virgin begins to spread westward from Byzantium following a decree of the Council of Ephesus recognizing Mary as the Mother of God (i.e., mother of Jesus Christ).

449

✗ Honoria, sister of the Roman emperor Valentinian III, sends her ring to the Hun leader Attila and asks for his protection in order to avoid marrying a man whom Valentinian is forcing upon her (year approximate). Attila claims that this is an offer of marriage, that Honoria is his affianced bride, and demands half the empire as her rightful inheritance (*see* 451).

450

✗ The eastern emperor Theodosius II dies at age 49 after falling from his horse while hunting. His sister Pulcheria, now 51, takes over the government and names the army chief of staff Marcian as emperor, placing the crown on his head before the Senate and taking him as husband, although she long ago took a vow of perpetual virginity and has never married.

The empress mother Galla Placidia dies at Ravenna November 27 at age 68. She served effectively as regent for her son, Valentinian, until court intrigue, rebellion, and invasion sapped her power.

451

✗ Attila marches westward into Gaul with a vast army of Huns and subject peoples after being refused the hand of Valentinian's sister, Honoria, and her half of the empire (*see* 449). Roman troops meet him on the Catalaunian plains, an indecisive battle is fought, Attila withdraws, but he will invade Italy again next year.

453

✗ The eastern empress Pulcheria dies at age 54, leaving her vast estates to the poor as evidence of her Christian devotion.

Attila the Hun dies after several years of pillaging Italian cities and towns. His hordes break up upon his demise, and subject German peoples rebel against their overlords.

455

✗ The Roman emperor Valentinian III is murdered March 16 by two of his guards, ending the dynasty begun by Theodosius in the last century. Valentinian's widow, Eudoxia, daughter of Theodosius II, sets up Petronius Maximus, a rich senator who outbids his competitors with his bounties to the troops and is proclaimed emperor the following day. When he, too, is killed by the crowd May 31 as he tries to escape, she calls the Vandal leader Gaiseric from North Africa. His troops attack Rome June 2 and methodically sack the city for 2 weeks.

460

✗ The Ostrogothic king Theodoric the Great has his daughter married to the son of Gaiseric, king of the Vandals. Gaiseric suspects her of trying to poison his son and sends the girl back to her father with her nose and ears cut off.

466

∞ Irish novitiate Bridget (or Brigid, or Bride), 13, enters a convent at Meath, beginning a career in which she will become a famous abbess (*see* 523).

491

✗ The eastern emperor Zeno dies at age 65 after a 17-year reign; his widow, the empress Ariadne, chooses a 61-year-old palace official as his successor, she marries him after his coronation, and he will reign until 518 as Anastasius I.

493

✗ Clotilda, 19, daughter of the Burgundian king Childeric, marries Clovis, 28, Merovingian king of the Franks.

496

✗ Frankish forces led by Clovis gain a mighty victory over the Alemanni near Cologne; Clovis's queen, Clotilda, persuades him to embrace Christianity, and, with 2,000 of his men, he accepts conversion Christmas Day in a mass baptism by the bishop of Reims.

6th Century

Clovis, king of the Franks, dies at age 46, his territories are divided among his four sons, and his widow, Clotilda, retires to the abbey of St. Martin at Tours, where she will devote her remaining 34 years to works of charity.

523

∞ The Irish abbess Bridget dies at age 70 after having founded four monasteries for women, most notably one at Kildare. She will be canonized and revered as St. Bridget.

526

The Ostrogothic king Theodoric the Great dies of dysentery August 30; his daughter Amalasuntha takes power as regent for her 10-year-old son, Atalaric. Equally fluent in Greek, Latin, and the language of her Gothic ancestors, Amalasuntha is a handsome, intelligent woman of great culture and strong will. She rules a kingdom that extends from its capital at Ravenna throughout the Italian peninsula, Sicily, Illyricum (Dalmatia), Corsica, and Sardinia. Amalasuntha makes her subjects—Romans as well as Goths—swear allegiance to young Atalaric and uses her power to rid her realm of dishonest government functionaries. She will curb the greed of corrupt landowners and effectively end the destructive incursions of barbarian tribesmen from the north.

527

Constantinople's Justinus I takes his nephew as co-emperor April 1 as an incurable wound saps his strength. He dies August 1 at age 77, and Justinian (Flavius Anicius Justinianus, or Flavius Petrus Sabbatius Justinianus) will reign until 565. His wife, Theodora, now 19, is the daughter of a circus bear-keeper and their marriage required a repeal of the law forbidding a patrician to wed an actress, but she will have a strong influence until her death in 545.

529

The Ostrogothic regent Amalasuntha receives a delegation sent by a council of disgruntled nobles urging that she have her son Atalaric, now 13, taught not by elderly schoolmasters, as in the past, but by men who will teach him to "ride, fence, and to be toughened, not to be turned into a bookworm, because 'he who fears the tutor's strap will never look unblinking at sword or spear.'" She reluctantly accedes, but will henceforth show little interest in the boy (see 534).

532

The Nika insurrection in January destroys large areas of Constantinople as crowds shouting "Nika!" (Victory!) set fires that destroy the city. Justinian panics, but his wife, Theodora, tells him, "Reflect whether, once you have escaped, you would not prefer death to safety." He is persuaded to remain. At least 30,000 rebels are put to the sword by the troops of Belisarius, and the young military commander helps Justinian begin an era of absolutism.

533

✗ The Ostrogothic regent Amalasuntha, who has lost her power to control the kingdom, sends a messenger to the emperor Justinian asking for asylum at Constantinople (*see* 529). Justinian quickly agrees, she ships the royal treasure by sea to the palace being prepared for her, and when she learns that her three chief enemies are plotting against her she has them murdered. Feeling more secure, she recalls the royal treasure ship, and when Justinian asks for an insignificant fortress in Sicily she puts him off with the suggestion that it would be "unfair in a great prince . . . to fasten a quarrel upon a boyish sovereign [Atalaric] unversed in public affairs" and an appeal that he "show kindness to an orphan boy." In secret, she negotiates to turn over her entire realm to Justinian (*see* 534).

534

✗ The Ostrogothic prince Atalaric, who has dissipated his youth in drink and debauchery, dies of tuberculosis at age 18 (*see* 529). His mother, Amalasuntha, proposes to her cousin Theodahad, the kingdom's largest landowner and her father's last male heir, that he share the throne with her but "swear an awful oath" that he will be king in name only. He readily accepts the offer, but she has forced Theodahad to return some land he appropriated, he hates her with a vengeance, and he has told Justinian's ambassador that he would be willing to turn over Tuscany in exchange for a large sum of money, the rank of senator, and permission to live at Constantinople (*see* 535).

535

 The new Ostrogothic king Theodahad revenges himself upon his cousin Amalasuntha. He has her

taken from Ravenna to a small island on Lake Bolsena, where she is strangled in her bath April 30. Her murder gives the emperor Justinian an excuse to invade Italy, and he sends his commander Belisarius on an expedition to Sicily.

 The *lex Julia* issued by the emperor Justinian (above) declares that a wife has no right to bring criminal charges of adultery against a husband, even though she may wish to complain that he has violated his marriage vow, but a husband has every right to bring such charges against a wife, and the Justinian Code makes adultery a capital offense. The Code revokes ancient penalties placed by Augustus against celibacy and childlessness, but it makes divorce almost impossible and places sexual self-denial above all else as the ethical way of life.

537

∞ Ravenna's Church of St. Vitale is completed in double octagonal shape with mosaic portraits of Justinian and his wife, Theodora, whose commander, Belisarius, has chased the Ostrogoths across the Alps and out of Italy.

⊖ Theodora (above), now 29, has introduced long white dresses, purple cloaks, gold embroidery, tiaras, and pointed shoes into Byzantine fashion.

541

⚥ The Great Plague of Justinian (bubonic plague) spreads from Egypt to Palestine and thence to Constantinople, where it kills from 5,000 to 10,000 each day for a while. The emperor Justinian himself contracts plague but recovers after a few months with help from his wife, Theodora.

548

 The influential Byzantine empress, Theodora, dies of cancer June 28 at age 40, leaving Justinian to rule alone at Constantinople (he will die in 565).

568

The Merovingian king Chilperic I of Soissons (Neustria) murders his second wife, Galswintha, and marries his mistress, Fredegunda, who has also persuaded him to reject his first wife, Audovera. Galswintha's sister Brunhilda is married to Chilperic's brother, Sigibert of Austrasia (both women are daughters of the Visigoth king Athanagild), and urges Sigibert to take action against his brother Chilperic.

Lombard forces invade Italy under the command of Alboin, who 2 years ago killed the Gepidae king Cunimund and married his daughter Rosamund. Lombard rule ends enforcement of the Code of Justinian promulgated in 535.

573

Sigibert of Austrasia (France) goes to war against his brother Chilperic of Soissons at the urging of his wife, Brunhilda. Sigibert appeals to the Germans on the right bank of the Rhine for help, and they obligingly attack the environs of Paris and Chartres, committing atrocities of all sorts.

The Great Plague of Justinian (bubonic plague) killed hundreds of thousands but spared the empress Theodora.

575

Sigibert of Austrasia pursues his brother Chilperic as far as Tournai. As the nobles of Neustria are raising Sigibert in triumph on the shield in the villa at Vitry near Arras, he is assassinated by hirelings of his brother's third wife, Fredegunda, who will engineer the deaths of her stepsons (the offspring of Chilperic's first wife, Audovera), whom she will accuse of killing her own three sons (who will actually die of plague). Sigibert is succeeded by his young son Childebert II, with the boy's mother, Brunhilda, as regent (*see* 584).

578

The Byzantine emperor Justinian II dies after several bouts of insanity. On the advice of his wife, Sophia, he has raised his general Tiberius to the rank of co-emperor, Tiberius has ruled jointly with Sophia since December 574, and he now begins a 4-year reign as Tiberius II Constantinus.

584

Chilperic I of Neustria is murdered; his wife, Fredegunda (or Fredegond), seizes his wealth, flees to Paris with her remaining son, Lothair (or Clotaire), and persuades the nobles to accept him as legitimate heir while she serves as regent, continuing her power struggles with Guntrum of Burgundy and her sister Brunhilda, queen mother of Austrasia (*see* 575).

592

The Japanese emperor Sushun is murdered after 5 years on the throne by agents of his uncle Umako Soga, who is jealous of the emperor's power. Sushun is succeeded by the widow of the late emperor Bintas; now 38, she will reign for 35 years beginning next year as the empress Suiko.

593

Japan's empress Suiko is the first to receive official recognition from China and begins a long reign

593

during a pivotal period in which Buddhism will take firm root.

596 ——————————————————

∞ The English king Aethelbert of Kent welcomes the Italian churchman Augustine and accepts baptism along with the rest of his court at the behest of his Christian Frankish wife, Bertha. He assigns Augustine and his 40 monks a residence at Canterbury and makes the town a center of Christianity.

597 ——————————————————

✗ The Frankish queen mother Fredegunda of Neustria defeats her old rival, Brunhilda of Austrasia, who supports the claims of her own son Childebert II to the Frankish throne against those of Fredegunda's son Clotaire.

✊ England gets her first written code of laws from Aethelbert of Kent. On the subject of women's property rights it says, "If she [the wife] bear a live child, let her have half the property, if the husband die first. If she wish to go away with her children, let her have half the property. If the husband wish to have them, [let her portion be] as one child."

The Franks (above) generally exclude women from the courts, bar them from inheriting certain ancestral lands, even keep them out of family counsels. A woman must have the consent of her parents to marry (eventually she will become attached to her land, with both her person and title used to purchase military loyalty). Adultery in a wife is punishable by death, whereas no penalty attaches to an adulterous husband.

598 ——————————————————

✗ Fredegunda of Neustria dies at Paris a few months after her victory over Brunhilda of Austrasia, who seizes Neustria and unites the Merovingian domains (*see* 613).

7th Century

607

The first Japanese envoy to China's Sui Court, sent by the empress Suiko, begins a long interchange that will lead to the sinoization of Japanese culture.

610

The prophet Mohammed at Mecca has a vision that he is a messenger of God and begins secretly to preach a new religion, to be called Islam. Now 40, he was orphaned at age 6, raised by an uncle, and hired in his early 20s by a rich widow, Khadija, to escort a caravan of her goods to Syria. She proposed marriage upon his return, and by one account got her uncle drunk so that he would approve. Although she was about 15 years his senior, Mohammed married her and became a merchant. Khadija's money gave him leisure to think, and after meditating for some years in a mountainside cave on the ignorance and superstition of his fellow Arabs, he has developed a faith with the encouragment of Khadija, who becomes his first disciple. He feels called upon to teach the religion, which will grow to embrace a major part of the world's population in the millennium ahead (*see* 619).

612

Arnulf, counselor to the Frankish king Clotaire II, becomes bishop of Metz, his wife enters a convent, and his son marries the daughter of Clotaire's mayor-of-the-palace Pepin of Landen.

A woman whose name will be remembered as Lady Zac-Kuk (it is recorded with the same glyph used to denote the First Mother) ascends the throne of the Mayan Empire at Palenque in the Yucatán October 22.

Mayans (above) use a 260-day calendar based on the length of a woman's gestation period, a calendar that would be impractical in geographical areas having more significant seasonal weather changes.

613

Clotaire II of the Franks unites Austrasia and Burgundy. He captures the queen mother, Brunhilda, now 80, widow of the late Sigibert, who was his uncle, and has her dragged to death behind a wild horse.

615

Pacal, 12-year-old son of Lady Zac-Kuk, becomes king of the Maya, but his mother will continue to wield the real power until her death in 640.

619

Mohammed's wife, Khadija, dies at age 64 after 24 years of marriage to her third husband. He has not taken any other wives, but will marry 12 in the next 12 years, mostly for political reasons.

Mohammed's wife, Khadija, supported his Islamic ideas; he took no other wives until after her death.

622 ———————————

∞ Mohammed's followers, who have been persecuted in Mecca, follow him July 16 to Medina, 200 miles away (his flight will be known as the *Hejira*), where he consolidates his growing forces.

628 ———————————

⚔ Mecca falls to the forces of Mohammed, who has fought his pagan enemies with troops that include women.

✊ Mohammed writes letters to all the world's rulers explaining the principles of the new monotheistic Muslim faith, as contained in his book, the Koran.

"Your women are a field for you to cultivate, so go to your field as you will," says the Koran (2:223). "Men are superior to women on account of the qualities in which God has given them preeminence, and because they spend of their property [for the support of women]" (4:34). It allows a man to have as many as four *kadins* (wives) if he is able to keep them all in the same style and accord each one the same amount of affection. Mohammed's intent is to eliminate the female infanticide that has been traditional among pagan Arabs and deal with the surplus of women. "If any of your women be guilty of whoredom, then bring your witnesses against them from among themselves; and if they bear witness to the fact, shut them up within their houses till death release them, or God make some way for them" (4). "Lo! The guile of women is very great" (12:28). But the Koran permits a husband to divorce a wife simply by saying three times, before a *kadi* (judge), "I divorce thee."

The Sharia (below) requires that women remain veiled and segregated, and orders severe punishments for crimes—murderers to have their hearts cut out, thieves to have a hand severed, adulterers to be tied in a sack and stoned to death. It permits women to manage their own property and keep money they earn without interference, but it condones castration to create eunuchs, it allows torture, slavery, and the rape of slaves, and it permits a man to own as many female slaves as he can afford.

Muslims (Mohammedans) will recognize the authority of the Sharia, a complex legal system much like that of the Jewish Talmud. It calls for circumcision of boys (but not girls) and forbids gambling, public entertainment, and art that portrays the human figure.

🎓 The Sharia (above) enjoins women as well as men to obtain secular and religious educations.

✗ The Sharia (above) forbids the eating of pork and thus follows the Mosaic law of Deuteronomy of 621 B.C., but permits camel meat. It prohibits consumption of alcohol, but Mohammed's followers circumvent his prohibition against wine by boiling it down to a concentrate and sweetening it with honey and spices.

632

∞ The prophet Mohammed dies June 7 at age 63 (or 65). His third (and favorite) wife, Aïshah, who married him at age 9, has not borne any children, and is still only about 19, resists claims by the prophet's son-in-law Ali (who has accused her of infidelity), and supports those of her father, Abu-Bakr, who becomes the first caliph. Mohammed's youngest daughter, Fatima (accent on first syllable), Ali's wife, dies at age 26, leaving two sons—Hassan and Hussein—who will found the Fatimid dynasty that will rule Egypt and North Africa from 909 to 1171.

641

✗ The Japanese emperor Jomei dies at age 48 and is succeeded by his widow, 47, who will reign until 645 as the empress Kogyoku.

654

✗ The Japanese emperor Kotoku dies at age 58, and the empress Kogyoku, who was removed in 645, is restored. Now 60, she begins a 7-year reign under the name Saimei.

656

✗ Ali, son-in-law of the late prophet Mohammed, becomes the fourth caliph. Mohammed's widow, Aïshah, leads a revolt against Ali but is defeated and captured at the Battle of the Camel at Basra. Ali exiles her to Medina.

657

∞ Hilda, 43, the Northumbrian abbess of Hartlepool, founds a monastery at Streaneshalch (Whitby) that she will head until shortly before her death in 680. She was baptized at age 13 by Paulinus, the first archbishop of York.

661

✗ Ali, the fourth caliph, is assassinated January 24 in Mesopotamia by a former supporter. His sons Hassan and Hussein (al-Husayn) by the late Fatima survive him, and his supporters will be called Shiites.

680

✗ Mohammed's grandson al-Husayn is killed in battle October 10 at Karbala. His followers, who considered his father, Ali, divinely chosen to transmit the faith of his father-in-law, claim that only Mohammed's descendants have the right to interpret the Koran; they are inspired by the martyrdom of al-Husayn to begin a new fundamentalist sect, the Shiites, which will impose strict rules on women.

682

Lady Wac-Chanil-Ahau, daughter of the Flint Sky-God K of Dos Pilas, arrives at Naranjo in the Yucatán and reestablishes its royal house.

683

✗ The Mayan king Pacal the Great of Palenque dies at age 71 after a 59-year reign.

686

✗ The Japanese emperor Tenmu dies after a 14-year reign and is succeeded by his widow (and niece), 40, who has her late husband's son executed for alleged treason in order that she may be succeeded by Kusakabe, her own son by Tenmu, but Kusakabe takes ill and dies before he can become emperor. His mother will reign until 697 as the empress Jito.

690

✗ The onetime concubine Wu Zhao proclaims herself ruler of China as "Holy and Divine Emperor." She has destroyed most of the Tang princes, over-thrown two of her own sons, and demonstrated remarkable abilities as an administrator, albeit a cruel one (she had the arms and legs of a rival in love chopped off) (*see* 705).

697

✗ The empress Jito, who has established the foundations of Japanese law, abdicates in favor of her 15-year-old grandson, who will reign until 707 as the emperor Momu. Jito's trusted lady-in-waiting Michiyo Tachibana, who has served as Momu's wet-nurse and governess, will exercise great power over the court. She has left her first husband and married Fuhito Fujiwara, a government minister whose

daughter Miyako by a previous wife will have children by Monmu.

 Poems by the empress Jito (above) will be included in the 20-volume *Manyoshu* (*Ten Thousand Words*) and *Hyakuninisshu* (*One Hundred Most Famous Poets*), which will be classics of Japanese literature.

698

✗ Berber forces led by resistance fighter al-Kahina ("The Diviner") are crushed by Arab invaders at Aures in North Africa and she is killed in battle. She has rallied the Berbers since the collapse of Byzantine power in the area but has accused the Byzantine landowners who once supported her of having betrayed the Aures people.

8th Century

705

✘ The Chinese empress Wu is deposed in a coup d'état organized by her ministers, who rebel against her excesses and install the son she deposed 15 years ago, restoring the Tang dynasty.

707

✘ The Japanese emperor Momu dies at age 24 after a 10-year reign and is succeeded by his aunt, 46, who will reign until 715 as the empress Gemmei. She is the sister of the former empress Jito and, like Jito, was also the late emperor Tenmu's niece and wife.

711

✘ Moors (Arabs and Berbers) from North Africa invade the Iberian Peninsula and defeat the Visigoth king Roderick, who dies fighting in July. Córdoba and Toledo fall to the Moors, who will take Seville next year and Lisbon in 716.

715

✘ The Japanese empress Gemmei abdicates at age 54 after an 8-year reign in which she has built a replica of the Chinese imperial palace at Japan's new capital, Nara. She is succeeded by her daughter, 35, who will reign until 724 as the empress Gensho.

722

✘ The British warrior-queen Aethelburg of Ine builds a fort at Taunton to oppose invading Danes.

724

✘ The Japanese empress Gensho abdicates in favor of her 23-year-old nephew (son of the late Momu by Fuhito Fujiwara's daughter Miyako), who will reign until 749 as the emperor Shomu.

732

✘ The Battle of Tours near Poitiers October 11 ends the menace of a 90,000-man Moorish army that has crossed the Pyrenees, invaded southern France, and burned Bordeaux. The Frankish leader Charles Martel (Charles the Hammer), 44, routs the Moors, killing their Yemenite general and sending them back into Iberia.

✊ The Moors continue to harry the coasts of Europe, taking slaves—women along with men—that are sold in the markets of Venice.

749

✘ The Japanese emperor Shomu abdicates at age 48 after a weak 25-year reign that has been dominated by his wife (and aunt), Komyo, a commoner whom he married at age 16. Their daughter, 31, will reign until 758 as the empress Koken, but Komyo and

749

her nephew, Nakamaro Fujiwara, control the government.

∞ The empress Komyo (above) has founded the Todai Temple at Nara, which is completed after 6 years of construction.

750

✘ The Abbasid caliphate, which will rule most of the Islamic empire for 350 years, is inaugurated by a descendant of the prophet Mohammed's uncle.

753

∞ The Anglo-Saxon missionary Boniface (Wynfrith) at Mainz writes a letter to the English king Aethelbald saying, in part, "Your contempt for lawful matrimony, were it for chastity's sake, would be laudable, but since you wallow in luxury and even in adultery with nuns, it is disgraceful and damnable. . . . We have heard that almost all the nobles of the Mercian kingdom, following your example, desert their lawful wives and live in guilty intercourse with adulteresses and nuns."

756

✘ The Chinese emperor Xuanzong abdicates after a 44-year reign following the death of his favorite concubine, Yang Guifei, who had been his daughter-in-law. She was the patron of his Mongol general An Lushan, who has rebelled, forcing Xuanzong and Yang Guifei to flee. The emperor's bodyguards have blamed Yang Guifei for their plight and demanded her death, and the emperor has permitted her to be strangled by his chief eunuch to appease the bodyguards.

The Donation of Pepin begins the temporal power of the papacy. Pepin III, king of the Franks, has taken lands that legally belong to the eastern empire and gives them to Pope Stephen II.

758

✘ The Japanese empress Koken abdicates in favor of her father's cousin, a grandson of the late Tenmu,

who will reign until 764 as the emperor Junin. Her mother, Komyo, and Komyo's nephew, Nakamaro Fujiwara, continue to hold the reins of government, but Komyo will die in 760.

761

✘ The former Japanese empress Koken, who has never married, is "cured" of a disease by the priest Dokyo, who has used prayers and potions; he becomes Koken's court favorite, arousing the jealousy of the emperor Junin.

764

✘ A revolt against the Japanese empress mother, Koken, and her favorite, Dokyo, is led by Nakamaro Fujiwara, but the revolt is suppressed, the emperor Junin is forced into exile, and Koken reassumes the imperial throne. She takes the name Shotoku, appoints Dokyo prime minister, and begins a new reign that will continue until 770.

768

✘ The Frankish king Pepin the Short dies September 24 at age 54. His son Charles, 26, who will be called Charles the Great, or Charlemagne, and will reign until 814, stands well over 6 feet tall, is a superb athlete, can speak Latin and understand Greek, but cannot learn to write. He inherits half of Pepin's realm, his brother Carloman the other half, but Charles has come to loathe his wife, Himeltrud, who has borne him a hunchbacked son and a daughter. He regards with a certain awe the Church doctrine that marriage is an inviolable sacrament but is not willing to discipline his own appetites, so while he prays forgiveness for his sins he does not let his marriage vows interfere with his fleshly pleasures.

770

✘ The Frankish queen mother Bertrada suggests to her son Charlemagne that he marry a Lombard princess, telling him that he can divorce his wife, Himeltrud, for reasons of state without mentioning his personal reasons for the divorce. Desiderius, king of the Lombards, whose daughter Liutberga is married to Charlemagne's cousin Tassilo, duke of Bavaria, desires a marital alliance with the Franks, with his daughter marrying Charlemagne while Charlemagne's only sister, Gisla, marries his son and co-ruler Adelchis. Bertrada travels to the Lombard court at Pavia, concludes the arrangements, and returns with the Lombard princess. Pope Stephen II gets wind of the forthcoming nuptials and writes to the Frankish court, "This would not be a marriage but disgraceful concubinage. . . . Would it not be the height of madness if the glorious race of the Franks . . . were to be contaminated by a union with the perfidious and stinking Lombards, who cannot even be called a nation and who have brought leprosy into the world?" Instead of having his sister marry Adelchis, Charlemagne sends her to a convent (she will become abbess of Chelles but continue to be a frequent guest at Charlemagne's secular court), and while he does marry the Lombard princess he will divorce her next year and send her back to Pavia.

The Japanese empress Shotoku (formerly Koken), now 53, abdicates in favor of a great-grandson of the late emperor Tenji, who will reign until 781 as the emperor K nin. She soon thereafter dies.

771

✗ Charlemagne becomes king of all the Franks December 4 upon the death of his brother Carloman, king of Austrasia, whose widow, Gaberga, flees with her two sons to the court of the Lombard king Desiderius at Pavia, where she finds a warm welcome (Desiderius is furious at Charlemagne for having divorced his daughter). Charlemagne, having repudiated his two previous marriages, has taken as his new wife a 13-year-old Swabian girl, Hildigard, who will bear him nine children.

774

✗ Charlemagne becomes the first Frankish king to visit Rome. He confirms the Donation of Pepin made in 756 while making it clear that he is sovereign even in papal lands.

780

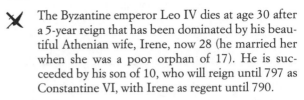

✗ The Byzantine emperor Leo IV dies at age 30 after a 5-year reign that has been dominated by his beautiful Athenian wife, Irene, now 28 (he married her when she was a poor orphan of 17). He is succeeded by his son of 10, who will reign until 797 as Constantine VI, with Irene as regent until 790.

∞ The queen mother Irene (above) restores image worship.

783

✗ Charlemagne's wife, Hildigard, dies in childbirth April 30 after her ninth confinement in less than 13 years of marriage. His mother, Bertrada, dies in mid-July and is buried with great ceremony beside his father in the Abbey of St. Denis. Needing a mother for his many children by Hildigard and Himeltrud, Charlemagne marries Fastrada, the young daughter of an East Frankish count named Radolf, and makes her his queen at Worms, where she will interfere in affairs of state and make herself generally unpopular.

785

✊ The Synod of Paderborn states that it is a deception produced by the devil to believe that a woman can voluntarily join the legions of the devil and be granted magical powers. It sets the death penalty for any who burn a woman on the grounds that she is a "witch," and Charlemagne confirms the ordinance. But Augustine and other founders of the Church wrote about the existence of succubi and other evil female spirits, and although the Church has discouraged the belief in witches there are occasional accusations that women possessed of evil spirits have stolen semen from sleeping men, caused waning powers, impotence, sterility, and miscarriages, inflicted the private parts with diseases and deformities, and caused nightmares and dreams of forbidden activities (*see* 1324).

789

✗ Offa II, king of Mercia, marries off his daughter Eadburgh to Beorhric, king of Wessex, who will prove no match for her intrigues. She involves herself in court matters and will soon have all her husband's favorite courtiers removed, by either denouncing them or personally poisoning them (*see* 802).

794

 Charlemagne's fourth wife, Fastrada, dies August 10 after 11 years of marriage. He consoles himself with Liutgard, a beautiful young Alemannian girl whom he marries and moves into his new palace at Aachen, where he will live for his remaining 20 years. Liutgard shares Charlemagne's interest in the liberal arts and is his first intellectual wife.

797

The Byzantine emperor Constantine VI, 27, is seized and blinded in July on orders from his mother, Irene, who has been placed in control of the empire by a new army uprising. Observing her son's infatuation with her attendant, Theodote, she has manipulated him into a bigamous marriage that has antagonized the public as well as the Church (from whom she has concealed her belief in image worship). Now 45, she deposes Constantine, has him flogged, and begins a 5-year reign as first Byzantine empress.

800

Charlemagne is crowned head of the western Roman Empire at Rome on Christmas Day, but the coronation is not recognized by Irene, empress of the eastern Roman Empire. Charlemagne's fifth wife, Liutgard, has taken ill in the spring and died childless. He sends a proposal of marriage to the Byzantine empress Irene, who at 50 is still considered the most beautiful woman in Europe.

9th Century

802

The Byzantine empress Irene, who has blinded her own son, is deposed by a conspiracy of patricians upon whom she has lavished honors and favors in a 5-year reign of prosperity. They exile her to Lesbos, where she is obliged to support herself by spinning (she will die there next year), and replace her with the minister of finance, who will reign until 811 as Nicephorus I, restoring iconoclasm. The fall of Irene destroys Charlemagne's fantasy of uniting the eastern and western empires.

Beorhric of Wessex dies after drinking a chalice of poison intended by his wife, Eadburgh, for one of the king's favorites. Left with no protection in court, she seizes whatever gold and jewelry she can and flees to the court of Charlemagne, who accepts a portion of her wealth and makes her abbess of a powerful convent. She will break her vow of chastity, be driven from the convent, and die poverty-stricken in Italy.

814

Charlemagne dies of pleurisy January 28 at age 71. His son Lothair, 36, whose twin brother died in infancy, becomes Holy Roman Emperor and will reign until 840 as Louis I (the Pious), a name derived from Clovis, to begin the Carolingian Empire.

860

The Hiragana alphabet becomes popular among Japanese women. This phonetic alphabet will be further simplified and reduced to 51 basic characters that will be used to supplement the Konji (Chinese) alphabet, which contains thousands of ideographic characters.

10th Century

904

The Saracen corsair Leo of Tropoli storms Thessalonica July 31, loots the town, and carries off 20,000 of its men and women into slavery.

907

China's Tang dynasty comes to an end after 289 years as the Khitan Mongols begin to conquer much of the country. Five different dynasties will assert imperial authority in the next 52 years; none will exercise much power beyond the Yellow River Basin (*see* 960).

911

Mercian forces in Britain rout Danish invaders at a battle near Tettenhall. Commanding the Mercians are their ealdorman Aethelred and his wife, Aethelflaed, eldest daughter of the late Alfred the Great, who becomes leader of her husband's people upon his death later in the year.

914

England's Warwick Castle near Stratford-upon-Avon is fortified by Aethelflaed, who leads the fight against Danish invaders.

918

Aethelflaed is killed in June at age 48 while fighting the Danes. She has united Mercia, conquered Wales, and become *de facto* ruler of the Danes and Mercians. Her daughter Aelfwyn inherits the crown.

919

Aelfwyn loses her throne to her mother's brother Edward, who will rule England until 924.

921

Ludmilla, wife of Bohemia's first Christian duke, is murdered by her pagan daughter-in-law, Drahomira. She will be canonized and become the patron saint of Bohemia.

922

France's Charles III (the Simple) is deposed by rebellious barons and replaced as king of the Franks by a usurper. Charles gathers an army to march against him.

923

The Battle of Soissons June 15 ends in defeat for Charles III, who is imprisoned by the barons and will die in 929. He has killed the usurper Robert, and the barons elect Rudolf, duke of Burgundy, king of the Franks.

924

 Edward, son of England's Alfred the Great, dies July 17 and is succeeded by Athelstan, who will reign until 940.

936

 Rudolf, duke of Burgundy, dies and is succeeded as king of France by a nephew of England's Athelstan, whose mother fled with him after the imprisonment of her husband, Charles, in 922. The new king will reign until 954 as Louis IV d'Outremer.

The German king Henry the Fowler dies July 2 at age 60 after a 17-year reign in which he has established Saxon town life. His son of 23 will be crowned Holy Roman Emperor in 962 and reign until 973 as Otto I.

940

 The Anglo-Saxon king Athelstan of England dies after a 16-year reign and is succeeded by his son, who will reign until 946 as Edmund. Irish-Norse Vikings led by Olaf conquer York and force Edmund to cede territory to them.

944

 Danish settlers help the Anglo-Saxon king Edmund regain the territory he ceded to Olaf in 940.

950

 Berengar II, 50, is crowned king of Italy upon the death of Lothair, son of Hugh of Italy. Berengar imprisons Lothair's widow, Adelaide (Adelheide), 19, a daughter of Burgundy's Rudolf II, but she is rescued by the German king Otto I of Saxony, 38, who will marry her next year as his second wife (he

married Edward the Elder's daughter Edith in 930) (*see* 962).

954

 France's Louis IV dies September 10 at age 33 and is succeeded by his son Lothair, 13, who will reign until 986.

955

 Otto I of Saxony defeats the Magyars August 10 in the Battle of Lechfeld, ending 50 years of Magyar threats to the West.

960

 The Northern Song dynasty, which will rule China until 1279, begins to restore China's unity.

962

Otto I (the Great) is crowned Holy Roman Emperor February 2 and his wife, Adelaide, is crowned empress. He will revive the western empire and come into growing conflict with Constantinople.

963

The dissolute Byzantine emperor Romanus II dies at age 25, probably of poison administered by his wife, Theophano.

969

The Byzantine emperor Nicephorus is murdered at the palace in Constantinople by his Armenian general John Zimiskes, who has been his wife's lover.

973

The Holy Roman Emperor Otto I dies May 7 at age 60 after an 11-year reign. Survived by his widow,

Adelaide, now 42, he is succeeded by their son, 18, who last year took as his wife the Byzantine princess Theophano, daughter of Romanus II. Adelaide will exert great influence on the new emperor, although her lavish philanthropies will be a source of contention between them, and he will reign until late 983 as Otto II.

Cloves, ginger, pepper, and other Eastern spices are available for purchase in the marketplace at Mainz, reports the Moorish physician-merchant Ibrahim ibn Yaacub, who has visited that city. The spices have been brought to Mainz by itinerant Jewish merchants, known as "Radanites," who have kept some international trade channels open in the three centuries of conflict between the Christian and Islamic worlds. In addition to spices, the Radanites have traded in numerous other commodities, transporting furs, woolen cloth, Frankish swords, eunuchs, and white female slaves to the Orient, while returning to Christian Europe with musk, pearls, precious stones, aloes, and spices that include cinnamon.

975

The mother of Japanese aristocrat Michitsuna Fujiwara completes her *Day-Fly Diary* (*Kagero Nikki*), relating the difficulties of married life in the years since 954.

978

England's Edward II is assassinated March 18 at Corfe Castle in Dorsetshire at age 15 in a conspiracy engineered by his stepmother, Elfthryth, who wants the crown for her son of 10. The boy succeeds Edward the Martyr and will reign until 1016 as Ethelred the Unready.

983

The Holy Roman Emperor Otto II dies suddenly in his palace at Rome December 7 at age 28. He is succeeded by his son of 3, who is crowned German king Christmas Day at Aix-la-Chapelle by Germans unaware of the emperor's death and will reign until

1002 as Otto III with his mother, Theophano, exercising power until 991 and his grandmother, Adelaide (Adelheide), now 52, and Archbishop Willigis of Mainz taking over until 996.

984

The German boy-king Otto III is seized early in the year by the deposed duke of Bavaria, Henry the Quarrelsome, 33. Henry (Heinrich der Zanker) claims the regency as a member of the reigning house but is forced to hand over the boy to his mother, Theophano, who arrives with the boy's grandmother, Adelaide (Adelheid).

987

Louis V of the Franks dies in May, and it is alleged that his mother, Emma, poisoned him. His death at age 20 ends the Carolingian dynasty founded by Charlemagne in 800, and the Capetian dynasty that will rule until 1328 comes to power in the person of Hugh Capet, now 49.

996

Otto the Great's grandson, now 16, is crowned Otto III at Rome May 21, and his grandmother, Adelaide (Adelheide), retires to a convent that she has founded at Seltz in the Alsace, where she will die in 999.

1000

The Japanese emperor Ichijo, now 20, makes his wife Sadako (Teishi), 25, empress, but she dies after 10 months and Akiko, 12, becomes empress.

 Nonfiction: *The Pillow-Book of Seish nagon* will be compiled in the next 15 years by a lady-in-waiting to the late Japanese empress Sadako (above). Daughter of the wit Mutosuke Kiyowara, Seish nagon, now 37, will fill her notes and comments with scathing criticisms and polished indelicacies that will make her diaries popular for centuries.

11th Century

1015

 Fiction: *The Tale of Genji* (*Genji monogatari*) by Japanese baroness Shikibu Murasaki, 35, will be a classic of world literature. Widowed at age 21, the baroness has become a lady-in-waiting to the empress Akiko and has probably written her long novel to be read as entertainment for the empress (*see* 1939).

Japanese women, not men, wrote their great medieval classics, including The Tale of Genji.

1028

 The Byzantine emperor Constantine VIII dies at age 68 and is succeeded by his daughter Zoë, 48.

She marries Romanus III Argyrolpolus, 60, and makes him co-emperor.

1032

 Robert II, Duke of Normandy, helps France's Henri I defeat his mother, Constance, and her younger son Robert, ending the French civil war.

1034

 The Byzantine empress Zoë poisons her husband, Romanus III, and marries the epileptic weakling Michael IV Paphiagonian, with whom she will reign until 1041.

1040

Lady Godiva rides naked through the streets of Coventry to persuade her husband, Leofric, earl of Mercia, to remit the heavy taxes that oppress the citizens (year approximate). The earl has said that he would grant his wife's request if she would ride naked through the streets, Lady Godiva (Godgifu) has issued a proclamation asking all citizens to remain indoors with their windows shut, she has only her long hair to cover her on the ride, her husband keeps his word and abolishes the taxes, but a local tailor is reputedly struck blind because he peeped.

Did Lady Godiva really ride naked through the streets of Coventry to spare its citizens from heavy taxes? LIBRARY OF CONGRESS

1042

✗ The Byzantine emperor Michael V Kalaphates shuts the empress Zoë up in a cloister, but Constantinople's nobility rises against him, locks him up in a monastery, and releases Zoë. She marries the scholarly Constantine IX Monomachus, 42, with whom she will reign until 1050.

1050

✗ The Byzantine empress Zoë dies at age 70, and her older sister, Theodora, who has shared the throne since 1042, is left to rule with Constantine IX. He has spent huge sums of money on luxuries and public buildings with a profligacy that has weakened the empire.

1051

✗ William, duke of Normandy, 23, marries Matilda, 17, daughter of Baldwin V, count of Flanders, and granddaughter of France's King Robert (year approximate). Baldwin's wife, Adela, is a daughter of the French king. The Council of Reims 2 years ago forbade the marriage, possibly for reasons of slight consanguinity, but Baldwin takes his daughter to Eu, the wedding takes place, and William takes his bride to Rouen. Standing only four feet two (he is five feet ten), she will bear him four sons and at least five daughters (*see* 1059).

1059

∞ Pope Nicholas II, at the second Lateran Council, sanctions the marriage in 1051 of William, duke of Normandy, with Matilda of Flanders, allegedly on condition that each endow a monastic house at Caen.

✒ The daughter of Japanese nobleman Takasue Sugawara loses her husband, Toshimitsu Tachibana, and, at age 50, begins her autobiography *Sarashina nikki* (*Sarashina Diary*), describing the life of an aristocratic family of the period.

1066

✗ England's Edward the Confessor dies January 5, his brother-in-law Harold Godwinson succeeds to the throne January 6 as Harold II, but William, duke of Normandy, lands with an invasion fleet September 28 at Pevensey. The Battle of Hastings October 14 ends in victory for William, Harold II is killed, William is crowned king of the English December 25, he will be known as William the Conqueror, and he will reign until 1087 as William I.

1068

✗ William the Conqueror brings his wife, Matilda, over to England, where she is crowned queen at Westminster in a great Whitsuntide gathering of English nobility.

1071

✗ A two-pronged fork is introduced to Venice by a Greek princess who marries the doge. Rich Venetians adopt the new fashion.

1077

✗ His barefoot penance in the snow at Canossa January 21 wins absolution for the German king Henry IV, 26, who has come to the stronghold of Matilda, the "Great Countess" of Tuscany, 30, to make rapprochement with Pope Gregory VII (who has excommunicated him). Matilda, whose husband, Godfrey the Hunchback, duke of Lorraine, died last year, is a strong supporter of the pope and has led her troops against Henry, whose "submission" is only a tactical ploy.

1081

✗ The German king Henry IV invades Italy and places Matilda, marchioness of Tuscany, under the imperial ban for supporting Pope Gregory VII. She refuses to make peace.

1083

∞ Matilda, queen to England's William the Conqueror, dies November 2 at age 49 and is buried at the nunnery that she has founded at Caen.

1085

∞ Pope Gregory VII dies May 25 at Salerno, discredited in most eyes. Allies of the German emperor Henry IV ravage her lands, but Matilda of Tuscany refuses to recognize the antipope Clement III, favoring instead Pope Urban II, who will enjoy her support until his death in 1099.

1100

 Diseases of Women by Italian gynecologist Trotula Platearius will remain a major textbook on the subject for the next 7 centuries (year approximate). Professor of medicine at the University of Salerno, Platearius is far ahead of her time in understanding the need for cleanliness and exercise.

12th Century

1107

Urraca of Aragon succeeds to the throne of León-Castile upon the death of her father. A widow of 27 with two infant sons, she will reign until 1126, warring for 13 of those 19 years against her coarse second husband, Alfonso of Aragon.

1118

Japan's emperor Toba, 15, takes as his wife the pretty 17-year-old mistress of his grandfather, the ex-emperor Shirakawa. Shoshi is a daughter of Kimizane Fujiwara and is pregnant with Shirakawa's son Sutoku.

1121

The Concordat of Worms condemns French theologian-philosopher Pierre Abélard, 42, for his teachings of the Trinity, and he is castrated by the hirelings of one Fulbert, whose niece Héloïse he has secretly married. Abélard withdraws to a monastery, pursued by his former student, Héloïse, and begins a persecuted life of wandering from one monastery to another, founding the priory of the Paraclete at which Héloïse will be prioress (see 1140).

1126

León-Castile's queen Urraca dies after a 19-year reign and is succeeded by her son, who will reign until 1157 as Alfonso VII.

Melissande succeeds to the throne of Jerusalem upon the death of Baldwin; eldest daughter of the Crusader king Baldwin II and his Armenian wife, Morphia, she marries Fulke V of Anjou, 24, with whom she will reign jointly beginning in 1131.

1133

The German king Lothair II arrives at Rome in March with Pope Innocent II, who crowns him emperor at the Church of the Lateran June 4 and hands over to him as papal fiefs the vast estates of Matilda, marchioness of Tuscany, which he secures for his daughter Gertrude and her husband, Henry the Proud of Bavaria.

1135

Melissande of Jerusalem is reconciled with her husband, Fulke V of Anjou, after a period of estrangement occasioned by her growing power and rumors that she has had adulterous relations with a rebel youth (see 1129; 1143).

England's Henry I dies December 1 at age 67 after a 35-year reign (his brother Curthose has died earlier as a prisoner at Cardiff). He is succeeded by his nephew Stephen of Blois, 38, who asserts his claim to the throne in opposition to claims by Henry's daughter Matilda, 33, widow of the late emperor Henry V, whose succession was accepted by England's barons in 1126 (her father made them all swear fealty to her) and who was married 2 years later to Geoffrey Plantagenet of Anjou (see 1138).

1136

∞ German nun Hildegard von Bingen, 38, becomes abbess of a Benedictine monastery at Disibodensberg upon the death of her mentor, the recluse Jutta of Spanheim, to whom she was sent at age 8 by her parents (they had promised their tenth child to the Church). Hildegard began having visions in childhood, they intensified later, and she took the veil at age 15 (*see* 1148).

✒ *Historia calamitatus mearum* by Pierre Abélard describes his love affair with Héloïse (*see* 1121; 1140).

1137

✗ William X, duke of Aquitaine and count of Poitou, dies, leaving his daughter Eleanor of Guienne, 15, as duchess of Aquitaine and countess of Poitou. Her feudal overlord Louis VI (Louis the Fat) sends his son of 16, Louis Capet, to Bordeaux to marry her but dies a few weeks later, August 1, at age 56 after a 29-year reign. Eleanor of Aquitaine becomes queen of France; her husband will reign until 1180 as Louis VII, but her own destiny will be different (*see* 1146).

1138

✗ The Battle of the Standard fought in August near Northallerton ends in defeat for Scotland's David I, who has invaded England in support of Matilda against the usurper Stephen of Blois, but David does take possession of Northumberland.

1139

✗ England's Bishop of Winchester assembles a synod at Westminster to hear charges of impiety against the usurper Stephen of Blois. Princess Matilda lands September 22 on the south coast of England and asserts her right to the throne of her late father, joining forces with Henry I's widow, Adeliza (Adelais), in an insurrection. Adeliza, who had expected Matilda to bring a larger force, grows fearful. Matilda holds Arundel Castle but, to ease her stepmother's fears, gives it up to Stephen, who allows her to leave for Bristol and thence to join her half brother Robert, earl of Gloucester (*see* 1135; 1138).

1140

✗ The Holy Roman Emperor Conrad III captures the fortress of Weinsberg from the Welf in December but permits the women of the town to leave. Each is permitted to take with her as much property as she can carry on her back, and each comes out bearing on her back a husband, father, or son, who thus escapes.

∞ Pierre Abélard is condemned for his "heresies" by the Council of Sens and sets out for Rome to present his defense.

1141

✗ England's King Stephen is surprised and captured February 2 while laying siege to Lincoln Castle (*see* 1139). Queen Matilda (or Maud) reigns for 6 months as "Domina of the English" while Stephen is held captive, but Stephen's supporters secure his release in exchange for the earl of Gloucester (*see* 1142).

1142

✗ Stephen of Blois lays siege to Oxford Castle, where England's Matilda and her supporters are brought to the edge of starvation. In late December, with the Thames River frozen and snow covering the region, they steal out of the castle dressed in white, get past Stephen's pickets, and travel six miles on foot to Abingdon, whence they are able to ride to Wallingford. A 5-year period of anarchy begins.

∞ Pierre Abélard dies at age 63 while en route to Rome. His body will be given to his widow, Héloïse, who will be buried beside him in 1164 (both will be reentombed at Paris in 1817).

1143

✗ Melissande of Jerusalem becomes regent for her son, Baldwin III, 13, upon the death of her husband, Fulke V of Anjou. They are crowned together, and she acts as queen (*see* 1152).

1143

England's Matilda retires to Normandy, which has submitted to the earl of Anjou during Stephen's captivity.

1146 ——————————————

 Eleanor of Aquitaine, now 24, announces at Vézelay on Easter Sunday that she is turning over her thousands of vassals to the Abbé Bernard of Clairvaux for a Second Crusade, which she vows to lead herself. On the day of the Crusaders' departure, she rides up on a white horse, clad in gilded buckskin boots and armor, surrounded by Sybelle, countess of Flanders; Mamille of Roucy; Florine of Bourgogne; and Faydide of Toulouse, themselves all armored. She meets with the Byzantine emperor Manuel Comnenus at Constantinople, proceeds by sea to Syria, which is ruled by her uncle, Raymond of Poitiers, and continues on to Jerusalem, where she is welcomed by Melissande, queen of the Christians.

1147 ——————————————

 France's Louis VII seizes his wife, Eleanor of Aquitaine, and takes her prisoner in order to get her away from her uncle, Raymond of Poitiers, prince of Antioch. She has found the sensuous indulgence of life as practiced by eastern Christians in Raymond's court far more attractive than the tedious routines of Paris.

1148 ——————————————

 Hildegard von Bingen founds a new monastery at Rupertsberg in the Rhine Valley near Bingen and settles there with 18 sisters (date approximate). She has been working since 1141 on her book *Scivias,* recording the 26 revelations she has received, and will not complete it until 1151 (*see* 1136; 1163).

1152 ——————————————

 France's Louis VII has his marriage to Eleanor of Aquitaine annulled on grounds of consanguinity and returns her lands and titles. Eleanor, now 30, has produced two daughters in 15 years but no

Eleanor of Aquitaine married Louis VII and, later, England's future Henry II, who laid claim to French lands. LIBRARY OF CONGRESS

male heir; within 2 months she marries Henry Plantagenet, now 19, count of Anjou, Maine, and Touraine and—by consent of his mother, Matilda—duke of Normandy, who is Louis's most dangerous rival in northern France and who gains by marriage domains that make him master of more than half of France. In the next 15 years Eleanor will bear Henry eight children (see 1154).

Rivalry between Melissande of Jerusalem and her son, Baldwin III, becomes so intense that they divide their realm, with Baldwin reigning in the north while Melissande rules Judea and Sumeria (see 1143; 1154).

1154

✗ Melissande of Jerusalem and her son, Baldwin III, end their hostilities and will rule together until her death in 1160 at the convent she has founded at Bethany.

England's king Stephen dies October 25 at age 54 and is succeeded by his adopted son, Henry Plantagenet, who is crowned at age 21 and will reign until 1189 as Henry II, inaugurating a Plantagenet dynasty that will rule England until 1399. Eleanor of Aquitaine, formerly queen of France, becomes queen of England.

✗ England's domestic wine industry begins to decline as cheap French wines are introduced by Eleanor of Aquitaine (above).

1155

♄ Physica (Liber simplicis medicinae, or Book of Simple Medicine) by Hildegard von Bingen lists nearly 300 medicinal herbs, explaining when to pick them and how to use them (year approximate). Causae et curae (Liber compositae medicinae, or Book of Medicine Carefully Arranged) by Hildegard catalogues 47 diseases, noting that women tend to miscarry or produce defective infants if they conceive before age 20 or after age 50. She advises a pregnant woman to hold a jasper (a piece of quartz) in her hand throughout her 9-month term and during the birth because "the tongue of the ancient serpent extends itself to the sweat of the infant emerg-

ing from that mother's womb, and he lies in wait for both mother and infant at the time."

1159

✗ An English army invades Toulouse to assert the rights of Henry II's wife, Eleanor of Aquitaine, but Louis VII drives the English off.

1163

∞ A letter of protection drawn up April 16 by the Holy Roman Emperor Frederick Barbarossa refers to Hildegard von Bingen, now 65, as "abbess." Hildegard, whose books Physica and Causae et curae appeared in the last decade, completes her book Liber vite miridorum.

1165

∞ Hildegard von Bingen founds a daughter house at Nibingen on the opposite bank of the Rhine from Rupertsberg near Rüdesheim (date approximate; see 1163). She has begun making extended missions through the German states (see 1170).

1169

✗ England's Henry II makes an effort to end the strife between him and his wife, Eleanor of Aquitaine, in order that he may dally in western Herefordshire with his mistress, Rosamund Clifford, daughter of Walter de Clifford. He divides the succession to his lands among his sons and allows Eleanor to retire to Poitiers, placing her in control of her French domains. Her second son, Richard, accompanies her and is made heir to to both Aquitaine and Poitou.

1170

♠ Hildegard von Bingen completes her book Liber divinorum operum—three works on the trilogy of apocalyptic, prophetic, and symbolic visions. Known as the "Sybil of the Rhine," she has long

il auff come tour espanier ples in
racles q il uit
Ci commce la bataille de Rocenaus r
la mort de Ro

Pus q klm li trespuissanz emp et
tres renomez or conquise toute ga
lice r toute espagne r sozmise ala foi
cristiene alonoz de dieu r de mo seign
s Jaq il retorna en stance r fist sesoz

The writings of Hildegard von Bingen illuminated a dark age; kings and popes sought her advice.

been consulted by popes, emperors, kings, archbishops, abbots, abbesses, the lower clergy, and laymen, carrying on extensive correspondence with all.

Eleanor of Aquitaine and her daughter Marie establish a "Court of Love" at Poitiers to teach concepts of courtly love.

1172

Eleanor of Aquitaine raises Aquitaine against her faithless husband, Henry II, and he is forced to reconcile his differences with the pope (*see* 1169).

Alrude, Countess of Bertinoro, leads an army to lift the siege of Aucona. She scatters the forces that have invested the town and defeats ambushers on her way home.

1173

The English princes Richard and Geoffrey lead a rebellion against their father, Henry II, with support from Eleanor of Aquitaine, but the House of Commons gives hearty support to the king (*see* 1172; 1174).

1174

Henry II crosses the Channel and captures his wife, Eleanor of Aquitaine, as she tries to flee Poitiers disguised as a man. She has been conspiring with French lords on behalf of her sons Richard and Geoffrey, whom Henry is unable to catch, but she will be imprisoned in various castles for the next 15 years.

Marie, countess of Champagne, daughter of Eleanor of Aquitaine by Louis VII, issues a proclamation: "We declare and we hold as firmly established that love cannot exert its powers between two people who are married to each other, for lovers give each other everything freely, under no compulsion or necessity, but married people are in duty bound to give in to each other's desires and deny themselves to each other in nothing."

1178

Georgia's Giorgi III has his daughter Tamara, 19, crowned as co-ruler of the Caucasian kingdom. He defeated his great-nephew Demna, the rightful ruler, in battle 4 years ago at Hereti, and had him blinded and then castrated.

1179

German abbess Hildegard von Bingen dies at Rupertsberg near Bingen September 17 at age 81 after a career in which she has founded a monastery and written scientific and medical treatises, accounts of her revelations, and lyrical poetry. Her visions and miracles have made her famous throughout Europe.

🎼 Motets and songs composed by Hildegard von Bingen (above) will be performed for much of the next millennium.

1180

✗ France's Louis VII dies September 18 at age 59 and is succeeded by his son of 15, who will rule until 1223 as Philip II Augustus.

1184

✗ Georgia's co-ruler Tamara, now 25, becomes sole ruler upon the death of her father, Giorgi III; last of the direct line of the Bagrationis who have ruled since 975, Queen Tamara (she is consecrated as such by the Archbishop of Kutaisi and also proclaimed "King of Kartli") begins a 24-year reign that will raise Georgia to the peak of its political power.

1185

✗ The Japanese emperor becomes the puppet that he will remain until 1868. The Minamoto family defeats the Taira clan at the Battle of Danoura April 24 on the Inland Sea, and Japan enters a centuries-long period of feudal wars among the feudal lords (*daimyo*) who rule under the shōguns with support from retainer-knights (*samurai*). Masako Hōjo, now 28, married Yoritomo Minamoto 8 years ago against her father's wishes (Minamoto had been exiled to Izu and had no title), but her father, Tokimasa Hōjo, has allied his forces with those of the Minamoto family.

1186

✗ The Kamakura period, which will dominate Japan until 1333, begins under the Minamoto leader Yoritomo, now 39, whose family is based in Kamakura. His power derives in large part from that of his wife's father, Tokimasa Hōjo.

1187

✗ Georgia's Queen Tamara, who has ruled under the guardianship of her father's sister Rusudani, marries George Bobolyubski, son of the Grand Prince of Kiev, but the overbearing prince devotes himself to waging war against the Muslims, drinking, and debauching with slaves and concubines.

1189

✗ England's Henry II dies July 6 at age 54 after paying homage to France's Philip II, and his widow, Eleanor of Aquitaine, finally gains her release after 15 years' imprisonment. Henry's son Richard Coeur de Lion will reign until 1199 as Richard I, spending only one year of his reign in England and visiting the British Isles only twice. Richard refuses to honor his contract to marry Alais, sister of the French king, to whom he has been betrothed since age 3, but at year's end he and Philip exchange pledges of good faith as they prepare to join the Third Crusade. Richard's mother, Eleanor of Aquitaine, now 67, will serve as regent in his absence.

Queen Tamara of Georgia allows her husband, Prince George Bobolyubski, to go into exile and takes a new husband, the Ossetian prince David Sosland, by whom she will have a son, Giorgi, in 1194 and a daughter, Rusudani, in 1195.

A papal bull forbids women to join the Third Crusade, but some will go with the knights to fight in the Holy Land despite the bull, just as they did in the first two crusades.

1190

✗ Richard the Lion-hearted rescues his sister Joanna, queen of Sicily, 25, while en route to the Holy Land. She has been held hostage by the usurper Tancred of Lecce since the death of her husband, William II of Sicily, to whom she was married at age 11.

1191

✗ The Russian prince George Bobolyubski leads a rebellion of disaffected Georgian noblemen against his ex-wife, Queen Tamara, but her forces win two pitched battles, the prince is captured, and Tamara allows him to withdraw to Byzantium.

Richard the Lion-hearted marries Berengaria of Navarre, 19, who is escorted to Cyprus for the wedding by Richard's mother, Eleanor of Aquitaine. Berengaria accompanies Richard and his sister Joanna to Palestine, where it is suggested that Joanna marry Saladin's brother and rule the kingdom of Jerusalem jointly with him.

1192

✗ Richard the Lion-hearted loses 95,000 of his 100,000 Third Crusaders in the Palestinian desert but makes an honorable peace with Saladin and leaves Jerusalem October 9. Traveling in flimsy disguise, he is captured December 20 at Vienna by Leopold, duke of Austria (*see* 1193).

1193

✗ Leopold, duke of Austria, surrenders Richard the Lion-hearted to the Holy Roman Emperor Henry VI, who demands a ransom of 130,000 marks for his return (*see* 1192). Richard's mother, Eleanor of Aquitaine, works to raise the ransom money (*see* 1194).

✊ Licensed prostitution begins in Japan (*see* Yoshiwara, 1617).

1194

✗ Richard the Lion-hearted returns to England briefly in March following payment of the first installment of his ransom, raised by his mother,

Eleanor of Aquitaine, who has traveled to Austria to gain his release (*see* 1193). His wife, Berengaria, remains in France (she will never set foot in England), and he arranges the marriage of his sister Joanna to Raymond, comte de Toulouse.

Marie of Champagne, daughter of Eleanor of Aquitaine (above), dies at age 53. She has reestablished at her court at Troyes the practices that Eleanor has sponsored, patronizing writers who will explain the system of courtly love. *Treatise on Love and Its Remedy* (*Tractatus de amore et de amoris remedio*) by Andreas, chaplain to Marie of Champagne, expounds earnestly on the theory and practice of courtly love (date approximate; *see* 1277).

1199

✗ Richard the Lion-hearted dies April 6 at age 32 after being wounded in the shoulder by a crossbow bolt. His brother John Lackland (or Softsword), 20, will reign until 1216.

The Japanese shōgun Yoritomo Minamoto dies at age 51, and his widow, the former Masako Hōjo, becomes the power behind her son, Yoriie, who becomes shōgun subject to the decisions of a council headed by Masako's father, Tokimasa Hōjo.

1200

✗ Eleanor of Aquitaine, now 78, leads an army that crushes a rebellion in Anjou against her second son, England's King John.

Prince George Bobolyubski tries once again to wrest the throne of Georgia from his ex-wife, Tamara. This time he has support from the Seljuk Turks, but again he is repulsed.

13th Century

1203

The Japanese shōgun Yoriie becomes ill, and fears arise that his son will gain dominance. Yoriie has married Wakasa Hiki, daughter of a powerful family that rivals the Hōjo and Minamoto families. Masako Hōjo and her father incarcerate Yoriie in a castle.

1204

Eleanor of Aquitaine dies April 1 at age 83 after a notable career in which she has been queen of both France and England. The bulk of her Aquitanian domains go to France's Philip Augustus.

The Japanese shōgun Yoriie is assassinated along with his wife and son; his younger brother, Sanetomo, 12, will be shōgun until 1219.

1205

Georgian forces led by Queen Tamara rout a Turkish army at the Battle of Basiani. She has marched with her men to the Turkish encampment on the eve of battle and been hailed with the cry "To our king!"

1206

The Beguine movement that begins to develop in Switzerland, the Rhineland, northern France, and the Low Countries brings together laywomen—all pledged to chastity, poverty, manual labor, and communal worship—into all-female, self-governing communities (year approximate). A surplus of females in this century and the next will make it impossible for many young women to marry unless they have dowries, and whereas one must have a dowry to join a convent, a beguinage has no such requirement.

1208

Pope Innocent preaches an Albigensian Crusade against the "heretic" Catharists of Albi, most of them women. The Catharist sect, which began in the 11th century, has flourished in France's Languedoc and spread into Italy, the Rhineland, and the Low Countries. Followers of Gnostic doctrine, Catharists believe that Eve was not at fault in the fall of Eden, being merely Satan's tool, that Mary Magdalene was the wife or concubine of Jesus, and that in heaven all creatures will be angels without sexual differentiation. They reject marriage for those of their number who attain perfection and refuse to consume meat or milk, which they regard as the fruits of copulation.

1209

Carcassonne surrenders after a siege by the crusader Simon de Montfort, 49, earl of Leicester and comte de Toulouse, who captures the Albigensian "heretics." A massacre of "heretic" women and children at Beziers takes a terrible toll.

The emir of Ardabil crosses the Arak mountains, slaughters 12,000 Georgians, and takes thousands more into slavery, enraging Queen Tamara.

1210

✗ Queen Tamara has her revenge upon the emir of Ardabil, taking him by surprise, killing him along with 12,000 of his people, and carrying off thousands as slaves. Her troops conduct daring raids into northern Persia, returning with booty from Marand in Azerbaijan, Tabriz, and Kazvin to her capital at Tiflis.

✊ Albigensian crusaders order "heretic" Catharists at Minerve to either renounce their faith or be burned; 140 women and men leap into the flames.

1212

✗ Queen Tamara of Georgia dies January 18 after a glorious 24-year reign and is buried in the tomb of her ancestors at Gelati.

∞ The Order of the Poor Clares (Franciscan nuns) is founded by Italian nun Clare of Assisi, 18, with help from her sister Clara and Friar Giovanni Francesco Bernardone, whose convent they joined last year over the violent objections of their parents.

A Children's Crusade sets out for the Holy Land under the leadership of a French shepherd boy known only as Stephen and a child from Cologne named Nicholas. Slave dealers kidnap Stephen's army and sell it into Egypt, Nicholas's crusade is aborted in Italy, and some 50,000 children are lost (many are sold into slavery at Marseilles).

1213

✗ The English Parliament has its beginnings in the Council of St. Albans.

1214

✗ England's King John (Lackland) imprisons his queen, Isabella of Angoulême, at Gloucester, where she gives birth to a daughter, Isabella (see 1216).

The Battle of Bouvines July 27 establishes France as a major European political power, brings Flanders under French domination, and gains the imperial crown for Frederick II, 19, who has been king of Sicily since age 3 and was married at 14 to the daughter of Aragon's Alfonso II (widow of Hungary's late Emeric).

1215

✗ The Magna Carta signed at Runnymede in mid-June limits the powers of England's monarchy. Barons meeting with John Lackland exact major concessions reaffirming traditional feudal privileges.

German nobles crown the Hohenstaufen king Frederick II at Aix-la-Chapelle July 25.

✊ Chapters VI and VII in the Magna Carta (above) say, "A widow, after the death of her husband, shall forthwith and without difficulty have her marriage portion and inheritance (*maritagium et hereditatem*); nor shall she give any thing for her dower, or for her marriage portion, or for the inheritance which her husband and she shall have held on the day of the death of that husband . . ." "Let no widow be compelled to marry, so long as she prefers to live without a husband; provided always that she gives security not to marry without our [royal] consent, if she holds of us, or without the consent of the lord of whom she holds, if she holds of another." Adult single women and widows in England have for more than a century been the equal of men in all business affairs, with laws of inheritance showing only a small bias toward male heirs, but laws with respect to married women are more complicated, women having their own dowries and property, men having the use of their wives' lands and command over their wives' chattels.

1216

✗ Genghis Khan invades the Near East with 60,000 Mongol horsemen, destroying ancient centers of civilization, ruining irrigation works, and eliminating everyone in his path—man, woman, or child.

England's John Lackland dies of dysentery October 19 at age 38 after crushing French-supported resistance to his rule in the north. His widow, Isabella of Angoulême, returns to France, where she will marry a former lover, the comte de la Marche. Her son of 9 will reign until 1272 as Henry III, but Louis VIII's wife, Blanche of Castile, 29, granddaughter of the late Eleanor of Aquitaine, tries to organize naval forces at Calais with a view to mounting an invasion force.

1218

 Genghis Khan conquers Persia, crushing all resistance and laying waste the countryside.

The Peace of Worcester ends hostilities between England's Henry III and the Welsh.

1219

Minamoto family control of the Japanese shōgunate ends in January with the assassination of the ruling shōgun, Sanetomo. His uncle, Yoshitoke Hojo, 57, installs a member of the Fujiwara family as shōgun, but he and his sister Masako hold the real power, and their family will rule Japan until 1333.

1221

Genghis Khan plunders Samarkand in his march to the West. Reports of rape and pillage reach eastern Europe, terrorizing the people.

1222

The Mongols make their first appearance in Europe as Genghis Khan invades Russian territories.

1223

The Battle of the Kalka River shows Europe the power of the Mongols. Their leader, Subutai, defeats a Russian army, but he does not press his victory and withdraws back into Asia.

1226

 France's Louis VIII dies November 8 at age 39 after conquering the South in a renewal of the crusade against Albigensian heretics. His 12-year-old son will reign until 1270 as Louis IX with the boy's mother, Blanche of Castile, now 39, serving as regent. She will effectively block efforts by ambitious vassals to weaken royal authority and return the nation to feudal anarchy.

1227

Genghis Khan dies August 18 at age 65, and his vast empire is divided among his three sons.

 Sunday crowds gather April 25 on the mainland near Venice to watch a procession advertised in advance by a messenger bearing an open letter to the effect that the goddess Venus would arise from the sea April 24 near Venice and begin to travel north toward Bohemia, breaking lances with any who would meet her in the lists. Preceded by a dozen squires dressed in white, two maids-in-waiting, and half a dozen musicians, the knight errant and minnesinger Ulrich von Lichtenstein, 26, rides up dressed as a woman, heavily veiled in a white gown with pearl headdress. He learned his knightly skills from Henry, margrave of Austria, was made a knight in 1222, and took a secret vow to devote his newly won knighthood to serving a woman whom he had never met but whom he had seen during the wedding festival of the duke of Saxony. She has spurned his offer to be her secret knight, but he challenges all the knights of Lombardy, Austria, and Bohemia to break lances with "Venus." It will take Ulrich 15 years to win the lady's love, and 2 years later she will hurt him in some cruel way, after which he will continue to find new women to whom he can play the courtly lover, the ideal knight (*compare* Dante, 1307).

1228

A Sixth Crusade embarks for the Holy Land in midsummer under the leadership of the excommunicated Holy Roman Emperor Frederick II, who uses diplomacy to achieve his ends.

1229

✠ Frederick II signs a treaty February 18 with the Egyptian sultan, who surrenders Bethlehem, Nazareth, and Jerusalem plus a corridor for use by Christian pilgrims. He enters Jerusalem March 12 and assumes the monarchy by right of his marriage in November 1225 to the late Iolande (Isabella), daughter of Jerusalem's titular king John.

✊ The Inquisition of Toulouse imposed by Albigensian crusaders forbids laypersons to read the Bible.

1230

✠ Pope Gregory and Frederick II end their hostilities in July: the emperor promises to respect papal territory, the pope absolves Frederick from excommunication.

1231

✊ The Japanese shōgun orders his people not to sell their children into slavery, but poor farmers will continue for centuries to sell their daughters, as will poor farmers in China, India, and many other parts of the world.

1233

🕐 A Japanese royal family adopts the ancient custom of staining teeth black (ohaguro). The practice begins to gain wide acceptance as a sign of beauty.

1234

✊ Armed women in several French communities rally male support to prevent the arrest of female "heretics" as the Albigensian Crusade continues.

1235

✠ The Mongols annex the Qin empire despite Qin efforts to resist them with explosive bombs.

1236

✠ Delhi's sultan Iltutmish dies and is succeeded by his daughter, Raziya, who becomes the first woman to head a Muslim state (see 1988). She will reign until 1240.

Georgia's Queen Rusudani, 41, daughter of the late Tamara, who was proclaimed "King of Kartli" upon the death of her brother, Georgi, flees Tiflis as Mongolian invaders ravish the once-great empire.

England's Henry III, now 29, marries Eleanor of Provence, 13, daughter of Raymond Berengar IV, count of Provence. The generosity of France's Louis IX has enabled Henry to keep some of England's Continental territories despite repeated military losses.

1237

✠ Mongol forces use gunpowder and possibly firearms to conquer much of eastern Europe. They devastate Poland but will fail in their efforts at conquest (see 1241).

Blanche of Rossi fights beside her husband, Battista of Padua, to defend Ezzelino in a war between the Guelfs and Ghibellines. When her husband falls in battle, the victors demand Blanche as part of the booty, but she throws herself on his tomb, causing its stone door to collapse upon her.

1239

✠ Pope Gregory IX excommunicates the Holy Roman Emperor Frederick II for a second time March 20, calling him a rake, a heretic, and the anti-Christ. The pope has taken exception to a projected marriage between Frederick's bastard son Enzio and Adelasia, heiress to Sardinia.

1240

✠ Turkish-backed Hindu troops murder the Muslim ruler Sultana Raziya and her husband, Altuniyya, October 13 after a surprise attack near Kaithal while en route to Delhi (see 1236). She was deposed early in the year and imprisoned, has married her jailer, and has persuaded him and his army to travel with her to Delhi.

Mongols of the Golden Horde conquer Kiev as they sweep through southern and central Russia.

with the bishop to give them the *consolamentum* in the event that they are wounded and cannot speak, they fight alongside the men, the bishop makes good on his promise as their situation becomes hopeless, and while the castle's military defenders are permitted to withdraw unharmed some 200 male and female Catharists are burned on a pyre.

1241

✗ The Battle of Liegnitz in Silesia ends in victory for the Mongols of the Golden Horde, who cut down the feudal nobility of eastern Europe but retire to Karakorum upon the death of their khan Ughetai (Ogadai) at age 56 in December.

1242

✗ The Mongol Golden Horde regroups on the lower Volga under the command of Batu, a grandson of the late Genghis Khan.

✊ *Il Statuto Veneto* (or *Il Statuto Giacomo Tiepolo*), promulgated for Venice under the rule of its doge Giacomo Tiepolo, requires that a husband render to his wife an account of his use of her dowry, with control of the capital sum remaining in her hands; an unfaithful wife forfeits her dowry, a widow enjoys her husband's patrimony until she remarries or dies, and should a couple renounce secular life their combined property is shared equally, with each free to do what he or she likes with the money and with parents providing for any underaged children on an equal basis (year approximate).

💲 Venice's grand doge Giacomo Tiepolo (above) carries on naval and military expeditions while settling factional disputes; his wife, Valdrada, devotes her time to supporting trading companies (year approximate).

⚕ The Mongols (above) have introduced eyeglasses and distilled alcoholic beverages into Europe.

1243

✊ Albigensian crusaders in France lay siege to Montsegur Castle, last stronghold of the Catharists. The castle's noblewomen make an arrangement

1244

✗ Jerusalem falls to Muslim mercenaries of the Egyptian pasha Khwarazmi. It will remain in Egyptian hands until 1517 and under Muslim control until 1918.

1245

✗ A council at Lyons deposes Frederick II July 27, finding him guilty of sacrilege and possible heresy. War breaks out in the German states as Pope Innocent IV orders the election of a new king.

1248

✗ A Seventh Crusade embarks for Egypt in August under the command of France's Louis IX.

1249

✗ The Seventh Crusade invades Egypt in the spring, takes Damietta without a blow, marches on Cairo, but is stopped outside Mansura.

1250

✗ The Battle of Fariskur April 6 ends in victory for Egyptian forces, who rout the scurvy-weakened crusaders of Louis IX, capture the king, massacre his men, and agree to release Louis only after he agrees to evacuate Damietta and pay a ransom of 800,000 gold pieces.

The Holy Roman Emperor Frederick II dies December 13 at age 55 after a 38-year reign. His son of 22 will reign briefly as Conrad IV.

1250

 Cinnamon, cloves, coriander, cumin, cubebs, ginger, mace, and nutmegs carried back by returning crusaders are now to be found in rich English and European houses but are in many cases valued more for their supposed medicinal value than for culinary purposes.

sack Baghdad February 10, massacre tens of thousands in a single week, and end the caliphate that has ruled from Baghdad since 762 and made the city a world center of learning and culture. Hülegu withdraws at news that his brother Mangu died late last year.

1251

 Shepherds and farmworkers in northern France abandon flocks and fields in a widespread insurrection. Marked by riots and bloody demonstrations, the revolt spreads to England and even as far as Syria before being ruthlessly suppressed.

1252

 Blanche of Castile dies at age 65 as her son, France's Louis IX, expels the nation's Jews. He led the ill-fated Seventh Crusade against her advice and fell into the hands of the Egyptian caliph (*see* 1250).

1254

 The German king Conrad IV dies in Italy May 21 at age 26. The death of the last Hohenstaufen king begins a 19-year Great Interregnum in the Holy Roman Empire.

Eleanor of Castile, 9-year-old daughter of Ferdinand III, is married to England's 15-year-old heir apparent, who will become Edward I in 1272 (*see* 1265).

1256

 Hülegu Khan's Mongols wipe out Persia's Assassins; Hülegu begins a 9-year reign, inaugurating the Ilkhan dynasty, which will rule Persia until 1349.

1258

 Persia's Hülegu Khan routs the last army of the eastern Abbasid caliphate January 17. His Mongols

1260

 The Yuan dynasty, which will rule China until 1368, is founded by a grandson of the late Genghis Khan. Kublai Khan, 44, has himself crowned emperor.

1261

 English women gain improved rights to control their own lands and money but do not have the same rights as men by any means (*see* 1215).

1264

 England's Henry III wars with the country's barons and is captured by the earl of Leicester, Simon de Montfort, after an ignominious defeat at the Battle of Lewes. Henry's wife, Eleanor of Provence, now 44, raises her own army of mercenaries to support her husband in the Baron's War, but her son Edward, 25, who has contributed to his father's defeat, is forced to give up his earldom of Chester.

1265

 Edward, Prince of Wales, escapes from his custodians, gains support from lords of the Welsh march, kills the earl of Leicester, Simon de Montfort, August 4 at Evesham, and will dictate government policy for the remaining 7 years of his father's reign.

1270

 France's Louis IX leads an Eighth Crusade, arrives at Carthage after a 17-day voyage, but dies of plague August 25. His son of 25 will reign until 1285 as Philip III.

1272

 England's Henry III dies at Westminster November 16 at age 65 after a 56-year reign. His son Edward, now 33, is away on the Eighth Crusade, together with Eleanor of Castile, princess of Wales, who will be said to have saved the prince's life by sucking the poison from a wound. Edward hears of his father's death late in the year in Sicily (*see* 1273).

1273

 England's new king Edward I pays homage to his cousin, France's Philip III, at Paris en route home from the crusade with his wife, Eleanor of Castile (*see* 1272; 1274).

The Great Interregnum, which has left the Holy Roman Empire without a ruler since 1254, ends September 29 with the election of Rudolph, count of Hapsburg, as German king.

1274

 England's Edward I lands at Dover August 2 and is crowned at Westminster August 16 together with his wife, Eleanor of Castile. His mother, Eleanor of Provence, retires to a convent, and Edward will reign until 1307.

China's Kublai Khan sends an invasion fleet to conquer Japan, but a typhoon November 20 sinks more than 200 Mongol ships along with 13,000 men sleeping aboard; the terror-stricken survivors retreat to the mainland (*see* 1281).

1277

∞ The bishop of Paris condemns the *Tractatus* of Andreas (*see* 1194), calling it an instrument of heresy and social disorder.

1278

✕ The Hapsburg family gains sovereignty over Austria to begin a dynasty that will continue until 1918.

1280

⚕ The Council of Boulogne decrees that when a mother dies in childbirth her mouth shall be held open so that the baby will not suffocate before an attempt is made to deliver it by cesarean section. The term "cesarean," or "caesarean," comes from the Latin *a caeso matris utero,* meaning to cut the mother's womb. Contrary to popular belief, Julius Caesar was delivered vaginally when he was born in 100 B.C.; cesarean section was used then only to take a baby from the body of a dead or dying mother, and Caesar's mother lived long after his birth. Ancient medical practitioners, given the choice between the survival of the mother or the baby, traditionally chose the mother. The fetus was killed inside the mother by fracturing its skull or by craniotomy—opening up the infant's skull and removing its brain. The body was then dismembered and removed. The Roman Catholic church prohibits abortion, dismemberment, or craniotomy intended to save the life of the mother (*see* 1916).

1281

✕ Kublai Khan sends a second invasion fleet to conquer Japan, but once again, as in 1274, a typhoon destroys most of the Mongol fleet, scarcely one-fifth of the invasion force survives, and the Japanese begin calling typhoons *kamikaze* (divine winds).

1282

✕ The Sicilian Vespers rebellion, which begins in a church outside Palermo at the hour of vespers March 31, leads to a wholesale massacre of the French and triggers a war that will continue for years. A French soldier has allegedly insulted a Sicilian woman, but the real basis of the rebellion is the heavy taxation imposed by Charles I (Charles d'Anjou) to equip an expedition against Constantinople.

1285

 The king of the Two Sicilies Charles I (Charles d'Anjou) dies at Foggia January 7 at age 55 as he prepares to invade Sicily again with a new fleet from Provence.

France's Philip III (the Bold) dies of plague October 5 while retreating from Gerona. His son of 17 will rule until 1314 as Philip IV.

1286

✖ Scotland's Alexander III falls from his horse March 16 while riding in the dark to visit his new queen at Kinghorn. He dies at age 43 after a 35-year reign, two sons and a daughter have predeceased him, and his only living descendant is the infant daughter of his own late daughter by the Norwegian king Eric Magnusson. Guardians are appointed to govern in the name of Margaret of Norway, but some clans rebel (*see* 1290).

1290

✖ Scotland's titular queen Margaret, Maid of Norway, reaches the Orkneys but dies there in September at age 7 under mysterious circumstances (*see* 1286). She had been betrothed to Edward, 6-year-old son of England's Edward I, and her death leaves Scotland without a monarch (*see* 1292).

1292

✖ England's Edward I resolves the question of Scottish succession, selecting John of Balliol, 43, to succeed the late Margaret, Maid of Norway.

1294

✖ China's Kublai Khan dies February 12 at age 78 after a 35-year reign that has established the Mongol (Yuan) dynasty. His grandson Timur Ojaitu continues the family rule.

1295

✳ Venetian traveler Marco Polo, 41, returns home after 17 years (1275 to 1292) in the service of the late Kublai Khan. He brings home spices, Oriental cooking ideas, and wondrous tales of the Far East.

1296

✖ The Battle of Curzola gives Genoa a victory over the Venetian fleet. The Genoese take 7,000 prisoners, including Marco Polo, who has commanded a galley. He will dictate his *Book of Various Experiences* in the next 3 years to a fellow prisoner.

1297

✖ The Confirmation of Charters reaffirms the Magna Carta of 1215. English barons and middle-class groups force Edward I to agree that the Crown may not levy a nonfeudal tax without a grant from Parliament. Edward invades northern France.

The spinning wheel began to revolutionize textile production, but most women still used distaffs and spindles.

Scotland's "Hammer and Scourge of England," William Wallace, 25, ravages Northumberland, Westmoreland, and Cumberland. He routs an English army of more than 50,000 in September at Stirling Bridge.

Wool or linen thread is usually left in its natural grey or brown but sometimes is dyed with roots, leaves, birch bark, madder, goldenrod, barberry, blackberry, woad, walnuts, flag iris, or lichens collected from the forest.

1298 ——————————————

 The invention of the spinning wheel begins to revolutionize textile production, but women in most of the world will continue for 7 centuries to hold their distaffs (long sticks, sometimes of metal) in one hand and the spindles they use as spools in the other as they spin raw wool or flax into thread.

1300 ——————————————

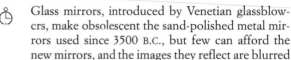 Glass mirrors, introduced by Venetian glassblowers, make obsolescent the sand-polished metal mirrors used since 3500 B.C., but few can afford the new mirrors, and the images they reflect are blurred and distorted.

14th Century

1305

Scottish patriot Sir William Wallace is betrayed and captured August 5 near Glasgow. Taken to London in fetters, he is hanged and his body drawn and quartered.

1306

The Japanese Buddhist nun Nijō, 49, begins writing her five-volume autobiographical work *Unasked Words* (*Towazugatari*) relating her love affairs beginning at age 14 with the 89th emperor Gofukakusa and, later, his brother. She became a nun in 1290 at age 32, and, since she was unable as such to attend Gofukakusa's funeral, she went disguised as a lady-in-waiting in the imperial household. Since she uses real names, her work will be kept secret in the imperial library until 1940.

1307

England's Edward I dies July 7 near Carlisle at age 68 while preparing to take the field against Scotland's Robert Bruce. His fourth and only surviving son, who assumes the throne as Edward II at age 23, immediately recalls his homosexual lover, Piers Gaveston, from exile, abandons the campaign against Robert Bruce, and devotes himself to frivolity.

The *Commedia*, which will become immortal as *The Divine Comedy* (*Divina commedia*) is begun by Italian poet Dante Alighieri, 42, who will immortalize his Florentine friends and enemies, including the late noblewoman Beatrice Portinari de' Bardi, who died in 1290, when she was 24 and Dante 25. In his *Vita nuova,* he tells of how he first saw Beatrice in 1274 when he was 9 and began to worship her although he never spoke a word to her, made no efforts to meet her, and saw her only at rare intervals. She knew nothing of his feelings toward her. Admirers of Dante will for generations accept his disembodied courtly love of Beatrice as a romantic ideal of the male-female relationship.

1308

England's Edward II journeys to France and on January 25 marries Isabella, 15, daughter of Philip IV, while his lover, Piers Gaveston, rules as regent at home. Gaveston marries the king's niece Margaret of Gloucester and receives the earldom of Cornwall.

1312

The Gascon knight Piers Gaveston, favorite of England's Edward II, is kidnapped by English barons and treacherously executed. Edward is forced to stand aside and permit 21 lords ordainers to govern the country under a series of ordinances drawn up last year.

1314

The Battle of Bannockburn June 24 assures Scottish independence. An English force of 100,000 commanded by the effeminate Edward II meets defeat at the hands of 40,000 Scotsmen under Robert Bruce, 40, who take Stirling Castle, the last Scottish castle still held by the English.

1317

 France adopts the Salic Law to exclude women from succeeding to the throne (*see* 1322; 1328).

1318

 German poet Heinrich Frauenlob von Meissen dies at age 68. Founder of a meistersinger school at Mainz, von Meissen has been called "Frauenlob," meaning "praise of women"' because he has used the word "Frau" for woman rather than the word "Weib."

1320

 The Declaration of Arbroath April 6 asserts Scottish independence in a letter from the Scottish Parliament to Pope John XXII.

1322

 France's Philip V dies at Longchamp January 2 at age 28 after a 6-year reign and is succeeded by his brother, 27, who will reign until 1328 as Charles IV, last of the direct line of Capetian kings. The accession of Charles IV establishes in principle the Salic Law adopted 5 years ago that the French throne can pass only through males; it excludes England's 9-year-old prince Edward, grandson of France's late Philip IV.

1323

 The Treaty of Northampton between Scotland and England recognizes Robert Bruce's title as Scottish king and provides for the marriage of his son David to Edward II's daughter Joanna.

1324

 Irish housewife Alice Kyteler is accused of witchcraft (*see* 785). Her first three husbands have died under allegedly mysterious circumstances, leaving their entire estates to her and her son, William Outlawe, thus enraging their other potential heirs. Her fourth is "afflicted with a wasting disease." One of her servant women swears that Kyteler is a witch and that she, herself, has participated in satanic rites on orders from her mistress; Kyteler is excommunicated, she flees to England, and her servant is burned at the stake.

1325

 England's Queen Isabelle travels to her native France and arranges the marriage of her son Edward, 12, to Philippa of Hainault, 11.

 Illiterate French "heretic" Prous Boneta is arrested at Montpellier, made to confess before the Inquisition at Carcassonne, and burnt at the stake there August 6.

1326

 The French queen of England's Edward II invades her husband's realm, which is effectively ruled by the earl of Winchester, Hugh le Despenser, and his son Hugh. Vowing revenge for the execution of the earl of Lancaster in 1322, Isabelle has the support of her paramour, Roger de Mortimer, 39, earl of March, who has been outlawed by Edward at the urging of the earl of Winchester, and Edward's supporters desert him. The king flees London October 2, taking refuge on the Glamorgan estates of the earl of Winchester. Isabelle's forces capture both Despensers and put them to death. Edward tries to escape by sea, Isabelle's men capture him November 16, and they imprison him at Kenilworth Castle.

1327

England's Edward II is effectively deposed by his wife, Isabelle, and her lover, Mortimer, who have the Parliament of Westminster force the king's abdication and replace him with his son of 14, who will reign until 1377 as Edward III. The deposed Edward II is imprisoned at Berkeley Castle in Gloucestershire and put to death with cruelty September 21; it is announced that he has died of natural causes.

1328

 France's Charles IV dies February 1 at age 33, and his death without an heir ends the direct line of Capetian kings descended from Charlemagne. An assembly of French barons confirms the Salic Law that "no woman nor her son may succeed to the monarchy," so Charles the Fair is succeeded by his cousin, 35, who will reign until 1350 as Philip IV, establishing the Valois dynasty, which will rule until 1589.

1329

 Robert Bruce, king of Scotland, dies of leprosy June 7 at age 54. His 5-year-old son will reign until 1371 as David II (but *see* 1332).

1332

✘ England's Edward III and Edward de Balliol invade Scotland. Edward installs Balliol as king, forcing Robert the Bruce's son David to flee to France.

1333

✘ The Battle of Halidon Hill gives England's Edward III revenge for his father's defeat at Bannockburn in 1314. His forces disperse a Scottish army marching to relieve his siege of Berwick.

Japan's Kamakura period ends after 148 years as the emperor Godaigo regains power and the power of Japanese women wanes. Heretofore a woman inherited her husband's property upon his death and took full responsibility for his debts.

 The Black Death begins in China as starvation weakens much of the population, making it vulnerable to a form of bubonic plague (*see* 1343).

1334

✘ Lady Agnes Randolph, 34, wife of Patrick, fourth earl of Dunbar and second earl of March, holds her Scottish castle for 5 months against the earl of Salisbury, whose English siege force includes many engineers with elaborate equipment. She will be remembered as "Black Agnes."

1337

✘ A "Hundred Years' War" between England and France begins as Philip VI contests English claims to Normandy, Maine, Anjou, and other French territories.

1341

💲 Venice's new doge Messir Giovanni Sorenzo and his wife, Franchesina, continue policies established under the preceding regime, dominated by the dogearessa Agnese. They support the local silk industry by discouraging importation of Oriental brocades and block import of German mirrors and Greek hanging lamps. Venetian glassmaking will flourish under the Sorenzos, who will hold down living costs. Dogaressas have worked for the past century—and will continue for the next 50 years or more—to develop Venetian crafts while also encouraging art and literature, but the commercial opulence growing out of trade with the East will lead to a decline in the state's industrial vitality.

 Increased Venetian trade with the East (above) will bring plagues, killing much of the population and weakening the survivors' physical vigor (*see* 1343).

1342

✘ Thessalonica has a popular uprising against the Byzantine emperor John V and his regent mother.

The religious zealots (Hesychasts) who support John Cantacuzene in the civil war establish a nearly independent state that will continue until 1347.

Louis of Bavaria acquires the Tyrol and Carinthia by marrying the "ugly duchess" Margaret of Tyrol.

1343

The Black Death that began in China 10 years ago strikes marauding Tatars who attack some Genoese merchants traveling from Cathay with silks and furs in baggage that may harbor rats. The plague, called bubonic because of its characteristic buboes, or enlarged lymph glands, is transmitted by fleas, carried by rats (see 1347).

1345

∞ The monastery of Vadstena, founded by Swedish visionary Birgitta Gudmarsson, 42, will give rise to the new Augustinian order of Birgittines (date approximate). Birgitta, whose husband, Ulf, died last year after fathering her eight children, began having visions of the Virgin Mary at age 7, married Gudmarsson at age 13, and has made pilgrimages to Norway and Spain (see 1349).

1346

✗ The Battle of Crécy August 26 establishes England as a great military power, reorients English social values by making yeomanry and aristocrats joint participants in the victory, and begins the end of the era of feudal chivalry (cavalry).

1347

✗ English forces under Edward III take the French port of Calais after a long siege and make it a military and commercial outpost that will be English for 211 years. Edward celebrates the end of the long siege by taking as servants six of the city's leading burghers, whose lives he has spared only at the request of his wife, Philippa.

The Black Death reaches Cyprus, whence it will spread to Florence and find thousands of victims weakened by famine and vulnerable to the plague (see 1343, 1348).

Jane I, queen of both the Sicilies and countess of Provence, opens a house of prostitution at Avignon in an effort to reduce venereal disease. "The Queen commands that on every Saturday the Women in the House be singly examined by the Abbess and a Surgeon appointed by the Directors, and if any of them has contracted any Illness by their Whoring, that they be separated from the rest, and not suffered to prostitute themselves, for fear the Youth who have to do with them should catch their Distempers."

1348

The Black Death (bubonic plague) reaches Florence in April and spreads to France and England, where it arrives in July or August, although London is spared until November. It will kill nearly two-thirds of the population in some parts of Europe.

1349

✗ A Scottish army invades England in the fall but withdraws after being stricken with plague.

The Black Death (bubonic plague), transmitted by rat-borne fleas, killed almost everybody in some European towns.

The Black Death spreads through England, where it will kill one-third to one-half the population. The English call a truce in their hostilities with plague-stricken France.

The Swedish visionary Birgitta travels to Rome, founds a hospice, and collects a following of disciples (*see* 1345; 1372).

English landlords offer high wages to field hands. Reapers and mowers spared by the Black Death eat better than they ever have or ever will again.

1350

France's Philip VI dies August 12 at age 57 after a 22-year reign. His son of 31 will reign until 1364 as John II.

Scotland's returning soldiers infect their families and villages with the Black Death, which also reaches into Wales.

1355

Inês Pires de Castro, mistress of Portugal's crown prince Pedro, is murdered with the connivance of King Afonso IV, who wants to preserve the legitimate succession to the throne and is fearful that her brothers in Galicia will gain control of the government. Pedro, who claims that he has married Inês, organizes a revolt and lays siege to Oporto.

1356

The Battle of Poitiers (or Maupertuis) September 19 ends in defeat for France's John II, whose army is cut to ribbons by the forces of Edward, 26, the Black Prince of Wales. John is taken prisoner to England along with a crowd of French aristocrats, and John's son Charles, 18, is unable to prevent civil chaos.

1360

The Peace of Bretigny signed at Calais brings a brief truce in the Hundred Years' War, which has exhausted both England and France.

1364

France's John II dies April 8 at age 45 in England, where he has been held captive since the Battle of Poitiers in 1356. His body is sent home with royal honors, and his son, now 27, will reign until 1380 as Charles V.

1368

The Ming dynasty founded by Qu Yuanzhang, 40, will rule until 1644 and begin a resurgence of Chinese nationalism. Qu, who drives the Mongols out of Beijing, will himself rule until 1398 under the name Hung-wu.

1369

Tamurlane (Timur the Lame, or Tamburlaine) makes himself master of Samarkand at age 33. A descendant of Genghis Khan, he begins to develop an armed horde that will conquer much of the world.

1371

Castile's Enrique Trastámara takes Zamora February 26 and forces Portugal's Fernão I to renounce his claims to Castile in the Treaty of Alcoutin. Fernão agrees to marry Enrique's daughter Leonora.

1372

The Swedish visionary Birgitta, now 69, makes a pilgrimage to Cyprus and Jerusalem (*see* 1349). She will die at Rome upon her return next year, but her Birgittine order will grow to have more than 80 convents throughout Europe.

1375

The Truce of Bruges brings a pause in the Hundred Years' War between England and France.

Denmark's Waldemar IV dies, survived by his 22-year-old daughter, Margrethe, Margrethe's 5-year-old son Olaf, her sister Ingeborg, and Ingeborg's son Albert. Waldemar betrothed Margrethe to Norway's Haakon VI when she was 7 to cement an alliance between the two countries, hoping that her son would rule over both kingdoms, but she has lived apart from Haakon and has been obliged to borrow money from the Norwegian treasury in order to support herself and her son (*see* 1376).

Buckles come into general use for footwear, which will inspire the nursery rhyme, "One, two, buckle my shoe" (date approximate).

1376

Denmark's tenants-in-chief meet at Odense in May and choose Margrethe as regent for her son, Olaf, who is titular king of both Denmark and Norway (*see* 1375).

1377

England's Edward III dies June 21 at age 64 and is succeeded by his 10-year-old grandson, son of the late Black Prince Edward of Wales, who will reign until 1399 as Richard II.

Parliament levies a 4-shilling poll tax that will lead to widespread rioting in 1381.

The "Babylonian Exile" of the papacy, which began in 1306, ends January 17 with the entry into Rome of Pope Gregory XI, who left Avignon in September of last year at the persuasion of Italian mystic Caterina Benincasa, 30, a Dominican nun who will be remembered as Catherine of Siena.

Population estimates based on the English poll tax (above) suggest that the nation's population has fallen to little more than 2 million, down from at least 3.5 million and possibly 5 million before the Black Death.

1380

France's Charles V dies in his manor at Beauté beside the forest of Vincennes September 16 at age 43 after eating poisonous mushrooms. Survived by his queen, Jeanne de Bourbon, he has ruled since the capture of his father at the Battle of Poitiers in 1356. His son of 12 will reign until 1422 as Charles VI, despite increasing bouts of insanity.

Catherine of Siena (Caterina Benincasa) has died at Rome April 29 at age 33 after a stroke that has left her paralyzed for 8 days from the waist down (*see* 1377). She has been tireless in her devotion to the Church and to those in need.

1382

Anne of Bohemia, 15, daughter of the Holy Roman Emperor Charles IV, is married at Westminster Abbey to England's Richard II, also 15.

Hungary's Louis the Great dies suddenly at Nagyszombat September 10 after a 40-year reign that also has included nearly 12 years as king of Poland. He is succeeded in Hungary by his daughter Maria of Anjou, whose husband, Sigismund of Luxembourg, will rule Hungary for 50 years beginning in 1387. Louis will be succeeded in Poland by his daughter Jadwiga (Hedwig).

1383

Sardinian troops commanded by Eleonora of Arborea, 33, repel an invasion force from Aragon. She becomes regent of Arborea for her infant son, Frederick (*see* 1395).

Portugal's Fernão I dies without male issue October 22 at age 38 after having antagonized Juan of Castile by canceling the betrothal of his daughter Beatrix to Juan, who lays claim to the Portuguese throne. Fernão's widow, Leonora, rules as regent for Beatrix, who marries Juan.

1384

Lisbon is besieged by forces sent by Castile's Juan, who has married the Portuguese infanta, Beatrix, but the people of Portugal resist his claims to the throne.

1385

✖ Portugal gains independence August 14 by defeating Castile in the Battle of Aljubarrota. The bastard son of the late Pedro has taken power with unanimous support from the cortes at Coimbra, disease forces the Castilians to withdraw, and João I, 28, will reign until 1433, establishing the Avis dynasty.

1386

✖ The Treaty of Windsor May 9 allies England and Portugal by joining Portugal's João I in marriage with John of Gaunt's daughter Philippa.

Jadwiga, queen of Poland, marries Jagiello, grand duke of Lithuania. He will be titular head of Poland until 1434 as Vladislav V, but it is Jadwiga who will control the country.

1387

✖ Denmark's Olaf II dies suddenly in August at age 17 after a 12-year reign and is succeeded by his mother, Margrethe, now 34, who will unite Scandinavia under her rule. Olaf's burial stone is inscribed, "Here rests Olaf, son of Queen Margrethe, whom she bore to Norway's King Haakon." Margrethe has served as regent of Denmark since her father's death in 1375.

✒ Poetry: *Troilus and Criseyde* by English poet Geoffrey Chaucer, 47, whose patron, John of Gaunt, last year helped him secure election as one of the two knights of the shire of Kent. Chaucer's *The Book of the Duchess* was an elegy to John of Gaunt's first wife, Blanche, who died in 1369. Chaucer's wife, Philippa, is a sister of Katherine Swynford, who has married John of Gaunt, but his connections have not sufficed to prevent him from losing his positions as controller of the customs for wool and controller of the petty custom on wines.

1388

✖ Norwegians elect Margrethe of Denmark queen in February, making her "the kingdom of Norway's mighty Lady and rightful Master."

France's Charles VI begins his personal reign at age 19 following the death of the duke of Anjou, which leaves Philip of Burgundy in a position of great power. Charles replaces Philip with his own brother Louis, duc d'Orléans, but Louis is an unpopular dandy and Philip, who poses as a reformer, gains the support of the king's wife, Isabelle of Bavaria.

1389

✖ Margrethe of Denmark has her 7-year-old grandnephew Eric of Pomerania proclaimed her successor; he will reign until 1439 as Eric of Norway. Disaffected Swedish magnates offer her the Swedish throne, her forces defeat the Swedish king, Albert of Mecklenburg, at Falköping, and they take Albert prisoner.

1390

✖ Scotland's first Stuart king, Robert II, dies May 13 at age 74. His legitimized son John, 50, changes his baptismal name and will reign until 1406 as Robert III.

✊ Paris "witch" Jehenna de Brigue, 34, is arrested on charges brought by her neighbor, Jean de Ruilly, who has come to her for medical assistance (*see* 1324). She has allegedly performed a ritual to protect him from witchcraft, reportedly allowing two toads to suck from her breasts, and he has apparently been cured of whatever ailed him. Brigue claims that she is not a witch but is acquainted with a witch named Marion who has taught her some charms (*see* 1391).

✒ Venetian-born French widow Christine de Pisan, 25, begins intensive studies in history, science, and poetry. Her husband of 10 years, a courtier who has encouraged her to continue her education (she has called him a man "whom no other could surpass in kindness, peacefulness, loyalty, and true love"), has died at age 35, leaving her the sole support of her mother, three children, and a niece. She will gain some fame in the next few years with her poetry, her biography of France's Charles V, her book on etiquette for women, books on pacifism and the arts of government and war, criticisms of misogynist literature, and biblical commentary: "There Adam slept, and God formed the body of woman from one of his ribs, signifying that she should stand at his side as a companion and never lie at his feet like a slave, and also that he should love her as his own flesh. . . . I don't know if you have already noted this: she was created in the image of God. How can any mouth dare to slander the vessel which bears such a noble imprint? . . . God created the soul and placed wholly similar souls, equally good and noble, in the feminine and masculine bodies" (*see* 1405).

1391

 Alleged "witch" Jehenna de Brigue tells a Parisian judge that her aunt has taught her to summon the devil (*see* 1390). She is sentenced to be burned, but the execution is delayed when she appears to be pregnant. It is then discovered that she is not pregnant, she appeals her case, a new hearing is held, de Brigue is stripped and tortured, and she changes her story, claiming that her neighbor Jean de Ruilly's wife, Macette, hired her to bewitch and poison her husband so that she could run off with another man. Macette is arrested, confesses after torture on the rack, and is sent along with de Brigue to "the Châtelet aux Halles [to be] mitred as sorcerers, put in the pillory; then led to the Pig Market to be burned alive."

1394

 England's Queen Anne of Bohemia dies of plague at age 28. Her husband, Richard II, will remarry in 1396.

1395

 The Swedish king Albert of Mecklenburg renounces the throne and retires to Mecklenburg as Margrethe of Denmark continues to take over his realm.

 Eleonora of Arborea in Sardinia introduces the *Carta di Logu,* a humanitarian code of laws that anticipates legal codes that will not be seen elsewhere for many years to come.

1396

 England's Richard II remarries, taking as his second wife Isabella, daughter of France's Charles VI.

1397

 Margrethe of Denmark completes her conquest of Sweden and has her grandnephew Eric crowned king of a united Scandinavia. Her dynastic Union of Kalmar will continue at least nominally until 1523, and Margrethe herself will rule as the "Semiramis of the North" until her death in 1412.

1398

 England's Richard II moves the country toward totalitarian government, packing the House of Commons with his adherents, who vote him a lifetime income, and delegating Parliament's powers to a committee friendly to his own interests. He imposes heavy taxes and pursues a reign of terror.

1399

 Henry of Bolingbroke, 32, a cousin of England's Richard II, defeats, captures, and deposes the king, who abdicates September 29. Parliament hails the usurper, who will reign until 1461 as Henry IV, founding the Lancastrian dynasty.

1400

 England's deposed king Richard II dies in February in Pontefract Castle, where he has probably been murdered. His supporters rise against the Lancastrian king Henry IV.

 Poetry: *The Canterbury Tales* by Geoffrey Chaucer, who dies October 25 at age 60, leaving the work incomplete. His Saintly Constance says in "The Man of Law's Wife," "Wommen are born to thraldom and penance/ And to ben under mannes governance." His Wife of Bath says, "In wifehood I intend to use my instrument as generously as my Maker sent it. If I am niggardly, may God give me sorrow! My husband shall have it morning and night when it pleases him to come forth and pay his debt." (She is depicted as a compendium of all women's vices.)

 "The Nun's Priest's Tale" by Chaucer (above) criticizes those who have sex "moore for delit than world to multiplye," an implication that people are using coitus interruptus, sponges, or other ways to avoid pregnancy.

15th Century

1402

✗ England's Henry IV, now 35, takes time off from battling the Welsh to marry the widow Joanna of Navarre, 32, whose first husband, the duke of Burgundy, died in 1399. The mother of eight, she becomes stepmother to Henry's 15-year-old son by his first wife, the late Mary de Behun.

1403

✗ England's Henry IV subdues Percy of Northumberland, who has joined a Welsh revolt begun in 1399.

∞ Bologna passes a law forbidding citizens to loiter about convents conversing and playing music with the nuns.

1405

✗ Tamerlane dies suddenly at Atrar February 17 at age 68 while planning a campaign against China. The Tatar chief has conquered Persia, Mesopotamia, Afghanistan, and much of India, but his empire quickly begins to dissolve.

⚱ Nonfiction: *The Book of the City of the Ladies* by Christine de Pisan attempts to record the history of women, based largely on what she has read in Scripture, and gives a lively defense of women against misogynists who would relegate them to inferior positions (some will call her work the first true feminist treatise). "You ask whether woman possesses any natural intelligence," she writes in her prologue. "Yes. It can be developed to become wisdom, and then it is most beautiful. . . . If it were customary to send little girls to school and to teach them the same subjects that are taught to boys, they would learn just as fully and would understand the subtleties of all arts and sciences. Indeed, maybe they would understand them better . . . for just as women's bodies are softer than men's, so their understanding is sharper."

1406

✗ Scotland's Robert III dies April 4 at age 65 after sending his son James, 11, to safety in France and then hearing that James has been captured by English sailors. James I will remain in English hands until 1424.

1407

✗ Louis, duc d'Orléans, is murdered after a night of drinking and wenching on orders from John the Fearless, duke of Burgundy, who becomes the toast of Paris. The promiscuous French queen, Isabelle of Bavaria, whose lovers have included Burgundy, had transferred her support to the unpopular spendthrift duc d'Orléans, and his murder begins a civil war between Burgundians and Armagnacs (the count of Armagnac is the father-in-law of Charles, the new duc d'Orléans) (*see* 1419).

1412

✗ Margrethe of Denmark dies suddenly October 28 at age 59 aboard her ship in Flensborg harbor. Her grandnephew Eric of Pomerania continues his reign as Eric VII of Denmark and Norway, Eric XIII of Sweden, but the death of the "lady king" (as delegates from Lübeck have called her) begins a long period of dissension as Eric assumes personal power and begins an oppressive rule.

1413

 England's Henry IV dies the evening of March 29 at age 45 and is succeeded by his son, now 25, who will reign until 1422 as Henry V. The new king's stepmother, Joanna of Navarre, now 43, is imprisoned on charges of witchcraft and will remain incarcerated for 3 years.

Yolande of Anjou marries her 10-year-old daughter, Marie of Aragon, in December to Charles, the 12-year-old third son of France's insane king Charles VI and his dissolute wife, Isabelle of Bavaria. Yolande takes young Charles with her to Provence and treats him as if he were her own son.

1414

 Sicily's king Ladislas dies after a 28-year reign in which he has expanded into central Italy. His widowed sister will reign until 1435 as Joanna (Giovanna) II, keeping Italian diplomacy in turmoil with her amorous intrigues as she plays off rival claimants to the throne.

1415

 The Battle of Agincourt October 25 ends in defeat for the French by English archers under the command of Henry V. France's nobility is shattered, the feudal system is discredited, and Normandy lies open to reconquest by England in the continuing Hundred Years' War.

1418

 France's royal family flees to the south as Burgundian forces regain power and massacre Armagnacs at Paris.

1419

 John the Fearless, Duke of Burgundy, is murdered September 1 while conferring on the bridge of Montereau with the French dauphin, Charles, whose older brothers Louis and John have died in 1415 and 1417, respectively. The murder is in reprisal for the 1407 killing of the duc d'Orléans. The new duke of Burgundy, Philip le Bon (whose 24 mistresses will bear 15 illegitimate children), reaffirms his country's alliance with England, and the Treaty of Brétigny, forced on the French October 14, provides for English sovereignty over Guines, Ponthieu, Poitou, Saintonge, Angoumois, Limousin, Périgord, Agenois, Quercy, Rouergue, and Bigorre.

1420

 The Treaty of Troyes, signed in May by France's insane king Charles VI under pressure from his wife, Isabelle, and Burgundy's Philip le Bon, allows the English to retain all of their conquests as far as the Loire, abolishes the Salic Law, which excludes women from the throne, and provides for the marriage of the French princess Catherine to Henry V. Her brother, the dauphin Charles, is declared illegitimate, and is driven south of the Loire by Henry's forces.

Yolande of Anjou marries her son René to Isabelle of Lorraine at Nancy. Charles I, duke of Lorraine, has lent support to the English; Yolande aims to tie him by blood to the House of Valois. René will lay claim to the throne of Sicily.

1422

England's Henry V dies of dysentery in France August 3 at age 35. His 8-month-old son inherits the crown and will reign until 1461 as Henry VI.

France's Charles VI dies at Paris October 1 at age 53 after a 42-year reign. The dauphin, now 19, was disinherited under the terms of the Treaty of Troyes signed in 1420 and will not be crowned until 1429; England's infant king, Henry VI, is proclaimed king of France. The rejected dauphin abandons himself to debauchery and is easy prey for his mistresses, but Yolande of Anjou will remove the mistresses along with her son-in-law's greedy counselors.

1424

 Scotland's James I gains his freedom at age 29 after nearly 18 years in English hands. The earl of Somerset remits 10,000 marks in ransom money as a dowry for his daughter Jane, who marries James February 12 at Southwark. James is crowned at Scone May 21 and will reign until 1437.

Yolande of Anjou arranges a meeting between her son-in-law, Charles, and Arthur, earl of Richmond and sovereign lord of Brittany, in an effort to detach Brittany from the English cause. Charles signs an agreement October 21 under pressure from Yolande to accept whatever conditions Richmond wishes for his support.

1425

 Yolande of Anjou writes a letter to the people of Lyons June 28 advising them that the council will "take the necessary steps towards the relief of the kingdom and the union of the princes of the blood, to carry out justice, and put an end to all plunder and pillage."

1427

The duke of Bedford leaves in March to resume the war with France, trying to restore prosperity to the French districts under his rule.

Venice inaugurates a new doge with costly ceremonies as the city-state glories in wealth and prosperity. A jeweled *corno* is placed on the head of the new dogaressa Marina Nani-Foscari.

1428

English forces lay siege to Orléans beginning in October with the reluctant consent of the Duke of Bedford.

1429

 Joan of Arc (Jeanne d'Arc) becomes the heroine of France and changes the course of history. A shepherd girl of 17 from Lorraine, she has heard voices and seen visions of the Archangel Michael, Saint Catherine, and Saint Margaret, who told her that since France was lost by a woman (Isabelle of Bavaria) it must be saved by a virgin. They pledged her to seek out the dauphin and deliver Orléans from the English. Having resisted the voices for 3 years, she persuades an uncle to conduct her to the sieur de Baudricourt, commander of Vaucouleurs, and although Baudricourt laughs her off he reports her visit to his superiors. Word of the visit reaches the duke of Lorraine, who tells Yolande of Anjou, mother-in-law of the dauphin. Baudricourt receives

Voices called Joan of Arc to lead the French to victory over their English invaders; she was burned at the stake. LIBRARY OF CONGRESS

orders from Chinon that Joan is to be conducted to the court. She is outfitted in a black jerkin, trunk hose fastened by aglets, a short black tunic, black hat, leggings with spurs, and a sword. Thus garbed, she meets with Yolande and Queen Marie at Chinon, where she is told what she must say to the dauphin.

"I tell you from my Lord that you are the true heir of France and son of the king," Joan of Arc (above) tells the dauphin. He provides her with a small army, and she writes a letter to the English, saying, "Surrender to the Maid sent hither, by God the King of Heaven, the keys of all the good towns you have taken and laid waste in France. . . . And to you, King of England, if you do not thus, I am a chieftain of war and whenever I meet your followers in France, I will drive them out; if they will not obey, I will put them all to death." Joan's leadership inspires her 4,000 men to liberate Orléans April 28. Charles is crowned at Reims July 17 and will reign until 1461 as Charles VII.

Joan of Arc, La Pucelle d'Orléans, has a standard embroidered for her bearing the fleur-de-lys and the words "Jesus Maria."

Poetry: Christine de Pisan, now 65, hears in July that the siege of Orléans has been lifted (above) and writes verses comparing Joan of Arc to such biblical heroines as Esther, Judith, and Deborah: "Ah, what honor to the feminine sex!/ Which God so loved/ That he showed/ A way to this great people/ By which the kingdom, once lost,/ Was recovered by a woman,/ A thing that men could not do."

1430

Joan of Arc enters Compiègne outside Paris May 23 and is taken prisoner along with her brothers. She is delivered to Jean de Luxembourg and thence to the English, who imprison her in a tower at Rouen, intending to discredit her. Charles VII makes no effort to save Joan, nor does the duke of Bedford intervene in her behalf.

1431

Joan of Arc is handed over to the former bishop of Beauvais Pierre Cauchon by the English, who vow to seize her again if she is not convicted of high treason against God. She is tried by an ecclesiastical court on charges that include inappropriate physical appearance: "Not only did she wear short tunics, but she dressed herself in tabbards and garments open at the sides, besides the matter is notorious since when she was captured she was wearing a surcoat cloak of gold, open on all sides, a cap on her head, and her hair cropped round in man's style. And in general, having cast aside all womanly decency, not only to the scorn of feminine modesty, but also of well instructed men, she had worn the apparel and garments of most dissolute men, and, in addition, had some weapons of defense." Convicted, the maid of Orléans is burned at the stake in the Old Market Square of Rouen May 30.

Charles, duke of Lorraine, dies. His daughter Isabelle, now 22, becomes duchess and her husband, René, the new duke at Nancy. (René calls himself also king of Naples but will never enforce his claims to the Neapolitan throne.) René's cousin Antoine de Vaudémont claims the throne, a war begins, and René is taken prisoner in the field at Bulgnéville. Yolande of Anjou advises her daughter-in-law to summon the council of Lorraine, rally her army, and demand help from France's Charles VII.

1432

Yolande of Anjou visits her daughter, Marie, and Charles VII at Chinon, bringing along her companion Agnès Sorel, 22, who is widely considered the most beautiful woman in France. Her beauty and wit have graced the luxurious court at Nancy of Yolande's son, René, who remains a prisoner of war (the duke of Burgundy will eventually pay his ransom) while Yolande's daughter-in-law, Isabelle, rules. Agnès charms not only the king but also his wife, Marie, and when it comes time for Yolande to leave the king insists that Agnès remain. His impoverished court is full of rough soldiers, with none of the intellectual stimulation that Agnès knew at Nancy, but her heart is touched by Charles's need for companionship and she soon responds to his passion for her. Yolande sees an opportunity to attain her ambitions for Charles by means of Agnès's diplomatic skills.

English mystic Margery Kempe (*née* Brunham), 65, begins dictating her autobiography to two Lancashire scribes, recounting her life beginning with her childhood as the daughter of a prosperous East Anglian family in Lynn (her father was the mayor) who married a local merchant, thought she was near death as she gave birth to her first child, had a vision of Christ, recovered, and felt that she was "bound to God and would be his servant." Failing as a brewer after 3 years, she failed again as a miller, bore 14 children, persuaded her husband, John, to go on a pilgrimage with her, and after 8 weeks of voluntary chastity told him that she would rather he were dead than to have sex with him ever again. He agreed not to "meddle with" her thereafter on condition that they continue to lie in the same bed and that she stop fasting on Fridays. For most of her ascetic life thereafter she went on pilgrimages alone to various German duchies and principalities, Rome, and Jerusalem, dressed always in white, defying those, including the archbishop of York, who accused her of heresy and tried to stop her from preaching. Having sought out the anchoress Julian of Norwich for long conversations, she will finish dictating in 1436, but her manuscript, in which she claims to have performed miracles, will not be discovered until 1934.

1433

 Agnès Sorel gives birth to a daughter, Charlotte, who is acknowledged by the king as a daughter of France and sister of the 10-year-old dauphin Louis. Agnès begins to attend the king and queen in both public and private, sharing the life of the court, and receives as a gift from Charles a manor at Beauté built by the late Charles V at the edge of the forest of Vincennes with a commanding view of the Marne. Called by the poet Christine de Pisan "a very remarkable domain," it has been deserted since Charles V died there in 1380.

1434

 African slaves are introduced into Portugal by a caravel returning from the southern continent (*see* 1441).

1435

 The duke of Bedford dies in France September 19. Philip le Bon, duke of Burgundy, breaks with the English and signs a treaty September 21 recognizing Charles VII as France's true and only king, but only after Charles has got down on his knees and atoned in public for the murder of John the Fearless in 1419 at Montereau. Charles's mother, Isabelle of Bavaria, has recently died. Paris remains in English hands, and England refuses to make peace on terms acceptable to the French.

Disbanded soldiers roam the French countryside, plundering villages to feed themselves, cutting down vineyards and grainfields, violating the women, and torturing the children, but Charles VII rallies his troops under the fleur-de-lys. The people of Cherington, Vincennes, Corbeil, Brie, Comte Robert, and St.-Germain-en-Laye welcome the army as liberators, Parisians who have supported the English take refuge in the Bastille, the king arrives at Montereau October 1, and he enters Paris November 12.

Agnès Sorel, who has helped Charles effect reconciliations with the feudal lords, takes part in his triumphal entry procession, wearing a gold-adorned bodice of red velvet, a mantle of ermine, a long azure veil, a gold-and-emerald necklace, and shoes *à la poulaine* (pointed at the toes). Pamphlets circulated by the English at Paris say that her presence disturbs the queen, who, in fact, loves the young woman whose smiles and kindness have had such a good influence on the king and his policies.

 German "witch" Agnes Bernauer is drowned in the Danube at Straubing. Daughter of a poor surgeon in Augsburg, she was secretly married 3 years ago to Albrecht, only son of Bavaria's duke Ernst, and the duke has her drowned while Albrecht is away. He takes up arms against his father but will agree after a year of warfare to marry Anna of Brunswick.

1436

 Agnès Sorel helps arrange the marriage of France's dauphin, Louis, now 13, to Margaret, 12-year-old daughter of Scotland's James I. The wedding in the cathedral of St. Gétienne at Tours is attended by more splendor than has been seen in France since the last century, when Charles's mother, Isabelle of Bavaria, arrived as a bride. Agnès is not present because she is expecting a child; the queen, also pregnant, gives birth soon afterward to a prince and becomes godmother to Agnès Sorel's second daughter, who is named Marie in the queen's honor. But the dauphin resents his father's attention to Agnès and will always be hostile to her. The king gives Margaret 2,000 livres to buy silks and furs but gives nothing to his son.

Scottish forces defeat the English near Berwick.

1437

 Agnès Sorel leaves Paris May 10 and will not be seen there again. Her friend Yolande of Anjou enlists the services of the Norman knight Pierre de Brezés, 23, who has become Seneschal of Anjou and commander of Angers. A friend of Agnès Sorel, he will fight for the king in all his battles.

1440

 The Battle of Anghiari gives the condottiere Niccolo Piccinino, 65, overlord of Bologna, a victory over the forces of Milan's Filippo Maria Visconti. Florence's Cosimo de' Medici backs the claims of Francesco Sforza to the duchy of Milan and supports a coalition of Venetians and Florentines who then defeat Piccinino.

 The late Joan of Arc's erstwhile companion in arms Gilles de Rais is executed October 20 near Nantes. Made marshal of France at age 25, he became so addicted to alcohol and consumed by lust that he has been enticing young beggars and women to follow him and then having them taken to his châteaux at Tiffauges, Machecoul, and Champtoce, where he allegedly violated them, tortured them, cut their throats, or hanged them. Charged with committing more than 140 crimes, he has been arrested, tried, and convicted.

1441

 Pierre de Brezés replaces the count of Maine as first minister to France's Charles VII and becomes a member of France's royal council along with the merchant Jacques Coeur (*see* below).

 African slaves are sold in the markets of Lisbon. A trade begins that will see more than 20 million African men and women transported in the next 460 years to Europe and—more especially—to the New World (*see* 1511).

 Agnès Sorel has introduced Jacques Coeur (above) to the French court. Married in his youth to the daughter of the mayor of Bourges, he has gained the protection of Yolande of Anjou and will soon become guardian of mines, keeper of the king's purse, and superintendent of finances, in which capacity he will collect taxes and revenues. He has trading companies all over France and a Mediterranean fleet of seven galleys, in which he undertakes numerous voyages, bringing back sugar from Cyprus, cloves from Alexandria, perfumed cinnamon, Persian carpets, and Egyptian velvets and satins, giving him an income said to be greater than that of all other French merchants combined. Agnès Sorel will advertise his wares, helping him to become the richest man in France, and he will advance funds to reorganize the kingdom and build a proper army and fleet.

Charles VII bestows upon Pierre de Brezés (above) the châteaux and seigneuries of Nogent-le-Roi, Anet, Brievel, and Monchauvet. A courtier protests that the "Seneschal spoils all, destroys all. He holds the king in subjection by the help of this Agnès, who is above the queen."

1442

 Agnès Sorel gains for merchant Jacques Coeur the dominant place on France's Grand Council. Yolande of Anjou dies soon thereafter at the Château de Saumur, diminishing the role of Agnès in France's affairs of state (which was never to initiate policy but merely to induce Charles VII to accept Yolande's decisions). The true head of the house of Anjou, Yolande has for more than a decade acted through Agnès to guide the monarch's hand and supply the means for his efforts to follow up on Joan of Arc's triumph at Orléans and drive the English out of France.

1443

✗ Agnès Sorel is made official mistress (*maîtresse-en-titre*) to France's Charles VII, becoming the first woman to be possessed of that title. "La belle Agnès," who is said to rule the king, begins a pat-

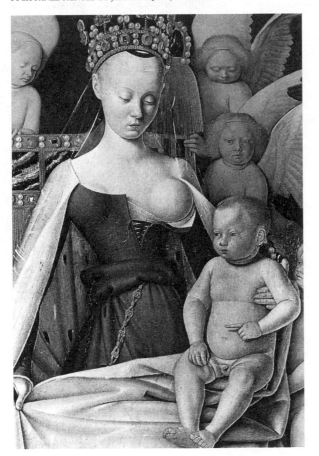

Agnès Sorel became mistress to France's Charles VII. She was considered the most beautiful woman in his realm. FROM A DIPTYCH PANEL PAINTED BY JEAN FOUQUET, CIRCA 1450

tern that will be followed by a number of women in centuries to come as France produces cleverly influential women and complaisant male rulers.

1444

✗ Margaret of Anjou, the beautiful daughter of Lorraine's King René, is betrothed to England's feeble Henry VI May 1 in St. Martin's Church at Tours. Yolande, René's second daughter, takes part with Agnès Sorel in a ballet at Châlons in June.

1445

✗ The duke of Suffolk arrives in February with a train of courtiers to escort Margaret of Anjou to England and is entertained with feasts and tournaments.

Agnès Sorel bears a third daughter at Beauté sur Marne. The king presents her with the Château d'Issoudoun.

1446

✗ The French dauphine Margaret of Scotland dies at Châlons of a lung inflammation August 16 after saying, *"Fi de la vie."* She has avoided the dauphin's bed and done her best to avoid having children, drinking vinegar, eating green apples, and lacing herself tightly in the belief that these measures will prevent pregnancy. Her death grieves the king and his mistress, Agnès Sorel, but does not trouble the dauphin, who will remarry in 1450. The queen gives birth at Tours December 18 to a boy who is named after his father.

1447

✗ The French dauphin Louis, now 23, sets out for the Dauphiné, a territory of villages, isolated castles, and wild country stretching for 125 miles along the Rhône, bordered by Savoy and Provence, and extending to the Alps. He arrives January 13 and will make his home near Grenoble, never to see his father again.

Milan establishes an Ambrosian republic upon the death of the last of the male line of Viscontis. Francesco Sforza, who has married Bianca Maria Visconti, is hired as military leader.

Jacques Coeur makes an agreement with the sultan of Egypt in an effort to annex Genoa; he uses Agnès Sorel as the channel for arranging and concluding agreements between the king and the new pope Nicholas V.

 Dresses in Europe's royal courts have tight-fitting bodices and sleeves, with revers turned back at the shoulders. Bosoms are exposed, and girdles placed beneath the breasts support them as if presenting them as temptations. Wide bands of linen are worn over women's hips to hold in their flesh; their skirts are drawn tight over the abdomen while in back they are full and very long, trimmed with fur, usually ermine (the width of the fur trimming is the measure by which a woman's status is judged).

1449

✗ France's Charles VII leaves Chinon August 14 in armor, leaving behind his *maîtresse-en-titre* Agnès Sorel, who is once again with child. In large part

Men regarded the "gentler sex" as companions in pleasure, exploited their talents, but denied them rights and dignity.

through her efforts, he has built the world's first regular army, making treaties with the Swiss and Scots to supply troops who are dependent not on feudal lords but on the king himself. Succeeding rapidly in his reconquest of Normandy, Charles enters Rouen November 10.

1450

✗ Agnès Sorel rejoins Charles VII at the manor of Mesnil, country villa of the abbots of Jumièges, is delivered of a daughter February 9, but suffers an attack of dysentery and dies that night at age 40 (the infant also dies). She is mourned as much by Queen Marie, who will henceforth live apart from Charles, as by the king himself.

Louis the dauphin, now 27, is married March 9 to Charlotte, 12-year-old daughter of the duke of Savoy. His father has not given his blessings to the marriage and is furious.

Charles's troops halt the English advance on Cherbourg, crushing the enemy at Formigny, as factional quarrels begin to tear England apart. Charles, who has now become the most powerful ruler in Christendom, is seduced by Antoinette de Maignelais, a cousin of the late Agnès Sorel. He marries her off to André de Villequier, comte de Sauveur, a complaisant courtier with whom he caroused in his youth, and remains with his new mistress through October and November, giving her the château d'Issoudon, which he previously gave to Agnès Sorel, plus the Château La Guerche in Touraine.

Bianca Maria Visconti, 26, wife of Milan's Francesco Sforza, overthrows the Ambrosian Republic and consolidates several territories into a powerful new duchy that controls the north of Italy. She has defended Cremona against the Venetians and led a naval attack against them.

1451

 France's Charles VII deprives his son Louis, the dauphin, of his pension for having married without the king's permission.

Jacques Coeur says to his wife, "Whatever people may say . . . I am as well with the king as ever I have been." He is thrown into prison a few days later on the preposterous charge of having poisoned the late Agnès Sorel.

1453

✘ Constantinople falls to the Ottoman Turks, who end the Byzantine empire, which has ruled since 476. The Turks force an entry May 29, sack the city, and make it their capital.

The Hundred Years' War, which has continued off and on since 1377, ends with the expulsion of English forces from every part of France except Calais, which they will hold for more than a century. Thanks to the late Joan of Arc, Yolande of Anjou, and Agnès Sorel, Charles VII has regained his realms.

Jacques Coeur is judged guilty of *lèse-majesté,* fined 400,000 crowns, committed to prison at Poitiers, and stripped of all his holdings.

1454

✘ France's Charles VII shuts himself up with his mistress, Antoinette de Maignelais, following the death of her husband, André de Vellequier, July 1. Charles gives Antoinette the right to inherit the château plus 2,000 livres to maintain herself in queenly style.

Jacques Coeur escapes from confinement in the château at Poitiers in October, finds refuge in a monastery at Montmorillon, and makes his way to Rome, where he receives a hearty welcome from Pope Nicholas V.

1455

✘ Margaret of Anjou arrives in England, where the Wars of the Roses erupt in a civil conflict that will continue until 1471 between the houses of York and Lancaster.

1456

✘ Athens falls to the Ottoman Turks, who will rule Greece and the Balkans for most of the next 4 centuries.

Jacques Coeur commands a fleet of 16 galleys on a crusade undertaken by Pope Calixtus III (Alonso Borgia), arrives at Chios, but dies there November 26.

Tomiko Hino, 16, daughter of a powerful Japanese family, marries the shōgun Yoshimasa Ashikaga, whose regime she will soon control.

✒ The Gutenberg Bible, published at Mainz by local printer Johann Gutenberg, 56, is a Vulgate bible that marks one of the earliest uses of printing from movable type in Europe.

1459

✘ Antoinette de Maignelais leaves the ailing Charles VII to become mistress to François, comte d'Etampes, who will become duke of Brittany. She secretly corresponds with Charles's son Louis, the dauphin, and supplies him with information that may help him in his intrigues against the king.

1460

✘ Margaret of Anjou, wife of England's deranged Henry VI, raises an army in northern England following the capture of her husband July 10 at the Battle of Northampton 66 miles from London by Yorkists wearing white roses, who defeat the royal Lancastrians wearing red roses. Her forces defeat those of Richard Plantagenet, third duke of York, 49, who has asserted his hereditary claim to the throne but is killed December 30 by Margaret's men, who surprise him at Wakefield in West Riding. Margaret has brought men from Scotland.

1461

✘ Edward of York, 19, avenges the death of his father, Richard, last year by defeating Lancastrians at Mortimer's Cross but is himself defeated at the second battle of St. Albans February 17. Margaret of Anjou regains possession of her husband, Henry VI. Edward beats the Lancastrians at Towton and is crowned in June as Edward IV after Parliament declares the Lancastrians to be usurpers.

Scotland's queen, Mary of Guelders, 28, who has continued the war against England following the death of her husband, James II, forces the surrender of Berwick. She has had the support of troops supplied by Margaret of Anjou.

France's Charles VII dies July 22 at age 58 after a 32-year reign in which his late mistress, Agnès Sorel, had a major influence, as, briefly, did Joan of Arc, in restoring the power of a nation that had been virtually destroyed by English invaders and internal wars between feudal lords. His son Louis, 38, who was banished in 1447 and has not seen *le roi* for 14 years, is crowned at Reims August 15 and will reign until 1483 as Louis XI. His patient, submissive wife, Charlotte, who surrounds herself with her sisters and ladies of the court at the château d'Amboise on the Loire, gives birth to a daughter, Anne.

1464

 England's Edward IV, now 22, marries Elizabeth Woodville, 27, provoking the rage of Richard Neville, earl of Warwick; when news of the secret marriage is made public, Edward's bride obtains many favors for her family (*see* 1483).

1465

 Yorkists recapture England's Lancastrian king Henry VI and imprison him in the Tower of London as the Wars of the Roses continue.

1467

 A Japanese civil war begins over the succession to the Ashikaga shogunate. The shōgun Yoshimasa appointed his brother Yoshimi Fujiwara as his suc-

cessor before the birth last year of his son Yoshihisa; the boy's mother wants Yoshihisa to be her husband's heir, so she enlists the support of Gen. Sōzen Yamana while her brother-in-law enlists the support of Gen. Katsumoto Hosokawa. Kyoto is destroyed in the fighting, which will spread throughout Japan and continue for 11 years.

1468

 Charles the Bold, duke of Burgundy, effects an alliance against France's Louis XI by marrying Margaret, sister of England's Edward IV.

1469

 The Spanish crowns of Aragon and Castile join in alliance October 19 at Valladolid, where the infante Ferdinand of Aragon and León, 17, marries the infanta Isabella of Castile, 18.

1470

 London goldsmith's wife Jane Shore becomes mistress to England's Edward IV without objection from her husband. She will enjoy the king's favors until his death in 1483, after which she will become mistress to other leading political figures.

1472

 Muscovy returns to the Roman Church through the marriage of the grand duke Ivan III to Zoë (Sophia) Palaeologa, niece of Constantinople's last Greek emperor Constantine XI Palaeologus. Zoë's father, Thomas, is despot of the Morea, Pope Sixtus IV has arranged the marriage, later Russian rulers will use it as the basis of their claim to be the protectors of Orthodox Christianity, Ivan will establish a Byzantine autocracy in Russia, and he will take the title czar (caesar).

A Franciscan commissioner reports that many nuns are living "unreligious and unbridled" lives.

Painting: *The Annunciation* by Florentine painter Leonardo da Vinci, born out of wedlock 20 years ago at Vinci to a peasant girl and fathered by a prominent local notary who has taken the youth to Florence and apprenticed him to the master Andrea del Verrocchio.

The grand duke of Muscovy Ivan III (above) will use Italian architects brought in by his wife, Zoë, to rebuild Moscow's grand ducal palace, the Kremlin.

1473

 The *Dispositio Achilles,* signed by the elector of Brandenburg Albrecht III, 59, legalizes the custom of primogeniture that has existed for centuries and helped motivate younger sons of Europe's nobility to join the Crusades in quest of lands. Albrecht is known as Achilles, and his "Dispositio" makes the eldest surviving male in a family the heir to the power and fortune of his father.

Japan's civil war continues despite the deaths of Gen. Katsumoto Hosokawa and Sōzen Yamana. Tomiko Hino's son Yoshihisa, now 8, becomes shōgun following the resignation of her husband, and Tomiko Hino, who has grown rich by loaning money at high interest to the combatants, imposing tolls, and speculating in rice, is the power behind the throne.

1474

Isabella succeeds to the throne of Castile and León December 13 upon the death of her half brother, who has ruled since 1454 as Enrique IV. But the succession 5 years after Isabella's marriage to Ferdinand of Aragon is challenged by Enrique's daughter, who is married to Portugal's Afonso V.

1475

Portugal and Castile go to war over the succession to Enrique IV (*see* 1474), but the cortes at Segovia recognizes Isabella's right to the throne with her husband, Ferdinand of Aragon.

1476

Wallachia returns Vlad Tepes (Dracula) to the throne January 31. Now 43, Dracula has married the sister of Hungary's Matthias Corvinus.

Milan's tyrant Galeazzo Maria Sforza is assassinated December 26 at age 32 by three young noblemen on the porch of the city's cathedral. He is succeeded by his 7-year-old son, Gian Galeazzo, under the regency of the boy's mother, Bona of Savoy (*see* 1450). She acknowledges that her late husband wronged the noblemen who killed him, asks the pope to issue a bull absolving Galeazzo's many and grievous sins, offers to make reparations and to build churches and monasteries and perform works of mercy, and endeavors to restore Milan's alliance with Ferrara by arranging a marriage between her daughter Anna and the newborn son and heir of Ferrara's Ercole d'Este. The pope tries to capitalize on the situation by pushing the marriage of Catharina Sforza, Galeazzo's daughter, to his own nephew, a match that had been arranged by Galeazzo (Bona has brought up Catharina with her own children) (*see* 1480).

1477

The Hapsburgs acquire the Netherlands August 18 through the marriage at Ghent of Maximilian, 18, son of the Holy Roman Emperor Frederick III, to Mary, 20, daughter of the late Charles the Bold.

The diamond engagement ring tradition has its beginnings as the counsel to the court of the Holy Roman Emperor Frederick III has the young archduke Maximilian (above) use the gold and silver pressed upon him by villagers as he sets out for Burgundy to have a jeweler create a gold ring set with diamonds forming the letter M.

1478

 Isabella of Castile launches an Inquisition against converted Jews who secretly practice their original faith, persecuting the so-called Marranos (the word originally meant pigs). The Inquisition will be broadened to cover all "heretics," including Muslims.

1479

✗ Aragon's Juan II dies January 20 at age 81 and is succeeded by his son Ferdinand, who at age 26 assumes the throne as Fernando II of Aragon and—through his 1469 marriage to his cousin Isabella—as Fernando V of Castile and León, uniting the major crowns of Spain to begin a reign that will continue until 1516.

1480

✗ Lodovico Sforza, 29, duke of Bari and a power at Milan, asks Ercole I of Ferrara for the hand of his daughter Isabella d'Este, 6. Lodovico is a powerful *condottieri*—a soldier of fortune who lives by hiring himself and whatever troops he can gather to the highest bidder among the constantly warring Italian city-states (the Republic of Florence, Duchy of Milan, Republic of Venice, papal states, and Kingdom of Naples are Italy's major powers, but there are many smaller powers). Ercole has promised Isabella to Gian Francesco Gonzaga, elder son of Mantua's marquis Federico, and unwilling to offend his close neighbor yet reluctant to miss the chance of so attractive an alliance, offers Lodovico the hand of Isabella's younger sister, Beatrice, 5 (*see* 1490; 1491).

1481

✗ Milanese power changes hands as Lodovico Sforza (Il Moro), uncle of Gian Galeazzo Sforza, ousts the boy's mother, Bona of Savoy, from her regency and takes over (*see* 1494).

1482

✗ Mary of Burgundy, daughter of the late Charles the Bold, dies March 27 at age 27 after a hunting accident in Flanders. Her husband, Maximilian of Austria, claims power over the Lowlands as regent for their infant son Philip; Brabant and Flanders reject his claims.

1483

✗ England's Edward IV dies April 9 at age 40 after a tyrannical reign in which he has enriched himself by confiscating the estates of his enemies and going into partnership with London merchants. His 1464 marriage to Elizabeth Woodville was invalid, Parliament rules June 5, and the two sons by that marriage are illegitimate. Edward's capable brother Richard, duke of Gloucester, is proclaimed king, Elizabeth's two sons are found smothered in the Tower of London, it is widely believed that they were murdered on Richard's orders, and Elizabeth flees to safety while the late king's mistress, Jane Shore, finds a new protector (*see* 1470; 1486).

France's Louis XI (the Spider) dies August 10 at age 60 after a 22-year reign in which the nation's prosperity has revived despite oppressive taxes. His wife, Charlotte, dies December 1. The tyrannical Louis is succeeded by his ugly, deformed son of 13, who will reign until 1498 as Charles VIII.

1484

✊ Pope Innocent VIII succeeds to the papacy and inveighs against witchcraft and sorcery. The bull *Summis desiderantes affectibus* issued December 5 initiates harsh measures against German "witches" and magicians. Any self-assured, independent woman risks being labeled a witch.

⚕ While clerics cite the Old Testament ("Thou shalt not suffer a witch to live," said Exodus [22:19]), so-called witches (above) are often midwives, detested by physicians for encroaching on their obstetrical practice.

1485

✗ The Battle of Bosworth August 22 ends England's Wars of the Roses, which have continued since 1460. French and Welsh forces help Henry, earl of Richmond, defeat Richard III, whose crown is found hanging on a bush and passes to the earl. He is crowned at Westminster October 30 and will reign until 1509 as Henry VII, inaugurating the Tudor dynasty, which will rule for 117 years (*see* 1486).

A mysterious "sweating sickness" forces postponement of Henry VII's coronation. It closes down Oxford for 6 weeks, spreads quickly to London, and within a week has killed thousands (*see* 1507).

Le Morte d'Arthur by the late Sir Thomas Malory is published by the English printer William Caxton and includes such lines as "there syr launcelot toke the fayrest lady by the hand, and she was naked as a nedel."

1486

England's Henry VII marries Elizabeth, daughter of the late Edward IV and his consort, Elizabeth Woodville (*see* 1483).

1489

Malleus maleficarum (*The Witches' Hammer*, i.e., the hammer with which to strike witches) by the inquisitors Hendrich (or Heinrich) Kramer and Jacob Sprenger in northern Germany is a handbook on witch-hunting that will be used to justify the burning and shackling of innocent midwives and countless mentally ill people (*see* 1484): "All witchcraft comes from carnal lust, which in women is insatiable. . . . Wherefore for the sake of fulfilling their lusts they consort even with devils"; "They have slippery tongues, and are able to conceal from their fellow-women those things which by evil arts they know; and, since they are weak, they find an easy and secret manner of vindicating themselves by witchcraft." The University of Cologne endorses the work, which has much to say about the sexual problems (infertility, impotence, painful coitus, nymphomania, and satyriasis) caused by "witches" and is studied throughout western Europe (*see* Wier, 1563).

1490

Isabella d'Este, now nearly 16, is married February 11 at Ferrara to Gian Francesco Gonzaga, 24, marquis of Mantua, whose sister Elizabetta is duchess of Urbino and will be a close friend of Isabella's.

"Witches" were persecuted by the superstitious, often with encouragement from jealous physicians.

The beautiful and learned Isabella has been raised partly at Ferrara and partly at the royal court of her grandfather Ferrante of Naples.

Beatrice d'Este turns 15 June 29 and sets out from Ferrara December 29 to marry Lodovico Sforza, duke of Bari and regent of Milan.

Tomiko Hino becomes a Buddhist nun. She effectively ruled as shōgun from 1474 until last year, when her son died.

1491

Beatrice d'Este marries Lodovico Sforza in the Castello of Pavia January 17, a date chosen as propitious by Il Moro in consultation with his court physician and astrologer. Cecilia Gallerani, his former mistress, gives birth May 1 to a boy, Cesare; Il

Moro gives her a stately mansion near the duomo at Milan, built originally by his ancestor Filippo Maria Visconti; he tells his bride the news of his son's birth and repeats his vow never to renew his liaison with Cecilia.

France's Charles VIII annexes Brittany by marrying Anne, duchess of Brittany. He thereby offends the German king Maximilian I, to whose daughter Margaret he was affianced as a dauphin by his late father, Louis XI (*see* 1492).

England's Henry VII goes to war to prevent the French annexation of Brittany (above), making peace with Scotland to release his troops for action on the Continent.

Lodovico Sforza, sends Beatrice 4 months later on a diplomatic mission to Venice, accompanied by a retinue of 1,200 that includes her mother, the duchess of Ferrara; still under 18, she sails down the Po and into the Adriatic, is entertained at Venice with a regatta, boat races, banquets, balls, and a torchlight procession, achieves few tangible results, but impresses the old Venetian councillors with her quickness, wisdom, and eloquence. She and her mother leave Venice June 2 and return to Ferrara, where she is reunited with her infant son. Her mother, Leonora, dies of a gastric infection October 11.

The German king Frederick III has died August 19 at Linz; his successor, Maximilian I, now 34, is married by proxy November 30 to Bianca Maria Sforza, 21, in the duomo at Milan (his first wife, Mary of

1492

Castile's Queen Isabella, who has borrowed the wherewithal from Luis de Santangel by putting up her jewels as security, finances navigator Christopher Columbus, who crosses the Atlantic to make the first known European landing in the Western Hemisphere since early in the 11th century.

Anne of Brittany crowned queen of France at St. Denis, February (*see* 1491). German king Maximilian tries to form a coalition against Anne's husband, Charles VII, to avenge his injured honor, seeks help from England's Henry VII, and Henry sends a letter to Lodovico Sforza, urging him to lead his Milanese forces in a southern invasion of France.

A decree issued March 31 by Ferdinand and Isabella (above) extends the Spanish Inquisition begun by Isabella in Castile in 1478. It orders Granada's 150,000 Jews to sell up and leave by July 31 "for the honor and glory of God."

Cecilia Gallerani, former mistress to Lodovico Sforza (Il Moro), is married in July to Count Lodovico Bergamene of Cremona.

Castile's Queen Isabella pledged her jewels as security to finance Columbus on his voyage of discovery. LIBRARY OF CONGRESS

1493

Beatrice d'Este gives birth at Milan January 25 to a son, who is given the name Ercole. Her husband,

Burgundy, died in 1482). The bride soon leaves to cross the Alps with Maximilian's ambassadors, accompanied as far as Como by an entourage that includes Lodovico and Beatrice (d'Este) Sforza, who rename their son Ercole Maximilian in honor of his godfather.

Isabella d'Este gives birth December 30 to her first child, a girl who is named Leonora.

1494

 King Ferrante of Naples dies January 25 at age 70. He has tried to get his son-in-law Lodovico Sforza to join him against France's Charles VII.

Bianca Maria Sforza reaches Vienna in March; her husband, Maximilian I, arrives, and they finally consummate their marriage. He treats her kindly at first but quickly finds fault with her extravagant habits and will soon leave her mostly to her own devices as her health begins to fail (she dies in 1510).

The duc d'Orléans crosses the Alps July 10 in the vanguard of a French army. Lodovico Sforza goes to meet him 3 days later, Orléans asks for a loan of 60,000 ducats, Lodovico undertakes to arrange the loan, but they soon have a falling-out.

Gian Galeazzo, duke of Milan, dies at Pavia October 21 at age 25, and there are false rumors that he was poisoned by his uncle, Lodovico Sforza, who becomes duke in his own right (see 1476). The young man's mother, Bona of Savoy, departs for Amboise and will return in 1499 to Savoy, where she will remain until her death in 1504. Isabella d'Este arrives at Milan November 28 to be with her sister, the duchess, and will remain in complete retirement for the next 2 years.

 Queen Isabella of Castile suspends a royal order for the sale of more than 500 Carib "Indians" into slavery. Christopher Columbus has brought the Caribs home from the West Indies, but the queen suggests in a letter to Bishop Fonseca that any sale await an inquiry into the causes for the imprisonment of the docile Indians and the lawfulness of their sale. When theologians differ on the lawfulness, Isabella orders the Caribs returned to their island.

1495

 Beatrice d'Este at Milan gives birth in February to a second son, who will be known as Francesco Sforza.

France's Charles VIII sends home for reinforcements to help him in his Italian campaign; his wife, Anne of Brittany, replies that there are no Frenchmen left to send—only widows grieving for their lost husbands. Lodovico Sforza arrives in September at the French camp with his wife, Beatrice, who impresses the French with her cleverness and tact.

The Spanish infanta Juana, 15-year-old daughter of Ferdinand and Isabella, marries Philip the Handsome, Count of Flanders, and settles with him at Ghent (see 1504).

Syphilis may have come back to Europe with Columbus from the New World—or perhaps it had always been there.

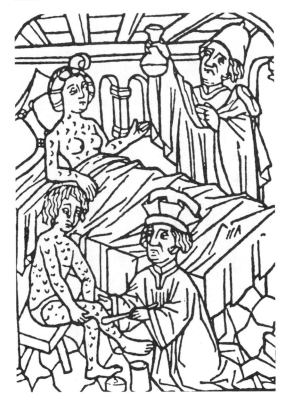

1495

 Syphilis strikes Naples in history's first recorded outbreak of the disease that will appear throughout Europe in the next 25 years, but the disease may have existed for years and been confused with leprosy. A more virulent form of syphilis than the disease of later centuries, the "new" malady infects the army of France's Charles VIII, who has laid siege to the city. Frenchmen call it the Neapolitan disease, Italians the French disease.

1496

 The count of Angoulême dies suddenly January 1 at age 41 after twice having made his young wife (and cousin), Louise, now 19, and his longtime mistress, Jeanne de Polignac, pregnant at the same time. Louise's daughter, Marguerite, will play a significant role in French politics, and her infant son, François, born in September 1494, will become king.

1497

 Beatrice d'Este gives birth to a stillborn son January 3 and dies at Milan a few hours later at age 21. Her husband, Duke Lodovico Sforza, loses the voice of reason and wisdom that has curbed his impetuosity, he antagonizes Venice, the pope turns against him, and he will soon come to grief (see 1500).

Lucrezia Borgia, 17, duchess of Ferrara, has her father, Pope Alexander VI (Rodrigo Borgia), annul the marriage that he arranged for her 4 years ago to Giovanni Sforza, lord of Pesaro. He betrothes the golden-haired beauty to Alfonso of Aragon, a nephew of the king of Naples; the match appalls Alfonso's sister, Isabella d'Este, but the pope almost completely cancels the annual fee that Ferrara pays as a fief of the Church (see 1501).

1498

 France's Charles VIII dies April 8 at age 27 after accidentally cracking his head on the lintel of a passageway in the castle of Amboise. Having no male heir, he is succeeded by his Valois cousin the duc d'Orléans, now 36, who will reign until 1515 as Louis XII.

1499

 France's Louis XII obtains a divorce from his barren wife of 16 years, Jeanne, daughter of the late Louis XI. He marries Anne of Brittany, widow of the late Charles VIII, to keep the duchy of Brittany in the French crown.

Lucrezia Borgia is appointed governor of Spoleto. Her father, Pope Alexander VI, confiscates the castles of the Gaetani family on the frontier between Naples and the Papal States; Lucrezia is able to buy them for 80,000 ducats.

1500

 France's Louis XII annexes Milan on the basis of his being the great-grandson of Gian Galeazzo Visconti. Lodovico Sforza has been captured April 10 and thrown into a French prison, where he will die in 8 years in a subterranean dungeon at Loches despite efforts by his sister-in-law Isabella d'Este to obtain his release. Isabella gives birth May 26 to a son, Federico, whose godfather is Cesare Borgia (see 1512).

 Portuguese navigator Gaspar de Corte-Real (or Corterreal), 50, makes the first authenticated European landing on the northern continent of the Western Hemisphere since Leif Ericsson 500 years ago and Thorfinn Karlsefni a few years later.

16th Century

✠ Ferdinand of Aragon declares Granada a Christian kingdom but encounters resistance from the Moors.

Lucrezia Borgia is married at Christmastime for the third and last time at age 21 to Alfonso d'Este, duke of Ferrara. The proxy wedding at Rome follows several rounds of debauched partying in which her father and her brother Cesare have been involved. Isabella d'Este and her two younger brothers escort the bride back to Ferrara, where the city sees a procession of 75 liveried archers, 80 trumpeters, 24 pipers, and numerous noblemen, squires, gentlemen, bishops, and ladies in carriages. Isabella's father puts on six comedies in a new theater large enough to seat 5,000.

✊ Spanish settlers at Santo Domingo introduce African slaves into Hispaniola—the first importation of blacks to the New World (*see* 1511).

1502

✠ Cesare Borgia, 26, attacks Urbino in north-central Italy while the duchy's artillery is away helping Cesare's father, Pope Alexander VI. Guidiobaldo di Montefeltro, duke of Urbino, 30, and his wife, Elizabetta, flee and Cesare adds Urbino to the pope's possessions. Pope Alexander offers Elizabetta an annulment of her marriage to the ailing duke and a potent French husband to replace him, Cesare Borgia promises her a pension, but although she is living on Venetian charity in exile with her husband she refuses the offer (*see* 1503).

Castile expels the last of the Moors, who have been in the country since 711.

1503

✠ Pope Alexander VI dies of malaria August 18 at age 72 after a papacy in which he has flaunted his mistresses (including, most recently, the teenaged blonde Giulia Vernese) and even had a painting of his chief mistress, Rosa Vanozza de' Catanei, dressed as the Virgin Mary, executed over the door to his bedroom. He has publicly acknowledged his four illegitimate children by Rosa, including his son Cesare and his daughter Lucrezia, who had her first two husbands while still in her teens.

Cesare Borgia's power crumbles following the death of his father, Pope Alexander (above). The people of Urbino drive out Borgia's soldiers and welcome back Duke Guidiobaldo and his faithful wife, Elizabetta, who surround themselves with the leading poets, painters, musicians, and writers of Italy, conducting endless discussions about life, ethics, manners, poetry, and love. The duke's soldiers include Count Baldassare Castiglione, 25, who adores Elizabetta and will soon serve the court as resident intellectual and ambassador (*see* 1516).

1504

✠ Ferdinand II of Aragon completes his conquest of Naples January 1 with the surrender of French forces at Gaeta. France controls northern Italy from Milan, the Spanish southern Italy, Sicily, and Naples, which they will hold until 1707.

Castile's Isabella the Catholic dies November 24 at age 53 after a 30-year reign in which she has financed the voyages of Columbus and persecuted non-Christians with the Inquisition. She is succeeded by her daughter Juana, now 25, and Juana's husband, Philip the Handsome (Felipe el Hermoso), but they remain in Flanders (*see* 1506).

1506

✗ Philip the Handsome dies suddenly at Burgos September 25 at age 28. His wife, Juana, lapses into profound melancholia and is declared unfit to govern (she will be known as "Juana la loca" and, along with her youngest daughter, Catalina, will be held under close surveillance at Tordesillas until her death in 1555); her father, Ferdinand II of Aragon, becomes regent of Castile and marries Germaine de Fox, niece of France's Louis XII. He will rule Castile until 1516 as Ferdinand V.

1507

✗ Maximilian I appoints his daughter Margaret of Austria, 26, guardian of her nephew the archduke Charles, 7, who is betrothed by treaty to the daughter of England's Henry VII. Maximilian makes Margaret regent of the Netherlands to serve until Charles is of age.

✊ The Portuguese capture Zafi in Morocco and begin commerce in captive Moors, Berbers, and Jews. Many are women, all are called white slaves.

⚕ The sweating sickness that struck London in 1485 strikes again (*see* 1518).

🎨 Painting: *Mona Lisa* by Leonardo da Vinci, who has been making sketches at Milan since 1505 of Lisa di Anton, Neapolitan wife of local businessman-politician Francesco del Giocando, 46. His model departs in the spring for Calabria on a long business trip with her husband, and the portrait is left incomplete.

The enigmatic smile of Leonardo da Vinci's Mona Lisa *raised questions that would defy answers down the centuries.* LOUVRE MUSEUM, PARIS

1508

✗ Maximilian I assumes the title of Roman Emperor-elect February 4 at Trent, and Pope Julius II decrees that the German king shall hereafter automatically become Holy Roman Emperor.

Isabella d'Este tries to send her son Federico, now 8, to safety in Genoa (she has remained at Milan despite Lodovico Sforza's urgings that she leave). Louis XII seizes the youth and does not allow him to return to his mother, and when he leaves Milan for France November 7 he takes Federico with him.

1509

✗ England's Henry VII dies April 22 at age 52 after a reign of nearly 24 years. His tall (6 feet 2 inches), athletic, well-educated son of 17 is married June 11 to Catherine of Aragon, 23, widow of his late brother and daughter of Ferdinand II. The new king will reign until 1547 as Henry VIII.

🖋 Nonfiction: *Of the Nobility and Excellence of Women* (*De nobilitate et praecellentia feminei sexus*) by German occultist philosopher Henricus Cornelius Agrippa von Nettesheim, 23, employs the writings of historians, poets, theologians, and mythmakers to support his 30 chapters, which he has dedicated to Margaret of Burgundy (*see* 1529).

1510

✕ Parliament attaints two former House of Commons speakers, and they are beheaded in mid-August. Henry VIII has charged them with treason, but their real crime has been their use of extortion in administering Henry's arbitrary taxation system and enriching themselves in the process.

⚚ The Venetian painter Giorgione (Giorgio da Castelfranco) dies of plague at age 32, having caught the disease from "a certain lady."

⚲ Venetian women adopt a platform-style shoe called the *chopine,* worn by Turkish harem women for hygienic reasons when visiting the bath (date approximate). One version, worn by men, has an iron ring on top to make it easier for its wearer to lift his feet from the mud. Women wear shoes mounted on painted wooden stands that raise them from three to four inches to a foot above the ground, making it impossible to walk in extreme versions of the shoe unless supported by a maid on either side. Prostitutes wear more elevated *chopines* to display themselves as they parade about the Piazza San Marco.

1511

✕ The papal forces of Julius II take Modena and Mirandola from the French in January, the French take Bologna May 13, Pope Julius allies himself with Venice to drive the French out of Italy, and in October he enlists Castile's Ferdinand II and England's Henry VIII in his Holy League.

✊ African slaves arrive in Cuba. Spaniards have imported them as laborers because the native Carib population has dropped alarmingly.

⚚ Parliament licenses 37 London women to practice surgery, some of them in combination with other aspects of medicine such as midwifery.

1512

✕ Forces of the Holy League meet defeat in an Easter battle at Ravenna, but a coalition of Swiss, papal, and imperial forces drive the French and their 5,000 German mercenaries out of Milan in May and return the Sforzas to power in their duchy.

The Swiss take Locarno, Lugano, and Ossola as their reward for helping to drive the French out of Milan.

1513

✕ French forces in Italy suffer bad defeats June 6 at Novara and August 17 at Guinegate. The allies force Louis XII to end his Italian invasion.

The Battle of Flodden Field September 9 just south of the Scottish border ends in victory for an English army sent by Henry VIII against Scotland's James IV, who is killed at age 40 while fighting on foot.

1514

✕ Persia is invaded by the Ottoman sultan Selim the Grim, who has slaughtered an estimated 40,000 of his heretic subjects and is determined to impose Sunnism on the Shiite Persians. His 80,000 cavalrymen rout a Persian army August 23, wounding Shah Ismail and forcing him to flee, leaving behind the favorites of his harem. Selim enters Tabriz September 15 and massacres much of its populace.

France's Louis XII, whose second wife has died without bearing a male heir to the throne, is married October 9 to the English princess Mary Tudor, 18.

1515

✕ France's Louis XII dies January 1 at age 52 after a 15-year reign. His widow, Mary Tudor, feigns pregnancy by wrapping towels around her waist and fainting in public, but Louise of Savoy demands that Mary be given a thorough physical examination and doctors find no evidence that she is pregnant. Louis is succeeded by his robust son-in-law and cousin once removed, François of Valois-Angoulême, who is not quite 21. The new king, who will reign until 1547 as François I under the domination of his mother, Louise of Savoy, leads his troops through the Alps into Lombardy in September and wins the 2-day Battle of Marignano, enforcing his claim to the title duke of Milan.

1516

✗ The Hapsburg dynasty, which will rule Spain until 1700, is founded February 23 upon the death at age 63 of Ferdinand of Castile and León (Ferdinand II of Aragon). Ferdinand's grandson, 16, a student in Flanders, unites Catalonia and Valencia with the kingdoms of Ferdinand and will reign until 1556 as Carlos I (his mother, Juana, remains incarcerated at Tordesillas).

Pope Leo X deposes the nephew of Guidobaldo di Montefeltro from the ducal throne of Urbino. Count Baldassare Castiglione, now 39, returns to Mantua and marries a teenage girl with whom he will find considerable happiness until her death after bearing their third child (*see* 1503; nonfiction, 1528).

1517

∞ The Reformation of the Catholic Church begins October 31 at Wittenberg, 60 miles southwest of Berlin, on the Elbe. Augustinian monk Martin Luther, 34, nails 95 theses to the door of the cathedral, challenging the excesses and abuses of the Roman Church, notably the sale of indulgences. Luther's action begins a long period of religious and civil wars in Europe.

1518

✗ Lorenzo de' Medici, 26, a grandson of Lorenzo the Magnificent, journeys to France from his native Florence in March and is married in late May at the Château d'Amboise to Madeleine de La Tour d'Auvergne, 16, a match arranged by his uncle,

Pope Leo X, to cement relations with the new French king François I. The wedding banquet is held in a great hall, a fanfare announces each new course, and 72 graceful demoiselles of the court dance until well after midnight in German, French, and Italian costumes. Guests include Diane de Poitiers, 18, and her husband Louis de Brezés, 59, Grand Seneschal of Normandy, to whom she was married 3 years ago. The wastrel bridegroom, unfortunately, has an unhealed wound which saps his vigor. He also has syphilis, but by the time he reaches Florence in September with his bride she is pregnant.

 A third major epidemic of the sweating sickness spreads over England with more severity than in 1507. It wipes out most of the population in some towns, many important figures succumb at Cambridge and Oxford, the disease reaches Calais, but it affects only the English there (*see* 1529).

1519

✗ The Holy Roman Emperor Maximilian I dies January 12 at age 59, and Spain's Carlos I is elected emperor as Charles V after Augsburg merchants bribe some electors. Louise of Savoy has dispensed liberal tribes to swing the election to her son, France's François I, but has been outbid by the agents of Carlos I. The election plunges Europe into political turmoil that will culminate in war (*see* 1525).

Isabella d'Este's husband, Francesco Gonzaga, dies April 4, leaving her a widow of 44. Her son, Federico, now 20, is formally declared marquis of Mantua with Isabella as regent. He falls in love with Isabella Boschetti, a matron who will be his mistress.

Madeleine de' Medici gives birth to a baby girl, Catarina (Catherine), April 13 at Florence but dies April 28 at age 17. Her husband, Lorenzo, dies at Florence of syphilis and tuberculosis May 4 at age 27.

Lucrezia Borgia dies at Ferrara June 24 at age 39 after giving birth to a stillborn child.

 Spanish adventurer Hernando Cortez, 34, sails from Cuba with 500 Castilians, nearly 300 natives, and 16 horses to conquer New Spain. He pays a ransom to secure the release of Geronimo de Aguilar, who was shipwrecked off the coast of Yucatán in 1511 and has learned the Mayan dialect. Cortez discovers in March that a 15-year-old Tabascan slave girl named Malinali speaks not only Mayan but also her native language, Nahuatl, which is the tongue of the Aztecs and other subject people. She is baptized along with nearly 20 other women, given the name Doña Marina, and taken aboard ship when the Spaniards move north along the coast. By translating from Nahuatl to Mayan, she enables Aguilar to communicate with the Aztecs and soon finds herself speaking for Cortez himself in negotiations with the natives, who use the name *Malintzin,* or *Malinche,* both for Cortez and the woman who speaks for him. The Aztec king Montezuma II meets with them November 8 at the gates of his capital, Tenochtitlán, and Malinche persuades him that he will be safe under the protection of Cortez (*see* 1520).

1520

 Denmark's Christian II invades Sweden with a large army of French, German, and Scottish mercenaries. He has persuaded Pope Leo X to excommunicate Sten Sture the Younger and place Sweden under an interdict, he defeats Sture at Bogesund, Sture sustains a mortal wound January 19 at the Battle of Tiveden, and Christian advances without opposition on Uppsala, where the Swedish Riksraad has assembled. The Swedish senators agree to accept Christian as king provided that he rule according to Swedish laws and customs and without recriminations. The king signs a convention March 31, but Sture's widow, Dame Christina Gyllenstjerna, at Stockholm has rallied the peasantry to defeat the Danish invaders at Balundsas March 19. The bloody Battle of Uppsala April 6 (Good Friday) gives Christian a narrow victory over the Swedish patriots, the Danish fleet arrives in May, Christian lays siege to Stockholm, and Christina surrenders September 7 on the promise of a general amnesty. Christian is crowned hereditary king of Sweden at Stockholm's cathedral November 4, Danish soldiers seize some of the king's guests November 7. Convicted of heresy and violence against the church, the bishops of Skara and Stragnas are beheaded in the public square at Stockholm at midnight, November 8, and the Danes kill 80 other Swedes in the ensuing bloodbath.

Christian II (above) has his men exhume the body of Sten Sture and burn it along with that of Sture's small child. He has Sten's widow, Dame Christina, and other Swedish noblewomen sent to Denmark as prisoners and suppresses opposition on the pretense of defending the church.

Hernando Cortez leaves Tenochtitlán for the coast in early May with his interpreters Aguilar and Doña Marina and most of his men (*see* 1519). His garrison at Tenochtitlán comes under attack in his absence after killing many unarmed young noblemen, Cortez returns to the capital, Montezuma II is fatally injured in the fighting that ensues. Aztec forces attack the Spaniards, who lose 900 of their 1,300-man force; the remaining 400 are all wounded but escape the massacre along with Doña Marina and another Indian woman (*see* 1521).

1521

 The Battle of Vilialar April 23 gives the Holy Roman Emperor Charles V a victory over insurgent *communeros,* ending the last Spanish resistance to absolutism. French support of the *communeros* and French designs on Navarre precipitate a war between France and Spain that will continue for 8 years.

Hernando Cortez starves out Tenochtitlán, which falls to his siege forces August 13 (*see* 1520). A group of 800 Aztec women and children have been captured when they came out of hiding at night in search of food. Cortez becomes captain-general of New Spain and sole ruler of the Aztecs with help from his mistress, Doña Marina (*see* 1522).

∞ Martin Luther writes that the sexual impulse is both natural and irrepressible. He will argue that celibacy was invented by the Devil as a source of sin and will advance the view that marriage is not a sacrament at all but rather a civil matter subject to city and state regulations, not canon law (*see* 1524).

1522

💲 Hernando Cortez's mistress, Doña Marina, gives birth to the conquistador's son, and he rewards her for her services by bestowing upon her enough land, gold, and vassals to keep her comfortable for life, but he sends to Cuba for his young wife, the noblewoman Doña Catalina Suárez de Marcayda (*see* 1521; 1523).

∞ Swiss Reformation clergyman Huldreich Zwingli, 38, condemns celibacy and Lenten fasting, calls on the bishop of Constance to permit priests to marry (or at least wink at their marriages), and will himself marry in 1524.

1523

✖ England's Henry VIII tries to force a grant of funds from Parliament and provokes a rebellion that ends only when the king abandons his demand.

Hernando Cortez's wife, Doña Catalina, dies under mysterious circumstances soon after her arrival in New Spain. Doña Marina remains the conquistador's chief interpreter and his major ally in converting the people to Christianity, but she will die at age 24 in 1527 or early 1528, possibly of smallpox.

∞ Huldreich Zwingli at Zurich publishes his 67 articles January 19, attacking transsubstantiation and the authority of the pope.

1524

✖ The constable de Bourbon lays siege to Marseilles in a civil war against France's François I. Female reinforcements arrive under the leadership of Améliane de Glandèves, throw back the constable's forces, and, when the enemy lays mines, dig a trench to plant mines of their own.

∞ "Only one woman in thousands has been endowed with the God-given aptitude to live in chastity and virginity," Martin Luther writes in *Kritische Gesamtausgabe.* "God fashioned her body so that she should be with a man, to have and to rear children. No woman should be ashamed of that for which God made and intended her."

1525

✖ The Battle of Pavia February 24 gives Spanish and German forces a victory over France's François I and his Swiss mercenaries. François is taken to Madrid in chains and writes to his mother, Louise of Savoy, "There is nothing left to me but honor, and my life, which is saved."

∞ Martin Luther, now 42, marries former nun Katharina von Bora, 26, who ran away from the Cistercian convent of Nimptschen, near Grimma, 2 years ago after adopting Lutheran doctrines. He has urged some nuns to leave their convent and has helped them find husbands; Katharina's (Käte's) proposed match has fallen through, she has been forced to work as a domestic servant, and Luther marries her, although not out of love and with misgivings that marriage may lose him the respect of some followers. Katharina will bear him six children, run his farm, and prove efficient in running the former Augustinian monastery at Wittenberg that she and Luther will use as a home (*see* 1531).

1526

✖ France's François I signs the humiliating Treaty of Madrid January 14 after being held captive for nearly a year by the emperor Charles V. He abandons Burgundy and renounces his claims to Flanders, Artois, Tournai, and Italy; once released, he says the terms were extorted and the treaty is invalid, but his wife, Claude, has died and he does agree to take as his second wife the Spanish princess Eleanor. Some observers characterize the stiff and solemn Eleanor as an "Andalusian madonna"; the king, who much prefers the company of his mistress, Anne d'Heilly, duchesse d'Etampes, is not content with beauty but rather seeks out learned women, feeling flattered by their intellectual conversation (although critics say their influence is bad for the country).

1527

∞ England's Henry VIII appeals to Rome for permission to divorce Catherine of Aragon, who has had several miscarriages and is clearly not going to pro-

Catherine of Aragon was the first of Henry VIII's six wives and remained his wife from 1509 to 1532.

duce an heir, so that he may marry his young mistress, Anne Boleyn.

Marguerite d'Angoulême, 35, queen of Navarre and older sister of France's François I, makes writers such as Rabelais welcome at her Château de Nerac in Agen; she creates an intellectual court while writing poetry, moral tales, and letters that encourage religious liberty (*see* 1531).

1528

French forces lay siege to Naples in the war against Charles V. Imperial troops come close to starvation, but typhus forces an end to the siege in late August.

∞ Austrian evangelist Jacob Hutter founds a "community of love" whose Austrian, German, and Swiss members share everything communally.

Nonfiction: *The Courtier* (*Il cortegiano*) by Count Baldassare Castiglione, now 50, whose manual for courtiers in dialogue form has circulated privately for some years (*see* 1516). Castiglione was sent by the duke of Urbino in 1505 as an envoy to England's Henry VII (who made him a knight) and has since served as Mantua's ambassador to the papal court at Rome and as papal nuncio for Pope Clement VII in Spain. He recounts four evenings of conversation among several dozen lords and ladies at Urbino in March 1507. The ideal lady and ideal gentleman must be of aristocratic birth, he says, and his characters expound on concepts of love, courtship, and sexual conduct. "Love is the source of all sweetness and moral virtue and leads men to concentrate on beauty, and beauty leads the mind toward the contemplation of divinity." A lover must see his lady often and converse with her, says Castiglione in his neo-Platonic theory of ideal love, instead of going off on endless quests in the name of serving her, as in medieval times, but to be the finest and most ennobling their love must remain chaste. "If the gentleman shall be pert . . . she will give him such an answer that he may clearly understand he is causing her annoyance. Again, if he shall be discreet and use modest phrases and words of love covertly . . . the lady will feign not to understand and will reply to his words in another sense, always modestly trying to change the subject. . . . If again the talk is such that she cannot feign not to understand she will take it all as a jest, pretending to be aware that it is said to her more out of compliment to her than because it is true, deprecating her merits and ascribing the praises that he gives her to the gentleman's courtesy." A woman should never show her admirer any clear sign of love, either by words or gestures or any other means. Castiglione will die next year in Spain.

1529

Henry VIII removes Cardinal Wolsey as his lord chancellor October 17 for failing to secure a papal annulment of his marriage; he replaces Wolsey with Thomas More.

French housewife Desle la Mansenée, 22, is hanged at Anjeux December 18 after being convicted of murder, heresy, and renouncing the Catholic faith. She has been accused of witchcraft and tortured by squassation (tied with weights and dropped from a height) until she confessed to her prosecutors that the Devil has promised her wealth if she will turn from Jesus, has made love to her, made her attend witches' sabbaths, and given her powers not only to poison cattle but actually to alter the weather.

London has a severe epidemic of the sweating sickness in May, the first since 1518, and the disease spreads in 2 months to Hamburg, Lübeck, and Bremen, reaches Mecklenburg in August, Königsberg and Danzig in September, and then strikes Göttingen, where it rages so fiercely that bodies must be buried eight to a grave. The epidemic moves on to Marburg, Augsburg, Vienna, and Switzerland but somehow spares the French (see 1551).

Protestantism gets its name April 16 as followers of Martin Luther protest a ruling by the Diet of Speyer that forbids the teaching of Luther's ideas in Catholic states while permitting Catholics to teach in Lutheran states.

Nonfiction: *On the Nobility and Excellence of Women* by Cornelius Heinrich Agrippa von Nettesheim, 45, whose work is finally published (see 1509). He aroused hostility at Cologne nearly a decade ago by defending a woman charged with witchcraft, but has been doctor and astrologer to France's queen mother, Louise of Savoy, and historian to Margaret of Austria at Antwerp. "Woman does not have a soul of a different sex from that which animates man," he writes. "Both received a soul which is absolutely the same and of an equal condition. Women and men were equally endowed with the gifts of spirit, reason, and the use of words; they were created for the same end, and the sexual difference between them will not confer a different destiny."

1530

Spain's Carlos I is officially crowned Charles V of the Holy Roman Empire and king of Italy February 23 at Bologna by Pope Clement VII.

Cardinal Wolsey dies November 29 at age 55 after a political career in which he has amassed a fortune second only to that of Henry VIII.

1531

The Schmalkaldic League organized February 6 allies the majority of Europe's Protestant princes against the Holy Roman Emperor Charles V.

The Catholic cantons attack Zurich and defeat Protesant forces October 11 in the Battle of Kappel. Huldreich Zwingli is killed in the fighting.

Poetry: *Mirror of the Sinful Soul* (*Le Miroir de l'âme pécheresse*) by Marguerite d'Angoulême, queen of Navarre, is based on the assumption that a woman is every bit man's equal in relation to God. "A father will have compassion on his son. A mother will never forget her child. A brother will cover the sin of his sister. But what husband ever forgave the faithlessness of his wife?" A lifelong Catholic, Marguerite d'Angoulême is also a humanist, and her devotional poetry shows that the writings of John Calvin have had a strong influence on her.

Nonfiction: *Table-talk* by Martin Luther, who writes, "My wife is more precious to me than the kingdom of France and all the treasures of Venice" but says also, "Men have broad shoulders and narrow hips, and accordingly they possess intelligence. Women have narrow shoulders and broad hips. Women ought to stay at home; the way they were created indicates this, for they have broad hips and a wide fundament to sit upon (keep house and bear and raise children)."

1532

Brittany's duchess Anne signs the treaty of Plessis-Mace with her son-in-law, France's François I, who adds the duchy to his realm (final absorption of Brittany into France will come in 1547).

Nonfiction: *Table-talk* by Martin Luther, who advances the view that Jesus probably committed adultery with Mary Magdalene and other women so as to partake fully of the nature of man. "Get you a wife and then your mind, however fussy it is, will

Peasant women, like these painted by Breughel, worked in the fields alongside their men throughout the world.

become straight as a ribbon; it will be reduced to one idea: Do and think as *she* wishes." "No good ever came out of female domination. God created Adam master and lord of all living creatures, but Eve spoiled all."

1533

✘ England's Henry VIII marries Anne Boleyn, 26, who has been his mistress for the past 6 years. The ceremony is performed in secret January 25 by Thomas Cranmer, 43, who has advised Henry that his 1509 marriage to Catherine of Aragon is null and void because she was previously married to Henry's late brother Arthur, prince of Wales, even though that marriage was never consummated. Henry makes Cranmer archbishop of Canterbury March 30, and the new queen is crowned at Westminster June 1 (*see* 1536).

Catherine de' Medici of Florence, daughter of the late Lorenzo, marries Henri de Valois, 14, duc

d'Orléans, who will become France's Henri II in 1547. Catherine is also 14; her father's family, which has grown rich in the spice trade and by supplying alum to the textile industry, placed her in the care of her maternal aunt, Clarice Strozzi, as an infant, and she was tutored by Giulio Cardinal de' Medici.

♠ Marguerite d'Angoulême, queen of Navarre, sees to it that her brother, François I, gives her nieces Madeleine and Marguerite education in mathematics, Latin, and the arts; the king's new daughter-in-law, Catherine de' Medici, will far outdo them in her academic achievement, becoming as proficient in Greek as any man.

♦ Nonfiction: *Table-talk* by Martin Luther, who writes, "Girls begin to talk and to stand on their feet sooner than boys because weeds always grow up more quickly than good crops."

🌾 Catherine de' Medici (above) introduces to France such vegetables as broccoli, globe artichokes, savoy cabbage, and haricot beans—fagioli given her by her brother Alessandro.

✗ The double boiler, called by Italians the *bagno maria* after a legendary alchemist named Maria de Cleofa (Marie of Alexandria, or Maria the Jewess), is introduced to the French court by Catherine de' Medici. The French will call it a *bain-marie*. Stuffed guinea hen is introduced by Catherine, and the dish will be known to the French as pintade à la Médicis. Catherine also introduces truffles and starts the French digging enthusiastically for truffles of their own. Pastries such as frangipani, macaroons, and Milan cakes, introduced only recently to Florence, will be introduced to France by Catherine.

1534

✘ Mary of Lorraine, 19, daughter of Claude of Lorraine, first duc de Guise, marries Louis d'Orléans, duc de Longueville, who will soon die (*see* 1538).

∞ England's Henry VIII breaks with the Church of Rome because it has has voided the annulment of his 1509 marriage to Catherine of Aragon. The Act of Supremacy appoints the king Protector and Only Supreme Head of the Church and Clergy of England, a title to be handed down to his successors. Pope Clement VII, who has evaded Henry's demands for nullification of the 1509 marriage and refused to sanction his marriage to Anne Boleyn, dies September 25 after eating poisonous mushrooms.

English convents and their schools are closed by order of Henry VIII. Girls for the next half-century will have little education unless their parents can afford private tutors, send their daughters abroad, or risk persecution and stiff penalties by sponsoring unlicensed schools. Poor girls will attend charity schools, but such schools will be mostly for boys, and the closing of the convents with their resident nuns deprives the nation of female teachers.

1535

An Act of Union joins the principality of Wales to England (*see* Scotland, 1707).

Sir Thomas More is beheaded July 6 at age 57 by order of England's Henry VIII for refusing to swear an oath of supremacy as required by last year's law.

Dutch Anabaptist fanatic John of Leyden (Jan Beuckelszoon), 28, who last year established a theocratic kingdom of Zion at Münster and has shocked the world with his hedonistic orgies, beheads one of his four wives by his own hand in the town marketplace. He justifies all his arbitrary actions on the basis of having received visions of heaven. The besieged city falls June 24 after 12 months of profligacy, and the leading Anabaptists are imprisoned (*see* 1536).

1536

England's Henry VIII has his wife, Anne Boleyn, beheaded May 19 on charges of adultery and incest, although her guilt of anything more than arrogance is by no means clear. (It has also been suggested that she was a witch, the evidence being a rudimentary sixth finger on her left hand.) Henry has had witnesses tortured, and 16 have testified that she had incestuous relations with her brother George, swearing that they all clearly and at the same time saw her "alluring him with her tongue in the said

Ann Boleyn, Henry VIII's second wife, bore him a daughter but was beheaded for alleged infidelity. FROM THE PAINTING BY HANS HOLBEIN

George's mouth and the said George's tongue in hers." Five of her alleged lovers are also executed. "You have chosen me from a low estate to be your queen and companion, far beyond my desert or desire," Anne says in her final letter to Henry, and she tells her supporters, "The king has been very good to me. He promoted me from a simple maid to be a marchioness. Then he raised me to be a queen. Now he will raise me to be a martyr." She has borne the king a daughter, Elizabeth, but has recently miscarried, causing Henry to believe that there is a curse on the marriage. On May 20 he marries Anne's lady-in-waiting Jane Seymour, 27, whose brother is duke of Somerset. She takes as her motto "Bound to obey and serve."

France's dauphin the duc d'Orléans, now 17, becomes enamored of Diane de Poitiers, now 37, whose late husband, Louis de Brezés, died in 1531 at age 72. Despite the discrepancy in their ages, she will be the young man's mistress until his death in 1559.

☿ *Thrésor des remèdes secrets pour les maladies des femmes* by French physician Jean Liebault describes, among other things, regimens designed to overcome lack of fertility. Catherine de' Medici, wife of the dauphin (above), has been unable to conceive.

∞ John of Leyden and some of his more prominent followers are tortured with exquisite cruelty in January and then executed in the marketplace of Münster (*see* 1535). The Anabaptists are butchered wholesale and will hereafter lose their identify (the remains of their zealot leader will swing in a cage from a church rafter until the 20th century).

1537

✘ Henry VIII's third queen, Jane Seymour, dies October 24 at age 28 a few days after giving birth to a son who will become Edward VI in 1547.

1538

✘ The third war between France's François I and the Holy Roman Emperor Charles V ends June 18 with each side retaining possession of its conquests.

Mary of Lorraine, duchesse de Guise, now 23 and widowed, marries Scotland's widowed James V, 26 (*see* 1542).

✒ Nonfiction: *Table-talk* by Martin Luther, who writes, "Eloquence in women shouldn't be praised; it is more fitting for them to lisp and stammer. This is more becoming to them."

1539

✘ Isabella d'Este dies at Mantua February 13 at age 64 after a career in which she has used her diplomatic skills to sway rulers' decisions and influence politics. She has encouraged scholars, poets, and artists such as Ariosto, Castiglione, Leonardo, and Titian.

Charles V puts down a rebellion in his native Ghent, whose citizens have refused to pay taxes to finance the emperor's war with France. François I has not responded to their pleas for help, and they are stripped of their privileges.

1540

✘ England's Henry VIII marries Anne of Clèves at Greenwich January 6 less than a week after meeting her and 4 days after saying openly that she had no looks, spoke no English, and was "no better than a Flanders mare." Anne, 25, is the daughter of the German Protestant leader John, duke of Clèves, and the marriage has been arranged by the lord privy seal Baron Thomas Cromwell, 54, to give Henry an ally against the Holy Roman Emperor Charles V and France's François I, but Henry soon finds that he has no reason to fear an attack from either. The king says the marriage has not been (and cannot be) consummated; he makes Cromwell earl of Essex but has the duke of Norfolk charge him with treason June 10. Parliament sends Cromwell to the Tower of London and declares the king's marriage null and void July 9. Henry marries Norfolk's niece Catherine Howard, 25, and Cromwell is beheaded on Tower Hill July 28.

1541

✘ A fire at Constantinople burns much of the Old Palace, and the Ottoman sultan Suleiman II (the Magnificent) moves his harem into the seraglio, where it will remain until 1909 (he married his Russian slave Roxalena in 1530, becoming the first sultan to make one of his odalisques empress). Centered round the courtyard of the Valide Sultana and containing nearly 400 rooms, or *odas,* for the imperial odalisques, the seraglio is located between the sultan's private apartments and those of the chief black eunuch. Now 45, Suleiman has reigned since 1520 and will remain in power until his death in 1566, but moving his harem close to the court gives the women of the seraglio a dominant influence that will continue until 1687.

Odalisques of the harem at Constantinople controlled the Ottoman empire when sultans were weak.

Spanish conquistador Pedro de Valdivia in Chile founds the city of Santiago del Nuevo Extremo February 12. He has persuaded Francisco Pizarro to let him lead an expedition south from Peru, accompanied by the widow Inés de Suárez, 33, who came to South America 4 years ago in search of her husband, only to find in 1538 that he had died after the siege of Cuzco a year earlier. (Pizarro completes his conquest of Peru but is assassinated June 26.) Inés, who has saved Valdivia's expedition by finding a freshwater spring in the Atacama Desert, serves as Valdivia's nurse and overseer of the 1,000 Indian supply carriers. Valdivia leaves Santiago in early September with nearly 90 horsemen to subdue rebellious tribesmen to the south, the city is attacked September 11 by nearly 10,000 warriors; the Spaniards have taken seven native chiefs hostage, and Inés de Suárez proposes that all seven be decapitated and their heads thrown at the attackers while the city's defenders mount a cavalry charge. She herself beheads the first captive, the scheme works, Valdivia returns September 15, but the attackers have burned most of Santiago's houses and Inés has been able to save only two young sows, a boar, a hen, a cock, and two handfuls of wheat, which are planted to produce grain in the fertile valley (*see* 1543).

Nonfiction: *The Schoolhouse of Women* by English journalist Edward Gosynhill is an antifemale diatribe (*see* 1542).

1542

England's Henry VIII has his fifth wife, Catherine Howard, beheaded February 13 on charges of adultery. She has admitted to having had premarital intimacies with her cousin Thomas Culpepper and with Francis Dereham; she has had clandestine meetings with both since her marriage to the king, and they have been beheaded earlier.

The Battle of Solvay Moss November 25 gives Henry VIII a victory over Scotland's James V. James dies December 14 at age 30 and is succeeded by his week-old daughter Mary, Queen of Scots, who was born to his second wife, Mary of Guise, as he lay dying.

Nonfiction: *The Praise of All Women* by Edward Gosynhill, who reverses the arguments he made last year.

1543

England's Henry VIII, now 52, marries Catherine Parr, 31, July 12. She will have a chastening influence on the king in his final years.

A ship from Peru arrives at Santiago in September with clothing, iron goods, and military supplies to relieve the Spanish encampment headed by Pedro de Valdivia (*see* 1541). Inés de Suárez has raised thousands of pigs and chickens to feed the city's inhabitants, and although most of the first year's wheat crop has been used for seed grain the new crop harvested in December is large enough to provide abundant supplies of bread (*see* 1549).

1544

Parliament recognizes two daughters of Henry VIII as heirs to the English throne in the event that Henry's son Edward should die without issue. Mary is Henry's daughter by Catherine of Aragon, Elizabeth his daughter by Anne Boleyn.

An English army invades Scotland in May and sacks Edinburgh; the Scots refuse to surrender.

1545

Scottish forces defeat their English invaders February 25 at Ancrum Moor. The English withdraw but invade once again in September.

The Byrth of Mankynde, an English birth manual, counsels that the midwife shall "sit before the labouring woman and shall diligently observe and wait, how much and after what means the child stireth itself. Also shall with hands anoynted with the oyle of those white lillies, rule and direct everything as shall seme best. Also the midwife must instruct and comfort the party, not only refreshing her with good meat and drink, but also with sweet words, giving her hope of a good speedie deliverance, encouraging and enstomaching her to patience and tolerance, bidding her to hold her breath as much as she may, also stroking gently with her hands her belly above the navel for that helps to depress the birth downward." Midwives also apply warm clothes to the stomach, administer enemas to widen the birth canal, employ belladonna as an antispasmodic, and give women sneezing powder in the belief that sneezing will help dislodge the infant. Christians believe that pain in childbirth is woman's punishment for Eve's sin, and efforts to ease the pain are often condemned. Alcohol, opium, Indian hemp, and mandrake root are used in surgery but generally not in childbirth, even though protracted labor can sometimes last 48 hours and more (the longer a birthing woman labors, the more her own life is put at risk).

1546

Pope Paul meets with Charles V June 7 and promises money and troops to help squelch the Protestant movement.

The Proverbs of John Heywood by English epigrammatist Heywood, 47, includes "Butter would not melt in her mouth"; "Half a loaf is better than none"; "Haste makes waste"; "The green new broom sweepeth clean"; "Look before you leap"; "Love me, love my dog"; "Many hands make light work"; "Two heads are better than one"; "Out of the frying pan into the fire"; "To tell tales out of school"; and "More things belong to marriage than four bare legs in a bed."

1547

François I dies March 31 at age 52 (his unpopular mistress, Anne d'Heilly, duchesse d'Etampes, reportedly cries out, "O earth, swallow me!" and flees to Limoges). He is succeeded by his son of 28, who will reign until 1559 as Henri II. Catherine de' Medici is queen of France, but the new king is

Catherine de' Medici was queen but had to put up with her husband's mistress, Diane de Poitiers. D. MCN. STAUFFER COLLECTION

Diane de Poitiers was 20 years older than France's Henri II but had charms he could not resist. FROM A PAINTING BY FRANÇOIS CLOUET, NATIONAL GALLERY, WASHINGTON, D.C.

dominated by his beautiful mistress Diane de Poitiers, now 48, who will have great influence over him throughout his reign (*see* 1536). Brittany is fully united with the French crown under Henri II.

Henry VIII has died January 28 at age 55 of syphilis and liver cirrhosis. News of the king's death has been kept from his 10-year-old son by the boy's uncle Edward Seymour, earl of Hertford, until he has obtained the boy's consent to become protector of England with power to act with or without advice of counsel. The Battle of Pinkie September 10 ends in victory for the earl of Hertford, who routs a much larger force, crushing Scottish resistance to the new boy king. King in all but name, the protector (who is now Baron Seymour, duke of Somerset) defeats James Hamilton, 32, second earl of Arran, duke of Châtelherault, and regent of Mary, Queen of Scots.

Although beaten at Pinkie (above), the Scots thwart a plan by Somerset to enforce a marriage treaty between young Edward and his 4-year-old half sister. They hastily arrange a marriage between Mary, Queen of Scots and the 2-year-old French dauphin.

Henry Howard, 29, earl of Surrey, has been beheaded January 19 on trumped-up charges of treason. He had blocked the projected marriage of his sister, the duchess of Richmond, to Thomas Seymour, 39, the lord high admiral, who now plots to displace his older brother, Edward, as guardian of the king.

Poetry: *Les Marguerites de la Marguerite des princesses* by Marguerite d'Angoulême, queen of Navarre, now 55.

France's new king Henri II (above) gives the Château de Chenonceaux in the Loire valley to his mistress, Diane de Poitiers, who will add an Italian garden and a bridge over the Cher River.

1548

Poland's Sigismund I dies April 1 at age 81 after a 42-year reign that has established Catholicism in the country. He is succeeded by his only son, 28, who will reign until 1572 as Sigismund II while the Protestant Reformation spreads to Poland. The new king refuses the diet's demand that he repudiate his second wife, the beautiful Lithuanian Calvinist Barbara Radziwill, and she will die under mysterious circumstances 5 days after her coronation in early December 1550.

Catherine Parr, Henry VIII's widow, who last year married Thomas Seymour, dies in childbirth at age 36.

Painting: *Self-Portrait* and *Girl at the Spinet* by Flemish painter Catherina van Hemessen, 20, at Antwerp.

1549

English authorities arrest the lord high admiral Thomas Seymour in January and send him to the Tower of London on charges of having schemed to marry Edward VI to Lady Jane Grey, 12, daughter of the duke of Suffolk, and gain as his own bride Henry VIII's daughter Elizabeth, 16. Seymour is baron Seymour of Sudeley and brother of the protector, but he is convicted of treason and executed March 20. The lord protector himself is sent to the

Tower October 14, having provoked aristocratic opposition, and will be executed early in 1552 after a trial on trumped-up charges.

 Inés de Suárez at Santiago, Chile, marries Rodrigo de Quiroga, one of Pedro de Valdivia's chief lieutenants, after Valdivia returns with orders barring him from living in the same house with Inés (*see* 1543). Now 42, she will be given land and money early next year to build the Church of Our Lady of Monserrate on Cerro Blanco Hill, Valdivia will send to Spain in 1552 for his wife, Marina Ortiz de Gaete, on orders from the king, but he will be killed fighting the Araucanian Federation in December 1553, and when his wife arrives in 1554 she will find herself responsible for debts of 200,000 pesos that he has accumulated.

1550

 England and France make peace in March under terms of the Treaty of Boulogne: England receives 400,000 crowns, France regains Boulogne, English troops withdraw from Scotland.

1551

 France's Henri II renews war against the Holy Roman Emperor Charles V, seizing the bishoprics of Toul, Metz, and Verdun (*see* 1552).

 A fifth epidemic of the sweating sickness strikes England in April, starting at Shrewsbury (*see* 1529). Foreigners are somehow spared, but English men and women who flee to the Continent die there of the disease, even though the French and Lowlanders are not affected.

 Painting: *Portrait of a Nun* (her sister Elena) by Italian painter Sofonisba Anguissola (Sophonisba Anguisciola), 19, at Cremona; *Portrait of a Lady* by Catherina Van Hemessen.

1552

 The Treaty of Chambord signed by France's Henri II January 15 with Maurice of Saxony pledges him to supply troops and money for the war against Charles V.

 Painting: *Self-Portrait* by Sofonisba Anguissola; *Portrait of a Man* by Catherina van Hemessen.

1553

 England's Edward VI dies of tuberculosis at Greenwich July 6 at age 15 and is succeeded by his Catholic half sister Mary, 37, who has been raised by her mother, Catherine of Aragon. A treaty of marriage is arranged between Mary and Spain's Philip, 26, son of Charles V, who is to be given the title king of England but to have no hand in government and no right to succeed Mary.

England's new queen (above) faces an insurrection led by Henry Grey, duke of Suffolk, who has married his daughter Lady Jane Grey, now 16, to Lord Guildford Dudley as part of a plot to alter the succession (Dudley induced the late Edward VI to sign letters of patent making Lady Jane Grey heir to the crown). Lady Jane is proclaimed queen July 9, but forces loyal to Mary disperse Suffolk's troops and imprison Lady Jane July 19.

Mary enters London August 3 to begin a harsh 5-year reign. She has the duke of Northumberland arrested, tried for treason, and executed August 22.

1554

 England's Queen Mary releases the duke of Suffolk from prison in a show of clemency toward those who took arms against her last year, but she hardens her position when Suffolk again proclaims his daughter Lady Jane Grey queen and tries to rally Leicestershire to her support.

Lady Jane Grey and her husband, Guildford Dudley, are executed February 12, 5 months after the execution of Dudley's father, the duke of Northumberland.

Princess Elizabeth, now 20, is sent to the Tower of London in March as the Spanish cry for her execution. Edward Courtenay, 28, earl of Devonshire, has been released from the Tower after 15 years of imprisonment in connection with his father's aspirations to the crown. Foiled in his effort to marry the new queen, he has plotted to marry Elizabeth and join her on the throne. Elizabeth is released from the Tower in May, Mary and the Spanish infante, Felipe, are married July 25. Felipe receives the kingdoms of Naples and Sicily plus the duchy of Milan from his father, Charles V.

An officer of the Inquisition named Paramo writes that the Holy Office has burned at least 30,000 "witches" in the past 150 years, thus saving the world from destruction.

Painting: *Self-Portrait* by Sofonisba Anguissola.

1555

Bloody Mary returns Roman Catholicism to England and persecutes Protestants. Hugh Latimer, bishop of Worcester, and Nicholas Ridley, bishop of London, have been imprisoned for 2 years on charges of heresy, and the queen has them burned at the stake October 16 at Oxford.

Poetry: *Oeuvres* by French poet Louise Labé (or Charlieu), 35, who donned a man's armor at age 22 and fought at the siege of Perpignan. Married 5 years ago at Lyons to Ennemond Perrin, a rich ropemaker, she is known as "the beautiful ropemaker" (*"la belle cordière"*).

Painting: *The Chess-Game* and *Portrait of a Dominican Astronomer* by Sofonisba Anguissola; *The Rest on the Flight into Egypt* by Catherina van Hemessen, who last year married the organist of Antwerp's cathedral.

1556

The Holy Roman Emperor Charles V resigns his Spanish kingdoms and Sicily January 16, resigns Burgundy soon after, and leaves the empire to his brother Ferdinand. His inept son Felipe (Philip) is left to rule Spain, the Netherlands, Milan, Naples, Franche-Comté, and the rich Spanish colonies. Philip makes peace with France's Henri II February 5.

Mary Tudor persecuted English Protestants and tried to restore Catholicism in her five-year reign.

Painting: *Portrait of Asdrubale Anguissola* (her baby brother), *Portrait of a Lady* (her mother, Bianca Ponzoni Anguissola), and *Portrait of a Dominican Monk* by Sofonisba Anguissola.

The Château d'Anet is completed for Diane de Poitiers by French architect Philibert Delorme, 46, after 9 years of construction.

1557

England's Mary Tudor declares war on France June 7 in support of her husband, Spain's Philip II, in a conflict provoked by Pope Paul IV.

Painting: *Portrait of Massimiliano Stampa* (third marquese of Sansino) by Sofonisba Anguissola.

1558

✗ England's glorious Elizabethan age begins November 17 as Mary Tudor dies at age 42 and is succeeded by her half sister Elizabeth, now 25. Daughter of Henry VIII by the late Anne Boleyn, Elizabeth will reign until 1603 in a golden period of English arts and letters.

✒ *First Blast of the Trumpet Against the Monstrous Regiment of Women* by Scottish clergyman John Knox, 53, says, "The nobility both of England and Scotland are inferior to brute beasts, for they do that to women which no male among the common sort of beasts can be proved to do with their females; that is, they reverence them, and quake at their presence; they obey their commandments, and that against God." "Promoting a woman to regiment [rule], superioritie, dominion, or empire above any realme, nation, or citie is repugnant to nature; contumelie to God, a thing most contrarious to His revealed will and approved ordinance; and finallie, it is the subversion of good order, of all equitie and justice. . . . Their sight in civile regiment is but blindnes: their strength, weakness: their counsel, foolishnes." Knox fled to the Continent at Mary Tudor's accession in 1553 and has been at Geneva since 1556, meeting occasionally with John Calvin.

🎨 Painting: *Portrait of Amilcare, Minerve, and Asdrubale Anguissola* and *Self-Portrait* by Sofonisba Anguissola.

1559

✗ Queen Elizabeth replies February 6 to a petition from the House of Commons: "To me it shall be a full satisfaction both for the memorial of my name, and for the glory also, if when I shall let my last breath, it be engraven upon my marble tomb, 'Here lieth Elizabeth, who reigned a virgin and died a virgin.'" Elizabeth raises her court favorite, Robert Dudley, to the privy council.

The Treaty of Cateau-Cambrésis April 3 ends the last war between the late Charles V and France. The treaty confirms Spanish possession of the Franche-Comté and the Italian states of Milan, Naples, and Sicily. Spain's Philip II marries the eldest daughter of Catherine de' Medici and Henri II, Elizabeth de Valois, 14, amidst great ceremony June 22 (the Spanish will call her "Isabel de la Paz" and take her to their hearts).

France's Henri II sustains a head wound June 30 in a tournament celebrating the Treaty of Cateau-Cambrésis (above) and his daughter's marriage. His younger sister, Marguerite, marries Emmanuel Philibert, comte de Savoie, at Henri's insistence July 8. The king, who has worn the colors of his aging mistress, Diane de Poitiers, in the joust, dies in agony July 10 at age 40. The king's eldest son, 14, who was married last year to Scotland's Mary Stu-

Elizabeth's 45-year rule of England saw the nation prosper and the arts flourish. ATTRIBUTED TO WILLIAM SEGAR, 1585

art, begins an 18-month reign as François II, with his uncles François, duc de Guise, and Charles, cardinal of Lorraine, as regents.

Mary Stuart, Queen of Scots (above), assumes the title Queen of England (*see* 1560).

Painting: *Holy Family* by Sofonisba Anguissola, who travels 85 miles in autumn from Milan to Genoa, embarks for Barcelona, and makes her way to Madrid, where she will be lady-in-waiting to the new Spanish queen, Isabel (Elizabeth) de Valois.

1560

The Conspiracy of Amboise, organized by the French Huguenot Louis de Bourbon, comte de Condé, tries to overthrow the Catholic Guises, but the queen mother, Catherine de' Medici, declares herself regent and helps thwart the Huguenots. Some 1,200 are hanged at Amboise in March, and Louis is imprisoned.

French troops in Scotland try to assert the claims of France's queen Mary Stuart, now 17, against Elizabeth of England, whom Catholics consider illegitimate. English troops besiege the French at Leith, Mary's mother, Marie of Lorraine, dies in June, and the Treaty of Edinburgh July 6 ends French interference in Scotland.

France's François II dies December 5 at age 16. His brother of 10 will reign until 1574 as Charles IX with his mother, Catherine de' Medici, ruling his realm.

Painting: *Portrait of Don Carlos* by Sofonisba Anguissola, who gives painting lessons to the new Spanish queen, Isabel de Valois, upon her recovery from an attack of smallpox.

The Château de Chenonceaux passes into the hands of France's queen mother, Catherine (above), who ousts her late husband's mistress (giving her the Château de Chaumont in exchange) and engages an architect to design a two-story gallery on the bridge erected by Diane de Poitiers. Catherine has reputedly said to Diane, "I have read the histories of this kingdom, Madam, and I have found in them from time to time at all periods whores have managed the business of kings," to which Diane only laughed.

1561

Mary, Queen of Scots returns from France August 19, landing at Leith because England has refused her passage. She becomes embroiled in argument with Calvinist John Knox, who last year drew up a Confession of Faith denying papal authority in Scotland.

Painting: *Portrait of Queen Isabel de Valois* and *Self-Portrait* by Sofonisba Anguissola.

1562

A massacre of Huguenots at Vassy March 1 by order of François, duc de Guise, begins a series of French civil wars. The Huguenots retaliate by murdering priests and raping nuns.

Spanish nun Teresa of Avila, 47, founds at Avila a convent for Discalced Carmelites, which will be followed by many such convents in which practicality will be combined with the most sublime spirituality.

1563

The Peace of Amboise signed by Catherine de' Medici March 19 is an edict ending the year-long conflict between French Catholics and Huguenots. It follows by 1 month the murder of François, duc de Guise, by a Huguenot, leaving Catherine in control of Catholic forces. She grants limited toleration, but the peace will not be lasting.

Mary, Queen of Scots sends her secretary William Maitland of Lethington, 35, to England to claim the right of succession to Elizabeth, but she receives no declaration from her cousin.

Queen Elizabeth tolerates English dissenters but persecutes Catholics, Unitarians (who deny the Trinity), and Brownists—Puritan extremists who will form the nucleus of the Congregational Church.

"If any African were carried away without his free consent," says Queen Elizabeth, "it would be detestable and call down the vengeance of Heaven upon the undertaking" (but *see* 1564).

An English Statute of Artificers sets women's wages at one-third to one-half those of men, even though the women work the same number of hours and perform tasks just as difficult.

De Praestigiis Daemonum by Flemish physician Johann Wier, 47, maintains that witches are merely miserable people with distorted minds. "Since witches are usually old women of melancholic nature and small brains (women who get easily depressed and have little trust in God) there is no doubt that the devil easily affects and deceives their minds by illusions and apparitions that so bewilder them that they confess to actions that they are very far from having committed." But much of the world will for centuries remain under the influence of the 1489 handbook on witch-hunting *Malleus Maleficarum* (*see* Loudon, 1634; Salem, 1692).

 A sixth (and final) epidemic of the sweating sickness devastates London, killing more than 17,000 in a population of 66,000. Possibly a form of influenza, the mysterious disease will not be seen again.

 The Tuileries Palace is built at Paris for the queen mother, Catherine de' Medici.

1564

 England's Elizabeth takes shares in John Hawkins's second slave-running venture and loans him one of her ships as her avarice overcomes the humane antipathy to slavery she expressed last year.

 A sheath to be worn by men as a protection against syphilis or other sexually transmitted disease is mentioned for the first time in medical literature. Designed by Italian anatomist Gabriel Fallopius of the University of Padua, it is made of linen, a dried bladder, or a section of an animal's intestine, fits over the glans, and is secured by the foreskin. Sheaths for circumcised men, eight inches long and tied at the base with a pink ribbon to make them more acceptable to women, are soon available. Fallopius says that his "overcoat," as it is popularly called, has been tested on more than 1,000 men "with complete success."

∞ The Council of Trent decrees, "Whoever saith that marriage is to be put above virginity and that it is not more blessed to remain chaste than to marry, let him be anathema."

 The sheath, or condom (above), will not be used for purposes of contraception until the 18th century.

1565

 Ottoman forces lay siege to Malta in May. Some 700 Knights of St. John hold out until September, when Spanish forces arrive and drive 31,000 Turks into the sea.

France's Charles IX, now 15, is married at the cathedral of Mézières November 27 to Elizabeth of Austria, 15, daughter of the Holy Roman Emperor Maximilian, in a match arranged by Catherine de' Medici. She has failed in her efforts to have her son married to England's Elizabeth, who at 32 is more than twice the young king's age.

Advisers to England's Elizabeth (above) entreat her to marry and produce an heir to the throne. She has been heard more than once to say that she would "live and die a virgin," and while she dances quadrilles with eligible French and Austrian princes, London gossip has it that a physical defect prevents her from marrying. Elizabeth nevertheless uses her feminine charms to manipulate her male advisers.

 Europe has poor harvests. Catherine de' Medici decrees that meals shall be limited to three courses.

1566

 The Italian secretary to Mary, Queen of Scots is seized the evening of March 9 by the earls of Morton and Lindsay, who invade Mary's supper chamber with armed men, hack David Rizzio, 33, to death with daggers, and throw his body into the courtyard at Holyrood. The noblemen act on orders from Mary's husband, Lord Darnley, who will himself be murdered next year.

 Calvinists ransack monasteries and churches in Antwerp and Ghent and throughout Flanders and the northern provinces as grain prices soar following a bad harvest. Margaret of Parma, regent for the Lowlands, receives a petition signed by 300 noblemen April 2 demanding abolition of the Inquisition. She promises to forward their petition to her natural brother Philip of Spain but raises an army instead.

1567

 Lord Darnley, husband to Mary, Queen of Scots, is found murdered February 10 at Kirk o' Field, Edinburgh, and the queen is suspected of complicity. She is kidnapped April 24 by James Hepburn, 31, fourth earl of Bothwell, who marries her in a Protestant church May 15. The marriage provokes a rebellion by Scottish noblemen, who desert the queen at Carberry Hill in June, force her to dismiss Bothwell, and make her sign an abdication in favor of her 13-month-old son, who is proclaimed James VI of Scotland July 24. The young king will be raised at Stirling Castle by the earl and countess of Mar.

1568

 The Peace of Longjumeau signed by Catherine de' Medici with the Huguenots March 23 ends a second French religious war.

Mary, Queen of Scots escapes from captivity in May but is defeated at Langside May 13 and placed in confinement after fleeing to England.

The Spanish queen Isabel de Valois has a miscarriage and dies at Madrid October 3 at age 23, leaving the Hapsburg dynasty without a male heir.

1569

 French Catholic forces under Henri, duc d'Anjou, defeat Huguenot forces March 13 at the Battle of Jarnac.

1570

 Japanese strongman Oda Nobunaga defeats his brother-in-law, the *daimyo* Nagamasa Asai, who has challenged the supremacy asserted by Nobunaga

2 years ago. Asai married Nobunaga's sister Oichi, now 22, for political reasons in 1566, and she has used her wiles to help her brother avoid a trap (*see* 1573).

Ivan the Terrible, czar of Muscovy, enters the city of Great Novgorod January 8 and begins a 5-week reign of terror. Having ravaged the approaches to the second richest city in his realm, he has batches of Novgorodians from all classes of society massacred each day, and his men plunder every church, monastery, manor house, warehouse, and farm within a radius of 100 miles, destroying all cattle and leaving the structures roofless. He does not permit rebuilding until February 13.

England's Elizabeth, now 37, tries in September to reopen marriage negotiations with the archduke Charles but finds that he has lost patience and become betrothed to the daughter of the duke of Bavaria. France's Charles IX has also recently been married, and while his younger brother Henri, duc d'Anjou, is eligible, he is only 19 and a notorious womanizer (although he will later be better known as a homosexual and transvestite). Catherine de' Medici is excited by the prospect of her younger son marrying Elizabeth, but, like his mother, he is a staunch Catholic and refuses to embrace Protestantism.

Spain's Philip II, now 42, chooses his 21-year-old niece Anne of Austria, daughter of the emperor Maximilian II, as his third wife and they are married November 12 at Segovia.

 Painting: *Portrait of Queen Anne of Austria* (above) by Sofonisba Anguissola, whose other works this year include *Portrait of the Infantas Isabella Clara Eugenia and Catalina Micaela* (daughters of the late Isabel de Valois).

1571

 Catherine de' Medici relays to the French minister Le Mothe Fénelon in February her son the duc d'Anjou's complaint that England's Elizabeth appears to be extremely immoral and that he would be universally ridiculed if he were to marry "so depraved a bride." Fénelon writes that there is no truth in the slurs cast upon Elizabeth, but Anjou, when sounded out, says he would not dream of giving up his faith.

The Battle of Lepanto October 7 in the Gulf of Lepanto near Corinth ends in defeat for an Ottoman fleet of 240 galleys. The Maritime League of 212 Spanish, Venetian, Genoese, and Maltese ships captures 130 vessels with their stores and provisions, takes 4,000 prisoners, frees 12,000 Christian galley slaves, and kills 25,000 Turks while suffering the loss of about 5,000 oarsmen and soldiers.

 Painting: *Portrait of Marguerita Gonzaga* by Sofonisba Anguissola, now 39, who has married the Spanish nobleman Don Fabrizio.

1572

 The Ottoman sultan Selim II rebuilds his navy following last year's defeat at the Battle of Lepanto.

Dutch insurgents capture Brill as their revolt against Spanish rule spreads to the north. Spanish forces lay siege to Haarlem, where patriot Kenau Hesseider and her corps of women volunteers hold off 30,000 Spaniards.

France's Princess Margot (Marguerite), 14, is married August 18 to the Huguenot Henri of Navarre in a political match arranged by her mother, Catherine de' Medici, with the idea of healing the nation's Catholic-Huguenot animosities. Four days of festivities follow, with balls, masquerades, state suppers, and performances by poets, musicians, and Italian comedians, but tensions are not eased.

The Massacre of St. Bartholomew August 23 and 24 kills an estimated 50,000 Huguenots at Paris and in the provinces. Urged on by the queen mother Catherine de' Medici, Catholics commit terrible atrocities, Catherine receives congratulations from all the Catholic powers, and Pope Gregory XIII orders that bonfires be lighted to celebrate the massacre. Catherine's role in the massacre increases public distrust of her as a duplicitous, manipulative Florentine.

Painting: *Portrait of Don Sebastian of Portugal* by Sofonisba Anguissola.

1573

Venice makes peace with the Turks March 7 at Constantinople, breaking with Spain, abandoning Cyprus, and agreeing to pay an indemnity of 300,000 ducats.

France's queen mother Catherine de' Medici pays a fortune to have her son Henri d'Anjou, brother of Charles IX, elected May 11 as first king of Poland. The new king signs a pact acknowledging strict limits on royal power and recognizing the right of Poland's nobility to elect kings.

The Ashikaga shōgunate that has ruled Japan since 1336 is ended as the shōgun Yoshiaki takes arms against the strongman Oda Nobunaga. He has the support of Nobunaga's brother-in-law Nagamasa Asai (*see* 1570), but Nobunaga sacks Asai's castle (permitting his own sister Oichi and her children to escape), Asai commits *seppuku* (ritual suicide), and Nobunaga ousts Yoshiaki (*see* 1582).

1574

France's Charles IX dies May 30 at age 24 and is succeeded by his brother Henri d'Anjou, now 23, who vacates the Polish throne (the Poles are happy to see him go), returns to France, and will reign until 1589 as Henri III under the domination of his rotund mother, Catherine de' Medici.

Leyden in the Lowlands comes under siege by Spanish forces. Willem of Orange (the Silent), who has lost two brothers in the Battle of Mookerheide in April, cuts the dike in several places to flood the land, and his ships sail up to Leyden's city wall October 3 to relieve the siege.

 Painting: *Portrait of Doña Maria Manrique de Lara y Pernstein and One of her Daughters* by Sofonisba Anguissola.

1575

Protestant rebels in the Lowlands meet at Breda in February with the Spanish governor-general, who agrees to withdraw his troops and officials from the Netherlands. The Holy Roman Emperor Maximilian II has mediated the settlement.

France's Henri III dresses in sweeping skirts, paints his face, douses himself in perfume, and surrounds himself with homosexual mignons following the death from puerperal fever of his *maîtresse-en-titre*, the princess of Condé. His sister Marguerite and her husband, Henri of Navarre, are dependent on the king for money, and he is so profligate with the mignons that he has little left for Marguerite and Henri (whose mistress, Charlotte de Suaves, is also the mistress of many other men).

1576

✗ The "Spanish Fury" erupts in November at Antwerp, where 6,000 men, women, and children are massacred by the mutinous Spanish garrison, which has been left unpaid and without food while charged with suppressing rebellious Protestants.

1577

✗ Willem the Silent enters Brussels in triumph September 23 and becomes lieutenant to the new governor, Archduke Mathias of Hapsburg.

1578

✗ Spain's Philip II sends an army to the Lowlands under the command of his Italian cousin Alessandro Farnese, 32, who defeats a patriot army at Gemblours January 31 and takes over Spanish and Austrian forces in the region. Philip's wife, Anne of Austria, gives birth to a son, who will succeed to the throne as Philip III.

🖌 Painting: *Portrait of the Infanta Isabella Clara Eugenia* and *Portrait of Giorgio Julio Clovio* by Sofonisba Anguissola, who has stopped with her husband, Don Fabrizio, at Rome en route from Spain to Palermo, where Don Fabrizio will die early next year.

1579

✗ The United Provinces established by the Union of Utrecht January 23 marks the birth of the Dutch

Republic. The Dutch sign a military alliance with England.

🖌 Painting: *Self-Portrait Seated at Her Desk* by Bolognese painter Lavinia Fontana, 27, whose portraits are commissioned by aristocrats and prominent clergymen.

1580

✗ Spain and Portugal unite under one crown following the death of Portugal's cardinal Henri after a 2-year reign as king. Spanish forces invade his country, prevail at the Battle of Alcantara near Lisbon August 25, and proclaim Spain's Philip II Portugal's Philip I. His wife, Anne of Austria, dies at age 31, having given birth to five children, four of whom died in childhood.

🖋 Nonfiction: *Essais* by French writer Michel Eyquem de Montaigne, 47, is published in its first two volumes. "Women are not altogether in the wrong when they refuse the rules of life prescribed to the World, for men only have established them and without their consent," Montaigne will write (III, v), and "The daughter-in-law of Pythagoras said that a woman who goes to bed with a man ought to lay aside her modesty with her skirt, and put it on again with her petticoat." *On the Demon Worship of Sorcerers* (*Démonomanie des sorciers*) by French political philosopher Jean Bodin, 50, who writes, "All authorities on witchcraft have made it clear that for every male witch there are fifty female witches. . . . This is the case not because of their frailty (since most of them are incorrigibly obstinate), but because of their bestial cupidity. . . . We note that Satan first approached the woman, who then seduced the man. For it was God's plan to humble Satan by giving him power generally and primarily over the least worthy creatures, such as snakes and vermin and other beasts that God's law calls foul; and next over other beasts rather than over men; and then over woman rather than man. . . . Thus Satan makes use of wives in order to ensnare their husbands."

🖌 Painter Sofonisba Anguissola, now 47, is married in January to ship's captain Orazio Lomelino, who fell in love with her last year on the passage from

Palermo to Livorno (Leghorn) following the death of her husband, Don Fabrizio.

1581

💲 English seaman Francis Drake captures the richest prize ever taken on the high seas, returning with Spanish gold, silver, and gemstones worth as much as the Crown's total revenues for a year; the Spanish ambassador demands restitution, but Elizabeth, after a 9-month delay, confers knighthood on Drake.

🎼 Ballet: *Ballet Comique de la Reyne* at Paris with music by the Italian composer Baltasarini, who is known in Paris as Beaujoyeulx. Presented for the queen mother, Catherine de' Medici, the ballet represents the first use of dance and music to convey a coherent dramatic idea.

1582

✘ Japan's Taira strongman Oda Nobunaga travels to join his general Hideyoshi, 46, who has conquered much of Honshu from the Mo'ori family (*see* 1570). His enemy, Gen. Akechi Mitsuhido, 56, sets fire to a monastery where Nobunaga has halted for the night, and Nobunaga, who has destroyed the power of the Buddhist priests, either dies in the flames or commits *seppuku* (ritual suicide) June 21 at age 46. Hideyoshi kills Mitsuhido, gains support from Nobunaga's *daimyo* Ieyasu, 39, at Edo, and begins to eliminate the Nobunaga family in a great struggle for power (*see* 1573). Mitsuhido's daughter Otama, 19, is married to the *daimyo* Tadaoki Hosokawa, who sends her into hiding for her own protection (*see* 1584).

∞ The ascetic and mystic nun Teresa of Avila dies at Albe de Tormes October 4 after a career of reforming the monastic movement. Daughter of a Jewish convert whose wife was a Castilian aristocrat, Sister Teresa has insisted that the chief role of nuns is to pray for souls in peril and intercede for others.

🖋 Poetry: A discourse on feminine virtue by Italian poet Torquato Tasso, 38, says that women who do not seek love out of unbridled passion are to be praised like the queen of Sheba, who came to Solomon.

🕐 A new Gregorian calendar instituted by Pope Gregory abolishes the ancient Julian calendar because its error of one day in every 128 years has moved the vernal equinox to March 11. Gregory restores the equinox to March 21, his calendar takes effect in Roman Catholic countries October 5 (which becomes October 15). Protestant countries will adhere to the Old Style Julian calendar of 45 B.C. until 1700 or later (*see* Britain, 1752), and the Russians will retain it until 1918.

1583

✘ Dutch forces from the seven United Provinces sympathetic to Spain occupy the mouth of the Scheldt River, blocking Antwerp from sea trade.

🖋 Nonfiction: *The Perfect Wife* (*La perfecta casada*) by Spanish poet-theologian Fray Louis (Ponce) de León, 56, is a handbook on the duties of a wife. Fray Louis was imprisoned by the Inquisition in 1572 but was absolved in 1576.

⬤ Sculpture: *Rape of the Sabine Women* by Giovanni da Bologna for the court of the Medicis at Florence. The marble work stands 13 feet 6 inches high.

1584

✘ Willem of Orange is murdered at Delft July 10 at age 51. Spain's Philip II has for 3 years offered a large reward to anyone who would rid the world of the man he calls a traitor. Ghent falls to Philip's forces, but Dutch and English volunteers set forth to liberate the city, one of the columns being led by Captain Mary Ambree.

Hideyoshi gains hegemony over central Japan and on August 8 moves into a great castle at Osaka.

⬤ Painting: *The Gozzadini Family* by Lavinia Fontana.

1585

✘ France is embroiled in another civil war as the Holy League vows to bar Henri of Navarre from inheriting the French throne.

Antwerp surrenders August 17 to the duke of Parma, who sacks Europe's chief commercial center, exiles its Protestants, and secures the Netherlands, Flanders, and Brabant for Spain.

1586

A plot to assassinate England's queen is discovered by spies of Elizabeth's secretary of state Francis Walsingham (whose daughter is married to Sir Philip Sydney). Anthony Babbington, 25, a page to Mary, Queen of Scots, has conspired with Jesuit priest John Ballard, who is executed along with Babbington and five others. Mary is convicted October 25 of involvement in the scheme, and her life hangs in the balance.

English butcher's wife Margaret Clitherow (*née* Middleton), 30, is tried at York on charges of harboring priests in her house. Converted to Catholicism at age 18, she is found guilty and crushed to death. She will be revered by Catholics as the "Pearl of York" and canonized in 1970.

1587

Mary, Queen of Scots is beheaded February 8 by order of her cousin Elizabeth, who has been persuaded that Mary Stuart's existence poses a continuing threat to the Protestant crown of England.

Japan's strongman Hideyoshi Toyotomi invades Kyushu to subjugate a defiant *daimyo* (*see* 1584). He is refused a beautiful woman with whom to sleep because all the women have embraced Christianity, which continues to gain Japanese converts, including Otama Hosokawa, daughter of the late Gen. Mitsuhido. Furious, Hideyoshi issues an edict forbidding foreign missionaries.

Virginia Dare is born August 18 on Roanoke Island to the daughter of John White and is the first English child to be born in North America. White lands 150 new settlers including 17 women in the Virginia colony on orders from Sir Walter Raleigh, but the new arrivals land too late to plant crops for fall and winter, so White returns to England for supplies to see them through (*see* 1586; 1591).

"Many pregnant women in confinement and small children of noble as well as of common rank are often miserably neglected, injured, harmed, and crippled at the time of the birth or in the following weeks, all through the clumsiness, arrogance, and rashness of the midwives and assisting women," writes German medical practitioner Anna of Saxony (date approximate). "Few sensible midwives are to be found in this country."

Painting: *Mystical Marriage of Saint Catherine* by Sofonisba Anguissola.

1588

An "invincible" Spanish Armada of 132 vessels sails against England, whose naval forces engage the enemy July 31. A great storm blows up the following week, and the elements help the English defeat the Armada August 8, scoring a victory that opens

Mary Stuart, Queen of Scots, laid claim to the English throne and was beheaded by order of Queen Elizabeth. NATIONAL PORTRAIT GALLERY, LONDON

the world to English trade and colonization. Queen Elizabeth travels by river August 8 to Tilbury, spends the night at Edward Ritche's house Saffron Garden, reviews her troops the next morning wearing a silver breastplate over her white velvet dress, mounts a horse, and addresses the men: "My loving people, we have been persuaded by some that are careful of our safety, to take heed how we commit ourselves to armed multitudes for fear of treachery; but I assure you I do not desire to live to distrust my faithful and loving people. Let tyrants fear. I have always so behaved my self, that under God, I have placed my chiefest strength and safeguard in the loyal hearts and goodwill of all my subjects, and therefore I am come amongst you, as you see, at this time, not for my recreation and disport, but being resolved in the midst and heat of the battle, to live or die amongst you all, to lay down for my God, and for my kingdom, and for my people, my honor, and my blood, even in the dust. I know I have the body but of a weak and feeble woman, but I have the heart and stomach of a king, and of King of England too, and think foul scorn that Parma or Spain, or any prince of Europe, should dare to invade the borders of my realm; to which, rather than any dishonor shall grow by me, I myself will take up arms, I myself will be your general, judge, and rewarder of every one of your virtues in the field. I know already for your forwardness, you have deserved rewards and crowns; and we do assure you, in the word of a Prince, they shall be duly paid you."

Painting: *Madonna Nursing Her Child* by Sofonisba Anguissola.

1589

Catherine de' Medici dies of pneumonia at Blois January 5 at age 69. Her son, France's Henri III, murders Henri of Guise and his brother, the Catholic party revolts at hearing the news, the king flees to the Huguenot camp at St. Cloud, and he is murdered there by a Dominican monk. The Bourbon dynasty, which will rule France until 1792, is founded by the recklessly promiscuous Henri of Navarre, whose wife, Marguerite d'Angoulême, has long since given up hope of regaining his affections.

He forces recognition of his claims and will rule until 1610 as Henri IV.

The Danish princess Anne of Denmark, 15, daughter of Frederik II, marries Scotland's James VI, 23.

More than 130 witches are reportedly burned in a single day in the German town of Quedlendburg. Witch-hunts in many of the German states, encouraged by Church dignitaries, create hysteria that will continue for much of the next decade.

Painting: *Holy Family* by Lavinia Fontana, who has been commissioned by Spain's Philip II to paint it for the Escorial Palace that he is completing at Madrid.

1590

The Battle of Ivry March 14 secures the French throne of Henri IV as the king defeats the Catholic League. His 15,000-man army lays siege to Paris in mid-May, and the resulting starvation kills thousands (*see* below).

Rebecca Lamp of Nördlingen, Swabia, is burned at the stake as a witch in March after months of imprisonment and torture. She was arrested in the absence of her husband, Peter, a respected accountant; his eloquent defense of her piety and innocence have been ignored, and more than 30 other well-respected women of the town meet the same fate, which will be ascribed to the ambitions of two local lawyers and a burgomaster.

Painting: *Queen Luisa of France Presenting Her Son Francis I to S. Francesca di Paolo* by Lavinia Fontana.

The siege of Paris (above) brings hunger and malnutrition that kill 13,000. Food supplies are inadequate for the city's 30,000 inhabitants and its 8,000-man garrison; by mid-June the Spanish ambassador has proposed grinding the bones of the dead to make flour; by July 9 the poor are chasing dogs and eating grass that grows in the streets.

1591

French royalists besiege Rouen with help from Robert Devereux, 25, earl of Essex. The resulting starvation in Normandy's richest city resembles that seen in Paris last year.

1592

✖ Rouen is relieved in April after months of siege have killed many and reduced the rest to skin and bones.

● Painting: *Holy Family with Saints Anne and John* by Sofonisba Anguissola.

🎭 Theater: *Two Gentleman of Verona* by English playwright William Shakespeare, 28: "Who is Sylvia? what is she?/ That all our swains commend her? Holy, fair, and wise is she;/ The heavens such grace did lend her" (IV, ii); *Titus Andronicus* by Shakespeare: "And easy it is/ Of a cut loaf to steal a shive" (II, i, meaning that adultery is easily arranged and likely to go unnoticed).

1593

✖ Elizabeth reminds England's Parliament February 27 that she has the right to "assent to or dissent from anything" it may do. Statutes are pending that will impose stiff new penalties on Catholics who refuse to attend Church of England services and make it a crime to attend Catholic services.

Marguerite d'Angoulême, wife of France's Henri IV, accepts her husband's offer to pay off her debts of 250,000 écus, grant her a yearly pension of 14,000 écus, and give her the castle of Usson at Auvergne; she agrees in April to proceed with a divorce (*see* 1599). Henri formally rejects Protestantism July 25 at Paris, is accepted into Catholicism, makes confession, and hears Mass.

✒ Poetry: "Venus and Adonis" by William Shakespeare: "Love keeps his revels where there are but twain," "Love surfeits not, Lust like a glutton dies./ Love is all truth, Lust full of forged lies." Poet-playwright Christopher Marlowe is killed May 30 at age 29 in a tavern brawl at Deptford where his companion Ingram Frizer stabs him in the eye in self-defense. Marlowe is survived by lines of verse that include "Come live with me and be my Love/ And we will all the pleasures prove/ That hills and valleys, dale and field,/ And all the craggy mountains yield" (from "The Passionate Shepherd to His Love").

1594

✖ France's Henri IV obtains the surrender of Paris March 22, is crowned at Chartres, and continues his campaign to win over each French province, either by negotiation or by force of arms. He has discarded his most recent mistress, Corisande, and found younger girls with whom to amuse himself.

✒ Fiction: *Promenade with M. de Montaigne* (*Le Proumenoir de M. de Montaigne*) by French professional writer Marie de Gournay (*née* le Jars), 28, who has edited the later *Essais* of the late Michel Eyquem de Montaigne and will publish them next year. He was mayor of Bordeaux when she met him in 1588, and he died in September 1592: "The common man believes that in order to be chaste a woman must not be clever: in truth it is doing chastity too little honor to believe it can be found beautiful only in the blind."

1595

✖ The Ottoman sultan Murad III dies January 6 at age 49 after a 21-year reign of debauchery in which he has sired 102 children (20 sons and 27 daughters survive). His eldest son, 27, will reign until 1603 as Mohammed III, furthering the empire's decline. He has his 19 brothers murdered in accordance with the "law of fratricide" and has 10 of his father's concubines drowned because they are pregnant and might bear sons. Mohammed's mother, the sultana Valide Baffo, is the power behind his throne.

🎭 Theater: *Romeo and Juliet* by William Shakespeare, whose "star-cross'd lovers" belong to the rival Montague and Capulet families of Verona: "What's in a name? That which we call a rose/ By any other name would smell as sweet" (II, ii); *A Midsummer Night's Dream* by Shakespeare: "The course of true love never did run smooth" (I, i).

1596

✖ The War of the Catholic League ends as France's Henri IV allies himself with the English and Dutch against Spain's Philip II, whose forces capture Calais in April.

Painting: *Portrait of Paolo Morigia* and *Judith and Her Handmaid* by Italian painter Fede Galizia, 18.

 Theater: *The Taming of the Shrew* by William Shakespeare and collaborators: "Crowns in my purse I have and goods at home/ And so am come abroad to see the world" (I, ii); "Kiss me, Kate" (II, i); "Such duty as the subject owes the prince/ Even such a woman oweth to her husband" (V, ii); "Thy husband is thy lord, thy life, thy keeper,/ Thy head, thy sovereign, one that cares for thee,/ And for thy maintenance commits his body/ To painful labor both by sea and land,/ To watch the night in storms, the day in cold,/ While thou liest warm at home, secure and safe;/ And craves no other tribute at thy hands/ But love, fair looks and true obedience,/ Too little payment for so great a debt" (V, ii).

1597

 Spain's Philip II sends a second armada against England, but a storm scatters the ships just as in 1588.

 Clara Geissler, 69, of Geinhausen is arrested on suspicion of witchcraft, tortured until she "confesses" whatever her inquisitors demand, names 20 other women who have been with her at her alleged sabbats, but recants immediately after the instruments of torture are removed. The women she has fingered are thereupon arrested, they too are tortured, and when one of them "confesses" Geissler is tortured again, recants again, and is subjected to another round of torture, during which she dies.

1598

 Spain's Philip II dies at the new Escorial Palace September 13 at age 71 after a 42-year reign. His indolent 20-year-old son by the late Anne of Austria will reign until 1621 as Philip III.

Japanese strongman Toyotomi Hideyoshi dies September 18 at age 62, leaving no legitimate sons. His son Hideyori, now 5, was borne to his mistress, Ochacha, now 31, who is known as Yodogimi (Lady Yodo). A power struggle begins among Hideyoshi's former vassals.

 The Edict of Nantes issued April 15 by France's Henri IV gives Protestant Huguenots equal political rights with Catholics. While it does not establish complete religious freedom, it does permit Huguenots to practice their religion in a number of cities and towns (*see* 1685).

 Poetry: "Hero and Leander" by the late Christopher Marlowe: "Who ever loved that loved not at first sight?"

1599

 England's earl of Essex is sent by Elizabeth to subdue Ireland's rebellious earl of Tyrone but is defeated at Arklow, makes a truce with Tyrone, and leaves his post as governor-general of Ireland to vindicate himself before the queen.

The Spanish infanta Isabella Clara Eugenia, now over 30, marries her cousin, the Archduke Albrecht of Austria, a cardinal who has received papal dispensation to marry.

Marguerite d'Angoulême's marriage to France's Henri IV is pronounced null and void November 10. The king now has two sons by his mistress, Gabrielle d'Estrées, who has insisted that his divorce be finalized; the Vatican opposes a new marriage because of Gabrielle's relationship to leading Protestants, the king's courtiers oppose it lest her two sons be legitimized and she bear more sons after becoming queen; Gabrielle resolves the matter by dying in childbirth, and Henri, after insisting that he is inconsolable, finds solace with Henriette d'Entragues, 18. Under pressure from her father, he signs a document agreeing to marry Henriette if she should become pregnant within 6 months and give birth to a son (*see* 1600).

 English women gain greater freedoms by an October act of Parliament.

 Painting: *Portrait of the Spanish Infanta Isabella Clara Eugenia* by Sofonisba Anguissola, now 67, who has known the princess (above) since her infancy. Isabella Clara has stopped at Genoa en route to her wedding in order to have Anguissola paint her betrothal portrait.

 Theater: *Much Ado about Nothing* by William Shakespeare: "Sigh no more, ladies, sigh no more,/

Men were deceivers ever, / One foot in sea and one on shore, / To one thing constant never" (II, iii).

1600

 France's ex-queen Marguerite warns her ex-husband Henri IV about her nephew Charles d'Angoulême, comte d'Auvergne, saying, "This badly counseled boy holds many places in this locality, houses which he has usurped from the late queen my mother as well as many castles, forts, and defenses which, for your sake, would be better demolished." Son of the late Charles IX by his Huguenot mistress, Marie Touchet, the nephew is a stepbrother of Henri's mistress, Henriette d'Entragues, and and opposes the Bourbon regime (*see* 1602).

Henri IV marries his niece Marie de' Medici, 27, in October. Despite his written agreement with Henriette d'Entragues and her father (above), he has made the match to the overweight Marie in order to satisfy his financial obligations to her father, the grand duke of Tuscany.

A new civil war erupts in Japan; the Toyotomi general Mitsunari Ishida tries to take the wives and children of the *daimyos* hostage, but Otama Hosokawa, whose husband is off fighting on the side of the *daimyo* Ieyasu Tokugawa, refuses to be taken prisoner. Since her Christian faith prevents her from taking her own life, she has a retainer kill her after she has set fire to the family home.

 Opera: *Euridice* 10/6 at Florence's Pitti Palace with music by Jacopo Peri: the world's first grand opera is presented on the occasion of the wedding of Marie de' Medici to France's Henri IV (above).

17th Century

1601

✖ Queen Elizabeth tells a deputation from the House of Commons November 30, "Though God hath raised me high, yet this I count the glory of my crown: that I have reigned with your love. . . . Of myself I must say this, I never was any greedy, scraping grasper, nor a strait fast-holding prince, nor yet a waster; my heart was never set on worldly goods, but only for my subjects' good."

⚕ French midwife Louyse Bourgeois, 38, attends Marie de' Medici at Fontainebleau for the delivery of the queen's first child before an audience of 200. Bourgeois is one of the first graduates of the Hôtel-Dieu, founded at a monastery as a school for midwives and gaining renown throughout Europe. The first great woman practitioner of obstetrics, she has replaced the official royal midwife (see 1608).

🎭 Theater: *Twelfth Night, or What You Will* by William Shakespeare: "Youth's a stuff will not endure" (II, iii); "O mistress mine! Where art thou roaming?/ Oh, stay and hear, your true love's coming . . . (II, iii); "She never told her love,/ But let concealment, like a worm i' th' bud,/ Feed on her damask cheek" (II, iv).

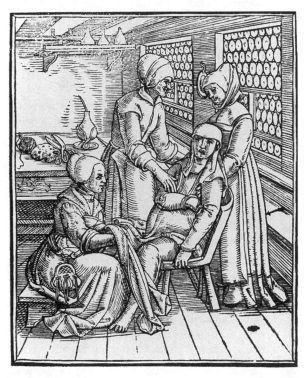

Midwives knew more about childbirth than most physicians, but neither knew much about hygiene. NATIONAL LIBRARY OF MEDICINE

1602

✖ Charles d'Angoulême, comte d'Auvergne, obtains Spanish backing for a scheme to have his stepsister Henriette's bastard son by Henri IV made heir to the French throne. Henri's second wife, Marie de' Medici, has produced a legitimate heir, the scheme amounts to high treason, Henriette and her father surrender the paper promising her the throne if she bears a son, and Charles d'Angoulême goes to the Bastille, where he will remain for 11 years.

1602

Theater: *Hamlet, Prince of Denmark* by William Shakespeare, who writes, "Frailty, thy name is woman!" (I, ii).

1603

Queen Elizabeth dies March 24 at age 69 after an extraordinary 45-year reign, ending 118 years of Tudor monarchy in England. She is succeeded by the Stuart son of the late Mary, Queen of Scots; now 36, he will reign until 1625 over a united kingdom as James I with his wife, Anne of Denmark, as queen until her death in 1619.

The Ottoman sultan Mohammed III dies of plague December 25 at age 37 after an 8-year reign. His son of 14 will reign until 1617 as Ahmed I, but women will hold the reins of power for the next few decades in the absence of any mentally stable sultan.

Japan's Kabuki theater has its beginnings in April at Kyoto where women led by Okuni Izumo dance at the Kitani shrine playing men's roles as well as women's (but *see* 1629).

1604

England's James I makes peace with Spain and directs his efforts to American colonization.

Hidetada, son of Japan's Tokugawa shōgun Ieyasu, hires Ofuku, 25, as wet nurse and governess. She has recently given birth to a third child of her own but will not see her children for many years as she joins the shōgun's household as Lady Kasuga. She will raise this first son of Hidetada's, and he will become shōgun in 1623 under the name Iemitsu.

Theater: *The Honest Whore*, Part I, by English playwrights Thomas Dekker and Thomas Middleton is performed by the Children of St. Paul's: "Were there no women, men might live as gods"; "The calmest husbands make the stormiest wives" (V, i).

1605

Marguerite d'Angoulême, now 50, leaves the castle of Usson in early July after nearly 20 years of exile,

is met at the Auvergne border by the duc de Sully, to whom she conveys news of a conspiracy by her onetime lover against the king, picks up her bastard half sister Diane de France at Longjumeau, and arrives at Paris, where she is greeted at her new residence, the Château de Madrid, by her onetime lover, Harlay de Chanvallon. The king calls upon her a week after her arrival, finds her bloated in body, an eccentric whose once-black hair is now concealed beneath a towering blond wig made from the hair of her footmen, and wearing outdated clothes. Henri stays for more than 3 hours and asks her to keep more sensible hours and be less extravagant in her gifts and entertainments, to which she replies that she is too old to change her habits.

India's Mughal emperor Akbar dies October 17 at age 62 after a 49-year reign. His son of 36, a drunk, will reign until 1627 as Jahangir ("Conqueror of the World") (*see* 1611).

A "Gunpowder Plot" to blow up the Houses of Parliament in revenge against harsh penal laws enacted against Roman Catholics comes to light when English Catholic Guy Fawkes, 35, is arrested the night of November 4 while entering the gunpowder-filled cellar under the building. He and his confederates will be hanged next year.

Catherine de Vivonne de Savelli, 17, marquise de Rambouillet, finds herself annoyed by the coarseness of Parisian society under Henri IV, packs her husband off to the country, and makes her home a center for refined and witty conversation—the first great Paris salon.

1606

A Virginia Charter granted by England's James I establishes the Plymouth Company and the London Company and authorizes them to establish settlements at least 100 miles apart in the North American area named for England's late "virgin queen."

1607

Jamestown, Virginia, is founded May 14 by Capt. Christopher Newport of the London Company, who has come up the river that he has named the James in honor of his king.

∞ Spanish novitiate Catalina de Erauzo, 15, escapes from her convent in handmade boys' clothing, calls herself Antonio Ramírez de Guzmán, and begins an adventurous life in which she will develop a reputation for purse-snatching, gambling, dueling, and womanizing (*see* 1623).

🏃 English boys at Jamestown (above) are challenged by Pocahontas, a native girl of about 12 whose father heads the Powhatan Confederacy, to leave their fort and compete with her in turning hand-springs.

👤 Jamestown's colonists are sick and starving by autumn, having buried at least 50. Capt. John Smith goes up the Chickahominy River in December to trade for corn with the Algonquins (*see* 1608).

1608

⚔ Capt. John Smith of the Jamestown colony is captured by the Powhatan chief Wahunsonacook, who is about to have him executed when (according to the account that Smith will give in his 1624 *General Historie of Virginia*), "Pocahontas, the king's dearest daughter, when no entreaty could prevail, got his head in her arms, and laid her own upon his to save him from death. Whereat the emperor was

Pocahontas, daughter of a Powhatan chief, saved colonist Captain John Smith's life, or so he would claim. LIBRARY OF CONGRESS

contented he should live to make him hatchets . . ." (*see* 1613).

☿ *Observations diverses sur la stérilité, perte de fruit, fécondité, accouchements et maladies des femmes et enfants nouveaux naîz* (*Divers Observations on Sterility, Miscarriage, Fertility, Childbirth and Illnesses of Women and Newborn Infants*) by midwife Louyse Bourgeois, now 45, is a treatise on childbirth with illustrations and explanations of the causes of miscarriage and premature birth (she advises bed rest to stop hemorrhaging) (*see* 1601). Although her patron, the duchesse d'Orléans, has died of puerperal fever, Bourgeois replies to her critics with an attack on male doctors. By next year she will have attended more than 2,000 births; her book, which will be plagiarized by English writers, will be translated into German and Dutch (*see* 1626).

1609

⚔ Spain's Philip III signs a truce with the Dutch April 9 after mediation by France's Henri IV and recognizes the independence of the Netherlands.

∞ English lay sister Mary (originally Joan) Ward, 24, who entered a convent of the Poor Clares at St. Omer 3 years ago and adopted the name Mary, founds a religious community of women in France that includes a school for girls. She will go on to start communities at Liège, Cologne, Vienna, Prague, Rome, Naples, and elsewhere, each with a school for English refugee boarding students and poor local girls (*see* 1619).

1610

⚔ Marie de' Medici is crowned queen of France May 13 in the royal church of St. Denis. Her husband, Henri IV, is assassinated the next day at Paris by a fanatic, her 9-year-old son will reign until 1643 as Louis XIII, but she will act as regent until he is of age and will exercise power for long after. Diane de France, duchesse d'Angoulême, now 72, has superintended the education of the new king (she is the illegitimate daughter of the late Henri II and, possibly, Diane de Poitiers). The queen mother, Marie, has become a great friend of her late husband's first queen, Marguerite d'Angoulême, but while Marguerite advises her on social matters it is probably on someone else's advice that she removes the duc de Sully from office and installs her favorite, Concino Concini, in a position of power, ushering in an era of cruelty and oppression for the peasantry.

The Hausa queen Amina dies at age 34 after an 18-year reign that has expanded her realm to the mouth of the Niger. She is said to have taken a new lover in every city she captured, having him beheaded the next day.

Hungarian noblewoman Elizabeth Báthory, Countess Nádasdy, a niece of Poland's Stephen Báthory, is found to have murdered 650 young girls in order to keep her youth by bathing in their warm blood. Her accomplices are burned at the stake, and she is confined to her fortress (*see* 1613).

Painting: *Self-Portrait* by Sofonisba Anguissola, now 78.

1611

India's Mughal emperor Jahangir marries Nur Jahan ("Light of the World"), who will control the realm of her drunken husband.

∞ The Authorized (King James) version of the Bible is published for the Church of England after 7 years of scholarly effort.

1612

The Holy Roman Emperor Rudolf II dies January 20 at age 59 after a reign of more than 35 years. His brother Matthias, 54, will reign until 1619.

Italian painter Artemisia Gentileschi, 19, accuses her tutor, Agostino Tassi, in May of having repeatedly raped her. Tassi has been convicted of conspiring to murder his wife, but it is his accuser who goes on trial. She is tortured with thumbscrews for 5 months to make her confess that she must have allowed the rapes, but Tassi is convicted in the end (he will spend 8 months in prison before being acquitted), and Gentileschi is married in November to Pietro Antonio di Vincenzo, a Florentine gentleman. Her talents as a painter of narrative scenes,

female nudes, and portraits of contemporaries will make her world-famous, but her accusation that she was raped will brand her as a woman of questionable character.

1613

The Romanov dynasty, which will rule Russia until 1917, is inaugurated July 22 with the crowning in the Kremlin at Moscow of Michael Romanov, 17, a grandnephew of Ivan IV. His election February 22 has ended the "time of the troubles" that has persisted since the death of Boris Godunov in 1605.

Bethlen Gábor (Gabriel Bethlen von Iktar), 33, becomes prince of Transylvania, ending the cruel Catholic reign of Gabriel Báthory, who is killed at age 24 (his cousin will die in prison next year) (*see* crime, 1610).

Pocahontas is taken hostage and brought to Jamestown, where the Virginia colonists hold her for ransom (which is not forthcoming) (*see* 1608). She is instructed in the Christian religion, baptized, and christened Rebecca.

1614

Virginia colony widower John Rolfe is married April 5 to Pocahontas, now about 18. Rolfe has been the main force in persuading the colonists to grow tobacco, whose smoke is detested by Capt. John Smith (and by King James in England) but whose exports are making the colony commercially viable.

Italian painter Lavinia Fontana dies at Rome August 11 at age 62. Daughter of a Bolognese artist whose work was inferior to hers, she married a fellow painter, Gian Paolo Zappi, who gave up his career to look after their 11 children when it became apparent that her talents were greater than his.

1615

France's Estates-General dissolves February 23 after 4 months in session. It has failed to gain concessions from the Crown with regard to taxation.

Former Queen Marguerite dies at Paris March 27 at age 61, the last survivor of the Valois dynasty. She has continued to gather young men about her, and one, a singer known as Villars, has been nicknamed "le roi Margot."

Anne of Austria, 14, eldest daughter of Spain's Philip III, is married to France's Louis XIII, also 14, in an ill-starred match arranged by the queen mother Marie de' Medici.

Osaka falls June 4 to the Japanese *daimyo* Ieyasu after a 6-month siege. Lady Yodo, now 49, commits *seppuku*, as does her son, Hideyori (both are then burnt in the flames that consume the castle). Survivors include Princess Sen, 18, a granddaughter of Ieyasu, who was married at age 7 to Hideyori, and Hideyori's 6-year-old daughter by one of his concubines.

✒ Fiction: *El ingenioso hidalgo don Quixote de la Mancha* by Spanish novelist Miguel de Saavedra Cervantes, 68, whose writing has been published since 1585. His burlesque of romantic chivalry contains the line "A woman's advice has little value, but he who won't take it is a fool" (II, 7).

Poetry: "Shepherd's Hunting" by English Cavalier poet George Wither, 27, who wrote the pastoral while imprisoned in Marshalsea for his libelous satire "Abuses Stript and Whipt" ("Little said is soonest mended"); *The Author's Resolution* by Wither contains the sonnet "Fidelia": "Shall I, wasting in despair, / Die because a woman's fair?/ Or make pale my cheeks with care/ 'Cause another's rosy are?/ Be she fairer than the day,/ Or the flowery meads in May,/ If she think not well of me,/ What care I how fair she be?"

1616

✗ Japan's Tokugawa shōgun Ieyasu dies June 1 at age 74. His son Hidetada, now 38, will marry a daughter of the emperor Gomizno (all her siblings will be killed or aborted) and reign until 1623. The late Hideyori's daughter, who survived last year's burning of Osaka Castle, becomes a nun at Tokei Temple in Kamakura, near Tokyo, and takes the name Tenshuni. Tokei Temple has a reputation for giving refuge to abused women, enabling them to get

divorces at a time when divorce is otherwise impossible; when the Tokugawa shogunate strips other temples of their privileges it will exempt Tokei, whose nuns will raise Tenshuni. Last surviving descendant of Toyotomi Hideyoshi, she will become chief priestess when she is about 30.

✊ John Rolfe and his wife, Rebecca (*née* Pocahontas), voyage to London, where Rebecca is lionized and presented at court. More than one publican capitalizes on her popularity by renaming his tavern "La Belle Sauvage."

💲 Mitsui begins its rise toward becoming the world's largest business organization. Rebelling against his noble caste, Japanese samurai Mitsui Sokubei Takatoshi opens a sake and soy sauce establishment, and his wife, Shuho, finds that patrons will pawn their valuables for a drink of sake.

✒ Poetry: "A Select Second Husband for Sir Thomas Overburies' Wife" by English poet John Davies, 51, of Hereford: "Beauty's but skin deep."

1617

✗ France's chief minister Concino Concini is arrested April 24 and executed on orders from Louis XIII, now 16, who banishes his mother, Marie de' Medici, to Blois. He has little to do with his wife, Anne of Austria, and they live apart.

✊ Rebecca Rolfe (Pocahontas) is taken ill while preparing to embark on a return voyage to Virginia and dies, probably of smallpox, which next year will also kill her father. Her son, Thomas Rolfe, will return to the colony.

Japan's Yoshiwara prostitute section is established at Edo. A local vice lord has persuaded shogunate authorities to license him to operate an area of supervised brothels in exchange for his surveillance of suspicious strangers (*see 1657*).

☿ *Instructions to My Daughter* by midwife Louyse Bourgeois, now 54, urges that it should be so arranged that the woman in labor shall neither see the male physician nor know that he is there.

✒ Nonfiction: *The Bride-Bush* by English writer William Whately, who says, "Whosover, therefore, doth desire to be a good wife, or to live comfortably, let her set down this conclusion within her soul: mine husband is my superior, my better; he hath authority and rule over me, nature has given it to him . . . [and] God hath given it to him." "A Mouzell for Melastomus, the Cynicall Bayer of, and foule mouthed Barger against Evahs Sex. Or an apological Answere to that Irreligious and Illiterate Pamphlet made by Jo[seph] Sw[etnam] and by him intituled, The Arraignement of Women" by English author and poet Rachel Speght, 20, says, "Man was created of the dust of the earth, but woman was made of a part of man, after that he was a living soule; yet was shee not produced from Adam's foote, to be his too low inferiour; nor from his head to be his superiour, but from his side, neare his heart, to be his equall. . . . Husbands should not account their wives as their vassals, but as those that are heires together of the grace of life."

1618

 The Defenestration of Prague (two governors are thrown from a window in the Palace of Hradcany) May 23 precipitates a Thirty Years' War that will devastate central Europe, putting women in constant danger of losing their husbands and sons, threatening even cloistered nuns with rape, pitting Catholics against Protestants in pitched battles, and disrupting agriculture to such an extent that millions will starve.

France's queen mother, Marie de' Medici, returns from exile following the negotiation of a treaty between her and the duc de Luynes. The duc de Richelieu, who has arranged the treaty, is exiled to Avignon for conspiring with her.

1619

 The Holy Roman Emperor Matthias dies at Vienna March 20 at age 62 and is succeeded by Bohemia's Ferdinand, 40, who will reign until 1637 as Ferdinand II.

✊ Three African women and 17 men are put ashore from a Dutch frigate at Jamestown to give the Virginia colony its first slaves.

✳ Some 90 young women arrive at Jamestown from England to marry settlers who pay 120 pounds of tobacco each for the cost of transporting their brides.

🎓 Mary Ward tries to start girls' schools in England like those she has opened on the Continent, emphasizing the study of Latin but denying charges that her intent is to have women preach sermons and administer the sacraments (see 1609; 1630).

1620

✳ The 180-ton vessel *Mayflower* out of Southampton arrives off Cape Cod November 11 with 100 Pilgrims plus two more born at sea during the 60-day voyage. English Separatists, they have obtained a patent from the London Company to settle in America.

 Painting: *Self-Portrait* by Sofonisba Anguissola, now 88.

1621

 Spain's Philip III dies March 31 at age 42 after a 23-year reign. His son of 16 will reign until 1665 as Philip IV, leaving affairs of state to his prime minister (who breaks the 1609 truce with Holland and resumes war).

The House of Commons petitions England's James I not to permit his son Charles to marry the Spanish infanta (see 1623). James angrily rebukes the Commons for meddling in foreign affairs and Commons asserts its rights December 18 in a Great Protestation (see 1622).

🖋 *The Anatomy of Melancholy* by English clergyman Robert Burton, 41, is a treatise on the causes, symptoms, and cure of melancholy. Says the vicar of St. Thomas's at Oxford, "Man's best possession is a loving wife" (III).

🖤 Sculpture: *Rape of Prospero* by Italian sculptor-painter Gian (or Giovanni) Lorenzo Bernini, 22, who will gain the patronage of Sweden's Queen Christina.

🎭 Theater: *A New Way to Pay Old Bills* by English playwright Philip Massinger, 38: "The sum of all that makes a just man happy/ Consists in the well choosing of his wife" (IV).

1622

✘ England's James I tears out the page in the journal of the Commons bearing the Great Protestation of last December, dissolves Parliament February 8, and imprisons his critics.

✒ Nonfiction: *Egalité des hommes et des femmes* by Marie de Gournay, now 56, attacks the hypocrisy of society's attitude toward women, who are expected to be submissive; *Historia di donna Camilla da Bruno Gonzaga* by Italian writer Camilla Faà Gonzaga, 23, will not be published until 1895.

1623

✘ England's Prince of Wales travels in secret to Spain with the duke of Buckingham, who has persuaded him to seek the hand of the infanta Maria, sister of Philip IV. "Mr. Smith" and "Mr. Brown" arrive at Madrid March 7 but find the infanta and Spanish court unenthusiastic and distrustful of young Charles's promise to change English penal laws against Catholics. Charles, now 22, returns October 5 and is soon betrothed instead to Henrietta Maria, 14, sister of France's Louis XIII, with marriage terms that require him to let her practice her Catholic faith freely and raise any children in that faith until they reach age 13 (*see* 1625).

Japan's Tokugawa shōgun abdicates at age 45; his son Iemitsu, now 19, will reign until 1651, raising the shōgunate to its greatest glory, with Lady Kasuga continuing to exercise considerable influence over him until her death in 1643. They will be married by proxy in February 1625.

Ndongo princess Nzinga in Angola succeeds to the throne after poisoning her brother. Her small monarchy is dwarfed by the neighboring Portuguese colony of Angola, but she is determined to resist the depredations of slave traders. She travels to Angola, where she negotiates with the governor and allows herself to be baptized into Christianity as Dona Aña de Souza (but *see* 1624).

✒ Nonfiction: *The Mother's Legacy to her Unborn Child* by English author Elizabeth Josceline (*née* Brooke), 26, expresses fear of childbirth and anxiety about the fate of her child should she die in childbirth. She worries that education might make her daughter less useful in the home. Josceline does, in fact, die after giving birth; her work will go through three editions by 1625 and will be reprinted in 1684. *The Countess of Lincoln's Nursery* by Elizabeth Knyvet, wife of the third earl of Lincoln, urges mothers to suckle their own children (she herself has borne 18 and lost at least one through the neglect of an incompetent nurse). Refuting suggestions that nursing is "troublesome . . . noisome to one's clothes, makes one look old, [or] endangers health," the countess reminds her readers that biblical mothers, beginning with Eve, nursed their infants.

▦ Antonio Ramírez de Guzmán (Catalina de Erauzo) is convicted of murder (date approximate) (*see* 1607). She killed her brother accidentally in a nighttime fight 2 or 3 years ago, hid out in a church for 8 months before making her escape, and has been tried for a different murder altogether. On the day she is to be executed she confesses all her crimes and reveals her true sex to a clergyman, who takes her to a convent for examination by the nuns. They discover that she is not only a woman but also a nun and a virgin, whereupon she is freed, given permission to wear men's clothing, and absolved of her sins by the new pope Urban VIII.

🌾 Pilgrim women and children at the Plymouth colony join with the men to plant corn and increase production after each family is assigned its own parcel of land, forsaking the communal Mayflower Compact with an incentive system.

👫 A Spanish edict offers rewards and special privileges to encourage large families, but the offer has little effect on birthrates.

1624

✘ Ndongo's Nzinga creates the new kingdom of Matamba after being driven out of Ndongo by the Portuguese (*see* 1623). She begins to train an elite army that she will lead against the Portuguese, first in alliance with the Jaga people, later in alliance with the Dutch (*see* 1641).

France and England sign a treaty providing for the marriage of Charles, prince of Wales, to Henrietta

Maria, daughter of Henri IV and Marie de' Medici (*see* 1623; 1625).

💲 Spain's Philip IV publishes sumptuary laws in response to popular criticism of his court's extravagance.

1625

⚔️ England's James I dies March 5 at age 58 and is succeeded by his son of 24 who ascends the throne March 27 and will reign until 1649 as Charles I. The new king is married by proxy May 1 to the bright-eyed French princess Henrietta Maria, now 16, and receives her at Canterbury June 13 (*see* 1623).

🎨 Painting: *Judith and Maidservant with Head of Holofernes* by Artemesia Gentileschi, now 32;

A portrait of France's queen mother Marie de' Medici by Rubens showed her to have a small goiter, considered a mark of beauty.
LOUVRE MUSEUM, PARIS

Marie de' Medici by Peter Paul Rubens; *The Procuress* by Dutch painter Gerrit van Honthorst, 34. Sofonisba Anguissola dies at Palermo in November at age 92 during a plague that will eventually wipe out half the city's population.

🍎 Rubens depicts a goiter in his portrait of Marie de' Medici (above). The thyroid gland swelling in the neck is esteemed as a mark of beauty when only moderate in size.

1626

✳️ Dutch colonists purchase Manhattan Island from Canarsie chiefs of the Wappinger Confederacy for fish hooks and trinkets valued at 60 guilders.

French colonists establish their first settlements in Madagascar and try to drive out the Hovas, who have lived on the African island for 600 years.

⚕️ Midwife Louyse Bourgeois, now 63, writes that at least three times "in the last 4 or 5 years" Paris midwives have hauled out the uterus along with the placenta when delivering infants, killing the mothers.

🖋️ Fiction: *The Shadow of Mlle. de Gournay* (*L'Ombre de la demoiselle de Gournay*) by Marie de Gournay.

1627

⚔️ The Mughal emperor Jahangir dies in October at age 58 while returning to Delhi from Kashmir. His son of 35 will reign until 1658 as Shah Jahan.

1628

⚕️ Bubonic plague kills half the population of Lyons. In the next 2 years it will kill a million in the northern Italian states, even more than are being killed in the continuing Thirty Years' War elsewhere in Europe.

1629

⚔️ Transylvania's Bethlen Gábor dies November 15 at age 49 after marrying a sister-in-law of Sweden's Gustavus Adolphus in hopes that the Swedes would help him obtain the Polish crown. He will be succeeded next year by George Rákóczi, who will reign until 1648.

🖌 Painting: *The Serenade* and *Jolly Toper* by Dutch painter Judith Leyster, 20, at Haarlem.

🎭 Japan's Kabuki theater becomes an all-male affair in October by order of the Tokugawa shōgun Iemitsu, who has decided that it is immoral for women to dance in public (*see* 1603). Women's roles are performed by men as in Elizabethan England, but the Japanese will take extraordinary measures to make the men playing female roles appear as women even to other Kabuki players. (The young female impersonators are soon selling their favors to admirers, just as the actresses had done.)

1630

⚔ England makes peace with France in April and with Spain in November, but the Thirty Years' War continues to take a heavy toll of lives in Europe.

☿ Bubonic plague kills 500,000 Venetians, hastening the decline of Venice.

Repeated epidemics in the decade ahead will reduce America's Huron tribe to one-third of its estimated 30,000 population.

∞ English authorities suppress Mary Ward's schools for girls but she will continue to operate them, defying persecution (*see* 1619; 1631).

🖌 Painting: *Standing Cavalier*, *Carousing Couple*, *Violinist with a Skull*, and *The Rommel-Pot Player* by Judith Leyster; *At the Greengrocer* and *Basket of Fruit with a Bunch of Asparagus* by French painter Louise Mouillon, 20.

🏛 The Palais de Luxembourg, completed at Paris for the queen mother Marie de' Medici after 15 years' work, was designed by French architect Salmon de Brosse to resemble the Florentine Pitti Palace, where she grew up.

1631

⚔ Cardinal Richelieu brings France into the war against the Hapsburgs by pledging subsidies Jan-

uary 13 to Sweden's Gustavus Adolphus and the duke of Saxe-Weimar.

Catholic soldiers take Magdeburg by storm May 20 and sack the city, massacring the citizenry and committing terrible atrocities. Fires break out in scattered places simultaneously, and only the cathedral escapes the flames. The Battle of Breitenfeld September 17 breaks the strength of revived Catholicism in central Europe as a Saxon-Swedish army of 40,000 defeats a German army of equal size.

✊ *Cautio criminalis* by German Jesuit poet Friedrich von Spee, 40, is published anonymously. Von Spee, who has often ministered to condemned witches, and he attacks the mentality behind witch-hunts and the legal use of torture to extract confessions (*see* Wier, 1563; Loudon, 1634; Salem, 1692).

🎓 Pope Urban VIII issues a decree dissolving Mary Ward's Institute of Women but orders Ward's release when he learns that she has been imprisoned by order of the Church in a small, airless German prison cell (*see* 1630). She will live in Rome until her return to England in 1639 (*see* 1642).

🖌 Painting: *The Rejected Officer*, *The Proposition*, *The Game of Tric-Trac*, and *Young Woman with a Lute* by Judith Leyster.

1632

⚔ The Battle of Lützen November 16 pits 20,000 Swedes against 18,000 Catholics. The Swedes win, but Gustavus II Adolphus is killed at age 38. His beautiful (but sickly and neurotic) widow, Maria Eleanora of Brandenburg, confines her only surviving child, Christina, 6, with her as Count Axel Gustaffson, 49, takes power as chancellor (*see* 1636).

✊ An English legal manual for women states that wife beating is still a husband's legal right against which the wife has no redress. Under English law, a woman's personal belongings, money, furniture, linens, and the like become the absolute property of her husband when she marries, and he is under no obligation to pass them on to her designated heirs. Her dowry does pass to her heirs; her husband enjoys the use of it only during his lifetime. If she predeceases him, he can continue to use her land until his own death. Most other Western countries have similar laws and customs.

1632

Painting: *Children with a Cat* by Judith Leyster; *King Charles I and Queen Henrietta* by Dutch painter Anthony van Dyck, 33, who visited Sofonisba Anguissola at Palermo 9 years ago and has now been named court painter.

English Puritan William Prynne, 32, attacks the London theater in his pamphlet "Histriomastix": "It hath evermore been the notorious badge of prostituted Strumpets and the lewdest Harlots, to ramble abroad to plays, to Playhouses; whither no honest, chaste or sober Girls or Women, but only branded Whores and infamous Adulteresses, did usually resort in ancient times." Prynne's lines are construed as an aspersion on Queen Henrietta Maria, who has taken part in a performance of a play at court. Prynne will be branded and heavily fined, have his ears cut off, and serve 8 years of a life sentence beginning in 1634 (London's theaters will be closed in 1642).

French courtesan Anne Lenclos, 16, takes her first lover to begin a 70-year career in which she will be mistress to two marshals of France, two marquises (including the marquis de Sévigné), the great Condé, the duc de La Rochefoucauld, and at least one abbé. A religious skeptic known as much for her taste and style as for her beauty, Ninon de Lenclos, as she is called, will be asked by some of the most respectable women to give their children lessons in good manners (her own two sons will be brought up without knowing that she is their mother; one of them will be sexually attracted to her and, when informed of their relationship, commit suicide). The salons over which she will officiate until her death in 1706 will attract the greatest wits, savants, writers, poets, playwrights, diplomats, and military officers of France.

1633

Italian scientist Galileo Galilei, 69, goes on trial at Rome April 12 for "heresy." He has dared to defend Copernican theory that the earth revolves about the sun and is threatened by the Inquisition with torture on the rack if he does not retract. He yields and is sent to his villa outside Florence, where he will be confined for the remaining 9 years of his life.

Painting: *Mother Sewing with Children by Lamplight, Mother Cleaning a Child's Hair, Soldier's Family, Card Players,* and *Self-Portrait* by Judith Leyster, now 24, who opens her own studio after several years of studying under Frans Hals and accepts students of her own. When Hals appropriates one of her apprentices, thus cheating her out of her fee for the young man's training, she sues Hals and, to everyone's surprise, wins.

1634

French witch-hunters at Loudon crush the legs of local curate Urbain Grandier, 44, and burn him alive August 18. The vain and handsome priest of the Huguenot St.-Pierre-du-March church is a notorious seducer of virgins and widows in the prosperous walled city of 20,000; he has insulted Cardinal Richelieu in a matter of church protocol, and been accused and found guilty of bewitching the convent of Ursuline nuns, whose hysterical, blasphemous fits have for years attracted morbid sightseers from all over Europe. Grandier protests his innocence to the end, the nuns are exorcised, Richelieu razes the fortified castle of Loudon to prevent its use by the Huguenots, but the descendants of the judges who sent Grandier to the stake will lead tormented lives and it will be said that Grandier put a curse on them.

1635

The Peace of Prague May 30 resolves differences between the Holy Roman Emperor Ferdinand II and the elector of Saxony. The Thirty Years' War becomes a conflict between the Franco-Swedish alliance and the Hapsburgs.

The Japanese Tokugawa shōgun Iemitsu acts to prevent any feudal lord from becoming too rich and powerful. He orders that each *daimyo* must visit Edo every other year, leave his wife and children at Edo for the year he is absent, and pay all the expenses of maintaining two places of residence.

Painting: *Portrait of a Woman, Girl with a Coral Necklace, Portrait of a Lutanist,* and *Young Flute Player* by Judith Leyster, who marries Jan Miense Molenaer, a fellow artist.

1636

✖ Sweden's Queen Christina, now 10, is removed from her obsessive mother's care and sent to live with her late father's sister, Catherine. After Catherine's death she will be raised by several different ladies of the court—but raised very much as a boy (*see* 1632; 1644).

The conde-duque de Olivares, who effectively rules Spain, invades France in a desperate gamble to restore Spanish power. His soldiers burn villages in Beauvais and Picardy, plunder crops, and force peasants to flee with food, livestock, and belongings. The French win a narrow victory at Corbie, forcing Spain into a war of attrition that will drain her for 23 years.

🎓 Harvard College has its beginnings in a seminary founded by the Great and General Court of Massachusetts at Newtowne (*see* 1638).

1637

✖ The Holy Roman Emperor Ferdinand II dies at Vienna February 15 at age 57. He is succeeded by his son of 28, who will reign until 1657 as Ferdinand III.

💲 Dutch tulip prices collapse after years of speculation in which a single Viceroy bulb has fetched as much as 1,000 pounds of cheese, four oxen, eight pigs, 12 sheep, a bed, and a suit of clothes.

✒ Fiction: *Novelas amorosas y exemplares* (ten short prose narratives) by Spanish novelist María de Zayas y Sofomayor, 36, gain wide readership with their stories of horror and melodrama, each with a happy ending.

🎨 Painting: *Still Life with Grapes and Vine Leaves* by Louise Mouillon.

1638

✊ Japanese peasants who have occupied Hara Castle near Nagasaki for nearly 3 months yield February 28 for lack of food and musket ammunition. Most of the 37,000 people are Christians, and most are annihilated by the Tokugawa shōgun Iemitsu, who

expels Japan's Portuguese traders, forbids construction of large ships that might carry anyone abroad, and orders that any farmer who cannot pay taxes be hanged as if he were a Christian.

✳ Colonial American religious leader Anne Hutchinson, 47, and her husband acquire territory from the Narragansett in the 2-year-old Rhode Island colony, where they establish a democratic community. They came to Boston 4 years ago from England, she held biweekly meetings with women at which she denounced Massachusetts Bay Colony clergymen as being "under the covenant of works, not of grace" for not permitting women to have a voice in church affairs, and she was tried for heresy and sedition. One of her accusers has said, "You have stepped out of your place. You have rather been a husband than a wife, and a preacher than a hearer, a magistrate than a subject." Hutchinson has been banished by Gov. John Winthrop, who has described her as "a woman of haughty and fierce carriage, a nimble wit and active spirit, a very voluble tongue, more bold than a man" (*see* 1643).

🎓 English clergyman John Harvard, 31, dies of tuberculosis September 14 after 1 year in the Massachusetts Bay Colony and leaves his library and half his estate of £800 to the "seminary" established at New Towne in 1636. Because he is a Cambridge graduate, New Towne will be renamed Cambridge, colonist Ann Radcliffe will contribute funds to the school, and by 1650 Harvard will have established the 4-year program that will become standard for American colleges (*see* Radcliffe, 1879).

✒ German poet Sibelle Schwartz dies of dysentery July 31 at at 17. Writer Samuel Gerlach, who will edit and publish two volumes of her work totaling more than 150 pages, will call her the "Tenth Muse," echoing Schwartz's statement in defense of women writing, "Weren't the Muses women?" (*see* Bradstreet, 1650).

1639

✖ Scottish Presbyterians seize Edinburgh Castle and raise an army but make peace June 18 with England's Charles I, who has marched to meet them near Berwick. A new Scottish Parliament assembled after the armies have disbanded is intractable in its opposition to English episcopacy (*see* 1640).

1640

✕ Scottish forces cross the Tweed August 20, defeat the English at Newburn August 28, occupy Newcastle and Durham, but cease hostilities October 21 when the English agree in the Treaty of Ripon to pay Scotland £850 per day to maintain her army.

Charles I convenes the "Long Parliament" November 5 and sets free members of Parliament he imprisoned earlier for refusing to loan him money.

💲 Inflation in England reduces the value of money to one-third its 1540 value; food prices outpace wage increases.

🎨 Painting: *Children with a Cat and a Slow-Worm* by Judith Leyster.

1641

✊ England's "Long Parliament" abolishes the Star Chamber and the Court of High Commission in July as it struggles to effect a revolution against the excesses of the English constitution. Both have been used to root out Calvinism and Presbyterianism.

Dutch forces in Africa take Luanda with help from Nzinga, queen of Ndongo and Matamba (*see* 1624). The Portuguese, who founded Luanda in 1576, have been using it as a base from which to export 10,000 slaves per year, most of them to Brazil (*see* 1643).

Kyoto's Shimabara district becomes a licensed brothel area (*see* Yoshiwara, 1617; 1657). The prostitutes belong to different ranks according to their beauty and education; each wears a special kimono that denotes her rank.

✒ Fiction: *Ibrahim ou l'illustre Bassa* by French novelist Madeleine de Scudéry, 33, whose first work is published under the name of her brother, Georges, 40. Both belong to the literary society of Catherine de Vivonne, marquise de Rambouillet, now 53, whose Hôtel Rambouillet is a gathering place for the nation's talent and wit (*see* 1605).

1642

✕ Civil war begins in England as Charles I sends his Cavaliers against the Puritan Parliament at York. The middle classes, great merchants, and much of the nobility oppose the king.

Brilliana, Lady Harley (*née* Conway), 42, third wife of Sir Robert Harley, is left in charge of Brampton Bryan Castle near Hereford when her husband goes to London for consultations with the Parliamentarians, whom he supports against the Royalist forces of Charles I. The Royalists approach the castle in December and order Lady Harley to surrender, but she places her seven children and nine stepchildren in relative safety and prepares for a siege (*see* 1643).

🎓 Mary Ward opens a school in her hometown of York despite the civil war that is disrupting classes at her other schools (*see* 1630). Now 57, she will continue to run the school at York until her death in 1645 (*see* 1686).

Lady Brilliana Harley defended her husband's castle in England's civil war between Roundheads and Cavaliers. LIBRARY OF CONGRESS

Nonfiction: *Matrimonial Honour* by English Puritan preacher Daniel Rogers says, "Husbands and wives should be as two sweet friends, bred under one constellation, tempered by an influence from Heaven, whereof neither can give any great reason save that Mercy and Providence first made themselves and then made their match." He calls married love a "sweet compound" of spiritual affection and carnal attraction, and a nice blend of the two is the "vital spirit and heart blood of wedlock."

English Puritan scholar-poet John Milton, 33, marries Mary Powell, 16, whose parents are Royalists. Milton, who is writing polemic tracts in behalf of the Puritan cause, has met Mary while on holiday in Oxfordshire (he has known her family for some years); their marriage quickly degenerates into petty bickering, she leaves in the fall to visit her family, and she will not return (*see* 1643).

1643

France's Louis XIII dies May 14 at age 43 after a 33-year reign dominated by his mother, Marie de' Medici, and Cardinal Richelieu. His son of 4 will reign until 1715 as Louis XIV, initially under the aegis of Giulio Mazarin, 41, a Sicilian who was naturalized as a Frenchman 4 years ago, was made cardinal 2 years ago, succeeded Cardinal Richelieu as prime minister, and has been retained by the queen regent, Anne of Austria.

The Battle of Rocroi May 19 gives a French army of 23,000 victory over a 20,000-man army of Spaniards, Dutch, Flemish, and Italian mercenaries, the first great French military success in decades.

Blanche, Lady Arundel, 60, defends Wardour Castle in the absence of her Cavalier husband, resisting the Parliamentary forces of Sir Edward Hungerford and others who have united against her in May. She has only 25 men to help her, and they inflict more than 60 casualties on the enemy.

Parliamentary forces try to take Lathom House, country seat of James Stanley, seventh Earl of Derby, while the earl is absent on a visit to the Isle of Man. His wife, Charlotte (*née* de la Tremoille), 7 years his senior and mother of his seven children, refuses to accept the local general's offer of safe

conduct and determines to defend the place, refusing to negotiate, defying artillery bombardment, and ignoring her neighbors' pleas and the insults shouted by the parliamentary soldiers. When the latter try to cut off her water supply, she sends out a party to steal their biggest gun and holds out for 3 months until a Royalist force arrives to lift the siege, permitting the countess to join her husband on the Isle of Man (*see* 1645).

Mary, Lady Bankes (*née* Hawtrey), holds out in Corfe Castle on the Dorset coast, refusing to surrender (the enemy has promised no mercy for the women and children that make up much of her army). More than 500 men attack her ten-foot-thick walls with small artillery June 23 and try to climb up with ladders, but Lady Bankes, who has only five soldiers to protect her daughters and many maidservants, leads a successful defense of the upper ward, pelting her attackers with stones and hot embers. (She later obtains an additional garrison of more than 50 men from the Royalist commander Prince Maurice; *see* 1646.)

Royalist siege forces bring up added strength against Brampton Bryan Castle July 26 (*see* 1642). Fowlers have been forbidden to supply the castle with game since January, its cattle have been driven off, its horses commandeered, and its servants intimidated from venturing into town. Brilliana, Lady Harley, holds out against a siege force of 700 Cavaliers, who attack her walls three times daily. Although short of food and in failing health, she has promised her husband to protect his holdings during his long absence in the civil war; some of her women are killed in the conflict, but she holds the enemy at bay for three months before dying in October. The castle's small garrison will surrender early next year, some £13,000 worth of property will be seized, and while no one in the Harley family will be harmed the castle will be destroyed.

Nzinga, queen of Ndongo and Matamba, routs Portuguese forces outside Mbaka (*see* 1641; 1647).

Anne Hutchinson, now 53, is killed by Indians in August or September along with all but one of the 15 members of her family (*see* 1638). Her husband died last year, and she has moved from the Rhode Island colony to a new settlement at what will become Pelham Bay in New York.

"The Doctrine and Discipline of Divorce" by poet John Milton is a 42-page pamphlet addressed to Parliament with the purpose of facilitating divorce (*see* 1642). He will write three more such tracts in the next few years, antagonizing Presbyterians by urging that canon law be revoked to authorize divorce on the grounds of "contrariety of mind" (*see* 1645; 1655).

"The Midwives' Just Petition," published at London in January, calls for a cessation of England's civil war in order that men may return to their wives so as to "bring them yearly under the delivering power of the midwife" (*see* 1646).

Painting: *Tulip* by Judith Leyster.

1644

The Ming dynasty, which has ruled China since the 1380s, ends in April with the suicide of Chongzhen, the last Ming emperor. Manchu forces begin the Qing (Ch'ing) dynasty, which will rule until 1912, imposing on the people the shaven head with queue (pigtail).

The Battle of Marston Moor July 2 ends in victory for Oliver Cromwell's English Roundheads over the Cavaliers of Charles I, winning the north country for the Puritan parliamentary forces. Women rally to the support of both sides in the civil war, depending largely on their husbands' sympathies. Charles sends his 14-year-old son and namesake to safety in France, but while in the Channel Islands en route the boy meets Lucy Walter, also 14, who will become his mistress and, in 1649, under the name "Mrs. Barlow," bear his son, James, who will be legitimized as the duke of Monmouth.

Sweden's Queen Christina ascends the throne on her 18th birthday, December 8 (*see* 1632; 1648).

1645

The Battle of Naseby June 14 seals the fate of Charles I's Cavaliers as England's middle class and merchants triumph (with support from many of the country's great noblemen).

Lady Bankes resists another Parliamentary siege force at Corfe Castle in December (her husband, Sir John, died in December 1644; *see* 1643; 1646).

Parliamentary forces resume their siege of Lathom House in December (*see* 1643). Its garrison, lacking the presence of the countess of Derby to encourage them, surrenders, and Parliamentarians say, "Three women ruined the Kingdom: Eve, the Queen, and the countess of Derby."

English "witches" Elizabeth Clarke and another woman are condemned and hanged after a trial at Chelmsford. Matthew Hopkins of Manningtree has led the witch hunt and accused 36 women, of whom 19 will eventually be executed, nine will die in prison, and only one will be acquitted after giving evidence against the others. Hopkins has hounded the poor, elderly, disabled Clarke day and night, not permitting her to sleep until she confesses to having received visits from Satan's "imps." Clarke is accused of having used witchcraft to cause the death of the son of Richard Edwards, a local landowner.

The family of John Milton's wife arrives at London as refugees from Oxfordshire following the Battle of Naseby (above), Mary is sent to a relative of Milton's, she begs her husband's pardon for her 3-year absence, and in the next 7 years will bear four children, although Milton will profess to enjoy no fulfillment in his marriage. When Mary dies in 1652 she will leave him with three living daughters (*see* 1643; 1657).

1646

Lady Bankes is obliged to surrender Corfe Castle to Oliver Cromwell's Roundheads in February after being betrayed by one of her officers, and although she is allowed to leave in safety along with her children the castle is sacked and destroyed (*see* 1645). England's 4-year civil war ends March 26, Charles I surrenders himself to the Scots May 5, but in July he rejects Parliament's proposals that he take the Covenant, support the Protestant establishment, and let Parliament control the militia for 20 years.

"The Midwives' Just Complaint," published September 22 at London, says that "whereas many miseries do attend upon civil wars," none is worse than the interruption of childbirth: "For many men, hopeful to have begot a race of soldiers, were there killed on a sudden, before they had performed anything to the benefit of midwives. . . . We were formerly well paid and highly respected in our parishes for our great skill and midnight industry; but now our art doth fail us, and little getting have we in this age, barren of all natural joys, and only fruitful of bloody calamities."

 "Rape is an accusation easily to be made, hard to be proved, and harder to be defended by the party accused, though never so innocent," says English barrister Matthew Hale, 37, who entered Lincoln's Inn at age 19 and was called to the bar 9 years ago.

1647

 The Scots surrender Charles I to Parliament January 30 in return for £400,000 in back pay.

Retreating Portuguese forces in Africa drown Kifunji, sister of Nzinga, queen of Ndongo and Matamba (see 1643; 1648).

 The Massachusetts and Connecticut colonies execute 14 women convicted of being "witches."

English nonconformist Sarah Wright reportedly fasts for 53 days.

 Fiction: *Parte segunda del sarao y entretenimiento honosto* (ten more short prose narratives; see 1637) by María de Zayas y Sofomayor, whose stories are bound together by a common thread as in Bocaccio's *The Decameron*.

1648

 Parliament renounces its allegiance to Charles I January 15 following revelations of a secret treaty that he has signed with the Scots. A second civil war begins, a Scottish army invades England but is defeated by Oliver Cromwell in mid-August at the Battle of Preston, Cromwell's "Roundheads" seize Charles December 1, Parliament expels 96 Presbyterian members by force December 6 and 7, and the remaining "Rump Parliament" of 60 members votes December 13 that Charles be brought to trial.

The Fronde (literally, "slingshot") uprising against France's Cardinal Mazarin and the queen regent Anne of Austria is an effort by the nobility to oppose the court by armed resistance. Anne, duchesse de Longueville, 28, whose position as mistress to the duc de La Rochefoucauld has given her an interest in politics, tries without success to persuade her younger brother, Louis, the Great Condé (a great grandson of Louis I), to the cause and will be called "the soul of the Fronde" (see 1651).

Europe's Thirty Years' War ends October 24 in the Peace of Westphalia.

Portuguese forces commanded by the Brazilian landowner Salvador de Sá regain Luanda August 10, defeating a Dutch garrison of 200 despite support from Nzinga, queen of Ndongo and Matamba (see 1647; 1650).

 English-born Maryland landowner Margaret Brent, 48 (approximate), appears before the Maryland Assembly January 21 and demands the right to cast two votes, one for herself and one as attorney for Lord Calvert, son of the colony's founder (he died last year, and she was named sole executrix under his will). When her demand is denied, she demands that all proceedings of the assembly be held invalid. Brent received the first land grant ever vested in a woman and has gone on to become one of the largest landowners in the colonies, earning the title Lord with the right, generally denied to women, to conduct business and sign contracts. She and her sister are proprietors of a large manorial estate, acquired through family connections. She has acted, and will continue to act, as attorney for her friends and neighbors in the Maryland colony.

 Swedish Army officers back from the Thirty Years' War receive land grants from Queen Christina, now 21. The grants will double the land held by the nobility as of 1611, and freehold peasants will face eviction as the expanding nobility applies German customs and attitudes toward the peasantry. In 2 years the nation will be faced with a food crisis.

 Poetry: *Hesperides, or The Works Both Human and Divine of Robert Herrick, Esq.,* by English poet Robert Herrick, 57, whose Royalist sympathies cause him to be evicted from his post as vicar of Dean Prior in Devonshire: "Gather ye rosebuds while ye may,/

Old Time is still a-flying:/ And this same flower that smiles today,/ Tomorrow will be dying" (from "To the Virgins, to Make Much of Time").

First performance: Singspiel *Neuerfundenes Freuden-Spiel genandt Friedens-Sieg* by German composer Marie Sophia, duchess of Brunswick-Lüneburg, 34, who received her first musical training at her father's court of Mecklenburg-Güstrow, fled the area in 1629 to escape the ravages of the Thirty Years' War, married the Duke of Brunswick-Lüneburg in July 1635, established an orchestra for their Brunswick residence in 1638, and reorganized it 4 years ago when they moved into his ancestral castle at Wolfenbüttel. Composer Heinrich Schütz has been her musical adviser, and she will engage him as Kapellmeister in 1655.

The Taj Mahal completed outside Agra in India is a red and white sandstone and marble mosque, meeting hall, and mausoleum built by the Mughal emperor Shah Jahan, now 56, for his favorite wife, Mumtaz Mahal (Jewel of the Palace) (*née* Arjumand Banu), who died in childbirth some 17 years ago at age 34 after bearing him 14 children.

1649

England's Charles I is sentenced to death and beheaded January 30 at Whitehall. Parliamentarian Alicia Lisle (*née* Beckenshaw), 35, will say that her "blood leaped within her to see the tyrant fall" (*see* 1685). The king's son of 18 is proclaimed Charles II at Edinburgh, in parts of Ireland, and in the Channel Islands (where his mistress, Lucy Walter, gives birth to his son; *see* 1644), but England becomes a republic headed by the Lord Protector Oliver Cromwell.

Japan's Tokugawa government saddles farmers with a new tax that requisitions virtually all their rice and obliges them to subsist on millet. They are forced to put their wives to work weaving cloth and to send surplus children to work in the city. A young girl selected to save her family from financial ruin by accepting employment in a brothel is regarded with pity and respect, not scorn, and a young prostitute is not without a certain honor.

An official proclamation of the Tokugawa government decrees that a farmer must divorce his wife,

however attractive she may be, if she does not rise very early in the morning, does not go out and collect hay to feed the livestock, does not work in the rice fields during the day, does not make rope or rice containers from rice straw in the evening, does not take good care of her husband, does her work carelessly, drinks too much tea, or takes too much time for leisure.

Fiction: *Artamène, ou le grand Cyrus* by Madeleine de Scudéry with some help from her brother Georges appears in the first of 10 volumes that will appear between now and 1659.

Poetry: "To Lucasta, on Going to the Wars" by English poet Richard Lovelace, 31, who has devoted his fortune to the Royalist cause, was wounded at Dunkirk while serving in the French army, and was imprisoned again upon his return to England: "I could not love thee, dear, so much/ Loved I not honour more."

1650

Nzinga, queen of Ndongo and Matamba, makes peace with the Portuguese after 30 years of warfare in which tens of thousands have died, hundreds of thousands taken into slavery (*see* 1648). She agrees to cease hostilities in October and give the Portuguese 130 slaves in order to obtain the release of her sister Mukumbu (*see* 1663).

England's new Puritan regime enforces church attendance, Parliament passes strict laws making adultery punishable by death and fornication by 3 months' imprisonment and limiting the elegance of clothing, but judges and juries will not enforce the laws and few people will be convicted; by 1657 the laws will have become virtually inoperative.

The Massachusetts colony changes its law making adultery a capital offense, making it punishable instead by whipping and the lifelong wearing of the scarlet letter "A" (*see* Hawthorne novel, 1850).

Britain has a typhus epidemic that by one account converts "the whole island into one vast hospital."

Poetry: *The Tenth Muse Lately Sprung Up* in America by English colonist Anne Bradstreet (*née* Dudley), 38, is published at London with metaphysical

Puritan poems that include "To My Dear and Loving Husband." Derivative and conventional (her later work, published posthumously, will be more original), it is the first book of poetry from the New World. But few women are possessed of the courage to have their work published, and Puritan Thomas Parker writes to his sister, who has such courage, "Your printing of a Book beyond the customs of your Sex, doth rankly smell."

 English physician William Harvey, 73, who was physician to Charles I until 1648, writes in *De Generatione Animalium*, "All animals, even those that produce their young alive, including man himself, are evolved out of the egg." It has been thought that a fetus was produced by the mixture of semen with menstrual blood, but Harvey, who has condemned the practice of stretching the labia vulvae in the hope of facilitating childbirth, says that the female egg contains within itself the substance and means to develop into an animal.

1651

✗ Charles II is crowned at Scone January 1, but Oliver Cromwell takes Perth in early August and defeats Royalist forces September 3 in the Battle of Worcester. Disguised as a servant to the daughter of a Royalist squire, Charles escapes to France October 17, and England's civil wars are ended.

France's queen mother Anne of Austria gives her reluctant consent to Parlement in February to dismiss Cardinal Mazarin, who flees the country but returns in December with 7,000 German troops to put down the Fronde rebellion (*see* 1648; 1652).

Japan's Tokugawa shōgun Iemitsu dies at age 47 after a 28-year reign. His son Ietsuna, 10, will reign until 1680, but Otama, a greengrocer's daughter who became one of Iemitsu's concubines at age 16, gave birth 6 years ago to another boy, who will ultimately gain power (*see* 1680).

Nonfiction: *The Mysteriousness of Marriage* by English essayist Jeremy Taylor, who writes, "When a man dwells in love, then the breasts of his wife are pleasant as the droppings upon the hill of Hermon, her eyes are fair as the light of Heaven, she is a fountain sealed, and he can quench his thirst, and ease his cares, and lay his sorrow down upon her lap, and can retire home as to his sanctuary and refectory, and his garden of sweetness and chaste refreshment."

First performances: *Cantate, Ariette e Duetti* by Venetian singer-composer Barbara Strozzi, 31, adopted daughter of local librettest-poet-playwright Giulio Strozzi, 68, a relative of the Florentine banking family. She is a member of the Accademia degli Unisone, which meets at her father's house.

1652

✗ Marshal Turenne intercepts the duc de Lorraine, buys him off, and hems in the Frondeurs July 2 in the Faubourg St. Antoine outside Paris as the Fronde uprising continues. Anne-Marie-Louise d'Orléans, 25, duchesse de Montpensier, persuades Parisians to open the city gates to the Fronde army (which has her father's support), she turns the guns of the Bastille on Turenne's royal forces, an insurrectionist government is proclaimed, Cardinal Mazarin flees France, but the Parisian bourgeoisie quarrels with the Fronde and permits Louis XIV to enter the city October 21.

Theater: Regents of the Japanese shōgun Ietsuna prohibit young boys from taking roles in the Kabuki theater. Mature men will hereafter play all roles (*see* 1629).

First performance: Singspiel *Glückwünschende Freudensdarstellung . . . Herrn Augesten Hertzogen zu Brunschweig und Lüneburg* by the duchess of Brunswick-Lüneburg.

1653

✗ Cardinal Mazarin returns to Paris unopposed, the Fronde uprising is ended, and France enters into a golden age, albeit one of absolutist rule.

Oliver Cromwell is proclaimed Lord Protector of the Commonwealth of England, Scotland, and Ireland December 15.

Poetry: *Poems, and Fancies: Written by the Right Honourable, the Lady Margaret Countess of Newcas-*

tle by English poet-playwright Margaret Cavendish (*née* Lucas), 30, who includes "A True Relation of My Birth, Breeding and Life," ending it with the statement that she has written it "to tell the truth, lest after ages should mistake, in not knowing I was daughter to one Master Lucas of St. Johns, near Colchester, in Essex, second wife to the Lord Marquis of Newcastle; for my Lord, having had two wives, I might easily have been mistaken, especially if I should die and my Lord marry again." She hopes that "my readers will not think me vain for writing my life, since there have been many that have done the like, as Caesar, Ovid, and many more, both men and women, and I know no reason I may not do so as well as they." She boldly admits to writing it for her own sake as well as to be remembered.

Sweden's defiantly unfeminine queen Christina reigned for 22 years before she quit to live in Rome.

1654

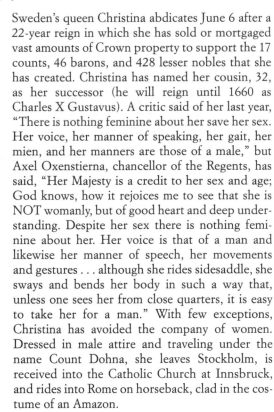

Sweden's queen Christina abdicates June 6 after a 22-year reign in which she has sold or mortgaged vast amounts of Crown property to support the 17 counts, 46 barons, and 428 lesser nobles that she has created. Christina has named her cousin, 32, as her successor (he will reign until 1660 as Charles X Gustavus). A critic said of her last year, "There is nothing feminine about her save her sex. Her voice, her manner of speaking, her gait, her mien, and her manners are those of a male," but Axel Oxenstierna, chancellor of the Regents, has said, "Her Majesty is a credit to her sex and age; God knows, how it rejoices me to see that she is NOT womanly, but of good heart and deep understanding. Despite her sex there is nothing feminine about her. Her voice is that of a man and likewise her manner of speech, her movements and gestures . . . although she rides sidesaddle, she sways and bends her body in such a way that, unless one sees her from close quarters, it is easy to take her for a man." With few exceptions, Christina has avoided the company of women. Dressed in male attire and traveling under the name Count Dohna, she leaves Stockholm, is received into the Catholic Church at Innsbruck, and rides into Rome on horseback, clad in the costume of an Amazon.

Fiction: *Clélie* by Madeleine de Scudéry appears in the first of 10 volumes that will appear between now and 1660. It is as artificial and clumsily constructed as her previous works.

First performance: *Cantate e Ariette* by Barbara Strozzi at Venice.

1655

Swedish forces invade Poland as Charles X Gustavus takes advantage of that country's struggle to save the Ukraine from Russia.

Parliament gives English magistrates the power to grant divorces but only on the grounds of desertion, impotence, or adultery.

Select Ayres and Dialogues by English composer Henry Love is dedicated to Mary Harvey, Lady Dering, 26, who married Sir Edward Dering 7 years ago, has studied with Love, and has herself written a few of his "Ayres." "Some of which I esteem the best of these Ayres, were of your own Composition," he writes, "and if your Noble Husband was pleased to give the Words . . . I beg leave to declare, for my own honour, that you are not only excellent for the time you spent for the practise of what I *Set* but are yourself so good a Composer, that few of any sex have arriv'd to such perfection."

The first known reference to the use of a sheath for contraception is made in an anonymous Parisian publication. *L'Ecole des filles* recommends a linen sheath to prevent passage of semen into the uterus, but while contraception will be widely employed among the upper-class French by the end of the century, intrauterine sponges will be favored over condoms (*see* Mme. de Sévigné, 1671).

1656

Swedish forces triumph over Poles at the Battle of Warsaw. Russia, Denmark, and the Holy Roman Empire declare war on Sweden's Charles X Gustavus.

1657

The Holy Roman Emperor Ferdinand II concludes an alliance with Poland to check Swedish aggression, his forces help drive out Charles X Gustavus, but he dies April 2 at age 48. His son of 16 will reign until 1704 as Leopold I.

Edo's Yoshiwara brothels move to a new area that will be known as Shin Yoshiwara. Its prostitutes have developed a language of their own to conceal the dialects that betray their peasant origins (*see* 1617; 1689). Yoshiwara will flourish until 1958.

Poet John Milton, now 49, remarries, this time to Catherine Woodcock, whose death within 2 years will inspire his sonnet "Methought I saw my late espoused Saint" (*see* 1645; 1662).

First performance: *Ariette a Voce Sola* by Barbara Strozzi at Venice with the composer singing the solo.

1658

Oliver Cromwell dies September 3 at age 58 after nearly 5 years as Lord Protector.

Painting: *Judith Triumphant* by Italian painter Elisabetta Sirani, 20, of Bologna, who has been commissioned for the past few years to portray clergymen, senators, and members of the nobility. Elisabetta is the eldest daughter of painter Andrea Sirani, whose crippling gout prevents him from supporting his family.

1659

The Treaty of the Pyrenees November 7 ends the ascendancy of Spain, which has been exhausted by war and by domestic misgovernment that has produced the revolt in Catalonia which ends this year. Under terms of the treaty, the Spanish infanta Maria Theresa, 21, is betrothed to France's Louis XIV with a dowry of 500,000 crowns (she renounces her claims upon her inheritance for herself or for any issue she may have by Louis).

First performance: *Di Porte Uterbe, e Ariette a Voce Sola* by Barbara Strozzi at Venice.

The Spanish infanta Maria Theresa (above) brings cocoa to France, where it will be endorsed by the Paris faculty of medicine and received with enthusiasm until it becomes surrounded with suspicion as an aphrodisiac in some circles and as a mysterious potion in others. (Mme. de Sévigné will write to her daughter that "the marquise de Coetlogon took so much chocolate, being pregnant last year, that she was brought to bed of a little boy who was as black as the devil.")

1660

Sweden's ex-queen Christina returns following the death of her cousin Charles X Gustavus February 12 at age 37 but fails to regain the throne and goes back to Rome.

England's civil war ends May 8 after 11 years as the son of the late Charles I is proclaimed king. Now 29, he lands at Dover May 26, arrives at Whitehall May 29 amid universal rejoicing, and will reign until 1685 as Charles II. He takes as his mistress Barbara Villiers, 20, daughter of the Second Viscount Grandison, and makes her husband, Roger

Palmer, earl of Castlemaine. The king's brother James, duke of York, receives royal permission to marry Anne Hyde, a commoner (to whom he was married last year).

English-born Quaker Mary Dyer is publicly hanged on Boston Common June 1. She came to America with her husband, William, about 25 years ago, was banished from the Massachusetts Bay colony for her antinomian views in 1638 along with her husband and Anne Hutchinson (*see* 1643), went back to England in 1650, joined the Society of Friends, returned to New England in 1657 and engaged in missionary work, was imprisoned at Boston that year after the passage of anti-Quaker laws, expelled from New Haven in 1658, imprisoned briefly once again at Boston last year, and then banished on pain of death. She defied the ban in order to minister to other Quakers who had been imprisoned at Boston, was arrested again and saved from the gallows only by the intercession of her son, returned to Boston last month, and has refused to comply with her banishment decree. Her death will help lead to an easing of anti-Quaker statutes in the colony.

Painting: *The Penitent Magdalene in the Wilderness* by Elisabetta Sirani. Judith Leyster dies at Heemstade February 8 at age 50; much of her work is now attributed to male painters.

First performance: *Di Porte Euterpe, o Vero Madrigale a Due Voci* by Barbara Strozzi at Venice.

France's Louis XIV, king since age 5 and now 22, assumes full power over state affairs March 9 upon the death of Cardinal Mazarin, having spent the last 5 years hunting game and pursuing women. He was waylaid while returning from his bath at age 18 and seduced by a Mme. Beauvais, one of his mother's ladies-in-waiting, and then fell in love with Mazarin's niece, Marie Mancini, to whom he proposed in 1658. Informed by his mother, Anne of Austria, that he must marry Marie Thérèse (Maria Theresa), the Spanish infanta, he reluctantly agreed, and she has just given birth to a son, but he takes as his mistress Louise-Françoise de Labaume Leblanc, 17, duchesse de La Vallière, who has been brought to the court by her mother and will bear the king four children.

Cookbook: *The Ladies' Directory and Choice Experiments and Curiosities of Preserving and Candying Both Fruit and Flowers* by English author Hannah Woolley (or Wolley), 38, who was orphaned at age 14, widowed last year after 13 years of marriage, and obliged to support herself and her children.

England's Charles II marries the Portuguese princess Catherine da Braganza, 23, who provides him with £300,000 in sugar, cash, and Brazilian mahogany plus the port of Tangier, the island of Bombay, and valuable trading privileges for English mariners in the New World. The May 20 marriage begins a lasting alliance between Portugal and England, but England's new queen is obliged to suffer the humiliation of accepting her husband's mistress, Barbara Villiers, who will embrace Roman Catholicism next year but continue to have amorous affairs. The beautiful Scottish noblewoman Frances Teresa Stewart, now 15, is appointed maid of honor to the new queen (*see* 1667).

Nonfiction: *Orations of Diverse Persons* by Margaret Cavendish, countess of Newcastle, now 39, declares that women are the more powerful sex, even though they are able to dominate men only through the wiles of love; *The Life and Death of Mistress Mary Frith* purports to tell the story of the late "Moll Cutpurse," who died 3 years ago at age 74. Having dressed herself as a man, free in her language and prone to drink and smoke, she organized a gang of robbers and established a pawnshop at which she sold stolen goods back to their original owners, using some of her vast profits to visit jails each Sunday and feed the inmates. By giving them lifetime freedom from pickpockets, she acquired powerful patrons, was never convicted of any crime, and died rich.

Poetry: *Geistliche Sonnette/Lieder und Gedichte/ zu Gottseeligem Zeitvertreib* by self-educated German poet Catharina von Greiffenberg, 28, is published in the spring at Nuremberg. It contains 250 sonnets, 52 songs (*Lieder*), and 48 other poems of varying quality, some of which have been published earlier under masculine names because society looks askance at women authors. Von Greiffenberg, whose father died when she was a child, was raised by his half brother, whom she will marry in 1664.

Poet John Milton, now 54, marries for a third time, taking as his wife Elizabeth Minshull, who will care for him until his death in 1674.

Theater: *The School for Wives* (*L'Ecole des Femmes*) by the French playwright Molière (Jean-Baptiste Poquelin), 40, 12/26 at the Palais-Royal, Paris.

Catherine da Braganza (above) introduces to the London court the Lisbon fashion of drinking tea; she also introduces the sweet Chinese orange.

1663

Matamba and Ndongo's queen Nzinga Mbandi dies at age 80 (approximate) after a career in which she has blocked the Portuguese from taking slaves (while participating in the trade herself at times), created the neigboring kingdom of Matamba, and helped the Dutch defeat her Portuguese enemies. Having abandoned Christianity, she has been reconverted, but her corpse is displayed in jewel-bedizened robes, a bow and arrow in her right hand, to inspire her people with awe, apprehension, and grief.

France's Louis XIV employs a court physician rather than the traditional midwife to attend the delivery of his favorite mistress, Louise de La Valiere. Obstetrical forceps, invented earlier in the century by the Huguenot Peter Chamberlen, Surgeon to the Queen, are not available to midwives (the instruments will remain the proprietary secret of the Chamberlens until the 1730s), and physicians who can use them are in demand because it is known that they can shorten labor and extract a child alive when manual skills might not suffice to save it (*see* 1682).

Fiction: *Christmas in Madrid, or Entertaining Nights, and Eight Tales* (*Navidades de Madrid, y noches, en ochos novelas*) by Spanish writer Mariana de Carvagal, 63.

1664

Nieuw Amsterdam becomes New York August 27 as 300 English soldiers take the town at the foot of Manhattan Island from the Dutch on orders from Charles II (*see* 1626). They rename the town after the king's brother James, duke of York.

Two English women are condemned as witches on professional evidence by Norwich physician-author Thomas Browne.

Nonfiction: *Sociable Letters* by Margaret Cavendish, who writes, "Many times married women desire children, as maids do husbands, more for honor than for comfort or happiness, thinking it a disgrace to live old maids, and so likewise barren." "But nature be thanked, she has been so bountiful to us as we oftener enslave men than men enslave us. They seem to govern the world, but we really govern the world in that we govern men. For what man is he that is not governed by a woman, more or less?"

Theater: *The Indian Queen* by John Dryden and Sir Robert Howard in January at London's Theatre Royal in Bridges Street; *The Forced Marriage* (*Le Mariage Forcé*) by Molière 1/29 at the Palais-Royal, Paris; *The Royal Ladies* by John Dryden in June at London's Royal Theatre in Bridges Street.

First performance: *Arie a Voce Sola* by Barbara Strozzi at Venice.

Cookbook: *The Cook's Guide* by Hannah Woolley.

1665

English naval forces defeat a Dutch fleet off Lowestoft June 3 as a second Anglo-Dutch war begins. Charles II's brother James, duke of York, 32, is lord high admiral and although married since 1659 to Anne Hyde, daughter of the Earl of Clarendon, takes as his mistress Arabella Churchill, 17, a lady-in-waiting to his wife. She will bear two sons by the Duke (who will inherit the throne in 1685).

Spain's Philip IV dies September 17 at age 60 after a weak reign. His son, now 4 and nearly crippled by rickets, will reign until 1700 as Charles II, last of the Spanish Hapsburgs, with his mother, Mariana of Austria, serving as regent until 1675.

London has its last large outbreak of the Black Death. Some two-thirds of London's 460,000 inhabitants leave town to avoid contagion, but at least 68,596 die plus a few thousand at Norwich, Newcastle, Portsmouth, Southampton, and Sunderland, most of them poor people who are imprisoned in their houses (which are marked by large red crosses) and given food handed in by constables. A rumor that contracting syphilis will serve to ward off the more deadly plague drives the men of London to storm the city's brothels.

Réflexions ou sentences et maximes morales by French writer François de La Rochefoucauld, 52, is published anonymously. Wise, witty, and never without a wise and witty mistress, La Rochefoucauld will be quoted for centuries: "When we think we hate flattery we only hate the manner of the flatterer." "The head is always the dupe of the heart." "We would rather speak ill of ourselves than not talk of ourselves at all." "The reason why so few people are agreeable in conversation is that each is thinking more about what he intends to say than about what others are saying, and we never listen when we are eager to speak." "One can find women who have never had one love affair, but it is rare indeed to find any who have had only one." "There are few chaste women who are not tired of their trade." "Few people know how to be old."

Painting: *Juno* by Dutch painter Rembrandt van Rijn, 59, who has used his common-law wife, Henrickje Stoffels, as his model; *The Jewish Bride* by Rembrandt. Elisabetta Sirani is stricken with stomach pains during Lent and dies at Bologna August 28 at age 27, possibly of poison administered by a jealous maid.

1666

France's queen mother, Anne of Austria, dies of breast cancer at Paris January 20 at age 64.

Nonfiction: *Women's Speaking Justified, Proved, and Knowed of the Scriptures* by English widow Margaret Fell, mother of nine, explains the ideas she shares with George Fox, leader of the Society of Friends, whom she will soon marry. She has supported Fox, a Leicestershire cobbler, and 3 years ago was sent to prison for refusing to take the Oath of Allegiance after pleading with Charles II to release a group of Quakers. Woman, like man, was created in God's image, Fell writes, and while she may be weak she was chosen for his purposes. To deny women their role is to act in behalf of the Devil, fulfilling the enmity decreed by God between woman and the serpent.

Theater: *The Misanthrope* by Molière 6/4 at the Palais-Royal, Paris: ". . . twenty, as everyone well knows, is not an age to play the prude" (III, v).

The Great Fire of London, which begins September 2, spreads through the crowded wooden houses near the Thames warehouses and continues for 4 days and nights until it has consumed four-fifths of the city, including some 13,200 houses.

Louis XIV issues an edict encouraging large families. Drafted by Jean-Baptiste Colbert, it will prove ineffectual.

1667

Louis XIV, now 28, takes as his mistress Françoise-Athénais Rochechouart, marquise de Montespan, 26, who married the marquis de Montespan 4 years ago and has become a lady-in-waiting to the queen. The duchesse de La Vallière removes herself to a Carmelite nunnery (*see* 1661), and Mme. de Montespan proceeds to bear the first of seven children that she will have by the king (all will be legitimized). Her husband is thrown into the Bastille, and his marriage to the marquise will be annulled in 1676.

Frances Stewart, maid of honor to England's Queen Catherine, marries the third duke of Richmond and flees the court. Now 20, she has posed for the face and torso of Britannia on English coins, but she is believed to have had an affair with King Charles.

Fiction: *Mathilde de Anguilon* by Madeleine de Scudéry, now 59, whose brother Georges dies at age 66.

Poetry: *Paradise Lost* by John Milton, who writes, "Oh! why did God,/ Creator wise, that peopl'd/ highest Heav'n/ With Spirits Masculine, create at

Theater: *She Would If She Could* by English playwright George Etherege 2/26 at the Lincoln's Inn Fields Theatre, London. *The Sullen Lovers (or, The Impertinents)* by English playwright Thomas Shadwell, 26, 5/2 at the Lincoln's Inn Fields Theatre; Shadwell has adapted the 1661 Molière play *Les Fâcheux. George Daudin, or The Abused Husband (Georges Daudin, ou le Mati Confondu)* by Molière 11/19 at the Palais-Royal, Paris.

1669

Crete falls to the Ottoman Turks, who take Candia September 27 after a 21-year siege. Venice loses her last colonial possession; the Turks will rule the island until 1898.

 Mexican Creole novitiate Juana Inés de Asbaje, 18, takes her final vows and becomes Sor Juana Inés de la Cruz. One of six illegitimate children born to an illiterate mother, she learned to read at age 3, consumed all the books in her grandfather's library, could write by age 6, and at age 8 was sent to Mexico City, where she received 20 lessons in Latin and went on to study the language by herself. Doña Leonor Carreto, wife of the Spanish viceroy, brought her to court, made her a lady-in-waiting and, later, court poet. Sor Inés wrote comedies and a religious play before deciding to leave the viceroy's court and join the Order of St. Jerome because ". . . considering the total negative opinion that I had of matrimony, it was the least unsuitable and the most decent station that I was able to select in order to bring about my salvation." Father Antonio Nuñez, her confessor, has censured her in public for writing poetry and socializing with the grandees, but she has replied, "Who has forbidden women to engage in private and individual studies? Have they not a rational soul as men do? Well, then, why cannot a woman profit by the privilege of enlightenment as they do? . . . What divine revelation, what rule of the Church, what reasonable judgment formulated such a severe law for us women?" Her viceregal protection has gained her special dispensation at the convent to keep books in her cell, receive visitors, and continue her literary life (*see 1690*).

 Painting: *Vase of Tulips, Roses, and Other Flowers with Insects* by Maria van Oosterwyck.

The marquise de Montespan, mistress to France's Louis XIV, influenced the roi du soleil *only to a point.*

last/ This noveltie on Earth, this fair defect/ of Nature, [Woman] . . . ?" Elsewhere in the poem he writes, ". . . Both/ Not equal, as their sex not equal, seen;/ For contemplation he in valour formed/ For softness she in sweet attractive grace;/ He for God only, she for God in him./ His fair large front and eyes sublime declared/ Absolute rule . . ." (IV, 295–301).

Theater: *Secret Love, or The Maiden Queen* by John Dryden in March at London's Theatre Royal in Bridges Street, which escaped the Great Fire that destroyed so much of the city last year.

1668

Spanish conquistadors in the Pacific rename the Islas de los Ladrones found by Magellan in 1521. They call them Las Marianas to honor Maria Anna of Austria, widow of Spain's Philip IV.

1670

France's Louis XIV makes a defensive alliance with Bavaria and with England's Charles II, whose sister Henrietta, duchesse d'Orléans, obtains the signatures of the English ministers to the secret Treaty of Dover in May. She returns to France and dies at St. Cloud June 30 at age 26, allegedly the victim of poison administered by order of her estranged husband, Philip, duc d'Orléans, brother of the Grand Monarch, but more probably of a ruptured appendix.

Charles II (above) makes his mistress, Barbara Villiers, duchess of Cleveland, although she has been criticized for trafficking in the sale of offices.

Nonfiction: *Pensées* by the late French philosopher-mathematician Blaise Pascal, who died in August 1662 at age 39 (the book is garbled, and no clearly edited version of Pascal's jaundiced thoughts will appear for 175 years): "Cleopatra's nose: had it been shorter, the whole aspect of the world would have been changed"; "The heart has its reasons which reason cannot know."

Fiction: *Zaïde* by French novelist Marie-Madeleine de La Vergne (*née* Pioche), 36, comtesse de La Fayette, who 4 years ago began a liaison with the duc de Rochefoucauld that will continue until his death in 1680.

English Proverbs by naturalist John Ray, 43, includes "Haste makes waste, and waste makes want, and want makes strife between goodman and his wife," "A cheerful wife is the joy of life," "A wife that expects to have a good name/ Is always at home, as if she were lame," "It's a good horse that never stumbles,/ And a good wife that never grumbles," "There is one good wife in the country, and every man thinks he has her," and "The misery is wide that the sheets will not decide."

Theater: *The Forc'd Marriage* by English playwright Aphra Behn (*née* Ayfara Amis), 30, who traveled to Surinam as a child, returned in 1658, married a London merchant named Behn who probably died of plague in 1666, volunteered to serve as a spy for Charles II in order to support herself, was sent to the Netherlands, never received pay for her services, and served time in debtors' prison before starting a writing career, which she begins with ribald stage comedies. Forced by her widowhood to earn a living, she will be the first woman in England to support herself by her writing, and some of her plays will remain as stock pieces well into the next century. "Who is't that to women's beauty would submit,/ And yet refuse the fetters of their wit?" (Prologue).

"Orange Girls" in English theaters sell Spanish Seville oranges, which are popular despite their sourness. One Orange Girl, Eleanor "Nell" Gwyn, 20, has become an actress and mistress to Charles II (above).

Nell Gwyn, the actress who was mistress to England's Charles II, bore the king two sons but died young.

Cookbook: *The Queen-like Closet* by Hannah Woolley contains recipes for preserving, cooking, physicking, and serving at table.

1671

 Maryland colony landowner-lawyer Margaret Brent dies at age 71 (approximately) after a career that will make her remembered in history as probably the first American feminist (*see* 1648).

Midwives' Book by Mrs. Jane Sharp of London, Practitioner in the Art of Midwifery above Thirty Years is the first English treatise on the subject. Addressing herself to other English midwives, Sharp rebukes male practitioners, "many professing the Art [without any skill in anatomy, which is the Principal part effectually necessary for a Midwife] meerly for Lucres sake." She pokes fun at such men for their pretension in using Greek and Latin words: it is not "hard words that perform the work as if none understood the 'Art of Midwifery' that cannot understand Greek." Sharp, who opposes attempts to speed up labor, warns about the difficulty of breach presentation and the dangers of hemorrhage and of removing the placenta. She believes in sustaining a woman's strength during labor and keeping her warm afterward, but the book is full of superstitious old wives' tales.

French writer Marie de Rabutin-Chantal, marquise de Sévigné, now 45, disparages use of the condom as a means of contraception. She describes it to her daughter the comtesse de Grignan as "an armor against enjoyment and a spiderweb against danger" (*see* 1655; Kennett, 1723).

1672

King Philip's War erupts in New England as Chief Metacum rebels against a 1671 order requiring his Narragansett and Wampanoag tribespeople to pay an annual tribute of £100. Hundreds of colonists will be killed in the next 4 years.

Theater: *The Country Wife* by English playwright William Wycherley in January at London's Theatre Royal in Drury Lane: "Good wives and private soldiers should be kept ignorant" (I); *The Mistaken Husband* by John Dryden in September at London's Drury Lane Theatre.

England tries to suppress the coffeehouses that have become gathering places for men who neglect their families to discuss business and politics over coffee.

Cookbook: *The Ladies' Delight* by Hannah Woolley.

1673

Willem III of Orange saves Amsterdam and the province of Holland from France's Louis XIV by opening sluice gates to flood the country.

England's royal mistress Barbara Villiers moves to Paris, having been supplanted in the king's favor by the duchess of Portland. He has acknowledged paternity of five of Villiers's seven children. His Catholic brother James, duke of York, now 40, whose first wife, Anne Hyde, died 2 years ago, marries Mary of Modena (*née* d'Este), 15, only daughter of Alfonso IV, duke of Modena.

Mitsukoshi department stores have their beginnings in the Echi-go-ya dry-goods shop opened at Edo by the Mitsui family (*see* 1616). By introducing fixed prices (*Kanane-nashi*) and cash-down installment buying (*Gen-gin*), Mitsukoshi (the name will be adopted in 1928) will become the largest store on the Ginza and Japan's largest department store chain.

Nonfiction: *The Ladies Calling* by English clergyman Richard Allestree, who writes, "As a Daughter is neither to anticipate, nor to contradict the will of her Parent, so (to hang the balance even) I must say she is not obliged to force her own, by marrying where she cannot love; for a negative voice in the case is sure as much the Child's right, as the Parents'." For a young woman to make a vow of marriage to someone she positively hated would be sacrilege, Allestree says, and his opinions reflect the new view of matrimony that now prevails.

Theater: *The Dutch Lover* by Aphra Behn is a tragicomedy of intrigue based on a Spanish novel.

1674

The Treaty of Westminster February 9 ends Anglo-Dutch hostilities, freeing England to expand her trade and grow prosperous while continental Europe becomes embroiled in depleting warfare. Parliament has cut off funds, forcing Charles to make peace.

1675

King Philip's War devastates New England. Called King Philip of Potanoket by the colonists, Chief Metacum leads the Narragansett and Wampanoag in attacks on 52 American settlements, destroying at least a dozen of them and killing 600 of New

England's finest men, but the British raid the Narragansett's winter home in the swamps of Rhode Island in November and massacre 600 men, women, and children (*see* 1672; 1676).

"Essay to Revive the Antient Education of Gentlewomen in Religion, Manners, Arts, and Tongues—With an Answer to the Objections against This Way of Education" by English educator Basua (or Bathshua) Makin (*née* Pell), 67, a onetime tutor to the children of the late Charles I, calls for an inclusive course of studies for girls. Daughter of a Sussex rector, Makin knew some Latin, Greek, Hebrew, French, and Italian by age 9; she has corresponded in Greek of late with the Dutch scholar Anna van Schurman; and although she demanded 12 years ago that young women be permitted to study not only painting and poetry but also grammar, rhetoric, logic, mathematics, physics, geography, history, and languages (especially Greek and Latin), she has modified that demand.

1676

Warriors from the Nipmuck, Wampanoag, and Narragansett tribes surround the English settlement of Lancaster in the Massachusetts colony at first light February 20, seeking revenge for the massacre of last November. They break into some houses, set others afire, and by midafternoon have killed at least a dozen settlers and taken 24 captive. Mary White Rowlandson is captured along with her 14-year-old son and her two daughters, Mary, 10, and Sarah, 6 (the latter is wounded and dies a week later in her mother's arms). The Native Americans have a reputation for respecting the chastity of their prisoners; Rowlandson is placed in the care of a Narragansett warrior and his wife, who take them along on a journey of nearly 12 weeks through the Connecticut River Valley. She is ransomed May 3 for clothing and food (*see* nonfiction, 1682).

King Philip's War ends in August after 4 years of hostilities. Colonial militiamen kill Chief Metacum in battle, break up his confederacy, and take his head to Plymouth, where it will be exhibited for the next 20 years. "King Philip's" widow and children

are sold as slaves to the West Indies despite Increase Mather's vote that they be executed.

Theater: *The Man of Mode, or Sir Fopling Flutter* by George Etherege 3/11 at London's Dorset Garden Theatre: "Next to coming to a good understanding with a new mistress, I love a quarrel with an old one" (I, i); *Abdelazer* by Aphra Behn.

1677

Willem of Orange turns 27 on November 4 and is married that day at London to the duke of York's daughter Mary, 15, a niece of England's Charles II (*see* "Glorious Revolution," 1688).

Christianized Mohawk religious leader Kateri Tekakwitha, 21, takes her first communion. Her conversion 2 years ago has aroused the hostility of her fellow Mohawks, who are suspicious of her piety and refusal to marry, so she has fled to the mission of St. Francis Xavier at Sault St. Louis, near Montreal. After her death in 1680, devotion to the "Lily of the Mohawks" will spread among the French and Indians of the area, and miracles will be credited to her intervention.

Theater: *Phaedra* (*Phèdre*) by French playwright Jean Racine, 37, 1/1 at the Hôtel de Bourgogne, Paris (in the long absence of her husband, Theseus, Phaedra falls in love with her stepson Hippolytus, who has fallen in love with the captive princess Aricie. Theseus returns, hears the stepson falsely accused of leading Phaedra into infidelity, and calls upon the God Neptune to destroy Hippolytus, but Phaedra is consumed with remorse and kills herself). *The Town-Fopp, or Sir Timothy Tawdrey* by Aphra Behn, whose mismatched lovers solve their problems by divorcing: "The Devil's in her tongue, and so 'tis in most women's of her age; for when it has quitted the tail, it repairs to the upper tier." *The Rover, or The Banish't Cavaliers* (Part I) by Behn, whose heroine, Hellena, says of matrimony, "What shall I get? A Cradle full of Noise and Mischief, with a Pack of Repentance at my Back." *The Rover* will be Behn's most popular play, but she will be accused of plagiarizing from Thomas Killegrew's play *Thomaso* (the first editions are published without her name).

The doctorate of philosophy conferred by the University of Padua June 25 upon scholar Elena Lucrezia Cornaro Piscopia, 32, is the first university degree ever received by a woman. Born to a noble Venetian family that has produced four doges, three popes, eight cardinals, and a queen of Cyprus, Piscopia began her classical education at age 7, studying Latin, Greek, Hebrew, Spanish, and French plus mathematics, philosophy, and astronomy. Theology has been the subject closest to her heart, and her disputations in Latin and Greek at Padua have drawn scholars from all over Europe, but while the university's rector has approved her application for the doctorate of theology, the Church has raised objections to granting this degree to a woman. She has been obliged to apply, instead, for the doctorate in philosophy, and her examination has drawn such a crowd of academic, religious, and political luminaries that the ceremony has had to be moved to the cathedral of Padua for lack of space at the university (see 1684).

Nonfiction: *The Lady's New-Year's-Gift or Advice to a Daughter* by George Savile, 45, first marquis of Halifax, acknowledges the injustice of many laws and customs relating to women but does not approve of attempts to change them, saying, "It is one of the *Disadvantages* belonging to your *Sex*, that young Women are seldom permitted to make their own *Choice*; their Friends' Care and Experience are thought safer Guides to them, than their own *Fancies*; and their *Modesty* often forbiddeth to them to refuse . . . when their *inward Consent* may not entirely go along with it. In this case there remaineth nothing for them to do, but to endeavour to make that easie which falleth to their *Lot*, and by a wise use of every thing they dislike in a *Husband*, turn out by degrees to be very supportable, which, if neglected, might in time begin an *Aversion*. You must first lay it down for a Foundation in general, That there is *Inequality* in the *Sexes*, and that for the better Oeconomy of the World, the *Men*, who are to be the *Lawgivers*, have the larger share of *Reason* bestow'd upon them; by which means your Sex is the better prepar'd for the *Compliance* that is necessary for the better performance of those *Duties* which seem to be most properly assign'd to it. This looks a little uncourtly at the first appearance; but

upon Examination it will be found that *Nature* is so far from being unjust to you, that she is partial on your side. . . . You have more strength in your *Looks*, than we have in our *Laws*, and more power by your *Tears* than we have by our *Arguments*."

Lord Halifax (above) concedes that the laws of marriage are harsher toward women than toward men but says that the sacredness of the institution necessitates this even though injustice may be done to some women. He takes to task the useless woman who thinks the care of a family beneath her or fears to weight her mind with duties lest she bring wrinkles to her face. He ridicules "*Girls of Fifty*, who resolve to be always *Young*, whatever *Time* with his Iron Teeth hath determined to the contrary." (The book gains immediate popularity and will go through 25 editions.)

Fiction: *La Princesse de Clèves* by the comtesse de La Fayette, now 44: "Force your husband to take you away. Do not fear that you are taking measures too harsh and too difficult: however terrible they may appear at first, they will be more pleasant in the end than the evils of an illicit love-affair."

Poetry: English poet Andrew Marvell dies August 16 at age 57 after taking an overdose of an opiate for his ague. He leaves behind verses that include the lines "To His Coy Mistress": "had we but world enough, and time,/ This coyness, lady, were no crime . . ."; "But at my back I always hear/ Time's winged chariot hurrying near."

Theater: *Sir Patient Fancy* by Aphra Behn is an intrigue play noteworthy for the loose moral fiber of its characters.

The Peace of St.-Germaine-en-Laye forced upon the elector of Brandenburg June 29 by France's Louis XIV obliges the elector to surrender to Sweden practically all of his conquests in Pomerania and receive practically nothing in return.

The Habeas Corpus Act passed by Parliament in May obliges English judges to issue upon request a writ directing a jailer to produce the body of any prisoner or show cause for his imprisonment.

🎭 Theater: *The Feign'd Curtezans, or A Nice Intrigue* by Aphra Behn, whose heroine, Cornelia, says to Galliard, "I rather fear you wou'd debauch me into that dull slave call'd a Wife."

🎼 Italian composer Alessandro Scarlatti, 20, gains the protection of Sweden's former Queen Christina at Rome and begins a 44-year career in which he will virtually create the language of classical music.

1680

✗ Japan's Tokugawa shōgun Ietsuna dies at age 39 after a 29-year reign. His half brother, now 34, whose mother became a nun in 1651 and is now known as Keishoin, will reign until 1709 as Tsunayoshi. Obedient to Confucian laws instructing respect for parents, Tsunayoshi will be influenced by his mother, who, in turn, will be influenced by Buddhist priests to give more importance to animals, birds, fish, and even insects than to people.

✊ Bohemian peasants stage a major revolt following a shift from soil tillage to dairy farming in the wake of the Thirty Years' War. An era of endemic unrest begins among the serfs.

Pueblo tribesmen at Taos and Santa Fe rise against the Spaniards August 11, destroy most of the Spanish churches, and drive 2,500 colonists from their territory.

🖋 Poetry: *First Dream* by Mexican poet Juana Inés de la Cruz, now 29.

▦ French poisoner Catherine Monvoisin is burned to death following her conviction by a secret tribunal on charges that she grew rich by concocting poisons and selling them to ladies at the court of Louis XIV. The king's mistress, Mme. de Montespan, has allegedly been one of La Voisin's customers; one of her attendants, the Italian beauty Olympe Mancini, comtesse de Soissons, 41, who has been a mistress to Louis XIV, is accused of having poisoned both her husband and the queen of Spain (she flees to the Netherlands), and her sister Marie Anne Mancini, duchesse de Boullon, 31, is banished from the court for her involvement in the affair (their sister Marie Mancini, princess de Colonna, 40, has also been a mistress of Louis XIV but now lives in Spain; their sister Laura Mancini, duchesse de Mercoeur, 44, is married to Louis de Vendôme; and their sister Hortense Mancini, duchesse de Mazarin, 34, adorns the court of England's Charles II).

1681

✗ Russia confiscates Tatar territories on the Volga, forcing the people to convert to Christianity.

🖋 Nonfiction: *La vie de la reine Christine faite par elle-même, dédié à Dieu* by Sweden's former queen (date approximate).

🎭 Theater: *The Rover, or The Banish't Cavalier* (Part II) by Aphra Behn, whose courtesan Angela Bianca spurns anyone who cannot meet her price; *The Roundheads* by Behn is staged in December.

1682

✗ Russia's Fedor III dies April 27 at age 21, his half brother Peter, 9, succeeds to the throne in preference to Fedor's mentally and physically defective brother Ivan, 15, but Ivan's sister Sophia Alekseevna, 25, instigates the musketeers (*Strelitzi*) to invade the Kremlin and murder Peter's supporters. Ivan is proclaimed tsar with Peter as his associate and begins a nominal 7-year reign in which Sophia will serve as regent and exercise the power.

⚕ France's Louis XIV employs physician Jules Clement as *accoucheur* for the dauphine Anne-Victoire, who, after a difficult birth, is confined to a darkened room without a light for 9 days (*see* 1663); courtiers begin to emulate *le roi de soleil*, increasing the move among rich families away from using midwives, who continue to attend most deliveries but whose activities among the aristocracy will be limited to births that appear to present no complications.

🖋 Nonfiction: *A True History of the Captivity and Restoration of Mrs. Mary Rowlandson* is published at Boston (*see* 1676). Her book defies Puritan sanctions against women making public statements; four editions are sold out.

Theater: *Venice Preserved, or A Plot Discovered* by English playwright Thomas Otway, 30, 2/9 at London's Dorset Garden Theatre: "O woman! lovely woman! Nature made thee/ To temper man: we had been been brutes without you;/ Angels are painted fair, to look like you;/ There's in you all that we believe of Heaven,/ Amazing brightness, purity, and truth,/ Eternal joy, and everlasting love" (I); *The City-Heiress* by Aphra Behn is staged in the spring.

1683

 The Great Treaty of Shackamaxon, signed by English colonist William Penn with Delaware chiefs, permits Penn to purchase territories that will become southeastern Pennsylvania. Penn's wife, Giulielma Maria, helps him administer the colony.

 Viennese die by the thousands in a 58-day siege by 300,000 Ottoman troops. Survivors sustain themselves by eating cats, donkeys, and everything else edible.

1684

 French troops occupy Lorraine; Louis XIV signs a truce with the Holy Roman Emperor Leopold at Regensburg allowing him to retain Lorraine plus all the territories he has obtained up to August 1, 1681, including Strasbourg.

 Scholar Elena Lucrezia Cornaro Piscopia dies at age 38, probably of tuberculosis (*see* 1678). Citizens of Venice and Padua hear of her death from cries in the street, "The Saint is dead!" She has spent the past 6 years ministering to the poor while continuing her studies and devoting herself to religious observance.

1685

England's Charles II dies February 6 at age 54 saying, "Let not poor Nelly starve," a reference to actress Nell Gwyn, now 34, who has often referred to herself openly as "the king's whore." She made her last stage appearance in 1682, has borne the king two sons, but will die in 2 years. Charles has made a profession of the Catholic faith on his deathbed, his Catholic brother James, now 51, succeeds him to begin a brief reign as James II, but the new king's nephew James, duke of Monmouth, claims "legitimate and legal" right to the throne.

Monmouth (above) is the acknowledged son of Charles (he has taken the surname Scott of his wife Anne, countess of Buccleuch); his mistress, Henrietta Maria, Baroness Wentworth, 28, has supplied funds, and he lands at Lyme Regis, Dorsetshire, with 82 supporters. English troops loyal to James II easily defeat Monmouth July 6 at the Battle of Sedgemoor, the last formal battle on English soil, and he is captured and beheaded.

 Alicia Lisle, now 71 and the widow of one of Cromwell's lords, is beheaded at Winchester by order of the infamous judge George, First Baron Jeffreys, 37, for giving shelter to two of Monmouth's rebels (above) after the Battle of Sedgemoor (*see* Lisle, 1649).

 The revocation of France's Edict of Nantes October 18 after 87 years of religious toleration forbids the practice of any religion but Catholicism and forbids Huguenots to emigrate (although 50,000 families do begin emigrating).

 Painting: *Still Life with Flowers and Insects in a Landscape* by Dutch painter Rachel Ruysch, 21.

1686

 The League of Augsburg is created July 9 to oppose France's Louis XIV allies the Holy Roman Emperor Leopold I, Spain's Carlos II, Sweden's Charles XI, and the electors of Bavaria, Saxony, and the Palatine. Last year's revocation of the Edict of Nantes has aroused Protestants against Louis (*see* 1689).

England's first convent school for girls is publicly recognized at York, where it has opened along lines established by Mary Ward in 1642.

The school for young ladies that opens August 1 at Saint-Cyr on the outskirts of Versailles is France's first state-supported school. Louis XIV bought the

Louis XIV's mistress, Françoise d'Aubigné, Mme. de Maintenon, opened France's first state-supported school.

property for 3 million francs 2 years ago as a gift for his second wife, Françoise d'Aubigné, Mme. de Maintenon, 50, who was governess to his children before becoming his mistress. She began founding small boarding schools for girls in 1680 but has been told by the king that her new one must not be a convent because France needs more good mothers, not more nuns. Its 250 students, aged 7 to 12 and expected to remain until age 20, have been personally selected by the king; each has proved that she has four noble ancestors on her father's side, that she is impoverished, and that she is free of epilepsy and the vapors. The headmistress, Mme. de Brinon, has a staff of 12, none of whom has been required to take the vows of any religious order but rather an oath to devote her life to educating the young women in her charge. The staff will be increased to 16, with four dames, or teachers, having three assistants each and with the student body divided into four groups of about 60 girls each. Girls 7 to 10 (the Reds) study reading, writing, arithmetic, elementary sacred history, catechism,

and music; girls 11 to 13 (the Greens) study the same subjects plus geography and mythology; girls 14 to 16 (the Yellows) take more advanced courses in French and religion, with extra classes in deportment and dancing; and girls 17 to 20 (the Blues) have far fewer academic studies but receive moral instruction and lessons in advanced needlework (*see* 1688; cookery, below).

Fiction: *Five Women Who Chose Love* (*Koshoku gonin onna*) and *A Woman Who Devoted Her Entire Life to Lovemaking* (*Koshoku ichidai onna*) by Saikaku Ihara, a widower whose realistic fiction reflects the sentiments and manners of Japan's masses.

"Cordon Bleu" cookery has its origin in the Institut de Saint-Louis (above). Cooking is among the subjects taught, and the school will become known for its cooking lessons and for the *cordon bleu* (blue ribbon) that the girls wear beginning at age 17 to show that they are members of the senior class (*see* 1895).

1687

Ukrainian cossack Ivan Stepanovich Mazepa-Koledinsky, 43, visits Moscow, wins the favor of the prime minister Vasili Vasilievich Golitsyn, 44, and virtually purchases the hetmanship of the Cossacks July 25. Educated at the court of the late Polish king John II Casimir, Mazepa was caught in bed with a married Polish woman, her husband tied him naked to the back of a wild horse, Dnieperian Cossacks rescued him on the steppe, and he has risen to leadership among them.

Traité de l'éducation des filles by French clergyman François de Salignac de la Mothe-Fénelon, 36, shows a rare insight into psychology. Fénelon was appointed at age 27 to head a Paris institution for women converts; his book, written for the daughters of French noblemen, expresses his belief that women should be prepared for their special roles in life, with those of the nobility being taught religion, the economics of contract law, and how to manage estates and servants. Instructors, he writes, must win the trust and affection of their pupils, setting just a few rules and exercising discipline by explaining those rules clearly and then adhering to them strictly, using punishment only as a last resort and never when either teacher or pupil has lost her temper. He proscribes reading of romantic novels, since they bear no resemblance to real life, and forbids instruction in Italian or Spanish lest girls read dangerous literature in those languages.

Music is a "corruptive influence," says Fénelon (above), but he concedes that if a girl is decidedly musical it is better that she be allowed church music than be denied music altogether.

1688

A "Glorious Revolution" ends nearly 4 years of Roman Catholic rule in England. England's James II issues a proclamation in April ordering clergymen to read from their pulpits the king's Declaration of Indulgence of last year exempting Catholics and Dissenters from penal statutes. The birth of a son to James's queen, Mary of Modena, June 10 suggests the likelihood of a Catholic succession. England's Whig leaders send an invitation to the king's son-in-law William of Orange June 30, William issues a declaration to the English people September 21, lands at Tor Bay November 5, and moves to assume the throne with his wife, Mary. Her deposed predecessor, Mary of Modena, escapes with her infant son to France, where she will be joined by James and will live until her death in 1718 at St. Germain.

Mme. de Maintenon dismisses the headmistress of her Saint-Cyr school December 10 and orders her to retire to a neighboring convent. Mme. de Brinon has dared to question the judgment of the king's wife (*see* 1686; 1692).

Nonfiction: *Les Caractères de Théophraste . . .* by French moralist-satirist Jean de La Bruyère, 43, whose portraits and aphorisms point out the arrogance and immorality of France's stupid ruling class: "When a beautiful woman approves the beauty of another woman, you may be sure that she has more of the same kind herself."

Fiction: *Oroonoko* by Aphra Behn, whose work (the first English philosophical novel) introduces the figure of the noble savage.

 Theater: English actress Anne Bracegirdle, 25, makes her stage debut in Thomas Shadwell's play *The Squire of Alsatia* in May at London's Drury Lane Theatre. Shadwell has adopted the Terence comedy *Adelphoe* of 160 B.C.

1689

The War of the League of Augsburg against France's Louis XIV widens as England's new king William III forms a Grand Alliance May 12 with the Dutch and with the League of Savoy. King William's War begins in North America as an outgrowth of the European conflict.

Russia's regent and czarina Sophia Alekseevna, 32, is deposed following exposure of a conspiracy to seize her half brother Peter, now 17, who is crowned czar in September and will reign until 1730 as Peter I. The new czar was forced into a marriage January 27 with the beautiful but stupid Eudoxia Lopukhina, but the marriage collapses by year's end.

Edo's Yoshiwara brothels have 2,800 prostitutes, according to an official census. The "happy field" moved to the city's Asakusa district after a fire in 1656 (*see* 1617; 1789).

Novelist-playwright Aphra Behn dies at London April 16 at age 48 and is honored by burial in Westminster Abbey (but in the Cloister rather than in Poets' Corner). She has produced several novels but is best known for her 17 plays.

 Theater: *Esther* by Jean Racine 1/26 at Mme. de Maintenon's School for Young Ladies at Saint-Cyr. Mme. de Maintenon has objected to "worldly amusement," so the king has asked Racine to write a play without love scenes that might tempt the cast of young ladies. His audience includes the royal family and England's deposed king James II with his wife, Mary, but the pit is packed with young officers, and Mme. de Maintenon is shocked at overhearing them compare the charms of the performers, who, in turn, are so preoccupied with the court and the young men that discipline at the school begins to break down.

Opera: *Dido and Aeneas* 12/30 at the Chelsea boarding school for girls operated by English danc-

Prostitutes in Tokyo's Yoshiwara district flourished for three centuries, selling "springtime." FROM A UKIYOE PRINT BY KIYOHIRO

ing master Joseph Priest, with music by English composer Henry Purcell, 30, libretto by Irish-born poet Nahum Tate, 37.

1690

✗ The Battle of the Boyne July 1 completes the Protestant conquest of Ireland, but Limerick resists and William III is forced to lift his siege of the city.

An essay by Mexican nun Juana Inés de la Cruz in New Spain is critical of a sermon delivered in 1650 by a prominent Jesuit priest (*see* 1669). Fernández de Santa Cruz, bishop of Puebla, has the essay published at his own expense, but without her knowledge, and sends her a copy with a letter signed "Sor Philotea" remarking, "It is a pity that so great a mind should stoop to lowly earthbound knowledge and not desire to probe what transpires in heaven. But since it does lower itself to ground level, may it not descend further still and ponder what goes on in hell." Sor Juana replies to "Sor Philotea" with a defense of women's right to education and intellectual growth, recounting her personal history, citing a long list of learned biblical women from whom she says she gained inspiration, and making a case for older women teaching younger ones.

1691

✗ The marquise de Montespan, now 50, leaves the court of France's Louis XIV and retires to a convent, having been supplanted by Mme. de Maintenon.

The Battle of Aughrim July 12 gives William and Mary's Dutch-born general a victory over French-supported Irish rebels. Limerick surrenders October 3 after another siege; the Treaty of Limerick ends the Irish rebellion.

∞ Sor Juana Inés de la Cruz, now 40, reaffirms her vows to the Church after a brouhaha over her 1690 essay and her reply to "Sor Philotea," in which she has criticized the Inquisition and argued for women's rights and education. In 21 years of Mexican convent life she has written poems, ballads, sacramental plays, and comedies while collecting 4,000 books—the largest library in the New World—which she now sells for charity on orders from the archbishop after being refused confession by her confessor, Father Nuñez, for lacking humility (*see* 1693).

Theater: *Athaliah* (*Athalié*) by Jean Racine in February at Mme. de Maintenon's School for Young Ladies at Saint-Cyr, with students playing the roles.

1692

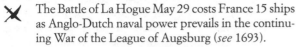 The Battle of La Hogue May 29 costs France 15 ships as Anglo-Dutch naval power prevails in the continuing War of the League of Augsburg (*see* 1693).

 Accusations of witchcraft by English-American clergyman Samuel Parris, 39, result in dozens of alleged witches being brought to trial at Salem in the Massachusetts colony in April as Parris reminds his neighbors of the Old Testament command "Thou shalt not suffer a witch to live" (Exodus 22:18). Tituba, Parris's female slave, has entertained neighborhood girls, including his daughter Elizabeth, 9, and Mary Warren, a 20-year-old servant with tales from her native West Indies. Her storytelling has led to descriptions of spirits, fortune-telling, and voodoo rituals, she has performed bits of magic, and her listeners, excited, have reacted with strange behavior that the Rev. Parris ascribes to witchcraft. One farmer's crops did poorly, and it is recalled that his neighbor, Sarah Good, was seen loitering near his property. Hearings on charges of witchcraft begin March 1, the suggestible girls are quick to level accusations against scores of "witches," and Rebecca Nurse (*née* Towne), 71, mother of eight and having many grandchildren, is arrested March 24, protests her innocence, but is placed in chains and kept in filthy jails at Salem and Boston until June 30, when

Witch trials in the Massachusetts colony exposed the superstitious ignorance and intolerance of the Puritan fathers.

she is tried and found guilty despite petitions signed on her behalf by 40 citizens, including members of the Putnam family. She is hanged on Gallows Hill July 19 with four others. A total of 19 are hanged and one pressed to death, many of them on the testimony of 12-year-old Anne Putnam (who in 1706, seeking church membership, will confess that it "was a great delusion of Satan in that sad time" and ask special forgiveness for her accusations against Rebecca Nurse). The last execution takes place September 22. Tituba herself, although sentenced to death, will be held in jail until May of next year, when the governor of the Massachusetts Bay Colony will order the release of all those accused and awaiting trial, but since she is unable to pay for her 13 months' maintenance in prison she will be sold to raise money for the expenses of keeping her for 13 months (*see* 1664; Mather, 1693; Sewall, 1700).

 Scots-American sea captain William Kidd, 38, marries New York widow Sara Oart and increases his holdings by £155 14s.

 Mme. de Maintenon begins transforming her school at Saint-Cyr into a convent school, the Institute de Saint Louis, after hearing scurrilous charges that it has become a training school for courtesans (*see* 1688; Theater, 1689). "It is I who have spread the sin of pride through our house," she professes, "and I shall be very fortunate if God does not punish me for it. . . . I wanted that the girls should have intelligence, that their hearts should be uplifted, and they are prouder and more haughty than is becoming in the greatest princesse. . . . A simple Christian education would have made them good girls, out of whom we could make good wives; we have made *beaux-esprits*, whom we ourselves cannot endure" (*see* 1713).

1693

French naval forces defeat an Anglo-Dutch fleet off Cape St. Vincent May 26 to 27, avenging the defeat suffered last year in the Battle of La Hogue, but Louis XIV's military advisers persuade him that great fleets are a waste of money and France will leave England and the Dutch to dispute supremacy of the sea. The French sack Heidelberg in the continuing War of the League of Augsburg.

∞ Sor Juana Inés in New Spain makes an abject public confession after giving away or selling for charity all of her books except three religious texts (*see* 1691). She begs forgiveness from her sister nuns, and next year will renounce all other aspirations, rededicating herself in a vow signed in her own blood (*see* 1695).

✒ *The Wonders of the Invisible World* by Boston Congregationalist minister Cotton Mather, 30, analyzes with scientific detachment the work of devils among the Salem witches (*see* 1692).

🎭 Theater: *The Old Batchelour* by English playwright William Congreve, 23, in March at London's Drury Lane Theatre: "She is too proud, too inconstant, too affected, too witty and too handsome for a wife" (I); "Oh thou delicious, damned, dear, destructive Woman" (III, ii); "Thus grief still treads upon the heels of pleasure,/ Marry'd in haste, we may repent at leisure" (V, iii); "Courtship [is] to marriage, as a very witty prologue to a very dull play" (V, x).

1694

✗ The Elector of Hanover George William divorces his wife, Sophia Dorothea, on grounds of adultery with the Swedish nobleman Philipp Christoph, count von Königsmark, 29 (who disappears suddenly, probably because he has been murdered). George has Sophia Dorothea imprisoned in the grange at Ahlden, her name is stricken from state prayers, every evidence of her presence is removed, neither of her two children is allowed to visit, her father will not try to do so, and her mother will gain permission only after repeated entreaties. George also imprisons Eleanora von Knesebeck in the fortress of Scharzfels.

Marie Aurora, countess of Königsmark and younger sister of the count (above), becomes mistress to Saxony's Augustus II ("the Strong"), by whom she will have a son, Maurice.

England's Mary II dies of smallpox December 28 at age 32, leaving her husband, William, to rule alone.

✒ Nonfiction: *A Serious Proposal to the Ladies for the Advancement of their True and Greatest Interest* by English merchant's daughter Mary Astell, 28, who writes, "Since God has given women as well as men intelligent souls, why should they be forbidden to improve them?" Astell proposes an academic, Protestant convent for women who cannot or will not marry, denigrates frivolous women, and praises "good devout women" who read books and do charitable work. Women, she says, "need not take up with mean things, since (if they are not wanting to themselves) they are capable of the best." "There is no reason why they should be content to be Cyphers in the World, useless at the best, and in a little time a burden and nuisance to all about them."

1695

✗ French siege forces bombard Brussels in August as the War of the League of Augsburg continues. England's William III recaptures Namur from the French in September.

∞ Spanish nun Juana Inés de la Cruz dies of plague in New Spain at age 44 after nursing victims of the disease.

🎭 Theater: *Love for Love* by William Congreve 4/30 at the Lincoln's Inn Fields Theatre, London: "You must not kiss and tell" (II); "Women are like tricks by sleight of hand,/ Which, to admire, we should not understand."

1696

✊ Parliament suspends the Habeas Corpus Act of 1679 following discovery of a plot to assassinate William III.

English journeymen strike for higher wages and better working conditions.

💲 The Navigation Act passed by Parliament April 10 forbids England's American colonists to export directly to Scotland or Ireland (*see* Woollens Act, 1699).

✒ Mme. de Sévigné dies of smallpox April 17 at age 70 after nursing her daughter, Françoise-Marguerite, now 50, through a long illness. She has written more than 1,500 extraordinary letters over the course of 25 years.

Theater: *Love's Last Shift, or The Fool in Fashion* by English playwright Colley Cibber, 24, in January at London's Royal Theatre in Drury Lane: "One had as good be out of the world as out of the fashion"; "We shall find no fiend in Hell can match the fury of a disappointed woman, —scorn'd! slighted! dismiss'd without a parting pang!" (IV) (compare Congreve, 1697). *The Relapse, or Virtue in Danger* by English playwright John Vanbrugh, 32, 11/21 at London's Drury Lane Theatre: "Once a woman has given you her heart you can never get rid of the rest of her" (II); *Woman's Wit, or The Lady in Fashion* by Cibber in December at London's Drury Lane Theatre.

1697

✗ Sweden's Charles XI dies April 5 at age 40 after a brilliant 37-year reign. His son of 14 will reign until 1718 as Charles XII, eclipsing the successes of his father.

The Treaty of Ryswick September 30 ends the 11-year-old War of the League of Augsburg. France recognizes William III as king of England with his sister-in-law Anne as heiress presumptive.

✒ Nonfiction: *A Serious Proposal to the Ladies for the Advancement of their True and Greatest Interest* by Mary Astell (second volume) is dedicated to Princess Anne, who has evidently pledged £10,000 toward the establishment of the first English college for women. Other women of means will contribute to the venture, but Gilbert Burnet, 54, bishop of Salisbury, says the scheme smacks of a revival of nunneries, and Princess Anne withdraws her offer. "The Foundation of Education, on which in a great measure all depends, shou'd be laid by the Mother," Astell writes, "for Fathers find other Business, they will not be confined to such a laborious work, they have not such opportunities of observing a Child's Temper nor are the greater part of them likely to do much good, since Precepts contradicted by Example seldom prove effectual."

🎭 Theater: *The Mourning Bride* by William Congreve 2/20 at the Lincoln's Inn Fields Theatre, London, with Anne Bracegirdle, now 34, creating the role of Almeria: "Music hath charms to soothe a savage breast,/ To soften rocks, or bend a knotted oak" (I, i); "Heav'n has no rage, like love to hatred turn'd,/ Nor hell a fury like a woman scorn'd" (III, viii) (compare Cibber, 1696); *The Provoked Wife* by John Vanbrugh in May at the Lincoln's Inn Fields Theatre, London: "I'll sooner undertake to teach sincerity to a courtier, generosity to an usurper, honesty to a lawyer, nay, humility to a divine, than discretion to a woman I see has once set her heart upon playing the fool" (II).

1698

✗ A Treaty of Partition signed by the European powers October 11 attempts to deal with the question of the Spanish succession. Spain's Carlos II is childless, and the Spanish house of Hapsburg is doomed (*see* 1700).

✊ Parliament opens the slave trade to British merchants, who will in some cases carry on a triangular trade from New England to Africa to the Caribbean islands to New England.

1699

💲 The Woolens Act passed by Parliament under pressure from the English wool lobby forbids any American colony to export wool, wool yarn, or wool cloth "to any place whatsoever." The act works a certain hardship on rural New Englanders, but while nearly every New England family keeps sheep and nearly every woman has a spinning wheel, few Americans are eager to enter the woolen manufacturing industry.

1700

✗ The Great Northern War begins in Europe as Russia, Poland, and Denmark join forces to oppose Swedish supremacy in the Baltic.

Spain's Carlos II dies November 1 at age 39 after a 35-year reign. He has named as his heir Philip of Anjou, 17, grandson of France's Louis XIV. The first Bourbon king of Spain will reign until 1746 as Philip V (but *see* War of the Spanish Succession, 1701).

Smallpox will kill an estimated 60 million Europeans in the century ahead and leave millions of others disfigured with pockmarks.

 Nonfiction: "Reflections upon Marriage Occasioned by the Duke and Duchess of Mazarine's Case" (pamphlet, published anonymously) by Mary Astell accepts marriage as a divinely appointed state of subjection for women. A lady of quality should not fall in love, she says. "It is the hardest thing in the World for a Woman to know that a Man is not Mercenary." Commenting on her Chelsea neighbor, the duchess of Mazarin, who has recently published an account of her marital troubles, she writes, "If Mme. Mazarine's Education made right improvement of her Wit and Sense, we should not have found her seeking Relief by such imprudent, not to say Scandalous, Methods, as the running away in Disguise with a Spruce Cavalier." "She then who Marries, ought to lay it down for an indisputable Maxim that her Husband must govern absolutely and intirely, and that she has nothing else to do but Please and Obey. She must not attempt to deny his Authority, or so much as dispute it; to struggle with her Yoke will not only make it gall the more, but she must believe him Wise and Good in all respects the best, at least he must be so to her. She who can't do this is no way fit to be a Wife . . ."

Poetry: "Annie Laurie" by Scottish poet William Douglas, 28, whose song is addressed to Anne, daughter of Sir Robert Laurie of the Maxwellton family: "Maxwellton's braes are bonnie/ . . . and for bonnie Annie Laurie/ I'd lay me down an' dee."

 Theater: *The Way of the World* by William Congreve in March at the Lincoln's Inn Fields Theatre, London: "I like her with all her faults; nay, like her for her faults" (I, iii); " 'Tis better to be left/ Than never to have loved" (II); *The Ambitious Stepmother* by English playwright Nicholas Rowe, 27, in December at the Lincoln's Inn Fields Theatre.

18th Century

1701

The first Prussian king crowns himself at Königsberg January 18. The Holy Roman Emperor Leopold I has given the elector of Brandenburg Frederick III, 42, sanction to assume the monarchy in return for a promise of military aid. The elector is married to Sophia Charlotte of Hanover and will reign until 1713 as Prussia's Frederick I.

An Act of Settlement provides for the succession to England's throne. William III, childless, is to be succeeded by his sister-in-law, Anne, and she, in turn, by the elector of Hanover, a great-grandson of the late James I.

The War of the Spanish Succession begins in Europe as Philip of Anjou gains recognition as king of Spain, especially in Castile, and the Holy Roman Emperor Leopold I moves to take over Spain's Dutch and Italian possessions (*see* 1700). England and Holland, fearful of having the France of Louis XIV joined with Spain, form a Grand Alliance with the emperor, and Eugene, prince of Savoy, joins the alliance September 7.

perity of England," she says March 11 in her first speech to Parliament. The House of Stuart's last monarch, Anne will reign until 1714. She names John Churchill, 52, husband of her court favorite Sarah (*née* Jennings), 42, and younger brother of the late James II's mistress, Arabella, as captain-general of England's land forces in Flanders and raises him from earl of Marlborough to duke of Marlborough December 14 after he has forced the surrender of Kaiserswerth on the Rhine, Venlo on the Meuse, and Liège. His wife has been managing his estates at Sandrich with great efficiency in his absence.

The *Daily Courant* begins publication at London March 11. Published by Elizabeth Mallet, it is the first English-language daily.

Theater: *The Inconstant, or The Way to Win Him* by George Farquhar in February at London's Drury Lane Theatre; *She Wou'd and She Wou'd Not, or The King Imposter* by Colley Cibber 11/26 at the Drury Lane.

England's Queen Anne gives royal approval to horse racing and originates the sweepstakes idea of racing for cash prizes (*see* Ascot, 1711)

1702

Queen Anne ascends the English throne March 8 at age 37 upon the death at age 51 of her brother-in-law, William III, who has fallen from his horse and suffered a chill. "As I know my heart to be entirely English, I can very sincerely assure you that there is not one thing you can expect or desire of me, which I shall not be ready to do for the happiness or pros-

1703

The duke of Marlborough invades the Spanish Netherlands as the War of the Spanish Succession continues.

St. Petersburg is founded May 1 by Russia's Peter the Great on reclaimed marshlands at the mouth of

the Gulf of Finland. Peter makes the new city his capital, turning Russia's focus to the West.

Painting: *Still Life with Flowers and Plums* by Rachel Ruysch, who married portrait painter Juriaen Pool 10 years ago and will bear 10 children by him.

A great storm strikes England November 26–27, killing thousands.

A Japanese earthquake December 30 sets fire to Edo and kills an estimated 200,000.

1704

The Battle of Blenheim (Blindheim or Hochstadt) August 13 ends in triumph for Queen Anne's favorite the duke of Marlborough, who leads the cavalry charge that breaks the enemy's resistance. Fighting as a "man" in his army is Irish soldier Christian "Mother" Ross, 37, who has enlisted under the name Christopher Welsh in an effort to find her husband, Richard, with whom she will be reunited in 1706. A French-Bavarian-Prussian coalition is defeated with help from Eugene, prince of Savoy (whose realm is overrun in his absence by French forces under the duc de Vendôme), only 16,000 French survivors return home, and the loss brings dismay to France's wives and mothers as well as to Louis XIV, whose military supremacy is gone forever.

The "Cassette girls" arrive at Mobile on the Gulf Coast in quest of husbands. The 25 young French women sent aboard a "brides' ship" carry small trunks (*cassettes*) filled with dowry gifts from Louis XIV, but when they see the primitive conditions in the Louisiana colony they refuse to marry any of the settlers, staging what will be called a "petticoat rebellion."

Boston housewife-shopkeeper Sarah Campbell Knight, 38, sets out on horseback for New York in December, securing guides and stopping at various post houses, inns, and homes in the towns through which she passes en route to settle a relative's estate. She will return early next year, the first woman ever to accomplish the journey on her own (the journal that she keeps will be published in 1865).

The "Cassette girls" (above) are persuaded to remain and will use okra obtained from African slaves to develop a cuisine that will expand the local fare of maize products, beans, sweet potatoes, and local game and seafood.

1705

The Holy Roman Emperor Leopold I dies May 5 at age 54 after a 47-year reign. His son of 26 will reign until 1711 as Josef I.

Metamorphosis Insectorum Surinamensium by German-born Dutch painter-entomologist Maria Sibylla Merian, 58, is published at Amsterdam in Latin and Dutch with 60 plates engraved from watercolors made by Merian during two years spent with her younger daughter, Dorothea, in the Dutch colony of Surinam beginning in 1699.

Other painting: *Young Girl Holding a Dove* by Venetian miniaturist Rosella Carriera, 29.

Blenheim Palace goes up at Woodstock in Oxfordshire for the duke of Marlborough. Queen Anne has commissioned the palace as a tribute to the victor of last year's great battle.

Famine strikes France, causing widespread distress that will continue for years (*see* 1709).

1706

The duke of Marlborough gains another victory over the French May 23 at the Battle of Ramillies in the continuing War of the Spanish Succession.

Theater: *The Beaux' Stratagem* by George Farquhar 3/8 at London's Haymarket Theatre: "How a little love and conversation improve a woman!" (IV, ii); *The Lady's Last Stake, or The Wife's Revenge* by Colley Cibber 12/13 at the Haymarket Theatre.

1707

The United Kingdom of Great Britain created May 3 unites England and Scotland under the Union Jack.

Queen Anne, the last Stuart monarch, saw England join Scotland to become the United Kingdom of Great Britain. FROM THE PAINTING BY SIR GODFREY KNELLER

1708

✗ The duke of Marlborough defeats French forces again July 11 at the Battle of Oudenarde with help from Eugene of Savoy. Lille surrenders in December after a nearly 4-month siege in which 30,000 combatants have lost their lives.

🎨 The elector Palatine invites Dutch still-life painter Rachel Ruysch, now 44, and her portraitist husband, Juriaen Pool, to live at his court in Düsseldorf. Ruysch continues to paint prolifically, signing her works with her maiden name.

🍴 Fortnum & Mason's opens in Piccadilly, London. William Fortnum, a former footman to Queen Anne, joins with Hugh Mason to start an enterprise that will provision better English households with comestible delicacies for generations.

1709

✗ The Battle of Maplaquet September 11 is the bloodiest in the War of the Spanish Succession, with the allies losing 20,000 lives. The duke of Marlborough (whose Tory political opponents call him a bloody butcher) and prince of Savoy triumph, but the French retreat in good order. Christian Ross's husband, Richard, is killed in the battle, and she marries Hugh Jones, a grenadier (*see* 1704; 1710).

☣ The Black Death kills 300,000 in Prussia, creating far more misery than any war.

🖊 Nonfiction: *An English-Saxon Homily on the Birthday of St. George* by self-educated English scholar Elizabeth Elstob, 26, is a translation of a medieval work published with an apologetic preface: "I know it will be said, What has a Woman to do with learning. . . . Where is the Fault in Womens seeking after Learning? why are they not to be valu'd for acquiring to themselves the noblest ornaments? what hurt can this be to themselves? what Disadvantage to others? But there are two things usually opposed against Womens Learning. That it makes them impertinent, and neglect their household affairs. Where this happens it is a Fault. . . . I do not observe it so frequently objected against Womens Diversions, that They take them off from Household Affairs . . ."

Poetry: *The Ladies Defence: or, The Bride-Woman's Counsellor Answered: A Poem in a Dialogue between Sir John Brute, Sir Wm. Loveall, Melissa, and a Parson* by English author Lady Mary Chudleigh, 53, says that marriage is virtual slavery, that "wife and servant are the same, but only differ in the Name," and argues for women's education; "January and May" by English poet Alexander Pope, 21, who writes, "All other goods by fortune's hand are given:/ a wife is the peculiar gift of Heav'n" and "To please a wife, when her occasions call,/ Would busy the most vigorous of us all./ And trust me, sir, the chastest you can choose/ Will ask observance, and exact her dues."

🧴 Eau de Cologne, introduced at the German city by Italian barber Jean-Baptiste Farina, is an alcohol-based blend of lemon spirits, orange bitters, and minto oil from the bergamot fruit. Much cheaper than perfume, it will gain wide popularity.

Europe has its coldest winter in memory. Temperatures begin falling January 6, the Seine and other French rivers freeze over, as do the canals of Venice and the mouth of the Tagus at Lisbon, huge blocks of ice make the English Channel unnavigable, and although there is a respite beginning January 25, when snow falls, some 24,000 Parisians die of the cold from January 5 to February 2. A second frost begins February 6 and continues for a month, freezing ink in pens even as people are writing and wine in bottles and killing fruit trees, vines, vegetables, and the seed grain needed for planting dies in the ground.

 Britain's Mediterranean fleet intercepts French grain supplies from North Africa, and market women from Paris march on Versailles to complain about the lack of bread. Mme. de Maintenon, now 73, is falsely accused of having bought up all the grain available (she has, in fact, made a point of eating only black bread to set an example).

1710

 English political preacher Henry Sacheverell, 36, is tried and convicted in March after attacking the Whig ministry. Sidney Godolphin, 65, lord high treasurer and an ally of Marlborough, has instigated the attack on Sacheverell and is dismissed by Queen Anne, who has gradually been soured on Marlborough through the subtle intrigues of Abigail, Lady Masham (*née* Hill), a cousin of the queen's onetime court favorite, Sarah Churchill. Lady Marlborough introduced Cousin Abigail to the court but has now been displaced by her as confidante to the queen and the power behind the throne. The Tory party wins a clear majority in the House of Commons in November and ousts Marlborough's Whig government in Britain's first clean-cut and peaceful transfer of power.

English grenadier Hugh Jones is killed fighting with the duke of Marlborough's forces on the Continent; his widow, Christian, is presented to Queen Anne, returns to her native Dublin, and marries a soldier named Davies (*see* 1709). She will die in 1739 at the Chelsea Pensioners' Hospital for old soldiers.

 English woman of letters Lady Mary Pierrepont, 21, writes July 10 to Bishop Burnet, "I am not now arguing for an equality of the two sexes. I do not doubt God and nature have thrown us into an inferior rank; we are a lower part of the creation, we owe obedience and submission to the superior sex, and any woman who suffers her vanity and folly to deny this, rebels against the law of the Creator, and the indisputable order of nature." Daughter of the fifth earl of Kingston, Lady Mary has taught herself Latin, speaks it as well as any man, and is better read than most. To her suitor, Edward Wortley Montagu, 32, who has tried to determine the size of her dowry, she writes in November, "People in my way are sold like slaves; and I cannot tell what price my master will put on me." Wortley Montagu is a close friend of London essayists Joseph Addison and Sir Richard Steele (*see* 1712).

 A British copyright law established by Queen Anne will be the basis of all future copyright laws.

1711

 Russia's Peter I, now 38, divorces his imbecilic wife, Eudoxia (or Eudokia) Loupokhina, and is married March 6 to his Latvian mistress Marta, 27, who will be known as the empress Catherine (Ekaterina). She has lived with the czar for the past 7 years and borne five children by him, including his surviving daughters, Anna and Elizabeth, who are now legitimized.

The Holy Roman Emperor Josef I dies of smallpox at age 32 April 17 and is succeeded by his brother, 26, who will reign until 1740 as Charles VI.

Queen Anne dismisses the duke of Marlborough at year's end as his Tory enemies increase their influence on her, accusing the duke of enriching himself through speculation.

 Queen Anne establishes the Ascot races. The Royal Enclosure at Ascot will used by the monarchy for years.

1712

 French forces gain a victory over British and Dutch forces at Denain. The Congress of Utrecht meets to find a resolution to the War of the Spanish Succession.

Colonist William Penn, now 67, suffers a massive stroke and is rendered virtually helpless. His second wife, Hannah Callowhill Penn, 41, who was 4 months pregnant with their second child (they have had eight) when she left England with him for a 3-month voyage to the New World in 1699, bribes officials to look the other way while she guides Penn's hand in signing colonial documents (*see* 1718).

Lady Mary Pierrepont resists her father's pressures to marry Clotworthy Skeffington, a rich but dull Irish nobleman 8 years her senior, and elopes in late August with the more learned (but insensitive) Edward Wortley Montagu (*see* 1710). Her father, who has spent £400 on her wedding outfit, gives her no dowry.

Poetry: *The Rape of the Lock* by Alexander Pope is a mock-heroic poem describing a day at Hampton Court where Queen Anne does "sometimes counsel take—and sometimes tea."

1713

Prussia's Frederick I dies February 25 at age 55. His son of 24 has married Britain's princess Sophia Dorothea and will reign until 1740 as Frederick Wilhelm I.

The Treaty of Utrecht April 11 ends the War of the Spanish Succession (called Queen Anne's War in North America).

Lettres sur l'Education des Filles by Mme. de Maintenon says, "There is little point in girls of common extraction learning to read as well as young ladies or being taught as fine a pronunciation or knowing what a period is, etc. It is the same with writing. All they need is enough to keep their accounts and memoranda; you don't need to teach them fine handwriting or talk to them of style; a little spelling will do. Arithmetic is different. They need it" (*see* 1686).

Queen Anne commissions German composer George Frideric Handel to write seven works to celebrate the Peace of Utrecht (above) and grants him a handsome lifetime pension of £200 per year. His *Te Deum* and *Jubilate* are performed 7/7 at St. Paul's Cathedral, London.

1714

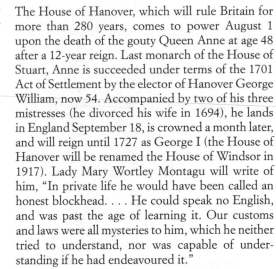

The House of Hanover, which will rule Britain for more than 280 years, comes to power August 1 upon the death of the gouty Queen Anne at age 48 after a 12-year reign. Last monarch of the House of Stuart, Anne is succeeded under terms of the 1701 Act of Settlement by the elector of Hanover George William, now 54. Accompanied by two of his three mistresses (he divorced his wife in 1694), he lands in England September 18, is crowned a month later, and will reign until 1727 as George I (the House of Hanover will be renamed the House of Windsor in 1917). Lady Mary Wortley Montagu will write of him, "In private life he would have been called an honest blockhead. . . . He could speak no English, and was past the age of learning it. Our customs and laws were all mysteries to him, which he neither tried to understand, nor was capable of understanding if he had endeavoured it."

Japanese philosopher-teacher Ekiken Kaibara dies at age 84. His booklet for students, *Onnadaigaku*, contains Confucianist ethical principles that will guide treatment of women for centuries: young people are to be segregated by sex beginning at age 7, and marriages are to be arranged for them; until she is married, a woman must obey her father; after marriage, she must obey her husband; and after his death, she must obey her oldest son; a marriage not condoned by the parents is deemed an adulterous relationship; to be considered virtuous, a woman must be obedient and submissive; women with ability, brains, or talent are troublesome, but a woman is expected to be good at weaving, sewing, cooking, and washing; above all, she is a child-producing machine: in rural areas, marriages will often not be registered until the bride has proven her ability to bear children, and if she cannot bear children she is expected to leave (although she may be permitted to remain if she is good-natured and her husband is able to sire a child by his mistress). A wife's duty is to serve her husband with absolute obedience and never to criticize or disparage him. She may not complain if he visits brothels and is even expected to pay his brothel bills.

Fiction: *The Adventures of Rivelle* by British writer Mary Manley (née de la Rivière), 42, who at age 16, after the death of her father, governor of Jersey, was lured into a bigamous marriage with a cousin, John

Manley, M.P., who soon deserted her. She later went to England and had some success as a London playwright and scandalmonger. Her *Adventures* is a semiautobiographical *roman à clef*.

1715

France's Louis XIV dies September 1 at age 76 after a 72-year reign. His great-grandson, 5, will reign until 1774 as Louis XV.

The death of the *roi de soleil* weakens the position of James Francis Edward Stuart, the Jacobite pretender, who has challenged the House of Hanover's claim to Britain's throne. The Scottish Jacobite John Erskine, 40, earl of Mar, whose wife, Frances, is Lady Mary Wortley Montagu's younger sister (they were married last year), raises a rebellion against George I but is halted by Royalist forces November 13 in his march on Edinburgh and loses 500 of his 12,000 men in the Battle of Sheriffmuir (the Royalists lose an equal number).

Nonfiction: *The Rudiments of Grammar* by Elizabeth Elstob is the first Anglo-Saxon grammar. Published by subscription, it goes to 250 Anglo-Saxon scholars, half of them women, but the vast majority of English women remain illiterate.

New Jersey colony Quaker Sybilla Masters (née Righton), 44, receives a patent (No. 401) at London November 25 for a machine to prepare "Indian corn." (England has been issuing patents since 1624.) Married in 1690 to Masters, a rich merchant who served as mayor of Philadelphia in 1708, Mrs. Masters voyaged to England in 1712 to refine her process for processing maize, or "Tuscarora rice," as she calls it, by stamping the grain instead of grinding it. Her device, consisting of wooden cogwheels, mortars, and trays, can be powered by water or horses (*see* 1716).

1716

Scottish Royalists disperse Jacobite troops in January to suppress the uprising against Britain's George I; captured Jacobite leaders are beheaded. Countess Mar, whose husband has fled to France, continues to live in her house in the Privy Gardens

of London's Whitehall Palace, and although overzealous patriots sometimes attack her she is protected by the fact that her family is solidly Whig and her husband insists that she had no part in his political activities.

Sybilla Righton Masters obtains a second British patent (No. 403) for "the Sole Working and Weaving" and a "New Method, Palmetto Chips, and Straw, for Covering hats and bonnets, and other improvements in the ware." The patent is actually issued to her husband, Thomas, who receives a monopoly on the importation of palmetto leaves from the West Indies. Mrs. Masters sets up shop in London to sell products made from the fiber, but the couple will return to Philadelphia in a year.

New York City's Common Council passes an ordinance requiring midwives to take out licenses and swear a version of the traditional midwives' oath.

Painting: *Fruit, Flowers, and Insects* by Rachel Ruysch, now 52, who returns from Düsseldorf to Amsterdam following the death of the elector Palatine.

Opera: Italian soprano Faustina Bordoni, 16, makes her debut at Venice singing in the C. F. Pollarolo opera *Ariodante*. She is engaged by the Elector Palatine to perform at his court.

1717

Prussia makes school attendance compulsory, but few families send their daughters to school.

Theater: French actress Adrienne Lecouvreur, 25, makes her debut at the Comédie-Française and attracts admirers who will soon include the author François-Marie-Arouet de Voltaire, 23, Marshal de Saxe, 21, and Charles Mordaunt, third earl of Peterborough, 59 (*see* 1730).

1718

Russia's Peter the Great has the ex-czarevich, Eudoxia, dragged from her monastery and publicly tried for alleged adultery. His son Aleksei is given 25 lashes with the knout June 19 (nobody has ever survived 30), given 15 more June 24, and dies June

26 at age 28 in the guardhouse of the citadel at St. Petersburg, 2 days after being condemned by the senate for "imagining" rebellion against his father. His death increases the power of Peter's wife, the empress Catherine (Marta Ekaterina), who gives birth to another daughter, Natalia, and will spend the next 7 years trying to keep the czar away from vodka and other women.

Colonist William Penn dies July 30 at Ruscombe, Berkshire, at age 73. His widow, Hannah, inherits control of the Pennsylvania colony (his will passes over the children by his first wife) and she will keep it intact for 14 years, resisting pressure from the Crown to surrender it and from some colonial factions to abandon it (*see* 1712). Penn's oldest son by his first marriage initiates legal action to nullify Penn's will and obtain the colony for himself, but Hannah will have the son's claims dismissed a week before her death from a stroke at age 55 in 1726.

Sweden's Charles XII is shot through the head December 11 as he peers over the parapet of the foremost trench 280 paces from the fortress of Fredriksten during a military expedition to Norway (one of his own men has evidently assassinated the bellicose king in order to avoid further loss of life). Dead at age 36, Charles is succeeded by his sister Ulrika Eleanora, 30, who accepts the crown on condition that the riksdag be allowed to draft a new constitution. She brings the Great Northern War to a close.

"Innoculation Against Smallpox" by Lady Mary Wortley Montagu reports a workable method known in the East since ancient times. Lady Mary, now 29, is in Constantinople, where her husband is the English minister, and although she married for love she has taken at least two lovers despite the fact that her own face is deeply pitted from smallpox she contracted in December 1815. She describes inoculation parties she has witnessed at which a small wound is made in the arm, a few drops of smallpox pus inserted, and a walnut shell tied over the infected area, a procedure that produces a true case of smallpox but one so mild that 98 percent of those inoculated recover (*see* 1721).

Marie de Vichy-Chamrond, 21, marries the marquis de Deffand, from whom she will soon be separated.

Lady Mary Wortley Montagu learned about inoculation at Constantinople and introduced it to Britain. NATIONAL LIBRARY OF MEDICINE

As witty as she is beautiful, she will preside over a salon that will attract the leading literary figures of Paris.

Opera: Italian soprano Francesca Cuzzoni, 20, makes her Venetian debut as Delinda in C. F. Pollarolo's opera *Ariodante* (Faustina Bordoni sings the role of Ginevra, and the two women begin a rivalry that will continue for the next decade).

1719

The Peace of Stockholm November 20 ends hostilities between Sweden's queen Ulrika Eleanora and Britain's George I.

A British slaver anchors off Port Natal and buys 74 Xhosa girls and boys for the Virginia colony's Rappahannock plantations. The Xhosa (called Bantu) are considered "better slaves for working than those of Madagascar, being stronger and blacker."

1720

Sweden's Ulrika Eleanora abdicates in favor of her husband, Frederick of Hesse, 44, who will reign until 1751 as Frederick I, but a new constitution strips the new king of much of his power.

1721

A London smallpox epidemic takes a heavy toll, but Lady Mary Wortley Montagu has her 5-year-old daughter inoculated in the presence of some leading physicians (*see* 1718). The child has a mild case of smallpox that immunizes her, the physicians are impressed, and George I has two of his grandchildren inoculated—but only after the procedure has been tested on 11 charity school children and on 6 inmates of Newgate Prison who volunteered in return for having their death sentences commuted.

Lady Mary Wortley Montagu (above) will later advise her daughter, "Hide your learning . . . as if it were a physical defect."

Theater: *The Refusal, or The Ladies' Philosophy* by Colley Cibber 2/4 at London's Drury Lane Theatre. *The Love Suicides at Sonezaki* (*Sonezaki Shinju*) by Monzaemon Chikamatsu, now 68, at Osaka. The play is the first of several domestic pieces based on actual incidents that Chikamatsu will write about the love affairs of Japan's increasingly important middle class.

1722

Manchester, New Hampshire, has its beginnings in a settlement established by Massachusetts colonists at Amoskeag on the Merrimack River 55 miles northwest of Boston.

1723

The Treaty of Charlottenburg October 10 between Britain and Prussia provides that the grandson of George I shall marry a Prussian princess and that Prussia's prince Frederick shall marry the daughter of the prince of Wales.

Opera: Francesca Cuzzoni makes her London debut 1/12 singing the role of Teofane with Italian soprano Margherita Durastanti, now 37, in the new Handel opera *Ottone* at the King's Theatre. Half-guinea tickets for the second night fetch 2 and even 3 guineas as word spreads of Cuzzoni's prowess; she will sing at the King's Theatre at £2,000 per season until the Royal Academy closes in June 1728.

The condom can emancipate young English wives from fear of "big belly, and the squalling brat," writes White Kennett, son of the bishop of Peterborough, in his satirical poem "Armour" (*see* 1655; 1671).

1724

The Rhode Island colony establishes property ownership qualifications for voters, but owning property does not qualify a woman to vote.

The Female Physician by English physician John Maubray observes that the "Politer Part of the World" has already begun to put itself in the hands of men physicians rather than midwives, and that the "middling classes" are doing likewise, but says of his colleagues, "I know some Chirurgeon-Practioners are too much acquainted with the Use of INSTRUMENTS to lay them aside; no, they do not (it may be) think of themselves in their Duty or proper Office, if they have not their cruel Accoutrements at Hand. And what is most unaccountable and unbecoming a Christian is that, when they have perhaps wounded the MOTHER, kill'd the INFANT, and with violent *Torture* and inexpressible *Pain*, drawn it out Piece-meal, they think no reward sufficient for such an extraordinary piece of mangled work."

Fiction: *Roxana* by English novelist-journalist Daniel Defoe, now 64, who writes, "I thought a woman was a free agent, as well as a man, and was born free, and could she manage herself suitably, might enjoy that liberty to as much purpose as the men do; that the laws of matrimony were indeed otherwise . . . and those such that a woman gave herself entirely away from herself, in marriage, and capitulated only to be, at best, but an upper servant."

1725

✗ Russia's Peter the Great dies January 28 at age 52 after a 42-year reign. His consort, now 41, will reign until 1727 as Catherine I while her daughter Elizabeth Petrovna, 14, pleasures herself with handsome young military officers (see 1741; Anna Ivanova, 1730).

France's Louis XV, now 15, is married August 15 to Marie Leszczynska, 22, daughter of Poland's former king Stanislas Leszczynski, who was deposed in 1709 and has been living in impoverished exile. The marriage has been arranged by the inept Louis Henri, duc de Bourbon, and although the queen will bear him ten children, including (in 1729) a son, she looks upon physical relations with a sense of duty rather than a pleasure, and her husband's feelings toward her will cool (see 1732).

✒ Fiction: *Memoirs of a Certain Island Adjacent to Utopia* by English novelist Eliza Haywood (née Fowler), 32, a onetime actress whose *roman à clef* scandalizes London society. Her periodical *The Female Spectator* will appear from 1744 to 1746 and will be followed the following year by *The Parrot*.

Theater: French dancer Marie Sallé, 18, appears at the Lincoln's Inn Fields Theatre, London, 10/23 in a revival of Colley Cibber's 1696 play *Love's Last Shift, or The Fool in Fashion*.

1726

✗ France's Louis XV dismisses Louis Henri, duc de Bourbon, and makes Bishop André-Hercule de Fleury, 73, a cardinal and virtual prime minister July 12. Fleury will hold power until his death in 1743, giving France peace, economic growth, and an upsurge of religious revivalism.

Sophia Dorothea of Celle dies November 13 after falling ill of a fever in which she has raved about her ex-husband's cruelty and wickedness (see 1694). George I, who will himself die next year, does not allow her name or that of her mother even to be inscribed on their coffins.

☿ Edinburgh's Town Council strengthens its law regulating midwives and appoints Dr. Joseph Gibson

professor of midwifery, the first such appointment in the British Isles.

🎼 Opera: Faustina Bordoni makes her London debut 5/5 singing the role of Rossane in the Handel opera *Alessandro* with Francesca Cuzzoni.

Ballet: Franco-Flemish dancer La Camargo (Marie-Anne Cupis), 16, makes her debut at the Paris Opéra 5/5 in J.-F. (Jean-Féry) Rebel's *Les caractères de la Danse*, written to display the talents of the dancers in the Académie Royale, especially Mme. François Prévost, now 46, who will come to resent the success of La Camargo.

1727

✗ Russia's extravagant, illiterate (but shrewd) Catherine I dies May 16 at age 44 after a brief reign and is succeeded by her son Peter, 12, who will reign until 1730.

Britain's George I dies of apoplexy at 67 the night of June 10 while en route by carriage to Hanover. He is succeeded by his son George Augustus, 44, elector of Hanover, who will reign until 1760 as George II with the guidance of his ministers and his wife, Caroline of Brandenburg-Ansbach, also 44, to whom he was married in 1705. Far more cultured and disciplined than he, she stops the new king from discharging the prime minister, Robert Walpole, with whom she enjoys discussing politics.

🎼 Opera: Faustina Bordoni creates the role of Alcestis in Handel's new opera *Admeto* 1/31 at the King's Theatre, London; she and her rival Francesca Cuzzoni exchange blows onstage 6/6 at the King's Theatre in the presence of the princess of Wales at a performance of the Bononcini opera *Astianatte*; she creates the role of Pulcheria in Handel's *Riccardo Primo* 11/11 at the King's Theatre; dancer Marie Sallé makes her Paris Opéra debut 9/14 in the Mouret opera *Les Amours des Dieux*.

1728

✗ British forces relieve Gibraltar in March after a 14-month Spanish siege.

Opera: Faustina Bordoni and her rival Francesca Cuzzoni are satirized as Polly and Lucy in J. C. Pepusch and John Gay's *The Beggar's Opera*, which has its first performance 1/29 at the Lincoln's Inn Fields Theatre, London. Bordoni creates the role of Emira in Handel's *Siroe, Re di Persia* 2/28 at London's Haymarket Theatre and the role of Elisa 5/4 in Handel's *Tolomeo, Re di Egitto* at the Haymarket. The Royal Academy closes prematurely in June when Bordoni falls ill, and the fortunes of Cuzzoni begin to decline (notoriously extravagant and improvident, she will die in obscurity, totally impoverished, in 1770 at Bologne). Marie Sallé dances a *pas de trois* in June with her great rival La Camargo and Mlle. Petit in *Hypermnestra*. She and La Camargo will appear together in numerous performances.

1729

The Treaty of Seville November 9 ends a 2-year war between Spain and an Anglo-French alliance. The allies agree to the Spanish succession in the Italian duchies; Britain retains Gibraltar.

Ballet: Marie Sallé creates a sensation 2/17, dancing with Laval in *Les Caractères de la Danse* and discarding the mask traditionally worn by dancers.

1730

The Russian czar Peter II dies of smallpox at age 14 January 30, the very day on which he was to have married Catherine, second daughter of Aleksis Dolgoruki. The Supreme Privy Council elects Peter's cousin Anna Ivanovna, 36, to the throne but with strict limits on her power, she enters Moscow February 26, her personal friends overthrow the Supreme Privy Council in a coup d'état March 8, and she summons her former lover Ernst Johann Biren, 39. Grandson of a groom to a former duke of Courland, Biren gained favor with Anna when she was duchess of Courland (her husband died in 1711, a year after she married him), she names Biren duke of Courland, grand chamberlain, and a count of the empire, and he adopts the arms of the French ducal house of Biron. The new czarina gives him an estate at Wenden with 50,000 crowns a year, and he will dominate her 10-year reign, antagonizing most Russians with his rapacity and treachery as together the czarina and Biron exile thousands to Siberia.

Denmark's Frederick IV dies at Odense October 12 at age 59 after a 31-year reign in which he has been forced to give up some German territories. He is succeeded by his narrow-minded son of 31 who will reign until 1746 as Christian VI, following the whims of his wife, Sophie Magdalene of Brandenburg-Kulmbach.

Painting: *The Dancer La Camargo* by French painter Nicolas Lancret, 40.

Actress Adrienne Lecouvreur dies at Paris March 20 at 37, and there are rumors that she has been poisoned by a rival, the duchesse de Bouillon. Passionately adored by many men, including Voltaire and Marshal de Saxe, she is refused a Christian burial by the Church because she has been an actress, so she is buried secretly, at night, by Voltaire and some friends in the rue de Boulogne.

1731

The Holy Roman Emperor Charles VI signs a second Treaty of Vienna March 16. He is 45, has no male offspring, and has decreed in a Pragmatic Sanction that if he should die without a male heir the empire shall devolve upon his daughters (the eldest, Maria Theresa, is now 14) and to their heirs by the law of primogeniture. If his daughters should die without heirs, the empire shall go to the heirs of his late brother Josef, who died in 1711. Britain recognizes this Pragmatic Sanction in the treaty, and the Dutch agree (but *see* 1740).

Parma and Piacenza pass to the son of Spain's Philip V following the death at age 52 of Antonio Farnese, head of the Farnese family, without male issue. Philip's son Carlos has taken Elizabeth Farnese as his second wife, and Spain's recognition of the Pragmatic Sanction (above) aids the succession of Charles to the Italian duchies.

Scotland's lord justice clerk James Erskine, Lord Grange, 52, bristles at criticism from his shrewish wife, Rachel (*née* Chiesley), who threatens to expose his conspiratorial Jacobite views, and spirits her away to the Hebrides. Her death is announced at Edinburgh, and a funeral is held. She will be kept incommunicado on various remote islands until 1742, when she will smuggle a letter to her cousin, the lord advocate, but although he will send a gunboat to look for her no trace of her will be found, and she will die in isolation in 1745.

French novitiate Catherine Cadière, 22, goes on trial at Aix after bringing charges of seduction against Father Jean-Baptist Girard, 50, who heads the Third Order of St. Theresa, and being countercharged with accusations of witchcraft. The trial will last a year, Cadière's lawyers will produce 10 other secular devotees and nuns who claim that Father Girard seduced them, he will call her a fraud and say that she invented the visions and ecstasies which she claims to have experienced, half the judges will vote to burn him, half will vote to hang her, they will wind up sending her to her mother and him to the ecclesiastical courts, and both will live out their days without further ado.

Fiction: *Histoire du Chevalier des Grieux et de Manon Lescaut* by the Abbé Prévost (Antoine-François d'Exiles), 35, whose work is condemned by French authorities. The story of an aristocrat who gives up everything in his passion for a demimondaine will be the basis of romantic novels, plays, and operas in the next century.

Painting: *A Harlot's Progress* by English painter William Hogarth.

Opera: Italian soprano Anna Maria Strata del Po sings the role of Cleofide in the new George Frideric Handel opera *Poro* 2/2 at London's Haymarket Theatre.

her off to the marquis de Vintimille, who removes himself to the provinces right after the ceremony (conjugal love is rare in France and quite unfashionable). While the comtesse de Mailly continues to live at Versailles, Louis buys her sister Pauline the Château de Choisy-le-Roi near the Forest of Sénart, furnishing it in silver and gold, but Pauline, after giving birth to a son, is seized with convulsions and dies in agony (her son, who is given the title comte du Lac, will bear such an uncanny resemblance to the king that he will become known as *le demilouis*) (*see* 1734).

Poor Richard's Almanack begins publication at Philadelphia. Printer-publisher Benjamin Franklin, 26, will publish new editions for 25 years, offering practical suggestions, recipes, advice on personal hygiene, and folksy urgings to be frugal, industrious, and orderly ("God helps those who help themselves," "You cannot pluck roses without fear of thorns, nor enjoy a fair wife without danger of horns," "Never leave till tomorrow that which you can do to-day," "A house without a woman and firelight is like a body without soul or spright") which are credited to a fictional "Richard Saunders." Circulation will reach 10,000, and colonial housewives will quote it as often as they do their Bibles. Franklin took as his common-law wife one Deborah Read 2 years ago, not being willing to marry her because her previous husband, while believed to have died, might turn up, making Deborah's new husband potentially liable for any debts he might have.

Oratorio: Anna Maria Strata del Po sings in the first performance of Handel's *Esther* 5/2 at the King's Theatre, London; she will be his leading soprano until 1737.

1732

France's Louis XV, now 22, takes as his first *maîtresse-en-titre* the Comtesse de Mailly (*née* de Nesle), also 22 (*see* 1725). Poor but not mercenary, she loves the king with more selfless sincerity than will any of her successors, but her scheming younger sister Pauline soon seduces the susceptible king and becomes pregnant by him. Louis marries

1733

The War of the Polish Succession begins in Europe following the death of Poland's August II February 1 at age 62. Austria, France, Russia, and the Holy Roman Empire are all soon involved.

Savannah, Georgia, is founded by English philanthropist James Edward Oglethorpe, 37, who arrives with a charter from George II for lands between the

Altamah and Savannah rivers and settles at the mouth of the latter with 120 men, women, and children. Creek native Mary Musgrove, 33, who at age 16 married white trader John Musgrove in Alabama, serves as Oglethorpe's principal interpreter and his trusted emissary in his dealings with the Indians. (Her father took her to South Carolina as a child to be educated, and she was baptized into the Church of England and given the name of Mary.) Related to leading chiefs of the Creek Nation, she will lend her support to the British in their struggles against the Spanish and, later, the French.

The design of the obstetrical forceps invented by Peter Chamberlen before the middle of the last century and guarded as a family secret is finally made public, although forceps of other designs have been available to male (but not female) practitioners of midwifery for some time. Using the forceps makes it possible not only to shorten labor but also to deliver live infants in cases where without them either the mother, or child, or both would have died (but *see* Nihell, 1758).

Oratorio: Anna Maria Strata del Po sings in the first performance of Handel's *Deborah* 3/17 at the King's Theatre, London.

Opera: La Camargo dances in Jean-Philippe Rameau's new opera *Hippolyte et Aricie* 10/1 at the Académie Royale in Paris. She is the first dancer to shorten the skirts of her costumes above the instep, which is considered immodest but permits her to create the entrechat and other innovations while allowing greater freedom of leg movement.

1734

The War of the Polish Succession spreads through Europe, with Spain, Naples, and the Two Sicilies involved.

France's Louis XV becomes infatuated with his mistress's surviving younger sister Marie Anne de Nesle, the widowed marquise de la Tournelle. She has persuaded Mme. de Mailly (who has never received gifts to match those given her late sister Pauline) to invite her to Versailles, but before she will yield to the king she insists that he banish her

sister Mme. de Mailly and make her, Marie Anne, duchesse de Châteauroux (*see* 1744).

Ballet: Marie Sallé appears 2/13 in the ballet *Pygmalion* at London's Drury Lane Theatre without pannier, skirt, or bodice; apart from her corset and petticoat, she wears only a simple muslin robe draped in the style of a Greek statue. It is the first time that a dancer has ventured totally to abandon the cumbersome and often inappropriate regalia of baroque stage costume; the simpler style of dress allows Sallé greater freedom, and she dances with her hair down, disdaining to wear any ornament on her head.

Opera: Marie Sallé dances at Covent Garden 11/8 as Terpsichore in the prologue of Handel's opera *Il Pastor Fido*; she appears 12/18 in Handel's opera *Oreste*.

1735

The War of the Polish Succession ends October 5 with the Treaty of Vienna, which will be ratified in 1738.

Scarlet fever strikes New England in a devastating epidemic.

Newport printer Ann Franklin (*née* Smith), 39, in the Rhode Island colony takes over the business of her husband, James, to publish the *Newport Mercury*, almanacs by her brother-in-law Benjamin and others, and colonial documents.

Fiction: *Les Memoires de Comte Comminges* by French courtesan and novelist Claudine-Alexandrine Guérin de Tencin, 54, who came to Paris in 1714 at age 33 after having lived a religious life, attracted a string of lovers with her wit and beauty, and used her influence to further the fortunes of her older brother, Cardinal Pierre Guérin de Tencin, who died 9 years later. She was imprisoned briefly in the Bastille after one of her lovers shot himself in her house in 1726, but she went on to maintain one of the most glittering salons in Paris.

Opera: Anna Maria Strata del Po sings the role of Genebra and Marie Sallé dances at London's Covent Garden 1/19 in Handel's new opera *Ariodante;* Sallé appears at Covent Garden dressed as a man 4/27 in Handel's new opera *Alcina* (the audience shows its disapproval of her attire).

✊ Britain repeals her statutes against witchcraft after centuries of oppressing women, many of them midwives who compete with physicians.

🎼 Oratorio: Anna Maria Strata del Po sings in the first performance of G. F. Handel's *Alexander's Feast* 2/19 at London's Covent Garden.

Opera: Anna Maria Strata del Po sings the title role in Handel's new opera *Atalanta* 5/23 at London's Royal Theatre in Covent Garden; French soprano Elisabeth Duparc performs several dances to the satisfaction of the royal family at Kensington Palace 11/15 and makes her operatic debut 11/23 at the King's Theatre in Johann Hasse's opera *Siroe*.

⌛ Mary Wortley Montagu, 18, daughter of Lady Mary, is married August 13 to the young, handsome, but impecunious earl of Bute, a nephew of the duke of Argyll, who has tried to persuade the young man to break off the match because the bride's father has withheld her dowry of £20,000 in an effort to prevent the marriage. Lady Mary writes to her brother-in-law, Lord Gower, "I hope by her future conduct she will atone for her past, and that her choice will prove more happy than you and Mr. Wortley expect." Lady Mary herself has begun a friendship with Count Francesco Algarotti, 24, a handsome Venetian scientist who is not particular about the gender of his lovers.

⚗ *Genera Plantarum* by Swedish botanist Carolus Linnaeus (Carl von Linné), 30, establishes the modern binomial system of taxonomy (*see* 1745).

🎭 A British Licensing Act restricts the number of London theaters and requires that all plays be subjected to the lord chamberlain for censorship before they may be presented. It will not be repealed until 1968.

🎼 Oratorio: Anna Maria Strata del Po sings in the first performance of G. F. Handel's *Il Triompho*

del Tempo e della Verità 3/23 at London's Covent Garden.

Opera: Marie Sallé dances at the Paris Opéra 10/24 in Jean-Philippe Rameau's new opera *Castor et Pollux*.

⚔ The Treaty of Vienna that ended the War of the Polish Succession in 1735 is ratified November 13.

⚗ *Propositions of Philosophy* by Italian prodigy Maria Agnesi, 20, contains 190 essays on philosophy, logic, mechanics, elasticity, celestial mechanics, Newton's theory of universal gravitation, and the need for higher education for women. As the eldest daughter of 21 children, she has been obliged to raise her siblings since the death of her mother but has nonetheless found time to pursue her studies. She has developed a mathematical formula (it will become known as "the witch of Agnesi") describing the curve that duplicates precisely the volume of a cube, thus solving an age-old puzzle.

Italian prodigy Maria Agnesi was a scholar and mathematical wizard who urged higher education for women. LIBRARY OF CONGRESS

1739

 The Cato Conspiracy at Stono in the South Carolina colony takes the lives of 44 blacks and 30 whites as slaves near Charleston arm themselves by robbing a store and set out for Florida, gathering recruits and murdering whites on the way. A hastily assembled force of whites crushes the rebellion, but slaveowners and their wives fear for their lives.

"Woman Not Inferior to Man" (pamphlet) by "Sophia, a Person of Quality" is published in England. Says its anonymous author, "It is a very great absurdity to argue that learning is useless to women, because, forsooth, they have no share in public offices. . . . Why is learning useless to us? Because we have no share in public offices. And why have we no share in public offices? Because we have no learning."

Fiction: *Le Siège de Calais* by Claudine de Tencin.

Oratorio: Elisabeth Duparc sings in a performance of G. F. Handel's 1736 work *Alexander's Feast*.

and science. As beautiful as she is learned, the marquise has been the mistress of Voltaire, now 46, since 1734, when he came to live with her in a ménage à trois and work at her husband's château of Cirey in Champagne. (The arrangement will continue for 16 years, until her death, and when she tries to break it off in order to devote herself to a new affair Voltaire will forbid it, saying that it would be improper.)

 Theater: Irish actress Margaret "Peg" Woffington, 20, makes her London debut at the Drury Lane Theatre in the role of Sylvia in the late George Farquhar's 1706 play *The Recruiting Officer*, winning every heart in the house with her lively beauty. She will remain at the Drury Lane until 1746, appear at Covent Garden until 1750, and then return to Dublin, where she will perform until 1754 (*see* 1756).

Oratorio: Elisabeth Duparc sings in a March performance at Covent Garden of G. F. Handel's 1732 work *Esther*.

1740

Prussia's Frederick Wilhelm I dies May 31 at age 51 after a 27-year reign in which he has built up a standing army of 83,000—enormous for a country of 2.5 million. His scholarly son of 28, who will reign until 1786 as Frederick II, has married Elizabeth Christina of Brunswick-Wolfenbüttel. He invades Silesia, precipitating a conflict with Austria that will continue for 15 of the next 23 years.

The Russian czarina Anna Ivanovna adopts her 8-week-old nephew October 5, declares him her successor, and dies October 17 at age 47 (*see* 1741).

The Holy Roman Emperor Charles VI dies October 20 at age 55, the last of the Hapsburg line, which began in 1516. His daughter Maria Theresa is queen of Hungary and Bohemia, but the king of Saxony, the elector of Bavaria, and Spain's Philip V contest her right to succeed Charles (*see* 1731). The War of the Austrian Succession will involve most of Europe's great powers in the next 8 years.

Institutions de physique by French scholar Gabrielle-Emilie, marquise du Châtelet-Lomont, 34, displays the author's learning in mathematics

1741

Peter the Great's daughter Elizabeth Petrovna, now 31, drives with her supporters to the barracks of the Preobrazhensky Guards the night of December 6, arouses their sympathies with a stirring speech, and leads them to the Winter Palace for a coup d'état. She seizes the new regent, Anna Leopoldovna, and her children, including the infant czar Ivan VI, banishes Anna and her husband, deposes the czar and has him imprisoned, and ascends the imperial throne to begin a reign that will continue until her death early in 1762. A Russian commission has found the regent Count Biron guilty of treason April 11 and sentenced him to death by quartering. The sentence has been commuted to banishment for life to Siberia, and the count's vast property has been confiscated, including diamonds worth £600,000. The French ambassador, plotting to destroy the Austrian influence dominant at St. Petersburg, has played on Elizabeth's fears that she would be confined to a convent for life.

 South Carolina colonist Elizabeth Lucas, 19, introduces indigo cultivation. The daughter of a British colonel who was stationed in the West Indies

before being called off to fight the Spaniards, Eliza has been managing his three South Carolina rice plantations since she was 16, taking care of her sick mother and younger sister, Polly, as well. Wappoo, the largest of the three properties, contains 600 acres and has 20 slaves. Worms and frosts will keep her from harvesting a decent indigo crop until 1744, but she will then find a ready market in Britain for the blue dye derived from it (*see* 1744).

1742

✗ Maria Theresa makes an alliance with Britain, raises two armies, and drives her allied invaders out of Bohemia.

⚕ Irish physician Fielding Ould gives the first description of episiotomy—an "incision towards the anus with a crooked pair of probe-sizars; introducing one blade between the head and the vagina . . . and the business is done in one pinch, by which the whole body will easily come forth" (*see* 1748).

𝄞 Oratorio: Susanna (Maria) Cibber (*née* Arne), 28, sings the contralto part (Elisabeth Duparc the soprano) in the first performance of George Frideric Handel's *The Messiah* 4/13 at the Dublin Cathedral in a charity concert for the benefit of "the Prisoners in several Gaols, and for the support of Mercer's Hospital in Stephen Street, and of the Charitable Infirmary on the Inn's Quay." Sister of the composer Thomas Arne, she was married 8 years ago to Theophilus Cibber, profligate son of the playwright–theatrical manager Colley Cibber, and 3 years ago was disgraced in a sex scandal that culminated in a trial that revealed the adulterous relationship forced upon her by her husband. He virtually sold her favors to John Sloper, a country squire who admired her, and when she eloped with Sloper he sued for £5,000 but was awarded only £10. Cibber's threats of reprisal forced her to hide out at Sloper's country house in Berkshire, where she has borne Sloper's children and led a quiet life. The chancellor of the cathedral, Dr. Delany, rises after her moving aria "He was despised" describing Christ's suffering and cries out, "Woman, for this all thy sins be forgiven thee," the concert raises enough money to free 142 prisoners from debtors' prison, and performances of the oratorio will become an annual Christmas tradition.

The Holy Roman Empress Maria Theresa gave Austria, Hungary, and Bohemia imperious leadership.

1743

✗ Austrian armies drive French and Bavarian troops out of Bavaria as the War of the Austrian Succession continues in Europe. An allied Pragmatic army of English, Hessian, and Hanoverian troops defeat the French June 27 in the Battle of Dettingen, the emperor Charles VII is forced to take refuge at Frankfurt, and the Dutch Republic throws in its lot with Britain in alliance with Austria's Maria Theresa, who makes an alliance with Saxony.

⚘ Poetry: *The Sorrowing of Turtledove* (*Den sörjande turdufvan*) by Swedish feminist Hedvig Charlotta Nordenflycht, 25, whose Platonist clergyman husband, Jacob Fabricius, has died at an early age, leaving her desolated.

Opera: English singer-actress Kitty Clive (*née* Raftor), 31, creates the role of Dalila in G. F. Handel's new opera *Samson* 2/18 at London's Drury Lane Theatre.

Oratorio: Mrs. Cibber creates the role of Mica in the new G. F. Handel work *Samson* 3/23 at London's Covent Garden.

1744

Prussia's Frederick II starts a Second Silesian War by marching through Saxony with 80,000 troops. He invades Bohemia in August and takes Prague in September before the Hapsburg forces of Maria Theresa drive him back into Saxony.

France deserts Frederick II (above) and declares war on both Britain and Maria Theresa. Mme. de Châteauroux, mistress to Louis XV, insists that the indolent king emulate the late Louis XIV and take personal command of his army in Flanders. He complies, taking along the haughty duchesse and her sister, Mme. de Lauragais, a fat, jolly woman with whom Louis sometimes goes to bed in preference to Mme. de Châteauroux. His immorality outrages his troops, and he removes himself with his companions to Metz, where he falls deathly ill August 8. The bishop of Soissons threatens to withhold the last rites unless the king gets rid of the unpopular Mme. de Châteauroux and Louis agrees; the bishop then announces that *le roi* is sincerely penitent and "asks pardon of God and man. He is informed that the lady is now some leagues from here, and he commands that in future she shall remain at a distance of fifty leagues from the Court." Mme. de Lauragais is also banished. Louis recovers, Queen Marie arrives at Metz to find him convalescent, he apologizes for having caused any unhappiness, but he has no intention of resuming sexual relations with her. Now 34 and the handsomest man in France if not in all of Europe, Louis the Well-Beloved (*le Bien-Aimé*; a popular poet named Vadé has coined the soubriquet) enters Paris in triumph November 13. He soon effects a reconciliation with Mme. de Châteauroux and recalls her to Versailles, but she falls ill, probably of typhus, and dies in a delirium December 8.

King George's War breaks out between France and Britain in the Caribbean and in North America—an offshoot of the War of the Austrian Succession.

Maria Theresa launches a pogrom to drive the Jews out of Bohemia and Moravia.

Dissertation sur la nature et la propagation du feu by the marquise du Châtelet-Lomont is published at Paris.

Theater: Mrs. Cibber becomes David Garrick's leading lady at London's Drury Lane Theatre, forming a partnership that will continue until her death in January 1766.

Oratorio: Elisabeth Duparc sings in a November performance of G. F. Handel's 1733 work *Deborah* at Covent Garden and in a performance there of his 1743 work *Samson*.

Eliza Lucas in the South Carolina colony produces a successful indigo crop and ships 17 pounds of dye to London, where merchants find it equal to the dye they have been importing from the French colonies (*see* 1741). Parliament approves a 6-pence-per-pound bonus on indigo produced in British colonies, and France makes it a capital crime to export indigo seeds from her islands. Eliza marries Charleston planter Charles Pinckney, 41, a widower. She distributes seeds from her crop to any South Carolina planter who wants them, and by 1746 the colony will be exporting 40,000 pounds of dye to Britain (*see* 1749).

1745

The Holy Roman Emperor Charles VII dies at Munich January 20 at age 47 after a 3-year reign. His son Maximilian Joseph, 17, succeeds as elector of Bavaria, signs the Treaty of Füssen April 22 with the empress Maria Theresa to end the Second Silesian War, and regains the land conquered by Austria by renouncing any claim to Austria's throne and supporting the imperial election of Maria Theresa's husband, Franz Stefan. Franz Stefan is elected Holy Roman Emperor and will reign until 1765 as Francis I.

The French dauphin, now 15, is married February 25 at Versailles to the Spanish infanta in a match intended to heal the estrangement between the two branches of the Bourbon family that has existed since Louis XV tactlessly rejected a proposed marriage to the infanta's older sister. At a masquerade ball to celebrate the nuptials, Louis meets the intelligent bourgeois beauty Mme. Charles-Guillaume Le Normant d'Etioles (*née* Jeanne Antoinette Poisson), 23. He makes love to her beginning in late February or early March, she pretends that her husband will be insanely jealous unless Louis makes her *maîtresse-en-titre,* Louis promises to present her at court upon his return from the army, and he buys her the marquisate of Pompadour, an estate in Limousin with annual revenues of 12,000 livres. The king and his son arrive May 10 at the headquarters of Maurice, comte de Saxe, and participate the next day in the Battle of Fontenoy, which ends in victory for the French over an allied army of British, Austrian, and Dutch troops. Louis and the dauphin return to Paris September 7, Mme. de Pompadour travels by closed carriage to Versailles September 10, and she is presented at court September 14 wearing a brocaded petticoat that weighs 40 pounds, meeting for the first time Queen Marie. The king and Mme. de Pompadour withdraw a few days later to Choisy, a château that he purchased originally for the late Mme. de Vintimille.

Scotland has an uprising of Highland peasants who have been driven off the land by "lairds" who want to break up the clans and use the Highlands for sheep raising. Flora Macdonald, 24, on the Isle of Skye lends her support to Charles Edward "Bonny Prince Charlie" Stuart, 25, who lands in the Hebrides July 25 and raises the Jacobite standard to proclaim his father James VIII of Scotland and James III of England. The Young Pretender leads 2,000 men into Edinburgh September 11 (*see* 1746).

 Fauna Suecica by Carolus Linnaeus places humans and all other animals that nourish their young with milk secreted by mammary glands in a class he names *Mammalia*, partly because wet-nursing is a controversial social issue (*see* 1737). Linnaeus is among those who are trying to convince women of quality that breast-feeding their own babies is the "natural" thing to do, whereas Lady Mary Wortley Montagu and others have favored the use of wet nurses (*see* Paris, 1780).

 German-born Frisian midwife Catharina Geertuida Schrader dies at age 88 after a career in which she has attended 3,060 deliveries, including 64 sets of twins and three sets of triplets. Widowed in 1689, she had to go to work to support her six children. Her memoirs, relating her work from 1693 to 1740, will be published posthumously.

Dublin's Lying-in Hospital (later to be called the Rotunda Hospital) is founded. Charity patients at lying-in hospitals are generally unmarried girls ashamed of their condition; most married women are delivered at home.

 Oratorio: Mrs. Cibber creates the role of Lichas in G. F. Handel's new work *Hercules* 1/5 at the King's Theatre, London.

1746

 The Battle of Falkirk January 17 gives the Jacobite pretender Charles Edward Stuart and his Highlanders a victory over the British dragoons, but the Battle of Culloden Moor April 16 ends Stuart efforts to regain the British throne. "Bonnie Prince Charlie" escapes to the Isle of Skye June 29 disguised as Betty Burke, maid to Flora Macdonald, who conducts him to safety from Benbecula to Portree at great risk to her own life. The Young Pretender gets away to France September 20, the British imprison Macdonald briefly in the Tower of London and will hold her for the next year aboard a troopship in Leith Roads and at London. They forbid anyone to wear the tartan, a ban that will continue until 1782.

France's dauphine, the former Spanish infanta, dies in July after giving birth to a daughter.

1747

 France's widower dauphin, still only 18, is remarried at Versailles February 9 to Marie-Josèphe of Saxony, 15, a niece of Marshal Saxe, who has obtained the help of Mme. de Pompadour in gaining the king's consent to the marriage. Etiquette requires that the entire court witness the bridal couple being put to bed together.

The Royal Navy scores smashing victories against French naval forces in the Caribbean, jeopardizing France's huge convoys of sugar.

Fiction: *Les malheurs de l'amour* by Claudine de Tencin, now 66. She will die in 1749.

1748

✗ The Treaty of Aix-la-Chapelle signed October 18 halts the War of the Austrian Succession after 8 years. Mme. de Pompadour, whose menstrual difficulties and repeated miscarriages are the talk of Paris, has participated in the negotiations leading up to the peace treaty, which gains nothing for

Louis XV's mistress, Mme. de Pompadour, ruled France virtually as prime minister, exercising great power. FROM A PAINTING BY DROUAIS IN THE NATIONAL GALLERY, LONDON

France and in fact requires that French sea defenses at Dunquerque be dismantled, and that the Young Pretender Bonny Prince Charlie be expelled. Hostilities will resume in 1756.

💲 "The only principle of life propagated among the young people is to get money," writes Scots-American Cadwallader Colden, 60, "and men are only esteemed according to what they are worth—that is, the money they are possessed of."

🧪 *Analytical Institutions* by Maria Agnesi (*see* 1738) proposes new methods for algebra, geometry, and differential and integral calculus. Using its author's skill with languages (she speaks Latin, Greek, French, and other languages as well as Italian), it correlates the work of many writers and mathematicians and will be the standard mathematical text for half a century. The book establishes Agnesi's reputation, and the empress Maria Theresa sends her a casket of jewels in recognition of her scholarship.

⚕ Fielding Ould in Ireland prescribes opiates for women undergoing difficult labor (*see* 1742). He is the first to advise episiotomy when it looks like the perineum is about to tear, but he regards cesarean section as a "detestable, barbarous, illegal piece of humanity."

✒ Fiction: *Clarissa, or the History of a Young Lady* by English novelist Samuel Richardson, 59, whose seven-volume novel will establish his lasting reputation and that of his heroine, Clarissa Harlowe, who resists her father's pressure to marry a rich, ugly man, disregards the advice of a friend who tells her, "Marry first, and love will come after," elopes from a country house with her lover, Lovelace, despite his libertine past, and comes to grief. Lady Mary Wortley Montagu, now 59 and living in lonely retirement in Italy, reads the work and writes to her daughter, "This Richardson is a strange fellow. I heartily despise him, and eagerly read him, nay, sob over his works in a most scandalous manner. The two first tomes of Clarissa touched me, as being very resembling to my maiden days."

1749

💲 South Carolina indigo exports to Britain reach 120,000 pounds, thanks to the efforts of Eliza

Pinckney (*see* agriculture, 1744). Pressing the indigo to produce dye creates an extremely obnoxious odor, but slave labor spares planters any unpleasantness.

Scottish physician William Hunter is appointed surgeon-midwife to the British Lying-In Hospital (he holds a similar position at the Middlesex Hospital) and will consult in the delivery of Queen Charlotte, although a midwife will make the actual delivery.

France's royal physicians warn Louis XV and Mme. de Pompadour that they must end their sexual relations. She has had another miscarriage during Lent, her bulging eyes indicates that she suffers from thyroid gland problems, and she is plagued also by chronic fatigue and an irregular heartbeat.

Nonfiction: *Rational Thoughts on Education of the Fair Sex* by German widow Dorothea Erxleben, 34, who has interrupted her medical studies to nurse her father and bear four children.

Oratorio: Elisabeth Duparc sings in an April performance at Covent Garden of G. F. Handel's 1742 work *The Messiah.*

Mme. de Pompadour (above) persuades Louis XV to turn over to her a small porcelain works at Vincennes, set up in 1741 but now so neglected that it has nearly stopped production. The marquise organizes a new company, transfers operations to Sèvres, and begins building up an establishment that will employ 60 painters and 440 other skilled artisans. Using soft paste rather than the hard paste employed at Dresden, they create colorful dinnerware (Mme. de Pompadour selects the *de roi*, *bleu turquoise*, and pale raspberry, which will be called *rose pompadour*) that is costlier than its Dresden counterpart but so popular that the Crown will purchase the works in 1760 and make it the Royal Porcelain Factory at Sèvres.

1750

The Iron Act passed by Parliament prohibits Britain's American colonists from manufacturing iron products while permitting them to produce bar and pig iron from their ore deposits, using the fuel which they have in abundance, and exchanging the iron for manufactured articles. The mercantilist act is designed to restrict the colonies to producing raw materials that the mother country can process or resell, using the colonies as a captive market, but colonists generally ignore the new law.

Nonfiction: *The Female Soldier* by British Army veteran Hannah Snell, 27, who in 1723 left her child and, disguised as a man, joined the army to look for her sailor husband. Having marched to Carlisle with her infantry regiment to fight supporters of Bonnie Prince Charlie, she deserted after being flogged, joined a Marine ship bound for India, was shot in the groin by the French at Pondicherry, found a woman doctor to remove the bullet, and thereafter somehow reached Portugal, where she learned that her missing husband had been executed in Italy. She promotes her book by performing military drill in full dress uniform onstage at the Sadler's Wells Theatre.

Painting: Rachel Ruysch dies at Amsterdam at age 86, having continued her still-life painting right to the end.

Theater: *The Rehearsal, or Bays in Petticoats* by soprano-playwright Kitty Clive 3/15 at London's Drury Lane Theatre.

1751

France's Louis XV mourns the loss of his first mistress, Mme. de Mailly, who dies in April at age 41. Since leaving Versailles she has atoned for her youthful wantonness with the king by devoting herself to charitable works, and she is found to be wearing a hair shirt and to have left instructions that she be buried in Potter's Field.

Benjamin Franklin discovers the electrical nature of lightning while flying a kite in a thunderstorm. He works to develop a lightning rod that will prevent the fires that so often begin in thunderstorms.

Fiction: *The History of Betsy Thoughtless* by Eliza Haywood, who was denounced by Alexander Pope in his *Dunciad*, published in 1728, and no longer satirizes London society figures.

1752

Public street lighting begins in Philadelphia. New York and Boston continue to light streets by placing a lamp in the window of every seventh house, but Philadelphia installs globe lamps imported from London.

Pope Benedict XIV appoints Maria Agnesi to fill the chair of mathematics at the University of Bologna but she declines, preferring to remain at Milan (*see* 1748; 1799).

Treatise on Midwifery by Scottish midwifery teacher William Smellie (with help from physician-novelist Tobias Smollett) gives a clear account of the mechanism of labor and sets forth sound rules for obstetrical practice, correcting many errors found in previous works. Smellie notes that an illiterate Irish woman, Mary Donally, is "emminent among the common people for extracting dead births," having saved both mother and baby in 1738 by using a sharp razor to make an incision in the side of the midline of the belly (*see* 1754; Nihell, 1758).

The Jermyn Street Hospital, founded at London, quickly comes to be called the General Lying-in Hospital (*see* Dublin, 1745). It will be renamed the Queen's Hospital, and, ultimately, Queen Charlotte's Hospital.

Fiction: *The Female Quixote, or The Adventures of Arabella* by English novelist-poet Charlotte Ramsay Lennox, 32.

Britain and her colonies adopt the Gregorian calendar of 1582. Thursday, September 14, follows Wednesday, September 2, by decree of Parliament, the change confuses bill collectors, rumors spread that salaried employees are losing 11 days' pay and that everybody is losing 11 days of her or his life, and there are riots to protest the calendar change.

1753

The Hardwicke Marriage Act passed by Parliament forbids marriage by "unauthorized persons." It requires parental consent for minors to marry and invalidates marriages performed without license or publication of the banns. Errant husbands and wifes of the lower classes have heretofore been able to disappear and contract bigamous marriages.

Nonfiction: *The Whole Duty of Woman* by English writer William Kenrick gives a definition of modesty which includes "diffidence in voicing an opinion and a low, gentle voice." The conduct book will go through nearly 20 editions by 1815.

Fiction: *The History of Jemmy and Jenny Hessamy* by Eliza Haywood.

1754

Paris recalls colonial administrator Joseph-François Dupleix, 57, from India, leaving the British in firm control of the subcontinent.

Treatise on Midwifery by English physician Benjamin Pugh advises that a woman be delivered while standing, kneeling, or sitting on a pillow in the lap of a strong woman in an armchair (*see* Smellie, 1752). Pugh discourages delivery while lying down, especially if there are complications.

German widow Dorothea Erxleben, now 39, graduates from Halle University with the approval of Prussia's Frederick the Great.

1755

British forces in North America take Fort Beauséjour in French Canada June 16 after a short siege; some 6,000 Acadian men and women who refuse to swear allegiance to George II are sent to the Georgia and South Carolina colonies with instructions that they are to be "disposed of in such manner as may best answer our design of preventing their reunion," and the property of the 9,000 remaining Acadians is for the most part confiscated.

Theater: English actress Frances Abington (*née* Barton), 18, makes her debut at London's Haymarket Theatre after a career as flower girl, street singer, milliner, and kitchen maid. She will perform at the Haymarket until 1759, play in Dublin, and return to London to join David Garrick's company at the Drury Lane, excelling in comic roles.

The Lisbon earthquake November 1 produces a seismic wave that makes the Tagus River overflow its banks, fire breaks out, and it takes 10,000 to

30,000 lives (60,000 by some accounts), shaking the confidence of Europe.

1756

 A Seven Years' War begins in Europe as Prussia's Frederick the Great invades Saxony. Austria, France, Russia, and Sweden are quickly involved. French widows will blame the king's mistress, the marquise de Pompadour, now 34, for having brought France into the war, but she has merely encouraged an alliance between France and Austria.

The French and Indian War brings British and French forces into conflict in an offshoot of the European War (above).

Theater: Peg Woffington and George Anne Bellamy, 35, as the queen of Babylon and the daughter of Darius, respectively, in Nathaniel Lee's *Alexander and the Rival Queens* 1/15 at London's Covent Garden. The two leading ladies squabble in the greenroom.

1757

 The Battle of Plassey June 23 establishes British sovereignty in India as Robert Clive defeats a Bengalese nabob who has played him false.

The Battle of Rossbach November 5 gives Prussia's Frederick the Great a crushing victory over the French. Louis XV (or his mistress, Mme. de Pompadour) says, *"Aprés moi, le déluge"* (After me, the flood), an expression already proverbial.

Theater: Peg Woffington falls ill May 17 at London's Covent Garden Theatre while playing the role of Rosalind in the epilogue of Shakespeare's *As You Like It*; her acting career is ended, and she will devote her final 3 years to charitable works.

1758

France suffers reverses in the continuing Seven Years' War, losing the Battle of Crefield near the Rhine June 23, giving up her West African ports to the British, and yielding control of Canada's Cape Breton Island.

South Carolina planter Charles Pinckney dies at age 55, leaving his widow, Eliza, to manage his seven plantations and look after the four children she has borne in five years (*see* 1744). Within a few years, the colony will be producing more than a million pounds of indigo dye annually.

A treatise on the art of midwifery by English midwife Elizabeth Nihell is a 400-page polemic alleging that men misuse forceps in deliveries, employing them too often to speed up delivery unnecessarily to impress women's families and enable the men to demand higher fees (*see* 1733). One of the few foreign midwives to have studied at France's prestigious Hôtel-Dieu school, she writes that use of the forceps leaves many children with disabilities, and their use increases child mortality rather than reducing it. She accuses William Smellie (*see* 1752) of having turned unsuccessful barbers, tailors, and even pork butchers into man-midwives (she suggests that they be called *pudendists*), many of whom do not wait for the full dilation of the cervix before applying the forceps, or use the forceps when some part other than the head is presenting. Male doctors, she charges, use the forceps unnecessarily to hasten deliveries and save their own time, concealing their errors with "a cloud of hard words and scientific jargon" that deceive their patients into thinking they are superior to midwives. The doctors, for their part, depict midwives as ignorant beldames who ply their patients with cordials, subject them to violent shakings, and make fun of their distress.

Childbirth was fraught with peril through most of history, as arrogant physicians competed with ignorant midwives. NATIONAL LIBRARY OF MEDICINE

First performances: A Mass by Austrian singer-pianist-composer Marianne (Anna Katherina) von Martínez, 17, is sung at Vienna's Court Church of St. Michael.

1759

French Canada falls to the British September 13 as the Seven Years' War continues in Europe. Former British colonial army officer George Washington, 26, has married Virginia widow Martha Dandridge Custis, 27, January 6 at her estate in Kent County.

Silhouette becomes a term of derision meaning a figure reduced to its simplest form. The demands of war and the luxury of the court have drained France's treasury, Etienne de Silhouette, 50, has been named controller-general through the influence of Louis XV's mistress, Mme. de Pompadour, he has attempted reforms that include a land tax on the estates of the nobility, a reduction of pensions, and the melting down of table silver for use as money, but his efforts arouse a storm of opposition and ridicule.

The translation of Isaac Newton's landmark 1687 work *Philosophiae Naturalis Principia Mathematica* by the marquise du Châtelet-Lomont is published posthumously (the marquise died in 1749 at age 43).

1760

A Russian army surprises Berlin October 9 and burns it in 3 days before retreating at news that Frederick the Great is rushing to relieve the city.

Britain's George II dies October 25 at age 77. His grandson George William Frederick, 22, assumes the throne as George III to begin a disastrous 60-year reign.

Theater: Peg Woffington dies at London March 26 at age 42 (approximate) (*see* Reade novel, 1853).

The first practical roller skates are introduced at London by Belgian musical instrument maker Joseph Merlin, who rolls into a masquerade party at Carlisle House in Soho Square playing a violin. Strapped to his feet, his *skaites* each have two

wheels in line attached to their soles, but the wheels have no ball bearings and are almost impossible to control. Unable to stop or turn, Merlin crashes into a large mirror valued at more than £500, smashes it to pieces, breaks his fiddle, and severely injures himself (*see* 1863).

1761

Britain's new king, George III, marries Charlotte Sophia, 16, niece of the Duke of Mecklenburg-Strelitz, who will bear him 15 children. He threatens to withdraw the subsidies that have enabled Prussia's Frederick the Great to withstand coalition forces in the Seven Years' War, which has cost hundreds of thousands of lives.

American Quakers exclude slave traders despite that fact that many in the Society of Friends are slave owners.

Fiction: *La Nouvelle Héloïse* by French philosopher Jean-Jacques Rousseau, 49, is about a man of low position who marries a young woman of higher station. Rousseau himself took a fancy in his early 30s to one Thérèse Levassour, a servant at the inn where he lived, seduced her, told her that while he would not marry, he would not desert her (she was neither pretty, clever, nor charming, was barely literate, could not tell time, count money, or name the months of the year in proper order, but bore him five children, who were turned over to a foundling home. He will marry her in 1768). Like Voltaire and many other French intellectuals and artists, Rousseau has received support from the king's mistress, Mme. de Pompadour.

1762

The Russian czarina Elizabeth Petrovna dies January 5 at age 52 after a 20-year reign and is succeeded by her imbecilic son of 33, who ascends the throne as Peter III. A military coup overthrows Peter in July; put to death July 18, he is succeeded by his widow Sophia-Augusta of Anhalt-Zerbst, 33, a convert to the Orthodox church who has changed her name to Catherine (Ekaterina Alekseevna) and will reign with "benevolent despotism" until 1796 as "the Semiramis of the North" (in Voltaire's phrase).

Lady Mary Wortley Montagu returns to England in mid-January after nearly 23 years abroad but dies of breast cancer August 21 at age 73.

Nonfiction: *The Social Contract* (*Contrat social*) by Jean-Jacques Rousseau, who writes, "Man is born free, and everywhere is in chains."

Fiction: *Emile, ou Traité de l'education* by Jean-Jacques Rousseau, who writes, "A perfect man and a perfect woman should no more resemble each other in mind than in countenance. . . . It is the part of one to be active and strong, and of the other to be passive and weak. Accept this principle and it follows in the second place that woman is intended to please man. . . . For this reason [women's] education must be wholly directed to their relations with men. To give them pleasure, to be useful to them, to win their love and esteem, to train them in their childhood, to care for them when they grow up." Of the ideal wife, he says, "Her dignity consists in being unknown to the world; her glory is in the esteem of her husband; her pleasures in the happiness of her family" (I); "It is not enough that a wife should be faithful: her husband, along with his friends and neighbors, must believe in her fidelity" (V).

"There is nothing that so much seduces reason from vigilance as the thought of passing life with an amiable woman," British lexicographer Doctor (Samuel) Johnson, 53, writes December 21 in a letter to Joseph Baretti.

Le Petit Trianon goes up at Versailles as a gift from Louis XV to his mistress, Mme. de Pompadour, who has diverted the king by installing at Trianon a farmyard and dairy, a menagerie, and a botanical garden that includes a conservatory planted with specimens brought from all over the world, including orange, lemon, olive, and oleander trees and the first strawberries grown in France.

1763

The Treaty of Paris signed February 10 ends Europe's Seven Years' War. Mme. de Pompadour, who has been vested with virtually all the powers of

a prime minister, sees France regain territories in Africa and India, plus the sugar-rich islands of Guadeloupe and Martinique in the West Indies, while losing to Britain her territories in Canada, plus Grenada in the West Indies and Senegal in West Africa.

"Sir, a woman preaching is like a dog's walking on his hind legs. It is not done well; but you are surprised to find it done at all," says Doctor Johnson July 31 (as quoted by his biographer, James Boswell).

Poetry: "On a Hyacinth" (*"Over en hyancint"*) by Hedvig Nordenflycht, who dies at age 45. The first Swedish feminist, she has used poetry purely to express her inner feelings without restraint. Nordenflycht fell in love late in life with Johan Fischerström, nearly 20 years her younger, but he could not reciprocate her feelings.

English potter Josiah Wedgwood, 33, perfects a vitrified "cream-color ware" that is not true porcelain but gives Britain a hard tableware more durable than earthenware if not as handsome as the porcelain produced at Sèvres or Dresden.

1764

Mme. de Pompadour, still *maîtresse-en-titre* to France's Louis XV (although he has had many casual liaisons since 1749), falls ill with bronchial pneumonia at Choisy in late February and dies April 15 at age 42 after a career in which she has wielded enormous influence over the nation's foreign and domestic affairs.

The Sugar Act passed by Parliament April 5 cuts in half the sixpence per gallon duty on molasses imported into British colonies from non-British islands in the West Indies. London sends customs officials to America and orders colonial governors to enforce the new law, but Boston lawyer James Otis, 39, denounces "taxation without representation" May 24 and urges the colonies to unite in opposition to any new British tax laws. Boston merchants organize a boycott of British luxury goods in August, initiating a policy of nonimportation.

Mme. de Pompadour (above) is possessed of only 37 gold louis in cash at her death, having spent nearly 37 million livres on châteaux, estates (she has owned 17 at various times, some purchased as investments), houses, trees, flowers, furnishings, lavish gifts, and the like. Much of her income was derived from investments in industrial enterprises, gambling, and shares in the prize money of privateers that she helped fit out to prey upon British shipping.

Painting: *Bacchus and Chloë* by neoclassicist Swiss painter and graphic artist Angelica Kauffmann, 23, who is a protégée of Sir Joshua Reynolds.

1765

The Quartering Act passed by Parliament May 15 orders colonists to provide barracks and supplies for British troops in America.

Commentaries on the Laws of England by English jurist William Blackstone, 42, says in its chapter "Of Husband and Wife," "By marriage, the husband and wife are one person in law; that is, the very being or legal existence of the woman is suspended during the marriage, or at least is incorporated and consolidated into that of the husband; under whose wing, protection, and *cover*, she performs every thing; . . . Upon this principle, of an union of person in husband and wife, depend almost all the legal rights, duties, and disabilities that either of them acquire by marriage. . . . A man cannot grant any thing to his wife, or enter into covenant with her: for the grant would be to suppose her separate existence; . . . A woman indeed may be attorney for her husband; for that implies no separation from, but is rather a representation of her lord. And a husband may also bequeath any thing to his wife by will; for that cannot take effect till the coverture is determined by his death. The husband is bound to provide his wife with necessaries by law, as much as himself: and if she contracts debts for them, he is obliged to pay them; but for any thing besides necessaries, he is not chargeable. . . . If the wife be indebted before marriage, the husband is bound afterward to pay the debt; for he has adopted her and her circumstances together. The husband also (by the old law) might give his wife moderate correction. For, as he is to answer for her misbehaviour, the law thought it reasonable to intrust him with this power of restraining her, by

domestic chastisement. . . . But, with us, in the politer reign of Charles the second, this power of correction began to be doubted: and a wife may now have security of the peace against her husband; or, in return, a husband against his wife. . . . These are the chief legal effects of marriage during the coverture; upon which we may observe, that even the disabilities, which the wife lies under, are for the most part intended for her protection and benefit. So great a favourite is the female sex of the laws of England."

The Westminster New Lying-in Hospital is founded at London, where wives of tradesmen and artisans are turning more and more to male physicians rather than midwives to deliver their infants.

Irish-American religious leader Barbara Heck (*née* Ruckle), 31, organizes the first Methodist Church in America, at New York.

Doctor Johnson, the English lexicographer, meets the tall, taciturn brewer Henry Thrale, 37, and his "Blue Stocking" wife Hester Lynch (*née* Salusbury), 24, in January and is invited to take up residence in their house at Streatham, Surrey, where he will continue to live for 16 years, attracting figures such as Sir Joshua Reynolds, Oliver Goldsmith, David Garrick, Fanny Burney, and Edmund Burke as the short, plump, lively, intelligent Mrs. Thrale makes her home an intellectual salon. ("Blue Stockings"—so called because they wear ordinary clothes to their meetings—will have no part of cards, gambling, and other foolish pastimes but rather try to imitate French salons.)

1766

Denmark's Frederick V dies January 14 at age 42 and is succeeded by his semi-idiot son of 16, who marries Caroline Matilda, 15-year-old daughter of the prince of Wales, and sinks into debauchery. He will reign at least nominally until 1808 as Christian VII.

Russia's Catherine the Great grants freedom of worship.

Nonfiction: *Sermons to Young Women* by English clergyman James Fordyce, who writes, "Men of the best sense have been usually adverse to the thought of marrying a witty female." His conduct book will go through 14 editions by 1815.

"Let them eat cake" [if there is no bread], writes Jean-Jacques Rousseau in his *Confessions*. He attributes the remark to "a great princess," but it will be widely ascribed in the 1780s and '90s to the Viennese princess Marie-Antoinette, now 11, who will become queen of France in 1774.

the powers of landowners over their serfs and plans for comprehensive education.

 Painting: *Portrait of Sir Joshua Reynolds* by Angelica Kauffmann.

1767

 Russia's Catherine the Great appoints a commission of 564 deputies—landowners, burghers, administrators, Cossacks, and ethnic minorities (but no clergymen or serfs)—to make recommendations for the modernization of the empire, with limits on

Catherine the Great gave Russia benevolent despotism, extending her country's borders and opening them to the oppressed.

1768

 France purchases Corsica from Genoa May 15, but Louis XV has lost most of his colonial empire, has taxed the people heavily to maintain his luxurious lifestyle, and is widely hated. He has recently become enamored of a Paris seamstress's bastard daughter, the beautiful Jeanne Bécu, 22, who worked as a prostitute for the roué Guillaume du Barry before meeting the king and is known as the comtesse du Barry (*see* 1769).

 Le Petit Trianon is completed at Versailles, where it was designed for the late Mme. de Pompadour.

 The price of bread at Paris reaches 4 sous per pound and a placard appears in the city: "Under Henri IV bread was sometimes expensive because of war and France had a king; under Louis XIV it sometimes went up because of war and sometimes because of famine and France had a king; now there is no war and no famine and the cost of bread still goes up and France has no king because the king is a grain merchant." Critics deplore government regulations that discourage French farmers from increasing their grain acreage and demand free circulation of grain.

1769

 France's Louis XV installs the comtesse du Barry as his *maîtresse-en-titre* April 23—4 days after her 23rd birthday (the king is 59). Although snubbed by the court, she gains such power that for the next 6 years she will virtually reign as the uncrowned queen. Queen Marie Leszczynska dies June 25 at age 66, plunging the court into mourning.

 Virginia's House of Burgesses issues resolutions May 16 rejecting Parliament's right to tax British colonists. The body is dissolved by the angry governor but its members meet privately and agree not to import any dutiable goods.

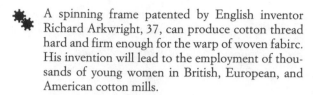 A spinning frame patented by English inventor Richard Arkwright, 37, can produce cotton thread hard and firm enough for the warp of woven fabirc. His invention will lead to the employment of thousands of young women in British, European, and American cotton mills.

Painting: *Interview of Hector and Andromache* by Angelica Kauffmann, who has become a fashionable London portrait painter and decorator. She is a member of the newly-founded Royal Academy of Art, headed by her mentor, Sir Joshua Reynolds.

1770

The Boston Massacre March 5 leaves three dead, two mortally wounded, and six injured following a fracas between colonists and British troops. Agitators use the incident to arouse rancor against the British.

Marie-Antoinette, 14, daughter of the Austrian empress Maria Theresa, marries the 15-year-old grandson of Louis XV May 16 at Versailles.

The Royal Society's *Journals and Observations, Physical and Literary* publishes a description of the gardenia species that will be credited to Scottish naturalist Alexander Garden but was actually discovered and named by the late colonial botanist Jane Colden (Mrs. William Farquar), who died 4 years ago at age 42 shortly after the death of her only child. Trained in botany by her father, Cadwallader Colden, who studied medicine in Scotland before emigrating to the New York colony (he served several times as royal acting governor), she had catalogued more than 300 regional plant specimens by 1757, illustrating many of them, but her father did not teach her Latin because he did not think women capable of learning the language.

Painting: *Vortigern and Rowena* by Angelica Kauffmann, who was secretly married in 1767 to the adventurer "Count Van Horn"; the revelation of his bigamy has led to her public humiliation; *Allegory of Music* by French painter Anne Vallayer-Coster, 26, who wins unanimous acceptance as a member of the Académie Royale.

Marie-Antoinette, the Austrian princess, married the ill-fated French dauphin who became Louis XVI. FROM A PAINTING BY MARIE ELISABETH VIGÉE-LEBRUN

Britain's 13 American colonies have an estimated population of 2.2 million, up from 1.6 million in 1760.

1771

English agriculturist Arthur Young writes, "Everyone but an idiot knows that the lower classes must be kept poor or they will never be industrious . . . they must like all mankind be in poverty or they will not work."

Painting: *The White Soup Bowl* by Anne Vallayer-Coster.

Scottish physician-novelist Tobias Smollett dies September 17 at age 50 after completing his novel *The Expedition of Humphry Clinker*, in which his hero, Matthew Bramble, writes to a friend that "the bread I eat in London is a deleterious paste, mixed up with chalk, alum, and bone-ashes, insipid to the taste, and destructive to the constitution. The good people are not ignorant of this adulteration, but they prefer it to wholesome bread because it is whiter than the meal of corn: thus they sacrifice their taste and their health and the lives of their tender infants, to a most absurd gratification of a misjudging eye."

1772

The Royal Marriage Act passed by Parliament requires the king's consent to the union of any member of the royal family and makes an unsanctioned marriage invalid.

Boston patriot Samuel Adams, 50, and local physician Joseph Warren, 31, organize a Committee of Correspondence November 2; similar committees spring up throughout the colonies, relaying the anti-British polemics of Adams and others.

The *Massachusetts Spy* publishes in two installments *The Adulateur*, an anonymous drama lampooning colonial governor Thomas Hutchinson. Its author will prove to be Mercy Otis Warren, 43.

The worst epidemic of puerperal (childbed) fever ever seen kills women all over Europe (*see* White, 1773).

1773

Virginia's House of Burgesses appoints a Provincial Committee of Correspondence March 12 to keep Virginia in touch with the other colonies.

The Tea Act passed by Parliament May 10 lightens duties on tea imported into Britain but permits tea to be shipped at full duty to the American colonies and to be sold directly to retailers, eliminating colonial middlemen and undercutting their prices. The Boston Tea Party December 16 demonstrates against the new law: men disguised as Mohawks board East India Company ships at Griffen's Wharf and throw 242 chests of tea, valued at more than £9,650, into Boston Harbor.

The *Boston Gazette* publishes *The Defeat*, an anonymous drama by propagandist Mercy Otis Warren that continues the theme begun last year in *The Adulateur*.

Treatise on the Management of Pregnant Women and Lying-in Women, and the Means of Curing, But More Especially of Preventing the Principal Disorders to Which They Are Liable by English surgeon Charles White at Manchester devotes its first chapter to "The Causes and Symptoms of the Puerperal or Child-bed Fever" (*see* 1772). White describes the customary practices following birth, saying, "As soon as she is delivered, if she be a person in affluent circumstances, she is covered up close in bed with additional clothes, the curtains are drawn round the bed and pinned together, every crevice in the windows and doors is closed, not excepting even the keyhole . . . and the good woman is not permitted to put her arm or even her nose out of bed for fear of catching cold. She is constantly supplied out of the spouts of a teapot with large quantities of warm liquors, to keep up perspiration and sweat, and her whole diet consists of them. She is confined to the horizontal position for many days together, whereby both the stools and the lochia are prevented from having a free exit. . . . The lochia, stagnating in the womb and the folds of the vagina, soon grow putrid . . ." Denouncing such practices, White advocates adequate ventilation and scrupulous cleanliness on the part of all attendants and also of towels, bed linens, and instruments. After birth, he says, a woman should be placed in an upright position so that her uterus can drain and she should be allowed to get up as soon as possible, usually on the second day. His advice is regarded as revolutionary (*see* Gordon, 1795).

Poetry: *Poems on Various Subjects, Religious and Moral, by Phillis Wheatley, Negro, Servant to Mr. John Wheatley of Boston, in New England* is published at London (no American edition will appear until 1784). Brought to Boston from her native Senegal when she was 7 or 8 and purchased as a slave at Boston, Wheatley is now about 20. She was frail and asthmatic as a child, and her owners, defy-

Phillis Wheatley came to Boston as a slave, learned to read, and became a celebrated poet. LIBRARY OF CONGRESS

ing the law and local custom, began to teach her to read. She was reading Scripture and English classics by age 12 and last year was given her freedom. John Wheatley finances her voyage to London, where she is presented to society.

1774

France's Louis XV dies of smallpox May 10 at age 64 after a reign of nearly 59 years, mourned by his final mistress, Mme. du Barry, now 31, who bravely kissed his hands May 3 when she first noticed the pustules on them. His grandson, now 19, will rule until 1792 as Louis XVI with his wife, Marie-Antoinette, as queen. Cardinal de la Roche Aymon, grand almoner of France, has forced the dying king to dictate a *lettre de cachet* ordering that the comtesse du Barry be sent as a prisoner of state to

the ancient Abbaye de Pont aux Dames, where she will remain for nearly a year, winning the friendship of the nuns and even of the stern abbess.

A new Quartering Act passed by Parliament June 2 updates the 1765 act. The coercive new law requires American colonists to house British troops in their barns or public inns where barracks are not available.

The first Continental Congress assembles at Philadelphia September 5 with all colonies except Georgia represented.

New York colony administrator William Johnson dies, bequeathing his estate to his "prudent & faithfull Housekeeper" Mary (Kaonwatsi-tsiaienni), 38, and the eight children she has borne him since 1759, the year his first wife, Katherine (*née* Weisenburg), died. A Mohawk woman, she and her family have helped Johnson manage the Six Nations and hold them to the British cause against the French. She will be a staunch Loyalist in the next 7 years, keeping the Iroquois on the side of the British.

Use of ergot, the *Claviceps purpura* (clubheaded purple) fungus that grows on rye and other stored grains, is reported for the first time in medical literature as a means of inducing labor in childbirth. It has long been employed by midwives for that purpose because it produces strong and unremitting cervical contractions (*see* 1822).

English religious mystic Ann Lee, 38, settles on a tract of land northeast of Albany in the New York colony and introduces "Shakerism" into America. A member of the Shaking Quaker sect, Lee abandoned her Manchester blacksmith husband after losing four children in quick succession. She is given to hysterics, convulsions, and hallucinations, denounces sex as a "filthy gratification," calls a consummated marriage "a covenant with death and an agreement with hell," preaches celibacy, and establishes a following (*see* 1784).

Letters to His Son by the late Philip Dormer Stanhope, fourth earl of Chesterfield, are published (against his wishes) by his widow a year after the earl's death at age 79. Chesterfield was married at age 39 to Melousina von Schlumberg, an illegitimate daughter of the late George I who was herself nearly 40 and had as her only attraction the fact that she was possessed of £50,000 plus an annual income of £3,000 (they lived from the start in adjoining houses, and Chesterfield celebrated his marriage by taking as his mistress Lady Frances Shirley, a great beauty). The earl's illegitimate son Philip, born of an intimacy with Elizabeth du Bouchet while he was serving as ambassador to The Hague, died in 1668 at age 36, leaving an unattractive widow of whose existence (and humble origin) his father had been blissfully unaware until the young man's death. His witty and cynical letters helped his son fill diplomatic posts and a seat in Parliament obtained for him by Lord Chesterfield: "Women who are either indisputably beautiful, or indisputably ugly, are best flattered upon the score of their understandings; but those who are in a state of mediocrity, are best flattered upon their beauty, for every woman who is not absolutely ugly thinks herself handsome" (9/5/48); "Women are only children of a larger growth; they have an entertaining tattle, and sometimes wit, but for solid, reasoning good sense, I never in my life knew one that had it, or who reasoned or acted consequentially for four-and-twenty hours together. A man of sense only trifles with them, plays with them, humours them, and flatters them, as he does with a sprightly, forward child; but he neither consults them about, nor trusts them with, serious matters, though he often makes them believe that he does both" (9/5/48); "Women are to be talked to as below men, and above children" (9/20/48); "Women are much more like each other than men: they have, in truth, but two passions, vanity and love; these are their universal characteristics" (12/19/49); "To take a wife merely as an agreeable and rational companion will commonly be found to be a grand mistake" (10/12/65). Since women have such great influence on other men that they can make or break one's reputation, Chesterfield has advised his son, "it is therefore absolutely necessary to manage, please, and flatter them and never to discover the least marks of contempt, which is what they never forgive." "He who flatters them most pleases them best, and they are most in love with him who they think is most in love with them."

"If Fate had given me in youth a husband whom I could have loved, I should have remained always true to him," Russia's Catherine the Great writes in a letter to her favorite, Prince Potemkin. "The trouble is that my heart would not willingly remain one hour without love."

 Painting: *Vase of Flowers with a Bust of Flora* by Anne Vallayer-Coster.

 Theater: *The Inflexible Captive* by English playwright Hannah More, 29, who has come to London from her native Bristol and joined the "Blue Stocking" set of Elizabeth Montagu. She was betrothed 7 years ago, her fiancé kept her dangling for 6 years and then settled £200 per year on her and took his leave.

1775

The American War of Independence begins at the Battle of Lexington April 19—just 2 weeks after publication of "The Group," a pamphlet by Mercy Otis Warren. John Adams has arranged for its printing and will later verify its authorship.

Cherokee chief Nancy Ward, 37, discourages her people from participating in the conflict on either side. She will save lives on both sides by warning the colonists of impending raids.

Mme. du Barry is released from the Abbaye de Pont aux Dames in May and purchases St. Vrain, a moated château with a lake on a large estate south of Paris, where she helps feed poor villagers through the cold winter. To visit the comtesse there risks incurring the wrath of Queen Marie-Antoinette, but one who takes that risk is Louis-Hercule-Timoléon de Cossé, 40, whose father, the duc de Brissac, is one of France's richest men.

 George III signs an order releasing from bondage the women and young children in British coal and salt mines. Many of the children are under 8, work like the women for 10 to 12 hours per day, and have been transferable with the collieries and saltworks when the properties changed hands or their masters had no further use for them.

Stop discrimination against women, says English-American pamphleteer Thomas Paine, 38, in his *Pennsylvania Magazine*. Paine has failed as a corsetmaker and tax collector in England, twice failed in marriage, and arrived at Philadelphia late last year with letters of introduction from Benjamin Franklin and encouragement to try his luck in America.

Painting: *Portrait of Count Shuvaloff* by Parisian painter (Marie-Louise) Elisabeth Vigée-Lebrun (*née* Vigée), 20, who has married local art dealer Jean-Baptiste-Pierre Lebrun (a chronic gambler, he will take much of her earnings). Her subject is the chamberlain to Russia's Catherine the Great at St. Petersburg.

Theater: Mrs. Malaprop delights audiences with "malapropisms" such as "headstrong as an allegory on the banks of the Nile" (III, iii) in *The Rivals* by Irish playwright Richard Brinsley Sheridan, 23, 1/17 at London's Royal Theatre in Covent Garden: "Thought does not become a young woman," says Mrs. Malaprop, but Sheridan says in an epilogue: "Through all the drama—whether damn'd or not—/ Love gilds the scene, and women guide the plot"; English actress Sarah Siddons (*née* Kemble), 20, makes her London debut in December playing the role of Portia in Shakespeare's 1596 tragedy *The Merchant of Venice* but is not well received and will work in the provinces until 1782.

Opera: Viennese soprano Catarina Cavalieri (Franziska Helena Appolonia Kavalier), 15, makes her debut 4/29 as Sandrina in Anfossi's *La finta giardiniera* at Vienna's Kärntnerthortheater.

Mrs. Thrale and her husband take Doctor Johnson to Paris on his only visit abroad. They visit Fontainebleau and see young Louis XVI and Marie-Antoinette at dinner.

Denmark's Queen Juliane Marie goes into partnership with some Copenhagen entrepreneurs to found the Royal Copenhagen Porcelain Manufactory, whose wares will be trademarked with three wavy blue lines. The queen will acquire full ownership in 1779.

1776

The Declaration of Independence is signed at Philadelphia July 4 (*see* 1777). Abigail Adams (*née* Smith), 31, at Boston has several months earlier written to her husband, John, at Philadelphia, "This intelligence will make a plain truth for you,

though a dangerous one. I could not join today in the petitions of our worthy pastor for a reconciliation between our no longer parent state, but tyrant state, and these Colonies. Let us separate: they are unworthy to be our brethren. Let us renounce them; and instead of supplications, as formerly, for their prosperity and happiness, let us beseech the Almighty to blast their counsels, and to bring to nought all their devices." Adams has written to her April 14, "Depend upon it. We know better than to repeal our Masculine systems. . . . We have only the Name of Masters, and rather than give up this, which would compleatly subject us to the Despotism of the Peticoat, I hope General Washington, and all our brave Heroes would fight."

Gen. William Howe, 46, lands with a British force at Kips Bay September 15 to occupy New York City. He stops in his pursuit of George Washington long enough to take tea with Mary Murray (*née* Linley), whose husband, Robert, is a successful merchant and loyal to the Crown. Their elegant farmhouse is on the Heights of Inklenberg, later to be called Murray Hill, and although she will be credited with having delayed Gen. Howe 2 hours or more by serving him and his aides cake and wine, thus permitting 3,500 men under Gen. Israel Putnam to escape with their guide, Aaron Burr, to Washington's lines on Harlem Heights, her intentions are to help the British, not the rebels.

New Jersey adopts a constitution July 2 which reaffirms the right of women worth $250 or more to vote, a privilege that they will enjoy until 1807 (but *see* New York, 1777).

Abigail Adams (above) writes to her husband, John, "[A]nd by the way, in the new code of laws which I suppose it will be necessary for you to make I desire you would Remember the Ladies, and be more generous to them than your ancestors. Do not put such unlimited power into the hands of the husbands. Remember, all men would be tyrants if they could. If particular care and attention is not paid to the ladies, we are determined to foment a revolution, and will not hold ourselves bound by any laws in which we have no voice or representation." When John Adams denies her petition and calls her saucy, she retorts, "I can not say that I think you very generous to the Ladies for whilst you are proclaiming peace and goodwill to Men, Eman-

Abigail Adams cautioned her husband, John, to be mindful of women in drawing up laws for a new nation. FROM A 1766 PAINTING BY BENJAMIN BLYTH

English courtesan Elizabeth Chudleigh, 56, is adjudged guilty of bigamy. Beautiful but illiterate, she had several affairs with courtiers of George II before being secretly married at age 24 to Augustus John Hervey, brother of the second earl of Bristol. She concealed the birth and death of a son, obtained a separation, denied the marriage on oath when being courted by the second duke of Kingston, married him in 1769, and inherited his estates when he died 3 years ago. His nephew has brought suit, and her marriage to Hervey (who has succeeded his brother as third earl of Bristol) will be declared valid next year.

The cocktail is invented (by some accounts) at an Elmsford, N.Y., tavern, where barmaid Elizabeth "Betsy" Flanagan decorates the bar she tends at Halls Corner with discarded tail feathers from poultry that has been roasted and served to patrons. An inebriated guest demands that she bring him "a glass of those cocktails," and Flanagan serves him a mixed drink garnished with one of the feathers.

Edinburgh surgeon John Hunter oversees the first successful attempt at human artificial insemination. He instructs a linen draper who suffers from hypospadias in how to impregnate his wife, using a warm syringe for the purpose.

cipating all Nations, you insist upon retaining absolute power over Wives."

"A woman of fortune, being used to the handling of money, spends it judiciously; but a woman who gets the command of money for the first time upon her marriage has such a gusto in spending it that she throws it away with great profusion," says Doctor Johnson March 28.

The comtesse du Barry receives permission in October to return to Paris and Louveciennes after 2½ years in exile. Having a huge income, she spends money lavishly on gifts to friends and family as she transforms Louveciennes into a country house for her relatives.

Poetry: A 42-line poem by Phillis Wheatley appears in the *Pennsylvania* magazine. It is addressed to Gen. Washington, with whom she has corresponded.

1777

The first official version of the Declaration of Independence, bearing the names of all signatories, appears in January at Baltimore. The Continental Congress, which fled to Baltimore from Philadelphia in December, has commissioned local printer Mary Katherine Goddard, 38, to print the document. Her brother William started the city's first newspaper, the *Maryland Journal*, 3 years ago, brought Mary in to run it while he served time in debtor's prison (he has gone broke trying to organize the colonial postal service). She is Baltimore's postmaster and its only printer, running not merely the newspaper but also the print shop, operating the presses herself. She pays post riders to have the Declaration delivered throughout the colonies.

The American garrison at Fort Ticonderoga abandons the fort in early July at news that British forces under Gen. Burgoyne are approaching, and he defeats the Continentals easily July 7 at Hubbarton, Vermont. One of Burgoyne's lieutenants, David Jones, is courting Jane McCrea, 22, the orphaned daughter of a Presbyterian minister, whom he has known since childhood. She has been living with her oldest brother at Fort Edward, down the Hudson from Fort Ticonderoga, and despite his pleas she elects to stay behind when most of the rebel sympathizers leave Fort Edwards for Albany. Visiting her friend, Mrs. Sarah McNeil, on the morning of July 27, she finds Mrs. McNeil frantically packing for the journey to Albany. Burgoyne has bribed the Iroquois to support him, a band of Iroquois arrives at the McNeil house, they turn Mrs. McNeil over to the British, but Jane McCrae's body is later found, naked, on a hill not far away. She has been scalped (the Indians later present her three-foot-long blonde scalp of hair to the British), shot four times, and bears numerous stab wounds. News of her death creates an outcry at London, Edmund Burke rises in the House of Commons to demand that the British Army stop using Indian agents, and thousands of colonists whose sympathies were uncertain are now moved to support the cause of the Revolution. Men flock to the colors of Gen. Benedict Arnold and Gen. Horatio Gates, who hand Burgoyne's now far-outnumbered forces a decisive defeat at Bemis Heights, near Saratoga, October 7. When news of the victory reaches Paris in September, the Americans are assured of French support, which will prove crucial in their struggle for independence.

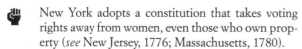 New York adopts a constitution that takes voting rights away from women, even those who own property (see New Jersey, 1776; Massachusetts, 1780).

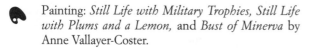 Painting: *Still Life with Military Trophies, Still Life with Plums and a Lemon,* and *Bust of Minerva* by Anne Vallayer-Coster.

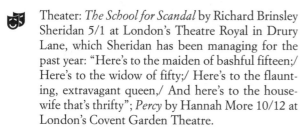 Theater: *The School for Scandal* by Richard Brinsley Sheridan 5/1 at London's Theatre Royal in Drury Lane, which Sheridan has been managing for the past year: "Here's to the maiden of bashful fifteen;/ Here's to the widow of fifty;/ Here's to the flaunting, extravagant queen,/ And here's to the housewife that's thrifty"; *Percy* by Hannah More 10/12 at London's Covent Garden Theatre.

"Molly Pitcher" won her soubriquet at the Battle of Monmouth in the American Revolution. LIBRARY OF CONGRESS

1778

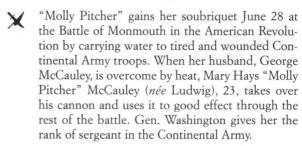 "Molly Pitcher" gains her soubriquet June 28 at the Battle of Monmouth in the American Revolution by carrying water to tired and wounded Continental Army troops. When her husband, George McCauley, is overcome by heat, Mary Hays "Molly Pitcher" McCauley (*née* Ludwig), 23, takes over his cannon and uses it to good effect through the rest of the battle. Gen. Washington gives her the rank of sergeant in the Continental Army.

Virginia property owner Hannah Lee Corbin writes to her brother, Gen. Richard Henry "Lighthorse Harry" Lee, 46, to protest the taxation of women since they are not permitted to vote. He replies that Virginia women, like women in some other colonies, do have that right (*see* 1777).

Fiction: *Evelina, or the History of a Young Lady's Entry into the World* by English novelist Fanny (Frances) Burney, 26, is published anonymously. Burney, who has been encouraged by Mrs. Thrale and Doctor Johnson, virtually invents the social novel of domestic life.

The comtesse du Barry, now 35, begins an affair with Henry Seymour, 50, a nephew of the duke of Somerset and half brother to the earl of Sandwich, who occupies a small château near Louveciennes with his French wife, an infant son, and a grown daughter by a previous marriage.

English novelist Fanny Burney's Evelina, *published anonymously when she was 26, broke new ground.*

1779

Gen. James Clinton participates in a punitive expedition against the Iroquois allies of Britain in the continuing American Revolution and concludes, "Bad as the savages are, they never violate the chastity of any women their prisoners" (*see* 1777).

Painting: *Marie-Antoinette* by Elisabeth Vigée-Lebrun, whose charm and beauty have won the queen's friendship as well as her patronage.

1780

Maria Theresa of Austria, Hungary, and Bohemia dies of smallpox November 28 at age 63, leaving her son Josef free to rule alone (he has visited Russia's Catherine the Great in April against his mother's wishes).

The Holy Roman Emperor Josef II abolishes serfdom in Bohemia and Hungary, completing work begun by his late mother.

Massachusetts adopts a constitution that deprives women of their voting rights (*see* New York, 1777; New Hampshire, 1784).

London dancer Emma Hart (*née* Emily Lyon), 19, is billed as the "goddess of health" and directs the sensuous revels at a Temple of Health opened by English saddler's son James Graham with incense burners, flame-breathing dragons, lascivious paintings, and a Celestial Bed erected on 40 glass pillars with numerous electrical devices intended to rejuvenate the impotent and permit the childless to conceive. Graham, who has visited Philadelphia and heard about Benjamin Franklin's experiments with electricity, has obtained backing from the duchess of Devonshire (*see* marriage to Hamilton, 1791).

Of 21,000 children born in Paris, 17,000 are sent to the country to be wet-nursed, 3,000 placed in nursery homes, 700 wet-nursed at home, and only 700 suckled by their own mothers, who risk the scorn of society.

Fiction: *The Chapter of Accidents* by English writer Sophia Lee, 30, whose novel is so successful that she is able to open a school for girls at Bath.

The death of the duc de Brissac, Maréchal de France, at year's end makes his only surviving son, the duc de Cossé, now 46, one of the nation's richest men; the new duc de Brissac takes as his mistress Mme. du Barry, whose relationship with Henry Seymour has become strained.

1781

The American Revolution ends October 19 with the surrender of Gen. Cornwallis at Yorktown, Virginia, but only after some bloody encounters (*see* 1782).

Russia's Catherine the Great signs a treaty with the Holy Roman Emperor Josef II promising him the entire eastern half of the Balkans. She seeks to drive the Ottoman Turks out of Europe and establish her 2-year-old grandson Constantine as head of a new Greek empire.

💲 Doctor Johnson, now 71, is obliged to move out of his friend Mrs. Thrale's house in Surrey following the death in March of her husband, Henry, who has squandered a fortune trying to manufacture an antifouling compound for preserving ships' bottoms and trying to brew beer without hops. Mrs. Thrale, who determined years ago to overlook her husband's marital infidelities, helped Henry's accountant recover from the financial disaster. An executor of the brewer's will, Johnson helps arrange the sale of his Anchor Brewery. Mrs. Thrale, who nearly suffers a nervous breakdown, will marry Gabriel Piozzi, an accomplished musician.

1782

✗ Massachusetts schoolteacher Deborah Samson, 21, outfits herself in men's clothing and joins Capt. Nathan Thayer's company of volunteers under the name "Robert Surtlieff." She will serve for 18 months and be wounded twice before "brain fever" takes her out of action and her sex is discovered.

British forces evacuate Savannah in July and Charleston in December but will continue to occupy New York until November of next year.

✒ Fiction: *Cecilia* by Fanny Burney; *Sara Burgerhart* by Dutch novelists Elisabeth Wolff (*née* Bekker), 44, and Agatha Deken, 41.

🎭 Theater: Sarah Siddons returns to London's Drury Lane Theatre in October as Isabella in David Garrick's adaptation of Thomas Southerne's 1694 play *The Fatal Marriage,* scores an immediate success, and will be hailed as the queen of the London stage for the next 30 years (*see* 1775; 1803).

🎼 Opera: Catarina Cavalieri creates the role of Constanze in W. A. Mozart's new opera *The Abduction from the Seraglio* (*Die Entführung aus dem Serail*) 7/16 at Vienna.

Sarah Siddons reigned for 30 years as queen of the London stage, famous for her tragic roles. LIBRARY OF CONGRESS

1783

✗ Parliament votes February 24 to abandon further prosecution of the war against Britain's American colonies; Congress proclaims victory in the American War of Independence April 19.

Russia's Catherine the Great annexes the Crimea, which her favorite, Grigori Aleksandrovich Potemkin, 44, has conquered from the Ottoman Turks, expels the Turks, and offers a large grant of land to the Mennonites, promising them religious freedom and exemption from military service.

🎨 French painters Adelaïde Labille-Guiard, 33, and Elisabeth Vigée-Lebrun are admitted to membership in the Académie Royale May 31 (the Académie has a rule against allowing more than four female members at any one time). Labille-Guiard, who first exhibited her work 9 years ago at the Académie de

San Luc in Paris with support from Mme. du Barry, has taken a number of female pupils and is building a network of women artists. She separated from her husband, Louis Nicolas Guiard, in 1779 after 10 years of marriage but continues to sign her work "Labille f[emme] Guiard" (*see* 1785).

1784

✗ The U.S. Congress, meeting at Annapolis, ratifies the Treaty of Paris January 14, bringing the War of Independence to a formal end.

✊ New Hampshire adopts a constitution that deprives women of their right to vote (*see* Massachusetts, 1780).

∞ Shaker leader Mother Ann Lee dies at Watervliet, N.Y., September 8 at age 48, disappointing zealous followers who had believed her to be immortal. Shakerism will continue in America, setting an example with inventive, orderly methods of building, toolmaking, and furniture making, animal husbandry, cooking, and production of woodenware, yarns, textiles, and botanical herbs. They will develop the Poland China hog and innovate the practice of retailing garden seeds in small, labeled paper packets.

✒ Poetry: "Green Grow the Rashes" by Scottish poet Robert Burns, who writes, "What signifies the life o' man,/ And 'twere na for the lasses?"

🎨 Painting: *The Family of King Ferdinand IV and Queen Maria Carolina* by Angelica Kauffmann.

🎼 Italian violinist Regina Strinsacchi (Strina Sacchi), 20, scores a great success at Vienna with two concerts after several years of traveling through the Italian states. W. A. Mozart performs with her in her second Vienna concert and composes one of his finest sonatas for the occasion.

👪 Abortion and infanticide become common among the poor of Japan as famine discourages large families.

1785

✗ The affair of the diamond necklace creates a sensation in France beginning August 15 when Cardinal de Rohan-Guémenée, 51, is arrested as he prepares to officiate at Assumption Day services for Louis XVI and Marie-Antoinette. His mistress, Jeanne de Valois, comtesse de La Motte, 29, has led him to believe that the queen is enamored of him and has authorized him to buy a necklace of diamonds collected by the Paris jewelry firm Boehmer and Bassenge, intended originally for Mme. du Barry. The comtesse has presented the jewelers with notes signed by the cardinal, they have complained to the queen, she has told Boehmer that she never ordered the necklace and certainly never received it, the comtesse is also arrested, and much of France chooses not to believe the queen. The case will be tried before the parlement next year.

English widow Maria Anne Fitzherbert (*née* Smyth), 29, is married secretly in mid-December to the Prince of Wales, 23, although the marriage is invalid under terms of the 1772 Royal Marriage Act since it was contracted without the king's permission. Because she is a Roman Catholic, the danger of Mrs. Fitzherbert's bearing a child who may one day claim the throne will be a source of gossip and concern for years to come (*see* 1795).

💲 Congress establishes the dollar as the official currency of the new United States, employing a decimal system devised by Thomas Jefferson.

✒ Fiction: *Willem Leevend* by Elisabeth Wolff and Agatha Deken.

🎨 Painter Adelaïde Labille-Guiard leads a protest against the Académie Royale's rule limiting female membership to four, fails to overturn the rule, and holds an exhibition of her own for women artists, whose work is thereupon attacked by critics (*see* 1783). She has lobbied for government-subsidized art education for women.

🎼 Opera: Italian soprano Maria Mandini creates the role of Marcellina in Wolfgang Amadeus Mozart's opera *The Marriage of Figaro* (*Le Nozze de Figaro*) 5/1 at Vienna's Burgtheater; Mozart has written the role (and the aria "Il capro e la capretta") with Mandini's singing voice in mind; Italian mezzo-soprano Celeste Coltellini, 25, comes to Vienna at the urging of the emperor Josef II and sings 8/6 in the Cimarossa opera *La Contadina in Spirito* (W. A. Mozart will write soprano parts for her in a quartet and a trio).

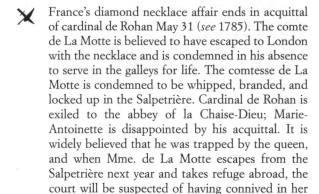

A *Classical Dictionary of the Vulgar Tongue*, published at London, defines a condom as "the dried gut of a sheep, worn by men in the act of coition, to prevent venereal infection." No mention is made of the condom's use to prevent pregnancy, that being regarded as a woman's concern, not a man's.

1786

France's diamond necklace affair ends in acquittal of cardinal de Rohan May 31 (*see* 1785). The comte de La Motte is believed to have escaped to London with the necklace and is condemned in his absence to serve in the galleys for life. The comtesse de La Motte is condemned to be whipped, branded, and locked up in the Salpetrière. Cardinal de Rohan is exiled to the abbey of la Chaise-Dieu; Marie-Antoinette is disappointed by his acquittal. It is widely believed that he was trapped by the queen, and when Mme. de La Motte escapes from the Salpetrière next year and takes refuge abroad, the court will be suspected of having connived in her escape (she will die in a drunken fall from a third-floor window in 1791).

1787

A Constitutional Convention that has been meeting at Philadelphia draws up a Constitution for the new United States of America. It establishes a bicameral legislature rather than a parliament and provides for legislators and a chief executive to be elected for limited terms rather than for life.

Russia's Catherine the Great begins a second war with the Ottoman Empire, using Turkish intrigues with the Crimean Tatars as an excuse to pursue her objective of obtaining Georgia.

Painting: *Marie-Antoinette and Her Children* and *The Marquise de Pezé and the Marquise de Rouget and her Two Children* by Elisabeth Vigée-Lebrun; *The Piano Lesson* (date approximate) by French painter Marguerite Gérard, 26, a sister-in-law of Jean Honoré Fragonard, 55.

1788

The Parlement at Paris presents Louis XVI with a list of grievances as the country suffers its worst economic chaos of the century. The king calls the Estates-General to assemble in May of next year for the first time since 1614.

The United States Constitution takes effect June 21 as New Hampshire becomes the ninth state to ratify it.

Observations on the New Constitution and on the Federal Union by "A Columbian Patriot" expresses the anti-Federalist views of Mercy Otis Warren, now close to 60, who would have preferred "a union of the states on the free principles of the late Confederation."

Nonfiction: *Thoughts on Society* by Hannah Moore; *Lettres sur le caractère et les ecrits de J.-J. Rousseau* by French libertine Mme. Germaine de Staël (*née* Anne-Louise-Germaine Necker), 22, whose 2-year-old marriage to the Swedish ambassador has turned sour. Daughter of the finance minister Jacques Necker, Mme. de Staël is becoming notorious for her love affairs.

Painting: *Portrait of Hubert Robert* by Elisabeth Vigée-Lebrun; *An Architect and His Family* by Marguerite Gérard (date approximate).

Opera: Catarina Cavalieri sings the role of Donna Elvira in a performance of W. A. Mozart's 1787 opera *Don Giovanni* 5/7 at Vienna. Now 28, Cavalieri has one eye, is considered spectacularly ugly, and is a poor actress, but Mozart has written an extra aria for her.

1789

A French revolution begins July 14 as a mob of 32,000, including hundreds of women, storms the Bastille prison, symbol of royal tyranny.

A Paris mob riots from October 5 to 6 and a revolutionary band, mostly women, marches to Versailles. Gen. Lafayette rescues the royal family and moves it to Paris. The price of bread reaches 4.5 sous per pound at Paris in July, and in some places it is 6 sous per pound. Widespread unemployment has reduced the people's ability to avoid starvation, but the National Assembly permits duty-free grain imports to relieve the hunger.

Japan bans streetwalkers and requires prostitutes at Edo to move into the Yoshiwara section established in 1617. Some 2,000 move into the area within a few days (mixed bathing is also prohibited, and public bathhouses separate men from women).

Fiction: *The Castles of Athlin and Dunbayne* by English Gothic novelist Ann Radcliffe (*née* Ward), 25, whose Oxford-educated husband, William, owns and edits the weekly *English Chronicle*.

Painter Elisabeth Vigée-Lebrun leaves for Italy at the outbreak of the Revolution (above). She will arrive at London in 1802, paint celebrities including Lord Byron and the Prince of Wales, and not return to Paris until 1805.

1790

France's marquis de Condorcet proposes July 3 that women be granted civil rights.

"On the Equality of the Sexes" by Boston writer Judith Sargent Murray, 39, appears in the *Massachusetts* magazine. "It is true," she says, "some ignoramuses have, absurdly enough, informed us, that the beauteous fair of paradise, was seduced from her obedience, by a malignant demon, *in the guise of a baleful serpent*; but we, who are better informed, know that the fallen spirit presented himself to her view, *a shining angel still*; for thus, saith the criticks in the Hebrew tongue, ought the word to be rendered. Let us examine her motive. . . . It doth not appear that she was governed by any one sensual appetite, but merely by a desire of adorning her mind; a laudable ambition fired her soul, and a thirst for knowledge impelled the predilection so fatal in its consequences. Adam could not plead the same deception; assuredly, he was not deceived; nor ought we to admire his superior strength, or wonder at his sagacity, when we so often confess that example is much more influential than precept . . ." Murray will claim that she wrote it in 1779.

The colony of "Jerusalem" is founded in upstate New York by U.S. religious leader Jemima Wilkinson, 39, who favors celibacy (year approximate).

Letters on Education by English reformer Catherine Macaulay, 59, expresses the notion that when the two sexes receive equal education the outcome will be intellectual equality. "Moreover, whenever significantly intellectual sex differences emerge they can be readily explained in terms of differences in education."

Fiction: *A Sicilian Romance* by Ann Radcliffe.

Poetry: *Fugitive Verses* by Scottish poet Joanna Baillie, 28; "Beacon Hill" by Boston poet Sarah Wentworth Morton (*née* Apthorp), 31, whose husband, Perez, had an affair 2 years ago with her sister, Frances, that ended with Frances taking her own life. Her poem in the *Columbia Centinel* December 4 celebrates events that transpired at Boston Hill during the War of Independence.

Painting: *Portrait of Madame de Cenlis* by Adelaïde Labille-Guiard; *Innocence between Virtue and Vice* by French painter Marie Guillemine Lerouix de la Ville, 22, a student of Jacques Louis David, who will marry royalist Pierre Vincent Benoist in 1793; *Queen Charlotte and Miss Farren* (actress Elizabeth Farren, 29) by English painter Thomas Lawrence, 21.

1791

France enacts a law providing for the state to take over the responsibility for feeding abandoned children as the end of feudal rights also ends feudal obligations. Another law permits civil marriages, and there is agitation for legalized divorce.

Fiction: *The Romance of the Forest* by Ann Radcliffe. *Justine* by French pervert Donatien-Alphonse-François de Sade, 51, marquis de Sade, who has been confined for much of his life in prisons, partly for using Spanish fly made from the pulverized bodies of the blister beetle *Lytta vesicatoria,* which irritates the bladder and urethra. Sexual gratification by inflicting pain on a loved one is described by the marquis in his obscene novel and will be called "sadism." *Charlotte Temple—A Tale of Truth* by English-American novelist Susanna Caswell Rowson, 29, whose heroine is an English schoolgirl who is seduced by a British officer and taken to America, where she gives birth to a child and is abandoned.

Sir William Hamilton, the British ambassador to Naples, is persuaded by his mistress, Emma Lyon, now 30, to make her his wife (*see* Medicine, 1780). She and her mother, who called herself Mrs. Cadogan, came to London from their native Cheshire in the late 1770s, Emma became mistress to Sir Harry Fetherstonehaugh, someone impregnated her, Sir Harry suspected one of his guests of being the father, the guest introduced her to his rich uncle, Sir William, who offered to pay the nephew's debts in exchange for Emma, and he has taken her and her mother to Naples, where she has become a close friend of Queen Maria Carolina (*see* 1793).

Camembert cheese is invented, or reinvented, by French farmer's wife Marie-Fontaine Harel at Vimoutiers in the Department of Orne.

1792

A Parisian mob storms the Tuileries Palace August 10 at the instigation of Georges-Jacques Danton, 33, after Louis XVI orders his Swiss guards to stop firing on the people. Some 600 guardsmen are massacred, the king is confined in the Temple, and the Paris commune takes power under Danton.

Many French women enlist in the army to fight the Austrians (who have laid siege to Lille) and Prussians (who are defeated at Valmy September 20 with women, often dressed in rags, fighting in the front ranks alongside men). Heroines of the army include Reine Chapuy, Rose Bouillon, Catherine Pocheta, and the young Fernig sisters (*see* 1793).

The duc de Brissac is killed by the knives, scythes, and sabers of a mob en route to Versailles in late September; his mistress, the comtesse du Barry, now 51 (although she insists that she is 42), leaves for Calais October 19 together with the duchesse de Brancas, whose passport is in order, and the widowed duchesse d'Aiguillon, who has no passport and disguises herself as a maid. The group reaches London, where Mme. du Barry will remain for nearly 6 months.

Vindication of the Rights of Women by English writer Mary Wollstonecraft, 33, at London is a blunt attack on convention. Rejecting the notion, advanced by Rousseau, that women are inferior to men, Wollstonecraft argues that women should have the same opportunities in education and employment as men and be able to consort with them on equal terms. Daughter of a drunkard and wife beater who squandered his fortune, Wollstonecraft, who is largely self-educated, started a school 10 years ago but without success. She meets U.S. timber merchant Capt. Gilbert Imlay at Paris, where she goes to witness the Terror for a book, and will bear a daughter by him in 1794.

Mary Wollstonecraft asserted the rights of women, refuting the idea that they were intellectual inferiors. FROM A PAINTING BY JOHN OPIE, NATIONAL PORTRAIT GALLERY, LONDON

Paris has 5 days of rioting in January as the cost of living soars.

Katherine Greene (*née* Littlefield), 37, widow of Revolutionary War hero Gen. Nathanael Greene, who died 6 years ago at age 43, meets mechanical genius Eli Whitney, 26, aboard ship while he is en route to the Carolinas for a tutoring position. She invites him to her Georgia plantation, Mulberry Grove, on the Savannah River, and when she complains that her embroidery frame doesn't fit right he devises a new tambour that pleases her. She remarks that the locally grown upland short-staple cotton has green seeds that are difficult to separate from the lint, quite unlike the long-staple sea island cotton, whose black seeds are easily separated and which has long been a staple of American commerce. It takes a slave woman a full day to clean the seeds out of the fiber and produce one pound of clean cotton. Whitney studies the problem and after 10 days has constructed a model for a cotton "gin." With Mrs. Greene's encouragement, he works on his gin for the next 6 months, but although it pulls the seeds from the cotton it has a problem: the loose seeds get clogged in the rollers. Mrs. Greene hands him a brush from the hearth, Whitney installs it in his cotton gin, and it sweeps away the seeds. His perfected gin, which enables planters to produce far more cotton for the textile mills, will revolutionize the economies of the United States and Britain.

Yale denies admission to would-be freshman Lucinda Foote, 16, noting that she is qualified in all respects "except for her sex."

Painting: *Self-Portrait* by French painter Marie Geneviève Bouliar, 30.

Music: *Three Sonatas for Violin and Pianoforte* by English soprano-composer Elizabeth Billington (*née* Weichsell), 26, is published at London, but James Ridgeway's scurrilous *Memoirs of Mrs. Billington from Her Birth* titillates gossips and makes life uncomfortable for the young woman. Her German-born father is chief oboist at the King's Theatre, she and her brother Carl have given recitals since 1774, and she married at age 18 against her family's wishes (*see* 1794).

1793

Louis XVI goes to the guillotine January 21 in the Place de la Revolution, which will later be called the Place de la Concorde.

The comtesse du Barry returns from London March 3 against the advice of her English friends, saying that she has "a debt of honor to be settled in France." The Convention introduces a law in July authorizing local authorities to arrest anyone suspected of "uncivic behavior such as lack of patriotism or aristocratic tendencies," and Mme. du Barry is imprisoned.

French patriot Charlotte Corday (Marie-Anne-Charlotte Corday d'Armont), 25, assassinates the radical Jacobin Jean-Paul Marat July 13. Girondists have attacked Marat and brought him to trial. Acquitted April 24, he has joined with Danton and Robespierre of the *Comité de Salut Public* in overthrowing the power of the Girondists, 31 Girondist deputies have been arrested June 2, and Corday, who has been horrified by the excesses of the Jacobin terrorists, stabs Marat to death in his bath, where he nurses a persistent skin disease. She has gained entrance to his rooms at 20 rue de Cordeliers, by claiming to have detailed knowledge about a group of Girondin conspirators in the Calvados area. An ardent royalist and daughter of an impoverished aristocrat, she lives with an aunt in Caen and is involved with the same Girondin group that

Charlotte Corday assassinated the radical Jacobin Jean-Paul Marat as the French Revolution stirred passions.

she has pretended to betray. Corday makes no effort to escape but stands calmly at the window, watching the mob that gathers, and offers no resistance to the police when they arrive to arrest her.

France's Convention decrees that women may no longer join the army but offers only 5 sous per kilometer to help volunteers return home.

The Reign of Terror gathers force at Paris and elsewhere. Marie-Antoinette's aristocratic superintendent of household and intimate companion Marie-Thérèse-Louise de Savoie-Carignan, princesse de Lamballe, 45, escaped to England in 1791 but returned to share the queen's imprisonment in the Temple. She refuses to take the oath declaring her detestation of the monarchy and is torn to pieces by the mob as she leaves the courtroom. Marie-Antoinette herself goes to the guillotine October 16.

Poet Jeanne-Manon Philipon Roland, 39, goes to the guillotine November 8, and her Girondist husband Jean-Marie Roland de La Platiere, 59, commits suicide a week later in Normandy at news of Mme. Roland's death. Her last words are reported to have been "O Liberty! Liberty! how many crimes are committed in thy name!"

The comtesse du Barry goes to the guillotine December 7 after a trial that has taken up most of the previous day.

A purge of priests in the Vendée and efforts to conscript peasants into the revolutionary army incites a popular uprising. Generals Louis-Marie Turreau and François Westermann suppress the revolt with unbridled brutality, killing 300,000 to 600,000 men, women, and children. Jacobin judge Jean-Baptiste Carrier executes 13,000 at Nantes (many are drowned in the Loire in specially built boats). Gen. Westermann routs the Vendée rebel army at Savenay December 23.

A British fleet puts in at Naples, where the ambassador's wife, Lady Hamilton (*née* Emma Lyon), now 32, is introduced to Admiral Horatio Nelson. She becomes Nelson's mistress (*see* 1800; music, 1794).

A cotton thread is perfected by the wife of Samuel Slater, who has opened the first U.S. cotton mill at the falls of the Blackstone River at what later will be

Mme. du Barry fled to England to escape the Reign of Terror but returned to Paris and went to the guillotine. NEW YORK PUBLIC LIBRARY

called Pawtucket, R.I. Now 25, Slater spent 6½ years as apprentice to a partner of English inventor Richard Arkwright, committed plans for textile machinery to memory, posed as a common laborer, and arrived at Providence 4 years ago.

 Nonfiction: *Réflexions sur le procès de la reine* by Mme. de Staël, who has fled to the Necker family estate at Coppet on Lake Geneva to escape the Reign of Terror and written her *Réflexions* in the vain hope of saving Marie-Antoinette (above).

 Painting: *Painting at Rest, Little Girls at a Crossroads,* and *Concealed Love* by French painter

Jeanne Philiberte Ledoux, 26; *The Death of Marat* by French painter Jacques-Louis David, 45, portrays Marat's assassin, Charlotte Corday, wielding her knife.

 Massachusetts repeals its Puritanical antitheater laws after a fight led by Sarah Wentworth Apthorp Morton and her husband, Perez.

Fashionable young Parisian women wear sheer gauze draperies in December, adopting a fashion that critics say displays "insolent luxury amidst public wretchedness." The women, who wear blond wigs, have fans in their belts and purses at their bosoms to provide some concealment but are otherwise barely clothed.

Indigo-cultivation pioneer Eliza Pinckney dies of cancer May 26 at age 71. President Washington serves as a pallbearer at his own request.

Australian pioneer John Macarthur, who arrived with his wife, Elizabeth (*née* Veale), then 23, in New South Wales 4 years ago with the second British fleet, receives a grant of land near Parramatta and names it Elizabeth Farm. Probably the first woman in Australia with any education, Elizabeth will have seven surviving children, manage her husband's complex business ventures in his frequent absences from the colony, and introduce merino sheep, conducting successful breeding experiments that will lay the foundation for Australia's wool industry (*see* 1816).

1794

 Robespierre crushes his rivals at Paris, has Danton and the others guillotined in late March, but is himself toppled July 27 in the Conspiracy of 9 Thermidor and sent to the guillotine with his companions.

Princess Caroline Amelia Elisabeth of Brunswick-Wolfenbüttel is married by proxy December 4 to Britain's prince of Wales, with the earl of Malmesbury standing in for the prince (*see* 1795).

Fiction: *The Mysteries of Udolpho* by Ann Radcliffe. *Charlotte Temple* by Susanna Rowson is about an English schoolgirl's unsuccessful struggle to defend her virtue against a seducer who is abetted by a Frenchwoman at her school. It will be a best seller for decades.

Poetry: Swedish poet Anna Maria Lenngren, 40, begins having her poems published in her husband's newspaper, the *Stockholms Posten,* and quickly charms the paper's readers, who have never before seen such works in Swedish.

 Painting: *Aspasia* by Marie Geneviève Bouliar.

 Opera: English soprano-composer Elizabeth Billington goes abroad with her brother and husband to escape London gossips (*see* 1792). Sir William Hamilton at Naples has her sing at a private party and persuades her to perform at the San Carlo Opera House, she makes a brilliant debut in May in Bianchi's opera *Inez de Castro* (written especially for her), her husband dies of apoplexy soon afterward, she becomes a great friend of Emma, Lady Hamilton, and remains at Naples for another 16 months, singing in operas composed for her by Paisiello, Paer, and Himmel.

1795

 Britain's Prince of Wales, now 32, is formally married at London April 8 to Princess Caroline Amelia Elisabeth of Brunswick-Wolfenbüttel, 26, although he still considers himself married to Mrs. Fitzherbert (*see* 1785; 1794; 1814).

The French Convention, threatened by a royalist revolt, calls upon the dissolute rake Paul-François-Jean Nicolas, 40, comte de Barras, to defend it. Barras met the Corsican artillery officer Napoleon Bonaparte, 26, during the siege of Toulon in 1793, has installed his creole mistress, Joséphine, in Bonaparte's bed (*see* 1796), and gives Bonaparte and other Jacobin officers command of forces defending the convention. Bonaparte drives the Paris mob from the streets with a "whiff of grapeshot" on "The Day of the Sections" October 5 (13 Vendemiaire).

 The Female Society of Philadelphia for the Relief and Employment of the Poor is founded by local Quaker spinster Ann Parrish.

A Treatise on the Epidemic of Puerperal Fever of Aberdeen by Scottish surgeon Alexander Gordon suggests that the fever is contagious. It is not, he writes, "a miasma in the air," as is commonly believed because it is not indiscriminate, but is suffered only by a woman visited by a practitioner who has previously attended a woman with the fever. "By observation, I plainly perceived the channel by which it was propagated, and I arrived at that certainty in the matter, that I could venture to foretell what women would be affected with the disease upon hearing by what midwife they were to be delivered, or by what nurse they were to be attended, during their lying in; and almost in every instance, my prediction was verified" (*see* White, 1773). Gordon recommends fumigation of hospital wards, clothing, and bedding (*see* Holmes, 1843).

 Nonfiction: *Réflexions sur la paix intérieure* by Mme. de Staël, who has returned to Paris to start a salon but is advised to go back to Coppet.

 Painting: *Daphne and Phyllis* by French painter Pauline Auzou (*née* Desmarquets), 20.

1796

 Napoleon Bonaparte is married March 9 at Paris to Joséphine de Beauharnais (*née* Marie-Josèphe-Rose Tascher de la Pagerie), 33, Martinique-born widow of the late vicomte de Beauharnais, who was blamed for the fall of Mainz to the Prussians in 1793 and went to the guillotine in July 1794 (she has for more than a year been mistress to the comte de Barras). Joséphine accompanies Bonaparte as he invades Italy but soon returns to Paris as he defeats the Austrians and Piedmontese in April, enters Milan May 16, and conquers all of Lombardy as far as Mantua.

Russia's Catherine the Great dies of apoplexy November 10 at age 67 after a 34-year reign. She is succeeded by her mentally unbalanced son of 42, who will reign until 1801 as Paul I.

 The *North Carolina Minerva* and *Fayetteville Advertiser* for March 31 carries a manifesto that says, in part, "Too long the male sex usurped to themselves the title of lords of the creation, enacted laws and enforced statutes at large, without consulting or

Joséphine de Beauharnais married Napoleon Bonaparte but found he cared more about la gloire *than* l'amour.

considering women worthy of being their coadjustors."

 English physician Edward Jenner, 47, pioneers the use of vaccination against smallpox, which disfigures so many women. He takes lymph from cowpox pustules on the hand of dairymaid Sarah Nelmes at Berkeley, Gloucestershire, scratches it into the skin of an 8-year-old schoolboy, and a few weeks later inoculates the boy with matter from a smallpox pustule; the boy does not develop even a mild case of smallpox (*see* 1798).

Nonfiction: *The Influence of the Passions* (*De l'Influence des passions*) by Mme. de Staël, who has borne two children by her lover, Vicomte Louis de Narbonne, and begun an affair with the courtier Benjamin Constant, 28, who has left his wife to join her; *The Science of Rights* by German philosopher Johann Fichte, 34, who writes, "In an uncorrupted woman the sexual impulse does not manifest itself at all, but only love; and this love is the natural impulse of a woman to satisfy a man."

Painting: *Portrait of Chevalier Alexandre-Marie Lenoir* and *Portrait of Alelaïde Binard* (Mme. Lenoir) by Marie Geneviève Bouliar; *Mother of Alcibiades* by Pauline Auzou; *Portrait of Christian-Georg von Schantz* (a Swedish sea captain) by French painter Gabrielle Capet, 35; *Interior of the Atelier of a Woman Painter* (a tribute to Vigée-Lebrun; oil on canvas) by French painter Marie Victoire Lemoine, 42.

American Cookery by Amelia Simmons ("an American orphan") is the first cookbook to contain native American specialties. Simmons includes Indian pudding, Indian slapjack (pancakes), jonny-cake, pickled watermelon rind, Jerusalem artichokes, spruce beer, and a gingerbread that is much softer than the thin European variety.

Opera: Italian soprano Angelica Catalani makes her debut at Venice's Teatro la Fenice.

The "Veuve Clicquot" (Widow Cliquot) begins improving French champagne production. Nicole-Barbe Cliquot, 20, whose father is the mayor of Reims and whose vintner husband, whom she married 3 years ago, has just died following the birth of their daughter, determines to carry on his business. She will pioneer the process of *remuage* (moving) in which champagne bottles are stored upside down (*sur pointe*), shaken periodically, and turned over a period of months until the sediment in the wine drops down to coat the cork, and then uncorked for an instant to permit pressure to expel the sediment, whereupon a clean cork is quickly reinserted. Veuve Cliquot will create pink champagne simply by pressing the grapes as soon as they are picked (*see* 1820).

English utilitarian philosopher-economist Jeremy Bentham, 49, says in *The Annals of Agriculture* that population can be controlled not by a "bribatory act" or a "dead letter" but by "a sponge." His middle-class readers are aware of several ways to avoid pregnancy.

1797

Gen. Bonaparte gains his first decisive victory at the Battle of Rivoli in mid-January, takes Mantua February 2 after a 6-month siege, and intimidates Pope Pius VI into ceding Romagna, Bologna, and Ferrara. Austria is obliged to cede her Belgian provinces to France and make other concessions under terms of the Treaty of Campo Formio signed October 17.

Mary Wollstonecraft marries political writer-novelist William Godwin, who has impregnated her; they decide to live and work in separate lodgings, and she dies September 10 at age 38 after giving birth to a daughter, Mary, who will become a noted writer (*see* Fiction, 1818).

Fiction: *The Italian* by Ann Radcliffe; *The Coquette* by U.S. novelist Hannah Foster is about Eliza Wharton, a woman in her 30s who has an affair with a rake and dies in childbirth.

1798

The Battle of Frauenbrün March 3 ends in victory for the French over a Swiss force that includes 280 women under the leadership of Martha Glar, 64, who is killed along with the men in her family, her two daughters, three granddaughters (the youngest is only 10), and 154 other women. Survivors carry the wounded and mutilated from the field.

Inquiry into the Cause and Effects of the Variolae Vaccine by Edward Jenner announces his discovery of vaccination—a much safer means of protection against smallpox than inoculation (*see* 1796).

Practical Education by English writer Maria Edgeworth, 32, and her father, Richard, 54, is based on recorded conversations of children with their elders to illustrate a child's chain of reasoning.

Nonfiction: *Alcuin: A Dialogue on the Rights of Women* by U.S. writer Charles Brockden Brown, 27. The first American professional writer, Brown has been influenced by the ideas of William Godwin and Mary Wollstonecraft in England.

Fiction: *Juliette* by the marquis de Sade, whose comte de Belmor says, "Our so-called chivalry, which consists in absurdly venerating an object intended to serve our needs, derives from the fear of witches that once plagued our ignorant ancestors. Their terror was transmuted first into respect, then into worship; thus gallantry was miraculously born from the womb of ignorant superstition. But such respect is fundamentally unnatural, since Nature nowhere gives a single instance of it. *The natural inferiority of women* to men is universally evident, and nothing intrinsic to the female sex naturally inspires respect."

Poetry: *Plays on the Passions* by Joanna Baillie contains dramas in blank verse, each one focusing on a particular emotion. "A Few Words to My Dear Daughter" (*"Nagra ord till min köra dotter"*) by Anna Maria Lenngren advises her imagined daughter to avoid both learned activities and political interests, cultivating instead the everyday virtues of "prudence" and a "sensitive cheerfulness." Lunngren will henceforth write only occasionally, avoiding any subjects with political implications.

Theater: *Speed the Plough* by English playwright Thomas Morton, 34: "Be quiet, wull ye [says farmer Ashfield]. Always ding, dinging Dame Grundy into my ears—What will Mrs. Grundy say? What will Mrs. Grundy think?"

The advent of smallpox vaccinations (above) will decrease demand for "beauty patches"—star-, crescent-, moon-, and heart-shaped black silk or velvet patches worn as camouflage since the last century, sometimes a dozen at a time, by pockmarked women. The patches have been used as signals: one on her right cheek meaning that a woman is married, on her left that she is betrothed, near her mouth that she is willing to flirt, at the corner of her eye that she is in the grip of a smoldering passion.

1799

Welsh industrialist Robert Owen, 28, marries the daughter of Scottish industrialist David Dale, 60, and becomes manager and co-owner of Dale's cot-

ton mill in England's Lancashire. He determines "to make arrangements to supersede the evil conditions [of the millhands] . . . by good conditions" (*see* 1824).

Mathematician Maria Agnesi dies in May at age 81. She turned her home into a hospital and has spent the last 15 years of her life administering the Po Alberto Trivulzio Public Institution for Care of the Elderly and Homeless.

Strictures on a Modern System of Female Education by Hannah More rejects the doctrine of paternal austerity because "it drives the general spirit to artifice and the rugged to despair. It generates deceit and cunning, the most hopeless and hateful of the whole category of female failings." More advocates the early establishment of paternal trust, encouraging the child's sense of dependency while circumventing secrecy; "the dread of severity will drive terrified children to seek, not for reformation but for impunity. A readiness to forgive them promotes frankness; and we should, above all things, encourage them to be frank in order to get at their faults." She seeks to define female potential in terms of the capacity to transcend the stereotyping that consigns women to weakness and folly.

Fiction: Claire d'Albe by French writer Sophie Cottin (*née* Risteau), 29, who married a Parisian banker at age 17, was widowed without children at 20, and has taken up writing verses and romances to divert herself.

Painting: *Young Woman Reading* by Pauline Auzou.

1800

Lord Nelson, whose naval victories over the French have made him a national hero, moves his mistress, Emma, Lady Hamilton, to England (she has borne him a daughter, Horatia). Polite society is appalled by the relationship, which is widely viewed as "a harlot's corruption of a great man." Her husband will die in 1803, leaving her his fortune, and Lord Nelson will be killed 2 years later at the Battle of Trafalgar (*see* 1812).

Nonfiction: *The Influence of Literature upon Society (Literature et Ses Rapports avec les Institutions*

Lady Hamilton dallied with Admiral Horatio Nelson, the great naval hero, and bore him a daughter. FROM THE 1800 PAINTING BY JOHANN SCHMIDT

Sociales) by Mme. de Staël, who writes, "The entire social order . . . is arrayed against a woman who wants to rise to a man's reputation." She was permitted by Napoleon to return to Paris 3 years ago but soon antagonized him and retreated once again to Coppet.

Fiction: *Castle Rackrent* by Maria Edgeworth, who writes about Irish life.

Painting: *Portrait of a Young Woman Playing a Prelude on a Piano* by Pauline Auzou.

Opera: Angelica Catalani sings at Trieste in the 1796 Cimarosa opera *Gli Orazi ed i Curiazi.*

19th Century

1801

 The Female Association for the Relief of Women and Children in Reduced Circumstances is founded at Philadelphia by philanthropists who include Rebecca Gratz, 20, whose father is a prominent fur trader and shipper.

Philadelphia philanthropist Rebecca Gratz helped "Women and Children in Reduced Circumstances."

$ German-American fur trader John Jacob Astor, 38, travels through upstate New York bartering "firewater" (whiskey) and flannel with the Iroquois and Seneca to obtain animal pelts, chiefly beaver for use in hats. Some he sells in the Albany market but the best go to his wife, Sarah (*née* Todd), in New York, where he married her in 1785 (she was cleaning the doorstep of her widowed mother's boardinghouse when they met, he was selling cakes in the street, her $300 dowry helped him get started in the fur business, and she has borne eight children). A better judge of fur than her husband, Sarah beats the smelly pelts and does her best to sell them to customers of her successful music store. Distantly related to the Brevoorts, she will help her husband make profitable connections.

Nonfiction: *How Gertrude Teaches Her Children* (*Wie Gertrud ihre Kinder lehrt*) by Swiss educationalist Johann Heinrich Pestalozzi, 55, shows that to educate a woman is to educate a family community.

Fiction: *Quixotism: Exhibited in the Romantic Opinions and Extravagant Adventures of Dorcasina Sheldon* by U.S. novelist Tabitha Tenney (*née* Gilman), 39.

Painting: *Melancholy* by French painter Constance Charpentier, 34; *Portrait of a Father and Daughter* by French painter Constance Mayer, 23.

Opera: Angelica Catalani sings at Milan's Teatro alla Scala in the Cimarosa opera *Clitennestra*.

1802

A school for midwives opens at the Paris-Maternité. A similar school will soon be set up by the Prussian government at Berlin.

Fiction: *Delphine* by Mme. de Staël, who says in her preface, "I was, and I still am convinced that women, being the victims of all social institutions, are destined to misery if they make the least concession to their feelings and if, in any way whatever, they lose control of themselves." Her liberalism enrages Napoleon Bonaparte (he will exile her and her lover, Benjamin Constant, next year to her family estate on Lake Geneva).

Painting: *Two Young Girls Reading a Letter* by Pauline Auzou.

Mme. de Staël antagonized the emperor Napoleon with her writings and her scandalous lifestyle.

Theater: Irish comic actress Julia Glover (*née* Betterton), 23, makes her Drury Lane Theatre debut to begin a notable career. She first appeared onstage at age 10 and was sold by her father in 1798 to Samuel Glover.

Mme. Tussaud's wax museum opens at London. Swiss wax modeler Marie Gresholtz Tussaud, 42, was commissioned during the Reign of Terror at Paris 9 years ago to make death masks of famous guillotine victims, using the heads of decapitated bodies, and has recently inherited the wax museum of her uncle, J. C. Curtius. She will settle her collection in Baker Street in 1833 and connect it with a chamber of horrors containing relics of criminals and instruments of torture.

1803

The Louisiana Purchase April 30 doubles the size of the United States, extending her western border to the Rocky Mountains with 828,000 square miles of territory. Needing money for Napoleon's military adventures, France sells the vast area for 80 million francs ($15 million) (*see* Lewis and Clark, 1804).

Fiction: *Valérie* by Russian mystic-novelist Barbara Juliana von Krüdener (*née* von Vietinghoff), 39, whose 1782 marriage to the Russian ambassador at Venice ended after less than 3 years; *Thaddeus of Warsaw* by English romance novelist Jane Porter, 27.

Poetry: *Poems* by Scottish poet Anne Grant (*née* MacVicar), 48, who was widowed in 1801.

Theater: Sarah Siddons leaves the Drury Lane Theatre for Covent Garden, where she will perform until her retirement in 1812 (*see* 1782).

Parliament enacts the first British abortion law, earlier laws having been enacted in ecclesiastical courts but not civil courts. The new law outlaws abortion after 4½ months, when the fetus is deemed to have "quickened" (*see* 1867).

1804

The emperor Napoleon's mother, Marie Letizia (*née* Romolino), 55, is given special status in May as

"Madame Mère de l'Empereur." Of her 12 children, seven survived infancy; he was her fourth (*see* 1814).

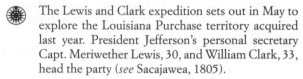 The Lewis and Clark expedition sets out in May to explore the Louisiana Purchase territory acquired last year. President Jefferson's personal secretary Capt. Meriwether Lewis, 30, and William Clark, 33, head the party (*see* Sacajawea, 1805).

Fiction: *St. Clair* by Irish novelist Sydney Owenson, 21, who went to work as a governess to support the family after her father, a theatrical manager, encountered financial problems.

Painting: *The First Feeling of Coquetry* by Pauline Auzou.

English jockey Alicia Meynell rides against Capt. William Flint in a four-mile race at York August 25—the first woman jockey.

1805

The Lewis and Clark expedition engages as guide and interpreter one Toussaint Charbonneau, 46, a French-Canadian *voyageur* whose wife, Sacajawea, has given birth in February in the Mandan villages (*see* 1804). Charbonneau, who won Sacajawea in a gambling game 11 years ago when she was about 14

Sacajawea saved the Lewis and Clark expedition from starvation and helped guide it to the Pacific. LIBRARY OF CONGRESS

and married her along with another Shoshone girl captured by the Crow, brings along his wife and infant son. The first band of Shoshone they encounter is headed by her brother, Cameahwait, who helps the expedition obtain the horses and supplies they need to cross the high mountains into the Columbia River basin. Lewis, who calls her "Jenny," and Clark, who calls her "Janie," learn from Sacajawea how to find and eat wild roots, which enable them to survive a bitter winter. She often serves as guide as well as interpreter, and with her help the expedition reaches the Pacific Coast November 7.

Fiction: *Mathilde* by Sophie Cottin.

1806

Former British Prime Minister William Pitt the Younger dies January 23 at age 46, leaving an annual pension of £1,200 to his housekeeper, Lady Hester Stanhope, 30, who in 1810 will leave Britain with a female companion, survive a shipwreck off the island of Rhodes in the eastern Mediterranean, and eventually settle in the Middle East, where she will wield considerable power for some 20 years.

Prussia's Friedrich Wilhelm III declares war on France at the instigation of his wife, Queen Louisa, but his forces will be no match for those of Napoleon.

The Orphan Asylum Society is founded at New York by Canadian-born schoolteacher Joanne Bethune, 36.

Fiction: *Elisabeth, ou les exiles de Sibérie* by Sophie Cottin; *The Wild Irish Girl* by Sydney Owenson.

Poetry: *Letters from the Mountains* by Anne Grant; *Original Poems for Infant Minds* by English poets Ann and Jane Taylor, 21 and 23, respectively, includes Jane's nursery rhyme "Twinkle, twinkle, little star,/ How I wonder what you are!/ Up above the world so high,/ Like a diamond in the sky."

Painting: *Angelica Catalani* by Elisabeth Vigée-Lebrun; *A Blind Man Surrounded by His Children Being Consoled for His Loss of Vision by the Pleasures of His Four Other Senses* by Constance Charpentier.

Lady Hester Stanhope went off to the Middle East and wielded considerable power over the Arab tribes. FROM AN ENGRAVING BY C. HULLMANDEL AFTER R. J. HAMERTON

Récamier (*née* Bernard), 30, who has presided over the most interesting salon in Paris but whose banker husband, Jacques, has suffered financial reverses; *The Hungarian Brothers* by English novelist Anna Maria Porter, 27, younger sister of Jane.

Juvenile: *Tales from Shakespeare* by English essayist-critic Charles Lamb, 32, and his sister Mary Ann, 43. Lamb has been taking care of Mary Ann since she killed their invalid mother in a fit of insanity 11 years ago and has given up his own projected marriage to devote his efforts to that responsibility, although he himself has been mentally unbalanced and was confined to an asylum from age 20 to 21.

Painter Angelica Kauffmann dies at Rome at age 66.

1808

French forces invade Spain in January, by mid-March they number more than 100,000, and Madrid falls March 26 to Gen. Joachim Murat, who forces Carlos IV to abdicate. But when 12,000 French troops lay siege to Saragossa, a 20-year-old woman who will be remembered only as Augustina, the Maid of Saragossa, places a match to an artillery piece and rallies the city's disheartened defenders with the cry, "So long as the French are near, Saragossa has one defender!"

Nonfiction: *Memoirs of an American Lady* (essays) by poet Anne Grant, who lived as a child in North America.

Painting: *Portrait of Mme de Staël as Corinne* by Elisabeth Vigée-Lebrun. *Coquetry Punished, or The Broken Mirror* by Pauline Auzou; *The First Care of a Young Doctor* by Constance Charpentier; Goya paintings owned by the Spanish prime minister Manuel de Godoy, 41, are inventoried, and the list includes *The Naked Maja* and *The Maja Clothed*, painted nearly life-size and possibly showing the duchess of Alba, who died in 1802. The word "Maja" is derived from "maya," title of the queen of the May; it means something between "wanton" and "wench," and the work is so scandalous that Godoy is able to keep it only by virtue of his position as prime minister and lover of the queen Maria Luisa. *La Grande Baigneuse* by French painter Jean-Auguste-Dominique Ingres, 28.

1807

The emperor Napoleon meets at Tilsit July 6 with Prussia's young Queen Louisa, who, although she has no political power (the Prussian army has been virtually wiped out), pleads with him to treat her conquered country justly. "I am a wife and mother and it is by these titles that I appeal for your mercy on behalf of Prussia," she says. He will call her "the most admirable queen and at the same time the most interesting woman I had ever met" (but *see* 1810).

New Jersey revokes woman suffrage, granted in the constitution it adopted July 2, 1776. Women have not been voting for the state legislators who hold power at Trenton, and the legislators strip them of their voting powers.

Fiction: *Corinne* by Mme. de Staël is based on the court beauty Jeanne-Françoise-Julie-Adélaide

Blind Viennese singer, concert pianist, organist and composer Theresia von Paradis, 49, opens a school to train talented young musicians.

1809

 The emperor Napoleon announces to his wife, Joséphine, that he is compelled to divorce her for reasons of state, saying, "I still love you, but in politics there is no heart, only head." She has contributed to his power by attracting the cream of French intellectual society to Malmaison, the Luxembourg Palace, and the Tuilleries, but has not borne any children. The emperor's lawyers find a slight technical irregularity (no parish priest was present) in the religious marriage ceremony of December 1, 1804, which they use to have the marriage declared null and void (*see* 1810).

Napoleon dumped Joséphine to marry the Austrian princess Maria Louisa because he hoped to found a dynasty. FROM A PAINTING BY FRANÇOIS GERARD

Napoleon makes his sister Elisa (Marie-Anne-Elisa), 32, grand duchess of Tuscany in recognition of the profitable way that she has managed the economy of Lucca since 1805. She travels with her husband, Felix Bacciochi, to Florence, where she establishes a magnificent court in the Pitti Palace.

 South Killingly, Conn., inventor Mary Kies (*née* Dixon), 57, is awarded a U.S. patent May 5 for "a new and useful improvement in weaving straw with silk or thread." She is the first woman to receive a U.S. patent, but her invention will soon be outmoded (*see* Woodhouse, 1821).

 Danville, Ky., surgeon Ephraim McDowell, 38, performs the first recorded U.S. gynecological operation to remove a 22½-pound ovarian tumor. His procedure on Jane Crawford (*née* Todd), 47, at Greensburg, performed December 25 in 25 minutes without anesthesia (assistants held down her arms and legs), demonstrates that surgery of the abdominal cavity need not be fatal. The patient, who has ridden 60 miles on horseback to Danville despite severe pain, endures the operation fully dressed, is up and about 5 days later, and is able to return home in 3 weeks.

 The first U.S. parochial school is founded near Baltimore by English-American widow Elizabeth Ann Seton, 36, a recent convert to Roman Catholicism who is joined by other Catholic women in starting the Sisters of Charity, a religious order that will be allied in 1850 with France's Daughters of Charity of St. Vincent de Paul. Mother of five, "Mother Seton" will be credited with several "miracles" and be canonized in 1975 as the first American saint.

 Fiction: *Coelebs in Search of a Wife* by Hannah More; *The Absentee* by Maria Edgeworth.

1810

 Napoleon is married March 11 by proxy at Vienna to the Austrian archduchess Maria Luisa, 18, in a match arranged by Austrian foreign minister von Metternich. The "little corporal," now 40, hopes to father an heir to his vast empire.

The "dragon lady" of the South China Sea surrenders April 20 to China's governor-general Bai Ling.

A former prostitute, Zheng Yi Sao replaced her late husband, Zheng Yi, as head of the pirates upon his death 3 years ago. Backed by her lover and adopted son Zhang Bao, she has led a confederation of some 70,000 men and women whose 1,800 pirate junks prey on commercial shipping. So great is her power that she is able to negotiate a deal that gives her and some of her senior commanders high-ranking posts in the Chinese military while pardoning all of her pirates.

Prussia's Queen Louisa dies of a pulmonary embolism July 19 at age 34. Napoleon has tried to destroy her reputation, but his charges have only endeared her to her people. She has borne eight children and is called "the mother of the nation" (*Landesmutter*).

Mexican rebels led by the Creole priest Miguel Hidalgo y Costilla, 57, capture Guanajato, Guadalajara, and Valladolid from the Spaniards to begin an insurrection that will culminate in independence in 1821. Patriot Gertrudis Bocanegra, 45, who has persuaded her soldier husband to quit the Spanish Army, joins a rebel group led by Manuel Muñiz, taking along her husband and their 10-year-old son. She raises an army of women, persuades her daughters to join, carries vital messages between rebel groups, and plays a major role in the attack on Valladolid (*see* 1817).

Nonfiction: *De l'Allemagne* by Mme. de Staël appears in the first of its three volumes, introducing German romanticism to French literature.

Fiction: *The Scottish Chiefs* by Jane Porter.

Painting: *The Sons of Marshal Ney* by French painter Marie Eléonore Godefroid, 32; *The Arrival of the Archduchess Marie Louise in the Gallery of the Château de Compiègne* by Pauline Auzou; *Portrait of a Woman* by Gabrielle Capet.

Music: Polish pianist Maria Agata Szymanowska (*née* Wolowska), 20, makes her debut as a concert pianist at Warsaw and then at Paris, winning the admiration of the Italian composer Luigi Cherubini (who will dedicate his Fantasia in C Minor for Piano to her).

The Munich Oktoberfest has its beginnings in a festival staged to celebrate the marriage of Bavaria's crown prince Ludwig (Louis), 24, to princess Therese of Saxe-Hildburghausen, 18, who will bear him seven children.

France makes abortion a criminal offense (*see* 1814).

1811

The Regency Act passed by Parliament February 5 authorizes the prince of Wales, now 49, to reign in place of his father, George III, who is blind and has become permanently mad after losing his favorite daughter, Amelia.

Nonfiction: *Superstitions of the Highlanders* by Anne Grant, now 56, who moved to Edinburgh last year and will gain the support of Walter Scott.

Fiction: *Sense and Sensibility, A Novel by a Lady* is published anonymously at London. Its author is Jane Austen, 36, a spinster whose depiction of manners and mores in English country society will rank her as one of the world's great novelists.

Napoleon decrees that foundling hospitals in France shall be provided with turntable devices (*tours*) so that parents can leave unwanted infants without being recognized or questioned. Millions of infants have been drowned, smothered, or abandoned, depriving the French army of potential recruits. By 1833, the number of infants left at such hospitals will have increased from 63,000 to 127,000, but the hospitals will be closed by government order a few years later.

1812

Lady Hamilton, now 47, is sent to an English debtor's prison, having squandered her late husband's fortune in just 9 years (*see* 1800; Lord Chesterfield, 1774). A friend helps her escape to Calais, where she will die in 1815.

Painting: *A Mother Receiving the Confidences of Her Daughter* by Constance Charpentier; *Time of Her Departure from Vienna, Distributing Her Mother's Diamonds to Her Brothers and Sisters, March, 1810* by Pauline Auzou; *The Children of the Duke of Rovigo* by Marie Eléonore Godefroid.

Theater: Sarah Siddons, now 57, appears at Covent Garden June 29 as Lady Macbeth in Shakespeare's 1606 tragedy and bids farewell to the stage, although she will continue to make occasional appearances and give readings.

1813

 English Quaker Elizabeth Fry, 33, begins working to improve the conditions of women in Newgate Prison, where inmates are not segregated by sex. Fry will be instrumental in introducing education and employment into British prisons and will open soup kitchens for London's poor.

 Fiction: *Pride and Prejudice* by Jane Austen. Published anonymously, as was last year's *Sense and*

Jane Austen wrote just six novels about English country society but they made her name immortal.

Sensibility, her new novel tells the story of Elizabeth Bennet, one of many daughters of a foolish, husband-hunting mother: "It is a truth universally acknowledged, that a single man in possession of a good fortune must be in want of a wife";"Happiness in marriage is entirely a matter of chance" (Chapter 6); "One cannot always be laughing at a man without now and then stumbling on something witty" (Chapter 40); "Unhappy as the event must be for Lydia, we may draw from it this useful lesson: that loss of virtue in a female is irretrievable; that one false step involves her in endless ruin; that her reputation is no less brittle than it is beautiful; and that she cannot be too much guarded in her behavior towards the undeserving of the other sex" (Chapter 47).

 U.S. First Lady Dolley Madison (*née* Payne), 40, serves ice cream at the inauguration party for her husband, James, on March 4.

1814

 The emperor Napoleon is exiled to the Isle of Elba following his abdication April 11. His wife, Marie-Louise, returns to Vienna and is awarded the duchy of Parma. His ex-wife, Joséphine, who has continued to bear the title empress, dies at Malmaison. His mother, Marie Letizia, now 65, supports him in his exile (*see* 1804), and his critics, who include Mme. de Staël, return to Paris.

Caroline, princess of Wales, now 46, leaves England August 16, to the relief of her husband and his ministers, and visits with her brother at Brunswick before going on to Frankfurt, Strasbourg, Bern, Lausanne, and Geneva.

The Battle of Bladensburg 4 miles from Washington, D.C., August 24 ends in a rout of 7,000 untrained state militiamen by 3,000 British regulars, who march into the city and burn most of its public buildings, including the executive mansion. Admiral Cockburn of the Royal Navy has announced his intention of taking President Madison's wife, Dolley, hostage and parading her through the streets of London. With the enemy closing in and her husband away with his troops, Dolley, who by some accounts took over some of the president's duties when he fell deathly ill last

Dolley Madison eluded the British in the War of 1812 and saved the executive mansion's valuables.

weave cotton cloth in an enterprise that is soon producing some 30 miles of cloth per day.

Fiction: *Mansfield Park* by Jane Austen; *O'Donnel* by novelist Sydney Morgan (*née* Owenson), now 32, who 2 years ago married surgeon Thomas C. Morgan.

Ballet: English soprano Mme. (Lucia Elizabeth) Vestris (*née* Bartolozzi), 18, makes her stage debut 7/10 at the King's Theatre, London, singing the title role in the ballet *Il Ratto di Proserpina*, a role created by the Italian soprano Josephine Grassini (Bartolozzi was married at age 15 to Armand Vestris, then 25 and the lead dancer at the King's Theatre). When the season closes in August, she and her husband go to Paris.

France prohibits abortion under a new law that permits the procedure only "when it is required to preserve the life of the mother when that is gravely threatened" (*see* 1810).

1815

The emperor Napoleon leaves Elba, raises an army, marches on Paris, enters the city March 20, and begins a new 100-day reign. The Battle of Waterloo June 18 ends the Little Corporal's threat once and for all, and he is exiled to the island of St. Helena in the South Atlantic.

Caroline, princess of Wales, journeys to Rome, Genoa, Milan, Venice, and the Italian lakes before embarking for Tunis.

Fiction: *The Pastors' Fireside* by Jane Porter.

1816

Caroline, princess of Wales, travels in April to Greece, Ephesus, and Jerusalem while her husband dallies at home with his mistresses.

The Académie Française awards its gold medal to French mathematician-physicist Sophie Germain, 40, who has twice been denied the prize because of her sex. Her paper on the mathematical laws that apply to the elasticity of surfaces inspires another mathematician to write, "It is a work which few men are able to read and which only one woman

year, orders that the Gilbert Stuart painting of George Washington be removed from its frame and given to some friends for safekeeping, collects copies of vital state documents, gathers up whatever silver she can, disguises herself as a farm wife, and escapes through Georgetown. The British set fire to the mansion, which is gutted (a rainstorm saves the outer walls, which will be repainted to create the "White House").

Massachusetts becomes a cotton cloth producer to meet the pent-up demand for the cloth that came from England before the War of 1812. Francis Cabot Lowell, 39, raises $100,000 for a company he started with Patrick Jackson in 1812, uses power from the Charles River to power machines he installs in an old paper mill at Waltham, employs farm girls to run the machines, and houses them six to a room while they earn their dowry money. Lowell and Jackson card and spin cotton thread and

was able to write." As a woman, Germain could not be admitted to the Ecole Polytechnique, so she collected professors' lecture notes from other students, submitted a paper to mathematician Joseph Lagrange under a pseudonym, and impressed him so much that he became her mentor. She has carried on correspondence with mathematician Karl Gauss, also using a pseudonym. The Académie's award makes her name known throughout France, and she is the first woman ever invited to attended sessions at the prestigious Institut de Paris.

∞ The Female Union Society for the Promotion of Sabbath-Schools is founded at New York by schoolteacher Joanne Bethune.

Fiction: *Emma* by Jane Austen: "A single woman with a narrow income, must be a ridiculous, disagreeable old maid, the proper sport of boys and girls, but a single woman of fortune is always respectable, and may be as sensible and pleasant as anybody else." Austen will die next year at age 41, leaving her novels *Persusasion* and *Northanger Abbey* to be published posthumously.

Opera: Italian soprano Giuditta (Maria Costanza) Pasta (*née* Negri) Italian soprano, 18, makes her Paris debut at the Théâtre des Italiens in Baer's *Il Principe di Taranto* and goes on to sing the role of Donna Elvira in the 1787 Mozart opera *Don Giovanni*; Mme. Vestris makes her Paris debut under the name Lucia Bartolozzi-Vestris 12/7 as Proserpina at the Théâtre des Italiens.

Lachian Macquarie, governor of New South Wales, gives Elizabeth Macarthur, now 49, and her husband, John, a new grant of 600 acres near Camden in recognition of Elizabeth's work toward the improvement of agriculture in the Australian colony (*see* 1793).

Caroline, princess of Wales, travels in the spring to Innsbrück, going on to Karlsruhe and Vienna. She has produced a daughter, Charlotte, but no male heir.

The Austrian princess Maria Leopoldina, 20, is married by proxy May 13 at Vienna to Portugal's crown prince Pedro, 18, whose father, João VI, has ruled by proxy from Brazil since 1807. Pedro's real father may be the courtly marquês of Marialva, a middle-aged bachelor who was for many years the lover of Queen Carlota Joaquina, and it is the marquês who came to Vienna as João's emissary last year to make the match with Leopoldina. She leaves Vienna June 21 with a large entourage, makes her way to Livorno (Leghorn), and embarks on a Portuguese frigate for Rio de Janeiro, which she reaches after an 82-day voyage (*see* 1819).

Mexican patriot Gertrudis Bocanegra is tried by the Spaniards, sentenced to death, and executed October 10 at age 52 (*see* 1810). Her husband has been killed in battle, she has been sent to her native Pátzcuaro to obtain military information and persuade royalist troops to come over to the rebel side, the Spaniards have caught her, and they have imprisoned her along with her daughters.

Colombian patriot La Pola (Policarpa Salavarrieta), 22, is executed by a Spanish firing squad in mid-November at Santa Fe, east of Bogotá. She has worked since age 15 in the cause of independence for New Granada, which will be achieved in 2 years through the efforts of Simon Bolívar and others.

Napoleon, in exile on the island of St. Helena in the South Atlantic, writes January 9 to Gaspard Gourgaud, "Nature intended women to be our slaves. . . . They are our property, we are not theirs. . . . They belong to us, just as a tree which bears fruit belongs to the gardener. What a mad idea to demand equality for women! . . . Women are nothing but machines for producing children." He will die in 1821, and his widow, Marie-Louise, will contract a morganatic marriage the following year with count von Neipperg (her 6-year-old son by the emperor lives with her at Vienna but will die of tuberculosis in 1832).

Fiction: *Ormond* by Maria Edgeworth, whose father, Richard, dies at age 73. Like her 1809 novel *The Absentee,* it is about Irish life.

Painting: *Still Life with a Lobster* by Anne Vallayer-Coster, now 73.

Opera: Giuditta Pasta sings the role of Telemachus in the Cimarosa opera *Penelope* 1/11 at the King's Theatre, London, and goes on to sing the roles of

Cherubino in the 1786 Mozart opera *Le Nozze di Figaro*, Fiordiligi in the 1790 Mozart opera *Così Fan Tutte*, and Servlia in the 1790 Mozart opera *La Clemenza di Tito*.

A fifth edition of his 1798 *Essay on the Principles of Population* by English authority Thomas Malthus, now 51, rejects artificial devices, saying that the misery of overpopulation is necessary to "stimulate industry" and discourage "indolence."

1818

Britain's Queen (Sophia) Charlotte dies in September at age 74, having borne 15 children to George III, who has been deranged for the past decade. News of her death comes as a shock to Caroline, princess of Wales, who is still on the Continent.

A surgeon pressing his ear against a woman's corset first hears the fetal heartbeat, inaugurating medical surveillance of embryonic development.

Nonfiction: *Observations on the Real Rights of Women, with Their Appropriate Duties, Agreeable to Scripture, Reason, and Common Sense* by Boston writer Hannah Mather Crocker, 46, a granddaughter of preacher Increase Mather. Every "female," she writes, has the "right" to cover the faults of those around her with the "mantle of meek charity." Women have "rights" to be virtuous, loving, religious, and sympathetic, thus supporting and improving human society. It was the "mutual virtue of common energy, and fortitude of the sexes" that won the American Revolution. But she contends that the female mind has powers equal to those of the male, that women are capable of making their own judgments and acting for themselves ("The wise Author of nature has endowed the female mind with equal powers and facilities, and given them the same right of judging and acting for themselves, as he gave to the male sex"), and that the sexes share equally in divine grace under Christianity. *Ten Years of Exile* (memoir) by Mme. de Staël.

Fiction: *Frankenstein, or The Modern Prometheus* by English novelist Mary Wollstonecraft Godwin Shelley, 21, gains instant success with its story about a scientist who takes parts of corpses to manufacture a living creature. Author Shelley is the wife of poet Percy Bysshe Shelley and daughter of the late women's rights champion Mary Wollstonecraft by the philosopher William Goodwin. Her book will go through at least two printings per year for 40 years, it will be translated into 30 languages, millions of copies will be sold, and it will make the word "Frankenstein" a common noun meaning any work that controls its originator. *The Bride of Lammermoor* by Scottish poet-novelist Walter Scott, 47. *Marriage* by Scottish novelist Susan Edmonstone Ferrier, 36, who has developed a close friendship with Scott.

Theater: *Sappho* by German playwright Franz Grillparzer, 27, 4/21 at Vienna's Burgtheater. Grillparzer's Sappho is the ruler of Lesbos. She returns with laurels from the competition at Olympia, accompanied by young Phaon, whom she loves and proposes to make her co-ruler. When she discovers that he is in love with Melitta, a slave, she arranges to have the girl secretly removed from the island, but Phaon manages to flee with Melitta. They are captured and returned to Sappho, Phaon tells her he loves her but only as a goddess, and Sappho realizes that she was not meant for an ordinary existence. She announces that her place is with the gods, bestows her blessings on Phaon, and throws herself into the sea, where she drowns.

1819

The Portuguese princess Maria Leopoldina gives birth at Rio April 4 to a girl, Maria da Glória, who will grow up to rule Portugal as Maria II (*see* 1817). Maria Leopoldina suffers a miscarriage in December (*see* 1821).

Hawaii's Kamehameha dies May 8 at age 82 after a 24-year reign that has consolidated the Sandwich Island kingdom. His favorite wife, Kaahumanu, an Amazonian warrior who will survive until 1832, succeeds as co-ruler with the new king, a youth of 22, and his mother, Keopuloani. The two widows persuade him to dine publicly with them at Kailua and to permit food for both sexes to be cooked in the same oven, defying traditional taboos. The new king will reign until 1824 as Kamehameha II.

The stethoscope invented by French physician René-Théophile-Hyacinthe Laënnec, 38, is a roll of paper that avoids the indelicacy of having to place the physician's ear to the heaving bosom of a female patient.

Middlebury, Vt., educator Emma Hart Willard, 32, presents her "Plan for Improving Female Education" to Gov. De Witt Clinton and sends copies to prominent men throughout America. Printed at her own expense, it argues that the current system of privately financed education is inadequate because most schools are operated by their proprietors only as commercial ventures, many (especially those for girls) have no entrance requirements, they have few regulations, and their curricula are shallow. Willard has evolved her own teaching methods, after being denied admission because of her sex by Middlebury College to study its curriculum, methods, and standards, and has run her own school since 1814. Education, she says, "should seek to bring its subjects to the perfection of their moral, intellectual, and physical nature, in order that they may be of the greatest possible use to themselves and others." Since women give society its moral tone, Willard concludes, the country will benefit from quality female education. The New York State Legislature rejects her plan, but Gov. Clinton is more receptive (*see* 1821).

Fiction: *Ivanhoe* by Walter Scott, whose heroine, Rebecca, is modeled on Philadelphia philanthropist Rebecca Gratz, now 39, who 10 years ago nursed Washington Irving's dying fiancée (*see* 1801). Irving met Scott 2 years ago on a visit to Britain and spoke about Gratz.

Poetry: *Poetic Attempts* (*Skaldeförsök*) by the late Anna Maria Lenngren, who died 2 years ago at age 63.

Painting: *Young Boy Near an Apple with a Fistful of Sticks* by Jeanne Philiberte Ledoux, now 52; *The Dream of Happiness* by Constance Mayer, who will take her own life in 1821.

Theater: *Altorf* by Scottish heiress and social reformer Frances "Fanny" Wright, 24, 2/6 at New York. Wright, who inherited a fortune at age 2 when her parents died, arrived last year in America with her sister, Camilla, now 22, and toured the northern and eastern states. She has written a tragedy about the Swiss struggle for independence

(starring James Wallach in the title role, it closes after three performances). The Wright sisters will return next year to Britain after a winter in Philadelphia (*see* 1824; Nonfiction, 1821).

1820

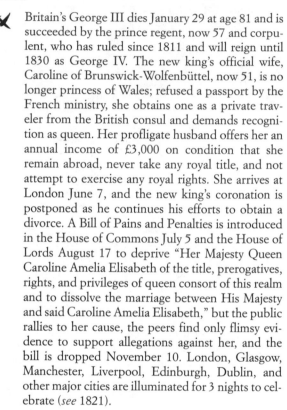

Britain's George III dies January 29 at age 81 and is succeeded by the prince regent, now 57 and corpulent, who has ruled since 1811 and will reign until 1830 as George IV. The new king's official wife, Caroline of Brunswick-Wolfenbüttel, now 51, is no longer princess of Wales; refused a passport by the French ministry, she obtains one as a private traveler from the British consul and demands recognition as queen. Her profligate husband offers her an annual income of £3,000 on condition that she remain abroad, never take any royal title, and not attempt to exercise any royal rights. She arrives at London June 7, and the new king's coronation is postponed as he continues his efforts to obtain a divorce. A Bill of Pains and Penalties is introduced in the House of Commons July 5 and the House of Lords August 17 to deprive "Her Majesty Queen Caroline Amelia Elisabeth of the title, prerogatives, rights, and privileges of queen consort of this realm and to dissolve the marriage between His Majesty and said Caroline Amelia Elisabeth," but the public rallies to her cause, the peers find only flimsy evidence to support allegations against her, and the bill is dropped November 10. London, Glasgow, Manchester, Liverpool, Edinburgh, Dublin, and other major cities are illuminated for 3 nights to celebrate (*see* 1821).

The first boarding school for black girls in Washington, D.C., opens under the direction of teacher Maria Becraft, 15.

Opera: Mme. Vestris makes her Drury Lane debut 2/19 singing the role of Lilla in Cobb's opera *The Siege of Belgrade* and opens there 5/30 singing the role of Don Giovanni in W. T. Moncrief's *Giovanni in London*, a burlesque version of the 1786 Mozart opera *Don Giovanni* that plays to packed houses every night until 7/8, when the season closes.

French champagne bottler Veuve Clicquot, now 43, retires to her Château de Boursin, where she will live for the next 50 years until her death (*see* 1797).

1821

✗ The Portuguese princess Maria Leopoldina gives birth at Rio de Janeiro March 6 to a boy, Dom João Carlos, who becomes heir to the thrones of both Brazil and Portugal but will die early next year (*see* 1819). Her father-in-law, João VI, leaves for Lisbon in late April, never to return, and her husband, Pedro, now 22, begins an absolutist rule in Brazil (*see* 1822).

Caroline of Brunswick-Wolfenbüttel dies August 7 at age 53 after years of efforts by Britain's George IV to vilify, persecute, and humiliate her (he barred her from Westminster Abbey on coronation day in July, and she was taken ill the next evening). She has left instructions that she is to be buried at Brunswick and that her coffin is to be inscribed with the words "Here lies Caroline, the injured Queen of England." George IV, who has increased Mrs. Fitzherbert's annuity to £10,000 in April, rejects the City of London's decision to pay honor to the late queen; hoping to avoid public demonstrations, he swears that Caroline's funeral cortege will not pass through the City even if he has to call out the Life Guards to stop it, but even though his troops actually fire into the crowds at one point they assemble in such dense throngs that it is impossible to control them.

💲 The Daughters of Africa mutual benefit society is founded at Philadelphia by 200 working-class women.

✿ Wethersfield, Conn., inventor Sophia Woodhouse is awarded a U.S. patent for using different varieties of grass, notably redtop and spear grass gathered from riverbanks, to make bonnets (*see* Kies, 1809).

🎓 The Emma Willard School has its beginnings in the Troy Female Seminary at Troy, N.Y., whose Common Council has appropriated $4,000 to finance the institution (*see* 1819). Educator Willard, who moved her Middlebury, Vt., school to Waterford, N.Y., at Gov. Clinton's invitation, now moves it to Troy and offers a serious course of study equivalent to that at the best men's high schools and better

than what is found at some colleges; she will prove that young women can master subjects such as mathematics and philosophy without losing their health or charm.

✒ Nonfiction: *Views of Society and Manners in America* by Fanny Wright is published anonymously at London and, when its author becomes known, wins Wright the friendship of such luminaries as Jeremy Bentham and the marquis de Lafayette: "The prejudices still to be found in Europe . . . which would confine . . . female conversation to the last new publication, new bonnet, *pas seul* are entirely unknown here. The women are assuming their places as thinking beings."

🎼 Opera: Giuditta Pasta makes her triumphant return to the Théâtre des Italiens 6/5 singing the role of Desdemona in the first Paris performance of the 1816 Rossini opera *Otello*. She goes on to sing the roles of Donna Anna in the 1786 Mozart opera *Don Giovanni* and Giulietta in *Romeo et Giulietta*.

👫 A British census shows that women outnumber men and are longer-lived than men.

1822

✗ The Portuguese princess Maria Leopoldina at Rio de Janeiro persuades her husband, Dom Pedro, to defy his father's orders to return to Lisbon (*see* 1821). He announces January 9 that he will remain in Brazil, proclaims independence, is crowned emperor December 1 and will reign until 1831 as Pedro I. He has met the voluptuous beauty Domitila de Castro, 25, at São Paulo and begun an adulterous affair that he will make little effort to conceal from Maria Leopoldina (*see* 1824).

⚕ Upstate New York physician John Stearns publishes a paper on the uses of ergot for inducing labor in childbirth and thus saving the doctor's time as well as avoiding the distress of prolonged labor. President of the State Medical Society, Stearns has learned from an immigrant German midwife about ergot and states that it has no ill effects, but he cautions that it produces an incessant action, leaving no time to turn the child in the uterus or birth canal, and should be used only after the fetus is well positioned for easy delivery. The fungus, which contains several alkaloid drugs for which there is not yet any antidote, begins to come into wide use in the medical profession and by the end of the century will be routinely employed to stimulate uterine muscles, speed up labor, quicken the expulsion and the placenta, and stem postpartum hemorrhage by forcing the uterus to contract, although if used without proper care, or if the fetus does not move as expected, it can cause the uterus to mold around the body of the infant, rupturing the uterus and killing the child, or prevent expulsion of the placenta (*see* 1774; ergotamine, 1918).

Opera: Giuditta Pasta dazzles audiences at Paris in the Rossini operas *Tancredi* (1813) and *Mosè in Egitto* (1818).

Ballet: Italian ballerina Marie Taglione makes her debut at age 8 at Vienna and is soon dancing at the Paris Opéra. Within a few years she will be setting the standard against which all other dancers are judged, and by the time she retires in 1847 she will be world-famous for her choreography as well as her dancing.

Maria Szymanowska is awarded the title First Pianist to the Russian Court (*see* 1810; 1828).

English reformer Francis Place, 51, recommends contraception in his pamphlet *To the Married of Both Sexes of the Working People*. Dropped in quantities throughout London and handed out in the marketplace, it advises coitus interruptus or the insertion of a soft wool or cotton sponge "as large as a green walnut, or a small apple" and "tied by a bobbin or penny ribbon."

New York City's population reaches 124,000; a family of 14 can live comfortably on $3,000 per year.

1823

Virginia gentleman-farmer's wife Anne Royall (*née* Newport), 54, finds herself penniless when her husband dies after 16 years of marriage and his relatives cheat her out of his estate (she met him when her mother went to work as a servant in his house). She petitions Congress for a widow's pension, since her late husband was a prominent Continental Army general, but to earn a living Mrs. Royall begins traveling about the country, writing about her experiences, and giving her readers scathing insights into the lives of prominent visitors, such as Gen. Lafayette, and citizens (*see* 1830).

Nonfiction: *My Mind and Its Thoughts* by Sarah Wentworth Morton, now 64, whose essay "The Sexes" says, "To man belong professions, dignities, authorities, and pleasures; for woman, there remain only duties, domestic virtue, and perhaps as the result of these, the happiness of tranquil submission."

Fiction: *Valperga* by Mary Wollstonecraft Shelley.

Opera: Giuditta Pasta makes her second London debut in April as Desdemona in the Rossini opera *Otello* and goes on to sing the role of Semiramis in the Rossini opera *Semiramide*, both times with the composer conducting; German soprano Henrietta (Henriette Gertrud Walpurgis) Sontag (Sonntag), 17, sings the title role in Carl Maria von Weber's new opera *Euryanthe* 10/25 at Vienna.

1824

Domitila de Castro, mistress to Brazil's Pedro I, gives birth in May to her first child by the emperor, who continues to sleep with his wife, Maria Leopoldina, while flaunting his infidelities (*see* 1822). He will bestow titles and lands on Domitila and make her a lady-in-waiting to Maria Leopoldina next year (*see* 1826).

Hawaii's Kamehameha II and his wife die of measles July 14 on a state visit to Britain (*see* 1819; 1825).

Women weavers at Pawtucket, R.I., join with men May 29 in the first joint strike by U.S. men and women.

Fanny Wright makes a second voyage to America, following in the wake of the Marquis de Lafayette, and joins him on visits to Thomas Jefferson and James Madison. She champions women's rights and free public schools in America (*see* 1821; 1825).

English reformer Robert Owen promotes women's liberation, abolition of slavery, and free progressive education. He purchases New Harmony, Ind., from the German Lutheran Rappites who founded it 10 years ago. Owen is starting communes in England, Ireland, Mexico, and the United States, all of them doomed to fail (*see* 1825).

U.S. missionaries, who arrived in the Sandwich Islands 4 years ago, gain support from Hawaii's high chiefess Kapiolani, who hikes nearly 100 miles in December to the 4,000-foot peak of Mauna Loa on the big island (Hawaii), descends 500 feet into the Kilauea Volcano's crater, and—ignoring the pleas of her husband—defies the steaming, hissing lake of red-hot lava, saying, "I fear not Pele" (the pagan god still worshipped by most Hawaiians). (When she is found to have breast cancer in the 1840s, Kapiolani will undergo a mastectomy without anesthesia.)

Nonfiction: *A Narrative of the Life of Mrs. Mary Jemison Who Was Taken by the Indians in the Year 1755 When Only about Twelve Years of Age and Has Continued to Reside Amongst Them to the Present* by upstate New Yorker Mary Jemison, 81, whose book will outsell works by Sir Walter Scott and James Fenimore Cooper until the end of the decade (she has dictated her story to schoolteacher James Everett Seaver). Jemison married a member of the Delaware tribe, who "soon gained my affection" and "Strange as it may seem, I loved him." Her Seneca captors sided with the British during the Revolution and deeded land to her when they were removed to reservations following independence.

Fiction: *Hobomok: A Tale of Early Times* by Massachusetts writer Lydia Maria Francis, 22, depicts consensual marriage between a white woman and an Indian; *A Winter in Washington* by U.S. novelist Margaret Bayard Smith, 45, who in 1800 married the editor of the *National Intelligencer*, a Jeffersonian newspaper in the nation's capitol; *Redwood* by Miss (Katherine Maria) Sedgwick, 34, who will become the best-known U.S. woman novelist of her day; *The Inheritance* by Susan Edmonstone Ferrier; *Duke Christian of Lüneburg* by Jane Porter.

Poetry: *Don Juan* by English poet George Gordon, Lord Byron, who dies of marsh fever at Missolonghi April 19 at age 36 while helping the Greeks in their fight for independence: "Man's love is of man's life a thing apart, 'Tis woman's whole existence," Byron has written.

Painting: *View of a Portion of the Château of Fontainebleau* and *Scene from the Novel of Gil Blas of Santillane* by Adrienne Grandpierre-Deverzy.

Japanese *ikebana* (flower arranging) master Ippo Mishosai dies at age 63 after having founded the Misho school at Osaka. Originally a simple offering of floral arrangements to the gods and, later, to Buddha, *ikebana* was formalized as an art form in the late 15th century and by the early 17th century had developed into a complex style called Rikka with rigid rules. Nageire, a more flexible and natural style, has gained popularity, and Mishosai has combined characteristics of both styles into a style called Kakubana, which tries to give free expression to the feelings and emotions of the arranger and will gain widespread acceptance, especially in the western part of Japan (*see* 1927).

First performances: Henrietta Sontag sings in Ludwig van Beethoven's new Symphony No. 9 in D minor (*Choral*) 5/7 and in his Missa Solemnis 5/13, both at Vienna.

Opera: Spanish mezzo-soprano Grace Vallemaria (Felicia) García, 17, makes her London debut 6/17 at the King's Theatre singing the role of Rosina in the 1816 Rossini opera *Il Barbiere di Seviglia*, voyages to America with her despotic father and the family, opens the New York season 11/29 at the Park Theatre singing the same role, but next year will marry Eugène Malibran, a French merchant, in order to free herself from her father's demands.

The Virginia Housewife by Mary Randolph (*née* Randolph), 72, is the first regional American cookbook. It contains recipes for such Southern specialties as Virginia ham, turtle soup, and gooseberry fool.

1825

Hawaii's Kamehameha III becomes king at age 12 upon news of his brother's death last year in England. Kaahumanu, widow of Kamehameha I, will rule as regent until her death in 1832, the new king will be crowned the following year, and he will reign until 1854.

Fanny Wright publishes a pamphlet under the title "A Plan for the Gradual Abolition of Slavery in the United States Without Danger of Loss to the Citizens of the South," urging Congress to set aside large tracts of public land for emancipated slaves. In December, she purchases 640 acres near Chickasaw Bluffs (later Memphis), Tenn., and establishes the Nashoba (Chickasaw for "wolf") community with a Scottish plantation overseer (see 1828).

Scottish social reformer Robert Dale Owen, 24, accompanies his father to the New Harmony community in Indiana that Robert Owen purchased last year. After a visit to Britain late in 1827, the son will return to America and remain there, and although New Harmony will not survive beyond 1828 it will be the first of many American communes.

Pennsylvania ironworks owner Rebecca Lukens, 31, takes over the works on the Brandywine Creek left to her by her late husband, who has just died after winning a navy contract to make the boiler plate for the U.S.S. *Codorus*, which is to be the first U.S.-built metal-hulled vessel. The job is behind schedule and the business in debt, but Lukens, who has a newborn child, rejects her mother's advice and makes up her mind to see the job through. She hires her brother-in-law to manage the workmen, handles all the paperwork herself, sets piece rates, watches costs, and sets prices high enough to yield a profit. The *Codorus* is completed with plate from her mill, and the ironworks will grow to become Lukens Steel, a major supplier of plate for locomotives, steamboats, and machinery.

Nonfiction: *Memoirs* (Part I) by English courtesan Harriette Wilson (*née* Dubochet), 39, whose lovers since age 15 have included the earl of Craven, the duke of Argyll, the marquis of Worcester, and the duke of Wellington (who has spurned suggestions that he pay to have the revelations suppressed, snarling, "Publish and be damned!").

Poetry: *Das Hospiz am grossen Sant Bernard* by German poet Annette von Droste-Hülsoff, 28.

Painting: *Slice of Watermelon* by Philadelphia painter Sarah Miriam Peale, 25, whose father, James, paints miniatures and whose uncle, Charles Willson Peale, is famous for his portraits of George Washington. She travels to Washington, D.C., where she does a portrait of the marquis de Lafayette, who is visiting America.

Theater: Mme. Vestris plays the leading role of Phoebe in the three-act James Job Poole comedy *Paul Pry* at London's Haymarket Theatre, singing the song "Cherry Ripe."

Opera: Giuditta Pasta sings in Rossini's new opera *Il Viaggio a Reims* 6/19 at Paris; Henrietta Sontag makes her Berlin debut at the Königstädter 8/3 as Isabella in the 1813 Rossini opera *L'Italiana in Algeri*.

Every Woman's Book: Or, What Is Love? by English physician Richard Carlile is the first book on birth control in Britain. It recommends coitus interruptus (partial or complete withdrawal) for contraception or use of the sponge, which is "certainly effectual in all cases; but not so easily observed by all persons." Carlile mentions an English duchess who "never goes out to dinner without being prepared with a sponge." He speaks of French and Italians who "wear them fastened to their waists, and always have them at hand." Carlile also recommends that a man wear a *baudruche*, or "glove."

1826

Brazil's Pedro I celebrates his 28th birthday in October by granting patents of nobility to the father, brothers, and a distant cousin of his mistress, Domitila (see 1824). Pedro's empress, Maria Leopoldina, asks the Austrian minister to convey news of her situation to her father, the emperor Franz, in Vienna, and orders Pedro to send Domitila away. Pedro refuses, she suffers a miscarriage December 2, and 6 days later she dictates a letter to her sister Marie-Louise, saying, "For almost four years . . . , for the love of a seductive monster, I have been reduced to the state of greatest slavery and totally forgotten by my adored Pedro. Lately I have received final proof that he has forgotten me completely, mistreating me in the presence of that very one who is the cause of all my afflictions." She dies December 11 of puerperal fever at age 29, survived by four of her six children, including a year-old son who will rule Brazil from 1841 to 1889 as Pedro II.

The British Lying-in Hospital establishes courses for "monthly nurses"—women who will nurse mothers during the lying-in period but who are not, at least officially, supposed to deliver children.

New York opens its first high schools for girls, but they will soon be closed.

Juvenile Miscellany, founded by Lydia Maria Francis, is the first monthly magazine for children. It will continue only until 1833.

Nonfiction: *Sketches of History, Life and Manners of the United States* by Anne Newport Royall, who calls on booksellers at Baltimore, Philadelphia, New York, Albany, New Haven, Springfield, Hartford, Worcester, and Boston to push sales; *Diary of an Ennuyée* by Irish critic Anna Brownell Jameson (*née* Murphy), 32.

Opera: Giuditta Pasta sings at Paris in March in the new Rossini opera *Zelmira*; Henrietta Sontag makes her Paris debut 5/15 at the Théâtre des Italiens singing the role of Rosina in the 1816 Rossini opera *Il Barbiere di Siviglia*.

A sixth edition of the 1798 *Essay on Population* by Thomas R. Malthus expands the original pamphlet into a massive book which points out that in an industrialized society national income tends to outpace population growth. The size of the family becomes a function of choice through adequacy and prevalence of contraceptive measures. Poor laws, says Malthus, encourage large families with doles. He recommends late marriage and "moral restraint" to relieve mankind, at least briefly, of its inevitable fate.

1827

The first free school for infants opens at New York under the direction of Joanne Bethune, now 57, to free working-class parents from some of the burdens of child care. Bethune is a disciple of Swiss educator Johann Heinrich Pestalozzi, and her school, which is soon followed by eight others, is open to children of 18 months to five years of age.

Fiction: *Hope Leslie* by Miss Sedgwick; *The O'Briens and the O'Flahertys* by Sydney Morgan.

Theater: *Marriage for Money* (Le Mariage d'Argent) by French playwright Eugène Scribe, 35, 12/3 at the Théâtre-Française, Paris.

Music: German composer (Jakob Ludwig) Felix Mendelssohn (-Bartholdy), 18, has his Overture to *A Midsummer Night's Dream* performed for the first time 2/17 at Stettin. Mendelssohn's talents as a pianist and composer are surpassed by those of his sister Fanny, 21, who was told at age 14, "Music will perhaps be Felix's profession, while for you it can and must be only an ornament, never the root of your being and doing . . . and your very joy at the praise he earns proves that you might, in his place, have merited equal approval." She has not been permitted to publish her many choral and piano pieces, six of which Felix will publish under his own name (*see* 1842).

1828

President John Quincy Adams resists exhortations from his wife, Louisa, to get out of the house and campaign actively for reelection. She has been angered to read of an Irish immigrant girl who was sexually abused by her master and has written two fictional poems about a girl who commits suicide when her hopes are dashed of marrying the young master who took advantage of her. Despite her own vigorous efforts, her husband loses to war hero Andrew Jackson, whose overweight wife, Rachel (*née* Donnelson), has been accused of bigamy and adultery in a smear campaign of speeches and handbills (her first husband had filed for divorce and she had believed herself free to marry Jackson even though, technically, she was still married).

Madagascar's Hova king Radama I dies after an 18-year reign that has encouraged the spread of British influence. He is succeeded by his queen Ranavaloana I who will reign for 33 years, remaining throughout hostile to both French and British influence and the efforts of missionaries.

Fanny Wright, now 32, arrives in January at her Nashoba community with English barrister's wife Frances Trollope (*née* Milton), 47, whose husband is trying to develop a Cincinnati business after the failure of his legal practice. They find that Wright's overseer and his mulatto mistress have set up a colony of free love and let the plantation go to ruin, Mrs. Trollope hurries back to Cincinnati, and Wright publishes an article in the *Memphis Advocate* attacking racially segregated schools, organized religion, racial taboos in sexual relations, and the institution of marriage: "The marriage law existing without the pale of the institution [Nashoba] is of no force within that pale. No woman can forfeit her individual rights or individual existence, and no man assert over her any rights or power whatsoever beyond what he may exercise over her free and voluntary affection. . . . Let us inquire—not if a mother be a wife, or a father a husband, but if parents can supply, to the creatures they have brought into being, all things requisite to make existence a blessing." About sex she writes, "Let us not teach that virtue consists in the crucifying of the affections and appetites. . . . Let us attach ideas of purity to monastic chastity, impossible to man or woman without consequences fraught with evil." She spends the summer at the failing New Harmony community, making plans to terminate her Nashoba community (it will become Germantown), transport its slaves to Haiti, and free them (*see* 1825; 1829).

Girls and women at Dover, N.H., organize the first strike of U.S. women wage earners after the cotton-mill owners post new regulations, which include: "The bell to call the people to work will be rung 5 minutes and tolled 5 minutes; at the last stroke the entrance will be closed and a fee of 12½ cents exacted of anyone for whom it may be opened"; "No person can be allowed to leave work without permission of the overseer"; and "No talking can be permitted while at work, except on business." The 12½-cent fine for tardiness represents one-third of a day's wage. Several hundred women join in the strike, but they return to work after a few days (*see* 1834).

English paleontologist Mary Anning, 29, discovers the bones of a prehistoric pterodactyl, the first such find ever. As a child she discovered the fossil skeleton of an icthyosaurus in a cliff at her native Lyme Regis.

The Royal Astronomical Society awards English astronomer Caroline Lucretia Herschel, 78, its gold medal. She has discovered eight comets and three nebulae, but the medal is for arranging the catalog of star clusters and nebulae discovered by her late brother William (originally Friedrich Wilhelm), who in 1781 discovered the planet Uranus, using a telescope in his backyard at Bath, and became private astronomer to the king.

An English physician suggests that the word *obstetrician*, from the Latin "to stand before," be used to denote a specialist in childbirth in place of such terms as male midwife, man midwife, midman, *accoucheur*, and even androboethogynist.

Fanny Wright (above) hears that religious revivalism is sweeping Cincinnati. She goes to the city and delivers a series of anticlerical lectures.

The *Ladies' Magazine* begins publication at Boston in January with the avowed aim "to make females better acquainted with their duties and privileges." Editor of the new 50-page magazine is onetime schoolteacher Sarah Josepha Hale (*née* Buell), 39 (*see* 1834).

Fiction: *Sketches from Everyday Life* (*Teckninger utur Hvardagslivet*) by Swedish writer Fredrika Bremer, 24, has been written to help finance the charitable work she is doing among the cottagers on her family's estate just south of Stockholm; *The Field of Forty Footsteps* by Jane Porter.

Opera: Grace Malibran makes her Paris debut 4/8 in the role of Sémiramide at the Théâtre des Italiens; Henrietta Sontag makes her London debut at the King's Theatre 4/19 singing the role of Rosina.

Music: German piano prodigy Clara (Josephine) Wieck, 9, makes her first public appearance 10/30 at Leipzig's Gewandhaus. She returned to Europe alone last year. Maria Szymanowska ends her performing career, settles at St. Petersburg, and devotes herself to teaching, heading a salon that attracts the capital's social and artistic elite, Glinka and Pushkin included.

America's Shakers drop their permissive attitude toward alcohol, forbidding the use of "beer, cider, wines, and all ardent liquors . . . on all occasions; at house-raisings, husking bees, harvestings, and all other gatherings" (*see* 1774).

1829

✕ President Andrew Jackson takes the oath of office March 4 amid gossip about the new wife of Sen. John Eaton (D., Tenn.), Jackson's choice for secretary of war. Margaret "Peggy" Eaton (*née* O'Neale), 28, has been the center of gossip for years. She was first married in 1816, at age 16, to John Timberlake, a naval purser by whom she bore three children, but he proved unreliable, lost several jobs, and began drinking heavily. Sen. Eaton, a rich young widower who in 1818 had taken a room at the boardinghouse run by Peggy's father, helped Timberlake obtain a navy commission and began escorting Peggy to Washington parties. Timberlake died last year in the Mediterranean, Eaton has married Peggy January 1 in a ceremony performed by the Senate chaplain; Tennessee's entire congressional delegation has called on the White House to urge that Jackson name someone other than Eaton as secretary of war, Jackson defies them (his own wife, Rachel, has died of a heart attack a few weeks before the inauguration), most of official Washington snubs the Eatons, Peggy forbids her new husband to accept an ambassadorship that would remove them from the country, and Jackson calls a Cabinet meeting in September specifically to discuss the Eaton affair (*see* 1831).

✊ British authorities in India abolish the practice of *suttee* whereby Hindu women burn themselves on their husbands' funeral pyres. While the practice varies from one part of the country to another, in some places it is considered a noble act while in Bengal it is rarely voluntary: widows are dragged screaming to the pyres by sons wishing to avoid the burden of having to support aged relatives.

Charleston reformers Sarah Moore Grimké, 36, and her sister Angelina Emily, 24, leave for the North. Members of a slaveholding family, they will become convinced Quakers and take active roles in the antislavery movement while writing and lecturing also on women's rights (*see* 1836).

Fanny Wright purchases a small church in New York's Broome Street, near the Bowery, early in the year and turns it into a Hall of Science, giving lectures (*see* 1828).

Robert Dale Owen and Fanny Wright (above) move their newspaper, the *Free Enquirer* (formerly the *New Harmony Gazette*), to New York and use it to condemn capital punishment and demand improvements in women's rights, including liberal divorce laws, legal rights for married women, and equal educational opportunities.

✒ Nonfiction: *The Frugal Housewife* by Lydia Maria Francis will go through 21 editions in the next decade.

Poetry: *The Sorrows of Rosalie* by Irish poet Caroline Elizabeth Sarah Norton (*née* Sheridan), 21, who 2 years ago married a 27-year-old member of Parliament, has borne three sons, has taken up writing because her dissolute barrister husband does not provide for them, and gains some measure of economic independence (*see* 1836); "Retrospection" is published under the name "Helen" in the 2-year-old *Ladies' Magazine*, edited by Sarah Josepha Hale, who encourages its author, Sarah Ellen Power Whitman, 26, to make further contributions.

🎭 Theater: English actress Fanny (Frances Anne) Kemble, 19, makes her debut in October at London's Royal Theatre in Covent Garden playing the role of Juliet with the company headed by her father, Charles, and mother, Maria Theresa De Camp Kemble. An immediate success, she is soon able to recoup her family's failing fortunes and revive the popularity of the Royal Theatre.

👫 Fanny Wright (above) urges easier access to safe methods of contraception; opponents call her "the great red harlot of infidelity."

1830

✕ Britain's debauched George IV dies childless June 26 at age 67 and is succeeded by his childless brother William, 64, duke of Clarence, who will reign until 1837 as William IV. His consort, 38, whom he married in 1818, is the daughter of George, duke of Saxe-Coburg-Meiningen, and will reign as Queen Adelaide, but her own two daughters died in infancy and she, too, is childless.

✊ Fanny Wright returns from the Caribbean in June after having transported slaves from her Nashoba community to Haiti at great expense and personal discomfort. She has emancipated the slaves and made arrangements for their housing and employment (*see* 1828). She sails in July for Europe, her sister will die next year, and she will return in 1835 to America, where she will continue until her death at Cincinnati in December 1852 to write and lecture on such causes as more equitable distribution of property, the gradual emancipation of slaves and settlement of freedmen outside the United States, and women's rights.

The Church of Jesus Christ of Latter-Day Saints is founded April 6 at Fayette, N.Y., by local farmhand Joseph Smith, Jr., 25, who has *The Book of Mormon* published in 522 pages at Palmyra, N.Y. The book claims that the Indians of the New World were originally Jews who sailed from the Near East in the 6th century B.C. and who received a visit from Jesus Christ after his resurrection. Smith says he has translated the book with miraculous help from strange hieroglyphics on some golden tablets buried near Palmyra and revealed to him by an angel named Moroni. Mormons will practice polygamy, and their marriages will make Smith and his followers unwelcome in many communities.

Paul Pry begins weekly publication at Washington, D.C., with gossip unearthed by journalist Anne Newport Royall (*see* 1823). Carrying a green umbrella and a newspaper subscription book, she lays siege to local politicians, who may incur her vitriol if they do not subscribe to the paper that she will rename *The Huntress*.

Godey's Lady's Book begins publication at Philadelphia under the name *Lady's Book*. Publisher Louis Antoine Godey, 26, will acquire Sarah Josepha Hale's magazine in 1837.

Poetry: "Mary Had a Little Lamb" by Sarah Josepha Hale, whose verse in Lydia Maria Francis's magazine *Juvenile Miscellany* will be set to music from the song "Goodnight, Ladies" in 1867.

Birds of America by French-American artist and naturalist John James Audubon, now 45, is published in the first of its several editions (*see* 1813). His wife's financial support has enabled Audubon to pursue his passion for painting birds from life; his work began appearing in London 3 years ago (*see* 1839).

Theater: Mme. Vestris leases London's Olympic Theatre from John Scott 12/6 at an annual rental of £1,000. Built in 1806 from the timbers of a French man-o'-war, the Olympic is a few steps from Drury Lane at Castle and Wych streets and has a capacity of 1,800. Mme. Vestris obtains a license from the Lord Chamberlain to present "entertainments of music, dancing, bulettas, spectacle, and pantomime from Michaelmas to Easter" (a "buletta" is a short, light musical piece in verse similar to French vaudeville). Maria Foote, a popular soubrette, agrees to perform for a number of evenings before going on tour, and Mme. Vestris hopes to make the Olympic a theater of the beau monde.

Opera: Italian mezzo-soprano Giuditta Grisi, 24, creates the role of Romeo in the new opera *I Capuleti e i Montecchi* by composer Vincenzo Bellini, 28, 3/4 at Venice's Teatro a la Fenice; Italian soprano Eugenia Tadolini (*née* Savonari), 21, makes her Paris debut 10/23 at the Théâtre des Italiens in the Rossini opera *Ricciardo e Zoraide*; Giuditta Pasta creates the title role in the new Gaetano Donizetti opera *Anna Bolena* 12/26 at the Teatro Carcano in Milan and is largely responsible for making the work so successful.

Music: Clara Wieck gives her first complete piano recital 11/8/30 at Leipzig's Gewandhaus. By 1835 she will be acclaimed throughout Europe as a phenomenon, admired by Goethe, Mendelssohn, Chopin, Paganini, and Robert Schumann.

"In whatever proportion the cultivation of potatoes prevails . . . in that same proportion the working people are wretched," writes English political journalist William Cobbett, 67, in *Rural Rides*. Domestic baking and brewing skills have been forgotten by the English peasantry, he says. "Nowadays all is looked for at shops. To buy the thing ready made is the taste of the day: thousands who are housekeepers buy their dinners ready cooked."

Congress makes abortion a statutory crime.

1831

U.S. Secretary of War John Eaton submits his resignation in April, Secretary of State Martin Van Buren (a widower who has been kind to Eaton's wife, Peggy, when others were not) resigns as well, and President Jackson then demands the resignations of three Cabinet members whose wives have snubbed Mrs. Eaton, thus leaving all Cabinet posts empty except one (*see* 1859).

Boston orator Maria W. Stewart (*née* Miller), 28, addresses a crowd at Franklin Hall and becomes the first U.S. woman to deliver a political speech in public before a mixed audience comprised of blacks and whites of both sexes. She will lecture at the meetinghouse for the next 2 years, mostly on the rights of her fellow black Americans, and her talks to the African-American Female Intelligence Society of America will be published, first in the *Liberator* and then in pamphlets.

Nonfiction: *The Mother's Book* by Lydia Maria Francis; *The History of Mary Prince, a West Indian Slave* is the first slave narrative by a woman to be published in America.

Fiction: *Mothers and Daughters* by English novelist Catherine Grace Gore (*née* Moody), 32; *Destiny* by Susan Edmonstone Ferrier is a Highland romance; *The H. Family (Familjen H . . .)* by Fredrika Bremer represents the second and third volumes of her 1828 book *Sketches from Everyday Life*.

Theater: Mme. Vestris opens her Olympic Theatre at London 1/3 with W. H. Murray's *Mary, Queen of Scots*—four one-act plays beginning with *The Escape from Loch Leven*; Fanny Kemble, now 22, voyages to America with her father, now 57, and, among other roles, plays Juliet to her father's Romeo.

Opera: Giuditta Pasta creates the role of Amina in Vincenzo Bellini's new opera *La Sonnambula* 3/6 at Milan's Teatro Carcano and the title role in Bellini's opera *Norma* 12/26 at Milan's Teatro alla Scala, with soprano Giulia Grisi, 20, younger sister of Giuditta.

Moral Physiology; or, A Brief and Plain Treatise on the Population Question by Robert Dale Owen is published at New York. Son of the English socialist factory owner, Owen tries to popularize contraceptive measures more effective than the widely employed coitus interruptus method. He favors using a small, damp sponge tied to a ribbon, because it gives the woman some control, but warns that it is not always effective. French women douche or use a bidet in addition to the sponge (*but see* 1832).

The Female Anti-Slavery Society of Salem, Mass., is founded by free women of color who include Mary A. and Dorothy C. Battys, Charlotte Bell, and Eleanor C. Harvey.

A modern sewing machine devised by New York inventor Walter Hunt, 36, has a needle with an eye in its point that pushes thread through cloth to interlock with a second thread carried by a shuttle. Hunt does not obtain a patent, and when he suggests in 1838 that his daughter Caroline, then 15, go into business making corsets with his machine, she will protest that it would put needy seamstresses out of work.

Nonfiction: *Domestic Manners of the Americans* by Frances Trollope, now 52, who says of her subject, "I do not like them. I do not like their principles, I do not like their manners, I do not like their opinions" (she spent 3 years in the United States collecting material for her book; *see* 1827); *Characteristics of Shakespeare's Women* by Anna Jameson.

Fiction: *Indiana* and *Valentine* by French novelist George Sand (Amandine-Aurore-Lucile Dupin, Baronne Dudevant), 28, who at age 16 inherited her family's estate at Nohant, at 18 married a retired army officer to whom she has borne two children, but has lived independently at Paris for the past year, collaborating under the pen name Jules Sand with author Jules Sandeau, 21, on pieces for *Le Figaro* and shocking Paris by going about in trousers.

Theater: *The Hunchback* by Irish playwright (James) Sheridan Knowles, 48, 4/5 at London's Royal Theatre in Covent Garden, with Knowles as the hunchback and Fanny Kemble as his daughter Julia.

Opera: Giulia Grisi sings the role of Adelina with Giuditta Pasta in the premiere of Gaetano Donizetti's opera *Ugo, Conte di Parigi* 3/13 at Milan's Teatro alla Scala; unable to break a contract she made as a minor, Grisi leaves for Paris, where she makes her debut in October in the title role of Rossini's *Semiramide*.

An Enquiry into the Principles of Population by English scholar Thomas Rowe Edmonds says, "Amongst the great body of the people at the

French novelist George Sand shocked people as much by her amours and attire as by her books.

present moment, sexual intercourse is the only gratification, and thus, by a most unfortunate concurrence of adverse circumstances, population goes on augmenting at a period when it ought to be restrained. To better the condition of the labouring classes, that is, to place more food and comforts before them, however paradoxical it may appear, is the wisest move to check redundancy. . . . When [the Irish] are better fed they will have other enjoyments at command than sexual intercourse, and their numbers, therefore, will not increase in the same proportion as at present."

"Fruits of Philosophy" by Cambridge, Mass., physician Charles Knowlton, 32, is a Malthusian pamphlet advocating contraception. Its author, who claims to have pioneered vaginal douching with a syringe "to destroy the fecundating property of the sperm by chemical agents," is prosecuted for

obscenity, convicted, and imprisoned for 3 months. Knowlton says that douching with solutions of alum, sulfate of zinc, saleratus, vinegar, or liquid chloride is harmless, cheap, will not cause sterility, does not impede coitus, and keeps control of conception in the hands of women, but he stresses the need for an acidic or restringent agent in the douche solution, not just cold water. Douches will soon be readily available at pharmacies and apothecary shops and sold by respectable mail-order houses, purportedly for hygienic use. Not for well over a century will scientists learn that sperm can sometimes move in less than 10 seconds from the vaginal canal into the cervix, where douching is of no avail.

1833

Spain's Ferdinand VII dies at Madrid September 29 at age 48 after a repressive 19-year reign. His 2-year-old daughter will reign until 1868 as Isabella II, dominated first by Ferdinand's fourth wife, Maria Christina of Naples (who 3 years ago persuaded Ferdinand to abolish the Salic Law in Spain by pragmatic sanction) and then by profligate courtiers.

Portugal's Maria II is restored to the throne by her father, Dom Pedro, who has returned from Brazil and defeated her brother Dom Miguel with French and British aid. A quadruple alliance of Britain, France, Spain, and Portugal will expel Miguel from Portugal at the end of May 1834 following the death of Dom Pedro, and Maria will reign until 1853 through two insurrections.

 Parliament orders abolition of slavery in all British colonies by August 1 of next year in a bill passed August 23. Children under 6 are to be freed immediately, slaves over 6 given a period of apprenticeship that will be eliminated in 1837. Slave owners are to be given £120 million in compensation.

A factory act voted by Parliament August 29 forbids employment of children under age 9, forbids factory owners to work children between 9 and 13 for more than 48 hours per week, requires that children under 13 be given at least 2 hours' schooling per day, limits working hours for children between 13 and 18 to 12 per day, 69 per week. But

Tories have opposed the measure, as have many Whigs; it applies only to textile mills; and its safeguards will prove inadequate.

"An Appeal in Favor of That Class of Americans Called Africans" by Boston abolitionist David Lee Child and his bride, Lydia Maria (Francis) Child, now 31, proposes that blacks be educated. The idea is considered outrageous in most circles, but the "Appeal" converts many supporters of slavery to the abolitionist cause.

Lydia Maria Child helped sway supporters of slavery to the cause of abolition, outraging her critics.

Canterbury, Conn., schoolmistress Prudence Crandall, 29, admits a black girl to the private girls' academy which she opened 2 years ago and immediately comes under fire for violating a special act of the legislature directing her not to admit black girls. On the advice of abolitionist William Lloyd Garrison, 28, and others, she establishes a new school for "young ladies and little misses of color." Outraged neighbors pressure the state legislature in May to enact enact a bill forbidding the establishment of schools for nonresident blacks without permission from local authorities. Crandall is indicted, convicted, and placed in prison, where she will remain until July of next year, when her conviction will be reversed on a technicality. Local pressure will force her to close her school 2 months later.

The American Anti-Slavery Society is founded at Philadelphia December 4 by abolitionists who include James Mott, 45. The Female Anti-Slavery Society is founded at Philadelphia under the leadership of James's wife, Lucretia (née Coffin), 40, after she finds that her husband's group is for men only.

Lucretia Mott began her feminist-abolitionist-temperance career by speaking out at Quaker meetings. SMITHSONIAN INSTITUTION PHOTOGRAPH FROM A PAINTING BY JOSEPH KYLE

South Carolina's Stephens College has its beginnings in the Columbia Female Academy founded by local families, who engage Lucy Wales as preceptress. Her students receive the same education as men except that the young men are taught Greek and Latin and the women are not.

Nonfiction: *Beauties of the Court of Charles II* by Anna Jameson.

Fiction: *Lélia* by George Sand, whose novel *Indiana* last year asserted the right of women to love and independence. Sand begins a love affair with playwright-poet Alfred-Louis-Charles de Musset, 23.

Opera: Eugenia Tadolini makes her Milan debut at the Teatro alla Scala 10/1 in the Donizetti opera *Il Furioso*.

The diaphragm contraceptive, invented by German physician Friedrich Adolphe Wilde, is a cervical cap, made of ivory, silver, gold, or latex from a wax mold of the patient's cervix, that will never gain much popularity. Women have used sponges for contraception since biblical times; the diaphragm is only marginally more effective (*see* 1880).

instruments—improvements developed recently in France and Germany.

Sarah Josepha Hale's 6-year-old *Ladies' Magazine* renames itself *American Ladies Magazine*; it will be merged into *Godey's Lady's Book* in 1837.

Fiction: *The Cousins* (*Cousinerna*) by Swedish novelist Sophie von Knorring, 37, who will turn out novels at the rate of nearly one per year for the next decade; *Jacques* by George Sand; *Helen* by Maria Edgeworth, now 67.

Theater: Fanny Kemble, now 24, retires from the stage after her June marriage to Pierce Butler, a Philadelphian who owns a rice plantation with 700 slaves on Butler's Island, Georgia, in the Altamaha delta (but *see* 1846).

Opera: Grace Malibran makes her La Scala debut 5/15 singing the title role of the 1831 Bellini opera *Norma*.

Ballet: Ballerina Marie Taglioni, now 29, adopts the bell-like skirt (worn in *Sylphide*) that will become standard for classical dancers worldwide. She has popularized dancing *en pointe* and will initiate the system of ballet examination at the Paris Opéra.

1834

Women cotton-mill workers organize a strike at Lowell, Mass., in February after the owners announce a 15 percent wage cut and some 800 women at Dover, N.H., join the walk-out (*see* 1828).

The Connexion of the Physical Sciences by Scottish astronomer and scientific writer Mary Somerville (*née* Fairfax), 54, advances original ideas conceived after translating Pierre-Simon de Laplace's *The Mechanism of the Heavens* (*Mécanique Celeste*), which she published 3 years ago. Her new work secures her reputation and will win her an annual government pension of £300.

French obstetrician Marie Durocher uses methods developed by midwives at La Maternité hospital in Paris to reduce infant mortality rates in Rio de Janeiro. The first woman obstetrician licensed to practice in Rio, Dr. Durocher believes in as little intervention as possible in normal childbirth but uses the most modern monitoring and measuring

1835

Democracy in America (*De la Démocratie en Amérique*) by French aristocrat Alexis-Charles-Henri-Maurice Clérel de Tocqueville, 35, attributes the prosperity and growing strength of the American people to "the superiority of their women," noting significant differences between the status of women in America and in Europe: "In Europe there are people who, confusing the divergent attributes of the sexes, claim to make of man and woman creatures who are, not equal only, but actually similar. They would attribute the same functions to both, impose the same duties, and grant the same rights; they would have them share everything—work, pleasure, public affairs. It is easy to see that the sort of equality forced on both sexes degrades them both, and that so coarse a jumble of nature's works could produce nothing but feeble men and unseemly women. . . . That is far from being the American view . . . of democratic equality . . .

between the man and woman. They think that nature . . . clearly intended to give their diverse faculties a diverse employment. . . . The Americans have applied to the sexes the great principle of political economy which now dominates industry. . . . In America, more than anywhere else in the world, care has been taken constantly to trace clearly distinct spheres of action for the two sexes."

De Tocqueville (above), who traveled for 9 months in 1831 through eastern Canada, New England, New York, Philadelphia, Baltimore, Washington, Cincinnati, Tennessee, and New Orleans on a commission to study the U.S. penitentiary system, writes that the "inexorable opinion of the public carefully circumscribes woman within the narrow circle of domestic interests and duties, and forbids her to step beyond it" (he does not know that this was far less true of women in colonial America).

Boston physician Harriot Kezia Hunt, 34, and a sister begin a practice devoted primarily to treating women and children. She has studied anatomy and physiology with a local physician for the past 2 years but is otherwise untrained; good nursing, proper diet, bathing on a regular basis, exercise, and rest are her chief recommendations (*see* 1850; Blackwell, 1849).

Nonfiction: *History and Condition of Women in Various Ages and Nations* by Lydia Maria Child; *Goethe's Correspondence with a Child* (*Goethe's Briefwechsel mit einem Kinde*) by German writer Bettina Brentano von Arnim, 50, who in her youth was a friend of Goethe's mother.

Opera: Giulia Grisi creates the role of Elvira in the premiere of Vincenzo Bellini's opera *I Puritani* 1/24 at the Théâtre des Italiens, Paris, and the role of Elena in Gaetano Donizetti's opera *Marino Faliero* at the same theater.

1836

George Eden, Lord Auckland, arrives at Calcutta March 4 to take up his position as Britain's governor-general of India. His devoted sisters Emily, 39, and Fanny, 35, accompany him to join the *memsahibs* whose husbands will soon be fighting Afghan tribesmen on the northwestern frontier (*see*

1841). Emily Eden will find India's heat oppressive, the brutality of some British colonials toward the natives intolerable, and the condition of Indian women—never educated in any way, never allowed outside their houses, and treated as chattels by their men—impossible.

English poet Caroline Norton, now 28, leaves her boorish and abusive husband, George, who is still an unsuccessful barrister (*see* Poetry, 1829). He sues Lord Melbourne, 58, the onetime prime minister, who has been calling upon her each evening, for "alienating his wife's affections," and is awarded £10,000 in damages. Under British law, children belong to their father, and Mrs. Norton is not permitted even to see her sons except in the presence of a lawyer (*see* 1837).

A Married Woman's Property Act is introduced in the New York State legislature but fails (*see* Mississippi, 1839).

Abolitionist Angelina E. Grimké issues a pamphlet under the title "Appeal to Christian Women of the Southern States" (*see* 1829; 1838).

Lowell, Mass., mill owners permit boardinghouses to raise board rates, effectively reducing by more than 12 percent the wages they pay their women workers, virtually all of whom live in boardinghouses. The workers strike in protest, but the strike is short-lived (*see* 1834; 1844).

Comanche warriors attack Fort Parker, Texas Territory, May 19 and kill five members of the Parker family before riding off with 9-year-old Cynthia Ann Parker. She will live happily with the tribe for 24 years (until "rescued" against her will early in 1861 by the Texas Rangers), marry the great chief Nacona, and bear two children—a daughter, Topsannah (Prairie Flower), and a son, Quanah, who will be known as Quanah Parker, the greatest Comanche chief in history.

U.S. missionary Marcus Whitman, 34, takes his wife, Narcissa (*née* Prentiss), 28, and Eliza Spalding to the Pacific Northwest. They are the first white women to cross the continent (*see* below).

Georgia's Wesleyan College has its beginnings in the Georgia Female College chartered at Macon December 23—the world's first college chartered

Pioneer women braved the hardships—hunger, thirst, disease, and hostile natives—of the Oregon Trail. LIBRARY OF CONGRESS

to grant degrees to women. An article by "A Lady" in the *Georgia Messenger* urging establishment of the school has said, "Let the young ladies of this republic continue another half century to receive what has, during the last 20 years, been considered a genteel education, and there will not be energy enough in the country, mental or physical, to guide the helm of state or to defend its priceless institutions." But one man, asked to contribute a starting fund for the new college, has said, "No, I will not give a dollar; all a woman needs to know is how to read the New Testament, and to spin and weave clothing."

Fiction: *Mrs. Armytage* by Catherine Gore; *The Illusions* (*Illusionerna*) by Sophie von Knorring depicts life in Stockholm's high society.

Poetry: *Voice from the Factories* by Caroline Norton (above) is an attack on child labor.

Theater: Boston-born actress Charlotte Cushman, 20, who has failed as an opera singer, makes her New York acting debut 9/12 at the 10-year-old, 3,500-seat Bowery Theatre playing Lady Macbeth to theater manager Thomas Hamblin's Macbeth in the 1606 Shakespearean tragedy; Ann Waring, who plays Lady MacDuff, suffers a serious injury in a fall 9/21, the theater goes up in flames 9/22, and Cushman retreats to Albany (*see* 1837).

Opera: Grace Malibran suffers a severe injury in a riding accident while pregnant, sings in September at the Manchester Festival despite her condition, but dies shortly thereafter at age 28 (the French poet Alfred de Musset writes a poem in tribute); English soprano Elizabeth Rainforth, 21, makes her stage debut 10/27 singing the role of Mandane in Arne's 1762 opera *Artaxerxes* at the St. James's Theatre, London. She will sing at Covent Garden until 1843.

Ballet: Danish ballerina Lucile Grahn, 17, appears in a new version of the 1832 ballet *La Sylphide* staged by August Bournonville, 31, at Copenhagen. She created the role of Astrid in his 1835 ballet *Valdemar* but will move to Paris to escape Bournonville's influence.

Narcissa Whitman (above) praises frontier food, writing, "I wish some of the feeble ones in the States could have a ride over the mountains; they would say like me, victuals even the plainest kind never relished so well before."

1837

Queen Victoria succeeds to the British throne at age 18 upon the death June 20 at age 71 of her uncle, William IV, after a 7-year reign. William's widow, Caroline Adelaide of Saxe-Coburg Meiningen, 44, who married him in 1818 and is credited with having turned a middle-aged rake into a respectable (albeit dull) gentleman, is devasted with grief. Salic law forbids female succession in Hanover, and that kingdom is separated from Britain. A granddaughter of George III, Victoria will reign until 1901.

Mrs. Fitzherbert, mistress to the late George IV, has died with all the rites of Roman Catholicism Easter Monday at age 80.

Japan's Tokugawa shōgun Ienari resigns at age 64 after a 44-year rule marked by widespread disturbances produced in part by Ienari's efforts to reform government and improve education. Ienari has had 40 mistresses; half of his 54 children have died in infancy.

Caroline Norton persuades a friend in Parliament to introduce an Infant Custody Bill, the first piece of

Economic depression begins in the United States following the failure in March of a New Orleans cotton brokerage firm. New York banks suspend specie payment May 10, financial panic ensues, 39,000 Americans go bankrupt, and many thousands more are reduced to starvation.

Tiffany & Co. has its beginnings in a New York "Stationery and Fancy Goods Store" that opens September 18 near City Hall. Merchant Charles Lewis Tiffany, 25, has borrowed $1,000 from his father in Connecticut, he and his partner stock Chinese bric-a-brac, pottery, and umbrellas as well as stationery, total sales for the first 3 days are $4.98, profits the first week total 33¢, but the firm will grow to be one of the world's most prestigious jewelery retailers. Tiffany will start manufacturing its own jewelry in 1848 and add gold jewelry that year, open a Paris branch in 1850, adopt the firm name Tiffany & Co. in 1853, and open a London branch in 1868.

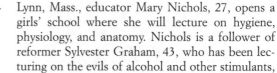 Lynn, Mass., educator Mary Nichols, 27, opens a girls' school where she will lecture on hygiene, physiology, and anatomy. Nichols is a follower of reformer Sylvester Graham, 43, who has been lecturing on the evils of alcohol and other stimulants, meats, fats, mustard, catsup, pepper, and—most especially—white bread. He has called them injurious to health and stimulating to carnal appetites.

Oberlin College opens at Oberlin, Ohio, and admits qualified blacks. Founded 4 years ago, its stated objectives included "the elevation of the female character, by bringing within reach of the misjudged and neglected sex all the instructive privileges which have hitherto unreasonably distinguished the leading sex from theirs." Four women are admitted on an equal basis beginning September 6, making Oberlin the first coeducational U.S. college, but female students, whose "literary" course is considered easier than that of the men, are required to wash the clothes of male students, clean their rooms, and serve them at meals. Women are not permitted to recite in public or work in the fields with the other students.

Mount Holyoke Female Seminary, which opens November 8 in a plain brick building at South Hadley, Mass., is the first U.S. college for women (although it will not institute collegiate standards

Victoria was only 18 when she inherited the British throne. She would reign as queen and empress for 64 years.

women's rights legislation ever brought before the House of Commons (*see* 1836). It proposes merely that judges consider the position of the mother in cases of separation and divorce, but Norton writes in an essay, "The Natural Claim of a Mother to the Custody of Her Children," "You may teach a child to hush his little voice to a whisper when he utters [his mother's] forbidden name . . . but nature's great instinct will remain nevertheless, strong and unchangeable. He will love and honor his mother, he will sometimes wonder at her absence, and sometimes pine for her return" (*see* 1838).

U.S. educator Catharine Esther Beecher, 36, issues a pamphlet under the title "Essay on Slavery and Abolitionism with Reference to the Duty of American Females." Beecher, whose fiancé has been lost at sea, is a daughter of the Calvinist clergyman Lyman Beecher, president of the Lane Theological Seminary at Cincinnati.

for many years to come). Local educator Mary Mason Lyon, 40, proposes to give the best possible education to women of modest means. She has combed the countryside seeking contributions from women, who have given anywhere from 6¢ to a few hundred dollars (but more often have offered quilt scraps for students' sewing baskets or feathers for their pillows). Her goal is to make each student "a handmaid to the Gospel and an efficient auxiliary in the great task of renovating the world." Providing courses in botany, chemistry, composition, geography, geology, history, and logic, charging a tuition of $64, and requiring each student to do 1 hour's housework per day, she is so successful with her 80 students (116 by year's end) that she will have to turn away 400 applicants next year for lack of space.

Catharine Beecher (above) estimated 2 years ago that America needed 30,000 new teachers. "Because few men will enter a business that will not support a family," she wrote, "females must be trained and educated for this employment." She has given up teaching herself in order to promote "the duty of American women to their country," which is to go west and teach the children in frontier towns. Most U.S. schoolteachers are now men, but by the time Beecher dies in 1878 most will be women.

The Pitman shorthand system devised by Englishman Isaac Pitman, 24, is the first scientific shorthand system. It is based on phonetics and employs lines, curves, and hooks with contractions and "grammalogues" for frequently occurring words (see Gregg, 1888).

Nonfiction: *Society in America* by feminist English writer and critic Harriet Martineau, 35, who visited the United States from 1834 to 1836 and writes, "While woman's intellect is confined, her morals crushed, her health ruined, her weakness encouraged, and her strength punished, she is told that her lot is cast in the paradise of women: and there is no country where there is so much boasting of the 'chivalrous' treatment she enjoys. . . . Her husband's hair stands on end at the idea of her working, and he toils to indulge her with money. . . . In short, indulgence is given her as a substitute for justice. Her case differs from that of the slave, as to

the principle, just so far as this: that the indulgence is large and universal, instead of petty and capricious"; "Is it to be understood that the principles of the Declaration of Independence bear no relation to half of the human race?" "Persecution for opinion, punishment for all manifestations of intellectual and moral strength, are still as common as women who have opinons and who manifest strength"; "Nobody, I believe, defends the arrangement by which . . . divorce is obtainable only by the very rich. The barbarism of granting that as a privilege!"

Fiction: *Mauprat* by George Sand; *The Vicar of Wrexhill* by Frances Trollope, who was widowed 2 years ago; *The Neighbors* (*Grannarna*) by Fredrika Bremer.

Poetry: "To an Infant" by Lowell, Mass., poet Jane Erminia Starkweather Locke, 32, who has given birth to her first daughter and writes her verses August 11 about a female child inheriting the wearisome toil of woman's daily existence.

Theater: The February issue of *Godey's Ladies Book* carries actress Charlotte Cushman's "Extracts from My Journal: The Actress." Mme. Vestris at London announces 4/19 that she is bankrupt. Her creditors agree to settle at 4 shillings to the pound; her furniture and other effects are auctioned off at Belgrave Square. Charlotte Cushman opens 8/26 at New York's 2,500-seat Park Theatre playing the role of Patrick in *The Poor Soldier*.

Procter & Gamble is founded at Cincinnati by English-American candle maker William Procter, 35, and his Irish-American brother-in-law James Gamble, 34, a soap boiler. They peddle candles in the street and to the Ohio River trade, grossing $50,000 their first year despite competition from local soap and candle factories and from housewives who make their own soap from grease, fat, and clean wood ashes boiled in backyard kettles (see Ivory Soap, 1878).

Harriet Martineau (above) says of corn on the cob, "The greatest drawback is the way in which it is necessary to eat it. . . . It looks awkward enough: but what is to be done? Surrendering such a vegetable from considerations of grace is not to be thought of."

Parliament passes the Infant Custody Bill, largely through efforts by Caroline Norton (*see* 1837), but their father has sent her sons to school in Scotland, where the new law does not apply (*see* 1842).

Abolitionist Sarah Moore Grimké, now 46, issues a pamphlet under the title "Letters on the Equality of the Sexes and the Condition of Woman; Addressed to Mary Parker, President of the Boston Female Anti-Slavery Society." She rejects any suggestion that women should not speak out on moral issues; as morally responsible individuals, she says, they cannot do otherwise, and she urges that women become ministers. Her sister Angelina has married abolitionist Theodore Dwight Weld (*see* 1836; 1839).

English lighthouse keeper's daughter Grace Darling, 23, rescues the survivors of the foundering ship *Forfarshire* September 7 with help from her father, William, 43, and wins plaudits for her heroism.

Iron in the blood is what enables blood to absorb so much oxygen, concludes Swedish chemist Jöns Jakob Berzelius, 59, who pioneers an understanding of hemoglobin and the iron-deficiency anemia common in women, who lose blood in their menstrual cycle.

Boston schoolgirl Mary Ashton Rice, 18, and five other young women ask Harvard's president Josiah Quincy for admittance as freshmen (year approximate). They demonstrate their qualifications, Quincy admits that they are "unusually capable," but he insists that a woman's place is in the home. Infuriated, Rice tells him, "I wish I were God, for the instant, that I might kill every woman from Eve down and let you have a masculine world all to yourselves and see how you would like that!"

Philadelphia's Hebrew Sunday School is founded by philanthropist Rebecca Gratz, now 57, who has modeled it after schools in "other religious communities." The first of its kind, it uses prayers written by Gratz, who teaches classes and will continue as president of the institution until 1864, when she will retire at age 83. Jewish congregations at New York, Charleston, and Richmond will establish Sunday schools of their own in the next few years.

Fiction: *Spiridion* by George Sand, who begins a 9 year liaison with composer Frédéric Chopin 4 years after her estrangement from poet-playwright Alfred de Musset (he has taken to drink after failures to achieve reconciliation and will never recover, but despair has inspired his most creative work). Chopin at 28 is tubercular and, like Musset, 6 years younger than Sand, who continues to have her novels published while scandalizing Europe with her masculine attire and cigar smoking.

Theater: French actress Rachel Félix, 17, makes her Paris debut in June at the Comédie-Française in the role of Camille in Corneille's *Horace*, leaves the audience spellbound, and begins a career as *la grande Rachel*. Mme. Vestris, now 41, is married July 8 to actor Charles James Mathews, 34, and sails with him a week later aboard the *Great Western* to America. They open at New York's Park Theatre 9/17 in *The Drama's Levee*, *One Hour*, and *The Loan of a Lover* but play to nearly empty houses for 2 weeks before going on to Philadelphia, where business is so poor that the manager of the theater at Baltimore cancels their engagement.

Opera: Anglo-Swedish soprano Jenny (*née* Johanna Maria) Lind, 17, makes her debut at Stockholm singing the role of Agathe in the 1821 von Weber opera *Der Freischutz*.

Music: Pianist Clara Wieck, now 19, is appointed kammervirtuoso to the Austrian court. Playwright Franz Grillparzer writes a poem in her honor entitled "Clara Wieck und Beethoven."

Popular songs: "Annie Laurie" by Scottish composer Alicia Ann Spottiswoode, 28, Lady John Scott, lyrics from the 1700 poem by William Douglas.

Mississippi passes the first U.S. married woman's property law, giving wives the right to hold property—including income from their employment—in their own names.

The U.S. antislavery movement splits into two factions, largely because of abolitionist William Lloyd Garrison's advocacy of women's rights, including their right to participate in the antislavery movement (*see* 1840).

"Appeal to the Christian Women of the South" by Angelina Grimké is published in September in the *Anti-Slavery Examiner*: "I know that you do not make the laws but I also know that you are the wives and mothers, the sisters and daughters of those who do."

Angelina Grimké (above), her sister, Sarah, and Sarah's husband, Theodore Dwight Weld, compile *American Slavery as It Is: Testimony of a Thousand Witnesses*. They suggest that one of the chief monstrosities of slavery is concubinage—the rape and sexual coercion of black women by white masters.

The first state-supported normal school (teacher's college) is founded at Lexington, Mass., through the efforts of Board of Education Secretary Horace Mann, 33.

Nonfiction: *The Wives of England* by English writer Sarah Ellis, who says in her conduct book, "To make her husband happy, to raise his character, to give dignity to his house, and to train up his children in the path of wisdom—these are the objects which a true wife will not rest satisfied without endeavouring to obtain." Her book will be republished in 1849.

Fiction: *The Widow Barnaby* by Frances Trollope; *Deerbrook* by Harriet Martineau; *The Home, or Family Cares and Chores* (*Hemmet*) by Fredrika Bremer.

John James Audubon returns to America, where he will remain permanently after 13 years of shuttling back and forth to Europe (*see* 1830). In 1831, at Charleston, he met John Bachman, a Lutheran minister who was interested in natural history, and Bachman's sister-in-law, Maria Martin, then 35, who has painted branches, plants, flowers, and insects—each as detailed as Audubon's birds—that complement Audubon's work and appear as backgrounds in his new *Ornithological Biography*, whose text she and her brother-in-law have compiled.

Opera: Jenny Lind makes her English debut singing the role of Alice in the 1831 Meyerbeer opera *Robert le Diable*; Giulia Grisi sings the title role in Gaetano Donizetti's 1833 opera *Lucrezia Borgia* in its first London performance 6/6 opposite tenor Giovannio Mario, who will become her professional partner and lifelong companion; Italian soprano Giosapina (Amelia Maria Josepha) Straponi, 23, makes her debut at Milan's Teatro alla Scala and is in large part responsible for the theater's agreeing to produce the opera *Oberto, Conte di San Bonifacio* by composer Giuseppe Verdi, 26, 11/17.

Ballet: U.S. ballerina Augusta Maywood becomes the first American to dance at the Paris Opéra (*see* 1947).

1840

Queen Victoria marries her first cousin Albert February 10 wearing only items of British manufacture. Her husband, 3 months her junior, is a son of the duke of Saxe-Coburg-Gotha and a nephew of the king of the Belgians Leopold I.

Willem I of the Netherlands abdicates October 7 at age 68 after a 26-year reign in order to marry the Roman Catholic Belgian comtesse d'Oultremont, who is unpopular with the Dutch.

Johnstown, N.Y., lawyer's daughter Elizabeth Cady, 24, is married in May to Henry Brewster Stanton, 34, a prominent abolitionist, despite her family's vehement opposition to abolitionists, who are considered fanatics. (Wendell Philips and his wife, Ann, have been influential in converting Stanton to the abolitionist cause.) The word "obey" is omitted from the wedding ceremony at the bride's insistence, and the couple travels the next day to New Jersey for a visit with retired abolitionist Theodore Dwight Weld, his wife, Angelina Grimké Weld, and Angelina's sister Sarah, who lives with them.

The American Anti-Slavery Society holds its annual meeting; Abby Kelley is admitted to the business committee with the support of Boston abolitionist William Lloyd Garrison, now 35. Lucretia C. Mott, now 44, and Lydia Maria Child, now 38, are given places on the executive committee, but more conservative members walk out of the meeting, saying that Garrison's insistence on women's equality muddies the issue of slavery by raising an "extraneous novelty." Abolitionists like Garrison and Wendell Phillips are called "Aunt Nancy Men" and hermaphrodites for their support of women's rights.

that black females, especially if barren, are subjected to considerable physical and psychological abuse (children of slaves being considered the master's property), and returns at year's end more affected by the treatment of women than by the plight of slaves (*see* first Woman's Rights Convention, 1848).

Fiction: *The Widow Married* by Frances Trollope, who will not herself remarry and whose 115 books will scarcely be read after her death in 1863.

Poetry: *The Dream* by Caroline Norton.

Opera: English soprano Sophie Anne Thillon (*née* Hunt), 21, makes her Opéra-Comique debut at Paris 8/11 in the title role of Grisar's opera *Lady Melvil.*

Pianist Clara Wieck marries composer Robert Schumann September 12—the day before her 21st birthday—after a 3-year battle with her father, who has opposed the marriage and tried to prevent communication between the two. She will give birth to eight children in the next decade while continuing to perform at concerts as far away as Copenhagen, teaching with her husband at the Leipzig Conservatory, and giving private lessons at Dresden and Düsseldorf.

Popular songs: "Rocked in the Cradle of the Deep" by English composer Joseph P. Knight, 28, lyrics by Emma Willard, who retired 2 years ago from her Emma Willard School.

The polka is introduced to the United States by Viennese ballet dancer Fanny Eissler, 30, who introduced the dance to the Paris stage 6 years ago and who begins a U.S. tour that will add to her fortune.

Afternoon tea is introduced by Anna, duchess of Bedford. The tea interval will become a lasting British tradition, but the English still drink more coffee than tea.

1841

Jessie Benton, 17, daughter of U.S. Senator Thomas Hart Benton (D., Mo.), marries Lieut. John Charles Frémont, 28, who has just returned to Washington after leading his own exploratory party along the

Female slaves often fetched high prices at auction. Sexual abuse by slave owners was not uncommon. HARPER'S WEEKLY

The World's Anti-Slavery Convention opens at London. Lucretia C. Mott is among the seven women in the U.S. delegation, but the British reject the women's credentials and refuse to seat them on the convention floor. A British clergyman says that including women would subject the convention to ridicule (decorum and social usage as much as any biblical injunction have in this century dictated that women remain silent in public meetings, although Quaker women like Lucretia Mott have always resisted this dictate and spoken out). William Garrison arrives a few days later and joins the women in the curtained gallery at one end of the hall, saying that a meeting which begins by barring representatives of half the human race makes mockery of its claim to be a "world's" convention (*see* 1839). Elizabeth Cady Stanton (above), who has accompanied her husband to London (he is the only New Yorker to speak out in favor of seating the women delegates), meets Lucretia Mott, hears witnesses testify

Des Moines River. Sen. Benton had opposed the marriage, and, in fact, had arranged to have him sent west on his first expedition, but Frémont obtains his father-in-law's support for a survey of the route of the Oregon Trail, and when he returns next year it is Jessie who will write the vivid reports that will capture the imagination of government bureaucrats and the general public (*see* 1847).

Afghans at Kabul rebel against the British garrison in early October, assassinate the puppet ruler Shah Shuja in December, murder British envoys Sir Alexander Burnes and Sir William Macnaghten, and lay siege to the British cantonments, which house officers' wives and children along with soldiers (*see* 1842).

 Queen Victoria replies to Leopold I of the Belgians, who has sent her good wishes on the birth of a child, "You cannot really wish me to be the '*mamma d'une nombreuse famille*' . . . men never think, at least seldom think, what a hard task it is for us women to go through this very often."

A Manual of Midwifery by English physician Michael Ryan says of menstruation, "The hygienic precautions relating to menstruation are scarcely ever duly attended to in this country. The young female, at the age of puberty, is not informed as to the change which is to occur to her; she is left ignorant on the subject; she is much astonished at the first eruption of the uterine secretion. . . . She is not cautioned to avoid, during each periodical evacuation, exposure to cold, humidity, all strong emotions, violent exertions, walking, riding, dancing, etc., exciting aliments and drinks, etc., unless by the Hebrew persuasion."

The *Lancet* for December 11 contains a letter from a country doctor, who complains about a husband who "persisted in being at the bedside [while his wife was delivering]. I confess it did not square with my old-fashioned notions of delicacy or propriety." But the following week's issue contains a letter from a Dr. John Chatto, who writes, "I think a medical man steps far beyond his province when he endeavours to prevent a husband being present at the accouchement of his wife. Man and wife are one, and it is a matter between themselves with which we have nothing whatever to do."

 Brook Farm is founded at West Roxbury, Mass., by New England intellectuals who join former Unitarian minister George Ripley, 38, and his wife, Sophia (*née* Dana), also 38, in forming a commune and school that will pursue truth, justice, and order. Shares of stock in the enterprise are sold to members who include teachers, farmers, carpenters, printers, and shoemakers, with each man and woman receiving a dollar a day for his or her labors and with housing, food, clothing, and fuel provided at cost to all members and their families. By 1844 the commune, whose leading spirit is Sophia Ripley, will have grown to include four houses, workrooms, and dormitories with an infant school, primary school, and 6-year college preparatory course whose classes in botany, philosophy, Greek, Latin, Italian, German, music, and drawing will attract students from as far away as Havana and Manila.

Manhattanville College of the Sacred Heart is founded at New York.

 Theater: Rachel Félix becomes a full-time member of the Comédie-Française, starring in one role after another. She will have two children but no husband, saying, "I will have renters, but not owners."

Opera: Sophie Thillon creates the role of Catarina in Auber's new opera *Les Diamants de la Couronne* 3/6 at the Opéra-Comique, Paris.

Ballet: Neapolitan dancer Carlotta Grisi, 22, appears in the premiere of Adolphe-Charles Adam's classic tragedy *Giselle, ou les Wilis* 6/28 at the Théâtre de l'Académie Royal et de Musique, Paris.

 A Treatise on Domestic Economy for the Use of Young Ladies at Home and at School by Catharine E. Beecher elevates the subject of women's role in the kitchen to new heights and begins a movement toward serious education in the household arts. The *Treatise* will be reissued 15 times in the next 15 years.

1842

Afghans at Kabul permit the British garrison there to leave for India January 6 along with wives and children (*see* 1841). Some of the women have only thin dresses to wear in the bitter cold, some have babies only a few days old, four give birth en route, there is no food, and the women and children are sent back to Kabul January 9 under the escort of Dost Mohammed's son Akbar Khan (the 4,000 men are attacked in the Khyber Pass and only one survives). Prime Minister Peel has appointed Edward Law, 51, first earl of Ellenborough, to replace Lord Auckland as governor-general of India; Lord Ellenborough, who has been deserted by his wife, Jane Digby, arrives February 28; Emily Eden and her sister Fanny leave for England with their brother George March 12; British forces retake Kabul in September and rescue the women and children who have survived.

Britain's Mines Act takes effect, prohibiting employment in mines of women, girls, and boys under age 10. The new law implements recommendations made by an investigative commission, appointed 2 years ago, which found children as young as 5 working underground to haul trucks in passages too narrow for men. Women and girls have been harnessed like horses to pull coal trucks.

One of Caroline Norton's three sons dies after falling from a pony, and her husband finally permits her to see the other two (*see* 1838). She is able to reestablish relations with the boys (both of whom will predecease her), but despite their separation George still controls her earnings, will often balk at giving her an allowance, will delay her publishing contracts, and in 1853 will take her to court in an effort to make her pay debts that are not hers (*see* 1857).

Lynn, Massachusetts, abolitionist Gulielma Maria Estes is asked to leave the Methodist Church because she has befriended former slave Frederick Douglass, 25, with whom she has been seen walking. Female abolitionist groups paid $711.96 to buy Douglass his freedom 4 years ago and bought him a printing press, which he has used to publish an antislavery journal whose first issue employed the slogan, "Right is of no sex."

The British government rejects the calculating machine on which mathematician Charles Babbage, 50, has been working since 1833 after it has advanced £17,000 to help Babbage develop the machine (he has spent some £20,000 of his own capital). Prime Minister Robert Peel has joked,

"How about setting the machine to calculate the time at which it will be of use?" but Italian engineer Luigi Menabrea publishes an account of Babbage's "difference engine" in French and it is read by Augusta Ada Lovelace, 27, the only legitimate daughter of the late Lord Byron, who sees possibilities in Babbage's calculator, translates the account into English, has it published over her initials, A. A. L., in Taylor's *Scientific Memoirs*, and shows the translation to Babbage. He asks why she did not write an original paper, and Lady Lovelace responds with an extension of the Italian's paper that is three times longer, corrects some serious errors in Babbage's own work, and compares his machine with the Jacquard loom of 1801, which is also programmed with punched cards. "It weaves algebraic patterns just as the Jacquard loom weaves flowers and leaves," she writes, but Babbage and Lady Lovelace will lose heavily with an "infallible" betting system for horse races that employs the "difference engine." (Lady Lovelace, who has become addicted to the laudanum and morphine used to treat her chronic asthma, will die of cancer in 1852 at age 36.)

Nonfiction: *The London Journal of Flora Tristan* by feminist French writer Tristan, 39, who writes, "Of course the fate of the married woman is very much sadder than that of the spinster; at least the unmarried woman enjoys a certain freedom, she can enter society, and travel with her family or with friends, whereas once a woman is married, she cannot stir from the house *without the permission of her husband*"; "Prostitution is a blight on the human race . . . for if you men did not impose chastity on women as a necessary virtue while refusing to practice it yourselves, they would not be rejected by society for yielding to the sentiments of their hearts, nor would seduced, deceived, and abandoned girls be forced into prostitution."

Fiction: *The Jew's Beech* (*Die Judenbuche*) by Annette von Droste-Hülsoff, whose only prose work is a fictional study of a murder in a Westphalian village much like the one in which she spent her Roman Catholic girlhood; *Clementine* by German novelist Fanny Lewald, 31, who converted from Judaism to Lutheranism at age 17 to marry a theologian and entered a Lutheran convent when he died just before their wedding; *The Rose of Tistelön* (*Rosen på Tistelön*) by Swedish novelist Emilie Flygare-Carlém, 35.

Painting: *Notre-Dame du Rosaire* (for a church in Senegal) by Marie Eléonore Godefroid, now 64, who will die of cholera in 1849.

Theater: Charlotte Cushman takes over as manager of Philadelphia's Walnut Street Theater in August and opens 9/22 as Mrs. Rankin in *The Belle's Strategem* with Claire Meader as Letitia.

First performances: Giulia Grisi takes part in the first complete public performance of Rossini's *Stabat Mater* 1/7 at Paris.

Felix Mendelssohn visits Queen Victoria, who sings him a song that she believes to be one of his. He writes to his sister Fanny, "It was really charming . . . then I was obliged to confess that Fanny had written the song (which I found very hard, but pride must have a fall), and beg her to sing one of mine also."

Opera: Giosapina Straponi sings the role of Abigaille in the new Verdi opera *Nabucco* (*Nebuchadnazzar*) 3/9 at Milan's Teatro alla Scalla; she first met Verdi late last year, her approval has been decisive in getting *Nabucco* produced, she will retire in February 1846 and begin living with Verdi in July 1847, although she will not become his second wife legally until 1859; Eugenia Tadolini, who is also among the first to embrace Verdi's cause, appears at Vienna's Kärtnortheater 5/19 in the first performance of the Donizetti opera *Linda di Chamounix* and creates the title role of the Donizetti opera *Maria di Rohan* 6/15 at the Kärtnortheater, both times with the composer conducting.

His wife's illness inspires Florida physician John Gorrie, 39, to pioneer air-conditioning (and mechanical refrigeration) with a method for lowering the temperature in her sick room at Apalachicola. Having waited in vain for ice from Maine that has been lost in the wreck of the schooner that was carrying it, Dr. Gorrie takes measures to alleviate the unbearable heat. He sets a vessel of ammonia atop a stepladder, lets it drip, and thus invents an artificial ice-making machine whose basic principle will be employed in air-conditioning (and in refrigeration).

The curette, an instrument invented by a Frenchman in 1723 for scraping wounds clean, is adapted by a Dr. Recamier for scraping the uterus to remove fungal growth or afterbirth. Dilation (of the cervix) and curettage will be widely used to terminate pregnancies, especially in the early weeks of gestation, but the procedure carries a considerable risk of infection.

1843

Abolitionist Sojourner Truth (Isabella [or Isabel] Baumfree or Van Wagener), 46, takes to the road June 1 as an itinerant preacher, speaking out for woman suffrage as well as against slavery. Born in Ulster County, N.Y., and freed by the New York Emancipation Act of 1827, she says she has been

Sojourner Truth adopted that name and toured the North with eloquent orations on the evils of slavery. SCHOMBURG CENTER, NYPL

moved by God to rename herself Sojourner Truth and will defy repeated attempts by mobs to silence her as she electrifies audiences in Connecticut, Massachusetts, Ohio, Indiana, and Kansas, often sharing the podium with Frederick Douglass and rivaling him in eloquence despite the fact that she is illiterate.

Former Boston schoolteacher Dorothea Lynde Dix, 41, reveals inhumane treatment of mental patients to the Massachusetts legislature. She has seen disturbed people imprisoned with criminals and left unclothed regardless of age or sex in cold, dark, unsanitary facilities, chained to the walls in some cases and often flogged. Her detailed, documented report encounters public apathy, but the legislature is moved to enlarge the Worcester insane asylum, and Dix will spend the next 40 years persuading state legislators and foreign officials to build 32 new hospitals and restaff existing facilities with intelligent, well-trained personnel.

Boston physician-poet Oliver Wendell Holmes, 34, publishes an indignant paper on the contagiousness of childbed (puerperal) fever (*see* 1847).

A Guy's Hospital, London, physician named Lever discovers albumin in the urine of women with eclampsia, the toxemia in pregnancy that produces edema, headaches, nausea, and even convulsions.

Miss Porter's School for Girls is founded at Farmington, Conn., by local schoolteacher Sarah Porter, 30, who will head the institution until her death in 1900. It will be the first to introduce science into its curriculum, and will maintain a reputation for academic excellence, but Miss Porter will emphasize "docile, amiable, and respectful manners" and claim that examinations and grades impede a spontaneous love of learning.

Fiction: *The Mayflower* by Cincinnati seminary professor's wife Harriet Beecher Stowe, 32, is a collection of stories and sketches written for periodicals to supplement her husband, Calvin's, meager income; *The Banker's Wife* by Catherine Gore; *Jenny* by Fanny Lewald, whose fiction expresses her support of women's rights; *The Peasant and His Landlord* (*Torparen och hans omgivning*) by Sophie von Knorring; *Consuelo* by George Sand.

Theater: Charlotte Cushman takes her last bow as full manager of Philadelphia's Walnut Street The-

Charlotte Cushman of Boston failed as an opera singer but became world famous as a Shakespearean actress. LIBRARY OF CONGRESS

ater 7/10 (despite her well-schooled swordsmanship, she has antagonized some people by playing the role of Romeo, and the theater has lost money); Cushman opens 10/23 at Philadelphia's Chestnut Theater in the role of Lady Macbeth to English actor William Macready's Macbeth. In December she acts at both the Chestnut and Walnut theaters in Philadelphia while traveling by train to New York every other day to appear with Macready at the Park Theatre.

Opera: Giulia Grisi creates the role of Norina in the premiere of Gaetano Donizetti's opera *Don Pasquale* 1/4 at the Théâtre des Italiens, Paris, and goes on to appear in two other Donizetti operas; *A Midsummer Night's Dream* 10/14 at Potsdam's Neues Palais, with music by Felix Mendelssohn which includes a "Wedding March" that will be used in a British royal wedding in 1858 and will remain popular for generations; Elizabeth Rainforth joins the company of London's Drury Lane Theatre, where she creates the title role 11/17 in Michael W. Balfe's new opera *The Bohemian Girl*.

Dancer Lola Montez (Irish-born adventuress Marie Dolores Eliza Rosanna Gilbert) makes her London debut as a "Spanish dancer" and leaves audiences cold. She eloped at age 19 with Capt. Thomas James and returned with him to India, where she had spent much of her girlhood, but the marriage ended last year in divorce (*see* 1844).

Frédéric Chopin continues his 5-year-old liaison with George Sand, but he has tuberculosis of the larynx and will die in the autumn of 1849 at age 39.

Japan's capital city of Edo has a population of 1.8 million and is second in size only to London, but the nation's total population of nearly 30 million is controlled by infanticide (the Japanese call it *mabiki,* using an agricultural term that means "thinning out"). Hundreds of thousands of second- and third-born sons are killed each year, but daughters are generally spared since they can be married off, sold as servants or prostitutes, or sent off to become geishas (professional entertainers).

1844

A prize-winning essay on Britain's "National Distress" by English author Samuel Laing, 31, reveals the effects of machinery on the country's working class: "About one-third plunged in extreme misery, and hovering on the verge of actual starvation; another third, or more, earning an income something better than that of the common agricultural labourer, but under circumstances very prejudicial to health, morality, and domestic comfort—viz. by the labour of young children, girls, and mothers of families in crowded factories; and finally, a third earning high wages, amply sufficient to support them in respectability and comfort."

"The Song of the Shirt" by English poet Thomas Hood, 44, appears in *Punch* as a protest against sweated labor: "O! men with sisters dear,/ O! men with mothers and wives!/ It is not linen you're wearing out,/ But human creatures' lives!"

The Lowell Female Labor Reform Association founded at the Massachusetts mill town by organizer Sarah G. Bagley and five associates calls on all women to join the struggle for a 10-hour day. Writes Bagley, "In the strength of our united influence we will show these driveling cotton lords, this mushroom aristocracy of New England, who so arrogantly aspire to lord it over God's heritage, that our rights cannot be trampled upon with impunity." The Association will have more than 600 members within a year as branches spring up in every New England textile center (*see* 1845).

Cotton mills at Lowell, Mass., employed girls who lived in dormitories and earned money for their dowries. FROM THE 1868 WINSLOW HOMER DRAWING *BELL-TIME*

Jefferson, Ga., physician Crawford Long, 29, makes the first use of ether in childbirth. He administers it to his wife during the delivery of their second child (*see* Simpson, 1847).

Charles Dickens, in his novel *The Life and Adventures of Martin Chuzzlewit*, shocks readers with his account of the drunken midwife Sairey (Sarah) Gamp. Most infants continue to be delivered at home by midwives, not in hospitals by physicians (*see* Midwives' Institute, 1881).

Nonfiction: *Summer on the Lake* by U.S. transcendentalist (Sarah) Margaret Fuller, 34, who has been giving public "conversations" at Boston since 1839 to further the education of women and become editor of the transcendentalist magazine *The Dial*. Horace Greeley invites her to become literary critic of his *New York Tribune*. *Letters to Young Ladies* by U.S. writer Lydia Sigourney.

Poetry: *Lyrics and Ballads* by Annette von Droste-Hülsoff; "The Boy's Thanksgiving Day" by Boston abolitionist Lydia Child begins, "Over the river, and through the woods/ To Grandfather's house we go . . ."

Theater: *The Drunkard, or The Fallen Saved* by U.S. playwright William H. Smith (originally Sedley), 37, and an anonymous "Gentleman" 2/12 at the Boston Museum. Showman P. T. (Phineas Taylor) Barnum, 34, picks up the morality play about the evils of drink and presents it at Philadelphia, New York, and other cities, where it attracts many women whose husbands have drinking problems.

Opera: Eugenia Tadolini creates the role of Elvira in the new Verdi opera *Ernani* 3/9 at Venice's Teatro la Fenice; Sophie Thillon makes her London debut 5/2 at the Princess's Theatre in the role of Catarina in the 1841 Auber opera *Les Diamants de la Couronne*.

Lola Montez dances at the Paris Opéra and finds the audience no more enthusiastic than that in London last year, but she will receive more heartening receptions at Berlin, Warsaw, and St. Petersburg (*see* 1846).

Pianist Clara Schumann makes a concert tour of Russia, leaving her young children in the care of her husband, Robert.

1845

Mexico severs relations with the United States March 28 following U.S. Senate ratification of a treaty to annex the 9-year-old Republic of Texas, which becomes the 28th state December 29.

The Massachusetts Committee on Manufactures headed by *Lowell Courier* owner William Schouler hears testimony from Sarah Bagley, Eliza Hemingway, Judith Payne, and other textile-mill workers about the evils of the 14-hour work day at low wages in unhealthy conditions. They give the example of 150 people working in one large room lighted by 293 small lamps and 61 larger lamps, with as many as 30 girls per day overcome by the fumes of the lamps. It is the first investigation into working conditions in U.S. history. The employer committee issues a report stating that the factory girls are healthy: "The remedy [for long hours] does not lie with us," it says. "We look for it in the progressive improvement in art and science, in a higher appreciation of man's destiny, in a less love for money, and a more ardent love for social happiness and intellectual superiority." But the women press for the defeat of Shouler, and even though women cannot vote he is defeated in his bid for reelection in the fall.

Nonfiction: *Woman in the Nineteenth Century* by Margaret Fuller, whose work for the *New York Tribune* has made her the leading U.S. critic: "As men become aware that few have had a fair chance, they are inclined to say that no women have had a fair chance."

Massachusetts feminist Margaret Fuller made herself the leading American literary critic of the 1840s.

Fiction: *Eine Lebensfrage* by Fanny Lewald, who meets a Berlin critic with whom she will live until he is free to marry her in 1855; *Comtesse de Rudolstadt* and *Le Meunier d'Angibault* by George Sand.

Theater: Charlotte Cushman makes her London debut 2/14 at the Princess's Theatre playing the role of Bianca in the tragedy *Fazio* by clergyman Henry Hart Milman and goes on 2/17 in the role of Emilia to U.S. actor Edwin Forrest's Othello. *Fashion* by U.S. novelist-playwright Anna Cora Mowatt, 26, 3/24 at New York's Park Theater. Mowatt has been forced by her husband's business failure to earn a living, a friend has suggested that she write a play, and her witty satire on New York society, whose parvenue women fawn obsequiously over what they think of as titled foreigners (in this case a former barber and cook), enjoys an unprecedented 3-week run.

Opera: Eugenia Tadolini creates the title role in the new Verdi opera *Alzira* 8/12 at Naples.

First performances: Concerto for Pianoforte and Orchestra in A minor by Robert Schumann, now 35, 12/4 at Dresden, with Clara Wieck Schumann, now 26, playing the work developed by her husband from a "Fantasy" he composed shortly after their marriage in 1839.

"Infanticide is practiced as extensively and as legally in England as it is on the banks of the Ganges," writes English politician-novelist Benjamin Disraeli, 40, in his novel *Sybil*. Disraeli is criticizing the use of laudanum, the opium preparation commonly employed by British mothers and "nannies" to quiet their infants.

1846

A Mexican war precipitated by President Polk begins January 13, hostilities begin April 25, Californians revolt against Mexican rule in mid-June, and the war escalates as U.S. forces occupy Monterey, Tampico, and other Mexican cities.

The word *osteoporosis* is introduced in medicine to delineate a condition, especially common in postmenopausal women (but also seen in men over age 60), marked by decrease in bone mass with concomitant increase in porosity and fragility. Caused by a disturbance of calcium metabolism, it can drain calcium deposits from the bone matrix until anywhere from 10 to 40 percent of the mineral is gone, making a woman prone to fractures that are slow to mend, giving her "dowager's hump," and causing her to lose several inches in height (*see* 1868).

The Putney Community organized in Vermont by clergyman John Humphrey Noyes, 34, and his followers antagonizes its neighbors. Noyes preaches promiscuity and free love in what he calls the communism of the early Christian church, he opposes monogamy as "idolatrous" and makes child-rearing a group undertaking, his neighbors have him arrested, and they try to break up his communal society (*see* Oneida Community, 1848).

Brook Farm at West Roxbury, Mass., celebrates the completion of a large new central building with a dance the night of March 2, but the building catches fire and burns to the ground. The commune has attracted such eminent visitors as Mar-

She called herself Lola Montez, danced, and captured the heart of Bavaria's mad king Ludwig (among others). RESIDENZ MUSEUM, MUNICH

garet Fuller, but the new building consumed all available funds and the Brook Farm experiment will end next year.

 Fiction: *La Mare au diable* by George Sand.

 Actress Fanny Kemble, who has been horrified by the treatment of slaves on Georgia plantations and consequently disenchanted with her rich husband, returns to the London stage (*see* 1834; Nonfiction, 1863).

Lola Montez, now 28, visits Munich on a European tour and seduces the eccentric Bavarian king Ludwig I, with whom she proceeds to have a scandalous affair (*see* 1844). He offers to make her a countess and provide her with a castle (*see* 1848).

 New Jersey housewife Nancy Johnson invents a portable, hand-cranked ice cream freezer. Her Johnson Patent Ice-Cream Freezer will be patented in 1848 by inventor William G. Young.

Miss Beecher's Domestic Receipt Book by Catharine E. Beecher will go through many printings.

1847

 Explorer John C. Frémont is court-martialed for having helped to lead a revolt against Mexican rule in California; his wife, Jessie, now 23, goes to President Polk to plead his case, but to no avail (*see* 1841; 1861).

 Parliament enacts legislation June 8 limiting working hours of British women and children aged 13 to 18 to 10 per day.

Mormon Brigham Young arrives at the Great Salt Lake July 24 with 143 men, 70 wagons, 93 horses, 52 mules, 66 oxen, 19 cows, three women—Harriet Wheeler Decker Young (*née* Page), Clarissa Decker Young, and Ellen Kimball (*née* Saunders)—and two children.

Cayuse warriors in Oregon country kill Marcus Whitman November 27 along with his wife, Narcissa, and 12 other settlers, who are blamed for the measles epidemic which has wiped out most of the tribe. Peter Skene Ogden, 53, of the Hudson's Bay Company rescues remnants of the group in Decem-

ber after they have been held for ransom for more than 2 weeks (*see* 1836).

 Butterick Patterns have their beginnings in a technique invented by U.S. tailor-shirtmaker Ebenezer Butterick, 21, for printing and cutting paper dressmaking patterns that can be used with sewing machines (*see* Demorest, 1860).

 Massachusetts librarian and amateur astronomer Maria Mitchell, 29, discovers a new comet with her two-inch rooftop telescope October 1, thereby winning a gold medal offered by the king of Denmark and infuriating university astronomers with costly observatories. Other women rally to Mitchell's support, buying her a larger telescope and obtaining press coverage of her achievement.

 Ether is used as an anesthetic in obstetrics for the first time by Scottish physician James Young Simpson, 36, who also discovers the anesthetic properties of chloroform and introduces it into obstetric practice (*see* 1831). Soporific agents including opiates and alcohol have been used in the past, as have pain-relieving remedies such as bloodletting and purges, but all have tended to stop labor or affect the newborn infant. Many physicians and clergymen, while accepting the potential value of anesthesia in surgery, are reluctant to see it used in childbirth, partly on the Calvinistic ground that it may inject a sense of pleasure, which they consider unseemly and even immoral in what should be a woman's painful duty.

Oliver Wendell Holmes becomes dean of the Harvard Medical School, and his 1843 paper on childbed fever finally gains attention.

Hungarian obstetrician Ignaz Philips Semmelweis, 29, shows in May that childbed fever (puerperal fever) is contagious and introduces a strict protocol of cleanliness at a Viennese hospital, requiring attendants to wash their hands in a solution of chloride of lime before examining, touching, or delivering a patient. By year's end, the death rate in his obstetric ward has fallen dramatically but hospital administrators do not accept the validity of his procedures (*see* 1850).

 Oberlin College graduate Antoinette Louise Brown, 22, enters the school's theological course despite efforts by many, including undergraduate Lucy Stone, 29, to dissuade her. Oberlin officials will try for 3 years to make her quit the program, they discourage her from preaching, and they will not award her a degree or a license. She will persevere, nonetheless, and become the first U.S. woman minister (if not the first to be officially ordained).

Fiction: *Wuthering Heights* by English novelist Ellis Bell (Emily Jane Brontë), 29, is a romance about Catherine Earnshaw and Heathcliff; *Jane Eyre* by Currer Bell (Emily's sister Charlotte Brontë), 31, reflects the penury and unhappiness of Brontë's life as governess and schoolteacher in the story of an orphan girl who becomes a governess and falls in love with her sardonic employer, a married man named Rochester: "I grant an ugly *woman* is a blot on the fair face of creation; but as to the *gentlemen*, let them be solicitous to possess only strength and valour: let their motto be:—Hunt, shoot, and fight: the rest is not worth a fillip"; *Agnes* by Acton Bell (Anne Brontë), 27, a third sister; *Edna Etheril, the Boston Seamstress* by Cambridge, Mass., writer

Charlotte Brontë's novel Jane Eyre *reflected her own unhappy life as a poor governess and schoolmarm.*

Mary Andrews Denison, 21, whose work will often appear under the pen names Clara Vance and N. I. Edson.

Poetry: *Evangeline* by Boston poet Henry Wadsworth Longfellow, 40. *The Princess Ida* by English poet Alfred Tennyson, 38, who writes, ". . . This is fixt/ As are the roots of earth and base of all,—/ Man for the field and woman for the hearth;/ Man for the sword, and for the needle she;/ Man with the head, and woman with the heart;/ Man to command, and woman to obey;/ All else confusion" (V, 1). Tennyson's heroine founds a college for women only in which male intruders are subject to the death penalty. Students receive a cross-cultural survey of the oppression of women, including Islam, Indian suttee, and Chinese foot binding, with a view to freeing women from their social conditioning. Princess Ida accepts the fact that some of her students will marry, but urges that they do so on a more equitable basis. A prince betrothed to Ida in childhood disguises himself as a woman and, with two friends, enters the college to persuade her to honor her agreement; his identity is discovered, he openly declares his love, his father and Princess Ida's raise an army to rescue him, they fight a battle with the army of Ida's brother, the college becomes a hospital, the students become nurses, they fall in love with the wounded soldiers, Ida falls in love with the wounded prince, he declares his support of her educational cause but insists that she is wrong to deny love and marriage for it and make it independent of men. Tennyson approves of higher education for women, but only when it serves the purposes of marriage.

Opera: Giulia Grisi sings the title role in the 1823 Rossini opera *Semiramide* 4/6 at the opening of the Royal Italian Opera at London's Covent Garden.

Two Parisian physicians find a way to extract the essence of parsley seeds, obtaining a substance which they call *apiol*. It has little effect on malaria, for which it was intended (quinine being very expensive), but proves to affect women whose menstrual periods have stopped. Prescribed for "menstrual irregularity," apiol is most effective in small doses and will gain popularity as an emmenagogue; by the 1920s it will be sold over the counter at pharmacies to produce abortion, becoming the most favored self-administered abortifacient other than lead plaster (diachylon, or black stick), which is perhaps even more effective albeit more dangerous (it can damage the nervous system and be fatal in large doses). Apiol will be withdrawn from over-the-counter sale for safety reasons in the 1950s and made available by prescription only.

1848

✗ Europe has revolutions as the *Communist Manifesto* written last year by Karl Marx and Friedrich Engels is translated into every language and distributed among working people everywhere. The Cabinet of Bavaria's Ludwig I has come to be called the "Lolaministerium" because of the influence of dancer Lola Montez, countess of Lansfeld, who has persuaded the king to inaugurate liberal policies; he abdicates in March, his son takes over, and Lola Montez flees the country.

The Treaty of Guadelupe Hidalgo February 2 ends the Mexican War, which began in 1846. Mexico loses 35 percent of her territory, including California, in return for $15 million and other concessions.

✊ The first Woman's Rights Convention opens at Seneca Falls, N.Y., July 19 under the leadership of Elizabeth Cady Stanton and Lucretia C. Mott. Attended by 300 delegates, the convention ends 2 days later with resolves to fight for woman suffrage and legal equality in marriage, work, and education. Stanton's husband, who has helped her draft the convention's resolution, gives her free rein in her reform activities but does not attend the convocation in which his wife introduces the resolution for woman suffrage (*see* 1850).

A Declaration of Sentiments read at the Woman's Rights Convention (above) says in part, "The history of mankind is a history of repeated injuries and usurpations on the part of man toward woman, having in direct object the establishment of absolute tyranny over her. . . . He has created a false public sentiment by giving to the world a different code of morals for men and women, by which moral delinquencies which exclude women from society are not only tolerated, but deemed of little account in man. He has endeavored in every way

The first Woman's Rights Convention, at Seneca Falls, N.Y., elicited ridicule from this cartoonist. LIBRARY OF CONGRESS

that he could to destroy her confidence in her powers, to lessen her self-respect, and to make her willing to lead a dependent and abject life." Many women consider the Declaration too daring, and it is adopted only by a narrow margin.

New York State passes a Married Women's Property Act which allows divorced women to retain some of their possessions. Polish-born feminist Ernestine L. Rose (*née* Potowski), 38, who has addressed the state legislature at least five times to urge passage of the bill, is jubilant, as is Quaker reformer Susan Brownell Anthony, 28. A rabbi's daughter who dissociated herself from Judaism at age 14, Rose went to court 2 years later to regain her late mother's inheritance, which her widowed father had contracted to pay an older man as her dowry, traveled to England, married a watchmaker, and at age 26 came with him to America. She has been one of Susan B. Anthony's chief lieutenants in New York, and she says, "Freedom, my friends, does not come from the clouds, like a meteor; it does not bloom in one night; it does not come without great efforts and great sacrifices; all who love liberty have to labor for it." Enacted in April (the State Senate has voted for it 23 to 1, the Assembly 93 to 9), the New York law will be amended repeatedly (*see* Mississippi, 1839; Massachusetts, 1854).

Ernestine Rose, daughter of a Polish rabbi, became a leader in the American suffragist movement. LIBRARY OF CONGRESS

Susan B. Anthony helped to lead the struggle for suffrage and other women's rights. MESERVE COLLECTION

The Oneida Community is founded in central New York State by sawmill owner Jonathan Burt, and preacher John Humphrey Noyes, who has been pressed by his neighbors to leave Vermont and has moved with 25 male and female adherents to the Perfectionist communal association founded earlier by Burt and others. They have asked Noyes to join them and by year's end the Oneida Association has 87 members, including children, although most have come with no idea that husbands and wives are expected to have multiple sexual partners (*see* 1846; 1851).

Physical Geography by Mary Somerville, now 68, will be used as a university textbook until the end of the century. Somerville moved to the Continent 8 years ago.

The *Lancet* for January 1 contains a letter from a Dr. G. T. Gream, who writes of labor pains in childbirth, "That women will die from their effect, no one will deny, and that they *have* done so is certainly true; but to esteem this as a proof of the usefulness of anaesthesia is showing an ignorance of the means always at the command of those who scientifically practice midwifery, which, if properly employed, will, in all cases, effectually prevent the occurrence of death from the prolonged pains of labor."

Females and Their Diseases by U.S. physician Charles Meigs of the Jefferson Medical School at Philadelphia contains the author's remarkable statement, "I am proud to say . . . that there are women who prefer to suffer the extremity of danger and pain rather than waive those scruples of delicacy which prevent their maladies from being fully explored." False modesty keeps many women from seeing (or being seen by) doctors; it also encourages doctors to put Victorian prudishness ahead of sound medical practice (many avert their eyes when they reach under a patient's skirts to examine her, often making misdiagnoses as a result). In a lecture last year, Dr. Meigs said of woman, "She has a head almost too small for intellect and just big enough for love."

New England Female Medical College is founded as a homeopathic school for midwives by Samuel Gregory. It will quickly become a regular medical school and will be merged in 1874 with Boston University.

Queen's College for women receives a royal charter and opens May 1 in Harley Street, London. The principal of King's College began classes for women 3 years ago and, with help from author-poet Charles Kingsley and others, has founded Queen's College with funding from The Governesses' Benevolent Institution and a maid of honour to Queen Victoria. They began raising money 2 years ago after the Taunton Commission criticized female education as dreary and superficial. The first English women's institution of higher learning, it is open to young women from age 12 and upwards, with preparatory classes for girls aged 9 to 12, and will have 50 students by 1850 plus evening classes for governesses already employed. The school offers training in mathematics, the classics, and sport to ensure a livelihood for what are known as "redundant" or "surplus" women—meaning those who cannot find husbands.

"One of the greatest improvements in education is that teachers are now fitted for their duties by being taught the art of teaching," writes Mary Somerville in *Physical Geography* (above).

Fiction: *Mary Barton* by English novelist Elizabeth Cleghorn Gaskell (*née* Stevenson), 38, who gains immediate success with her realistic portrayal of Manchester factory life (which is published anonymously); *The Tenant of Wildfell Hall* by Acton Bell (Anne Brontë), whose second novel is the story of a young mother seeking asylum from her husband, a drunken profligate (Anne's sister Emily dies in December of tuberculosis, which will take Anne's life next year); *Vanity Fair* by English novelist William Makepeace Thackeray, 37, introduces the unscrupulous, self-seeking adventuress Becky Sharp, who claws her way up the social ladder with "only herself and her own wits to trust to," but Thackeray's essential point is that society puts a

premium on hypocrisy, and that a person without money or position can succeed only by violating the ethical principles to which society pays lip service: ". . . it was only from her French being so good, that you could know she was not a born woman of fashion" (XXIX); *François le Champi* by George Sand; *La Dame aux camélias* by French novelist-dramatist Alexandre Dumas, 24, bastard son of Alexandre Dumas père, whose doomed tubercular heroine, Marguerite Gautier, and her lover, Armand Duval, will appear on the stage in 1852.

Fanny Kemble's husband, Pierce Butler, divorces her on grounds of abandonment. She has come back to the United States and is attracting good crowds with her readings from Shakespeare, which she will continue for more than a decade.

Opera: Eugenia Tadolini makes her London debut 5/20 in the 1842 Donizetti opera *Linda di Chamounix* and goes on to sing in the 1843 Donizetti opera *Don Pasquale*. She will retire in 1851.

Popular songs: "Oh! Susanna!" by Pittsburgh songwriter Stephen Collins Foster, 21, is sung February 25 by G. N. Christy of the Christy Minstrels. Foster's nonsense song will be in the repertoire of every minstrel show, and gold seekers will sing it en route to California.

Americans dance the polka to show sympathy with Europe's revolutionists (above).

The Oneida Community (above) will popularize a variation on coitus interruptus for avoiding pregnancy: in coitus reservatus, the male refrains completely from ejaculating, but the technique is risky and requires a high degree of cooperation between man and woman.

1849

Maryland slave Harriet Tubman, 29, escapes to the North and begins a career as "conductor" on the Underground Railway, which started in 1838. Southern planters will put a bounty of $40,000 on her head, but Tubman will make 19 trips back to the South to free upwards of 300 slaves, including her aged parents, whom she will bring North in 1857.

Harriet Tubman led so many slaves out of bondage that she was called "the Moses of her people."

"Discourse on Woman" by Lucretia Coffin Mott responds to a lecture by novelist Richard Henry Dana: the present position of woman is neither her natural nor her original one, Mott writes. God established her natural equality with man, and the lives of great women have demonstrated her natural abilities, yet, like a slave, she has no liberty but is rather in subjection everywhere to man. She is subject to laws that are not of her making, and excluded from a pulpit that disciplines her and binds her to a marriage contract that degrades her.

The first U.S. woman M.D. graduates at the head of her class at Geneva Medical College in Syracuse, N.Y., January 23 after having been ostracized by other students. English-born physician Elizabeth Blackwell, 28, will return to the United States in August 1851 after interning at St. Bartholomew's Hospital, London, and taking a midwifery course at Paris, and although American hospitals will refuse to hire her because she is a woman she will nevertheless play an important role in U.S. medicine (*see* Hunt, 1835, 1850; New York Infirmary, 1857).

Harriet Beecher Stowe, now 38, visits her father, Calvinist seminary president Lyman Beecher, now 73, at Cincinnati with her six children and writes to her husband, Calvin, in Vermont, "Cholera in the city has been malignant. Common vehicles are employed to remove the dead. . . . The haste, the absence of reverent decency, whether we will or no, bring very doleful images to our mind. On Tuesday, 116 deaths. July 10: Yesterday little Charlie was taken ill, not seriously. At any other time I should not be alarmed. July 12: About 1 o'clock this morning Miss Stewart opened my door, crying, 'Mrs. Stowe, Henry is vomiting.' Charlie is getting better and is suspiciously cross. July 17: A Negro servant, Anne Frankie, died yesterday morning and our poor little dog Daisie, that had been ailing the day before, was suddenly seized with frightful spasms and died in half an hour. July 23: At last my dear the hand of the Lord has touched us. Little Charlie is gone, and I write as though there were no sorrow like my sorrow, yet there has been in this city as in the land of Egypt scarce a house without its dead."

Bedford College (The College for Women in Bedford Square) opens at London, the second English women's institution for higher learning (*see* Queen's, 1848; Newnham, 1871; Girton, 1873).

The *Lily* begins publication January 1 at Seneca Falls, N.Y., as a temperance newspaper—the first paper owned, edited, and controlled by a woman and dedicated exclusively to women's interests. Amelia Bloomer (*née* Jenks), 30, who omitted the word "obey" from her marriage ceremony last year, uses the printing press next door to her house to publish a paper that quickly departs from campaigning against the evils of drink to address such issues as unjust marriage laws, woman suffrage, and women's education (*see* 1851).

Nonfiction: *Moral Beginnings* (*Esquisses morales*) by French writer Daniel Stern (Marie de Flavigny, comtesse d'Agoult), 44, a close friend of novelist George Sand. She married the count in 1827, left him 7 years later for composer Franz Liszt, and has had three daughters by Liszt (the youngest, Cosima, will marry first pianist-conductor Hans von Bülow and then composer Richard Wagner).

Fiction: *La Petite Fadette* by George Sand; *Shirley* by Currer Bell (Charlotte Brontë); *Passages in the Life of Mrs. Margaret Maitland* by Scottish novelist Margaret Oliphant, 21, who uses her mother's name rather than that of her father, Francis Wilson;

The Ogilvies by English novelist Dinah Maria Mulock, 23; *Brothers and Sisters* (*Syskonlif*) by Fredrika Bremer.

Poetry: "Annabel Lee" by Edgar Allan Poe, who dies October 7 at age 40 after a final spree in Baltimore; "The Ballad of the Tempest, or the Captain's Daughter," by Boston publisher James Thomas Fields of Ticknor, Reed & Fields, whose poem will be published in the McGuffey *Readers*: " 'We are lost!' the captain shouted,/ As he staggered down the stairs./ But his little daughter whispered,/ As she took his icy hand,/ 'Isn't God upon the ocean,/ Just the same as on the land?' "

Painting: *Plowing with Oxen* by French painter Rosa (Marie-Rosalie) Bonheur, 27.

Opera: Jenny Lind gives her final operatic performance in May and turns to concert and oratorio singing, partly to avoid celebrity (*see* Barnum, 1850).

Popular songs: "Nelly Was a Lady" by Stephen C. Foster.

1850

The first installments of *Uncle Tom's Cabin* by Harriet Beecher Stowe appear in the antislavery weekly *National Era* (*see* 1851). Stowe has been horrified at the prospect of a new Fugitive Slave Act, which Congress passes September 18.

The first National Convention for Women's Rights opens October 23 in Brinley Hall at Worcester, Mass., largely at the inspiration of Lucy Stone, who was graduated 3 years ago from Oberlin College and will organize annual conventions for years to come (*see* 1848; Bloomer, 1851). Ernestine Rose, one of the speakers, declaims, "Who has ever heard of the Pilgrim Mothers? Did they not endure all— as the Pilgrim Fathers did?"

Women make up only 13 percent of America's paid labor force, with most of them employed in agriculture or as domestic servants despite growing opportunities for employment in textile mills and other factories; middle-class women find such employment suitable only for immigrants.

Margaret Fuller, Marchioness Ossoli, dies July 19 at age 40 when her ship is wrecked off Fire Island,

N.Y., and founders with all hands, including Fuller's husband, the Marchese Angelo Ossoli, and their child. Fuller married the impoverished nobleman 2 or 3 years ago at Rome but fled with him to Florence last year when the revolutionary republic that they supported was crushed.

The Singer Sewing Machine invented by U.S. actor-mechanic Isaac Merrit Singer, 38, will become the world's largest-selling machine of its kind (*see* Howe, 1843). A boiler explosion has destroyed Singer's patented wood-carving machine, he has watched some Boston mechanics trying to repair a primitive sewing machine, and he has been inspired to devise a better one.

Mr. Singer's sewing machine was a blessing to women, and also a curse—for many it would mean sweatshop labor.

Only half the children born in the United States until now have reached the age of 5. The percentage will increase dramatically.

Ignaz Semmelweis enforces antiseptic practices in the obstetric ward of Budapest's St. Rochus Hospital (*see* 1847). He has returned to Budapest after failing to convince Viennese hospital authorities of the need for sterile conditions but will die in 1865 of the puerperal fever that he has devoted his career to preventing.

The vaginal speculum introduced into medical practice permits full visual examination of the cervix, but it is generally regarded as an affront to modesty and many physicians refuse to use it lest it sexually arouse their patients (*see* Carter, 1853).

The *American Journal of the Medical Sciences* publishes a paper by Montgomery, Ala., surgeon James Marion Sims, 37, describing his success in repairing a vesico-vaginal fistula, an unpleasant and not uncommon tear between the bladder and the vagina that causes urine to leak into the vagina. Usually produced by prolonged or difficult labor or bad midwifery, the wound may heal itself, but if it does not it may doom a woman to suffer discomfort and isolation for the rest of her life. Sims has developed a special speculum for use in the operation, his breakthrough establishes his reputation, and he moves to New York. He will later state that his education at Philadelphia's Jefferson Medical College, considered one of the best in the country in 1835, gave him absolutely no idea of how to treat his first cases (*see* 1855).

Harvard Medical School dean Oliver Wendell Holmes admits the first black students and the first woman—Harriot Kezia Hunt, now 44 (*see* 1835). Male students riot in protest, and Hunt, who has repeatedly tried for admittance over the years, is obliged to withdraw. Only 2 percent of Boston physicians are women; by 1890, 18 percent will be women.

Woman's Medical College of Pennsylvania is founded at Philadelphia, initially as an Eclectic school, with support from Quaker feminist Lucretia Mott, now 57. Its moving spirit is Dr. Ann Preston, another Quaker (*see* Flexner Report, 1910).

Thoughts on Self-Culture, Addressed to Women by English writers Emily Anne Eliza Shirreff, 36, and her sister Maria Georgina Gray, encourages women to educate themselves.

North London Collegiate School for girls is founded by English educator Frances Mary Buss, 23, with support from the Rev. David Laing of the Governess's Benevolent Institution. It will be her personal property until 1870, when it will become vested in trustees and merge with the Lower Camden School, and by 1872 the two will have a combined enrollment of 470 pupils, with those in the higher school paying tuitions of 15 guineas per year

(4 to 6 guineas in the lower school) at a time when parents of young ladies pay £100 and even £300 per year to have their daughters instructed in the so-called "accomplishments."

Half the women in 274 English parishes can read and write, up from 36 percent in 1750, as a result of the growth of public education for girls (the percentage of literate men is 65 percent, up from 64 percent in 1750). For all parishes, the percentage of literate women is 55 percent, of literate men 70 percent (*see* 1911).

The Falloux law passed by France's Parlement provides for the opening of primary schools for girls in towns with populations of more than 800. It also reinstitutes the letter of obedience, which allows a person who has spent some time in a convent near a mother superior to teach without the diploma required of secular woman teachers. The minister of education retains a monopoly in the distribution of teaching diplomas.

U.S. journalist Jane Cannon Swisshelm, 34, visits Washington, D.C., to hear Congress debate disposition of Mexican territory acquired through the 1846–48 war, which she opposed. Horace Greeley of the *New York Tribune* engages her as the paper's Washington correspondent, she becomes the first woman to secure a seat in the congressional reporters' gallery, but she leaves after a brief stay.

Nonfiction: "Woman and Her Needs" by U.S. social worker Elizabeth Oak Smith (*née* Prince), 44, is a monograph by a participant in the women's rights convention (above); *Thoughts on Self Culture Addressed to Women* by English educational reformer Maria Georgina Grey (*née* Shirreff), 34, who will found the Women's Education Union and the Girls' Public Day School Company to provide "moral and intellectual training," which, she says, is as necessary to girls as to boys and "must be conducted on the same principles and by the same methods"; *Histoire de la révolution de 1848* by Daniel Stern (Marie de Flavigny, comtesse d'Agoult).

Fiction: *The Scarlet Letter* by Salem, Mass., novelist Nathaniel Hawthorne, 46, is about inhumanity in Puritan New England (*see* human rights, 1650). He begins with the observation that Puritan women of the 17th century, with their "broad shoulders and well-developed busts," were hardier than their descendants; every "successive mother has transmitted to her child a fainter bloom, a more delicate and briefer beauty, and a slighter physical frame..." His heroine, Hester Prynne, is forced to wear the letter "A" as evidence of her adultery. *The Moorland Cottage* by Mrs. Gaskell. *Olive* by Dinah Craik.

Poetry: *Sonnets from the Portuguese* by English poet Elizabeth Barrett Browning, 44, expresses hesitation at burdening poet Robert Browning with an invalid wife. She married Browning 4 years ago despite her infirmity, the result of an injury sustained while saddling a horse at age 15 (she also spent 6 years in bed following her brother's death in a sailboat accident): "How do I love thee? Let me count the ways./ I love thee to the depth and breadth and height/ My soul can reach..." (Sonnet 43). "In Memoriam" by Alfred Tennyson, who began the elegy 17 years ago upon the death of his sister's fiancé, Arthur Hallam: " 'Tis better to have loved and lost,/ Than never to have loved at all."

Painting: *Labourages Nivernais* by Rosa Bonheur.

Opera: Henrietta Sontag creates the role of Maretha in Jacques Halévy's new opera *La Tempestà* 6/8 at Her Majesty's Theatre, London; Richard Wagner's new opera *Lohengrin* 8/28 at the Weimar Theater includes a "Wedding March" (*see* royal wedding, 1858).

Coloratura soprano Jenny Lind, now 30, signs a contract in January with U.S. showman P. T. Barnum, who guarantees the "Swedish nightingale"

Poet Elizabeth Barrett Browning took the "masculine" sonnet form and gave it a woman's interpretation. LIBRARY OF CONGRESS

Jenny Lind had completed her operatic career when P. T. Barnum promoted her as the "Swedish nightingale." LIBRARY OF CONGRESS

$1,000 per night plus all expenses, allows her to select her own concert repertory, and frees her to perform for charity. The contract is revised to give Lind a share in the profits when it becomes clear that proceeds will exceed Barnum's original projections. A crowd of more than 30,000 is on hand to greet her when she arrives at New York September 1, she opens at New York's Castle Garden September 11 in a concert that grosses $17,864.05, donates nearly $15,000 (her share of the receipts from her first two concerts) to charity, and departs November 25 on a 2-year tour that will take her to Baltimore, Washington, south to Havana, and west to St. Louis in which she will earn $130,000, of which $100,000 will go to charities.

President Millard Fillmore and his wife, Abigail (*née* Powers), install the first White House cooking stove. Cooks at the executive mansion quit in protest, preferring to use the fireplace until an expert from the Patent Office spends a day showing them how to regulate the heat with dampers.

1851

Phra Chom Klao Mongkut, 47, becomes king of Siam at age 47 upon the death of his half brother (*see* Anna Leonowens, 1862).

An observation study of 700 homes in a working-class London area reveals that the average housewife works 75 hours per week—15 hours per day—cooking, cleaning, and looking after the children. She spends one-quarter of her day in the kitchen.

British economist-philosopher John Stuart Mill, 45, marries his longtime confidante, widow Harriet Taylor (*née* Hardy), 44, whose essays and suggestions have helped him for more than 20 years. Her latest essay, "Enfranchisement for Women," says, in part, "We deny the right of any portion of the species to decide for another portion . . . what is and what is not their 'proper sphere.' The proper sphere for all human beings is the largest and highest which they are able to attain." The Mills have drafted a formal protest against repressive marriage laws but will live together for only 7 years before Harriet dies at age 51 in Avignon.

Lucretia C. Mott and Elizabeth Smith sponsor a Philadelphia tailoring cooperative that gives employment to women, and they participate in a second women's rights convention.

Men and women are treated equally and all classes of work are viewed as equally honorable in the Oneida Community, which has 300 converts living in communal buildings made of timber from the community's farms (*see* 1848). John Humphrey Noyes lectures each Tuesday on love, sex, and the etiquette of complex marriage; children are reared in the "children's house" operated by men and women considered best qualified.

On the Preservation of the Health of Women by British physician John Edward Tilt, 36, is published at London: "Man was created independent because destined to govern the family, society, and nature," he writes, "while woman was made dependent, tied to hearth and home by a long chain of never-ending infirmities."

Antoinette Louise Brown, now 28, is ordained as a minister in the Congregational Church (*see* Oberlin, 1847).

Sarah Josepha Hale organizes the Ladies' Missionary Society of Philadelphia (*see* 1853).

The District of Columbia Teachers College at Washington has its beginnings in the Normal School for Colored Girls started by New York teacher Myrtilla Miner, who opens the first school to train young black women as teachers. Her six pupils will grow to number 40 as she gains financial support from abolitionists (Harriet Beecher Stowe contributes $1,000), and while her school will be the target of racial violence and Miner's health will be frail she will insist, "There is no law to prevent my teaching these people, and I *shall* teach them, even unto death." She will continue until 1860.

Nonfiction: *The Female Volunteer: Or the Life and Wonderful Adventures of Miss Eliza Allen, A Young Lady of Eastport, Maine* by Eliza Allen, 25, who was refused permission while in her teens to marry the young man she loved, dressed herself as a man, and fought in the Mexican War, sustaining wounds. *Homes of the New World* (*Hemmen i den nya bärlden*) is a collection of letters to her sister Agathe by Fredrika Bremer, now 50, who has returned to

Sweden after 2 years in America, stopping en route for 2 months in England. Wishing to study U.S. social and political conditions, with special reference to the status of women, Bremer has visited St. Paul in the Minnesota Territory and many places in the deep South, many places on the Atlantic Coast, and in New England.

Fiction: *Uncle Tom's Cabin, or Life among the Lowly* (further installments) by Harriet Beecher Stowe, now 40, whose sentimental tearjerker about slavery will have record sales (*see* 1852); *The Wide, Wide World* by U.S. novelist Elizabeth Wetherell (Susan Bogert Warner), 32, whose novel is the first book in the United States to have sales of more than 1 million copies but will be far outsold by Stowe's book; *The Sunny Side; or, The Country Minister's Wife* by U.S. novelist Elizabeth Wooster Phelps (*née* Stewart), 36, whose book, published at Edinburgh, has sales of 100,000 copies by year's end and will be translated into French and German; *The Head of the Family* by Dinah Mulock.

Poetry: *Das geistliche Jahr* by the late Annette von Droste-Hülsoff, who died in May 1848 at age 51; her cycle of religious poems, begun in 1820 and completed in 1839, reflects her doubts as well as her piety.

Painting: *Returning from the Fields* by Rosa Bonheur.

Sculpture: *The Greek Slave* exhibited at the London Great Exhibition is a marble figure completed in 1843 by U.S. sculptor Hiram Powers, now 45, who started his career in a Cincinnati waxworks and moved in 1837 to Florence, where he will live until his death in 1873. Inspired by reports that Greek prisoners were sold in slave markets by the Turks during the 1821–1829 war for Greek independence, the neoclassical nude attracts great attention and authorities set aside special hours for women who are embarrassed at viewing it in the presence of men.

Amelia Bloomer urges reform of women's clothing in her newspaper the *Lily*. She will be ridiculed for going about in public wearing full-cut trousers, or pantalettes ("bloomers"), under a short skirt—a costume designed by Elizabeth Gerrit Miller (*née* Smith), now 28, and introduced 3 years ago at the

Amelia Bloomer tried to popularize pantaloons but few women were about to give up their hoopskirts.

Woman's Rights Convention at Seneca Falls, N.Y. Miller, who married a New York lawyer at age 21, designed what she called a "short dress" with "Turkish trousers" extending to the ankle for the feminine task of gardening. She visited Elizabeth Cady Stanton, who liked the costume, as did her houseguest, Amelia Bloomer, and both began wearing the pantelettes everywhere, although they were often thrown out of public places for their immodest appearance. Stanton's husband is one of the few husbands who has not refused to be seen with his wife when she was wearing her bloomer costume in public, but Elizabeth now refuses to endorse the costume, saying that women, for their own protection, should wear trousers, jackets, and coats. Sarah Josepha Hale of *Godey's Lady's Book* takes a dim view of the pantelettes; Bloomer and Miller will both give them up before 1860.

1852

 The National Woman's Rights Convention at Syracuse, N.Y., hears speeches from feminists who include Elizabeth Cady Stanton and Matilda Gage (*née* Joslyn), 26.

An editorial in the *New York Herald* September 12 asks, "How did woman first become subject to man as she now is all over the world?" It goes on to answer, "By her nature, her sex, just as the negro is and always will be, to the end of time, inferior to the white race, and, therefore, doomed to subjection; but happier than she would be in any other condition, just because it is the law of her nature. The women themselves would not have this law reversed."

Uncle Tom's Cabin by Harriet Beecher Stowe (below) ends with an appeal to mothers—"you, who have learned by the cradles of your own children, to love and feel for all mankind"—to intervene against slavery's injustices. Her book stirs up public opinion in the North against slavery as no book ever has done before. It also stirs up animosity in the South against its author.

 French merchant Aristide Boucicaut and his wife, Marguerite, open Au Bon Marché, a Paris piecegoods and *nouveautés* shop occupying 30 square meters in the faubourg St. Germaine of the 7th Arondissement that they will turn into the world's first true department store. They institute revolutionary retailing principles that include firm and visible prices, markups of no more than 13 percent (other stores mark factory prices up 40 percent, but high volume and rapid turnover compensate for smaller gross margins), and free entrance with no moral obligation to buy. Customers think there must be imperceptible faults in the merchandise to explain such low prices, but the Boucicauts will soon begin extending the right to exchange merchandise or obtain a cash refund, sales will increase from less than half a million gold francs this year to 5 million by 1860, 7 million 1863. By 1870, the Boucicauts will have bought neighboring buildings and the Bon Marché will occupy an entire city block with sales of 20 million gold francs in dresses, coats, underwear, shoes, millinery, and the like.

 The fictional Marie St. Clare in *Uncle Tom's Cabin* (below) satirizes the role of delicate invalid so popular among U.S. women. Stowe's half-sister, Isabella Beecher Hooker, 40, has a prolapsed uterus and is one of many middle-class women who spend weeks taking "water cures" at hydrotherapy institutions. Pregnant women in America are commonly said (in an excess of modesty not generally known in Victorian Britain) to be in "an interesting condition" or to be "visiting in the country." Newborn infants are said to have been "discovered under the gooseberry bush" or in the "cabbage patch."

 Antioch College, founded at Yellow Springs, Ohio, by Massachusetts educator Horace Mann, will claim to be "the first American college of high rank to grant absolutely equal opportunities to women and men." In his lengthy inaugural address, President Mann says that female education must "be rescued from its present reproach of inferiority, and advanced to an equality with that of males." Antioch's first students will include 11 transferees from Oberlin, including three women who have seen seniors at that college denied the right to sit on the platform at commencement and read their essays because they were women (*see* Oberlin, 1833; Iowa, 1856).

Abolitionist Sarah Moore Grimké, now 60, writes December 31 to Harriot Hunt lamenting her lack of educational opportunities: "The powers of my mind have never been allowed expansion." In an undated essay she will write, "With me, learning was a passion. . . . Had I received the education I craved and been bred to the profession of law, I might have been a useful member of society, and instead of myself and my property being taken care of, I might have been a protector of the helpless. . . . Many a woman shudders . . . at the terrible eclipse of those intellectual powers which in early life seemed prophetic of usefulness and happiness. . . . It is because we feel we have powers which are crushed, responsibilities which we are not permitted to exercise . . . rights vested in us as moral and intellectual beings which are utterly ignored and trampled upon . . . it is because we feel this so keenly we now demand an equal education with men."

 The *Pioneer* at San Francisco begins publishing copies of letters written to her sister Mary Jane in Amherst, Mass., by Louisa Amelia Smith Clapp (*née* Knapp), 33, who came around Cape Horn with her husband, Dr. Fayette Clapp, in 1849, and has lived in a mining camp at the north fork of the Feather River. Her 23 letters will give a vivid picture of life in the mining camps, and male writers will borrow heavily from them in years to come. She will teach school in San Francisco for 20 years before returning east.

 Fiction: *Uncle Tom's Cabin* (above) is published in book form March 15 and goes through 120 U.S. editions within a year (*see* 1851); 300,000 copies are sold in America with similar sales abroad, a popular success never before seen in publishing and rarely to be seen again; *The Blithedale Romance* by Nathaniel Hawthorne is a critique of the 1841–1847 Brook Farm experiment and analyzes the urge to seek Utopia and the possibly tragic effects of feminist emancipation (his heroine, Priscilla, is a delicate, sickly type "whose impalpable grace lay so singularly between disease and beauty"); *A Peep at "Number 5," or, a Chapter in the Life of a City Pastor* and *The Angel over the Right Shoulder; or, The Beginning of a New Year* by Elizabeth Wooster Phelps, who gives birth to her third child in August and dies of "brain disease" November 30 at age 37; *Queechy* by Elizabeth Wetherell (Susan Bogert Warner).

Harriet Beecher Stowe wrote the book that inflamed opinion against slavery: Uncle Tom's Cabin. FROM AN 1853 PORTRAIT BY ALANSON FISHER, STOWE-DAY FOUNDATION

 Theater: *Camille, the Lady of the Camellias* (*La Dame aux Camélias*) by Alexandre Dumas fils 2/2 at the Théâtre du Vaudeville, Paris. Based on Dumas's 1848 novel, it romanticizes the notion of delicate, sickly beauty (the play about a tubercular prostitute was published in 1848, but censors have delayed its production); *Uncle Tom's Cabin* by George L. Aiken, 22, 9/27 at the Troy, N.Y., Museum. Adapted from Harriet Beecher Stowe's novel (above), the play will be produced throughout the country with enormous success in the North.

 Opera: Russia's grand duchess Helena Pavlovich hears the premiere of court pianist Anton Grigorev Rubinstein's opera Dmitri Donskoi 4/30 at St. Petersburg and invites him to be music director at Michael Palace and spend the summer with her on Kammeney Island in the Neva River, where he will write Melody in F, played primarily with the thumbs.

1853

 The French emperor Napoleon III is married at Notre Dame Cathedral, Paris, January 30 to the Spanish beauty Eugénie, 26, second daughter of Don Cipriano, count of Teba, and his wife (who is of Scottish descent).

Portugal's Maria II (Maria de Glória) dies November 15 at age 34 after a 27-year reign marked by insurrections in 1846 and 1851 and interrupted by a 5-year civil war during which the queen lived in England.

 The Massachusetts Constitutional Convention receives a petition to permit woman suffrage. The appeal comes from the wife of educator and social reformer Amos Bronson Alcott and 73 other women (see Lucy Stone, 1850; Elizabeth Cady Stanton, 1860).

The United States Review predicts that "within half a century "machinery will perform all work—automata will direct them. The only tasks of the human race will be to make love, study, and be happy." Meanwhile, drudgery remains a way of life for all but a tiny handful of the world's women.

 Leipzig gynecologist Karl Siegmund Franz Credé, 34, develops a method of expressing the placenta in

childbirth by massaging the uterus for 15 to 30 minutes after delivery, beginning gently and gradually increasing the amount of compression until the placenta is expelled naturally.

On the Pathology and Treatment of Hysteria by British physician Robert Brudenell Carter, 25, says that "no one who has realized the amount of moral evil wrought in girls . . . whose prurient desires have been increased by Indian hemp and partially gratified by medical manipulations, can deny that remedy is worse than the disease" (*see* Hippocrates, 429 B.C.). "I have . . . seen in unmarried women, of the middle class of society, reduced by the constant use of the [vaginal] speculum [*see* 1850] to the mental and moral condition of prostitutes; seeking to give themselves the same indulgence by the practice of solitary vice; and asking every medical practitioner . . . to institute an examination of the sexual organs."

∞ Two young women supported by the 2-year-old Ladies' Missionary Society of Philadelphia near completion of their training at the Female Medical College of Philadelphia, but the Denominational Missionary Board refuses to employ them unless they go out as the wives of missionaries, fearing that troubles may otherwise arise that will prejudice the mission's cause. The two women refuse to be forced into wedlock, but Sarah Josepha Hale helps find "useful positions" for them abroad.

Nonfiction: *England in 1851, or Sketches of a Tour in England* by Fredrika Bremer is based on her 2-month visit en route home from America.

Fiction: *Passion and Principle* by Maria Grey and her older sister, Emily Anne Elizabeth Shireff, 39; *Peg Woffington* by English novelist-playwright Charles Reade, 39 (he has adapted last year's play *Masks and Faces* at the suggestion of actress Laura Seymour, who will be his housekeeper beginning next year); *Cranford* and *Ruth* by Mrs. Gaskell; *Villette* by Currer Bell (Charlotte Brontë), who will marry Arthur Bell Nichols, her father's curate, next year but will die in 1855; *Agatha's Husband* by Dinah Mulock; *Liberia* by *Godey's Lady's Book* editor Sarah Josepha Hale sets forth her "solution" to the slavery problem, to wit, that slaves be educated to the responsibilities of emancipation, that their freedom be purchased either by the U.S. government or with funds earned by the slaves themselves, and that, once liberated, they be resettled in the African colony of Liberia since "among us" they have "no home, no position, and no future" since "two races that do not intermarry can never live together as equals."

Juvenile: *The Heir of Redclyffe* by English author Charlotte Mary Yonge, 30, who since 1851 has been editing the girls' magazine *Monthly Packet*, which she will continue to do until 1890 as she writes dozens of adult and juvenile novels (part of the profits from her book will go toward outfitting a missionary schooner).

Painting: *The Horse Fair* by Rosa Bonheur.

Sculpture: Emigrée U.S. sculptor Harriet Goodhue Hosmer, 22, in Rome creates an original bust of Daphne and begins selling busts based on figures from classical mythology. A friend of actress Charlotte Cushman; she was denied admission to Boston Medical School on account of her sex (she had applied in order to study anatomy), but has attended the Medical College of St. Louis (*see* 1856).

Theater: English-born U.S. actress Laura Keene, now 33, becomes manager of Baltimore's Charles Street Theater December 24.

Opera: *La Traviata* 3/6 at Venice's Teatro la Fenice, with a libretto based on last year's Alexandre Dumas play, *La Dame aux Camélias*, music by Giuseppe Verdi, who has completed it in 4 weeks (the production in modern dress is a dismal failure); French soprano Hortense (Catherine [Caroline-Jeanne]) Schneider, 20, makes her debut 5/15 at Agen singing the role of Inèz in Donizetti's 1840 opera *La Favorita*.

English divorcée Jane Digby, now 46, travels to Damascus after having lived for years in Paris, Munich, and Greece. Sheik Abdul Medjuel El Mazrab serves as guide for the 9-day camel caravan that takes her across the Syrian desert to view the archaeological remains of ancient Palmyra. After further journeys with El Mazrab to Baghdad, Digby will marry him, become queen of his tribe, and adopt native dress.

U.S. abolitionist Sarah Grimké, now 62, leaves the household that she has shared with her sister Angelina and Angelina's husband, Theodore Dwight Weld, in an effort to pursue a career of her own. She works in public libraries with the idea of compiling a list of laws in various states that she considers unfair to women.

The Massachusetts legislature enacts a Married Women's Property Act at the prodding of feminist Mary Ferrin (*née* Upton), who has been petitioning the lawmakers since 1848 and gaining support for the measure from able men and like-minded women. The law gives control of their property to women who marry after the law takes effect, empowers a wife to make a will without her husband's consent (except as it applies to one-half her personal property), and gives her certain fixed rights in the estate of her husband should he die intestate.

"A Brief Summary in Plain Language of the Most Important Laws Concerning Women" by English educator Barbara Leigh Smith, 27, is a pamphlet documenting the consequences of not permitting married women to own property and raising questions about other laws that discriminate against women. Smith attended the Ladies College in Bedford Square in 1849 and last year founded an experimental primary school for London boys and girls (*see* 1857).

A typhus epidemic in the Russian army spreads to the British and French in the Crimea, where war has begun March 14. Florence Nightingale, 34, superintendent of a London hospital for invalid women, takes 34 London nurses to Scutari. She left her rich, upper-class family in her 20s to train as a nurse at Kaiserwerth Institute, near Düsseldorf. Doctors at Scutari stubbornly refuse her help until casualties from the Battle of Inkerman spill into their rat-infested corridors, but she has been charged by the secretary of state for war to take complete charge of nursing British soldiers. Nightingale organizes a barracks hospital, where she introduces sanitary measures that will reduce the toll of cholera, dysentery, and typhus (but disease will nevertheless take more lives in the Crimean War than will battle casualties). Although loaded with problems of administration and supply, Nightingale always takes her turn at nursing. At night, she walks through the wards with her lamp, giving encouragement, comfort, and advice to the patients.

A Vatican ruling that makes the Immaculate Conception of the Virgin an article of faith implies papal "infallibility" in all matters. The papal bull *Ineffabilis Deus*, issued by Pius IX December 8, declares: "From the first moment of her conception the Blessed Virgin Mary was, by the singular grace and privilege of Almighty God, and in view of the merits of Jesus Christ, Saviour of Mankind, kept free from all stain of original sin."

Florence Nightingale brought her nurses to the Crimea to care for British soldiers down with cholera and typhus. LIBRARY OF CONGRESS

New Jersey schoolmistress Clara (Clarissa Harlowe) Barton, 33, quits the free school that she has founded and goes to work at Washington, D.C., for the U.S. Patent Office, where she becomes the only female employee of the federal government. The school has grown so large that the townsmen have decided to install a man as principal; Barton has declined to subordinate herself to a man (*see* 1861).

Fiction: *Clara Morrison* by Scottish-born Australian writer Catherine Helen Spence, 29, who started her novel while working as a governess. She will write five more novels and become an outspoken feminist, making lecture tours in Britain and America.

Poetry: *Poems on Miscellaneous Subjects* by U.S. poet Frances Ellen Watkins Harper, 29, whose book has an introduction by abolitionist William Lloyd Garrison.

Lucy Stone married Henry Blackwell but retained her maiden name, a decision almost unheard of.

 Opera: Giulia Grisi appears at New York's Castle Garden in the title role of the 1833 Donizetti opera *Lucrezia Borgia* and, later, at the city's new Academy of Music in the title role of the 1831 Bellini opera *Norma*; Henrietta Sontag travels to Mexico City with an Italian company for an engagement at the local opera house, appears in the title role of *Lucrezia Borgia*, falls ill with cholera, and dies June 17 at age 48.

Popular song: "Jeanie with the Light Brown Hair" by Stephen C. Foster.

 Feminist Lucy Stone gives a speech in mid-October in which she says, "In education, in marriage, in religion, in everything, disappointment is the lot of women. It shall be the business of my life to deepen this disappointment in every woman's heart until she bows down to it no longer."

The Massachusetts legislature amends the state's divorce law to make it more equitable for women.

The Young Women's Christian Association (YWCA) is founded at London to improve the condition of working girls by providing good food and a decent place to sleep for young women living away from home.

Woman's Hospital opens in New York May 4 at 29th Street and Madison Avenue. The world's first institution established by women "for the treatment of diseases peculiar to women and for the maintenance of a lying-in hospital," it has a capacity of 40 beds, one surgeon (the now-famous J. Marion Sims; *see* 1850), a nurse, and two matrons—one to administer to the sick, one to supervise domestic arrangements. It will later move to 49th Street, between Park and Lexington avenues, and then to 114th Street, between Columbus and Amsterdam avenues, where it will become part of St. Luke's Hospital.

Dr. Elizabeth Blackwell notes that "the midwife has become entirely supplanted by the doctor" but does not mourn the fading of the "old midwife," who was "an imperfect institution" that will "disappear with the progress of society. The midwife must give way to the physician. Woman, therefore, must become physician."

Mary Walker, 22, is graduated from Syracuse Medical College and becomes the first practicing U.S. woman M.D. (*see* 1865; Blackwell, 1849).

 The first U.S. kindergarten opens at Watertown, Wis., where the wife of German immigrant Carl Schurz, 26, has started the school for children of other immigrants (*see* Peabody, 1860).

Elmira Female College, founded at Elmira, N.Y., will be the first U.S. institution to grant academic degrees to women (*see* Mount Holyoke, 1837; Antioch, 1852; Vassar, 1861).

Fiction: *Ruth Hall* by U.S. novelist Sara Payson Willis, 44, relates the struggles of a widow to support herself. The author's first husband, a bank cashier, died, and in 1849 she was married to a Boston merchant, who soon left her. *The District Governor's Daughters* (*Amtmandens døttre*) by feminist Norwegian novelist Camilla Collett (*née* Wergeland), 42, is Norway's first modern novel: it deals with the inhibiting influences of society and family on the growth of young women.

Juvenile: *The Two Guardians; or Home in This World* by Charlotte M. Yonge.

Laura Keene opens her own theater in New York under the name Laura Keene's Varieties.

New York–born entertainer Lotta Mignon Crabtree, 8, makes her first public appearance in late November at the Sierra mining settlement of Rapid Creek. She and her mother, Mary Ann, arrived at San Francisco 2 years ago to join her father at the Grass Valley mining camp. Prospectors pay heavily to hear her sing and watch dance numbers taught her by her San Francisco neighbor Lola Montez, now 37, who has toured America with her divertissement *Lola Montez in Bavaria* and claims to have had lovers who included not only King Ludwig but also an Irish lord, the Russian emperor, a Polish prince, writer Alexandre Dumas, and pianist-composer Franz Liszt (*see* 1848; Crabtree, 1864).

Italian tragedienne Adelaide Ristori, 33, performs in the works of Corneille and Racine, capturing Parisian audiences despite competition from "*la grande Rachel*" (Félix).

Opera: Hortense Schneider makes her Paris debut 8/31 at the Bouffe-Parisienne.

1856

The new British governor-general for India Charles Viscount Canning, 43, arrives at Bombay January 29 with his wife, Charlotte Elizabeth (*née* Stuart), 38, after a two-month journey from England and reaches Calcutta a month later. Charlotte Canning has endured her husband's philandering for the past decade and welcomes the opportunity to separate him from his mistress, but he remains distant (*see* Sepoy Mutiny, 1857).

The beautiful Chinese imperial concubine Cixi, 21, bears a son, is made empress to the Qing emperor Xianfeng, and immediately gains control of the throne, beginning a ruthless and reactionary regime that will continue until her death in 1908.

U.S. medical student Elizabeth Garrett Anderson passes the examination of Britain's Society of Apothecaries, but English student Jessie Meriton White, who has applied to the Royal College of Surgeons in the University of London for admittance to their examinations, is turned down.

The University of Iowa, founded at Ames, is open to women as well as men (*see* Antioch, 1852; Swarthmore, 1864).

Nonfiction: *A Chronological History of the United States* by Boston historian Elizabeth Palmer Peabody, 52 (*see* kindergarten, 1860).

Fiction: *Hertha* by Fredrika Bremer is a social pamphlet in fictional form; *Dred: A Tale of the Great Dismal Swamp* by Harriet Beecher Stowe expands on the author's antislavery views; *Rose Clark* by Sara Payson Willis tells of a reluctant widow being tricked into marriage by a gross sensualist, who then slanders her and leaves her penniless.

Poetry: "A Farewell" by English novelist-poet Charles Kingsley, 37, is a satiric poem containing the line "Be good, sweet maid, and let who will be clever."

Juvenile: *The Daisy Chain; or Aspirations, a Family Chronicle* and *Beechcroft* by Charlotte M. Yonge, whose ideas about feminine girlhood and young womanhood reflect those deemed appropriate for upper-middle-class girls.

Sculpture: *Puck* by Harriet Goodhue Hosmer meets with such success that 50 replicas are sold at $1,000 each.

Laura Keene moves into a new New York theater— Laura Keene's Theatre—as manager and leading lady.

Ballet: Danish ballerina Lucile Grahn, now 37, retires from dancing and will serve as ballet mistress, first with the Leipzig State Theater, then with the Munich Court Opera (*see* 1836).

Popular songs: "Darling Nelly Gray" by Otterbein College student Benjamin Russell Hanby at Westerville, Ohio, whose song does much to arouse sympathy for America's slaves; "Gentle Annie" by Stephen C. Foster.

1857

 The Sepoy Mutiny that begins May 10 at Meerut ends the British East India Company's control of India. The Brahmin patriot Lakshmibai (*née* Manikarnika Tambe), 22, who was married at age 8 to the rajah of Jhansi and buried him 4 years ago, joins up with the rebels, trains an army of women, and defends the fortress at Jhansi against the British, whose forces are massacred at Delhi May 11. Native regiments at Cawnpore revolt June 5, the British there are forced to surrender, and although they are promised safe conduct to Allahabad for their women and children, the party is fired on by sepoys June 27 as it piles aboard boats; those left unhurt, including 15 young ladies, are later slaughtered, and news of their fate brings horror to Charlotte Canning and her husband at Calcutta as they await the outcome of the siege of Lucknow. Fresh British troops arrive in September and relieve Lucknow November 17 (*see* 1858).

 New York seamstresses stage a demonstration March 8 to demand higher pay and better working conditions (*see* 1908).

Britain's Matrimonial Causes Act, passed by Parliament in July, makes it easier to obtain a divorce: "It shall be lawful for any wife to present a petition to the said Court, praying that her marriage may be dissolved, on the ground that since the celebration thereof her husband has been guilty of incestuous adultery, or of bigamy with adultery, or of rape, or of sodomy or bestiality, or of adultery coupled with such cruelty as without adultery would have entitled her to a divorce *a mensa et toro*, or of adultery coupled with desertion, without reasonable excuse, for two years or upwards." While it requires that a man merely prove adultery on the part of his wife, whereas a wife must show evidence of desertion as well, the new law does provide for the establish-

ment of divorce courts, gives divorced and separated women the right to their own earnings, grants them the same property rights as single women, and establishes that a husband's responsibility as provider continues in perpetuity after a marriage is ended; judges receive the right to require a man to support his ex-wife, and the law orders the world's first alimony payments. Caroline Norton, now 49, has written essays to support her cause, notably "A Letter to the Queen," published in 1855, and Parliament has changed the original bill somewhat in light of Mrs. Norton's case (*see* 1842).

The *Englishwoman's Review* begins campaigning for women's rights.

London has an estimated 6,000 houses of prostitution (one house in every 60), girls as young as eleven are offered to male passersby in the street, and syphilis is rampant (*see* Contagious Diseases Act, 1864).

 The New York Infirmary for Indigent Women and Children opens on Florence Nightingale's birthday, May 12, under the direction of Elizabeth Blackwell, her younger sister, Emily, 30, and Polish-American physician Marie E. Zakrzewska, 27, who has been head midwife at Berlin's Royal Maternity Hospital (*see* 1849). The loss of an eye has prevented Blackwell from achieving her ambition to practice as a surgeon, she has been unable to find a place on any other hospital staff because of her sex, and has started the new hospital that will be run entirely by women, partly for the benefit of the poor, partly to give women physicians opportunities to gain clinical experience. Located at Stuyvesant Square and 15th Street, it will move in November 1875 to 321 East 15th Street and remain there until 1981 (having become a gender-neutral infirmary in the 1960s and merged with Downtown Hospital in 1979), but while women physicians will be prominent in some European countries, they will remain an insignificant minority in U. S. medicine for more than a century.

New Orleans has a yellow fever epidemic that lasts for months and takes upward of 7,000 lives. Death carts rattle through the streets to the cry "Bring out your dead."

 Nonfiction: "Women and Work" (essay) by schoolmistress Barbara Leigh Smith, who marries Eugene

Bodichon but says that wifely dependency is degrading to women and that every woman should be allowed to obtain an education and occupation in order to secure a decent living (*see* 1853).

George Eliot was her pen name—her novels were glorious, but her private life kept society's doors closed to her.

Fiction: *The Professor* by the late Charlotte Brontë, who died in 1855. "The Sad Fortunes of the Rev. Amos Barton" by English writer George Eliot (Mary Anne, or Marian, Evans), 37, who 3 years ago began living openly with philosopher-critic George Henry Lewes, 40, a married man who cannot divorce his wife because he has failed to condemn her for having had a child by another man. Eliot, whose story is published in *Blackwood's* magazine, is a puritan at heart and calls herself Mrs.

Lewes, as does Lewes, but she is shunned by proper Victorian wives. *John Halifax, Gentleman* by Dinah Mulock. *Married or Single* by Miss Sedgwick, now 67, who has written it "to lessen the stigma placed on the term 'old maid.' " *Madame Bovary* by French novelist Gustave Flaubert, 36, who is prosecuted for immorality but wins acquittal.

Poetry: *The Flower* (*La flor*) by Spanish poet Rosalía de Castro, 20, who writes in Galician; "Santa Filomena" by Henry Wadsworth Longfellow is a tribute to Crimean War nurse Florence Nightingale: "Lo! in that house of misery/ A lady with a lamp I see . . ." (*see* 1854).

The first Currier & Ives prints are issued as New York lithographer Nathaniel Currier, 44, takes into partnership his bookkeeper of 5 years, James Merritt Ives, 33, and begins signing all his prints with the new firm name. Currier has been issuing lithographs since 1835 that illustrate U.S. manners, personages, and events. His most prolific talent since 1849 has been English-born artist Frances Flora "Fanny" Bond Palmer, now 45, who draws directly on the stones used to make her lithographs. Her views of Manhattan, one from Brooklyn Heights and the other from Weehawken, N.J., have been among Currier's best sellers; her *American Farm Scenes* (1853), *American Winter Scenes* (1854), and *American Country Life* (1855) have also won wide acclaim, and although she will travel no farther than Long Island or up the Hudson River, she will produce *Midnight Race on the Mississippi* in 1860, *The Rocky Mountains, Emigrants Crossing the Plains* in 1861, and *Across the Continent, Westward the Course of Empire* in 1868.

Opera: Giulia Grisi, now 45, reappears at the Théâtre des Italiens, Paris, 1/11 after a long absence singing the role of Leonora in the 1853 Verdi opera *Il Trovatore.*

Scottish gentlewoman Madeleine Hamilton Smith, 22, stands trial at the High Court of Edinburgh on charges of having murdered her ex-lover Pierre-Emile l'Angelier, a clerk whom she met at Glasgow 2 years ago. The prosecution shows that she became engaged to William Kinnock, a richer suitor, and that she purchased arsenic on three occasions, but it cannot show that she met l'Angelier in the week prior to his final violent illness. The verdict is "not proven," Smith's family nevertheless ostracizes her, and she moves to London, where she will marry George Wardle in 1861. She will later divorce him, emigrate to America, and live until 1928.

✕ "To make good bread or to understand the process of making it is the duty of every woman; indeed an art that should never be neglected in the education of a lady," writes Sarah Josepha Hale in her book *Receipts for the Millions.* "The lady derives her title from 'dividing or distributing bread'; the more perfect the bread the more perfect the lady." More than 95 percent of the bread consumed in America is home-baked.

♟♟ Parliament enacts legislation limiting explicit advertising of contraceptives.

1858

✕ Britain's princess royal Victoria is married at London January 25 at age 18 to Prussia's crown prince Friedrich Wilhelm (*see* music, below).

Jhansi falls in April to British forces, but the rajah's widow, Lakshmibai, escapes with most of her troops (*see* 1857). She manages to gain control of 300 horsemen but is unable to impress upon the male rebel leaders that their situation is perilous, and despite her own careful preparations for battle the swift attack of the British overwhelms her men and she is killed in battle. George Canning is elevated from governor-general to viceroy, the East India Company is abolished November 1, and the British government rules most of India directly.

✊ Queen Victoria writes to her daughter Victoria, the crown princess of Prussia (above), March 24, "In a reply to your observation that you find a married woman has much more liberty than an unmarried one; in one sense of the word she has,—but what I meant was—a physical point of view— . . . aches— and sufferings and miseries and plagues—which you must struggle against—and enjoyments, etc. to give up . . . you will feel the yoke of a married woman! Without that—certainly it is unbounded happiness—if one has a husband one worships! It is a foretaste of Heaven. . . . I had nine times for eight

months to bear with those above-named enemies and real misery . . . and I own it tried me sorely; one feels so pinned down—one's wings clipped—in fact, only half one's self—particularly the first and second time. This I call the 'shadow side.' "

Feminist Lucy Stone at Orange, N.J., returns her property-tax bill without payment, saying that she and other women "will cheerfully pay our taxes" when they receive the right to vote but rebel against "taxation without representation." The tax collector sells off her household goods, including her year-old daughter Alice's cradle, to raise the tax money; a sisterly neighbor buys back the goods and returns them.

∞ French schoolgirl Bernadette Soubirous, 14, at Lourdes has a vision February 11 of "a lady" dressed in a white robe with a blue sash, the first of 18 such visions that she will have through mid-July. The asthmatic daughter of a poor farmer, Bernadette lives with her parents and six siblings in a one-room stone house. She is cured of her asthma, tells local priests that "the lady" has urged her to "tell the priests to build a chapel here" at the grotto near a bend in the Gave de Pau River, and is called a sorceress, but there are reports of miraculous cures at the grotto and a chapel will be built (*see* 1866).

❙❙ The *Englishwoman's Journal* begins publication at London with support from women who include Barbara Leigh Smith Bodichon. Jessie Boucherett, 33, buys a copy at a railway station bookstall, goes to the new periodical's office in Langham Place, and offers her services.

✒ Nonfiction: *Intellectual Education and Its Influence on the Character and Happiness of Women* by novelist Emily Shireff.

Fiction: *Real Life* by French novelist Mathilde Bourdon, 41.

Poetry: *Legends and Lyrics* by English poet Adelaide Ann Procter, 33, whose lyric poem "The Lost Chord" begins "Seated one day at the organ,/ I was weary and ill at ease,/ And my fingers wandered idly/ Over the noisy keys . . ." (*see* song, 1877).

🎭 Theater: Rachel Félix (*La grande Rachel*) dies of consumption at a villa in the south of France January 3 at age 36. Her funeral procession to Père-

Lachaise cemetery in Paris brings out a crowd of 40,000 mourners and more than 600 carriages.

Both the 1843 Mendelssohn "Wedding March" from *A Midsummer Night's Dream* music and the 1850 Wagner "Wedding March" from the opera *Lohengrin* are played at Britain's royal wedding (above), beginning a tradition that will endure for weddings of royalty, nobility, and commoners in much of the world.

Opera: Giulia Grisi sings the role of Valentin (Giovanni Mario is Raoul) in the 1836 Meyerbeer opera *Les Huguenots* 5/15 at London's Covent Garden Theatre, which has been rebuilt after a fire in 1856.

The Mason jar, patented by New York metalworker John Landis Mason, 26, is a glass container with a thread molded into its top and a zinc lid with a threaded ring sealer. Mason's reusable jar, made at first by Whitney Glass Works of Glassboro, N.J., will free farm women from having to rely on pickle barrels, root cellars, and smokehouses to get through the winter. Urban women, too, will use Mason jars to put up surplus fruits and vegetables, especially tomatoes, berries, relish, and pickles, and the jars will soon be sealed with paraffin wax, a by-product of kerosene (*see* Ball brothers, 1887).

1859

Prussia's Crown Princess Victoria bears a son (the future kaiser) January 27 after a difficult birth.

The Society for Promoting Employment of Women is founded by Jessie Boucherett and Adelaide Proctor to expand opportunities for British women in areas from bookkeeping to shoemaking.

French schoolteacher Julie Daubié, 35, wins first prize in a contest given by the Académie Impérial and the Lyons Chamber of Commerce on how to improve women's salaries. Daubié's winning paper, "The Impoverished Woman by an Impoverished One," examines the reasons for women's inability to support themselves, explores every field of work open to women, shows the inequality of salaries paid to men and women doing the same work, discusses the apprenticeships available only to young men, and denounces with acerbic wit the exploitive

practices, injustices, and lack of humanity that she has found among employers. The paper will not be published until 1866 (*see* 1862).

Elizabeth Cady Stanton inherits $50,000 from her father and founds the National Woman's Suffrage Association (NWSA) May 15 with help from feminists who include Matilda Joslyn Gage, now 33 (*see* 1848; 1860).

"All marriage is such a lottery," Queen Victoria writes to her daughter (above). "The happiness is always an exchange—though it may be a very happy one—still, the poor woman is bodily and morally the husband's slave. That always sticks in my throat. When I think of a merry, happy, free young girl—and look at the ailing, aching state a young wife generally is doomed to—which you can't deny is the penalty of marriage."

The discovery of oil at Titusville, Pa., August 28 launches a new era of lighting by kerosene, a name coined 4 years ago. The new lighting will be cheaper than that obtained from sperm-oil lamps and more pleasant than that from candles made of lard wax.

India gets her first power looms, which some women see as a threat to their livelihoods.

Narragansett Bay lighthouse keeper Idawalley Zoradia Lewis, 17, rescues four Newport boys, sons of rich summer families, after their small sailboat capsizes. (None can swim, and all would have drowned without her aid.) Lewis took over the light 2 years ago after her father suffered a stroke. In addition to tending the light and caring for her ill parents, she has been rowing a skiff 300 yards to the mainland and back twice each day, in all kinds of weather, to take her three younger siblings to school and home again (*see* 1869).

Prussia's crown princess (above) receives a letter in March from her mother, the queen of England: "Poor dear darling! I pity you! It is indeed too hard and dreadful what we have to go through and men ought to have an adoration for one, and indeed do everything to make up, for what after all they alone are the cause of!" The queen owes her position to the fact that in 1817 Britain's royal physician, Sir Richard Croft, permitted Crown Princess Charlotte to die during labor rather than dismember the future king who, in the event, was

Queen Victoria knew something about birthing babies: she learned from having nine accouchements.

women, largely through the efforts of Florence Nightingale, but does not recommend midwifery as suitable, even though Nightingale wants to see the status of midwives improved.

British gynecologist Isaac Baker Brown advocates clitoridectomy—surgical removal of the skin hood above the clitoris—for the relief of nervous or sexual disorders. He will be expelled from the London Obstetrical Society in 1866 for reviving the practice and will die soon afterward, but U.S. practioners will perform the procedure from 1867 until well after the turn of the century despite attacks by the American medical profession on "female castration."

Fiction: *Adam Bede* by George Eliot gives its author her first wide success; *Round the Sofa* by Mrs. Gaskell; *Les malheurs de Sophie* by Russian-born French author Sophie Rostopchine, comtesse de Ségur, 60; *Daughter of the Sea* (*La hija del mar*) by Rosalía de Castro, who has married the historian-art critic Manuel Martínez Murguía; *Southwold* by feminist U.S. novelist Lillie Devereux Olmsted, 26, whose protagonist is embittered at being rejected by the man she loves, expresses "bold and even unfeminine opinions," shocks her friends and relatives by not taking every word of Scripture literally, claims that Christianity has been harmful to women's status, and ultimately takes her own life; *Our Nig; or, Sketches from the Life of a Free Black, in a Two-Story White House, North, Showing that Slavery's Shadows Fall Even There* by New Hampshire writer Harriet E. Wilson (*née* Adams) is a fictionalized account of her life that some will call the first novel published by a black American.

Juvenile: *Ben Sylvester's Word* by Charlotte M. Yonge.

Opera: Spanish-American soprano Adelina (*née* Adela Juana Maria) Patti, 16, makes her debut 11/24 at New York's Academy of Music singing the title role in Donizetti's 1835 opera *Lucia di Lammermoor*.

Widow Peggy Eaton, now 59, shocks Washington again by marrying her grandchildren's 19-year-old Italian dancing teacher (*see* 1829). Mrs. Eaton's husband, John, died three years ago, and she has been raising the four children of one of her daughters, who has also died. She and her new husband will

stillborn. (Sir Richard soon afterward committed suicide, and King William died in 1837 without an heir.) British women going into childbirth now often demand that they be given chloroform à la reine; Queen Victoria was given the anesthesia 6 years ago to help her in her eighth accouchement. Writing in mid-June, the queen says, "I positively think those ladies who are always enceinte quite disgusting; it is more like a rabbit or a guinea-pig than anything else. Really it is not very nice. There is Lady Kildare who has two a year, one in January and one in December—and always is so, whenever one sees her!"

The Society for Promoting Employment of Women (above) includes nursing as a desirable career for

move to New York in 1865, and in 1866 he will steal her fortune and marry her youngest granddaughter.

1860

✘ South Carolina adopts an Ordinance of Secession December 20 following the election of Abraham Lincoln, who has won 40 percent of the popular vote. Mary Chesnut (*née* Boykin), 37, whose husband, James, has been one of South Carolina's two U.S. senators, returns to the Chesnut family plantation at Camden and begins keeping a diary.

✊ Elizabeth Cady Stanton urges woman suffrage in an address to a joint session of the New York State Legislature (*see* 1859; Equal Rights Association, 1866).

An antislavery pamphlet written by Lydia Maria Child cites the exploitation of black women under slavery.

Lynn, Mass., shoe factory workers walk off the job March 7 in a strike for higher pay. Dressed in hoopskirts, carrying parasols, and led by the Lynn City Guards, some 800 women parade through a snowstorm carrying a banner that reads "AMERICAN LADIES WILL NOT BE SLAVES GIVE US A FAIR COMPENSATION AND WE WILL LABOUR CHEERFULLY" (*see* 1869).

"The Annual 'Pigmarkend' [girl-market] [was] held for three successive Sabbaths in July, on the square of Västeras," writes English traveler Horace Marryat in his book *One Year in Sweden*. "Hundreds of girls stand marshalled in rows to be hired out by the month or year; each with book in hand containing certificates of her former master as to her honesty and sobriety—morality not alluded to."

💲 The Oneida Community grosses $100,000 from sales of the Newhouse trap, named for Community member Sewell Newhouse, who invented the device that is fast becoming the standard in North America and will eventually become so for most of the world. The major enterprise of the 12-year-old Community is making traps, and men of the Community have developed dishwashers and machines for paring apples and washing vegetables to spare themselves the tedium of kitchen chores.

Nantucket schoolteacher Margaret Getchell, 19, is obliged by a childhood injury to wear a glass eye and resigns to seek a less demanding job. She travels to New York, where a distant cousin, Rowland Hussey Macy, a onetime Nantucket whaler, opened a dry-goods store 2 years ago on Sixth Avenue, just south of 14th Street. Macy hires her as a cashier, she takes a room across the street and works late to help balance accounts. At her suggestion, Macy will expand his line of ribbons, laces, and other accessories to include toiletries, hats, specialty clothing, and, later, books, china, silver, home furnishings, jewelry, and—most successfully—groceries (*see* 1866).

Mme. Demorest's Emporium opens in New York to sell dry goods. Ellen "Nell" Demorest (*née* Curtis), 35, who has opened millinery shops at Philadelphia and Troy, N.Y., married dry-goods merchant William Jennings Demorest 2 years ago. After watching her maid cut out a dress pattern from pieces of wrapping paper, she has come up with the idea of creating accurate patterns that can be copied and used for dressmaking at home, her husband has suggested a fashion quarterly that will incorporate her idea, and they begin publishing *Mme. Demorest's Mirror of Fashions*, with a tissue-paper dressmaking pattern stapled to each copy (*see* Butterick, 1847). The magazine will develop into a monthly, and by 1876 will be selling 3 million patterns per year. Demorest will hire large numbers of women to help her in her enterprise, urging them to seek employment in such "unladylike" occupations as bookkeeping, typesetting, and telegraphy (*see* 1865).

⚕ The Nightingale Nurse Training School is founded at St. Thomas's Hospital, London, where a select few will study, without expense, for one year each (*see* 1854). Florence Nightingale, now 40, makes plans to open a school for midwifery nurses at King's College Hospital, also in London.

🎓 Elizabeth Palmer Peabody opens the first U.S. English-speaking kindergarten at Boston, a school for preschoolers that follows the lead set by Mrs. Carl Schurz in 1855. Mrs. Peabody's sisters are married to Horace Mann and Nathaniel Hawthorne.

Ⅱ London feminist Emily Faithfull, 25, establishes a printing house whose compositors are all women and is appointed printer and publisher-in-ordinary to Queen Victoria. She will start *Victoria Magazine* in 1863 and use it to promote the claims of women to gainful employment.

 Fiction: *The Mill on the Floss* by George Eliot: "The happiest women, like the happiest nations, have no history"; "I should like to know what is the proper function of women, if it is not to make reasons for husbands to stay at home, and still stronger reasons for bachelors to go out"; *Right at Last* by Mrs. Gaskell; *Maleska: The Indian Wife of the White Hunter* by Ann S. Winterbotham Stephens, 50, is the first "dime novel" and a runaway best-seller; *The Mad Hunter* by Mary Andrews Denison (who will write at least eight "dime novels" in the 1860s) is a murder mystery.

Poetry: "Rock Me to Sleep, Mother" by New England poet Florence Percy (Elizabeth Chase Akers), 28, who writes, "Backward, turn backward, O time in your flight,/ Make me a child again just for tonight."

Virginia adopts a code providing for a prison term of up to 20 years for a white man convicted of rape with possible death for any freed black man found guilty of the same crime, but few white men will be convicted (*see* Hale, 1646).

1861

 The U.S. Civil War begins April 12 as Confederate guns bombard Fort Sumter in Charleston harbor. "The War Powers of the Government," a pamphlet by Maryland political activist Anna Ella Carroll, 45, sets forth President Lincoln's legal justification for sending the U.S. Army against the Confederacy. Carroll has been a prominent spokesperson for the anti-Catholic, anti-immigration American Party, called by E. Z. C. "Ned Buntline" Judson the "Know-Nothing Party," but Lincoln has her pamphlet distributed to every member of Congress, Assistant Secretary of War Thomas Scott pays her $1,250 out of his own pocket and has 10,000 copies printed, she travels in the fall to St. Louis, discovers that control of the Tennessee River is more essential to a Union victory than controlling the Mississippi, and upon her return in November submits a plan to Scott for implementing a Tennessee strategy that will prove decisive to the successful conduct of the war.

Varina Howell Davis, 35, wife of Confederate President Jefferson Davis, confides in a letter to her mother in Mississippi that "the North has a great advantage in manufacturing power" and that her husband is "depressed" about the Confederacy's prospects. She follows President Davis to Montgomery, Ala., and then, when the capital is moved, to Richmond, where her husband's political enemies criticize her as being "imperious" and society women scorn her "unladylike" western dress and manners.

Canadian-born runaway Sarah Emma Edmonds, 19, who ran away 2 years ago from the New Brunswick farm of her hard-driving father and has been selling books door to door in Michigan dressed as a man, enlists in the Union Army under the name Frank Thompson along with her male friends. Rejected at first as too small (an officer calls the five-foot-six girl a "beardless boy"), she is soon allowed to join and is sent with her regiment to the Potomac. She will spend most of her time behind the front lines, nursing the sick and wounded, will provide Union officers with information regarding Confederate troop movements, and will identify Rebel spies in the Union camps. Several hundred other women will try to pass as men for service in the Union Army, and some will succeed.

John C. Frémont fails to put down disturbances in Missouri and is fired from his post as head of the Department of the West; his wife, Jessie, calls upon President Lincoln to ask for his reinstatement, she is refused, Frémont will soon lose the fortune he made in California mining with unwise speculations in railroad stocks, and Jessie will be forced to support the family with her writing.

English-American entrepreneur Katherine Prescott Wormley, 31, at Newport, R.I., forms a local chapter of the Woman's Union and obtains a government contract to manufacture uniforms, thus providing employment for soldiers' wives who would otherwise be destitute.

Washington, D.C., widow Rose O'Neal Greenhow, 46, is arrested on her doorstep August 23 by detective Allan Pinkerton as she tries to swallow a coded message. Union forces have been routed July 21 at the Battle of Bull Run near the Manassas railway junction across the Potomac, and Greenhow is suspected of having passed three messages to the Confederacy giving information on the strength they would face and when the attack would begin. Greenhow and one of her daughters are placed under house arrest, and when they manage to slip more notes out to Rebel agents they are confined in the Old Capitol Prison, where Greenhow waves a Confederate flag from her window (*see* 1862).

The U.S. Sanitary Commission created by Secretary of War Simon Cameron June 9 is an outgrowth of the Ladies Central Relief founded April 25 by Dr. Elizabeth Blackwell, now 40. Former educator Clara Barton, also now 40, quits her job at the U.S. Patent Office to distribute food and supplies sent by their families in Massachusetts to troops stationed at the capital. After the first Battle of Bull Run, she sees that men brought to the Potomac docks are dying for want of prompt medical attention, gains permission to pass through the battle lines (although she is well aware that women on a battlefield are regarded as nuisances or even prostitutes), and attends to survivors of the carnage. Barton will raise thousands of dollars to buy food and medicine for Union soldiers, create and direct facilities for recovering soldiers' lost baggage, and run an agency to locate missing men that will continue until 1869 (*see* American Association of the Red Cross, 1881).

Clara Barton quit her job in the patent office to nurse the wounded in America's bloody Civil War. LIBRARY OF CONGRESS

 Dorothea Dix, now 59, wins an appointment as superintendent of women nurses for the Union.

Britain's Prince Albert dies of cancer (diagnosed as typhoid fever) September 14, leaving Queen Victoria desolate.

Charlotte Elizabeth, Countess Canning, dies of malaria at Calcutta November 18 at age 44. Her husband, the viceroy, will leave India in March of next year and die 3 months later.

The Nightingale Nurse Training School, founded last year at London, opens an annex in which Florence Nightingale hopes to train midwives to serve the working poor, but an outbreak of puerperal fever, stemming from a woman who has been delivered while suffering from erysipelas, forces the annex to close.

Richmond heiress Sally Louisa Tompkins, 27, turns her large house into a 22-bed clinic at her own expense and operates it as the Robertson Hospital.

President Jefferson Davis issues an order in late summer discontinuing all nonmilitary hospitals but commissions Tompkins a captain in the cavalry to circumvent his own order. "Cap'n Sally" and her hospital will care for nearly 1,300 wound cases in the next four years, and only 73 men will die.

 Vassar Female College is chartered at Poughkeepsie, N.Y., by local brewer Matthew Vassar, 69, who has made a fortune in land speculation. "It is my hope," he will say, "to inaugurate a new era in the history and life of woman. I wish to give one sex all the advantages too long monopolized by the other. Ours is, and is to be, an institution for women—not men" (*see* 1865).

 Fiction: *Silas Marner, or the Weaver of Raveloe* by George Eliot; *A Merchant House in the Archipelago* (*Ett köpmanshus i skärgarden*) by Emilie Flygare-Carlém; *Flavio* by Rosalía de Castro.

Dancer Lola Montez, former mistress to Bavaria's Ludwig I, dies in obscurity at Astoria, N.Y., January 17 at age 42.

Opera: U.S. soprano Clara Louise Kellogg, 18, makes her operatic debut 2/27 at New York's 7-year-old Academy of Music singing the role of Gilda in the 1851 Verdi opera Rigoletto; Adelina Patti, now 18, makes her European debut at London's Covent Garden 5/14 singing the role of Amina in the 1831 Bellini opera La Sonnambula and goes on to sing at Berlin in December.

Venezuelan piano prodigy Teresa Carreño, 8, gives her first New York recital.

Book of Household Management by English journalist Isabella Mary Beeton (*née* Mayson), 25, gives precise recipes for Victorian dishes in a thick, three-pound volume whose contents appeared originally in periodicals. Mrs. Beeton gives costs and cooking times as well as ingredient quantities.

The Book of Nature, Containing Information for Young People Who Think of Getting Married, on the Philosophy of Procreation and Sexual Intercourse showing How to Prevent Conception and To Avoid Child-bearing by James Ashton, M.D., is published at New York.

British-ruled Ireland makes abortion a criminal offense.

President Lincoln and his wife, Mary, lose their son Willie, 11, in February on the night of a rare White House ball. Mary has convulsions, and the president hires a nurse to watch her. She was the target only 4 days earlier of a poem, written by Eleanor Donnelly, that was published under the title "The Lady-President's Ball" and juxtaposed the small compensation given to families of dead soldiers with the lavish lifestyle of Mrs. Lincoln. An editorial by journalist Mary Clemmer Ames has claimed that while American women "sewed, scraped lint, made bandages," the First Lady "spent her time rolling to and fro between Washington and New York, intent on extravagant purchases for herself . . ." Mrs. Lincoln, who receives few letters of sympathy after Willie's death, suffers a breakdown and severe depression.

Rose Greenhow is tried for treason March 25 (*see* 1861). Gen. George McClellan says she "knows my plans better than Lincoln or the Cabinet, and has four times compelled me to change them." Lacking solid evidence of her guilt, the judges release her to Confederate officials across the Potomac and order her to remain away from Washington. Greenhow goes to Richmond, where President Jefferson Davis awards her $2,500 for her services, saying, "But for you there would have been no Battle of Bull Run." The information she has amassed will be instrumental in gaining further victories for Confederate generals (*see* 1863).

Yankee sympathizer Elizabeth Van Lew, 44, at Richmond uses her high social position to obtain valuable information for the Union, which she openly supports. She and her rich mother have freed their own slaves and purchased those of others in order to free them (*see* 1865).

The Union Navy under the command of Capt. David Farragut silences Confederate guns below New Orleans April 25, Gen. Benjamin F. Butler enters the city May 1 with occupation forces that rule with a heavy hand, a woman on a balcony in the French Quarter dumps the contents of a chamber pot on Farragut's head, and Gen. Butler issues an order May 15 that any woman who persists in insulting Union soldiers "shall be regarded and held liable to be treated as a woman plying her avocation." He intends the humiliating order to intimidate civilians into compliance with occupation orders, but it is interpreted as giving license to his troops to treat ladies as prostitutes. Lord Palmerston delivers a message to the House of Commons calling Butler's conduct "infamous," but Charles Francis Adams, American ambassador to Britain, protests that the Confederacy holds 2 million women in slavery.

Confederate forces under Gen. T. J. "Stonewall" Jackson and Richard B. Ewell take Fort Royal, Va., May 23 with help from Confederate spy Belle (*née* Isabelle) Boyd, 18, of Martinsburg, the "Siren of the Shenandoah." Familiar with every inch of the countryside, she has engaged in systematic pilfering of Union sabers, pistols, and ammunition, which are sorely needed by the Rebels and have been smuggled through the Southern lines. She carried messages last year from Rose Greenhow in Washington that came via Betty Duvall and will become Jackson's aide-de-camp and courier. Union authorities arrest Boyd July 30 by order of Secretary of War Stanton and take her to Washington, where she is held in the Old Capitol Prison until August 29, when she is released—perhaps to break her ties with other Confederate sympathizers in the Capitol—and sent south with some 200 other prisoners aboard the steamship *Juniata* down the Potomac.

"Does anybody wonder so many women die?" writes Mary Chesnut in her diary June 9. "Grief and constant anxiety kill nearly as many women as men die on the battlefield."

First Lady Mary Todd Lincoln regains possession of herself in summer and becomes an abolitionist, diverting funds that had been allocated to her for soldier care to her work in behalf of "all the oppressed colored race." She is the first First Lady to welcome blacks as White House guests, letting a Sunday School festival group use the South Lawn for a picnic and ordering the staff to "have everything done in the grand style" for them.

The Woman's Loyal National League, organized with help from Elizabeth Cady Stanton's husband, Henry, mounts a petition to end slavery.

U.S. women take the places of men in factories, arsenals, bakeries, retail shops, and government offices throughout the Union and the Confederacy as military draft calls create labor shortages.

New York retail merchant A. T. (Alexander Tierney) Stewart, 59, contributes $100,000 to the Union cause, sells uniforms at cost to the Union Army, and erects the world's largest department store at 10th Street and 4th Avenue. Stewart has introduced a revolutionary one-price system with each item carrying a price tag, an innovation that permits him to employ women salesclerks, who can be hired more cheaply than men. Having amassed a fortune of $50 million, Stewart gives a 10 percent discount to wives and children of clergymen and schoolteachers.

Women on both sides of the War of Secession scrape lint and roll bandages for the wounded, mostly in haphazard fashion. Northern women hold charity fairs to benefit the Sanitary Commission.

Iowa widow Annie Wittenmyer (*née* Turner), 35, works with the Sanitary Commission to devise a system for feeding Union soldiers in field hospitals. Women volunteers have scrounged milk, eggs, and vegetables for soldiers too sick to eat the regular pork-and-beans ration, but Wittenmyer's system ends confusion by establishing a diet kitchen in each hospital with "dietary nurses" who provide appropriate meals for every patient (*see* 1871).

The New England Hospital for Women and Children is founded by Marie E. Zakrzewska, now 33, who has practiced midwifery at Elizabeth Blackwell's New York Infirmary (*see* 1857).

Women replace men in schoolteaching positions as more men are called up to serve in the Union and Confederate armies.

Julie-Victoire Daubié receives her baccalaureate degree May 17 after 9 months of opposition from the French minister of education and the dean of the University of Lyons (*see* 1859). The University of Paris has refused to let her take the baccalaureate examinations, but the University of Lyons has agreed to let her do so, the Empress Eugénie has put pressure on Parlement, and the education minister, Gustave Rouland, has finally agreed to sign the baccalaureate despite his fears that opening universities to women will subject the schools to ridicule. Daubié, who is largely self-taught (in the absence of any secondary schools for girls), has maintained that there is nothing in the law to restrict a woman's right to education, and has demonstrated that intellectual improvement is a woman's key to emancipation.

"The Education of Women, and How It Would Be Affected by University Examinations" (essay) by Irish-born English journalist Frances Cobbe (*née* Power), 40, is published at London: "The natural constitution of the female mind renders a solid education peculiarly desirable, and even necessary, to bring out all womanly powers and gifts in proper balance and usefulness. I verily believe that a *man* can infinitely better dispense with sound mental training than a woman. Among the essential differences between the mental constitutions of the two sexes, one of the most odious is the preponderance in [women] of the intuitive over the reasoning faculties. Thus it has been facetiously expressed, 'When a man has laboriously climbed up step by step to the summit of his argument, he will generally find a woman standing before him on the top but of how she got there, neither he nor she can give the smallest explanation.' This rapid intuition of women may or may not prove a defect. Properly trained and balanced by that carefulness of truth which comes of conscientious study, it is no defect at all, but a great advantage; but unregulated quickness is a peril and misfortune. Jumping at conclusions is a favorite species of feminine steeplechase, with whose results we are all too familiar. . . . Women need solid mental training, not only to amend their reasoning and open their minds to argument, but also to correct the terribly inaccurate and superficial knowledge they now usually think sufficient. . . . High education does not make women *less* able and willing to perform their natural duties, but better and more intelligently able to do so." Cobbe points out that at the University of Padua "women learned and taught by the side of Galileo, Petrarch, and Columbus."

Welsh-born Singapore schoolteacher Anna (Harriette) Leonowens (*née* Crawford), 27, arrives in Bangkok at the invitation of King Mongkut to take up a position as governess to his children, bringing along her own 6-year-old son, Lewis, but leaving her 7-year-old daughter, Avis, in Singapore. Her parents sailed for India when she was 6, leaving her behind; her father died fighting for the queen, her mother remarried, Anna rejoined her at Bombay when she was 15, she married Major Thomas Lewis Leonowens in 1851 and returned with him to England, accompanied him to Singapore 6 years ago, and lost her fortune in the Sepoy Rebellion of 1857 as banks failed throughout India. Major Leonowens died after a tiger hunt in 1858, and she opened a school for officers' children in Singapore, attracting the attention of the Siamese consul, who had been instructed to secure an English governess. After lengthy negotiations, Anna received a letter in March from King Mongkut saying, "We are in good pleasure and satisfaction in hearing that you are willingness to undertake the education of our beloved royal children. . . . We hope that in doing your education on us and on our children (whom English call inhabitants of benighted land) you will do your best endeavor for knowledge of English language, science, and literature, and not for conversion to Christianity." The king of Siam, she finds, is quixotic and unpredictable, but she indignantly rejects suggestions that she join his harem and will remain at his court until 1867.

Philadelphia teacher Charlotte Forten, 25, moves in August to the sea islands off South Carolina to educate "contraband" slaves who have escaped to the Union lines. The daughter of a prominent free family, she sets up a one-room schoolhouse in which she gives children the rudiments of a formal education while teaching adults moral and social behavior to prepare them for life as free Americans.

Nonfiction: *Life in the Old World* (*Lif i gamla verlden*) by Fredrika Bremer appears as the last of six volumes that have been published since 1860 relating details of her extensive travels in Switzerland, Italy, and the Near East.

Fiction: *Margret Howth: A Story of To-day* by U.S. novelist Rebecca Davis (*née* Harding), 31; *St. Elmo* by Mobile, Alabama, novelist Augusta Jane Evans, 27, whose pious heroine, Edna Earl, becomes a celebrated author and a luminary in the New York literary scene; *Lady Audley's Secret* by English novelist Mary Elizabeth Braddon, 25, is a thriller about a blond murderess.

Poetry: *Goblin Market and Other Poems* by English poet Christina Georgina Rossetti, 31, gives the Pre-Raphaelites their first great literary success. The poet's brother Dante Gabriel Rossetti, 34, is a leader of the Pre-Raphaelite Brotherhood and its rebellion against the Royal Academy of Art, but his wife of 2 years succumbs to an overdose of the laudanum that she has been taking to dull the pain of her tuberculosis; *The Lady of Garaye* by Caroline Norton.

Sculptor Harriet Hosmer, now 31, sues for libel. Her statue *Zenobia* is on display at London, it is credited to an Italian artist, and a critic says, "As for Miss Hosmer, her want of modesty is enough to disgust a dog. She has casts for the entire *female model* made and exhibited in a shockingly indecent manner to all the young artists who call upon her."

Theater: *East Lynne, or The Elopement* 4/21 at Boston is an adaptation of the 1861 novel by English novelist Ellen Price Wood, 48, whose story has been running in the *Baltimore Sun*. The melodrama will be perennially revived, becoming the most popular play in U.S. stage history; *Mazeppa* 6/16 at New York's New Bowery Theater, with poet-actress Adah Isaacs Menken, 27, strapped half nude to a horse in a melodramatic adaptation of the 1819 Byron poem that creates a sensation.

Opera: U.S. soprano Geneviève (*née* Genbevra Guerrabella) Ward, 23, sings the role of Violetta in a New York production of the 1853 Verdi opera *La Traviata* but will soon lose her singing voice after contracting diphtheria on a visit to Cuba.

"The Battle Hymn of the Republic" appears in the February *Atlantic Monthly* with lyrics by Julia Howe (*née* Ward), 43, who helps her husband, Samuel Gridley Howe, 61, in publishing the Boston abolitionist journal the *Commonwealth,* which is dedicated also to prison reform, improved care for the feeble-minded, and abolition of imprisonment for debt. Julia Howe, who has received $4 for the lines she wrote one night late last year at Washington's Willard Hotel after visiting Massachusetts troops at a nearby army camp, sees her verse set almost immediately to the tune "Glory, Glory, Hallelujah" (or "John Brown's Body") attributed to one William Steffe.

1863

Confederate forces under Gen. Bragg move south January 3 after defeating a Union Army under Gen. Rosecrans at Stones River (Murfreesboro), Tenn., as Federal reinforcements pour in from Nashville. Union spy Pauline Cushman, 29, posing as an actress in search of her older brother in the Confederate Army, obtains a room at the Evans House, a hotel in Shelbyville, where she quickly makes friends with a Confederate captain of engineers. She steals his plans and drawings of defense fortifications, smuggles some out in the handles of butcher knives and others inside the craw of a chicken, which a woman farmer carries across the lines. Discovered and court-martialed, Cushman is found guilty, but Federal troops arrive and release her before she can be hanged and she is commissioned a major in the Union Army.

Union forces suffer defeat at Chancellorsville, Va., from May 1 to May 4, but Gen. T. J. "Stonewall" Jackson is wounded by one of his own sentries May 2 and dies of pneumonia May 10. News of his death reaches Belle Boyd at Mobile, Ala., she hurries back to Martinsburg, Va., and when Union forces attack Winchester June 14 she is only 4 miles away (*see* below).

The Battle of Gettysburg and the fall of Vicksburg in early July seem to doom the Confederacy's chances, but Rose Greenhow sails for Europe in August to raise money for the Southern cause (*see* 1862). Her book *My Imprisonment and the First Year of Abolition Rule in Washington* enjoys brisk sales abroad, and she is presented at court at both London and Paris (where she is given a private audience with Napoleon III) (*see* 1864).

Mary Todd Lincoln hears of the fighting at Gettysburg while visiting the Soldiers' Home, where she has been going almost daily to walk through the hospital aisles, distributing fresh fruit and bouquets of flowers. She heads home to be with her husband, and suffers an accident in which she cracks her skull on a rock. Someone has sabotaged her carriage, which has become detached, and she has been thrown out of it. Rushed to a nearby medical unit for treatment, she suffers for months (her wound, which has exposed her skull, becomes infected and must be reopened).

An order for the arrest of Belle Boyd (above) is issued July 23; she is held under house arrest owing to the grave illness of her mother, but when her mother improves she is taken to Carroll Prison at Washington and then to the Old Capitol Prison. After engineering the escape of three other prisoners in October, she is removed December 1 to Fortress Monroe, where she meets with Gen. Benjamin F. Butler, known in the South as "Beast" Butler (*see* 1862).

President Lincoln signs the Emancipation Proclamation January 1 in part at the urging of his wife, Mary, who has insisted that he do it not just for reasons of political necessity but as a matter of right.

Quaker orator Anna Dickinson, 20, speaks in May at the Great Hall of New York's Cooper Union after lecture tours through New Hampshire and Connecticut, stirs an audience of 5,000, and pockets a fee of $1,000 for her eloquence in the causes of women, blacks, interracial marriage, and an end to double standards.

The National Women's Loyalty League is founded May 14 to oppose slavery.

The Troy, N.Y., Collar Laundry Workers headed by Irish-American laundress Kate Mullaney strike for higher wages. The women work 12- to 14-hour days

Mary Todd Lincoln encouraged her husband to push for abolition of slavery. MATTHEW BRADY PHOTOGRAPH, LIBRARY OF CONGRESS

at temperatures close to 100° F. and earn scarcely $2 to $3 per week (*see* 1866).

Frontierswoman Sarah Wakefield is taken prisoner during a Sioux uprising. In *A Narrative of Indian Captivity* she will say of her 6 weeks "in Sioux tepees" that "the Indians were as respectful towards me as any white man would be towards a lady: and now, when I hear all the Indians abused, it aggravates me, for I know some are as manly, honest, and noble, as our own race."

$ Mrs. Lincoln (above) is well enough by autumn to make a shopping trip to New York, where she runs up huge bills at Lord & Taylor (*see* 1864).

 Singer Manufacturing Co. is incorporated by sewing machine inventor I. M. Singer and Edward Clark. Family incomes in America average only $500 per year and a new Singer sewing machine sells for $100, but Clark's $5-per-month installment plan persuades customers to buy Singer machines, which cost perhaps $40 to make, including all overhead.

Union warships in the ongoing Civil War have the advantage of newly patented chemical flares for communicating over long distances and pinpointing the location of shipwrecks. The flares will be called "Very lights" in 1877 after navy lieutenant Edward Wilson Very, now 15, who will make small improvements, but they are actually the invention of Martha "Mattie" Costan (*née* Hunt), 37, who eloped at age 14 with 19-year-old Benjamin Costan. He died of pneumonia 7 years later, in 1847, after the birth of their fourth son, and she found in an old trunk his plans for a prototype signal flare. After working for nearly a decade on perfecting the flares, she had managed to get a bright white and a vivid red chemical fire but needed a blue for the standard maritime codes. Having corresponded (under a man's name) with fireworks manufacturers, she saw a display celebrating completion of the first Atlantic cable in mid-August 1858, obtained the blue that she required, was awarded patents for "Costan Telegraphic Night Signals" in the United States, Britain, France, the Netherlands, Austria, Denmark, Sweden, and Italy, and executed a U.S. government order for $6,000 worth of the flares that have been instrumental in saving thousands of Union seamen's lives.

New York Medical College for Women, founded with help from Elizabeth Cady Stanton, is a homeopathic institution.

∞ The Universalist Church ordains feminist Olympia Brown, 28, as a minister.

President Lincoln proclaims the first national Thanksgiving Day October 3 and sets aside the last Thursday of November to commemorate the feast given by the Pilgrims in 1621 for their Wampanoag benefactors. The president has acted partly in response to a plea from *Godey's Lady's Book* editor Sarah Josepha Hale, now 74, who has campaigned since 1846 for Thanksgiving Day observances and by 1852 had persuaded people to celebrate Thanksgiv-

Sarah Josepha Hale edited Godey's Lady's Book, *giving her enormous influence on society.*

Poetry: *Gallician Songs* (*Cantares gallegos*) and *To My Mother* (*A mi madre*) by Rosalía de Castro.

Painting: *Le Déjeuner sur l'Herbe* by French painter Edouard Manet, 31, is exhibited May 15 at the Salon des Réfusés in Paris and creates a furor with its depiction of a nude picnicking with two clothed men. Other paintings: *Mlle. Victorine in the Costume of an Espada* and *Olympia*, both by Manet, whose model for all three is redhead Victorine Meurent, a painter herself, who will live until 1928.

Teresa Carreño, now 10, performs for President Lincoln on the White House piano (*see* 1861). Her keyboard talents will make her the toast of four continents in the next 5 decades.

Opera: Clara Kellogg sings the role of Marguerite in the 1859 Gounod opera *Faust* 11/25 at New

Venezuelan piano prodigy Teresa Carreño performed for President Lincoln and the crowned heads of Europe. LIBRARY OF CONGRESS

ing on the same day in 30 of the 32 states, in U.S. consulates abroad, and on U.S. ships in foreign waters.

Nonfiction: *Journal of a Residence on a Georgia Plantation* by actress Fanny Kemble is adapted from her diaries of 1838–1839. Now 53, Kemble has written several plays, a volume of poems, and other books of reminiscences but none so influential as this one, whose accounts of slavery—15-year-old mothers and 30-year-old grandmothers housed in squalid slave quarters, men and women punished with the lash, and all fed meager rations—are credited with dampening British interest in intervening on the side of the Confederacy in the Civil War. Kemble has bought a cottage at Berkshire, Mass., and although she will make frequent trips home will not return to England to live until 1877.

Fiction: *Romola* by George Eliot; *Sylvia's Lovers* by Mrs. Gaskell; *The Rector and the Doctor's Family* and *Salem Chapel* by Margaret Oliphant, now 35, who in 1852 married her artist cousin Frances Oliphant but was widowed 4 years ago and left not only with a debt of £1,000 but also with relatives to support and educate; *Held in Bondage* by English novelist Ouida (Marie Louise de la Ramée), 24.

York's Academy of Music. It will be her most famous role until her retirement in 1887.

Sarah Josepha Hale (above) maintains her pink-and-white complexion with old-fashioned home-made "wrinkle eradicators." She keeps sheets of heavy brown butcher paper in an upper drawer of her bureau and a bottle of fresh apple vinegar atop the bureau. Before going to bed at night she takes little strips of the paper, soaks them in vinegar, and applies them to her temples to ward off "crows' feet." To keep her hands soft, she has compounded a mixture of lard, rose water, and coconut milk, a bottle of which is always on her office desk as well as on her dressing table, and she never washes her hands without using it. Hale usually wears silk "because it shakes the dust," indulges in lace at the throat, but abhors tight lac-ing, calling it injurious to health, and will not wear earrings.

General Tom Thumb is married February 10 at New York's Grace Church on Broadway and 10th Street to Lavinia Warren (Mercy Bunn), who stands 2 feet 8 inches in height. Heavily promoted by showman P. T. Barnum, the wedding attracts huge crowds that jam the streets (the wedding party stands on a grand piano to receive guests at the Metropolitan Hotel).

Britain's Prince of Wales is married March 10 to Princess Alexandra of Denmark.

The first four-wheeled roller skates are patented by New York inventor James L. Plimpton, whose small boxwood wheels are arranged in pairs and cushioned by rubber pads, making it possible to maintain balance while executing intricate maneu-vers (*see* 1760). Plimpton's roller skates will lead to a widespread roller-skating fad later in this decade, and the craze will sweep Europe in the 1870s.

Edinburgh obstetrician Sir James Young Simpson, now 52, describes a method of "menstrual regula-tion," saying, "I have made frequent use of a tube resembling in length and size a male catheter, with a large number of thickly-set small orifices stretch-ing along for about two inches from its extremity, and having an exhausting syringe adapted to its lower extremity, by which air could be withdrawn after it had been introduced into the cavity of the uterus. The use of this instrument is in some cases attended with striking results."

1864

Union Army surgeon Mary Edwards Walker, 31, is captured in enemy territory (she has slipped behind Confederate lines to treat civilians) and held in a Richmond, Va., prison for 4 months before being exchanged for a male Confederate surgeon who has been held prisoner in the North (*see* medicine, 1865).

Confederate spy Belle Boyd tries to run the Union blockade aboard the Anglo-Rebel steamer *Grey-hound* out of Wilmington, N.C., the ship is seized by Union naval forces, and she meets Ensign Samuel Wylde Hardinge, Jr., of Brooklyn, N.Y., who is arrested June 8 and dismissed July 8 for neglect of duty in permitting the captain of the *Greyhound* to escape. Boyd has reached London and is married there August 25 to Hardinge, who leaves in November, makes his way to his wife's home in Martinsburg, Va., but is arrested a second time in December and held prisoner, first at Wash-ington, then 16 miles away at Fort Delaware (*see* Nonfiction, 1865).

Confederate spy Rose Greenhow collects her book royalties in gold coin and embarks from England with fresh funds for the Southern cause, but her ship is wrecked by a violent storm September 30 and she is drowned near Wilmington, N.C., at age 49, pulled down by the leather bag full of gold pieces round her neck (*see* 1863).

Abraham Lincoln wins reelection in November as Union forces score victories. First Lady Mary Todd Lincoln has gone to New York behind the presi-dent's back, run up debts totaling $27,000 at dry-goods stores, and then tried to get Republican politicians to pay them, arguing that they grew rich from her husband's patronage. A. T. Stewart and other merchants have offered her unlimited credit, and she has feared that news of her profligacy would be used to defeat her husband in his reelec-tion bid.

Parliament passes a Contagious Diseases Act, mak-ing any woman suspected of prostitution in a garrison town subject to police "inspection" for venereal disease. If she is menstruating, she may be detained until an examination is possible. Doctors who perform the examinations are said to rape their patients, and if they say a woman is diseased she may be held in confinement and treated with mercury until deemed cured. A woman who refuses to submit to examination may be imprisoned at hard labor. More Contagious Diseases Acts will be passed in 1866 and 1869 (see 1882).

Kamehamea IV of the Sandwich Islands sells the island of Niihau to Mrs. Elizabeth Sinclair, an émigrée Scotswoman whose late husband acquired large holdings in New Zealand before being lost at sea. Feeling the property insufficient to keep her large family together, she has sold it, loaded her family, livestock, and movable possessions aboard her own clipper ship, and visited several places before deciding on Hawaii. The 12-mile-long, 46,000-acre island—plus the 65,000-acre Great Makaweli estate on Kaui—will remain in her family for more than a century after Mrs. Sinclair's death in 1890, being used to graze sheep and cattle.

The Ladies' Medical College is founded by the 2-year-old Female Medical Society at London with the purpose of forcing the admittance of women into medical practice but, more immediately, to establish midwifery as a suitable occupation for gentlewomen.

The Women's Medical College is founded by Dr. Elizabeth Blackwell and her sister Emily at their New York Infirmary for Women and Children. It has America's first professorship of hygiene, or preventive medicine (Elizabeth Blackwell holds the chair).

Swarthmore College, founded outside Philadelphia, is open to women as well as men (see Iowa, 1856). By 1879, nearly half of all U.S. colleges will be coeducational.

Nonfiction: *Woman and Her Social Relationships* (*La donna e suoi rapporti sociale*) by Italian feminist Anna Maria Mozzoni, 27, urges other young middle-class women to discard the tradition of indolent, vacuous parasitism and open themselves to a wider life; *Woman and Her Era* by onetime Sing Sing prison matron Liza W. (Eliza Woods Burhans)

Farnham, 48, who writes that women are not only morally superior to men but also biologically superior: "Life is exalted in proportion to its Organic and Functional complexity; Woman's Organism is more complex in her totality of Function, larger than those of any other being inhabiting our earth; Therefore her position in the scale of Life as the most exalted, the Sovereign One"; *Hospital Sketches* by U.S. writer Louisa May Alcott, 32, whose father, Amos Bronson Alcott, failed in his Fruitlands commune experiment of 1844 and who was herself forced for a time to perform menial work in order to support her family (she has lately been working as a nurse in a military hospital).

Fiction: *The Perpetual Curate* by Margaret Oliphant.

Poetry: *In War Time* by U.S. poet John Greenleaf Whittier, 56, whose "Barbara Fritchie" contains the lines "'Shoot, if you must, this old gray head,/ But spare your country's flag,' she said." It is based on an apocryphal story that is widely believed.

Juvenile: *A Book of Golden Deeds in All Times and All Lands* by Charlotte M. Yonge.

English housewife Julia Margaret Cameron (*née* Pattle), 46, produces a photographic portrait of a little girl and proclaims it her "first success." She will become Britain's best-known photograher, not only capturing the likenesses of such notables as Alfred Tennyson, Charles Darwin, actress Ellen Terry, and Alice Liddell (for whom mathematician Charles Dodgson is now writing his *Alice's Adventures in Wonderland*), but also allegorical, religious, and sentimental scenes.

Theater: Lotta Crabtree, now 17, makes her debut June 5 at Niblo's Saloon at Broadway and Prince Street, New York, which her mother, Mary Ann, has rented for the month of June after coming east from San Francisco with 14 gold watches and a valise full of gold nuggets. A protégée of Lola Montez, who taught her how to dance, she toured the mining camps as a child, enthusiastic audiences showered the stage with nuggets and silver dollars when she sang, "How Can I Leave Thee?" and she made her San Francisco debut 5 years ago, but while some goldfield veterans who had cheered "Lotta the Unapproachable" in San Francisco cheer her in New York, she does not impress the rest of the audience, leaves the stage in tears, and closes after 6 nights. Crabtree has more success in Chicago, where she opens August 1 at McVicker's Theater in *The Seven Sisters*, an extravaganza in which she plays the role of Tartarine in blackface, strumming the banjo, dancing breakdowns, jigs, and hornpipes, and playing four other roles for a 3-week run.

Opera: Hortense Schneider creates the title role in Jacques Offenbach's new opera *La Belle Hélène* 12/17 at the Théâtre des Variétés, Paris.

Oregon settler Asa Mercer goes back east and arranges for the transportation of several dozen unmarried females to the Puget Sound area. "I had been taught to believe, and did believe," he will later explain, "that practically all the goodness in the world came from the influence of pure-minded women. At that time there was not a single woman of marriageable age on Puget Sound . . . [and] the baser element was almost beyond the reach of female influence and its wholesome results." A college graduate, Mercer will make another such trip in 1866, and his efforts will win him election to the Oregon Legislative Assembly.

1865

General Grant takes Richmond April 3 with help from local Yankee sympathizer Elizabeth Van Lew, who has brought supplies to imprisoned Union officers and helped many to escape (*see* 1862). Affecting peculiar dress and behavior in order to divert suspicion, "Crazy Bet" has maintained five relay stations between the Confederate capitol and Grant's headquarters.

The War of the Rebellion ends April 9 with Lee's surrender at Appomattox Court House in Virginia. The Union has lost 360,222 men (110,000 of them in battle), the Confederacy 258,000 (94,000 in battle), with 471,427 wounded on both sides. Men with missing arms and legs are everywhere to be seen, the nation is full of widows and orphans, and marriageable young women have trouble finding husbands.

President Lincoln is shot at Ford's Theatre in Washington April 14. Actress Laura Keene, now

45, recognizes actor John Wilkes Booth as the assassin and holds the dying president's head in her lap until he is taken from his box at the theater to a house across the street. Police search the boarding-house of Mrs. Mary E. Jenkins Surratt, 45, and she is arrested April 17 on conspiracy charges in connection with the president's murder. Her son John, a Confederate courier, has met in the house with Booth and others but has evidently distanced himself after learning of Booth's plan. Booth has been killed trying to escape. His alleged conspirators, including Mrs. Surratt, are tried beginning May 12, found guilty, and hanged July 7.

Mrs. Lincoln has left town for Chicago, where she puts up at a genteel but cheap hotel. Her husband has left a substantial estate but no will, and pending settlement she is obliged to subsist on about $1,500 per year while she employs a lobbyist and writes to every influential man she has ever known, pressing Congress to pay her the $100,000 that Lincoln would have received for the 4 years of his second term (it will wind up giving her $25,000 less taxes). Friends and acquaintances have reduced the $27,000 in bills that she has run up, but she still owes $15,000 and will not retire the debt for some years, and then only with help from her son Robert (*see* 1870).

The Ku Klux Klan organized at Pulaski, Tenn., is a secret social club of young white men who hope to recapture the comradeship and excitement of the war. Members, who are sworn to protect Southern womanhood from the "black menace," adopt a uniform that is soon discovered to terrorize superstitious blacks, and Klan members will rape black women as one means of intimidating newly enfranchised black voters while they try to return local and state government to white, Democratic party control. A majority of Southern whites will join the KKK in the next few years.

The Salvation Army has its beginnings in a London mission founded in Whitechapel by English humanitarian Catherine (*née* Mumford) Booth, 36, and her evangelist husband, William, also 36, who have been moved by the plight of the poor. Enduring the taunts of critics, who will beat her, kick her, and pelt her at times with mud, paint, stones, dead cats, and even live coals, she will enlist other women in an evangelical crusade against social evils, including prostitution. She and her husband will turn a group of converted criminals into a "Hallelujah Band," he will say, "The best men in my army are the women," and she will bear eight children, all of whom will be active in the Salvation Army.

London physician James Barry dies July 25 at age 70 and is discovered by undertakers to be a woman. Her real name is Miranda Stuart, she studied at Edinburgh College of Medicine, and she has traveled the world since age 18, working her way up through the medical ranks to reach the top of her profession without ever revealing her sex. During her service in South Africa she discovered a plant that has been widely used to treat syphilis and gonorrhea.

Mary Walker, M.D., has served as assistant surgeon in the Union Army (see 1864) and is awarded the Congressional Medal of Honor, the first woman ever to be thus distinguished (but see 1916). She has taken to wearing a frock coat and trousers during the Civil War, will be arrested several times in the next few years for appearing that way in the street, and will be active in the Mutual Dress Reform and Equal Rights Association.

Vassar Female College, which opens at Poughkeepsie, N.Y., September 20, is the first true women's college in America (see 1861; Holyoke, 1837). Of its 30 faculty members, 22 are women. Maria Mitchell, who has discovered a comet that bears her name, is professor of astronomy and will remain in that position for 23 years (she was admitted to membership in the American Academy of Arts and Sciences 15 years ago, becoming the first woman member) (see Smith, 1871).

A school for freed blacks opens in South Carolina's Sea Islands under the direction of educator Martha Schofield, 26, who has organized the enterprise.

Nonfiction: *Belle Boyd in Camp and Prison, Written by Herself* by the Confederate spy, still in London. She has been warned that publishing the book will endanger the life of her husband, Samuel Hardinge; she has warned that she will expose Union atrocities if any harm befalls him, he is released from Fort Delaware February 3 by

order of Secretary of War Stanton and sails aboard the Cunard steamer *Cuba* February 8 for Liverpool, and her two-volume book appears in London 3 months after his arrival February 19 (his health has been damaged by imprisonment, and he will die within 18 months). *Sesame and Lilies* by English writer John Ruskin, 46, who says, "You cannot hammer a girl into anything. She grows as a flower does,—she will wither without sun; she will decay in her sheath as a narcissus will if you do not give her air enough; she may fall and defile her head in dust if you leave her without help at some moments of her life; but you cannot fetter her; she must take her own fair form and way if she take any."

Fiction: *Cousin Phillis* and *Wives and Daughters* by Mrs. Gaskell; *Alice's Adventures in Wonderland* by English mathematician Lewis Carroll (Charles Lutwidge Dodgson), 33, who has written his fantasy for the entertainment of Alice Liddell, second daughter of classical scholar Henry George Liddell, 54, dean of Christ Church; *Our Mutual Friend* by Charles Dickens, now 53: "The question [with Mr. Podsnap] about everything was, would it bring a blush into the cheek of the young person [Podsnap's daughter Georgiana]" (xi).

Poetry: "The Hand That Rocks the Cradle Is the Hand That Rules the World" by U.S. lawyer-poet William Ross Wallace, 46, who has gained fame with his Civil War songs.

Juvenile: *Hans Brinker, or The Silver Skates* by New York author Mary Elizabeth Mapes Dodge, 34.

Theater: London actress Marie Effie Wilton, 25, who has appeared in some Strand Theatre burlesques, purchases the Queen's Theatre in January and renames it the Prince of Wales's Theatre, begins its second season 9/25 and opens 11/11 in Thomas W. Robertson's new comedy *Society* with Miss Larkin, scoring such a success that another row of stalls has to be added and the prince of Wales makes his first visit.

Mme. Demorest has 300 women agents selling her paper dress patterns throughout America (see 1860). Her business has grown despite the war and will soon have agents in Europe.

1866

✘ Washington demands removal of French forces from Mexico February 12. Having failed to gain U.S. recognition, the emperor Maximilian sends his Belgian-born wife, Carlota, to seek aid from Pope Pius IX and Napoleon III, but she soon finds that his cause is hopeless. He will go before a firing squad next June, thus ending Napoleon III's dream of establishing an empire in Latin America.

✊ The American Equal Rights Association founded May 10 at New York is an outgrowth of the Woman's Rights Society (*see* 1848; 1869).

Memphis has a race riot as police join with white citizens in an attack on the black community: 46 blacks and five whites are killed as Reconstruction roils the South in the wake of the Civil War. Congressional hearings held after the Memphis riot produce testimony from several black women that they were brutally raped by their white attackers.

Elizabeth Cady Stanton runs for Congress as an independent, opposing Republican protectionist economic policies, accusing Republicans of helping the rich at the expense of the masses and trying to establish a new aristocracy, and opposing woman suffrage bills presented by Democrats.

Troy, N.Y., iron molders go on strike and receive $1,000 from the women of the growing Collar Laundry Workers Union (*see* 1863). When New York bricklayers walk off the job later in the year, they receive $500 from Kate Mullaney's laundry workers (*see* 1868).

💲 R. H. Macy, who 3 years ago promoted Margaret Getchell to bookkeeper, makes her superintendent of his store (*see* 1860). She is the first woman in the city to have charge of what is becoming a major department store (*see* 1869).

⚕ A London dispensary for women opens under the direction of local physician Elizabeth Garrett Anderson, now 31, who pioneers the admission of women to the professions, including medicine. The extent of female invalidism, Anderson argues, is much exaggerated by male physicians: women's natural functions are not all that debilitating, she says, pointing out that among the working classes women continue to work during menstruation "without intermission, and, as a rule, without ill effects" (*see* Jacobi, 1877).

Bernadette Soubirous of Lourdes enters the convent of Saint Gildard at Nevers, where she will die of tuberculosis in 1879 despite administration of water from the grotto at Lourdes (*see* 1858). Reports of cures from the grotto will nevertheless continue to attract sick, blind, and infirm visitors (*see* 1926).

The Western Health Reform Institute is founded at Battle Creek, Mich., by Seventh-Day Adventist prophet Ellen Gould White (*née* Harmon), 38, whose sanitorium treatment combines vegetarian diet and hydrotherapy with some accepted medical methods. Alcohol, coffee, tobacco, meat, and sugar are all detrimental to the body and mind, White maintains, echoing sentiments expressed earlier by Amelia Bloomer and Elizabeth Cady Stanton. The "San" will incubate the infant U.S. breakfast-food industry.

∞ Cincinnati's Plum Street Temple is completed for the city's B'nai Yeshurun congregation, whose Austrian-American rabbi Isaac Meyer Wise, 47, is pioneering a Reform movement in U.S. Judaism by abandoning dietary laws and other Orthodox practices such as segregating women.

✒ Nonfiction: *The Higher Education of Women* by English reformer Sarah Emily Davies, 36.

Fiction: *Felix Holt the Radical* by George Eliot; *Wives and Daughters* by Mrs. Gaskell; *Miss Majoribanks* by Margaret Oliphant; "Life in the Iron Mills" by Rebecca Harding Davis appears in *Atlantic Tales*.

Juvenile: *The Dove in the Eagle's Nest* by Charlotte M. Yonge.

🎭 Theater: Lotta Crabtree opens in January at Boston's Howard Athenaeum, dances the MacGowan Reel, sings "Mickey Dear" in an Irish brogue, burlesques the late Lola Montez, plays Topsy in *Uncle Tom's Cabin*, appears in Dion Boucicault's *Irish Assurance and Yankee Modesty*, begins the second week with *The Seven Sisters*, and enjoys a run of 18 performances, giving a final performance February 10; Crabtree opens in June at Washington's National Theater under the management of John T. Ford, whose Ford's Theater has been closed since the

Washington debutante Belle Boyd parlayed her exploits as a daring Confederate spy into a stage career. LIBRARY OF CONGRESS

Broadway musicals: Italian-born dancer Marie Bonfanti, 19, in *The Black Crook* 9/12 at Niblo's Garden, with a Faustian plot by U.S. playwright Charles M. Barras, 40, a cast of 100 dancing girls in pink tights (clergymen denounce their costumes and indelicate postures, as does James Gordon Bennett in his *New York Herald*), music adapted from various sources, 474 perfs. The first true Broadway musical, it runs 5½ hours on opening night, will see many revivals, and will tour for more than 40 years.

Popular songs: "Come Back to Erin" by London songwriter Claribel (Charlotte Allington Barnard); "When You and I Were Young, Maggie" by Detroit composer J. A. Butterfield, lyrics by Canadian-American journalist George Washington Johnson of the *Cleveland Plain Dealer*.

Vassar College undergraduates form two baseball teams. Baseball remains an amateur sport, even for men (professional ball will not begin until 1869), and although women professionals will barnstorm the country in the 1890s, the women's game will gradually become softball.

Swiss entrepreneur Henri Nestlé, 50, formulates a combination of farinaceous pap and milk for infants who cannot take mother's milk and starts a firm under his own name to produce the new infant food (*see* formula, 1921).

1867

assassination last year of President Lincoln, and goes on to make appearances at Buffalo, Cincinnati, and Columbus, Ohio, before making her Philadelphia debut at the Arch Street Theater; Belle Boyd makes her acting debut at the Theatre Royal in Manchester in the role of Pauline in *The Lady of Lyons* (she has been coached by emigrée U.S. actress Aponia Jones, 26, who was a star in America before the war and has become a favorite at London's Drury Lane Theatre); Marie Wilton in T. W. Robertson's comedy *Ours* 9/15 at the Prince of Wales's Theatre, London, with Miss Larkin and Squire Bancroft, 25.

Opera: Hortense Schneider creates the role of Boulotte in the new Offenbach opera *Barbe-bleue* 2/5 at the Théâtre des Variétés, Paris.

Elizabeth Cady Stanton addresses the New York State Senate Judiciary Committee January 23 urging that women be permitted to vote for delegates to a convention that will rewrite the state constitution of 1777: "From a recent examination of the archives of the State of New Jersey we learn that, owing to a liberal Quaker influence, women and negroes exercised the right of suffrage in that State 31 years—from 1776 to 1807—when 'white males' ignored the constitution, and arbitrarily assumed the reins of government. This act of injustice is sufficient to account for the moral darkness that seems to have settled down upon that unhappy State. During the dynasty of women and negroes, does history record any social revolution peculiar to that period? Because women voted there, was the institution of marriage annulled, the sanctity of the home invaded, cradles annihilated . . . ? Did the men of that period become mere satellites of the dinner-pot, the wash-tub, or the spinning-wheel? Were they dwarfed and crippled in body and soul, while their enfranchised wives became giants in stature and intellect?"

Parliament debates a Reform Bill that would expand suffrage. Economist-philosopher John Stuart Mill, now 61, argues that giving even a minority of women the vote would be of benefit to all: "They would no longer be classified with children and lunatics, as incapable of taking care of themselves or others, and needing that everything should be done for them." But Caroline Norton, whose divorce and custody battle led to passage of the Matrimonial Causes Act 10 years ago, does not support woman suffrage, believing that women need special legal protection precisely because they *are* inferior. The Reform Bill passes with help from Liberal M.P. Henry Fawcett, 44, who was blinded in an 1858 shooting accident but became professor of political economy at Cambridge in 1863 and this year marries physician Elizabeth Garrett Anderson's younger sister, Millicent, 20. He will support her woman-suffrage efforts.

The Scottish Women's Suffrage Society holds its first meeting June 11.

The Kansas legislature proposes an amendment enfranchising women and presents it to voters for ratification. Suffragists Susan B. Anthony and Elizabeth Cady Stanton (above) persuade feminist Lucy Stone, now 49, and her husband, Henry Blackwell, to campaign for ratification and the couple enjoys some success in May. Anthony and Stanton launch their own effort in August, receiving aid from George Francis Train, a handsome, charming, and abstemious millionaire who has made a fortune in foreign ventures, harbors presidential aspirations, and supports women's rights (along with Irish independence, free trade, monetary inflation, and central banking) while opposing extension of the franchise to the illiterate. Attired always in purple gloves and full dress, Train pleads the case of woman suffrage to the New York State constitutional convention. Kansas voters defeat the amendment, but Anthony and Stanton, financed by Train, speak at major cities en route home to New York (see the *Revolution*, 1868).

English physicians perform the first "radical" mastectomy for breast cancer, removing not only the breast but also the chest muscles and various lymph nodes. The long, complicated operation, impossible before the invention of nitrous oxide and sulfuric ether anesthesia, will remain popular in Europe until the 1930s (see Halsted, 1889).

The North of England Council for Promoting Higher Education of Women is founded by reformers who include Josephine (Elizabeth) Butler (*née* Grey), 39, (Anne) Jemima Clough, 47, and Manchester schoolmistress Elizabeth Clark Wolstenholm-Elby, 33. They begin to press for women's examinations at the university level but encounter opposition from Emily Davies, who opposes separate examinations and is fighting for the right of women to have the same examinations as men (see 1869).

Anna Leonowens sails from Bangkok July 5 after 5 years as governess and teacher to the king of Siam's royal children (see 1862); she reaches England in September, places her son, Lewis, in a school in Ireland, and sails for New York with her daughter, Avis (see 1868).

Howard University for Negroes is founded by white Congregationalists outside Washington, D.C. The founders, who include Gen. O. O. Howard, director of the Freedmen's Bureau, arouse ridicule with their proposal to admit students of all ages, male or female, married or single, informed or ignorant.

Milwaukee printer Christopher Latham Sholes, 48, invents the first practical "writing machine" while seeking a way to inscribe braille-like characters for use by the blind. Asked to test the machine's efficiency, court reporter Charles Weller types, "Now is the time for all good men to come to the aid of the party." Sholes will call his machine a "typewriter" (see 1868).

Fiction: *The Village on the Cliff* by English novelist Anne Isabella, Lady Ritchie (*née* Thackeray), 30, who has been part of her father's literary circle; *The Night of the Blue Boots* (*El caballero de las botas azules*) by Rosalía de Castro; *Under Two Flags* by Ouida (Marie-Louise de la Ramée); *Thérèse Raquin* by French novelist Emile (Edouard-Charles-Antoine) Zola, 27.

Juvenile: *Ragged Dick, or Street Life in New York* is serialized in the periodical *Student and Schoolmate* published at New York. Signed "Oliver Optic," the book is actually by Unitarian minister Horatio Alger, 35, whose more than 100 rags-to-riches novels in the next 30 years will dramatize virtues of pluck, honesty, hard work, and marrying the boss's daughter.

Painting: *Deer in Repose* and *Stag Listening to the Wind* (both oil on canvas) by Rosa Bonheur.

Theater: Lotta Crabtree opens at Crosby's Opera House, Chicago, as Little Nell in *The Marchioness*, a loose adaptation by Irish-American actor-playwright John Brougham of Charles Dickens's 1841 novel *The Old Curiosity Shop*, and goes on to appear in nine other plays in a 17-day engagement; Marie Wilton and Miss Larkin in T. W. Robertson's *Caste* 4/6 at the Prince of Wales's Theatre, London, with Squire Bancroft and Lydia Foote; Lotta Crabtree opens at Wallack's Theater, New York, playing six parts in *Pet of the Petticoats* and the role of Lydie Larrigan in *Family Jars*, begins the second week with *The Marchioness*, packs the house each night, earns nearly $10,000 in 28 days, and by September is back in Chicago, playing Little Nell in *The Marchioness* at McVicker's Theater as she continually invents new business and improvises new lines; Marie Wilton and Lydia Foote in Dion Boucicault's *How She Loves Him* 12/21 at the Prince of Wales's Theatre with Squire Bancroft and Mrs. Leigh Murray.

Opera: Hortense Schneider creates the title role in the new Offenbach opera *La Grande-Duchesse de Gerolstein* 4/12 at the Théâtre des Variétés, Paris, and draws enormous crowds—including virtually all the crowned heads of Europe—throughout the exhibition year; Clara Kellogg makes her London debut singing the role of Marguerite in Gounod's 1859 opera *Faust*.

New York's Knickerbocker Base Ball Club establishes the last Tuesday of each month in the season as "Ladies' Day," offering free admission to wives, daughters, and girlfriends with "suitable seats or settees."

Overpopulation is a red herring invented by the capitalists to justify poverty among the working class, says German socialist Karl Marx, 50, in *Das Kapital*. He rejects the idea of contraception and favors enhanced production and more equitable distribution of wealth as better ways to improve the lot of the working class.

Parliament makes clear for the first time that a woman can be tried for precipitating her own miscarriage (*see* 1803; 1937).

1868

Spain's prime minister Ramón María Narváez, duke of Valencia, dies April 23 at age 68, and a revolutionary proclamation issued at Cádiz September 18 by Admiral Juan Bautista Topete y Carballo, 47, ends absolutist rule. The press has attacked Isabella II for making her court favorite (an actor) Spain's minister of state, and her royal forces are defeated September 28 at Alcolea by Marshal Juan Prim y Prats, 54. Isabella flees to France September 29, her enemies declare her deposed, and Marshal Prim forms a provisional government October 5 under the regency of the former governor of Cuba Francisco Serrano y Domínguez, 58. The new regime annuls reactionary laws, abolishes religious orders, including the Jesuits, and establishes universal suffrage and a free press (*see* 1870).

Madagascar's Hova queen Rashoherina dies after a 5-year reign and is succeeded by Ranavalona II, who will reign as queen until 1883. True power remains in the hands of her husband and first minister, Rainilaiarivony, a Christian who was married to Rashoherina and will retain power until 1896 by marrying Ranavalona's successor.

Siam's king Mongkut (Rama IV) dies of fever October 1 at age 64 after a 17-year reign, leaving generous bequests to Anna Leonowens and her son, Lewis (the king's executors will withhold their inheritances). The king's own son of 15, Somdeth Phra Paraminda Maha Chulalongkorn, who will reign until 1910 as Rama V, studied under Mrs. Leonowens from 1862 to 1867 and promised her that if he ever became king he would rule over "a free, not an enslaved, nation." The new king of Siam is crowned November 11 after recovering from the same fever that killed his father.

The first meeting of Britain's National Society for Woman Suffrage (NSWS) convenes October 30.

Congress enacts an 8-hour law for federal employees, but workers in private industry continue to work 10 to 12 hours per day and often more.

The 2-year-old National Labor Union headed by William H. Sylvis, 40, of the Iron-Moulders Union admits four women to its Congress and urges women to "learn trades, engage in business, join our labor unions or form protective unions of your own, and use every honorable means to persuade or force employers to do justice to women by paying them equal wages for equal work." Sylvis praises Kate Mullaney for her "indefatigable exertions on behalf of female laborers," calls her "the smartest and most energetic woman in America," and proposes that she be appointed assistant secretary and national organizer for women, but Mullaney will lead another strike of her laundresses next year, she will lose, and her union will be destroyed despite widespread support from the fledgling labor movement.

U.S. women hired for factory, office, and retail-store jobs during the Civil War continue in such work (New York City alone has nearly 30,000 working women) but are almost universally relegated to menial positions or are paid less than men doing the same work. Elizabeth Cady Stanton founds the Working Woman's Association September 17 with help from militant trade union women attracted by the prolabor position of her newspaper (below). Those attending the first meeting include printer Augusta Lewis, who is famous for being able to set the entire text of Washington Irving's "Rip Van Winkle" in 6½ hours (*see* 1869).

Elizabeth Cady Stanton (above) and Susan B. Anthony take up the cause of Hester Vaughan in December. Born in England, Vaughan came to Philadelphia to be married, found that her fiancé was already married, took a job as a domestic, and was seduced by her employer, who fired her when he discovered that she was pregnant. Unable to find a new job, she was discovered with her dead infant, close to starvation and suffering from puerperal fever. Vaughan has been tried by an all-male jury, convicted of the murder of her illegitimate child, and sentenced to death. The judge has said that infanticide was so common that "some woman must

be made an example of." Stanton and Anthony hold a meeting at Philadelphia to protest the verdict, defying the convention that requires respectable women to shut their eyes and ears to such cases. They present a petition to the governor of Pennsylvania, who will eventually pardon Vaughan on the grounds that there was no evidence that the woman was responsible for her child's death.

Karl Marx writes to a friend December 12, "Social progress can be measured exactly by the social position of the fair sex, the ugly ones included."

 An employment agency for women is established at London, mostly to fill domestic positions.

 Guy's Hospital, London, physician Samuel Wilks, 44, gives the first clinical description of osteoporosis, or spongy hypertrophy of the bones, a kind of osteitis deformans (*see* 1846).

L'Amour by French historian Jules Michelet, 70, says that every century produces its own terrible malady—e.g., leprosy in the 13th, the Black Death in the 14th, syphilis in the 16th. The 19th, he says, is the "age of the womb" because it is so concerned with women's health. Popular medical literature caricatures women as the victims of a variety of "female complaints"—fallen wombs, hysteria, "venereal excess," and the like. For 15 to 28 days each month, almost always, "woman is not only an invalid, but a wounded one. She ceaselessly suffers from love's eternal wound."

 Wells College has its beginnings in the Wells Seminary for the Higher Education of Young Women incorporated March 28 at Aurora, N.Y., by Wells, Fargo Co. and American Express Co. co-founder Henry Wells, 62, who believes that women are capable of higher learning and should be instructed in language, science, mathematics, the humanities—in short, all the subjects taught to men. Wells is a close friend of Ezra Cornell and his college will always have close ties with Cornell University, founded 3 years ago at nearby Ithaca; the seminary, which opens in September with 36 girls, will change its name in 1870 to Wells College and will grow to have more than 400 students.

England's first salaried woman journalist, Eliza Linton (*née* Lynn), 46, opposes higher education for women. She characterizes "The Girl of the Period"

as "hard, unloving, mercenary, ambitious without domestic faculty and devoid of healthy natural instincts.... Men are afraid of her; and with reason. They may amuse themselves with her for an evening, but they do not readily take her for life." Linton castigates those of her sex who are "bold in bearing" and "masculine in mind" rather than "tender, loving, retiring, [and] domestic."

La Donna begins publication on a fortnightly basis at Venice under the direction of Gualberta Beccari, daughter of a patriot of Italy's Risorgimento, who will move it to Bologna in 1878 and in 1892 to Turin, where she will continue publishing it until her death in 1906, giving voice to northern poets and correspondents but mainly to Anna Maria Mozzoni (*see* 1888).

The newspaper *Revolution*, founded by suffragist Susan B. Anthony and Elizabeth Cady Stanton with financial backing from George Francis Train (*see* 1867) has as its slogan, "Men, their rights and nothing more; women, their rights and nothing less." Taking up the cause of Hester Vaughan (above), the paper publishes reports that thousands of infants are being abandoned each year on New York doorsteps and in alleys.

A patent for a typewriter is issued to Christopher Sholes, Carlos G. Glidden, and Samuel W. Soule (*see* Sholes, 1867). Businessmen James Densmore and George Washington Yost encourage Sholes to construct a machine whose most commonly used keys will be widely separated on the keyboard to avoid jamming, and Sholes aligns the letters in an arrangement that will permit rapid fingering:

QWERTYUIOP
ASDFGHJKL
ZXCVBNM

Densmore and Yost will buy the patent and persuade Remington Fire Arms Co. to produce the machine (*see* 1874).

The *Chicago Legal News* begins weekly publication under the direction of local lawyer Myra Blackwell, 37, who has learned law in her husband's office and will use her publication—the first such periodical in the West—to reform the courts (*see* 1872).

Nonfiction: *Criminals, Idiots, Women, and Minors* by Frances Power Cobbe is an analysis of—and protest against—the engineering of women's dependence in order to allow male supremacy.

Fiction: *Love Sacrifice* by Maria Grey and her sister Emily Shireff; *The Minister's Wife* by Margaret Oliphant, who is awarded a Civil List pension; *Waiting for the Verdict* and *Dallas Galbraith* by Rebecca Harding Davis.

Juvenile: *Little Women: Or Meg, Jo, Beth and Amy* (first volume) by Louisa May Alcott, whose book will give the Alcotts financial security; *Elsie Dinsmore* by U.S. author Martha Farquharson (Martha Finley; Farquharson is Gaelic for Finley), 40, who will write the seven-volume *Mildred* series and the 12-volume *Pewit's Nest* series in addition to 26 *Elsie* novels.

Theater: Belle Boyd makes her New York debut 1/9 as Juliana in *The Honeymoon* with Bowery star Robert Johnston and in *Faint Heart Never Won Fair Lady*, at the Théâtre Français (14th Street Theater), where Adelaide Ristori has been appearing nightly but interrupts her engagement because it is the opening night of Pike's Opera House (later the Grand Opera House) at 23rd Street and 8th Avenue; Lotta Crabtree opens in January at the 4,300-seat Broadway Theater playing the role of Little Nell in *The Marchioness*; Marie Wilton and Lydia Foote in T. W. Robertson's new comedy *Play* 2/15 at the Prince of Wales's Theatre, with Squire Bancroft and H. J. Montague; Lotta Crabtree opens in the summer at Wallack's Theater, New York, in *Firefly; or The Friend of the Flag*, a spectacle with five acts, 17 scenes, French legionnaires, Arabs, marching bands, cannon, and wild ponies. Based on last year's Ouida novel *Under Two Flags*, it moves to Philadelphia and then to the 3,150-seat Boston Theatre.

Opera: Hortense Schneider appears in the new Offenbach opera *La Périchole* 10/6 at the Théâtre des Variétés, Paris.

The Brahms Lullaby is published at Berlin with words from "Des Knaben Wunderhorn" (a Mrs. Natalia Macfarren writes English lyrics).

1868

The All-England Croquet Club founded at Wimbledon holds its first championship matches. Played in England for the past 12 to 15 years by women as much as men, the 13th-century game will yield in popularity to tennis in the next 10 years (*see* 1874).

Badminton is invented at England's Badminton Hall, the Gloucestershire residence of the duke of Beaufort, Henry Charles Fitzroy Somerset, 44. The new racquet game is played with a feathered shuttlecock, which is batted back and forth across a net and will be popular with women as well as men.

 The *Revolution* (above) does not shy away from reporting incidents of rape, infanticide, prostitution, and wife beating, despite the fact that respectable Americans avoid mentioning such subjects.

 The *Revolution* (above) runs stories about New York's thinly disguised abortionist offices and the easy availability of abortifacients, including patent medicines which, it points out, are often highly alcoholic or laced with laudanum.

1869

The Subjection of Women by John Stuart Mill, now 63, demands the emancipation of women and their acceptance on completely equal terms with men (*see* 1866). Mill's wife, Harriet, has had a great influence on the work, which contains the line "To understand one woman is not necessarily to understand any other woman." Writing July 14 to Scottish philosopher Alexander Bain, 51, Mill says, "The most important thing women have to do is stir up the zeal of women themselves."

A new British Contagious Diseases Act permits police constables to arrest female prostitutes but takes no action against their male customers (*see* 1864; 1882).

Tokyo authorities in August order all prostitutes confined to the Yoshiwara, Shinagawa, Shinjuku, and Itabashi districts; Osaka authorities permit reopening of the city's red light districts.

The American Woman Suffrage Association (AWSA) is founded at Boston by Lucy Stone and her husband, Henry Blackwell, who favor obtaining suffrage on a state-by-state basis.

Susan B. Anthony breaks with the 3-year-old American Equal Rights Association to campaign and lecture on the need for a constitutional amendment that will give all U.S. women the right to vote. She and Elizabeth Cady Stanton found the National Woman Suffrage Association (NWSA), which gains support from Isabella Beecher Hooker. Stanton castigates men who refuse to support woman suffrage. Women, she says, are held in slavery by their constant fear of rape and recommends that every woman buy a big Newfoundland dog for protection and carry a gun and learn to use it. She gains support from her husband, Henry, for her proposal that the AWSA membership should be limited to women, convincing him that women can do the job better alone (*see* 1848; 1872).

Boston-born suffragist Mary Ashton Livermore (*née* Rice), 49, begins publishing the *Agitator*, a journal to promote the cause of women's voting rights. It will be merged into the *Woman's Journal*.

The 22-man legislature of the new Wyoming Territory adopts a constitution December 10 at Cheyenne with a provision giving women the right both to vote and to hold office. Local suffragist Esther Mcquigg Slack Morris (*née* Hobart), 55, has given a tea party September 2 for legislative candidates and extracted promises from both Democrats and Republicans to support woman suffrage. It is the first time in the world that men have given women the right to vote (*see* Utah, 1870).

The Women's Typographical Union Local #1 is founded by Augusta Lewis as an outgrowth of the Working Women's Association (*see* 1868). The president of the international union says, "Though most liberal inducements were offered to women compositors to take the place of men on strike, not a single member of the union could be induced to do so" (*see* 1871).

The Noble Order of the Knights of Labor is founded by U.S. union organizers as National Labor Union president William H. Sylvis dies in July (*see* 1868).

The Daughters of St. Crispin (DOSC), founded July 28 at a convention of 30 delegates in Lynn, Mass., is the first U.S. national women's labor organization (*see* strike, 1860). The women shoemakers at Lynn demand equal pay for equal work. Lodges in San Francisco, Chicago, Philadelphia, New York, Maine, and Massachusetts have sent delegates, they elect Carrie Wilson president, but the group will survive only until 1876.

$ New York's R. H. Macy Co. has sales of more than $1 million and employs 200 people. Store superintendent Margaret Getchell has attracted crowds with stunts such as dressing a pair of cats in doll's clothing and letting them sleep in the twin cribs placed in a show window. She has moved in with Macy's family and marries Abiel LaForge, who served as a captain in the Union Army and is a friend of Macy's son (Macy hires him as a lace buyer). The couple takes up residence in a five-room apartment right over the store where, in the next 8 years, Margaret will give birth to six children, including twins (see 1874).

The world grows smaller with the completion of America's first transcontinental railroad May 10 and the opening of the Suez Canal to traffic November 17. The empress Eugénie has traveled to Cairo in October to represent France at the ceremonies inaugurating the canal, which has been engineered by her cousin, Ferdinand de Lesseps, for the khedive of Egypt.

U.S. Baptist minister Jonathan Scobie at Yokohama invents the rickshaw to transport his invalid wife about town. Improved models will provide employment for Scobie's converts, and the ginrickshaw will be popular in many Oriental cities.

Narragansett Bay lighthouse keeper Ida Lewis, now 27, gains national attention after rescuing two soldiers from the raging sea on a raw, snowy March afternoon (see 1859). Lewis, who has been sitting wrapped in a blanket with her feet in the oven to help her recover from a bad cold, has somehow heard the cries of the men, who hired a 14-year-old boy to row them from the mainland to Fort Adams. Their boat has capsized, the boy has drowned, and Lewis, barefoot and without any hat or coat, rows half a mile to reach them. Helped by her younger brother, she hauls in the two men, one of them unconscious, and rows them back to the lighthouse, where she works for an hour to revive the unconscious soldier. *Harper's* magazine, which describes her as "slender, blue-eyed, with light brown hair, frank and hearty," asks, "Are we to believe that it is 'feminine' for young women to row

boats in storms? Is it 'womanly' to tug and strain through a tempest and then pull half-drowned men into a skiff?" It concludes, "No man will be such an—let us say donkey—as to insist that it was unfeminine in Ida Lewis to pull off in her boat to save men from drowning" (see 1879).

On Molecular and Microscopic Science by Mary Somerville, now 89, caps the career of the Scottish scientific writer.

Cambridge University agrees to offer an examination for women at the university level following petitions by women who include Jemima Clough (see 1867; 1871).

Kansas City's Central Female College is founded with women professors and a feminist philosophy: "Let us elevate the standard of female education and then, when a lady has attained to a broad and elegant mental culture, and asks for a position in which she may help those of her own sex that are aspiring to the same degree of culture, let us not turn her away and give this place to a man."

Nonfiction: *Pro Aris et Focis* by Elizabeth Harding Davis, published in England, is a collection of essays, some of which take issue with "a certain number of voices . . . high, shrill, and occasionally discordant" being raised over the question of women's rights. Although it was the Christian religion that raised women from a slave status in pagan society, she says, the wheel has now turned full circle and many "modern women" are now boasting of their freedom from the very faith that made them free. On the subject of woman suffrage, she observes that many women are more interested in dress and amusement than in political issues, most are occupied entirely with their domestic duties, and very few would vote in opposition to the wishes of their husbands. Although she herself is a career woman, she writes that women of refinement and modesty could not survive for long the shocks in store for them in the study of medicine, and if women do insist on having public careers she hopes that they will not be potential wives and mothers but rather "some of that surplus female population . . . [who] have no chance of rest in a husband's house, and many of whom, unhappily, have no provision for the actual wants of life." It is no reproach to women, she argues, to admit that they are unfitted for men's work just as men are unfitted for theirs. A woman's brain, being, "like the rest of her frame, of more delicate organization, is not capable of such sustained and continuous mental exertion as man's"; "The True Story of Lady Byron's Life" by Harriet Beecher Stowe in the *Atlantic Monthly* magazine refutes vicious interpretations of the character of the poet's late widow, representing her as a Christ-like figure who saved a tormented genius, but her revelation of the secret confided in her by Lady Byron (that Lord Byron was guilty of incest) raises a storm of fury on both sides of the Atlantic (*see* 1870).

Juvenile: *Little Women* (second volume) and its sequel *Good Wives* by Louisa May Alcott.

Painting: *The Sisters* by French painter Berthe Morisot, 28.

Theater: Marie Wilton, Augusta Wilton, Carlotta Addison, and Mrs. Buckingham White in T. W. Robertson's comedy *School* 1/16 with Squire Bancroft and H. J. Montague. Robertson's sister Margaret Shafto Robertson, 20, marries actor William Hunter Kendal (Grimstone) and will soon be famous as the actress Madge Kendal. Lotta Crabtree returns to San Francisco for the first time in 5 years, appearing in late July at the new $150,000 California Theater in a 6-week engagement that begins with *The Marchioness* followed by Tom Taylor's *Ticket of Leave Man*. Audiences give her a diamond tiara.

Opera: Hortense Schneider creates the title role in Offenbach's new opera *La Diva* at the Théâtre des Variétés, Paris.

Popular songs: "Sweet Genevieve" by U.S. composer Henry Tucker, lyrics by George Cooper, 31.

The American Woman's Home by Catherine E. Beecher and her sister Harriet Beecher Stowe deplores the popularity of store-bought bread, which accounts for perhaps 2 percent of all bread eaten in America. "The true housewife makes bread the sovereign of her kitchen." Defenders of store-bought bread say that home-baked bread sits heavy on the stomach, but lightness is not the only criterion for judgment, say the Beecher sisters; commercially baked bread is "light indeed, so light that [its loaves] seem to have neither weight nor substance, but with no more sweetness or taste than so much cotton wool."

Campbell Soup Co. has its beginnings in a cannery opened at Camden, N.J., by Philadelphia fruit wholesaler Joseph Campbell, who goes into partnership with an icebox maker to can small peas and fancy asparagus (*see* 1898).

H. J. Heinz Co. has its beginnings at Sharpsburg, Pa., where Henry John Heinz, 24, goes into partnership with another entrepreneur to pack processed horseradish in clear bottles (the competition's green bottles often disguise the fact that their product contains turnip filler). Heinz has employed several local women for nearly a decade to help him supply Pittsburgh grocers with the surplus from his garden (*see* ketchup, 1876).

A speaker at the annual meeting of the British Medical Association condemns "beastly contrivances" for limiting the numbers of offspring (*see* U.S. "Comstock Law," 1872).

Pope Pius IX declares abortion of any kind an excommunicatory sin (*see* 1930).

1870

Spain's Isabella II, now 39, is persuaded to abdicate June 25 at Paris after a 27-year reign.

France declares war on Prussia July 19 following release by count von Bismarck of a telegram from Napoleon III that has tried to humiliate the kaiser. Three German armies invade France, French socialist Paule (Paulina) Mink (*née* Mekarska), 31, organizes the defenses of Auxerre, but the Germans triumph over the French at Metz, Napoleon III surrenders with 80,000 men, the empress Eugénie arrives in England September 8, the Germans lay siege to Paris beginning September 19, and Eugénie finds a house at Chislehurst 2 weeks later while her husband is held prisoner at Wilhelmshöhe (*see* 1871).

"Appeal to Women Throughout the World" by Julia Ward Howe of 1862 "Battle Hymn of the Republic" fame calls for an international women's conference on efforts to avoid war in the future. She will become the first president next year of the U.S. branch of the Woman's International Peace Association.

A New York City jury acquits sometime lawyer Albert McFarland of the murder in the *Tribune* office of reporter James Richardson. The prosecution has contended that McFarland was an alcoholic who could not hold a job and periodically beat his wife, Abby Sage. She took up dramatic reading and moved the family into a boardinghouse, met Richardson there, obtained a divorce in Indiana, and was planning to marry Richardson when he was murdered. *Tribune* editor Horace Greeley married them before Richardson died. The defense has contended that Abby Sage was a loose woman, that her divorce was not valid, and that she could not therefore testify against her husband even though she was the key witness to his alleged alcoholism and violence. The all-male jury rules that McFarland is innocent by reason of temporary insanity. He is released and given custody of the couple's child. The *Tribune* publishes Abby Sage's account of their marriage, which she was not allowed to present in court.

Elizabeth Cady Stanton and Susan B. Anthony call a public meeting in the spring to protest the outcome of the McFarland-Richardson case (above), attracting 1,000 women—the largest crowd ever assembled in New York. Stanton calls it "the Dred Scott decision of the woman's movement," comparing it to the 1857 Supreme Court ruling that supported slave owners. She asserts that it will bring a new phase to women's rights: "As personal liberty, in the true order, comes before political freedom, woman must first be emancipated from the old bondage of a divinely ordained allegiance to man before her pride of sex can be so aroused as to demand the rights of citizenship." Stanton attacks the 14th Amendment (ratified 2 years ago) and 15th Amendment (ratified March 30) because they do not extend voting rights to women, and she promises to work toward the "alteration and modification of our divorce laws."

An August act of Parliament allows women to retain money they have earned on their own rather than turn it over to their husbands. Author of the first Married Women's Property Act is Manchester barrister Richard Marsden Pankhurst (*see* 1882). But Queen Victoria, in her letter of May 29 to Sir Theodore Martin, has said, "The Queen is most anxious to enlist every one who can speak or write to join in checking this mad, wicked folly of 'Woman's Rights,' with all its attendant horrors, on which her poor feeble sex is bent, forgetting every sense of womanly feeling and propriety."

Says *Punch*, the London comic weekly, "The rights of women who demand,/ Those women are but few:/ The greater part had rather staid/ Exactly as they do./ Beauty has claims for which she fights/ At ease with winning arms;/ The women who want women's rights/ Want mostly, women's charms."

A new Japanese law establishes two kinds of kinship: that between parent and child is kinship of the first degree, that between husband and wife *or husband and mistress* is of the second degree, and a man is permitted as many mistresses as he can afford (*see* 1872). Adultery is punishable in the case of wives, but a husband may be punished only if his sexual partner is someone else's wife and the woman's husband takes the matter to court. A Japanese couple wishing to get married must obtain permission from all four parents and from the head of each household, the *koshu*, who may be a grandfather but is in any case a man; nobody can be married into the family, or adopted by anyone in the household, or divorced without the permission from the *koshu*, who is obligated to support his grandparents, parents, wife, children, and siblings, and to provide the children with an education (*see* 1873).

Women gain full suffrage in the Territory of Utah (*see* Wyoming, 1869; Anthony, 1872). Roxey Snow Young, 66, who has worked to get women the vote, was secretly married in 1842 to the late Joseph Smith (she was his fourth or fifth wife), and 5 years later was married along with several other of Smith's widows to Brigham Young, but while a defender of polygamy she has tried to dispel the myth that Mormon wives must bow to their husbands' wills.

 Congress votes to give former First Lady Mary Todd Lincoln a $3,000 annual pension (it will later increase the amount to $5,000). Her son Robert has had her committed for insanity, but has gained her freedom and with her pension she is able to travel to Europe, resume her old ways of buying clothes, and live in style.

Spiritualist Victoria Claflin Woodhull, 32, and her "magnetic healer" sister Tennessee Celeste Claflin,

24, establish the first woman's brokerage firm on Wall Street. Daughters of an itinerant Ohio peddler and his spiritualist wife, they have grown up with their eight siblings in a world of medicine shows and theatrical troupes. Scandalous stories have circulated about them, but they have gained support from railroad magnate Cornelius Vanderbilt, and their offices, opened February 4 at 44 Broad Street, attract a crowd of some 4,000 curious visitors. Within a few months they have raked in over $500,000.

British physician Henry Maudsley observes that "the forms and habits of mutilated men approach those of women. But while woman preserves her sex, she will necessarily be feebler than man, and having her special bodily and mental characters, will have, to a certain extent, her own sphere of activity." Regarding a woman as a "mutilated male" permits doctors to judge her as unfit for the demands of the larger world and thus justify limiting her activities. Even as her reproductive organs restrict these activities, they determine the pattern of her life. The uterus is considered the "controlling organ" in the female body; a prolapsed uterus, caused by a bungling obstetrician who has left the damaged perineum unsewn and weakened, is not uncommon, and in some cases the fallen organ may protrude beyond the vulva, dragging the vagina behind it (hard physical labor, repeated pregnancies, and poor diet are also often responsible; doctors are inclined to blame it on tight corset lacing, sexual abuse, singing, dancing, riding horseback, and skating). Women with pelvic pains are often misdiagnosed as having prolapse, when they actually have ulceration or inflammation of the uterus, and are treated with manipulation, injections, and intravaginal supporters called pessaries, some of which are so large and complicated that they can only be worn under a large hoopskirt. Many physicians have developed nonsurgical techniques for treating "problems" such as a "displaced" uterus and leucorrhea (vaginal discharge, which may be treated with daily douches or even cauterization with local applications of nitric and chromic acid).

A Chinese mob at Tianjin attacks a Roman Catholic orphanage June 21 and kills 24 foreigners, including the French consul and some French and Belgian nuns accused of kidnapping children.

A British Education Act expands elementary education for girls as well as boys.

Women enter the University of Michigan for the first time since its founding at Ann Arbor in 1817. By the end of the 1870s there will be 154 U.S. coeducational colleges, up from 24 at the close of the Civil War (see Oberlin, 1833).

The 9-year-old Massachusetts Institute of Technology admits Vassar graduate Ellen Swallow Richards, 28, as a special student in chemistry. She will be M.I.T.'s first woman graduate, will marry a professor, and when he undertakes to make the first analyses of water for the State Board of Health, it is she who will do most of the work (without pay) (see 1908).

New York's Hunter College has its beginnings in the Normal College for Women established on Fourth Avenue. The school, which will train countless teachers for the city's public school system, will be renamed Hunter in 1914 to honor its longtime president Thomas Hunter.

Kappa Alpha Theta, the first Greek-letter sorority, is founded at Indiana Asbury University (later De Pauw) in Greencastle, Indiana.

The *Revolution* suspends publication at New York with outstanding debts of $10,000 (George F. Train withdrew his support last year, and the paper has refused to accept patent medicine advertising, which is the mainstay of most newspapers). Susan B. Anthony is stuck with the bills; Elizabeth Cady Stanton, disclaiming any obligation, advises Anthony to ignore the debt, give up feminist activity for a while, and amass some personal savings.

Woodhull & Claflin's Weekly begins publication May 14 at New York (see brokerage firm, above). "Progress! Free Thought! Untrammeled Lives! Breaking the Way for Future Generations!" shouts its masthead; backed by Commodore Vanderbilt, the paper exposes stock and bond frauds and political corruption, advocates women's rights, and promotes clairvoyant healing and free love.

Nonfiction: *The Impoverished Woman in the XIXth Century: Her Economic, Moral, Professional Condition (La femme pauvre au XIXe siècle: Sa condition économique, morale, professionale)* (three volumes) by Julie Daubié acquaints readers with the problems of prostitutes and the conditions that force women into prostitution (*see* education, 1862); *Political Economy for Beginners* by Millicent Garrett Fawcett, now 23; *The English Governess at the Siamese Court, Being Recollections of 6 Years in the Royal Palace at Bangkok* by Anna Leonowens, who had an article on her experiences published in the June 1869 *Atlantic Monthly* (*see* 1867); *Lady Byron Vindicated* by Harriet Beecher Stowe tries to prove that the lady suffered humiliation in a man's world of drunken jokes, licentiousness, and unequal "justice" which allots to women only the virtue of suffering. British readers object to the book, and it has little success in Britain, although the charges against Lord Byron will later be substantiated (*see* 1869).

Fiction: *The Mystery of Edwin Drood* by the late Charles Dickens, who has died June 9 at age 58 leaving the work unfinished (and providing in his will for his longtime mistress, Ellen "Nelly" Ternan, now 31); *An Old Fashioned Girl* by Louisa May Alcott.

Poetry: "Curfew Must Not Ring Tonight" by U.S. poet Rose Hartwick Thorpe, 20; *The House of Life* by Dante Gabriel Rossetti, who has been persuaded to exhume the unpublished poems he buried with his wife in 1862 and whose work establishes his reputation.

Juvenile: *A Flat Iron for a Farthing* by English author Julianna Horatia Ewing (*née* Gatty), 29, whose mother launched *Aunt Judy's Magazine* 4 years ago; *The Caged Lion* by Charlotte M. Yonge.

Painting: *The Artist's Sister Edma and Their Mother* by Berthe Morisot; *The Little Soldier* and *The Passer-by* by French painter Eva Gonzalès, 21, who will die in April 1883 after giving birth to a son (her bereaved husband will marry her sister Jeanne, who will raise the boy).

Theater: Marie Wilton (Mrs. Squire Bancroft) and Carlotta Addison in T. W. Robertson's new comedy *M. P.* 4/23 at the Prince of Wales's Theatre, London, with Squire Bancroft.

Opera: *Die Walküre* 6/26 at Munich, with music by Richard Wagner, who marries the divorcée Cosima Liszt von Bülow.

One of every three Boston families, one in every four New York and San Francisco familes, and one in every five Philadelphia and Chicago families has a live-in servant.

U.S. architects incorporate rear entrances, back stairways, and servant's quarters when designing middle-class houses so that domestics can perform their chores without disturbing the family.

New York City gets its first luxury apartment house. Built by Rutherford Stuyvesant in East 18th Street from designs by Richard Morris Hunt, 43, the five-story walk-up building is modeled on Parisian apartment buildings, complete with concierge, but a New Yorker says, "Gentlemen will never consent to live on mere shelves under a common roof." Rents for six rooms with bath range from $83 to $125 per month—far beyond the means of New York's boardinghouse and tenement-dwelling masses.

1871

Paris capitulates to German troops January 28 after a war with Prussia that has left many widows on both sides. French radical Louise Michel, 40, becomes increasingly militant at the urging of her lover, Théophile Ferré, she has the support of the city's poor in Montmartre, and when the Commune of Paris is established in March she heads the Women's Vigilance Committee of the 18th *arondissement*. Louis Thiers, who has been elected president of a Third Republic, sends troops to seize the Commune's cannon, but they have refused to fire and have fraternized with the crowd, which has seized and executed two generals along with hostages, who include the archbishop. "Bloody Week" in the closing days of May ends with 20,000 to 30,000 Parisians dying on the barricades (not even the Reign of Terror in 1793–1794 saw so much bloodshed). Paule Mink, who has worked in the provinces to rally support for the Commune, escapes to Switzerland, but Michel, who is among the last defenders in Montmartre Cemetery, gives herself up in place of her mother, to whom she is devoted, and is imprisoned at Versailles, tried, convicted, and sentenced in December to exile. She is locked in a cage with anarchist Natalie Lemel aboard the prison ship *Virginie* and sent on a

4-month voyage to New Caledonia, where she is to serve life imprisonment (*see* 1880).

Napoleon III arrives at Dover March 20 and is reunited with his wife, Eugénie. He devotes his efforts to teaching the prince imperial about French politics but will die early in 1873 of bladder disease.

Victoria Woodhull electrifies the convention of the National Woman Suffrage Association at Washington in January by arranging through her congressional connections to speak in support of woman suffrage before the House Committee on the Judiciary. She meets in May with Elizabeth Cady Stanton, who confirms what she has heard about an alleged adulterous affair between Brooklyn clergyman Henry Ward Beecher and his parishioner Elizabeth Tilton. Beecher's sisters (Catharine, Harriet Beecher Stowe, and Isabella Beecher Hooker) have taken conservative positions on women's issues, and Stowe's recent novel *My Wife and I* has parodied both Woodhull and Stanton. Stanton, who has privately characterized Catherine Beecher as a "narrow, bigoted, arrogant" woman who might have become humane if she had ever "loved with sufficient devotion, passion, & abandon," cautions Susan B. Anthony against any involvement with Woodhull.

Typographical Union corresponding secretary Augusta Lewis, the first woman to hold office in an international union, issues a statement to the union's annual convention: "We refuse to take the men's situations when they are on strike, and when there is no strike if we ask for work in union offices we are told by union foremen that 'there are no conveniences for us.' We are ostracized in many offices because we are members of the union, and although the principle is right, disadvantages are so many that we cannot much longer hold together. . . . It is the general opinion of female compositors that they are more justly treated by what is termed 'rat' foremen, printers, and employers than they are by union men" (*see* 1869; 1878).

Suffragist Isabella Beecher Hooker receives a letter dated October 24 from a Norfolk, Conn., woman who says she has no children and "only the dreary routine of household cares to occupy my mind. My husband is an old-fashioned farmer, and plods contentedly on year after year without a mower or reaper, without books or anything to make home pleasant. His amusement is to go to the village store to spend his evenings and rainy days, while I *amuse* myself by mending his old pants, or some other equally agreeable occupation. . . . Of course, such a man is bitterly opposed to 'woman's rights' and loses no opportunity for the usual sneer. I have no money and but few clothes. He forbids my giving anything away, as everything is *his* and nothing mine. In short I am nothing but a housekeeper without wages, doing *all* the work of the family. I have no fondness for this kind of life. . . . Would it be wrong for me to go to Hartford this winter for a few weeks or to some other place where people *live*? . . . I can sew or do anything that is necessary to be done,—can take care of children and teach them, as this was formerly my employment. I must get away from here for a while or go crazy. . . . My husband's father buried his *fourth* wife a few days since. She laid down the burden of life willingly, at sixty-two years of age. He will doubtless marry again soon, as it *costs too much* to hire a housekeeper."

Japan's Meiji government passes a law permitting intermarriage between people of different social classes. Up to now, the *shi* (samurai), the *no* (farmers), the *ko* (craftsmen), and the *sho* (merchants) have been kept separate, the groups being distinguished by different clothing, different haircuts, different food, different houses, and different ways of speaking. Under the new law, any girl can marry a *samurai,* but as with all brides, any money or property she inherits belongs automatically to him, and should anything happen to her their children belong to the husband's family. So long as her mother-in-law is alive, her husband may turn his earnings over to his mother, the mother determines how the money is to be spent, and she may order her son to divorce his wife. The law permits anyone to cut hair but is soon amended to prohibit women from cutting hair.

Mormon leader Brigham Young, now 70, is arrested at Salt Lake City in Utah Territory on charges of polygamy (he has 27 wives). The polygamy issue will delay Utah statehood until 1896.

Greek archaeologist Sophia Schliemann (*née* Engastrontenos), 19, helps her husband in excavations that begin October 11 on the hill of Hissarlik, site of ancient Troy. German-American businessman Heinrich Schliemann, 51, married her in September 1868 after studying photographs of possible candidates (she frankly admitted that she was marrying him to please her parents and because he was so rich), and has helped her learn French and German (she will later teach herself English as well). The Schliemanns will antagonize professionals with their destructive, amateur diggings, it will turn out that they missed Priam's Troy, but beginning in 1874 they will uncover at Mycenae the world's greatest golden treasure trove. Schliemann acquired U.S. citizenship in California in 1850, amassed a large fortune in the next 13 years through usurious banking and Crimean War profiteering, and has devoted himself in the past 2 years to studying sites mentioned in the writings of Homer.

Amherst College, chartered in 1825 in Massachusetts, rejects some women applicants. Applauding the move, an undergraduate writes in the college newspaper, "Amherst College was never intended for the education of females. . . . Widely different educational means and methods ought to be employed in fitting men and women for totally different spheres of duty and usefulness." But another undergraduate replies, "For the sake of the thoughtless many who constantly need restraint, we ask for the presence of women in our midst. We believe it is not only possible but certain that her presence would effect a complete reformation in many of those immoralities which now disgrace our college."

Smith College is established at Northampton, Mass., near Amherst (above). The late Sophia Smith, who died last year at age 73, inherited a fortune from her brother Austin in 1861, having outlived five other siblings, and left $393,105 at her own death to endow a college for women that will open in 1875. Deaf beginning at age 40, Smith had planned originally to found a school for deaf-mutes, but after such a school was started by someone else in 1868 she decided instead to endow a college for women. Her pastor and two Amherst professors helped draft her will, which declared, "It is my opinion that by the higher and more thorough Christian education of women, what are called 'wrongs' will be redressed, their wages adjusted, their weight of influence in reforming the evils of

society will be greatly increased, as teachers, as writers, as mothers, as members of society, their power of good will be incalculably enlarged." Her purpose, she said, was not to "render my sex any the less feminine" but simply to "furnish women with the means of usefulness, happiness, and honor now withheld from them."

U.S. schoolteacher Frances Elizabeth Caroline Willard, 31, accepts the presidency of the Evanston College for Ladies at Evanston, Ill. It will be merged into Northwestern University in 1873, and she will become dean of women at the university (*see* WCTU, 1874).

Julie-Victoire Daubié, now 47, becomes the first French woman to obtain a master's degree in humanities (*see* 1862). The Sorbonne does not permit women on its benches, but Daubié has secured a tutor and passed the required examinations during the Prussian occupation of Paris. She begins studying for her doctorate but will die of tuberculosis in August 1874, a few months before her final examinations.

Newnham College has its beginnings in Merton Hall, which is opened in the village of Newnham, outside Cambridge, for women who come to the town to attend lectures in preparation for the new examination (*see* 1869). Millicent Garrett Fawcett, now 24, is one of the founders, and Jemima Clough, who begins with five students, will remain principal of the college until her death in 1892. Students are allowed to study for as short or as long a period as they wish, and to take what exams they like or none at all, an arrangement condemned by Emily Davies, who says that women should be offered no such "soft" options and makes Greek compulsory. By the end of the decade, half of Newnham's students will be taking the tripos (final examinations) in mathematics or the classics, but many women will hate the school because it repudiates the accepted role of a middle-class woman and is thought to violate the laws of God, of health, and of social conduct.

Elizabeth Wolstenholm submits a report to the Royal Commission on the Education of Girls proposing a scheme for setting up girls' schools (*see* 1867). The National Union for Improving the Education of Women is founded, as is the Public Day

School Company, which will open its first school for girls at Chelsea in 1873. By 1887 it will have 32 schools with 6,185 pupils.

The *Christian Woman* is founded and edited by Annie Turner Wittenmyer, now 44, who campaigns for temperance. Wittenmyer was head of Union Army kitchens during the Civil War and also worked with the sick and wounded (*see* 1862).

The weekly paper *New Northwest* begins publication at Portland, Oregon, under the direction of Abigail Scott Duniway, 36, whose father decided to emigrate in the spring of 1852 and whose invalid mother died of cholera in the Black Hills of Wyoming Territory, leaving her and eight other children to proceed with their father on the Oregon Trail (her baby brother Willie died 10 weeks later). She herself became a schoolteacher, got married, and has had six children; her husband has lost his farm near Salem and been disabled by a runaway wagon, she opened a millinery shop to support the family, heard stories of women abandoned by their husbands and powerless to keep their homes from being sold out from under them, and has been persuaded by her husband that women's lot will never improve until they can vote. She has moved to Portland to start the paper, whose type is set by her two sons (*see* human rights, 1872).

Nonfiction: *Origin, Tendencies, and Principles of Government* by Victoria Woodhull is a collection of articles on socialism and free love; *A Few Words about Women* (*Kilka słów kobietach*) by Polish feminist-novelist Elja Orzeszkowa (*née* Elzbieta Pawlowska), 30, who champions a woman's right to self-expression outside the home. Married at age 16, she agitated among her neighbors in the Kobryn district before the uprising of 1863, divorced her husband after he was exiled to Siberia, and has found herself ostracized. She has moved to Grodno, where she is compared to George Sand, now 67.

Fiction: *Folle-Farine* by Ouida; *Birth of the Sewing-Machine Girl, or Death at the Wheel*, a melodramatic serial, appears in Street & Smith's *New-York Weekly*.

Juvenile: *Little Men* by Louisa May Alcott; *A Dog of Flanders* by Ouida.

Poetry: "There was a little girl,/ Who had a little curl/ Right in the middle of her forehead;/ And when she was good/ She was very, very good,/ But when she was bad she was horrid," writes Henry Wadsworth Longfellow, now 64.

Sculpture: A full-scale marble statue of Abraham Lincoln unveiled at Washington is the work of sculptor Vinnie Ream, now 24, who 6 years ago was commissioned by Congress to create the work that will stand in the Capitol.

Popular songs: "Chopsticks" ("The Celebrated Chop Waltz") by English composer Arthur de Lulli (Euphemia Allen), 16.

The Chicago Fire that rages from October 8 to 9 destroys 3.5 square miles of the city, killing perhaps 250 and leaving 100,000 homeless. It has allegedly

Sculptor Vinnie Ream was only 18 when Congress commissioned her to make a bust of the late President Lincoln. LIBRARY OF CONGRESS

been started on the warm Sunday evening by a cow kicking over a kerosene lantern belonging to Mrs. Patrick O'Leary, a working-class wife with five children, in DeKoven Street on the Southwest Side, and did, in fact, start in the O'Leary barn. Burned to the ground in the general conflagration is the Palmer House, a $3.5 million hostelry built by local merchant Potter Palmer, 45, who made a fortune from dry goods and cotton during the Civil War and has put up the grand hotel as a wedding present for his Kentucky-born wife, Bertha (*née* Honoré), now 22. She persuades him not to leave Chicago but to stay and help rebuild it, he will erect an even more luxurious new Palmer House, and she will become the city's society queen, as prominent as Mrs. Astor in New York, while making it fashionable for women to give their time and money to civic and charitable causes (*see* 1889).

Abortion is punishable by up to 5 years in prison under the criminal code enacted by the new German Empire proclaimed January 18.

Elizabeth Cady Stanton (above) calls infanticide and abortion "disgusting and degrading crimes" but does not condemn women for resorting to them, saying that the problem lies in men being unable to control their desires and women's inability to resist.

Victoria Woodhull made money on Wall Street and had the temerity to aspire to be President. LIBRARY OF CONGRESS

1872

 Victoria Claflin Woodhull announces that she will be a candidate for the U.S. presidency on the People's party ticket with freedman Frederick Douglass as her running mate. She calls on all activist women to register and vote, contending that the 14th Amendment, ratified in 1868, actually enfranchised women, since it made no mention of gender in its provision asserting the rights of citizenship, and there is therefore no necessity for a 16th Amendment that would grant woman suffrage. Woodhull has made a fortune in Wall Street but is unable to get onto the ballot. Susan B. Anthony and other women's rights advocates are arrested at Rochester, N.Y., for attempting to vote in the November 5 election (Anthony is tried for breaking the law and is supported chiefly by Matilda Joslyn Gage, now 46). President Grant, who has the support of Elizabeth Cady Stanton, wins reelection with 54 percent of the popular vote. Stanton's husband, Henry, has supported *New York Tribune* editor Horace Greeley, an early supporter of the woman's movement, who dies November 29 at age 61.

Chicago lawyer Myra Blackwell secures passage of a state law making it illegal to discriminate in employment on the basis of sex (*see* 1868). She lost her law library in last year's fire but has taken the Illinois bar examination and passed with distinction; being a woman has kept her from entering practice, and the new law opens the profession to women lawyers. Blackwell's *Legal News* will become a major force in effecting the retirement (and pensioning) of superannuated judges, better treatment of witnesses at trials, codification of professional standards, and other legal reforms.

A ship carrying Chinese slaves bound for Peru stops at Yokohama and is denied clearance. When the Japanese government insists that the slaves be returned to China, the ship's captain replies that Japan's houses of prostitution also involve the selling of people (*see* 1869). The Meiji government thereupon enacts a law October 2 forbidding people to sell their daughters as prostitutes or geishas and decrees that existing prostitutes are free to leave without having to pay for their freedom. According to the law, the women have no rights as human beings, but since horses and cows do not have to repay debts, neither do the prostitutes. The law is flexible and will prove unenforceable: since a poor farmer may, in bad times, have no choice but to sell his daughter, the goverment may give approval after looking into the case.

Keio University founder Yukichi Fukuzawa publishes a book in which he critizes Japan's 1870 law permitting mistresses to belong to a man's household and have rights comparable to those of his wife. Fukuda's followers are called *Meirokusha* (*see* 1880).

Congress passes a law guaranteeing equal pay for equal work in U.S. federal employment after lobbying by feminist lawyer Belva Ann Lockwood, 42, who has spoken at New York's Cooper Union in behalf of Victoria Woodhull (above) but has then stumped the South to get votes for Horace Greeley.

Victoria Woodhull (above) has demanded that women be given the right to vote. But the cause of women's rights is damaged by *Woodhull & Claflin's Weekly*, which advocates free love and socialism and recommends licensing and medical inspection of prostitutes. It also publishes the first English translation of *The Communist Manifesto* written by Karl Marx and Friedrich Engels late in 1847.

Portland, Ore., newspaper publisher Abigail Duniway addresses a joint session of the Oregon legislature and persuades the men to pass a law allowing married women to go into business for themselves and protecting their property if their husbands leave them (*see* 1871). She will later win Oregon women the right to sue and to control their own earnings (*see* 1883).

💲 Japan's first silk-reeling factory begins operation in Gunma Prefecture with young women workers

Lawyer Belva Ann Lockwood persuaded Congress to guarantee equal pay for equal work in federal employment. LIBRARY OF CONGRESS

(most of them daughters of former *samurai*) who include the manager's 13-year-old daughter. He has put her to work to set an example and facilitate recruitment, which has initially proved difficult. The government has imported equipment and engineers from France to start the operation, which will soon be run mostly by poor farmers' daughters aged 12 to 20 working 12-hour days on 3- to 5-year contracts to help their families financially and prepare for marriage (*see* 1904).

New York actress Josie Mansfield, mistress of Wall Street speculator James Fisk, is the subject of a quarrel between Fisk and his business rival Edward S. Stokes, who is also a rival for Mansfield's favors. Stokes shoots Fisk January 6, and the Erie Ring, which had been headed by Fisk and Jay Gould collapses.

Bloomingdale's has its beginnings in New York's Great East Side Store opened at 938 Third Avenue by merchant Lyman G. Bloomingdale, 31, and his brothers Joseph and Gustave (*see* 1886).

U.S. inventor Luther Chicks Crowell patents a machine to make flat-bottomed paper bags that will become familiar to every housewife. Springfield, Mass., inventor Margaret E. "Mattie" Knight, now 34, obtained a patent 2 years ago for an attachment to bag-folding machines and produced the first square-bottom bags but sold the patent to her employers. (At age 12, after witnessing an accident in a cotton mill, when a shuttle slid out of its loom and pierced a man with its steel tip, she invented a stop-motion device that could have prevented such an occurrence.) Knight rejects an offer of $50,000 for her rights, will assign most of her patents to her employers for spot cash in lieu of royalties, and will die in 1914 leaving an estate of only $275. Crowell's machine will be improved in 1883 by one that will make the automatic, or "flick," bag—a self-opening bag with a flat bottom and side pleats.

An Encouragement of Learning (*Gakumon no susume*) by Yukichi Fukuzawa (above) begins, "Heaven created no man above another, and no man below another," which contradicts Confucian philosophy, and includes a chapter on women, saying of women's education that the world cannot exist without both men and women, and that women are just as human as men.

Compulsory education for Japanese children begins in August, but relatively few girls show up. Monthly tuition is 15 to 25 sen (100 sen can buy about 57 quarts of rice), and girls are generally considered better off without education, which many believe actually to be harmful to women. Poor families sometimes send their daughters off to work as maids in respectable households, where they can learn how to behave in polite society and prepare themselves for marriage and motherhood (*see* 1873).

Russia begins opening institutions of higher learning to women, partly to keep young women from going off to Zurich and other cities, where they may become radicalized.

The University of Wisconsin gives women full access to a college curriculum for the first time but allows female students to register for a course only if it does not have enough males and requires coeds to use the library on different days from male students.

Cornell University, which opened 4 years ago at Ithaca, N.Y., becomes coeducational.

Nonfiction: *Woman's Worth and Worthlessness* by U.S. writer Mary Abigail Dodge, 39, says that a woman is not "supported" by a man "when she works as hard in the home as he does out of it"; *The Romance of the Harem* by Anna Leonowens is based on stories she heard as governess to the king of Siam's children.

Fiction: *Middlemarch* by George Eliot.

Juvenile: *What Katy Did* by U.S. author Susan Coolidge (Sarah Chauncey Woolsey), 37.

Painting: *Paris Seen from the Trocadero* by Berthe Morisot; *The Artist's Mother* (*Mrs. George Washington Whistler, or Arrangement in Grey and Black No. 3*) by émigré U.S. painter-etcher James A. McNeill Whistler, 38.

Theater: Lotta Crabtree plays New Orleans in February, is invited to a private banquet given in her honor by the six-foot four-inch Grand Duke Alexis of Russia, 23, goes on to play Memphis, is back in San Francisco in April at the newly renovated Metropolitan Theater, and leaves in the fall for a tour of England and the Continent.

Sarah Bernhardt (*née* Rosine Bernard), 28, begins a 10-year career with the Comédie-Française at Paris. "The Divine Sarah" will gain world renown and continue acting even after having a leg amputated in 1914.

Italian actress Eleonora Duse, 13, begins a 27-year career by appearing at Verona as Juliet in the Shakespeare tragedy of 1595.

Opera: Canadian soprano Emma Albani (Marie Louise Emma Cécile Lajeunesse), 20, makes her London debut 4/2 at Covent Garden singing the role of Amina in the 1831 Bellini opera *La Sonnambula*. Albani will perform at Covent Garden nearly every season until 1896, notably as Elsa of Brabant in the 1870 Wagner opera *Lohengrin* (1875) and Elisabeth in the 1845 Wagner opera *Tannhäuser* (1876).

Boston has a fire that begins November 9 with an explosion in a warehouse stocked with hoopskirts. The blaze, which rages for 3 days before burning itself out, consumes 65 acres in the richest part of the city, destroying 776 buildings that include granite and brick warehouses (*see* Simmons College, 1902).

 Upstate New York weaver's daughter Amanda Theodosia Jones, 37, is awarded five patents (she will receive a sixth next year) for a process that she has developed for preserving food by means of a vacuum process. She places the food in a container, drains air out through a series of valves, adds water heated to a temperature of between 100° and 120° F., and immediately seals the container (*see* 1890).

 The Ebers papyrus discovered at Thebes by German Egyptologist Georg Moritz Ebers, 35, is the oldest known compendium of ancient Egyptian medical writings. It contains a formula for a tampon medicated to prevent conception.

The "Comstock Law" enacted by Congress November 1 makes it a criminal offense to use the mails to import or transport in interstate commerce "any article of medicine for the prevention of conception or for causing abortion." The law, which also makes it illegal to use the mails to communicate any information regarding contraception or abortion, takes its name from New York moralist Anthony Comstock, 28, an agent of the U.S. Post Office who heads the New York Society for the Suppression of Vice (*see* 1874; Mme. Restell, 1878).

1873

 Divorced women in Britain gain the right to claim custody of their children.

A Japanese law enacted in May gives women the right to divorce. Another law provides that a woman without a husband or son may be a *koshu* (head of household) on a temporary basis until she marries a man who will adopt her family name (a *muku-iri*) or until her daughter marries such a man (*see* 1870; 1878).

Susan B. Anthony goes on trial for voting in a Rochester, N.Y., election and tells a court June 18,

"As when the slaves who got their freedom had to take it over or under or through the unjust forms of the law, precisely so now must women take it to get their right to a voice in this government." She will, she says, "earnestly and persistently continue to urge all women to the practical recognition of the old Revolutionary maxim, 'Resistance to tyranny is obedience to God.' " Fined $100, she says, "I shall never pay a penny of this unjust claim."

Indiana Women's Prison opens at Indianapolis with a woman superintendent and 17 prisoners transferred from State Reformatory at Jeffersonville, where the degrading treatment of female inmates outraged a group of Quaker women. They saw the women forced to strip naked and take outdoor baths in front of whip-cracking male guards, heard about nocturnal visits made by the guards to women's prison cells, and have demanded the construction of a separate facility for women. It is the first U.S. penal institution operated exclusively by and for women.

 Puerperal fever has reached epidemic proportions, reports U.S. physician Fordyce Barker, and is 20 times more prevalent than last year, striking rich women twice as often as the poor and killing four times as many women in home deliveries than in hospitals. The fever takes 130 lives at Cincinnati, where in earlier years it never took more than 20.

New York's Bellevue Hospital establishes the Nightingale system of nurse's training (*see* Nightingale, 1854). Nursing and schoolteaching are the only professions open to respectable U.S. women.

 Sex in Education, or A Fair Chance for Girls by Harvard physician Edward H. Clarke says that "woman, in the interest of the race, is dowered with a set of organs peculiar to itself, whose complexity, delicacy, sympathies, and force are among the marvels of creation. If properly nurtured and cared for, they are a source of strength and power to her. If neglected and mismanaged, they retaliate upon their possessor with weakness and disease as well of mind as of body." Clarke opposes coeducation at Harvard, and his book amounts to a polemic expounding his idea that women who undertake serious study are ruining their health and destroying their reproductive abilities as their wombs atrophy.

Bennett College for Women has its beginnings in the Bennett Seminary, founded as a coeducational school for blacks in the basement of a Methodist Episcopal church in Greensboro, N.C., with financial support from Troy, N.Y., donor Lyman Bennett (*see* 1926).

The University of Mt. Allison College at Sackville, New Brunswick, opens its doors to women. It is the first Canadian college to admit women to all its courses and degrees on the same basis as men (*see* 1882).

Girton College opens in October on a 16-acre site about two miles from Cambridge under the direction of educational reformer Emily Davies, now 43, who established the small college for women under another name 4 years ago at Hitchin with Emily Shirreff to prepare women for the university examination. The women have excelled in the tripos (final examinations) for classics and mathematics. Equipped to accommodate about 21 students, the first building is one side of a proposed quadrangle. Davies will be mistress of the school until 1875, and Shirreff will succeed her (*see* 1874).

Only 16 percent of school-age Japanese girls are in elementary school as compared with 46 percent of school-age boys (*see* 1872; 1874).

St. Nicholas Magazine begins publication under the editorship of Mary Elizabeth Mapes Dodge of 1865 *Hans Brinker* fame, who will run the new periodical for children until her death in 1905 at age 74.

Juvenile: *Lab-Lie-by-the-Fire* by Juliana Ewing.

Painting: *A Portrait of Mrs. Robert Simpson Cassatt* (mother of the artist) by emigrée U.S. painter Mary Cassatt, 29, who has taken up residence at Paris.

Theater: Irish-born, Brooklyn-raised actress Ada Rehan (originally Crehan), 13, makes her stage debut at Newark, N.J., in *Across the Continent*. Her name will be misspelled when she appears at Louisa Lane Drew's Arch Street Theater in Philadelphia, and she will retain Rehan as her stage name (*see* 1879).

Opera: German soprano Therese Malten, 18, makes her debut singing the role of Pamina in the 1791 Mozart opera *Die Zauberflöte* at Dresden, where she will sing for the next 30 years.

French perfume makers at Grasse revolutionize the industry with a new process that extracts a solid essence from flower roots or from substances by placing them in contact with volatile fluids which dissolve essential ingredients and isolate them as they evaporate.

Japan's empress Shōken stops staining her teeth black and wearing her hair in the traditional manner that for centuries has identified a married woman in order to set an example. Inaugurator of the new fashion has been feminist Kajiko (originally Katsuko) Yajima, 40, who married at age 25, bore three daughters, but left her husband 10 years after their marriage because he was a heavy drinker and abused her.

British traveler Isabella Bird, 41, stops at the Sandwich Islands in January, disdains to stay at the only hotel on Oahu, embarks for other islands, and remains until August 7, when she sails from Honolulu for San Francisco after having given up the sidesaddle to ride astride her horse through high, grassy hills wearing a MacGregor tartan flannel outfit made up of Turkish trousers and an ankle-length tunic, a broad-brimmed Australian hat, and boots with jangling Mexican spurs.

1874

The Dublin Women's Suffrage Society is founded by local feminists, but the suffrage movement will be slow to spread in Ireland.

Massachusetts enacts the first effective 10-hour day law for women May 8 (*see* Supreme Court decision, 1908).

New York social worker Etta Angel Wheeler finds a little girl wandering naked through the city's slums after having been beaten, slashed, and turned out by her drunken foster mother. Appeals are made to the 8-year-old ASPCA for lack of any other agency, the American Society for the Prevention of Cruelty to Animals decides that the child is an animal and deserving of shelter, the ASPCA prosecutes the foster mother for starving and abusing the 9-year-old girl, and the American Society for the Prevention of Cruelty to Children (ASPCC) is organized.

A Cheyenne war party attacks the wagons of a settler's family 10 miles south of Monument, Kansas, September 11, killing Lydia German (*née* Cox), 49, her husband, John, their son, Stephen, and their daughters Rebecca Jane, 25, who has raised an axe in self-defense, and Joanna C., 20. Daughters Catherine E., 22, Sophia L., 17, Julia, 12, and Nancy Adelaide "Addy," 10, are carried off to the Canadian River country in the Texas Panhandle. An army unit attacks a Cheyenne camp of 100 lodges November 10, routes the Cheyennes, and finds Julia and Addy German dirty, cold, and hungry but safe (*see* 1875).

New York's R. H. Macy Co. follows Margaret Getchell LaForge's suggestion and displays its doll collection in the world's first Christmas windows, beginning a tradition that other stores will follow (*see* 1869).

The London School of Medicine for Women is founded by Elizabeth Blackwell, now 53, and Scottish medical student Sophia Jex-Blake, 34, whose brother Thomas, 42, has just been named headmaster of Rugby. Jex-Blake will obtain her medical degree from the University of Bern with a thesis on puerperal fever and gain the legal right to practice medicine in Britain in 1877 (*see* 1878).

Britain's Female Medical Society closes, ending the hope of women like Florence Nightingale that the nation can produce midwives having scientific skills equal to those of European midwives (*see* 1861).

U.S. medical authority Lucien Warner writes that "it is not . . . hard work and privation which make the women of our country invalids, but circumstances and habits intimately connected with the so-called blessings of wealth and refinement." He notes that "the African negress who toils beside her husband in the fields of the south, and Bridget, who washes, and scrubs and toils in our homes at the north, enjoy for the most part good health, with comparative immunity from uterine disease."

U.S. physicians, male and female, continue as they will until the end of the century to obtain medical diplomas after as little as 4 months' attendance at schools that often have no laboratories, no dissection facilities, and no clinical training.

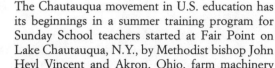

The Chautauqua movement in U.S. education has its beginnings in a summer training program for Sunday School teachers started at Fair Point on Lake Chautauqua, N.Y., by Methodist bishop John Heyl Vincent and Akron, Ohio, farm machinery maker Lewis Miller: they begin an institution 10 miles from Lake Erie that will develop into a traveling tent show of lecturers bringing culture to small-town America. President Grant's appearance at Chautauqua next year will lend prestige to the movement, more than 100,000 people will sign up for home-study correspondence courses by 1877, the Chautauqua Normal School of Languages will start in 1879, and the Chautauqua Press will list 93 titles by 1885, by which time there will be Chautauquas in more than 30 states.

The London School Board grants degrees to women for the first time after agitation by reformers who include Board member Emily Davies, mistress of Girton College at Cambridge (*see* 1873).

Japan's Ministry of Education founds a teacher's school for women in Tokyo's Ochanomizu (the word means "water for tea") district but has trouble finding girls who are qualified, or willing, to be teachers (only 80 students apply for 100 places, and only 15 will be in the first graduating class of 1878, because teaching is considered a suitable occupation only for unattractive girls from families without means). Ochanomizu Women's College, opened in March, will become a liberal arts college under that name in 1949.

About 33 percent of school-age Japanese girls are in elementary school as compared with 54 percent of school-age boys (*see* 1873).

The Remington typewriter introduced by F. Remington & Sons Fire Arms Co. begins a revolution in written communication. Philo Remington, 68, has acquired sole rights to the Sholes typewriter of 1868 for $12,000, but the $125 price of the Remington typewriter is more than a month's rent for many substantial business firms, and Remington produces only eight machines (*see* 1875).

Nonfiction: *Recollections of a Tour Made in Scotland AD 1803* by the late English writer Dorothy Wordsworth, only sister of the late poet, who survived him by 5 years, dying in 1855 at age 84.

Early typewriters had only capital letters, but improved machines opened new opportunities for women.

Fiction: *Fettered for Life; or, Lord and Master* by Lillie Devereux Olmsted, whose protagonist is a successful reporter who turns out to be a woman in disguise. Donning trousers and jacket, the reporter finds that "my limbs were free; I could move untrammelled, and my actions were free; I could go about unquestioned; no man insulted me, and when I asked for work, I was not offered outrage"; *Kitty's Choice: A Story of Berrytown* by Rebecca Harding Davis, who has become far more a journalistic commentator than a novelist; *Old Kensington* by Lady Ritchie.

Juvenile: *Two Little Wooden Shoes* by Ouida, who settles at Florence, where she will live for the next 20 years.

Painting: *Mme. Boursier and Her Daughter* by Berthe Morisot, now 33, who marries Edouard Manet's brother and joins the French "Impressionists," whose work is rejected by the Salon and who hold their first exhibition at Paris in an "independent" show of canvases which include a harbor scene entitled *Impression: Sunrise* by Claude Monet, now 40. His work prompts art critic Louis Leroy to call the painters "Impressionists," an epithet that will soon lose its pejorative overtone. The group will include the émigrée U.S. painter Mary Cassatt beginning in 1879; *Calling the Roll after an Engagement, Crimea* by English painter Elizabeth Thompson, 24.

Theater: Dion Boucicault's *Bellelamar* 8/10 at Booth's Theater, New York, is about Confederate spy Belle Boyd, who retired from the stage at New Orleans at age 24 in March 1869 after appearing with stock companies under the name Nina Benjamin. She married English tea merchant John Swainston Hammond a few days later in the Crescent City (*see* 1886).

Lawn tennis is patented under the name *Spharistike* (Greek for "playing ball") by British sportsman Walter Clopton Wingfield, 41, who has codified rules for a game played indoors for at least 5 centuries. The new game is introduced in Bermuda and from there into the United States, but more vigorous sportsmen dismiss it as suitable only for ladies.

Jennie Jerome, 20, daughter of Wall Street speculator Leonard Jerome, is married April 15 at the British embassy in Paris to Lord Randolph Henry Churchill, 24, third son of the seventh duke of Marlborough and newly elected member of Parliament. The father of the beautiful dark-eyed bride has suffered financial reverses but provides the couple with an income of £3,000 per year, the Duke (who does not attend the ceremony) has had to sell off family treasures but pays Lord Randolph's debts of £2,000 and raises his allowance to £1,100 per year, Lord Randolph makes his maiden speech in the House of Commons May 22, and Jennie gives birth November 30 to a son, Winston Leonard Spencer Churchill (*see* 1895).

The Women's Christian Temperance Union (WCTU) is founded at Cleveland, where 135 women meet November 18 at the Second Presbyterian Church and dedicate themselves to ending the traffic in liquor. President of the WCTU is Annie Turner Wittenmyer, editor of the *Christian Woman*; Northwestern University dean Frances Willard, now 35, resigns her position to become the WCTU's corresponding secretary.

U.S. postal inspectors seize more than 60,000 "rubber articles" and 3,000 boxes of pills under terms of the 1872 Comstock Law.

1875

✗ China's Tonghzi emperor Mu Zung dies in January at age 19 after a 12-year reign in which the dowager empress Cixi (Ziaoqin) was co-regent until 1873 (*see* 1856). She adopts her nephew Zaitian, a cousin of Mu Zung, who formally ascends the throne February 25 at age 4 and will reign until 1908 as the Guangxu emperor.

✊ Britain's Trades Union Congress admits its first women delegates.

✴ Some 850 Cheyenne surrender to U.S. Army forces March 6 and turn over Catherine and Sophia German, who were taken nearly 6 months ago along with their two younger sisters (*see* 1874). One of the girls is reportedly pregnant, and the surviving members of the German family are reunited at Fort Leavenworth, Kansas. Gen. Nelson Miles secures a congressional appropriation of $10,000 to set up a fund for their care. All of the girls will marry, all will live well into the 20th century, and Julia will survive until 1959, dying at age 92.

∞ *Science and Health with Key to the Scriptures* by New England divorcée Mary Baker, 54, claims that biblical teachings have helped her recover from the effects of a bad fall and explains a system of faith healing. Sickly since childhood, she met a faith healer in 1862, followed his methods for a while, and began her own "Christian Science" movement in 1866 (*see* 1879).

The Theosophical Society is founded by charismatic Ukrainian-American mystic Helena Blavatsky (*née* Helena Petrovna Hahn), 44, who arrived at New York in steerage 2 years ago, claims to have received knowledge from "masters" on a trip to Tibet, and has charmed millionaire Col. Henry Steel Olcott into abandoning his family to devote all his time (and money) to his spiritualist studies with her. Chaired by Olcott, the Society's avowed purpose is to encourage the "universal Brotherhood of Humanity" and to reveal "unexplained laws of Nature and the psychical powers latent in man" (*see* 1884).

🎓 Wellesley College for Women, founded in 1870, opens September 8 in a lavishly landscaped park around Lake Waban at Wellesley, Mass., with a main building whose central hall has a four-story glass-roofed central hall. Built by Boston lawyer Henry Fowle Durant with profits made in the Civil War, the college has an initial enrollment of 314 and a faculty made up entirely of women (its president will always be a woman). Durant has said, "Women can do the work. I give them the chance." His wife, Pauline, who was herself denied an education, laid the cornerstone of the main building and serves on Wellesley's board of trustees.

Smith College opens at Northampton, Mass., 24 hours after the opening of Wellesley (above), but with only 14 students (*see* 1871). Smith is the first U.S. woman's college whose admissions standards and curriculum are the equivalent of those at male institutions (*see* Vassar, 1865; Bryn Mawr, 1885).

⏸ New York inventor Thomas A. Edison, 28, devises the first duplicating machine to employ a wax stencil. Edison, who has been experimenting with paraffin paper for possible use as telegraph tape, will receive a patent next year for "a method of preparing autographic stencils for printing" and will obtain a second for an improved method in 1880 (*see* Mimeograph, 1887).

"Mere girls are now earning from $10 to $20 a week with the 'Type-Writer,' " says an advertisement placed by Remington Fire Arms Co. in the New York newspaper the *Nation* December 15, "and we can secure good situations for 100 expert writers on it in counting-rooms in this City" (*see* 1874; 1876).

🖋 Poetry: *Preludes* by English poet-essayist Alice Christiana Gertrude Thompson, 28, who will marry author-journalist Arthur Meynell, 5 years her junior, in 1877. *An Idyl of Work* by New England poet Lucy Larcom, 51, whose mother ran a boarding-house for Lowell factory girls and who herself, at age 11, went to work in the mills as a bobbin girl, laboring from 5 in the morning until 7 at night changing the bobbins on spinning frames; her work deals with the factory women she knew in the 1840s. "There were compensations for being shut in to daily toil so early," Larcom will write in *A New England Girlhood*. "The mill itself had its lessons for us. But it was not, and could not be, the right sort of life for a child, and we were happy in the knowledge that, at the longest, our employment was only to be temporary. . . . To me, it was an incalculable help to find myself among so many working-girls, all of us thrown upon our own resources but thrown much more upon each other's sympathies."

Painting: *Quatre Bras, 1815* by Elizabeth Thompson, a sister of the poet-essayist Alice Thompson (above).

Theater: Lotta Crabtree entertains audiences at New Orleans and Cincinnati as her performances remain wildly popular (and remunerative); Charlotte Cushman makes her final appearance 11/7 at Booth's Theatre, New York, in the role of Lady Macbeth.

Opera: *Carmen* 3/3 at the Opéra-Comique, Paris, with music by Georges Bizet, who dies June 3 at age 36 of a throat ailment. Girls from a cigarette factory smoke on stage in Act I, but no self-respecting woman in the audience is a smoker.

Hoopskirts go out of fashion in America after nearly half a century as bustles come in to replace them (although not all women have worn hoopskirts and nobody has ever worn them all the time). The hoops have become so large as to require at least 25 yards of material for a single dress, and the weight of so much fabric has so taxed the strength of a young woman with the 18-inch waist mandated by fashion that she has often worn supporting pads to relieve her back by throwing some of the weight onto the backs of her hips. The gathers of the skirt have gradually been pushed forward, and the "back pannier," which has bunched the skirt over the rear of the hoops, has evolved into the bustle.

Brooklyn, N.Y., Congregational minister Henry Ward Beecher, now 62, wins acquittal July 2 when a sensational 6-month adultery trial ends in a hung jury (*see* Woodhull, 1871). Beecher has clearly been guilty of having sex with a parishioner's wife in the late 1860s, and while his older sisters, Catharine and Harriet, have staunchly defended his innocence in the affair, his younger half sister, Isabella Beecher Hooker, has publicly questioned it.

San Francisco officials dedicate a fountain September 9 at the intersection of Geary, Market, and Kearney streets. Actress Lotta Crabtree (above), who is fulfilling an engagement at Cincinnati, has paid $10,000 to have a 30-foot shaft of iron cast at Philadelphia and shipped in sections across the country to mark the fountain that is designed to relieve the thirst of horses and men. She will not see it until 1879.

1876

The new British viceroy for India Robert Lytton, 45, son of the novelist Bulwer-Lytton, arrives at Bombay April 7 with his wife, Edith (*née* Liddell), 34, who is unsettled by the immorality she finds among colonial bureaucrats and their *memsahibs* (*see* 1877).

Tasmania's four-foot-three-inch aborigine queen Trucanini dies at Hobart May 11 in her 60s. She saw white men stab her mother to death as a child, was raped by white convicts at age 16, and then sold herself for food at work camps until she met a white builder, who with her help recorded the customs of her tribe.

The National Woman Suffrage Association (NWSA) issues a protest in January against the forthcoming centennial celebrations, calling the United States "an oligarchy of sex, and not a true republic" since it "has refused to one-half its citizens the only means of self-government—the ballot . . ." NWSA members resolve "that we meet in our respective towns and districts on the Fourth of July, 1876, and declare ourselves no longer bound to obey laws in whose making we have had no voice, and, in presence of the assembled nations of the world gathered on this soil to celebrate our nation's centennial, demand justice for the women of this land."

A "Declaration of Rights of the Women of the United States" written by Elizabeth Cady Stanton and Matilda Joslyn Gage is presented to the acting U.S. vice president July 4 at Philadelphia by Gage and Susan B. Anthony. It includes "Articles of Impeachment" which begin, "The introduction of the word 'male' into all the State constitutions, denying to women the right of suffrage, and thereby making sex a crime . . ." and include the statement "We ask justice, we ask equality, we ask that all the civil and political rights that belong to citizens of the United States, be guaranteed to us and our daughters forever" (*see* 1887).

1876

The Battle of Little Big Horn June 25 has ended in the massacre of a 264-man U.S. Seventh Cavalry Force under Lt. Col. George Armstrong Custer, 37, at the hands of Sioux chief Sitting Bull, 42, and his tribesmen, who have been angered by the encroachments of whites on their buffalo hunting grounds in the Black Hills of Montana Territory. Custer's widow, Elizabeth (*née* Bacon), 34, will write and lecture extensively in her efforts to defend the reputation of her late husband.

 San Francisco's I. Magnin Co. has its beginnings in the Yankee Notions Store opened by Dutch-American seamstress Mary Ann Magnin, 27, whose husband, Isaac, is a woodcarver and gilder. Her needles, pins, threads, and buttons have no special distinction, but Magnin will attract a wide following with the bridal trousseaux and infant layettes that she will make while raising seven children and running the shop.

Emigré German physician Emil Noeggerath angers the newly formed American Gynecological Society by insisting that 90 percent of sterile women suffer from gonorrhea contracted from husbands who in many cases have been treated for the disease and been pronounced cured. Latent gonorrhea in men, he says, explains why so many healthy young women begin to suffer from "female complaints" shortly after marriage and why so many remain childless (*see* 1879).

The *Transactions of the American Gynecological Society* carries a paper entitled "Extirpation of the Functionally Active Ovaries for the Remedy of Otherwise Incurable Diseases" by Rome, Ga., physician Robert Battey, who urges the removal of healthy ovaries as an effective treatment for menstrual complaints and sexual disorders such as "mania." While healthy, he says, an ovary may nevertheless be "viciously or abnormally performing its functions." By putting an end to ovulation entirely, maintains Battey, a physician can "uproot and remove serious sexual disorders and re-establish . . . general health." But of Battey's first 10 cases, two patients have died and only one, a 38-year-old mother faced with "threatening mania," has become so tractable after the procedure that he can pronounce it an unqualified success. "She now does unaided the house-work of her family." Elizabeth Blackwell will

campaign vigorously against Battey's operation, calling it "the castration of women," but ovariotomy will lead to further drastically invasive gynecological operations; within 15 years hysterectomies will be common and some doctors will even be performing clitoridectomies for cases of "nymphomania" and "excessive masturbation" (*see* Brown, 1859).

A label for "Mrs. Lydia E. Pinkham's Vegetable Compound" is patented by Lynn, Mass., housewife Lydia Estes Pinkham, 57, whose husband, Isaac, lost all his money in the 1873 financial panic. Mrs. Pinkham has for more than a decade been buying unicorn root, life root, black cohosh, pleurisy root, and fenugreek seed from local suppliers, macerating them in her kitchen, and suspending them in about 19 percent alcohol (although she and her children belong to the local temperance society) to create a medicine for "woman's weakness" and related ills.

Lydia Pinkham's Vegetable Compound—18 percent alcohol—was promoted as a cure for "women's complaints."

She insists that at the recommended dosage of three spoonfuls a day her vegetable compound is not an intoxicating beverage, and she will continue to brew the nostrum in her own kitchen and write her own homely advertising until her death in 1883. Distrust of doctors, who dose patients indiscriminately with "mineral" medicines such as calomel (a cathartic which contains mercury and sometimes produces mercury poisioning) has made self-dosage with "botanical" folk remedies widely popular. Pinkham's bright blue paper label claims that her Vegetable Compound is a sure cure for "Prolapsis Uteri, or falling of the Womb, and all Female Weaknesses, including Leucorrhea, painful menstruation, inflammation and ulceration of the womb, irregularities, floodings, *etc.*" (*see* 1879).

The American Medical Association admits its first woman member—Sarah Stevenson, 35—after 29 years as an all-male organization. But even in such specialties as obstetrics, gynecology, and pediatrics, U.S. medical practitioners will, with few exceptions, continue to be virtually all male for another century.

A November 8 act of Parliament permits registration of women medical practitioners in Britain.

The Remington typewriter introduced at the Philadelphia Centennial Exposition (above) does not yet have a shift key (*see* 1874; 1878).

Stenotypy begins to facilitate courtroom reporting and make records of legal proceedings more accurate. New York inventor John Colinergos Zachos patents a "typewriter and phonotypic notation" device with type fixed on 18 shuttle bars, two or more of may be placed in position simultaneously, the device has a plunger common to all the bars for making impressions, and it permits printing a legible text at a high reporting speed.

McCall's magazine begins publication in April under the name *The Queen*. Scots-American entrepreneur James McCall started McCall Pattern Co. in 1870 with a small shop at 543 Broadway, New York, and uses the eight-page pattern and fashion periodical to promote his dress patterns, but it will grow to become a major magazine for women.

"A Classification and Subject Index for Cataloguing and Arranging the Books and Pamphlets of a Library" by Amherst College librarian Melvil Dewey, 25, originates the Dewey decimal system.

Fiction: *Daniel Deronda* by George Eliot; *Pheobe [sic] Junior* by Margaret Oliphant.

Juvenile: *Aunt Charlotte's Stories of Greek History for the Little Ones* by Charlotte M. Yonge.

Painting: *Balaclava* by Elizabeth Thompson.

Theater: Lotta Crabtree in *Musette* 11/27 at New York's 1,000-seat Park Theater, which she has leased. The play runs for 3 weeks and is followed by a revival of *The Marchioness* (audiences come more to see "Lotta the Inimitable" than the plays in which the cigar-smoking actress appears). Charlotte Cushman has died of pneumonia at her native Boston February 11 at age 59.

Opera: Adelina Patti sings the title role in the first London performance of the 1871 Verdi opera *Aida* 6/22 at Covent Garden.

Popular songs: "I'll Take You Home Again, Kathleen" by U.S. songwriter Thomas P. Westendorf, 28.

Daredevil Maria Spelterina becomes the first woman to cross Niagara Falls on a cable.

The Bissell Grand Rapids carpet sweeper patented by Grand Rapids, Mich., china shop proprietor M. R. Bissell is the world's first carpet sweeper (*see* vacuum cleaner, 1901). Bissell suffers from allergic headaches caused by the dusty straw in which china is packed and has devised a sweeper with a knob that adjusts its brushes to variations in floor surface and a box to contain the dust. His wife, Anna, will take charge of the company after Bissell's death in 1880, establish national distribution, and head the firm until her own death in 1934.

"Harvey Girls" begin bringing civilized manners to the American frontier as the first Fred Harvey restaurant opens in the Santa Fe Railroad depot at Topeka, Kan. English-American restaurateur Frederick Henry Harvey, 41, has worked as a freight agent for J. F. Joy's Chicago, Burlington & Quincy Railroad, Joy has turned down his proposal that clean, well-run restaurants be opened for the benefit of passengers, but the Santa Fe has been receptive to the idea and Harvey's Topeka restaurant will soon be joined by others along the Santa Fe line and at other major rail depots and junctions. By the time of Harvey's death in early 1901 there will be 47 Fred Harvey restaurants, all serving good food on Irish linen, with Sheffield silverware, served by well-trained Harvey Girls.

Glasgow grocer Thomas Johnstone Lipton, 26, opens his first shop and has two fat pigs driven through the streets bearing on their scrubbed sides the words "I'm going to Liptons, The Best Shop in Town for Bacon." Lipton sailed to America at age 15 to spend 4 years learning the merchandising methods employed in the grocery section of a New York department store, he will open more stores, and he will be a millionaire by age 29 (*see* tea, 1890).

Heinz's Tomato Ketchup is introduced by H. J. Heinz of Pittsburgh (*see* 1869). Heinz packs pickles and other foods as well as the ketchup, which is 29 percent sugar.

1877

 Queen Victoria is proclaimed empress of India January 1 at a Great Assemblage, or Durbar, held by the viceroy, Lord Lytton, and his wife, Edith, on a grassy plain north of Delhi. While thousands die of hunger in famine-stricken Bombay and Madras, the British Raj entertains officials, rajahs, and subalterns at a fancy ball. The viceroy and vicereine arrive at Government House, Calcutta, January 13, and Edith Lady Lytton settles down to a round of visiting soldiers' wives in their barracks and nurses in their hospitals, charming local society while her husband raises eyebrows with his undignified manner and open flirtations.

A U.S. electoral commission appointed January 29 resolves the disputed 1876 presidential election March 2 in favor of Ohio's Republican governor Rutherford Birchard Hayes, whose pious wife, Lucy (*née* Webb) is a graduate of Cincinnati Wesleyan Female College and becomes the first college-educated First Lady. They move into the White House March 4.

Victoria Woodhull and her sister, Tennessee Claflin, move to England to escape puritanical criticism of their views and behavior (*see* 1872).

 English explorer Lady Ann Blunt (*née* King), 40, daughter of Ada Byron, Countess Lovelace, travels across the desert from Aleppo to Baghdad, skirting the Bedouin tribes that inhabit the region.

Physician Mary Putnam Jacobi disputed the idea that a woman's menstrual cycle was a disabling handicap. LIBRARY OF CONGRESS

 Question of Rest for Women During Menstruation by English-American physician Mary Jacobi (*née* Mary Corinna Putnam), 35, disputes the notion that women must leave off their pursuit of everyday activities during their menstrual periods (*see* Anderson, 1866). The first woman to receive a degree from New York City's College of Pharmacy at a time when no regular U.S. medical school would accept women, Jacobi entered the Female Medical College of Pennsylvania, completed her studies at the Ecole de Médécine in Paris, where she was the first woman student, and has been practicing at Elizabeth Blackwell's New York Infirmary for Women and Children.

The Association for the Higher Education of Women in Glasgow is founded.

The first telephone switchboard is installed May 17 in the Boston office of Edwin T. Holmes, proprietor of Holmes Burglar Alarm Service. Telephone inventor Alexander Graham Bell, 30, loans Holmes 12 telephones, and the switchboard at 342 Washington Street is used for telephone service by day and as a burglar alarm at night. Men operate the switchboard in shifts, but within a few years, thousands of American women will be employed as switchboard operators (see 1878).

Britain's remaining restrictions on freedom of the press end with the court trial at London of Annie Wood Besant (Ajax), 30, and Charles Bradlaugh, 44, who have republished Charles Knowlton's Malthusian 1835 pamphlet "Fruits of Philosophy" advocating contraception (see below). Their case is heard in July, their pamphlet is described in court as "indecent, lewd, and obscene," and although Besant and Bradlaugh are acquitted Besant is socially ostracized and loses custody of her daughter because a judge fears that she might contaminate the child with her ideas. The suffragette movement has given her no support lest it jeopardize its case for enfranchising British women.

The central branch of New York's YMCA offers the world's first typing course—a 6-month program for women.

Fiction: *Deephaven* (stories) by South Berwick, Me., author Sarah Orne Jewett, 27; *From the Camp of the Silent* (*Fra de stummes leir*) by Camilla Collett; *Anna Karenina* by Russian novelist Leo Tolstoy, 48, who writes, "They resumed the conversation started at dinner—the emancipation and occupations of women. Levin agreed with Dolly that a girl who did not marry could always find some feminine occupation in the family. He supported this view by saying that no family can get along without women to help them, that every family, poor or rich, had to have nurses, either paid or belonging to the family."

Juvenile: *Black Beauty* by English author Anna Sewell, 57, whose "Autobiography of a Horse" will be a worldwide best-seller and remain popular for more than a century. Sewell gets a flat £20 for her manuscript and will receive no royalties; *That Lass o' Lowrie's* by English-American author Frances (Eliza) Burnett (*née* Hodgson), 28.

Painting: *The Reader* by Mary Cassatt; *Inkermann* by Elizabeth Thompson, who marries Sir William Francis Butler and becomes Lady Butler; *Nana* by Edouard Manet.

Opera: Adelina Patti makes her La Scala debut at Milan 11/3 in the 1853 Verdi opera *La Traviata*.

Popular songs: "In the Gloaming" by English composer Annie Fortescue Harrison, 26, who has recently married the comptroller of Queen Victoria's household, Sir Arthur Hill, lyrics by Meta Orred; "The Lost Chord" by Gilbert & Sullivan's Arthur Sullivan, who has been inspired by the fatal illness of his brother Frederick, lyrics by the late poet Adelaide A. Procter, whose verse was published in 1858 and who died 6 years later at age 39.

British entomologist Eleanor A. Ormerod, 49, begins publishing *Annual Report of Observations of Injurious Pests*, beginning a 20-year career in which she will make herself an international clearinghouse for entomological information. Ormerod's efficient and inexpensive methods for eradicating insect pests (saline solution for turnip moths, car grease and sulfur applied to infested areas of the hide for maggots that plague livestock) will be credited with saving half the cows in Britain (see 1889).

The new U.S. First Lady Lucy Hayes (above) is a teetotaler and will be derided by her detractors as "Lemonade Lucy." Her husband uses her aversion to alcohol as an excuse to ban liquor from the White House.

The taboo subject of contraception comes into the open at the Bradlaugh-Besant trial (above). Many poor women, desperate for relief from continual pregnancies, have bought the 1832 manual "Fruits of Philosophy" after hearing publicity about the trial, and the acquittal of Bradlaugh and Besant will lead to an end of the ban against disseminating contraceptive advice. But Besant is contemptuous of condoms, saying that they are "used by men of loose character as a guard against syphilitic diseases, and occasionally recommended as a preventive check." She prefers that the woman remain in control by using the sponge.

The Malthusian League is founded in England by George and Charles Drydale to spread the teachings of the late Thomas Malthus.

1878

 A trial of 193 young Russian revolutionaries ends January 23 with the acquittal of a great many of the accused, but the police, using special powers of "administrative exile," pick up most of the men and women who have been acquitted and send them off to Siberia or elsewhere. St. Petersburg's chief of police Gen. F. F. Trepov is shot and wounded in January by revolutionary Vera Zasulich, 26, as an act of protest against the flogging of a prisoner ordered by Gen. Trepov. Zasulich is clearly guilty, but a jury of her peers acquits her on the ground that her action was a legitimate form of political protest, a crowd cheers her as she leaves the courthouse, the authorities permit her to go abroad, and she will become an associate of Karl Marx.

A British Factory and Workshop Act gives more protection to women.

Augusta Lewis's Women's Local #1 collapses after 9 years, and women are accepted into the printer's union on the same basis as men (*see* 1871). No other U.S. trade union except the Cigar Makers admits women equally with men, and women are accepted only begrudgingly in both unions.

Kita Kasuse, a Japanese widow in Kochi Prefecture, tries to vote in a local election, arguing that she is the *koshu* of her household under terms of the 1873 law and a taxpayer. She is told that only men may vote, and that this is justified since men serve in the military. Kasuse poins out that *koshu* do not have to serve, nor do oldest sons, but she is still not permitted to vote. When her tax notice arrives, she refuses to pay and writes to the minister of the interior (*see* 1879).

 The New York Exchange for Woman's Work is founded in early March at the 108 East 31st Street home of Mary (Mrs. William Gardner) Choate (*née* Atwater), 39, a federal judge's wife who has invited a few friends to meet for the purpose of discussing a plan to give opportunities to women by creating "a market for the sale of any wares which they would have it in their power to offer, which neither the stores nor any existing benevolent societies now furnish them" (*see* 1883).

 Sophia Jex-Blake of the London School of Medicine for Women clashes with Elizabeth Garrett Anderson and returns to her native Edinburgh (*see* 1874). Women have gained the right to obtain clinical instruction at the Royal Free Hospital.

Dutch suffragist leader Aletta Jacobs, 29, becomes the first woman physician to practice in Holland (*see* birth control clinic, 1882).

Frontier prostitute "Calamity Jane" proved true blue in a Dakota Territory smallpox epidemic. LIBRARY OF CONGRESS

A smallpox epidemic strikes Deadwood in the Black Hills of Dakota Territory. Frontier prostitute Martha Jane Cannary, 26, works heroically in men's clothing to nurse the ill and renders service that will help make her legendary as "Calamity Jane." In a letter written to her daughter late last year she said,

"There are thousands of Sioux in this valley. I am not afraid of them. They think I am a crazy woman and never molest me. . . . I guess I am the only human being they are afraid of."

The University of London receives permission March 28 to grant academic degrees to women.

Emma Nutt is hired September 1 as the first woman telephone switchboard operator (*see* switchboard, 1877, 1879).

Remington Arms Co. improves the Remington typewriter of 1876 by adding a shift key system that employs upper- and lowercase letters on the same type bar. Wyckoff, Seamens, and Benedict buy Remington's typewriter business and found Remington Typewriter Co. (*see* Underwood, 1895).

Fiction: *A Law unto Herself* by Rebecca Harding Davis; *The Leavenworth Case* by U.S. mystery novelist Anna Katherine Green, 31.

Juvenile: *Aunt Charlotte's Stories of German History for the Little Ones* by Charlotte M. Yonge.

Painting: *Girl in a Blue Armchair* and *Mr. Robert S. Cassatt* (father of the artist) by Mary Cassatt; *Head of a Dog* by Rosa Bonheur.

Theater: *The Girl with No Dowry* (*Bespridannitsa*) by Russian playwright Aleksandr Ostrovsky, 55, November 10 at Moscow's Maly Theater. Larisa Dmitriyevna Ogudalovna has no dowry because she has lost her father. She is nevertheless highly desirable and deeply in love with Sergey Paratov, an adventurous nobleman. She consents, however, to marry a poor clerk who loves her. Other suitors continue to seek her favors. Paratov returns after a year's absence, shows up at Larisa's engagement dinner, and although engaged to marry an heiress persuades Larisa to join him in a picnic on the banks of the Volga. She soon realizes that his intentions are not honorable. Her fiancé comes after them with a gun, discovers that Paratov has abandoned Larisa, and vows to protect her from her other suitors. She mocks him for his lack of pride, and he shoots her. Dying, she thanks him for ending her life.

Opera: German contralto Ernestine Schumann (*née* Rossler), 17, makes her debut at the Dresden Royal Opera singing the role of Cucena in the 1853 Verdi opera *Il Trovatore*. She will marry in 1882 and become famous as Mme. Schumann-Heink.

President Hayes and his wife, Lucy, invite the children of Washington, D.C., to an Easter egg roll on the White House lawn, beginning a tradition.

Ivory Soap has its origin in the White Soap introduced by Cincinnati's 51-year-old Procter & Gamble, whose chemists have perfected a hard, white, floating soap. Harley Procter, now 21, will be inspired to rename the soap Ivory while reading a psalm in church in 1882, and beginning in December of that year Ivory will be aggressively advertised with the slogan "99 and 44/100% pure."

The Woman's Home, a residential hotel for working women, opens in April on the west side of New York's Fourth Avenue between 32nd and 33rd streets. Built with funds provided by the late merchant prince A. T. Stewart, who died 2 years ago, the seven-story structure with penthouse has 502 sleeping rooms, a large interior garden graced with ornate fountains, amd eight reception rooms, parlors, and dining rooms, but rates are $6 to $10 per week at a time when working girls earn only $5 to $15 per week. Residents may not bring in pets, sewing machines, pianos, memorabilia, or other expressions of individuality, and they are not permitted to entertain gentlemen callers. "Stewart and Vanderbilt are both dead," says the comic periodical *Puck*, ". . . but in one thing the dry-goods man has the advantage of the Commodore. His executors are men after his own heart. If the old Philistine [meaning Cornelius Vanderbilt] were alive to-day, he couldn't suggest one additional item of meanness and petty tyranny in the management of the 'Woman's Home.'" The *Daily Tribune* announces in late May that the Woman's Home will be converted into the Park Avenue Hotel, open to both sexes, and it will continue as such until it is razed in 1927.

Antivice crusader Anthony Comstock of 1872 Comstock Law fame approaches a reputed New York abortionist who has a luxurious mansion at 657 Fifth Avenue (52nd Street). Hiding his identity, he says he is desperately poor and will be ruined if his wife has another child. English-born brothelkeeper Anna A. Trow Somers Lohman, 65, alias Mme. Restell, supplies Comstock with drugs and contraceptives. He has her indicted and refuses a $40,000 offer to drop his charges, Mme. Restell posts bail and returns to her house, newspaper stories convince her that she will be convicted, and she slits her throat in her bathtub April 1.

1879

 The newspaper *Tokyo Nichinichi Shimbun* runs a story January 31 about Kita Kasuse (*see* 1878). It calls her an eccentric woman, but she gains fame as the *minken oba-a-san*—the civil rights grandmother.

Congress gives women the right to argue before the U.S. Supreme Court. Belva Ann Lockwood, now 48, whose second husband died 2 years ago at age 73, has previously been denied a petition to plead a case in the high court on the basis of custom but has persuaded sympathetic congressmen to support a measure, insisting that if women have the right to practice law they are entitled to pursue legal matters to the country's highest courts. She argues a case before the Supreme Court March 3, becoming the first woman to do so.

 F. W. Woolworth Co. has its beginnings at Watertown, N.Y., where store clerk Frank Winfield Woolworth, 27, persuades his employer to install a counter at which all goods are priced at 5¢. He then induces one of the firm's principals to lend him $400 with which to open a Utica store at which all items are priced at 5¢. The store fails in 3 months, but the same partner stakes Woolworth to try a five-and-dime store at Lancaster, Pa. which opens June 21 and proves successful. Stores opened by Woolworth at Philadelphia, Harrisburg, and York, Pa., and at Newark, N.J., will have indifferent success, but when he opens five-and-dimes at Buffalo, Erie, Scranton, and some other cities Woolworth will tap the low-income market and begin to build a worldwide chain of open-shelf, self-service stores that will employ thousands of women (*see* Barbara Hutton, 1924).

The May Company is started at Leadville, Colo., by German-American merchant David May, 26, who has left his Hartford City, Ind., clothing store job with $25,000 and gone West to seek a cure for his asthma. Starting with a store of board framework covered with muslin, May sells out his stock within a few weeks as Leadville booms overnight from a town of 500 to one of 25,000 in the wake of a silver strike in 1874.

National Cash Register (NCR) has its beginnings in a register patented November 4 by Dayton, Ohio, saloon keeper James J. "Jake" Ritty, whose health has been undermined by his bartenders' pilfering. Ritty took a sea voyage to Europe to recover and was inspired by a recording device on the steamship marking the revolutions of the vessel's propeller and giving its officers a complete and accurate daily record of the ship's speed. "Ritty's Incorruptible Cashier" in its first version merely registers the amount of each cash transaction on a dial, but a second model elevates a small plate to display the amounts so both clerk and customer can see it. The inventor and his brother will develop an improved model that records each day's transactions on a paper roll that can be checked by a store owner against the amount of cash in the cashbox, and thousands of women will be employed as cashiers.

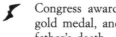 Congress awards lighthouse keeper Ida Lewis a gold medal, and she is finally—7 years after her father's death—granted the official title keeper of the light (*see* 1869). She has saved the lives of 13 people and will save five more, the last one in 1906 when, at age 64, she will rescue a woman who falls out of a boat when coming to visit her.

California stagecoach driver "Cockeyed Charlie" Parkhurst dies of cancer December 29 at age 67 in a cabin near Watsonville. An autopsy reveals that "Charlie" was a woman—Charlotte Darkey Parkhurst—and it develops that she grew up in a New Hampshire orphanage after being abandoned by her parents, ran away in boy's clothing, hooked up with a Worcester livery stabler, became a husky five-foot seven-inch teenager, learned to handle a team, and after working at Providence and in Georgia left in 1851 for California, where her taste for cigars and chewing tobacco helped her pose successfully as a man. A horse had damaged her left eye, and she wore a patch over it as she drove stage routes through the mother-lode country of the Sierras. A baby's red dress in her trunk suggests that she may once have borne a child.

The gonococcus bacterium involved in the sexual transmission of gonorrhea is discovered under the microscope by German physician Albert Ludwig Siegmund Neisser, 24. Doctors generally believe that gonorrhea is endemic in women and that vaginal discharges are evidence of the disease. They dismiss suggestions that women contract gonorrheal infections from their husbands, saying rather that it is the product of crowded city conditions, excessive masturbation, or exposure to the cold. So-called "pox" doctors, who treat men for gonorrhea and syphilis, often conspire with their patients to keep the men's wives and fiancées unaware of the nature of the men's illness (see 1876).

U.S. physician George Beard delivers an address before the Baltimore Medical and Chirurgical Society on the subject of "American Nervousness: Its Philosophy and Treatment." He calls the new disease "neurasthenia" and says it affects particularly "brain workers" and those obliged to live under the stress of disadvantageous circumstances; it will soon become a mark of status in America, with fashionable women comparing symptoms, physicians, and health spas as they conform to the idealized view of woman as invalid. Many a woman uses neurasthenia as a way to play on her husband's sympathy, avoiding the need to satisfy his sexual demands.

Lydia Pinkham's face appears for the first time on the label of her patented Vegetable Compound, which bears the statements "The Health of Woman is the Hope of the Race" and "A Woman Can Sympathize with Women" (see 1876). Advertisements invite readers to write to Mrs. Pinkham (see 1881).

"Chlorosis," which combines the symptoms of iron-deficiency anemia and mild hysteria, affects many Western women, but pulmonary tuberculosis remains the leading cause of death among both women and men in most countries. Tuberculosis is romanticized, and healthy women drink vinegar or eat arsenic in an effort to attain the pallor and blazing eyes of the tuberculosis victim.

The Church of Christ, Scientist is chartered at Boston by Mary Baker Eddy to propagate the spiritual and metaphysical system of Christian Science (see 1875).

John Humphrey Noyes of the Oneida Community decamps for Canada June 23 after 31 years of religiously defying laws against adultery and fornication (see 1851). His community has prospered by selling traps and spoons of its own manufacture; its members have been free to have sexual relations without regard to marriage; Noyes himself, now 67, has been the "first husband" to most of the Community's 12- and 13-year-old girls; young men and women have been expected to accept older members as sexual partners at least some of the time; women generally have had sexual relations only when and with whom they pleased and to have only as many children as suited them; couples who fell in love and stopped circulating sexually have been accused of "idolatry"; and some have rebelled against the Association's rules.

Somerville College opens at Oxford for the education of women, taking its name from the late Scottish scientific writer Mary Somerville, who died 7 years ago at age 92. Lady Margaret Hall opens at Oxford.

Radcliffe College has its beginnings in classes for women started at Cambridge, Mass., by Elizabeth Cary Agassiz, 51, widow of the late naturalist Louis Agassiz, who died 6 years ago at age 66 (see 1894).

The multiple switchboard invented by U.S. engineer Leroy B. Firman will make the telephone a commercial success and help increase the number of U.S. subscribers from 50,000 in 1880 to 250,000 in 1890 (see 1877; dial telephone, 1919).

The Union School of Stenography and Typewriting opened at New York by schoolteacher Mary Foot Seymour, 33, is the first U.S. secretarial school whose students are all women. Only 5 percent of copyists, bookkeepers, accountants, and office clerks are women, but Seymour has taught herself shorthand and become a court reporter. She has hired women to transcribe her notes into longhand, but sees that it will save time if they can be transcribed directly on a typewriter. By the end of the century, women office workers will far outnumber men.

La Nouvelle Revue is founded at Paris by French writer Juliette Adam (née Lamber), 43, whose husband, a senator, died 2 years ago at age 61. Her salon during the Empire attracted the city's progressive politicians and its best artists and wits.

Telephone switchboards created even more jobs for women than did typewriters.

Nonfiction: *Woman and Socialism* (*Die Frau und der Sozialismus*) by German socialist Ferdinand August Bebel, 39, whose work will be translated into all leading languages. It holds capitalism responsible for woman's historic subjection to man, and while it supports feminist demands for legal and political rights it argues that complete emancipation can come only through the overthrow of the capitalist system. Class antagonisms among women, Bebel says, are mitigated somewhat by the fact that all women share certain common interests, and while they "march in separate armies" they may nevertheless "strike a united blow" in the fight for equal rights.

Juvenile: *Under the Window* by English illustrator Catherine "Kate" Greenaway, 33, of the *Illustrated London News*. Her "toy-book" will popularize early-19th-century costumes for children's wear.

Painting: *The Cup of Tea, Woman and Child Driving* (Lydia Cassatt with a niece of Edgar Degas), *Lydia in a Loge Wearing a Pearl Necklace*, and *Lydia Leaning on Her Arms Seated in a Loge* by Mary Cassatt; *Weaning the Calves* by Rosa Bonheur; *The Remnants of the Army* by Lady Elizabeth Butler; *Female Life Class* by U.S. painter Alice Barber Stephens, 21.

Theater: *A Doll's House* (*Et Dukkehjem*) by Norwegian playwright Henrik Ibsen, 50, 1/21 at Copenhagen's Royal Theater. Torwald, the bank-manager husband of Ibsen's heroine, Nora, has indulged her every wish, calling her his "little songbird," "little scatterbrain," or "little squirrel," she charges that he has made her into a doll, just as her father did, and in the end she deserts him and her children for no better reason than to assert her freedom. "It's your fault that I have made nothing of my life," Nora tells him, and when he says that she has failed in her duty as a wife and mother she replies, "I have another duty—to myself." There cannot be a marriage unless there can be "communion between us," she says. And slams the door. Audiences express shock. Ada Rehan, now 19, makes her New York debut in May in *L'Assommoir* and soon becomes the leading lady for Augustin Daly's repertory company, playing opposite John Drew. Lotta Crabtree returns to San Francisco, appears at the Academy of Music in *Musette*, and keeps most of the audience in its seats at her first matinee despite the excitement caused when *Chronicle* editor Charles De Young, 32, shoots and kills a clergyman who has declared his candidacy for mayor and denounced De Young's candidate (De Young is removed to safety but will himself be shot dead by the mayor's son next year).

Opera: Maine-born soprano Lilian Nordica (*née* Norton), 22, makes her debut in June at Milan singing the role of Donna Elvira in the 1787 Mozart opera *Don Giovanni*.

The first milk bottles appear at Brooklyn, N.Y., where the Echo Farms Dairy delivers milk in glass bottles instead of measuring it into the pitchers of housewives and serving maids from barrels carried in milk wagons. Some competitors will soon follow suit.

1880

France grants amnesty to those arrested and sentenced after the fall of the Paris Commune 9 years ago. Anarchist Louise Michel (she was converted to the anarchist cause by Natalie Lemel en route to New Caledonia) returns to Paris, where she is hailed variously as *"la grande citoyen"* and the "red virgin," organizes her followers, and once again worries police, although she envisions an anarchism that does not include terrorism (*see* 1890).

Russia's pious czarina Wilhelmina (Maria Aleksandrovna of Hesse-Darmstadt) dies of tuberculosis June 6 at age 56 in the Winter Palace at St. Petersburg. Aleksandr II's mistress since she was 17 has been Katharina Dolgorukova, Princess Yourieffskaia, now 33, and he marries her July 18 in a private ceremony at Czarskoe Seloe, knowing that his life is in danger from terrorist attacks and that he may be killed at any time (*see* 1881).

Japanese mistresses cease to enjoy official recognition under a new law (*see* 1870), but many men, including the emperor, continue to take mistresses, just as in Europe. Famous geisha sometimes become mistresses to rich noblemen.

Leadville, Colo., storekeeper Horace A. W. "Hod" Tabor, 53, takes as his mistress the blond, blue-eyed divorcée Elizabeth "Baby Doe" McCourt, 23, by buying off her previous protector. He has grubstaked two starving prospectors to $64.75 worth of provisions and wound up 10 months later owning silver mines, including the Matchless, that will earn him as much as $4 million per year. Tabor soon divorces his wife, Augusta, and marries Baby Doe in a lavish wedding at Washington, D.C. He will build her a Denver opera house and a mansion graced with nude statuary and 100 peacocks, but when silver prices drop in 1893 he will be bankrupted and will die a pauper 6 years later, having left Baby Doe the now worthless Matchless mine.

Woodward & Lothrop's Boston Dry Goods House opens at Washington, D.C. Former Chelsea, Mass., merchants Samuel Walter Woodward, 32, and Alvin Mason Lothrop, 33, will move in January of next year from 705 Market Street to a five-story building with steam-powered elevators at 921 Pennsylvania Avenue, and in 1887 they will take over a new $100,000 building at 11th and F streets.

Southall, Barclay, & Co. of Birmingham introduces sanitary napkins for women, each containing a pad of absorbent cotton wool. They are considered a convenience for women who may be traveling when their monthly periods come on and cannot

wear the diapers used when they are at home (*see* Kotex, 1918).

Italian nun Frances Xavier Cabrini, 30, founds the Missionary Sisters of the Sacred Heart and is named Mother Superior of the new order. Mother Cabrini, who took her vows 3 years ago, is assigned by the Church to supervise an orphanage at Codogno. By 1887 her order will have seven convents, and the following year it will gain formal recognition from the Vatican (*see* 1889).

English-born U.S. Methodist preacher and temperance lecturer Anna Howard Shaw, 33, wins ordination as a minister of the Methodist Protestant Church. She used the proceeds of lecture fees to finance her studies at Boston University divinity school, will be pastor of two Cape Cod churches, and will obtain an M.D. from B.U.'s medical school in 1886 before resigning to devote all of her efforts to woman suffrage (*see* 1916).

Newnham College is created at Cambridge University as a second hall opens and merges with the one opened in 1871. The new building will be called Sidgwick Hall by 1889 in honor of its proctors, Mr. and Mrs. Henry Sidgwick (*see* 1889).

Women account for 32 percent of all U.S. college undergraduates, up from 21 percent in 1870 (*see* 1910).

Women account for 60 percent of the teachers in U.S. elementary and secondary schools, up from 25 percent before the Civil War.

Britain's first high schools for girls open.

France opens her first secondary schools for girls.

The *Girl's Own Paper* begins publication in January at London under the aegis of the Religious Tract Society. It will enjoy far more success than the *Boy's Own Paper*, introduced last year, and by 1884 will have the largest circulation of any illustrated English magazine.

Nonfiction: *History of Woman Suffrage* by Elizabeth Cady Stanton, Susan B. Anthony, and Mathilda Joslyn Gage, who write, "The prolonged slavery of women is the darkest page in human history"; "The queens in history compare favorably with the kings"; "The woman is uniformly sacrificed to the wife and mother"; "Wherever the skilled hands and cultural brains of women have made the battle of life easier for man, he has readily pardoned her sound judgment and proper self-assertion"; "But when at last woman stands on an even platform with man, his acknowledged equal everywhere, with the same freedom to express herself in the religion of government of the country, then, and not until then . . . will he be able to legislate as wisely and generously for her as for himself."

Fiction: *Nana* by Emile Zola, now 40, exposes the misery of life as a Parisian prostitute; "Boule de Suif" by French short-story writer Henri-René-Albert-Guy de Maupassant, 30, is about a patriotic prostitute in the Franco-Prussian War; it will be followed by even better stories, but its author is already ill with the syphilis that will put him into a straitjacket and then kill him at age 43, just 4 years after his younger brother dies in an insane asylum of the same disease.

Poetry: *New Leaves* (*Follas novas*) by Rosalía de Castro.

Juvenile: *The Peterkin Papers* by Boston author Lucretia Peabody Hale, 60, whose book *The Last of the Peterkin* will appear in 1886; *Kate Greenaway's Birthday Book* by Catherine Greenaway; *Burnt Out: A Story for Mother's Meetings* by Charlotte M. Yonge.

Painting: *Lydia Cassatt Knitting in the Garden at Marly* by Mary Cassatt.

Opera: Polish soprano Marcella Semprich (Prakseda Marcellina Kochanska), 22, makes her London debut at Covent Garden 6/12 in the title role of the 1835 Donizetti opera *Lucia di Lammermoor*.

Half of New York's population is packed into tenements on the Lower East Side, an area that accounts for a disproportionate 70 percent of the city's deaths.

A pharmacy to dispense soluble pessaries (vaginal contraceptive suppositories based on quinine in cocoa butter) opens at Clerkenwell, England, under the management of Walter John Rendell. Dr. Henry Arthur Allbutt of Leeds will popularize the commercial pessaries, but inventive housewives throughout Europe and America will devise home-made spermicidal barriers of cocoa butter and glycerine, douching afterward as an added precaution (*see* Place, 1822; Wilde, 1833; Allbutt, 1887).

German physician Wilhelm P. J. Mensinga introduces the Mensinga Pessary, an improved diaphragm, as vulcanization (invented in 1839) and other advances make rubber more practical to use. Circular in shape, the soft rubber shield is held in place over the cervix by a spring which pushes it firmly against the wall of the vagina, blocking entry to the uterus; it can be left in for a month but requires fitting by a qualified medical practitioner. Mensinga's avowed intent is to protect women from pregnancies that may jeopardize their lives because of pelvic malformations or other health problems (*see* 1882; Wilde, 1833).

Pope Pius XI declares abortion of any kind an excommunicatory sin.

1881

Russia's Czar Aleksandr II is killed March 13 at St. Petersburg when a bomb tears off his legs, rips open his face, and mutilates his face in an assassination engineered and carried out by Sophia Perovskaya, who heads a band of Nihilist terrorists of a populist fringe group. The leadership of the People's Will (*Narodnaya Volya*) is arrested and the group is taken over by Vera Nikolaevna Figner, 28, who has organized a resistance movement within the army and navy, written propaganda, and plotted to blow up the czar's train (*see* 1880; 1883).

The Householders in Scotland Act gives Scottish women the right to vote in local elections.

A Century of Dishonor by U.S. author Helen Maria Hunt Jackson (*née* Fiske), 49, records government wrongs in dealing with Indian tribes. Jackson, whose first husband and son both died in the Civil War, has lived in Colorado Springs since remarryng in 1875. She will be appointed a special commissioner next year to investigate conditions among California's Mission Indians.

A Chicago and North Western Railroad freight train plunges off a washed-out Iowa bridge in a torrential rainstorm on the night of July 6. Kate

Shelley, 15, sees the accident from her widowed mother's cottage, braves violent winds and rain to make her way across a treacherous wooden trestle and reach the Moingona Station a mile away, the station agent flags down the midnight express, and Shelley's warning saves the passengers' lives. The Iowa state legislature will grant her a $200 reward and a Tiffany medal next year, Frances Willard will give her a 1-year college scholarship, she will herself become a station agent, and when she dies in 1912 the Chicago and North Western will send a private railcar to convey family and friends to her funeral.

The American Association of the Red Cross is founded by Clara Barton of Civil War fame, who did relief work in Europe during the Franco-Prussian War and has campaigned to have the United States sign a Geneva Convention. Now 59, Barton will serve as president of the American National Red Cross until 1904, when lack of public support will require a congressional appropriation to keep the Red Cross from folding.

Britain's Midwives' Institute has its beginnings in the Matron's Aid or Trained Midwives' Registration Society, founded to improve the quality of attendants at childbirth (*see* Dickens, 1844; Midwives' Act, 1902).

Sales of Mrs. Lydia E. Pinkham's Vegetable Compound reach nearly $200,000 (*see* 1879). Mrs. Pinkham's son Dan dies of tuberculosis in October at age 32, despite her recommendations that he take her liver pills; his brother Will has contracted the same disease, is too ill to attend Dan's funeral, and dies within 2 months in Los Angeles at age 28 (*see* 1883).

The University of Cambridge agrees to admit women on a formal basis to its honor examinations and grants certificates to women in lieu of degrees (*see* 1874).

Spelman College has its beginnings in the Atlanta Baptist Female Seminary. The school will be renamed in 1924 to honor oilman John D. Rockefeller's mother-in-law, Lucy Henry Spelman, and will be the leading U.S. college for black women.

Tuskegee Normal and Industrial Institute is founded at Tuskegee, Ala., where local blacks have invited Booker T. Washington, 25, to start the pioneer school for blacks. Washington, who has been instructor to 75 Native American youths at the Hampton Normal and Agricultural Institute in Virginia, gets help from Hampton graduate Olivia America Davidson, 27, who will become his second wife in August 1886 following the death of his first wife, Fannie, and will bear two sons before her death in May 1889.

Dana Hall School opens September 8 at Wellesley, Mass., to serve as a preparatory school for Wellesley College (only 30 of the college's first 314 students were able to pass a placement examination in 1875). Local businessman Charles P. Dana has given his friend Henry F. Durant a boarding house (formerly a church) to serve as home to the new school, whose headmistresses, Julia and Sarah Eastman, charge $325 per year for tuition and board, stress individual development, and will have 78 boarders and 38 day students by 1893 (*see* 1899).

The *U.S. Companion* sends Anna Leonowens to Russia following the assassination of the czar (above) to write a series of articles. Her son, Lewis, will return to Siam next year and will be made an officer in the cavalry.

Nonfiction: *Handbook for Women Engaged in Social and Political Work* by Irish-born London reformer Helen Blackburn, 39, who since 1874 has been secretary of the National Society for Women's Suffrage and now begins a decade as editor of the *Englishwoman's Review*; *Narrative of My Captivity among the Sioux Indians* by Dakota settler Fanny Kelly (*née* Wiggins), 36, who was captured by the Oglala Sioux near Fort Laramie in July 1864 along with Sara Larimer, who was held only briefly whereas Kelly became the servant of Chief Ottawa, learned to speak his language, was fairly treated, and tended to the wounds of braves hurt while fighting the whites before she effected her daring escape.

Fiction: *Sick Heart* (*Cuore Infermo*) by Neapolitan novelist-journalist Matilde Serao, 25, who joins the staff of *Capitan Fracassa* at Rome; *Lotti, die Uhrmacherin* by Austrian poet-novelist Marie von Ebner-Eschenbach (*née* von Dubsky), 51; *A Village Commune* by Ouida.

Poetry: *Xantippe and Other Verse* by English poet Amy Levy, 18, whose title poem appeared in the *Universal Magazine* in May 1880. Levy has been studying at Newnham College, London.

Juvenile: *Five Little Peppers and How They Grew* by U.S. author Margaret Sidney (Harriett Mulford Stone Lathrop), 37; *Daddy Darwin's Dovecote* by Julianna Ewing; *Heidi* (*Heidis Lehr- und Wander-jahre, Heidi kann brauchen, Was es gelernt hat*) by Swiss author Johanna Heusser Spyri, 54.

Painting: *Femme à la Tapisserie* (her sister Lydia working at a tapestry frame), *Woman Seated before a French Screen*, and *Master Robert Kelso Cassatt* by Mary Cassatt; *Scotland for Ever!* by Lady Elizabeth Butler.

Opera: Vienna-born U.S. soprano Emma (Johanna) Juch, 17, makes her debut in June at Her Majesty's Theatre, London, singing the role of Philine in the 1866 Ambroise Thomas opera *Mignon* and sings the same role in her New York debut at the Academy of Music 10/21; Australian-born soprano May Witty, 16, makes her operatic debut in the chorus at the Liverpool Court Theatre.

Stage musicals: Lillian Russell (*née* Helen Louise Leonard), 19, plays D'Jemma in the comic opera *The Great Mogul* (or *The Snake Charmer*) with music by French composer Edmond Audran, 39. Russell adopted her stage name last year while appearing at Tony Pastor's Opera House in New York and has toured California in *The Great Mogul*, which she will follow with roles in *Patience* and other Gilbert and Sullivan operettas. Her clear soprano voice and well-upholstered beauty will make her popular for more than 20 years.

1882

British authorities in Ireland release nationalist leader Charles Stewart Parnell, 35, from Kilmain-ham Prison May 2 after he agrees to cooperate with the Liberal Party and stop inciting Irishmen to intimidate tenant farmers who cooperate with land-lords. Fenians murder Lord Frederick Cavendish, the new undersecretary, and a companion May 6 in broad daylight in Dublin's Phoenix Park, Parnell repudiates the act and disavows the campaign of Irish terrorism that has involved dynamiting public buildings in England, but the British suspend trial by jury. Parnell, who was elected chairman of the Irish Parliamentary Party in May 1880, has since that time been having a love affair with Katharine Wood O'Shea, now 37, and has helped advance her husband's political career (*see* 1889).

Parliament passes a second Married Women's Property Act in August, allowing married women to own property in their own right. Passage of the measure follows efforts by women's rights champion Richard Marsden Pankhurst, who 3 years ago married Emmeline Goulden, now 25 (*see* 1903).

Parliament hears an address from Josephine Butler, now 54, who has been touring the country in a crusade against the Contagious Diseases Acts of 1864, 1866, and 1869, taking her case to workingmen whose daughters have been forced into prostitution. "I am not here to represent virtuous women alone," she declares. "I plead for the rights of the most virtuous and the most vicious equally, and I speak for the womanhood of the world. . . . The moral character of a woman, though it be of the lowest, does not alter the sacrilegious character of an independent assault upon her person." Parliament will repeal the Contagious Diseases Acts in 1886.

German obstetrician Max Sänger revives cesarean deliveries for women with deformed pelvises (often the result of rickets), using aseptic methods and suturing the uterine wall as well as the abdominal wall with silk thread. Sänger enjoys an 80 percent success rate (*see* 1894).

French chemist Louis Pasteur has recently demonstrated that microbial chains he first discovered in 1860 and called *streptococci* are the major cause of the virulent infection puerperal fever, which remains a problem, especially for parturient women with wounded genitalia. Hospitals will not generally use antiseptic practices until 1885, and physicians will continue to cover up puerperal fever deaths by ascribing them to other causes.

Japan's first girls' high school opens but teaches mostly sewing, housekeeping, and poise. The private school will become a government-operated public school in 1886 but will still put its emphasis on preparing girls to be good wives, teaching them how to relate to a husband and a mother-in-law, raise children, keep house, treat servants, and behave in polite society.

The University of Mississippi opens its doors to women, becoming the first Southern state institution of higher learning to do so.

The University of Mt. Allison College, New Brunswick, grants a degree to Hattie S. Stewart, 22, who becomes the first woman to receive a degree from a Canadian college (see 1873). The University of Toronto and Queen's University, at Kingston, Ontario, soon follow Mt. Allison's example, but Dalhousie (which admitted women for the the first time last year), McGill, and others will be slower to grant women degrees.

Wesfield College for women opens at Hampstead, England.

St. Timothy's School opens September 14 in an old house at Catonsville, Md., outside Baltimore. Sarah Randolph "Miss Sally" Carter, 23, has founded the "Select School for Young Ladies" with $500 in capital; her cousin Sarah Nichols teaches spelling, her sister Mary Coles "Miss Polly" Carter will join the faculty next year, and enrollment will grow to 142 by 1970.

Nonfiction: *Alexandre II, Détails inédits sur sa vie intime et sa mort* by Victor Laferté (Katharina Dolgorukova, the late czar's mistress). The St. Petersburg government will suppress her 1890 *Memoires*.

Fiction: *Anne* by U.S. novelist Constance Fenimore Woolson, 42, a grandniece of the late James Fenimore Cooper, whose novel has been serialized in *Harper's* magazine; *Petit Bob* by French novelist Gyp (the comtesse de Mirabeau de Martel), 33; *Maremma* by Ouida; *The Bishop* (*Brynjólfur Sveinsson biskup*) by Icelandic novelist Torf Hildurhólm, 37; *Fantasia* by Matilde Serao.

Juvenile: *A Book of Worthies Gathered from the Old Histories* by Charlotte M. Yonge.

Painting: *Floreat Etona!* by Lady Elizabeth Butler.

Theater: The "Jersey Lily" Lillie (Emily Charlotte Le Breton) Langtry, 30, who made her London stage debut last year, makes her first U.S. appearance in Tom Taylor's *An Unequal Match* 11/6 at Wallack's Theater, New York. Mrs. Langtry gained her soubriquet from the painting "The Jersey Lily" by Sir John Everett Millais, for whom she posed. Sarah Bernhardt in Victorien Sardou's *Fedora* 12/11 at the Théâtre du Vaudeville, Paris. Written especially for Bernhardt, the melodrama provides the name for a fashionable new soft felt hat with a high roll on its side brim and a lengthwise crease in its low crown.

Opera: German soprano Rosa Sucher (*née* Hasselbeck), 33, makes her London debut in May at the Drury Lane Theatre singing the role of Elsa in the 1850 Wagner opera *Lohengrin*, appears 5/30 in the first London production of Wagner's 1868 opera *Die Meistersinger von Nürnberg*, and sings the role of Isolde 6/20 in the first London production of Wagner's 1865 opera *Tristan und Isolde*; Therese Malten accepts Wagner's invitation to share a role in his new opera *Parsifal*, which has its first performance 7/26 in the Festpielhaus at Bayreuth.

The Andrew Jergens Co., founded at Cincinnati by Dutch-born entrepreneur Jergens, 30, in partnership with a local soapmaker, makes a luxury toilet soap. A onetime lumberjack, Jergens will formulate a hand lotion whose popularity will make him rich.

The world's first electric flatiron is patented June 6 by New York inventor Henry W. Weely, but his iron heats up only when plugged into its stand and quickly cools down when in use. Since few homes have electricity anyway, Weely's iron is not a success (see 1906).

Only 2 percent of New York homes have water connections, and while tenements have some rudimentary plumbing facilities nearly every private house has a backyard privy.

The world's first birth control clinic is opened at Amsterdam by Aletta Jacobs, now 33, who has been won over by neo-Malthusians on a visit to London (see 1878). She equips women with the Mensinga Pessary, which will come to be called the "Dutch cap," but because it requires medical fitting it will never be popular with working-class women (see 1880; Bradlaugh and Besant, 1877; Sanger, 1914).

1883

Russian revolutionary Vera Nikolaevna Figner is arrested and condemned to death (*see* 1881). The sentence is commuted, she is imprisoned for a year, and she will spend 20 years in solitary confinement at the notorious Schlüsselburg Prison on an island in the Neva River, writing poetry: and memoirs (*see* 1917).

Oregon newspaper publisher Abigail Duniway persuades the state legislature to approve a constitutional amendment providing for woman suffrage, but voters reject the measure (*see* 1872; 1912).

The 5-year-old New York Exchange for Woman's Work takes rooms at 4 East 20th Street, formerly occupied by the Decorative Arts Club, and holds its first fund-raising event. The Exchange is gaining recognition as "a successful school as well as a business house for all women who are in earnest in their desire to be independent, and to help those depending on them for a home, the comforts of life, a better education, and the assistance necessary in beginning a business life . . ." (*see* 1894).

The Working Girls' Vacation Society, founded by philanthropists at New York, is one of the first such organizations.

A lasting machine patented by West Indian immigrant Jan Matzeliger, 31, revolutionizes the U.S. shoe industry.

Russian mathematician-scientist Sofia Kovalevskaia (*née* Sofia Vasilevna Korvin-Kruvovskaia), 33, who was graduated *summa cum laude* at Göttingen but has been prevented by her sex from obtaining a teaching job in Russia, accepts a position as lecturer in mathematics at the University of Stockholm. The playwright August Strindberg says, "A female professor of mathematics is a pernicious and unpleasant phenomenon—even, one might say, a monstrosity," but Kovalevskaia (her husband, whom she married only that she might travel abroad, has just committed suicide) will gain fame for her Caucy-Kovalevsky Theorem of Differential Equations, and her essay "On the Rotation of a Solid Body about a Fixed Point" will win the Prix Bordin of the Académie Française (*see* 1889).

Lydia Pinkham dies May 17 at age 64, less than 5 months after suffering a paralytic stroke, but letters bearing her "signature" continue to be sent to customers writing in for advice (*see* 1879; 1898).

The Church of England Day School Company is founded. It will have at least 12 schools for girls under its care by 1890.

The *Ladies' Home Journal* begins publication at Philadelphia under the name *Ladies' Journal*. Maine-born publisher Cyrus H. K. (Herman Kotzschmar) Curtis, 32, offers cash prizes to readers who submit the most names of possible subscribers.

More than 3,000 Remington typewriters are sold, up from about 2,350 last year. By 1885 sales will reach 5,000 per year (*see* 1878; Underwood, 1895).

Fiction: *Aldersyde* by Scottish novelist Annie S. (Shepherd) Swan, 24, who marries a schoolteacher (he will later become a physician). *Hester* by Margaret Oliphant. *Treasure Island* by Scottish novelist-poet Robert Louis Stevenson, 23, who has returned to Scotland after having traveled across the Atlantic in steerage and across America in an emigrant train to pursue Fanny Van de Graft Osbourne, a married woman 11 years his senior and mother of three. He met her 7 years ago at Fontainebleau, France, married her at San Francisco in 1880, and thereafter took her to a western mining town. *For the Major* (novelette) by Constance Fenimore Woolson.

Poetry: *Poems of Passion* by Wisconsin-born poet Ella Wheeler Wilcox, 33, whose poem "Solitude" begins, "Laugh, and the world laughs with you;/ Weep, and you weep alone" (her book was originally rejected by publishers because of the "immorality" of some of its poems).

Painting: *Self-Portrait* by Parisian model and Post-Impressionist Suzanne (originally Marie-Clémentine) Valadon, 18, who has an affair with Catalan journalist-painter Miguel Utrillo y Molius and gives birth December 26 to a son, Maurice, whom Utrillo will acknowledge in 1891 although the child may have been fathered by another man; *Portrait of Young Woman in Black*, *Portrait of Mrs. Robert Simpson Cassatt*, and *Elsie Cassatt* (the artist's niece) by Mary Cassatt; *Parisienne* (pastel) and *Jean et Jacques* (oil on canvas) by Russian painter Marie Bashkirtseff, 24.

Theater: Lotta Crabtree in *Musette* 12/22 at the Opéra-Comique, London; audiences are not responsive.

Opera: Marcella Semprich makes her Metropolitan Opera debut 10/24—second night of the Met's first season—in the title role of the 1835 Donizetti opera *Lucia di Lammermoor*. She will be a regular at the Met from 1898 to 1909.

The New York Gothams baseball team holds the first Ladies' Day in professional ball June 16, allowing women into its ballpark at a reduced rate (*see* 1867). Spectators at public sporting events have been virtually all men up to now.

The most lavish party yet held in America is staged March 26 at the $2 million Gothic mansion of railroad magnate William Kissam Vanderbilt, 34, on the northwest corner of New York's Fifth Avenue at 53rd Street. Vanderbilt is chairman of the Lake Shore & Michigan Southern, and the *New York World* estimates that his wife has spent $155,730 for costumes, $11,000 for flowers, $4,000 for hired carriages, $4,000 for hairdressers, and $65,270 for catering, champagne, music, and the like to make the $250,000 fancy dress ball a success.

Buffalo-born California widow Harriet W. R. Strong, 39, whose husband has recently committed suicide after losing the family fortune in a silver-mining venture, inherits 20 acres of semi-arid land in southern California. Always sickly in her youth and prone to nervous breakdowns, she marshals her energies, studies crops that are doing well, and plants walnut trees. When lack of water threatens to ruin her first harvest, she will design and patent a flood control/storage dam system incorporating a series of dams that regulate water flow and ensure safety in case of a break. Engineers as far away as Central America will adopt her ideas, she will pioneer in winter irrigation, her walnut orchard will become the largest in the world, extending for 25 miles, and she will grow citrus fruits, pomegranates, and pampas grass as well.

German-American entrepreneur Julius Schmid, 18, begins making condoms, using the tissue of lamb ceca, which he has been using to make "goldbeater" capping shins for bottles of perfume and other volatile liquids. A cripple who came to New York 2 years ago from Scherndorf, Schmid competes with the relatively low-priced rubber condoms that have been available in America since the 1850s, and he, himself, will switch to the manufacture of "rubbers." But even if washed and reused the condoms are too costly for working-class people, and because their reliability is suspect they must be tested first by inflating them with air or water. Most women find them unacceptable because of their known associations with prostitution and disease prevention (*see* 1723; Youngs, 1920).

1884

The Fabian Society founded in January by young London intellectuals aims to reconstruct society "in accordance with the highest moral responsibilities." Recognizing that deciding what courses to pursue will require "long taking of counsel," they adopt the name Fabian from the 3rd century B.C. Roman statesman Quintus Fabius Maximus, called "Cunctator" (delayer) because of his cautious delaying tactics against Hannibal. Irish-born critic George Bernard Shaw, 27, joins in May, London economist Sidney James Webb, 25, and writer Beatrice Potter, 26, will soon join, Webb will marry Potter, and the Webbs will set up a socialist salon, attracting celebrated thinkers and writers.

Woodstock, Tenn., schoolteacher Ida Bell Wells, 22, boards a Chesapeake & Ohio Railroad train May 4, taking a seat in the first-class "Ladies' Car" for the short trip between Woodstock and Memphis. The U.S. Supreme Court ruled last year that the civil rights acts of 1875 were unconstitutional and that blacks could be effectively banned from public accommodations, including hotels, restaurants, theaters, barbershops, and the like. The C&O conductor orders Wells to vacate the Ladies' Car and take a seat in the second-class smokers' section. She refuses, bracing her feet against the seat in front of her, and when the conductor reaches for her she bites him. He gets help from two train workers, and they manage to push her off the train to a standing ovation from the white passengers. Born into slavery at Holly Springs, Miss., Wells was left an orphan after a yellow fever epidemic in 1878 and has had to raise her seven younger siblings. Humiliated, her dress torn in the struggle, she vows to take the railroad (and segregation) to court. The C&O tries to bribe her to drop the case, but she refuses. The judge, who turns out to be an ex-Union soldier from Minnesota, rules in her favor, awarding her $500 in damages; the *Memphis Daily Appeal* reports the story under the headline "A Darky Damsel Obtains a Verdict for Damages," but the railroad appeals the verdict (*see* 1887).

Gynecologist Karl S. F. Credé at Leipzig, now 65, discovers that a few drops of silver nitrate solution in the eyes of a newborn infant will almost always prevent blindness from gonorrheal infection (ophthalmia neonatorum is the leading cause of preventable blindness among newborns) (*see* Howe Act, 1890).

Japanese midwife Mitsuko Takahashi, 33, applies for admittance to Tokyo's Saiseigakusha Medical School but is rejected. She sits in front of the school's gate for 3 days and 3 nights until its administrators decide to be make the institution coeducational (*see* Tokyo Women's Medical School, 1900).

Spiritualist Helena Blavatsky is summoned to England to face challenges to her authority (*see* 1875). A report labels her a fraud, describing her as "one of the most accomplished, ingenious, and interesting imposters in history," but by the time of her death in 1891 Blavatsky will have 100,000 followers.

Ireland's first women college graduates receive their degrees October 22.

Mississippi State College for Women has its beginnings in the Mississippi Industrial Institute and College for the Education of White Girls of the State of Mississippi (*see* 1982).

New York's Brearley School opens with 50 girls in a brownstone house at 6 East 45th Street under the direction of educator Samuel Brearley, Jr., 33, who studied at Phillips Andover, received his bachelor's degree from Harvard in 1871, attended Oxford's Balliol College for 3 years, and has been persuaded by Mrs. Joseph H. Choate to start a good private school for girls. Brearley, who has borrowed a few thousand dollars from his Harvard classmate Charles Bonaparte, a great-nephew of the emperor, will die late in 1886, but his school will grow to

have about 550 girls (*see* Spence, 1892; Chapin, 1901).

Nonfiction: *Public Relief and Private Charity* by New York State Board of Charities commissioner Josephine Shaw Lowell, 40, advocates a state-administered philanthropy.

Fiction: *Ramona* by Helen Hunt Jackson, whose novel about the treatment of Native Americans has an even greater impact than did her 1881 book (the author slips on the staircase of her home, breaks her leg in several places, and will die next year at age 53); *Carlowie* by Annie Swan; *Ishmael* by Mary Elizabeth Braddon; *In the Tennessee Mountains* (stories) by U.S. writer Mary Noailles Murfree, 34; *Regaldina* by Italian novelist Nera (Anna Radius Zuccari), 38.

Poetry: *Beside the River Sar* (*En las orillas del Sar*) by Rosalía de Castro, who has cancer and will die in July of next year at age 48; *A Minor Poet and Other Verse* by Amy Levy.

Juvenile: *The Armourer's Prentices* by Charlotte M. Yonge.

Painting: *Alexander J. Cassatt and his Son Robert Kelso Cassatt* by Mary Cassatt, whose brother Alexander is a Pennsylvania Railroad executive.

Theater: Lotta Crabtree in *The Old Curiosity Shop* 1/12 at London in an adaptation of his late father's 1841 novel by Charles Dickens the younger. The prince of Wales attends 1/15 to hear Crabtree play the mandolin in her American interpretation of Little Nell, and she continues through April, drawing bigger audiences than Henry Irving. Lotta Crabtree 5/12 in the comic vaudeville *Mam'zelle Nitouche*.

Opera: Therese Malten appears as Leonore in the 1806 Beethoven opera *Fidelio* 11/10 at London's Drury Lane Theatre.

Popular songs: "Rock-a-bye Baby" by U.S. composer I. Canning (Effie I. Crockett), 15, who uses lyrics from *Mother Goose's Melodies* of 1765.

English tennis player Maud Watson, 21, takes the first women's singles title at Wimbledon, where men have competed each year since 1877. U.S. tournament competition is still for men only.

Reaper inventor Cyrus H. McCormick dies at Chicago May 13 at age 75. His widow, Nancy "Nettie" Fowler McCormick, 50, who has served as his private secretary and business counsel, takes over management of the McCormick Harvesting Machine Co., which she will run until it is merged in 1902 with Deering to form International Harvester.

Mrs. Lincoln's Boston Cook Book by Boston Cooking School director Mary Johnson Lincoln (*née* Bailey), 40, contains recipes developed at her school.

1885

The "Bicyclette Moderne" designed by French engineer G. Juzan makes bicycle riding appropriate for women. It has two wheels of equal size with a chain-driven rear wheel employing a drive chain stronger than the one on the first rear-drive "Bicyclette" designed by André Guilmet in 1868 and manufactured by Meyer et Cie. The Rover Co. of Coventry, England, introduces the "safety" bicycle designed by the late J. K. Starley, whose vehicle has wheels of equal size, a departure from the "ordinary," whose front wheel is much larger than its rear wheel. Sewing machine inventor James Kemp Starley died in 1881 at age 51 after having designed the bicycle that has wheels 30 inches in diameter with solid rubber tires (*see* United States, 1889; pneumatic bicycle tire, 1888).

Davenport, Iowa, patient Mary Gartside, 22, undergoes the first successful U.S. appendectomy (by some accounts) January 4. Local physician William West Grant has diagnosed a perforated appendix and is the first U.S. physician deliberately to open the abdomen and sever the appendix from the cecum.

A New York physician estimates that 75 percent of deaths in childbirth are the result of puerperal fever and guesses that they may be 40 per 1,000 in private practice.

Japan gets her first licensed female medical practitioner: Ginko Ogino, 34, has studied at a medical *juku* and passed the tests of the Ministry of Health. Married at age 16, she contracted a sexually transmitted disease from her husband, was treated by male physicians, and vowed to become a physician herself to treat similarly infected female patients, but she has had to use all her powers of persuasion to convince the ministry that it should permit women to take its licensing examination.

St. Hilda's College, opened at Cheltenham, is England's first training college for women. Cheltenham Ladies' College principal Dorothea Beale, 54, who won appointment in 1857 as head teacher of the Clergy Daughters' School in Westmoreland and strongly supports woman suffrage, has founded the teachers' college. She will sponsor St. Hilda's Hall for women teachers at Oxford in 1893.

Bryn Mawr College for Women opens outside Philadelphia. Founded by former Quaker minister Joseph Taylor, the new school employs the only four women PhDs in the United States and along with Radcliffe (*see* 1894) will be the only college to prepare women for the PhD for more than 50 years. British mathematician Charlotte Scott Angas, 27, is invited to teach math at the new institution. Cornell alumna Martha Carey Thomas, 28, who has done postgraduate work at Johns Hopkins, Leipzig, Zurich (where she received her PhD), and the Sorbonne, is professor of English and the first woman faculty member in America to have the title "dean," in which capacity she organizes the undergraduate studies program and the first graduate program at any women's school. She also founds the Bryn Mawr School for Girls at Baltimore (*see* 1895).

Mills College is incorporated as such outside Oakland, Calif. It is an outgrowth of the Young Ladies' Seminary founded at Benicia in 1852, headed beginning in 1854 by Mary Atkins (who warned her charges not to "tarry before a mirror for more than 3 seconds"), and purchased in 1855 by the late Cyrus Mills, who died last year at age 65, and his wife, Susan (*née* Tolman), now 59, who will head the school until her retirement in 1909. The couple went to Ceylon as missionaries in 1848, came home in 1854 after she fell ill, later taught a school for the children of missionaries at Honolulu in the Sandwich Islands, and settled after the Civil War in California, where Mills prospered in real estate speculations. His Christian Female Seminary, opened in August 1871 at a time when the new University of California accepted no women, and by

1873 had 270 students and 20 teachers. Mills will become known in time as the "Vassar of the West."

Tokyo Women Teachers School adopts Western dress as uniforms for students.

Good Housekeeping magazine begins publication in May at Springfield, Mass.

Nonfiction: *Boots and Saddles, or Life with General Custer in Dakota* by Custer's widow, Elizabeth, who will outlive anyone who can refute her defense of her late husband (*see* 1876) (she will live until 1933).

Fiction: *Constance Ring* by Norwegian novelist Amalie Skram (*née* Alver), 38, who has lived at Copenhagen since her marriage; *A Divided House* by Annie Swan.

Poetry: "The Betrothed" by English journalist-poet Rudyard Kipling, 20, whose satirical poem contains the lines "A woman is only a woman, but a good Cigar is a Smoke." Chauvinist Kipling went to India at age 15 and has worked since age 17 on the editorial staff of the *Civil & Military Gazette and Pioneer* at Lahore.

Painting: *Lady at the Tea Table* and *Alexander J. Cassatt* by Mary Cassatt; *After the Battle, Tel el Kebir* by Lady Elizabeth Butler. Sarah Peale dies at Philadelphia at age 84.

Theater: Lotta Crabtree in *Mam'zelle Nitouche* in March at Daly's Theater, New York.

U.S. markswoman Annie Oakley (Phoebe Anne Oakley Mozee Butler), 25, joins the 2-year-old *Buffalo Bill's Wild West Show*. Growing up in Ohio, she shot game and sold it in the Cincinnati market with such success that she was able to pay off the mortgage on the family farm. She married vaudeville marksman Frank E. Butler at age 15 after beating him in a shooting match. Now she amazes *Wild West Show* audiences with her accuracy—splitting a playing card held edge-on at 30 paces, hitting dimes tossed into the air, and so forth. Punched complimentary tickets will be called "Annie Oakleys" after the playing cards that she shoots full of holes before they touch the ground. "The Peerless Lady Wingshot" will remain one of the *Wild West Show*'s star attractions for 17 years (*see* 1922).

English music hall entertainer Marie Lloyd (Matilda Alice Victoria Wood), 15, makes her debut at London's Royal Eagle Music Hall (later the Grecian). She will continue performing until shortly before her death in 1922, touring America, South Africa, and Australia with her off-color songs and skits.

U.S. violinist Maud Powell, 18, makes her European debut with the Berlin Philharmonic Orchestra and goes on to make her U.S. debut with the New York Philharmonic under Theodore Thomas.

Annie Oakley, the "Peerless Lady Wingshot," attracted crowds to Buffalo Bill's Wild West Show. BUFFALO BILL HISTORICAL CENTER, CODY, WYO.

BUFFALO BILL'S WILD WEST.
CONGRESS, ROUGH RIDERS OF THE WORLD.

MISS ANNIE OAKLEY,

Opera: German soprano Lillie Lehmann, 37, makes her Metropolitan Opera debut 11/25 singing the title role in the 1875 Bizet opera *Carmen* and goes on to sing Brünnhilde in the 1870 Wagner opera *Die Walküre* and a variety of other roles.

 Maud Watson takes her second women's singles title at Wimbledon.

 Texas rancher's wife Henrietta Maria Morse King (*née* Chamberlain), 53, and her daughter, Alice Gertrudis King, inherit the 600,000-acre King Ranch upon the death of its co-founder Richard King April 14 at age 59. Mrs. King will be instrumental in adding to her late husband's vast holdings, inducing a railroad to build through her property, solving the problem of water by importing a new kind of well-drilling rig that taps an artesian reservoir, and helping to develop a new breed of cattle—the Santa Gertrudis strain (a cross between a shorthorn and a Brahman). King's lawyer, Robert Justus Kleberg, now 30, will marry Alice next year and assume management of the ranch, which now employs 1,000 hands and grazes 100,000 head (he will also assume a $500,000 debt left by King, who borrowed money to buy more land).

 India has a population of some 265 million, up from 203.4 million in 1850. British physicians in this century have introduced Western medicine into India to reduce the death rate, and moralists have reduced the slaughter of female infants and other customs that once held India's population growth in check, measures that include *suttee*, the custom of burning wives along with their dead husbands on funeral pyres (*see* 1829).

1886

Parliament enacts a Guardianship of Infants bill recognizing a mother's role in child care.

Parliament repeals the Contagious Diseases Act in April following a campaign by Josephine Butler.

Congressional investigations into the Ku Klux Klan produce testimony to the effect that Klansmen have raped black women as a means of intimidation (*see* 1865).

The Noble Order of the Knights of Labor establishes a Woman's Department to "investigate the abuses to which our sex is subjected by unscrupulous employers and agitate the principle to which our order teaches of equal pay for equal work." Irish-American hosiery-mill worker Leonora Barry of Amsterdam, N.Y., is named head of the new department; a widow with three children, her only experience has been running a machine, but in the next 2 years she will travel from Rhode Island to Colorado and from Toronto to Alabama compiling statistics on women's work (*see* 1888).

Japan's Association of Silk Mills establishes a 15-hour day (from 4:30 in the morning until 7:30 at night) for workers, most of them young women, and cuts wages by 10 sen per day (*see* 1872). (Silk thread is Japan's biggest export.) Companies pay parents a given amount when they hire their daughters (who are sometimes only 7 or 8 years of age), and deduct more than half the girl's wages to pay for her food. An additional amount is deducted for the parents, and the girls are left with almost nothing.

More than 100 women workers at the Amamiya Silk-Reeling Works in Kofu, Yamanashi Prefecture, go on strike in June after the owner announces that working hours will be increased from 14 hours to 14½, daily wages for the best workers reduced from 32.3 sen to 22.3 sen, and wage deductions made when a girl leaves her machine to get a drink of water or go to the toilet. It is the first organized strike by female workers in Japan, newspapers publicize it, and it ends June 16 when the owner agrees to reduce working hours and discuss better working conditions. Workers at three other factories follow the lead of the girls at the Amamiya Works (Kofu has 73 factories employing a total of 4,400 girls).

 A model Bloomingdale's department store opens on New York's Third Avenue at 59th Street near a station of the Third Avenue El that opened 8 years ago (*see* 1872). Bloomingdale brothers Lyman, Joseph, and Gustave have built up a thriving enterprise, specializing in whalebone for corsets, yard goods, ladies' notions, and hoopskirts with help from the El, which has contributed to an uptown movement of the city's middle class. By the turn of the century, Bloomingdale's will cover 80 percent of the block from 59th to 60th Street between Third and Lexington avenues and by 1927 will occupy the entire block.

Nonfiction: *Castle Nowhere: Lake Country Sketches* by Constance Fenimore Woolson.

Fiction: *A White Heron and Other Stories* by Sarah Orne Jewett, now 36, who 4 years ago began a relationship (known as a "Boston marriage") with Annie Fields, a widow, that will continue until Jewett's death in 1909 at age 59; *East Angels* and *Rodman the Keeper: Southern Sketches* by Constance Fenimore Woolson; *The Mayor of Casterbridge* by English novelist Thomas Hardy, 46, includes a shocking episode wherein a man sells his wife at a country fair; *Effie Ogilvy* by Margaret Oliphant; *The Romance of Two Worlds* by English novelist Marie Corelli (Mary Mackay), 31, whose sentimental, self-righteous works will be the favorite reading of Queen Victoria and Italy's Queen Margherita; *Conquest of Rome* (*Conquista di Roma*) by Matilde Serao; *Teresa* by Nera.

Juvenile: *Little Lord Fauntleroy* by Frances Hodgson Burnett, whose story of an American boy who inherits a vast estate in England is based on an actual event; *Jo's Boys* by Louisa May Alcott.

Painting: *Girl Arranging Her Hair* and *Child in a Straw Hat* by Mary Cassatt.

Sculpture: *The Kiss* (*Le Baiser*) by French sculptor Auguste Rodin, 45, whose sensuous white marble work represents the illicit Italian lovers Paolo Malatesta and Francesca da Rimini, of the 13th century, whose story was told by Dante Alighieri (Francesca's husband, Giovanni Malatesta, murdered her because she was in love with his brother Paolo).

Theater: Belle Boyd, now 41, in *The Rebel Spy* 2/22 at the People's Theater, Toledo, Ohio, reciting a dramatic narrative of her Civil War activities. Her second husband, John S. Hammond, granted her a divorce in 1884 after she had borne two daughters and a son, she was remarried in January 1885 to an actor 15 years her junior, she has evidently fired upon and wounded a young man who was calling upon her daughter Grace and had refused to marry her. Boyd will give the recitals for more than 14 years until her death in Wisconsin at age 56 of a heart attack in June 1900.

Blanche Bingley, 22, wins in women's singles at Wimbledon.

President Grover Cleveland, a bachelor of 49, is married in the Blue Room of the White House June 2 to his ward, Frances (*née* Frank) Folsom, 21, a week after her return from a trip to Europe with her mother, Emma. Cleveland has for 25 years been a friend of the bride's mother, whose investments he has managed since she lost her husband, and gossip had it that he would marry her, not her daughter. On a presidential visit to New York to review the annual Decoration Day parade, every marching band has struck up the song, "He's Going to Marry Yum-Yum," from Gilbert and Sullivan's latest opera, *The Mikado*.

Johnson's Wax is introduced at Racine, Wis., by local parquet flooring peddler Samuel C. Johnson, who has diversified into paste wax. S. C. Johnson & Son will become the world's leading producer of floor wax.

Avon Products has its beginnings in the California Perfume Co. founded by Brooklyn, N.Y., door-to-door book salesman David H. McConnell, 28, whose firm will become the world's largest cosmetic company. McConnell has been gaining admission to his customers' parlors by offering free vials of perfume, which he has formulated in five different fragrances—Violet, White Rose, Heliotrope, Lily-of-the-Valley, and Hyacinth. He has found more response to the perfume than to *Pilgrim's Progress* or *The American Book of Home Nursing*, so he abandons book selling and concentrates on selling perfume, hiring Mrs. P. F. E. Albee of Winchester, N.H., who has sold books for him, to develop a door-to-door selling strategy. Believing that women are more likely to trust other women, she creates an all-woman sales force and by 1897 will have 12 women selling 18 fragrances (*see* 1898).

A dishwasher patented in December by Illinois politician's wife Josephine Cochrane is crude but effective. Tired of having her servants break her good china after her formal dinners, Cochrane has crafted individual wire compartments for plates, saucers, and cups, fastened them round the circumference of a wheel resting in a large copper boiler, and used a motor to turn the wheel while hot; soapy water squirts up from the bottom of the boiler, bounces off the top, and rains down on the china. Hotels and restaurants will be Cochrane's best customers, since relatively few private houses have the quantities of hot water that her machine requires (*see* 1914).

 The Virginia Supreme Court upholds the conviction of a man who raped his 14-year-old stepdaughter (*Bailey* v. *Commonwealth*). The girl felt herself to be in the power of her attacker's authority, the Court rules, and the fact that she offered no physical resistance does not signify consent (*see* Nebraska, 1889).

 Coca-Cola goes on sale May 8 at Jacob's Pharmacy in Atlanta, where local pharmacist John Styth Pemberton has formulated a headache and hangover remedy whose syrup ingredients include fruit syrup plus dried leaves from the South American coca shrub and an extract of kola nuts from Africa. He has been advertising his Coca-Cola "esteemed Brain Tonic and Intellectual Beverage" since March 29, claiming that it will cure (among other things) "hysteria in the female."

Salada Tea has its beginnings in the Golden Tea-Pot Blend of the Salada Ceylon Tea Co. introduced by Canadian wholesale grocery salesman Peter C. Larkin, who is convinced that Ceylon teas will replace China teas in America as they have in England.

The Japanese Christian Temperance Union is founded at Tokyo by feminist Kajiko Yajima, now 53.

 The Statue of Liberty dedicated October 28 on Bedloe's Island in New York Harbor has been designed by French sculptor Frédéric-Auguste Bartholdi, 52, and presented by the people of France. Joseph Pulitzer's *New York World* has raised $100,000 for a pedestal that Congress had refused to fund for the copper statue "Liberté Eclairant le Monde," which stands more than 151 feet tall. The pedestal will be inscribed in 1903 with words written in 1883 by philanthropist Emma Lazarus, 37: "Give me your tired, your poor,/ Your huddled masses, yearning to breathe free,/ The wretched refuse of your teeming shore./ Send these, the homeless, tempest tossed, to me:/ I lift my lamp beside the golden door."

New York's Statue of Liberty, created in Paris, became a beacon of hope to U.S. immigrants. FROM *LE JOURNAL ILLUSTRÉ* FOR MAY 28, 1876

1887

 The Tennessee Supreme Court rules in April that Ida Wells's intent in 1884 was to harrass, not to obtain a comfortable seat for the short ride between Woodstock and Memphis, thus reversing the lower court's decision against the C&O Railroad (*see* 1892).

Lancashire women miners march to London May 17 demanding the right to work.

A "Protest" dated September 17 and presented to President Cleveland on the centennial of the Constitution by feminist writer Lillie Devereux Blake (*née* Olmsted), now 54, is less militant in its language than the NWSA's "Declaration" of 1876 but says that its signers "cannot allow the occasion to pass without reminding you that one-half the people who obey the laws of the United States are unjustly denied all place or part in the body politic. . . . This denial of our chartered rights, this injustice of which we complain, is inflicted in defiance of the provisions of the Constitution you profess to honor. . . ." Signers include, in addition to Blake, Susan B. Anthony, Matilda Joslyn Gage, Rachel G. Foster, and Mary Wright Sewall.

The Perkins Institution founded in 1829 receives a request from telephone pioneer Alexander Graham Bell to examine 6-year-old Helen Adams Keller, who lost her sight and hearing at 19 months of age. The Institution had a similar patient beginning in 1836, when 7-year-old Laura Dewey Bridgman, a New Hampshire farmer's daughter, was brought in, having lost her sight, hearing, and sense of smell at age 2 in a scarlet fever epidemic that killed her two older sisters. Bridgman, now 58, is still at the Institute, which dispatches Anne Mansfield Sullivan, 20, to the Keller home. She starts work with young Helen March 2 and quickly teaches her to feel objects and associate them with words spelled out by finger signals on the palm of her hand; Helen soon can feel raised words on cardboard and make her own sentences by arranging words in a frame (see 1904).

Sophie Newcomb (The H. Sophie Newcomb Memorial College for Women) opens in September at New Orleans as an adjunct to Tulane University. Philanthropist Josephine LeMounier Newcomb, 70, whose late husband, Warren, a grocery wholesaler, died in 1866, gave Tulane $100,000 last year to found a women's college to be named for her late daughter, Harriott Sophie, who died of diphtheria at age 15 in 1870. She will give Tulane another $3.5 million for the school.

The A. B. Dick Diaphragm Mimeograph goes on sale March 17. Thomas Edison has licensed Chicago lumberman Albert Blake Dick, 31, to use his stencil invention, Dick has constructed a flat-bed duplicator suitable for office use, employing a strong stencil fabric made from a species of hazel bush that grows only on certain Japanese islands, and his machine will soon be used by women in offices worldwide (see 1875; Xerox, 1937).

Nonfiction: *Ancient Legends of Ireland* by London author–salon hostess Lady Jane Francesca Wilde, 61, whose poetry and prose has for years been published at Dublin (under the name "Speranza") and whose son Oscar has gained fame as a wit.

Fiction: *Sjur Gabriel* and *Two Friends* (*To venner*) by Amalie Skram are the first two of seven novels in her series *The People of Hellemyr* (*Hellemyrsfolket*), which will continue until 1898; *Child of the Parish* (*Das Gemeindekind*) by Marie von Ebner-Eschenbach; *Ricardo Joanna* by Matilda Serao; *Thelma* by Marie Corelli; *The Gates of Eden* by Annie Swan.

Juvenile: *The Birds' Christmas Carol* by U.S. writer Kate Douglas Wiggin (*née* Smith), 31.

Painting: *Relay Hunting* (oil on canvas) by Rosa Bonheur; *A Little Girl* by French painter Cecila Beaux, 32.

Theater: Lotta Crabtree in *Pawn Ticket 210* by David Belasco and Clay Green in September at McVicker's Theater, Chicago; Sarah Bernhardt in Victorien Sardou's *La Tosca* 11/24 at the Théâtre de la Porte-Saint-Martin, Paris.

Opera: Australian soprano Nellie Melba (Helen Mitchell), 26, makes her operatic debut at the Brussels Opera singing the role of Gilda in the 1851 Verdi opera *Rigoletto*.

Charlotte "Lottie" Dod, 15, wins in women's singles at Wimbledon; Ellen F. Hansel wins the first women's singles title at Newport.

The first U.S. social register is published by New York golf promoter Louis Keller, 30, the son of a patent lawyer who owns a farm at Springfield, N.J., on which he has founded the Baltusero Golf Club. Keller has earlier helped start the scandal sheet *Town Topics*. His 100-page book sells for $1.75, contains roughly 3,600 names based largely on telephone listings which it prints in larger type than that used in the phone company directory, draws on the membership list of the Calumet Club at 29th Street and Fifth Avenue, and will be followed by social registers published in most major U.S. cities, with preference given to white, non-Jewish, non-divorced residents considered respectable by the arbiters who compile the books.

Ball-Mason jars are introduced by Ball Brothers Glass Manufacturing Co. of Muncie, Ind. (*see* Mason, 1855). William Charles Ball, 35, and his brothers Lucius Lorenzo, Frank C., Edmund Burke, and George Alexander began making tin oilcans at Buffalo, N.Y., 10 years ago, switched to glass oil and fruit jars in 1884, and have moved to Muncie, where natural gas has been discovered and which has offered free gas and a generous land site.

Arthur Allbutt, an English physician at Leeds, is struck off Britain's Medical Register for publishing *The Wives' Handbook*, a pamphlet that has been heavily subsidized by the new and growing contraceptive industry.

1888

The Knights of Labor receives a report from investigator Leonora Barry showing that women workers typically earn $2.50 to $3 for an 84-hour week (*see* 1886). She describes a Paterson, N.J., linen mill in which "women stood on a stone floor with water from a revolving cylinder flying constantly against the breast. They had in the coldest weather to go home with underclothing dripping because they were allowed neither space nor a few moments of time in which to change their clothing. Men's pants that retail at prices from $1 to $7 per pair are taken by the contractor at 15¢ per pair. Operatives are then employed and huddled together in a close, stifling backroom, where the machine operatives furnish their own machines and, in most cases, thread, and do all the machine work on pants . . . for 5¢ a pair; 6 pairs is an average day's work."

Leonora Barry (above) addresses the Knights of Labor with a speech urging that "more consideration be given, and more thorough educational measures be adopted, on behalf of the working women of the land, the majority of whom are entirely ignorant of the economic and industrial question which is to them of vital importance." A Catholic priest has denounced her as a "lady tramp" and called the Knights "a vulgar, immoral society" for encouraging women to act as organizers, but Barry fiercely defends her right as "an Irishwoman, a Catholic, and an honest woman" to serve the cause of her fellow workers.

Terence V. Powderly, General Master Workman of the Knights (above), says, "The working man has struggled down through the centuries for a recognition of his toil, and within the last 10 years has received more of recognition than ever before. But, while securing that recognition for himself he has selfishly ignored the woman worker, and she, through the same necessities which compelled him to part with his labor at a sacrifice, is now obliged to do the same by hers. The only logical result of that is it eventually reduces the wages of all, for the work of the future will be done by far more delicate hands than the past ever saw manipulating the implements of labor. The rights of the sexes are coequal. Their privileges should be the same." But the Knights of Labor is in decline, its Woman's Department will be disbanded in 1890, and the rising American Federation of Labor is far less concerned with women workers.

Women workers at Britain's Bryant and May match factory go on strike July 17 demanding higher pay and better working conditions.

The first patent for a pneumatic bicycle tire is awarded October 31 to Scottish veterinary surgeon John Boyd Dunlop, 47, at Belfast, Ireland. Advised by a physician to have his sickly son ride a tricycle, Dunlop has devised the tires to cushion the boy's ride on Belfast's cobblestone streets, using rubber sheeting and strips of linen from an old dress of his wife's. Pneumatic tires will make bicycle riding more attractive to women (*see* 1885).

Matilde Serao attacks the 20-year-old publication *La Donna* for holding up the "foreign" woman as a model for Italy's women at a time when the nation is at war with Libya, but Gualberta Beccari, Anna Maria Mozzoni, and others seek to emulate the women's journals, women's clubs, women's associations, and women participation in charity, education, and reform that they see in France, Britain, and America while Italy remains backward with regard to literacy.

U.S. inventor John Robert Gregg introduces a new shorthand system he calls "Light Line Phonography." It will largely replace the Pitman system in America (*see* 1837).

Nonfiction: *Some Successful Women* by U.S. writer Sarah Knowles Bolton, 47; *Books and Men* by U.S. essayist Agnes Repplier, 33, whose essay "Children, Past and Present" appeared 2 years ago in the *Atlantic Monthly* with humorous comments on how certain well-known figures were disciplined in their childhood.

Fiction: *Lucie* by Amalie Skram. *The Romance of a Shop* and *Reuben Sachs* (her only Jewish novel) by Amy Levy. *Robert Elsemere* by English novelist–

social worker Mrs. Humphry Ward (*née* Mary Augusta Arnold), 37, whose spiritual romance will inspire philanthropist Passmore Edwards in 1897 to found a settlement for the poor in London's Tavistock Square. *The Book of the Thousand Nights and a Night* by English Orientalist Richard Burton, 67, who in 1853 visited Mecca disguised as a Pathan; he has translated in its entirety the Arabian Nights stories known in the West until now only through expurgated stories such as "Aladdin and the Lamp." Sources of the stories are largely Persian, not Arabic, and are presented within the framework of a situation involving the 10th-century Persian monarch Shahriyar and his wife, Shahrazad (Scheherazade). Having had faithless wives in the past, Shahriyar has been taking a new one each night and ordering her put to death in the morning, but Scheherazade ends this practice by keeping the monarch fascinated with stories, many of them bawdy. Burton writes about the circumcision of Arab women in his notes: "After the operator has cut out the clitoris and the lips of the labia . . . she then sews up the parts with a pack needle and a thread of sheepskin, while a tin tube is inserted for the passage of urine. Before marriage the bridegroom trains himself for a month on beef, honey, and milk; for if he can open the bride with his natural weapon he is a mighty sworder. If he fails, he tries penetration with his fingers, and by way of last resort, whips out his knife and cuts the parts open. The suffering of the bride must be severe." Burton's 16-volume work enjoys great success, but after his death in 1890 his wife, Isabel, will burn the manuscript containing his full translation of *The Perfumed Garden of Cheikh Nezaoui: A Manual of Arabian Erotology. The Hidden Hand* by Washington, D.C., mystery writer E.D.E.N. (Emma Dorothy Eliza Nevitte) Southworth, 69.

Theater: English actress Violet Augusta Mary Vanbrugh, 21, and her sister Irene, 16, make their debuts at Margate as Ophelia and Phoebe, respectively, in the 1600 Shakespeare comedy *As You Like It*. Both women, but most especially Irene, will have long and illustrious acting careers.

Opera: Shanghai-born U.S. soprano Emma Hayden Eames, 22, makes her debut 3/13 at the Paris Opéra singing the role of Juliette in the 1867 Gounod opera *Roméo et Juliette*; Adelina Patti sings the same role 10/28 at the Paris Opéra with Gounod himself conducting (she has sung it at Madrid, Lisbon, Buenos Aires, and Montivideo earlier in the year, receiving her usual fee of £1,000 per performance).

The Fadette Ladies' Orchestra of Boston founded by Caroline B. Nichols, 22, will be the first professional all-woman orchestra to gain national recognition. It begins with six players performing at house parties in town and at summer resorts in Maine (*see* 1895).

Lottie Dod wins in women's singles at Wimbledon, Bertha Townsend, 19, in U.S. women's singles.

There are only about four hundred people in New York Society," says social arbiter (and climber) Ward McAllister, 60, in a *New York Tribune* interview (*see* social register, 1887). McAllister failed in a San Francisco law practice and traveled east to Newport, R.I., at age 22 to marry the heiress to a steamboat fortune. In 1872 he organized the Patriarchs, a group comprised of the heads of New York's oldest families on whose approval social aspirants depend, and he has become social adviser to Caroline Astor (*née* Schermerhorn), 58, who at age 22 married real estate heir William Backhouse Astor and whose Fifth Avenue mansion has a ballroom that can accommodate 400 people (but, please, no clergymen, physicians, Jews, blacks, musicians, or actors).

The National Council of Women is founded.

Mum antiperspirant—an oily cream containing zinc—is introduced in U.S. pharmacies, but the product does not dry readily and most women use perfume or cologne to mask armpit odors (*see* 1902).

Jack the Ripper makes headlines. London East End streetwalkers Mary Ann Nicholls, Annie Chapman, Elizabeth Stride, and their neighbors Catherine Eddowes and Mary Kelly die at the hands of one or more killers who feed the women poisoned grapes and then disembowel them. Scotland Yard can find no solution to the mystery, and it will later be alleged that agents of Queen Victoria murdered the women to hush up a scandal involving the queen's grandson Albert, duke of Clarence.

Austria's Archduke Rudolph, 31, is found dead January 30 with his mistress Baroness Marie Vetsera, 17, at Rudolph's hunting lodge Mayerling outside Vienna. The beautiful Marie has been shot by the crown prince, who has then taken his own life, leaving the Hapsburg emperor Franz Josef without an heir.

The London County Council gets its first woman alderman as Emma Cons takes her seat.

Irish M.P. Capt. William O'Shea files for divorce on grounds of adultery December 24 and cites as corespondent Charles Stewart Parnell, who has helped O'Shea advance his political career (*see* 1882). O'Shea's wife, Katherine, has been living more or less openly with Parnell for years and has evidently borne two children by him (*see* 1890).

A new Japanese Constitution adopted in February makes it impossible for a woman to become empress as in centuries past and denies women the right to participate in politics.

Chicago's Hull-House opens in the South Halsted Street slums under the direction of social worker Jane Addams, 29, with financial help from her Rockford College classmate Ellen Gates Starr, 30. Having visited London's Toynbee Hall, she rents the rundown Charles Hull mansion in the center of the city's ghetto and opens a settlement house in September that will help the poor immigrants of the neighborhood with problems such as sweatshops, child labor, truancy, juvenile delinquency, industrial safety, and political corruption. Within a year, Hull-House volunteers and a small resident staff will have helped more than 50,000 people with education, recreation, child care, and other services.

Bertha Palmer lends her support to Hull-House (above) and will soon be seen—fur coat and all—performing volunteer duties there amid poor immigrants (*see* Chicago Fire, 1871). Mrs. Palmer, whose husband, Potter, has converted North Shore swamplands into roads and houses and built a magnificent Norman-style Gold Coast mansion for his family on Lake Shore Drive, will also be instrumental in organizing the city's millinery workers and take an active role in the Women's Trade Union League (*see* 1893).

U.S. state legislatures begin to tighten divorce laws to discourage marital separation following revelations that the United States has the world's highest divorce rate. From now until 1906, grounds for divorce will be reduced from more than 400 to fewer than 20; only three states will continue to permit courts to grant divorces on any grounds they see fit; North Carolina will prohibit divorce altogether; New York will grant divorces only for reasons of adultery; New Jersey only for adultery or desertion.

Baltimore bookkeeper Mary Richmond, 28, takes a $50-per-month job on a trial basis as a fund raiser for the local Charity Organization Society, a community clearinghouse. To see how the money is being spent, she visits the poor and begins to develop the casework method of determining applicants' individual needs. Richmond will help save from bankruptcy a secret fraternal society for blacks that provides life and burial insurance for former slaves at a time when insurance companies will not accept such people as policyholders. She will set objective standards for giving to the poor that will make social work a paid profession.

 First Lady Caroline Harrison (*née* Scott), 56, has electricity installed in the White House.

I. M. Singer Co. introduces the first electric sewing machines, based on a patent issued January 25, 1887, for a motor developed by Philip Diehl, head of Singer's experimental department at Elizabethport, N.J. The company sells a million machines (many of them to sweatshop operators), up from 539,000 in 1880 (*see* 1903).

 The "safety" bicycle patented in 1885 is introduced in the United States. Within 4 years, more than a million Americans, many of them women, will be riding the new bikes.

Nellie Bly leaves Hoboken, N.J., November 14 in an attempt to outdo the hero of the 1873 Jules Verne novel *Le Tour du Monde en Quatre-Vingt Jours*. Reporter Elizabeth "Nellie Bly" Cochrane, 22, of the *New York World* has earlier feigned madness in a successful attempt to gain admission for 10 days to New York's insane asylum on Blackwell's Island. She has persuaded her editor to give her a

The "safety" bicycle made cycling popular with women as well as men, once they got the hang of it.

bold new assignment and leaves at just after 9:40 in the morning to break the fictional record of Phileas Fogg (*see* 1890).

The University of Stockholm makes mathematician Sofia Kovalevskaia a tenured professor, and Russia's Imperial Academy of Sciences changes its rules against women to permit her election to membership (*see* 1883; Fiction, 1895).

Johns Hopkins surgeon William Stewart Halsted, 38, performs his first radical mastectomy (*see* 1867). A stickler for hygiene who pioneered the practice of local anesthesia 7 years ago by injecting a patient with cocaine, Halsted sends his shirts to Paris to be laundered. His procedure will in some cases involve removal of several ribs as well as the breast, chest muscles, and lymph nodes; it will be the universally accepted treatment for breast cancer in America for nearly a century, although it will be discredited in Europe by the 1930s and replaced by a modified operation in which the chest muscles are left intact (*see* 1971).

Pope Leo XIII sends Mother Cabrini to the United States to work with poor Italian immigrants (*see* 1880). She opens a school, returns to Italy to oversee her convents, but will return next year to America and found a New Orleans convent, school, and orphanage. She will also start a hospital in New York and establish additional convents in Denver,

Seattle, Los Angeles, Central America, South America, and Europe (*see* 1946).

Barnard College opens near New York's Columbia University after 3 years of effort by Annie Nathan Meyer, 24, who has charmed and cajoled Columbia trustees and alumni. Columbia has had a Collegiate Course for Women in which members of the opposite sex could study independently for the same examinations as men; Meyer passed the entrance exam for the Collegiate Course in 1885, and when her father discovered what she had done he warned her that she would never marry, since "men hate intelligent wives." The new woman's college is named for Columbia's late president Frederick August Porter Barnard, who died 6 months ago at age 80 after a long career in which he favored extending the university's educational opportunities to women. Its first dean is Bryn Mawr graduate Emily James Putnam, 24, a classics scholar who has done postgraduate work at Girton College, Cambridge.

Newnham College, Cambridge, opens a third hall June 9 (*see* 1880).

Holloway College opens in October to prepare women students for the London degree and the Oxford examinations.

Nonfiction: *Some Eminent Women of Our Time* by Millicent Garrett Fawcett.

Fiction: *An Irish Cousin* by Irish novelist Edith (Anna Oenone) Somerville, 31, and her cousin Violet Florence Martin, 27, who writes under the name Martin Ross (their books will be published under the names Somerville and Ross); *Miss Meredith* by Amy Levy; *Sentry on the Alert* (*All' erta sentinella*) by Matilda Serao; *L'Indomanai* by Nera; *Along the Niemnem* (*Nad Niemnem*) by Elja Orzeszkowa, whose stories of peasant life have changed her public image, giving people cause to call her "the good lady of Grodno" (*see* 1871); *Lady Car* by Margaret Oliphant.

Poetry: *A London Plane-Tree and Other Verse* by Amy Levy, who takes her own life at London September 10 at age 27, a week after the volume is published.

Painting: *The Circus* by Suzanne Valadon; *Col. William F. "Buffalo Bill" Cody* by Rosa Bonheur, who portrays the showman riding a gray horse. He has come to Paris with bronco riders and Indians for the Paris Exposition, she has invited him to her estate at By to inspect her own horses, and he has given her two broncos; *Little Angèle* by Boston poet-painter Lilla Perry (*née* Cabot), 41.

Theater: Siri von Essen (the playwright's wife) plays the title role in August Strindberg's *Miss Julie* (*Frøken Julie*) 3/14 at Copenhagen's Studentersamfundet. The play about a sexual liaison between a young woman of good birth and her father's valet (Strindberg is himself a housemaid's son) creates a scandal. *Helene* by U.S. novelist-playwright Martha Morton, 24, 10/29 at New York's Union Square Theatre (the drama ran for just one performance last year but has been revived by actress Clara Morris and will run for 2 years, earning Morton $50,000).

Opera: Emma Juch establishes the Emma Juch Opera Company, which will tour for several years, giving performances in Havana and in Mexico as well as in many U.S. cities.

The Chicago Auditorium opens December 9 with Adelina Patti, now 46, singing "Home, Sweet Home" to an audience that includes President Harrison. The new auditorium seats 3,500.

Blanche Bingley Hillyard wins in women's singles at Wimbledon, Bertha Townsend in U.S. women's singles.

Former Texas outlaw Belle Starr (*née* Myra Belle Shirley) is shot dead February 3 in Oklahoma Territory by person or persons unknown 2 days short of her 41st birthday.

The Nebraska Supreme Court reverses a rapist's conviction on grounds that "voluntary submission by the woman, while she has power to resist, no matter how reluctantly yielded, removes from the act an essential element of the crime of rape . . . if the carnal knowledge was with the consent of the woman, no matter how tardily given, or how much force had theretofore been employed, it is no rape" (*see* Virginia, 1886; Missouri, 1892).

English gardener Gertrude Jekyll, 46, publishes an article deploring the "bedding out" which has started in large gardens and almost submerged "the beauties of the many little flowering cottage plots of our English waysides." In the next few decades she will help to establish the herbaceous border throughout the country; her own garden at Munstead Heath, Surrey, will attract visitors for more than a century.

British entomologist Eleanor A. Ormerod, now 61, receives an urgent request from the U.S. Department of Agriculture's chief entomologist for help in dealing with the Mediterranean caterpillar, which threatens worldwide destruction of stored flour inventories. She advises him to have the managers of flour mills turn on the steam and scald the critters.

1890

Charles Stewart Parnell denies Capt. William O'Shea's charges of adultery (*see* 1889). Katherine O'Shea files charges of neglect and cruelty against her husband in June, claiming that he had had an affair with her sister Anna and that he encouraged her to have an affair with Parnell. Katherine's beloved Aunt Ben (Anna Maria Wood) died last year at age 95, leaving her considerable estate to her favorite niece, who has been trying to avoid a scandal that might jeopardize her inheritance; Katherine's siblings are contesting the will. The case of *O'Shea* v. *O'Shea and Parnell* goes to trial November 15, it is grist for the mills of music hall comedians and cartoonists as well as newspaper reporters worldwide, a special jury finds in the plaintiff's favor, Parnell loses his leadership of the Irish Nationalist party December 2, and Katie O'Shea comes under attack as "the Political Princess— O'Shea Who Must Be Obeyed," "the were-wolf woman of Irish politics," and the evil genius who has set back the cause of Irish home rule. Newspapers publish letters referring to Mrs. O'Shea as "the Uncrowned Queen of Ireland," and one woman writes, "It seems horrible that the weakness of a woman old enough to take care of herself, and belonging to a class that should be refined and worthy of being called 'the elite,' should be able to ruin a career. . . . It is such women as she who lead men into the belief that we are weak, frail dolls, virtuous only for fear or lack of opportunity . . ." (*see* 1891).

French anarchist Louise Michel, now 60, hears of a plot to commit her to an insane asylum and takes refuge in England, where she will continue until her death in 1905 to be a symbol of the radical struggle (*see* 1871).

Willem III of the Netherlands dies November 23 at age 73 after a 34-year reign. He is succeeded by his daughter Helena Pauline Maria of Orange-Nassau, 10, whose mother, Emma, will rule as regent until 1898 but who will herself reign through two major wars until 1948 as Wilhelmina I.

The Consumers League of New York, first organization of its kind, is founded by former State Board of Charities commissioner Josephine Shaw Lowell, now 46, and Maud Nathan, 27, sister of reformer Annie Nathan, who was largely responsible for the founding of Barnard College last year (*see* National Consumers League, 1900).

Nellie Bly boards the S.S. *Oceanic* at Yokohama January 7 and sails for San Francisco after having crossed the Atlantic, Europe, and Asia in her well-publicized attempt to girdle the earth in less than 80 days (*see* 1889). The *New York World* reporter is advised at San Francisco that the purser has left the ship's bill of health at Yokohama and that nobody may leave the ship for 2 weeks, she threatens to jump overboard and swim, she is put onto a tug and taken ashore, her train across the continent detours to avoid blizzards and is almost derailed when it hits a handcar, but she pulls into Jersey City at 3:41 in the afternoon of January 25 after a journey of 72 days, 6 hours, 11 minutes, 14 seconds.

The Howe Act adopted by the New York State legislature requires physicians to apply prophylactic drops to the eyes of newborn infants in order to combat infections caused by gonorrheal infections (*see* Credé, 1884; Barnes, 1902).

The National Florence Crittenden Missions of the United States and Abroad is founded by New York patent medicine dealer Charles N. Crittenden with help from Frances Willard of the Women's Christian Temperance Union.

The University of Chicago is founded with women admitted on the same basis as men. Former Wellesley president Alice Freeman Palmer, who raised that college's academic standing in her 6-year

Elizabeth Cochrane outdid Jules Verne's fictional Phileas Fogg by girdling the earth in little more than 72 days.

tenure before retiring to marry Harvard philosophy professor George Herbert Palmer, serves as Chicago's dean of women and assistant professor of history. She has accepted the positions on condition that Chicago also hire her friend Marion Talbot as assistant professor of sociology and assistant dean (Talbot founded the Association of Collegiate Alumnae following her graduation from Boston University in 1881).

Only 3 percent of Americans age 18 to 21 attend college. The figure will rise to 8 percent by 1930, but male students will still far outnumber females.

Rosemary Hall opens on a family estate of that name at Wallingford, Conn., under the direction of English scholar Caroline Ruutz-Rees, 25, who has been hired as headmistress by founder Mary Choate (*née* Atwater). She and her husband, Judge William G. Choate, will start the Choate School for boys in 1896; Ruutz-Rees will move the boarding school for girls to Greenwich in 1900; it will return to Wallingford in 1971, and by 1993 Choate-Rosemary Hall will have 1,029 students, 516 of them girls.

Cambridge undergraduate Philippa Fawcett out-scores her male classmates. St. Margaret's College opens at Glasgow, Scotland. Wales has three women's colleges—at Aberystwyth, Bangor, and Cardiff—and Ireland has Alexander College for Women.

Britain gets her first woman newspaper correspondent as Flora Shaw Lugard goes to work for the *Times* of London.

Japan gets her first women telephone operators. Ministry of Communication officials put their daughters to work as operators when advertisements fail to produce female applicants, and by next year all operators will be women. As in Western countries, Japanese switchboards will provide a major source of employment for women.

Fiction: *Tales of Florence* (*Florence Novellen*) by German poet–story writer Isolde Kurz, 37; *S. G. Myre* by Amalie Skram.

Poetry: *Poems by Emily Dickinson* is published at the urging of Lavinia Dickinson, whose late sister Emily Elizabeth died at her native Amherst, Mass., 4 years ago at age 55 without ever having had any of her work appear under her own name. Edited by Amherst resident Mabel Loomis Todd, 33, the book receives a cool reception from critics but has a good enough public response to warrant publication of more Emily Dickinson poems. New volumes will appear in 1891 and 1896, and by 1945 nearly all of her many hundreds of poems will have been published and her reputation as a major U.S. poet will be secure: "Because I could not stop for Death,/ He kindly stopped for me;/ The carriage held but just ourselves/ And Immortality."

Juvenile: *Heart of Gold* by English author L. T. Meade (Elizabeth Thomasina Smith [*née* Meade]), 36; *Timothy's Quest* by Kate Douglas Wiggin.

Painting: *Mother and Child* (Mme. de Fleury and her daughter) by Mary Cassatt.

The "Gibson Girl" created by New York illustrator Charles Dana Gibson, 22, makes her first appearance in the humor weekly *Life*, which has been buying Gibson drawings since 1886. Millions will share Gibson's conception of the ideal American girl, which reflects the looks of Southern belle Irene

The "Gibson girl" epitomized feminine pulchritude in the 1890s and early twentieth century.

Langhorne, now 17 and at finishing school in New York. She will marry Gibson in 1895.

Opera: Italian soprano Gemma (Matilda) Bellincioni, 25, creates the role of Santuzza in the new Pietro Mascagni opera *Cavalleria Rusticana* 5/17 at Rome's Teatro Constanzi. Bellincioni's popularity will be eclipsed by that of Emma Calvé (*see* 1893).

Helen Bertha Grace "Lena" Rice, 24 (Ireland), wins in women's singles at Wimbledon, Ellen C. Roosevelt in U.S. women's singles.

The Colonial Dames of America is founded May 23 by women who can show that their ancestors came to America before 1776 (*see* National Society, 1893).

The Daughters of the American Revolution (DAR) is organized at Washington, D.C., by four women who include two government clerks. The Sons of the American Revolution, founded last year, has voted not to admit women's auxiliaries, so Mary Smith Lockwood has written a letter to the *Washington Post* in July announcing a meeting for the formation of a women's group. Lockwood meets in August with Eugenia Washington and Ellen Hardin Walworth at Walworth's house, they make Walworth secretary-general, and they name First

Lady Caroline Lavinia Harrison (*née* Scott) president of the group, whose membership is based on heredity (*see* 1939).

The National Council of Women's Clubs is founded.

Populist party leader Mary Elizabeth Cylens Lease, 36, tells Kansas farmers they should "raise less corn and more hell." Having begun speaking in behalf of Irish home rule in 1885, she now makes 161 speeches as she stumps the state. Told by "the Kansas Python" that Kansas suffers "from two great robbers, the Santa Fe Railroad and the loan companies," the farmers vote against the Republicans and elect independent-party candidates to Congress.

The U.S. Women's Pure Food Vaccum Preserving Co. founded by Amanda Jones uses her methods to preserve rice, tapioca pudding, and a line of luncheon meats (*see* 1872). Officers, employees, and stockholders are all women, and although Jones, now 55, will be forced out of management in 1893 and will sell her interests to a meatpacking company, the concern she starts will continue in business until 1923.

Thomas Lipton enters the tea business to assure supplies of tea at low cost for his 300 grocery shops (*see* 1879). He offers "The Finest the World Can Produce" at 1 shilling 7 pence per pound when the going rate is roughly a shilling higher.

Cambridge University scientist (and antifeminist) Walter Heape carries out the first succesful embryo transplant in rabbits, presaging artificial human reproduction.

1891

Hawaii's king David Kalakahua dies January 20 at age 54 after a 16-year reign and is succeeded by his sister, 52, who will reign until 1893 as Queen Lydia Liliuokalani. The white elite which owns 80 percent of arable lands in the islands has united in the Hawaiian League to oppose Kalakahua, who has favored the interests of sugar magnate Claus Spreckels, and the sugar planters form an Annexation Club in a plot to overthrow the queen, who tries to restore the rights of the Hawaiian people (*see* abdication, 1893).

Katherine O'Shea, now 46, is married June 25 to Charles Stewart Parnell, but Parnell, rheumatic and exhausted after addressing crowds bareheaded in pouring rain, dies at Brighton October 6 at age 45. His widow will receive half her aunt's estate (minus court costs) next year, with some of it going to her ex-husband, a lawyer will abscond with much of the fortune in 1906, and "Kitty" O'Shea Parnell will live to age 76, dying in February 1921.

The Australian Woman Suffrage League is founded at Sydney by local feminist Rose Scott, 44, who will lobby not only for enfranchisement but also for raising the age of consent, shortening hours of shop assistants, and similar causes. She will not marry, saying, "Life is too short to spend on the admiration of one man."

Britain has 1.25 million women in "service" jobs; domestic servants are employed even in middle-class households.

Physician Anna Wessel Williams, 27, obtains her M.D. from the Women's Medical College of New York and accepts a position in the newly created diagnostic laboratory of the city's Health Department, the first such lab in America. New York is in the grip of a diphtheria epidemic (the disease is called "diphtheria"—from the Greek word for leather—because of the tough, yellowish-gray membrane formed in the throats of victims; it causes inflammation of the heart and nervous system and is a leading killer of children). An antitoxin has been developed but is too weak to be effective and impossible to manufacture in the massive quantities needed (*see* 1894).

Pembroke College is established as the women's annex of Brown University, the Rhode Island College that moved to Providence in 1770 after 16 years at Warren and took the name Brown in 1804.

Nonfiction: *Common Sense in the Household: A Manual of Practical Housewifery* by U.S. writer Marion Harland (Mary Virginia Terhune [*née* Hawes]), 60, becomes a best-seller that will be translated into French, German, and Arabic; *Ancient Cures* by Lady Jane Francesca Wilde.

Fiction: *The Story of Gösta Berling* (*Gösta Berlings saga*) by Swedish novelist Selma (Ottiliana Lovisa) Lagerlöf, 32; *Frue Inés* by Amalie Skram; *The Country of Cocaigne* (*Il paese di Cuccagna*) by

Matilde Serao; *Your Son, My Lord* by U.S. novelist Ellen Hamilton Gardener, 38; *A New England Nun and Other Stories* by U.S. author Mary Eleanor Wilkins Freeman, 39; *The Railway Man and His Children* by Margaret Oliphant; *Tess of the d'Urbervilles* by Thomas Hardy portrays human tragedies rooted in the conflict between the changing society of industrial England and the rural ways of an earlier age.

Juvenile: *A Sweet Girl Graduate* by L. T. Meade.

 Painting: *The Bath*, *The Fitting*, *The Letter*, *The Parrot*, and *La Toilette* by Mary Cassatt.

Sculpture: *Memorial to Mrs. Henry Adams* by U.S. sculptor Augustus Saint-Gaudens for Washington's Rock Creek Park. Local historian Henry Brooks Adams has commissioned the work in memory of his wife, Clover (*née* Marian Hooper), to whom he was married in June 1872 and who killed herself in December 1885 at age 42 by swallowing potassium cyanide, which she used in her photographic darkroom. The sculpture is an approximation of Kwannon, the Buddhist goddess of compassion, which Adams has seen on a visit to the Japanese Imperial Shrine at Nikko.

 Theater: *Hedda Gabler* by Henrik Ibsen 2/26 at Oslo's Christiania Theater.

Sarah Bernhardt embarks on a world tour in which she will perform the roles of Phaedra, Marguerite Gautier (in *La Dame aux Camélias*), Fedora, Tosca, and Cleopatra for audiences in North and South America and Australia (*see* 1872).

 Stage musicals: *Cinder-Ellen Up-too-late* 12/24 at London's Gaiety Theatre, with Lottie Collins in the last successful presentation of burlesque, the light musical entertainment that has been popular for half a century but that will be replaced by musical comedy (U.S. forms of burlesque will make the term disreputable with nudity and vulgarity), music and lyrics by Canadian-American songwriter-minstrel show manager Henry J. Sayers, 38, songs that include "Ta-ra-ra-boom-der-ay: did you see my wife today? No, I saw her yesterday: ta-ra-ra-boom-der-ay," 236 perfs.

U.S. circus entertainer Loie (Marie Louise) Fuller, 29, becomes a stage dancer and creates a sensation with an exotic solo skirt dance in which she wears

yards of swirling silk and uses multidirectional colored lights to illuminate them (*see* 1892).

Opera: Emma Eames makes her London debut at Covent Garden 4/7 and her Metropolitan Opera debut 12/14 singing the role of Marguerite in the 1859 Gounod opera *Faust*; Lillian Nordica, now 34, makes her Metropolitan Opera debut singing the role of Leonora in the 1853 Verdi opera *Il Trovatore* (*see* 1879).

 Lottie Dod wins in women's singles at Wimbledon, Mabel E. Cahill in U.S. women's singles.

"No human law can abolish natural and inherent rights of marriage," says Pope Leo XIII in *Rerum novarum*, "or limit in any way its chief and principal purpose . . . which is to increase and multiply."

1892

Queen Victoria's unsavory grandson Prince Eddy (Albert Victor, duke of Clarence) dies of pneumonia January 14 at age 28—less than 6 weeks after having become affianced to Princess May (Mary of Teck), 26, who will marry the prince's younger brother George next year.

The Austrian Society of Friends of Peace founded last year by writer-pacifist Bertha Félice Baroness von Suttner (*née* Kinsky), 49, and others begins publishing its journal *Lay Down Your Arms* (*Die Waffen nieder*) that baroness von Suttner will edit until 1899 (*see* 1905).

Ida Wells hears at Natchez March 10 that her friend Thomas Moss and two of his business partners were taken from their jail cells, put onto a train, and lynched the day before one mile outside of Memphis. They had owned a grocery store that was taking business away from a white competitor and had shot three whites who wanted to raze the store. Wells returns to Memphis and launches an anti-lynching campaign, urging blacks to arm themselves in self-defense. She herself begins wearing a pistol, and, quoting her friend's last words, urges Memphis blacks to emigrate west. She travels to the newly opened Oklahoma Territory so that she can report back on conditions there, and in 2 months some 6,000 blacks have followed her advice, some ministers leading their entire congregations to

Oklahoma. The white business community of Memphis watches in alarm as its black customers abandon the city, by wagon if they cannot afford train fare, and Wells urges those who remain to boycott the local trolley car system. The boycott is so effective that owners of the traction company come to visit with her and and beg that she call off the action. Wells follows newspaper reports and visits scenes of lynchings, interviews eyewitnesses to document the circumstances of the 728 lynchings over the preceding decade, and finds that only one-third of the victims were even accused of rape. She writes an editorial that is published May 21 in *Free Speech*, saying, in part, "Nobody in this section of the country believes the threadbare lie that Negro men rape white women. . . . If Southern white men are not careful . . . a conclusion will be reached which will be very damaging to the moral reputation of their women." White men burn down the offices of the paper, its co-owner is chased out of town, and there are lynch threats against Wells herself. She has gone to Philadelphia and proceeds to New York.

Elizabeth Cady Stanton, now 76, addresses Congress in a speech demanding absolute independence—physical, emotional, financial, intellectual, and legal—for women. Women must be permitted to take responsibility for their own lives, she argues, and not have to wait until they are widows to take charge of their own lives (she herself has been a widow since age 71, but was emotionally and financially independent before her husband's death). Grossly overweight, lame, her eyesight failing, and her activities limited by heart disease, Stanton continues to write and speak out for the cause that has occupied her since 1848.

"If every demand raised by these [equal rights feminists] were granted today, we working women would still be just where we were before," declares English socialist Eleanor Marx, 36, youngest daughter of the late Karl. "Women-workers would still work infamously long hours, for infamously low wages, under infamously unhealthful conditions . . ." She notes that women's rights advocate Millicent Fawcett, whose husband, Henry, a Liberal M.P., first opposed limiting women's working hours in 1873, has "declared herself expressly in opposition to any legal reduction of working hours for female workers."

Italy raises to 12 the minimum age for marriage for girls.

British women gain entry to more institutions of higher education, but most colleges bar their doors to women.

New York's Sacred Heart of Jesus School opens in four West 51st Street brownstone houses purchased by Father Joseph Mooney of the church by that name. Staffed by the Sisters of Charity and headed by Sister Marie Austin (who keeps clothing in a closet for needy girls and goes from house to house Sunday mornings to rouse children for Mass), the school for daughters of working-class families will move to a large building in West 52nd Street and accept boys as well (keeping them separate until the 1970s) as it grows into the largest school on the West Side, with nearly 3,000 pupils, before shrinking with demographic changes to fewer than 300.

New York's Spence School for girls has its beginnings in Miss Spence's School, opened by educator Clara Beebe Spence, 30, whose private school will grow to have an enrollment of 350 in kindergarten through 12th grade (*see* Brearley, 1884; Chapin, 1901).

Vogue magazine begins publication late in the year at New York as a society weekly, devoting its first issues largely to coming-out parties, galas, betrothals, marriages, travel itineraries, golf, theater, concerts, and art. Its editor, Josephine Redding, is never without a hat but does not wear corsets (*see* Condé Nast, 1909).

The Addressograph invented by Sioux City, Iowa, engineer Joseph Smith Duncan prints addresses automatically and will soon be used by women in offices all over America. Duncan's first model employs a revolving, hexagonal block of wood to which he has glued rubber type torn from rubber stamps; a new name and address advance to the printing point each time the block is turned, and the process of turning the block re-inks the type. Duncan will put a more refined model into production in July of next year from a back office in Chicago.

Nonfiction: *A Voice from the South by a Black Woman of the South* by Washington, D.C., schoolteacher Anna Julia Haywood Cooper, 34, whose mother was a slave but who has herself obtained B.A. and M.A. degrees from Oberlin; *Eve's Daughters, or Common Sense for Maid, Wife, and Mother* by Marion Harland expresses the view that U.S. mothers have an obligation to bear "troops" of children lest the country be overrun by "massed filth— Irish cotters, and German boors, and loose and criminal fugitives from everywhere."

Fiction: "The Yellow Wall-Paper" by Boston feminist writer Charlotte Stetson (*née* Perkins), 32, a niece of the late Harriet Beecher Stowe, appears in the January issue of the *New England Newspaper* (Stetson was treated for neurasthenia shortly after her marriage in 1885, her depression became intolerable after the birth of her child, a specialist in nervous disorders forbade her to write or engage in any intellectual pursuit, but she divorced her husband, resumed her writing career, and has written a story about the helpless frustration of a female patient, a would-be writer, whose madness has been brought on by the patronizing attitude of her doctor-husband and who secretly keeps a diary in the attic where she is confined); *Helen Brent, M.D.* by Annie Nathan Meyer, whose novel is published anonymously: its heroine refuses to give up her career for marriage, insisting that she has as much right to ask a man to abandon his ambition as he has to make the same demand on her, and declares that she will forgo marriage until she can find a man willing to accept a wife who will continue her career; *Pray, Sir, Whose Daughter?* by Ellen Hamilton Gardener renounces an attempt by the New York State Legislature to lower the age of consent, criticizes the low wages paid to working women, and attacks the inferior position of women in the marital relationship; *Iola Leroy; or, Shadows Uplifted* by Frances Ellen Watkins Harper, now 67, is the first novel by a black American woman; *Silhouettes of American Life* by Rebecca Harding Davis; *The Soul of Lillith* by Marie Corelli; *Seino* by Nera; *Betrayed* (*Forraadt*) by Amalie Skram shocks her contemporaries with its pessimism and concern with the erotic problems of women.

Poetry: *Fate and Other Poems* (*Fatalità*) by Italian poet Ada Negri, 22, who since age 18 has been teaching school in the small Pavian village of Motta-Visconti. Her poems about the virtues of the hardworking, long-suffering proletariat as compared with the parasitic bourgeoisie make her an instant celebrity, and the government makes her professor of Italian literature at the normal school (teachers' college) in Milan. *Mr. Bassyr in Brazil* (*Pan Balcer w Brazylji*) by Polish poet Marja Konopnicka (*née* Wasilowska), 42. *Women: 1862* by Constance Fenimore Woolson.

Juvenile: *Bashful Fifteen* by L. T. Meade.

Theater: Lillie Langtry in *Lady Windermere's Fan* by Irish playwright Oscar Wilde 2/22 at the St. James's Theatre, London (a play written especially for "The Jersey Lily"); Lotta Crabtree, now 45, starts out in the fall for a tour but cancels after 6 agonizing weeks and will never act on stage again (she has made herself the richest American actress).

Ballet: Dancer Loie Fuller makes her Paris debut and wins even greater acclaim than she did last year in America.

Lottie Dod wins in women's singles at Wimbledon, Mabel Cahill in U.S. women's singles.

The Missouri Supreme Court convicts a man of rape without demanding that his victim demonstrate "utmost resistance" since she was being intimidated with a pistol (*see* Nebraska, 1889).

The *Ladies' Home Journal* announces that it will accept no more patent medicine advertisements. The *Journal* has been edited since 1889 by Dutch-American editor Edward William Bok, 29 (*see* 1883).

The Woman's Baking Co. of Chicago advertises, "No man shall touch the bread before the consumer does." Men may harness the delivery wagon horses and handle the reins, but a woman in uniform does the actual handling. Other bakeries compete by hand-wrapping their loaves in kraft paper and tying each with a string.

1893

Romania's diffident Crown Prince Ferdinand, 27, is married January 10 at Sigmaringen to Marie Alexandra Victoria, 17, a granddaughter of Britain's Queen Victoria and of the late Russian Czar Alexander II. She had hoped to marry Victoria's grandson George, now duke of York, who is married at Buckingham Palace July 6 to his late brother's fiancée, Mary of Teck.

Queen Liliuokalani of Hawaii abdicated reluctantly, yielding to the armed might of U.S. Marines. UNITED PRESS

Hawaiian annexationists overthrow Queen Liliuokalani with support from U.S. minister John Leavitt Stevens. Armed marines from the U.S.S. *Boston* are landed January 16 to "protect" U.S. interests, the queen abdicates under duress January 17 after reigning for less than 2 years, and the annexationists block U.S. efforts to restore the monarchy. "I yield to the superior forces of the United States of America, whose minister plenipotentiary . . . has caused United States troops to be landed in Honolulu and declared that he would

support the . . . provisional government." Grover Cleveland begins a second term as president March 4 and opposes the annexation of Hawaii. An investigation shows that most Hawaiians have not supported the coup, and that Hawaiians and Americans in the pineapple and sugar industries have played a leading role in opposing the queen. Cleveland tells Congress he will try to restore the queen to her throne in return for clemency for those who organized the coup, but the queen and the provisional government refuse the deal and Cleveland abandons the idea. The islands will be annexed to the United States in 1898.

The Columbian Exposition, which opens at Chicago features a Woman's Building designed to illustrate women's growing role and the problems they still face. Filled with exhibits from 47 nations, it has been organized by local philanthropist and society queen Bertha Palmer, now 43, who has been personally responsible for obtaining many of the exhibits. The Woman's Building is a highlight of the world's fair and propels Mrs. Palmer into national prominence.

Russian-American anarchist Emma Goldman, 24, makes a speech in New York's Union Square August 21 urging striking clockmakers to steal bread if they cannot afford to buy food for their families in the economic depression (below). There is little practical difference, she says, between the cruelties of U.S. plutocracy and those of czarist Russia. Police arrest her for inciting to riot, and she is sentenced to 1 year's imprisonment (*see* 1901).

Emma Goldman (above) will define anarchism as "the philosophy of a new social order based on liberty unrestricted by man-made law; the theory that all forms of government rest on violence and are therefore wrong and harmful." As for feminism, she will say, "True [female] emancipation begins neither at the polls nor in courts. It begins in woman's soul. History tells us that every oppressed class gains true liberation from its masters through its own efforts. It is necessary that woman learn that lesson, that she realize that her freedom will reach as far as her power to achieve her freedom reaches."

New Zealand adopts woman suffrage September 19 and becomes the first country to do so. A petition signed by a third of New Zealand's women has persuaded the House of Representatives to pass the act, Women's Christian Temperance Union franchise department head Katharine Sheppard has petitioned for the reform three times in the last 3 years, and the number of names on the petition has grown by 10,000 each time until it has reached 31,872 (*see* 1898).

Colorado's male electorate votes for woman suffrage.

New York's Henry Street Settlement House has its beginnings in the Nurses' Settlement founded by trained nurse and social worker Lillian D. Wald, 26, to help immigrants on the city's Lower East Side, most of them poor Jews. She will soon add a nurses' training program, community educational programs, and youth clubs (*see* Chicago's Hull-House, 1889).

Denison House is opened in Boston's South End by social worker Helena Dudley and Wellesley College professor Vita Scudder, 31.

The National Council of Jewish Women is founded at Chicago by local reformer Hannah Solomon (*née* Greenebaum), 35. She and her sister, Mrs. Henry Frank, were the first Jewish women invited in 1877 to join the Chicago Women's Club, and she was asked to participate in the Parliament of Religions at the World's Columbian Exposition (above). The Parliament included representatives of religions from all over the world, and Solomon was appalled to find that the women were expected merely to serve tea. A friend of Jane Addams, she has written to rabbis of Reformed congregations in major cities asking them to suggest women who may help organize volunteers to address their efforts to solving problems of women's rights, child welfare, anti-Semitism, community needs, and the like. The NCJW, whose first president is Hannah Solomon, will develop research and education programs designed to help people of all faiths improve the quality of life for women, children, and families. Solomon, herself, will find time, as well, to help found Chicago's Juvenile Court, serve on the board of the Civic Federation, and help start the Associated Charities of Chicago.

Wall Street stock prices take a sudden drop May 5, the market collapses June 27, 600 banks close their doors, more than 15,000 business firms fail, and 74 railroads go into receivership in an economic depression that began last year and will continue for 4 more years. The average U.S. worker earns $9.42 per week, and immigrants often receive less than $1 per day. Millions of unemployed workers roam the streets, begging for help, and abandoned children are often left to live by their wits.

The Gleason Gear Planer perfected by U.S. inventor Kate Gleason, 27, with her father produces beveled gears faster and more cheaply than any comparable machine. Detroit's fledgling auto industry will buy the Planer, and Henry Ford will call it "the most remarkable machine work ever done by a woman" (*see* housing, 1919).

English naturalist (botanist, entomologist, ichthyologist)-ethnographer-linguist-geographer Mary Henrietta Kingsley, 30, explores West Africa on the first of two journeys, spanning 17 months, in which she will go with Fang tribesmen down the Ogowe (or Ogooué) River through cannibal country that has been called "the white man's grave," photographing wildlife, and collecting for the British Museum beetles never before catalogued plus 18 species of reptiles and 65 fish. A niece of the late novelist-poet Charles Kingsley, she nursed her parents until they died within 6 weeks of each other last year and felt useless afterwards (her father, a footloose physician, married her mother, his cook, 4 days before Mary was born, and Mary, like her late mother, tends to drop her g's and h's when she speaks). She wears long black Victorian skirts at all times, remarking that "one would never want to go about in Africa in a way that would embarrass one to be seen in Piccadilly," and Rudyard Kipling will say of her, "Being human, she must have been afraid of something. But one never found out what it was" (*see* medicine, 1900).

Johns Hopkins Medical School at Baltimore admits women on the same basis as men—the first medical school to do so. Funds allocated to start the school have been invested in Baltimore & Ohio Railroad stock, which has fared poorly; Mary Garrett, daughter of the B&O's president, has donated $300,000 to the school on condition that women be admitted. But within 10 years all but three of the 17 U.S. medical schools now operating will have closed due to efforts to make them coeducational (*see* Flexner Report, 1910).

Lillian Wald in New York (above) will develop a visiting nurse program that within 13 years will have 100 nurses making 227,000 house calls per year.

Geologist Florence Bascom, 31, receives her doctorate from Johns Hopkins University (above), the first woman to be so honored.

New York City's Woman Teachers' Association petitions the state legislature to place them "on an equal financial footing with men," who receive $3,000 per year as compared to $1,700 for the women.

Nonfiction: *Woman's Place To-day* by Lillie Devereux Blake is based on lectures that she has given in response to a misogynist theologian and deals with dogmatic theology based on a masculine interpretation of the Bible; *Woman Suffrage and Politics* by former Iowa Woman Suffrage Association organizer Carrie Chapman Catt (*née* Lane), 34 (with Nettie Rogers Shuler); *Public Assistance of the Poor in France* by U.S. economist–social scientist Emily Greene Balch, 26; *The Rhythm of Life* (essays) by Alice Meynell.

Fiction: *Recollections of Ludolf Ursleu the Younger* (*Erinnerungen von Ludolf Ursleu dem jüngeren*) by German feminist novelist Ricarda Huch, 29; "Aunt Fountain's Prisoner" by Rebecca Harding Davis appears in *Stories of the South*; *Maggie: A Girl of the Streets* by New York newspaper reporter Stephen Crane, 21, who has the naturalistic portrayal of slum life published at his own expense.

Poetry: *In This Our World* by Charlotte Perkins Stetson, who has been separated from her husband since 1888 and will obtain a divorce next year.

Juvenile: *Jill, a Flower Girl* and *A Young Mutineer; A Story for Girls* by L. T. Meade; *Beechcroft at Rockstone* by Charlotte M. Yonge.

Painting: *The Boating Party* by Mary Cassatt; *Two Horses* by Rosa Bonheur.

The White House by U.S. photographer Frances Benjamin Johnston, 29, who has photographed interiors of the executive mansion at Washington, D.C., and now photographs the "White City" of the World's Columbian Exposition at Chicago. Like most of her work, the pictures have been taken on commission (*see* 1900).

Theater: *The Girl I Left Behind Me* by David Belasco and *New York Sun* critic Franklin Fyler 1/25 at New York's Empire Theatre, 208 performances; *A Woman of No Importance* by Oscar Wilde 4/14 at London's Haymarket Theatre; Mrs. Patrick Campbell (Beatrice Rose Stella Tanner), 28, in Arthur Wing Pinero's *The Second Mrs. Tanqueray* 5/28 at the St. James's Theatre, London (the daughter of an Italian beauty who spoke no English when she met Tanner's father in Bombay and he no Italian, Tanner herself was married at age 20 to a man of 19).

First performances: *Dramatic Overture* (Opus 12) by U.S. composer Margaret Ruthven Lang, 25, 4/7 at Boston in a performance by the Boston Symphony. She is the first American composer to have one of her works played by a major orchestra, and her overture *Witichis* (Opus 10) receives three performances at the World's Columbian Exposition in Chicago (above).

Violinist Maud Powell, now 26, gives two performances with the New York Philharmonic at the World's Columbian Exposition under the direction of Theodore Thomas. She also delivers a paper entitled "Women and the Violin" to the Women's Musical Congress.

Opera: French soprano (Rosa-Noémie) Emma Calvé (originally Calvet de Roquer), 35, makes her Metropolitan Opera debut 11/29 in the 1875 Bizet opera *Carmen*; Nellie Melba makes her Metropolitan Opera debut 12/4 in the title role of Donizetti's 1835 opera *Lucia di Lammermoor*.

Popular songs: Queen Liliuokalani (above), now 55, has written a number of songs, including "Farewell to Thee" ("Aloha Oe"); "Happy Birthday to You" ("Good Morning to All") by Louisville, Ky., private kindergarten teacher Mildred Hill, 34, lyrics by her sister Patty Smith Hill, 25.

Lottie Dod wins in women's singles at Wimbledon, Aline M. Terry in U.S. women's singles.

The British Ladies' Golf Union is formed under the direction of Lady Margaret Scott, 18, whose title helps give the game respectability for other women. She will be women's champion for 3 years until her retirement from competitive play in 1895.

Paris students witness the world's first striptease February 9 at the Bal des Quatre Arts. Gendarmes seize the artist's model who has disrobed for the art students, a court fines her 100 francs, the ruling provokes a riot in the Latin Quarter, students besiege the Prefecture of Police, and military intervention is required to restore order.

Japanese entrepreneur Kokichi Mikimoto, 35, pioneers cultured pearls. He has learned from a Tokyo University professor that if a foreign object enters a pearl oyster's shell and is not expelled the oyster will use it as the core of a pearl. Five years ago he established the first pearl farm in the Shinmei inlet, and when he pulls up a bamboo basket for routine inspection July 11 he finds a semispherical pearl—the world's first cultured pearl. The natural Oriental pearl business will fade in the next few decades as Japanese women dive for oysters seeded by Mikimoto.

Lizzie Borden makes headlines in June when she goes on trial at Fall River, Mass. Spinster Lizzie Andrew Borden, 32, is charged with having killed her stepmother and then her father on the morning of August 4 last year, she testifies that she was out of the house at the time, her sensational trial boosts newspaper circulation figures to new heights, the jury finally rules to acquit, but street urchins chant, "Lizzie Borden took an axe/ And gave her mother forty whacks./ And when she saw what she had done/ She gave her father forty-one."

The Woman's Building at the Columbian Exposition in Chicago (above) has been designed by M.I.T. architecture school graduate Sophia Gregoria Hayden, 25, who was the first woman to enter M.I.T.'s graduate school but could not obtain work as an architect and has been teaching drawing at a Boston high school. Her Renaissance Revival design won the contest for the Woman's Building, she traveled to Chicago to complete the working drawings, she has been the first to complete her fair pavilion, but she is paid only $1,500 where the Exposition's male architects receive between

$4,500 and $15,000, and she will not be offered further commissions. Rumors will spread that she has had a breakdown, and the *American Architect and Building News* will call this "breakdown" "a much more telling argument against . . . women entering this especial profession than anything else could."

Aunt Jemima pancake mix is promoted at the Chicago fair by St. Joseph, Mo., miller R. T. Davis, who has acquired another man's formula and improved it by adding rice flour, corn sugar, and powdered milk so that it can be prepared by adding only water. Davis sets up a 24-foot-high flour barrel, arranges displays inside the barrel, and engages former Kentucky slave Nancy Green, 59, to demonstrate the Aunt Jemima mix at a griddle outside the barrel.

1894

The Local Government Act passed by Parliament March 1 increases the rights of British women to vote, but they still have no voice in national elections (*see* WSPV, 1903).

The Union for Industrial Progress is founded at Boston by Women's Education and Industrial Union director Mary Kimball Kehew, 34, and Mary Kenney, 30, who marries John O'Sullivan, labor editor of the *Boston Globe* (*see* WTUL, 1903).

Women bustle makers at Boston work from 8:30 in the morning until 6 at night to earn 25¢ per dozen—a day's output. Men do much better.

Japanese factories (most of them textile mills) employ 308,000 workers, of whom 240,000 are women (*see* 1886; 1904).

The New York Exchange for Woman's Work, which has moved to 329 Fifth Avenue, issues its first catalogue of handmade goods—tea sandwiches, cookies, jams, children's wear, "fancy and useful articles" for gifts, and a collection of gems and cameos donated by "an anonymous gentleman" (*see* 1883). The Exchange will move in 1901 into its own brownstone at 334 Madison Avenue (43rd Street), in 1920 into two houses at 541 Madison Avenue (54th Street), in 1980 to 660 Madison Avenue (61st Street), and in 1991 to 1095 Third

Avenue (64th Street) as it becomes increasingly well known for its hand-smocked children's clothes, handmade gifts, and wedding cakes.

The Japanese Army employs its first female nurses to work in hospitals treating wounds sustained in the nation's successful war against Russia.

The first successful U.S. cesarean section delivery is performed at Boston on a woman with a tiny pelvis who has previously lost two infants (*see* 1882; 1980).

Anna Wessel Williams in New York isolates an unusually powerful and prolific strain of diphtheria toxin and produces an antitoxin which will bear her name and continue in production for at least a century (*see* 1891). It will make diphtheria a rare disease in most of the world.

Radcliffe College for Women opens at Cambridge, Mass., after 15 years of opposition by Harvard president Charles William Eliot to the classes given since 1879 by Elizabeth Cary Agassiz. The college, whose students are taught by Harvard professors, is named for Anne Radcliffe, who in the 17th century became the first woman to make a gift to Harvard (*see* Comstock, 1923).

Nonfiction: *Safar Nameh: Persian Pictures, a Book of Travel* by English traveler Gertrude Margaret Lowthian Bell, 26, who visited Persia 2 years ago with Sir Frank and Lady Lascelles, her stepmother's sister and brother-in-law. One of the first women to matriculate at Oxford, Bell has mastered several European languages and has studied Farsi.

Fiction: *The Real Charlotte* by Somerville and Ross (Edith Somerville and Violet Martin); *Marcella* by Mrs. Humphry Ward; *Pembroke* by Mary Eleanor Wilkins Freeman; *Horace Chase* by the late Constance Fenimore Woolson, who has died at Venice January 24 at age 53 after falling or jumping from her bedroom window; "New Year's Eve" ("Otsugomori") by Japanese writer Ichiyō (*née* Natsu) Higuchi, 22; *The Soul of an Artist* (*Anima sola*) by Nera; *Mariage de Chiffon* by Gyp.

Juvenile: *Seven Little Australians* by English-born Australian author Ethel Sibyl Turner, 22, whose book will remain in print through most of the next century.

Painting: *The Boating Party* and *Summertime* by Mary Cassatt. German graphic artist Käthe Kollwitz (*née* Käthe Ida Schmidt), 27, completes the first in a series of prints, *Der Weberaufstand*, inspired by last year's Gerhart Hauptmann play *The Weavers*.

Theater: *How to Get Rid of Your Mistress* (*Un Fil à la Patte*) by French playwright Georges Feydeau, 31, 1/9 at the Théâtre du Palais-Royal, Paris; *The Land of Heart's Desire* by Irish poet-playwright William Butler Yeats, 28, 3/29 at London's Avenue Theatre in a production financed by tea heiress and patron Annie Elizabeth Fredericka Horniman, 34, who also finances a production at the same theater of George Bernard Shaw's *Arms and the Man*, which has its premiere 4/21. Horniman will sponsor construction of Dublin's Abbey Theatre in 1904 and purchase Manchester's Gaiety Theatre in 1908, turning it into a repertory theater.

Violinist Maud Powell becomes the first woman to form and lead a string quartet (*see* 1893).

Blanche Bingley Hillyard wins in women's singles at Wimbledon, Helen R. Helwig in U.S. women's singles.

A London Building Act voted by Parliament limits the height of buildings to 150 feet. A development called Queen Anne's Mansions has disturbed Queen Victoria's view, and no skyscrapers will be erected in London for nearly 60 years.

French chef August Escoffier, 47, creates Pêche Melba at London's 5-year-old Savoy Hotel to honor the Australian grande cantrice Mme. Nellie Melba, now 33, who is singing at Covent Garden. Inspired by the swan in Richard Wagner's 1850 opera *Lohengrin*, Escoffier tops a scoop of vanilla ice cream on a cooked peach half with a purée of raspberries and almond slivers.

Mme. Melba (above) breakfasts on tea and dry toast; knowing that she is always concerned about her weight, Escoffier slices white bread as thin as he can and toasts it to create what will come to be known as Melba Toast.

Minute Tapioca is introduced at Boston by the Whitman Grocery Co., which has acquired rights to a process invented more than a decade ago by local housewife Susan Stavers. She obtained South American manioc (cassava) roots, imported duty-free since 1883 for use as starch, and ran them through her coffee grinder to produce translucent granules that made a smooth pudding, selling the product in paper bags (Whitman sells it in boxes).

1895

The word *feminist* appears for the first time in the April 27 issue of the *Athenaeum*, an English literary weekly, in describing a woman who "has in her the capacity of fighting her way back to independence" (*see* West, 1913).

The National Federation of Afro-American Women is founded July 21 at Washington, D.C. (*see* 1896).

Utah adopts a Constitution granting women suffrage after a campaign by the *Woman's Exponent*, a Mormon journal edited since 1877 by Blanche Woodward Wells, 67.

Dr. Mary Putnam Jacobi, now 53, writes, "I think, finally, it is in the increased attention paid to women, and especially in their new function as lucrative patients, scarcely imagined a hundred years ago, that we find explanation for much of the ill-health among women, freshly discovered today . . ."

Bryn Mawr Dean of Faculties M. Carey Thomas, now 37, takes over as president of the college, a position that she will hold until her retirement in 1922 (*see* 1885). Whereas Smith and Wellesley emphasize "domestic values" to prepare graduates for marriage and motherhood, Bryn Mawr's Thomas tells her "sisterhood" of students that they must be able to participate in the workplace and the professions on an equal basis with men. She champions women's causes and plays an active role in the Association of College Alumnae (which helps young women pursue undergraduate degrees and promotes opportunities for graduates). When Harvard's Charles Eliot upholds the segregation of women from men in 1899 on grounds of "Darwinian" theory, Thomas will ridicule him in public, suggesting that he is suffering from "sun spots on his brain."

Underwood Typewriter Co. is founded by New York ribbon and carbon merchant John Thomas Underwood, 38, to develop and market a machine patented 2 years ago by Brooklyn inventors Franz X. and Herman L. Wagner, whose typewriter enables the typist to see what is being typed.

Nonfiction: "A Red Record" (pamphlet) by Ida B. Wells, who writes, "True chivalry respects all womanhood, and no one who reads the record, as it is written in the faces of the million mulattoes in the South, will for a minute conceive that the southern white man had a very chivalrous regard for the honor due the women of his race or respect for the womanhood which circumstances placed in his power" (Wells does not say so, but most of the 10,000 lynchings that she calculates to have taken place since 1865 have been justified on the grounds of trumped-up charges of black-on-white rape; now 33, Wells marries Chicago publisher Ferdinand Barnett and becomes Ida Wells-Barnett); *Famous Leaders among Women* by Sarah Knowles Bolton.

Fiction: *From a Good Family* (*Aus guter Familie*) by German novelist Clara Viebig, 35; *Vera Brantzova* by mathematician Sofia Kovalevskaia; *Professor Hieronymus* by Amalie Skram arouses controversy over its depiction of how the mentally ill are treated; *The Sorrows of Satan* by Marie Corelli; *Sir Robert's Fortune* by Margaret Oliphant; *The Front Yard, and Other Italian Stories* by the late Constance Fenimore Woolson; "Growing Up" ("*Takekurabe*"), "Turbid Painting:" ("*Nigorie*"), "Forked Road" ("*Wakareaichi*"), and "The Thirteenth Night" ("*Jusanya*") by Ichiyo Higuchi, whose stories are published in *Bungaku* magazine.

Opera: Rosa Sucher makes her Metropolitan Opera debut 1/25 with the Damrosch Opera Company singing the role of Isolde in the 1865 Wagner opera *Tristan und Isolde*.

The Fadettes give a performance at Boston's Chickering Hall (*see* 1888). By 1898 the all-woman orchestra will have 40 players.

A poem by Wellesley College English professor Katharine Lee Bates, 36, will be set to the music of Samuel A. Ward's "Materna" and become "America the Beautiful," an unofficial national anthem. A climb up Pike's Peak inspired Bates to write her poem on July 22, 1893, about America's "amber waves of grain" and "purple mountain majesties above the fruited plain . . . from sea to shining sea." Revised versions will appear in 1904 and 1911.

Charlotte Cooper, 24, wins in women's singles at Wimbledon, Juliette P. Atkinson in U.S. women's singles.

Lord Randolph Churchill dies of syphilis January 24 at age 43 after returning to England from a voyage to the Orient with his wife, Jennie, who stood by him after he revealed the nature of the disease that exacerbated his already reckless and impetuous behavior, obliging him to resign from the Commons in December 1886 (see 1874). Their son Winston, now 20, is graduated from Sandhurst, gazetted to the 4th Hussars, and travels in the fall to Havana via New York to witness Spanish efforts to suppress a Cuban rebellion.

Mary Victoria Leiter, 25, the beautiful daughter of retired Marshall Field department store tycoon Levi Z. Leiter of Chicago, is married at the family's Washington, D.C., house on Dupont Circle April 23 to Parliamentary undersecretary of state for India George Nathaniel Curzon, 36, Lord Curzon of Kedleston. The bridegroom has spent 2 days with his prospective father-in-law's lawyers and been assured that his bride has been given $700,000 and he, himself, will have a guaranteed income of £6,000 per year. The couple sails for England 4 days later, Curzon will become viceroy of India (see politics, 1898), and Mary will never see America again.

Consuelo Vanderbilt, daughter of railroad magnate William K. Vanderbilt, turns 18 March 2, is given a "Bal Blanc" August 28 in the ballroom of the family's $11 million Marble House "cottage" at Newport (footmen in powdered wigs usher in the 500 guests, who dance to the music of three orchestras, dine at midnight, sup at 3), and is married November 6 at St. Thomas's Episcopal Church on New York's Fifth Avenue to Charles, ninth duke of Marlborough, who is 25 and has had to give up the woman he loved to wed Consuelo. Her match with the impoverished "Sunny" has been arranged by her mother, Alva, now 43, who in 2 months will become Mrs. Oliver H. P. Belmont (marrying a man

5 years her junior) and work for woman suffrage. Consuelo, whose intent to marry Winthrop Rutherfurd has been thwarted and whose $2.5 million dowry produces $100,000 per year in interest, will separate from the duke in 1911, obtain a divorce in 1920, set up homes for unwed mothers, and advocate woman suffrage.

Britain's National Trust for Places of Historic Interest or Natural Beauty is founded by reformers who include Octavia Hill, 57. Funded by the taxpayers, it will preserve country houses, landscaped parks, and gardens and protect 150 "stately homes," 17 entire villages, more than 2,000 farms, and some nature reserves.

The Cordon Bleu Cooking School opened by Marthe Distel at the Palais-Royal in Paris takes a name derived from the blue ribbon worn by older girls at the school opened by Mme. de Maintenon in 1686. The Grand Diplôme of the new school on the rue Champ de Mars will become the highest credential a chef can have (see 1934).

1896

Utah is admitted to the Union as the 45th state after Mormons agree to give up polygamous marriage.

Idaho women gain suffrage through an amendment to the state Constitution. Speeches by Portland, Ore., suffragist Abigail Dunniway (see 1883) are credited with having helped gain passage of the amendment.

The National Association of Colored Women is created by a merger of the 2-year-old Colored Women's League and the year-old National Federation of Afro-American Women, both of which have held conventions in July at Washington, D.C. Memphis-born Oberlin-educated schoolteacher Mary Eliza Terrell (née Church), 32, will head the new NACW until 1901, working to establish kindergartens, day nurseries, and Mother Clubs, whose purpose is to improve the moral standards of the "less favored and more ignorant sisters," because the world "will always judge the womanhood of the race through the masses of our women" (see Berlin Conference, 1904).

Russian revolutionary Aleksandra Mikhailovna Kollontai (*née* Domantovich), 24, visits a textile factory with her husband, is appalled at the working conditions and by her husband's callous attitude toward those conditions, becomes an active Marxist, and embarks on a career of distributing leaflets, writing, publishing, and speaking out both in Russia and abroad (*see* 1917).

A gold rush to Canada's Klondike near the Alaskan border begins following the discovery of gold there August 17 (*see* 1897).

A paper on the treatment of eclampsia, read at Dublin's Rotunda Hospital, condemns induction of labor, saying that delivery can be speeded up only if the cervix shows signs of dilation. It recommends the use of morphia, venesection, purgation, and oxygen if necessary, with no food or drugs to be given by mouth, and the patient to be placed on her side in order that secretions may flow out of her mouth and not collect in her lungs.

Nonfiction: *Misused Feminine Power* (*Missbrukad kvinnokraft*) by Swedish reformer Ellen Karolina Sophia Key, 47, who says that since woman is by nature primarily a mother, if she persists in modern claims of "individualism" and equal rights with man to the point where she denies her fundamental, natural function she will not only destroy her own physical and spiritual development but also endanger the entire future of the race; *The Colour of Life* by Alice Meynell.

Fiction: *Oh! What a Plague Is Love* by Irish novelist Katharine Tynan, 35, who is a great friend of Alice Meynell (above) and will write more than 100 novels; *The Green Graves of Balgowrie* by Scottish novelist Jane Findlater, 31; *Sir George Tressady* by Mrs. Humphry Ward; *Country of the Pointed Firs* (stories) by Sarah Orne Jewett, who portrays the loneliness of the isolated and declining coastal town of South Berwick, Me.; *Dorothy, and Other Italian Stories* by the late Constance Fenimore Woolson; *Doctor Warrick's Daughters* by Rebecca Harding Davis; "This Child" ("*Konoko*") and "Forked Road" ("*Wakaremichi*") by Ichiyō Higuchi, who dies of tuberculosis November 23 at age 24.

Poetry: *Tempeste* by Ada Negri, who marries a rich Piedmontese industrialist.

Juvenile: *The Little Colonel* by U.S. writer Annie Fellows Johnson, 33, begins a series of "Little Colonel" books; *A Princess of the Gutter* and *Dr. Rumsey's Patient: A Very Strange Story* by L. T. Meade.

Painting: *Ellen Mary Cassatt in a White Coat* (niece of the artist) by Mary Cassatt; *Haystacks, Giverny* by Lilla Cabot Perry (date approximate).

Theater: French comedienne Anna Held, 23, makes her U.S. debut September 21 at New York's Herald Square Theatre in a lavish production of the 1884 Charles H. Hoyt play *A Parlor Match* mounted by Florenz Ziegfeld with help from Charles Dillingham.

Films: French filmmaker Alice Guy-Blaché, 23, directs *La Fée aux Choux*, the first fictional film ever (it lasts only a few minutes). She has worked as a secretary for cinema pioneer Léon Gaumont and by 1905 will be directing all of his films.

Opera: Emma Albani, now 44, has the last and greatest triumph of her stage career 6/26 at Covent Garden singing the role of Isolde in the 1865 Wagner opera *Tristan und Isolde*.

The Women's String Orchestra of New York is founded by professionally trained instrumentalists who have been denied traditional employment opportunities because of their sex. Considered amateurs because they receive no pay, they will number between 18 and 45 and give three concerts per year at Mendelssohn Hall until they disband in 1906.

"Little Egypt" dances nude on the table at a private dinner given at Louis Sherry's by New York playboy Barnum Seeley, grandson and heir of the late circus promoter P. T. Barnum, who died 5 years ago at age 80. But while Fahrida Mahszar is widely thought to have performed the *danse du ventre*, or hootchy-kootchy, on the Midway Plaisance of Chicago's 1893 Columbian Exposition under the name "Little Egypt," she never in fact appeared there.

Popular songs: "Sweet Rosie O'Grady" by New York songwriter Maude Nugent, 19, who has been unable to find a publisher and introduces the song herself at Tony Pastor's Opera House.

Charlotte Cooper wins in women's singles at Wimbledon, Elizabeth H. Moore in women's U.S. singles.

Fannie Farmer's Boston Cooking-School Cookbook by the 39-year-old head of a teacher training institution uses a precise measuring system that will make the 700-page book an enduring best-seller in America (but not in Europe). Farmer suffered a paralysis of the left leg at age 16 and has been considered unmarriageable. Miss Farmer's School of Cookery will survive until 1944.

"Dainty Desserts" by Johnstown, N.Y., entrepreneur Rose Knox (*née* Rosetta Markward), 39, is a booklet containing recipes which she has developed using the Knox Gelatine that she and her husband, Charles, produce at Johnstown. They invested their savings of $5,000 to buy the company 6 years ago, and after Charles's death in 1908 she will take over the business, whose sales will have mushroomed thanks in large part to her recipe booklet, and continue to run it until she is 88.

The *Ligue de la Régéneration Humaine* is founded by French libertarian Paul Robin, who came into contact with English neo-Malthusians while in exile during the 1870s.

Madagascar's Hova queen Ranavalona is deposed at the end of February by Gen. Joseph Gallieni, the French soldier who last August proclaimed the country a colony of France and who now ends the 110-year-old Hova dynasty, exiling Queen Ranavalona to the island of Réunion, from which she will be relocated to Algeria.

Queen Victoria, now 78, celebrates her Diamond Jubilee June 22, braving the heat in her usual black silk moiré dress and wearing a a wreath of acacia leaves and an aigrette of diamonds in her black lace bonnet as she reviews regiments who have come from all over the Empire. Her daughter-in-law, Alexandra, princess of Wales, sits beside the queen in the carriage during the tedious 3-hour procession through London (still beautiful but now virtually stone-deaf, the princess has long since learned to overlook the flagrant infidelities of her husband, whose mistresses have included the actresses Sarah Bernhardt and Lillie Langtry and the socially

Madagascar's Queen Ranavalona III, last of the 110-year-old Hova dynasty, fell victim to French colonial ambitions.

prominent Lady Aylesford and Lady Brooke, later countess of Warwick).

 Japan's Meiji government confers a medal in March upon Toku Komagata, 57, of Niigata Prefecture, making her the only woman out of 618 people who have received the medal since it was inaugurated in 1882. Komagata attracted attention during the Sino-Japanese War of 1894–1895 by advising the government that she wanted to donate ¥1 for the war effort and then working night and day to earn the money. Betrothed in 1860 at age 20, she discovered that her fiancé's family had lost most of its property and had barely enough to eat; advised not to go through with the marriage, she replied that she had given her word—and then proceeded to take care of her in-laws, working harder than any man to raise her six children. Up before dawn, she had worked by candlelight at night, spinning, weaving, cooking, cleaning, working in the fields in summer, raising silkworms, collecting firewood in winter. When her husband died she did not remarry, and her second and third sons have joined the army.

The Associazione Nazionale per le Donne is founded at Rome to advance the cause of Italian women (*see* 1899).

"There never will be complete equality until women themselves help to make laws and elect lawmakers," writes Susan B. Anthony in "The Status of Women, Past, Present and Future," published in the May issue of the *Arena*.

News of last year's Klondike gold discoveries reaches the United States in January and starts a new gold rush. Wisconsin-born widow Harriet Pullen (*née* Smith), 38, whose fur-trader husband has died, leaving her with four children and no money, joins the rush to Skagway, Alaska, where she sets up a stove on the beach, bakes dried apples for hungry gold seekers, and makes $3 per day—enough to open her own restaurant. By year's end, "Ma" Pullen has bought a team of horses and begun a freight service along the gold trail; she will rent a house next year and turn it into a hotel, will buy the place outright in 1900, and will run it until her death in 1947.

Kansas City's Children's Mercy Hospital is founded by two sisters, Alice Berry Graham, a widowed dentist, and Katharine Berry Richardson, a widowed surgeon, whose first patient is a crippled girl of 6 whom they have found crying in the street. They cure her and will found the Free Bed Fund Association for Crippled, Deformed, and Ruptured Children, which treats patients regardless of their families' ability to pay. Dr. Graham will die in 1913 and her sister Katharine will launch a fundraising drive to build a permanent home for the hospital.

French nun Thérèse of Lisieux (Thérèse Martin) dies of tuberculosis at age 24 in the Carmelite convent of Lisieux, Normandy, that she entered at 15. Her *History of a Soul* (*Histoire d'une âme*), published posthumously, will illustrate her "little way" of simple, trusting Christianity, it will gain wide popularity, she will be canonized in 1925, and in 1947 she will be associated with Joan of Arc as patron saint of France.

The PTA (Parent-Teachers' Association) has its beginnings in the National Congress of Mothers founded by 2,000 U.S. women February 17.

The *Woman's Home Companion* begins publication at Springfield, Ohio. Publisher John S. Crowell started the magazine in 1873 under the name *Home Companion*, renamed it the *Ladies' Home Companion* in 1886, and has changed its name to avoid confusion with Cyrus H. K. Curtis's magazine, published since 1883. It will continue until 1956.

New York Sun reader Virginia O'Hanlon of 115 West 95th Street writes to the paper's editor saying, "I am 8 years old. Some of my little friends say there is no Santa Claus. Papa says, 'If you see it in The Sun it's so.' Please tell me the truth; is there a Santa Claus?" Former *New York Times* Civil War correspondent Francis Parcellus Church, 58, childless himself, replies in an unsigned front page editorial published September 21: "Virginia, your little friends are wrong. They have been affected by the skepticism of a skeptical age. They do not believe except they see. . . . Yes, Virginia, there is a Santa Claus. He exists as certainly as love and generosity and devotion exist. . . . Not believe in Santa Claus? You might as well not believe in fairies. . . . No Santa Claus! Thank God, he lives, and he lives forever." The *Sun* will reprint the editorial each year until the paper is merged with the *World-Telegram* in January 1950.

Nonfiction: *Travels in West Africa* by Mary Kingsley; *Eighty Years and More* (autobiography) by Elizabeth Cady Stanton, now 81.

Fiction: *Children of the Eifel* (*Kinder der Eifel*) by Clara Viebig; *Patience Sparhawk and Her Times* by U.S. novelist Gertrude (Franklin Horn) Atherton, 39; *A Daughter of Strife* by Jane Findlater; *Amuleto* by Nera.

Painting: *Breakfast in Bed* by Mary Cassatt; *The Woman in Business* by Alice Barber Stephens.

Theater: U.S. actress Maude Adams (Maude Kiskadden), 25, who has adopted her mother's maiden name, in James M. Barrie's *The Little Minister* 9/27 at New York's Empire Theater, 300 perfs.

Broadway musicals: Edna May, 17, as the Salvation Army girl Violet Gray and Harry Davenport in *The Belle of New York* 9/18 at the Casino Theatre, with Gustave A. Kecker–Hugh Martin songs that include "The Anti-Cigarette Society," 56 perfs.

Opera: Viennese soprano Fritzi Scheff, 18, makes her debut at the Munich Royal Opera singing the role of Maria in the 1840 Donizetti opera *La Figlia del Reggimento*.

Blanche Bingley Hillyard wins in women's singles at Wimbledon, Juliette Atkinson in U.S. women's singles.

The United All-English Croquet Association is founded as improved mallets, wickets, and balls revive the popularity of the game (*see* 1868).

Red Cross shoes for women are introduced by a new Cincinnati firm that will sell out to United States Shoe Corp. in 1923.

Lifebuoy soap is introduced under the name Lifebudy by English soapmaker W. H. Lever, who has been expanding his Sunlight Soap business since 1888. He has acquired a controlling interest in a Cambridge, Mass., company and will promote Lifebuoy as a safeguard against body odor.

Jell-O is introduced by LeRoy, N.Y., cough medicine manufacturer Pearl B. Wait, whose wife, Mary, gives the product its name. Wait's gelatin dessert is made from a recipe adapted from one developed by Peter Cooper in 1845. The powder is 88 percent sugar.

More than 60 cases of champagne are consumed by 900 guests in Louis XV period costumes at a $9,000 ball given February 10 by Mrs. Bradley Martin, daughter of Carnegie Steel magnate Henry Phipps, who has had a huge Waldorf-Astoria suite decorated in the manner of Versailles despite the national economic depression that has persisted since 1893.

1898

Spain's Queen Marie-Amelie acts on the advice of Pope Leo XIII and orders a suspension of hostilities against Cuban rebels in early April, but U.S. newspapers have stirred up passions against the Spaniards, accusing them of having blown up the battleship *Maine* in Havana harbor February 15 with a loss of 258 men and two officers. A Spanish-American war begins April 22 and continues for 112 days.

An Italian anarchist stabs the Austrian empress Elizabeth September 10 at Geneva as she walks from her hotel to the steamer. She dies within a few hours at age 60.

China's dowager empress Cixi moves September 21 to crush the reform movement which threatens to sweep aside her corrupt Manchu bureaucracy. She stages a palace coup and imprisons the boy emperor Guangxu, who has listened to those who would have China follow the reforms enacted under Japan's Meiji emperor.

The new British viceroy to India, George Nathaniel Curzon, Baron Curzon of Kedleston, now 39, arrives at Bombay December 30 with his wife, Mary, the Chicago department store heiress, now 28, who will entertain lavishly and be far more popular than the stuffed-shirt viceregent (but make no effort in her 7 years as vicereine to span the gap between native Indians and the Raj).

New Zealand women gain the right to vote on the same basis as men, becoming the world's first women to enjoy equal suffrage (*see* 1893).

Chicago glove maker Agnes Nestor, 18, leads a strike at the Eisendrath Glove factory, whose management, after seeing production halted through 10 days of picketing, accedes to the (nonunion) workers' demands. Nestor has been working in factories since age 14, putting in 10 hours a day six days a week (*see* 1902).

Irish women are permitted to sit on district councils beginning December 22.

Polish-born French physical chemist Marie (Marja) Curie (*née* Sklodowska), 31, and her husband, Pierre, 39, isolate radium, the first important radioactive element. Married 3 years ago, they have endured extreme poverty, have earlier discovered a highly radioactive and dangerous element which they called polonium, after Marie's native land, and have now detected radium while extracting pure substances from pitchblende ore (*see* 1903).

Anita Newcombe McGee, 34, is appointed assistant surgeon in the U.S. Army at the outbreak of the Spanish-American War (above). She is the first woman to hold that position and in 3 years will draft the section of the Army Reorganization Bill establishing the Nurse Corps as a permanent part of the army.

Anna Wessel Williams uses her efforts to obtain enough rabies vaccine to begin large-scale production in America (*see* 1891). Together with Italian physician Adelchi Negri, she has identified the distinctive brain cell peculiar to an animal with rabies and will develop a method that quickly detects the so-called "Negri bodies."

Lydia Pinkham's Vegetable Compound is widely advertised as "The Greatest Medical Discovery Since the Dawn of History" (*see* 1881). It will continue to be made and sold for another 76 years (*see* 1905).

Central Hindu College is founded at Benares by English reformer Annie Besant, now 51, who embraced theosophy in 1889 and has been campaigning for nationalism in India.

Miss Hall's School for girls opens at Pittsfield, Mass., where Smith College graduate Mira Hinsdale Hall, 35, will teach boarding and day students in the belief that "a secondary school should seek to develop in every student the power to think independently and clearly, to discriminate between the gaudy and the real, and to be tolerant of others, while holding oneself to a high standard." Her school will grow to have 180 students.

Nonfiction: *Loom and Spindle* by New England author Harriet Train Hanson Robinson, 73, who went to work at age 10 as a bobbin doffer in a Lowell, Mass., cotton mill, worked 14-hour days, and then attended evening classes until she could go to Lowell High School for 2 years.

Fiction: *Offspring (Afkom)* by Amalie Skram completes her seven-volume series *The People of Hellemyr (Hellemyrsfolket)*; *American Wives and English Husbands* and *The Californians* by Gertrude Atherton; *Prisoners of Hope* by New York novelist Mary Johnston, 22 (approximate), who has written the work, mostly in Central Park, out of financial need.

Poetry: *In This Our World* by Charlotte Perkins Stetson.

Juvenile: *The Rebellion of Lil* by L. T. Meade.

Opera: Croatian soprano Milka Ternina (Trnina), 34, makes her Covent Garden debut 6/3 in the role of Isolde and goes on to sing the Wagnerian roles of Sieglinde in *Die Walküre*, Brünhilde in *Siegfried* and *Götterdämmerung*, and Leonore in the 1805 Beethoven opera *Fidelio* (she will sing next year at the Bayreuth Festival); Czech soprano Emmy Destinn (Ema Destinnová), 20, makes her debut 7/19 in the role of Santuzza in the 1890 Mascagni opera *Cavalleria Rusticana* at the Berlin Krolloper; Fritzi Scheff makes her Metropolitan Opera debut as Marcelline in *Fidelio*.

Charlotte Cooper wins in women's singles at Wimbledon, Juliette Atkinson in U.S. women's singles.

California Perfume Co. has 5,000 door-to-door saleswomen offering not only perfume but also cologne, Sweet Sixteen Face Powder, Rose Lip Pomade, headache cures, shaving soap, tooth-cleaning tablets, shoe cleaner, furniture polish, spot remover, mothproofer, food flavorings, and cookbooks (*see* 1885; 1929).

Jos. Campbell Preserve Co. introduces double-strength "condensed" soups developed by researcher John T. Dorrance, 25, a nephew of the company's president, who has degrees from MIT and the University of Göttingen (*see* 1869). Marketed with red-and-white labels, the new soups will revolutionize the canned-soup business.

Annual British tea consumption reaches 10 pounds per capita, up from two pounds in 1797, as prohibitively high coffee prices encourage tea consumption.

1899

Polish-born Berlin Marxist Rosa Luxemburg, 28, attacks arguments that labor's working conditions have improved and that reforms must come from within the system. Only international revolution can help the workingman, says "Bloody Rosa" in April, and she will continue to agitate until her death in 1919 (*see* 1914).

The first International Women's Congress opens June 26.

The Unione Femminile Nazionale is founded at Milan to advance the cause of Italian women (*see* 1897; 1903).

The Chicago Institute is founded by reaper heiress Anita Eugénie McCormick Blaine, 33, with Francis W. Parker to train teachers and educate children using progressive methods. Philanthropist Blaine was married 10 years ago to Emmons Blaine, son of onetime presidential candidate James G. Blaine.

Former Rutland, Vt., schoolteacher Helen Temple Cooke, 34, borrows $52,125 from the father of a former student and buys the Dana Hall school that she will head until her death in 1955 (*see* 1881; Pine Manor, 1930).

The *Anglo-Saxon Review* begins publication at London. Lady Randolph Churchill (Jennie Jerome) edits and finances the gold-tooled leather-bound quarterly.

Nonfiction: *From Polotzk to Boston* by Russian-American author Mary Antin, 18, recounts her experiences as an immigrant (the work has been translated from its original Yiddish edition); *The Theory of the Leisure Class* by University of Chicago social scientist Thorstein Bunde Veblen, 42, says that society adopts decorum (or etiquette) and refined tastes as evidence of gentility because such things can be acquired only with leisure. Veblen introduces such concepts as "conspicuous consumption," "conspicuous waste," and "vicarious" consumption and waste to explain social behavior that has either defied explanation or gone unexamined. He speaks of the burden placed upon women by the struggle to meet standards of "decency" imposed to bring order to the confused and transient social structure of a highly organized industrial community. *West African Studies* by Mary Kingsley.

Fiction: *The Awakening* by St. Louis–born New Orleans novelist Kate Chopin (*née* Katherine O'Flaherty), 48, whose heroine, Edna Pontellier, is married to a respectable merchant but falls in love with another man, leaves her husband, finds that there is no place for her in society, and commits suicide. Critics deplore the book about a woman awakening to her own sexuality and autonomy, and

it will earn its author royalties of only $145. *Rachel* by Jane Findlater. *Some Experiences of an Irish M.P.* by Somerville and Ross (Edith Somerville and Violet Martin). *She Walks in Beauty* by Katharine Tynan.

Poetry: *Gedichte* by Isolde Kurz.

Juvenile: *The Story of Little Black Sambo* by Scottish writer-illustrator Helen (Brody) Bannerman (*née* Watson), 37, who 10 years ago married a physician in the Indian Medical Service and accompanied him to Madras; her East Indian hero thwarts his tiger pursuers by turning them to butter; *The Story of the Treasure Seekers: The Adventures of the Bastable Children in Search of a Fortune* by English writer E. (Edith) Nesbit, 41.

Painting: *Mrs. Horace O. Havemeyer* by Mary Cassatt. Rosa Bonheur dies May 5 at her estate near the Forest of Fontainebleau at age 77 and is buried at her request in Père-Lachaise cemetery, Paris, in the same vault as her lifelong friend, Nathalie Micas, who died in her 50s.

Theater: Julia Marlowe in Clyde Fitch's *Barbara Fritchie* 10/23 at New York's Criterion Theatre, 83 perfs.

Stage musicals: *Floradora* 11/11 at London's Lyric Theatre, with music by Leslie Stuart, lyrics by Ernest Boyd-Jones and Paul Rubens, songs that include the second-act number beginning, "Tell me, pretty maiden, are there any more at home like you?. . ." 455 perfs.

Opera: Mme. Schumann-Heink makes her Metropolitan Opera debut 1/9 singing the role of Ortrud in the 1850 Wagner opera *Lohengrin*. She will continue at the Met until 1932.

Blanche Bingley Hillyard wins in women's singles at Wimbledon, Marion Jones in U.S. women's singles.

"Elegant dress serves its purpose of elegance not only in that it is expensive, but also because it is the insignia of leisure," writes Thorstein Veblen (above). "It not only shows that the wearer is able to consume a relatively large value, but it argues at the same time that he consumes without producing. The dress of women goes even farther than that of men in the way of demonstrating the wearer's abstinence from productive employment. . . . The substantial reason for

Women wore corsets to show the world that they didn't have to do heavy work, said sociologist Thorstein Veblen.

our tenacious attachment to the skirt is just this: it is expensive and it hampers the wearer at every turn and incapacitates her for all useful exertion. The like is true of the feminine custom of wearing the hair excessively long." Women wear corsets and white gloves to show the world that they need not scrub floors, Chinese bind girls' feet so that they will be unable to walk properly when they grow up, and men in Western societies resist having their wives work because a nonworking wife is emblematic of "vicarious leisure" (the man of the house may not be a gentleman of leisure, but heaven forbid that his genteel wife, too, should have to work). She "still, quite unmistakably, remains his chattel in theory, for the habitual rendering of vicarious leisure and consumption is the abiding mark of the unfree servant." "The high heel, the skirt, the impractical bonnet, the corset, and the general disregard of the wearer's comfort which is an obvious feature of all civilized women's apparel, are so many items of evidence to the effect that in the modern civilized scheme of life the woman is still, in theory, the economic dependent of the man."

"Conspicuous consumption" and "conspicuous waste" require such large expenditures that they are "probably the most effectual of the Malthusian prudential checks" on population growth and make for low birthrates in some classes of society, writes Thorstein Veblen in his *Theory of the Leisure Class* (above).

 "The sacrifice of suffering, of doubt, of obloquy, which has been endured by the pioneers in the woman movement will never be fully known or understood," says suffragist Carrie Chapman Catt in a February speech.

The International Ladies' Garment Workers' Union is founded June 3 by cloakmakers who meet in a small hall on New York's Lower East Side. The union's seven locals represent 2,310 workers in New York, Newark, Philadelphia, and Baltimore. By 1904 the ILGWU will have 5,400 members in 66 locals in 27 cities (*see* 1909 strike), and by 1913 it will be the American Federation of Labor's third largest affiliate. Only 3.5 percent of the U.S. workforce is now organized. Employers are free to hire and fire at will and at whim.

Storyville in New Orleans has more than two dozen ornate Basin Street "sporting palaces" in two blocks set aside 3 years ago under a plan devised by alderman Sidney Story. Mahogany Hall, a four-story marble mansion at 235 Basin Street built for $40,000 and operated by famed madam Lulu White, is the most elaborate establishment, with five lavish parlors and 15 bedrooms, each having mirrors at the head and foot of its bed. White, who calls herself the "Queen of the Demi-Monde," is so powerful that the city's tax assessors value her mansion with its furnishings at a mere $300 and she is never arrested. Poorer prostitutes operate out of "cribs" behind the "palaces" (*see* 1917).

Chicago's Everleigh Club opens at 2131–33 Dearborn Street, where local entrepreneur Minna Everleigh, 23, and her sister Ada, 21, have bought and refurbished a bordello with an inheritance of $40,000 each from their late father, a Kentucky lawyer. Visitors, who require letters of introduction, are entertained by string quartets and other pleasures (*see* 1911).

Kansas City has 147 houses of pleasure, the most elegant being that of Annie Chambers. Her $100,000 mansion is graced with a larger-than-life portrait of Annie dressed in a swirl of roses and gauze but little else.

The National Consumers League has its beginnings in the Consumers League for Fair Labor Standards

Paris demi-mondaines *caught the eye of Toulouse-Lautrec.*
They had their counterparts in every city. FROM TOULOUSE-
LAUTREC'S *RUE DES MOULINS,* CHESTER DALE COLLECTION

founded by New York social worker Florence Kelley, 41, who last year joined the Henry Street Settlement after 8 years at Chicago's Hull-House (*see* 1893; Addams, 1889; New York Consumers League, 1890). Conscientious consumers, says Kelley, will not want to buy goods made in substandard factories, or by child labor, or finished in tenements. She is joined by Josephine Goldmark and others in a campaign against child labor and tenement sweatshops. The League will work for minimum wage laws, shorter hours, improved working conditions, occupational safety, better conditions for migrant farm labor, and consumer protection in the form of pure food and drug laws.

 Only 19 percent of U.S. factory workers are women, down from 25 percent in 1850. Most are employed in the northern textile and garment industries, but the number of women in southern

factories has tripled since the Civil War. And whereas 41 percent of black women work outside the home for wages (most of them in agriculture or as domestic servants), only 17 percent of white women—chiefly immigrants—work for wages. Women employees overall receive 53 percent of what men are paid for the same work, and in some industries they receive only one-third as much.

 Naturalist Mary Kingsley goes to Africa to serve as a nurse in the Boer War but contracts typhoid fever in Simonstown and dies June 1 at age 37 (*see* science, 1893).

Tokyo Women's Medical School is founded by local physician Yaei Yashioka (*née* Washiyama), 29, who rejected traditional early marriage in order to pursue a career like that of her father, a country doctor in Shizuoka Prefecture. When she was graduated at age 14 after 9 years' education, she was one of two girls in a class of 102. She gained admittance 4 years later (1889) to Saiseigakjusha Medical School, the same Tokyo medical school that her two brothers attended (it was the only coeducational medical school and has since given up coeducation), became a licensed physician in 1892, went home to help her father, returned to Tokyo in 1894, married, and opened a clinic and school with her husband. Her new medical school will become a college in 1947.

Infant mortality in the United States is 122 per 1,000 live births, in England and Wales 154, and in India 232 (*see* 1951).

Average age at death in the United States is 47.

The U.S. College Entrance Examination Board is founded to screen applicants to colleges. College Board Scholastic Aptitude Tests (S.A.T.s) will be graded on a scale of 200 to 800, and colleges will use S.A.T. scores as a supplement to secondary school records and other relevant information in judging qualifications of applicants, but the scores will never be more than approximate and will have a standard error of measurement in the area of 32 points.

Tokyo's Tsudajuku College has its beginnings in a school founded by teachers Umiko Tsuda and Sutematsu Oyama, who were among a group of students sent to the United States for study in 1871. Tsuda returned to Japan in 1882, taught English to

Japanese girls, and in 1889 entered Bryn Mawr College to commence another 7 years' study in America. The new school will become a college in 1948.

San Francisco Examiner reporter Winfred Black, 36, rushes to Galveston, Texas, at news that a September 8 hurricane has killed upwards of 6,000 people. Disguising herself as a boy to get into the city, she is the first reporter—and the only woman journalist—to cover the disaster story.

Nonfiction: *Women and Economics: A Study of the Economic Relation Between Men and Women as a Factor in Social Evolution* by Charlotte Perkins (Stetson) Gilman, who writes, "The women whose splendid extravagance dazzles the world, whose economic goods are the greatest, are often neither houseworkers nor mothers, but simply the women who hold most power over the men who have the most money" (*see* Veblen, 1899); *The Higher Edu-*

cation of Women by Bryn Mawr College president Martha Carey Thomas, now 43, who is prominent in the struggle for woman suffrage; *The Century of the Child* (*Barnets Århundrade*) by Ellen Key, who has taught school at Stockholm for 19 years and is now a lecturer at the People's Institute for Workingmen.

Fiction: *The Village of Women* (*Das Weiberdorf*) and *Our Daily Bread* (*Das tägliche Brot*) by Clara Viebig; *To Have and to Hold* by Mary Johnston, whose mother died last year, leaving her in charge of the household: her story of the wives of Jamestown colonists has been serialized in the *Atlantic Monthly* (it will be filmed in 1915 and again in 1922); *Sister Carrie* by U.S. novelist Theodore Dreiser, 29: publisher Frank N. Doubleday hastily withdraws the book when his wife says it is too sordid, the small edition goes almost unnoticed, and Dreiser suffers a nervous breakdown; *The Master Christian* by Marie Corelli; *The Flame of Life* (*Il fuoco*) by Gabriele D'Annunzio has been inspired by the actress Eleonora Duse, now 41, with whom D'Annunzio has had a long affair; *The Old House* (*La vecchia casa*) by Nera.

Juvenile: *Claudine at School* (*Claudine à l'ecole*) by French author Colette (Sidonie-Gabrielle-Claudine Colette), 27, is a semiautobiographical series of stories that will have many sequels.

Painting: *Portrait of a Young Girl* by Mary Cassatt; *The Wyndham Sisters* by U.S. painter John Singer Sargent, 44.

Japan's Women's College of Art has its beginnings in a Tokyo academy founded by Shizu Sato; it will become a college in 1949.

Josephine B. Johnston wins a gold medal at the Paris Exposition for her before-and-after photographs documenting the benefits of progressive education at the Hampton Institute in Virginia (*see* 1893). She is the only U.S. woman photographer at the third International Photographic Congress at Paris, and she goes on to take photographs at the Carlisle Indian School in Pennsylvania.

Broadway musicals: Lillian Russell, Joe Weber, Lew Fields, De Wolf Hopper, and David Warfield in *Fiddle-dee-dee* 9/16 at Weber & Fields Music Hall, with songs that include "Rosie, You Are My Posie

Charlotte Perkins Gilman said that women's economic dependence was their chief barrier to progress. LIBRARY OF CONGRESS

(Ma Blushin' Rosie)" by John Stromberg, lyrics by Edgar Smith, 262 perfs.

Opera: German soprano Johanna (Amelia Agnes) Gadski, 27, makes her debut 1/6 as a regular member of New York's Metropolitan Opera company, singing the role of Senta in the 1843 Wagner opera *Der Fliegende Holländer*. She will remain with the Met until 1917; Scottish soprano Mary Garden (Mary Davidson), 25, creates the title role in the new Gustave Charpentier opera *Louise* 1/12 at the Opéra-Comique, Paris; Milka Ternina sings the title role in the new Puccini opera *Tosca* at Covent Garden 7/12 in its first London production.

 Blanche Bingley Hillyard wins in women's singles at Wimbledon, Myrtle McAteer in U.S. women's singles.

Lady Randolph Churchill (Jennie Jerome), now 46, remarries July 28, taking as her second husband George Cornwallis-West, 26, a lieutenant in the Scots Guard whom she met last year (*see* 1895; 1913).

The Junior League of the New York College Settlement is founded by postdebutante Mary Harriman, daughter of financier Edward Harriman, who organizes a group to aid a local settlement house. Debutantes flock to join the league, which will be followed by Junior Leagues of Baltimore, Brooklyn, Philadelphia, and (in 1906) of Boston. By 1920, there will be 39 Junior Leagues engaged in civic improvement projects, and Dorothy Whitney (Mrs. Willard) Straight will organize them into the Association of Junior Leagues of America.

One U.S. home in seven has a bathtub; showers are even rarer.

Mead Johnson Co. is founded at Evansville, Ind., to produce the infant cereal Pablum, which will be sold through physicians' recommendations.

Typical U.S. food prices: sugar 4¢ lb., eggs 14¢ doz., butter 24¢ to 25¢ lb. Boardinghouses offer turkey dinner at 20¢ and supper or breakfast at 15¢, but a male stenographer earns $10 per week and an unskilled girl $2.50. Half of all U.S. working women are farmhands or domestic servants.

Kansas prohibitionist Carry (Amelia) Nation (*née* Moore), 54, declares that since the saloon is illegal

Temperance advocate Carry Nation went on a fierce hatchet-wielding rampage against saloons. ITHACA, N.Y., *SATURDAY GLOBE,* FEBRUARY 1901

in Kansas, any citizen has the right to destroy liquor, furniture, and fixtures in any public place selling intoxicants. Standing six feet tall and weighing 175 pounds, she raids a "bastion of male arrogance" December 27, beginning a campaign of hatchet wielding through Kansas cities and towns, and although she will be arrested for taking the law into her own hands, fined, imprisoned, clubbed, and shot at, she will persevere (her husband will divorce her next year on grounds of desertion).

White mothers in America have 3.56 children on average, down from more than seven a century ago when infant mortality was higher, girls married slightly younger, and women knew less about contraception and abortion. The birthrate will decline by another third in the next 30 years.

Metal catheters for use in abortion are widely available in France. A physician writes that a woman can perform the procedure without assistance, saying that he believes "the average French woman can locate her uterine os [bone] as certainly as she can touch the tip of her nose." He suggests dilating the cervix "by rotary onward motion . . . until the sensation of rupture occurs and by the escape of bloody fluid proves the success of the operation." A woman nervous about using a catheter (although many are encased in rubber) will often terminate a pregnancy by taking a long rubber nozzle to inject water under high pressure into her uterus, irritating the uterine walls to dislodge the placenta. Abortionists earlier in the century have employed this method, and although many women now understand how to do it themselves, such use of a syringe can damage the vagina or uterus if the apparatus is not properly sterilized and not used with meticulous care to prevent peritonitis or creating air bubbles which may travel to the lungs or heart. Most women, in France and elsewhere rely on vaginal douching, which is safer, albeit far less effective.

A new German criminal code includes provisions against obscene advertisements, including those promoting the sale of contraceptives.

20th Century

1901

Queen Victoria dies January 22 at age 81 after a reign of nearly 64 years in which the United Kingdom has grown from a nation of 25 million to one of 37 million and the Empire has grown to cover much of Africa and Asia. Victoria's son, the prince of Wales, now 59, will reign until 1910 as Edward VII; he has formed a liaison with Alice Keppel, whose husband, George, has no objection (neither does Queen Alexandra), and she will remain the king's only mistress until his death.

Russian revolutionary Konstantinovna Nadezhda Krupskaya, 32, becomes secretary of the Bolshevik faction of the Social Democratic party, a post that she will hold until 1917.

Anarchist Emma Goldman is accused of having had a hand in the assassination of President William McKinley, who has been shot in the stomach at point-blank range September 6 during a visit to the Pan-American Exposition at Buffalo, N.Y. (*see* 893). Goldman, who has actually renounced the use of violence as a tactic, is deprived of her U.S. citizenship (*see* 1917).

Utah Governor Heber M. Wells vetoes a bill that would have eased restrictions on polygamy, which was officially outlawed when Utah gained statehood in 1894. The March 14 veto comes within days of passage by the legislature of a measure which would make it virtually impossible to prosecute people accused of multiple marriages.

The first chapter of the College Equal Suffrage League is founded by Boston suffragists Maud May Park (*née* Wood), 30, and Inez Gillmore (*née* Haynes), 28, to get more young women involved in the struggle for voting rights. Park, who was graduated summa cum laude from Radcliffe in 3 years, secretly married a Boston architect while still in college and met Gillmore, who entered Radcliffe as a special student after her marriage. Park will travel across the country organizing chapters of the CESL.

Average life expectancy at birth for U.S. white females is 51.08 years, for white males 48.23 years.

Girls in Western cultures menstruate for the first time at about age 14, down from age 17 in the late 18th century. The average age of menarche will decline to 13 in this century.

Scottish surgeon Elsie Maud Inglis, 37, opens an Edinburgh maternity hospital staffed entirely by women. She has been horrified both by the lack of proper maternity facilities and by her male colleagues' prejudice against women physicians.

Johns Hopkins Hospital research physician Dorothy Reed, 27, disproves the theory that Hodgkin's disease is a form of tuberculosis by demonstrating that a particular blood cell is present in every case and is a distinctive characteristic of the disease. It will became known as the Reed (or Sternberg-Reed or Reed-Sternberg) cell. A Johns Hopkins graduate, Reed has studied under William Osler and William H. Welch.

The Instructive Nursing Association begins making antenatal visits to outpatients of Boston's Lying-In Hospital. By 1912 it will be making at least three such visits to every patient. Most hospitals now offer "painless" birth not readily available in home deliveries, but puerperal fever remains a hazard in both hospital and home deliveries, obstetricians casually "sterilizing" needles and probes by running them through bars of soap and cleaning their hands by wiping them on towels.

Argyrol, introduced by Philadelphia chemists Albert C. Barnes and Herman Hille, both 31, is a silver-gelatin colloid that will come into almost universal use for protecting newborn infants from blindness caused by gonorrheal infection (*see* Howe Act, 1890). Stored in bottles, however, Argyrol can become contaminated, and evaporation often raises its concentration to dangerously high levels (*see* Baker, below).

New York physician Sarah Josephine Baker, 28, gives up her private practice after 1 year and obtains a position as a city medical inspector at an annual salary that is double the $185 she earned last year (although her patients included actress Lillian Russell). Baker, who was graduated second in her class of 18 from the Women's Medical College of New York 3 years ago, works in the West Side slum known as Hell's Kitchen, where she inspects for contagious diseases such as influenza, dysentery, smallpox, and typhoid fever (*see* 1903).

Dr. Baker (above) will solve the problems of contaminated and overconcentrated Argyrol (above) by placing silver nitrate in beeswax capsules, each containing just enough solution for one eye. Her method will be adopted throughout the world.

Japan Women's College opens at Tokyo. Many of its graduates will participate in the nation's fledgling feminist movement.

Texas Women's University is founded at Denton.

New York's Chapin School has its beginnings in Miss Chapin's School for Girls and Kindergarten for Boys and Girls opened in the fall by former Brearley primary classes director Maria Bowen Chapin, 38. Her primary school for 75 pupils in a townhouse at 12 East 47th Street will move to 48–50 East 58th Street in 1905, add an upper school in 1909, move into two brownstones at 32–34 East 57th Street in 1910, become a girls-only school in 1915, have 318 students by 1925, move into its own building at 100 East End Avenue in

1928, add a kindergarten in 1974, and grow to have an enrollment of 575. Miss Chapin will head the school until 1932.

"Dorothy Dix Talks" begins appearing as a column in William Randolph Hearst's *New York Evening Journal*. "Dix" is former *New Orleans Picayune* women's page columnist Elizabeth Merriwether Gilmer, 29, who accepts the reality of a sexual double standard and counsels her readers on how to deal with this reality. "The young girl who lets any one boy monopolize her, simply shuts the door in the face of good times and her chances of making a better match," she will write. She will advise women to develop a positive self-image and to work at jobs without sacrificing their femininity, good nature, and adaptability, but she will also champion the cause of woman suffrage with three pamphlets that will appear from 1912 to 1914.

Fiction: *My Brilliant Career* by Australian novelist (Stella Marian Sarah) Miles Franklin, 22, who writes under the pseudonym Brent of Bin Bin (a fifth-generation Australian, she will emigrate to America in 1906 and work as a secretary for the Women's Trade Union League but will return to her homeland for good in 1927); *The Child: Andrea* (*Barnet*) (stories) by Danish novelist Karen Michælis, 29, whose work will be translated into 15 languages; *Regine Vosgerau* by German novelist-poet Helene Voigt-Diederichs, 26; *The Doomswoman, An Historical Romance of Old California* by Gertrude Atherton.

Poetry: *The Innumerable Heart* (*Le Coeur innombrable*) by French poet Anna Elisabeth de Brancovan, comtesse de Noailles, 25, who was married 4 years ago to Count Mathieu de Noailles and last year gave birth to a son, Anne-Jules; *Undercurrent* (*Unterström*) by Helene Voigt-Diederichs (above); *Tangled Hair* (*Midaregami*) by Japanese poet Akiko Yosano (*née* Ōtori), 23, who breaks the centuries-old literary ban against a woman expressing her emotions in print.

Juvenile: *Mrs. Wiggs of the Cabbage Patch* by U.S. writer Alice (Caldwell) Hegan, 31; *The Would-Be Goods* by Edith Nesbit; *A Sister of the Red Cross: A Tale of the South African War* and *Girls of the True Blue* by L. T. Meade.

Painting: *Portrait of a Sick Girl* by German painter Paula Modersohn-Becker (*née* Becker), 25, who has married landscape artist Otto Modersohn; *Antoine Holding a Child by Both Hands, Fillette au Grand Chapeau,* and *Mother and Boy* by Mary Cassatt; *Portrait* by Cecilia Beaux.

Photograph: "Marsh at Dawn" by U.S. photographer Imogen Cunningham, 18.

Theater: Amelia Bingham in Clyde Fitch's *The Climbers* 1/21 at New York's Bijou Theater, 163 perfs.; *The Three Sisters (Tri Sestry)* by Russian playwright Anton Chekhov, 41, 1/31 at the Moscow Art Theater; Minnie Maddern Fiske (*née* Marie Augusta Davey), 34, in *Miranda of the Balcony* by U.S. playwright Ann Crawford Flexner, 27, 9/24 to open Harrison Grey Fiske's new Manhattan Theater, 62 perfs.; Elsie de Wolfe in Fitch's *The Way of the World* 11/4 at Hammerstein's Victoria Theater, New York, 35 perfs.; Annie Russell in Fitch's *The Girl and the Judge* 12/4 at New York's Lyceum Theater, 125 perfs.

Opera: Milka Ternina makes her Metropolitan Opera debut 2/4 singing the title role in the 1900 Puccini opera *Tosca* (she will retire in 1906 to teach at Zagreb); U.S. soprano Geraldine Farrar, 19, makes her debut 10/15 at the Berlin Royal Opera singing the role of Marguerite in the 1859 Gounod opera *Faust.*

Popular songs: *Seven Songs as Unpretentious as the Wild Rose* by Janesville, Wis., songwriter Carrie Bond (*née* Jacobs), 39, includes "I Love You Truly."

Charlotte Cooper Sterry wins in women's singles at Wimbledon, Elizabeth Moore in U.S. women's singles.

Texas ranch owner Anna Edson Taylor, 43, goes over Niagara's Horseshoe Falls in a barrel October 24. She wears a leather harness inside the barrel, which is four and a half feet long, three feet in diameter, and cushioned inside. The former Bay City, Mich., schoolteacher suffers only shock and minor cuts in the 167-foot drop, wins a reward that helps pay an installment on her ranch loan, and is the first person to go over the falls and survive.

The first practical electric vacuum cleaner is invented by British bridge builder and wheel designer Hubert Booth. His Vacuum Cleaner Co. Ltd. sends vans around to houses and uses the Booth machine to suck out dust via tubes to the street (*see* Spangler, Hoover, 1907; Electrolux, 1921).

A new tenement house law is passed in New York, whose 83,000 "old law" masonry-and-wood tenements house 70 percent of the city's population. Strung end to end like railroad cars, the rooms in the old six-story tenements have only tiny air shafts to provide light and air to their 90-foot lengths, they crowd 10 families into 25- by 100-foot lots, and their minimal communal plumbing is indoors only because outhouses would consume land used for building.

The Settlement Cookbook by Milwaukee settlement house worker Lizzie Black (Mrs. Simon Kander) is published with funds raised by volunteer women through advertisements after the settlement house directors have refused a request for $18 to print a book that would save students in a class for immigrants from having to copy recipes off the blackboard. Using the slogan "The way to a man's heart," the book will earn enough money in 8 years to pay for a new settlement house building and be a perennial best-seller.

1902

Women textile workers in Britain present a suffrage petition to Parliament February 18 (*see* WSPU, 1903).

Glasgow outlaws barmaids beginning April 22, creating a storm of controversy.

Irish-born journalist Daisy (May) Bates (*née* O'Dwyer), 38, sets out riding sidesaddle April 23 to help her husband, Jack, drive 770 head of Hereford cattle 600 to 700 miles through parched western Australia to the Ethel Creek station that she has purchased on the Murchison River. Some 200 head are lost en route, the Bates's rocky marriage is further strained (it will effectively end next year), but Daisy, who has heard about aboriginal women being forced by pearlers to dive in the latter months of pregnancy, discovers caves containing traces of prehistoric life. She will educate herself in anthropology, live in the bush with the aborigines, and devote her efforts to improving their lives (*see* 1912).

Chicago glovemaker Agnes Nestor helps organize the International Glove Workers Union (A.F. of L.) and founds Local #1 of the IGWU (*see* 1899; 1903).

Greenwich House is founded in New York's Greenwich Village by Boston heiress and social reformer Mary Simkovitch (*née* Kingsbury), 35, who 3 years ago married a Russian-born Columbia University professor of economic history whom she had met in Berlin.

U.S. feminists mourn the loss of suffragist Elizabeth Cady Stanton, who dies at New York October 26 at age 87.

History of the Standard Oil Company by journalist Ida Minerva Tarbell, 44, begins appearing in *McClure's* magazine installments, revealing that John D. Rockefeller controls 90 percent of U.S. oil-refining capacity and has an annual income of $45 million. Raised in Titusville by a father who made a fortune building barrels for the oil trade, Tarbell has uncovered facts about the secretive Rockefeller

Ida Tarbell's "muckraking" exposed the machinations of pioneer oilman John D. Rockefeller. LIBRARY OF CONGRESS

that will lead to the breakup of his Standard Oil trust by the Supreme Court in 1911.

U.S. astronomer Henrietta Swan Leavitt, 34, joins the staff of the Harvard College Observatory and is soon appointed head of its department of photographic photometry. A colleague of Annie Jump Cannon, 39 (both are extremely deaf), she will observe in her study of Cepheid variable stars that the brighter they are the longer the period of their light variation, and by 1912 she will show that the apparent magnitude decreases linearly with the logarithm of the period, a simple relationship that will point the way to a method for measuring the distance of stars (*see* Cannon, 1930).

The Midwives' Bill passed by Parliament July 31 requires licensing of midwives. They are required to send for physicians when complications arise in labor, and physicians are bound to respond to such calls. Women's organizations have pushed for the legislation following well-publicized stories of childbirth fatalities last year, when physicians refused to attend cases because they did not want to follow where a midwife had been in charge. Unqualified midwives are given until 1910 to obtain qualification, and even the best midwives remain subject to regulation by the medical profession. The measure arrests the decline of midwifery in Britain (but *see* 1905); in America, midwives will survive only in the poorest segments of society.

Twilight Sleep is introduced by the German physician Von Steinbuchel of Graz to eliminate the pain of childbirth. Based on the principle that it is the knowledge of pain rather than the pain itself that damages women, the technique will be refined by two other Germans and used most notably at Freiburg's Frauenklinik, which will attract women from other countries. Beginning only after labor contractions are well established in order to avoid having sleep stop the labor before it really begins, obstetricians inject 1/150 grain of scopalomine (an amnesiac) with ½ grain of narcophin or morphine (narcotic analgesics) After 45 minutes, a second injection of 1/150 grain of scopalomine is given, with subsequent injections of scopalomine only depending on results of memory tests given to the patient, who receives only enough medication to remain in an amnesiac or semiconscious state and not enough to cause any serious complications such as infant respiratory depression at birth or uterine inertia, which may prolong labor or cause post-partum hemorrhage (many variations of the technique will evolve). Ideally, the patient remains drowsy and sleeps between contractions, feeling some pain during contractions but remembering little or nothing afterward (*see* 1909).

Northwestern University Medical School closes its women's division in a backlash against feminism; by 1910, scarcely 3 percent of students at Michigan Medical School will be women, down from 25 percent in 1890.

Rhodes scholarships are established under the will of British gold- and diamond-mine magnate Cecil J. Rhodes, who dies in Africa March 26 at age 49 leaving $10 million to endow 170 3-year scholarships at Oxford University. Awarded each year to 60 young men from the British colonies, 100 from the United States, and 15 from Germany, the scholarships pay £250 per year; the trustees will increase the amount but will not award any scholarships to women until 1976.

Simmons College for Women opens October 9 at Boston and soon has 132 students, half of whom hold jobs as clerks, bookkeepers, and stenographers, one-quarter of whom are teachers and the rest having various other occupations. Money for the new college has come from the estate of the late John Simmons, who pioneered before 1835 in producing ready-made men's suits (which were stitched by women, many of them farmers' wives who worked on them during the long winter months), quit the clothing business in 1854 to devote his energies to real estate, was inspired by the example of Matthew Vassar to found a women's college, and died in August 1870 at age 75. The Boston fire of 1872 destroyed all of his buildings, the insurance companies could not meet their obligations, and his estate was left with nothing but the property on which the buildings had stood. It has taken nearly 30 years to build the estate back to its original value and provide for the college, which next year will acquire the Boston Cooking School and make its director, Maria Willett Howard, head of its Department of Cooking. In addition to college-level academic courses and vocational courses in bookkeeping, shorthand, and typing (many of them night courses), Simmons offers a 1-year domestic science program that will come to be called the "diamond ring" course. Its school for social workers will open in 1904.

Nonfiction: *Harriet Hubbard Ayer's Book of Health and Beauty* by skin cream manufacturer Ayer, 53, who married Herbert Copeland Ayer in 1865, lost a child in the Chicago fire of 1871, divorced her husband in 1886, met a chemist who claimed to have the formula for a face cream that his grandfather had invented for the legendary Mme. Récamier (a beauty in the court of Napoleon I), borrowed enough money to buy the formula, and started making the cream, selling it under the Recamier name. She wrote advertising that employed testimonials from prominent entertainers, including Lily Langtry, and socialites but was victimized by her financial backers, her ex-husband, and her daughter (who discredited her, seized her business, slandered and sued her, and had her committed to a mental asylum). She has lectured on her "14 Months in a Madhouse," and written beauty columns for newspapers.

Fiction: *After the Divorce* (*Dopo il divorzio*) by Italian novelist Grazia Deledda, 30; *Aus der Triumphgasse* by Ricarda Huch; *The Watch on the Rhine* (*Die Wacht am Rhein*) by Clara Viebig; *The Story of a Mother* by Jane Findlater; *The Conqueror* by Gertrude Atherton is a fictional biography of Alexander Hamilton and pioneers the biographical novel; *Audrey* by Mary Johnston, whose novel will be turned into a play starring Eleanor Robson.

Poetry: *The Shadow of Days* (*L'Ombre des jours*) by Anna, comtesse de Noailles.

Juvenile: *The Tale of Peter Rabbit* by English artist-writer-naturalist Beatrix Potter, 36, who has been the first person in England to establish the fact that lichens represent a merging of algae and fungi but whose efforts in botany have been frustrated by the male scientific establishment. Written as an illustrated letter to the son of her former governess, *Peter Rabbit* was written in 1900 but is published now by F. Warne and Co., whose editor, Norman Warne, will be engaged to Potter but will die in 1905 before they can marry. Peter, Mopsy, Flopsy, and Cottontail will be followed by 22 more books that Potter will write and illustrate in the next 11 years. *Five Children and It* by Edith Nesbit. *A World of Girls: The Story of a School* by L. T. Meade.

Painting: *Jeanette in a Green Bonnet* (*La Chapeau au Fillette Vert*) and *Child in Orange Dress* by Mary Cassatt; *Tent Pegging* by Lady Elizabeth Butler.

Crayola brand crayons are introduced by the Easton, Pa., firm Binney & Smith. Founder's son Edwin Binney has developed the crayons by adding oil and pigments to the black paraffin and stearic acid marking devices sold by the firm, and his mother has suggested the name Crayola.

Boston's Fenway Court opens New Year's Eve with a concert by 50 Boston Symphony musicians and a crowd of socialites who have come to see the art collection of department store heiress Isabella Stewart (Mrs. John Lowell) Gardner, 62, and its diamond-and-pearl-bedizened owner, whose husband died in 1898. Novelist Henry James has compared her with "a figure on a wondrous cinquecento tapestry." She has had an ancient mosaic floor from Rome, stone lions from Florence, and balconies from Venice imported to grace her Italianate palace, under construction since 1899, which she will bequeath to the public along with its art treasures upon her death in 1924.

Theater: *Her Lord and Master* by Martha Morton 2/24 at New York's Gaiety Theater, with Effie Shannon and Douglas Fairbanks, 69 perfs.; *The Diplomat* by Martha Morton 3/20 at New York's Madison Square Garden, 76 perfs.; English-born Irish actress-patriot Maud Gonne, 36, in *Cathleen ni Houlihan* by William Butler Yeats, now 36, and Isabella Augusta, Lady Gregory (*née* Persse), 50, 4/2 at St. Teresa's Total Abstinence Hall, Dublin; Canadian-born actress Lucile Watson, 23, in Clyde Fitch's *The Girl with the Green Eyes* 12/25 at New York's Savoy Theatre, 108 perfs.

Opera: Mary Garden creates the female lead in the new Debussy opera Pélleas et Mélisande 4/30 at the Opéra-Comique, Paris.

Broadway musicals: Lillian Russell in *Twirly Whirly* 9/11 at the Weber and Fields Music Hall, songs that include "Come Down Ma Evenin' Star," 244 perfs.

Paris entertainer Mistinguett (Jeanne Bourgeois), 29, performs the Apache dance with Max Dearly at the Moulin Rouge music hall (year approximate). She started her career singing in restaurants while selling flowers.

Muriel Evelyn Robb, 24, wins in women's singles at Wimbledon, Marion Jones in U.S. women's singles.

The Teddy Bear introduced by Russian-American candy store operator Morris Michtom and his wife of Brooklyn, N.Y., has movable arms, legs, and head. The Michtoms have seen a cartoon by Clifford Berryman in the November 18 *Washington Evening Star* showing President "Teddy" Roosevelt refusing to shoot a mother bear while hunting in Mississippi. They obtain the president's permission to use his nickname, and their brown plush toy Teddy Bear creates a sensation (*see* 1903).

The brassiere, invented by French fashion designer Charles R. Debevoise, will have little popularity until the introduction of elastic (*see* 1914).

Everdry, a new deodorant cream, improves on Mum (*see* 1888) by adding aluminum chloride to the zinc to expedite drying (*see* 1919).

Paris jeweler Louis Cartier creates 27 diamond tiaras for the coronation of Britain's Edward VII. Cartier opens a London branch in New Bond Street with his brother Jacques in charge.

Rosecliff is completed at Newport, R.I., by New York architect Stanford White for Mrs. Hermann Oelrichs (*née* Fair), daughter of the late San Francisco mining and banking magnate James Fair. Last of the great Newport "cottages," Rosecliff is a 40-room French château with a Court of Love designed by sculptor Augustus Saint-Gaudens after one at Versailles.

Whitehall is completed at Palm Beach by Carrère and Hastings for Florida East Coast Railway magnate Henry M. Flagler and his third bride. Flagler has told the architects to "build me the finest home you can think of," they have put up a 73-room, $2.5 million Spanish-inspired temple with massive Doric columns and gigantic urns, the 6-acre waterfront home has been finished in 8 months, and the *New York Herald* calls it "more wonderful than any palace in Europe, grander and more magnificent than any other private dwelling in the world."

1903

 The Oregon state legislature enacts a law February 19 prohibiting employment of women for more than 10 hours per day in any factory or laundry (*see* Supreme Court decision, 1908).

Agnes Nestor and Elizabeth Christman lead female glove makers out of the International Glove Workers Union and form their own women's local (*see* 1902); Nestor, now 23, is elected president. Sweatshop workers are obliged to accept whatever treatment they are given and have no means of redress. They are penalized not only if their stitches are crooked or they stain goods with machine oil, but also if they talk or laugh while at work. They may be charged 50¢ per week for the use of a machine and electricity, 5¢ per week for the use of a mirror and towel, 5¢ per week for drinking water.

The National Women's Trade Union League (WTUL) is founded by Women's Educational and Industrial Union director Mary Kimball Kehew, now 44, Mary Kenney O'Sullivan, Jane Addams, and a group of middle-class U.S. reformers who want to help working women organize themselves into trade unions. Kehew serves as president, Addams as vice president, and members include Chicago social worker Mary Eliza McDowell, 49, who 4 years ago joined with Addams and Ellen Starr at Hull-House. Social worker Lillian Wald of New York's Henry Street Settlement will work vigorously for the WTUL, Agnes Nestor (above) will be a member of its executive board beginning in 1907, and the group's research teams will develop detailed statistical reports to back up campaigns for legislation in such areas as minimum wages, sanitation, and old-age pensions (*see* Schneiderman, 1905).

The Women's Social and Political Union (WSPU) is founded at London October 3 by reformers who include Emmeline Goulden Pankhurst, now 46, whose husband, Richard, died in 1898 (*see* 1882). She gathers like-minded women at her house, and they begin to work through the Independent Labour party to achieve their goal of voting rights for women (*see* 1905).

The Consiglio Nazionale delle Donne Italiane, organized at Rome, will quickly become Italy's leading feminist group (*see* 1899; 1908).

Mme. Marie Curie helped isolate radium, the first radioactive element. It won her a Nobel Prize in physics. LIBRARY OF CONGRESS

 Marie Curie is awarded the Nobel Prize December 10 together with her husband, Pierre. She is the first woman recipient of the prize (*see* 1911).

 "Typhoid Mary" gets her name as New York has an outbreak of typhoid fever with 1,300 cases reported. City medical inspector Sarah Josephine Baker helps trace the epidemic to one Mary Mallon, a carrier of the disease (but not a victim), who takes jobs that involve handling food, often using assumed names. Typhoid Mary refuses to stop, will be placed under detention in 1915, and will remain confined until her death in 1938.

Sarah Josephine Baker (above) is appointed assistant health commissioner (*see* 1901). Her all-male staff resigns en masse, but Baker will license midwives, standardize the inspection of schoolchildren for contagious diseases, teach mothers hygiene, proper ventilation, and nutrition, establish "milk stations" where mothers can obtain free pasteurized milk, distribute baby formula of limewater and milk sugar that any woman can make at home, and start a "Little Mothers League" that teaches infant care to children whose mothers leave them in charge of their siblings. Within 15 years, her efforts will cut the death rate in New York's slums from 1,500 per week to 300, enabling the city to claim the lowest infant mortality rate of any in the Western world (*see* 1916).

Skidmore College has its beginnings in the Young Women's Industrial Club of Saratoga Springs (N.Y.), founded by local philanthropist Lucy Scribner (*née* Skidmore), 50, for the "mutual instruction and improvement of the members and to establish a social center for the cultivation of such knowledge and arts as may promote their well-being." Its classes in domestic science, piano and vocal music, English literature, stenography, and physical culture attract 200 women and girls. Mrs. Scribner will build a clubhouse next year, will acquire the Temple Grove Seminary building in 1909, and in 1911 will turn the club into the Skidmore School of Arts with a gift of $300,000 (*see* 1922).

The *London Daily Mirror* begins publication. *Daily Mail* publisher Alfred C. W. Harmsworth and his brother Harold hire a woman editor, address the tabloid to women, but will make it a general-interest "picture newspaper" next year to pick up lagging sales. It will have a circulation of more than a million by 1909, A. C. Harmsworth will be made a baronet (Viscount Northcliffe) in 1905, his brother Viscount Rothermere.

Nonfiction: *The Woman Who Toils* by U.S. reformer Marie Van Vorst, 35, and her sister-in-law Bessie Van Vorst is an exposé of life in a Lynn, Mass., shoe factory and in South Carolina cotton mills: championing the cause of labor unions, it says, "Organize labor well . . . so that the work-woman who obtains her task may be able to continue it and keep her health and self-respect"; *The Home, Its Work and Influence* by Charlotte Perkins (Stetson) Gilman; *The Life of the Finnish Workers* by Aleksandra Kollontai, now 31, who has left her husband and child to devote her energies to social revolution.

Fiction: *The New Hope* (*La Nouvelle Espérance*) by Anna, comtesse de Noailles; *Kent Hampden* by

Rebecca Harding Davis, now 72, whose son Richard has become a celebrated war correspondent; *Mrs. Pendleton's Four-in-Hand* by Gertrude Atherton; *Elias Portolu* by Grazia Deledda; *Una passione* by Nera, now 57.

Juvenile: *Rebecca of Sunnybrook Farm* by Kate Douglas Wiggin, now 47 (her book is actually an adult best-seller); *The Tailor of Gloucester* and *The Tale of Squirrel Nutkin* by Beatrix Potter.

Painting: *Silent Mother and Old Peasant* by Paula Modersohn-Becker.

Theater: *The Hour-Glass* by W. B. Yeats and Lady Gregory 3/14 at Dublin's Moleworth Hall; *The King's Threshold* by Yeats and Lady Gregory 3/14 at Dublin's Moleworth Hall; "Give women the vote, and in five years there will be a crushing tax on bachelors," writes George Bernard Shaw in the preface to his play *Man and Superman* (which will have its stage premiere in 1905).

Opera: Adelina Patti begins her final American tour 11/4 at New York's Carnegie Hall.

Broadway musicals: Fritzi Scheff in *Babette* 11/16 at the Broadway Theater, 59 perfs.

Popular songs: "(You're the Flower of My Heart) Sweet Adeline" by U.S. composer Henry W. Armstrong, 24, lyrics by Richard H. Gerard (R. G. Husch), 27, whose words, inspired by the farewell tour of Italian prima donna Adelina Patti (above), will be sung by generations of barbershop quartets; "Waltzing Matilda" by Australian songwriter Marie Cowan, who has adapted the 1818 Scottish song "Thou Bonny Wood of Craigie Lee" ("Matilda" is Aussie slang for a knapsack; a "swagman" is a worker).

D. K. (Dorothea Katherine) Douglass, 30, wins in women's singles at Wimbledon, Elizabeth Moore in U.S. women's singles.

New York's Colony Club is founded by women who include society matron Mrs. J. (Jefferson) Borden Harriman (*née* Florence Jaffray Jones), 32, who was obliged to leave Newport last summer to run some errands in the city and found the Harriman town house full of painters and plasterers. It was unheard of for a proper woman to check into a hotel alone, and the city had no women's club with a proper clubhouse. She has persuaded Mrs. John Jacob Astor, Mrs. Payne Whitney, and some other women to join her in building a clubhouse with all the comforts of the Union Club. They fix an initiation fee of $150 and annual dues at $100, placing the Colony Club on the same level as the most expensive men's clubs, and set exclusive admission standards. J. P. Morgan, whose three daughters all join, agrees to subscribe $10,000 toward building the clubhouse if nine other men will do the same, William C. Whitney offers to put up $25,000 if the clubhouse is as large as the new Metropolitan Club, and Stanford White is commissioned to design the building at 120 Madison Avenue, between 30th and 31st streets (*see* 1907).

The Teddy Bear introduced last year by Morris Michtom and his wife encounters a challenge from the German firm Steiff Co., founded in 1880 at Giengen in Swabia by crippled seamstress Margarete Steiff, now 56. Her nephew Richard claims to have designed a plush bear last year with jointed limbs and a movable head, he shows it at the Leipzig Fair with little success, but a U.S. buyer sees the bear on the last day of the fair and orders 3,000.

President Roosevelt designates Florida's Pelican Island a National Wildlife Refuge, a seabird sanctuary where the fowl will be safe from the plume hunters who shoot birds to obtain feathers for milliners who use them for women's hats.

sessions in the 1871 Chicago Fire, she received help from the Knights of Labor and later went to work organizing for the union. Mine owners, including oil magnate John D. Rockefeller, have asked for her deportation (*see* 1925).

Polish-American garment worker Rose (*née* Rachel) Schneiderman, 22, is elected to the executive board of the United Cloth Hat and Cap-makers Union and involves herself in a strike against a "runaway" shop that has relocated to New Jersey in order to avoid paying union wages. Schneiderman went to work at age 16 lining caps at $6 per week, out of which she had to pay for her $30 sewing machine, thread, lunches, and transportation. Her mother warned her that "men don't want a woman with a big mouth," but she and two other women obtained a UCHCU charter by stationing themselves outside factories as workers came off their shifts and getting 25 signatures on membership blanks for their own local of the Jewish Socialist United Cloth Hat and Cap-makers' Union.

Chicago packinghouse workers go on strike. No effort has been made to organize women employees, known to the men as "petticoat butchers," but Irish-American workers Hannah O'Day and Maggie Condon have led a walkout of women. Their strike was quickly broken, some of its leaders were blacklisted, and the women, fearful of starting a

Fiery orators like Rose Schneiderman came out of the sweatshops to organize their sisters against exploitation. BROWN BROTHERS

1904

Japanese naval forces attack the Russian base at Port Arthur in southern Manchuria February 8, launching the first war in which armored battleships, self-propelled torpedoes, land mines, quickfiring artillery, and machine guns will be used. Japan declares war February 10, defeats the Russians at the Yalu River May 1, occupy Dairen May 30, occupy Seoul, and force the Russians to pull back to Mukden.

Colorado authorities accuse Irish-American labor agitator Mary Harris "Mother" Jones, 74, of stirring up striking coal miners and orders her out of the state March 27. A widow who lost all her pos-

union, formed the Maud Gonne Club, named in honor of the Irish patriot-actress. After hearing a speech by Mary McDowell of the University of Chicago Settlement about working conditions in the packing houses, they asked her for help—and began to transform their club into a union: Local 183 of the Amalgamated Meat Cutters and Butcher Workmen of North America. But employers (Swift, Wilson, and Cudahy) break the strike, and the union, including Local 183, is defeated.

Japanese factories employ 530,000 workers, 310,000 of them women, of whom 80 percent tend spindles in textile mills and earn wages based on whether their abilities put them into the first grade (27 sen per day) or second grade (14.3 sen per day) (one sho of rice [3.8 pints] costs 20 sen) (*see* 1872).

The International Council of Women holds a meeting at Berlin in June and forms the International Woman Suffrage Alliance with Carrie Chapman Catt as president. Delegates include National Association of Colored Women president Mary Terrell, who delivers a speech in German describing the numerous contributions made by blacks. Rosika Schwimmer, 26, another delegate, returns to her native Budapest, helps found Feministá Egyesülte, a feminist and pacifist association, and translates the 1899 Charlotte Perkins book *Women and Economics* into Hungarian (*see* 1913).

💲 Russian-American seamstress Lane Bryant (*née* Lena Himmelstein), 24, opens a New York store selling maternity clothes. The first merchant to sell ready-to-wear clothing for stout and pregnant women, she will build a chain of Lane Bryant stores.

⚕ Britain's Interdepartmental Committee on Physical Deterioration deplores the rapid decline in breastfeeding, due in part to the employment of married women in industry, but due mostly to the chronic ill health that makes women incapable of producing milk. The committee's report demonstrates the alarming extent of poverty and ill health in British slums, where in some areas one out of four infants dies in its first 12 months and 33 percent of the children surveyed are hungry.

🎓 Helen Keller is graduated magna cum laude from Radcliffe College at age 23 and begins to write

about blindness, a subject taboo in women's magazines because so many cases are related to venereal disease (*see* 1887). Keller has learned to speak at Boston's Horace Mann School for the Deaf by feeling the position of the tongue and lips of others, making sounds, and imitating the lip and tongue motions. She has learned to lip-read by placing her fingers on the lips and throat of the speaker while the words spoken were spelled out on the palm of her hand, her book *The Story of My Life* appeared in 1902, she will begin lecturing in 1913 to raise money for the American Foundation for the Blind, her teacher Anne Sullivan will remain with her until she dies in 1936, and Keller will continue to work for the blind and deaf until her own death in 1968.

Helen Keller could not see or hear but Anne Sullivan helped her become a famous writer. LIBRARY OF CONGRESS

Bethune-Cookman College has its beginnings in the Daytona Normal and Industrial Institute for the Training of Negro Girls opened October 3 by Mary McLeod Bethune, 29, in a rented four-room cabin rented at Daytona, Fla. Bethune makes potato pies for workmen building the nearby Clarendon Hotel, earns $5 for a down payment on some land, uses charred splinters for pencils, mashed elderberries for ink, and a packing case for a desk, and solicits funds from prominent millionaire vacationers to build Faith Hall. She will have 100 pupils with three assistant teachers next year, and within 2 years, her five pupils (four girls and her little son) will have grown to 250 (*see* 1923).

Nonfiction: *History of the Standard Oil Company* by Ida M. Tarbell (*see* 1901) says the corporation is guilty of "commercial sin" but regards John D. Rockefeller as a genius for recognizing that he had to control the transportation of oil if he was to control the oil industry.

Fiction: *Hendrik on the Hill* (*Hendrik i bakken*) by Danish novelist Marie Bregendahl, 37; *Jean Jílek* by Czech novelist Teréza Novaková (*née* Lanhausová), 51, is about an 18th-century Czech who emigrates because of religious scruples; *The Sleeping Army* (*Das schlafende Heer*) by Clara Viebig; *Freckles* by U.S. novelist Gene Stratton-Porter, 39; *Rulers of Kings* by Gertrude Atherton, whose newest novel has been serialized in *Lippincott's* magazine; *Bits of Gossip* by Rebecca Harding Davis; *Sir Mortimer* by Mary Johnston, whose historical romance about Elizabethan sea rovers has been serialized in *Harper's* magazine; *Ashes* (*Cenere*) by Grazia Deledda.

Poetry: "Please Don't Die" ("Kimi shinitamau-kotonakare") by Akiko Yosano is an anti-war appeal to her brother: its appearance in *Myojo* magazine creates a controversy in the midst of Japan's triumphant war against Russia (above); *The Amazed Face* (*Visage émerveillé*) by Anna, comtesse de Noailles is the diary of a nun's love.

Juvenile: *The Tale of Benjamin Bunny* and *The Tale of Two Bad Mice* by Beatrix Potter; *The New Treasure Seekers* by Edith Nesbit.

Painting: *Old Peasant Woman* by Paula Modersohn-Becker; *Ellen Mary as a Growing Girl* and *Mother and Child before a Window* by Mary Cassatt.

Theater: *The Triumph of Love* by Martha Morton Conheim 2/8 at New York's Criterion Theater; Eleonora Duse in Gabriele D'Annunzio's *The Daughter of Jorio* (*La figlia di Iorio*) 3/2 at Milan's Teatro Lirico; Kate Rorke in George Bernard Shaw's *Candida* 4/20 at London's Royal Court Theatre; Mrs. Fiske in C. M. S. McClellan's *Leah Kleschna* 12/12 at New York's Manhattan Theater, which Fiske and her husband, playwright Harrison Grey Fiske, have rented since 1901 in order to be independent of Charles Frohman's Theatrical Syndicate, 631 perfs.; *On Baile's Strand* by Lady Gregory and W. B. Yeats 12/27 at Dublin's new Abbey Theatre off O'Connell Street; Nina Boucicault in James M. Barrie's *Peter Pan, or The Boy Who Would Not Grow Up* 12/27 at the Duke of York's Theatre, London.

Opera: *Madama Butterfly* 2/17 at Milan's Teatro alla Scala, with music by Giacomo Puccini, who has seen John Luther Long's play *Madame Butterfly* at London. Staged originally by David Belasco in New York, the play about the opening of Japan is based on the short story "Madame Butterfly," which appeared in the January 1900 issue of *Century* magazine (the new opera is a fiasco in its initial production); Emmy Destinn makes her London debut at Covent Garden 5/2 as Donna Anna in the 1787 Mozart opera *Don Giovanni*.

Broadway musicals: Anna Held and Canadian-born actress Marie Dressler (Leila von Koerber), 34, in *Higgledy-Piggledy* 10/12 at the Weber Music Hall, 185 perfs.

D. K. Douglass wins in women's singles at Wimbledon, May Godfray Sutton, 16 (Br.), in U.S. women's singles (the first non-American to win).

An article by Richmond, Va., lawyer-novelist Thomas Nelson Page, 51, in the *North American Review* blames lynching on black men's unchecked propensity toward sexual crimes. Many of Page's stories are written in black dialect.

The Ladies' Home Journal launches an exposé of the U.S. patent medicine business (*see* 1905).

Pure Food Law advocates take space at the St. Louis Exposition to dramatize the fact that U.S. foods are being colored with potentially harmful dyes. North Dakota Food Commissioner Edwin F. Ladd reports that "more than 90 percent of the local meat markets in the state were using chemical preservatives, and in nearly every butcher shop could be found a bottle of 'Freezem,' 'Preservaline,' or 'Iceine'. . . . In the dried beef, in the smoked meats, in the canned bacon, in the canned chipped beef, boracic acid or borates is a common ingredient. . . . Of cocoas and chocolates examined about 70 percent have been found adulterated. . . . Ninety percent of the so-called French peas we have taken up . . . were found to contain copper salts. Of all the canned mushrooms, 85 percent were found bleached by sulphites. There was but one brand of catsup which was pure. Many catsups were made from the waste products from canners—pulp, skins, ripe tomatoes, green tomatoes, starch paste, coal-tar colors, chemical preservatives, usually benzoate of soda or salicylic acid. . . . While potted chicken and potted turkey are common products, I have never yet found a can in the state which really contained determinable quantities of either chicken or turkey."

 "The cook was a good cook, as cooks go, and as cooks go, she went," writes English author Saki (H. H. Munro) in his story "Reginald."

1905

 Russian revolutionists who include Aleksandra Kollontai demonstrate in front of the Winter Palace at St. Petersburg January 9 ("Bloody Sunday") and are machine-gunned on orders from the czar. Kollontai attends the inaugural meeting of the Union for Women's Equality in April, speaks out against "classless" feminism, and meets V. I. Lenin briefly in the fall as revolution engulfs the nation (*see* 1907).

Socialist women agitated for revolution against the czar in the wake of Russia's defeat by Japanese naval forces.

The fifth Nobel Peace Prize is awarded to Austrian feminist and pacifist Bertha, baroness von Suttner, now 62 (*see* 1892). Her journal *Lay Down Your Arms* (*Die Waffen Nieder*) ceased publication in 1899, but her 1889 book of the same title has been translated into many European languages. She is the first woman peace Nobelist (there will not be another one until 1931).

 The Women's Vote Bill fails in Parliament May 12; English suffragist Emmeline Pankhurst begins propagandizing her cause with sensationalist methods that will include arson, bombing, hunger strikes, and window smashing (*see* 1903). Her daughter Christabel (Harriette), 25, and suffragist Annie Kenney, 26, attend a Liberal party meeting in the Free Trade Hall in Manchester called to endorse the candidacy of Winston Churchill for Parliament, they unfurl a banner challenging foreign secretary Sir Edward Grey's suffrage policy, police arrest them October 4, and they become the first suffragists to draw prison sentences, creating a national sensation (*see* 1906).

French feminist Madeleine (*née* Anne) Pelletier, 31, becomes secretary of the Groupe de la Solidarité de Femme; she will join with anarchists in imitating the law-breaking tactics of Emmeline Pankhurst's WSPU.

"Sensible and responsible women do not want to vote," writes former president Grover Cleveland in the April *Ladies' Home Journal.* "The relative positions to be assumed by men and women in the working out of our civilization were assigned long ago by a higher intelligence than ours. . . . Legislators should never neglect the dictates of chivalry in their treatment of women; but this does not demand that a smirking appearance of acquiescence should conceal or smother a thoughtful lawmaker's intelligent disapproval of female suffrage. It is one of the chief charms of women that they are not especially amenable to argument; but that is not a reason why, when they demand the ballot as an inherent right, they should not be reminded that suffrage is a privilege which attaches neither to man nor to woman by nature. . . . I have sometimes wondered if the really good women who are inclined to approve this doctrine of female suffrage are not deluding themselves with purely sentimental views of the subject. Have they not in some way allowed the idea to gain a place in their minds that if the suffrage were accorded to women it would be the pure, the honest, the intelligent, and the patriotic of the sex who would avail themselves of it?"

The Harlem Equal Rights League is founded by Irish-born New York public librarian Maud Malone as part of the city's division of the National Women's Suffrage League.

Rose Schneiderman is elected to the executive board of the Woman's Trade Union League founded 2 years ago. She had her doubts at first that women who were not themselves wage earners could understand the problems faced by working women, but has changed her mind (see 1909).

A monograph by U.S. geneticist Nettie Stevens, 44, identifies the X and Y chromosomes, accurately pinpointing their role in determining the sex of an embryo (an XX combination produces a female, XY a male). Born in Vermont, Stevens entered Stanford at age 35 and received her bachelor's degree only 6 years ago. Her implicit suggestion that a father "allows" the birth of a daughter by contributing his X chromosome offends some men; a similar work published independently and simultaneously by Stevens's former colleague Edmund B. Wilson is less specific in defining X and Y chromosomes.

Three Essays on the Theory of Sexuality by Viennese psychoanalyst Sigmund Freud, published in December, creates heated controversy with the view that women are capable of orgasm, whereas women up to now have been expected to tolerate sex with clenched teeth but not to enjoy it. The high incidence of female frigidity, says Freud, is an emotional and psychological problem of "sexually immature women" that can be treated with analysis. There are two kinds of female orgasm, clitoral and vaginal, he says, and the former is "adolescent," whereas vaginal orgasm, the true, mature, womanly orgasm, can be achieved only through vaginal penetration by the penis, but women, recognizing their inferiority to men, are reluctant to accept their femininity (*see* Masters and Johnson, 1970).

The Midwives Roll in Britain contains 22,308 names, of whom 7,465 hold the Obstetrical Society certificate, 2,333 hold hospital certificates, and 12,521 are in "bona fide practice" holding no cer-

tificate at all (*see* 1902). Many are totally illiterate and must have required records filled in for them, others have trouble reading a clinical thermometer. In many parts of the country, illegal, uncertificated midwives—often preferred by poor women because they are cheap and not averse to helping with the housework—will continue to practice until the 1930s.

The *Ladies' Home Journal* charges that soothing letters from "Lydia Pinkham" often prevent women from seeking proper medical care (*see* 1898; 1904). It creates a scandal by publishing a photograph of Pinkham's grave as evidence that she died in 1883 and thus cannot still be writing letters to customers, but the proprietary medicine, whose 18 percent alcohol content does not draw any criticism from the Women's Christian Temperance Union, continues to enjoy good sales and will be a $3-million-per-year business by the 1920s (*see* 1926).

L. C. Smith & Brothers sells its first typewriter to the *New York Tribune* for the paper's newsroom. The Syracuse, N.Y., firm will for years be the largest producer of typewriters.

Royal Typewriter Co. is founded by New York financier Thomas Fortune Ryan, who puts up $220,000 to back inventors Edward B. Hess and Lewis C. Meyers. The Royal typewriter has innovations that include a friction-free ball-bearing one-track rail to support the weight of the carriage as it moves back and forth, a new paper feed, a shield to keep erasure crumbs from falling into the nest of type bars, a lighter and faster type bar action, and complete visibility of words as they are typed.

Nonfiction: *A Survey of the Woman Problem* (*Zur Kritik der Weiblichkeit*) (essays) by Austrian feminist Rosa Mayreder, 47, points out the importance of acknowledging individual variations independent of sex.

Fiction: *The House of Mirth* by New York novelist Edith Newbold Wharton (*née* Jones), 43, who gains her first popularity with a fictional analysis of the stratified society she knows so well as the wife of a rich banker (she married Wharton in 1885) and of that society's reaction to change; *The Scarlet Pimpernel* by Hungarian-born British novelist-playwright Baroness Emmuska Orczy, 43; *Letters from the Convent* (Levelek a za bárdából) (stories) by Hungarian poet–story writer Margit Kaffka, 25; *La Domination* by Anna, comtesse de Noailles; *Three-Quarters of an Hour Before Daybreak* (*Dreiviertel Stunde vor Tag*) by Helene Voigt-Diederichs; *Amanda of the Mill* by Marie Van Vorst.

Poetry: *Neue Gedichte* by Isolde Kurz.

Juvenile: *The Children of Wilton Chase*; *Dumps, A Plain Girl*; *Four on an Island*; *Girls New and Old*; *A Ring of Rubies*; and *Good Luck* by L. T. Meade.

Painting: *Girl among Birch Trees* by Paula Modersohn-Becker; *Family Group Reading* by Mary Cassatt.

Theater: English actress Gladys Cooper, 17, makes her debut to begin a notable career; *No Mother to Guide Her* by U.S. actress-melodramatist Lillian Mortimer 9/5 at Detroit's Whitney Theater, with Mortimer as the comic soubrette Bunco; Mary Shaw and Arnold Daly in George Bernard Shaw's *Mrs. Warren's Profession* 10/30 at New York's Garrick Theater (they are prosecuted for performing in an "immoral" play), 14 perfs. (London's Lord Chamberlain has refused to license the play about a woman whose income is derived from houses of prostitution; London will not see a production until 1926); Blanche Bates in David Belasco's *The Girl of the Golden West* 11/14 at New York's Belasco Theater, 224 perfs.; Annie Russell in Bernard Shaw's *Major Barbara*, a "discussion in three acts" about a Salvation Army officer, 11/28 at London's Royal Court Theatre.

Opera: German soprano Marie Wittich sings the title role in Richard Strauss's *Salomé* 12/9 at Dresden's Hofoper. The libretto is based on the 1896 play by the late Oscar Wilde, and Wittich had originally refused to sing a sensuous song to the imprisoned John the Baptist, praising his body, his hair, his mouth, saying, "I won't do it, I'm a decent woman" (after the opera's first performance at New York's Metropolitan Opera House January 22, 1907, J. P. Morgan will forbid further performances, and *Salomé* will not be revived at the Met until 1934).

(Angela) Isadora Duncan, 27, opens a dancing school for children at Berlin. The U.S. dancer, who gives birth to a child out of wedlock, has developed a spontaneous style that tries to symbolize music, poetry, and elements of nature instead of conforming to the "false and preposterous" strictures of classical ballet.

Broadway musicals: Fritzi Scheff in Victor Herbert's *Mlle. Modiste* 12/25 at the Knickerbocker Theater, with songs that include "Kiss Me Again" and "I Want What I Want When I Want It," 262 perfs.

Popular songs: Vaudeville star Eva Tanguy will popularize the song "I Don't Care" by Harry O. Sutton, lyrics by Jean Lewis.

May Sutton wins in women's singles at Wimbledon, Elizabeth Moore in U.S. women's singles.

President Roosevelt gives away the bride March 5 at New York when his cousin Anna Eleanor Roosevelt, 20, marries Columbia Law School student Franklin Delano Roosevelt, 23, her fifth cousin once removed. Orphaned since age 10, she has been raised by a grandmother and is considered an ugly duckling, while Franklin (Harvard '04) is one of the handsomest men in America (*see* medicine, 1921).

Sigmund Freud (above) says that memories of childhood seduction are fantasized stories used to mask sexual activities such as masturbation. He has written earlier that hysteria was caused by sexual abuse (he called it "seduction") of a child by a parent, but his theory of fantasized stories will be used to support the claim that women lie about having been raped, either to protect themselves or because of hysterical, masochistic proclivities.

1906

Mary, Baroness Curzon, former vicereine of India, dies of a heart attack at Carlton House Terrace, London, July 18, at age 36—7 months after returning to England. Her years in the tropics with an insensitive husband have undermined her health.

Finland grants women the right to vote on the same basis as men March 7, becoming the first European nation to do so (*see* New Zealand, 1898); all men and women 24 and older are enfranchised except those supported by the state (*see* 1907; Norway, 1913).

Britain's Labour party calls for woman suffrage April 17. A *London Daily Mail* writer coins the term "suffragettes" for women such as Emmeline Pankhurst and her daughters Christabel and (Estelle) Sylvia, 24, who campaign for woman suffrage (*see* 1905). Mrs. Pankhurst has said January 31 that women have to become violent and risk arrest if they are to achieve their goals. London barrister Frederick Pethick-Lawrence, 35, and his wife, Emmeline, 39, are introduced to the Pankhursts by Labour party leader Keir Hardie and offer their support. Annie Kenney interrupts a speech by the prime minister, Sir Henry Campbell-Bannerman, and is arrested again. Suffragettes are jailed October 24, and they refuse meals beginning December 25 (*see* 1912).

The *New York Times* editorializes that the British women's noisy hysteria is self-defeating. English-American novelist-playwright Israel Zangwill, 42, replies in a letter published October 29, "If you

Emmeline Pankhurst saw that ladylike behavior was not about to gain British women the vote. LIBRARY OF CONGRESS

mean that noisiness and hysteria are proofs of unfitness for public life then every Parliament in the world should close, every election meeting be prohibited, every sex be disenfranchised. Did Englishmen ever get their voting right save by noisiness and hysteria?"

French suffragists demand a reduction in taxes so that deputies opposed to letting women vote will receive no salaries from the state.

Mother Earth is founded by anarchist Emma Goldman, now 37, with Polish-American anarchist Alexander Berkman, who has just been released from prison after having served time for an attempt on the life of industrialist Henry Clay Frick in the Homestead Strike of 1892 (*see* 1917).

Mormon leader Joseph F. Smith is charged with polygamy November 23 after his fifth wife gives birth to his 43rd child. Descended from the founder of the Church of Jesus Christ of Latter-Day Saints, Smith pleads guilty and pays $300, the maximum fine, after telling the Salt Lake City district judge that he considers each of his marriages to be a solemn contract.

German cannon maker's daughter Bertha Krupp, 20, marries industrialist Gustav von Bohlen und Halbach, 34, who obtains an imperial edict permitting him to call himself "Krupp von Bohlen und Halbach" (*see* "Big Bertha," 1914).

The Wassermann test developed by German physician August Wassermann, 40, and (independently) by Hungarian physician Lazlo Detre is a specific blood test for syphilis. Its use in St. Louis and New York indicates that 10 percent of pregnant married women are actively syphilitic and 5 to 6 percent of infants born to poor families are congenitally syphilitic (*see* Ehrlich, 1909).

Former Cheltenham Ladies College headmistress Dorothea Beale dies at age 75, leaving an enormous financial legacy to the school that she headed beginning in 1858 (she has invested her money shrewdly while roaming the school grounds on her tricycle, asking passersby to push her up hills).

Sweet Briar College opens in September at Sweet Briar, Va., with Mary Kay Bennett as president.

The Madeira School has its beginnings in Miss Madeira's School, founded near Dupont Circle in Washington, D.C., by educator Lucy Madeira, 32, who herself attended public school in Washington, borrowed money for college, and has been teaching since her graduation from Vassar 10 years ago. Her all-girl preparatory school of 15 day students and 13 residents will move in 1931 to Greenway (later McLean), Va., and grow to have a 400-acre campus with 302 students.

New York's Nightingale-Bamford School has its beginnings in Miss Nightingale's Classes, given at girls' homes by educator Frances Nightingale, a Georgia-born spinster who has never been to college but has been encouraged by her New York cousins, the Delafields, to teach girls in the city (*see* 1920; Brearley, 1884; Spence, 1892; Chapin, 1901; Dalton, 1916).

Fiction: *A Woman at Bay* (*Una donna*) by Italian poet-novelist Rina Faccio, 30, who uses the pen name Sibilla Aleramo (her book will be translated into German, Dutch, French, English, Spanish, Swedish, Russian, and Polish); *The Ivy and the Alabaster* (*Vedera*) by Grazia Deledda; *Jirí Matlan* by Teréza Novaková traces the evolution of a fervent Protestant sectarian into an enthusiastic socialist; *The Ladder to the Stars* by Jane Findlater.

Poetry: *P. H. Buch* by German poet Else Lasker-Schüler, 30, is about the late vagabond poet Peter Hille, with whom she lived before his death 2 years ago at age 49.

Juvenile: *The Tale of Mr. Jeremy Fisher* and *The Story of Miss Moppet* by Beatrix Potter; *The Railway Children* by Edith Nesbit; *The Fortunes of Philippa* by English author Angela Brazil, 37.

Painting: *Seated Female Nude*, *Self-Portrait*, *Nude Girl with Apple*, and *Reclining Mother and Child* by Paula Modersohn-Becker; *Mother (Jeanne) Looking Down at Her Two Children Petting a Dog* by Mary Cassatt; *Self-Portrait* by Parisian painter Marie Laurencin, 22, whose seamstress mother has borne her out of wedlock; *Portrait of Gertrude Stein* by emigré Spanish painter Pablo Picasso whose subject is the American emigrée Stein, 33 (both live in Paris).

Theater: Shakespearean actress Ellen (Alicia) Terry, 59, in George Bernard Shaw's *Captain Brassbound's Conversion* (which he has written especially for her) 3/20 at London's Royal Court Theatre; Gertrude Elliott and Forbes Robertson in Shaw's *Caesar and Cleopatra* 3/31 at Berlin (in German), 10/31 at New York's New Amsterdam Theater, 49 perfs.; Mrs. Minnie Maddern Fiske in Elwyn Mitchell's (John Philip Varley's) *The New York Idea* 11/18 at New York's Lyric Theater.

Ballet: U.S. dancer-choreographer Ruth Denis, 29, produces her first ballet, *Radha*, and changes her name to St. Denis. She will tour Europe with the ballet for the next 3 years (*see* 1914).

Opera: *The Wreckers* (*Standrecht*) 11/11 at Leipzig, with music by English composer Ethel Smyth, 48; Geraldine Farrar makes her Metropolitan Opera debut singing the role of Juliet in the 1867 Gounod opera *Roméo et Juliette*; Italian soprano Amalita Galli-Curci, 24 (or 17) makes her debut at Trani 12/26 singing the role of Gilda in the 1851 Verdi opera *Rigoletto*.

Broadway musicals: "Mary's a Grand Old Name" makes a hit in George M. Cohan's *Forty-Five Minutes from Broadway* 1/1 at the New Amsterdam Theater, 90 perfs.; "Every Day Is Ladies' Day with Me" (*see* sports, 1883) brings down the house in Victor Herbert's *The Red Mill* 9/24 at the Knickerbocker Theater, 274 perfs.

Dorothea Chambers wins in women's singles at Wimbledon, Helen Homans in U.S. women's singles.

Harvard Physical Director Dudley Sargent, M.D., gives a speech March 30 warning women against playing contact sports. "Let woman rather confine herself to the lighter and more graceful forms of gymnastics and athletics, and make herself supreme along these lines as she has already done in aesthetic dancing," he says.

President Roosevelt's daughter Alice Lee, 21, is married in the East Room of the White House February 17 to Congressman Nicholas Longworth (R. Ohio), 39, who was with her in Secretary of War William Howard Taft's party last year on a trip to Hawaii and the Orient.

Teddy Roosevelt's daughter, Alice, married Nicholas Longworth in the White House and gained renown for her wit. LIBRARY OF CONGRESS

The permanent wave introduced by London hairdresser Charles Nessler, 34, takes 8 to 12 hours and costs $1,000. Only 18 women avail themselves of Nessler's service (*see* 1915; Buzzacchini, 1926).

Lux Flakes are introduced by Lever Brothers for chiffons and other fine fabrics.

Ontario, Calif., electric utility meter reader Earl Richardson begins manufacturing lightweight electric irons under the name Hotpoint. Homemakers have told him that they do their ironing on Tuesday, would use electric irons if they were not so heavy, but want to iron during daylight hours, not at night. Richardson persuades his plant supervisors to experiment with generating electricity all day on Tuesday as an experiment, and the plant gradually extends its hours of operation (*see* 1882; 1912; washing machine, 1907).

New York architect Stanford White, now 52, is shot dead June 25 at the roof garden restaurant atop Madison Square Garden, which he designed in 1889. His murderer is Pittsburgh millionaire Harry K. Thaw, whose wife, Evelyn Nesbit Thaw, was a chorus girl and White's mistress before her marriage. Thaw will win acquittal on an insanity plea.

The murder of Cortland, N.Y., factory girl Grace Brown, 19, makes world headlines in July. A capsized rowboat found in Big Moose Lake in the Adirondacks the morning of July 13 leads to a search, a boy of 13 spots a young woman's body in 8 feet of water early in the afternoon, police arrest Chester Gillett, 22, at a nearby resort July 14 and charge him with murder. Raised by missionary parents at Kansas City, young Gillett took a job last year as foreman at his uncle's shirtwaist factory in Cortland, where the employees included Grace Brown, daughter of a local farmer. Pregnant by Gillett, Brown wrote him pitiful letters begging him to marry her and finally threatening to go to his family with her story. Gillett has ambitions to marry a society girl whom he has met, and he wrote to Brown asking her to travel with him to the Adirondacks, where he said he would marry her. He signed the register at the Glenmore Hotel "Carl Graham and wife of Albany" upon his arrival by train the morning of July 12 and took Brown out on the lake that afternoon in a hired rowboat. Gillett will be executed next year at Auburn prison.

A Wisconsin court of appeals acquits an accused rapist despite evidence that the 16-year-old victim, attacked by a stranger, screamed, tried to get away, and was nearly strangled. She did not testify that she used her hands, feet, or pelvic muscles to demonstrate lack of consent, the court rules, and the facts that she was not bruised and had no torn clothing make any claim that she offered "utmost resistance" "well nigh incredible."

India's population nears 300 million, up from little more than 200 million in 1850. Mohandas Gandhi in South Africa takes a vow of sexual abstinence (*brahmacharya*) and will oppose other means to limit population in India. (In 1885, at 16, Gandhi had sex with his wife of 14 while his father died in another room of the house. British physicians in the last century introduced Western medicine to reduce India's death rate, and British moralists eliminated the slaughter of female children and other customs that held the population in check.)

The first commercially prepared spermicidal jellies are introduced.

1907

Russian revolutionary Aleksandra Kollontai organizes public meetings under the auspices of the Union of Textile Workers (whose members are mostly women), pretending that they are lectures on maternal hygiene and whatnot, but Czarist police break up the meetings when lecturers speak out against social exploitation and support woman suffrage (*see* 1905). Police arrest Bolshevik revolutionary Inessa Armand, 33, who, after bearing five children, has dedicated herself to social reform. She met V. I. Lenin on a long visit to Switzerland in 1903 and has since then subordinated her efforts in behalf of women's rights to working for the wider cause of emancipating the working class and all of society. The aborted revolution is suppressed.

Mounted London police ride into a deputation from the Women's Social and Political Union February 13 as they march on Parliament to demand voting rights. The suffragettes clash with police for 5 hours, 15 of them reach the House of Commons, and a record 57 are sent to Holloway Prison February 14. Some have had their clothes ripped and their bodies bruised, but Christabel Pankhurst says in court, "The women who asked for votes were in danger of their lives. We do not come here in any way to excuse our conduct. We feel yesterday was a great day for our movement." Suffragist Annie Kenney, 28, vows to lead 1,000 women onto the floor of the House of Commons if it does not grant women the vote by the end of its session, but Parliament kills the woman suffrage bill March 8.

Finnish women win their first seats in the nation's Parliament March 15 (*see* 1906).

Norway's Storting votes 95 to 26 June 14 to grant suffrage for women provided that they, or their husbands, pay taxes regularly. An estimated 300,000 Norwegian women are eligible to vote.

The Equality League of Self-Supporting Women is funded by U.S. suffragist Harriet Eaton Blatch (*née* Stanton), 51, daughter of the late Elizabeth Cady Stanton, who has lived in England and been impressed by the activities of the Women's Franchise League. She will found the Women's Political Union next year.

U.S. suffragists rally in New York's Madison Square December 31 to petition Congress for woman suffrage. Mrs. Boorman Wells, an English suffragist, addresses the crowd, asking, "Do you think it would be possible for women to make a worse mess of politics than the men have?"

Neiman-Marcus opens September 10 at Dallas, and its initial stock is practically sold out in 4 weeks. The two-story fashion emporium at the corner of Elm and Murphy Streets has been started by former Atlanta advertising agency president A. L. Neiman, his wife, Carrie, and his brother-in-law Herbert Marcus, who have been offered the choice of selling out for $25,000 in cash or receiving stock in the Coca-Cola Company plus the Missouri franchise for Coca-Cola syrup. They have opted for the cash, start the store with $30,000 in capital ($22,000 of it from Neiman), invest $12,000 in carpeting and fixtures for the premises they lease at $750 per month, and Carrie Neiman stocks it with $17,000 worth of tailored suits for women, evening gowns, furs, coats, dresses, and millinery for the women of Dallas, a city of 86,000 with 222 saloons.

Crimean War nurse Florence Nightingale, now 87, is awarded the British Order of Merit, the first woman to be thus honored.

Wilmington, Del., social worker Emily Bissell (*née* Perkins), 46, heads the first Christmas seal drive to aid tubercular children. She has hit on the scheme of designing and printing the seals, which she sells for 1¢ apiece at the Wilmington Post Office to raise money for combating the disease that takes more lives than any other. Her seals raise $3,000, and when they are sold nationwide beginning next year the revenue will increase to $120,000—easily enough to build a home for consumptives at Wilmington.

Ministry of Healing by Ellen G. White, now 79, of the Battle Creek Sanatorium condemns the overly decorative style of current women's fashions and recommends that "every article of dress should fit easily, obstructing neither the circulation of the blood nor a free, full, natural respiration. Everything should be so loose that when the arms are raised, the clothing will be correspondingly lifted" (*see* 1866).

The Chicago School of Civics and Philanthropy is founded by local social workers Julia Clifford Lathrop, 49, and Sophonisba Preston Breckenridge, 41.

Nonfiction: *Syria: The Desert and the Town* by Gertrude Lowthian Bell, now 39, who has learned Arabic, studied Byzantine history, and traveled widely in the Mideast on her own, venturing with only one servant among wild desert tribes and pretending at times to be German (she speaks the language passably well) because she knows that the Ottoman Turks, who control Palestine and Mesopotamia, prefer Germans to Britons (*see* politics, 1915).

Lady Ottoline Morrell (*née* Ottoline Violet Anne Cavendish Bentinck), 34, begins a career as literary hostess that will continue until 1938, inviting prominent writers and artists to the Bloomsbury house that she and her Liberal M.P. husband, Philip, bought last year at 44 Bedford Square. They will acquire a country house in Oxfordshire in 1914, and the tall (six feet), beautiful Lady Ottoline will cultivate admirers who will include Bertrand Russell and Lytton Strachey.

Fiction: *The Land of Children* (*Kinderland*) by Helene Voigt-Diederichs; *Ancestors* by Gertrude Atherton; *Ties* (*En*) by Japanese novelist Yaeko (*née* Yae) Nogami, 22; *Three Weeks* by English novelist Elinor Glyn (*née* Sutherland), 43, who knows little about grammar or syntax but gains wide readership for her "risqué" novel.

Juvenile: *The Wonderful Adventures of Nils* (*Nils Holgerssons underbara resa*) by Selma Lagerlöf; *The Enchanted Castle* by Edith Nesbit; *Three Girls in School*; *The Honourable Miss, A Story of an Old-*

What English Orientalist Gertrude Lowthian Belle learned on her Near Eastern travels would prove valuable.

Fashioned Town; and *The Little School Mothers: A Story for Girls* by L. T. Meade.

Poetry: *Sonnets to Duse and Other Poems* by U.S. poet Sara Teasdale, 23, whose dramatic monologue "Guenevere" has appeared in the May issue of *Reedy's Mirror*; *Bedazzlements* (*Les Eblouissements*) by Anna, comtesse de Noailles.

Painting: *Young Finnish Girl*, *Young Girl Sleeping*, and *Landscape at the Water's Edge* (all oil on canvas) by Ukraine-born St. Petersburg painter Sonia Terk (*née* Sophie Stern), 22, who was adopted at age 5 by her maternal aunt Anna and uncle Henri (né Gherman) Terk, a St. Petersburg banker and took his name but is determined to live in Paris; *Figured Composition*, *Self-Portrait with Camellia Branch*, and *Mother and Child* by Paula Modersohn-Becker, who gives birth to a daughter, Matilde, November

2, gets out of bed for the first time November 21, suffers a thrombosis of the leg, and dies of a heart attack at the north German artists' colony of Worpswede at age 31 just as she was beginning to receive some favorable notices.

Theater: *The Rising of the Moon* by Lady Gregory 3/9 at Dublin's Abbey Theatre; *The Movers* by Martha Morton 9/3 at New York's Hackett Theater, with Dorothy Donnelly; Antoinctte Perry, 19, and David Warfield in David Belasco's *A Grand Army Man* 10/16 at New York's new Stuyvesant Theater on 44th Street (Perry has been performing since before she was 17 but will give up the stage for 15 years beginning in 1909).

Opera: Russian soprano Xeniya Georgiyevena Derzhinskaya, 18, creates the role of Fevrona in the new Rimsky-Korsakov opera *The Legend of the Invisible City of Kitezh and of the Maiden Fevrona* 2/7 at St. Petersburg's Maryinsky Theater.

Broadway musicals: 50 "Anna Held Girls" appear in *The Follies of 1907* 7/18 at the Jardin de Paris on the roof of the New York Theater: the extravaganza has been staged by Florenz Ziegfeld, now 38, who married comedian Held 10 years ago. She writes lyrics to Vincent Scotto's song "It's Delightful to Be Married (The Parisian Model)," showgirls appear in a swimming pool in a simulated motion picture production, 70 perfs. (*see* below); Connie Edliss, Louise Dresser, Lew Fields, and Vernon Castle in *The Girl Behind the Counter* 10/1 at the Herald Square Theater, with Howard Talbot–Arthur Anderson songs, 260 perfs.

May Sutton wins in women's singles at Wimbledon, Evelyn Sears in U.S. women's singles.

New York's new Colony Club building opens formally March 11 (*see* 1903). Designed by the late Stanford White, it has been brightly and cheerfully decorated by Canadian-born socialite Elsie de Wolfe, 41, who ended her stage career in 1905 after playing against such actors as John Drew and has designed the interiors. A trendsetter who since 1887 has presided over a salon in the house that she shares with playwright's agent Elizabeth Marbury at 122 East 17th Street, de Wolfe will inaugurate the fashion of wearing little white gloves and, in 1924, will be the first woman to tint her gray hair

blue (*see* 1926). The club has 498 members and by next year will have 819.

Australian long-distance swimmer Annette Kellerman, 22, is arrested for indecent exposure at Boston's Revere Beach, where she has appeared in a skirtless one-piece bathing suit. Even infants will be required to wear complete bathing costumes on U.S. beaches for more than 25 years.

The *Ziegfeld Follies* (above) features a chorus line composed of beautiful Follies girls chosen with an eye to slenderness of figure as Ziegfeld creates a new physical ideal of feminine beauty to replace the ample figure now in vogue. Opulent new editions will appear almost every year until 1931.

Alice Babette Toklas, 30, meets Gertrude Stein at Paris in September and begins a 37-year relationship during which the two will be inseparable. She knew Stein's family in California and within a few years will have moved into the apartment that Stein shares with her brother at 27 rue de Fleurus, where the two women will have a salon that will be world-famous.

Persil, introduced by Henkel & Cie. of Dusseldorf, is the world's first household detergent but is not suitable for heavy-duty laundry use (*see* Tide, 1946).

The Thor washing machine, introduced by Hurley Machine Co. of Chicago, is the first complete, self-contained electric washer. Some U.S. power companies still turn on their generators only at sunset (*see* Hotpoint iron, 1906), but more now keep them on all day, making it possible for housewives to use electric appliances such as washing machines, irons, vacuum cleaners (*see* below) and fans during the day.

The Maytag Pastime washer introduced by Parsons Band Cutter and Self-Feeder Co. of Newton, Iowa, is a sideline to the farm equipment produced by the company which Frederick Louis Maytag, 50, has headed since 1893. The washer has a corrugated wooden tub with a hand-operated dolly inside, Maytag will add a pulley mechanism in 1909 to permit operation of the machine from an outside power source, he will introduce an electric washer in 1911, but Maytag's entry into the washer field is primarily to solve the problem of seasonal slumps in the farm implement business.

The Hoover Vacuum Cleaner has its beginnings in an electric vacuum cleaner invented by J. Murray Spangler, who has improved on the cleaner patented by H. C. Booth in 1901. U.S. industrialist W. H. Hoover, now 58, will manufacture Spangler's machine; his Hoover Suction Sweeper Co. will become the Hoover Co. in 1922, and his machine will be so successful that the word "hoover" will become a generic for vacuum cleaner in Britain.

Work by Philadelphia chemist Mary Engel Pennington, 34, attracts the attention of U.S. Department of Agriculture chemist Harvey W. Wiley, who has her take a civil service exam. She signs the exam paper M. E. Pennington and by the time her gender is discovered has become indispensable to Wiley, who makes her first chief of the U.S. Food Laboratory. She has been operating her own laboratory, specializing in bacteriological analysis, and Wiley assigns her to work on the problem of keeping refrigerated food fresh. Like outside air, air within a refrigerated locker loses its ability to hold moisture as it approaches the freezing point. Food in the locker dries out, and adding humidity just makes it moldy. Pennington's solution to the problem of humidity control in refrigeration will be widely adopted in industry.

1908

China's dowager empress Cixi dies of dysentery November 15 at age 73 after 52 years as the power behind the Qing throne.

Physician Elizabeth Garrett Anderson, now 72, is elected mayor of Aldeburgh, becoming Britain's first woman mayor.

 The U.S. Supreme Court sustains Oregon's 1903 10-hour day law for women in factories and laundries February 4 in *Muller* v. *State of Oregon*. The decision classes women with minors and rests on women's biological "inferiority," their potential maternity, and their "natural dependence on men." Says the Court, "That woman's physical structure and the performance of maternal functions place her at a disadvantage in the struggle for subsistence is obvious. This is especially true when the burdens of motherhood are upon her. Even when they are not, by abundant testimony of the medical fraternity continuance for a long time on her feet at work, repeating this from day to day, tends to injurious effects upon the body, and as healthy mothers are essential to vigorous offspring, the physical well-being of woman becomes an object of public interest and care in order to preserve the strength and vigor of the race."

New York women socialists demonstrate for equal rights and better working conditions March 8 to commemorate the demonstration of March 8, 1857. They demand voting rights and an end to sweatshops and child labor (*see* 1910).

A rumor that a black man has raped a white woman at Springfield, Ill., starts a riot August 14 that continues until the next day. An influx of black workers has created economic pressure, and whites go on a rampage in black residential areas, killing eight people and forcing 2,000 to run for their lives before state militia can restore order.

"We are not ashamed of what we have done," says Christabel Pankhurst March 19 in a speech at the Albert Hall, "because, when you have a great cause to fight for, the moment of greatest humiliation is the moment when the spirit is proudest." Suffragists 100,000 strong storm Parliament on the evening of October 13, and two dozen are arrested. Parliament immediately passes an order forbidding women access to the building. Emmeline Pankhurst speaks out in court October 21 to say, "We have taken this action, because, as women . . . we realize that the condition of our sex is so deplorable that it is our duty even to break the law in order to call attention to the reasons why we do so." She and Christabel draw prison sentences October 24 after a sensational trial in which two Cabinet members have testified for the defense.

"The true objection to woman suffrage lies far deeper than any argument," declaims Bryn Mawr president M. Carey Thomas, now 51, in an October address to the North American Woman Suffrage Assocation at Buffalo, N.Y. "Giving women the ballot is the visible sign and symbol of a stupendous revolution and before it we are afraid. Women are one-half the world but only a century ago the world of music and painting and sculpture and literature and scholarship and science was a man's world. The

Emmeline Pankhurst's daughter Christabel fought for suffrage as vigorously as did her mother. LIBRARY OF CONGRESS

world of trades and professions and of work of all kinds was a man's world. Women lived in a twilight life, a half-life apart, and looked out and saw men as shadows walking. It was a man's world. The laws were man's laws, the government a man's government, the country a man's country. . . . The man's world must become a man's and woman's world. Why are we afraid? It is the next step forward on the path toward the sunrise, and the sun is rising over a new heaven and a new earth."

The Consiglio Nazionale delle Donne Italiane, founded 5 years ago, holds its first national congress at Rome. The mayor, the minister of education, several countesses, even the queen attend the opening session, but wrangling over questions of divorce and religious education in the schools divides the delegates in bitter controversy.

The All-Russian Women's Congress meets in December, but Aleksandra Kollontai, who has played a leading role, then slips across the border into exile in order to avoid arrest.

The Animal Mind by Vassar psychologist Margaret Floy Washburn, 37, reviews current knowledge of animal behavior, taking a middle road between the preoccupation with behavior of her U.S. colleagues and the focus on consciousness that permeates the work of European pschologists.

Nara Women's College has its beginnings in a nursery school teacher's college founded in the ancient Japanese capital.

Alpha Kappa Alpha Sorority, founded January 15 at Howard University, is the first Greek-letter society for black women (*see* 1913; 1920).

Nonfiction: *The Breaking-in of a Yachtsman* by New York reformer Mary Heaton Vorse, 33, who moved with her husband 2 years ago to Greenwich Village, where they founded an experimental cooperative living arrangement that will attract such visitors as Theodore Dreiser, Maksim Gorky, Mother Jones, and Mark Twain.

Fiction: *The Norrtull Gang* (*Norrtullsligan*) by Swedish novelist Elin Mathilde Elisabeth Wägner, 26; *The Cross in Venn* (*Das Kreuz in Venn*) by Clara Viebig is about the suppressed hatred and secret patriotic longings of servile Polish peasants under German domination; *Crossrigs* by Jane Findlater and her older sister, Mary, 43; *La Retraite sentimentale* by Colette, who last year divorced Henri Gauthier-Villars; *The Elusive Pimpernel* by Baroness Orczy; *Holy Orders* by Marie Corelli; *June Jeopardy* by suffragist Inez Leonore Gillmore; *Lewis Rand* by Mary Johnston is less lushly romantic than her earlier novels.

Juvenile: *Anne of Green Gables* by Canadian novelist L. M. (Lucy Maud) Montgomery, 35, who begins a series of Anne books about the Canadian wilderness.

Sculptor Harriet G. Hosmer, who returned from Europe in 1900 to her native Watertown, Mass., dies there February 21 at age 77.

Painting: *View of the Murnau Marsh* by German painter Gabriele Münter, 31; *Group of Artists, Portrait of Picasso*, and *Women Dancing the Cancan* by Marie Laurencin, who last year was introduced by

Pablo Picasso to Guillaume Apollinaire (Wilhelm de Kostrowitzky), 28, a poet who, like her, was born and out of wedlock and whose love will influence her work just as her love will influence his (they will never live together, but she will officiate as hostess at dinner when they entertain); *Yellow Nude* (oil on canvas) by Sonia Terk, who is married in December at London to former banker Wilhelm Uhde, 33 (he moved last year to Paris with his French wife, and opened a small gallery, but has been divorced).

Theater: *Getting Married* by George Bernard Shaw 5/12 at London's Haymarket Theatre: "Women are called womanly only when they regard themselves as existing solely for the use of men," Shaw has written in a preface; *What Every Woman Knows* by James M. Barrie 9/3 at the Duke of York's Theatre, London: "It's a sort of bloom on a woman. If you have it, you don't need to have anything else; and if you don't, it doesn't much matter what else you have" (Maude Adams stars in the Broadway opening at the Empire Theater 12/23).

Opera: New York impresario Oscar Hammerstein announces March 30 that he has signed Italian coloratura soprano Luisa Tetrazzini, 36, to a 5-year contract. She had her first big success last year singing the role of Violetta in the 1853 Verdi opera *La Traviata*; English soprano Maggie Teyte (Tate), 19, makes her debut at the Opéra-Comique, Paris, having been chosen by composer Claude Debussy to succeed Mary Garden in the role of Mélisande in his 1902 opera *Pélleas et Melisande*. She has changed the spelling of her name to avoid mispronunciation by the French and will specialize in French songs, those of Debussy in particular.

Stage musicals: Comedian Nora Bayes (*née* Nora Goldberg), 28, in *The [Ziegfeld] Follies* 6/15 at New York's Jardin de Paris, with songs that include "Shine On, Harvest Moon" by Bayes, lyrics by her husband, Jack Norworth, 120 perfs.

(Penelope) Dorothea Harvey Boothby, 27, wins in women's singles at Wimbledon, Maud Bargar Wallach, 36, in U.S. women's singles.

British figure skater Madge Syers wins her event at the Olympic Games—the first woman Olympic gold medalist (Olympic events have been for men only since their revival in 1896, and this is the first competition open to women).

U.S. climber Annie Smith Peck, 57, makes it to the top of Mount Huascarán in the Peruvian Andes September 2—the first mountaineer of either sex to scale the 21,812-foot peak. When Peck climbed the Matterhorn in the Swiss Alps 13 years ago (she was the third woman to make the ascent) and the Singer Company gave away a picture of her in climbing gear with every machine it sold, a writer observed that "Ladies pumping away at the treadle could sigh with admiration at one of their sex who had launched into the world's most daring occupation." *Harper's* magazine has sponsored her expedition to South America.

Mother's Day is observed for the first time at Philadelphia. Suffragist-temperance worker Anna May Jarvis, 44, attended a memorial service last year at the Methodist Church in Grafton, W.Va., for her mother Anna Reeves Jarvis, who died at Philadelphia May 9, 1905, conceived the idea of an annual worldwide tribute to mothers, and will agitate for a national U.S. Mother's Day (*see* 1913).

New York's Sullivan Ordinance, enacted January 21, orders restaurant and hotel owners to forbid women to smoke in a public place. One Katie Mulcahey is arrested for lighting up a cigarette January 22 and says in night court, "I've got as much right to smoke as you have. I never heard of this new law and I don't want to hear about it. No man shall dictate to me." But when she cannot pay a $5 fine she is sent to jail.

The American Home Economics Association is founded with Ellen Swallow Richards, now 66, as president (*see* 1870). She has promoted the fledgling science of nutrition, writing some of the U.S. Department of Agriculture's first bulletins on the subject, setting up demonstration kitchens and pioneer school-lunch programs, testing products for adulterants, and encouraging other women to raise the status of homemaking. Through the efforts of her association (and those of other home economists), U.S. homemakers will boost consumption of oranges and otherwise improve the nutrition of their families.

Mrs. Baird's Bakeries, Inc., has its beginnings at Fort Worth, Texas, where Mrs. Ninnie L. Baird starts selling the bread she has baked for her neighbors since 1905. She still uses her small wood-fired kitchen oven but expands operations to a shed behind her house, and by 1910 will have purchased a commercial oven from a hotel, burning artificial "Pintsch" gas and baking 40 loaves at a time. Her husband, William, will die in 1911, by which time the family bakery will be a thriving concern, with cars lined up as early as 5 o'clock in the morning to buy fresh bread right out of the oven. Mrs. Baird will continue as active head of the business until her death in 1961, despite her "retirement" in 1920, and the company will be one of the nation's largest family-owned wholesale bakers.

 Anglican Bishops at the Lambeth Conference refer to contraception as "preventive abortion," but in the next two decades clergymen will gradually become convinced by the utilitarian argument that contraception spares society high social costs (*see* 1930).

1909

 The Fianna na hEireann is founded by Irish actress-patriot Constance (Georgina) de Markievicz (*née* Gore-Booth), 41, a landed aristocrat who in 1900 married the six-foot-four-inch Polish artist and playwright Count Casimir Dunin-Markievicz, a widower 6 years her junior. A paramilitary order, the Fianna's avowed purpose is to train boys to fight in the cause of Irish independence from Britain; the "Rebel Countess" (as she will be called) teaches her young men marksmanship and otherwise prepares them for military service in the cause of a free Ireland (*see* 1916).

 Eva Gore-Booth, sister of Countess Markievicz (above), has been active in the north of England, organizing the Manchester and Salford Women's Trades Council to fight for the rights of women workers, and last year (with the countess's help) defeated Winston Churchill in a parliamentary election fought over issues that included the right of women to work as barmaids.

Carrie Chapman Catt, now 50, presides at a London convention of the International Woman's Suffrage Alliance but refuses April 26 to take sides in the controversy over whether British women have been too militant in their fight to gain voting rights.

The Men's League for Woman Suffrage is founded by Columbia University doctoral candidate Max F. Eastman, 26, at the instigation of his older sister, Crystal. Their mother, Annis Eastman (*née* Ford), is a self-taught minister (she preaches from Thomas K. Beecher's old pulpit at Elmira, N.Y.), and Max will recall her high school graduation essay, "O Femina, Femina," saying, "I am sure it expressed the smiling wish that women would buck up and be something, and the opinion that it was their fault and men's loss as well as theirs if they did not."

The NAACP (National Association for the Advancement of Colored People) is founded at New York following a January meeting attended by social worker Mary White Ovington, 44. She joins with W. E. Walling, union leader Leonora O'Reilly, 38, immigrant leader Henry Moscowitz, and others in "a revival of the Abolitionist spirit," and the association holds its first conference May 30.

Emmeline Pankhurst arrives at New York October 19 aboard the White Star liner *Oceanic* and is

Constance, Countess Markievicz, was a valiant heroine in the cause of Irish nationalism.

greeted by a crowd of women holding a banner that reads, "Vote for Women." She declares that British women are on the verge of getting the vote.

New York garment workers assemble at Cooper Union on the night of November 22 to hear speeches by Samuel Gompers of the AF of L, Mary Dreier of the WTUL, and others about a proposed strike. Most are immigrant women under age 25 who work at piece rates in unheated lofts, and they are especially moved by Clara Lemlich, 19, who is recovering from a beating on a picket line but stands up on the floor, asks to be heard, makes her way to the platform, and says in Yiddish, "I am a working girl, one of those who are on strike against intolerable conditions. I am tired of listening to speakers who talk in general terms. What we are here for is to decide whether we shall or shall not strike. I offer a resolution that a general strike be declared—now." Her resolution is adopted, and a strike begins that will last more than 9 weeks and involve some 20,000 women wage earners.

The strikers (above), who belong to the Ladies' Waist Makers' Union Local 25 of the 9-year-old International Ladies' Garment Workers' Union (ILGWU), heed the exhortations of Rose Schneiderman, now 27, who walks the picket lines, harangues the crowds, and attends countless meetings, braving cold, hunger, police brutality and attacks by company-hired thugs. Society women including Alva Ertskin Belmont (née Smith), 56, and Anne Morgan (daughter of financier J. P. Morgan) join the picket lines in December to avert further violence, getting more press coverage for the strikers and contributions to their strike fund. The sight of rich suffragists on the picket lines persuades thousands of working-class women to join the suffrage movement, whose success will help them in their struggle for improved working conditions.

☤ Mrs. C. Temple Emmet of New York is at Frieburg, Germany, when her confinement ends and is the first American woman to have childbirth with Twilight Sleep (*see* 1902). A granddaughter of the Astors, she will return to Germany for two further deliveries and will spread the word about Twilight Sleep in America (*see* 1915; *McClure's*, 1914).

An arsenic compound formulated by German bacteriologist Paul Ehrlich to fight syphilis is the first antibacterial therapeutic drug and pioneers chemotherapy in medicine. Ehrlich's compound number 592 is effective in destroying the trypanosomes that cause syphilis in mice and produces no side effects or aftereffects, his purer, more soluble variant number 606 will prove effective next year in treating human victims of syphilis, and the drug will be marketed under the name Salvarsan. Ehrlich's arsphenamine will reduce the incidence of syphilis in England and France by 50 percent in the next 5 years, but while his work will lead to the discovery of new antibacterial agents, many will attack his syphilis cure on the ground that it encourages sin.

🎓 *Metodo della pedagogia scientifica* by Italian schoolteacher-physician Maria Montessori, 39, will have a remarkable influence on education worldwide. The first woman graduate of the University of Rome medical school, Dr. Montessori became interested some years ago in helping "slow" students. She was assigned to a group of 8-year-old "idiots" and soon had them outscoring "normal" students on state-administered proficiency tests (*see* 1912).

The National Kindergarten Association (National Association for the Promotion of Kindergarten Education) is founded at New York by local businesswoman Bessie Locke, 44, who herself attended a private kindergarten in 1870 at Boston (*see* Peabody, 1860). She has reportedly seen the success of a friend's kindergarten in a city slum area and quit the business world. In the next 30 years, Locke will help to open more than 3,000 kindergartens serving 1.5 million U.S. children.

🎓 The Westover School opens in April at Middlebury, Conn., and by autumn has 135 boarding students in buildings designed by Theodate Pope Riddle, 41, one of America's first women architects. Founder Mary Robbins Hillard, 47, will head the preparatory school for girls until her death in October 1932 at age 70, and it will grow to have an enrollment of 171, including day students.

Ashley Hall opens at Charleston, S.C., where Tennessee-born Smith graduate Mary Vardrine McBee, 30, has obtained a master's degree, bought a strip of land for $16,000, and converted a three-story mansion into a boarding school. She vows that her graduates will be prepared to enter the best Eastern colleges. The state's only all-girl elementary and secondary school, Ashley Hall will grow to be a day school with nearly 500 students.

The National Training School for Women and Girls opens October 19 at Washington, D.C., under the direction of Woman's Industrial Club manager Nannie Helen Burroughs, 31, who has scored high in the civil service examinations but been told that there were no government jobs available for "a colored clerk." She starts off with seven students and eight staff members, offers practical courses in sewing, shoe repair, home economics, laundering, interior decorating, gardening, bookkeeping, shorthand, typing, printing, nursing, and barbering, and by year's end has 31 students. She also emphasizes academic courses and insists that each student take at least one course in black history. Burroughs will die in 1961, and her institution will be renamed the Nannie Burroughs School 3 years later.

Condé Nast takes over *Vogue* magazine (*see* 1892). Now 35, the former *Collier's* advertising manager has organized a company to make and sell dress patterns under an arrangement with Cyrus Curtis's *Ladies' Home Journal. Vogue* has a circulation of only 22,500, but Nast will make it a monthly and in 1914 will name managing editor Edna Woolman Chase, now 32, as editor in chief; she will build circulation to more than 130,000, launching British and French editions and training a generation of fashion editors, including Carmel Snow, now 19, who will become editor in chief of Hearst's *Harper's Bazaar.*

Fiction: *Three Lives* by Gertrude Stein includes "The Good Anna," "The Gentle Lena," and—more notably—"Melanctha"; *Luzmela's Daughter* (*La niña de Luzmela*) by Spanish novelist Concha Espina de Serna, 32; *The Children of the Pure and Living* (*Deti cistého civého*) by Teréza Novaková; *Girl of the Limberlost* by Gene Stratton-Porter; *The Circular Staircase* by Pittsburgh mystery novelist Mary Roberts Rinehart, 32.

Selma Lagerlöf is awarded the Nobel Prize in literature, the first woman writer to be thus honored.

Poetry: *Poems* (*Kvoedi*) by Icelandic poet Hulda (Unnur Benediktsdóttir Bjarklind), 28; *A Quiet Crisis* (*Csendes vélsá gok*) by Margit Kaffka.

Nannie Helen Burroughs was "too black" to teach in a Washington, D.C., public school, so she started her own. LIBRARY OF CONGRESS

Juvenile: *The Tale of the Flopsy Bunnies* by Beatrix Potter.

Painting: *Apollinaire and His Friends* by Marie Laurencin; *Spring, Nude at the Mirror, After the Bath, Adam and Eve,* and *Summer* by Suzanne Valadon, now 44, who meets artist Andrea Utter, 23, one of her son Maurice Utrillo's friends, leaves her husband, files for divorce, and goes off to live with Utter; Sonia Terk Uhde at Paris gives dinner parties to which she invites Picasso, Gertrude Stein, Alice B. Toklas, Vlaminck, Van Donken, Derain, and Braque: Countess Berthe de la Rose Delaunay comes to dinner with her tall, vigorous, redheaded painter son Robert, and he begins an affair with the hostess (*see* 1910);

Theater: *The Goddess of Reason* by Mary Johnston 2/15 at Daly's Theater, New York's, with Julia Marlowe, 48 perfs.; *Seven Days* by Mary Roberts Rinehart (above) and Avery Hopwood 11/11 at New York's Astor Theater, with Hope Latham, Florence Reed and Lucille La Verne, 397 perfs.

Opera: Mme. Schumann-Heink creates the title role of Klytemnestra in the world premiere of Richard Strauss's opera *Elektra* 1/25 at Dresden's Königliches Operhaus; Romanian-American soprano Alma Gluck (*née* Reba Fiersohn), 25, makes her Metropolitan Opera debut singing the role of Sophia in the 1894 Massenet opera *Werther*.

Broadway musicals: Elsie Janis (Elsie Bierbover), 19, in *The Fair Co-ed* 2/1 at the Knickerbocker Theater, with Gustav Laders–George Ade songs, 136 perfs.; Nora Bayes, Eva Tanguy, and Russian-American actress-singer Sophie Tucker (*née* Sonia Kalish), 25, in *The [Ziegfeld] Follies* 6/14 at the Jardin de Paris, with songs that include "By the Light of the Silvery Moon," 64 perfs.; Helen Hayes (Brown), 9, makes her first New York appearance in Victor Herbert's *Old Dutch* 11/22 at the Herald Square Theater (she has been a professional actress since age 5), 88 perfs.

Popular songs: "Meet Me Tonight in Dreamland" by Leo Friedman, 40, lyrics by Beth Slater Whitson, 30.

Dorothea Boothby wins in women's singles at Wimbledon, Hazel V. Hotchkiss, 22, in U.S. women's singles.

Paris couturiers introduce fashions that flatter women by emphasizing hips and delineating waistlines. The new gowns employ high-busted corsets, but U.S. women prefer low-busted versions, which accentuate smaller bosoms while minimizing larger ones.

Viennese-American milliner Hattie Carnegie (*née* Henrietta Köningeiser), 23, goes into partnership with her seamstress neighbor Ruth Rose Roth. Carnegie (who has borrowed her name from the steel magnate Andrew Carnegie) left school at age 13 when her father died and went to work at Macy's. In 4 years she and Roth will have their own shop near Riverside Drive, with Roth designing clothes that Carnegie (who makes the hats) will model and sell (*see* 1919).

The "kewpie" (short for cupid) figure with a cherubic head that comes to a point is patented by New York author-illustrator Rose Cecil O'Neill, 35, whose creation is soon translated into buttons, cutouts, salt and pepper shakers, soap, curtain fabric, and birthday cards. Kewpie will be the basis of a mold that will be made in 1913 by Pratt Institute art student Joseph L. Kallus and manufactured as a doll, initially in Germany from bisque. Mass-produced in America from celluloid and other materials, the kewpie doll and other kewpie renditions will earn $1.5 million for O'Neill, who wears a toga at her Greenwich Village salons.

The Melitta drip coffeemaker invented by Dresden *hausfrau* Melitta Bentz is introduced at the Leipzig Fair and begins a movement away from percolators. She began experimenting with coffee filters 2 years ago, first cutting a circle out of a sheet of blotting paper from her son's schoolbook and sticking it into the bottom of a brass pot that she poked full of holes. By putting coffee grounds on top of the filter and pouring boiling water over it, she has obtained better-tasting coffee in less time and without the bother of wrapping loose grounds in a cloth bag and boiling water around it. Her husband, Hugo, hired a tinsmith last year to make pots based on her idea, and they sell more than 1,200 coffeemakers at the trade fair. By 1912 her company will be making a line of coffee filters that will soon be replaced by cone-shaped filters, and the metal pots will be replaced by porcelain and plastic models as her drip-coffee method gains worldwide popularity.

1910

Britain's Edward VII dies May 6 at age 68 after a 9-year reign and is succeeded by his second son, George, now 44, who will reign until 1936 with help from his wife, Mary, nearly 44 herself. She will be credited with helping the bluff king adapt to changing conditions and make himself popular with the people, although he will never be as popular as she.

Japanese police arrest 26 anarchists and socialists on charges of planning to assassinate the Meiji emperor Mutsuhito. All are men except revolutionist Suga Sugano, 29, who will be executed next year along with 11 other alleged conspirators after a secret trial without witnesses.

 English suffragist Lady Constance Lytton tells visitors to her Walton jail in January that she was allowed only 4 days without food on a hunger strike before a steel gag was pushed into her mouth and liquified food poured into her stomach via a four-foot tube.

The International Socialist Women's Congress at Copenhagen adopts the suggestion of German delegate Clara Zetkin (*née* Eissner), 53, to establish March 8 as International Women's Day—the female equivalent of May Day (*see* New York, 1908). The day will be observed for the first time next year with parades and demonstrations, bringing out crowds mostly in Europe and Asia, but not in North America.

The League of German Women's Organizations names *Die Frau* editor Gertrude Baumer, 37, president. She will found a socialist school for women in 1917, head the League until 1919, and gain election to the Reichstag in 1920 (*see* 1933).

The International Ladies' Garment Workers' Union (ILGWU) wins its 9-week strike for New York cloakmakers with help from Rose Schneiderman and the Woman's Trade Union League (*see* 1909). The New York strike will be followed in the next few years by similar job actions in Brooklyn, Philadelphia, Chicago, Boston, Cleveland, Muscatine (Iowa), Kalamazoo (Mich.), Lawrence (Mass.), and Paterson (N.J.) (*see* Dubinsky, 1932).

Russian-American garment worker and labor organizer Bessie Abramowitz, 21, leads a strike against Chicago's Hart, Schaffner and Marx. For 20 years she will be the only female union leader in Chicago's clothing industry (*see* 1914).

Work Accidents and the Law by New York suffragist Crystal Eastman, 29 (Vassar '03), will contribute to the passage of U.S. worker-safety legislation.

The Mann White Slave Traffic Act signed into law by President Taft June 25 discourages interstate transportation of women for immoral purposes. Newspaper stories about black prizefighter Jack Johnson and his white wife have inspired passage of the law, but Emma Goldman, in essays published by her Mother Earth Publishing Association, has written, "Our reformers have suddenly made a great discovery—the white slave traffic. . . . It is significant that whenever the public mind is to be diverted from a great social wrong, a crusade is inaugurated against indecency, gambling, saloons, etc. . . . How is it that an institution, known almost to every child, should have been discovered so suddenly? . . . Prostitution has been, and is, a widespread evil, yet mankind goes on its business, perfectly indifferent to the sufferings and distress of the victims of prostitution. As indifferent, indeed, as mankind has remained to our industrial system, to our economic prostitution. . . . Nowhere is woman treated according to the merit of her work, but rather as a sex. It is therefore almost inevitable that she should pay for her right to exist . . . with sex favors. Thus it is merely a question of degree whether she sells herself to one man, in or out of marriage, or to many men. Whether our reformers admit it or not, the economic and social inferiority of woman is responsible for prostitution."

Women in Washington State gain the right to vote in a constitutional amendment adopted November 8 (*see* California, 1911).

Half of all births in the United States are still attended by midwives, who deliver infants mostly of black and immigrant women.

The Flexner Report (*Medical Education in the United States and Canada*) shows that three out of four North American medical schools are inadequate. Funded by a $14,000 grant from the 8-year-old Carnegie Foundation, physician Abraham Flexner, 44, has inspected 155 medical schools and his findings will lead to the closing of every women's medical college except Woman's Medical College of Philadelphia.

A Paris fashion for imitation sable and sealskin encourages amateur Chinese hunters to trap Manchurian marmots, many of which are infected with bubonic plague. An epidemic of the plague transmitted by unhealthy marmots will kill 60,000 in

Manchuria and China in the next 2 years, and in the next 9 years will kill 1.5 million in China and India.

Christian Science founder Mary Baker Eddy dies at Chestnut Hill, Mass., December 3 at age 89. Her denomination has grown to number 100,000 but will never have more than about 250,000 followers.

Women account for nearly 40 percent of all U.S. college undergraduates, up from 32 percent in 1880 (see 1920). But Wesleyan College in Connecticut returns to being for men only after nearly 50 years as a coeducational institution, and many coed colleges establish quotas to limit female admissions.

Women's Wear Daily begins publication at New York July 13 under the direction of journalist Edmund Fairchild, 44, whose trade paper for the garment industry will be the basis of a publishing empire.

La Mujer begins publication in Puerto Rico. Editor of the feminist journal is Luisa Capetillo, 30, who has worked in factories for as little as 3¢ for a 10–12-hour day and 3 years ago participated in a strike at an Arecibo factory and became a member of the Free Federation of Puerto Rican Workers.

Nonfiction: *Diary of a Shirtwaist Striker* by Russian-American feminist Theresa Serber Malkiel, 36; *The Lady* by Barnard College dean Emily James Putnam, who writes, "The Lady is proverbial for her skill in eluding definition. . . . For the purpose of the present discussion she may be described merely as the female of the favored social class." Beginning with the upper-class woman of ancient Greece, she continues through the cultivated woman of the antebellum South in the United States. Humorist Mark Twain (Samuel Clemens) dies at Redding, Conn., April 21 at age 74 and is buried with a funeral oration written by feminist preacher Anis Ford Eastman. Some of Twain's friends recall that when he was asked, "What would men be without women?" he replied, "Scarce, sir. Mighty scarce."

Fiction: *The Penholder* (*Pennskaftet*) by Elin Wägner, whose new novel is based on the Swedish feminist movement; *A Dangerous Age* (*Den farlige alder*) by Karen Michælis is about the erotic crisis of a woman in her 40s; *Summer* (*Nyár*) (stories) by Margit Kaffka; *The Devourers* by London-born

Italian novelist Annie Vivanti, 42; *La Vagabonde* by Colette, who marries Henri de Jouvenal.

Poetry: *The Evening Album: Poems* (*Vechernii al'bom: Stikhi*) by Russian poet Marina (Ivanovna) Tsvetaeva, 18; *Dal profondo* by Ada Negri, who leaves her rich husband and takes her 12-year-old daughter, Bianca, to Switzerland; *The Eternal Forces* (*Les Forces éternelles*) by Anna, comtesse de Noailles.

Juvenile: *The Secret Garden* by Frances Hodgson Burnett; *The Tale of Mrs. Tittlemouse* and *The Tale of Jemima Puddle-Duck* by Beatrix Potter; *Maida's Little Shop* by suffragist Inez Gillmore; *Captain January* by Gardiner, Me., author Laura E. (Elizabeth) Richards (*née* Howe), 60, a daughter of Julia Ward Howe (who dies at Newport, R.I., October 17 at age 91).

Painting: *Joy of Living* by Suzanne Valadon, whose large canvas shows the influence of the late Pierre Puvis de Chavannes; *The Assembly* by Marie Laurencin. Sonia Terk Uhde realizes in June that she is pregnant, her husband, Wilhelm, agrees to divorce her, she contracts scarlet fever a month later but recovers, marries Robert Delaunay November 10, and will give birth in January to a son, who will be named after his paternal uncle Charles.

Photographer Imogen Cunningham, who has worked with Edward Curtis, opens a portrait studio in Seattle but is mainly interested in still-life flower studies.

Films: Pearl White in Joseph A. Golden's *The New Magdalene*; Canadian-born beauty Mary Pickford (originally Gladys Smith), 17, in D. W. Griffith's *Ramona*.

Ballet: Russian ballerina Tamara Karsavina, 25, dances the role of Ivan Czarevich in Igor Stravinsky's *The Firebird* 6/25 at the Paris Opéra, with choreography by Michel Fokine.

Broadway musicals: Marie Dressler in *Tillie's Nightmare* 5/5 at the Herald Square Theater, with songs that include "Heaven Will Protect the Working Girl" based on the 1898 song "She Was Bred in Old Kentucky," 77 perfs.; singer Fanny Brice (Fannie Borach), 18, appears in *The [Ziegfeld] Follies* 6/20 at the Jardin de Paris (Brice won a Brooklyn talent contest 5 years ago singing "When You Know You're Not Forgotten by the Girl You Can't Forget," left school to start a theatrical career, and has been hired at $75 per week by Florenz Ziegfeld), 88 perfs.; *Naughty Marietta* 11/7 at the New York Theater, with lyrics by actress manqué and songwriter Rida Young (*née* Johnson), 35, music by Victor Herbert, songs that include "Ah, Sweet Mystery of Life" and "I'm Falling in Love with Someone."

Opera: Italian soprano Claudia Muzio (Claudina Muzzio), 20, makes her debut at Arezzo 1/15 in the 1884 Massenet opera *Manon*; Emmy Destinn creates the role of Minnie in the new Puccini opera *The Girl of the Golden West* (*La Fanciulla del West*) 12/10 at New York's Metropolitan Opera with Enrico Caruso as Dick Johnson.

Popular songs: "A Perfect Day" by Carrie Jacobs-Bond; "Let Me Call You Sweetheart" by Leo Friedman, lyrics by Beth Slater Whitson.

Dorothea Chambers wins in women's singles at Wimbledon, Hazel Hotchkiss in U.S. women's singles.

The Camp Fire Girls of America is founded by Luther Halsey Gulick, 45, who helped James Naismith invent the game of basketball in 1891 at Springfield, Mass. Now director of physical education for New York City public schools and a social engineer for the Russell Sage Foundation, Gulick gets help from his wife.

The Girl Guides is founded by Boer War hero Robert Stephenson Smyth, Lord Baden-Powell of Gilwell, with his sister Agnes, 52 (*see* Girl Scouts of America, 1912).

Father's Day is observed for the first time June 19 at Spokane, Wash., where the local YMCA and the Spokane Ministerial Association have persuaded the city fathers to set aside a Sunday to "honor thy father." The idea has come from local housewife Mrs. John Bruce Dodd, 28, who has been inspired by the selflessness and responsibility of her father, William Smart, a Civil War veteran who raised his daughter and her five brothers after the early death of his wife.

The Elizabeth Arden beauty salon chain has its beginnings in a New York beauty treatment parlor started by Canadian-American beauty shop secretary Florence Nightingale Graham, 25, who first goes into business with Elizabeth Hubbard, has a falling out with her partner, borrows $6,000 from a cousin, and opens a Fifth Avenue shop under the name Elizabeth Arden, inspired by the 1864 Tennyson poem "Enoch Arden." Graham repays the loan within 4 months, will move farther uptown, and will open a Washington, D.C., branch in 1915. She will help formulate the first nongreasy skin cream and package it under the name Amoretta and introduce lipsticks in colors coordinated to skin tones and clothing; by 1938 there will be 29 Elizabeth Arden salons, 10 of them in foreign countries, while Graham's Maine vacation home will be operating as a health resort under the name Maine Chance Farm. Elizabeth Arden beauty products will be selling at major department stores.

Mme. C. J. Walker Manufacturing Co. moves into its own Indianapolis building and prospers in the business of making and marketing a hair straightener invented by Sarah Walker (*née* Breedlove), 42, who 5 years ago devised a formula for treating tightly curled hair and sold it by mail order. Orphaned before she was 6, Walker married at age 14, was widowed at 20, and worked as a St. Louis washerwoman to support herself and her daughter, A'Lelia, while educating herself in her spare time. She has sold her products door to door, set up factories to produce them at Denver and Pittsburgh, and recruited a sales force of "beauty analysts" who go from house to house dressed in white shirts and long black skirts. She will soon be the first black woman to make herself a millionaire.

American physician Hawley Harvey Crippen, 48, is arrested aboard the S.S. *Montrose* off Canada July 31 and charged with having murdered his second wife, Cora (*née* Turner), whose remains have been discovered buried in the basement of his London house. Dr. Crippen poisoned Cora, dissected the body, burned the bones, and buried the rest. He has been traveling as "Mr. and Master Robinson" with his secretary and mistress, Ethel le Neve, who has been disguised as his "son," but the ship's master has seen them holding hands, become suspicious, and sent a wireless message to Scotland Yard, whose chief inspector has crossed the Atlantic aboard a faster ship and come aboard the *Montrose* disguised as the St. Lawrence pilot. Both Crippen and le Neve will be tried at the Old Bailey, and Crippen will be executed.

 The National 4-H Clubs have their beginnings in a three-leaf-clover pin awarded by Iowa schoolteacher Jessie (*née* Celestia Josephine) Field Shambaugh, 29, who in 1901 formed a Boys Corn Club and a Girls Home Club to foster feelings of pride and self-worth in the students to whom she taught improved farming techniques and home management in her Page County, Iowa, school (she began 4 years ago to establish such clubs in each of the county's 130 schools). The pin has the letter H on each of its three leaves, symbolizing head, hand, and heart, with the word Page in its center. A fourth H will be added, first to represent home, then to represent health. 4-H will evolve into a national organization, sponsored by the U.S. Department of Agriculture, and Shambaugh will become known as the "Mother of 4-H."

1911

 China is proclaimed a republic in February, a revolution begins in October, unrest spreads through the country, young women leave a mission school to form a regiment, women go into battle at their own initiative, wearing men's clothes, and throw homemade bombs on Nanjing from a hill above the city, but bloodshed overall is minimal. A revolutionary provisional assembly at Nanjing elects physician Sun Yat-sen (Sun Zhong Shan), 45, president of the United Provinces of China December 30 (*see* 1912).

 China's political and social revolution (above) will end the 267-year Qing (Ch'ing) dynasty and begin the decline of selling young women into matrimony and binding girls' feet in childhood, a practice that has been popular in much of the country since the 16th century. All toes except the big toe of girls aged four to six, sometimes younger, are bent under the foot and pulled back toward the heel by binding them so tightly that toes may putrefy and sometimes even drop off. The foot is painful for a year, until it is withered into a stump, making walking difficult

without assistance. Often a foot is broken or permanently crippled, and once maimed it cannot be unbound without great pain. Especially in northern China, where fewer women are needed to work in the rice fields, girls' feet are subjected to the painful deformation partly to symbolize women's dependence on men, partly to signify a family's wealth and status (although many poor families bind their daughters' feet in hopes that it will make her attractive to a rich suitor), and partly because men find the gait of woman taking tiny, delicate steps on "lily feet" erotic (somewhat like the gait of Western women wearing high heels); to touch such a foot is, for a Chinese, comparable to touching a woman's breast in Western society (*see* 1919).

The first International Women's Day March 8 produces rallies in Austria, Denmark, Germany, and Switzerland to protest lack of representation by women in trade unions.

Militant English suffragists continue their campaign to win the vote. "We are here to claim our rights as women, not only to be free, but to fight for freedom," says Christabel Pankhurst in a speech March 23. "It is our privilege, as well as our pride and our joy, to take some part in this militant movement, which, as we believe, means the regeneration of all humanity. . . . Nothing but contempt is due to those people who ask us to submit to unmerited oppression. We shall not do it." Composer Ethel Smyth, who has joined the movement, dresses in a Norfolk jacket and knickerbockers, smokes a pipe, and heaves a paper-wrapped brick through the ground-floor window of the home secretary, an action that sends her for 2 months to Holloway Gaol, where she writes "The March of the Women"—battle song of the WSPU. Other militants burn the words "Votes for Women" into the turf of golf courses, temporarily ruining greens and fairways to press their point.

"Feminism is a movement that seems to me self-condemned in its very name," writes Italian philosopher Benedetto Croce, 45. "It is a 'feminine' idea in the bad sense of that word. Men, too, have their particular problems, but they haven't invented 'masculinism' " (*see* West, 1913).

New York's Triangle Shirtwaist Factory in the Asch Building at Washington Place and Greene Street has a fire March 25 and 146 people are killed, most of them young sweatshop seamstresses who are unable to escape because the factory owner has locked all exits to the roof lest employees steal the shirtwaists, take them to the roof, and drop them to accomplices in the street below. Some 500 women and 50 men are employed in the factory, working from 7:30 in the morning until 6 at night, mostly for $6 to $8 per week, under conditions so crowded that their chairs are dovetailed and oil-soaked rags and lint lie on the floor beneath each sewing machine. Screaming young girls leap or fall from the burning 10-story loft building, and the tragedy brings new demands for better working conditions. Rose Schneiderman delivers a speech at the Metropolitan Opera House, saying, "I would be a traitor to these poor, burned bodies if I came here to talk good fellowship. . . . Every year thousands of us are maimed. The life of men and women is so cheap and property is so sacred" (*see* IWW Lawrence strike, 1912).

Social worker Gertrude Barnum, 45, goes to work raising funds for the International Ladies' Garment Workers' Union, an activity that will occupy her for the next 5 years.

Chicago's mayor closes the city's Everleigh Club following a campaign subsidized by rival madams to put the rich Everleigh sisters out of business (*see* 1900).

California women gain suffrage by constitutional amendment (*see* New York, 1917).

Portuguese women get the vote April 30.

The literary magazine *Seito* (*Bluestocking*), which begins publication in September at Tokyo, marks the start of a women's liberation movement launched by feminist Raicho (*née* Haru) Hiratsuka, 25. Her father helped draft the Constitution of 1889 and the Civil Code, which is so heavily weighted against women. After their first child was born, he sent his wife, Tsuya, to a small school for girls that later became a college, letting his mother take care of the baby. He has been taken aback by Tsuya's going behind his back and helping to finance their daughter's defiance of the Civil Code. Raicho has married a man 5 years her junior but has refused to register the marriage, since that would mean forfeiting all rights to her husband. She has registered her children under her own name and her husband has supported her in this, testifying that the children were his and were not illegitimate. The government had insisted that the couple was not legally married, but the issue has been decided in Hiratsuka's favor. The Shinto sun god Amaterasuomikami is a woman, and Hiratsuka writes in her first issue, "In the beginning, women were the sun. The sun was shining, and we were truly human beings. Now we are the moon, pale-faced like sick people, shining only as the reflection of others. We must take back our hidden sun. We must find our hidden talents . . ." *Seito* will be suppressed after its February 1916 issue, and the status of Japanese women will remain low (*see* 1919).

$ Missouri becomes the first state to provide public aid to mothers of dependent children; by 1913, 18 states will have aid-to-mothers statutes, but strict eligibility standards and the fact that few eligible women apply for assistance will make the laws applicable to only a small percentage of needy mothers (*see* medicine, 1921).

Leslie's Illustrated Weekly feature writer and drama critic Harriet Quimby, 36, passes her flying test August 1 in a 30-horsepower Blériot monoplane and becomes the first licensed U.S. woman pilot (French pilot Hélène Dutrieu is the world's only other woman with a pilot's license). Quimby wins $600 September 23 as the sole competitor in a 20-mile cross-country race for women over Nassau Boulevard on Long Island, N.Y. "In my opinion," she says, "there is no reason why the aeroplane should not open up a fruitful occupation for women. I see no reason why they cannot realize handsome incomes by carrying passengers between adjacent towns, why they cannot derive incomes from parcel delivery, from taking photographs from above, or from conducting schools for flying" (*see* 1912).

An electric self-starter for motorcar engines invented by C. F. Kettering makes automobiles safe for women to drive themselves without having to rely on men. Cadillac boss Henry M. Leland gives Kettering's Dayton Engineering Laboratories (Delco) a contract to supply 4,000 self-starters after losing a good friend who was killed trying to crank a woman's balky engine.

Mme. Curie wins her second Nobel Prize, this one for chemistry.

Literacy in England reaches 99 percent for both sexes, up from 55 percent for women and 70 percent for men in 1850. In many other countries, women remain largely illiterate.

The First Mexican Congress (el Primer Congreso Méxicanisto) is organized at Laredo, Texas, by Mexican-American journalist Jovita Idar, 26, and her family. She has written in the state's Spanish-language newspapers about the problems of Hispanics in Texas; the educational and cultural conference addresses those problems (*see* 1913).

Women account for 11 percent of students at Canadian colleges and universities (*see* 1882).

New York's Katherine Gibbs School is founded by local widow Gibbs, 46, who has sold her jewelry to raise the start-up funds for what will become America's most prestigious secretarial school. Without any experience but with two sons to support, Gibbs has recognized the need for a school that she will develop to include not only secretarial courses but also courses in business law and liberal arts.

Nonfiction: *The Immoral Effects of Ignorance in Sexual Relations* by English novelist-playwright Laurence Housman, 46, a younger brother of poet A. E. Housman, who writes, "I discovered how girls were sent ignorant through life into marriage, and pleaded that they, like men, had a right to know themselves and what was the nature of the contract to which they were giving themselves for life—then I remember I was told by one, who herself had the care of daughters, that that ignorance formed too valuable an addition to the virginal charm of womanhood in the marriage market"; *The Man-Made World; Or, Our Androcentric Culture* by Charlotte Perkins Gilman; *The Book of Woman's Power* by Ida M. Tarbell; *My Opinions on the Liberties, Rights, and Obligations of the Puerto Rican Woman* by *La Mujer* editor Luisa Capetillo; *Half a Man: The Status of the Negro in New York* by local activist Mary White Ovington, who played a leading role in the founding 2 years ago of the NAACP; *Search for the Apex of the World: High Mountain Climbing in Peru and Bolivia, Including the Conquest of Mount Huascarán* by Annie Smith Peck (*see* sports, 1908).

Fiction: *Ethan Frome* by Edith Wharton; *The Harvester* by Gene Stratton Porter; *The Case of Richard Meynell* by Mrs. Humphry Ward, now 60, who 3 years ago became first president of the Anti-Suffrage League; *Life Everlasting* by Marie Corelli; *In a German Pension* (short stories) by New Zealand–born writer Katherine Mansfield (Kathleen M. Beauchamp), 22, who left home for London 3 years ago, lived a bohemian life, married, divorced after 3 weeks, found herself pregnant by another man, was put up at a Bavarian hotel by her mother, and miscarried; *Abandonment* (*Akirame*) by Japanese novelist Toshiko Tamura (*née* Sato), 27; *The Woman in the Sea* (*Agua de nieve*) by Concha Espina de Serna; *The Long Roll* by Mary Johnston is a Civil War novel; *Mother* by U.S. novelist Kathleen Thompson Norris, 31, whose novels will be serialized in women's magazines for more than 30 years.

Juvenile: *Mother Carey's Chickens* by Kate Douglas Wiggin; *The Tale of Timmy Tip-toes* by Beatrix Potter; *The New Girl at St. Chance* and *A Fourth-Form Friendship* by Angela Brazil.

Poetry: "The Female of the Species" by Rudyard Kipling: "But the she-bear thus accosted rends the peasant tooth and nail/ For the female of the species is more deadly than the male."

Painting: *Woman Reading at a Window* by English painter Gwen (Gwendolen) John, 35, whose younger brother is the more famous painter Augustus John; *Still Life with Teapot* by Suzanne Valadon; *The Young Women* by Marie Laurencin.

Sculpture: *Russian Dancers* by U.S. sculptor Melvina Cornell Hoffman, 16, whose father died 2 years ago. Her mother took her to Europe, where she has studied under Auguste Rodin.

Theater: Mrs. Minnie Maddern Fiske in Harry James Smith's *Mrs. Bumpsted-Leigh* 4/3 at New York's Lyceum Theater, 64 perfs.; Christine Silve in Bernard Shaw's *Fanny's First Play* 4/19 at London's Little Theatre, 622 perfs.; ballet dancer Ida Rubinstein plays the lead role in Gabriele D'Annunzio's *The Martyrdom of Saint Sebastian* 5/22 at the Théâtre du Châtelet, Paris, with music by Claude Debussy, but D'Annunzio's works were placed on the index of forbidden books by the Vatican in early May and the archbishop of Paris warns

Roman Catholics not to attend performances on threat of excommunication.

Japanese actress Sumako Matsui (Masako Kobayashi), 25, plays the role of Ophelia in a translation of the 1602 Shakespeare tragedy *Hamlet* in what is called New Theater (*Shingeki*). Men have played female roles until now and will continue to do so in the Kabuki theater.

Films: Blanche Sweet in D. W. Griffith's *Fighting Blood* and *The Lonedale Operator*; Norma Talmadge, 18, and Maurice Costelli in William Humphreys's *A Tale of Two Cities*.

Broadway musicals: Hazel Dawn, 19, in Ivan Caryll's *The Pink Lady* 3/13 at the New Amsterdam Theater, 312 perfs. (the hit makes pink the year's fashion color); the Dolly Sisters (Viennese dancers Jennie [Jan Szieka] and Rosie [Roszka] Deutsch, both 18) in *The Ziegfeld Follies* 6/26 at the Jardin de Paris, 80 perfs.

The Society of Women Musicians is founded at London by musicologist-critic Marion M. Scott with Gertrude Eaton and others to represent the interests of women in music. It will give concerts, especially of works by women (*see* 1928).

Opera: Spanish soprano Conchita Supervia, 15, sings the role of Octavian in the Roman premiere of the new Richard Strauss opera *Der Rosenkavalier*; Maggie Teyte begins an engagement with the Chicago Opera company that will continue until 1914.

Popular songs: "Everybody's Doin' It" by Irving Berlin popularizes the Turkey Trot dance invented by dancer Vernon Castle and his bride, Irene Foote Castle, 18; "I Want a Girl (Just Like the Girl that Married Dear Old Dad)" by Harry von Tilzer, Oedipal lyrics by Will Dillon, 34; "Little Grey Home in the West" by English composer Hermann Lohr, 40, lyrics by Miss D. Eardley Wilmot, 28.

Dorothea Chambers wins in women's singles at Wimbledon, Hazel Hotchkiss in U.S. women's singles.

A black woman is raped and then hanged at Okemah, Okla., after allegedly having shot a sheriff. Florida adopts a statute making it "unlawful to publish or broadcast information identifying [a] sexual offense victim"; the law will stand for 80 years before it is ruled unconstitutional.

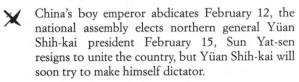

1912

China's boy emperor abdicates February 12, the national assembly elects northern general Yüan Shih-kai president February 15, Sun Yat-sen resigns to unite the country, but Yüan Shih-kai will soon try to make himself dictator.

An English suffragist gets married January 13 without using the words "I will obey" in her wedding ceremony (*see* Stanton, 1840). A Virginia woman is married in mid-February after having the words "obey and serve him" stricken from the ceremony.

English suffragists Emmeline Pankhurst and Emmeline and Frederick Pethick-Lawrence are arrested in early March after window-breaking demonstrations (Pankhurst and two others have broken the windows of Prime Minister Asquith's residence at 10 Downing Street after leaving a note for him), Annie Kenney takes over the WSPU while Pankhurst and the Pethick-Lawrences are in Holloway Gaol for 2 months, Pankhurst and her daughter Christabel, who has not been allowed to practice law, repudiate the Pethick-Lawrences after their release, they join the United Suffragists, and Emmeline Pethick-Lawrence voyages to America to support U.S. suffragists.

London pathologist Sir Almroth Edward Wright, 51, writes a letter to the *Times* headed "Militant Hysteria." "Peace will come again," he writes. "It will come when woman ceases to teach all manner of evil of man despitefully. It will come when she ceases to impute to him as a crime her own natural disabilities, when she ceases to resent the fact that man cannot and does not wish to work side by side with her. And peace will return when . . . the woman who remains in England comes to recognize that she can without sacrifice of dignity give a willing subordination to the husband or father, who, when all is said and done, earns and lays up money for her." Dr. Wright also publishes a monograph entitled "The Unexpurgated Case Against Woman Suffrage."

Newspapers report that the Chinese Parliament at Nanjing has granted equal suffrage to women March 21. Carrie Chapman Catt, who has founded and heads the International Woman Suffrage Alliance, arrives by train at New York November 15 after a 20-month world tour and tells reporters that Chinese women do not yet have the vote but "have a flourishing suffrage society, and if the franchise does not come to them soon they may be the next militant vote getters." She says that Chinese suffragists have headquarters in every city and have threatened to use force if they do not get voting rights, but Chinese women will not vote on the same basis as men until 1949. The suffragist movement in France and Germany has more strength and dignity than is generally known, Catt declares, and she predicts that practically all the world's women will be enfranchised within 50 years.

Italy's lower house of Parliament votes 209 to 48 against giving women the right to vote (but *see* 1919).

France's Parlement votes in November to repeal article 340 of the Napoleonic Civil Code, easing restrictions against women, but French women will not vote in general elections until 1945.

A mass meeting of the Wage Earner's League and the Collegiate Equal Suffrage League in the Great Hall of the People at New York's Cooper Union April 22 protests the New York State Legislature's failure to pass a resolution endorsing woman suffrage. Attacking the state senator who said that if women were to get "into the arena of politics with its alliances and distressing contests—the delicacy is gone, the charm is gone, and you emasculize woman," labor leader Rose Schneiderman rises to her full four feet nine inches and says, "I wonder if it will add to my height when I get the vote. I might work for it all the harder if it did. It is just too ridiculous, this talk of becoming less womanly, just as if a woman could be anything else except a woman. . . . It seems to me that the working woman ought to wake up to the truth of her situation; all this talk about women's charm does not mean working women. Working women are expected to work and produce their kind so that they too may work until they die of some industrial disease." She speaks of women in laundries standing 13 to 14

hours each day in terrible steam and heat with their hands in hot starch. "Certainly these women won't lose any more of their beauty and charm by putting a ballot in a ballot box once a year than they are likely to standing in the . . . laundries all year round."

New York suffragists including Maud Malone heckle presidential candidates Woodrow Wilson and Theodore Roosevelt, asking, "Shall the women vote?" (*see* 1917).

Male voters in four U.S. states—Michigan, Kansas, Oregon, and the new state of Arizona—vote in the November 6 elections to adopt constitutional amendments granting woman suffrage, but Wisconsin voters reject the proposal. Oregon's male electorate votes 57,000 to 51,000 to adopt the amendment, and suffragist Abigail Duniway, now 78 and confined to a wheelchair, is asked to write the official proclamation and sign it with the governor. Asked if she is excited, she replies, "Excited? No, I am not excited. I *knew* it would come."

Lawrence, Mass., woolen mills have a bitter strike beginning in January as women join with men in smashing machines. Women employees, who work the same hours as men but for less pay and do housework in addition, carry banners with the slogan "We want bread and roses too." A woman striker is killed January 30 in a street fight with police, and Industrial Workers of the World (IWW) organizer Elizabeth Gurley Flynn, 21, gets her first taste of labor-management violence. The strikers send about 150 children to New York to get them out of harm's way, but when police step in with billy clubs to stop the departure of a second group, the resultant national publicity puts pressure on the mill owners to settle the strike, and they meet most of the strikers' demands (*see* 1913).

A minimum wage law for women and children enacted by the Massachusetts legislature is the first state law of its kind.

Kalamazoo, Mich., corset makers strike against a company that they charge with immoral behavior. One striker, Josephine Casey, says, "The girls are compelled to pay for their own thread, and this is quite an item. It is a common practice for foremen to forget to charge them for the thread for several days and then to suggest a way in which these girls may repay them for this 'kindness.' " The striking women are arrested.

The Japanese newspaper *Manchoho Shimbun* publishes a letter June 8 addressed to the president of Tokyo Boseki, a large textile company. Written by a young woman employee, it says, "Please help me. I work at Tokyo Boseki. Until last year, we started work at 6 in the morning and worked until 6 in the evening, 12 hours. Starting in March, we have had to work 18 hours a day. We have had to start at 11 in the evening and work until 6 the next morning, with only one hour off to eat and rest. My body is so tired that I cannot sleep." Japan's economy is dependent on textile exports, and textile factories depend on cheap labor.

Daisy Bates applies for the position of Protector of Aborigines in Australia's Northern Territory; she has had more experience in living with the natives than anyone else, but her application for the salaried job is rejected on the ground that a woman would need a police escort, which would hamper her work among people who regard their wives as chattels that can be sold or traded and whose population is being ravaged by sexually transmitted diseases contracted from white settlers (*see* 1902). She is given the unpaid job of Honorary Protector in the Eucla district, but, having no money, is obliged in June to put her 183,000-acre cattle station up for sale in order to finance the work that will occupy her for more than 30 years (*see* 1938).

The International Ladies' Garment Workers Union (ILGWU) calls a strike in December (but *see* 1913).

The S.S. *Titanic* of the White Star Line scrapes an iceberg in the North Atlantic on her maiden voyage, sustains a 300-foot slash, and sinks in 2½ hours on the night of April 15. Only 711 of the 2,224 aboard survive, and the 1,513 lost include such prominent millionaires as R. H. Macy's boss Isidor Straus, 67, whose wife, Ida, also drowns, having refused to join other first-class women in the lifeboats. Survivors include Denver millionaire Molly (originally Margaret) Brown, 44, who has donned woolen underwear, heavy bloomers, two wool petticoats, a $4,000 sable muff, and a $60,000 chinchilla cape, marshaled dozens of shivering women and children into lifeboats, boarded the last one, and threatened to throw the only seaman aboard into the drink if he did not start rowing. She has picked up an oar herself, ordered the other 23 women in the boat to stop crying and start rowing, given most of her clothing to the others, and—now down to her underwear—threatened malingerers with a Colt pistol. She and her companions are rescued after 7 hours on the icy North Atlantic, and she is hailed as a national hero when she reaches New York.

Sylvia Pankhurst and other British suffragists say it was not male chivalry but simply the universal rule that women and children go first that was reponsible for the survival of so many women in the sinking of the *Titanic* (above). A *New York Times* editorial says the Pankhurst comment has set back the cause of woman suffrage.

Pilot Harriet Quimby takes off from Dover in a Blériot monoplane April 16, crosses the English channel at an altitude of 1,500 feet, circles Boulogne twice, and lands near Hardelot after 30 minutes in the air, becoming the first woman to fly the Channel (*see* 1911). During the third annual Boston aviation meet July 1 she flies the meet's manager in a Blériot monoplane to an altitude of 6,000 feet (no woman has ever flown that high), but the plane suddenly goes into a dive, neither Quimby nor her passenger is strapped in, and both are hurled to their deaths.

The Children's Bureau, founded at Washington, begins lobbying for federal legislation to fund education of women in prenatal and postnatal care (*see* Sheppard-Towner Act, 1921).

An article in the *Nation* on the U.S. servant shortage says that "it might be a very good thing for a woman's health to sweep her room, and make her bed, and dust her parlor, and get her dinner; but the attenuation of her physical energies has been carried so far by civilization that it will take a generation or two of golfing, boating, and bathing to give her sex back the strength of old days, when the domestic virtues went hand in hand with the domestic labors."

The Montessori Method by Italian educator Maria Montessori, now 42, describes her success at teaching slum children between the ages of 3 and 6 how to read (*see* 1909). She begins a movement of Montessori schools for teachers.

Buffalo, N.Y., heiress Mabel Ganson Dodge, 33, returns from Europe, takes a brownstone at 23 Fifth Avenue in New York's Greenwich Village, and is persuaded by journalist Lincoln Steffens to open her home to the local intelligentsia because "you have a centralizing, magnetic, social faculty. You attract, stimulate, and soothe people, and men like to sit with you and talk to you themselves. You make them think more fluently, and they feel enhanced." Dodge was married at age 21, lost her husband 3 years later in a hunting accident, sailed to Europe to recover from a nervous breakdown, met Edwin Dodge aboard ship, married him in 1905, lived with him in a villa at Florence, entertained American artists, and twice tried to commit suicide before leaving her second husband. Her "Salon Dodge" in New York will flourish on Wednesday evenings for 3 years, attracting such notables as Gertrude Stein, Emma Goldman, John Reed, Margaret Sanger, Alfred Stieglitz, and Walter Lippmann (*see* 1916).

Nonfiction: *Woman's Share in Social Culture* by U.S. feminist college professor Anna Spencer (*née* Garlin), 61, who says, "The failure of women to produce genius of the first rank in most of the supreme forms of human effort has been used to block the way of all women of talent and ambition for intellectual achievement in a manner that would be amusingly absurd were it not so monstrously unjust and socially harmful"; *The Business of Being a Woman* by Ida M. Tarbell; *Pathbreaking: The Story of a Pioneer* by Abigail Scott Duniway (above), who writes, "I, if not washing, scrubbing, churning, or nursing the baby, was preparing their meals in our lean-to kitchen. To bear two children in two and a half years from my marriage day, to make thousands of pounds of butter every year for market day, not including what was used in our free hotel at home, to sew and cook, and wash and iron; to bake and clean and stew and fry; to be, in short, a general pioneer drudge, with never a penny of my own, was not pleasant business for an erstwhile school teacher" (*see* 1871); *The Promised Land* by Mary Antin; *Journal* by English baroness Lady Alice Hillingdon, now 55, who has written, "I am happy now that Charles calls on my bedchamber

less frequently than of old. As it is, I now endure but two calls a week and when I hear his steps outside my door I lie down on my bed, close my eyes, open my legs, and think of England."

Fiction: *Mein Herz* (her only novel) by Else Lasker-Schüler; *A Night of Death* (*En dødsnat*) by Marie Bregendahl; *Pledge* (*Seigen*) by Toshiko Tamura; *Julia France and Her Times* by Gertrude Atherton; *Cease Firing* by Mary Johnston is another Civil War novel; *Daddy Long-Legs* by U.S. novelist Jean (*née* Alice Jane Chandler) Webster, 36.

Poetry: *A Dome of Many-Coloured Glass* by Boston poet Amy Lowell, 36, sister of Harvard president Abbott Lawrence Lowell, 56. Barely 5 feet tall and weighing 250 pounds, the poet defies convention by smoking cigars, cursing in public, and taking another woman into her life and home; *Colors and Years* (*Szinekésvek*) by Margit Kaffka; *The Magic Lantern* (*Volshebnyi fonar': Vtororaia knige stikhov*) by Marina Tsvetaeva; *Evening* (*Vecher*) by Russian poet Anna Akhmatova (Anna Andreyevna Gorenko), 24.

Poetry magazine begins publication in October. Founder Harriet Monroe, 51, received a $1,000 commission 20 years ago to write the "Columbian Ode" for the World's Columbian Exposition of 1893 in Chicago, has found backers and solicited work from more than 50 poets, and will continue publication until her death in 1936.

Juvenile: *The Tale of Mr. Tod* by Beatrix Potter.

 Painting: *The Future Unveiled* by Suzanne Valadon.

 Theater: Laurette Taylor (the playwright's bride) in J. Hartley Manners's *Peg o' My Heart* 12/20 at New York's Cort Theater, 692 perfs.

The Minsky brothers take over New York's Winter Garden Theater for bawdy burlesque productions.

Films: Sarah Bernhardt, now 57, in *Queen Elizabeth*, which is shown July 12 at New York's Lyceum Theater and is the first feature-length motion picture seen in America.

Other films: Mary Pickford, now 19, in D. W. Griffith's *Her First Biscuit*; Lillian Gish (originally Lillian Diana de Guiche), 15, in Griffith's *The Musketeers of Pig Alley*.

Lancashire comedienne-singer Gracie Fields (Grace Stansfield), 12, makes her debut in August at the Hippodrome in Rochdale.

Opera: Spanish soprano Lucrezia Bori, 24, makes her Metropolitan Opera debut singing opposite Enrico Caruso; German soprano Frieda Hempel, 27, makes her Metropolitan Opera debut 12/27 singing the role of the Queen in the 1836 Meyerbeer opera *Les Huguenots* (she is considered the natural successor to Sembrich and will remain with the company for 20 years).

Ballet: Tamara Karsavina dances the role of Chloé, Waslaw Nijinsky that of Daphnis in Maurice Ravel's *Daphnis et Chloé* 6/8 at the Théâtre du Châtelet, Paris, choreography by Michel Fokine.

Mrs. D. R. Larombe (*née* Ethel Warneford Thomson), 33, wins in women's singles at Wimbledon, Mary K. Browne, 15, in U.S. women's singles.

Australian swimmer Fanny Durack wins the 100-meter freestyle in 1 minute, 22.2 seconds at the Olympic Games in Stockholm; Swedish swimmer Greta Johansson wins the platform dive event.

The first commercially successful electric flatiron is introduced by Rowenta, a German manufacturer (*see* 1882; Schneiderman, above; Hotpoint, 1906). Laundries, which employ vast numbers of women worldwide, are Rowenta's major customers.

The Hadassah Study Circle at New York's Temple Emanuel reconstitutes itself February 24 under the leadership of Baltimore-born Zionist Henrietta Szold, 52, who will make the sisterhood of U.S. Jewish women a nationwide Zionist organization beginning in 1916 and head the group until 1926. Szold has been disappointed in love by Talmudic scholar Louis Ginzberg, 39, whose first books she translated but who 4 years ago met Adele Katzenstein in Berlin and married her.

The Girl Scouts of America has its beginnings March 12 at Savannah, Ga., where Juliette Gordon Low, 52, enrolls 18 girls in the first troop of Girl Guides in America (*see* England, 1910). The Girl Guides will be renamed Girl Scouts next year; their initial uniform—wide black bloomers, white middy blouses, and black stockings—will change to blue serge and, later, to green.

New York showgirl Bessie McCoy, 24, is married July 8 to correspondent Richard Harding Davis, 48, who has divorced his first wife June 18. McCoy is famous for the show-stopping song-and-dance number "The Yama Yama Man" in the 1908 musical comedy *The Three Twins*.

1913

"Humanity is like a bird with two wings—the one is male, the other female. Unless both wings are strong and impelled by some common force, the bird cannot fly heavenward," says Persian Baha'i leader 'Abdu'l-Bahá, 68, in a January speech at London to the Women's Freedom League. "According to the spirit of this age, women must advance and fulfill their mission in all departments of life, becoming equal to men. They must be on the same level as men and enjoy equal rights."

Rochester, N.Y., garment worker Ida Brayman, 17, dies February 15 of gunshot wounds sustained when she was shot by her employer during a labor-management struggle. Elizabeth Gurley Flynn is arrested February 25 at Paterson, N.J., in a strike called by local silk workers to protest the installation of improved machinery that will eliminate jobs. The IWW (International Workers of the World) has led the strike, which continues for 5 months (*see* Flynn, 1912).

A general strike of lingerie makers in Brooklyn and Manhattan brings out 35,000 young women, many still in their early teens, who march in picket lines organized by Rose Schneiderman. But the ILGWU strike that began last December is called off March 15 after 13 weeks.

U.S. suffragettes march 5,000 strong down Washington's Pennsylvania Avenue March 3 (the day before Woodrow Wilson's inauguration) following New Jersey Quaker social worker Alice Paul, 28, who was studying at the London School of Economics in 1908 when she became involved in the militant English suffrage movement and in the next 2 years was repeatedly imprisoned for demonstrating on behalf of the cause. Force-fed through her nose when she staged hunger strikes, she returned to America 3 years ago to fight for woman suffrage in her own country, only to find that most U.S. suffragette leaders were fearful of offending anyone. Suffragist lawyer Inez Boissevain (*née* Milholland), 27, rides a white horse. Crowds of angry, jeering men slap the demonstrators, spit at them, and poke them with lighted cigars, a brawl stops the march before it can reach the White House, 40 people are hospitalized, and it takes a cavalry troop from Ft. Myer to restore order (*see* 1916).

Norwegian women gain the right to vote on the same basis as men (*see* Finland, 1906; Russia, 1917).

English suffragist Emmeline Pankhurst draws a 3-year jail sentence April 3 for arson (she has incited her supporters to place explosives in the house of Chancellor of the Exchequer David Lloyd George) but will serve only 1 year and devote part of it to a hunger strike (*see* 1906). Pankhurst supporters invade the Manchester Art Gallery and mutilate 18 paintings. Parliament passes the Prisoners' Temporary Discharge for Ill Health Act in April to thwart hunger strikes; militant suffragists call it the Cat and Mouse Act (*see* 1918).

Suffragist Emily Davison, 41, who has been imprisoned several times for stone throwing, setting mailboxes afire, and attacking a Baptist minister whom she mistook for Prime Minister Lloyd George, is fatally injured June 4 when she runs onto the track at the Derby wearing a WSPU banner, tries to grab the reins of the king's horse, and is trampled. She had attempted suicide at Holloway Gaol to protest against force-feeding.

Sylvia Pankhurst is sentenced July 8 to 3 months in prison.

"I myself have never been able to find out precisely what feminism is," writes Irish-born English journalist Rebecca West, 20, in the November 13 issue of the *Clarion*. "I only know that people call me a feminist whenever I express sentiments that differentiate me from a doormat." Cicily Isabel Fairfield, who has been using the pen name "Rebecca West" since about 1911, when she went to work as reviewer for the feminist magazine *Free Woman*, joined the *Clarion* as a political writer last year.

Harriet Tubman has died in poverty March 10 at age 92 in the Harriet Tubman Home for Aged Negroes that she founded years ago at Auburn, N.Y.

New York's Grand Central Terminal opens February 1 at 42nd Street and Park Avenue, replacing a 41-year-old New York Central and New Haven train shed with the world's largest railway station. Trains under Park Avenue have been electrified since December 1906. Far bigger than Pennsylvania Station, Grand Central has 31 tracks on its upper level, 17 on its lower (which opened for commuter service in October 1912). Separate men's and women's waiting rooms and lavatories are at either end of the main waiting room off 42nd Street; the women's waiting room, at the east end, has amenities that include a hairdressing salon.

The Midwife in England by U.S. medical investigator Caroline Conant Van Blarkom, 34, says that half of all U.S. birth attendants are midwives and many are unfamiliar with the simple practice of applying silver nitrate solution to the eyes of newborn infants (*see* Argyrol, 1901). The United States, she notes, is the only civilized country in the world that does not protect its mothers and infants by providing for the licensing and training of midwives.

Romania's Crown Princess Marie, now 37, organizes an emergency cholera camp at Zimnicea to treat soldiers stricken with disease while fighting the Bulgarians in a Balkan war that began last October and continues until August 6. Wearing heavy riding boots, she works tirelessly for 2 weeks, winning the respect and admiration of doctors, orderlies, soldiers, officers, and sisters of charity.

The American Cancer Society has its beginnings in the American Society for the Control of Cancer, founded with support from philanthropist John D. Rockefeller, Jr. Nine out of 10 cancer patients die of the disease; the mortality rate will fall sharply, but the incidence of cancer will increase (*see* 1945).

Delta Sigma Theta Sorority is founded January 13 at Howard University, the second Greek-letter society for black women (*see* 1908; 1920).

The Liga Femenil Mexicanista is founded at Laredo, Texas, by Hispanic women concerned lest their cultural heritage be lost (*see* 1911). Founders, who include Jovita Idar, focus their efforts on educating poor children.

Harper's Bazar is purchased by William Randolph Hearst, who will change its name to *Harper's Bazaar* in 1929 and install Carmel Snow (*née* White), sister of his general manager, Thomas Justin White, as editor. The magazine for women has been published since 1867 by Harper Bros.

Condé Nast launches *Dress & Vanity Fair*, a new fashion magazine whose name is shortened after four issues simply to *Vanity Fair*; edited by Frank Crowninshield, it will be merged with *Vogue* in 1936 and not re-emerge under its own name until the 1980s.

Fiction: *O Pioneers!* by former *McClure's* magazine managing editor Willa Sibert Cather, 39, who grew up on the Nebraska frontier; *The Custom of the Country* by Edith Wharton (the custom being for a man to keep his wife totally in the dark about "the real business of life"); *Virginia* by Virginia novelist Ellen Anderson Gholson Glasgow, 39; *Hagar* by Mary Johnston is a feminist manifesto in novel form (Johnston took an active role 4 years ago in organizing the Equal Suffrage League of Virginia and, with her sisters, has just finished building Three Hills near Warm Springs, Va., where she will live until her death in 1936); *Pollyanna* by U.S. novelist Eleanor Porter (*née* Hodgman), 45, whose saccharine heroine always looks for the bright side of everything; *Reeds in the Wind* (*Cinna al vento*) by Grazia Deledda; *Woman Writer* (*Onna sakusha*) and *Mummy's Lipstick* (*Miira no kuchibeni*) by Toshiko Tamura.

Poetry: *From Two Books* (*Iz dvukh knig*) by Marina Tsvetaeva.

Juvenile: *Laddie* by Gene Stratton Porter; *The Tale of Pigling Bland* by Beatrix Potter.

Painting: *Cats* by Russian painter Natalia Sergeevna Goncharova, 32, who has her first one-woman show at Moscow, includes a Rayonist painting, and is invited to design settings and costumes for the Ballets Russe; *Tango au Bal Bullier* (oil on canvas), *Tango-Magic-City* (oil on canvas), and *Study of Colors* (colored pencil on paper) by Sonia Delaunay, who also designs ballet costumes and advertisements; *Nude Having Her Hair Done* by Suzanne Valadon.

Anthony Comstock of the New York Society for the Suppression of Vice sees a copy of last year's Paul Chabas painting *September Morn* May 13 in the window of a New York art dealer in West 46th Street (*see* Comstock Law, 1872). Now 69, Comstock demands that the picture (which is the basis of the world's first pinup calendar) be removed from the window because it shows "too little morning and too much maid," Chicago alderman "Bathhouse John" Coughlin vows that the picture will not be displayed publicly in Chicago, but oilman Calouste Gulbenkian will acquire the oil and it will wind up at New York's Metropolitan Museum of Art.

Theater: Doris Keane in Edward Sheldon's *Romance* 2/10 at Maxine Elliott's Theater, New York, 160 perfs; Sybil Thorndike, 30, in St. John Ervine's *Jane Clegg* 6/19 at London.

Films: Blanche Sweet, Mae Marsh, and Henry B. Walthall in D. W. Griffith's *Judith of Bethulia*, the first American-made four-reel film; Mabel Normand (originally Fortescue), 19, and Mack Sennett in Sennett's *Barney Oldfield's Race for Life*.

Broadway musicals: Irene and Vernon Castle do the Turkey Trot in *The Sunshine Girl* 2/3 at the Knickerbocker Theater, 160 perfs.; Charlotte Greenwood in *The Passing Show* 6/10 at the Winter Garden Theater, with a runway to bring the show's scantily clad chorus girls close to the audience, 116 perfs.; Ann Pennington makes her debut at age 15 with Fanny Brice and Leon Errol in *The Ziegfeld Follies* 6/16 at the New Amsterdam Theater, 96 perfs.

Ballet: *The Rite of Spring* (*Le Sacre du Printemps*) 6/13 at the Théâtre du Châtelet, Paris, with Serge Diaghilev's Ballet Russe, choreography by Waslaw Nijinsky with considerable help from Polish ballerina-choreographer Cyvia Rambam, 25, who will move to London, adopt the stage name Marie Rambert, and eventually start her own company. Outraged audiences react violently to the wild dissonances of composer Igor Stravinsky's score, but the ballet begins a new epoch in music.

English pianist Ethel Leginska (Liggins), 26, makes her New York debut after 10 years of European performances. She will be called the "Paderewski of women pianists," will begin composing her own music next year, and will go on to have a career as conductor.

Bulgarian violin prodigy Nedyalka Simeonova, 12, travels to America with her father and gives a number of concerts, most of them at Boston. She will study at New York under Auer beginning in 1921 and make a successful concert debut there in 1923.

Opera: Norwegian soprano Kirsten Flagstad, 18, makes her debut December 12 in the 1903 Eugen D'Albert opera *Tiefland* at Oslo's National Theater.

Popular songs: "Now Is the Hour (Maori Farewell Song)" by New Zealand songwriters Maewa Kaihan, Clement Scott, and Dorothy Stewart.

Dorothea Chambers wins in women's singles at Wimbledon, Mary Browne in U.S. women's singles.

Pennsylvania makes Mother's Day a state holiday (*see* Jarvis, 1908; Wilson, 1914).

The first U.S. deck shuffleboard game is played on a hotel court at Daytona, Fla. The game will become popular with elderly retirees.

The former Jennie Jerome, now 59, divorces George Cornwallis-West, who marries the actress Mrs. Patrick Campbell, 12 years his senior and even more impecunious than he (*see* 1900; 1919). Jenny's son Winston Churchill is now First Lord of the Admiralty.

London police arrest a woman July 15 for wearing a split skirt in Richmond Park.

Coco Chanel pioneers sportswear for women at a new boutique in Deauville that features berets and open-necked shirts in an age when women of fashion adorn themselves with feathers and huge hats. Gabrielle Chanel, 30, gained her nickname at age 20 while entertaining the 10th Light Horse Regiment in the small garrison town of Moulins, became a Paris milliner while mistress to Etienne Balsan, and is now mistress to English businessman Arthur Capel; her lovers will include England's second duke of Westminster, who owns 17 Rolls-Royces and has mammoth greenhouses in which pears and peaches ripen all year round, and she will make sweaters the fashion of the rich as Chanel knitwear gains world fame (*see* Chanel No. 5, 1921).

Brillo Manufacturing Corp. is founded by New York lawyer Milton B. Loeb, 26, whose client (a manufacturing jeweler) has developed a way to clean aluminum cooking utensils using steel wool

with a special reddish soap that gives the vessels a brilliant shine.

Swedish-American inventor Gideon Sundback, 33, develops the first dependable slide fastener and efficient machines to manufacture it commercially. He attaches matching metal locks to a flexible backing, each tooth being a tiny hook that engages with an eye under an adjoining hook on an opposite tape. He will patent improvements on his slide fastener in 1917 and assign the patents to the Hookless Fastener Co. of Meadville, Pa., which will manufacture the Talon slide fastener (*see* "zipper," 1926).

1914

(Geneviève Josephine) Henriette Caillaux (*née* Raynouard), 39, walks into the office of *Figaro* editor Gaston Calmette, 55, at Paris March 16 and shoots him dead. Her husband, finance minister Joseph Caillaux, nearly 51, is a former premier and one of France's richest men; Calmette has been running articles depicting him as a liar, grafter, blackmailer, thief, and secret ally of the Germans, and has threatened to print private letters that Henriette exchanged with him several years ago when she was married to Leo Claretie, the paper's literary critic (they were divorced in the spring of 1908, she was awarded custody of their daughter, Germaine, now 19, and Caillaux divorced his wife to marry her). Taken to St. Lazare Prison, Mme. Caillaux is asked to explain herself and says she shot Calmette "because there is no more justice in France. There is only the revolver." Her roomy cell is close to that in which Marie-Antoinette awaited trial in 1793, and she is permitted to wear her own clothing and order meals sent in from good restaurants. Caillaux resigns from the Cabinet March 17, Henriette's trial begins June 20, and a claque hired by her husband hisses or applauds on signals from a man with long black hair seated near the witness box. One witness is a Hungarian named Lipscher, whose mistress, Thérèse Duverger, serves as liaison between the German and Austrian spy systems, but Mme. Caillaux wins acquittal July 28 (*see* below).

The assassination of Austria's archduke Ferdinand and his wife at Sarajevo, Bosnia, June 28 precipitates a world war which begins August 1. European rallies marking the fourth International Women's Day March 8 have decried the saber rattling that presages a major war. Russian revolutionist Aleksandra Kollontai's pamphlet "Who Needs War?" ends with the words "our enemy is in the rear" and is widely translated.

German Marxist Rosa Luxemburg co-founds (with Karl Liebknecht) the Spartacus League (*Spartakusbund*) and will be in prison for most of the war (*see* 1919).

Hungarian pacifist Rosika Schwimmer, who has settled at London earlier in the year, sails for New York, goes with Carrie Chapman Catt to call upon Secretary of State William Jennings Bryan at Washington, meets with President Wilson September 18 to urge mediation in the European conflict, and finds him evasive. Schwimmer addresses the Nebraska legislature and speaks in more than 20 other states in a plea for mediation (*see* 1915).

Romania's first king, Carol I, dies of a heart attack October 9 at age 75 after a 48-year reign. His nephew Ferdinand, now 49, becomes king, beginning a 13-year reign that will be dominated by his wife, Marie, now nearly 39.

Mme. Caillaux and her husband (above) are riding in an open cab on the Boulevard des Capucines October 22 when a woman cries out, "Voilà, Caillaux, l'espion d'Allemand." A crowd surges toward the carriage, shouting, "A bas Caillaux" and "Mort pour le *traître.*" M. and Mme. Caillaux board the steamer *Perou* at Bordeaux November 14 and sail for Venezuela. Some observers claim that Mme. Caillaux has saved France, arguing that if her husband, who was building a French socialist party, had remained in the Cabinet he might have taken power as head of a commune and let Paris fall to the "Bosch."

German artillerymen bombard Paris using "Big Bertha," a long-range gun made by Krupp of Essen (*see* 1906).

Two women, 11 children, and eight men die in the Ludlow massacre April 20 as state militia near Trinidad, Colo., set fire to the tents of striking coal miners who are struggling for recognition of their United Mine Workers union.

U.S. suffragettes march on the Capitol at Washington June 28 to demand voting rights for women. The march is staged within hours of the assassination at Sarajevo (above).

Rosika Schwimmer (above) presents President Wilson with a petition representing about 1 million European suffragists.

International Woman Suffrage Alliance president Carrie Chapman Catt, now 55, inherits $9 million from the estate of *Leslie's Illustrated Newspaper* publisher Miriam Leslie, who has died at age 78. Leslie's husband, Frank, who started the paper in 1855, died in 1880, leaving her a bankrupt business which she made profitable, earning a fortune (Catt will not receive the money until 1917).

Crystal Eastman brings together the first meeting of the Woman's Peace Party at New York in November. English suffragist Emmeline Pethick-Lawrence, who has been invited to speak, has been imprisoned in Holloway Gaol and force-fed. She maintains that there is "no life worth living, but a fighting life" and that it is time for women to be angry and act angry, "active, and militant."

The Amalgamated Clothing Workers of America is founded by a dissident majority within the manufacturer-oriented United Garment Workers Union. Bessie Hillman (*née* Abramowitz), who led the 1910 strike against Hart, Schaffner and Marx, has married Lithuanian-American labor leader Sidney Hillman, 27, who becomes first president of the new union.

The June issue of *McClure's* magazine carries an article on the subject of painless childbirth; it describes the Twilight Sleep method of providing pain relief in labor (*see* 1909; 1915).

New York City has only 38 more public schools than in 1899 despite an increase of more than 300,000 in enrollment. The overcrowded schools turn away 60,000 to 75,000 children each year for lack of space.

The Foxcroft School is founded at Middleburg, Va. Charlotte Haxall Nowland, 29, a former gymnastics teacher at the 32-year-old St. Timothy's, opens the boarding school for girls at her ancestral estate.

Nonfiction: *They Who Knock at Our Gates* by Mary Antin, now 33, who campaigns against proposals in Congress to enact restrictive immigration laws; *Tender Buttons* by Gertrude Stein.

Fiction: *The Precipice* by U.S. journalist-novelist Ella Wilkinson Peattie, now 52, who at 22 became the *Chicago Tribune*'s first "girl reporter": her heroine is a social worker (modeled on Julia Lathrop, first head of the Children's Bureau), who seeks independence; *Angel Island* by Inez Gillmore, who left her husband last year; *The Witch* by Mary Johnston is set in 17th-century England; *Mariflor* (*La esfinge Maragata*) by Concha Espina de Serna; *Black Bread* (*Czarny chleb*) by Polish novelist Marja Rodziewiczówna, 51; *Drasar* by Teréza Novaková; *The Faults of Others* (*Le colpe altrui*) by Grazia Deledda; *Recaptured* (*L'Entrave*) by Colette.

Poetry: *Los Sonetos de la Muerte* by Chilean poet Gabriela Mistral (Lucila Godoy Alcayaga), 25; *The Rosary* (*Chetki*) by Anna Akhmatova; *Sword Blades and Poppy Seeds* by Amy Lowell, who has moved to England and become a leader of the Imagists.

Painting: *Electric Prisms* (oil on canvas) by Sonia Delaunay; *The Casting of the Net* by Suzanne Valadon, now 49, who marries Andrea Utter, now 28, before he joins his army corps; *Still Life on the Corner of Mantelpiece* by Vanessa Bell.

Theater: Stella (Mrs. Patrick) Campbell, now 47, plays the role of the Covent Garden flower girl Eliza Doolittle in George Bernard Shaw's *Pygmalion* 4/11 at His Majesty's Theatre, London (her shocker "Not bloody likely" in Act III helps give Shaw another commercial success), 118 perfs.; *Daddy Long-Legs* by Jean Webster 9/28 at New York's Gaiety Theater, with Boots Wooster, Ruth Chatterton, 20, Lillian Ross, Gladys Smith.

Films: Marie Dressler, now 44, Mabel Normand, and the Keystone Kops appear with Charles Chaplin in Mack Sennett's *Tillie's Punctured Romance*, the first U.S. feature-length comedy; Pearl Fay White, 22, and Crane Wilbur in Donald MacKenzie's *The Perils of Pauline*, produced by a Hearst-controlled company whose "cliff-hanger" serials ("To be continued . . .") are designed to bring audiences back each week to see "The Lady Daredevil of the Fillums"; D. W. Griffith's *The Mother and the Law* attacks factory owners who pose as public benefactors.

The first movie column appears in the *Chicago Record-Herald* under the byline Louella Parsons. Former *Chicago Tribune* reporter Parsons (Louella Oettinger), 21, has recently sold a film script for $25 (*see* 1918).

Opera: New Zealand–born U.S. soprano Frances Alda, 30, appears in the new Victor Herbert opera *Madeleine* 1/24 at New York's Metropolitan Opera House; Claudia Muzzo appears at Covent Garden's summer season singing such roles as Desdemona in the 1887 Verdi opera *Otello* and the title role in the 1900 Puccini opera *Tosca* (with Enrico Caruso); Austrian authorities intern soprano Emmy Destinn in the Bohemian castle of Stráznal Nezarkou, which she has purchased (she is an avowed sympathizer with the cause of Czech independence); Maggie Teyte joins the Boston Opera Company.

Japanese soprano Tamaki Miura, 29, appears at Berlin and at London's Albert Hall. She will sing with the Chicago opera next year and will gain fame in the role of Ciao-Ciao-San in the 1904 Puccini opera *Madama Butterfly*.

Dancer-choreographer Ruth St. Denis, now 37, marries dancer Ted Shawn, 22, and moves with him to Los Angeles, where they found the Denishawn School of Dancing and the Denishawn Dancers (*see* 1906). St. Denis created *O-Mika*, a Japanese dance-drama, last year, and is gaining prominence.

Japan's Takarazuka theater gives its first performance at Takarazuka City, a spa in the Osaka-Kobe-Kyoto area. It is the brainchild of entrepreneur Ichizo Kobayashi, who founded the Hankyu Railway in 1898 and is establishing Takarazuka City as a resort; he decrees that "charming," well-bred girls shall play male as well as female roles in sentimental, platonic love stories, most of them musicals. All-girl Takarazuka companies will entertain middle-class (and less affluent) audiences for more than 75 years, both in Takarazuka and in Tokyo, while the troupe also puts on small-scale shows and traveling shows that will play not only in Japan but also abroad.

Broadway musicals: Ann Pennington, Ed Wynn, and Leon Errol in *The Ziegfeld Follies* 6/1 at the New Amsterdam Theater, 112 perfs; Marilyn Miller makes her debut at age 14 in *The Passing Show* 6/10 at the Winter Garden Theater, with barelegged chorus girls, 133 perfs.; Irene and Vernon Castle do the Castle Walk and Fanny Brice sings in *Watch Your Step* 12/8 at the New Amsterdam Theater, with Irving Berlin songs that include "Play a Simple Melody," 175 perfs.

Popular songs: "Keep the Home Fires Burning" by London composer David Ivor Davies, 21, lyrics by American-born poet Lena Guilbert Ford, who will die in a zeppelin raid on London in 1918.

Dorothea Chambers wins in women's singles at Wimbledon, Mary Browne in U.S. women's singles.

The first national Mother's Day is proclaimed by President Wilson. The second Sunday in May will become the biggest business day of the year for U.S. restaurants and flower shops (*see* 1913; "M-O-T-H-E-R," 1915).

First Lady Ellen Louise Axson Wilson dies of kidney tuberculosis August 7 right after congressional passage of an alley-clearance bill that she has championed.

Helena Rubinstein challenges Elizabeth Arden for leadership in the fledgling U.S. cosmetics industry (*see* 1910). Now 44 (she claims to be 54 so that her products will seem more effective), Rubinstein left her native Poland after an unhappy love affair at age 19 to seek a husband in Australia, made $100,000 in 3 years near Melbourne selling sunburned Australian women a skin cream that she formulated from ingredients that included almonds and tree bark, has opened England's first beauty salon in London, opened another one in Paris, and is the reigning beauty adviser to French and British society. The four-foot-eleven-inch cosmetician, whose Maison de Beauté in Manhattan's 49th Street gains quick popularity, will introduce medicated face creams and waterproof mascara. Rubenstein will pioneer in sending saleswomen out on road tours to demonstrate proper makeup application as she builds a chain of beauty salons (*see* 1928).

The Paris Patriotic League of Women issues a manifesto March 10 against fashions that are too revealing; signed by several comtesses and marquises, it urges "elegant women and all the young women, who set the tone in France, not to yield to the present tendency, but to combine courageously to offset it by precept and example. Let them reflect upon their responsibility. What they do other women of more modest position, who have their eyes fixed upon them, will do in their turn. Let us also not forget that we must have a care for the reputation which France hitherto has borne for elegance and taste."

The elastic brassiere, which will supplant the corset now in common use, is patented in November by New York inventor Mary Phelps "Polly" Jacob, 21, who as a debutante found that the cover of her bulky corset, which hampered her freedom of movement, showed over her decolletage. Dressing for a dance, she asked her French maid, Marie, for two silk pocket handkerchiefs, some pink ribbon, and needle and thread, and the two devised the prototype bra, which flattens the bustline against the chest. A descendant of steamboat pioneer Robert Fulton, Jacob was asked by friends to make bras for them, a manufacturer requested a sample and enclosed a dollar, and with this encouragement she engaged a designer to make drawings, borrowed $100, rented two sewing machines, and hired two immigrant girls to stitch up a few hundred Backless Brassieres. She took them to New York's better stores but has met with little success. Through a family friend she will sell her patent to the corset maker Warner Brothers Corset Co. of Bridgeport, Conn., which for $1,500 will acquire all rights to a patent that will later be estimated to be worth $15 million. Jacob will marry her childhood sweetheart, Richard Peabody, next year, and will bear two children before getting a divorce (*see* 1927; Maiden Form, 1923).

A company founded by Josephine Cochrane to make dishwashers (*see* 1886) introduces a smaller machine but finds little acceptance. To wash just one evening's dinner dishes may require the entire contents of a family's hot-water tank, the water in much of the country is too "hard" for soap to create the suds needed for dishwashing, and a poll conducted next year will show that most women actually enjoy washing dishes as a relaxing chore at day's end. Cochrane's company will merge with an Ohio concern to produce the Kitchenaid dishwasher, but few homes will have such machines for another 40 years.

Postum Cereal founder C. W. Post commits suicide May 9 at his Santa Barbara, Calif., home in a fit of depression at age 59. Marjorie Merriweather Post, 27, his only child, inherits the company and will build it into General Foods Corp. (*see* 1926).

U.S. feminist Margaret Louise Sanger (*née* Higgins), 31, introduces the term "birth control" in her radical feminist magazine *The Woman Rebel*. Sanger has seen her mother worn out by having more than a dozen babies, and as a nurse she has seen the effects of self-induced abortions. On a visit to France last year she was impressed by the sexual sophistication of ordinary mothers with regard to preventing pregnancies. She exiles herself to England to escape federal prosecution for publishing and mailing *Family Limitation*, a brochure that describes the benefits to working-class couples of using douches, condoms, and pessaries for contraception (*see* Brooklyn clinic, 1916).

1915

Jane Addams, Carrie Chapman Catt, and some 3,000 other women meet at Washington, D.C., January 10 to call for the abolition of war. They organize the Women's Peace Party (*see* below).

The British Admiralty enlists the aid of Middle East expert Gertrude Lowthian Bell, now 47, who 2 years ago pushed south from Damascus into the Nejd area of central Arabia, where Lady Ann Blunt, by that time a septuagenarian horse trader resident in Egypt, had recently passed, probably on a horse-buying expedition (*see* 1877). Bell, traveling with only one servant, copied ancient inscriptions, took photographs, made notes, dealt with wild tribespeople, collected valuable information, and met T. E. Lawrence, now 26, an Orientalist with whom she now works briefly at Cairo before being sent to Delhi. There she serves for a few weeks as a liaison between the government of India and the newly formed Arab Intelligence Bureau, preparing a gazeteer, or geographical dictionary. She is then sent to Basra, where she compares her information on the desert tribes with that being received by the British Expeditionary Force in Mesopotamia (*see* 1916).

The pacifist views of Chicago social worker Jane Addams gained her few friends but that did not stop her. LIBRARY OF CONGRESS

An International Congress of Women meets at the Hague from April 28 to May 1 and forms an International Committee of Women for Permanent Peace (later to be called the Women's International League for Peace and Freedom). Some 2,400 delegates attend, including Jane Addams, Boston city planner Emily Greene Balch, 47 (a Quaker pacifist), Rosika Schwimmer, Emmeline Pethick-Lawrence, and Dr. Aletta Jacobs, and they endorse a plan for neutral mediation devised by Schwimmer and—independently—Julia Grace Wales, a Canadian English instructor at the University of Wisconsin.

Russian revolutionary Aleksandra Kollontai, now 43, tours the United States with a plea not to join the European conflict and to accept socialism.

German authorities in occupied Brussels arrest British Red Cross nurse Edith Louisa Cavell, 50, August 4 on charges of having assisted Allied military prisoners to escape. Tried and convicted, she is

Russian revolutionist Aleksandra Kollontai agitated against the "capitalist, imperialist" war. LIBRARY OF CONGRESS

executed by a firing squad October 12 along with a Belgian who has provided guides, and her last words are said to have been "I realize that patriotism is not enough. I must have no hatred or bitterness towards anyone." British propagandists use her death to inflame public sentiment against the savage Boche and ignore the fact that the French have shot a woman for a similar offense.

Rosika Schwimmer reaches Henry Ford November 17 and learns that he has chartered the Scandinavian-American liner *Oskar II* to carry a group of Americans to Europe on an unofficial mission of mediation. The ship leaves Hoboken, N.J., December 4 with more than 160 aboard, including Schwimmer, other social reformers, students, and reporters (most of whom ridicule Ford's "Peace Ship" and describe Schwimmer's behavior as "domineering"). Ford becomes ill, and when the ship arrives at Christiana, Norway, he turns about for home. The International Committee of Women for Permanent Peace (above) follows Jane Addams's lead in refusing to support the venture (*see* 1916).

President Wilson is remarried at Washington December 18 to Edith Bolling Galt, who will wield greater power than any previous First Lady.

Christabel Pankhurst tells an audience at New York's Carnegie Hall October 25, "What we suffragettes aspire to be when we are enfranchised is ambassadors of freedom to women in other parts of the world, who are not so free as we are."

Britain employs women transport workers, including bus conductors, as well as women clerks, farmhands, industrial workers, and domestics; more than 1 million more women now work full time than before the war, most visibly in transport but more signficantly in factories. Munitions factories are reportedly two and a half times more productive, thanks to women workers.

Scopolamine-Morphine Anaesthesia by Chicago physician Bertha Van Hoosen, 52, expounds on painless childbirth using Twilight Sleep, the German method with which Van Hoosen began experimenting in 1904 (*see* 1914). By 1908 she had delivered 2,000 healthy babies using scopolamine, and U.S. feminists have begun demanding that physicians recognize the right of every mother to choose painless childbirth. Mrs. C. Temple Emmet gains support from Mrs. John Jacob Astor (whose husband went down with the *Titanic* in 1912) to start the National Twilight Sleep Association at New York to disseminate information about the method and agitate "for the emancipation of women from the bondage of pain."

Barnard College professor Juliet Poyntz works with labor leader Rose Schneiderman and ILGWU leaders Fania Cohn, 30, and Pauline Newman to establish an education program for the union's dressmakers, largely young immigrant women of Local 25, to help them learn history, labor law, art, music appreciation, and public speaking.

Nonfiction: *The Ways of Women* by Ida Tarbell; *Woman of Yesterday and Today* and *Woman and Freedom* by Theresa Serber Malkiel; *The Story of a Pioneer* (autobiography) by Anna Howard Shaw, now 68, who heads the Women's Committee of the Council of National Defense.

Fiction: *The Song of the Lark* by Willa Cather; *The Bent Twig* by Vermont novelist Dorothea (Frances) Canfield Fisher, 36; *Fidelity* by Iowa-born novelist Susan Glaspell, 33; *In Mr. Knox's Country* by Somerville and Ross (Edith Somerville and Violet

Martin, who dies at age 53, leaving her cousin Edith, now 57 and master of foxhounds for the West Carberry Pack, to carry on alone); *The Fortunes of Garin* by Mary Johnston; *Dear Enemy* by Jean Webster; *Marianna Sirca* by Grazia Deledda.

Poetry: *Rivers to the Sea* by Sara Teasdale; "To the Soul of Progress" by U.S. poet Marianne Craig Moore, 27 (Bryn Mawr '09), whose brief satire on war appears in the *Egoist*, a London journal dedicated to the New Imagist movement in poetry; other of Moore's work is published in Harriet Monroe's magazine *Poetry: Songs of Angus* by Scottish poet Violet Jacob (*née* Kennedy-Erskine), 52.

Juvenile: *Pollyanna Grows Up* by Eleanor Porter; *Anne of the Island* by Maud Montgomery.

Painting: *Portrait of Mme. Gustave Coquiot* by Suzanne Valadon, who has a solo show at Bertha Weill's. Natalia Goncharova, now 34, leaves Paris with Mikhail F. Larionov, also 34, to design sets at Geneva for Sergei Diaghilev's ballets. She will marry Larianov, but not until her 74th birthday; *Portrait of Iris Tree* (oil on canvas) by Vanessa Bell.

Films: Lillian Gish, Mae (originally Mary) Marsh, 20, and Henry B. Walthall in D. W. Griffith's *The Birth of a Nation*, which has such cinematic innovations as the close-up, pan (panoramic shot), flashback, and use of a moving camera in addition to its element of racism. Also: Theda Bara (Theodosia Goodman), 25, is billed as "the vamp" in advertisements for Frank Powell's *A Fool There Was* ("Kiss me, my fool").

Opera: Soprano Geraldine Farrar, now 32, creates the role of Catherine Huebscher in Umberto Giordano's new opera *Madame Sans-Gêne* 1/25 at New York's Metropolitan Opera House; U.S. soprano Eva (Barnes) Mason, 22, makes her Metropolitan Opera debut 11/20 singing the role of Sophie in the 1911 Strauss opera *Der Rosenkavalier*.

Ballet: English ballerina Alicia Markova (*née* Lilian Alicia Marks) makes her debut at age 14.

The Houston Symphony Orchestra is founded with support from arts patron Ima Hogg, 33, who settled in Houston 6 years ago after studying piano in New York, Berlin, and Vienna. Her late father, Col. James Stephen Hogg, was governor of Texas from

1890 to 1894 and later made a fortune in the oilfields.

Broadway musicals: Marilyn Miller in *The Passing Show* 5/29 at the Winter Garden Theater, with baritone John Charles Thomas in his Broadway debut, 145 perfs.; Ann Pennington, W. C. Fields, and Ed Wynn in *The Ziegfeld Follies* 6/21 at the New Amsterdam Theater, 104 perfs.; Vivienne Segal in *The Blue Paradise* 8/5 at the Casino Theater, 356 perfs.

Popular songs: "I Didn't Raise My Boy to Be a Soldier" by Al Piantadosi, who has plagiarized a melody by Harry Haas), lyrics by Alfred Bryan; "M-O-T-H-E-R, a Word that Means the World to Me" by Theodore Morse, lyrics by Howard Johnson.

Wimbledon tennis is canceled for the duration of the war; Norwegian-American Molla Bjurstedt, 23, wins in U.S. women's singles.

Permanent wave pioneer Charles Nessler, who uses Nestle as his professional name, opens a New York shop (*see* 1906). He now employs a machine for heating and waving hair, applying hot alkali after the hair is porous enough to hold moisture so that it will hold its curl. Patrons, who will soon include President Wilson's second wife, Edith (above), pay up to $120 for a wave (*see* 1926).

1916

Rosika Schwimmer resigns in February from the International Committee of Women for Permanent Peace as charges increase that she has been dictatorial (*see* 1915; 1926). The Great War spreads and becomes more intense as all hope for neutral mediation ends.

An Irish Easter Rebellion involving about 1,500 insurgents leads to the proclamation of a republic, but it collapses in less than a week and the rebels, led by Michael Mallin and Countess Markievicz, now 48, surrender April 30 (*see* 1909). Wearing the green uniform of the Irish Citizen Army with breeches and puttees in imitation of her heroine, Joan of Arc, the countess walks up to the British captain outside Dublin's College of Surgeons, takes her pistol out of its holster, kisses it, and hands it to the captain, tells him she is ready, and refuses his offer of a ride to the jail, saying that she prefers to walk. She is held for a week in solitary confinement at Kilmainham jail while other rebel leaders go before firing squads, but her life and that of one other leader (the American-born Eamon De Valera) are spared, hers "solely and only on account of her sex" (British propagandists have exploited Germany's execution last year of Edith Cavell and do not want a woman's blood on their own hands). Countess Markievicz is sentenced to "penal servitude for life" (but *see* 1917).

Information supplied by Orientalist Gertrude Lowthian Bell helps the British foment an Arab revolt against the Ottoman Turks, beginning June 5 with an attack on the garrison at Medina (*see* 1915; 1921).

The Indian Home Rule League is founded by Annie Besant, now 69, who next year will become president of the Indian National Congress.

Congress purges the Congressional Medal of Honor list of 911 recipients who were not cited for specific acts of valor in a move to preserve the medal's special status. Among those stricken from the rolls is Civil War veteran Mary Edwards Walker, now 84, who will try until her death in 1919 to be reinstated, proudly wearing the medal everywhere she goes despite the revocation (*see* 1864). Her medal will be restored, but not until 1977.

Montana voters elect the first U.S. congresswoman. Republican Jeanette Rankin, 36, has crisscrossed the state on horseback and says that Montana women got the vote "because the spirit of pioneer days is still alive."

✊ Conservative U.S. suffragists expel Alice Paul from their organization; she renames her Congressional Union the National Woman's Party to spearhead the movement for woman suffrage using the more militant means employed in Britain, even if it means being imprisoned and force-fed when they go on hunger strikes (*see* 1913; 1917).

The Canadian provinces of Manitoba, Saskatchewan, and Alberta grant women voting rights (*see* 1917).

President Woodrow Wilson addresses a suffrage gathering at Atlantic City September 8 and assures his cheering listeners that women will get the vote "in a little while." Suffrage leader Dr. Anna Howard Shaw, now 69, replies that women have waited long enough and want the vote now.

Chinese reformer Xiang Jianyu, 21, is graduated from a school in Xhangsha, opens a girls' school, and campaigns against foot binding and feudal marriage (*see* 1922).

Japan's Diet enacts a law in September that forbids hiring girls and boys under age 12 except in special cases where the employer provides education. The law, which applies only to factories with 14 employees or more, limits working hours to 12 per day, with an hour off. It provides for 2 days off per month. Children aged 12 to 15 are considered *hogoshokko* (protected workers) and given special protection: they may not work night shifts except in alternate weeks, must have 4 days off per month, and must be paid each month, with the employer responsible for making sure that the child has saved some money. Where many young girls are employed, there must be a woman supervisor. Girls and boys must be kept separate in employee dormitories, and each worker must be provided with space equal to half a *tatami* mat with his or her own *futon*. Factory owners fight the new measure with such vigor that it will not become effective for 20 years.

💲 The Allies and Central Powers rely increasingly on women to produce munitions for the Great War, which continues in Europe. Those not employed directly in factories work on railways, as porters, and as trolley-car conductors.

Irish-American Typographical Union worker Maud Swartz (*née* O'Farrell), 37, becomes the first full-time secretary of the Women's Trade Union League at New York.

Hetty Green dies July 3 at age 80 leaving an estate of more than $100 million that has made her the richest woman in America. Henrietta Howland Green (*née* Robinson) inherited $10 million at age 29 from her father and a maternal aunt, members of a New Bedford, Mass., whaling-ship family, and kept her finances separate from those of her late husband, Edward H. Green, whom she married in

WOMEN OF BRITAIN

COME INTO THE FACTORIES

Women pitched in to help as war engulfed Europe in the bloodiest conflict history had ever seen.

1867. She multiplied her fortune with investments in stocks, government bonds, mortgages, and Chicago real estate while living penuriously; her son lost a leg because she would not hire a physician to treat him, and the eccentric "witch of Wall Street" dies in the small fourth-floor apartment at 1203 Washington St., Hoboken, N.J. (a quick ferryboat ride from Wall Street and with a rent below $20 per month), that she has occupied since 1895.

Married Love by English paleobotanist Marie (Charlotte) Stopes (*née* Carmichael), 36, says that married women have as much right to sexual pleasure as their husbands, making only incidental mention of birth control. "An impersonal and scientific knowledge of the structure of our bodies is the surest safeguard against prurient curiosity and lascivious gloating," she writes (Chapter 5), and "Each coming together of man and wife, even if they have been mated for many years, should be a fresh adventure; each winning should necessitate a fresh wooing" (Chapter 10). Married to Canadian botanist R. R. Gates in 1911, Mrs. Stopes did not realize until a year later that he was impotent and she still a virgin. She began studying sexuality, initiated proceedings for an annulment in 1914, and has written a huge best-seller (although banned in the United States, it goes through seven printings and will ultimately have sales of more than 1 million copies) (*see* 1918).

New York obstetrician Edwin Craig urges his colleagues in the New York Medical Society to be restrained in performing cesarean sections because "once a cesarean always a cesarean" (a mother who has had a C-section risks rupturing her scarred uterus if she goes into labor again, although rupturing is extremely rare). Fewer than 1 percent of U.S. infants are delivered by cesarean section, and a doctor with a high cesarean rate is considered either inexpert or a butcher. The procedure requires a vertical incision to remove the baby from its mother's uterus (*see* 1980).

Syphilis is responsible for the deaths of 73,000 U.S. infants, including 41,700 stillbirths. An estimated 25 to 50 percent of adult blindness is due to gonococcal infection at birth.

New York University invites the city's assistant medical director Sarah Josephine Baker to lecture but does not permit her to apply for its new doctorate degree in public health, which is open only to men.

Russell Sage College for Women is founded at Troy, N.Y., by philanthropist Margaret Olivia Slocum Sage, 88, whose late husband died 10 years ago at age 90, leaving her $70 million amassed as an associate of Jay Gould in his railroad security manipulations. Sage's second wife, she established the Russell Sage Foundation for improving social and living conditions in the United States with a $10 million gift in 1907 and has given liberally to Cornell, Princeton, Rensselaer Polytechnic Institute, and the Emma Willard School.

New York's Dalton School has its beginnings in a girls' school founded by U.S. educator Helen Parkhurst, 24, who studied at Rome with Maria Montessori early in 1914 (*see* Montessori, 1912). The school will take its name from the Dalton Plan applied to the Dalton, Mass., high school with encouragement from the wife of paper heir W. Murray Crane. Although its preschool and elementary grades are coeducational, it will not accept boys in its high school until 1969.

Fiction: *The Golden Arrow* by English novelist Mary (Gladys Meredith) Webb, 35; *Sussex Gorse* by English novelist Sheila Kaye-Smith, 29; *Greenmantle* by English novelist John Buchan, 41, who writes, "Mankind has a sense of humour which stops short of the final absurdity. There never has been, and there never could be a real Superman. . . . But there might be a Superwoman. Women have got a perilous logic which we never have, and some of the best of them don't see the joke of life like the ordinary man. They can be far greater than men, for they can go straight to the heart of things. There never was a man so near the divine as Joan of Arc" (Mrs. Patrick Campbell, the actress, will say, "Do you know why God withheld the sense of humor from women? That we may love you instead of laughing at you"); *The Jerneploog Family's Success* (*Släkten Jerneploogs framgang*) by Elin Wägner is an ironic arraignment of war; *Prosperity* (*Eiga*) by Toshiko Tamura; *A New Life* (*Atarashiki inochi*) and *Machiko* by Yaeko Nogami; *Mrs. Balfame* by Gertrude Atherton.

Poetry: *Twentieth Century Harlequinade and Other Poems* by English poet Edith Sitwell, 29, and her brother Osbert, 23; "Of Stravinsky's Three Pieces, Grotesques, for String Quartet" by Amy Lowell; *Sea Garden* by U.S. poet H.D. (Hilda Doolittle Aldington), 30, who married the English Imagist poet Richard Aldington in 1912 but will divorce him after the war and return to America; *La inquietud del rosal* by feminist Argentinia poet Alfonsina Storni, 24.

Juvenile: *Nursery Rhymes of London Town* by English author Eleanor Farjeon, 35.

Painting: *Jeune Fille au Botiron* (oil on canvas) and *Le Marché au Minho* by Sonia Delaunay.

Mabel Dodge leaves New York and settles in Croton-on-Hudson, where she meets and marries post-impressionist painter Maurice Stern, who will introduce her to the artistic community at Taos, New Mexico (*see* 1912; 1923).

Films: Lillian Gish, Robert Harron, Mae Marsh, and Constance Talmadge in D. W. Griffith's *Intolerance*. Also: Alla Nazimova in Herbert Brenon's *War Brides*.

Opera: Austrian soprano Maria Jeritza (Jedladecka), 28, creates the title role in the new Richard Strauss opera *Ariadne auf Naxos* 10/4 at Vienna; Amalita Galli-Curci makes her U.S. debut 11/18 at the Chicago Opera singing the role of Gilda in the 1851 Verdi opera *Rigoletto*; Claudia Muzio, now 27, makes her Metropolitan Opera debut 12/4 in the title role of the 1900 Puccini opera *Tosca*.

Stage musicals: Fanny Brice, Ina Claire (Ina Fagan), 23, Ann Pennington, and W. C. Fields in *The Ziegfeld Follies* 6/12 at New York's New Amsterdam Theater, 112 perfs. *Follies* girl Marion Davies (Marion Cecilia Douras), 19, meets publisher William Randolph Hearst, now 53 and the father of five (he married another chorus girl, Millicent Wilson, in 1903), with whom she will remain until his death in 1951; Hazel Dawn, Marie Dressler, and Elsie Janis in *The Century Girl* 11/16 at New York's Century Theater, with songs that include Irving Berlin's "You Belong to Me," 200 perfs.

Molla Burjsted wins the U.S. women's singles title in tennis.

The Women's International Bowling Congress has its beginnings in the Woman's National Bowling Association, founded November 29 by 40 women at St. Louis. It will become the world's largest women's sports organization.

The first large-scale study of iodine's effect on human goiter is conducted by U.S. physicians David Marine and E. C. Kendall. Girls in some Akron, Ohio, schools are given tablets containing 0.2 gram of sodium iodide, and the incidence of goiter is found to drop markedly in susceptible teenage girls who take the tablets.

1916

Birth control pioneer Margaret Sanger campaigned to give women some control over the size of their families.

✖️ Nathan's Famous frankfurters have their beginning in a Coney Island, N.Y., hot dog stand at the corner of Stillwell and Surf avenues opened by Polish-American merchant Nathan Handwerker, 25, who sells his franks at 5¢ each—half the price charged by Feltman's German Gardens on Surf Avenue, where Handwerker has worked weekends as a counterman while making $4.50 per week as a delivery boy on the Lower East Side. Handwerker has invested his life savings of $300 in the hot dog stand; works 18 to 20 hours per day with his 19-year-old bride, Ida, who laces the franks with her secret spice recipe; and prospers.

👪 The first birth control clinic outside Holland opens at 46 Amboy Street, Brooklyn. Margaret Sanger distributes circulars printed in English, Italian, and Yiddish to announce the opening (see 1914). Police raid the clinic, Sanger is jailed for 30 days, founds the New York Birth Control League after her release, and begins publication of the *Birth Control Review* (see 1921).

1917

✖️ The Women's Army Auxiliary Air Force organized in France by London botany professor and fungi expert Helen Charlotte Isabella Gwynne-Vaughan (*née* Fraser), 38, works to keep Britain's De Havillands, Farmans, and Sopworths in the air against the fighter planes flown by Baron von Richtofen's "Flying Circus."

Congress declares war on Germany April 6—4 days after President Wilson has sent a war message to the Senate. Congresswoman Rankin's is the lone dissenting voice. She will later say, "I felt at the time

Jeanette Rankin's was the lone dissenting voice when Congress voted to declare war in 1917. LIBRARY OF CONGRESS

that the first woman [in Congress] should take the first stand, that the first time the first woman had a chance to say no to war she should say it." Rankin will lose her bid for the Republican Senate nomination next year, and she will not be reelected to Congress until 1940.

Emma Goldman is arrested along with Alexander Berkman, their journal *Mother Earth* is suppressed, and they are sentenced to 2 years' imprisonment for leading opposition to U.S. military conscription (*see* 1906; 1919).

British authorities in Ireland release Countess Markievicz June 18 on orders from Prime Minister Lloyd George, who wants to reassure the Allies that London is trying to solve its Irish Home Rule problem (*see* 1916; 1918).

German radicals who include Clara Zetkin found the Independent Social Democratic party (Spartacus League) (*see* 1919).

Russia's provisional government chief Aleksandr Kerensky organizes a women's battalion of 300 young working-class women, some only 17 years old, who have had combat experience serving as frontline nurses. Lt. Marie Baktscharow (or Maria Bochkareva) (*née* Frotkova), 28, who heads the battalion, allegedly heard voices in 1914 telling her to "go to war to save the country." She joined the Tomsk Reserve Battalion as its only female regular, gained a reputation for bravery in rescuing wounded comrades in the face of machine-gun fire, was paralyzed for 5 months by a shell fragment in her spine, but has recovered from this and other wounds. Visiting St. Petersburg, she has proposed a "Woman's Battalion of Death," immediately received 1,500 applications, received another 500 the next day, and has chosen 300. Her group is sent to the northern front, where 29 are killed and 40 wounded; it will be followed by other "suicide battalions."

Dutch-born dancer Mata Hari (Gertrud Margarette [or Margaretha Geertruida] Zelle), 41, is convicted of having spied for the Germans and shot by a firing squad October 15 at St. Lazare. At 19, she married an army officer, one Capt. MacLeod, with whom she traveled to Java, where

Anarchist Emma Goldman encouraged resistance to military conscription in "the war to end wars." LIBRARY OF CONGRESS

she learned the rudiments of Balinese temple dancing. After her return to Europe she left her husband, went to Paris as "Lady MacLeod," and later entertained audiences under the name *Mata Hari* (Malay for "the sun" or "eye of the dawn"), doing semi-nude "Indian" dances until the novelty wore off and she turned to prostitution. It is doubtful that she sold the Germans anything more than her body.

The first U.S. woman governor takes office in Texas. Miriam Amanda "Ma" Ferguson (*née* Wallace), 42, fills the vacancy left by her husband, James, who has been impeached and removed from office (*see* 1924), but no woman will be elected to a state governorship in her own right until 1974.

 Russian women, who now make up half the nation's labor force (up from one-third before the war) observe the seventh International Women's Day February 23 (March 8 in Western calendars) by demonstrating against the excesses of the czarist government. It is the first day of the Russian Revolution.

Amanda "Ma" Ferguson took over from her husband as governor of Texas, becoming the first woman governor. LIBRARY OF CONGRESS

Russian women gain the right to vote on the same basis as men (*see* Norway, 1913; Canada, 1918).

"We want the vote so that we may serve our country better," says Emmeline Pankhurst April 23 in a speech at the Queen's Hall. "We want the vote so that we shall be more faithful and more true to our allies. We want the vote so that we may help to maintain the cause of Christian civilization for which we entered this war. We want the vote so that in future such wars if possible may be averted."

The Canadian provinces of British Columbia and Ontario grant women voting rights (*see* 1916). A Wartime Elections Act enfranchises Canadian women with close relatives in the armed services, and a Military Voters Act gives the vote to women who are themselves in active service (*see* 1918).

Alice Paul's National Woman's Party pickets the White House in October to urge presidential support of the woman suffrage amendment (*see* 1916). Demonstrators who include Paul, Maud Malone, and 265 others are arrested and and sentenced to 7 months' imprisonment in the filthy Occuquan Workhouse, where most will serve 60 days. Paul is placed in solitary confinement in the psychiatric ward in an effort to discredit her, and force-fed when she goes on a 3-week hunger strike.

President Wilson endorses equal suffrage October 25 when he speaks at the White House before a group from the New York State Woman Suffrage party, and 20,000 women march in a New York suffrage parade October 27.

New York adopts a constitutional amendment November 6 that makes it the first state to grant equal voting rights to women (*see* 1918). Labor leader Rose Schneiderman, who has made regular trips to the State Capitol at Albany, continues to lobby the legislature for passage of a 48-hour workweek law for women, and a minimum wage, which would benefit men as well as women, since employers would be less likely to replace male workers with lower-paid female workers.

Most Canadian provinces will enact equal guardianship laws in the next 6 years, giving mothers rights equal to those of fathers with regard to custody, control, and education of children. Divorce laws will be made less discriminatory, although property settlements will not recognize a housewife's contribution to a family's assets.

Federal authorities at New Orleans respond to America's entrance into the war (above) by shutting down Storyville, whose brothels now have fewer than 700 prostitutes (*see* 1900). Mahogany Hall's madam, Lulu White, has lost most of her money (she gave it to George Killishaw, her lover and trusted companion, to invest in Los Angeles real estate, and he disappeared with it); she has opened a saloon next door but has only a handful of octaroons to entertain customers when the Feds close her down.

Russian housewives waiting in endless bread-shop queues at Petrograd demonstrate in protest, they are joined by soldiers from the Petrograd garrison, sailors from Kronstadt, and the factory workers'

Red Guards, who seize government offices and storm the Winter Palace of the Romanovs, which the Battalion of Women (above) help to defend. A Bolshevik revolution begins the night of November 6 (October 24 by the Julian calendar still used in Russia). Aleksandra Kollontai, now 45 (*see* 1896), is appointed People's Commissar of Social Welfare, becoming the world's first woman political minister (*see* 1944).

Revolutionist Vera Nikolaevna Figner, now 65, is made chairman of the amnesty committee and becomes a national heroine (*see* 1883). Released from prison in 1904 and sent to Siberia, she returned after only 2 years and is celebrated for her memoirs, which have been published under the title *How the Clock of My Life Stopped*.

💲 Mary Pickford and other stars speak at bond rallies that will help sell $18.7 billion in Liberty Bonds this year and next despite their low 3.5 percent interest rate (railroad bonds yield 4.79 percent).

☿ A survey conducted for the Children's Bureau of the U.S. Department of Labor shows that maternity is the second leading cause of death (tuberculosis remains first) for women aged 15 to 44 and concludes that the United States is a particularly dangerous country in which to have a baby.

¶¶ U.S. journalist Dorothy Day, 19, quits her job on the IWW newspaper the *Call* and joins the *Masses*, a U.S. Communist party newspaper that is soon suppressed (*see* 1933).

Shufunotomo (*Housewife's Companion*) begins publication in March at Tokyo.

✒ Nonfiction: *Hearts of Controversy* by Alice Meynell, now 70.

Fiction: *Regiment of Women* by English novelist-playwright Clemence Dane (Winifred Ashton), 26; *Gone to Earth* by Mary Webb; *Prelude* by Katherine Mansfield, who begins to show symptoms of tuberculosis but next year will marry the critic John Middleton Murry, with whom she has lived since 1912; *Irish Memoirs* by Edith Somerville, who continues to write under the name Somerville and Ross (*see* 1915); *Le Solitarie* by poet Ada Negri; *Asa-Hanna* by Elin Wägner, whose heroine becomes involved by marriage with a family of sly, petty criminal types; *A Daughter in the Morning* by Milwaukee

journalist-suffragist Zona Gale, 43, is a fictionalized declaration of female awareness; *The Lady of Kingdoms* by Inez Gillmore Irwin, now 44, who obtained a divorce from Gillmore and last year married California journalist William H. Irwin; "Tales of a Polygamous City" by "An Elderly Spinster" is a fictionalized examination of the plight of women in a male-dominated society that is published in the *Atlantic Monthly*: Iowa-born writer Margaret (Wilhelmina) Wilson, 35, worked in India as a missionary for the United Presbyterian Church from 1904 to 1910, teaching at the Gujranwala Girl's School in the Punjab and helping at Sailkot Hospital before coming down with typhoid fever; *Ladies Must Live* by U.S. poet-novelist Alice Miller (*née* Duer), 43; *The Blue Envelope* by U.S. playwright-novelist Sophie Kerr, 37, whose novels will be serialized in the *Saturday Evening Post* and the women's magazines.

Poetry: *Renascence and Other Poems* by Maine-born poet Edna St. Vincent Millay, 25, whose title poem appeared 5 years ago and won her a sponsor who has put her through Vassar; *Love Songs* by Sara Teasdale (Pulitzer Prize); *Women Are People!* by Alice Duer Miller (above); *The White Flock* (*Belaya staya*) by Anna Akhmatova.

Juvenile: *Understood Betsy* by Dorothea Canfield Fisher; *Anne's House of Dreams* by Maud Montgomery.

🎨 Sculpture: *Bacchanal Russe* (ballet figures) by Melvina Hoffman, who has applied to Columbia University's College of Physicians and Surgeons to study dissection and anatomy.

🎭 Theater: *The Old Lady Shows Her Medals* and *Seven Women* by James M. Barrie 4/7 at London's New Theatre; English actress Estelle Winwood, 34, in Jesse Lynch Williams's *Why Marry?* 12/25 at New York's Astor Theater.

Films: Lillian Gish and her sister Dorothy, 19, in D. W. Griffith's *Hearts of the World* (financed by the British government to arouse U.S. sympathies against the Germans but released after U.S. entry into the war).

🎼 Ballet: U.S. ballerina Doris Humphrey, 21, makes her debut with the Denishawn Company founded by Ruth St. Denis and Ted Shawn.

Opera: English soprano Florence Easton, 35, makes her Metropolitan Opera debut 12/7 in the 1890 Mascagni opera *Cavalleria Rusticana*. She will be a Met regular until February 1936.

Broadway musicals: Louise Dresser in Jerome Kern's *Have a Heart* 1/11 at the Liberty Theater, 76 perfs.; Peggy Wood in Jerome Kern's *Love o' Mike* 1/15 at the Shubert Theater, 192 perfs.; Marion Davies and Edna May Oliver in *Oh, Boy!* 2/20 at the Princess Theater, with Jerome Kern songs that include "Till the Clouds Roll By," 463 perfs.; Marion Davies in *The Ziegfeld Follies* 6/12 at the New Amsterdam Theater; Peggy Wood in Sigmund Romberg's *Maytime* 8/17 at the Shubert Theater, with book and lyrics by Rida Johnson Young, songs that include "Will You Remember (Sweetheart)?"; dancer Fred Astaire (originally Austerlitz), 18, and his sister Adele make their Broadway debut in *Over the Top* (revue) 11/28 at the 44th Street Roof Theater, 78 perfs.

London comedienne (Esmeralda) Cicely Courtneidge, 34, appears at the Victoria Palace Music Hall, competing with stars such as Marie Lloyd (*see* 1885), Florrie Ford, Vesta Tilley (male impersonator Matilda Alice Powles, now 53), and Gertie Miller. Courtneidge has married comedian Jack Hulbert.

Molla Bjurstedt wins in women's singles at the Patriotic Tournament held in place of regular U.S. Lawn Tennis Association championships.

A *New York Times* story headlined "How to Save in Big Homes" infuriates Assistant Secretary of the Navy Franklin D. Roosevelt by telling readers that his wife does "the buying, the cooks see that there is no food wasted, the laundress is sparing in her use of soap; each servant has a watchful eye of evidences of shortcomings in others, and all are encouraged to make suggestions in the use of 'left overs.' " The story, which appears after Eleanor has left for vacation on Campobello Island, New Brunswick, reveals that the Roosevelt household of seven has 10 servants.

A British Public Meals Order provides for one meatless day per week at restaurants and hotels, 5 days without potatoes, and no more than 2 ounces of meat at breakfast, 5 ounces at lunch or dinner.

Beginning September 17, bread prices are fixed at 9d per 4-pound loaf, and even in this worst year of the war the British eat better than do their enemies and even than most neutrals.

France rations sugar and decrees that wheat flour shall be used only for bread; sale of fancy bread and pastries is forbidden. French restaurants are restricted in the number of dishes they may serve and forbidden to serve milk or cream after 9 in the morning.

U.S. bacteriologist Alice Evans, 36, begins work that will show the ability of the bacterium that causes contagious abortion (Bang's disease) in cattle to be passed to human beings, notably via raw milk, and produce undulant fever or brucellosis. The dairy industry and medical profession will oppose Evans, but compulsory pasteurization of U.S. milk in the late 1920s will be achieved largely through her efforts in the next 9 years.

1918

Russia's new Bolshevik regime signs the Treaty of Brest-Litovsk March 3, ending participation in the "capitalist-imperialist" war despite opposition by Left Communists (including Inessa Armand) to the capitulation. Armand, now 42, has shared living quarters at Paris and Cracow with V. I. Lenin and his wife, Krupskaya.

British authorities at Dublin rearrest Countess Markievicz May 18, take her to London, and imprison her in Holloway Gaol, where she is soon joined by Mrs. John McBride (actress Maud Gonne, whose late husband, John, was executed for treason in 1916) and Mrs. Thomas J. Clarke (Kathleen Daly, whose husband and brothers have been murdered). All are suspected of involvement in a German plot (*see* 1917; 1919).

Russia's royal Romanov family is shot to death July 16 at Ekaterinburg by order of the Bolsheviks 4 days after others of the Russian nobility have been assassinated elsewhere. Nicholas II, the czarina Aleksandra, their daughters Olga, Tatiana, Marie, and Anastasia, their son Alexis, Prince Dolgorolkoff, their physician, a nurse, and a lady-in-waiting are all put to death July 16 or within a few

Irish patriot Maud Gonne was an actress who wound up as a free nation's ambassador to Paris. LIBRARY OF CONGRESS

The Great War ends in an armistice November 11, leaving most participants drained and grieving. Killed in the conflict have been 1.8 million Germans, 1.7 million Russians, 1.4 million French, 1.2 million Austrians and Hungarians, between 750,000 and 950,000 British, 460,000 Italians, 325,000 Turks, and 115,000 Americans. Some 20 million have been blinded, maimed, mutilated, crippled, permanently shell-shocked, or otherwise disabled.

U.S. suffragist Alice Paul has been released from jail in January, and President Wilson has said that woman suffrage was urgently needed as a "war measure."

German, Austrian, and Polish women gain the right to vote on the same basis as men (*see* Russia, 1917; Britain, Canada, below; Netherlands, 1919).

U.S. war plants have employed 1 million women, but many suffragists have followed the lead of pacifists Carrie Chapman Catt and Jane Addams in opposing anything that supported the war effort. Few labor unions accept women, whose health is neglected and who generally receive less than men for equivalent work.

British women over age 30 gain the right to vote under terms of the Fourth Franchise Bill, passed last year, which also grants suffrage to all men over age 21. Emmeline Pankhurst has favorably influenced masculine opinion by persuading women to do war work and has helped obtain passage of the Franchise Bill (*see* 1913; 1928). An act passed November 21 permits women to be members of Parliament, and in the Irish elections December 14 Countess Markievicz (above), still in Holloway gaol, is elected to the Dail Eireann (*see* 1919). Women in England, Scotland, and Wales vote for the first time in a national election December 28.

Nova Scotia grants female suffrage (*see* 1917), and the Ottawa government grants full female suffrage in federal elections. Suffragist Clara MacDonald Denison, 51, has worked to persuade the provincial legislatures to let women vote (*see* New Brunswick, 1919).

A resolution providing for a U.S. Woman Suffrage Amendment has passed the House of Representatives in January, but the Senate rejects the resolu-

weeks of that date, but rumors will persist that one or more of the daughters has somehow been spared (*see* 1928).

Russian terrorist Fanya Kaplan (*née* Feiga Efimovna Roidman), 28, shoots at the Bolshevik leader V. I. Lenin August 30, says she did it because he betrayed the Revolution in making peace with Germany, and is executed soon thereafter despite Lenin's opposition. "A revolutionist executed in a revolutionary country! Never," Lenin's wife, Nadezhda Krupskaya, has said.

Rosika Schwimmer returns to her native Budapest in October, is elected to the National Council of Fifteen, and is appointed ambassador to Switzerland, becoming the first woman ambassador (*see* 1915; 1919).

tion for the third time October 1 despite a rousing speech that day from President Wilson, who asks the senators, "The strange revelations of this war having made many things new and plain to Governments as well as to peoples, are we alone to refuse to learn the lesson, are we alone to ask and take the utmost that our women can give, service and sacrifice of every kind, and still say that we do not see that they merit the title that gives them the right to stand by our side in the guidance of the affairs of their nation and ours? We have made partners of the women in this war. Shall we admit them only to a partnership of suffering and sacrifice and toil and not to a partnership of privlege and right?" (see 1919).

British Columbia becomes the first Canadian province to pass a law guaranteeing that women will not be paid less than a living wage. By 1922, all provinces except New Brunswick and Prince Edward Island will have women's minimum wage laws.

Inessa Armand (above) has differed with V. I. Lenin on questions of women's rights, arguing that women should be free to love and to escape from the constraints of "bourgeois marriage." Lenin has regarded her views as supporting unlimited promiscuity, and while the revolution will bring legal emancipation it will not bring women any closer to real freedom.

Wives of 43 Japanese fishermen gather on the beach at Namekawa in Toyama Prefecture July 23 to complain about the high price of rice. They go into town and demand that rice shops sell to them at lower prices, and their efforts begin a nationwide movement. Police arrest 7,813 protesters.

The "Spanish" influenza epidemic that sweeps through Europe, America, and the Orient is the worst pandemic to afflict mankind since the Black Death of the mid–14th century. It will kill 21.64 million—more than 1 percent of the world's population and more than twice the number killed in the Great War. The flu, which actually began in China, affects 80 percent of the population in Spain, has spread all over the U.S. East Coast by mid-September, and soon affects nearly 25 percent of Americans, forcing schools to close, hospitals to run out of beds, and coffin supplies to be exhausted.

The alkaloid drug ergotamine is extracted from the ergot fungus *Claviceps purpura*. Useful in small doses as a muscle and blood vessel contractant, the drug will be used to treat migraine attacks and induce uterine contractions in childbirth. It will also be used to induce abortion (see ergonovine, 1935).

The Maternity Center Association of New York is founded to provide prenatal care and education for pregnant women in poor neighborhoods (see 1932).

The International Church of the Four-Square Gospel is founded at Los Angeles by Canadian-American evangelist Aimee (Elizabeth) Semple McPherson (*née* Kennedy), 28, who accompanied her first husband as a missionary to Hong Kong, has walked out on the father of her second child, and comes to the city in a seven-passenger Oldsmobile whose doors carry the message "Jesus is coming soon—Get Ready. Where will you spend Eternity?" in six-inch-high letters. She conducts healing services for victims of the influenza epidemic (above), promises that the "deaf hear, the blind see, and the lame walk," and offers hope and salvation to southern and midwestern migrants newly arrived in southern California. McPherson will create a large following that will provide funds to build the huge Angelus Temple, from which her sermons will be broadcast over a radio station purchased with contributions from the faithful. Patriotic-religious music played by a 50-piece band will precede the sermons, and the McPherson movement, based largely on faith healing, adult baptism, and fundamentalist spectacle, will attract thousands (see 1923).

Tokyo Women's University has its beginnings in a school opened by U.S. and Japanese Protestants as an outgrowth of a 1910 Christian convention at Edinburgh that addressed the subject of higher education in Asia. The new school will gain university status in 1948.

Nonfiction: *The New Morality and the Working Class* by Aleksandra Kollontai; *Mobilizing Woman Power* by Harriet Eaton Blatch.

Fiction: *My Antonia* by Willa Cather; *Birth* by Zona Gale; *Foes* by Mary Johnston is set in 18th-century Scotland; *The Return of the Soldier* by Rebecca

West; *One's Own Fate* (*Svoya sudba*) by Russian poet-novelist Marietta Sergeyevna Shaginyan, 30.

Poetry: *Old Road to Paradise* by U.S. poet-novelist Margaret Widdemer, 33 (Pulitzer Prize); *Heart of a Woman and Other Poems* by U.S. poet Georgia Douglas Camp Johnson, 31, who will be the first black American poet to gain national recognition since Frances Harper in the 19th century; *The Ghetto* by Irish-American poet Lola (*née* Rose Emily) Ridge, 44; *The Sweet Loss* (*El dulce daño*) by Alfonsina Storni; *Ecstasy Collection* (*Skrizhal sbornik*) by Anna Akhmatova; *More Songs of Angus* by Violet Jacob.

Juvenile: *The Tale of Johnny Town-Mouse* by Beatrix Potter; *A Patriotic Schoolgirl* by Angela Brazil.

Films: Theda Bara in J. Gordon Edwards's *Salome* and *When a Woman Sins*; Constance Talmadge in Edwards's *A Pair of Silk Stockings*; Mabel Normand in F. Richard Jones's *Mickey*.

Louella Parsons loses her job at the *Chicago Record-Herald* when William Randolph Hearst acquires the paper but starts a new gossip column in the *New York Morning Telegraph* that catches Hearst's eye (*see* 1914; 1925).

Stage musicals: Marilyn Miller and Fred and Adele Astaire in *The Passing Show* 7/25 at New York's Winter Garden Theater, with songs that include "Smiles" and with June Caprice singing "I'm Forever Blowing Bubbles," 124 perfs.; Marilyn Miller and W. C. Fields in *The Ziegfeld Follies* 6/18 at New York's New Amsterdam Theater, 151 perfs.; vaudeville trooper Mae West, 26, in *Sometime* 10/4 at New York's Shubert Theater, with West singing songs that include "Any Kind of Man" by Rudolf Friml, 283 perfs.; Gracie Fields, now 20, in *Mr. Tower of London* 10/28 at Nottingham's Coliseum (created by impresario Archie Pitts, it will tour the country for 9 years).

Opera: U.S. soprano Rosa Melba Ponselle (Rosa Ponzillo), 21, makes her Metropolitan Opera debut 11/15 singing the role of Donna Leonora opposite Enrico Caruso in the 1862 Verdi opera *La Forza del Destino*. She is the first U.S. woman to become a Met prima donna without having trained in Europe.

Molla Burjsted wins the U.S. women's tennis singles title.

Boston tennis player Eleanora Randolph Sears, now 37, begins playing squash at the Harvard Club, even though women are officially forbidden to enter the building (*see* 1928).

The Raggedy Ann Doll introduced by a New York firm is based on a doll produced to promote sales of the first book of Raggedy Ann stories. *Indianapolis Star* political cartoonist John Gruelle, 37, found the handmade rag doll in his attic last year and gave it to his tubercular daughter Marcella, they named it Raggedy Ann through a combination of neighbor James Whitcomb Riley's "Little Orphan Annie" of 1885 and Riley's poem "The Raggedy Man," the doll inspired Gruelle to make up stories which he told to entertain Marcella, she died holding the doll in March of 1916 after being vaccinated by a contaminated needle, Gruelle's book will have 25 sequels, and the Raggedy Ann doll will grow to become a $20-million-per-year business.

Rinso, introduced by Lever Brothers, is the world's first granulated laundry soap (*see* Lux Flakes, 1906; detergent, 1946).

Kotex is introduced under the name "Celucotton" by Kimberly & Clark Co. of Neenah, Wis., whose German-American chemist Ernst Mahler, 31, has developed a wood-cellulose substitute for cotton to fill the desperate need for dressings and bandages in European field hospitals. When word reaches Wisconsin that Red Cross nurses are using Celucotton for sanitary napkins, the company begins development of the first commercial sanitary napkin; it will be sold as Kotex beginning in 1921 (*see* Kleenex, 1924; Tampax, 1936).

English researcher Edward Mellanby shows that cod-liver oil contains an agent that cures rickets, giving recognition to a treatment used by North Sea mothers for generations.

Wise Parenthood by Marie Stopes, whose 1916 book produced so many letters from women seeking ways to limit fertility that she has quickly written a new one, directly approaching the subject of birth control by providing diagrams of the reproductive organs and giving descriptions of various means of contraception. She marries aircraft manufacturer Humphrey Vernon Roe, 42, who will support her in her efforts (*see* 1921).

1919

 Berlin authorities arrest socialist agitators Rosa Luxemburg, now 49, and Karl Liebknecht, 48, after an insurrection inspired by their Spartacus party (*see* 1914). They are murdered January 15 while being transferred from military headquarters to prison and Luxemburg's body is thrown into the Landwehr Canal, where it is not found until June 1. Many women have joined the Spartacide revolt at Berlin (*see* Spartacus League, 1917), participating in atrocities there and in the city's suburbs; one woman is reported to have killed 20 soldiers, and many women are taken prisoner along with the men.

Feminist Adele Schreiber, who in 1910 founded the German Association for the Rights of Mothers and Children, is elected January 23 along with 33 other women as members of the first Reichstag of the new Weimar Republic.

Women in East Prussia are organized into militia to fight the Bolsheviks.

The German Communist party is founded by radicals who include Clara Zetkin, now 62.

Countess Markievicz is released from Holloway Gaol March 6 following the death of another prisoner from influenza in Gloucester Gaol, she returns to Dublin March 15, and is soon appointed secretary for labour in the De Valera government with the support of the Irish Women Workers Union headed by Helena Molony (*see* 1918). But the countess makes a speech in May at Newmarket urging a boycott of English manufacturers, authorities deem her remarks seditious, she is arrested June 13, and she is held in Cork jail until October 16 (*see* 1920).

Rosika Schwimmer quits her Hungarian government posts following the accession March 21 of Bolshevik revolutionary Béla Kun, who wants a dictatorship of Hungary's proletariat (*see* 1918; 1920).

Romania's Queen Marie pleads her country's cause at the Paris peace conference, where she is fêted by Clemenceaux, Poincaré, and British statesman Arthur Balfour. She was influential in bringing Romania into the war on the side of her British and Russian cousins, only to have her adopted country devastated by invading German and Hungarian armies. Hungarian forces invade Transylvania in July, Romanian forces drive them back and occupy Budapest August 4, 3 days after the overthrow of Béla Kun's government (above), and remain until November 14, when they withdraw under pressure from the Allies, taking with them everything they can carry (*see* 1920).

U.S. authorities release anarchists Emma Goldman and Alexander Berkman from prison but deport them with more than 200 others to Soviet Russia (*see* 1917). Justice Department lawyer J. (John) Edgar Hoover, 24, who handles deportation cases involving alleged Communist revolutionaries, calls Goldman "the most dangerous woman in America." She will disagree with policies of the Lenin government, leave Russia in 1921, and explain why in her 1923 book *My Disillusionment in Russia*.

The American Communist party is founded by socialists who include feminist Ella Bloor (*née* Reeve), 57, who took her name when she wrote pieces of investigative reporting for Upton Sinclair at the turn of the century and is known as "Mother Bloor." A fiery speaker for the party, she will be arrested more than 30 times.

The Women's International League for Peace and Freedom is founded with help from former Wellesley College economics and sociology professor Emily Greene Balch, now 52, who serves as international secretary. Her appointment at Wellesley was not renewed because of questions about her "patriotism."

Britain's House of Commons gets its first woman member as Virginia-born Viscountess Nancy Witcher Astor (*née* Langhorne), 40, is elected as a Conservative to succeed her husband as representive for Plymouth. A close friend of Romania's Queen Marie (above), she met and married emigré U.S. real estate heir (William) Waldorf, Third Viscount Astor, in 1906 and married him, becoming one of the richest women in England (he has moved to the House of Lords). "Obviously I can't say that the best man won," Lady Astor jokes, "but the best policy did."

Lady Astor, born in Virginia, won herself a seat in Parliament, becoming the first woman member. LIBRARY OF CONGRESS

President Wilson suffers a paralyzing stroke October 2 as isolationist Republican senators mount opposition to joining the League of Nations, which Wilson has championed. The president's second wife, Edith Bolling Wilson, now 47, has decoded secret messages and even attended peace talks in her husband's stead as small strokes have left him increasingly disabled, and she decides whom he will and will not see. She prevents his physician from announcing news of the president's condition and carries on in his place without public knowledge (some will call her the "first woman president").

The first Feminist Congress opens at New York March 1 with a statement by Crystal Eastman, who reminds her audience that four-fifths of the women in America are "still denied the elementary political right of voting."

A new Belgian electoral law adopted May 9 gives the franchise to certain classes of women.

Dutch women gain the right to vote on the same basis as men.

France's Chamber of Deputies adopts a bill May 9 granting women the right to vote in elections for members of communal and departmental assemblies. Former Prime Minister Aristide Briand tells reporters, "It is inadmissable that after this war the privileges of women shall be inferior to those of men." French women vote for the first time in legislative elections held November 30, but they will not vote on the same basis as men until 1944.

Sweden's parliament grants suffrage to women May 28 but they will not vote on the same basis as men until 1921.

The Canadian province of New Brunswick grants women suffrage (*see* Prince Edward Island, 1942; Quebec, 1940).

A "lame duck" House of Representatives has failed by one vote February 16 to pass a woman's suffrage bill, but the U.S. Senate votes 56 to 25 June 4 to submit a woman's suffrage amendment to the states for ratification (*see* 1918; 1920).

Italy's lower house of Parliament votes 174 to 55 September 9 to grant women the right to vote on a limited basis (*see* 1912; 1928).

Grand Duchess Charlotte of Luxembourg grants woman suffrage October 25.

Britain's Sex Disqualification (Removal) Act gives women access to the professions.

An International Congress of Working Women is founded at Washington, D.C., with WTUL secretary Maud Swartz as secretary. It will convene at Geneva, Switzerland, in October 1921, change its name to the International Federation of Working Women, and move its headquarters to London.

Southern leaders of the National Association of Colored Women, now headed by Mary Morris Talbert (*née* Burnett), 52, draw up a list of grievances associated with domestic servitude since Emancipation. They make polite reference to "exposure to moral temptations on the job" and cite the case of a black woman in Georgia who lost her job because she would not allow her employer to kiss her; when the case went to trial, the judge said, "This court will never take the word of a nigger against the word of a white man."

Japanese feminist Raicho Hiratsuka of 1911 *Bluestocking* fame joins with Fusae Ichikawa, 26, to start the organization New Women (*Atarashi Onna*) with the aim of amending a law that forbids women from listening or responding to political speeches. Daughter of a poor farmer, Ichikawa has managed to get through high school and attend teacher's college at a time when only 40 percent of girls went even to elementary school. Before coming to Tokyo she taught elementary school and then became a reporter for a newspaper in Aichi Prefecture. *Atarashi Onna* becomes an obscene term among Japanese men, who throw stones at Raichi Hiratsuka's house (*see* 1920).

A Chinese crusade against foot binding begins in December (*see* Xiang Jianyn, 1916).

$ The cost of living in New York City is 79 percent higher than it was in 1914, says the Bureau of Labor Statistics.

German mathematician (Amalie) Emmy Noether, 37, gains an official appointment at Göttingen University, where she will develop theories of ideals and of noncommutative algebras. Anti-Semitism and male dominance have hindered her academic career despite the major contributions that she has made to the development of abstract algebra (*see* 1933).

Harvard University names its first woman professor: toxicologist Dr. Alice Hamilton, 50, whose older sister is the classicist Edith Hamilton, becomes assistant professor of industrial medicine at the Medical School, where she will remain until 1935, pioneering in the study of hygiene and industrial diseases.

Physician Dorothy Reed Mendenhall (she married Charles Mendenhall in February 1906), now 45, conducts a comprehensive survey of war orphanages in Belgium and France, makes nutritional studies of children in England, and represents the Children's Bureau of the U.S. Department of Labor at the International Child Welfare Conference (*see* 1901). She has worked on a nationwide U.S. drive to weigh all children under age 6, found widespread evidence of malnutrition, and developed norms for height and weight for children up to age 6.

Baltimore Sun correspondent Marguerite E. Harrison (*née* Baker), 39, arrives at Berlin in January—the first English-speaking woman to reach the city since the November Armistice. Widowed in 1915 and left with a 13-year-old son (plus a debt of nearly $70,000), she has used her language skills and social connections to obtain an assignment from the War Department's Military Intelligence Division and plays a double role in a city racked by starvation, street fighting (above), and political intrigue. Harrison returns to Baltimore after the Versailles peace treaty is signed in June but sails for England early in November with instructions from MID to provide information on conditions in Warsaw, Kiev, and Moscow (she has paid off her late husband's debts with an inheritance received from the estate of her late father; *see* 1920).

Dial telephones are introduced November 8 at Norfolk, Va., by American Telephone & Telegraph Co., which has earlier rejected dial phones but accepts them now under threat of a telephone operators' strike. So many switchboard operators are needed to run the nation's telephone system that the growth of phone ownership will soon outstrip the supply of available labor.

Nonfiction: *The Seattle General Strike* by local journalist Anna Louise Strong, 31, who covered the strike that began February 6.

Fiction: *The Mother* (*Le madre*) by Grazia Deledda; *Legend* by Clemence Dane; *The Pot Boils* by English novelist (Margaret) Storm Jameson, 28; *The Lamp in the Desert* by English novelist Ethel Mary Dell, 38; *Tamarisk Town* by Sheila Kaye-Smith; *Michael Forth* by Mary Johnston is set in the postbellum South; *The Charm School* by Alice Duer Miller; *The See-Saw: A Story of Today* by Sophie Kerr.

Poetry: *Poems* by U.S. poet Michael Strange (Blanche Oelrichs), who has divorced Philadelphia millionaire Leonard Thomas and will marry John Barrymore next year; *Exile* (*Esilio*) by Ada Negri.

Painting: *Lake Placid* by U.S. painter Florine Stettheimer, 48; *The Tigress*, *Black Venus*, *Reclining Slave*, and *Utrillo at His Easel* by Suzanne Valadon, now 54, who has taught her son Maurice, now 35, everything she knows.

Theater: Norma Trevor in George Bernard Shaw's *Augustus Does His Bit* 3/12 at New York's Guild Theater, 111 perfs.; Alma Tell, 27, in George V. Hobart's *The Fall and Rise of Susan Lenox* 6/9 at New York's 44th Street Theater; Ina Claire and Ruth Terry in Avery Hopwood's *The Gold Diggers* 9/30 at New York's Lyceum Theater, 282 perfs.; *Aria da Capo* by Edna St. Vincent Millay 12/15 at New York's Provincetown Playhouse.

Films: Lillian Gish and Richard Barthelmess in D. W. Griffith's *Broken Blossoms*; Constance Talmadge and Elmer Layton in Griffith's *Fall of Babylon*; Carol Dempster and Barthelmess in Griffith's *Scarlet Days*; Gloria Swanson (Gloria May Josephine Svensson), 20, and Bebe (originally Virginia) Daniels, 18, in Cecil B. DeMille's *Male and Female* (film editor Anne Bauchens, 38, works 16 to 18 hours a day in the cutting room and will continue editing DeMille's work until his death in 1959).

United Artists is founded at Hollywood by D. W. Griffith, Charles Chaplin, romantic star Mary Pickford, and matinee idol Douglas Fairbanks, who have set up the firm to increase their share of the profits from the films they make. Now 36, Fairbanks will marry Pickford next year and both will continue making films selected, financed, and distributed (but not produced) by United Artists.

Broadway musicals: Blossom Seeley, Al Jolson, and George White in *The Whirl of Society* 3/5 at the Winter Garden Theater, with a runway across the pit that runs up the aisles, giving audiences a closer look at Seeley and the chorus girls, 136 perfs.; "dimple-kneed" Ann Pennington and White in (George White's) *Scandals* 6/2 at the Liberty Theater, 128 perfs.; Marilyn Miller, Eddie Cantor, and Eddie Dowling in *The Ziegfeld Follies* 6/16 at the New Amsterdam Theater, with Irving Berlin songs that include "A Pretty Girl Is Like a Melody,"

which will become the *Follies* theme, 171 perfs.; Fanny Brice, Will Rogers, and W. C. Fields in *The Ziegfeld Midnight Frolic* 10/2 at the New Amsterdam Roof with songs that include "Rose of Washington Square"; Fred and Adele Astaire in *Apple Blossoms* 10/7 at the Globe Theater, 256 perfs.; Peggy Wood in *Buddies* 10/26 at the Selwyn Theater, 259 perfs.; Edith Day in *Irene* 11/18 at the Vanderbilt Theater, with Harry Tierney–Joseph McCarthy songs that include "Alice Blue Gown," 670 perfs.

Opera: Maria Jeritza sings the role of the empress, German soprano Lotte Lehmann, 31, the role of the dyer's wife in the new Richard Strauss opera *Die Frau ohne Schatten* 10/10 at Vienna's Opernhaus.

Suzanne Lenglen, 20 (Fr), wins in women's singles at Wimbledon, Hazel Hotchkiss Wightman in U.S. women's singles.

Lenglen (above) appears wearing a one-piece pleated dress without a petticoat, a shocking departure from the traditional tennis dress.

Paris couturière Evelyn Vionnet, 42, reopens the salon that she ran briefly just before the Great War and will soon dominate the fashion scene with her bias-cut dresses and skirts of pointy handkerchief draperies. Paris holds its first fashion shows since the war, displaying feminine styles that in many cases do without corsets, use soft materials and panniers to emphasize hips, and introduce skirts that hang seven to eight inches from the ground. American visitors call the skirts too short and fill in backless evening gowns with lace.

The song "Alice Blue Gown" (above) takes its title from a color named for the outspoken Washington hostess Alice Roosevelt Longworth, now 35, daughter of the former president (who has died January 6 at age 60).

The former Jennie Jerome, now 65, marries for the third time, taking Montagu Porch, 32, as her husband (*see* 1913). She will die in 1921. Her son Winston Churchill is now secretary of state for war and air.

Hattie Carnegie, Inc., is incorporated by New York designer Carnegie, who has dissolved her partnership with Ruth Rose Roth and begun making trips to Paris (*see* 1909). She brings back sample fashions, which she redesigns to satisfy American tastes, and in 10 years will have annual sales of $3.5 million (*see* 1942).

Advertisements for the deodorant cream Odo-Ro-No introduce the term "B.O.," meaning body odor, to lure women concerned about armpit perspiration odor.

The pogo stick patented by U.S. inventor George B. Hansburg, 32, is a bouncing metal stick that thousands will ride in the 1920s and will be the basis of a dance number in *The Ziegfeld Follies*.

 Belgian food prices drop by 50 percent, British by 25 percent, but prices remain high elsewhere in Europe. German ports are blockaded until July 12. French beef, mutton, pork, and veal prices have increased nearly sixfold since 1914, reports *Le Petit Journal*, and egg, cheese, and butter prices have increased fourfold. France removes restrictions on the sale of beans, peas, rice, eggs, and condensed milk, and then on bread, but while the wartime ban on sugar imports is lifted the import duty on sugar is raised to almost prohibitive levels.

U.S. food prices remain far above 1914 levels. Milk is 15¢ qt., up from 9¢; sirloin steak 61¢ lb., up from 32¢, fresh eggs 62¢ doz., up from 34¢. President Wilson urges Congress in early August to extend the wartime Food Control Act, and Attorney General A. Mitchell Palmer says the government will prosecute food dealers engaged in price gouging.

 The Voluntary Parenthood League is founded under the direction of U.S. feminist Mary Ware Dennett to promote the notion that parenthood should be a matter of choice and bring about repeal of the 1872 Comstock Law.

Emma Goldman (above) has been defending in public the necessity of birth control on grounds of libertarianism, not neo-Malthusian economics.

1920

 Hungarians reject the Communist rule of Béla Kun, Admiral Nikolaus Horthy de Nagybanya forms a new royalist government March 1, Rosika Schwimmer finds her life endangered under Hungary's new

dictatorship, and she has herself smuggled onto a boat that carries her down the Danube (*see* 1919). She emigrates to America, where she is regarded as a Bolshevik spy (*see* 1926).

Romania's Queen Marie sees her diplomatic efforts of last year rewarded in the Treaty of Trianon, signed June 4, and other peace treaties by whose terms Greater Romania (*Romania Mare*) becomes a vast country of 122,282 square miles.

The former French empress Eugénie dies at Madrid's Palacio Liria July 11 at age 94.

British "Black and Tans" in Ireland arrest Countess Markievicz September 26 and hold her in Mountjoy jail (*see* 1919). Other political prisoners die in hunger strikes, martyrs to the cause of independence. The rebels shoot 14 British spies November 21, the Black and Tans retaliate that afternoon by firing at random during a football match at Croke Park, killing 12 women and men (including one of the players) and wounding 60. The countess is court-martialed December 2 and 3 on charges that she organized the Fianna in 1909, and she awaits her sentence at year's end (*see* 1921).

Sen. Warren G. Harding (R., Ohio), 54, a handsome, genial mediocrity, wins election to the presidency with help from women voters (below). His harsh-voiced wife, Florence (*née* Kling) (he calls her the Duchess), who is 5 to 8 years his senior, was deserted by her first husband, Henry de Wolfe.

 The Women's Bureau of the Department of Labor is created by an act of Congress signed into law by President Wilson June 5 "to formulate standards and policies to promote the welfare of wage earning women, improve their working conditions, increase their efficiency, and advance their opportunities for popular employment." Swedish-American labor organizer Mary Anderson, 47, the Bureau's first director, receives a salary of $5,000 (she came to America in steerage at age 16, spoke no English when she arrived, and has risen through the ranks of the labor movement).

U.S. woman suffrage is proclaimed in effect August 26 following Tennessee's ratification of the 19th Amendment to the Constitution: "1. The Right of citizens of the United States to vote shall not be denied or abridged by the United States or by any

State on account of sex. 2. Congress shall have the power to enforce this Article by appropriate legislation." Wisconsin has been the first state to ratify, Illinois the second, but some supporters of woman suffrage—including Kentucky suffragist Laura Clay, 71, whose father, Cassius Marcellus Clay, was an ally of Abraham Lincoln—have opposed a federal law because of their dedication to states' rights.

Carrie Chapman Catt, now 61, who has come to Nashville to combat the Men's Anti-Suffrage Association and other opposition groups, will later write, "Never in the history of politics has there been such a nefarious lobby as labored to block the ratification. . . . In the short time that I spent in the capital I was more maligned, more lied about, than in the 30 previous years I worked for suffrage. I was flooded with anonymous letters, vulgar, ignorant, insane. . . . Even tricksters . . . appropriated our telegrams, tapped our telephones, listened outside our windows and transoms." Suffragist (Anita) Lili Pollitzer, 25, has met with Tennessee State Legislator Harry T. Burn, 24, and persuaded him to cast the deciding vote. "I know that a mother's advice is always safest for a boy to follow," he says, "and my mother wanted me to vote for ratification." The amendment enfranchises 26 million women of voting age.

The League of Women Voters, founded by Carrie Chapman Catt (above), will give impartial, in-depth information on candidates, platforms, and ballot issues. An outgrowth of the National American Woman Suffrage Association (NAWSA), which Catt reorganized between 1905 and 1915, the non-partisan League aims to educate newly enfranchised women, study issues at all levels of government, and take positions on social issues. Its first president is Maud Park, now 59, who has worked since before the turn of the century to gain the vote for women.

Czech women gain the right to vote on the same basis as men.

Japan's Coalition of New Women (*Shinfujin Kyokai*) is founded by feminists who include Raicho Hiratsuka and Fusae Ichikawa (*see* 1919). The coalition includes the Bluestockings; groups of teachers, newspaper reporters, and housewives; and other reform organizations. It begins to publish a newspaper under the name *Josei Dōmei* (Women's League)

and in July sends a petition to the Diet requesting voting rights for women and an end to laws that forbid women from having political meetings and participating in politics (*see* 1945).

A. T. Stewart & Co. coat buyer Frieda Muller Loehmann, 47, and her son Charles invest $800 to open a Brooklyn specialty shop that will have little success until it becomes a discount store. Loehmann pays cash to buy surplus dresses at reduced prices from garment markers in Manhattan's cash-short Seventh Avenue, passes the savings on to her customers, will shift entirely to discounting in 1922, and will shop for bargains until 2 weeks before her death in 1962, by which time Loehmann's will have annual sales of $3 million. (Son Charles will open a Bronx store in 1930 that will develop into a 13-state chain of 34 stores, each with plain pipe racks, communal dressing rooms, and a cash-only, no-returns policy.)

Japan has 4 million gainfully employed women, but they earn only about one-third as much as men; only 12.5 percent work in offices, where they are expected to perform "womanly" duties such as serving tea and otherwise making conditions more pleasant for men.

 Tokyo buses start using women conductors.

 A landmark article by Chicago obstetrician Joseph DeLee, 51, recommends routine use of forceps, episiotomy (an incision of the perineum at the end of the second stage of labor), and early removal of the placenta to protect the baby's head from injury and conserve the woman's energy. An artifical cut is much cleaner and more controlled than a jagged natural tear, he writes, and the operation he recommends will shorten labor, produce less bleeding, lower the risk of infection, and prevent irreparable damage to mother and infant. He has often wondered, he writes, "whether Nature did not deliberately intend women to be used up in the process of reproduction, in a manner analogous to that of the salmon, which dies after spawning." DeLee suggests that it would be better for infants if all deliveries were by cesarean section, and calls extended labor "pathogenic," not only because it is painful to mothers and damages infants but also because husbands are so often left with "ailing, unresponsive"

wives. A woman ought to be as "anatomically perfect" after delivery as she was before, he writes, both for her own sake and her husband's, and he suggests that a woman's genitalia can be reconstructed to their "virginal state" by surgically incising the perineum before it has a chance to tear naturally. He recommends sedating the woman, allowing her cervix to dilate, giving her ether when the fetus enters the birth canal, making a cut of several inches through the skin and muscles of the perineum, and applying forceps to lift the fetus's head over the perineum while using a stethoscope to monitor the fetal heart, administering ergot or a derivative to contract the uterus, extracting the placenta with a "shoehorn maneuver," and, finally, stitching up the perineal cut.

The Rockefeller Institute assigns U.S. medical researcher Louise Pearce, 35, to a team that goes to Leopoldville in the Belgian Congo to conduct scientific tests of a compound (it will become known as tryparsmiva) isolated last year by Pearce and her colleague, Wade Hampton Brown. Sleeping sickness, which inflames the brain and keeps the victim in a state of constant drowsiness, is endemic in the Congo. Researchers have isolated the cause of the disease in a microscopic parasite transmitted by the bite of the tsetse fly. Pearce and Brown's compound effectively destroys the parasite in test animals. They conduct a scientifically planned program to determine the efficacy of tryparsmiva, and within weeks, even victims of the most severe cases are cured and the effects of sleeping sickness reversed. Pearce, whose work will save tens of thousands of lives (and make Congo workers far more productive) by eradicating the disease, is awarded the Order of the Crown of Belgium. She will be awarded the $10,000 King Leopold II prize in 1953.

St. Luke's College of Nursing has its beginnings in a school started at St. Luke's Hospital in Tokyo. It will become a junior college in 1954 and gain full college status in 1964.

∞ Joan of Arc is canonized by the Vatican and becomes St. Joan. She was designated "venerable" in 1904 and declared "blessed" in 1909.

Women account for 47 percent of all U.S. college undergraduates, up from less than 40 percent in 1910, and for the first time have as much access to a college education as men do.

Zeta Phi Beta Sorority is founded January 16 at Howard University, becoming the third Greek-letter society for black women.

Oxford moves May 18 to give women professors equal status with their male colleagues and on October 7 admits the university's 100 women to study for full degrees.

Miss Nightingale's School opens with 50 girls in New York, where Frances Nightingale was joined last year by university-educated Northern Irish teacher Maya Bamford, who came to the United States during the Great War and has taught at the Bryn Mawr School in Baltimore (*see* 1906). They have acquired a brownstone in East 92nd Street, and their school, which now includes a high school, will be renamed Nightingale-Bamford in 1929. It will grow to have 500 girls in grades kindergarten through 12th grade.

Baltimore Sun correspondent (and espionage agent) Marguerite Harrison slips out of Warsaw in January (*see* 1919). Accompanied by Dr. Anna Karlin, who is trying to return to her native Russia after having lived in America, Harrison arrives at Minsk, proceeds to Vilna, and sets out by sleigh from Minsk February 8 for Moscow, which they reach by rail within a few days despite their lack of visas. Harrison attends a lecture by V. I. Lenin and interviews Leon Trotsky and Aleksandra Kollontai through interpreters. Arrested by the Cheka (secret police) and charged with espionage, she agrees to serve as a counterspy but is finally sent to Lubyanka Prison October 24 (*see* 1921).

Time and Tide begins publication at London. It has been founded by Welsh feminist Margaret Haig Thomas, viscountess Rhondda, 37, who was arrested before the war for trying to chemical-bomb letters inside a mailbox, was released after refusing food, escaped the sinking of the *Lusitania* in 1915, worked in her father's business while he served as food controller, and after his death in 1918 tried unsuccessfully to take his seat in the House of Lords. She will take personal charge of her weekly journal of politics and literature in 1926, giving it a liberal right-wing bias.

"Winnie Winkle the Breadwinner" by cartoonist Martin Michael Branner, 31, begins in September in the 15-month-old *New York Daily News*.

Nonfiction: *A Woman's Point of View* by Harriet Eaton Blatch, now 64.

Fiction: *The Age of Innocence* by Edith Wharton (Pulitzer Prize); *Bridal Wreath* (*Kransen*; in England, *The Garland*) by Norwegian novelist Sigrid Undset, 38, is the first novel in her *Kristin Lavransdatter* trilogy; *Kasja* by Marja Rodziewiczówna; *The Metal of the Dead* (*El metal de los muertos*) by Concha Espina de Serna is about life in the Rio Tinto mines; *Women in Love* and *The Lost Girl* by D. H. Lawrence; *The House in Dormer Forest* by Mary Webb; *Bliss and Other Stories* by Katherine Mansfield includes "Je Ne Parle Français" and "Prelude"; *The Lee Shore* and *Potterism* by English novelist (Emilie) Rose Macaulay, 39; *Chéri* by Colette; *This Marrying* by U.S. novelist Margaret Banning (*née* Culkin), 29; *Youth and the Bright Medusa* (stories) by Willa Cather; *Painted Meadows* (stories from the *Saturday Evening Post*) by Sophie Kerr; *Miss Lulu Bett* by Zona Gale (*see* Theater, below).

Poetry: *A Few Figs from Thistles* by Edna St. Vincent Millay: "My candle burns at both ends;/ It will not last the night;/ But, ah, my foes, and, oh, my friends—/ It gives a lovely light."

Painting: *Painterly Construction* by Russian abstractionist Liubov Popova, 31, explores illusions of depth and energy. She will die of scarlet fever in 1924. *Young Italian Girl with a Doll* by Suzanne Valadon. *Women in the Forest* by Marie Laurencin, whose liaison with Guillaume Apollinaire ended in 1913, although he has celebrated their love in some of his most memorable poems; *Asbury Park South* by Florine Stettheimer; *Elsie de Wolfe* and *Miss Natalie Barney, "L'Amazone"* by Romaine Brooks.

New York's Société Anonyme is founded by Katherine S. Dreier, Marcel Duchamp, and others who will open the city's first modern art museum.

Theater: Moya Nugent and Noël Coward in Coward's *I'll Leave It to You* 7/21 at London's New Theatre, 37 perfs.; Effie Ellsier in *The Bat* by Mary Roberts Rinehart and Avery Hopwood 8/23 at New York's Morosco Theater, a dramatization of Rinehart's 1908 novel *The Circular Staircase*, 867 perfs.; Helen Westley and Dudley Digges in George Bernard Shaw's *Heartbreak House* 11/10 at New York's Garrick Theater, 125 perfs.; *Miss Lulu Bett* by Zona Gale 12/27 at New York's Biltmore Theater, with Carroll McComas as the abused spinster who rebels against her dense brother-in-law (Gale will rewrite the last act after a week to give the play a happy ending, and wits will say it should now be called *Miss Lulu Better*) (Pulitzer Prize).

Films: Clarine Seymour and Richard Barthelmess in D. W. Griffith's *The Idol Dancer*; Carol Dempster and Barthelmess in Griffith's *The Love Flower*.

Ballet: German dancer-choreographer Mary Wigman (Marie Wiegmann), 34, opens a school at Dresden that will grow to have branches throughout Germany and have an influence that will spread, through Wigman's star pupil, Hanya Holm, to New York (*see* 1931).

Broadway musicals: Ann Pennington in (George White's) *Scandals* 6/7 at the Globe Theater, with music by George Gershwin, 134 perfs.; Fanny Brice and W. C. Fields in *The Ziegfeld Follies* 6/22 at the New Amsterdam Theater, 123 perfs. (Brice has made headlines in February by refusing to turn over her husband, gambler Nicky Arnstein, to authorities on charges of having stolen $5 million in securities and passing bad checks unless the New York district attorney gives Arnstein immunity from questioning and releases him on $50,000 bail); Marilyn Miller in Jerome Kern's *Sally* 12/21 at the New Amsterdam Theater, with songs that include "Look for the Silver Lining," 570 perfs.; Marie Dressler and Janet Adair in *The Passing Show* 12/29 at the Winter Garden Theater, with songs that include "In Little Old New York," 200 perfs.

Popular songs: Mamie Smith (*née* Robertson), 37, records "That Thing Called Love" in place of Sophie Tucker, becoming the first black jazz-blues singer to cut a record, and she follows it with "Crazy Blues," which is so successful that it makes a fortune for Smith and her promoter.

Suzanne Lenglen wins in women's singles at Wimbledon, Molla Bjurstedt Mallory in U.S. women's singles.

British golf champion Joyce Wethered, 19, wins the English ladies championship to begin a decade of triumph in which she will be virtually unbeatable.

Swedish figure skater Magda Julin-Maurey wins her event in the winter Olympics. U.S. swimmer Ethelda Bleibtrey wins the 100-meter freestyle in 1 minute, 13.6 seconds at the summer Olympics at Antwerp and wins the 400-meter freestyle in 1 minute, 34 seconds; U.S. swimmer Aileen Riggin wins the springboard dive event, Danish swimmer Stefani Fryland the platform dive. Other events are for men only.

Antoine de Paris creates the mannish shingle bob haircut, which will replace the conventional bob introduced by dancer Irene Castle in 1914. Polish-born hairdresser Antek Cierplikowski, 35, calls himself Monsieur Antoine.

Hemlines rise on U.S. dresses; sleeves are shortened or eliminated as designers introduce long-waisted styles to give women a slender look.

The first Miss America beauty queen is crowned at Atlantic City, N.J., to begin a lasting tradition.

The ratio of U.S. domestic servants to the general population is half what it was in 1890. Middle-class women employ mostly day workers, who tend to be blacks rather than immigrants or native-born whites and who return to their own families at night; only relatively affluent households can afford live-in help.

U.S. architects design middle-class houses with "servant-less" kitchens in response to decreased employment of domestic help (above).

Kate Gleason of 1893 Gear Planer fame pioneers low-cost concrete development housing with a project at East Rochester, N.Y. Houses up to now have all been custom-built and relatively expensive, but young families can buy Gleason's mass-produced units for a small down payment plus $40 per month (see 1921).

France makes abortion illegal in order to compensate for the population loss experienced in the Great War. Severe fines and prison sentences are mandated for anyone who administers or receives an abortion, but the law will be widely flouted. Within 50 years the number of illegal abortions will climb to an estimated 500,000 per year, with bungled abortions causing an estimated 500 deaths per year.

"Any Protestant woman in her senses would object to marrying a Roman Catholic," writes Marie Stopes October 18 in a letter to an Irish Catholic. "They prohibit the use of proper hygienic Birth Control methods preferring that a woman's health should be entirely ruined and that she should bring forth feeble, dying, or imbecile infants rather than that proper hygienic methods should be used."

A new French legal ruling classes contraception with abortion and makes anything having to do with birth control illegal.

Youngs Rubber Co. is founded by U.S. entrepreneur Merle Leland Youngs, 33, to make Trojan brand condoms, which will compete with Julius Schmid's Sheik and Ramses brands (see 1883). Trojans will become the largest-selling condoms sold through U.S. drugstores, but while condoms became familiar to U.S. doughboys during the war in France, they were used mostly to avoid sexually transmitted diseases, and that association continues to hamper their acceptance for purposes of avoiding pregnancy in marriage (see 1923).

Russia legalizes abortion by a November decree of the Lenin government at Moscow, but while Russian physicians are not permitted to refuse an abortion where a woman is no more than 2½ months pregnant, they are ordered to discourage patients from having abortions, especially in first pregnancies. The decree's stated purpose is to combat illegal abortions by providing safe and legal ones, which will be free until 1936. Russian physicians employ a method of vacuum extraction called "dry cupping" (see 1936).

1921

President Harding is inaugurated March 4. Republican Alice Roosevelt Longworth, whose own husband is a notorious womanizer, says that Harding looks like "a debauched Roman emperor," and he quickly gets into poker games with his "Ohio Gang" in a little green house at 1625 K Street, where scandalized neighbors see women of dubious reputation entering and exiting (and even two naked women fighting out front with broken bottles in their hands). There are also reports that the president has impregnated Nan Britton, a high school newspaper reporter from Marion, Ohio. Harding's wife, Florence, and her friend Evalyn McLean (*née* Walsh) (who owns the Hope diamond) occupy themselves with buying clothes and jewelry and consulting fortune-tellers.

British authorities in Ireland sentence Countess Markievicz to 2 years' hard labor for having founded the Fianna in 1909 (*see* 1920). She writes to her sister, Mabel Gore-Booth, "It rather amused me to *see* that for starting Boy Scouts in England B. [Baden] Powell was made a baronet! . . . I bet he did not work as hard as I did from 1909 till 1913." A truce between the British and Irish armies takes effect July 11, and the countess is released July 24 (*see* 1923).

The Irish Free State appoints Mrs. John MacBride (patriot-actress Maud Gonne) as its first diplomat to France.

Australian voters elect their first woman member of Parliament March 13.

Canada's federal Parliament at Ottawa gets its first woman member following the election of Agnes Mcphail (*née* Campbell), 31, as representative of the United Farmers of Ontario. She will champion the cause of women in the workforce. Canadian feminist Nellie McClung is elected as a Liberal in Alberta; she will try without success to liberalize the province's divorce laws and will be defeated in 1925.

London issues a White Paper, *Review of the Civil Administration of Mesopotamia,* written by Gertrude Lowthian Bell, now 53, who serves as Oriental Secretary to the British high commissioner, Sir Percy Cox. (He has conducted a plebiscite showing 96 percent approval of installing Syria's Faisal I as king of Iraq.) When told by her mother that her work was well received, Bell replies, "The general line taken by the Press seems to be that it's most remarkable that a dog should be able to stand on its hind legs at all—i.e., a female write a White Paper [*see* Doctor Johnson, 1763]. I hope they'll drop that source of wonder and pay attention to the report itself."

 Six women are sworn in as jurors in a British divorce court January 25. They are the first women ever to serve in a case involving the breakdown of a marriage, but when letters described as "beastly" and "abominable" are produced in evidence they are read only by the six male jurors, the women choosing simply not to look.

Swedish women gain the right to vote on the same basis as men.

President Harding warns a Des Moines, Iowa, audience November 22 that it would be dangerous if women voters were to unite as a class.

The Lucy Stone League is founded to establish a woman's legal right to be officially known by her maiden name after marriage. New York journalist Ruth Hale (Mrs. Heywood Broun), 35, who has demanded that the State Department issue a passport in her maiden name, is elected president of the new organization, whose charter members include *New York Times* reporter Jane Grant (Mrs. Harold Ross); Hale promptly denounces a government ruling that married female federal employees must use their husbands' names.

 The British Medical Association estimates that a family of five needs 22s. 6½d. per week for food to maintain proper health, but as unemployment reaches its peak in July the dole is 29s. 3d. per week and rents in even the worst slum tenements average 6s. per week.

The National Federation of Business and Professional Women's Clubs holds its third annual convention in July and hears from the president of Mills College that 8 million American women— 1.9 million of them married—are gainfully employed: 50 percent are teachers, 37 percent have secretarial jobs, only 1,600 have law degrees. Only about 5 percent of medical students are women, and only 8 percent of U.S. hospitals accept female interns.

 Cincinnati aviatrix Laura Brownell, 23, sets a record for women in May by looping the loop 199 times but loses control of her plane June 5 and crashes to her death on Long Island.

 Viennese child psychologist Melanie Klein (*née* Reizes), 39, presents her first paper, "The Development of a Child," before the Hungarian Psycho-analytic Society. She will work on techniques for analyzing children using a psychoanalytic setting similar to that employed by Freud for adults, providing a child with a box of toys on the assumption that she or he will express herself/himself more eloquently in play than in words (see 1932).

The Sheppard-Towner Maternity and Infancy Protection Act, passed by Congress over opposition from the medical profession and signed into law by President Harding (above), aims to benefit poor women and their children by funding education in midwifery. Designed to aid mothers and infants and enacted after intense lobbying by women's reform organizations, it is the first federal health and welfare program, it establishes child-health and maternity consultation centers and "health mobiles" to educate mothers in prenatal care, it provides hospital facilities for problem pregnancies and deliveries, but Congress will not extend the act beyond 1929 (see Missouri, 1911; Children's Bureau, 1912).

More than half the children born in the District of Columbia, Hartford, Springfield, Mass., Minneapolis–St. Paul, Spokane, and San Francisco are delivered in hospitals; in Philadelphia, New York, and Cincinnati the figure is between 30 and 50 percent, but in Cleveland it is still only 22 percent.

The American Foundation for the Blind is founded with help from Helen Keller, now 41, and Anne Sullivan Macy, now 55.

Poliomyelitis (infantile paralysis) strikes former Assistant Secretary of the Navy Franklin Delano Roosevelt, now 39, in August at his vacation home on Campobello Island, New Brunswick. Roosevelt's wife, Eleanor, now 36, who has borne six children (one did not survive infancy), has not slept with him since 1918, when she discovered evidence confirming her suspicions that he was having an affair with her personal secretary, Lucy Page Mercer; when she offered to give him a divorce, his mother, Sarah, and political mentor, Louis Howe, said, respectively, that it would damage the family's reputation and weaken him politically. Eleanor loyally and compassionately nurses FDR through his illness, setting aside the hurt and resentment caused by his infidelity; since he will no longer be able to

walk, she will hereafter serve many times as his emissary.

The president of the U.S. Chamber of Commerce speaks out January 16 about the poor state of education, which he says has fallen below the standards of every other civilized country: of the 600,000 teachers in America, he tells the National Education Association, one-sixth are under 21, 30,000 have no education themselves beyond eighth grade, 150,000 have not gone beyond the third year in high school, and 450,000 U.S. children either have no classrooms or must learn in overcrowded classes.

The American Relief Administration obtains the release of Baltimore Sun correspondent Marguerite Harrison from a Russian prison in July (see 1920). Back home in Baltimore, she argues that Washington should recognize Russia's new Bolshevik government in America's own self interest.

The New York Times hires English-born U.S. freelance writer Anne O'Hare McCormick (née Anna Elizabeth O'Hare), 41, to write reports from Europe, to which she travels each year on her husband's business trips (see 1936).

"Tillie the Toiler" by U.S. cartoonist Russ Westover challenges the 2-year-old comic strip "Winnie Winkle."

Nonfiction: The Story of the Woman's Party by Inez Gillmore Irwin, who praises the courage of Alice Paul and Lucy Burns.

Fiction: The Mistress of Husaby (Husfrue) by Sigrid Undset; Morning Star (Stella matutina) by Ada Negri, whose autobiographical novel relates the struggles of her widowed mother, who worked 18-hour days at starvation wages in a silk factory to put her gifted daughter through normal school (teacher's college); Red Beacon (Dulze nombre) by Concha Espina de Serna; Tales and Legends by German poet-playwright Nelly Leonie Sachs, 30; Husband and Wife (Mann und Frau) by Helene Voigt-Diedrichs; Dangerous Ages by Rose Macaulay; Joanna Godden by Sheila Kaye-Smith; Mavis of Green Hill by U.S. novelist Faith Baldwin, 28, whose books will be serialized in magazines for women and be second in popularity only to those of Kathleen Norris (see 1911); Little Ships by Kathleen

Norris; *Half Loaves* by Margaret Culkin Banning; *Her Father's Daughter* by Gene Stratton Porter; *The Mysterious Affair at Styles* by English mystery writer Agatha (Mary Clarissa Miller) Christie, 30, introduces the detective Hercule Poirot, late of the Belgian Sûreté.

Poetry: *Nets to Catch the Wind* by U.S. poet-novelist Elinor Wylie (*née* Hoyt), 36; *Second April* by Edna St. Vincent Millay; *Poems* by Marianne Moore; *Hymen* by H.D. (Hilda Doolittle); *The Farmer's Bride* (*The Saturday Market*) by English poet Charlotte Mary Mew, 51; *At the Very Edge of the Sea* (*U samogo morya*) and *Anno Domini MCMXXI* by Anna Akhmatova, now 33, who has defied her father's objections to her career; *Mile II* (*Versty II*) by Marina Tsvetaeva.

Juvenile: *Rilla of Ingleside* by Maud Montgomery, who married a clergyman 10 years ago, moved to his manse in Ontario, and deals in her latest book with the impact of the Great War on a little island community; *Maida's Little House* by Inez Gillmore Irwin (above); *A Popular Schoolgirl* and *A Proper New Schoolgirl* by Angela Brazil.

Painting: *Femme-peintre and Her Model* by Marie Laurencin.

Etching: *Killed in Action* by Käthe Kollwitz.

Theater: Hazel Dawn in Wilson Collison and Avery Hopwood's *Getting Gertie's Garter* 8/21 at New York's Republic Theater, 120 perfs.; *A Bill of Divorcement* by Clemence Dane 3/14 at St. Martin's Theatre, London, with English actress Lilian Braithwaite, 48, as Margaret Fairfield, Malcolm Keen as her husband, Meggie Albanesi as her daughter, Sidney; Katharine Cornell, 23, plays the role of Sidney with Charles Waldron 10/10 at New York's George M. Cohan Theater 10/10, 173 perfs.; Pauline Lord plays the role of Anna Christopherson in Eugene O'Neill's *Anna Christie*, the story of a prostitute's fight for redemption, 11/2 at New York's Vanderbilt Theater, 177 perfs.

Britain's George V makes May Witty, now 56, a Dame of the British Empire in recognition of her success at raising money for the war effort in America and her native Australia. She is the first actress to be so honored.

Films: Carol Dempster and Ralph Graves in D. W. Griffith's *Dream Street*; Lillian Gish, Lowell Sherman, and Richard Barthelmess in Griffith's *Way Down East*; Mary Pickford in Alfred E. Green and Jack Pickford's *Little Lord Fauntleroy;* Jackie Coogan, Edna Purviance, 26, and Charlie Chaplin in Chaplin's *The Kid.*

Isadora Duncan opens a Moscow school for the dance at the invitation of the Soviet government (*see* 1905). Now 43, Duncan meets and marries Russian poet Sergei Aleksandrovich Esenin, 26, who 2 years ago founded the Imagist group and is known as the "poet laureate of the Revolution." He and Duncan, neither speaking the other's language, will tour the United States; many will call them Bolshevist spies (*see* 1927).

Stage musicals: Florence Mills, 25, and teenager Josephine Baker in the all-black revue *Shuffle Along* 5/23 at New York's 63rd Street Music Hall, with Eubie Blake–Noble Sissle songs that include "Love Will Find a Way" and "I'm Just Wild About Harry," 504 perfs.; Fanny Brice in *The Ziegfeld Follies* 6/21 at New York's Globe Theater, with Brice singing the torch song "My Man" published at Paris last year under the title "Mon Homme" and made poignant by the fact that Brice is married to gambler Nick Arnstein; Ann Pennington in (George White's) *Scandals* 7/11 at New York's Liberty Theater with music by George Gershwin, 97 perfs.; *The Greenwich Village Follies* 8/31 at New York's Shubert Theater, with Ted Lewis, songs that include "Three O'Clock in the Morning" by Spanish composer Julian Robledo, 34, lyrics by New York lyricist Dolly Morse (Dorothy Terrio), 31, 167 perfs.; *Blossom Time* 9/21 at New York's Ambassador Theater, with book and lyrics by Dorothy Donnelly, who has adapted the German operetta *Das Dreimädelhaus,* based on the life of composer Franz Schubert, music by Sigmund Romberg, 592 perfs.; Lenore Ulric, 24, in *Kiki* 11/29 at New York's Belasco Theater, with songs that include "Some Day I'll Find You," 600 perfs.

Opera: Amalita Galli-Curci makes her Metropolitan Opera debut 11/14 in the 1853 Verdi opera *La Traviata* (she will be a regular member of the Met company until January 1930).

Suzanne Lenglen wins in women's singles at Wimbledon, Molla Bjurstedt Mallory in women's singles at the West Side Tennis Club courts in Forest Hills, N.Y.

Chanel No. 5, introduced May 5 by "Coco" Chanel, has none of the "feminine" floral scent found in other fragrances and will become the world's leading perfume (*see* 1913).

Drano is introduced by Cincinnati's P. W. Drackett & Sons, whose drain cleaner consists of crystals containing sodium hydroxide (caustic lye). The company was founded in 1910 by Philip Wilbur Drackett to distribute chemicals (*see* 1933).

Electrolux vacuum cleaners are introduced by Swedish electric lamp salesman Axel Wenner-Gren, 40, who has founded the Electrolux Co. to produce the machines that will be the world's top-performing vacuum cleaners. Wenner-Gren's company will also be a major factor in refrigerators.

U.S. cigarette consumption reaches 43 billion, up from 10 billion in 1910 despite the fact that cigarettes are illegal in 14 states. Anticigarette bills are pending in 28 other states, college girls are expelled for smoking, but tobacco companies promote the addiction to nicotine.

A French court sentences Henri-Désiré Landru, 52, to death December 1. Nicknamed "Bluebeard," he has allegedly promised marriage to 10 women and then murdered them, although no bodies have been produced (he has also killed a boy). Landru will be executed in February of next year.

Kate Gleason sells six-room concrete-block houses for $4,000 (*see* 1920). Included are built-in mirrors, bookcases, ironing boards, and gas ranges (*see* 1927).

U.S. landscape gardener Beatrix Farrand (*née* Jones), 49, begins work on the gardens of Dumbarton Oaks—the Georgetown, D.C., estate purchased last year by diplomat Robert Woods Bliss and his wife, Mildred. A niece of novelist Edith Wharton, Farrand traveled in 1895 to England, where she visited the gardens of Gertrude Jekyll and Vita Sackville-West. She has designed gardens for Wharton's estate at Lenox, Mass., the White House, Princeton University, and her own Reef Point family estate at Seal Harbor on Mount Desert Island, Me. Farrand will continue work on Dumbarton Oaks until 1947 as she accepts commissions, also, from Yale, Oberlin, the University of Chicago, Vassar, Hamilton College, Occidental College, the California Institute of Technology, and millionaires such as Herbert Satterlee, Gerrish Milliken, and Abby Aldrich Rockefeller (whose estate at Seal Harbor, on Mount Desert Island, Me., is close to Reef Point).

U.S. women arrive at Moscow November 24 to assist in famine relief.

The name "Betty Crocker" is developed by Washburn, Crosby Co. of Minneapolis. The firm runs a contest to promote its Gold Medal Flour, and letters from contestants are answered by the fictitious food authority Betty Crocker (*see* 1936).

SMA, the first commercial infant formula, is introduced by Wyeth, a U.S. company that will become part of American Home Products. Competing brands (Similac, Enfamil, Isomil, etc.) will come onto the market, mothers will be encouraged to bottle-feed their babies, and breast-feeding will decline sharply (*see* La Leche League, 1956).

The Mothers' Clinic for Constructive Birth Control opens March 17 off the Holloway Road in North London. Founder of the first British birth control clinic is Marie Stopes (*see* 1918); her 1918 book *Wise Motherhood* called family planning the basis of a truly fulfilled marriage, her new Society for Constructive Birth Control and Racial Progress puts pressure on government officials to provide working-class women with effective means of family planning, and her clinic gives out free advice and contraceptive aids (sponges, cervical caps, and suppositories). Stopes says coitus interruptus is extremely unreliable, physically and psychologically dangerous, and has deleterious side effects; she opposes the douche as possibly harmful, calls the condom unromantic and unaesthetic, and makes her staff take an oath promising not to provide any information on how to induce miscarriage (*see* 1923).

British census results reported August 23 show a population increase of nearly 2 million, since 1911; women outnumber men by 2 million, but the ratio remains virtually the same as before the Great War.

Margaret Sanger and Mary Ware Dennet found the American Birth Control League November 2 (*see* 1916; 1923).

1922

Chinese Communist Xiang Jianyu, now 27, establishes a Women's Department in the Party and serves as its first director (*see* 1916). She participated in the 4th of May Movement in 1919, worked in a French textile mill the following year, studied the writings of Karl Marx, was married last year, and wrote a thesis on the emancipation and transformation of women (*see* 1927).

The U.S. Supreme Court rules unanimously February 27 that the 19th Amendment, granting suffrage to women, is not unconstitutional, as some opponents have charged (*see* 1920).

Women in the Canadian province of Prince Edward's Island gain the right to vote in provincial elections (*see* 1919; Quebec, 1940).

The Women's Trade Union League elects Maud Swartz, now 43, as its president in June. She has worked since last year as U.S. vice president of the International Federation of Working Women and is the first working-class head of the WTUL. (Her predecessor, Margaret Dreier Robbins, who held the job for 15 years, was a rich woman who could contribute money of her own and raise more from others; Swartz cannot play that role but will nevertheless prove an effective leader of the organization.)

The Cable Act signed into law by President Harding grants independent citizenship to married women.

Ida Wells Bennett, now 60, travels to Arkansas to investigate reports of black prisoners being tortured with electric prongs. Whites from neighboring states came to Helena and broke up a meeting of black sharecroppers attempting to form a union, the black men were tried and convicted, 67 were given long prison terms, 12 sentenced to death. No one but a family member is permitted to go inside the prison to see the convicts, but Bennnet, who has been writing about the case in the *Chicago Defender*, gets in touch with family members of the prisoners, poses as a cousin of one man to get inside, and gathers details of what happened. Within a year the Supreme Court will rule that the men did not get a fair trial, and subsequently all will be set free.

Britain gets her first woman barrister as Dr. Ivy Williams of Oxford is called to the bar. The nation has 3,619 divorces, up from 823 in 1911.

Japanese schoolteachers obtain maternity leave in October, but only a minority of pregnant working teachers take the maximum time off permitted before the birth of a child.

Globe circler "Nellie Bly" (Elizabeth Cochrane Seaman) dies of pneumonia at New York January 27 at age 54 (*see* Kilgallen, 1936).

A mail plane from San Francisco arrives at Long Island's Curtiss Field October 8 carrying Lilian Gatlin, who becomes the first woman to cross the continent by airplane. Gatlin has made the 2,680-mile flight in 27 hours, 11 minutes to publicize the National Association of Aviation Gold Mothers, which she has founded to honor flyers, male and female, who have given their lives "on the altar of patriotism and progress in pursuit of an ideal."

The Bas (Bat) Mitzvah ceremony introduced in America by the Society for Advancement of Judaism (the Reconstructionist movement) is a feminine version of the Bar Mitzvah that has honored 13-year-old Jewish boys since the 14th century. Used primarily in Conservative congregations, it will also be used to some extent in Orthodox synagogues and Reform temples, signifying an increase in young women's education and their broader role outside the home.

Skidmore College for Women is founded at Saratoga Springs, N.Y., as an outgrowth of an art school started in 1911 (*see* 1903). It granted its first bachelor's degrees in 1919, has changed its corporate name, and by 1925 will have 168 students housed in a cluster of old buildings. By the time of benefactor Lucy Skidmore Scribner's death in May 1931, Skidmore will have an enrollment of more than 600, a faculty of 79, and 16 buildings.

The *Reader's Digest* begins publication in February at New York. Canadian-born social worker Lila

Bell Acheson Wallace, 32, has helped her husband, De Witt, whom she married in October of last year, to condense articles "of lasting interest" and collect them in a pocket-size magazine, containing no advertising, whose circulation of 1,500 will grow to more than 200,000 by 1929 and eventually to 29 million in 13 languages. Although its readership will be overwhelmingly female, the *Digest* will not be averse to publishing off-color stories; for years to come it will show a marked bias in favor of Europe's rising totalitarian governments and against both Jews and Roman Catholics.

Former *Baltimore Sun* correspondent Marguerite Harrison sets sail for Yokohama from Vancouver in June with a magazine assignment to write a series about conditions in the Far East (*see* 1921). She spends 2 months in Tokyo, sails in late July for the town of Aleksandrovsk in northern Sakhalin, and proceeds to Vladivostok, Beijing, and—by automobile—across the Gobi Desert. Arrested at Chita on orders from Moscow, she is put aboard the Trans-Siberian Railway, returned to Lubyanka Prison, but eventually released through the agency, once again, of the American Relief Administration, which is supplying U.S. food to the famine-stricken Russians.

Nonfiction: *Etiquette—The Blue Book of Social Usage* by New York divorcée Emily Post (*née* Price), 48, who has found the manners of Americans far inferior to those of their social counterparts in Europe.

Fiction: U.S. bookseller Sylvia Beach, 35, publishes James Joyce's new novel *Ulysses* under the imprint of her Paris bookshop's name, Shakespeare & Co. All reputable publishers have refused the stream-of-consciousness account of a day in the lives of Dubliner Leopold Bloom and his wife, Molly, but Beach, whose talent for bringing French, English, and U.S. writers together is making her store an intellectual center, has helped Joyce edit his disjointed manuscript, which he has continued revising to the last, even adding another one-third when it was in page proofs. *One of Ours* by Willa Cather (Pulitzer Prize); *The Garden Party and Other Stories* by Katherine Mansfield; *1492* by Mary Johnston is about Christopher Columbus and is her most successful work; *Silver Cross* by Mary Johnston is about England's Henry VII; *The Cross* (*Korset*) by

Sigrid Undset completes her *Kristin Lavransdatter* trilogy (she will be converted to Roman Catholicism in 1924 and win the 1928 Nobel Prize for literature); *The Nameless One* (*Den namnlösa*) by Elin Wägner; *The Change* (*Bermena*) by Marietta Shaginyan; *Jacob's Room* by English novelist Virginia Woolf (*née* Stephen), 40, who 5 years ago set up the Hogarth Press with her husband, Leonard (they have made their London home the center of the Bloomsbury Group); *Seven for a Secret* by Mary Webb; *The Judge* by Rebecca West; *Man and Maid* by Elinor Glyn, who will spend the next 5 years in Hollywood; *The Clash* by Storm Jameson; *Spellbinders* by Margaret Culkin Banning; *One Thing Is Certain* by Sophie Kerr; *Jigsaw* by London postdebutante (Mary) Barbara (Hamilton) Cartland, 21, whose first novel enjoys huge success and launches her on a long career: "I think the reason my generation bobbed and shingled their hair, flattened their bosoms, and lowered their waists," she will say, "was not that we wanted to be masculine, but that we didn't want to be emotional. War widows, many of them still wearing crepe and widows' weeds in the Victorian tradition, had full bosoms, full skirts, and fluffed-out hair. To shingle was to cut loose from the maternal pattern; it was an anti-sentiment symbol, not an anti-feminine one."

Poetry: *Clouds* (*Moln*) by Swedish poet Karin Maria Boye, 22; *Mile I* (*Versty I*), *Poems to Blok* (*Stikhi k Bloku*), *The King-Maiden* (*Tsar' devitsa*), and *Parting* (*Razluka*) by Marina Tsvetaeva; *Bonnie Joann* by Violet Jacob; *Desolaçion* by Gabriela Mistral; *Maternità* by Ada Negri; *Bronze: A Book of Verse* by Georgia Douglas Camp Johnson.

Juvenile: *Gerry Goes to School* by English author Elinor Mary Brent-Dyer, 28, is the first of 98 "Chalet School" girls' stories; *The Velveteen Rabbit* by U.S. author Margery Bianco (*née* Williams). 41.

Painting: *Nude* by Suzanne Valadon.

Sculpture: *The Sacrifice* (war monument) by Melvina Hoffman.

Theater: U.S. actress Florence Eldridge (originally McKechnie), 20, and Henry Hull in John Willard's *The Cat and the Canary* 2/7 at New York's National Theater; *To the Ladies* by Marc Connelly and George S. Kaufman 2/20 at New York's Liberty

Theater, 128 perfs.; English actress Margaret Wycherley and Dennis King in George Bernard Shaw's *Back to Methusaleh* 2/27 at New York's Garrick Theater, 72 perfs.; *Abie's Irish Rose* by U.S. playwright Anne Nichols, 30, 5/23 at New York's Fulton Theater, a play about a mixed marriage, 2,532 perfs. (a new record); Mary Blair plays a butterfly, Vinton Freedly a male cricket in Karel and Josef Capek's *The World We Live In* (*The Insect Comedy*) 10/31 at New York's Al Jolson Theater, 112 perfs.; Jeanne Eagels (Aguilar), 30, plays the role of Somerset Maugham's Sadie Thompson in John Colton and Clemence Randolph's *Rain* 11/7 at New York's Maxine Elliott Theater, 321 perfs.; Ruth Gilmore, Howard Lindsay, and Ronald Young in Marc Connelly and George S. Kaufman's *The '49ers* 11/13 at New York's Cort Theater, 16 perfs.; *The Texas Nightingale* by U.S. playwright Zoë Akins, 36, 11/20 at New York's Empire Theater, 31 perfs.

"Texas" Guinan begins her career as Prohibition-era New York nightclub hostess. Mary Louise Cecilia Guinan, 38, goes to work as mistress of ceremonies at the Café des Beaux Arts and is soon hired away by Larry Fay of El Fey, from whose club she will move to the Rendezvous, 300 Club, Argonaut, Century, Salon Royal, and Club Intime, and to several Texas Guinan Clubs that will serve bootleg Scotch at $25 a fifth, bootleg champagne at $25 a bottle, plain water at $2 a pitcher. The clubs will charge from $5 to $25 cover to the "butter-and-egg men"; Texas Guinan ("Give the little girl a great big hand") will welcome customers from her seat atop a piano with the cry "Hello, sucker!"

Films: Dorothy and Lillian Gish in D. W. Griffith's *Orphans of the Storm*; Gloria Swanson in Cecil B. DeMille's *Beyond the Rocks* with Rudolph Valentino; Alice Terry and Lewis Stone in Rex Ingram's *The Prisoner of Zenda*.

Opera: Soviet mezzo-soprano Mariya Maxikova (*née* Petrovna), 20, makes her debut singing the role of Amneris in the 1871 Verdi opera *Aïda* at Moscow's Bolshoi Theater. Australian soprano Florence Austral (Florence Wilson), 28, makes her London debut 5/16 at Covent Garden singing the role of Brünnhilde in the 1870 Wagner opera *Die Walküre* (she has heretofore sung under the name

Prohibition was honored in the breach; women as well as men delighted in evading the law. LIBRARY OF CONGRESS

Fawaz, her stepfather's name). By the end of the season she has appeared in the Brünnhilde role in the entire Wagnerian Ring; Tamaki Miura makes her Metropolitan Opera debut.

Broadway musicals: Janet Adair, Fred Allen, and Eugene and Willie Howard in *The Passing Show* 9/20 at the Winter Garden Theater, with songs that include "Carolina in the Morning" by Walter Donaldson, lyrics by Gus Kahn, 95 perfs.; Elizabeth Hines in George M. Cohan's *Little Nellie Kelly* 11/13 at the Liberty Theater, 276 perfs.

Lillian Russell (Moore) dies at Pittsburgh June 5 at age 60.

Sharpshooter Annie Oakley, now 61, smashes 98 out of 100 clay pigeons March 5 at North Carolina's Pinehurst Gun Club, breaking all records. Her hair turned completely white in 17 hours after she was involved in a train accident 21 years ago, another such accident last year has put her into a brace, and she has melted down her hundreds of gold medals in order to raise money for a children's home in the South.

Suzanne Lenglen wins in women's singles at Wimbledon, Molla Bjurstedt Mallory in U.S. women's singles.

The U.S. Field Hockey Association is founded to govern standards of play for women in schools, clubs, and colleges. It will sponsor sectional and national tournaments.

Mah-jongg is introduced in America, where a nationwide craze begins for the ancient Chinese game. The 144-tile sets will outsell radios within a year.

French couturiers revive full-length skirts.

The Maytag Gyrofoam washing machine introduced by the Newton, Iowa, firm outperforms all other washing machines yet takes up only 425 square inches of floor space (see 1907). Now 65, F. L. Maytag has built his own aluminum foundry to cast the tubs for his new machine.

A San Francisco jury acquits film comedian Roscoe C. "Fatty" Arbuckle of murder April 12 after deliberating only one minute. After Arbuckle, 35, attended a Labor Day party at the St. Francis Hotel last year one of the other guests, actress Virginia Rappe, complained of stomach pains and died a few days later of a ruptured bladder. It is rumored that Arbuckle raped her with a champagne bottle, distributors have withdrawn his pictures, and Paramount has fired him.

The Hall-Mills murder case makes world headlines. Children looking for mushrooms in a field across the Raritan River from New Brunswick, N.J., early in the morning of September 16 find the bodies of overweight clergyman Edward H. Hall, 44, and a member of his church choir, Eleanor Mills, 34, wife of a local gardener and mother of two. Both have been shot in the head, they have been dead for 36

hours, and police find notes suggesting that they have been lovers (Hall's widow, Frances, is a Johnson & Johnson heiress and about 20 years his senior) (see 1926).

London housewife Edith Thompson goes on trial at the Old Bailey on charges of having, with her accomplice, Frederick Bywaters, stabbed her husband on his way home from the theater. The trial creates a tabloid sensation, both defendants are found guilty, and they will be executed next year despite repeated petitions for reprieve.

1923

Britain's moody, neurotic Prince Albert, duke of York, is married April 23 at Westminster Abbey to Elizabeth Bowes-Lyon, 22, who has overcome her initial reluctance to marry the prince with his speech defect and nervous tics. She is the first commoner to marry a prince of the realm since 1660, and he is the first son of a king to be married in Westminster Abbey since 1382.

President Harding dies August 23 and is succeeded by his laconic vice president, Calvin Coolidge, whose wife, Grace, is a onetime teacher of the deaf and mute. "That made it easier for her to live with Calvin," says Washington wit Alice Roosevelt Longworth, who will soon become a great friend of the new chief executive and his wife.

Turkish military leader Gen. Mustafa Kemal, 42, is elected president by an assembly at Ankara and begins turning Turkey into a modern nation in which women will no longer wear veils as they have since the founding of the now-defunct Ottoman Empire in 1290 and for centuries before that (although there was nothing in the Koran that required veils).

Scottish Conservative Katherine Marjory, duchess of Atholl, 49, is elected to Parliament as representative for Kinross and Perthshire. An early opponent of woman suffrage, she will become the first woman Conservative minister next year, serving until 1929 as parliamentary secretary to the board of education and then campaigning until 1939 for better treatment of women and children throughout the Empire.

Countess Markievicz, now 55, canvasses for signatures on a petition calling for the release of Irish Republican prisoners and is arrested November 20 by British detectives at Dublin (*see* 1921). A hunger striker dies that day at Newbridge Prison and the countess herself, who is held without charges, refuses food at the North Dublin Union, a detention camp for women that opened in June. She is released December 24 and will continue speaking for the Women's Prisoners Defense League, Fianna, labor, and other causes until her death from peritonitis following an appendectomy in July 1927.

The House of Commons votes 231 to 27 March 2 to adopt the Matrimonial Causes bill.

A minimum wage law for women in the District of Columbia passed by Congress in 1918 is unconstitutional, the Supreme Court rules April 9 in the case of *Adkins* v. *Children's Hospital* (*see* 1937).

The National Woman's party founded by Alice Paul in 1913 meets at Seneca Falls, N.Y., and endorses an Equal Rights Amendment drafted by Paul, who calls it the Lucretia Mott amendment. Suffragist and labor reformer Maud Younger, 53, works with young Lili Pollitzer and others to effect passage of the amendment.

Aimee Semple McPherson dedicates Angelus Temple of the Four-Square Gospel at Los Angeles January 1 with a plaque overhead that reads "Jesus Christ, the same yesterday, and today, and forever" and a large rotating illuminated cross visible for 50 miles (*see* 1918). McPherson uses special effects to produce thunder, lightning, and wind that illustrate her "foursquare gospel" and help fill her 5,300-seat auditorium. To fundamentalists who quoted I Timothy 2:11–12 ("Let the woman learn in silence with all subjection, but I suffer not a woman to teach, nor to usurp authority over the man, but to be in silence"), she has replied, "Woman brought sin into the world, didn't she? Then surely she should have the right to undo the wrong and lead the world to the Eden above. Woman's personality, her tender sympathies, her simple, direct message—the woman, motherheart, working over the world, yearning to help its wayward sons and daughters—these are all qualities in favor of her right to tell the story of God's love. . . . Women were co-laborers with Peter and Paul in their work. But did not the apostle say, 'Let your women keep silence in the churches'? Yes, but he did not refer to a godly woman's right to preach the eternal Gospel, for he also gives specific instructions as to how a woman should conduct herself while preaching or praying in public. The best reason in favor of a woman's right to preach the Gospel is that God's favor has attended it and blessed results follow" (*see* 1926).

Her faithful followers had no idea what Los Angeles evangelist Aimee Semple MacPherson did in private. LIBRARY OF CONGRESS

Bethune-Cookman College is founded at Daytona, Fla., by a merger of Mary McLeod Bethune's 19-year-old Daytona Normal and Industrial Institute for Negro Girls with the Cookman Institute for Men at Jacksonville. Bethune will head the college until 1942, making its slogan "Enter to Learn, Depart to Serve" (*see* 1936).

Mary McLeod Bethune pioneered education for Florida women of her race and fought for civil rights. GORDON PARKS PHOTO, LIBRARY OF CONGRESS

Radcliffe College gets its first full-time president: Smith graduate Ada Louise Comstock, 46, will serve until her retirement in 1943, whereupon she will marry her longtime suitor, Wallace Notestein, a Yale professor emeritus.

Washington, D.C., housewife Elisabeth May Craig (*née* Adams), 34, virtually takes over the newspaper column "On the Inside in Washington" after her husband, Donald, is severely injured in an auto accident. Dressed in blue and wearing flowered hats so that she will be remembered at press conferences, May Craig will be a prominent Capitol correspondent for decades.

Nonfiction: *Woman Suffrage and Politics, the Inner Study of the Suffrage Movement* by Carrie Chapman Catt (with N. R. Shuler); *His Religion and Hers; A Study of the Faith of Our Fathers and the Work of Our Mothers* by Charlotte Perkins Gilman.

Fiction: *A Lost Lady* by Willa Cather; *Black Oxen* by Gertrude Atherton is about a woman of a certain age who receives rejuvenating hormone injections and takes a lover 20 years her junior; *Jennifer Lorn* by Elinor Wylie; *The Dove's Nest and Other Stories* by the late Katherine Mansfield, who has died of tuberculosis in France January 9 at age 34; *The Conquered* by British writer Naomi Margaret Mitchison (*née* Haldane), 26, whose novels about ancient Greece, Sparta, and Egypt will be based on lore acquired in her travels; *The Innocents or the Wisdom of Women* (*Les Innocentes ou la sagesse des femmes*) by Anna, comtesse de Noailles; *Love of Worker Bees* (stories) by revolutionary Aleksandra Kollontai, who writes openly about sexuality and women's role in social and economic life; *Told by an Idiot* by Rose Macaulay; *The End of the House of Alard* by Sheila Kaye-Smith, now 36, who will marry a clergyman next year and convert to Roman Catholicism in 1929; *The Able McLaughlins* by Margaret Wilson, now 41 (Pulitzer Prize; Wilson, whose father has just died, freeing her from nursing cares, sails for Europe and marries George Douglas Turner, a onetime YMCA secretary whom she met at Lahore when she was a missionary in the Punjab; he served as a British spy in the Great War and has obtained a divorce from heiress Mary Borden); *Faint Perfume* by Zona Gale, who helps write the new Wisconsin Equal Rights Law; *Lummox* by U.S. novelist Fannie Hurst, 33; *Country Club People* by Margaret Culkin Banning; *Weeds* by Ontario-born U.S. novelist Edith Summers Kelley, 39, who completes the novel about impoverished Kentucky tobacco farmers on the alfalfa farm that she and her husband are running without much success in California's Imperial Valley (they failed in a Kentucky farming venture from 1914 to 1916; *see* 1974); *Croat* by Mary Johnston is about Sir Walter Raleigh's lost Virginia colony; *The Shoreless Sea* by English novelist Molly (Patricia) Panter-Downes, 17; *Whose Body?* by English novelist Dorothy L. (Leigh) Sayers, 30 (one of the first women graduates of Oxford), introduces the amateur detective Lord Peter Wimsey.

Poetry: *The Harp-Weaver and Other Poems* by Edna St. Vincent Millay, who marries and moves to

Austerlitz, N.Y., in the Berkshires: "Euclid alone has looked on Beauty bare" (Sonnet 22, II, 11–12); *Marriage* by Marianne Moore; *Body of This Death* by U.S. poet Louise Bogan, 26; *Knights Errant and Other Poems* by U.S. nun Sister Mary Madaleva (*née* Mary Evaline Wolff), who in 1908 joined the congregation of the Holy Cross, which runs St. Mary's College of Notre Dame in Indiana; *Psyche* (*Psikheia*) and *Craft* (*Remeslo*) by Marina Tsvetaeva.

Juvenile: *Real Fairies* by English writer Enid Blyton, 23.

Painting: *Still Life with Violin* by Suzanne Valadon; *Portrait of André Salmon* (a prominent art critic), *Portrait of Jeannot Salmon*, and *Portrait of Baronne Gourgaud* by Marie Laurencin.

Theater: Ann Trevor, Herbert Marshall, and Coward in Noël Coward's *The Young Idea* 2/1 at London's Savoy Theatre, 60 perfs.; Boots Wooster in Owen Davis's *Icebound* 2/10 at New York's Sam Harris Theater, 171 perfs.; Lucile Watson in Philip Barry's *You and I* 2/19 at New York's Belmont Theater, 140 perfs.; Helen Westley, Dudley Digges (as Mr. Zero), and Edward G. Robinson (as Shrdlu) in Elmer Rice's *The Adding Machine* 3/9 at New York's Garrick Theater, 72 perfs.; Annette Margules as Tondeleyo in Leon Gordon's *White Cargo* 11/5 at New York's Greenwich Village Theater, 678 perfs.; Winifred Lenihan in George Bernard Shaw's *Saint Joan* 12/28 at New York's Garrick Theater, 214 perfs.: "Woman [is] the female of the human species, and not a different kind of animal," Shaw has written in a preface.

Sarah Bernhardt dies at Paris March 26 at age 79.

George Burns and Gracie Allen form a new comedy team. Gracie (Grace Ethel Cecile Rosalie Allen), 17, has married Burns (Nathan Bimbaum), 27, and will play his stooge for 30 years.

Films: Natalie Talmadge and Buster Keaton in Keaton's *Our Hospitality*. Also: Blanche Sweet in John Griffith Wray's *Anna Christie*; Estelle Taylor, Nita Naldi, Theodore Robert, and Richard Dix in Cecil B. DeMille's *The Ten Commandments*; Alice Terry and Ramon Novarro in Rex Ingram's *Where the Pavement Ends*; Edna Purviance, 29, and Adolphe Menjou in Charles Chaplin's *A Woman of Paris*.

Paramount Studios names Edith Head, 18, chief designer. She will head the entire designing department beginning in 1938, will switch to Universal Pictures in 1967, and will continue working until well into the 1970s.

Ballet: Edith Sitwell reads her poetry in *Façade* 6/12 at London's Aeolian Hall, music by English composer William Walton, 21; Felicia Dubrovska dances in *Les Noces* (*The Wedding*) 6/14 at the Théâtre Gaiété-Lyrique, Paris, with music and lyrics by Igor Stravinsky, choreography by Bronislava Nijinska.

Stage musicals: Gertrude Lawrence (Gertrud Alexandra Dagmar Lawrence Klasen), 24, in André Charlot's revue *Rats* 2/21 at London's Vaudeville Theatre; Helen Ford in *Helen of Troy, N.Y.* 6/19 at New York's Selwyn Theater, 191 perfs.; seminude showgirls appear with Frank Fay in *Artists and Models* 8/20 at New York's Shubert Theater, 312 perfs.; Gertrude Lawrence and Noël Coward in André Charlot's revue *London Calling* 9/4 at the Duke of York's Theatre, London, music and lyrics mostly by Coward, songs that include Eubie Blake and Noble Sissle's "You Were Meant for Me"; Grace Moore in Irving Berlin's *The Music Box Revue* 9/22 at New York's Music Box Theater, 273 perfs.; Fanny Brice with Paul Whiteman and his Orchestra in *The Ziegfeld Follies* 10/20 at New York's New Amsterdam Theater, 233 perfs.

Popular songs: "Down-Hearted Blues" by U.S. songwriter-blues singer Alberta Hunter (Josephine Beatty), 24, lyrics by Lovie Austin (Philadelphia blues singer Bessie Smith, 23, records the song, which has sales of 2 million copies); blues singer "Ma" Rainey (*née* Gertrude Pridgett), 37, cuts her first recordings, including some songs whose lyrics she has written herself, others with lyrics by the Rev. Thomas A. Dorsey, and begins to gain a following among northern blacks (she and her husband, Will "Pa" Rainey, have toured the South with minstrel troupes for nearly 20 years); "Mexicali Rose" by Jack B. Tenny, lyrics by Helen Stone.

Dance marathons become a U.S. craze. A Cleveland girl dances for more than 50 hours, wearing out five male partners and losing 24 pounds (from 113 pounds to 89) while her ankles swell to twice their original size. Baltimore police stop a marathon after 53 hours.

Suzanne Lenglen wins in women's singles at Wimbledon, Helen Newington Wills, 17, in U.S. women's singles.

The Wightman Cup donated by Hazel Hotchkiss Wightman for the winner of a U.S.-British women's tennis tournament will do for women's tennis what the Davis Cup is doing for men's.

Maiden Form brassieres are introduced by four-foot-eleven-inch Russian-American entrepreneur Ida Rosenthal (*née* Kagonovich), 36, who last year bought a half interest in a fashionable dress shop in New York's West 57th Street (*see* 1914). She and her English-American partner Enid Bissett have given away sample brassieres with a little uplift because they did not like the fit of their dresses on flat-chested "flappers." Rosenthal, whose family changed its name to Cohen when it came to America in 1904, married William Rosenthal in 1906, and together they invest $4,500 to incorporate the Maiden Form Brassiere Co. He is an amateur sculptor, and as head of production he designs a precursor to cup sizing (*see* 1940). By 1938 their firm will have revenues of $4.5 million, and by the 1960s the gross will be $40 million.

U.S. fashion designers introduce new styles in November that emphasize corduroy, flannel, and knitted fabrics, with hemlines 10 inches from the floor.

Mabel Dodge, in Taos, N.M., falls in love with Tony Luhan, a Pueblo Indian. He becomes her fourth husband (*see* 1916). She tries to re-create her New York salon of 1912–1915, inviting visitors who include painter Georgia O'Keeffe and novelist D. H. Lawrence, with whose wife, Frieda, she will compete.

Paris bread prices rise in May to their highest levels since 1870.

British housewives boycott sugar and tea in May, saying they are overpriced.

 A supermarket of sorts opens in San Francisco, where a large steel-frame building opens on the site of a former baseball field and circus ground with 68,000 square feet of selling space and room to park 4,350 automobiles (shoppers are offered free parking for one hour). The Crystal Palace sells food, drugs, cigarettes, and jewelry and has a beauty parlor and dry cleaner.

The *Practitioner*, a British medical journal, deals openly with the subject of contraception for the first time in its July issue. Lady Florence E. Barrett writes, "To attempt to lower the number of the efficient while the inefficient multiply spells disaster in the future."

The American Birth Control League opens the Sanger Research Bureau with a birth control clinic in Sanger's New York house at 17 West 16th Street, where it will remain for 50 years. Sanger, who says birth control is essentially education for women, persuades ABCL president James F. Cooper and his associate Herbert Simonds to start Holland-Rantos, the first U.S. company to manufacture rubber diaphragm contraceptives for women (*see* Wilde, 1833; Sanger, 1921). While the diaphragm, like the sponge and the cervical cap, provides women with a means of avoiding pregnancy independent of a man's use of a condom, it must be professionally fitted by a physician and is too expensive for most women (*see* 1929).

Dr. Marie Stopes in London, who, like Sanger (above), opposes abortion, brings libel charges against Dr. Halliday Sutherland, who has alleged that her campaign encourages women's immorality and that she uses the poor as guinea pigs for her contraceptive experiments (*see* 1921). A jury brushes aside the summation by the judge, who calls her 1918 book *Married Love* "obscene," and awards Dr. Stopes £100 in damages. Stopes is actually just as interested in raising fertility among the upper classes as she is in lowering it among the lower classes, accepting the eugenic argument that the struggle for survial is being reversed with the "unfit" outbreeding the "fit" and thus putting the nation at risk of racial suicide. She views birth control as a means of elevating women among the ignorant and unskilled lower classes, limiting the growth of such classes; the working-class woman, she says, must be taught birth control because "such knowledge is not only essential to her private well-being, but essential to her in the fulfillment of her duties as a citizen," but her London clinic does not attract many women.

V. I. Lenin dies of sclerosis January 21 at age 53, survived by his widow, the former Nadezhda Konstantinovna Krupskaya (*see* 1901).

Former Texas governor Miriam A. "Ma" Ferguson, now 49, runs for governor in her own right and is elected, becoming the first woman to win a state governorship (*see* 1917). She has campaigned on promises to exonerate her husband, weaken the power of the Ku Klux Klan, and bring the state budget under control. Although she will not be able to reduce state spending, she will push through a law forbidding anyone (including a Klan member) to wear a mask in public, get the legislature to grant her husband "legislative amnesty" (which will later be ruled unconstitional), and grant executive clemency to 3,500 prisoners.

Nellie Tayloe Ross is inaugurated as governor of Wyoming, becoming the second woman governor.

French Orientalist Alexandra David-Neel (née David), 56, arrives at the forbidden Tibetan capital of Lhasa in February, becoming the first European woman to enter the city. A onetime opera singer who in 1904 married the chief engineer for French railways in Tunisia, she has had her travels financed by her husband, Philip, at Tunis. She was long ago converted to Buddhism and has learned the Tibetan language; disguised as a beggar and accompanied by a young man whom she has adopted in China's Yunan province, David-Neel has defied cold, hunger, dysentery, bandits, and British-Chinese orders barring Westerners from entering Tibet, but her weight has dropped from 180 pounds to a mere 90, and she leaves Lhasa after 2 months.

U.S. explorer Delia J. (Julia) Akeley (née Denning), 48, sets out with native porters October 24 to make the first foot safari across the African landmass. Having divorced her first husband at age 27 to marry explorer Carl Akeley, then 38, she divorced Akeley last year (he marries another woman October 26 and will die in November 1926 on an expedition for the American Museum of Natural History to collect mountain gorillas in the Belgian Congo). The white-haired Mrs. Akeley has obtained sponsorship from the Brooklyn Museum of Arts and Sciences but does not know her porters' language and is scarcely able to communicate with them (*see* 1925).

U.S. physician George Frederick Dick, 43, and his wife, Gladys Rowena (née Henry), 42, isolate the streptococcus that incites scarlet fever. They will devise the Dick skin test for susceptibility to the disease.

Princess Marie Bonaparte, now 42, travels to Vienna to obtain psychoanalysis from Sigmund Freud, whose work has attracted great attention in Parisian intellectual circles. She becomes Freud's friend and will be a founder of the Paris Psychoanalytic Society but will have no reply to Freud in the mid-1930s when he says, "The great question that has never been answered and which I have not yet been able to answer, despite my thirty years of research into the feminine soul, is *What does a woman want?*"

Lenin's widow, Nadezhda Krupskaya (above), now 54, remains active and will exert great influence in the area of education.

New York World editor Margaret Petheridge Farrar, 27, and two colleagues create the world's first crossword puzzle book. Published by Simon & Schuster, it has sales of 400,000 its first year (*see* 1942).

Nonfiction: *The First Time in History: Two Years of Russia's New Life* by Anna Louise Strong.

Fiction: *The Constant Nymph* by English novelist Margaret Kennedy, 28, who was trained as a historian; *When the Bough Breaks* by Naomi Mitchison; *Precious Bane* by Mary Webb; *Orphan Island* by Rose Macaulay; *The Silver Rapids (Silverforsen)* by Elin Wägner; *The Romance of Teresa Hennert (Romans Tersy Hennert)* by Polish novelist Zofja Nalkowska, 39; *Something Childish and Other Stories* by the late Katherine Mansfield; *So Big* by U.S. novelist Edna Ferber, 37 (Pulitzer Prize); "The Spring Flight" by Inez Gillmore Irwin, now 51, wins the O. Henry Memorial prize; *A Handmaid of the Lord* by Margaret Culkin Banning; *Country People* by U.S. novelist Ruth Suckow, 32; *The Ship Kaijinmaru (Kaijinmaru)* by Yaeko Nogami.

Poetry: *Ternura* by Gabriela Mistral; *The Swain (Molodets)* by Marina Tsvetaeva.

Juvenile: *Schoolgirl Kitty* and *Captain Peggy* by Angela Brazil.

Painting: *Beauty Contest* by Florine Stettheimer; *Una, Lady Troubridge* by Romaine Brooks.

Lithograph: *Never Again War!* by Käthe Kollwitz.

Sculpture: *Pavlova* (bust) by Melvina Hoffman.

Theater: Spring Byington and Osgood Perkins in George S. Kaufman and Marc Connelly's *Beggar on Horseback* 2/12 at New York's Broadhurst Theater, 164 perfs.; Evelyn Hope, Maud Gill, Cedric Hardwicke, and Melville Cooper in Eden Phillpotts's *The Farmer's Wife* 3/11 at London's Court Theatre, 1,329 perfs; Pauline Lord, Glenn Anders, and Richard Bennett in Sidney Coe Howard's *They Knew What They Wanted* 11/24 at New York's Garrick Theater, 414 perfs.; Australian actress May Robson, 56, Lilian Braithwaite, and Coward in Nöel Coward's *The Vortex* 12/16 at London's Royalty Theatre, 224 perfs.

Eleonora Duse dies of pneumonia at Pittsburgh's Hotel Schenley April 21 at age 65; Lotta Crabtree dies September 25 at age 76 in the Boston hotel that she has owned since 1909 (4 years after the death of her mother, Mary Ann, who invested her stage earnings in real estate and municipal bonds). She has bequeathed her estate, worth nearly $4 million, mostly to veterans of the Great War and their families.

Films: ZaSu Pitts, 26, and Gibson Gowland (as McTeague) in Erich von Stroheim's *Greed*. Also: Carol Dempster in D. W. Griffith's *Isn't Life Wonderful*; Mary Astor (Lucille Langhanke), 18, and John Barrymore in Henry Beaumont's *Beau Brummel*; Swedish actress Greta Garbo (Greta Louisa Gustafsson), 19, in Mauritz Stiller's *Gösta Berling's Saga*; Canadian-born actress (Edith) Norma Shearer, 22, Lon Chaney, and John Gilbert in Victor Seastrom's *He Who Gets Slapped*; Madge Bellamy and George O'Brien in John Ford's *The Iron Horse*; Betty Bronson in Herbert Brenon's *Peter Pan*; Lillian and Dorothy Gish with William Powell and Ronald Colman in Henry King's *Romola*.

Philadelphia's Curtis Institute of Music opens in October. Publishing heiress Mary Louise Curtis Bok, 48, who in 1896 married Louisa Curtis's suc-

cessor as editor of the *Ladies' Home Journal*, has given $500,000 to start the school. She will increase its endowment to $12.5 million by 1927, and it will be able to drop tuition charges.

Ballet: Russian dancer-choreographer Anna Pavlova, now 43, gives a farewell tour of America with a 42-member company; Russian ballerina Alexandra Danilova, 20, of the Maryinsky Theater goes on tour with choreographer George Balanchine and defects; she will be engaged by Sergei Diaghilev next year for his Ballets Russes and will never return to the U.S.S.R.

Broadway musicals: English comediennes Beatrice Lillie (Constance Sylvia Munston), 29, and Jack Buchanan in *André Charlot's Revue of 1924* 1/9 at the Times Square Theater, with songs that include "Limehouse Blues," 138 perfs.; Vivienne Segal and Will Rogers in *The Ziegfeld Follies* 6/24 at the New Amsterdam Theater, 520 perfs.; Mary Enis and Dennis King in Rudolf Friml's *Rosemarie* 9/2 at the Imperial Theater, with songs that include "Indian Love Call" and the title song, 557 perfs.; the Dolly Sisters in *The Greenwich Village Follies* 9/16 at the Shubert Theater, with Cole Porter songs that include "I'm in Love Again" and "Babes in the Woods," 127 perfs.; Florence Mills in the all-black revue *Dixie to Broadway* 11/22 at the Broadhurst Theater, 77 perfs.; Fred Astaire and his sister Adele in *Lady Be Good* 12/1 at the Liberty Theater, with George and Ira Gershwin songs that include "Somebody Loves Me," "The Man I Love," and "Fascinating Rhythm," 184 perfs.; *The Student Prince of Heidelberg* 12/2 at the Jolson Theater, with Sigmund Romberg–Dorothy Donnelly songs that include "Deep in My Heart, Dear," 608 perfs.

Kathleen "Kitty" McKane, 27, wins in women's singles at Wimbledon, beating Helen Wills, who wins in women's singles at Forest Hills, where a tennis stadium is completed for New York's West Side Tennis Club. The matches, which began in 1881, have been held for the past 3 years at Philadelphia's Germantown Cricket Club but will be held until 1980 at Forest Hills, in Queens.

Austrian figure skater Herma Szabo-Planck wins her event in the winter Olympics at Chamonix. U.S. swimmer Ethel Lackie wins the 100-meter freestyle in 1 minute, 12.4 seconds at the summer Olympics in Paris; U.S. swimmer Martha Norelius wins the 400-meter freestyle in 6 minutes, 2.2 seconds, U.S. swimmer Sybil Bauer the 100-meter backstroke in 1 minute, 23.2 seconds, British swimmer Lucy Morton the 200-meter breaststroke in 3 minutes, 33.2 seconds, U.S. swimmer Elizabeth Becker the springboard dive event, U.S. swimmer Caroline Smith the platform dive.

Polly's Apparel Shop at 2719 Broadway, New York, closes down as Polish-born New York retailer Polly Adler (originally Pearl), 24, who arrived in steerage at Ellis Island in 1914, goes back into business as a madam with a large apartment off Riverside Drive, paying heavy bribes to corrupt law enforcement officials to keep her establishment open. Raped at 17 by her supervisor in a Brooklyn shirt factory, Adler had an abortion, moved to Manhattan, worked in a corset factory, met a young actress who introduced her to gangsters and bootleggers on the upper West Side, met one who offered to pay her rent if he and his girlfriend could use her apartment as a meeting place, and began procuring for him and his friends. Soprano Rosa Ponselle was among the customers at her lingerie shop, whereas her brothel clients soon include actor Wallace Beery, playwright George S. Kaufman (who has a charge account), humorist Robert Benchley, business magnates, socialites, gambler Arnold Rothstein, and gangsters Al Capone, Jack "Legs" Diamond, and Dutch Schultz (Arthur Flegenheimer). Dark-haired, tall (five feet 11 inches), plump, flamboyantly dressed, and surrounded by her "girls," Polly is soon a familiar figure at the city's popular speakeasies, moving her operation to Saratoga Springs each summer as she builds her business with houses that always have paneled French-gray walls and are furnished with jade and rose quartz lamps, Gobelin tapestries, and Louis XVI furniture (see 1935).

F. W. Woolworth's Canadian-born widow Jennie (née Creighton) dies May 24, leaving her granddaughter Barbara Hutton, 12, $26 million—one-third of her $78.3 million estate. The girl's mother, Edna, committed suicide with strychnine at New York's Plaza Hotel in May 1917, leaving her $2.1 million (see 1926).

Kleenex, introduced under the name Celluwipes by Kimberly & Clark, is the first disposable handker-chief. Ernst Mahler of 1918 Kotex fame has developed the product from celucotton, the name will be changed to Kleenex 'Kerchiefs, and it will be shortened subsequently to the one word Kleenex.

Miami Beach promoter Carl Fisher hires publicity man Steve Hanagan, who will deluge newspapers with pictures of Florida "bathing beauties" to convey the idea that the Atlantic at Miami Beach in January is warmer than the Pacific at Los Angeles in August.

Paris milliner Lily Daché, 24, arrives at New York, sells hats for R. H. Macy's, works for 10 weeks in a small Broadway hat shop, saves her money, and then opens her own shop with a $100 down payment, selling American-made hats molded to the head in the latest fashion. Working for Riboud last year, she introduced the cloche, a new shape to go with women's short hair.

The U.S. National Council of Catholic Women launches a campaign in July urging modesty in dress.

30 percent of U.S. bread is baked at home, down from 70 percent in 1910.

1925

The Autobiography of Mother Jones by union organizer Mary Jones, now 95, says, "I am always in favor of obeying the law, but if the high-class burglar breaks the law and defies it, then I say we must have a law that will defend the nation and our people." Jones has grown up in the U.S. labor movement and been imprisoned on occasion for violent activities in behalf of West Virginia and Colorado coal miners, her slogan has been "Pray for the dead and fight like hell for the living," and to illustrate the abuses of child labor she tells of meeting a boy of 10 and asking him why he was not in school. "I ain't lost no leg," said the boy, and Jones tells her readers that "lads went to school when they were incapacitated by accidents" in the mines and mills.

"I am humbly following in your footsteps and having a row with the Government over the iniquity of the Marriage Tax," birth control advocate Marie Stopes writes to playwright George Bernard Shaw

June 29. "Our incomes being added together, [my husband and I] are liable for supertax, which we are refusing to pay on the grounds of morality, as I consider in a Christian country it is an immoral and outrageous act to tax me because I am living in holy matrimony instead of as my husband's mistress."

Explorer Delia Akeley crosses Kenya's Somali desert, battling tsetse flies and other insect pests to reach Nairobi, from which she dispatches specimens of wildlife to her sponsors at the Brooklyn Museum (*see* 1924). She visits with Pygmies in the Ituri Forest, reaches Wamba in the Belgian Congo May 4 with photographs she has taken of African women and children, arrives at the mouth of the Congo River on the Atlantic in September after an 11-month journey, and returns to New York with more than 30 specimens of game animals for the museum plus a wealth of adventure stories.

German physicist Ida (Eva) Noddak (*née* Tacke), 29, discovers element 43, which will be called technetium (she calls it masurium, because it was found at Masuria). She will also isolate element 75 (rhenium) and will be among the first to suggest the possibility of nuclear fission.

The National Academy of Sciences elects its first woman member. She is physician Florence Sabin, 54.

Australian physician (Annie) Jean Macnamara, 26, tests an immune serum for poliomyelitis (generally called "infantile paralysis") during an epidemic of the crippling disease. She becomes convinced of its value, will visit England and North America on a Rockefeller scholarship, and (with Melbourne virologist Frank McFarland Burnet, now 26) will discover that there is more than one strain of polio virus (*see* Salk, 1952). Macnamara will learn of the invention of the artificial respirator (iron lung) by a Harvard professor late in 1928, will introduce the first such device to Australia, and will be created a Dame of the British Empire in 1935 (*see* agriculture, 1951).

The Frontier Nursing Service of Hayden, Ky., is founded by nurse Mary Breckenridge, who has cared for children in wartime France, acquired midwifery training in England, and chosen upon her return to work among people in a remote area of Appalachia who are accessible only by horseback and are not served by any doctor or trained midwife. The Service, which will import trained English midwives and send some Americans to England for training, will not begin training its own midwives for another 20 years.

The *New Yorker* magazine begins publication in February. Founded by Harold Ross with help from his wife, *New York Times* reporter Jane Grant, it quickly attracts the talents of cartoonists who include Helen Hokinson, 26, and in October begins publishing a "Letter from Paris," signed Genêt but written by journalist Janet Flanner, 33, who will continue writing the "Letters" for nearly 50 years.

Cosmopolitan magazine is created by a merger of Hearst's *International Magazine* with an earlier *Cosmopolitan* under the editorship of Raymond Land, 47, who will publish fiction by Edna Ferber, Fannie Hurst, and Dorothy Parker, among others (*see* 1965).

Nonfiction: *What I Remember* by pioneer suffragist Millicent Garrett Fawcett, now 78; *Isles of Fear* by U.S. journalist Katherine Mayo, 57, exposes the evils of American colonial administration in the Philippines.

Fiction: *Mrs. Dalloway* by Virginia Woolf, who experiments with stream-of-consciousness technique; *Serena Blandish, or The Difficulty of Getting Married* by "A Lady of Quality" (English novelist Enid Bagnold, 36); *Pastors and Masters* by English novelist Ivy Compton-Burnett, 33; *The Big House at Inver* by Edith Somerville, now 67; *Cloud Cuckoo Land* by Naomi Mitchison; *Barren Ground* by Ellen Glasgow, who gains her first critical success at age 51; *The Professor's House* by Willa Cather; *The Making of Americans* by Gertrude Stein; *The Mother's Recompense* by Edith Wharton, whose nonfiction work *The Writing of Fiction* describes her approach; *The Rim of the Prairie* by U.S. novelist Bess Streeter Aldrich, 44, whose banker-lawyer husband has just died, leaving her the sole support of her four children; *The Crystal Cup* by Gertrude Atherton; *The Odyssey of a Nice Girl* by Ruth Suckow; *The House on the Meadows* (*Dom nad takami*) by Zofja Nalkowska; *The Life of a German Mother* (*Auf Marienhoff: Das Leben einer deutschen*

Mutter) by Helene Voigt-Diedrichs; *The Chase* by Molly Panter-Downes; *Gentlemen Prefer Blondes* by California novelist-scriptwriter Anita Loos, 32, who started writing scenarios for D. W. Griffith at age 15; her gold-digging Lorelei Lee says things like "So this gentleman said a girl with brains ought to do something with them besides think" and "Any girl who was a lady would not even think of having such a good time that she did not remember to hang on to her jewelry."

Poetry: *What's O'Clock* by Amy Lowell, who dies May 12 at age 51 (Pulitzer Prize, 1926); *Honey out of a Rock* by U.S. poet Babette Deutsch, 30; *Ocre* by Alfonsina Storni; *Vesperina* and *I canti dell'isole* (about Capri) by Ada Negri.

Juvenile: *The Childhood and the Enchanters* (*L'Enfant et les sortilèges*) by Colette; *Faithful Jenny Dove, and Other Tales* by Eleanor Farjeon; *The School at the Chalet* by Elinor Mary Brent-Dyer is about the founding of a school in the Austrian Tyrol by a young Englishwoman.

Painting: *Nymph and Hind* and *Young Dancer* by Marie Laurencin.

Proletariat (woodcut series) by Käthe Kollwitz.

Theater: Eleanor Parker and James Gleason in Gleason and Richard Taber's prizefight comedy *Is Zat So?* 1/5 at New York's 39th Street Theater, 618 perfs.; June Walker and George Abbott in John Howard Lawson's *Processional* 1/12 at New York's Garrick Theater, 96 perfs.; U.S. actress Tallulah Bankhead, 22, and Edna Best in Nöel Coward's *Fallen Angels* 4/21 at London's Globe Theatre, 158 perfs.; Marie Tempest and Ann Trevor in Coward's *Hay Fever* 6/8 at London's Ambassadors Theatre, 337 perfs.; Chrystal Herne in George Kelly's *Craig's Wife* 10/12 at New York's Morosco Theater, 289 perfs.; Laurette Taylor and Louis Calhern in Philip Barry's *In a Garden* 11/16 at New York's Plymouth Theater, 73 perfs., Jane Cowl, 35, and Joyce Carey (*née* Lawrence [Lilian Braithwaite's daughter]), 26, in Coward's *Easy Virtue* 12/7 at New York's Empire Theater, 147 perfs.; New York Neighborhood Playhouse set and costume designer Aline Bernstein (*née* Frankau), 44, does the sets for the first American production of *The Dybbuk*, meets would-be playwright Thomas Wolfe, 24, and begins a 5-year

love affair in which she will travel with him to Europe, persuade him to write novels instead of plays, back him financially, and serve as his unofficial agent.

Films: French actress Renée Adorée (Jeanne de la Fonte), 27, and John Gilbert in King Vidor's *The Big Parade*. Also: May McAvoy, Ramon Novarro, and Francis X. Bushman in Fred Niblo's *Ben Hur*; Hungarian-born actress Vilma Banky (Vilma Lonchit), 26, and Ronald Colman in George Fitzmaurice's *The Dark Angel*; Banky, Louise Dresser, and Rudolph Valentino in Clarence Brown's *The Eagle*; Betty Bronson and Esther Ralston in Herbert Brenon's *A Kiss for Cinderella*; Mae Murray and John Gilbert in Erich von Stroheim's *The Merry Widow*; Greta Garbo in G. W. Pabst's *Streets of Sorrow*, about girls being forced into prostitution; Jetta Goudal and Julian in Rupert Julian's *Three Faces East*; Polish-born actress Pola Negri (Appolonia Chalupek), 26, and Charles Emmet Mack in Malcolm St. Clair's *Woman of the World*.

Pola Negri starred in the silent film Woman of the World, *competing with Theda Bara and Gloria Swanson.*

Gossip columnist Louella Parsons contracts tuberculosis, is told she has only 6 months to live, retires to California, recovers her health, and becomes the Hearst syndicate's Hollywood columnist (*see* 1918; Sheila Graham, 1933; Hedda Hopper, 1936).

English pianist Ethel Liginska, now 38, makes her conducting debut 1/9 with the New York Symphony Orchestra and goes on later in the year to lead an orchestra at the Hollywood Bowl.

Polish-born French harpsichordist Wanda Louis Landowska, 46, opens a school of early-music interpretation at Paris. She is well known for her rendition of Bach's "Well-tempered Clavier."

Stage musicals: Binnie Hale (Beatrice Mary Hale-Munro), 25, in *No, No, Nanette* 3/11 at London's Phoenix Theatre, with Vincent Youmans–Irving Caesar–Otto Harbach songs that include "Tea for Two" and "I Want to Be Happy"; Hermione Baddeley and Nigel Bruce in Nöel Coward's revue *On with the Dance* 4/30 at London's Pavilion Theatre, 229 perfs.; Helen Ford in *Dearest Enemy* 9/18 at New York's Knickerbocker Theater, with a book by Herbert Fields based on the Revolutionary War legend about Mrs. Robert Murray delaying General Howe, Rodgers and Hart songs that include "Here in My Arms," 286 perfs.; Marilyn Miller, Jack Donahue, and Clifton Webb in *Sunny* 9/22 at New York's New Amsterdam Theater, with Jerome Kern–Otto Harbach–Oscar Hammerstein II songs that include "Who," 517 perfs.; emigrée U.S. entertainer Josephine Baker, now 19, in *La Revue Nigre* 10/7 at the Paris Théâtre des Champs-Elysées; Beatrice Lillie, Gertrude Lawrence, chorus girl Anna Neagle (Marjorie Robertson), 21, and Jack Buchanan in *The Charlot Revue* 11/10 at New York's Selwyn Theater, with songs that include Nöel Coward's "Poor Little Rich Girl," 138 perfs.; Margaret Dumont and the Four Marx Brothers in *The Cocoanuts* 12/8 at New York's Lyric Theater, with Irving Berlin songs, 218 perfs.; Queenie Smith, soprano Jeanette MacDonald, 18, and Robert Halliday in *Tip-Toes* 12/28 at New York's Liberty Theater, with George and Ira Gershwin songs that include "Sweet and Low-Down," 194 perfs.

"The Charleston" is introduced to Paris by "Bricktop," a redheaded American who arrived penniless from her native Harlem last year and has become hostess at a Place Pigalle nightclub. Ada Beatrice Queen Victoria Louisa Virginia Smith du Conge, 30, begins a half century as nightclub hostess.

Popular songs: "Yes, Sir, That's My Baby!" by Walter Donaldson and Gus Kahn; "I Love My Baby (My Baby Loves Me)" by Harry Warren, 32, lyrics

"Flappers" danced the Charleston and swigged bathtub gin as the 1920s roared and rollicked. JOHN HELD, JR., DRAWING FOR *LIFE*, LIBRARY OF CONGRESS

by Austrian-American writer Bud Green, 28; "Sleepy Time Gal" by Ange Lorenzo and Richard A. Whiting, lyrics by Joseph R. Alden and Raymond B. Egan; "Sweet Georgia Brown" by Ben Bernie, Maceo Pinkard, and Kenneth Casey; "Dinah" by Harry Akst, 31, lyrics by Sam M. Lewis and Joe Young; "Five Foot Two, Eyes of Blue" by Ray Henderson, lyrics by Sam M. Lewis and Joe Young; "Don't Bring Lulu" by Henderson, lyrics by Billy Rose and Lew Brown; "My Yiddishe Momme" by Jack Yellen and Lew Pollak, lyrics by Yellen (for Sophie Tucker); Bessie Smith records "Cake-Walking Babies (From Home)," "J. C. Holmes Blues," and W. C. Handy's 1914 hit "St. Louis Blues."

Suzanne Lenglen wins in women's singles at Wimbledon, Helen Wills in women's singles at Forest Hills.

British athlete Phyllis Green clears the 5-foot barrier in the high jump July 11, becoming the first woman to do so (*see* 1958).

Contract bridge begins to replace auction bridge. Railroad heir and yachtsman Harold S. Vanderbilt, 41, invents the variation while on a Caribbean cruise; it will eclipse auction bridge and whist beginning in 1930, when Romanian-American expert Eli Culbertson wins a challenge match at London's Almack's Club that will bring the game wide publicity (*see* Goren, 1936).

Lever Brothers introduces Lux toilet soap under the name Lux Toilet Form. The white milled soap will challenge Palmolive and Procter & Gamble's Cashmere Bouquet (*see* 1905; Lux Flakes, 1906; Rinso, 1918; Unilever, 1929).

Couturière Jeanne Lanvin, 58 (approximate), capitalizes on the U.S. demand for French perfumes by introducing her fragrance My Sin (*Mon Péché*), which has failed in Paris but will be a big success in America. Shalimar, introduced by Pierre and Jacques Guerlain, will also gain wide popularity.

U.S. tobacco magnate James Buchanan "Buck" Duke dies of pernicious anemia and pneumonia at New York October 10 at age 68, leaving his daughter Doris, nearly 14 and an A student at Brearley, more than $30 million of his $100 million estate (she is more than four times richer than Barbara Hutton).

U.S. cigarette production reaches 82.2 billion, up from 66.7 billion in 1923 as tobacco companies try to lure women smokers.

William Randolph Hearst opens his San Simeon castle La Cuesta Encantada overlooking the Pacific on 240,000 acres of ranch land plus another 90,000 for his American buffalo, giraffes, zebras, camels, and ostriches. His architect and interior designer is Julia Morgan, 53, who in 1898 was the first woman admitted to the College of Engineering at the University of California, Berkeley, and in 1902 became the first woman certified in architecture by the Ecole des Beaux-Arts at Paris. Encouraged by Hearst's mother to open her own architectural office, she gained recognition by designing a new Fairmont Hotel to replace the one destroyed in the 1906 San Francisco earthquake and met Hearst while completing his

mother's estate at Pleasanton, east of Berkeley, in 1915. Standing only five feet tall and weighing scarcely 100 pounds, Morgan has pioneered in bringing outside light into dark interior spaces. Hearst commissioned her in 1919 to design San Simeon, a project that will occupy her for another 14 years. He has spent an estimated $50 million to build the Hispano-Moorish Casa Grande and its adjoining buildings for himself and his mistress, Marion Davies (the place requires a staff of 50).

Birth control wins the endorsements of the New York Obstetrical Society, New York Academy of Medicine, and American Medical Association after persuasion by New York obstetrician Robert L. Dickinson, who obtains a $10,000 Rockefeller Foundation grant for research in contraception.

1926

British authorities in India grant women the right to vote, but only in provincial elections.

Hungarian feminist-pacifist Rosika Schwimmer, now 49, files final papers for U.S. citizenship but refuses to swear that she will bear arms for the country in the event of war. A district court denies her application, a ruling that will be reversed on appeal (*see* 1920; Supreme Court decision, 1929).

Lydia Pinkham Gove, 41, a granddaughter of the Vegetable Compound creator, hires an open plane and pilot at Los Angeles and, accompanied by a clergyman friend, flies to East Boston in July. Making frequent stops for fuel and overnight rest, she crosses the country in 7 days—the first commercial passenger on a transcontinental flight.

English-American astronomer Cecilia Payne, 26, of the Harvard College Observatory determines that helium is more abundant in the stars than on earth. Payne, who earned a PhD from Radcliffe last year after publishing six papers (the *Astronomical Union* described her doctoral dissertation as "undoubtedly the most brilliant ever written in astronomy"), has used data on 20 of the 25 most abundant elements in the earth's crust (*see* 1933).

Lydia Pinkham Gove (above) has taken over advertising responsibilities for the family patent medicine product but will herself die of ovarian cancer in 1948. (*see* 1905; 1950).

The grotto of Lourdes, which has been drawing hopeful patients since 1858, attracts new attention after French housewife Augustine Augault is relieved overnight of a fibroid tumor of the uterus that has swelled her weight from 77 pounds to 102. The tumor has been diagnosed as such by physicians, but after Mme. Augault is carried on a stretcher at the procession of the Blessed Sacrament at Lourdes it is found to have disappeared by 30 physicians, Catholic and non-Catholic—a "miracle" that will help lead to the canonization of Sister Bernadette in 1933 (*see* 1866).

California newspapers May 18 report that evangelist Aimee Semple McPherson has disappeared while swimming and is presumed to have drowned (*see* 1923). She has returned April 24 from a long vacation with her daughter, Roberta, through Europe and the Holy Land. Some 15,000 of her followers kneel in prayer for her soul at her Bible School auditorium, hundreds more pray on the sidewalks and lawns around her temple, pleading with her to return from the dead, but she has actually been having a tryst at Carmel with former *Los Angeles Times* radio station manager Kenneth Gladstone Ormiston, a married man and agnostic who in 1923 built radio station KFSG (Kalling Four-Square Gospel) atop her temple. She returns to Los Angeles June 27, receives a wild reception from city officials and thousands of cheering well-wishers, and announces the next day that she was kidnapped (Ormiston discreetly moves to Chicago). A grand jury meets July 8 to decide whether anyone should be indicted for kidnapping, but she appears outside the courthouse wearing a simple white crepe dress with a long blue cape, produces seven other women of similar build, hairstyle, and facial features wearing outfits identical to hers, and the grand jury decides July 20 that anyone claiming to have seen her at Carmel might have been mistaken. It finds insufficient evidence to warrant an indictment.

Catholic bishops in Italy ban scantily clad women from church and criticize women's participation in sports as "incompatible" with a woman's dignity.

Soviet Russian women of 19 have a literacy rate of 88.2 percent, men 24 to 25 a rate of 95.7 percent, up from an overall rate of only 78 percent in 1897, following a campaign by the Bolshevik government to teach children to read and write.

Sarah Lawrence College for Women is founded at Bronxville, N.Y., by local real estate developer William V. Lawrence, who names the liberal arts college for his wife.

Bennett College for Women at Greensboro, N.C., takes that name after 53 years as a coeducational school as the Woman's Home Missionary Society expands its educational programs to include black women (*see* 1873).

Parents magazine has its beginnings in *Children: The Magazine for Parents* started by New York bachelor George Joseph Hecht, 30, who has campaigned vigorously for child welfare programs and population control. He will marry a Baltimore schoolteacher in 1931 and become a father.

Fiction: *Adam's Breed* by English poet-novelist Marguerite Radclyffe Hall, 40; *Lolly Willowes; or, The Loving Huntsman* by English novelist Sylvia Townsend Warner, 32 (first selection of the new Book-Of-The-Month-Club); *Crewe Train* by Rose Macaulay; *The Black Knight* by Ethel Dell; *The Journey of the Seven Friars* (*Die Fahrt der sieben Ordersrüder*) (stories) by East Prussian poet–novelist Agnes Miegel, 47; *The Last of Chéri* by Colette; *The Orphan Angel* by Elinor Wylie; *A Brittle Heaven* by Babette Deutsch; *Show Boat* by Edna Ferber; *My Mortal Enemy* (stories) by Willa Cather; *The Women of the Family* by Margaret Culkin Banning; *Glass Houses* by *Chicago Tribune* publishing heiress–novelist Eleanor "Cissy" Gizycka (*née* Patterson), 45, who at age 23 married the Polish adventurer Count Josef Gizycki, from whom she obtained a divorce 5 years ago; *The Painted Room* by Margaret Wilson; *The Time of Man* by Kentucky novelist–lyric poet Elizabeth Madox Roberts, 40; *Iowa Interiors* (16 stories which have appeared in magazines such as *Smart Set*, *Century*, and *American Mercury*) by Ruth Suckow; *The Murder of Roger Ackroyd* by Agatha Christie; *Clouds of Witness* by Dorothy Sayers; Ernest Hemingway's *The Sun Also Rises* quotes Gertrude Stein in an epigraph that says, "You are all a lost generation," a line Stein heard her garageman use in scolding a young mechanic who did not make proper repairs on her Model T Ford.

Poetry: *The Close Couplet* by U.S. poet Laura Riding, 25; *Fiddler's Farewell* by U.S. poet Leonora Speyer (*née* von Stosch), 53 (1927 Pulitzer Prize, although Harriet Monroe of *Poetry* magazine criticizes the selection, politely praising Speyer's "extraordinary record" as a poet of "fine distinction" but noting that Sara Teasdale's *Dark of the Moon* is far superior); *The Land* by English poet-novelist V. (Vita; Victoria Mary) Sackville-West, 34; *Enough Rope* by U.S. poet-author Dorothy Parker (*née* Rothschild), 33, who is well known for her 1920 advertising line "Brevity is the soul of lingerie" and will be better known for "Men seldom make passes/ At girls who wear glasses," for putting down an actress with the line, "She ran the whole gamut of emotions from A to B," and for the verse "Guns aren't lawful;/ Nooses give;/ Gas smells awful;/ You might as well live."

Juvenile: *The Little Engine That Could* by U.S. author Watty Piper (Mabel C. Bragg), illustrations by George and Doris Haumon; *Maida's Little School* by Inez Gillmore Irwin.

The *New York Herald-Tribune* appoints Irita Bradford (Mrs. Carl) Van Doren, 35, head of its Book Review section following the death of Book Review editor Stuart Sherman. Her stewardship over the next 37 years will have a powerful influence on what America reads.

Radcliffe graduate Mary Woodard, 27, marries New York gallery owner Paul Reinhardt, her employer, and becomes the only art dealer on 57th Street with a degree in art history. Mary Cassatt dies at the Château de Beaufresne, her country house outside Paris, June 14 at age 81 (a diabetic, she has been blind for more than a decade).

Theater: Comedienne Sarah Hope Crews, English actress Margalo Gilmore, 25, and Earle Larimore in Sidney Howard's *The Silver Cord*, a play about mother-son love, 12/20 at New York's John Golden Theater, 112 perfs.

English actress Eva Le Gallienne, 27, founds the Civic Repertory Theatre of New York.

Films: Brigitte Helm, Alfred Abel, and Rudolf Klein-Rogge in Fritz Lang's *Metropolis*. Also: Lillian Gish, Renée Adorée, and John Gilbert in King Vidor's *La Bohème*; Vera Baranovskaia in Vsevlod Pudovkin's *Mother*; Lillian Gish, Lars Hanson, and Henry B. Walthall in Victor Seastrom's *The Scarlet Letter*; Mexican-American actress Dolores Del Rio (Dolores Asunsolo), 18, Victor McLaglen, and Edmund Lowe in Raoul Walsh's *What Price Glory?*

Ballet: Martha Graham makes her first solo appearance 4/18 at New York's 48th Street Theater. Now 31, Graham studied at Los Angeles with Ruth St. Denis, now 49, and Ted Shawn, 35; she performed as lead dancer in the ballet *Xochitl* in 1920, joined the *Greenwich Village Follies* in 1923, will form her own dance troupe, and will improvise a highly individual choreography. Graham will continue dancing until 1970.

Opera: U.S. soprano Marian Talley, 19, makes her Metropolitan Opera debut singing in the 1851 Verdi opera *Rigoletto*.

First performances: Wanda Landowska plays in the world premiere of Manuel de Falla's *Concerto for Harpsichord, Flute, Oboe, Clarinet, Violin, and Cello* 11/5 at Barcelona.

Broadway musicals: Ann Pennington in *George White's Scandals* 6/14 at the Apollo Theater introduces the Black Bottom dance step, which will rival the Charleston, songs that include "The Birth of the Blues," 424 perfs.; Yvonne D'Arle in *Countess Maritza* 9/18 at the Shubert Theater, with music by Viennese composer Emmerich Kalman, book and lyrics by Harry B. Smith, who has adapted a Viennese operetta, 318 perfs.; Pauline Mason, Kate Smith, and Eddie Dowling in *Honeymoon Lane* 9/20 at the Knickerbocker Theater, with songs that include "The Little White House (At the End of Honeymoon Lane)," 317 perfs.; Gertrude Lawrence in *Oh, Kay!* 11/8 at the Imperial Theater, with George and Ira Gershwin songs that include "Do, Do, Do," "Someone to Watch Over Me," "Heaven on Earth," and the title song, 256 perfs.; Vivienne Segal and Robert Halliday in *The Desert Song* 11/30 at the Casino Theater, with Sigmund Romberg–Oscar Hammerstein II–Otto Harbach songs that include "Blue Heaven" and "One Alone," 471 perfs.; Helen Ford in *Peggy-Ann* 12/27 at the Vanderbilt Theater, with Rodgers and Hart songs that include "Where's That Rainbow?" 333 perfs.; Belle Baker and Al Shean in *Betsy* 12/28 at the New Amsterdam Theater, with songs that include "Blue Skies" by Irving Berlin (who eloped in January with New York society girl Ellin Mackay, 22, daughter of Postal Telegraph president Clarence Mackay), 39 perfs.

Josephine Baker opens her own Paris nightclub at age 20 after having risen to fame in *La Revue Nigre* and starred at the Folies Bergère in a G-string ornamented with bananas. The U.S. emigrée darling of European café society will begin a professional singing career in 1930, be naturalized as a French citizen in 1937, and continue performing until shortly before her death in 1974.

Popular songs: "In a Little Spanish Town" by U.S. composer Mabel Wayne, lyrics by Sam M. Lewis and Joe Young; Bessie Smith records "Baby Doll."

Egyptian singer (Ibrahim) um Kalthum (originally Ibrahim Oum Koulsoum or Ibrahim Umm Kulthum), 18, gives her first successful Cairo concert, launching a career that will make her known as the "mother of Middle Eastern music." She has been influenced by the poet Ahmad Rami and will sing more than 250 of his songs.

Kitty McKane Godfree wins in women's singles at Wimbledon, Molla Bjurstedt Mallory at Forest Hills.

Miniature golf is invented by Tennessee entrepreneur Frieda Carter, part owner of the Fairyland Inn resort, who will patent her "Tom Thumb Golf" in 1929. By 1930 there will be 25,000 to 50,000 miniature golf courses.

Gertrude Caroline Ederle, 19, becomes the first woman to swim the English Channel. The New York Olympic champion failed in a Channel attempt last year but arrives at Dover August 6 after 14½ hours in the water, has been forced by heavy seas to swim 35 miles to cover the 21 miles from Cape Gris–Nez near Calais, still beats the world record by nearly 2 hours, and suffers a hearing loss that will prove permanent (*see* Chadwick, 1951).

New York stockbroker Franklyn Lawes Hutton, brother of E. F. Hutton, marries a divorcée from Detroit and sells 50,000 shares of his daughter Barbara's Woolworth stock, netting her more than $10 million, which he reinvests in a mixed portfolio (*see* 1924). He obtains permission from the surrogate court to buy two adjoining 26-room duplex apartments at 1020 Fifth Avenue, New York, one of them for Barbara, the other for himself and his new wife (*see* 1930).

Society decorator Elsie de Wolfe, now 60 and blue-haired, is married March 10 to British diplomat Sir Charles Mendl, whose wealth enables her to throw lavish parties at their homes in New York, Beverly Hills, and Versailles, which the new Lady Mendl has decorated with delicate 18th-century furniture and her usual glazed cotton chintz fabrics.

Italian hairdresser Antonio Buzzacchino invents a new permanent waving method that will make the "permanent" widely fashionable (*see* 1906).

Playwright George Bernard Shaw endorses the new fashion for shorter, lighter dresses, saying that they are for "real human beings" rather than "upholstered Victorian angels," but traditionalists deplore the rising hemlines, claiming that they bring a decline in morals, and physicians warn that the boyish new "flapper" look causes women to weaken their health by excessive dieting. British doctor J. S. Russell tells the Institute of Hygiene that women are turning to alcohol and drugs in a desperate effort to cope with their hectic lives.

Slide fasteners get the name "zippers" after a promotional luncheon at which English novelist Gilbert Frankau, 42, has said, "Zip! It's open! Zip! It's closed!" (*see* Sundback, 1913). Italian-born Paris couturière Elsa Schiaparelli, 46, will use zippers in her 1930 line and when the general patents expire the following year the zipper will come into wide use in men's trousers, jeans, windbreakers, and sweaters and in women's dresses and other apparel.

The first electric steam irons go on sale at New York department stores, but although their moisture helps prevent scorching they find few buyers at $10 when regular electric irons cost only $6.

"Blow some my way," says a woman to a man lighting a cigarette in billboards posted by Liggett & Meyers for its 13-year-old Chesterfield brand. The advertisements break a taboo by suggesting that women enjoy cigarette smoke (*see* Lucky Strike, 1928).

The Hall-Mills murder of 1922 makes new headlines. New Jersey police arrest Frances Stevens Hall September 29 and charge her with having murdered her husband and his mistress, the case goes to trial in October, a jury turns in a not-guilty verdict December 3, and the case remains a mystery.

Postum Cereal boss Marjorie Merriweather Post (Hutton), now 39, moves into a 54-room triplex apartment—the largest in New York—at 1107 Fifth Avenue. She has sold her town house at the southeast corner of 92nd Street on condition that the builder virtually re-create it atop the 14-story apartment house he erects on the site. Connected by two private elevators to the private foyer on the building's ground floor, the apartment, for which she pays an annual rent of $75,000 on a 15-year lease, has a swimming pool, gymnasium, ballroom, gown room for hanging ball gowns, cold-storage room for flowers and furs, silver room, wine room, bakery, sun porch, separate men's and women's guest closets, and separate laundry rooms for household and servants (*see* Mar-a-Lago, 1927).

Marjorie Merriweather Post (above) puts in at Gloucester, Mass., to have her yacht provisioned, her chef obtains a frozen goose from General Seafoods, she eats goose, and she seeks out owner Clarence Birdseye, who is selling quantities of frozen fish but is on the verge of bankruptcy. Birdseye's freezing process impresses Post, but her stockbroker husband, E. F. Hutton, and board of directors oppose paying $2 million to buy Birdseye's business. It will cost them more when Postum Co. acquires the business in 1929.

Ideal Marriage, Its Physiology and Technique by Dutch gynecologist Th. H. Van de Velde, 53, says that "a fundamental principle of the Roman Catholic sexual code, which corresponds with precepts in Protestant and Jewish doctrine, is the rejection of all actions to prevent conception," but he notes that the "methods of contraception known and practiced today often contravene the demands of Ideal Marriage by diminishing stimulation, disturbing and dislocating normal relations, offending taste . . ." Van de Velde assumes that families will limit their numbers under the guidance of physicians.

Tobacco companies targeted women at a time when most people considered smoking "unladylike."

"Blow some my way"

Chesterfield

Dictator Benito Mussolini pushes through repressive laws against birth control in Fascist Italy, departing from his 1913 neo-Malthusian position.

1927

Chinese warlord Generalissimo Chiang Kai-shek, 41, who succeeded to the leadership of the Guomindang in 1925, takes Hangchow in February, Shanghai and Ghangzhou (Canton) a few weeks later, and Nanjing March 24, ending the era of warlord rivalry. He negotiates with bankers and industrialists at Shanghai, where he once ran a brokerage business; promised $3 to $10 million if he will break with Moscow, he reverses his earlier political philosophy, overthrows the leftist government at Hangchow, establishes a rightist National Revolutionary Government at Nanjing with Communists and left-wing elements excluded, and launches a "White Terror" campaign to crush an "autumn harvest uprising" led by Communist Mao Zedong in September. Revolutionist Xiang Jianyu defies the White Terror, remaining in Hunan to organize labor unions and run an underground newspaper (but *see* 1928). Chiang marries the Christianized Wellesley graduate Song Mei-ling, 26, December 1, brushing aside questions as to the legality of his divorce from the mother of his son, and allies himself with one of China's richest, most powerful families. On December 15 he expels Russians from Shanghai following an attempted coup in Guangzhou.

The New York Stock Exchange seats a woman member for the first time January 13.

Charles A. Lindbergh makes the first solo transatlantic flight in late May. U.S. aviatrix Ruth Elder, 23, is less lucky; she and her co-pilot go down 520 miles west of Portugal October 13, their plane catches fire and sinks almost immediately, but they are rescued by a passing tanker (*see* Earhart, 1928; 1932).

Scripps College for Women opens in October at Claremont, Calif., as one of several associated, but autonomous, colleges built around the nucleus of Pomona College. Publisher-philanthropist Ellen Browning Scripps, 89, who moved to California in 1891 and built a house at La Jolla, near San Diego, 6 years later, has contributed more than $1.5 million to the new college and will add substantially to that figure in her will. She backed her brother James in starting the *Detroit Evening News* in 1873, helped her much younger half brother E. W. (Edward Willys) with six of his nine papers, and now owns shares in 16 papers nationwide.

Nonfiction: *My Journey to Lhasa* (*Pied et en Mandiant de la Cine à L'Inde à Travers le Thibet; Voyage d'une Parisienne à Lhassa*) by Alexandra David-Neel (see 1924); *Mother India* by Katherine Mayo attacks Indian social customs such as child marriage.

Fiction: *Jalna* by Canadian novelist Mazo de la Roche, 42; *To the Lighthouse* by Virginia Woolf; *The Left Bank* (stories) by Welsh-Creole author Jean Rhys (Gwen Williams), 33; *The Five Pearls* (*Pärlorna*) by Elin Wägner; *The Jackdaw* (*Choucas*) by Zofja Nalkowska is set in a Swiss sanitorium; *Death Comes for the Archbishop* by Willa Cather is based on the 19th-century French-American clergyman Jean-Baptiste Lamy, who built the first cathedral in the Southwest at Santa Fe; *Twilight Sleep* by Edith Wharton; *At the Charity Clinic* (*Seryoshitsu nte*) by Japanese proletarian novelist Taiko (*née* Tai) Hirabayashi, 22; *Pressure* by Margaret Culkin Banning; *Black April* by South Carolina novelist Julia M. Peterkin (*née* Mood), 46, who was raised by a Gullah nurse and is married to the manager of Lang Syne Plantation, one of the state's most productive, which employs 450 Gullah laborers; *The Immortal Marriage* by Gertrude Atherton; *Dusty Answer* by English novelist Rosamond Nina Lehmann, 24; *My Heart and My Flesh* by Elizabeth Madox Roberts; *The Lovely Ship* by Storm Jameson (her first real success); *Mr. Fortune's Maggot* by Sylvia Townsend Warner; *The Unpleasantness at the Bellona Club* by Dorothy Sayers.

Poetry: *First and Second Poems* by English poet Ruth Pitter, 30; *Northern Lights* by Violet Jacob; *The Honor of Suffering* (*L'Honneur de souffrir*) by Anna, comtesse de Noailles; *Collected Poetry* (*Gesammelte Gedichte*) by Agnes Miegel, who gives up her job with the *Königsberger Zeitung*.

Painting: *Radiator Building, New York* by U.S. painter Georgia O'Keeffe, 39, who married photographer Alfred Stieglitz of the 291 Gallery 3 years ago but has been spending more and more time in the Southwest while Stieglitz, now 63, devotes his attentions to Philadelphia-born photographer Dorothy Norman (*née* Sticker), 22, whose husband, Edward, is the son of a Sears, Roebuck founder.

The Sogetsu school of Japanese flower arrangement (*ikebana*) is founded by Sofu Teshigahara, 27, who has developed a systematic approach to traditional *ikebana* that makes it accessible to more people (*see* 1824). The Sogetsu school will grow to have branches throughout the world (*see* 1980).

Theater: U.S. actress Ruth Gordon (Jones), 30, in Maxwell Anderson's *Saturday's Children* 1/26 at New York's Booth Theater, 310 perfs.; Alfred Lunt, English-American actress Lynn (*née* Lillie Louise) Fontanne (Lunt), 39, Margalo Gilmore, and Earle Larimore in S. N. Behrman's *The Second Man* 4/11 at New York's Guild Theater, 178 perfs.; *Porgy* by U.S. novelist-playwright DuBose Heyward, 42, and his wife, Dorothy, 10/27 at New York's Guild Theater, 367 perfs. (*see* Gershwin opera, 1935); Jane Cowl and Joyce Carey in Robert Emmet Sherwood's *The Road to Rome* 11/31 at The Playhouse, New York, 440 perfs.; Hope Williams in Philip Barry's *Paris Bound* 12/27 at New York's Music Box Theater, 234 perfs.

Films (all silent): Norma Shearer and Ramon Novarro in Ernst Lubitsch's *The Student Prince in Old Heidelberg*; Janet Gaynor (Laura Gainor), 21, and George O'Brien in F. W. Murneau's *Sunrise*; Fay Wray, ZaSu Pitts, and Erich von Stroheim in von Stroheim's *Wedding March*. Also: Norma Talmadge, now 34, and Gilbert Roland in Fred Niblo's *Camille*; Laura LaPlante, 23, and Creighton Hale in Paul Leni's *The Cat and the Canary*; Albert Préjean and Olga Tschechova in René Clair's *Un Chapeau de Paille d'Italie*; Marion Davies in Sam Wood's *The Fair Co-Ed*; Greta Garbo in Clarence Brown's *Flesh and the Devil*; Janet Gaynor and Charles Farrell in Frank Borzage's *Seventh Heaven*; Jetta Goudal and George Bancroft in William K. Howard's *White Gold*; Clara (Gordon) Bow, 22, Charles "Buddy" Rogers, Richard Arlen, and Gary Cooper in William A. Wellman's *Wings*.

The Academy of Motion Picture Arts and Sciences is founded May 11 by Louis B. Mayer of MGM.

Annual awards of the Academy will be called "Oscars" by movie columnist Sidney Skolsky (now a press agent of 22); first winners of the gold statuette (which is 92.5 percent tin) include Janet Gaynor (above) for best actress.

Opera: *The King's Henchman* 2/17 at New York's Metropolitan Opera House, with music by U.S. composer Deems Taylor, 41, libretto by Edna St. Vincent Millay, who contributes proceeds of her pamphlet "Justice Denied in Massachusetts" to the defense of alleged murderers Sacco and Vanzetti, makes a personal appeal to the governor that he spare the men, and is arrested in the deathwatch outside the Boston Court House the night of their execution.

Broadway musicals: Torch singer Ruth Etting, 28, and dancer Claire Luce, 24, in *The Ziegfeld Follies* 8/16 at the Ziegfeld Theater, with Luce dancing atop a crystal ball, Irving Berlin songs, 167 perfs.; Constance Carpenter and William Gaxton in *A Connecticut Yankee* 11/3 at the Vanderbilt Theater, with Rodgers and Hart songs that include "My Heart Stood Still," and "Thou Swell," 418 perfs.; comedienne Patsy (*née* Sarah Veronica Rose) Kelly, 17, in *Delmar's Revels* 11/28 at the Shubert Theater, with Jimmy McHugh–Dorothy Fields songs, 112 perfs.; Helen Morgan (as Julie LaVerne) in *Show Boat* 12/27 at the Ziegfeld Theater, with book by Edna Ferber, Jerome Kern–Oscar Hammerstein II songs that include "Bill," "Can't Help Lovin' Dat Man," "Ol' Man River," "Only Make-Believe," "Life on the Wicked Stage," and "Why Do I Love You?" 527 perfs.

Dancer Isadora Duncan is strangled to death at Nice September 14 at age 49 when her long scarf is entangled in a rear wheel of the sports car being demonstrated to her by an automobile salesman of whom she has become enamored (*see* 1921).

Popular songs: Bessie Smith records "After You've Gone," "Backwater Blues," and Irving Berlin's 1911 hit "Alexander's Ragtime Band."

Helen Wills wins in women's singles at both Wimbledon and Forest Hills.

Denver bowler Floretta McCutcheon (*née* Doty), 39, challenges champion Jimmy Smith to a three-game set December 18 and beats him 704 to 697.

"She is simply the greatest bowler I have ever seen," Smith comments.

Frances Heenan "Peaches" Browning, 16, sues millionaire New York real estate operator Edward W. "Daddy" Browning, 52, for divorce in a White Plains, N.Y., courthouse after less than a year of marriage. The January trial produces testimony that titillates newspaper readers.

Boyish fashions for women dominate Paris fashion shows in May, reducing bustlines and emphasizing slim hips with oversized belts. By next year, the typical woman's dress will be made from just seven yards of fabric, down from 19 before the war.

Brassiere inventor Caresse Crosby (Polly Jacob Peabody Crosby) rides naked on a baby elephant down the Champs-Elysées, Paris, to promote an art students' ball (see brassiere, 1914). In 1921, at age 27, she left her husband and children and eloped with bachelor banker-poet Henry Sturgis "Harry" Crosby, then 21. He has recently quit his job with J. P. Morgan to devote himself to poetry, and she has changed her name to Caresse. They found the Black Sun Press to publish limited editions of works by James Joyce, Hart Crane, and Ezra Pound (see 1929).

Super Suds introduced by Colgate and Company is a laundry and dishwashing soap product composed of quick-melting hollow beads rather than flakes or powder (see Rinso, 1918; Tide, 1946).

The Snyder-Gray murder trial makes world headlines. Queens Village, Long Island, housewife Ruth Snyder and her corset salesman lover Henry Judd Gray kill New York magazine art editor Albert Snyder with a sash weight March 20 in a suburban sex triangle. A jury convicts the pair, and they will die in the electric chair at Sing Sing early next year.

Mar-a-Lago is completed at Palm Beach, Fla., for Postum Cereal head Marjorie Merriweather Post and her notoriously faithless husband, E. F. Hutton (they also have retreats in the Adirondacks, on the north shore of Long Island, and in Greenwich, Conn., along with their New York City triplex apartment). Surrounded by 17 acres of property extending from the ocean to Lake Worth, the 115-room mansion (second largest private residence in America) has taken 4 years to complete. Three

ships from Genoa have brought the Dorian stone for its outer walls, the ancient red roofing tiles have come from Cuba along with black and white marble inlay for the floors, Post has picked up 38,000 antique Spanish tiles for indoor wall decoration, and she has helped Palm Beach survive an economic depression by hiring all available local craftsmen to work on the $7 million project. Shaped like a crescent with a 75-foot tower, the house is surrounded by guest houses, staff quarters, cutting gardens, and a nine-hole golf course.

Contractor Kate Gleason, now 62, builds a concrete community at Sausalito, Calif., based on principles of Indian adobe construction (see 1921). Suburbs all over America have begun to follow her example.

Borden introduces homogenized milk; other U.S. milk is still sold with cream at the top that must be mixed in before the milk is poured.

Gerber Baby Foods has its beginnings at Fremont, Mich., where local food processor Daniel F. Gerber, 28, is told by doctors to feed his sick daughter, Sally, strained peas. Gerber finds that strained baby foods are commercially available but expensive, sold only in a few parts of the country, and available only at pharmacies only by doctor's prescription (see 1928).

German physiologists Bernard Zondek and S. Ascheim discover a sex hormone that will lead to the first early test for pregnancy.

Birth control pioneer Margaret Sanger organizes the first World Population Conference (see 1921; International Planned Parenthood, 1948).

1928

The Cunard liner *Berengaria* arrives in fogbound New York harbor February 6 with 1,136 passengers who include a woman who calls herself Anastasia Tchaikovsky and claims to be the youngest daughter of Russia's Nicholas II, thought to have been murdered at age 16 with the rest of the czar's family at Ekaterinburg in 1918. She tells reporters that she has come to have doctors reset her jaw, which she says was broken by a Bolshevik soldier in 1918, and to visit her third cousin, the former Princess Xenia, who is married to a rich American, William B. Leeds, but she does not speak Russian except when in a trance. Grand Dukes Boris and Cyril have denied that she was their niece, Grand Duchess Olga, sister of the late czar, has said that the young woman was not her niece, but an old nurse has positively identified her and Grand Duke Andrew says he is sure that she *is* Anastasia. Other women will claim to be Anastasia; none will prove it.

Nationalist Chinese forces arrest Communist agitator Xiang Jianyu and execute her in May, gagging her to prevent her from making a final speech (*see* 1927).

Scottish coalminer's daughter Jennie Lee, 24, is elected to represent North Lanark in the House of Commons and becomes the youngest M.P. She will set aside her feminist principles to marry Welsh politician Aneurin Bevan, now 31, in 1934, and will wind up as Baroness Lee of Ashridge.

Benito Mussolini's Italy abolishes woman suffrage May 12 under a new law that restricts the franchise to men 21 and over who pay syndicate rates or taxes of 100 lire (*see* 1919). The law reduces the electorate from nearly 10 million to only 3 million and requires that voters approve or reject in toto the 400 candidates submitted by the Fascist grand council.

The Representation of the People Act approved by Parliament May 7 reduces the age of women voters from 30 to 21. English suffragist Emmeline Pankhurst dies June 14 at age 69. Women gain the vote on the same basis as men under provisions of a July 2 act of Parliament (*see* 1918; Jennie Lee, above).

Ecuador and Guyana give women the right to vote on the same basis as men.

Alice Paul founds the World Party for Equal Rights for Women.

Rose Schneiderman, now 44, is elected president of the National Women's Trade Union League (she was the only eastern organizer of the League from 1917 to 1919). Schneiderman and ILGWU Education Secretary Fania Cohn convene the first Women's Auxiliary Conference to set priorities and plan strategies for an organized movement of working-class housewives that will be regionally based but national in scope. The conferees urge women to lose their timidity, stop clinging to ideas of women's "inferiority." Women, they say, have power as consumers and should exercise it, setting up cooperative buying arrangements to keep prices down and cooperative child care so that mothers will have time to be active in community-based organizations. "It is time the Women's Auxiliaries become something more than agencies for sick benefits, relief work, and tea parties," Schneiderman says, and she exhorts her listeners to learn how to lobby for legislation that affects working-class women. The next decade will see a radicalization of women's union auxiliaries across the country, especially in coal, steel, and automaking towns of western Pennsylvania, West Virginia, Kentucky, southern Illinois, and Michigan, where one major employer's outright ownership or domination of local housing, banks, and food stores means that women are oppressed by management just as much as their husbands are. Members of women's union auxiliaries in the next 10 years will walk picket lines, set up food kitchens, and fight with police and company goons.

Crystal Eastman dies of nephritis July 8 at age 47 after writing in the *Nation* magazine, "No self-respecting feminist would accept alimony. It would be her own confession that she could not take care of herself" (she has been married and divorced twice).

Women's Union Auxiliaries (above) will gather information about food prices and utility rates, using the data to build grass roots organizations that will lobby for social legislation. Within 10 years they will be demanding not only fair prices for food but also a greater say in the running of their lives and their children's lives.

Amelia Earhart, 30, and two male pilots fly a multi-engine Fokker from Newfoundland to Burry Port, Wales, June 17 in 15 hours, 48 minutes, but she denies that she was ever at the controls. The U.S. aviatrix is the first woman to fly the Atlantic (*see* 1932).

Coming of Age in Samoa by American Museum of Natural History anthropologist Margaret Mead, 26,

Amelia Earhart was the first woman to fly across the Atlantic, inspiring a generation with her courage. LIBRARY OF CONGRESS

is based on studies made while living with the natives. Mead's book on the development of social behavior among adolescents on the Pacific island stresses the impermanence of human values.

The Women's Auxiliary Conference (above) notes that women's role in their children's education should not be limited to the home. Mothers should demand a voice in shaping the curricula of public schools, run for local school boards, and make sure that prolabor people get onto the boards.

Nonfiction: *The Hammer and the Scythe: Communist Russia Enters the Second Decade* by *New York Times* foreign correspondent Anne O'Hare McCormick. *The New Russia* by U.S. journalist Dorothy Thompson, 34, who marries novelist Sinclair Lewis. Thompson did social work and campaigned for woman suffrage in New York before sailing for Europe in 1920. She decided on a career in journalism while aboard ship, worked first for the *Philadelphia Ledger* and then for the *New York Post*, married Hungarian author Joseph Bard in 1923, divorced him 4 years later, and headed the

Post's Berlin office from 1924 until this year. She and Lewis return to America, but she will travel to Europe again in the early 1930s. *Asia Reborn* by Marguerite Harrison is a political and economic analysis of the new movements in the Far East; *The Intelligent Woman's Guide to Socialism and Capitalism* by George Bernard Shaw; *Anarchy Is Not Enough* (essays) and *Contemporaries and Snobs* (essays) by poet Laura Riding.

Fiction: *The Diary of Miss Sophia* by radical feminist Chinese novelist Ding Ling (Jiang Bingzhi), 24, who writes openly about feminine psychology and sexual desires; *Black Sparta* by Naomi Mitchison; *The Well of Loneliness* by Radclyffe Hall, who calls herself "John" and whose novel about a lesbian attachment between a young girl and an older woman encounters censorship problems (the book is said to have no literary merit and is banned, despite testimonials from E. M. Forster and Virginia Woolf); *Orlando* by Virginia Woolf; *Lady Chatterley's Lover* by D. H. Lawrence, who is dying of tuberculosis at Florence; his explicit account of the sex relations between the wife of a crippled English peer and their lusty gamekeeper, Mellors, is privately printed because no English publisher will touch it (*see* 1959); *Keeping Up Appearances* by Rose Macaulay; *Poor Women* (stories) by Irish writer Norah Hoult, 30; *The House in the Forest* by Katharine Tynan, now 67; *Nobuko* by Japanese novelist Yuriko (*née* Yuro) Miyamoto, 29; *From the Candy Factory (Kyarameru Kojo Kara)* by Japanese novelist Ineko Sata (*née* Kubokawa), 24; *Peripatetic Diary* (Horoki) by Japanese novelist Fumiko Hayashi, 25, is a best seller; *Up the Country* by "Brent of Bin Bin" (*see* 1901), who served with the Scottish Women's Hospital in Macedonia during the Great War but will spend the rest of her life in Australia; *The Children* by Edith Wharton; *Brook Evans* by Susan Glaspell; *Nothing Is Sacred* by U.S. novelist Josephine Herbst, 36, who came to New York late in 1919 and early in 1920 began an adulterous affair with playwright Maxwell Anderson, then an editorial writer for the *New York Globe* (his wife will die in 1931, and he will marry two other women, but not Josie Herbst); *Money of Her Own* by Margaret Culkin Banning; *Trivial Breath* and *Mr. Hodge and Mr. Hazard* by Elinor Wylie; *A Lantern in Her Hand* by Bess Streeter Aldrich; *Scarlet Sister*

Mary by Julia Peterkin (Pulitzer Prize); *Jingling in the Wind* by Elizabeth Madox Roberts, who is awarded the John Reed Memorial Prize by *Poetry* magazine; *A President Is Born* by Fannie Hurst; *The Bonney Family* by Ruth Suckow; *Daughters of India* by Margaret Wilson; *The Single Standard* by former Hearst newspaper reporter Adela Rogers St. John, 34; *Fall Flight* by Eleanor Gizycka is, like her 1926 novel *Glass Houses*, autobiographical; *The Mystery of the Blue Train* by Agatha Christie.

Poetry: *Buck in the Snow* by Edna St. Vincent Millay; *After Russia* (*Posle Rossii, 1922–1925*) by Marina Tsvetaeva, now 36.

Juvenile: *Millions of Cats* by U.S. author-illustrator Wanda Gág, 35.

Painting: *Nightwave* by Georgia O'Keeffe.

Theater: *Noisy Late Spring Night* (*Banshun Soya*) by Japanese writer Fumiko (*née* Fumo) Enji, 23, at Tokyo's Tsukiji Theater propels Enji into the literary limelight; Lynn Fontanne, Glenn Anders, Earle Larimore, and Australian actress Judith (*née* Frances Margaret) Anderson, 29, in Eugene O'Neill's *Strange Interlude*, a Freudian study of women with Elizabethan monologistic asides, 1/30 at New York's John Golden Theater, 426 perfs.; Marguerite Churchill in Aurania Rouverol's *Skidding* 5/21 at New York's Bijou Theater, 448 perfs.; Lee Tracy, Osgood Perkins, and Dorothy Stickney (originally Dorothy Hugo), 28, in Ben Hecht and Charles MacArthur's *The Front Page* 8/14 at New York's Times Square Theater, 276 perfs. (MacArthur marries actress Helen Hayes 8/17); *Machinal* by Sophie Treadwell 9/7 at New York's Plymouth Theater, with Jean Adair, Clark Gable, and Zita Johnson is based on last year's Snyder-Gray murder case, 91 perfs.; Hope Williams in Philip Barry's *Holiday* 11/26 at New York's Plymouth Theater, 229 perfs.

Ellen Terry dies at her English home July 28 at age 81.

Films: Eleanor Boardman in King Vidor's *The Crowd* (silent); Maria Falconetti in Carl Theodor Dreyer's *The Passion of Joan of Arc*; Lillian Gish and Lars Hanson in Victor Seastrom's *The Wind*; Janet Gaynor in F. W. Murnau's *The Four Devils*; Colleen Moore (Kathleen Morrison), 28, and Gary Cooper in George Fitzmaurice's *Lilac Time*; Greta Garbo in Fred Niblo's *The Mysterious Lady*; Joan Crawford (Lucille Le Sueur), 19, and John Mack Brown in Henry Beaumont's *Our Dancing Daughters*; Gloria Swanson, Lionel Barrymore, and Raoul Walsh in Walsh's *Sadie Thompson* (Swanson, who is a petite four foot eleven inches, rejected a $17,500-per-week contract offered by Jesse Lasky and Adolph Zukor 2 years ago and started her own production company with help from Boston banker Joseph P. Kennedy, a frequent visitor to her 24-room Hollywood mansions whose staff numbers 11); Janet Gaynor in Frank Borzage's *Street Angel*; Marion Davies and William Haines in King Vidor's *Show People*; Raquel Torres and Monte Blue in W. S. Van Dyke's *White Shadows in the South Seas*; Greta Garbo in Clarence Brown's *A Woman of Affairs*.

Screen star Norma Shearer, now 26, converts to Judaism and is married September 29 at Los Angeles to the diminutive (but brilliant) Hollywood producer Irving Grant Thalberg, 29. Shearer will have mental problems beginning in 1933, and Thalberg will die in 1936.

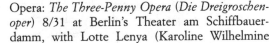

Opera: *The Three-Penny Opera* (*Die Dreigroschenoper*) 8/31 at Berlin's Theater am Schiffbauerdamm, with Lotte Lenya (Karoline Wilhelmine Blamauer Lenja), 27, as Jenny, music by her husband, Kurt Weill, libretto by Bertolt Brecht, who has transposed the *Beggar's Opera* of 1728 into the idiom of Germany's Weimar Republic.

U.S. soprano Grace Moore, 26, makes her Metropolitan Opera debut singing the role of Mimi in the 1896 Puccini opera *La Bohème*.

The Society of Women Musicians, founded in 1911, makes a successful appeal to the British Broadcasting Company for the inclusion of women in BBC orchestras (*see 1971*).

Stage musicals: Marilyn Miller, Frank Morgan, and Jack Donahue in *Rosalie* 1/10 at New York's New Amsterdam Theater, with music by George Gershwin and Sigmund Romberg, 335 perfs.; Vivienne Segal, Dennis King (as d'Artagnan), Reginald Owen (as Cardinal Richelieu), and Clarence Derwent (Louis XIII) in *The Three Musketeers* 3/13 at New York's Lyric Theater, with music by Rudolf

Friml, songs that include "March of the Musketeers," 318 perfs.; Jessie Matthews, Tilly Losch, and Melville Cooper in *This Year of Grace* 3/22 at the London Pavilion, with Nöel Coward songs that include "A Room with a View" and "World Weary," 316 perfs.; *Blackbirds of 1928* 5/9 at New York's Liberty Theater, with Bill "Bojangles" Robinson, Jimmy McHugh–Dorothy Fields songs that include "Digga Digga Do" and "I Can't Give You Anything but Love," 518 perfs.; Ann Pennington, Harry Richman, and Willie and Eugene Howard in *George White's Scandals* 7/2 at New York's Apollo Theater, 240 perfs.; Evelyn Herbert and Robert Halliday in *The New Moon* 9/10 at New York's Imperial Theater, with music by Sigmund Romberg, lyrics by Oscar Hammerstein II and others, songs that include "One Kiss," "Lover, Come Back to Me," "Softly, as in a Morning Sunrise," "Wanting You," and "Stout-Hearted Men," 509 perfs.; Irene Bordoni in *Paris* 10/8 at New York's Music Box Theater, with Cole Porter–Ray Goetz songs that include "Let's Fall in Love" with lyrics that begin "Birds do it . . ." 195 perfs.; Ona Munson, Bert Lahr, Jack Whiting, and Victor Moore in *Hold Everything* 10/10 at New York's Broadhurst Theater, with songs that include "You're the Cream in My Coffee," 413 perfs.; Margaret Dumont and the Four Marx Brothers in *Animal Crackers* 10/23 at New York's 44th Street Theater, 191 perfs.; Gertrude Lawrence and Clifton Webb in *Treasure Girl* 11/8 at New York's Alvin Theater, with Gershwin songs that include "I've Got a Crush on You," "I've Got a Feeling I'm Falling," and "Oh, So Nice," 68 perfs.

Hollywood musicals: Vilma Banky plays Marie in Victor Fleming's *The Awakening* with Walter Byron, Louis Wolheim, and Irving Berlin's song "Marie."

Helen Wills wins again in women's singles both at Wimbledon and at Forest Hills.

Eleanora Sears, now 46, wins the first U.S. women's national squash title (*see* 1918). She will continue to participate in tournament play until age 70.

Norwegian figure skater Sonja Henie, 16, wins her first Olympic gold medal in the winter games at St. Moritz. U.S. runner Elizabeth Robinson wins the 100-meter dash in 12.2 seconds in the summer games at Amsterdam, German runner Lina Radke

the 800-meter run in 2 minutes, 16.8 seconds, Canadian athlete Ethel Catherwood the running high jump at 5 feet, 3 inches, Polish athlete Helena Konopacka the discus throw (129 feet, 11 7/8 inches). U.S. swimmer Albina Osipowich wins the 100-meter freestyle event in 1 minute, 11 seconds, Martha Norelius the 400-meter freestyle in 5 minutes, 42.8 seconds, Dutch swimmer Marie Braun the 100-meter backstroke in 1 minute, 22 seconds, German swimmer Hilde Schrader the 200-meter breaststroke in 3 minutes, 12.6 seconds, U.S. swimmer Helen Meany the springboard dive event, U.S. swimmer Elizabeth B. Pinkston the platform dive.

Helena Rubinstein sells her enterprise for $3 million (*see* 1914). She will buy it back next year for $1.5 million and will have a $60 million business by the time of her death at age 94 in 1965.

American Tobacco Co. boss George Washington Hill, 44, promotes Lucky Strike cigarettes to women with the slogan "Reach for a Lucky instead of a sweet" in an effort to persuade women that candy is fattening while smoking is not.

Daniel Gerber improves baby foods with improved methods for straining peas and finds by a market survey that a large market exists for such foods if they can be sold cheaply through grocery stores (*see* 1927). Gerber offers six cans for a dollar (less than half the price of baby foods sold at pharmacies) to customers who will send in coupons filled out with the names and addresses of their grocers (*see* 1929).

Enduring Passion by Marie Stopes (whose book *Radiant Motherhood* is also published) reports that British working-class women have told her that they want to find ways to make their husbands less, rather than more, passionate. "The demand for a simple pill or a drug to solve such troubles is astonishingly widespread," she writes. "After lecturing to working-class audiences, in the question time, and even more when talking individually to members of the audience afterward, I am surprised by the prevalence of the rumour that there are drugs which can safely be taken to reduce the man's virility, and that such drugs act directly and only on the sex organs. I think it may not be out of place, even in a book specifically addressed to educated people, to explode this popular fallacy, and warn everyone that *no reliable drug of this nature exists.*"

Lucky Strike cigarette ads seduced women by appealing to their anxiety about putting on weight.

1929

The U.S. Supreme Court rules 6 to 3 against Rosika Schwimmer's application for citizenship May 27 because she has refused to swear that she will bear arms to defend her adopted country (*see* 1926). Chief Justice Oliver Wendell Holmes, in dissenting, says that Mme. Schwimmer "seems to be a woman of superior character and intelligence, obviously more than ordinarily desirable as a citizen of the United States," and adds, "If there is any principle of the Constitution that more imperatively calls for attachment than any other, it is the principle of free thought—not free thought for those who agree with us but freedom for the thought that we hate."

British voters elect 13 women members of Parliament May 31. Socialist Prime Minister Ramsay MacDonald appoints Margaret Bondfield minister of labor June 7 as more workers line up for the dole.

The Japanese Diet comes close to passing a women's civil rights bill, but Prime Minister Tomomasa Tanaka declares that it is still too early to extend civil rights to women. The minister of the interior says women should stay at home and wash diapers (*see* 1930).

Gastonia, N.C., textile worker Ella Mae Wiggins is murdered September 14 during a strike.

New York papers report February 3 that business girls average $33.50 for a 50-hour week, but wages will soon drop. The Department of Labor's Women's Bureau demands in July that housewives be included in a federal census on employment. The stock market crash in October begins an economic depression that will continue for the next decade.

Middletowne—A Study in Contemporary American Culture by U.S. sociologists Robert Staughton Lynd, 37, and his wife, Helen (*née* Merrell), 32, who break new ground by applying methods and approaches used in studying primitive peoples to the midwestern city of Muncie, Ind., comparing that city in 1894 and 1924, and allying sociology with anthropology.

Irish crystallographer Kathleen Lonsdale (*née* Yardley), 26, at University College, London, uses X-ray diffraction analysis of organic crystals to work out the structure of hexamethylbenzene. She will solve the structure of hexachlorobenzene in 1931, using Fourier analysis (*see* 1945).

Midwifery in Denmark by Dorothy Reed Mendenhall, now 55, favors greater reliance in childbirth on midwives and less intervention in the natural process. Dr. Mendenhall has examined Danish practices and concluded that Americans' fascination with technology is detrimental to maternal and child health.

The first Blue Cross nonprofit tax-exempt health insurance association is organized at Dallas, Tex., where local schoolteachers whose unpaid bills have been a burden to Baylor University Hospital make an arrangement with the hospital. Each teacher is guaranteed up to 21 days' annual free use of a semiprivate room and other hospital services on condition that small monthly fees be paid in advance on a regular basis. The program will quickly spread to all hospitals in the area, a central agency will collect the fees, and the Blue Cross trademark of the American Hospital Association (the national association of voluntary hospitals) will be used by agencies throughout the country that meet AHA standards. By 1935 Blue Cross will have half a million subscribers, and a Blue Shield program set up by medical societies and local doctors' guilds will provide surgical insurance.

The Seeing Eye is founded at Nashville, Tenn., by local philanthropist and dog fancier Dorothy Wood Eustis (née Harrison), 43, who breeds German shepherds. She saw a 1927 magazine article about a Swiss school that trained dogs for blinded war veterans, was asked by a blind Tennessee man to train a dog for him, and has opened the first Seeing Eye class. Her operation will move to Whippany, N.J., in 1932 and to Morristown, N.J., in 1965, training more than 4,500 Seeing Eye dogs (German shepherds, Laboradors, and golden retrievers) for the sightless.

"The so-called method of coeducation is false in theory and harmful to Christian training," proclaims Pope Pius XI December 31 in his encyclical *Divini illius magistri.*

Nonfiction: *Is Sex Necessary?* by *New Yorker* magazine essayist E. B. (Elwyn Brooks) White, 30, and his humorist-cartoonist colleague James (Grover) Thurber, 34, who write, "Woman, observing that her mate went out of his way to make himself entertaining, rightly surmised that sex had something to do with it. From that she logically concluded that sex was recreational rather than procreational. (The small hardy band of girls who failed to get this point were responsible for the popularity of women's field hockey.)"

Fiction: *The Last September* by Irish-born English novelist Elizabeth Bowen, 30; *The True Heart* by Sylvia Townsend Warner; *Harriet Hume: A London Fantasy* by Rebecca West, who has an illegitimate 14-year-old son, Anthony, fathered by novelist H. G. Wells; *Sido* by Colette; *The Fortunes of Richard Mahoney* by Australian novelist Henry Handel Richardson (Ethel Florence Roberta Richardson), 59; *Birth of an Individual* by Ding Ling; *Restaurant (Rakuyo)* by Ineko Sata; *A Ring about Roderick (Ring um Roderich)* by Helene Voigt-Diederichs; *Whiteoaks* by Mazo de la Roche; *Angels and Earthly Creatures* by Elinor Wylie; *The Fugitive's Return* by Susan Glaspell; *Hudson River Bracketed* by Edith Wharton, now 67; *Claudia* by U.S. novelist Rose Franken, 31; *Hitty: Her First 100 Years* by U.S. novelist Rachel Liman Field, 34; *Dido, Queen of Hearts* by Gertrude Atherton; *Cora* by Ruth Suckow; *Marcea-Maria* by Sophie Kerr; *Trousers of Taffeta* by Margaret Wilson; *The Black Dudley Murder* (in England, *Crime at Black Dudley*) by English mystery novelist Margery Allingham, 25, introduces the gentleman sleuth Albert Campion; *The Man in the Queue* by Scottish mystery novelist Josephine Tey (Elizabeth Mackintosh), 33.

Poetry: *Gold Coast Customs* by Edith Sitwell; *The Rambling Sailor* by the late Charlotte Mew, who died last year at age 58; *From a Garden in the Antipodes* by English-born New Zealand poet Mary Ursula Bethell, 55, is published under a pen name; *Dark Summer* by Louise Bogan includes her long poems "The Flume" and "Summer Wish."

Juvenile: *Magic for Marigold* by Maud Montgomery.

Painting: *Church of Saint Bernard in the Trees* by Suzanne Valadon; *Black Flower* and *Blue Larkspur* by Georgia O'Keeffe.

Chicago's Field Museum commissions sculptor Melvina Hoffman to make 110 bronze studies, 25 of them full figures, for a "Races of Mankind" Exhibition. Hoffman will travel to remote parts of the world in order to study primitive people in their native environments and will find bushwomen with buttocks so large that their babies can stand on them.

Theater: Mary Servoss, Leo Bulgakov, Erin O'Brien Moore, and Beulah Bondi in Elmer Rice's *Street Scene* 1/10 at The Playhouse in New York, 601 perfs.; Helen Wylie, French-American actress Claudette Colbert (Lily Claudette Chauchoin), 23, Dudley Digges, and Glenn Anders in Eugene O'Neill's *Dynamo* 2/11 at New York's Martin Beck Theater, 50 perfs.; Muriel Kirkland in Preston Sturges's comedy *Strictly Dishonorable* 9/18 at New York's Alvin Theater (Kirkland falls ill in December and is replaced by director Antoinette Perry's 17-year-old daughter, Marguerite), 557 perfs.; Margalo Gilmore and Leslie Howard in John L. Baldridge's *Berkeley Square* 11/4 at New York's Lyceum Theater, 229 perfs.; Sidney Fox as Dorothy Donovan in Aurania Rouverol's *It Never Rains* 11/19 at New York's Republic Theater, 185 perfs.

Radio drama: *The Goldbergs* 11/20 with Gertrude Berg (*née* Edelstein), 30, in the role of Molly Goldberg in a series initially entitled *The Rise of the Goldbergs* (*see* 1949).

Films: Louise Brooks, 23, in G. W. Pabst's *Pandora's Box* and *Diary of a Lost Girl*. Also: German actress Marlene Dietrich (*née* Maria Magdalena von Losch), 28, and Emil Jannings in Josef von Sternberg's *The Blue Angel*; George Arliss and Joan Bennett, 19, in Alfred E. Green's *Disraeli*; Daniel L. Haynes and Nina Mae McKinney in King Vidor's *Hallelujah*; Gloria Swanson in Erich von Stroheim's *Queen Kelly* (censored in the United States, the picture will be shown briefly in Europe).

Hollywood musicals: Joan Crawford, Norma Shearer, John Gilbert, John Barrymore, Marie Dressler, Marion Davies, Buster Keaton, Conrad Nagel, Jack Benny, and Rudy Vallée in Charles Riesner's *Hollywood Revue of 1929* with songs including "Singin' in the Rain"; Maurice Chevalier and Jeanette MacDonald sing "Dream Lover" and "The March of the Grenadiers" in Ernst Lubitsch's *The Love Parade*; Helen Morgan in Rouben Mamoulian's *Applause*; Janet Gaynor and Charles Farrell in David Butler's *Sunny Side Up* with songs that include "I'm a Dreamer" and the title song.

Stage musicals: Irene Delroy and Jack Haley in *Follow Thru* 1/9 at New York's 46th Street Theater, with songs that include "Button Up Your Overcoat," 403 perfs.; Fred Allen, Portland Hoffa, Libby Holman, Bettina Hall, Peggy Conklin, and Clifton Webb in *The Little Show* 4/30 at New York's Music Box Theater, with songs that include "I Guess I'll Have to Change My Plan," "Moanin' Low," "Caught in the Rain," and "Can't We Be Friends" (music by Kay Swift), 321 perfs.; Canadian-born dancer-actress Ruby (*née* Ethel) Keeler, 18, Jimmy Durante, and Duke Ellington and his Orchestra in *Show Girl* 7/2 at New York's Ziegfeld Theater, with music by George Gershwin that includes the ballet "An American in Paris," lyrics by Ira Gershwin and Gus Kahn, songs that include "Liza" sung by Al Jolson in the audience to his wife, Ruby Keeler, onstage, 111 perfs.; Peggy Wood in Noël Coward's *Bitter Sweet* 7/18 at His Majesty's Theatre, London, with songs that include "I'll See You Again" and "Zigeuner," 697 perfs.; Gracie Fields in *The Show's the Thing* at London's Victoria Palace Theatre (it will run for 18 months); Helen Morgan as Addie Schmidt in *Sweet Adeline* 9/3 at New York's Hammerstein Theater, with Jerome Kern–Oscar Hammerstein II songs that include "Why Was I Born?," "Don't Ever Leave Me," and "Here Am I," 234 perfs.

Opera: Rosa Ponselle makes her London debut at Covent Garden 5/28 singing the title role in the 1831 Bellini opera *Norma*. She will continue to sing until her retirement in April 1937. U.S. contralto Gladys Swarthout, 28, makes her Metropolitan Opera debut 11/15 singing the role of La Cieca in the 1876 Ponchielli opera *La Gioconda*. She will be a Met regular until 1945.

Popular songs: "Am I Blue?" by Harry Akst, lyrics by Grant Clarke (for Ethel Waters to sing in the film *On With the Show*); "Falling In Love Again" by German songwriter Friedrich Hollaender, 33 (for Marlene Dietrich to sing in the film *The Blue Angel*); Bessie Smith records "Nobody Knows You When You're Down and Out."

Helen Wills wins again in women's singles both at Wimbledon and at Forest Hills.

The Japanese Mah-jongg Association is founded as the Chinese game gains popularity.

Robert and Helen Lynd report in their sociological study *Middletowne* (above) that Muncie, Ind., men are preoccupied with earning a living and with such practical matters as car repairs that they take little part in household affairs, leaving it to their wives to care for and discipline the children, make social arrangements, and the like.

The first crease-resistant cotton fabric is introduced by Tootal's of St. Helens, England.

Nestlé Colorinse, introduced in 10 shades, is the first home-applied hair coloring; one shade is a blue-grey that will be popular among older women (*see* permanent wave, 1906; Clairol, 1931).

California Perfume Co. chief David McConnell, now 72, introduces a new line of products under the name Avon, inspired by Shakespeare's home-town Stratford-upon-Avon (*see* 1898). The door-to-door cosmetic company will rename itself Avon Products in 1939, and its saleswomen will be called Avon Ladies. It will grow to have 1.5 million Avon Ladies (plus 2,000 Avon Men) and be the world's largest employer of women.

Caresse Crosby (Polly Jacob), now 35, is widowed December 10 when her husband, Harry, kills his mistress, Josephine Bigelow (*née* Rotch), 22, and then takes his own life in an apparent suicide pact (*see* 1927). She and Harry, who have lived in France since 1922, have been visiting New York; she has been attending theater with poet Hart Crane and emerges to learn that Harry has killed himself in a friend's duplex apartment at the Hotel des Artistes in West 67th Street.

Daniel Gerber begins selling strained baby foods through grocery stores (*see* 1928). Using leads supplied by mail-order customers, Gerber salesmen drive cars whose horns play "Rock-a-Bye Baby," they sell 590,000 cans in 1 year, and other food processors are inspired to enter the baby food market.

German chemist Adolph Butenandt, 26, and U.S. biochemist Edward Adelbert Doisy, 36, isolate the sex hormone estrone—one of the three principal forms of estrogen (the others are estradiol and estriol; the most plentiful, estradiol, which is also the most powerful, is secreted by the ovaries, the placenta, the testes, and the outer cover of the adrenal glands, which also produces estrogens from steroid chemicals in body fat). Estrogen regulates the menstrual cycle, initiating the release of an egg from the ovaries each month, and it was reported last year by German obstetrician-gynecologist Bernhardt Zondek that pregnant women excrete large amounts of estrogen in their urine (*see* pregnancy test, 1930; androgen, 1931; progesterone, 1934).

Robert and Helen Lynd report in *Middletowne* (above) that use of contraceptives is almost universal among women in the professional and business classes but rare among working-class wives.

New York police raid Sanger's Clinic, but Margaret Sanger continues to campaign for birth control (*see* 1923; International Planned Parenthood, 1948).

1930

Magda Lupescu, 26, mistress to Romania's Carol II, joins him at Bucharest in June after his son, the boy king Michael, has been removed after a 3-year reign. The new king, 37, who has electrified the country by arriving from Paris by airplane, will reign until 1940, with Lupescu (her father, a Moldavian junk dealer, Latinized his name from Wolff) exercising great influence on his regime. Romanians hate the king's mistress because she is vulgar, ruthless, egocentric, and Jewish (anti-Semitism is endemic); Carol's mother, Queen Marie, refuses to meet with Lupescu, referring to her as that "lady of light repute."

A civil disobedience campaign against the British in India begins March 12. The All-India Trade Congress has empowered Mahatma Gandhi to begin the demonstration, and he sets out on a 165-mile march to the Gujarat Coast of the Arabian Sea to produce salt by evaporating seawater in violation of the law and as a gesture of defiance against the British monopoly in salt production. When authorities jail Gandhi, his Anti–Salt Law campaign is taken up by the prominent Brahmin poet Sarojini Naidu (*née* Chattopadhyaya), 51, who has studied in England, worked for woman suffrage, alienated her family by marrying out of her caste, headed a Bombay salon that has welcomed people of all colors and religions, and been arrested as many times as Gandhi himself.

France enacts a workmen's insurance law April 30.

South Africa's white women receive the vote May 19, but blacks of both sexes remain disenfranchised.

Some 35,000 Japanese textile workers, most of them women, strike the Kanebo factory in April. Tokyo Muslin has a strike of 1,500 women workers in June to protest layoffs and factory closings as economic depression deepens throughout most of the world; the women remain in their dormitory and refuse to leave.

Japanese feminist Itsue Takamure, 36, joins with Raicho Hiratsuka in forming a new group to publish the magazine *Fujinsensen* (*Women's Front Line*) and press for women's rights. Prime Minister Osachi Hamaguchi announces in July that the Diet has approved legislation extending civil rights to women, but the upper house fails to approve the new law (*see* 1929). The same thing will happen in February and March of next year.

Amelia Earhart flies her Lockheed Vega at 171 miles per hour January 15, setting a new women's speed record.

The first airline flight attendant begins work in mid-May for United Airlines. Boeing agent Steve Stimpson at San Francisco has suggested that commercial aircraft carry "young women as couriers," United has hired Ellen Church and told the registered nurse and student pilot to hire seven other nurses—all aged 25, all single, all with pleasant personalities, none taller than five feet four or heavier than 115 pounds—and they serve cold meals and beverages, pass out candy and chewing gum, and comfort airsick passengers. Women cabin attendants, generally called "stewardesses," will serve to help allay public fears of flying.

British aviatrix Amy Johnson, 27, arrives in Australia May 24 after making the first solo flight by a woman from London. She has piloted her de Havilland Tiger Moth through a thick fog over the English Channel and has been forced twice by violent storms to land—once in a Near Eastern desert, once between Java and Surabaya. Johnson has had to lay over in Rangoon and Bangkok for repairs. She follows the 19½-day flight to Australia with a record six-day solo flight from England to India.

Harvard astronomer Annie Jump Cannon, now 66, completes cataloging and classifying some 400,000 astronomical objects. The "Census Taker of the Sky" started her work in 1897.

Social Organization of Manua and *Growing Up in New Guinea* by Margaret Mead are published to wide acclaim.

The American Board of Obstetrics and Gynecology is established to give medical schools criteria by which to judge the capabilities of staff members and general practitioners.

Intellectual Growth in Young Children by English Freudian education specialist Susan Brierley Isaacs (*née* Fairhurst), 45, challenges some of the ideas set forth by Swiss psychologist Jean Piaget, 34, in his 1926 book *The Child's Conception of the World.*

Isaacs ran an experimental progressive school at Cambridge from 1924 to 1927, letting children learn for themselves rather than instructing them, and letting them give vent to emotional expression rather than imposing strict discipline. She will head the Department of Child Development at London's Institute of Education from 1933 to 1943.

Pine Manor Junior College is created out of the Dana Hall Post-Graduate School at Wellesley, Mass. (*see* 1899). It will move to its own Chestnut Hill, Mass., campus in 1965 and become independent of Dana Hill.

The *Moscow News* begins publication with Anna Louise Strong as editor-publisher. The English-language paper is for foreigners.

Heiress Eleanor "Cissy" Patterson Gizycka Schlesinger, whose second husband, Elmer, died last year, offers to buy William Randolph Hearst's *Washington Herald*, is hired instead as editor at $200 per week plus one-third of all profits, has her name legally changed to Eleanor Medill Patterson, and reports for work August 30 in a chauffeur-driven 16-cylinder Cadillac limousine. She gets editorial advice from her ex-son-in-law Drew Pearson and, emphasizing sex and gossip, will make the *Herald* Washington's largest-circulation morning paper within a year, but it will not turn a profit until 1937 (*see* 1937).

"Blondie" debuts September 8. Chicago cartoonist Murat Bernard "Chic" Young, 29, has been drawing "Dumb Dora." The antics of his Jazz Age flapper heroine and her playboy husband Dagwood Bumstead will make "Blondie" the most widely syndicated of all cartoon strips.

Nonfiction: "A Room of One's Own" (essay) by Virginia Woolf champions the cause of independence for women: "Women have served all these centuries as looking-glasses possessing the magic and delicious power of reflecting the figure of a man at twice its natural size"; "When one reads of a witch being ducked, of a woman possessed by devils, of a wise woman selling herbs, or even of a very remarkable man who had a mother, then I think we are on the track of a lost novelist, a suppressed poet, of some mute and inglorious Jane Austen or Emily Brontë who dashed her brains out on the moor or moped and mowed about the highways crazed with the torture her gift had put her to. Indeed, I would venture that Anon, who wrote so many poems without signing them, was a woman"; *Seductio ad Absurdum: The Principles and Practices of Seduction—A Beginner's Guide* by U.S. author Emily Hahn, 25; *The Greek Way* by former Bryn Mawr Preparatory School headmistress Edith Hamilton, 63; *Epistle to Prometheus* by Babette Deutsch; *The Practice of Philosophy* by Radcliffe philosophy professor Susanne (Katherina) Langer (*née* Knauth), 34.

Fiction: *East Wind, West Wind* by U.S. novelist Pearl Comfort Buck (*née* Sydenstricker), 38, who was raised in China by her Presbyterian missionary parents and wrote the book aboard ship en route to America; *A Woman* by Ding Ling, who joins China's League of Left-Wing Writers and becomes the editor of its journal (she will join the Communist party in 1932); *Years of Grace* by U.S. novelist Margaret Ayer Barnes, 64 (Pulitzer Prize); *Brothers and Sisters* by Ivy Compton-Burnett; *Time, Gentlemen, Time!* by Norah Hoult; *The Edwardians* by V. Sackville-West; *The Voyage Home* by Storm Jameson; *The Fool of the Family* by Margaret Kennedy is a sequel to her *Constant Nymph* of 1924 (it will be made into the 1934 play and 1947 film *Escape Me Never*); *Experts Are Puzzled* (stories) by Laura Riding; *Elinor Barley* (stories) by Sylvia Townsend Warner; *Mitsou* by Colette; *Cimarron* by Edna Ferber, who writes, "If American politics are too dirty for women to take part in, there's something wrong with American politics"; *The Great Meadow* by Elizabeth Madox Roberts; *Mixed Marriage* by Margaret Culkin Banning; *Bridal Pond* (stories) by Zona Gale; *The Kramer Girls* by Ruth Suckow; *The Office Wife* and *Make-Believe* by Faith Baldwin; *Murder at the Vicarage* by Agatha Christie, whose detective Jane Marple will appear in 14 other mystery novels; *Strong Poison* by Dorothy Sayers; *Mystery Mile* by Margery Allingham; *The Door* by Mary Roberts Rinehart; *While the Patient Slept* by U.S. mystery novelist Mignon Good Eberhart, 31.

Poetry: *Les Poésies de Gérard d'Houville* by French poet Marie-Louise-Antoinette de Heredia, 55, who has written under a *nom de plume*; *Land of Children* (*Kinderland*) by Agnes Miegel; *Poems: A Joking Word* and *Thirty Poems Less* by Laura Riding; *Laments for the Living* by Dorothy Parker.

Juvenile: *The Secret of the Old Clock* by Carolyn Keene (U.S. author Mildred Augustine Wirt Benson, 25) features the adventures of 16-year-old amateur detective Nancy Drew. The first woman to receive a master's degree from the University of Iowa, Benson has written the book on an old Underwood typewriter, received about $125, will write 22 more of the first 30 Nancy Drew mysteries, and will never receive any royalties from the Stratemeyer Syndicate, whose founder, Edward Stratemeyer, has died at Newark, N.J., May 10 at age 67 after developing the Nancy Drew character. His daughter, Harriet Stratemeyer Adams, 37, takes over the business of producing *Bobbsey Twins* books under the name Laura Lee Hope, *Tom Swift* books under the name Victor Appleton, *Hardy Boys* books under the name Franklin W. Dixon, and *Rover Boys* books as well. Insisting on moral stories with no epithets stronger than "gosh," Adams will update the Nancy Drew mysteries beginning in 1959 (changing their heroine's age to 18 so that she may drive legally in every state, eliminating ethnic slurs) and will still be writing when she dies in March 1982 at age 89.

Painting: *The Boat* by Marie Laurencin; *Self-Portrait* by New York painter Lee Krasner (Lena Krassner), 22.

Theater: Ruth Ford, Glenn Anders, and Earle Larrimore in Philip Barry's *Hotel Universe* 4/14 at New York's Martin Beck Theater, 81 perfs.; *The Barrets of Wimpole Street* by Dutch-English playwright Rudolph Besier, 52, at England's Malvern Festival (it will open next year at New York's Empire Theater with Katharine Cornell); Gertrude Lawrence, Noël Coward, and Laurence Kerr Olivier in Coward's *Private Lives* 9/24 at London's Phoenix Theatre, with Coward's song "Someday I'll Find You," 101 perfs.; Spring Byington and Kaufman in George S. Kaufman and Moss Hart's *Once in a Lifetime* 9/24 at New York's Music Box Theater, 401 perfs.; Dorothy Hull, Varree Teasdale, and Muriel Kirkland as three ex-Follies girls on the make in Zoë Akins's *The Greeks Had a Word for It* 9/25 at New York's Sam H. Harris Theater, 253 perfs.; Russian-American actress Eugenie Leontovich, 30, as the dancer Grusinskaya in *Grand Hotel* by W. A. Drake, who has adapted the Vicki Baum novel (it will appear next year), 11/13 at New York's

National Theater, 459 perfs.; *Alison's House* by Susan Glaspell, now 48, 12/1 at New York's Civic Repertory Theater, 41 perfs. (based on the life of poet Emily Dickinson; Pulitzer Prize).

Radio drama: *Death Valley Days* 7/30 on NBC Blue Network stations. New York advertising copywriter Ruth Cornwall Woodman has researched background for the show by visiting Panamint City.

Films: Greta Garbo in Clarence Brown's *Anna Christie* ("Garbo Talks," the advertisements shout); Jean Harlow (Harlean Carpenter), 19, and Ben Lyon in Howard Hughes's *Hell's Angels*; Louise Dresser, Will Rogers, and Joel McCrea in Henry King's *Lightnin'*; Marie Dressler and Wallace Beery in George Hill's *Min and Bill*; Marlene Dietrich, Gary Cooper, and Adolphe Menjou in Josef von Sternberg's *Morocco*; Norah Baring and Herbert Marshall in Alfred Hitchcock's *Murder*; Ruth Chatterton in Richard Wallace's *The Right to Love*; Ina Claire and Fredric March in George Cukor and Cyril Gardner's *The Royal Family of Broadway*; Jackie Coogan and Mitzi Green (Mitzi Keno), 10, in John Cromwell's *Tom Sawyer*.

Stage musicals: Ruth Etting in *Nine-Fifteen Revue* 2/11 at New York's George M. Cohan Theater, with Harold Arlen–Ted Koehler songs that include "Get Happy," 7 perfs.; Gertrude Lawrence and Harry Richman in *Lew Leslie's International Revue* 2/15 at New York's Majestic Theater, with Jimmy McHugh–Dorothy Fields songs that include "Exactly Like You" and "On the Sunny Side of the Street," 96 perfs.; Ruth Etting and Ed Wynn in *Simple Simon* 2/18 at New York's Ziegfeld Theater, with Richard Rodgers–Lorenz Hart songs that include "Ten Cents a Dance" and "I Still Believe in You," 135 perfs.; Eleanor Powell, Joe Cook, and Dave Chasen in *Fine and Dandy* 9/23 at New York's Erlanger Theater, with music by Kay Swift, 33, lyrics by Paul James (Swift's husband, James Warburg), songs that include "Can This Be Love?" 255 perfs.; Ethel Merman (originally Zimmerman), 21, in *Girl Crazy* 10/14 at New York's Alvin Theater, with Gershwin songs that include "I Got Rhythm," "Embraceable You," "Little White Lies," "But Not for Me," and "Bidin' My Time," 272 perfs.; Libby Holman, Fred Allen, and Clifton Webb in *Three's a Crowd* 10/15 at New York's Selwyn Theater, with

songs that include "Body and Soul" and "Something to Remember You By," 272 perfs.; Rosalind Russell, 19, Imogene Coca, and Sterling Holloway in *The Garrick Gaieties* 10/16 at New York's Guild Theater, with songs that include "I'm Only Human After All" and "Out of Breath and Scared to Death of You," 158 perfs.; Ethel Waters (*née* Howard), 34, and Cecil Mack's Choir in *Lew Leslie's Blackbirds of 1930* 10/22 at New York's Royale Theater, with songs that include "Memories of You" by Eubie Blake, lyrics by Andy Razaf, 57 perfs.; Fanny Brice and George Jessel in *Sweet and Low* 11/17 at New York's 46th Street Theater, with songs that include "Outside Looking In" and "Cheerful Little Earful," 184 perfs.; Marilyn Miller, Fred and Adele Astaire, Bob Hope, and Eddie Foy, Jr., in *Smiles* 11/18 at New York's Ziegfeld Theater, with songs that include "Time on My Hands" and "You're Driving Me Crazy," 63 perfs.; Jessie Matthews in *Ever Green* 12/3 at London's Adelphi Theatre, with Richard Rodgers–Lorenz Hart songs that include "Dancing on the Ceiling," 254 perfs.; Hope Williams, Ann Pennington, Jimmy Durante, Lew Clayton, and Eddie Jackson in *The New Yorkers* 12/8 at New York's Broadway Theater, with Cole Porter songs that include "Love for Sale," 162 perfs.

First performances: Piano Concertino by English composer Elizabeth Maconchy, 23, is played at Prague; her suite *The Land* is played at the Proms in London.

Popular songs: "It Happened in Monterey" by Mabel Wayne, lyrics by William Rose (for the film *King of Jazz* with Paul Whiteman); "Them There Eyes" by Maceo Pinkard, William Tracey, and Doris Tauber.

Jennie Kelleher of Madison, Wis., bowls a perfect 300 game February 12, becoming the first woman to do so.

Helen Wills Moody wins in women's singles at Wimbledon, Betty Nuthall, 19 (Br), at Forest Hills (the first non-American U.S. champion).

Woolworth heiress Barbara Hutton, who matriculated 2 years ago at Miss Porter's School for Girls at Farmington, Conn., turns 18 in November and makes her debut December 21 at a $60,000 ball for which the first floor of New York's Ritz-Carlton Hotel has been transformed with white birches, eucalyptus trees from California, mountain heather, scarlet poinsettias, and 10,000 American Beauty roses (workmen have labored for 2 days and nights to create the opulent bower). The 1,000 guests (among them, Brooke Astor, Doris Duke, Virginia Thaw, and Louise Van Alen) are greeted by Maurice Chevalier, dressed as Santa Claus, and helpers who hand out party favors—pocket-size gold jewelry cases containing unmounted diamonds, emeralds, rubies, and sapphires—while unemployed men sell apples on the sidewalks outside. Singer Rudy Vallee entertains the guests, who dance to music supplied by Meyer Davis, Howard Lanin, and two other orchestras. Hutton's aunt Marjorie Meriweather Post (Mrs. E. F. Hutton) has arranged the affair, which takes place on in the face of worsening economic problems. Despite Prohibition, 200 waiters serve 2,000 bottles of champagne plus 1,000 seven-course midnight suppers and 1,000 breakfasts (*see* 1924; 1931).

Birds Eye Frosted Foods go on sale for the first time March 6 at Springfield, Mass. General Foods introduces frozen peas, spinach, raspberries, cherries, loganberries, fish, and various meats, but the packets, kept in ice cream cabinets, are not readily visible and sell at relatively high prices (35¢ for a package of peas).

Sliced bread is introduced under the Wonder Bread label by Continental Baking. Battle Creek, Mich., inventor Otto Frederick Rohwedder perfected the commercial bread slicer in January 1928 after 15 years of work. Consumers are suspicious at first (sliced bread does grow stale faster) but soon accept the product enthusiastically.

The first true supermarket opens in August at Jamaica, Long Island, where former Kroger store manager Michael S. Cullen, 46, opens the King Kullen Market in an abandoned garage and meets with instant success (*see* 1923; Big Bear, 1932).

Benito Mussolini's Italy makes abortion a crime "against the integrity and health of the race," but illegal abortions continue at a rate of more than half a million per year.

A human egg cell is seen for the first time through a microscope (*see* spermatozoa, 1677). Japanese

researchers discover that human ovaries generally release eggs 12 to 16 days before menstruation, but about one woman in four will be found to be wildly erratic in her menstrual cycle and all women will be found to be erratic for a few months after the birth of a child.

Ascheim-Z (Zondek) pregnancy tests come into wider use: urine or blood from a woman suspected of being pregnant is injected into a female rabbit, which is killed a few days later; if the woman was pregnant, hormones in her urine or blood give the rabbit's ovaries an appearance of pregnancy. The tests will eventually be superseded by immunological or immunoassay methods.

A U.S. court decision extending trademark protection to contraceptive devices encourages production of better-quality condoms. The economic depression makes large families increasingly burdensome to breadwinners.

Anglican bishops meeting at the Lambeth Conference accord at least lukewarm acceptance to contraception (*see* 1908). But 16 British clinics and two private consultants have seen only 21,000 clients since 1921, and, since cervical caps and diaphragms are too costly or difficult for most women, their failure rate is distressingly high. Most couples continue to rely on sponges, douches, and coitus interruptus to avoid pregnancy. The birthrate in the U.K. will fall to 15.8 per thousand in the next 2 years, down from 34.1 in 1870–1872 and 24.5 in 1910–1912, but the reasons for the drop are largely economic.

The encyclical *Casti connubii* issued December 31 by Pope Pius XI prohibits taking an infant's life to save the mother's (although many cesareans are performed to remove an impacted fetus). It also says, "Any use whatsoever of matrimony exercised in such a way that the [sex] act is deliberately frustrated in its natural power to generate life is an offense against the law of God and of nature, and those who indulge in such are branded with the guilt of a grave sin." The statement of opposition to "artificial fertility regulation" is, in part, a response to the Anglicans' Lambeth Conference position (above). But the "rhythm" system of birth control favored by the Church is an inadequate form of contraception for the reasons suggested above (critics call it "Vatican roulette"), and increasing numbers of Roman Catholics are employing artificial methods of birth control, including abortion.

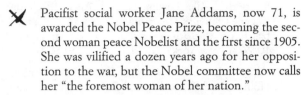

Pacifist social worker Jane Addams, now 71, is awarded the Nobel Peace Prize, becoming the second woman peace Nobelist and the first since 1905. She was vilified a dozen years ago for her opposition to the war, but the Nobel committee now calls her "the foremost woman of her nation."

Atlanta reformer Jessie Daniel Ames founds the Southern Commission on the Study of Lynching to combat the idea that lynching is necessary to protect the chastity of white women like herself. Her commission releases a study showing that only 16.7 percent of lynch victims between 1889 and 1929 were ever accused of attempted rape and only 6.7 percent were guilty of actual rape (*see* 1937).

The case of the "Scottsboro boys" creates a furor over sexual relations between white women and black men. A shouting mob surrounds the county courthouse at Scottsboro, Ala., where nine black youths are being tried on charges of having raped two white women aboard a freight car March 25 after having thrown some white hoboes off the train. Asked if they were raped, one woman says no, the other yes (but *see* 1933). A physician testifies that he examined Victoria Price, 21, and Ruby Bates, 17, of Huntsville shortly after the alleged rape, and that while he found dried semen he saw no live spermatozoa and no blood. The jury discounts this, and the 3-day trial ends April 9 with eight of the defendants sentenced to death and the ninth to life imprisonment. The Supreme Court will reverse the Scottsboro convictions, some indictments will later be dropped, the sentences will be commuted to life imprisonment, and the defendants will serve a total of 130 years behind bars (one will not be paroled until 1951).

Three San Jose, Calif., canneries cut wages, and workers organized by Communist party members walk out in the summer. Among the organizers is Dorothy Ray Healey, 16, who has dropped out of high school to work in the Santa Clara valley.

Spanish women gain the right to vote on the same basis as men.

The outbreak of war in Manchuria September 18 ends efforts to gain civil rights for Japanese women.

U.S. women take in boarders, do sewing, laundry, and dressmaking, provide $1 manicures, and set up parlor grocery stores to supplement their husbands' incomes as economic recession deepens.

New York's Lord & Taylor makes its fashion and interior decoration director Dorothy Shaver, 34, vice president in charge of advertising and publicity. Shaver will bring to prominence such fashion designers as Anne Fogarty, Lily Daché, Claire McCardle, Rose Marie Reid, and Pauline Trigère (*see* 1945).

Chicago medical researcher Florence Seibert, 34, and her colleagues isolate the active tuberculin protein after 8 years of effort. Left severely lame by an attack of poliomyelitis (infantile paralysis) at age 3, Seibert has invented a special filtration trap that eliminates the chemicals which remain in water after distillation. Sterilization kills the bacteria, but traces of toxic chemicals left behind reenter the water via steam droplets produced in distillation. Seibert's filter makes multiple distillations unnecessary, and the protein derivative that she obtains is far purer than the tuberculin bacillus isolated by German physician Robert Koch in 1882.

Nonfiction: *On Understanding Women* by U.S. historian Mary Beard (*née* Ritter), 55, who married Charles A. Beard in 1900; *Women and Politics* by Katherine Marjory, duchess of Atholl.

Fiction: *The Good Earth* by Pearl S. Buck (Pulitzer prize); *A Story of Honest Poverty* (*Seihin no sho*) and *The Town of the Accordion and the Fish* (*Fukin to sakana no machi*) by Fumiko Hayashi; *The Waves* by Virginia Woolf; *Corn King and Spring Queen* by Naomi Mitchison is about ancient Egypt, Scythia, and the Middle East; *After Leaving Mr. Mackenzie* by Jean Rhys; *Men and Wives* by Ivy Compton-Burnett; *Broome Stages* by Clemence Dane; *Tobit Transplanted* by English novelist and travel writer Stella Benson, 39, who will die of tuberculosis in 1933; *Apartments to Let* by Norah Hoult; *Without My Cloak* by Irish playwright-novelist Kate O'Brien, 34; *A Moral Ending and Other Stories* by

Sylvia Townsend Warner; *All Passion Spent* by V. Sackville-West; *The Hydroelectric Station* (*Gidrotsentral*) by Marietta Shaginyan; *The Walls of the World* (*Sciany swiata*) by Zofja Nalkowska is a study of prison life; *Shadows on the Rock* by Willa Cather; *Plagued by the Nightingale* by U.S. novelist Kay Boyle, 29; *Grand Hotel* by Austrian-American novelist Vicki Baum, 43 (*see* Theater, 1930); *The Town's Too Small* by Margaret Culkin Banning; *Penhally* by Kentucky-born novelist Caroline Gordon, 35, who married poet Alan Tate in 1924, worked as a secretary-typist from 1924 to 1928 for English novelist Ford Madox Ford, and has learned her craft from him (she will win a Guggenheim Fellowship next year and go with her husband to France, where they lived after he won a Guggenheim in 1928); *Children and Older People* by Ruth Suckow; *Back Street* by Fannie Hurst; *Babs: A Story of Divine Corners, Mary Lou: A Story of Divine Corners, Skyscraper*, and *Today's Virtue* by Faith Baldwin; *A White Bird Flying* by Bess Streeter Aldrich; *Calico Bush* by Rachel Field; *Police at the Funeral* and *The Girth Chalice Mystery* (in England, *Look to the Lady*) by Margery Allingham; *Walking Corpse* (in England, *Great Southern Mystery*) by London novelist Margaret Isabel Cole, 38, who (with her husband, G. D. H. Cole) is prominent in the socialist Fabian Society.

Poetry: *Death and Taxes* by Dorothy Parker.

Painting: *Portrait of Frida and Diego* by Mexican painter Frida Kahlo, 21, who married muralist Diego Rivera in 1929.

New York's Whitney Museum of American Art opens on 8th Street, Greenwich Village, to display works by young artists. Sculptor (and railroad heiress) Gertrude Vanderbilt Whitney, 56, whose husband, sportsman Harry Payne Whitney, died last year at age 58, will modestly wait 8 years before displaying any of her own works. The museum she founds will move in 1966 to Madison Avenue at 75th Street.

Theater: Helen Westley, Lee Strasberg, June Walker, and Franchot Tone in Lynn Riggs's *Green Grow the Lilacs* 1/26 at New York's Guild Theater, 64 perfs.; Lily Cahill in *As Husbands Go* by U.S. playwright Rachel Crothers, 59, 3/15 at New York's John Golden Theater, 124 perfs; *Autumn Crocus* by English playwright C. L. Anthony (Dorothy Gladys Smith), 33, 4/20 at London's Lyric Theatre, with Fay Compton, Jessica Tandy, 20, and Francis Lederer; Stella Adler, Franchot Tone, Clifford Odets, and Rose McClendon in Paul Green's *The House of Connelly* 10/5 at New York's Martin Beck Theater, 81 perfs.; Alla Nazimova and Alice Brady in Eugene O'Neill's *Mourning Becomes Electra*, a play based on the 5th-century B.C. Greek tragedies, 10/26 at New York's Guild Theater, 150 perfs.

Films: Sylvia Sidney (Sophia Kosow), 21, Phillips Holmes, and Frances (Jean) Dee, 24, in Josef von Sternberg's *An American Tragedy*; Marlene Dietrich in von Sternberg's *Dishonored*; Jean Arthur (Gladys Greene), 22, and Charles Boyer in Frank Borzage's *History Is Made at Night*; Hertha Thiele and Dorothea Wieck in Karl Froelich's *Mädchen in Uniform*; Annabella in René Clair's *Le Million*; James Cagney, Jean Harlow, and Mae Clark (who gets half a grapefruit in her face) in William Wellman's *Public Enemy*; Sylvia Sidney and William Collier, Jr., in King Vidor's *Street Scene*; Greta Garbo and Clark Gable in Robert Z. Leonard's *Susan Lenox: Her Fall and Rise*.

Radio: *The Easy Aces*, with comedian Goodman Ace, 32, and his wife, Jane (*née* Epstein), who will gain a reputation for witticisms such as "Time wounds all heels." *Easy Aces* will continue until 1945, *Mr. Ace and Jane* until 1955.

Kate Smith makes her radio debut May 1 singing "When the Moon Comes over the Mountain" on CBS stations. Kathryn Elizabeth Smith, now 22, has played comic fat girl roles in Broadway shows, has finally won a singing role at New York's Palace Theater, begins a radio career that will continue for nearly half a century, will sing Irving Berlin's "God Bless America" in a 1938 Armistice Day broadcast, and will acquire exclusive air rights to the song Berlin originally wrote for his 1918 show *Yip, Yip, Yaphank* but laid aside.

Opera: French-born U.S. soprano Lily (*née* Alice Josephine) Pons, 32, makes her Metropolitan Opera debut 1/3 singing the title role in the 1835 Donizetti opera *Lucia di Lammermoor*; English soprano Joan Cross, 30, makes her Covent Garden debut singing the role of Mimi in the 1896 Puccini opera *La Bohème*. The Old Vic company moves to the Sadler's Wells Theatre with English soprano Edith (Mary) Coates, 23, as its leading mezzo-soprano.

Ballet: Alicia Makarova, Antony Tudor, and Frederick Ashton in *Façade* 4/26 at London's Cambridge Theatre, with music by William Walton, choreography by Ashton (*see* 1923).

London's Royal Ballet has its beginnings in the Vic-Wells (later Sadler's Wells) Ballet founded by Irish ballerina Ninette de Valois (Edris Stannus), 33, whose small opera ballet ensemble will grow to become Britain's national ballet company.

Mary Wigman at Dresden sends her pupil and teacher Hanya Holm (Johanna Eckert), 38, to New York to establish a U.S. branch of her ballet school (*see* 1920). Wigman's school will be shut down by German authorities in a few years, and Holm will open her own studio in 1936, melding Wigman's disciplines and choreographic ideas with American approaches that will find expression in Broadway musical numbers.

Broadway musicals: Fanny Brice (Mrs. Billy Rose) in *Billy Rose's Crazy Quilt* 5/19 at the 44th Street Theater, with songs that include "I Found a Million Dollar Baby—in a Five and Ten Cent Store," 79 perfs.; Beatrice Lillie and Ernest Truex in *The Little Show* 6/1 at the Music Box Theater, with Nöel Coward songs that include "Mad Dogs and Englishmen," 136 perfs.; Fred and Adele Astaire make their last appearance together in *The Band Wagon* 6/3 at the New Amsterdam Theater, with the first revolving stage to be used in a musical, songs that include "Dancing in the Dark" and "I Love Louisa," 260 perfs.; Helen Morgan, Ruth Etting, and Harry Richman in *The Ziegfeld Follies* 7/1 at the Ziegfeld Theater, 165 perfs.; Lillian Roth and William Demarest in *Earl Carroll's Vanities* 7/27 at the new 3,000-seat Earl Carroll Theater on 7th Avenue at 50th Street, with naked chorus girls, Ravel's "Bolero," songs that include "Goodnight, Sweetheart" by English songwriters Ray Noble, James Campbell, and Reg Connelly, 278 perfs.; Ethel Merman, Willie Howard, Rudy Vallee, and Ray Bolger in *George White's Scandals* 9/14 at the Apollo Theater, with songs that include "Life Is Just a Bowl of Cherries," 202 perfs.; Ann Pennington and Harriet Lake (Georgia Sothern) in *Every-*

body's Welcome 10/13 at the Shubert Theater, with Tommy and Jimmy Dorsey, songs that include "As Time Goes By" by Herman Hupfield (*see* film *Casablanca*, 1942), 139 perfs.; Bettina Hall, Georges Metaxa, and Eddie Foy, Jr. in *The Cat and the Fiddle* 10/15 at the Globe Theater, with Jerome Kern–Otto Harbach songs that include "She Didn't Say 'Yes' " and "The Night Was Made for Love," 395 perfs.

Popular songs: "Sally" by English songwriters Harry Leon (Sugarman), Will E. Haines, and Leo Towers (for Maurice Elvey's film *Sally in Our Alley* with music hall star Gracie Fields, now 33).

Kentucky singer-songwriter Aunt Molly Jackson (Mary Magdalene Garlande), 51, travels to New York and joins a national music tour in support of striking miners; by 1939 she will have a repertoire of more than 200 songs, including "Dreadful Memories," "Coal Miner's Farewell," "Death of Harry Sims," and "I Am a Union Woman."

Minor league pitcher Jackie Mitchell, 17, signs a contract to pitch for the Memphis Lookouts in the Southern Association, takes the mound in April against the New York Yankees in an exhibition game at Chattanooga, Tenn., and strikes out Babe Ruth in four pitches, and Lou Gehrig in three.

Cilly Aussem, 22 (Ger), wins in women's singles at Wimbledon, Helen Wills Moody at Forest Hills.

Starr Faithfull, 25, makes lurid headlines June 8 when her body—clad only in a silk dress—washes up on the beach at Long Beach, N.Y. The beautiful woman has been dead since June 5, suicide notes are produced some weeks later, but the cause of her death will remain a mystery.

Lili de Alvarez appears in center court at Wimbledon June 23 wearing shorts—the first woman in Wimbledon history not to wear the traditional skirt.

The Nevada State Legislature enacts a 6-week residency law for divorce seekers in a move to generate revenue for the Depression-struck state, which has almost no tax base since most of its lands are federally owned. Nevada grants 5,260 divorces, up from 2,500 in 1928, and 4,745 of the decrees are handed down at Reno, which becomes the boomtown divorce capital of the world (*see* 1942).

Clairol hair dye is introduced by U.S. chemists' broker Lawrence Gelb, 33, who has acquired the formula in Europe (*see* Nestlé Colorinse, 1929). Gelb builds a research laboratory and plant at Stamford, Conn., and tries to create a U.S. market for hair dyes (*see* Miss Clairol, 1950).

British medical researcher Lucy Wills at Bombay discovers that pregnant women with nutritional megaloblastic anemia respond to diets containing autolyzed yeast.

The Supreme Court upholds a company that has been sued by the FTC for false advertising (*FTC* v. *Raladam*). The company has advertised its thyroid-extract product, Marmola, as "a scientific remedy for obesity," and while the Court agrees with the American Medical Association that the ads are dangerously misleading, it rules that such advertising is not unfair to competition.

Daniel Gerber's Fremont Packing Co. adds salt to its baby foods (*see* 1929). Infants' taste buds are not sufficiently developed to discern any difference, but sales resistance has come from mothers who taste their babies' food.

U.S. mechanical refrigerator production tops 1 million units, up from 5,000 in 1921. By 1937 the industry will be producing refrigerators at the rate of nearly 3 million per year.

Birds Eye Frosted Foods go on sale across the United States as General Foods expands distribution, but only a few retail grocers have freezer cases for displaying frozen foods (*see* 1930).

Adolph Butenandt isolates the male sex hormone androgen (*see* 1929).

1932

The U.S. Senate gets a woman member January 12 as Hattie Ophelia Carraway (*née* Wyatt), 53, of Arkansas takes the seat of her late husband, Thaddeus Horatius, who died in November. Sen. Carraway is elected in her own right in November and will serve until 1945.

Gov. Franklin D. Roosevelt promises a "new deal" for the American people and is elected president by a landslide. His wife, Eleanor, tells Associated Press staff writer Lorena Hickock, 38, "If I wanted to be selfish I could wish that he had not been elected, but I am deeply and sincerely glad. I wouldn't have had it otherwise. And now I shall start to work on my own salvation. I never wanted to be a President's wife, and I don't want it now. You don't quite believe me, do you? Very likely no one would—except possibly some woman who had had the job. Well, it's true just the same." Hickock portrays Eleanor as a career woman with a life of her own.

Brazil, Uruguay, Thailand, and the Maldives give women the right to vote on the same basis as men. Puerto Rican women gain voting rights for the first time.

David Dubinsky (originally Dobnievski) becomes president of the International Ladies' Garment Workers' Union (ILGWU) at age 40. The Polish-American organizer launches a membership drive that will triple the union's rolls in 3 years.

The average U.S. weekly wage falls to $17, down from $28 in 1929, and women generally are paid below average. Breadlines form in many cities. Unemployment reaches between 15 and 17 million by year's end, 34 million Americans have no income of any kind, and those who do work average little more than $16 per week.

Amelia Earhart lands in Northern Ireland May 21 after having made the first solo transatlantic flight by a woman. It has taken her 14 hours, 16 minutes.

Beech Aircraft is founded at Wichita, Kans., by Walter H. Beech and his wife, Olive Ann, 28, who will head the light-plane manufacturing company after her husband's death in 1950.

The Changing Culture of an Indian Tribe by Margaret Mead is about the Omaha, with whom she conducted fieldwork in 1930.

Cleveland obstetrician Arthur Bill notes that "the principle of the relief of pain [in childbirth] is almost universally accepted." "Analgesia to the point of amnesia" is becoming routine in most major U.S. hospitals, although a few infants are born with breathing difficulties, raising doubts about Twilight Sleep (*see* 1915; Read, 1933).

The Maternity Center Association of New York, founded in 1918, begins to train qualified public health nurses in midwifery, supervise any remaining immigrant midwives, and deliver infants among the poor in rural areas as well as in the city. The Association will merge in 1958 with King's County Hospital, Brooklyn, where nurse-midwives will continue to deliver many clinic patients.

The Psychoanalysis of Children by Melanie Klein advances theories developed by the Viennese child psychologist (*see* 1921).

The Benzedrine Inhaler introduced by Smith Kline & French is a nasal decongestant whose active ingredient is amphetamine. It will be used in treating hyperkinetic children, prescribed for obesity, and abused as "speed."

Bennington College opens at North Bennington, Vt., in September with a student enrollment of 86 freshmen and a faculty of 19 headed by Robert Devore Leigh, 42. Local philanthropist Elizabeth Jennings (Mrs. George S.) Franklin, 45, and her mother have donated 140 acres of their farmstead as a site for the college (its tenant house, large barn, and two chicken houses have been remodeled to house the school). As each new class is added in the next 3 years, more student houses will be built, and by the time the first class is graduated in 1936 enrollment will be 250 with a faculty of 42. The curriculum by then will be fully developed, with courses in the four divisions of language and literature, social studies, science, and the arts. Students will receive instruction in music, dancing, art, creative writing, biology, physics, chemistry, mathematics, and the social sciences. Early in 1941 Bennington will receive the Jennings stone mansion, which will become the auditorium and art gallery, and carriage barn, neither of which was included in the original donation, and will be able to increase its enrollment to 270 students. Another 60 acres of adjoining meadowland will be added subsequently.

The Highlander Folk School is founded at Monteagle, Tenn., by educator Zilphia Horton and her husband, Miles (*see* music, 1962).

Eleanor Roosevelt gives her first press conference March 6 to 35 women reporters.

Family Circle begins publication at Newark, N.J., early in September with 24 pages. The first magazine to be distributed exclusively through grocery stores, the weekly is given free to shoppers at two eastern chains and will have a circulation of 1.44 million by 1939 (*see* 1946; *Woman's Day*, 1937).

Nonfiction: *The Roman Way* by Edith Hamilton; *Diary* (*Dagbok*) by Selma Lagerlöf, now 73.

Fiction: *Save Me the Waltz* by Alabama-born writer Zelda Fitzgerald (*née* Sayre), 32, who married novelist F. Scott Fitzgerald in 1920 and has written many of the stories that have been published under his name; *Sons* by Pearl S. Buck; *The Wise and Foolish Virgins* by English novelist Marguerite Steen, 38; *Inheritance* by English novelist Phyllis Bentley, 38; *Bright Skin* by Julia Peterkin; *A Lesson in Love* (*La Naissance du jour*) by Colette; *Slow Dawning* by Australian novelist Eleanor Dark (*née* O'Reilly), 31, who completed it in 1923; *They Were Defeated* by Rose Macaulay; *An Invitation to the Waltz* by Rosamond Lehmann; *The Salutation* (stories) by Sylvia Townsend Warner; *Obscure Destinies* (stories) by Willa Cather; *The Haunted Mirror* (stories) by Elizabeth Madox Roberts; *A Sheltered Life* by Ellen Glasgow; *Hepatica Hawks* by Rachel Field; *Certain People of Importance* by Kathleen Norris; *Path of True Love* by Margaret Culkin Banning; *Self-Made Woman, Weekend Marriage, District Nurse,* and *Myra: A Story of Divine Corners* by Faith Baldwin.

Poetry: *Days of Autumn* (*Herbsttage*) by Agnes Miegel.

Juvenile: *Little House in the Big Woods* by Missouri novelist Laura Wilder (*née* Ingalls), 65, who begins a series of eight volumes that will appear in the next 11 years to recount the author's girlhood in the Midwest of the late 19th century: " ' It was harder for little girls. Because they had to behave like little ladies all the time, not only on Sundays. Little girls could never slide downhill, like boys. Little girls had to sit in the house and stitch on samplers' "; *The Cat Who Went to Heaven* by U.S. author Elizabeth Coatsworth, 39, is based on a Japanese folk story; *Perkit the Pedlar* by Eleanor Farjeon.

Painting: *What Do Young Women Dream About?* by Marie Laurencin.

Theater: Ilka Chase, William Gargan, and Leslie Howard in Philip Barry's *The Animal Kingdom* 1/12 at New York's Broadhurst Theater, 183 perfs.; Edna Best and Herbert Marshall in John Van Druten's *There's Always Juliet* 2/15 at New York's Empire Theater, 108 perfs.; Beatrice Lillie, Hope Williams, Leo G. Carroll, and Claude Rains in George Bernard Shaw's *Too True to Be Good* 4/4 at New York's Guild Theater, 57 perfs.; Margaret Hamilton, Margaret Wycherly, and Dorothy Stickney in Rose Franken's *Another Language* 4/25 at New York's Booth Theater, 344 perfs.; *Service* by C. L. Anthony (Dorothy Smith) 10/12 at Wyndham's Theatre, London; English actress Constance Collier, 50, in George S. Kaufman and Edna Ferber's *Dinner at Eight* 10/22 at New York's Music Box Theater, 232 perfs.; Irish actress Patricia Collinge, 38, and Francis Lederer in C. L. Anthony's *Autumn Crocus* 11/19 at New York's Morosco Theater, 210 perfs.; Ina Claire and Earle Larimore in S. N. Behrman's *Biography* 12/12 at New York's Guild Theater, 283 perfs.

Films: Greta Garbo as a fading ballerina, Joan Crawford, John and Lionel Barrymore, Lewis Stone, Wallace Beery, and Jean Hersholt in Edmund Goulding's *Grand Hotel*; Canadian-American actress Fay Wray, 25, and Bruce Cabot in Merian C. Cooper and Ernest Schoedsack's *King Kong*; Gracie Fields in Basil Dean's *Looking on the Bright Side*; Miriam Hopkins, 29, Kay Francis (Katherine Gibbs), 27, and Herbert Marshall in Ernst Lubitsch's *Trouble in Paradise*. Also: Greta Garbo and Melvyn Douglas in George Fitzmaurice's *As You Desire Me*; Katharine Hepburn (Bryn Mawr '28) and John Barrymore in George Cukor's *A Bill of Divorcement*; Marlene Dietrich, Herbert Marshall, and Cary Grant in Josef von Sternberg's *Blonde Venus*; Marie Dressler and Jean Hersholt in Clarence Brown's *Emma*; Greta Garbo and Ramon Novarro in George Fitzmaurice's *Mata Hari*; Kay Francis and William Powell in Tay Garnett's *One-Way Passage*; Paul Muni and Ann Dvorak (Anna McKim), 22, in Howard Hawks's *Scarface*.

Radio drama: *Today's Children* on NBC stations is a soap opera created by writer Irna Phillips, 31, in a revamping of the soap opera *Painted Dreams,* which she has been writing for Chicago's WGN radio station.

 Stage musicals: Mary Boland in *Face the Music* 2/17 at New York's New Amsterdam Theater, with Irving Berlin songs that include "Let's Have Another Cup of Coffee," 165 perfs.; Joyce Barbour, Ivy St. Helier, and John Mills in Nöel Coward's *Words and Music* 9/16 at London's Adelphi Theatre, with songs that include "Mad Dogs and Englishmen," "Mad About the Boy," "Journey's End," and "Let's Say Goodbye," 164 perfs.; Helen Broderick and Milton Berle in *Earl Carroll's Vanities* 9/27 at New York's Broadway Theater, with songs that include "I Gotta Right to Sing the Blues," 87 perfs.; Ethel Merman, Jack Haley, and Sid Silvers in *Take a Chance* 11/26 at New York's Apollo Theater, with songs that include "You're an Old Smoothie," 243 perfs.; Fred Astaire and Claire Luce in *Gay Divorce* 11/29 at New York's Ethel Barrymore Theater, with Cole Porter songs that include "Night and Day," 248 perfs.; Beatrice Lillie and Bobby Clark in *Walk a Little Faster* 12/7 at New York's St. James Theater, with Vernon Duke–Yip Harburg songs that include "April in Paris" and "That's Life," 119 perfs.

Ballet: Irina Baronova, Tamara Tommanova, and David Lichine in *Jeux d'Enfants* (*Children's Games*) 4/14 at Monte Carlo, with music by the late Georges Bizet, choreography by Leonide Massine.

Opera: U.S. soprano Rose (Elizabeth) Bampton, 23, makes her Metropolitan Opera debut 11/20 singing the role of Laura in the 1876 Ponchielli opera *La Gioconda*.

Hollywood musicals: Kate Smith, George Burns and Gracie Allen, the Mills Brothers, the Boswell Sisters, Cab Calloway, and Bing Crosby in Frank Tuttle's *The Big Broadcast*; Maurice Chevalier and Jeanette MacDonald in Rouben Mamoulian's *Love Me Tonight* with Rodgers and Hart songs that include "Lover," "Mimi," and "Isn't It Romantic."

New York's Radio City Music Hall opens December 27 in Rockefeller Center with 6,200 seats. A mighty Wurlitzer organ and a 100-piece orchestra accompany vaudeville acts presented by showman Samuel "Roxy" Rothafel, but the world's largest indoor theater fails to attract crowds and will not gain success until it renames its high-kicking "Roxyette" chorus girls "Rockettes" and shows motion pictures.

Popular songs: "Don't Blame Me" by Jimmy McHugh, lyrics by Dorothy Fields; "Willow, Weep for Me" by Radcliffe graduate songwriter Ann Ronell, 23.

The Andrews Sisters from Minneapolis form a trio that will gain wild popularity in the next dozen years: LaVerne is 17, Maxene (*née* Maxine) 15, and Patty (Patricia) 12.

Helen Wills Moody wins in women's singles at Wimbledon, Helen Hull Jacobs, 23, at Forest Hills.

Sonja Henie wins her second gold medal in figure skating at the winter Olympics in Lake Placid. The summer games at Los Angeles attract 2,403 contestants from 39 countries. California athlete Mildred Ella "Babe" Didrikson, 18, wins the javelin throw (143 feet, 4 inches) and sets a new record of 11.7 seconds for the 80-meter hurdles; Polish-American athlete Stella Walsh (Stanislawa Walasiewicz), 21, wins the 100-meter dash in 11.9 seconds, U.S. athlete Jean Shiley the running high jump event (5 feet, 5¼ inches), U.S. athlete Lilian Copeland the discus throw (133 feet, 2 inches), U.S. swimmer Helene Madison the 100-meter freestyle in 1 minute, 6.8 seconds and the 400-meter freestyle in 5 minutes, 28.5 seconds, U.S. swimmer Eleanor Holm the 100-meter backstroke in 1 minute, 19.4 seconds, Australian swimmer Clare Dennis the 200-meter breaststroke in 3 minutes, 6.3 seconds, U.S. swimmer Georgia Coleman the springboard dive event, U.S. swimmer Dorothy Poynton the platform dive.

Japan's Showa government encourages young women to learn the *chanoyu* (tea ceremony), traditional etiquette, and *ikebana* (flower arrangement). Many "bridal schools" spring up to show prospective brides how to be good wives and mothers.

Fashion designer Elsa Schiaparelli introduces the padded shoulder (*see* zipper, 1926). By 1935 she will be a leader in *haute couture*.

Irish-born *Vogue* fashion editor Carmel Snow, now 41, resigns to become fashion editor of Hearst's *Harper's Bazaar*, which she will head from 1934 until her retirement in 1958. Condé Nast, who has been grooming her to succeed Edna Woolman Chase, will never speak to her again.

Revlon is founded by New York cosmetics salesman Charles Revson, 26, with his brother Joseph, 28, and chemist Charles Lachman, 35. When employer Elka Cosmetics rejects his ultimatum that he be made national distributor, young Revson rents a loft in the New York garment district, borrows money at 2 percent per month, and with Lachman's help develops a superior opaque nail enamel which he promotes with exotic names such as Tropic Sky rather than with the descriptive identifications dark red, medium red, pink, etc., that have been traditional. Focusing on beauty salons, Revlon uses intimidation to obtain distribution. Volume for the first 10 months is only $4,055.09, but Revson will start selling through drugstores in 1937, employing salesmen who "accidentally" destroy displays set up by the competition; by 1941 Revlon will have a virtual monopoly on beauty salon sales.

A Phoenix court convicts Winnie Ruth Judd (*née* McKinnell), 27, of having killed two women friends, dismembering their bodies, and shipping the remains to Los Angeles in a trunk (blood seeping from the trunk has led to the discovery of its gruesome contents). Sentenced to be hanged, Judd will later be declared insane and sentenced to a mental institution for life, but she will escape seven times and be at large for 7 years from 1962 to 1969. She will be paroled in 1971.

Big Bear Super Market opens at Elizabeth, N.J., and is the first large cut-rate self-service grocery store (*see* King Kullen, 1930). Local entrepreneurs Robert M. Otis and Roy O. Dawson have put up a total of $1,000 to take over an empty car factory on the outskirts of town, their Big Bear the Price Crusher store has 50,000 square feet of pine tables displaying meats, fruit, vegetables, packaged foods, radios, auto accessories, and paints, and after 1 year they have made a profit of $166,000 selling Quaker Oats oatmeal at 3¢ a box, pork chops at 10¢ lb. Traditional grocers persuade local newspapers to refuse Big Bear advertising and push through a state law against selling at or below cost, but Big Bear is quickly imitated by Great Tiger, Bull Market, Great Leopard, and others as the supermarket revolution gathers force.

Adolf Hitler comes to power as chancellor of Germany January 30 on a rising tide of nationalism as economic depression continues to create worldwide political shock waves. Berlin piano maker's wife Helena Bechstein encouraged the rabble-rouser in the 1920s, taught him manners, and introduced him to people, including Cosima Wagner, the composer's widow, who could help him socially, politically, and financially. Manufacturer Gertrud von Seidlitz gave him money and got more for him from her friends in Finland.

Communist leader Clara Zetkin, now 75, has denounced Hitler (above) in the Reichstag and goes to Moscow, where she dies. Feminist Gertrude Baumer, now 59, loses the seat that she has held since 1920 in the Reichstag (which is destroyed by fire February 7), she is interrogated by Hitler's Gestapo (secret police), but she continues to edit her newspaper *Die Frau*.

President Franklin Delano Roosevelt is inaugurated March 4, saying, "The only thing we have to fear is fear itself." His secretary of labor is Frances (*née* Fannie Coralie) Perkins, 50, who directed studies of female and child labor as executive secretary of the Consumers League of New York from 1910 to 1912. She is the first woman Cabinet member and for the next 12 years will oversee an unprecedented program of government interest in labor while the trade union movement gains power and political influence.

 Turkey grants women the right to vote on the same basis as men.

One of the alleged rape victims in the Scottsboro case of 1931 writes a letter to her boyfriend, Earl. "I want too make a statment too you," writes Ruby Bates. "Mary Sanders is a goddam lie about those Negroes jazzing me those policemen made me tell a lie that is my statement because I want too clear myself that is all . . . those Negroes did not touch me or those white boys I hope you will believe me the law dont . . . i was drunk at the time and did not know what i was doing i know it was wrong too let those Negroes die on account of me i hope you will believe my statement because it is the gods truth . . . i was jazzed but those white boys jazzed me i

Frances Perkins served under Franklin D. Roosevelt as the first woman Secretary of Labor. LIBRARY OF CONGRESS

wish those Negroes are not Burnt on account of me it is those white Boys fault that is my statement and that is all i know i hope you tell the law . . ."

 San Rafael, Calif., socialite–arctic explorer Louise Arner Boyd, 46, leads a scientific expedition on the east coast of Greenland, which she will continue to explore until 1941. Boyd first visited the Arctic in 1926, when she chartered a Norwegian sealer for a polar-bear hunt in Franz Josef Land, and in 1928 played a prominent role in the effort to locate polar explorer Roald Amundsen, who was missing (she became the first non-Norwegian woman to be awarded the Order of St. Olaf, First Class; *see* 1955).

 Some 5,000 Chicago schoolteachers storm the banks for back pay April 24 after having been paid in scrip for 10 months. Public school teachers typically earn $1,227 per year. Other typical annual U.S. earnings: congressman $8,663, lawyer $4,218, physician $3,382, college teacher $3,111, engineer

$2,250, construction worker $907, sleep-in domestic servant $260 ($21.66 per month), hired farmhand $216. Incomes of doctors and lawyers have fallen as much as 40 percent since 1929, and the most competent New York stenographers make only $16 per week, down from $40. Chicago women mostly earn less than 25¢ per hour.

Amelia Earhart flies from Los Angeles to Newark July 1, making the flight in 17 hours, 17 minutes.

Life in Lesu by U.S. anthropologist Hortense Powdermaker, 37, examines life in a tiny village on the southwest Pacific island of New Ireland. Powdermaker, who has studied under Bronislaw Malinowski at the London School of Economics, wins funding from the Social Science Research Council to study the community at Indianola, Miss. (*see* 1939).

Astronomer Cecilia Payne receives her first regular academic appointment at Harvard, but her courses are not listed in the catalogue, and although she receives a salary (her mentor, Harlow Shapley, has been paying her out of his supplies budget) her pay is not commensurate with her abilities and responsibilities (*see* 1926). She meets fellow astronomer Sergei Gaposhkin, a political refugee, sponsors his entry into the United States, and will marry him next year (*see* 1956).

The White House Conference on Child Health and Protection report *Fetal, Newborn, and Maternal Mortality and Morbidity* concludes that maternal mortality remained as high in 1930 as in 1915 despite increased incidence of hospital deliveries, introduction of prenatal care, and greater use of aseptic techniques. Deaths of infants from birth injuries, usually from excessive and improperly performed intervention, actually rose in that 15-year period by 40 to 50 percent in the 11-state area surveyed, and most women either received no prenatal care or care that underestimated complications or simply overlooked them.

Natural Childbirth by British obstetrician Grantly Dick-Read, 43, expresses the notion that modern woman has been subjected since childhood to mental conditioning that exaggerates her fears of childbirth, causing muscular tensions in labor which exacerbate the pain. Read, who speaks of "mystical ecstasy" in childbirth, is ridiculed by his colleagues and finds little acceptance in England for his ideas, which in any case are not altogether original (but *see* 1936).

"Sister Kenny" opens her first clinic for treating victims of poliomyelitis. Australian Army Nurse Corps war veteran Elizabeth Kenny, 47 (the "Sister" denotes the rank of second lieutenant given her in 1916), has an income derived from royalties on the patent for a stretcher equipped with shock treatment appliances that she invented for patients en route to hospital. Polio has no known cure, but physicians have been immobilizing patients with splints and casts, which cause their muscles to atrophy. Sister Kenny uses warm wool compresses to relieve pain and spasms plus limb manipulation therapy. The medical establishment, especially in Australia, disdains her methods, but she will open a facility in Britain in 1937 and one at Minneapolis in 1940 as she travels the world demonstrating her treatment.

The *Catholic Worker* begins publication with the aim of uniting workers and intellectuals in joint efforts to improve farming, education, and social conditions. Founder Dorothy Day, now 36, has since 1922 supervised a shelter in New York's Bowery and published a penny newspaper that expresses her religious commitment to human rights. She gets support from French-American editor Peter Maurin, who has developed a program of social reconstruction he calls "the green revolution." The new monthly will be a voice for pacifism and social justice and will have a circulation of 150,000 within 3 years.

Nonfiction: *The Autobiography of Alice B. Toklas* by Gertrude Stein, whose book is actually her own autobiography rather than that of the woman who has been her companion and secretary since 1907: "Rose is a rose is a rose," writes Stein, who is famous for being more concerned with the sound and rhythm of words than with intelligibility. *The German Woman and National Socialism* (*Die deutsche Frau und der National Sozialismus*) by political evangelist Guida Diehl, who recalls Brünhilde, heroine of the *Niebelungenlied,* and says, "Never did Hitler [above] promise to the masses in his rousing speeches any material advantage what-

Adolf Hitler's Nazi regime came to power with women's help but valued women only as breeders of soldiers.

ever. On the contrary he pleaded with them to turn aside from every form of advantage-seeking and serve the great thoughts: Honor, Freedom, Fatherland! In his success is shown the power of great divine truths. . . . For us women it was almost unendurable to see the weakness of manhood in the last decades. Therefore the outbreak of the War was, despite all the hardships, a great experience for us: the upheaval of 1914 was a powerful breaking through of heroic manhood. All the more fearful to us was the breakdown. Then we called to German men: 'We implore you, German Men, among whom we have seen and admired so much heroic courage. . . . We long to see Men and Heroes who scorn fate. . . . Call us to every service, even to weapons!' " *Testament of Youth* by British writer Vera Brittain, 40, who records her early education and experiences as a nurse in the Great War; *Baghdad Sketches* by British travel writer Freya (Madeline) Stark, 40, who has become fluent in Arabic and Turkish and will go on to master other languages and dialects; *Congo Solo: Misadventures Two Degrees North* by Emily Hahn, who has worked with the Red Cross in the Belgian Congo; *Crowded Hours* (autobiography) by Alice Roosevelt Longworth.

German feminist novelist-historian Ricarda Huch, now 69, resigns from the Prussian Academy of Literature in protest against the expulsion of Jewish writers. She was admitted 2 years ago as the first woman member.

Fiction: *Rebecca* by English novelist Daphne du Maurier, 26; *Frost in May* by English journalist-novelist Antonia White (*née* Botting), 34; *More Women than Men* by Ivy Compton-Burnett; *Cold Comfort Farm* by English novelist Stella Dorothea Gibbons, 31, satirizes rural melodramas of the kind written by Sheila Kaye-Smith and the late Mary Webb; *La Chatte* by Colette; *Lamb in His Bosom* by Georgia novelist Caroline Miller (*née* Pafford), 30 (Pulitzer Prize, Prix Femina; the book has no coherent plot and no coherent sequence of episodes but tries to capture the monotonous rhythms of household activities and the fatalistic endurance of Mrs. Miller's pioneer ancestors in backwoods Georgia); *Pity Is Not Enough* by Josephine Herbst; *Imitation of Life* by Fannie Hurst; *The Third Son* by Margaret Culkin Banning; *Miss Bishop* by Bess Streeter Aldrich; *Let the Hurricane Roar* by U.S. novelist Rose Wilder Lane, 46; *White-Collar Girl* and *Love's a Puzzle* by Faith Baldwin; *Murder Must Advertise* and *Hangman's Holiday* by Dorothy Sayers; *Kingdom of Death* (in England, *Sweet Danger*) by Margery Allingham.

Poetry: *The Life of the Dead* and *Laura and Francesca* by Laura Riding; *The Sleeping Crew* (*Spiacazaooga*) by Polish poet-playwright Marja Jasnorszewska-Pawlikowska (*née* Kossak), 34.

Theater: Alfred Lunt, Lynn Fontanne, and Noël Coward in Coward's *Design for Living* 1/24 at New York's Ethel Barrymore Theater, 135 perfs.; Katharine Cornell in Sidney Howard's *Alien Corn* 2/20 at New York's Belasco Theater, 98 perfs.; Mary Phillips, Walter C. Kelly, and Morris Carnovsky in Maxwell Anderson's *Both Your Houses*, a polemic against political corruption, 3/6 at New York's Royale Theater, 120 perfs.; Rose McClendon in Langston Hughes's *Mulatto* 10/24 at New York's Theater, 270 perfs.; Eugenia Leontovich as Lilly Garland, Moffat Johnston as Oscar Jaffe in Ben Hecht and Charles MacArthur's *Twentieth Century* 12/29 at New York's Broadhurst Theater, 152 perfs.

Radio: *Oxydol's Own Ma Perkins* continues the soap opera serial genre with daily 15-minute shows sponsored by Procter & Gamble. Actress Virginia

Payne, 23, plays the title role that she will continue for 27 years; *The Romance of Helen Trent* 7/24 is a soap opera by Frank Hummert and Anne Ashenhurst, whose show is carried on CBS network stations beginning 10/3.

Sally Rand attracts thousands to the Chicago World's Fair, which opens May 27 to celebrate a Century of Progress. The fan dancer, 29, gets star billing at the "Streets of Paris" concession on the Midway, does a slow dance to Debussy's "Clair de Lune" wearing only ostrich plumes, and is credited with making the fair a success as jobless Americans flock to Chicago in search of fun.

Films: Diana Wynyard (Dorothy Cox), 27, Clive Brook, and Ursula Jeans in Frank Lloyd's *Cavalcade*; John Barrymore and Bebe Daniels (Mrs. Ben Lyon), now 32, in William Wyler's *Counsellor-at-Law*; John Barrymore and Jean Harlow in George Cukor's *Dinner at Eight*; May Robson and Warren William in Frank Capra's *Lady for a Day*; Katharine Hepburn, Joan Bennett, 23, Frances Dee, Jean Parker (Luise-Stephanie Zelinska), 21, Edna May Oliver, and Paul Lukas in George Cukor's *Little Women*; Greta Garbo and John Gilbert in Rouben Mamoulian's *Queen Christina* (a largely fictional version of the life of the 17th-century Swedish queen); Mae West, now 41, as Diamond Lil ("Come up and see me sometime"), Louise Beavers, 25, as her sassy maid, Pearl, and Cary Grant in Lowell Sherman's *She Done Him Wrong*. Also: Jean Harlow, Lee Tracy, and Louise Beavers, in Victor Fleming's *Bombshell*; Miriam Hopkins, Gary Cooper, and Fredric March in Ernst Lubitsch's *Design for Living*; Carole Lombard (Jane Alice Peters), 24, Fredric March, Cary Grant, and Jack Oakie in Stuart Walker's *The Eagle and the Hawk*; Mae West and Cary Grant in Wesley Ruggles's *I'm No Angel*; Peggy Hopkins Joyce, Stuart Erwin, George Burns, Gracie Allen, and W. C. Fields in A. Edward Sutherland's *International House*; Loretta (*née* Gretchen) Young, 20, and Spencer Tracy in Frank Borzage's *Man's Castle*; Myrna Loy (Myrna Williams), 28, and Warner Baxter in W. S. Van Dyke's *Penthouse*.

London-born journalist Sheila Graham (*née* Lily Shiel), 25, comes to New York and begins the syndicated gossip column "Hollywood Today" that will eventually appear in 180 newspapers, rivaling Louella Parsons (*see* 1925) and Hedda Hopper (*see* 1936). Married at age 17 to John Graham Gilliam, a man of 42 who encouraged her to perform in musical comedies, she debuted in the 1927 revue *One Damned Thing After Another* and has lately been writing theater articles for London periodicals (*see* nonfiction, 1958).

Hollywood musicals: Bebe Daniels, Dick Powell, Ruby Keeler, Warner Baxter, and George Brent in Lloyd Bacon's *42nd Street* with Al Dubin–Harry Warren songs that include "Shuffle Off to Buffalo" and "You're Getting to Be a Habit with Me"; Ginger Rogers (Virginia Katherine McMath), 22, Dick Powell, and Joan Blondell, 24, in Mervyn LeRoy's *Gold Diggers of 1933* with choreography by Busby Berkeley, Al Dubin–Harry Warren songs that include "We're in the Money" and "Shadow Waltz"; Bing Crosby and Marion Davies in Raoul Walsh's *Going Hollywood* with songs that include "Temptation"; James Cagney, Joan Blondell, Ruby Keeler, and Dick Powell in Lloyd Bacon's *Footlight Parade* with choreography by Busby Berkeley, Sammy Fain–Irving Kahal songs that include "By a Waterfall" and "Honeymoon Hotel"; Dolores Del Rio, Gene Raymond, and Fred Astaire and Ginger Rogers (a new dance team) in Thornton Freeland's *Flying Down to Rio* (with Rogers doing everything Astaire does except backwards, wearing high heels), songs that include "Carioca," "Orchids in the Moonlight," and the title song.

Broadway musicals: Lupe Velez, Jimmy Durante, and Hope Williams in *Strike Me Pink* 3/4 at the Majestic Theater, 105 perfs.; Marilyn Miller, Clifton Webb, and Ethel Waters in *As Thousands Cheer* 9/30 at the Music Box Theater, with Irving Berlin songs that include "Easter Parade," 400 perfs.; Fay Templeton, Tamara Geva, Ray Middleton, George Murphy, and Bob Hope in *Roberta* (initially *Gowns by Roberta*) 11/18 at the New Ambassadors Theater, with Jerome Kern–Otto Harbach songs that include "Smoke Gets in Your Eyes" and "The Touch of Your Hand" ("Lovely to Look At" will be added for a 1935 film version), 295 perfs.

Popular songs: "Who's Afraid of the Big Bad Wolf?" by Ann Ronell with Walt Disney's musical director Frank E. Churchill (for Disney's first animated feature, *The Three Little Pigs*); "Dolores" by Paramount songwriter Frank Loesser, 23, lyrics by

Louis Alter (for the film *Las Vegas Nights*); "Sophisticated Lady" by Duke Ellington, lyrics by Irving Mills and Mitchell Parish.

Opera: Australian soprano Marjorie Lawrence, 24, makes her debut 2/25 at the Paris Opéra as Ortrud in the 1850 Wagner opera *Lohengrin*. She will be the only singer to ride a horse on stage, as Richard Wagner intended, in the finale of *Götterdämmerung*; Bellorussia-born soprano Jennie Tourel (Davidovich; Tourel is an anagram based on Anna El-Tour, her teacher in Paris), 32, makes her Opéra-Comique debut in the title role of the 1875 Bizet opera *Carmen*.

Helen Wills Moody wins in women's singles at Wimbledon, Helen Jacobs at Forest Hills.

Helen Jacobs (above) is the first woman to wear shorts in tournament play. Others still wear skirts knee length or longer.

Woolworth heiress Barbara Hutton, now 20 and worth $42 million, is married at Paris June 20 to Prince Alexis Mdivani, 30, whom she met on the Riviera when he was honeymooning with his first wife, heiress Louise Van Alen, who married him at Newport, R.I., in May 1931 (*see* 1930). Hutton's father has sent her on a round-the-world trip, but Mdivani has pursued his pudgy prey to Bangkok. The bride wears a conservative pearl gray Chanel print dress, picture hat, and sable stole. Her black pearl engagement ring was purchased with part of the $1 million received in the groom's divorce settlement from Van Alen, he receives a dowry of $1 million from Hutton, and when he tells her she is too fat she goes on a strict diet, losing 40 pounds in 1 year (the drastic reduction in caloric intake will lead to years of illness) (*see* 1935).

The Dy-Dee-Doll that sucks water from a bottle and wets its diaper is introduced by New York's Effanbee Doll Co., which has acquired patent rights from the doll's Brooklyn inventor, Marie Wittman. More than 25,000 are sold in its first year.

Dreft is introduced by Procter & Gamble for dishwashing in hard-water areas west of the Appalachians. The hymolal-salt detergent is costlier than soap but will prove a popular addition to Ivory soap, Oxydol, Camay, and Crisco (*see* Persil, 1907; Tide, 1946).

Windex for cleaning windows is introduced by Drackett Co. of 1921 Drano fame.

British Colonial Medical Service physician Cicely D. Williams, 40, describes a deficiency disease with symptoms that include edema, bloated stomach, cracked skin, red or dirty gray hair, and even dwarfism. The disease is common among infants at Accra on the Gold Goast, and Williams will use its African name, *kwashiorkor*, in a 1935 report for the British medical journal *Lancet*, calling it the disease "the deposed baby gets when the next one is born," indicating that it may be caused by a lack of mother's milk. It will later prove to be a worldwide protein-deficiency disease that goes under different names in different countries.

Borden Co. introduces the first vitamin D–fortified milk. Children are the chief victims of vitamin D deficiency and the chief consumers of milk.

Typical U.S. food prices: butter 28¢ lb., margarine 13¢ lb., eggs 29¢ doz., oranges 27¢ cents doz., milk 10¢ qt., bread 5¢ per 20-oz. loaf, sirloin steak 29¢ lb., round steak 26¢, rib roast 22¢, ham 31¢, bacon 22¢, leg of lamb 22¢, chicken 22¢, pork chops 20¢, cheese 24¢, coffee 26¢, rice 6¢, potatoes 2¢, sugar 6¢ (but *see* earnings, above).

Chocolate-chip Toll House cookies are created at Whitman, Mass., by innkeeper Ruth Wakefield (*née* Graves), who figures that semisweet chocolate-bar pieces dropped into cookie batter will melt in the oven and thus save her the time and trouble of melting them separately beforehand. The chocolate stays firm, and the cookies turn out to be delicious. Wakefield and her husband, Kenneth, bought the inn, built in 1709, 3 years ago, and opened a restaurant. Nestlé Corp. will start distributing chocolate "morsels" for inclusion in Toll House cookies beginning in 1939 and will acquire rights to the Toll House name.

Former *Ziegfeld Follies* girl Helen Gallagher, widow of vaudevillian Ed Gallagher of Gallagher & Shean fame, opens Gallagher's Steak House at 228 West 50th Street in New York, serving steak, a baked potato, and salad for $1.75 but nothing stronger than 3.2 beer until December.

The prohibition against sale of alcoholic beverages in the United States that began early in 1920 ends

December 5 as Utah becomes the 36th state to ratify the 21st Amendment repealing the 18th Amendment after an estimated 1.4 billion gallons of hard liquor have been sold illegally.

Prohibition's "Texas" Guinan has died November 5 at age 49, leaving an estate of only $28,173, although she is known to have banked well over $1 million in the mid-1920s (*see* 1922).

 Germany's new chancellor Adolf Hitler outlaws abortion, orders the execution of abortionists, supresses information about contraception, and encourages production of more "Aryans" by offering cash incentives to Germans who marry and cash awards for each new infant born (*see Lebensborn,* 1935). Nazi authorities carry out 56,000 sterilizations of the "unfit" this year and will have sterilized 250,000 by 1940. German birthrates will increase in the next few years, but so will birthrates elsewhere as the world begins to climb out of economic depression.

1934

 President Roosevelt names Ohio Supreme Court justice Florence Ellinwood Allen, 59, to the U.S. Sixth Circuit Court of Appeals, making her the first women federal judge. Responding to criticism that she was given the appointment as a token, Attorney General Homer Cummings says, "Florence Allen was not appointed because she was a woman. All we did was to see that she was not rejected because she was a woman." She will serve until her retirement in 1959, and when it is suggested that she may be nominated for the Supreme Court she will say, "That will never happen to a woman while I am living" (*see* 1981).

Cuba gives women the right to vote on the same basis as men.

"The message of woman's emancipation is a message discovered solely by the Jewish intellect and its content is stamped with the same spirit," says Adolf Hitler in a speech at Nuremberg September 8. "Only when man himself is unsure in the perception of his task did the eternal instinct of self- and folk-preservation begin to revolt in women.... For her world is her husband, her family, her children,

and her home.... Reason is dominant in man. He searches, analyzes, and often opens new immeasurable realms. But all things that are approached merely by reason are subject to change. Feeling in contrast is much more subtle than reason and woman is the feeling and therefore the stable element. I am convinced that the [National Socialist] Movement is understood by none better than the German woman. When our opponents imply that we in Germany have instituted a tyrannical regimentation of women, I can only confess that without the endurance and really loving devotion of woman to the Movement, I could never have led the Party to victory."

German housewife Gertrude Schlotz-Klinke, 32, is named *Reichsfrauenführer* (National Women's Leader) and made head of the Nazi Women's Group. The mother of six, she will eventually have two more husbands and bear five more children (*see* 1945).

 New Zealand aviatrix Jean Batten, 25, flies a Gypsy Moth from England to Australia, beats Amy Johnson's 1930 speed by nearly 5 days, and becomes the first woman to complete the return trip. Batten abandoned a promising musical career in England 5 years ago, sold her piano, and studied for a pilot's license, which she obtained in 1930. Next year she will fly across the South Atlantic to Argentina.

French physicist Irène Joliot-Curie, 38, and her husband, Frédéric, 34, bombard aluminum with alpha particles (helium nuclei) from a naturally radioactive source and turn the aluminum into a radioactive form of phosphorus, but Mme. Joliot-Curie's mother, Marie Curie, dies July 4 of pernicious anemia at age 66 (*see* 1904).

Patterns of Culture by Columbia University social anthropologist Ruth Benedict, 47, breaks new ground. Benedict studied anthropology for the first time at age 32, enrolled at Columbia 2 years later to study under Franz Boas, and will replace Boas as head of the department upon his retirement in 1936.

 The Dionne quintuplets born May 28 at Callander, Ontario, are the world's first five infants on record to be born at one delivery and survive. Elzire Dionne, 24, who already has six children, is delivered of five girls by her physician, Allen R. Dafoe, 51; the infants—Emilie, Yvonne, Cecile, Marie, and Annette—average 2 pounds, 11 ounces each.

Mary Margaret McBride, 34, begins broadcasting over New York's WOR to begn a career of more than 20 years as First Lady of Radio. Using the name "Martha Deane," the newspaper and magazine writer is supposed to be a grandmother with a large family who gives out household hints, but on her third day she interrupts her own program to announce that she does not cook very well and dislikes housekeeping intensely. McBride will move to NBC in 1941, will draw 40,000 fans to Yankee Stadium in 1949 to celebrate 15 years on the air, and will move to ABC in 1950.

The first double-crostic puzzle appears in the weekly *Saturday Review of Literature*. Onetime Brooklyn, N.Y., schoolteacher Elizabeth Kingsley (*née* Seelman), 63, has created the variation on crossword puzzles, which she will continue devising for the next 17 years.

Nonfiction: *Woman in the New State* (*Die Frau im neuen Staat*) by Nazi writer Lydia Gottschewski, who says, "It is a curious fact that pacifism . . . is a mark of an age weak in faith, whereas the people of religious times have honored war as God's rod of chastisement. . . . Only the age of enlightenment has wished to decide the great questions of world history at the table of diplomats. . . . As far as this fight [by the Nazis to arouse the war spirit among men] attacked the old feminism it was rightful and healthy"; *Lectures on Philosophy* (*Leçons de philosophie*) by French philosopher and religious writer Simone Weil, 25, who works on farms and in factories to gain direct experience with working-class life when she is not teaching philosophy; *A Backwards Glance* (autobiography) by Edith Wharton, now 72; *The Valley of the Assassins and Other Persian Travels* by Freya Stark, who has mapped the valley in Luristan while working for the *Baghdad Times*: "The great and almost only comfort about being a woman," she writes, "is that one can always pretend to be more stupid than one is, and no one is surprised."

Fiction: *Seven Gothic Tales* by Danish novelist Isak Dinesen (Karen Christentze Dinesen, 49, Baroness Blixen) who married her cousin in 1914 (although it

was his cousin she really loved), lived with him until 1921 on the British East African coffee plantation her parents purchased for them, contracted a virulent case of syphilis from him, underwent a long and embarrassing course of treatment, had a passionate affair with English hunter Denys Finch-Hatton, was forced to leave Africa after her plantation went bankrupt, and, home again now in Denmark, abandoned by Finch-Hatton and divorced, has written her book in English; *The Master of Hestviken* by Sigrid Undset includes her novels *The Axe*, *The Snakepit*, *In the Wilderness*, and *The Son Avenger*; *Crisis* (*Kris*) by Karin Boye; *The Land of Elizabeth* (*Ziemia Elzviety*) by Polish novelist Pola (Apolonia) Gljawiczynska, 38; *The Green Parrot* (*Der grüne Babagei*) by Helene Voigt-Diederichs; *Seven Poor Men of Sydney* and *The Salzburg Tales* by Australian novelist Christina (Ellen) Stead, 32; *Prelude to Christopher* by Eleanor Dark; *House with Peony* (*Botan no aru ie*) by Ineko Sata; *Company Parade* by Storm Jameson; *A Modern Tragedy* by Phyllis Bentley; *The First Woman* by Margaret Culkin Banning; *Did She?* by Elinor Glyn; *Matador* by Marguerite Steen; *Jonah's Gourd Vine* by U.S. novelist Zora Neale Hurston, 43; *My Next Bride* by Kay Boyle; *The Executioner Waits* by Josephine Herbst; *Now In November* by U.S. novelist Josephine Winslow Johnson, 24 (Pulitzer Prize); *Aluck Maury, Sportsman* by Caroline Gordon; *The Folks* by Ruth Suckow; *The Unpossessed* by U.S. novelist Tess Slesinger, 29, who will move to Hollywood next year to become a screenwriter; *Innocent Bystander*, *Within a Year*, *Wife Versus Secretary*, and *Honor Bound* by Faith Baldwin; *A Man Lay Dead* by New Zealand–born mystery novelist Ngaio Marsh, 35; *Murder on the Orient Express* by Agatha Christie, whose new Hercule Poirot novel is published in the United States as *Murder on the Calais Coach*; *The Nine Tailors* by Dorothy Sayers; *Death of a Ghost* by Margery Allingham; *The Cases of Susan Dare* by Mignon G. Eberhart; *Death in the Quarry*, *End of an Ancient Mariner*, and *Murder in Four Parts* by Margaret Cole.

Poetry: *A Mad Lady's Garland* by Ruth Pitter; *Last Poems* (*Dernier Vers*) by the late Anna, comtesse de Noailles, who died last year at age 57; *Wine from These Grapes* by Edna St. Vincent Millay; *Bright Ambush* by Seattle-born poet Audrey (May) Wurdemann, 24 (Pulitzer Prize).

Juvenile: *Mary Poppins* by Australian-born English author P. (Pamela) Travers, 28, whose wonder-working English governess will appear in a series of books.

Theater: Ilka Chase, Earle Larimore, and Stanley Ridges in Eugene O'Neill's *Days Without End* 1/18 at Henry Miller's Theater, New York, 57 perfs.; *Touch Wood* by C. L. Anthony (Dorothy Smith) 5/16 at London's Theatre Royal Haymarket; Jessie Royce Landis, Mary Philips, and Kenneth McKenna in George S. Kaufman and Moss Hart's *Merrily We Roll Along* 9/9 at New York's Music Box Theater, 155 perfs.; Mildred Natwick, 26, English actress Sybil Thorndike, 51, and English actress Estelle Winwood (*née* Goodwin), 51, in John Van Druten's *The Distaff Side* 9/25 at New York's Booth Theater, 177 perfs.; *The Children's Hour* by U.S. playwright Lillian Hellman, 29, 11/20 at Maxine Elliott's Theater, New York, with Eugenia Rawls hints at sexual abnormalities, 691 perfs. (the play's set designer, Aline Bernstein, ended her affair with novelist Thomas Wolfe several years ago but will figure in the person of Esther Jack in his posthumous 1939 novel *The Web and the Rock*); Jane Cowl in S. N. Behrman's *Rain from Heaven* 11/24 at New York's Golden Theater and protests Nazi treatment of German Jews, 99 perfs.; Constance Cummings in Samson Raphaelson's *Accent on Youth* 12/25 at New York's Plymouth Theater, 229 perfs.

The Hays Office created by the U.S. film industry's MPPDA (Motion Picture Producers and Distributors of America, Inc.) employs former Postmaster General Will H. Hays to administer a production code established by the industry. It will enforce such prohibitions as: no exposure of female breasts, no suggestion of cohabitation or seduction, and no unconventional kissing.

Shirley Temple makes her first full-length film at age 6 and follows Hamilton McFadden's *Stand Up and Cheer* (in which she steals the show by singing "Baby Take a Bow") with Alexander Hall's *Little Miss Marker* and David Butler's *Bright Eyes* (in which she sings "The Good Ship Lollipop"). All dimples and curly hair, Temple will go on to star in half a dozen other Hollywood films in the next 4 years.

Other films: Claudette Colbert and Clark Gable in Frank Capra's *It Happened One Night*; Carole Lombard and John Barrymore in Howard Hawks's *Twentieth Century*. Also: New York–born actress Anne Shirley (originally Dawn Evelyeen Paris), 16, as Anne Shirley in George Nicholls, Jr.'s *Anne of Green Gables*; Robert Donat and Austrian-born actress Elissa Landi (Elisabeth-Marie-Christine Kühnelt), 29, in Rowland V. Lee's *The Count of Monte Cristo*; Margaret Sullavan (Margaret Brooke), 23, and Douglass Montgomery in Frank Borzage's *Little Man, What Now?*; Shirley Temple in Richard Wallace's *The Little Minister*; Gracie Fields in Maurice Elvey's *Love, Life, and Laughter*; Miriam Hopkins, Joel McCrea, and Fay Wray in William A. Seiter's *The Richest Girl in the World*, based on the early life of Woolworth heiress Barbara Hutton (who is not, in fact, nearly so rich as tobacco heiress Doris Duke but is far more extravagant); Johnny Weissmuller and Irish-American actress Maureen O'Sullivan, 23, in Cedric Gibbons and Jack Con-

Shirley Temple sang, tap-danced, and dimpled her way into the hearts of moviegoers the world over. CULVER PICTURES, INC.

way's *Tarzan and His Mate*; William Powell and Myrna Loy in W. S. Van Dyke's *The Thin Man*; Helen Hayes and Brian Aherne in Gregory LaCava's *What Every Woman Knows*.

Opera: *Four Saints in Three Acts* 2/20 at New York's 44th Street Theater, with music by U.S. composer Virgil Garnett Thomson, 37, libretto by Gertrude Stein, whose opera is not about saints, is not presented in three acts, but adds to the fame of Gertrude Stein with such bewildering lines as "Pigeons in the grass, alas."

The Glyndebourne Festival Opera has its first season 54 miles south of London on the 640-acre estate of Audrey and John Christie. The London Philharmonic provides music for the June-to-August performances in the Christies' 800-seat opera house.

Lotte Lehmann, now 46, makes her Metropolitan Opera debut 12/31 singing the role of Sieglinde opposite tenor Lauritz Melchior in the 1870 Wagner opera *Die Walküre*; Marjorie (Florence) Lawrence sings the role of Brünnhilde in her own debut at the Met.

Ballet: English ballerina Margot Fonteyn (Margaret Hookham), 15, makes her debut dancing in the *Nutcracker Suite* at London's Vic-Wells Ballet; Soviet ballerina Galina Sergeyevna Ulanova, 24, makes her debut with the Kirov Ballet.

The Berkshire Music Festival has its first season on a 210-acre estate outside Lenox, Mass., whose grounds can accommodate up to 14,000 concertgoers. It is an outgrowth of the South Mountain Chamber-Music Festival begun at Pittsfield in 1918 under the aegis of philanthropist Elizabeth (Penn) Sprague Coolidge, now 69.

Phil Spitalny and His All-Girl Orchestra is formed by Ukrainian conductor-composer Philip Spitalny, 43, whose wife, Evelyn, entertains audiences with solos on her "magic violin." The group's *Hour of Charm* radio show will air from 1935 to 1948.

Stage musicals: Fanny Brice, Jane Froman, Eve Arden (originally Eunice Quedens), 21, Vilma and Buddy Ebsen, and Eugene and Willie Howard in *The New Ziegfeld Follies* 1/4 at New York's Winter Garden Theater, a production staged by Ziegfeld's widow, Billie Burke, with songs that include "I Like

the Looks of You" by Billy Hill, 182 perfs.; Ethel Merman, William Gaxton, and Victor Moore in *Anything Goes* 11/21 at New York's Alvin Theater, with Cole Porter songs that include "The Gypsy in Me," "I Get a Kick Out of You," "You're the Top," "Blow, Gabriel, Blow," "All Through the Night," and the title song, 420 perfs.; Sheila Barrett, Bobby Clark, and Ray Dooley in *Thumbs Up!* 12/27 at New York's St. James Theater, with songs that include "Autumn in New York" by Vernon Duke and "Zing! Went the Strings of My Heart" by James Hanley, 156 perfs.

Film musicals: Gracie Fields and John Loder in Basil Dean's *Sing as We Go*; Bing Crosby, Miriam Hopkins, and Kitty Carlisle (Catherine Holzman), 18, in Elliott Nugent's *She Loves Me Not* with songs that include "Love in Bloom."

Popular songs: "Miss Otis Regrets" by Noël Coward, who has written it for Bricktop (*see* 1925); "Little Man, You've Had a Busy Day," by Mabel Wayne, lyrics by Maurice Sigler and Al Hoffman; "You Oughta Be in Pictures" by U.S. composer Dana Suesse, 22, lyrics by Edward Heyman; "On the Good Ship Lollipop" by Richard Whiting, lyrics by Sidney Clare (for the film *Bright Eyes*, above).

Jazz singer Ella Fitzgerald, 16, lands a job with the Chick Webb Orchestra and begins a notable career.

Blues singer Bessie Smith appears at Harlem's new Apollo Theater, opened by two entrepreneurs who have bought a failing burlesque theater, changed its name, and changed its policy of barring black patrons. It will become the leading U.S. showcase for black performers.

Dorothy Round, 24, wins in women's singles at Wimbledon, Helen Jacobs at Forest Hills.

The fourth International Women's Games end at London August 11; German women have won top honors.

The Washeteria that opens April 18 at Fort Worth, Tex., is the first launderette. Proprietor J. F. Cantrell has installed four washing machines and charges by the hour.

U.S. textile designer Dorothy Liebes (*née* Wright), 34, opens her own New York design studio. The most accomplished weaver of her time, she has been the first American to adapt intricate hand techniques to mass production. Broadening the horizons of textile design, she will create patterns for DuPont carpeting, American Airlines seat upholstery, world's fairs, New York's Plaza Hotel, and the traveling throne room of the king of Saudi Arabia.

New York hat designer Sally Victor (*née* Josephs), 29, opens her own salon, catering to socialites and entertainers (customers soon include Irene Dunne, Helen Hayes, and Merle Oberon). She will popularize the baby bonnet, the Flemish sailor hat, and the pompadour hat.

Heiress Gloria (Laura Morgan) Vanderbilt, 10½, inherits $100,000 upon the death of her grandmother, Alice Gwynne Vanderbilt, in April. She makes headlines October 24 by telling a New York court that she prefers to live with her aunt, Mrs. Harry Payne Whitney, rather than with her mother, Mrs. Gloria Morgan Vanderbilt, widow of Reginald Vanderbilt (the late brother of Gertrude Vanderbilt Whitney), who seeks control of the girl's $2.8 million trust fund but whose own mother, Mrs. Laura Kilpatrick Morgan, testifies that Mrs. Vanderbilt moved to Europe soon after giving birth to little Gloria and "never wrote or inquired as to the baby's condition." The court rules November 21 that Mrs. Vanderbilt is unfit to have custody of her daughter (*see* 1941).

Bonnie Parker and Clyde Barrow, 24, die in a hail of bullets May 23 on a road 50 miles east of Shreveport, La., after a 2-year career in which they have casually killed 12 people in Texas, Oklahoma, Missouri, and Iowa. Their most successful robbery netted them no more than $3,500, and the father of one of their gang members has told the police where to watch for them. A Texas ranger and five sheriff's deputies have set up an ambush, Bonnie and Clyde drive into the trap at 85 miles per hour, the lawmen riddle them with 50 bullets, and they die holding a machine gun and a sawed-off shotgun, respectively.

John Dillinger, 32, leaves the Biograph Theater in Chicago July 22, not knowing that his girlfriend's landlady has betrayed him. FBI agents shoot him

dead after a brief career in which he has robbed banks in Indiana, Ohio, Illinois, and Wisconsin.

Tillie Lewis Foods has its beginnings in Flotill Products, founded in California's San Joaquin valley by Brooklyn, N.Y., divorcée Myrtle "Tillie" Ehrlich, 28, with a $10,000 loan from Italian pomodoro tomato canner Florindo Del Gaizo. Advised by the U.S. Department of Agriculture that pomodoro Italian canning tomatoes could not be grown in the United States, Ehrlich took her savings, sailed for Italy, met Del Gaizo aboard ship, convinced him that the tomatoes could be grown in California, and has persuaded the Pacific Can Co. of Stockton to build a plant she can rent. When Del Gaizo dies in 1937, she will borrow $100,000 to buy out his interest in Flotill, she will marry AF of L western director Meyer Lewis in 1947, and she will sell her Tillie Lewis Foods to a conglomerate for $6 million.

Le Cordon Bleu outgrows its 39-year-old Paris quarters in the Palais-Royale and is moved by Mme. Distel to 120 Rue du Faubourg St. Honoré (*see* 1895; 1945).

Birth Control: Its Use and Misuse by U.S. birth control advocate Dorothy Dunbar Bromley says America could avoid 8,000 maternal deaths per year by legalizing abortion, at least until adequate contraceptives are made available. Condoms are now made of latex, making them more comfortable than earlier rubber condoms.

Scientists isolate the female sex hormone progesterone, secreted naturally after the monthly release of an egg from a woman's ovaries (*see* estrogen, 1929). It causes the lining of the uterus to firm and thicken, inhibits some of the effects of estrogen, prevents the release of a second egg (thus preventing more than one pregnancy per month), and, if a fertilized egg does not adhere to the thickened uterine wall, stimulates the shedding of endometrial tissue to produce menstrual bleeding (*see* Marker, 1943).

"Woman has her battlefield," declaims Adolf Hitler (above) in an address to women at Nuremberg September 14. "With each child that she brings to the nation, she fights her fight for the nation."

The United Front for the Rights of Woman (*Frente Unica pro Derechos de La Mujer*) is founded in Mexico to campaign for female suffrage (*see* 1946).

The Nuremberg Laws enacted by the Nazi party congress meeting at Nuremberg September 15 deprive Jews of German citizenship, forbid German citizens' intermarriage with Jews, and make intercourse between "Aryans" and Jews punishable by death to prevent "racial pollution." (The basic definition of a Jew published November 14 defines the categories of mixed offspring, or *mischlinge*. The first degree includes anyone with two Jewish grandparents, the second degree anyone with one Jewish grandparent.)

The National Council of Negro Women founded December 5 by Mary McLeod Bethune is the first national coalition of black women's organizations (*see* National Association of Colored Women, 1896). Bethune will head the NCNW until 1949, working with the YWCA, the NAACP, the League of Women Voters, and other groups to eliminate racism and sexism.

 The Social Security Act signed into law by President Roosevelt August 14 provides a system of old-age annuities and unemployment insurance benefits. It provides for state aid to be matched by federal aid, with employers and employees taxed equally to support the program. The tax is to begin in 1937 at 1 percent and rise by steps to 3 percent in 1949; qualified employees are to be able to retire at age 65 beginning January 1, 1942, and receive payments of $10 to $15 per month for the rest of their lives; widows and orphans are to receive benefits beginning in 1940.

 Aviatrix Jean Gardner Batten flies from England to New Zealand in a record 11 days (*see* 1934). She has been obsessed for more than a decade with accomplishing the feat; her father had wanted her to be a concert pianist, but she sold her piano to finance flying lessons.

"Air hostesses" begin flying on 14-passenger TWA DC-2s December 6 (*see* 1930). The Douglas DC-3, which makes its first flight December 21, has been designed for American Airlines to carry 21 passengers at nearly 160 miles per hour.

 Nylon, developed by E. I. du Pont chemist Wallace Hume Carothers, 39, is a synthetic polyamide that will replace silk, rayon, and jute in many applications. Carothers has combined adipic acid and hexamethylenediamine to form long filaments of what he calls "polymer 66." Drawing the filaments out to a certain length aligns the polymer chains and pulls them to their full extent, making the filaments strong and durable but giving them many of the characteristics found in silk and wool (*see* 1937).

 Sex and Temperament in Three Primitive Societies by Margaret Mead is about three New Guinea tribes—the Arapesh, Mundgumor, and Tchambuli. Critics will later question her good fortune in finding three tribes that illustrated the points she wanted to make about the cultural determination of sex roles.

Sulfa drug chemotherapy introduced by German biochemist Gerhard Domagk, 40, launches a new era in medicine that will revolutionize treatment of gonorrhea. Physicians have relied on prophylaxis, mercurial ointments, and antiseptics to combat the disease, whose symptoms often go undetected in women, who are therefore not treated before it has spread throughout their reproductive tracts. Even with sulfa drugs, gonorrhea continues to account for much of the high rate of pelvic operations.

Studies by the U.S. medical profession indicate that uneducated immigrant midwives in New York have septicemia rates no worse than those of physicians in home and hospital deliveries (37 percent of all births are now in hospitals; *see* 1945). Where surgical intervention is needed, infection is even more likely, as increased high- and midforceps operations and cesarean sections create the "traumatized, devitalized tissues that allow the anaerobic streptococci already present to develop into infections despite the creation of a sterile operating environment." Some hospitals have infection rates as high as 11 percent.

 "Little Lulu" makes her debut in the *Saturday Evening Post* in December. Created by Philadelphia cartoonist Marjorie "Marge" Buell (*née* Henderson), 31, the resourceful, courageous Lulu, who outwits neighborhood boys, will appear in a syndicated newspaper strip beginning in 1944. Her creator will retain rights to the character, licensing Lulu for comic books, 26 animated cartoons, dolls, greeting cards, puzzles, games, toys, coloring books, and advertising.

Nonfiction: *North to the Orient* by U.S. writer Ann Morrow Lindbergh, 29, who married pilot Charles A. Lindbergh in 1929 and has joined him on many flights; *I Change Worlds: The Remaking of an American* by Anna Louise Strong; *The Living of Charlotte Perkins Gilman* (autobiography) by Gilman, who has terminal cancer and dies by her own hand at Pasadena, Calif., August 17 at age 75; *There's Always Tomorrow* (autobiography) by Marguerite Harrison, now 56, who in 1926 married English actor Arthur Middleton Blake.

Fiction: *Flowering Judas and Other Stories* by U.S. writer Katherine Anne Porter, 45; *Lucy Gayheart* by Willa Cather; *More Joy in Heaven and Other Stories* by Sylvia Townsend Warner; *A Progress of Stories* (stories) by Laura Riding; *Confessions of Love* (*Ai no kokuhaku*) by Japanese novelist Chiyo Uno, 37, who defied tradition by refusing an arranged marriage (and subjection to a domineering mother-in-law), married a cousin at age 19, deserted him 5 years later, sold stories to magazines, married a writer, split from him in 1929, married a well-known Cubist painter, and is notorious for her Westernized profligacy; *Oyster* (*Kaki*) by Fumiko Hayashi; *The Boundary* (*Granica*) by Zofja Nalkowska; *The Girls from Nowolipki* (*Dziewczekta z Nowolipek*) by Pola Gljawiczynska; *The House in Paris* by Elizabeth Bowen; *A House and Its Head* by Ivy Compton-Burnett; *South Riding* by feminist English novelist Winifred Holtby, 37; *Holy Ireland* by Norah Hoult; *I Met a Gypsy* and *White Hell of Pity* by Irish novelist Norah Lofts (*née* Robinson), 31; *This Bed Thy Centre* by English novelist Pamela Hansford Johnson, 23; *Regency Buck* by English novelist Georgette Heyer, 34; *Love in Winter* by Storm Jameson; *Art Makers* by Jessica North MacDonald; *A House Divided* by Pearl S. Buck; *A Vein of Iron* by Ellen Glasgow; *The Iron Will* by Margaret Culkin Banning; *Miss J. Looks On* by Sophie Kerr; *Big Business Murder* by Margaret Cole; *Death in the Stocks* by Georgette Heyer (above).

Poetry: *Theory of Flight* by U.S. poet Muriel Rukeyser, 21, includes her poem "The Trial," based on her reporting of the 1931 Scottsboro trial in Alabama for the *Vassar Student Review*; *For the Tree's Sake* (*För trädets skull*) by Karin Boye.

Juvenile: *National Velvet* by Enid Bagnold, whose book is illustrated by her daughter Laurian, 13. *Little House on the Prairie* by Laura Ingalls Wilder, whose parents settled in a shanty at De Smet, South Dakota, in 1880. The author was married at age 18 to Almanzo Wilder, helped him run a farm near her parents' house, suffered through crop-destroying hailstorms and droughts, nearly died when both came down with diphtheria, and helped nurse her husband after he was partially paralyzed by a stroke.

Theater: *The Old Maid* by Zoë Akins (who has adapted an Edith Wharton novel) 1/7 at New York's Empire Theater, with Australian-born actress Judith (*née* Frances Margaret) Anderson, 36, and Helen Mencken, 305 perfs. (Pulitzer Prize); Alfred Lunt, Lynn Fontanne, and Broderick Crawford in Noël Coward's *Point Valaine* 1/16 at New York's Ethel Barrymore Theater, 55 perfs.; Stella Adler, Morris Carnovsky, and John Garfield in Clifford Odets's *Awake and Sing!* 2/19 at New York's Belasco Theater, 209 perfs.; Burgess Meredith, Richard Bennett, and Margo (Mexican-American actress Maria Marguerita Guadelupe Boldao y Castilla, 17) in Maxwell Anderson's *Winterset*, based on the Sacco-Vanzetti case, 9/25 at New York's Martin Beck Theater, 195 perfs.; Joseph Dowling and Sheila Trent in Sidney Kingsley's *Dead End* 10/28 at New York's Belasco Theater, 268 perfs.; *Call It a Day* by C. L. Anthony (Dodie Smith) 10/30 at London's Globe Theatre, with Fay Compton; *Boy Meets Girl* by U.S. playwrights Bella (*née* Cohen) and Samuel Spewack, both 36, 11/27 at New York's Cort Theater, with Jerome Cowan, Garson Kanin, and Everett Sloane, 669 perfs.; Helen Hayes in Laurence Housman's *Victoria Regina* 12/26 at New York's Broadhurst Theater, 517 perfs. (plus 452 after a summer closing).

Royal Academy of Dramatic Art graduate Joan Littlewood, 21, founds the Theatre Union, an experimental group, at Manchester. Director Littlewood will reorganize the Union in 1945 as the Theatre Workshop and open in 1953 at London's Theatre Royal with a production of Shakespeare's *Twelfth Night*.

Radio comedy and drama: *Fibber McGee and Molly* 4/16 on NBC Blue Network stations with Jim and Marian Driscoll Jordan (to 1952).

Films: Greta Garbo and Fredric March in Clarence Brown's *Anna Karenina*; English character actress Elsa Lanchester (Elizabeth Sullivan), 32, and Boris Karloff in James Whale's *The Bride of Frankenstein*; Charles Laughton, Mary Boland, and Charles Ruggles in Leo McCarey's *Ruggles of Red Gap*; Robert Donat and Madeleine Carroll (Marie Madeleine Bernadette O'Carroll), 29, in Alfred Hitchcock's *The 39 Steps*; Leni Riefenstahl's propaganda documentary *Triumph of the Will* extolling last year's Nuremberg rallies. Also: Miriam Hopkins and Frances Dee in Rouben Mamoulian's *Becky Sharp*; Margaret Sullavan and Herbert Marshall in William Wyler's *The Good Fairy*; Gracie Fields in Basil Dean's *Look Up and Laugh*; Leslie Howard and Tasmanian-born actress Merle Oberon, 24, in Harold Young's *The Scarlet Pimpernel*.

Hollywood musicals: Ginger Rogers and Fred Astaire in Mark Sandrich's *Top Hat* with Irving Berlin songs that include "Cheek to Cheek," "Isn't It a Lovely Day to Be Caught in the Rain," and "Top Hat, White Tie, and Tails"; Joan Bennett and Bing Crosby in A. Edward Sutherland's *Mississippi* with Rodgers and Hart songs that include "It's Easy to Remember but So Hard to Forget"; Ann Sothern (Harriet Lake), 23, Merle Oberon, and Maurice Chevalier in Roy Del Ruth's *Folies Bergère*.

Stage musicals: Madge Evans and Cyril Ritchard in *Spread It Abroad* at London, with songs that include "These Foolish Things Remind Me of You"; Beatrice Lillie, Eleanor Powell, Ethel Waters, and Eddie Foy, Jr. in *At Home Abroad* 9/19 at New York's Winter Garden Theater, with Arthur Schwartz–Howard Dietz songs that include "Hottentot Potentate," 198 perfs.; Mary Boland, Melville Cooper, and Montgomery Clift in *Jubilee* 10/12 at New York's Imperial Theater, with Cole Porter songs that include "Begin the Beguine" and "Just One of Those Things," 169 perfs.

Opera: Norwegian soprano Kirsten (Malfrid) Flagstad, 40, makes her Metropolitan Opera debut 2/2 singing the role of Sieglinde in the 1870 Wagner opera *Die Walküre* and 4 days later sings the role of Isolde; she made her debut at Oslo in 1913 at age

Ginger Rogers teamed up with Fred Astaire to keep movie audiences entertained through the Depression. CULVER PICTURES, INC.

15; U.S. soprano Anne Wiggins Brown, 20, as Bess, Todd Duncan as Porgy in George Gershwin's *Porgy and Bess* 10/10 at New York's Alvin Theater, with choral direction by Eva Jessye, 40, of the Eva Jessye Singers, songs that include "Bess, You Is My Woman Now" and "It Ain't Necessarily So," 124 perfs.; Italian soprano Licia Albanese, 22, makes her debut 12/10 at Parma.

Popular songs: "I'm in the Mood for Love" by Dorothy Fields and Jimmy McHugh; jazz singer Connee (*née* Connie) Boswell, 27, becomes a soloist after several years of performing with her sisters (she had polio as a child and must use a wheelchair); Arkansas-born singer Patsy Montana (Rubye

Blevins), 20, records "I Wanna Be a Cowboy's Sweetheart" and becomes the first woman in country music to have a record that sells more than 1 million copies.

Helen Wills Moody wins in women's singles at Wimbledon, Helen Jacobs at Forest Hills.

Tobacco heiress Doris Duke, now 21, is married February 13 at her Fifth Avenue New York mansion to James H. R. Cromwell, 38, who has been divorced from Delphine Dodge of the automaking family (a chronic alcoholic who will die at age 45, she had an income of $2 million per year from her father's $57 million estate). Duke met Cromwell at Bar Harbor 6 years ago; the word "obey" is omitted from the marriage vows (see 1940; real estate, 1937).

Woolworth heiress Barbara Hutton obtains a Reno divorce May 13 from Prince Alexis Mdivani, who is given another $2 million (see 1933). Now 22, she is remarried that evening at Lake Tahoe to Kurt Heinrich Eberhardt Erdman Georg Haugwitz-Reventlow, 40, a Prussian-born Danish count who has received $1 million prior to the wedding (Mdivani is killed August 1 when his Rolls-Royce strikes a culvert in Spain). The handsome groom, who earned an Iron Cross fighting with the Germans in the Great War, is a skier and mountain climber who speaks five languages fluently. Hutton tells reporters that she is now completely happy, renounces her U.S. citizenship, spends $4 million to buy the biggest mansion in Regent's Park, London, and staffs it with footmen attired in canary-and-blue livery (see 1941).

Max Factor of Hollywood opens a supercolossal salon in the film capital. Now 58, the Russian-born cosmetics magnate arrived in America at age 27, became a Hollywood makeup man in his late thirties, and has a factory that employs 250 people producing cosmetics and wigs.

Federal agents kill Kate "Ma" Barker (née Arizona Donnie Clark), 62, and her husband, Fred, of the notorious Karpis-Barker gang January 16 outside Oklawaha, Fla., in a 6-hour shootout. Mrs. Barker has masterminded a series of robberies, kidnappings, and murders which her sons Lloyd, 38, Arthur, 35, and Fred committed (Fred was killed in 1927 at age 31).

New York District Attorney Thomas E. Dewey, 33, raids Polly Adler's brothel as part of a crackdown on an alleged prostitution syndicate (see 1924). Adler is convicted on charges of possessing pornographic films and serves 24 days under the alias "Joan Martin" (see 1943).

Ireland makes it a felony to sell, import, or advertise any form of birth control device or method.

Use of sulfonamides (above) will make it far less hazardous for physicians to perform dilation and curettage, the most commonly employed means of terminating pregnancies. Economic pressures created by the Depression have created a record demand for abortions, most of which are performed illegally, often by unqualified practitioners under nonsterile conditions.

Nazi SS (*Schutzstaffel*) leader Heinrich Himmler starts a *Lebensborn* (life source) state breeding program to produce an "Aryan super race." He encourages young women of "pure blood" to volunteer their services as mates of SS officers to contribute blond, blue-eyed babies who will grow into thin-lipped, narrow-nosed "Nordic beings" to carry on the "thousand-year Reich."

1936

Britain's George V dies January 20 at age 70 after a reign of nearly 26 years and is succeeded by his son David, 41, who assumes the throne as Edward VIII. The new king has given up his longtime affair with Freda Dudley Ward and wants to marry the American-born socialite Bessie Wallis Simpson (*née* Warfield), 39, who has just divorced her second husband. Edward abdicates December 10 so that he may marry "the woman I love," and his diffident younger brother Albert assumes the throne as George VI. Marie of Romania, who as a girl was in love with the new king's father, writes to a friend, "Personally I am too royal not to look upon David as a deserter. Also, I can work up no feelings for Mrs. Simpson. There is something . . . about her which does not make it a clean, fine love-romance. She has too much to do with cocktails and night clubs. She is an uninteresting heroine. I dislike her face, her name, her attitude, her style, the world she represents." Most commoners share Marie's view.

A Spanish civil war begins July 18 as army chiefs in Spanish Morocco start a revolt against the weak government at Madrid. Most of the army and air force supports insurgent generals Francisco Franco, 44, and Emilio Mola, 49, and the revolt spreads rapidly to the garrisons of Cádiz, Seville, Saragossa, and Burgos in Spain. "The fifth column" will take Madrid, says Gen. Mola when asked which of his four columns will capture the city. He refers to sympathizers within Madrid, but resistance stiffens when Communist orator La Pasionaria (Dolores Ibarruri, 41), exhorts housewives to take lunch to their husbands in the trenches and pour boiling oil on any Fascists who enter the city. "They shall not pass" (*"No pasarán"*), she has said July 18, and she rallies support with the cry "It is better to die on your feet than live on your knees" (*see* 1977).

 New Jersey mother Mabel Eaton loses custody of her children January 29 because of her affiliation with the Communist party. Labor organizer Elizabeth Gurley Flynn joins the Party, convinced that "the full opportunity for women to become free and equal citizens with access to all spheres of human endeavor cannot come under capitalism, although many demands have been won by organized struggle."

A new family law adopted in the Soviet Union discourages divorce with fees and other restrictions, tightens requirements for alimony payments, and establishes an extensive system of maternity welfare, child care, and state financial support, especially for women in the workforce.

The Supreme Court rules June 1 that a New York minimum wage law for women passed in 1933 is unconstitutional. The Court hands down the decision in the case of *Morehead* v. *New York ex. rel. Tipaldo* (*see* Fair Labor Standards Act, 1938).

Eleanor Roosevelt gives a garden party on the White House lawn in May for 60 girls from Washington's National Industrial School. All except eight are black, and the school's black superintendent Dr. Carrie Weaver Smith says, "Mrs. Roosevelt knows what the word 'lady' means," but the action outrages southern sensibilities. One newspaper speaks of the president's wife having entertained a bunch of "nigger whores" at the White House.

Mary McLeod Bethune is named director of Negro affairs in the National Youth Administration June 24 (*see* education, 1923). She is the first black woman to receive a major federal appointment.

💲 38 percent of U.S. families (11.7 million families) have incomes of less than $1,000 per year. The Bureau of Labor Statistics places the "poverty line" at $1,330.

⚡ English aviatrix Beryl Markham (*née* Clutterbuck), 33, leaves Abingdon, England, September 4 and crash-lands safely the next afternoon in a swamp on

Pilot Beryl Markham flew over Africa, across the Atlantic, and straight in the face of convention.

Nova Scotia's Cape Breton Island. She has been forced by bad weather to fly blind, relying on instruments, and is nearly out of fuel when she comes down. Her 23-hour, 45-minute flight makes her the first woman to fly the Atlantic solo and non-stop from east to west (two other women have died attempting the feat). Raised in East Africa, Markham was taught to hunt and ride, mauled by a lion, and attacked by a baboon. She was married after World War I to a man 16 years her senior, became increasingly promiscuous until her husband finally divorced her, was remarried 9 years ago to Mansfield Markham, the second son of a baronet, remained in Africa after he returned to England, had affairs with men who included Karen Blixen's lover Denys Finch-Hatton, but has refused to get a divorce. She has been flying since 1931, earning good money by carrying mail, supplies, and passengers all over East Africa.

New York Evening Journal reporter Dorothy Kilgallen, 23, sets out in September to beat Nelly Bly's 1889–90 round-the-world speed record. She crosses the Atlantic in the German dirigible *Hindenburg*, makes her way across Europe and Asia, and returns via Manila, where she catches a Pan American China Clipper bound for San Francisco via Guam, Wake, Midway, and Honolulu, but she loses out to *New York Telegram* reporter Bud Ekins, who breaks the record by circling the earth in 18 days, 14 hours, 56 minutes—all by air over new passenger routes. Kilgallen writes out of Hollywood for a while and then returns to New York, where she launches a newspaper gossip column, "The Voice of Broadway."

Rates of maternal mortality in the United States will drop sharply in the next 20 years through routinization of better care in delivery, use of antibiotic drugs, and superior intervention procedures performed by better-qualified physicians. Women will be given analgesics to relieve pain in childbirth and scopolamine to erase the memory of pain.

The *Ladies' Home Journal* carries a series of articles on maternity by U.S. medical writer Paul de Kruif, 46, who makes reference to Grantly Dick-Read's natural childbirth ideas (*see* 1933; 1942).

Eleanor Roosevelt contracts with the United Features newspaper syndicate to write six columns a week under the title "My Day." It is the first time a sitting First Lady has undertaken a money-making media career, and her decision creates some controversy (the diary recording her incessant travels and lecture tours will continue until shortly before her death in 1962). By year's end, 60 newspapers (up from an initial 20) carry the column, including some owned by publishers who oppose FDR. Mrs. Roosevelt urges women to put family life first, but concedes that they have a right to work for personal as well as for economic reasons.

First Lady Eleanor Roosevelt had a common touch that would continue beyond her White House years. LIBRARY OF CONGRESS

The *New York Herald Tribune* gives Dorothy Thompson, now 47, her own column, "On the Record," which gains instant success. *Trib* vice president Helen Rogers Reid (the publisher's wife) appoints women to edit its book review and magazine.

The *New York Times* makes Anne O'Hare McCormick, now 56, its first regular woman editorial-page contributor.

Sutairu (*Style*), Japan's first fashion magazine, is launched by novelist Ghiyu Uno.

Life magazine begins publication at New York November 23 with a cover illustration by photographer Margaret Bourke-White, 30.

Nonfiction: *Ladies of the Press* by *New York Herald Tribune* reporter Isabel Ross, who notes that there are not enough newspaperwomen even now to make any difference: "They are remarkable only because they are exceptions"; *The Southern Gates of Arabia: A Journey in the Hadhramaut* by Freya Stark; *Buddhism: Its Doctrines and Its Methods (Le Bouddhisme, ces doctrines et ces methodes)* by Alexandra David-Neel.

Fiction: *Nightwood* by U.S. novelist Djuna Barnes, 44; *The Faithful Spouse (Den trofaste hustru)* by Sigrid Undset; *Too Little (För lite)* by Karin Boye; *Novel on Yellow Paper* by English poet Stevie (*née* Florence Margaret) Smith, 34, whose mother, Ethel, died at age 42 when she was 16 (after attending Birmingham University and teaching school, she took a secretarial course and became secretary to Sir Neville Pearson, head of a large publishing firm, who has rejected her poetry and advised her to write a novel instead); *The Weather in the Streets* by Rosamond Lehmann (sequel to her 1932 novel); *Jamaica Inn* by Daphne du Maurier; *Mary Lavelle* by Kate O'Brien; *Blessed among Women* by Pamela Hansford Johnson; *Summer Will Show* by Sylvia Townsend Warner; *The Thinking Reed* by Rebecca West; *Check to Your King* and *Passport to Hell* by New Zealand novelist-poet Robin Hyde (Iris Wilkinson), 30; *Jungfrau* by Australian novelist (Ellen) Dymphna Cusack, 34; *The Beauties and Furies* by Christina Stead; *All the Swagger* by Miles Franklin; *The White Horses of Vienna and Other Stories* by Kay Boyle, now 34, whose novel *Death of a Man* is also published; *None Turned Back* by Storm Jameson completes the trilogy begun with *Company Parade* in 1934; *The Talisman Ring* by Georgette Heyer; *The Fallen Crane (Tsuru wa yamiki)* by Japanese novelist Kanoko Okamoto (*née* Kano Onuki), 47; *A Husband's Virtue (Otto no teisō)* by Japanese novelist Nobuko Yoshiya, 40, begins serialization in Tokyo and Osaka newspapers; *Gone with the Wind* by Atlanta novelist Margaret Mitchell, 36 (1937 Pulitzer Prize): Macmillan editor Harold Latham, 49, has changed the title from *Tomorrow Is Another Day*, and the heroine's name from Pansy to Scarlett O'Hara, and the book will be translated into 30 languages and have sales of more than 30 million copies worldwide (*see* Films, 1939); *The Trouble I've Seen* (four novellas) by U.S. writer Martha Gellhorn, 27, who has worked as an investigator for the Federal Relief Agency; *Of Lena Geyer* by U.S. novelist Marcia Davenport, 33, daughter of opera singer Alma Gluck; *Honor Bright* by U.S. novelist Frances Parkinson Keyes (*née* Wheeler), 51; *The Rolling Year* by U.S. novelist Agnes Sligh Turnbull, 47; *Letters to Susan* by Margaret Culkin Banning; *The Moon's Our Home, Men Are Such Fools!*, *Private Duty*, and *Girls of Divine Corners* by Faith Baldwin; *Flowers for the Judge* by Margery Allingham; *Behold, Here's Poison* by Georgette Heyer (above); *A Shilling for Candles* by Josephine Tey.

Poetry: *A Trophy of Arms* by Ruth Pitter wins Britain's Hawthornden Prize; *Il dono* by Ada Negri, now 66; *Under a Clear Sky (Unter hellen Himmel)* by Agnes Miegel.

Juvenile: *Anne of Windy Poplars* by Maud Montgomery, whose heroine becomes a mother.

Painting: *The Rehearsal* by Marie Laurencin, who will be quoted after her death as having said, "Why should I paint dead fish, onions, and beer glasses? Girls are so much prettier."

Photography: *Migrant Mother* by U.S. documentary photographer Dorothea Lange (originally Nutzhorn), 41, captures the hardship of the life being experienced by America's Dust Bowl victims; *You Have Seen Their Faces* by Margaret Bourke-White (text by Erskine Caldwell) contains 70 photographs of poverty-stricken Americans in Alabama, Arkansas, Florida, Georgia, Louisiana, Mississippi, South Carolina, and Tennessee.

Theater: Gertrude Lawrence and Coward in Noël Coward's *Tonight at 8:30* (one-act plays: *We Were Dancing, The Astonished Heart, A Family Album*, and *"Red Peppers"*) 1/9 at London's Phoenix Theatre, followed 1/13 by *Hands Across the Sea, Fumed Oak*, and *Shadow Play*, followed 3/21 by *Star Chamber*, 5/5 by *Ways and Means*, and 5/18 by *Still Life*; Ina Claire, Osgood Perkins, and Mildred Natwick, 27, in S. N. Behrman's *End of Summer* 2/17 at New York's Guild Theater, 121 perfs.; Alfred Lunt and Lynn Fontanne in Robert Sherwood's antiwar drama *Idiot's Delight* 3/29 at New York's Shubert Theater, 300 perfs.; *The Women* by U.S. playwright Clare Boothe (Luce), 33, 7/9 at

Photographer Dorothea Lange portrayed a woman forced by drought to leave America's Dust Bowl. LIBRARY OF CONGRESS

New York's Ethel Barrymore Theater, with Ilka Chase, Jane Seymour, Margalo Gilmore, Arlene Francis (Arlene Kazanjian), 27, Audrey Christie, Doris Day (Doris von Kappelhoff), 22, Marjorie Main, 46, and Ruth Hammond, 657 perfs.; Tallulah Bankhead in George Kelly's *Reflected Glory* 9/21 at New York's Morosco Theater, 127 perfs.; Margaret Sullavan and Tom Ewell in George S. Kaufman and Edna Ferber's *Stage Door* 10/22 at New York's Music Box Theater, 169 perfs.; Josephine Hull (*née* Sherwood), 50, Ruth Attaway, Frank Wilcox, and George Tobias in George S. Kaufman and Moss Hart's *You Can't Take It with You* 12/14 at New York's Booth Theater, 837 perfs.

Films: John Huston, Paul Lucas, and Russian-American actress Maria Ouspenskaya, 60, in William Wyler's *Dodsworth*; Jean Harlow, Myrna Loy, William Powell, and Spencer Tracy in Jack Conway's *Libeled Lady*; Gary Cooper and Jean Arthur in Frank Capra's *Mr. Deeds Goes to Town*; Miriam Hopkins, Bombay-born actress Merle Oberon (Estelle Merle O'Brien Thompson), 25, and Joel McCrae in William Wyler's *These Three*. Also: Fredric March and English-American actress Olivia de Havilland, 20, in Mervyn LeRoy's *Anthony Adverse*; Greta Garbo, Robert Taylor, and Lionel Barrymore in George Cukor's *Camille*; Sylvia Sidney and Spencer Tracy in Fritz Lang's *Fury*; William Powell, Myrna Loy, and Frank Morgan in Robert Z. Leonard's *The Great Ziegfeld*; Tyrone Power, Freddie Bartholomew, and Madeleine Carroll in Henry King's *Lloyd's of London*; Katharine Hepburn, Florence Eldridge, Fredric March, and Anita Colby (originally Counihan), 22, in John Ford's *Mary of Scotland*; Danielle Darrieux, 19, and Charles Boyer in Anatole Litvak's *Mayerling*; Carole Lombard and William Powell in Gregory La Cava's *My Man Godfrey*; Leni Riefenstahl's documentary *Olympia*; Gracie Fields in Monte Banks's *Queen of Hearts*; Irene (Marie) Dunne (originally Dunn), 32, and Melvyn Douglas in Richard Boleslawski's *Theodora Goes Wild*; Katharine Hepburn as a young English suffragist in Mark Sandrich's *A Woman Rebels*.

Former Hollywood actress Hedda Hopper (Elda Furry), 46, who debuted in 1915, begins regular radio broadcasts dealing with the latest gossip of the film capital (*see* Kilgallen, above; Louella Parsons, 1925; Sheila Graham, 1933). Her newspaper gossip column, written at the suggestion of *Washington Herald* editor Cissy Patterson (who met her at William Randolph Hearst's San Simeon ranch), will begin appearing in 1938 (*see* 1942).

Hollywood musicals: Ginger Rogers, Fred Astaire, Randolph Scott, Harriet Hilliard, and Betty Grable, 20, in Mark Sandrich's *Follow the Fleet* with Irving Berlin songs that include "Let's Face the Music," "Let Yourself Go," and "We Saw the Sea"; Clark Gable, Jeanette MacDonald, and Spencer Tracy in W. S. Van Dyke's *San Francisco* with songs that include the title song; Ginger Rogers and Fred Astaire in George Stevens's *Swing Time* with Jerome Kern–Dorothy Fields songs that include "A Fine Romance" and "The Way You Look Tonight"; Canadian-born singer Deanna (*née* Edna May) Durbin, 13, in Henry Koster's *Three Smart Girls*; tap dancer Eleanor Parker and James Stewart in Roy Del Ruth's *Born to Dance* with Cole

Porter songs that include "Easy to Love" and "I've Got You under My Skin"; Eleanor Parker, Jack Benny, and Robert Taylor in Roy Del Ruth's *Broadway Melody of 1936* with songs that include "I Gotta Feelin' You're Foolin' " and "You Are My Lucky Star"; Paul Robeson, Irene Dunne, and Helen Morgan in James Whale's *Show Boat* with Jerome Kern–Oscar Hammerstein II songs from the 1927 Broadway musical.

Broadway musicals: Eve Arden (Eunice Quedens), 23, Josephine Baker, Judy Canova, Bob Hope, and Fanny Brice in *The Ziegfeld Follies* 1/30 at the Winter Garden Theater, with songs that include "I Can't Get Started" by Vernon Duke, lyrics by Ira Gershwin, 227 perfs. (after an interruption due to Fanny Brice's illness); Tamara Geva, Ray Bolger, and George Church dance in the ballet *Slaughter on Tenth Avenue* in *On Your Toes* 4/11 at the Imperial Theater, with Rodgers and Hammerstein songs, 315 perfs.; Ethel Merman, Jimmy Durante, Grace and Paul Hartman, and Bob Hope in *Red, Hot and Blue* 10/29 at the Alvin Theater, with Cole Porter songs that include "De-Lovely" and "Down in the Depths on the 90th Floor," 183 perfs.; *The Show Is On* 12/25 at the Ethel Barrymore Theater, with the same cast as *The Women* (above), songs that include George and Ira Gershwin's "By Strauss" and "Little Old Lady" by Hoagy Carmichael, lyrics by Stanley Adams, 202 perfs.

Opera: Spanish soprano Conchita Supervia, now 40 and at the height of her career, dies at London March 30 after childbirth.

Popular songs: Baltimore-born jazz singer Billie Holiday (Eleanora Fagan), 21, records "Did I Remember," "No Regrets," and "Billy's Blues." "Lady Day" cut her first records 3 years ago with Benny Goodman and others, went on to record with Teddy Wilson and members of the Count Basie band, and will tour with Basie next year. "The Night Is Young and You're So Beautiful" by Dana Suesse, lyrics by Billy Rose and Irving Kahal; Patsy Montana records "I Haven't Got a Pot to Cook In."

Helen Jacobs wins in women's singles at Wimbledon, Alice Marble, 22, at Forest Hills.

Sonja Henie wins her third Olympic gold medal in figure skating at the winter games in Garmisch-Partenkirchen. U.S. runner Helen Stephens wins the 100-meter dash in 11.5 seconds at the summer games in Berlin, Italian athlete Trebisonda Valla the 80-meter hurdles event in 11.7 seconds, Hungarian athlete Ibolya Csak the running high jump (5 feet, 3 inches), German athlete Gisela Mauermayer the discus throw (156 feet, 3 3/16 inches), German athlete Tilly Fleischer the javelin throw (148 feet, 2 3/4 inches), Dutch swimmer Hendrika Mastenbroek the 400-meter freestyle in 5 minutes, 26.4 seconds, Dutch swimmer Dina Senff the 100-meter breaststroke in 1 minute, 18.9 seconds, Japanese swimmer Hideko Maehata the 200-meter breaststroke in 3 minutes, 3.6 seconds, U.S. swimmer Marjorie Gestring the springboard dive event, Dorothy Poynton Hill the platform dive.

Winning Bridge Made Easy by Philadelphia lawyer Charles Henry Goren, 35, makes a radical departure from the dominant "honor-trick" method devised by Ely Culbertson for evaluating a hand (*see* Vanderbilt, 1925). Goren gives up the law to devote himself to refining his bidding system.

Bass Weejuns, introduced at $12 a pair by G. H. Bass & Co. of Wilton, Me., begin a unisex fashion for slip-on moccasin "loafers."

Tampax, Inc., is founded at New Brunswick, N.J., to produce a cotton tampon with string attached patented by Denver physician Earl Haas. Women since ancient times have used absorbent rags during their menstrual periods, but no commercial tampon has been available until now (*see* Kotex, 1918; Toxic Shock Syndrome, 1980).

Japanese authorities arrest Tokyo geisha Sada Abe, 31, May 21 on charges of having stabbed her unfaithful lover Kichizo Ishida to death in his sleep, castrating him, and carrying his penis about in her *obi* (sash) for 3 days while eluding police.

General Mills uses the name "Betty Crocker" as a signature for responses to consumer inquiries. The fictitious authority is portrayed as a gray-haired homemaker, an image that will see numerous revisions as Betty Crocker becomes a major brand name for various General Mills products (*see* 1929).

The Joy of Cooking by St. Louis housewife Irma Rombauer (*née* von Starkloff), 60, gives recipes in the most minute detail, telling the cook exactly what to do. Rombauer, whose lawyer husband taught her to cook after their marriage in 1899, had a private edition printed 5 years ago for her grown children; her daughter Marion Rombauer Becker, now, 33, will coauthor future editions.

 Moscow revokes the 1920 decree legalizing abortion. "We need men," Josef Stalin has written in the April 27 issue of the periodical *Labor.* "Abortion which destroys life is not acceptable in our country. The Soviet woman has the same rights as the man, but that does not free her from a great and honorable duty which nature has given her: she is a mother, she gives life." A new law adopted in May restricts abortions to cases in which pregnancy endangers the life of the woman or in which the child is likely to inherit a specified disease; women are taught nothing about birth control and have no access to contraceptives (*see* 1955).

A U.S. Circuit Court of Appeals judge rules that the purpose of the 1872 Comstock law, liberalized in 1929, "was not to prevent the importation, sale, or carriage by mail of things which might intelligently be employed by conscientious and competent physicians for the purpose of saving life or promoting the well-being of their patients." The ruling is made in a case brought by birth control advocate Hannah Stone (*see* Connecticut, 1965).

Women wanting to terminate pregnancies continue to rely mostly on vaginal douching, often with solutions of water, Lysol, carbolic soap, iodine, and turpentine. The bark of the American slippery elm tree, tightly rolled and slipped into the tight cervix, is used to open the cervix as it absorbs mucus and expands.

1937

U.S. women and children living in Shanghai are evacuated August 15 as Japanese forces prepare to launch an attack on the city. Japan has invaded China July in an undeclared war that will continue until 1945. The Japanese take Beijing July 28, Shanghai November 8, and Nanjing December 13 (*see* below).

 Spanish women observe the 27th International Women's Day March 8 by demonstrating against the rebel forces of Gen. Francisco Franco, who has obtained support from the Fascist regimes of Germany and Italy.

U.S. authorities in the Philippines grant women there the right to vote on the same basis as men.

The Supreme Court upholds the principle of a minimum wage for women March 29; its ruling in the case of *West Coast Hotel* v. *Parrish* reverses some earlier decisions (*see* 1923).

Wives and children of unarmed Republic Steel workers are brutally assaulted by Chicago police May 30 as strikers picket, singing "Solidarity Forever." Republic's $130,000-a-year boss Tom Girdler has said he would rather go back to hosing potatoes than give in to union organizers. He has ordered the police to fire on the demonstrators. Four are killed, three others mortally wounded, and 84 injured in the Memorial Day massacre.

The Southern Commission on the Study of Lynching founded 6 years ago by Jessie Daniel Ames begins naming sheriffs who permit unruly mobs to take away their prisoners, accusing the lawmen of contributing to the crime of lynching.

Britain liberalizes her divorce laws July 23, but a new Irish Constitution takes effect December 29 with a provision banning divorce and denouncing the idea of working mothers.

A German court at Waldenberg rules November 29 that the state may take children away from mothers and fathers who refuse to teach them Nazi ideology.

Japanese troops rape and murder more than 10,000 Chinese women in their march into Nanjing and massacre some 200,000 civilians inside the city. The Imperial Army authorizes the recruiting of "comfort girl" battalions of Korean girls and women to gratify the sexual needs of its soldiers (*see* 1941; 1991).

Lord & Taylor promotes Dorothy Shaver to president (*see* 1931), but while the press proclaims her $110,000 salary as the highest on record for any woman, *Life* magazine notes that men in comparable jobs earn four times that much. Shaver will boost current sales of $30 million up to $50 million by 1951, and they will reach $100 million by the time of her death in 1959.

Amelia Earhart disappears July 2 on a Pacific flight from New Guinea to Howland Island (*see* 1932). She was married in 1931 to New York publisher George Putnam.

Cooperation and Competition Among Primitive Societies by Margaret Mead is published.

The Neurotic Personality of Our Time by German-American psychoanalyst Karen Danielsen Horney, 52, attacks Freudian antifeminism. She blames the industrial civilization of America for the anxieties that plague modern men, women, and children.

The emergency three-digit telephone number 999 comes into use in Britain to summon police, fire-fighting, or ambulance aid. Britain's example will be followed in Europe, the Far East, and South America (*see* New York, 1968).

Xerography, pioneered by New York prelaw student Chester Floyd Carlson, 31, is a dry-copying process that will revolutionize duplication of papers in offices, schools, and libraries (*see* 1938).

Anne O'Hare McCormick of the *New York Times*, whose regular bylined column on foreign affairs has begun appearing February 1, receives a Pulitzer Prize for journalism, the second woman to win it.

Actress Marion Davies saves her longtime lover William Randolph Hearst from bankruptcy by giving him a certified check for $1 million. *Washington Herald* editor Cissy Patterson gives him an equal amount, but since he is still in dire straits she leases the paper from him August 7 and leases Hearst's *Washington Times* as well, both for a 5-year period with an option to buy (*see* 1930). Asked about the problems of a woman publisher, she tells an interviewer, "Men are not at all sensitive about taking a woman's money, but they don't like to work for her. Sometimes one can overcome this by persuasion, sometimes it takes violent methods, but the woman must not let herself be licked." Women have become especially interested in legislation banning child labor and laws protecting the consumer, she says, "including adequate food, drug and cosmetic laws." The *Herald* shows its first profit in November (*see* 1939).

Harper's Bazaar promotes columnist Diana Vreeland (*née* Dalziel), 37, to fashion editor. Born in Paris of a U.S. mother and Scottish father, banker's wife Vreeland came to New York in 1914, made her debut in 1922, and last year began writing a *Bazaar* column under the heading "Why Don't You?" with Depression-blind suggestions such as "Why don't you put all your dogs in bright yellow collars and leads like all the dogs in Paris?" and "Why don't you have a furry elk-hide trunk for the back of your car?" (*see* 1962).

Woman's Day appears in October as the A&P launches a 3¢ monthly women's service magazine for distribution in A&P stores. The food chain will sell the magazine to Fawcett in 1958.

Nonfiction: *This Is My Story* by Eleanor Roosevelt, who writes, "No one can make you feel inferior without your consent" (she naturally makes no mention of the pain that her husband's infidelity has caused her); *Everybody's Autobiography* by Gertrude Stein, now 63; *Eight Decades* (essays) by Agnes Repplier, now 82.

Fiction: *Their Eyes Were Watching God* by Zora Neale Hurston; *Noon Wine* by Katherine Anne Porter; *None Shall Look Back* (a Civil War novel) and *The Garden of Adonis* by Caroline Gordon; *Unmasked* (*Genomskadad*) by Elin Wägner, now 55, who shows her admiration for Ellen Key; *The Apple Tree of Paradise* (*Rajska jablon*) by Pola Gljawiczynska; *The Delineation of Mother and Son* (*Oyakojojō*) by Kanoko Okamoto; *Daughters and Sons* by Ivy Compton-Burnett; *Coming from the Fair* by Norah Hoult; *The Rising Tide* by Irish novelist Molly Keane, 33, who wrote her first novel at age 17 under the pen name M. J. Farrell and sold it to supplement her allowance; *Coronation Summer* by English novelist Angela (Margaret) Thirkell (*née* Mackail), 45, who will write more than 30 novels about the descendants of characters in Anthony Trollope's 19th-century "Barsetshire" novels; *I Would Be a Private* by Rose Macaulay; *The Delicate Monster* by Storm Jameson; *Here To-day* by Pamela Hansford Johnson; *The Heart Has Wings, That Man Is Mine, Twenty-Four Hours a Day*, and *Manhattan Nights* by Faith Baldwin; *Fine to Look At* by Sophie Kerr; *The Case of the Late Pig* and *Dancers in the Morning* by Margery Allingham.

Poetry: *Cold Morning Sky* by Russian-American poet Marya Zaturenska, 35 (Pulitzer Prize); *Crystallizations (Krystalizacje)* by Marja Jasnorszewska-Pawlikowska; *A Good Time Was Had by All* by Stevie Smith.

Painting: *Voyages Lointains* (gouache on paper) by Sonia Delaunay.

Sculpture: *Tower of Mothers* (bronze) by Käthe Kollwitz.

Changing New York by U.S. photographer Berenice Abbott, 39 (text by Elizabeth McCausland), records scenes of the city where she has taught at the New School for Social Research while photographing artistic and social circles. Born in Maine, Abbott returned to the United States in 1929 after having studied sculpture in Paris and photographing well-known artists and writers of the decade.

Theater: Burgess Meredith and Peggy Ashcroft in Maxwell Anderson's *High Tor* 1/9 at New York's Martin Beck Theater, 171 perfs.; Dudley Digges, Henry Hull, and Margo in Anderson's *The Masque of Kings* 2/8 at New York's Shubert Theater, 89 perfs.; Peggy Conklin and Lucile Watson in Mark Reed's *Yes, My Darling Daughter* 2/9 at The Playhouse, New York, 405 perfs.; Katherine Locke, Jules Garfield, and Cornell Wilde in Arthur Kober's *"Having Wonderful Time"* 2/20 at New York's Lyceum Theater, 132 perfs.; Sam Levine, Eddie Albert, and Betty Field, 19, in John Murray and Allen Boretz's *Room Service* 5/19 at New York's Cort Theater, 500 perfs.; *Susan and God* by Rachel Crothers, now 66, 10/7 at New York's Plymouth Theater, with Gertrude Lawrence, Douglas Gilmore, Vera Allen, and Nancy Kelly, 16.

Radio: *The Guiding Light* 1/25 over NBC features the Rev. John Rutledge (co-authored by soap-opera writer-actress Irna Phillips, now 35, who pioneered the genre in 1930 on Chicago's WGN, it will move to CBS radio in 1947, air on CBS until 1956, and go on TV in 1952 with Phillips still running the show); *Our Gal Sunday* by Chicago advertising agency writers Frank and Anne (Ashenhurst) Hummert 3/29: "the story of an orphan girl named Sunday from the little town of Silver Creek, Colorado, who in young womanhood married England's richest, most handsome lord, Lord Henry Brinthorpe—the story that asks the question, Can this girl from a mining town in the West find happiness as the wife of a wealthy and titled Englishman?" (to 1959); *The Road to Life* by Irna Phillips 9/13 on CBS stations (by 1943 Phillips will have five serials on the air and be earning $250,000 per year, with six assistants to crank out daily continuity).

Films: Vienna-born actress Luise Rainer, 25, and Paul Muni in Sidney Franklin's *The Good Earth*; Katharine Hepburn, Adolphe Menjou, Lucille (Desirée) Ball, 26, and Ginger Rogers in Gregory La Cava's *Stage Door*; Claude Rains and Lana Turner (Julia Jean Mildred Frances Turner, renamed Lana by director Mervyn LeRoy), 17, in LeRoy's *They Won't Forget*. Also: Irene Dunne and Cary Grant in Leo McCarey's *The Awful Truth*; Flora Robson (as Queen Elizabeth) and Laurence Olivier in William K. Howard's *Fire Over England*; Dorothy Lamour (Dorothy Kaumeyer), 22, Jon Hall, and Raymond Massey in John Ford's *The Hurricane*; Victor Moore and Beulah Bondi in Leo McCarey's *Make Way for Tomorrow*; Bette (originally Ruth Elizabeth) Davis, 29, and Humphrey Bogart in Lloyd Bacon's *Marked Woman*; Ronald Colman, Madeleine Carroll, and Douglas Fairbanks, Jr., in John Cromwell's *The Prisoner of Zenda*; Gracie Fields in Basil Dean's *The Show Goes On* with Cyril Ritchard and in Monte Banks's *We're Going to Be Rich* with Victor McLaglen and Brian Donlevy; Janet Gaynor and Fredric March in William Wellman's *A Star Is Born*; Constance Bennett, 33 (Joan's sister), Cary Grant, and Roland Young in Norman Z. McLeod's *Topper*; Anna Neagle, now 33, and Anton Walbrook in Herbert Wilcox's *Victoria the Great*.

George B. Seitz's *A Family Affair* with Mickey Rooney as Andy Hardy and Lionel Barrymore as Judge James Hardy is the first of a series that will continue off and on for 21 years, with Lewis Stone as Judge Hardy, Fay Holden as Mrs. Hardy, and girlfriends who will include Ann Rutherford, Judy Garland, Lana Turner, Esther Williams, Kathryn Grayson, and Donna Reed.

Hollywood musicals: Ginger Rogers and Fred Astaire in Mark Sandrich's *Shall We Dance?* with music by George Gershwin (who dies July 11 of a brain tumor at age 38), lyrics by Ira Gershwin, songs that include "They Can't Take That Away from Me," "They All Laughed," "Slap That Bass," "Let's Call the Whole Thing Off," and the title song; Deanna Durbin, Leopold Stokowski, and Adolphe Menjou in Henry Koster's *One Hundred Men and a Girl*.

Stage musicals: *Pins and Needles* 11/27 at New York's Labor Stage Theater, with Harold Rome songs that include "Nobody Makes a Pass at Me," 1,108 perfs. (the International Ladies' Garment Workers' Union [ILGWU] sponsors the production, and no cast member receives more than $55 per week); Cicely Courtneidge and Bobby Howes in *Hide and Seek* 12/6 at the London Hippodrome, with songs by Vivian Ellis; Jack Buchanan and Evelyn Laye in *Between the Devil* 12/22 at New York's Imperial Theater, with Arthur Schwartz–Howard Dietz songs that include "By Myself," 93 perfs.

Ballet: Margot Fonteyn, now 17, dances the title role in the 1841 Adam ballet *Giselle* 1/18 at the Sadler's Wells Theatre, London, and in *Les Patineurs (The Skaters)* 2/16 at the Sadler's Wells, with music by Meyerbeer, choreography by Frederick Ashton; Lyubov Tchernicheva in *Francesca da Rimini* 7/15 at London's Royal Opera House in Covent Garden, with music by Tchaikovsky, choreography by David Lichine, 36.

Opera: U.S. soprano Helen Traubel, 38, makes her Metropolitan Opera debut; Croatian soprano Zinka Milanov (*née* Kunc), 31, makes her Metropolitan Opera debut 12/17 singing the role of Leonora in the 1862 Verdi opera *La Forza del Destino* (she will be a Met regular until 1966).

Popular songs: The Andrews Sisters have their first big hit recording with "Bei Mir Bist Du Schön (Means I Love You)," with English lyrics by Sammy Cahn and Saul Chapin from Sholom Secunda's 1933 Yiddish musical; Patsy Montana records "Sweet Violence."

Dorothy Round wins in women's singles at Wimbledon, Anita Lizana at Forest Hills.

Nylon is patented by E. I. du Pont's W. H. Carothers, who assigns the patent to Du Pont (*see* 1935). The first completely man-made fiber will have wide uses not only in clothing but also as a substitute for canvas in sailboat sails, sisal in ships' hawsers, hog bristles in brushes, etc. (*see* stockings, 1940; Terylene-Dacron, 1941).

The Babee-Tenda infant chair invented by George B. Hansburg of 1919 pogo stick fame will not tip over. Now 50, Hansburg has devised the chair for his first granddaughter, Norma.

Former Chicago social worker Elizabeth Wood, 38, is named to head the city's new Housing Authority, which she will head until political pressures force her to resign in 1954. As "Chicago's largest landlord," Wood will develop the philosophy that housing works best when residents are mixed by race, economic class, and family size, and rather than high-rise developments she will favor small, dispersed projects where building heights are limited to the distance that a mother in a window can be heard when calling to a child in a playground below (*see* Jacobs, 1961).

Tobacco heiress Doris Duke builds a $1 million Hawaiian dream house and calls it Hele Kapu (she will later rename it Shangri-la). Two stone camels grace the entrance to the Moroccan-Persian mansion. (Duke also has a New York mansion at Fifth Avenue and 78th Street, a Tudor-style Newport, R.I. castle called Rough Point, and a 2,500-acre farm outside Somerville, N.J., with a 34-room stone house, movie theater, indoor swimming pool and tennis court, and 42 miles of road.)

Pepperidge Farm bread is introduced by Connecticut entrepreneur Margaret Rudkin (*née* Fogarty), 40, who sets up an oven in her stockbroker husband's former polo pony stable on the family's 120-acre Pepperidge Farm and makes whole-wheat bread, which she sells first to neighbors and then through a New York City fancy food retailer (*see* 1940).

Home freezers become commercially important for the first time in the United States as frozen food sales increase, but relatively few Americans have anything more advanced than an icebox. Icemen continue regular deliveries.

The supermarket shopping cart introduced at Oklahoma City June 4 begins a revolution in food buying. Sylvan N. Goldman, 38, who owns Standard Food Markets and Humpty Dumpty Stores, has created the cart to enable customers to buy more than can fit in the wicker baskets they carry; he has taken some folding chairs, put them on wheels, raised the seats to accommodate a lower shopping basket, placed a second basket on the seat, and used the chair back as a handle. Four U.S. companies will develop the shopping cart into a computer-designed chromed-steel cart that can be nested in a small area.

Cookbook *Serve it Forth* by Scots-Irish California gastronome and prose stylist M. F. K. (Mary Francis Kennedy) Fisher, 29.

Contraception receives virtually unqualified endorsement from an American Medical Association committee on birth control (*see* 1940).

The first state contraceptive clinic opens March 15 at Raleigh, N.C. The State Board of Health introduces a program for indigent married women in its regular maternity and child health service.

Islam's Grand Mufti issues a *fatwa* permitting Muslims to take any measure to avoid conception to which both man and woman agree.

Britain's Birkett Committee on Abortion reports, "Many mothers seem not to understand that self-induced abortion is illegal [*see* 1867]. They assumed it was legal before the third month, and only outside the law when procured by another person." Working-class women, especially, adhere to the view that life is not present until the fetus "quickens." They take pills not to abort but rather to "bring on the period."

Researchers at Pennsylvania State University discover that natural estrogen and natural progesterone both can suppress the release of an egg from the ovary of a laboratory rabbit.

1938

Spotlight on Spain by Katherine Marjory, duchess of Atholl, now 64, opposes on principle the idea of European "nonintervention" in the ongoing Spanish Civil War but does not advocate British assistance to the beleaguered Spanish Republic (*see* 1924). She has financed an unexpurgated translation of Adolf Hitler's 1925 book *Mein Kampf* to warn of the German dictator's intentions and opposes the September 29 Munich agreement in which Prime Ministers Chamberlain and Daladier "appease" Hitler by letting him take the Sudetenland, a 16,000-square-mile territory that covers nearly one-third of Czechoslovakia. Lady Marjory's Conservative constituents find another candidate for Parliament, she resigns her seat, her opponents caricature her as the "Red Duchess," she is defeated in the by-election, and she will work until her death in 1960 for the relief of refugees from totalitarianism.

English missionary Gladys Aylward, 36, escorts more than 100 children, most of them aged four to eight, on a 27-day march to escape Japanese invasion forces. Having quit school at age 14 to become a parlor maid, she spent all her savings 8 years ago on a railroad ticket to Tientsin and founded the Inn of the Sixth Happiness at Yangcheng, northern China, with Scottish missionary Jeannie Lawson. Aylward is nearly dead from typhus by the time she reaches her destination, but recovers to continue with her life, which she will spend lecturing, preaching, and working with lepers. After 5 years in England, she will return to the Orient in 1953 and head an orphanage in Taiwan.

The Women's Bureau of the U.S. Department of Labor issues its annual report February 20 criticizing companies that replace men with women employees to save money.

The Fair Labor Standards Act (wage and hour law) passed by Congress June 15 limits the working hours of some 12.5 million U.S. workers in the first national effort to place a floor under wages and a ceiling on hours. Working hours for the first year after the new law takes effect are limited to 44 per week with the limit to be reduced to 42 for the second year and 40 for every year thereafter. Longer workweeks are permitted only if overtime work is paid for at 1½ times the regular rate. Minimum wage is to be 25¢ per hour for the first year, 30¢ for the next 6 years, but domestic servants will not be included under the law until 1974 and live-in maids continue typically to earn $30 per month or less plus meals (*see* Minimum Wage Act, 1949).

The new minimum wage law (above) wipes out the needlework industry in Puerto Rico, where 25¢ has been the hourly rate for *skilled* workers among its 40,000 employees.

First Lady Eleanor Roosevelt presents U.S. aviatrix and cosmetics executive Jacqueline Cochran, 28, with the Marmon Trophy, awarded to the leading aviatrix by the Ligue Internationale des Aviateurs, in a ceremony held April 4. Cochran broke the international women's record for 1,000 kilometers last year and on three occasions established new national records for the 100-kilometer distance. She wins the Bendix Trophy, flying an untested Seversky pursuit plane in the trans-American Bendix Race. A trained beautician who took 6 weeks off from work in 1932 to take flying lessons and received her pilot's license within 2 weeks, Cochran started her own cosmetics company in 1934, the year that she flew to an altitude of 30,000 meters in a biplane with canvas wings and an unheated, unpressurized cockpit, trying to breathe oxygen through a tube (which burst) (*see* 1941).

Soviet aviatrix Valentina (Stepanovna) Grizodubova, 28, gains world fame when she and two female companions break the women's long-distance flying record, flying 4,000 miles—3,687 of them in one direction, from Moscow to the Far East, in their plane, the *Motherland*. Forced to land in a swamp after running out of fuel, the crew copes with three days of rain, has to deal with a lynx in the cockpit, and chases off bears. Grizodubova receives the Order of Lenin, is made a Hero of the Soviet Union, next year will be made head of women's aviation, and beginning in 1941 will command a regiment of long-range planes, flying on bombing missions, and surviving attacks by German fighter planes.

General Electric announces in December that it has developed a nonreflecting glass (the press calls it "invisible glass") that will find wide use in camera lenses, picture frames, store windows, and the like. Research physicist Katherine Burr Blodgett, 40, has found in experiments with an unusually oily substance developed by the late Irving Langmuir in 1923 that by repeatedly lowering a metal plate into it she can build up layers, each one molecule thick, to create what will be called Langmuir-Blodgett film. Since it reflects no light, it permits 100 percent of the light that falls onto a lens to pass through it,

whereas ordinary glass loses 8 to 10 percent of the light through reflection.

A strange fish brought up in the nets of a trawler December 22 from 40 fathoms in the estuary of South Africa's Chalumna River is identified by local natural history museum curator Marjorie Courtenay-Latimer, 28, as a coelacanth, believed to have been extinct for at least 70 million years. Nearly six feet long and weighing 150 pounds, the steely blue, lobe-finned fish will be named *Latimeria chalumnae* Smith (amateur ichthyologist J. L. B. Smith, 41, who teaches chemistry at Rhodes University College in Grahams town, will confirm Courtenay-Latimer's finding and take credit for making the initial identification).

Babies Hospital pathologist Dorothy Hansine, 37, at New York's Columbia Presbyterian Hospital publishes her findings on cystic fibrosis, a previously unrecognized disease which she has named. She has collected infants' hearts with congenital defects since 1935, will develop a method of diagnosing CF in living patients, describe the genetics of the disease, and, in 1959, publish a paper suggesting guidelines for the care of young adults with CF, which up to now has been invariably fatal in infancy.

Schering Pharmaceutical chemists create an estrogen pill; they find that by replacing one hydrogen atom on the estradiol molecule chain with a group of atoms (called an ethinyl radical) they produce a compound which can be taken orally instead of being injected for such purposes as relief of painful menstruation.

British steroid chemist Charles Dodds creates diethylstilbestrol (DES), the first synthetic estrogen.

A new U.S. Food, Drug and Cosmetic Act, signed into law June 27, requires drug manufacturers for the first time to test products for safety and efficacy before putting them on the market.

The first true Xerox image appears October 22 at Astoria, Queens (*see* 1937). The electrophotographic image is imprinted on wax paper which has been pressed against an electrostatically charged 2- by 3-inch sulfur-coated zinc plate that has been dusted with lycopodium powder. Chester Carlson, who has been helped by a German refugee physicist, will receive his first patent in 1940 for the process he will call "xerography," using the Greek word *xeros* for dry, but he will fail in his initial attempts to get financial backing (*see* 1946).

Nonfiction: *A Study of Matriarchy* (*Bokeisei kenkyu*) by Itsue Takamure, who has been reading history since 1931 and found that all the books were written by men and ignored women; *The Passing of the Aborigines* by Daisy Bates, now 74, is a best-seller in Europe (an Australian edition will not appear until 1946), and its author is hailed by one critic as "an entirely heroic woman," combining the qualities of "Father Damien, Florence Nightingale, Miss Edna May Oliver, Miss Cicely Courtneidge, and Dickens's Mrs. Jellyby" (*see* 1912); *China Fights Back: An American Woman with the 8th Route Army* by emigrée U.S. journalist Agnes Smedley, 46, who went to China 10 years ago and has dedicated herself to the Chinese revolutionary cause; *With Malice Toward Some* by U.S. writer Margaret Halsey, 28, who spent a year in Devon, England, where her husband was an exchange professor; *The Child and the State* (2 volumes) by Chicago social worker Grace Abbott, 59, who worked with the late Jane Addams at Hull-House.

Fiction: *The Death of the Heart* by Elizabeth Bowen; *Out of Africa* by Isak Dinesen; *Tropisms* (*Tropismes*) by Russian-born French novelist Nathalie Sarraute (*née* Tcherniak), 36; *Mysterious* (*Myhemlighetsfull*) by Elin Wägner, whose new novel, like her last, is partly autobiographical, pursuing the theme of unhappy marriage and identifying the heroine with a selfless woman's movement involved in humanitarian causes; *Pillars of Fire* (*Slupy ogniste*) by Pola Gljawiczynska is about the tribulations of woman in a man's world; *Over the Frontier* by Stevie Smith, who employs the same amusing, autographical, monologue style that made her 1934 novel a success; *The Lady and the Unicorn* by English novelist Rumer Godden, 30; *Pray for the Wanderer* by Kate O'Brien; *The Monument* and *World's End* by Pamela Hansford Johnson; *Requiem for Idols* and *Out of This Nettle: An American Colin Lowrie* by Norah Lofts; *Young Man with a Horn* by U.S. novelist Dorothy Dodds Baker, 31, has been inspired by the music, if not the life, of the late Bix Beiderbecke, who died of lobar pneumonia at age 28 in August 1931; *All This and Heaven Too* by Rachel Field; *Free*

Land by Rose Wilder Lane; *Field of Honor* by Adela Rogers St. John; *Remember the End* by Agnes Turnbull; *Dynasty of Death* by U.S. novelist Taylor Caldwell, 38, who 7 years ago obtained her bachelor's degree at the University of Buffalo, studying nights while working as a court stenographer by day; *Too Young to Marry* by Margaret Culkin Banning; *Hotel Hostess, Enchanted Oasis,* and *Rich Girl, Poor Girl* by Faith Baldwin; *Adventure with Women* and *Stay Out of My Life* by Sophie Kerr; *Dance of Death* by U.S. mystery novelist Helen McCloy, 34; *Artists in Crime* by Ngaio Marsh; *The Fashion in Shrouds* by Margery Allingham.

Pearl S. Buck wins the Nobel Prize for literature.

Poetry: *Mediterranean* and *U.S. 1* by Muriel Rukeyser; *Mascarillo y trébol* by Alfonsina Storni, who discovers that she has cancer and commits suicide at age 46.

Juvenile: *The Yearling* by U.S. novelist Marjorie Kennan Rawlings, 42 (Pulitzer Prize).

Painting: *Delores* by Marie Laurencin. Suzanne Valadon suffers a stroke in her Montmartre studio and dies April 7 at age 72 en route to Piccini Hospital.

Sculpture: *Forms in Echelon* (wood) by English sculptor Barbara Hepworth, 35, who attended Leeds School of Art with Henry Moore when she was 16 and he 21 at a time when, as Moore would later observe, a woman studying sculpture was not taken seriously. Hepworth has 4-year-old triplets plus an older son by a previous marriage.

Theater: Peggy Simpson and Helen Trenholme in Ian Hay's *Bachelor Born* 1/25 at New York's Morosco Theater, 400 perfs.; Sara Allgood, Julie Haydon, and Cedric Hardwicke in Paul Vincent Carroll's *Shadow and Substance* 1/26 at New York's Golden Theater, 274 perfs.; Dudley Digges, Dorothy Stickney, 37, and Dickie Van Patten in Paul Osborn's *On Borrowed Time* 2/3 at New York's Longacre Theater, 321 perfs.; Martha Scott, 23, Frank Craven, and Philip Coolidge in Thornton Wilder's *Our Town* 2/4 at New York's Henry Miller Theater, 336 perfs.; Ezra Stone as Henry Aldrich, Eddie Bracken, and Betty Field in Clifford Goldsmith's *What a Life* 4/13 at New York's Biltmore Theater, 538 perfs.; *Dear Octopus* by Dodie Smith 9/14 at the Queen's Theatre, London, with veteran

English actress Dame Marie Tempest (originally Marie Susan Etherington), 74, and John Gielgud; *Kiss the Boys Goodbye* by Clare Boothe (Luce) 9/28 at Henry Miller's Theater, New York, with Millard Mitchell, Helen Claire, and Benay Venuta, 286 perfs.; Eddie Dowling, Madge Evans, and Russell Collins in Philip Barry's *Here Come the Clowns* 12/7 at New York's Booth Theater, 88 perfs.; *Quiet Wedding* by English playwright Esther Helen McCracken (*née* Armstrong), 36, 12/12 at Wyndham's Theatre, London.

Radio: *Young Widder Brown* 7/26 over NBC stations. Created by Frank and Anne Hummert, the soap opera will continue daily until June 1956.

Films: Katharine Hepburn and Cary Grant in Howard Hawks's *Bringing Up Baby*; Michael Redgrave, Margaret Lockwood (Margaret Day), 21, Paul Lukas, and Dame May Witty in Alfred Hitchcock's *The Lady Vanishes*; Wendy Hiller, 26, and Leslie Howard in Anthony Asquith and Howard's *Pygmalion*. Also: Ginette Leclerc and Raimu in Marcel Pagnol's *The Baker's Wife*; Katharine Hepburn and Cary Grant in George Cukor's *Holiday*; Alice Faye (originally Leppert), 23, and Tyrone Power in Henry King's *In Old Chicago*; Bette Davis, Henry Fonda, and George Brent in William Wyler's *Jezebel*; Gracie Fields in Monte Banks's *Keep Smiling* with Roger Livesey; Margaret Sullavan, Robert Taylor, and Franchot Tone in Frank Borzage's *Three Comrades*; Jean Arthur, Lionel Barrymore, James Stewart, tap dancer Ann Miller (Lucille Ann Collier), 15, and Spring Byington in Frank Capra's *You Can't Take It with You*. Warner Brothers has suspended Bette Davis April 1 for refusing to rehearse her role in the new picture called for in her contract, saying the script is "atrocious."

Hollywood musicals: Olivia de Havilland and Dick Powell in Ray Enright's *Hard to Get* with Harry Warren–Johnny Mercer songs that include "You Must Have Been a Beautiful Baby."

Stage musicals: Peggy Wood in *Operette* 3/16 at His Majesty's Theatre, London, with Noël Coward songs that include "The Stately Homes of England," 133 perfs.; Berlin-born Norwegian ballet dancer Vera Zorina (Brigitta Hartwig), 21, Dennis King, and Vivienne Segal in *I Married an Angel* 5/11 at New York's Shubert Theater, with Rodgers

and Hart songs that include "Spring Is Here" and the title song, 338 perfs.; Cicely Courtneidge, Leonora Corbett, and Jack Hulbert in *Under Your Hat* 10/24 at London's Palace Theatre, with songs by Vivian Ellis; ingenue Mary Martin, 24, does a simulated striptease to Cole Porter's song "My Heart Belongs to Daddy" in *Leave It to Me* 11/9 at New York's Imperial Theater (other songs include "Most Gentlemen Don't Like Love"), 307 perfs.

Opera: Polish-born German soprano (Olga Maria) Elisabeth (Friederike) Schwarzkopf, 23, makes her debut at the Berlin Städtische Oper singing the role of the Flower Maiden in the 1882 Wagner opera *Parsifal* and is soon moved up from second soprano to singing leading roles.

Chicago-born dancer-choreographer Katherine Dunham, 28, wins an appointment as dance director of the Federal Theater Project.

Popular songs: Gracie Fields records "The Biggest Aspidistra in the World" by Jimmy Harper, Will Haines, and Tommy Connor; "I Get Along Without You Very Well (Except Sometimes)" by Hoagy Carmichael, lyrics by Jane Brown Thompson; "Camel Hop" by Mary Lou Williams; "A-Tisket, A-Tasket" by Ella Fitzgerald and Van Alexander; "The Flat Foot Floogie" by Slim Gaillard, Slam Steward, and Bud Green (who have been forced to change the word "floozie" to "floogie").

The samba and the conga are introduced to U.S. dance floors.

Helen Wills Moody wins in women's singles at Wimbledon, Alice Marble at Forest Hills.

Hattie Carnegie fashion designer Claire McCardell, 33, creates a tent dress based on an Algerian (or Moroccan) robe, it is included in the fall collection of Townley Sportswear, most buyers reject it, but a Best & Co. buyer orders 100, advertises it in New York's Sunday papers, and promptly orders 200 more. Seventh Avenue garment makers copy the "monastic" design, and McCardell soon finds herself famous as the designer of the "American Look."

Fashion Is Spinach by former New York designer Elizabeth Hawes, 35, pokes fun at the business that she entered 10 years ago after studying in Paris but has recently quit.

The case of *R.* v. *Bourne* arouses controversy over abortion in Britain. London gynecologist Alec Bourne has aborted a 14-year-old girl who was raped by four soldiers, his defenders argue that there are times when deliberate abortion should be lawful, the judge rules that under certain circumstances the surgeon has not only the right but the duty to terminate a pregnancy, and Dr. Bourne is acquitted.

1939

World War II begins September 1 as German troops invade Poland. The French have evacuated 16,000 children from Paris August 30 in anticipation of the conflict and declare martial law September 1. Britain, too, has evacuated city children to the countryside. Both countries declare war on Germany September 3. Unity Valkyrie Mitford, 25, a daughter of Lord Redesdale and a friend of Adolf Hitler, hears of London's action, fires two bullets into her head, but survives and returns to England.

The WRNS (Women's Royal Navy Service) has recruited 3,400 "Wrens" by November to serve in antiaircraft batteries and naval command centers. The ATS (Auxiliary Territorial Service, the women's branch of the British Army) has 24,000 women aged 18 to 35, the WAAF (Women's Auxiliary Air Force, linked to the RAF) 8,800 (it has raised its upper age limit to 50 for women with experience in radar plotting of enemy aircraft), and nursing services 8,000. Some 25,000 women have registered for the Women's Land Army, and recruiting has been suspended. Women in all the uniformed services are dismayed to find themselves assigned mostly to menial positions such as cooking, cleaning, and clerical work, but many are pressed into use as drivers and mechanics. The Women's Voluntary Service for Civil Defence (WVS) founded last year by the marchioness of Reading has had 500,000 volunteers.

Helen Douglas (*née* Gahagan), 38, a onetime opera singer, becomes chairwoman of the John Steinbeck Committee to Aid Migratory Workers. Wife of Hollywood actor Melvyn Douglas, she resigns in September as U.S. Communists begin objecting to the anti-Fascist stands of liberal organizations (Moscow and Berlin have signed a mutual nonaggression pact August 21). Douglas writes to her friend, Congressman H. Jerry Voorhis, that she finds herself "in the absurd position . . . of most liberals today. The Communists call us reactionary and the reactionaries call us Communists" (*see* 1944).

Marian Anderson tries to rent Constitution Hall at Washington, D.C., for a concert and is refused because of her race by the Daughters of the American Revolution, who own the hall. Now 42, the black contralto has been acclaimed by European critics as the world's greatest, Eleanor Roosevelt and other DAR members resign to show support, and Anderson draws an audience of 75,000 at the Lincoln Memorial Easter Sunday.

New York City Corporation Counsel lawyer Jane Bolin (Mizelle), 31, is summoned to the New York City Building at the World's Fair July 22 by Mayor La Guardia, who swears her in as a judge of the city's Domestic Relations Court. The first black woman to graduate from Yale Law School, the first to join the New York City Bar Association, and the first in the Corporation Counsel's office, Bolin becomes the nation's first black woman judge (she will serve until 1978).

Japan's Ministry of Labor permits mineowners to hire women as the war in China produces manpower shortages. Laws protecting women in the workplace are not enforced.

Filipino women gain the right to vote on the same basis as men.

The National Women's Party convenes at Washington December 16 and urges immediate congressional action on an Equal Rights Amendment.

President Roosevelt asks Congress January 16 to extend Social Security coverage to more women and children.

Austrian mathematical physicist Lisa Meitner, 61, and her nephew Otto Frisch, 35, at Stockholm publish a paper in February describing nuclear fission (and coining that term). They have worked out the implications of the discovery in December of last year by German chemist Otto Hahn and his colleague Fritz Strassman that the nucleus of certain uranium atoms can be split into two approximately equal halves, releasing not only energy but also neutrons that can, in turn, split other uranium atoms. Nazi persecution forced Meitner to flee Austria last year (she will remain in Sweden for the next 20 years), Hahn and Strassman have sent her their findings, and she has analyzed them, calculating the enormous amount of energy that splitting the atom would release.

After Freedom by anthropologist Hortense Powdermaker is a study of community life in Indianola, Miss. (*see* 1933). Powdermaker has founded the Department of Anthropology and Sociology at Queens College, New York, and will teach there until her retirement.

Viennese-born psychoanalyst Anna Freud, 43, champions the cause of analysis following the death at London of her father, Sigmund, from cancer September 23 at age 83.

Publisher Cissy Patterson exercises her option January 28 and buys the *Washington Herald* and *Washington Times* from William Randolph Hearst (*see* 1937). She merges the morning and afternoon papers to create the *Times-Herald*, which has 10 editions per day promoting her isolationist views, and she will continue to publish it until her death in July 1948.

Glamour magazine begins publication at New York in April. Street & Smith has launched the monthly to reach working women above the age of its 4-year-old *Mademoiselle*'s readership.

"Letter from London" by Molly Panter-Downes begins appearing in the *New Yorker* magazine.

Nonfiction: *How to Win and Hold a Husband* by Dorothy Dix (Elizabeth M. Gilman, now 68); *All in the Day's Work* by Ida Tarbell, now 82.

Fiction: *Pale Horse, Pale Rider* (stories) by Katherine Anne Porter; *Winter of Artifice* by writer Anaïs Nin, 36; *Mrs. Miniver* by English novelist-poet Jan Struther (Joyce Mastone Anstruther Graham), 38, who has written articles in the *Times* relating her fictional character's activities; *Black Narcissus* by Rumer Godden; *A Family and a Fortune* by Ivy Compton-Burnett; *Blossom like a Rose* by Norah Lofts; *Pioneers on Parade* by Dymphna Cusack and

Miles Franklin; *Sown among Thorns* by Ethel Dell; *Alberte* (trilogy) by Norwegian novelist Cora Sandel (Jara Fabricius), 59; *Woman Diver* (*Ama*) by Japanese novelist Yoko Ota, 36; *The Story of an Old Geisha* (*Rogisho*) and *River Light* (*Kawa akari*) by Kanoko Okamoto; poet Akiko Yosano, now 61, publishes a new version of *The Tale of Genji* (*Shinyaku Genji monogatari*) from 1015, translated into modern Japanese; *Moses, Man of the Mountain* by Zora Neale Hurston; *Rope of Gold* by Josephine Herbst completes a trilogy begun in 1933; *Seasoned Timber* by Dorothea Canfield Fisher; *Enough to Live On* by Margaret Culkin Banning; *White Magic, The Station Wagon Set, The High Road*, and *Career by Proxy* by Faith Baldwin; *Overture to Death* by Ngaio Marsh.

Juvenile: *Mike Mulligan and His Steam Shovel* by U.S. author Virginia Lee Burton; *By the Shores of Lake Silver* by Laura Ingalls Wilder.

Poetry: *Inner Landscape* by Belgian-American poet-novelist May (*née* Eléanore Marie) Sarton, 27; *Churning Wind: Poems* by Muriel Rukeyser; *Here Lies* by Dorothy Parker.

Painting: *Red, White, Blue, Yellow, Black* (collage of oil on paper) by Lee Krasner; Grandma Moses gains overnight fame after engineer–art collector Louis Caldor sees work by the primitivist Anna Mary Robertson, 79, displayed in a drugstore window at Hoosick Falls, N.Y. Caldor drives to Robertson's farm, buys all 15 of her paintings, and exhibits three of them at New York's new Museum of Modern Art in a show entitled "Contemporary Unknown Painters." Gwen John falls ill, takes the boat train to Dieppe, collapses on arrival, and dies September 18 at age 63.

Theater: Jessica Tandy, Barry Fitzgerald, and George Coulouris in Paul Vincent Carroll's *The White Steed* 1/10 at New York's Cort Theater, 136 perfs.; Fredric March and Florence Eldridge in George S. Kaufman and Moss Hart's *The American Way* 1/21 at New York's Center Theater in Rockefeller Center, 164 perfs.; *The Little Foxes* by Lillian Hellman 2/15 at New York's National Theater, with Tallulah Bankhead, Carl Benton Reid, Dan Duryea, and Patricia Collinge, sets and costumes by Aline Bernstein, 191 perfs.; *Family Portrait* by

Lenore Coffee and William Joyce Cowan 3/8 at New York's Morosco Theater, with Judith Anderson and Philip Truex, 111 perfs.; Katharine Hepburn, Lenore Lonergan, Shirley Booth (Thelma Booth Ford), 31, Van Heflin, and Joseph Cotten in Philip Barry's *The Philadelphia Story* 3/28 at New York's Shubert Theater, 96 perfs.; Katharine Cornell, Laurence Olivier, and Margalo Gilmore in S. N. Behrman's *No Time for Comedy* 4/17 at New York's Ethel Barrymore Theater, 185 perfs.; Gertrude Lawrence in Samson Raphaelson's *Skylark* 10/11 at New York's Belasco Theater, 250 perfs.; Eddie Dowling, Julie Haydon, Gene Kelly, Celeste Holm, 20, William Bendix, and Reginald Beane in William Saroyan's *The Time of Your Life* 10/25 at New York's Booth Theater, 185 perfs.; *Margin for Error* by Clare Boothe 11/3 at New York's Plymouth Theater, with Otto Preminger, 264 perfs.; Dorothy Stickney and Howard Lindsay in Lindsay and Russel Crouse's *Life with Father* 11/8 at New York's Empire Theater, 3,244 perfs.; José Ferrer, Paul Muni, and German actress Uta Hagen, 30, in Maxwell Anderson's *Key Largo* 11/27 at New York's Ethel Barrymore Theater, 105 perfs.; Dorothy Gish, Russell Collins, and Enid Marley in Paul Osborn's *Mornings at Seven* 11/30 at New York's Longacre Theater, 44 perfs.

Films: English actress Vivien Leigh (*née* Hartley), 25, as Scarlett O'Hara, Butterfly McQueen as her maid who "don't know nothin' 'bout birthin' babies," Hattie McDaniel, Clark Gable as Rhett Butler, Leslie Howard as Ashley Wilkes, and Olivia de Havilland as Melanie Hamilton in Victor Fleming's *Gone With the Wind.*

Other films: James Stewart and Marlene Dietrich in George Marshall's *Destry Rides Again*; Gary Cooper and Jean Arthur in Frank Capra's *Mr. Smith Goes to Washington*; John Wayne and Claire Trevor (originally Wemlinger), 30, in John Ford's *Stagecoach*; Michael Redgrave and Margaret Lockwood in Carol Reed's *The Stars Look Down*; Merle Oberon and Laurence Olivier in William Wyler's *Wuthering Heights*. Also: Bette Davis in Edmund Goulding's *Dark Victory* and *The Old Maid*; Henry Fonda and Claudette Colbert in John Ford's *Drums along the Mohawk*; Robert Donat and Irish actress Greer Garson, 30, in Sam Wood's *Goodbye, Mr. Chips*; Irene Dunne and Charles

English actress Vivien Leigh was a most convincing Scarlett O'Hara in Hollywood's Gone With the Wind. CULVER PICTURES, INC.

Boyer in Leo McCarey's *Love Affair*; Claudette Colbert, Don Ameche, and John Barrymore in Mitchell Leisen's *Midnight*; Greta Garbo and Melvyn Douglas in Ernst Lubitsch's *Ninotchka* ("Garbo Laughs," say the advertisements); Anna Neagle in Herbert Wilcox's *Nurse Edith Cavell*; Cary Grant, Jean Arthur, and Richard Barthelmess in Howard Hawks's *Only Angels Have Wings*; Bette Davis and Errol Flynn in Michael Curtiz's *The Private Lives of Elizabeth and Essex*; Gracie Fields in Monte Banks's *Shipyard Sally* (Fields is diagnosed with cancer, has a hysterectomy in June at London's Old Chelsea Hospital for Women, is unconscious for 3 days as a million letters and hundreds of bouquets and gifts pour in, but recovers, ends her 16-year marriage to Archie Pitts in July, and will live until 1979); Joan Crawford, Norma Shearer, Rosalind Russell, Mary Boland, English-American actress Joan Fontaine (Joan de Beauvoir de Havilland, Olivia's sister), 21 (she has taken her stepfather's name), Paulette Goddard (Marion Levy), 24, Lucile Watson, Marjorie Main, 49, Virginia Weidler, Ruth (Carol) Hussey (originally O'Rourke), 21, Phyllis Povah, Mary Beth Hughes, 21, Virginia Grey, 23, and Hedda Hopper in George Cukor's *The Women*.

Carole Lombard marries Clark Gable March 29 at Kingman, Arizona. Annabella marries Tyrone Power April 23 at Hollywood. Barbara Stanwyck (Ruby Stevens Fay) marries Robert Taylor (Arlington Spangler Brugh) May 14 at San Diego.

Movie stars like Barbara Stanwyck became familiar world-wide—a kind of international royalty.

♪ Hollywood musicals: Judy Garland (Frances Ethel Gumm), 17, as Dorothy Gale, Ray Bolger as the Tin Man, Bert Lahr as the Cowardly Lion, Jack Haley as the Scarecrow, Frank Morgan as the Wizard, and Margaret Hamilton as the Wicked Witch of the West in Victor Fleming's *The Wizard of Oz* with Harold Arlen–Yip Harburg songs that include "Somewhere Over the Rainbow," "Follow the Yellow Brick Road," "We're Off to See the Wizard," and "If I Only Had a Brain."

Judy Garland bearded the Wizard of Oz despite threats from the Wicked Witch of the West. CULVER PICTURES, INC.

Radio: *The Dinah Shore Show* 8/6 on NBC Blue Network stations with singer Dinah (*née* Frances, or Fanny, Rose) Shore, 18.

Opera: U.S. contralto Risë Stevens (Risë Steenberg), 26, makes her Metropolitan Opera debut in the 1866 Charles Ambroise Thomas opera *Mignon*.

First performances: Chamber Concerto No. 1 by English composer Elisabeth Lutyens, 33, whose father is the architect Sir Edwin Lutyens.

Broadway musicals: Portuguese-born Brazilian singer Carmen Miranda, 26, belts out "South American Way" in *The Streets of Paris* 6/19 at the Broadhurst Theater, 274 perfs.; Ann Miller, Ella Logan, Willie and Eugene Howard, Ben Blue, and the Three Stooges in the 13th and final edition of *George White's Scandals* 8/28 at the Alvin Theater, with Sammy Fain–Jack Yellen songs that include "Are You Having Any Fun?" 120 perfs.; Grace

McDonald, Jack Whiting, Eve Arden, June Allyson (Ella Geisman), 16, and Vera-Ellen (Vera Ellen Rohe), 13, in *Very Warm for May* 11/17 at the Alvin Theater, with Jerome Kern–Oscar Hammerstein II songs that include "All the Things You Are," 59 perfs.; Ethel Merman, Bert Lahr, and Betty Grable, 23, in *Du Barry Was a Lady* 12/6 at the 46th Street Theater, with Cole Porter songs that include "Friendship," and "Do I Love You?," 408 perfs.

Frank Sinatra joins bandleader Harry James at age 23 to sing with a new band that James is assembling. The New Jersey roadhouse singer will leave within a year to join the Tommy Dorsey band, will break his contract with Dorsey in 1942 and take an 8-week engagement at New York's Paramount Theater to begin a career as idol of teenage "bobby-soxers."

Popular songs: "I'll Never Smile Again" by U.S. songwriter Ruth Lowe, a former pianist in an all-girl band who has written the song in memory of her late husband; Billie Holiday records "Strange Fruit" and "Fine and Mellow"; The Andrews Sisters record "The Beer Barrel Polka" with new English lyrics by Lew Brown to a 1934 Czech song; Ella Fitzgerald records "Undecided" with the Chic Webb band, which she takes over upon the death of Webb and will lead for the next 3 years; New York singer-songwriter Carmen McRae, 19, writes "Dream of Life" for Billie Holiday (she will sing at a New York jazz club in the 1940s and appear briefly with Count Basie and Benny Carter's band in 1944); Patsy Montana records "I Love My Fruit."

Alice Marble wins in women's singles at both Wimbledon and Forest Hills.

Peruvian bullfighter Conchita Cintrón, 17, makes her debut in Mexico, where women are permitted to be *toreras* (she has ridden horses in the ring for Portuguese-style bullfighting—*rejoneo*—since age 12). Daughter of an Irish-American woman and a Puerto Rican father, Cintrón will have had 211 bullfights by 1943 and killed 401 bulls (*see* 1949).

Cup sizing (A, B, C, and D) for brassieres is introduced by Warner Brothers of Bridgeport, Conn., whose designer Leona Lax (*née* Gross), 48, has developed the concept (*see* 1914; Maiden Form, 1923).

Paris couturière Evelyn Vionnet, now 62, closes her House of Vionnet at the outbreak of war.

1940

 European hostilities escalate as Adolf Hitler launches a *blitzkrieg* (lightning war) against Belgium, the Netherlands, and France. Winston Churchill succeeds Neville Chamberlain as British prime minister as French defenses collapse.

First Lady Eleanor Roosevelt is sent by her husband to nominate Secretary of Agriculture Henry A. Wallace for the vice presidency at the Democratic party convention July 16. FDR wins an unprecedented third term in the White House.

British families in London, Glasgow, Liverpool, Birmingham, Bristol, Coventry, and other large cities seek shelter from Nazi bombs beginning in August as the Luftwaffe sends planes across the Channel in the Battle of Britain. RAF planes retaliate, and Hitler declares an all-out war on British cities September 4: 400 Londoners die in air raids September 9, another 200 die the next day, and thousands are injured, including many women and children. German bombers hit Coventry November 14 in the worst raid of all, and 1,000 are killed. Women's Auxiliary Air Force crews of 16 replace 10-man crews to handle heavy barrage balloons. Other WAAF members train as photographers, radio operators, and bomb plotters.

Journalist Dorothy Thompson makes a lecture tour urging U.S. entry into the European conflict, but Alice Roosevelt Longworth, who has allied herself with isolationists, says of Thompson, "She is the only woman who had her menopause in public and got paid for it."

 German SS troops surround a densely populated Jewish area in Czestochowa in January, herd thousands of half-naked Polish men and women into a large square, beat them bloody, and keep them standing for hours in the frosty night air while young girls are taken into the synagogue, forced to undress, raped, and tortured.

Jews in Germany and German-occupied countries come under growing persecution. Poet-playwright

Nelly Sachs escapes to Sweden through the intercession of novelist Selma Lagerlöf and the Swedish royal family, but not every Jewish woman is so lucky.

Québecois women finally gain the right to vote in provincial elections; most other Canadian women have had voting rights since 1918, and in many other respects the women of Quebec continue to have fewer rights than women in other provinces (*see* 1964).

💲 The first U.S. Social Security checks go out January 30 and total $75,844, a figure that will rise into the billions as more pensioners become eligible for benefits. The first check goes to Vermont widow Ida May Fuller, 35, who receives $22.54 and will collect more than $20,000 before she dies in 1975 at age 100 (*see* 1935). But women who retire at 65 now live on average only 10 more years.

U.S. unemployment remains above 8 million, with 14.6 percent of the work force idle.

✾ German girls are reported in May to be saving their hair for production of felt needed in the war effort.

⚗ *Statistical Mechanics* by German-American physicist Maria Goeppert Mayer 34, and her husband, Joseph, at Columbia University is a pioneering work that will lead Mrs. Mayer to conduct research on isotopes for an atomic-bomb project.

☤ German physician Ruth W. Tichauer, 30, who has fled Europe with her husband, sets up a practice in a barrio of La Paz, Bolivia. She will treat Indians in the jungle and mountains for the next 40 years, introducing insulin, "antibiótico," "tuberculina," and other instrumentalities of modern medicine, and cutting the death rate drastically as her patient load grows to number 6,000.

Only 37.6 of 10,000 U.S. women die after being delivered of live infants, down from 60.8 in 1915.

U.S. Blue Cross health insurance programs have 6 million subscribers, up from 500,000 in 1935, but Blue Shield surgical insurance covers only 260,000.

▌▐ *Newsday* begins publication at Long Island City, N.Y., where copper heir Harry F. Guggenheim and his third wife, Alicia Patterson, 34, start a daily paper with a name culled from contest submissions. Pub-

lishing heiress Patterson will later say that Guggenheim "emancipated me from purposelessness."

"Brenda Starr" by Chicago cartoonist Mrs. Dale Messick, 34, debuts June 30 in the *Chicago Tribune* and *New York Daily News* to depict the comic-strip adventures of a 23-year-old reporter for the *Flash.* Messick has tried for 4 years to sell syndicate editors on her cartoons. "Because I was a woman, they couldn't believe I could draw," she will later recall. "They'd set my drawings aside and say [with a leer], 'How about lunch?' " It has taken Mollie Slott of the Tribune-News Syndicate to give her the nod. Messick's five-foot-two-inch heroine, who looks like Rita Hayworth and has an endless wardrobe (but whom feminists will applaud as a role model), will meet Basil St. John in 1945 and marry him in 1975 without either having aged a day.

✒ Nonfiction: *My Native Land* by Anna Louise Strong; *A Winter in Arabia* by Freya Stark: *Salud: A South American Journal* by novelist Margaret Culkin Banning.

Fiction: *The Man Who Loved Children* by Christina Stead, who has one of her characters say, "I know your breed; all your fine officials debauch the young girls who are afraid to lose their jobs; that's as old as Washington"; *Gypsy, Gypsy* by Rumer Godden; *The Heart Is a Lonely Hunter* by U.S. novelist Carson Smith McCullers, 23; *Cherry Country (Sakura no kuni)* by Yoko Ota, wins the *Asahi Shimbun*'s 50th Anniversary prize; *Girl with Bare Feet (Suashi no musume)* by Ineko Sata; *Kallocain* by Karin Boye; *Esther Roon* by Norah Lofts; *No Man's Wit* by Rose Macaulay; *The Third Eye* by Elinor Glyn; *Out in Society* by Margaret Culkin Banning; *Letty and the Law* by Faith Baldwin; *Curtain Going Up* by Sophie Kerr; *The Cross-Eyed Bear* by U.S. mystery writer Dorothy B. Hughes (*née* Flanagan), 35; *Ten Little Niggers* by Agatha Christie, whose new detective novel will be published in America first as *And Then There Were None*, later as *Ten Little Indians*; *Black Plumes* by Margery Allingham.

Poetry: . . .*The White Cliffs* by Alice Duer Miller.

Juvenile: *Pat the Bunny* by U.S. author-illustrator Dorothy Kunhardt, 39, who has a felt bunny and other tactile objects affixed to her pages; *Miss Granby's Secret; or, The Bastard of Pinsk* by Eleanor

Farjeon; *The Naughtiest Girl in School* by Enid Blyton; *The Chalet School in Exile* by Elinor Brent-Dyer.

Painting: *Three White Squares* (paint on glass) by New York abstractionist I. (Irene) Pereira (*née* Rice), 38, who married Humberto Pereira in 1929, divorced him 1938, and next year will marry George W. Brown; *T. B. Harlem* by "bohemian" New York painter Alice Neel, 40; *Stump in Red Hills* by Georgia O'Keeffe; *Seated Nude* by Lee Krasner.

Photography: *Promenade des Anglais* by Vienna-born documentary photographer Lisette Model (*née* Seyberg), 33, contains photographs taken in 1937 on the French Riviera. She has applied for a darkroom job with the New York daily *P.M.*, whose picture editor, Ralph Steiner, has recognized the quality of her work and arranged for publication of her book, which brings her immdediate acclaim.

Theater: Gene (originally Gene Eliza Taylor) Tierney, 19, and Elliott Nugent in James Thurber and Nugent's *The Male Animal* 1/9 at New York's Cort Theater, 243 perfs.: *My Dear Children* by playwrights Catherine Turney, 33, and Jerry Horwin 1/31 at New York's Belasco Theater, with John Barrymore, 117 perfs.; Lenore Ulric, Lee J. Cobb, and Franchot Tone in Ernest Hemingway and Benjamin Glazer's *The Fifth Column* 3/26 at New York's Alvin Theater, 87 perfs.; Alfred Lunt and Lynn Fontanne in Robert Sherwood's *There Shall Be No Night* 4/29 at New York's Alvin Theater, 115 perfs.; Helen Craig and Horace McNally in Elmer Harris's *Johnny Belinda* 9/18 at New York's Belasco Theater, 321 perfs.; Ernest Truex and Jean Dixon in George S. Kaufman and Moss Hart's *George Washington Slept Here* 10/18 at New York's Lyceum Theater, 173 perfs.; Jane Cowl and Kent Smith in John Van Druten's *Old Acquaintance* 12/23 at New York's Morosco Theater, 170 perfs.; Shirley Booth, Jo Ann Sayers, and Morris Carnovsky in Joseph A. Fields and Jerome Chodorov's *My Sister Eileen*, a play based on Ruth McKinney's book, 12/26 at New York's Biltmore Theater, 865 perfs.

Films: Raymond Massey, Gene Lockhart, and Ruth Gordon in John Cromwell's *Abe Lincoln in Illinois*; Joel McCrae and Laraine Day (Laraine Johnson), 19, in Alfred Hitchcock's *Foreign Correspondent*; Henry Fonda and Jane Darwell (originally Patti Woodward), 61, in John Ford's *The Grapes of Wrath*; Rosalind Russell and Cary Grant in Howard Hawks's *His Girl Friday*, a new version of the 1928 stageplay *The Front Page*; Katharine Hepburn, Cary Grant, and James Stewart in George Cukor's *The Philadelphia Story*; Laurence Olivier, Greer Garson, Irish actress Maureen O'Sullivan, 29, and Edna May Oliver in Robert Z. Leonard's *Pride and Prejudice*; Joan Fontaine, Judith Anderson, and Laurence Olivier in Alfred Hitchcock's *Rebecca;* Sabu, Rex Ingram, and June Duprez in Ludwig Berger, Tim Whelan, and Michael Powell's *The Thief of Baghdad*. Also: Edward G. Robinson, Ruth Gordon, and Otto Kruger in William Dieterle's *Dr. Ehrlich's Magic Bullet*; Ginger Rogers and Dennis Morgan in Sam Wood's *Kitty Foyle*; Bette Davis and Herbert Marshall in William Wyler's *The Letter*; Tyrone Power and Linda (*née* Manetta Eloisa) Darnell, 19, in Rouben Mamoulian's *The Mark of Zorro*; Margaret Sullavan and James Stewart in Frank Borzage's *The Mortal Storm*; William Holden, Martha Scott, 25, and Frank Craven in Sam Wood's *Our Town*; George Raft, Humphrey Bogart, Ann (*née* Clara Lou) Sheridan, 25, and London-born actress Ida Lupino, 22, in Raoul Walsh's *They Drive by Night*; Vivien Leigh and Robert Taylor in Mervyn LeRoy's *Waterloo Bridge*.

Broadway musicals: Eve Arden, Betty Hutton (Betty Jane Thornburg), 18, Keenan Wynn, and Alfred Drake in *Two for the Show* 2/8 at the Booth Theater, with songs that include "How High the Moon" by Morgan Lewis, lyrics by Nancy Hamilton, 124 perfs.; Vera-Ellen, Marta Eggert, and Jack Haley in *Higher and Higher* 4/4 at the Shubert Theater, with Rogers and Hart songs that include "It Never Entered My Mind," 84 perfs.; William Gaxton, Victor Moore, Vera Zorina, and Irene Bordoni in *Louisiana Purchase* 5/28 at the Imperial Theater, with Irving Berlin songs that include "It's a Lovely Day Tomorrow," 444 perfs.; Ethel Waters, Todd Duncan, Dooley Wilson, and dancer Katherine Dunham, now 30, in *Cabin in the Sky* 10/25 at the Martin Beck Theater, with songs that include "Taking a Chance on Love," 156 perfs.; Ethel Merman, Vera-Ellen, Arthur Treacher, and Betty Hutton in *Panama Hattie* 10/30 at the 46th Street Theater, with Cole Porter songs that include "Let's Be Buddies," 501 perfs.; Gene Kelly, Vivienne Segal, and Canadian-born actress June Havoc (June Hovick), 30, in *Pal Joey* 12/25 at the Ethel Barrymore Theater, with Rodgers and Hart songs that include "Bewitched," "I Could Write a Book," and "Zip," 344 perfs.

Popular songs: Billie Holiday records "Loveless Love"; The Andrews Sisters record the 1920 Albert von Tilzer–Neville Fleeson song "I'll Be with You in Apple Blossom Time"; Little Esther (Esther Phillips [Esther Mae Jones]), 14, records "Double Crossing Blues" with the Johnny Otis band; "Beat Me, Daddy, Eight to the Bar" by Eleanore Sheehy, Don Raye, and Hughie Prince; "How Did He (She) Look" by U.S. composer Abner Silver, lyrics by Gladys Shelley.

Country singer Minnie Pearl (Sarah Ophelia Colley), 28, joins the cast of *Grand Ole Opry* at Nashville, Tenn., where she will be a fixture for decades.

Opera: Licia Albanese, now 26, makes her Metropolitan Opera debut 2/9 in the title role of the 1904 Puccini opera *Madama Butterfly* (she will have her greatest triumph in 1942 as Violetta in *La Traviata* and will continue at the Met until early 1966); U.S. soprano Eleanor Steber, 24, makes her Metropolitan Opera debut 12/7 singing the role of Sophie in the 1911 Strauss opera *Der Rosenkavalier* (she will continue with the Met until 1963).

Wimbledon tennis matches are canceled for the duration of the war. Alice Marble wins in women's singles at Forest Hills.

The first nylon stockings go on sale in the United States May 15. Hosiery makers have bought their yarn from E. I. DuPont, whose nylon production will go almost entirely into parachutes beginning next year (*see* 1937; Britain, 1946).

Cotton fabrics hold 80 percent of the U.S. textile market at the mills, down from 85 percent in 1930. Man-made fabrics, most of them cellulose fabrics such as rayon and acetate, have increased their market share to 10 percent (*see* 1950).

Former New York art dealer Mary Woodard Reinhardt, now 39, is remarried in June to Chicago advertising mogul Albert Lasker, 60. Since divorc-

ing Reinhardt she has developed the idea of "Hollywood Patterns"—inexpensive dress patterns sold with the cachet of *Vogue* magazine and the glamour of movie stars—which has enabled her to set herself up in business and live in a penthouse at 400 East 52nd Street (*see* 1926; 1941).

Tobacco heiress Doris Duke, now 28 and worth over $300 million, gives birth in July to a premature infant girl, who dies after 24 hours, and obtains a separation from her husband, James Cromwell (*see* 1934; 1947).

Demand for Pepperidge Farm bread obliges Margaret Rudkin to rent some buildings at Norwalk, Conn., and to expand her baking facilities (*see* 1937).

1941

World War II creates more widows as the Luftwaffe continues to bomb British cities, Nazi troops invade the Soviet Union, and Japanese planes attack Pearl Harbor. The House of Representatives votes 388 to 1 December 8 to approve a war resolution against Japan, with Rep. Jeanette Rankin, now 61, voicing the lone dissent. "As a woman I can't go to war," she will say, "and I refuse to send anyone else."

Panamanian women gain the right to vote on the same basis as men.

The Japanese Army recruits thousands of young girls—mostly from Korea and China—for the military brothels it has built since 1937 as its armies extend their reach into Southeast Asia and the South Pacific (*see* 1937; 1991).

Japan's Ministry of Labor opens more jobs to women that were formerly for men only (*see* 1939). The Patriotic Labor Corporation Order requires unmarried women aged 14 to 25 to participate in the war effort.

British Minister of Labour Ernest Bevin, 60, announces the first steps in a massive mobilization campaign March 11 and begins registering 20- and 21-year-old women for service in vital industrial and agricultural jobs as well as in the auxiliary ser-

"Your mother country appeals to you!": Soviet women exhorted their men to resist German invaders.

vices. Women work around the clock in war plants to free men for active service. Married women with young children are exempt from duty, but day and night nurseries spring up to care for children of working mothers.

Hollywood star Linda Darnell appears on the floor of the New York Curb Exchange November 18 to sell U.S. bonds and savings stamps for a fundraising effort.

British flyer Amy Johnson is drowned January 6 at age 37 when her plane ditches in the Thames estuary.

Jacqueline Cochran pilots a bomber to England, is commissioned a flight captain in the British Air Transport Auxiliary, and trains a group of women pilots for war transport service (*see* 1938; 1942).

"Never underestimate the power of a woman," say advertisements for the *Ladies' Home Journal*. N. W. Ayer copywriter Elizabeth "Bj" Kidd, 35, is credited with having coined the slogan, which will be used for more than 50 years.

Nonfiction: *The Alarm Clock* (*Väckarklocka*) by Elin Wägner is a feminist analysis of the horror that has befallen Europe; *Black Lamb and Gray Falcon* by English woman of letters Rebecca West, now 49, is a two-volume diary of her 1937 trip to Yugoslavia, a country whose Serbian population is being massacred by Croatians with help from German invasion forces; *Reveille in Washington* by U.S. historian Margaret Leech, 46.

Fiction: *Parents and Children* by Ivy Compton-Burnett; *Look at All Those Roses* (stories) by Elizabeth Bowen; *The Land of Spices* by Kate O'Brien; *Two Days in Aragon* by Molly Keane; *Come Wind, Come Weather* by Daphne du Maurier; *Dear For My Possessing* by Pamela Hansford Johnson begins a trilogy; *The Timeless Land* by Eleanor Dark; *The Seventh Cross* (*Das siebente Kreuz*) by emigrée German novelist Anna Seghers (Netty Radvanyi), 41; *A Curtain of Green* (stories) by Mississippi writer Eudora Welty, 32; *Reflections in a Golden Eye* by Carson McCullers; *In This Our Life* by Ellen Glasgow (Pulitzer Prize); *Saratoga Trunk* by Edna Ferber; *Green Centuries* by Caroline Gordon; *The Sun Is My Undoing* by Marguerite Steen; *Dear Me* by Agnes Turnbull; *Junior Miss* (stories) by U.S. writer Sally Benson (*née* Smith), 41 (*see* Theater, below); *Above Suspicion* by Scottish-American mystery novelist Helen Clark MacInnes, 33; *Traitor's Purse* by Margery Allingham. Virginia Woolf, who has had at least one nervous breakdown and fears another, drowns herself March 28 at age 69.

Poetry: *The Seven Deadly Sins* (*De sju dödsynderna*) by Karin Boye; *The Rose and the Burning Forest* (*Roza rói i lasy toonace*) by Marja Jasnorszewska-Pawlikowska. Marina Tsvetaeva, not yet 49, hangs herself August 31 at Yelabuga, a small town in the Tatar Autonomous Republic; evacuated from Russia in the path of approaching German forces, she and her teenage son are destitute.

Juvenile: *My Friend Flicka* by U.S. author Mary O'Hara (Mary O'Hara Alsop Stuart-Vasa), 56; *Little Town on the Prairie* by Laura Ingalls Wilder; *In*

My Mother's House by New Mexican author Ann Nolan Clark, 44; *Curious George* by German-American author Margaret (Elisabeth) Rey, 35, with illustrations by her husband, H. A. (Hans August) Rey, 43, whose monkey, George, will appear in six sequels (the Reys were living in Paris in June of last year but were able to bicycle south before the Wehrmacht arrived, reached Lisbon, sailed to Rio, where they had worked together and had married, and arrived at New York in October of last year).

Painting: *Self-Portrait with Bonito* (a parrot) by Frida Kahlo.

Theater: Josephine Hull, Jean Adair, and Boris Karloff in Joseph Kesselring's *Arsenic and Old Lace* 1/10 at New York's Fulton Theater, 1,437 perfs.; *Watch on the Rhine* by Lillian Hellman 4/1 at New York's Music Box Theater, with Paul Lukas, Mady Christians, Ann Blyth, 12, and George Coulouris, 378 perfs. (New York Drama Critics' Circle Award); Joyce Carey in Noël Coward's *Blithe Spirit* 7/2 at London's Piccadilly Theatre, 1,997 perfs.; Helen Hayes and Lotte Lenya in Maxwell Anderson's *Candle in the Wind* 10/22 at New York's Shubert Theater, 95 perfs.; Patricia Peardon, 16, as Judy Graves and Lenore Lonergan as Fuffy Adams in the Jerome Chodorov–Joseph Fields comedy *Junior Miss* (based on the Sally Benson book, above) 11/18 at New York's Lyceum Theater, 710 perfs.; Judith Evelyn, 28, and Vincent Price in Patrick Hamilton's *Angel Street* 12/5 at New York's Golden Theater, 1,295 perfs.

Films: Orson Welles, Agnes Moorehead, 34, Evelyn Keyes, 26, Joseph Cotten, Everett Sloane, and George Coulouris in Welles's *Citizen Kane*; Robert Montgomery and Evelyn Keyes in Alexander Hall's *Here Comes Mr. Jordan*; Sara Allgood, Roddy McDowell, Donald Crisp, and Walter Pigeon in John Ford's *How Green Was My Valley*; Wendy Hiller, now 29, and Rex Harrison in Gabriel Pascal's *Major Barbara*; Humphrey Bogart, Sydney Greenstreet, and Mary Astor in John Huston's *The Maltese Falcon*; Joan Fontaine, Laurence Olivier, and George Sanders in Alfred Hitchcock's *Rebecca*; Joel McCrae and Veronica Lake (Constance Ockleman), 21, in Preston Sturges's *Sullivan's Travels*. Also: Jean Arthur and Robert Cummings in Sam Wood's *The Devil and Miss Jones*; Paulette Goddard, Jack Oakie, and Chaplin in Charles Chaplin's *The Great Dictator*; Vienna-born actress Hedy Lamarr (Hedwig Kiesler), 27, Robert Young, and Ruth Hussey in King Vidor's *H. M. Pulham, Esq.*; Olivia de Havilland and Charles Boyer in Mitchell Leisen's *Hold Back the Dawn*; Ann Sheridan, Robert Cummings, and Ronald Reagan in Sam Wood's *King's Row*; Barbara Stanwyck, and Henry Fonda in Preston Sturges's *The Lady Eve*; Bette Davis in William Wyler's *The Little Foxes*; Bette Davis, Ann Sheridan, and Monty Woolley in William Keighley's *The Man Who Came to Dinner*; Martha Scott and Fredric March in Irving Rapper's *One Foot in Heaven*; Irene Dunne and Cary Grant in George Stevens's *Penny Serenade*; Edward G. Robinson, John Garfield, and Ida Lupino in Michael Curtiz's *The Sea Wolf*; Claudette Colbert and Ray Milland in Mark Sandrich's *Skylark*; Margaret Sullavan and Fredric March in John Cromwell's *So Ends Our Night*; Joan Fontaine and Cary Grant in Alfred Hitchcock's *Suspicion*; Vivien Leigh and Laurence Olivier in Alexander Korda's *That Hamilton Woman*; Ginger Rogers, George Murphy, and Burgess Meredith in Garson Kanin's *Tom, Dick and Harry*; Greta Garbo and Melvyn Douglas in George Cukor's *Two-faced Woman* (now 36, Garbo goes into "temporary" retirement, saying that she wants "to be let alone," and will never make another film; having earned $3 million in her 16-year career, she helps Britain by identifying high-level Nazi sympathizers in Stockholm, providing introductions, and carrying messages for British agents); Raimu, Fernandel, Josette Day, and Charpin in Marcel Pagnol's *The Well-Digger's Daughter*; Lon Chaney, Jr. and Chilean-born actress Evelyn Ankers, 23, in George Waggner's *The Wolf Man*; Joan Crawford in George Cukor's *A Woman's Face*.

English concert pianist Myra Hess, 51, is named Dame Commander of the British Empire.

Broadway musicals: Gertrude Lawrence and Danny Kaye in *Lady in the Dark* 1/23 at the Alvin Theater, with Kurt Weill–Ira Gershwin songs that include "Jenny (the Saga of)," 162 perfs. (Kaye, 28, has married Sylvia Fine while working in the Catskill Mountain "borscht circuit" and she has helped him with her witty lyrics); Rosemary Lane, Nancy Walker (*née* Ann Myrtle Swoyer), 20, and June Allyson in

Best Foot Forward 10/1 at the Ethel Barrymore Theater, with songs that include "Buckle Down, Winsocki," 326 perfs.; Danny Kaye, Eve Arden, and Nanette Fabray (originally Nanette Fabares), 21, in *Let's Face It* 10/29 at the Imperial Theater, with Cole Porter songs that include "You Irritate Me So," and Danny Kaye patter songs with lyrics by Sylvia Fine (above), 547 perfs.; Olsen and Johnson, Carmen Miranda, and Ella Logan in *Sons O'Fun* 12/1 at the Winter Garden Theater, with songs that include "Happy in Love," 742 perfs.

Popular songs: Billie Holiday records "God Bless the Child" and "Gloomy Sunday"; U.S. jazz singer Anita O'Day (Anita Belle Colton), 21, records "Let Me Off Uptown" with the Gene Krupa band; the Andrews Sisters record "Boogie Woogie Bugle Boy" by Don Raye and Hughie Prince; "Deep in the Heart of Texas" by U.S. songwriter June Swander, 32 (who has never been to Texas), and her husband, Don, 36; "Racing with the Moon" by Johnny Watson, lyrics by Pauline Pope (Watson's wife) and bandleader Vaughn Monroe.

Singer Jo Stafford, 23, joins the Tommy Dorsey band after several years' singing with the Stafford Sisters.

Sarah Palfrey Cooke, 18, wins in women's singles at Forest Hills.

Woolworth heiress Barbara Hutton obtains a legal separation at London July 28 from Count Haugwitz-Reventlow, who received $1 million prior to their marriage; he receives no alimony but is made trustee of a $1.5 million fund established by Hutton in the name of their London-born 5-year-old son, Lance, and will use part of the income to finance the boy's education (*see* 1935). Hutton will donate their London mansion to the U.S. government to use as an embassy residence (*see* 1942).

Railroad heiress Gloria Vanderbilt, now 17, defies her family December 28 to marry Pasquale John "Pat" Di Cicco, 32, a former Hollywood actors' agent who is on Howard Hughes's payroll at $1,500 per month. The ceremony is performed at the Mission of Santa Barbara (*see* 1934; 1945).

Claire McCardell quits Hattie Carnegie, takes her designs to a reorganized Townley Co., and will

remain there with her name on the firm's label (as a partner beginning in 1951) until her death in 1958.

Mary Lasker plants 2 to 3 million winter chrysanthemum seeds and grows plants which she presents to New York City for planting in Central Park and elsewhere as a memorial to her late mother, who died last year. She and her sister, Mrs. Allmon Fordyce, will import 40,000 bulbs from Holland after the war and persuade the city to plant them (along with some trees) on the Park Avenue center mall north of Grand Central Terminal.

A National Nutritional Conference for Defense convened by President Roosevelt examines causes for the physical defects found in so many young men called up by the draft. Mayo Clinic nutrition specialist Russell M. Wilder heads a group of experts in a study of the eating habits of 2,000 representative U.S. families (*see* 1943).

Only 30 percent of U.S. white bread is enriched with vitamins and iron. South Carolina becomes the first state to require enrichment.

Casserole Cookery by Baltimore author Marian Tracy will be the vademecum of young housewives for years to come.

Boston gynecologist George Smith and his epidemiologist wife, Olive, at the Free Hospital for Women note that women who have suffered spontaneous abortions have lower blood levels of estrogen than women who come uneventfully to term; believing that administering estrogen will protect developing fetuses, they will prescribe diethylstilbestrol (DES) to 515 pregnant women between 1943 and 1948; cooperating gynecologists in 48 other U.S. cities will give DES to 117 pregnant women in the same period, and by 1952 there will be more than 30 different brands of estrogen products on the market, including pills, injectable solutions, ointments, nasal sprays, and suppositories. Discovered by British researcher Sir Charles Dodds in 1938, the synthetic estrogen hormone DES has been used to promote quicker fattening of livestock and poultry and is now prescribed for the prevention of miscarriage (it is also used in doses of 25 mg. per day for 5 days after intercourse to prevent conception) (*see* medicine, 1971).

1942 ———————————————————

 The Women's Army Auxiliary Corps (WAAC) established by act of Congress in mid-May is headed by *Houston Post* editor Oveta Hobby (*née* Culp), 37, who in 1931 married Texas Governor William D. Hobby, 27 years her senior. Black women oppose her appointment because she is known to share the racist views prevalent in Texas, but 3,902 black women will serve in the WAAC. Rep. Edith Nourse Rogers, who has had the Corps in mind since 1917, has sponsored the legislation, which is designed to free men for active service by putting women into noncombat jobs.

The WAVES (Women Accepted for Voluntary Emergency Service), authorized by act of Congress July 30 to support the navy, is headed by Wellesley College president Mildred H. McAfee, 42. Only 68 black women will serve in the WAVES.

The Women's Auxiliary Ferrying Squadron, established September 10, is assigned to fly aircraft to bases in noncombat areas. Members have civilian status and earn $3,000 per year.

Jacqueline Cochran is named September 16 to direct the Women's Airforce Service Pilots—WASPS—which will supply more than 1,000 auxiliary pilots to the armed forces (*see* 1941). Upon her return from Britain she undertook a flight training program for the army air force. Her group absorbs the Auxiliary Ferrying Squadron (above) in November (*see* 1953).

 German troops burn the Czech village of Lidice in Bohemia June 6 after executing every male in reprisal for the assassination of Reinhard Heydrich. Only one man reportedly escapes; the female population is abused.

Some 30,000 Parisian Jews—women as well as men—are rounded up by 2,000 police officers July 16. The Germans bus them out of the city to Nazi concentration camps; only 30 will survive.

 More than 3.6 million American men remain unemployed, but the number has fallen from 9.5 million men and women in 1939. The ranks of the unemployed dwindle rapidly as war plants, shipyards, oil fields, and recruiting offices clamor for manpower and 2 million women enter the workforce. By November, 13 million women are working, 2.5 million of them in war industries, and experts say the nation will need another 6 million women workers by the end of 1943. Women who never worked before take factory and shipyard jobs previously reserved for men; "Rosie the Riveter" becomes a national symbol.

World War II brought women into the workplace as nothing before had ever done. Many remained.

 Keep Your Powder Dry: An Anthropologist Looks at America by Margaret Mead is published.

Revelation of Childbirth by Grantly Dick-Read expands on his 1933 book *Natural Childbirth* (*see* 1936). Working 2 years ago in London's slum areas, Dick-Read tried to help a Whitechapel woman in labor by putting a mask over her face to administer chloroform "when the head appeared and the dilation of the passages was obvious. She, however, resented the suggestion and firmly but kindly refused this help. . . . She shyly turned to me and said: 'It didn't hurt. It wasn't meant to, was it, Doctor?' " (*see* 1944).

Spinal anesthesia is introduced in U.S. obstetrics, allowing women to feel nothing from the waist down yet remain conscious. The technique, which will become routine at many hospitals, requires the use of forceps since the mother cannot push out the fetus (critics say the new technique merely helps health professionals justify higher fees).

The first *New York Times* Sunday crossword puzzle appears February 15. The *Times* has hired expert Margaret Petheridge Farrar, now 44, to design the puzzles, which will appear on a daily basis beginning in 1950. Farrar will continue in the job until she retires in 1968.

Nonfiction: *Letters from Syria* by Freya Stark, who works with the British Information Ministry to counter Axis propaganda in Aden, Yemen, Egypt, Iraq, and India; *Our Hearts Were Young and Gay* by former *Ladies' Home Journal* managing editor Emily Kimbrough, 42, and actress Cornelia Otis Skinner, 41; *West with the Night* by Beryl Markham (*see* 1936); *Generation of Vipers* by U.S. author Philip Gordon Wylie, 40, introduces the term "Momism" to describe what he calls an emasculating American matriarchy.

Fiction: *Return to the Future* by Sigrid Undset, who escaped to America 2 years ago when German forces invaded Norway; *The Road to the City* (*La Strada che va in città*) (two short novels) by Italian novelist Alessandra Tourninbarte (Natalia Ginzburg), 26, daughter of novelist–biology professor Carlo Levi; *The Company She Keeps* by U.S. novelist Mary McCarthy, 30; *The Robber Bridegroom* (novella) by Eudora Welty; *Breakfast with the Nikolides* by Rumer Godden; *Tales from Bective Bridge* (stories) by Irish short story writer Mary Lavin, 30 (with an introduction by Lord Dunsany, who has encouraged her); *The Brittle Glass* by Norah Lofts; *Frenchman's Creek* by Daphne du Maurier; *The Engagement* (*Das Verlöbnis*) by Helene Voigt-Diederichs; *The Puppet-Maker* (*Kyukichi tenguya*) by Chiyo Uno; *The Valley of Decision* by Marcia Davenport; *Gates of Allus* by U.S. novelist Gladys Schmitt, 33; *Dragon Seed* by Pearl S. Buck; *The Day Must Dawn* by Agnes Turnbull; *Meet Me in St. Louis* (stories) by Sally Benson; *The*

Horn of Life by Gertrude Atherton; *New Hope* by Ruth Suckow; *Assignment in Brittany* by Helen MacInnes; *Lay On, Mac Duff!* by U.S. mystery novelist Charlotte Armstrong, 37, whose detective MacDougal Duff is a former history professor.

Poetry: *For My People* by U.S. poet Margaret Walker (Alexander), 27; *Wake Island* by Muriel Rukeyser; *Street Songs* by Edith Sitwell, now 55.

Painting: *White Lines* by I. Rice Pereira; an *Art of This Century* exhibition opens at New York October 20 under the direction of copper heiress Marguerite "Peggy" Guggenheim, 44, who has married German painter Max Ernst.

Theater: Aline MacMahon and William Prince in Maxwell Anderson's *The Eve of St. Mark* 10/7 at New York's Cort Theater, 291 perfs.; Katharine Hepburn, Elliot Nugent, and Audrey Christie in Philip Barry's *Without Love* 11/10 at New York's St. James Theater, 113 perfs.; Florence Eldridge, E. G. Marshall, Fredric March, and Tallulah Bankhead in Thornton Wilder's *The Skin of Our Teeth* 11/18 at New York's Plymouth Theater, 359 perfs.

Films: Humphrey Bogart and Swedish-born actress Ingrid Bergman, 27, in Michael Curtiz's *Casablanca*; John Mills, English actress Celia Johnson, 34, Michael Wilding, and Noël Coward in Coward and David Lean's *In Which We Serve*; Joseph Cotten, Anne Baxter, 19, Dolores Costello, Tim Holt, and Agnes Moorehead in Orson Welles's *The Magnificent Ambersons*; Jean Arthur, Ronald Colman, and Cary Grant in George Stevens's *The Talk of the Town*. Also: Errol Flynn and Canadian-born actress Alexis Smith, 21, in Raoul Walsh's *Gentleman Jim*; Veronica Lake, Brian Donlevy, and Alan Ladd in Stuart Heisler's *The Glass Key*; French actress Michele Morgan (Simone Roussel), 22, and Paul Henreid in Robert Stevenson's *Joan of Paris*; Ginger Rogers and Ray Milland in Billy Wilder's *The Major and the Minor*; Henry Fonda and Olivia de Havilland in Elliot Nugent's *The Male Animal*; Greer Garson and Walter Pidgeon in William Wyler's *Mrs. Miniver*; Bette Davis, Paul Henreid, and Claude Rains in Irving Rapper's *Now, Voyager*; Massimo Girotti and Clara Calamia in Luchino Visconti's *Ossessione*; Claudette Colbert, Joel McCrae, and Rudy Vallée in Preston Sturges's *The Palm Beach Story*; Greer Garson and Ronald Colman in

Mervyn LeRoy's *Random Harvest*; Jack Benny and Carole Lombard (who has died at age 32 along with her mother and 20 other passengers in a TWA plane crash at Las Vegas January 16) in Ernst Lubitsch's *To Be or Not to Be*; Katharine Hepburn and Spencer Tracy in George Stevens's *Woman of the Year*.

The *Chicago Tribune–New York Daily News* syndicate acquires Hedda Hopper's Hollywood gossip column and gives it wide distribution (*see* 1936). Hopper feuds with Louella Parsons and others.

Hollywood musicals: Judy Garland and Gene Kelly in Busby Berkeley's *For Me and My Gal*; Bing Crosby, Fred Astaire, Marjorie Reynolds, and Louise Beavers in Mark Sandrich's *Holiday Inn*, with Irving Berlin's song "White Christmas"; Bing Crosby, Bob Hope, and Dorothy Lamour in David Butler's *The Road to Morocco* with Jimmy Van Heusen–Johnny Burke songs that include "Moonlight Becomes You" and the title song; Bing Crosby, Bob Hope, Dorothy Lamour, Ray Milland, Veronica Lake, Susan Hayward (Edythe Marrener), 23, Alan Ladd, Paulette Goddard, and Cecil B. DeMille in George Marshall's *Star-Spangled Rhythm* with songs that include "That Old Black Magic" by Harold Arlen, music by Johnny Mercer; Fred Astaire and Rita Hayworth (Margarita Carmen Cansino), 23, in William A. Seiter's *You Were Never Lovelier* with Jerome Kern–Johnny Mercer songs that include "Dearly Beloved," "I'm Old-Fashioned," and the title song; Dorothy Lamour, Betty Hutton, William Holden, and Eddie Bracken in Victor Schertzinger's *The Fleet's In* with Schertzinger–Johnny Mercer songs that include "Arthur Murray Taught Me Dancing in a Hurry" and "Tangerine"; Betty Grable, Carmen Miranda, Cesar Romero, Jackie Gleason, and Charlotte Greenwood in Irving Cummings's *Springtime in the Rockies* with songs that include "I Had the Craziest Dream" by Harry James, lyrics by Mack Gordon.

Ballet: Alicia Markova, Sono Osato, Jerome Robbins, Hugh Laing, and Antony Tudor in *Romeo and Juliet* 4/6 at New York's Metropolitan Opera House, with music by the late Frederick Delius, choreography by Tudor; Nora Kaye (as Hagar), Laing and Tudor in *Pillar of Fire* 4/8 at the Met,

with music by Arnold Schoenberg, choreography by Tudor; *Rodeo* 10/16 at the Met, with Agnes George de Mille, 37, music by Aaron Copland, choreography by de Mille; Tanaquil LeClerq and Todd Bolender in *Metamorphoses* 11/25 at New York's City Center, with music by Paul Hindemith, choreography by George Balanchine.

Opera: U.S. soprano Margaret Harshaw, 33, makes her Metropolitan Opera debut 11/22 singing the role of the second Norn in the 1876 Wagner opera *Götterdämmerung*. She will remain with the Met until 1963.

Elisabeth Schwarzkopf in Nazi Germany gives a debut recital at Berlin's Beethoven Saal; she will be the outstanding lieder singer for decades.

Broadway musicals: Stripteaser Gypsy Rose Lee (Rose Louise Hovick), 18, Bobby Clark, and Georgia Sothern in *Star and Garter* 1/24 at the Music Box Theater, with songs that include Harold Arlen's "Blues in the Night," 609 perfs.; Vera-Ellen and Ray Bolger in *By Jupiter* 6/2 at the Shubert Theater, with Rodgers and Hart songs, 427 perfs.

Popular songs: Peggy Lee (Norma Dolores Egstrom), 22, records Joe McCoy's "Why Don't You Do Right?" with Benny Goodman's band; The Andrews Sisters sing "Don't Sit Under the Apple Tree" by Lew Brown, Charlie Tobias, and Sam H. Sept in Edward Cline's film *Private Buckaroo*; Ella Mae Morse, 18, sings "Cow-Cow Boogie" for the newly-established Capitol Record label and has a million-copy best seller (she also records "Mr. Five-by-Five").

Pauline Betz, 22, wins in women's singles at Forest Hills.

U.S. marriage rates increase dramatically as women wed men of draft age (some of whom marry in hopes of getting deferment); wives of GIs receive $50 allotment checks and $10,000 life-insurance policies.

France's highest-paid screen star, Danielle Darrieux, 25, a known Nazi sympathizer, rescues Dominican playboy and sometime diplomat Porfirio Rubirosa, 35, from a German prison camp (the Resistance has placed him on its execution list) and marries him. The son of a Dominican general, he was married in

1932 to Flor de Oro, 16-year-old daughter of Gen. Rafael Trujillo, over her father's objections, but she obtained a divorce in 1936 and he was relieved of his diplomatic duties. The priapic Rubirosa has prospered by selling visas to would-be Jewish refugees and making love to rich women (*see* 1945).

Woolworth heiress Barbara Hutton marries Hollywood film star Cary Grant July 8 at Lake Arrowhead, Calif. Wags refer to the couple as "Cash and Cary," but Grant has insisted on signing a waiver relinquishing all claims to her fortune in the event of a divorce (*see* 1941; 1945).

The Supreme Court rules Nevada divorces valid throughout the United States.

The WAVES (above) wear uniforms designed by Mainbocher, who moved to New York 2 years ago. The WACS wear uniforms designed by Hattie Carnegie (*see* 1919), who has modified her "little Carnegie suit."

Claire McCardell designs stretch leotards to provide an extra layer of warmth for college girls living in dormitories that are chilly because of wartime fuel shortages (*see* 1938). She will soon design a denim wraparound housedress (she will call it the "popover") intended for women whose servants have left for jobs in war plants.

French designer Pauline Trigère, 29, goes into business with her brother and sister at New York, where she has worked since her arrival from Paris in 1937. She will become famous for the understated look of her long wool dinner sheaths and short-sleeved coats while favoring for her own attire a leopard-skin coat with leopard-skin skirt.

Millions of Europeans live in semistarvation as German troops cut off areas in the Ukraine and north Caucasus that have produced half of Soviet wheat and pork production. Food supplies fall to starvation levels in German-occupied Greece, Poland, and parts of Yugoslavia.

U.S. sugar rationing begins in May after consumers have created scarcities by hoarding 100-pound bags and commercial users have filled their warehouses. One-sixth of U.S. sugar supplies have come from the Philippines, which are in Japanese hands, U.S. householders are asked by ration boards to state how much sugar they have stockpiled, ration stamps are deducted to compensate, the weekly ration averages 8 ounces per person but will rise to 12 ounces.

Hoarding of coffee leads to coffee rationing, which begins in November with purchases limited to one pound every five weeks. Women pool and trade ration coupons.

American women cultivate "Victory Gardens" in backyards and communal plots as vegetables become scarce, especially in California, where two-thirds of the vegetable crop has been grown by Japanese-Americans, who are relocated to concentration camps under terms of Executive Order 9066. Forty percent of all U.S. vegetables are produced in nearly 20 million Victory Gardens, but the number will fall as interest flags.

British women "Dig for Victory" and raise vegetables in backyard gardens.

Milk deliveries in most U.S. cities are reduced to alternate days; in some cities horse-drawn milk wagons reappear.

How to Cook a Wolf by M. F. K. Fisher helps Americans cope with wartime food shortages.

Japan encourages large families by rewarding mothers who have borne many children and displays slogans urging women to reproduce. The government distributes maternity memoranda booklets to promote healthy deliveries and infant care.

1943

U.S.-born German Resistance fighter Dr. Mildred Harnack-Fish (*née* Fish), 40, is beheaded February 16 at Berlin's Plötzensee Prison. She joined her husband, economist Arvid Harnack, in his native Germany nearly 14 years ago and for the past 10 years has been working in a leftist Resistance group of 130 women and men to arrange the escape of dissidents and Jews, disseminate clandestine newsletters, and spy for the U.S. and Soviet embassies in Berlin. A military court sentenced her in December to 6 years' hard labor, but Adolf Hitler ordered a retrial and she was sentenced to death.

Medical student Sophie Scholl, 21, is executed at Munich along with her brother, three other medical students, and a professor for having published "The White Rose," a leaflet that called for "sabotage of the war effort and armaments and for the overthrow of the National Socialist way of life of our people . . . propagated defeatist ideas, and . . . most vulgarly defamed the Führer, thereby giving aid to the enemy of the Reich and weakening the armed security of the nation."

Italian resistance to the Germans begins in September. As U.S. and British forces put pressure on Axis troops in the south, women in Lombardy and the Piedmont form the Women's Defense Groups for Aid to the Fighters for Liberty (*Gruppi di Difesa della Donna e per l'Assistenza ai Combattenti per la Libertà*) (*see* 1944).

Distraught wives of Berlin Jews gather in Rose Street February 28 and succeed in blocking the deportation of their husbands to Nazi death camps. An estimated 27,000 Jews are married to non-Jewish women, and they have been given jobs in the armaments industry while other Jews were sent to their deaths. The crowd of women protesting the deportation grows to 1,000. "Give us back our men," they shout. "We want to see our men." Nearly 90 soldiers move in March 8, set up machine guns, and order the women to disperse, but they hold fast. Hitler's right-hand man Joseph Goebbels is forced in the end to order the release of 1,500 men, including 25 who have just been tattooed with numbers for Auschwitz.

Italian women observe the 33rd International Women's Day March 8 by demonstrating against the Fascist Mussolini government that has sent their sons to die in World War II.

British Minister of Labor Ernest Bevin, tells the House of Commons July 29 that he has stopped recruiting women for the uniformed services in order to make more women available for aircraft production. No further volunteers will be accepted for the ATS, WRNS, WAAF, or Women's Land Army, he announces, and women up to age 50 will be registered for war work later in the summer.

U.S. women join the workforce in vastly growing numbers as farms, factories, and shipyards con-

tribute to the effort that is turning the course of the war.

A "Pay-as-You-Go" Current Tax Payment Act voted by Congress June 9 provides for income taxes on wages and salaries to be withheld from paychecks by employers. Connecticut industralist Vivien Kellems, 47, refuses to withhold her employees' taxes and will serve time for tax evasion. She will later say, "The IRS has stolen from me over the past 20 years because I am single. It is unconstitutional to impose a penalty tax of 40 percent on me because I have no husband."

Kate Smith completes a radio marathon to promote war bonds September 22. Singing "God Bless America," she has sold $39 million worth of bonds.

A U.S. federal rent control law takes effect in November. The controls will expire in 1950 but will be continued by New York State and some other states.

The medical establishment recognizes the "Pap" test for detecting cervical cancer after 15 years of work by Greek-American physician George Nicholas Papanicolaou, 60, who developed the vaginal smear test at Cornell in 1928 to diagnose the cancer that has been the leading cause of death among U.S. women. It is based on exfoliative cytology (microscopic study of cells shed by bodily organs), and within 20 years will have reduced cancer of the cervix to number three as a cause of death among U.S. women.

The Infant and Child in the Culture of Today by Yale University psychoclinician Arnold L. Gesell, 63, and his assistant Frances Ilg says the infant should not be subjected to totalitarian rule but rather given autonomy (*see* Spock, 1946).

The comic-book *Wonder Woman* launched by All-America Comics with help from tennis star Alice Marble relates the deeds of a "female Superman" who, wearing a swimsuit and riding astride a circus horse, hunts down Hitler and his Nazi cohorts.

Nonfiction: *Battle Hymn of China* by Agnes Smedley, who has never joined the Communist party but nevertheless champions the cause of insurgent leader Mao Zedong: "I have always detested the belief that sex is the chief bond between man and woman," she writes. "Friendship is far more human."

Fiction: *The Fountainhead* by Russian-American novelist Ayn Rand, 38, who emigrated to the United States in 1926, married U.S. author Frank O'Connor 3 years later, became a U.S. citizen in 1931, and argues earnestly in defense of enlightened self-interest while attacking democratic selflessness and sacrifice for the common good; *A Tree Grows in Brooklyn* by New York novelist Betty Wehner Smith, 47; *Two Serious Ladies* by U.S. novelist Jane Bowles (*née* Auer), 25, who married novelist Paul Bowles on the eve of her 21st birthday in 1938; *The Walsh Girls* by U.S. novelist Elizabeth Janeway (*née* Hall), 29; *Hungry Hill* by Daphne du Maurier; *Cloudless May* by Storm Jameson; *Growing Up* by Angela Thirkell; *The Last of Summer* by Kate O'Brien; *Take Three Tenses: A Fugue in Time* by Rumer Godden; *Michael and All Angels* (in America, *The Golden Fleece*) by Norah Lofts; *Winter Quarters* by Pamela Hansford Johnson; *Who Killed Chloë?* by Margery Allingham; *The Case of the Weird Sisters* by Charlotte Armstrong.

Juvenile: *Johnny Tremain: A Novel for Young and Old* by U.S. author Esther Forbes, 52; *Those Happy Golden Years* by Laura Ingalls Wilder; *Thunderhead* by Mary O'Hara; *Little Navajo Bluebeard* by Ann Nolan Clark.

Painting: *The Thanksgiving Turkey* by Grandma Moses. Peggy Guggenheim presents the first display of paintings by Jackson Pollock beginning November 9 at her New York gallery.

Theater: *Dark Eyes* by Elena Miramova and Eugenia Leontovich 1/14 at New York's Belasco Theater, with Miramova, Leontovich, and Ludmilla Toretzka as three female Russian refugees trying to survive in New York, 174 perfs.; Madge Evans and Francis Reid in Sidney Kingsley's *The Patriots* 1/29 at New York's National Theater, 157 perfs.; *The Good Woman of Sechuan* (*Der gute Mensch von Sezuan*) by Bertolt Brecht 2/4 at Zurich's Schauspielhaus; Helen Hayes as Harriet Beecher Stowe in F. Ryerson and Cohn Claues's *Harriet* 3/3 at New York's Henry Miller Theater, 377 perfs.; (Beatrice) Joan Caulfield, 21, as Corliss Archer, Robert White as Dexter Perkins in F. Hugh Herbert's *Kiss and Tell* 3/17 at New York's Biltmore Theater, 103

perfs.; Shirley Booth, Ralph Bellamy, and Skippy Homeier in James Gow and Arnaud d'Usseau's *Tomorrow the World* 4/14 at New York's Ethel Barrymore Theater, 500 perfs.; Joyce Carey and Noël Coward in Coward's *Present Laughter* 4/29 at London's Haymarket Theatre, 38 perfs. (plus 528 beginning 4/16/47) and in Coward's *This Happy Breed* 4/30 at the same theater, alternating with *Present Laughter*; *Lovers and Friends* by Dodie Smith 11/29 at New York's Plymouth Theater, with Katharine Cornell, and Raymond Massey; Margaret Sullavan, Audrey Christie, and Elliott Nugent in John Van Druten's *The Voice of the Turtle* 12/8 at New York's Morosco Theater, 1,557 perfs.

Films: Roger Livesey and Scottish actress Deborah Kerr (Deborah Jane Kerr-Trimmer), 22, in Michael Powell and Emeric Pressburger's *The Life and Death of Colonel Blimp*; Jennifer Jones (originally Phyllis Isley), 24, in Henry King's *The Song of Bernadette*. Also: Joan Fontaine, Alexis Smith, and Charles Boyer in Edmund Goulding's *The Constant Nymph*; Pierre Fresnay and Ginette Leclerc in Henri-Georges Clouzot's *Le Corbeau*; Thorkild Roose and Lisbeth Movin in Carl Theodor Dreyer's *Day of Wrath*; Gary Cooper, Ingrid Bergman, and Greek actress Katina Paxinou, 43, in Sam Wood's *For Whom the Bell Tolls*; Gene Tierney and Don Ameche in Ernst Lubitsch's *Heaven Can Wait*; Walter Huston and Ann Harding (Dorothy Gatley), 42, in Michael Curtiz's *Mission to Moscow*; Loretta Young and Brian Aherne in Richard Wallace's *A Night to Remember*; Jane Russell, 22, in Howard Hughes's *The Outlaw* (Hughes designs a special brassiere that shows Russell's bosom to advantage); Teresa Wright, 24, and Joseph Cotten in Alfred Hitchcock's *Shadow of a Doubt*; Bette Davis and Paul Lukas in Herman Shumlin's *Watch on the Rhine*; Claire Trevor in George Archainbaud's *The Woman of the Town*.

Hollywood musicals: Joan Leslie, Fred Astaire, and Robert Benchley in Edward H. Griffith's *The Sky's the Limit* with Harold Arlen–Johnny Mercer songs that include "My Shining Hour" and "One for My Baby"; Dorothy Lamour and Bing Crosby in Edward Sutherland's *Dixie* with songs that include Jimmy Van Heusen and Johnny Mercer's "Sunday, Monday or Always."

Jane Froman entertains wounded servicemen in Europe but is seriously injured on a USO tour when her plane crashes into the Tagus River at Lisbon. Numerous operations, estimated to cost more than $500,000, restore the use of her legs and arms.

Broadway musicals: Ethel Merman in *Something for the Boys* 1/7 at the Alvin Theater, with a book by Harold and Dorothy Fields, Cole Porter songs that include "Hey, Good Lookin'," 422 perfs.; Celeste Holm and Alfred Drake in *Oklahoma!* 3/31 at the St. James Theater, with Rodgers and Hammerstein songs that include "Oh, What a Beautiful Morning," "People Will Say We're in Love," "Kansas City," "I Cain't Say No," "Pore Jud," "The Surrey with the Fringe on Top," and the title song (lyrics by Otto Harbach), 2,212 perfs.; Mary Martin and Kenny Baker in *One Touch of Venus* 10/7 at the Imperial Theater, with Kurt Weill–Ogden Nash songs that include "Speak Low" and "West Wind," 567 perfs.; Muriel Smith in *Carmen Jones* 12/2 at the Broadway Theater, with music by Georges Bizet, book and lyrics by Oscar Hammerstein II, 503 perfs.

Popular songs: "You'd Be So Nice to Come Home To" by Cole Porter (for the film *Something to Shout About*); "They're Either Too Young or Too Old" by Arthur Schwartz and Frank Loesser (for the film *Thank Your Lucky Stars*); "No Love, No Nothin'," by Harry Warren and Leo Robin (for the film *The Gang's All Here*).

Opera: U.S. soprano Patrice Munsell, 18, makes her Metropolitan Opera debut 12/4 singing the role of Philine in the 1866 Ambroise Thomas opera *Mignon*.

English jockey Judy Johnson rides Lone Gallant to a 10th-place finish April 27 in a steeplechase field of 11 horses at Baltimore's Pimlico racetrack. She is the first woman steeplechase rider at a major U.S. track.

Pauline Betz wins in women's singles at Forest Hills.

New York madam Polly Adler, now 43, is arrested in January, but she is ill with pleurisy and charges are dismissed (*see* 1935). She retires to the Los Angeles area (*see* Nonfiction, 1952).

Americans are told to "use it up, wear it out, make it do or do without." Shoes are rationed beginning February 7, but while Britons are allowed only one pair per year, the U.S. ration is three pairs, only slightly below the 3.43 bought on average in 1941.

Sneakers are impossible to find; schoolgirls have to buy shoes with reclaimed rubber soles that leave black marks on gymnasium floors.

Rubber, metal, paper, silk, and nylon are all collected for recycling; housewives wash and flatten tins for recycling and save kitchen fats to be exchanged for red ration points at the butcher's (*see* below).

Tobacco heiress Doris Duke, who received the last installment of her father's estate, estimated at $17 million, when she turned 30 in November of last year, obtains a Reno divorce from James H. R. Cromwell October 21. Cromwell contests the divorce in a New Jersey court on grounds that she was not a bona fide resident of Nevada (*see* 1940; 1944).

Rent controls (above) prevent landlords from raising rents by more than a small percentage each year and will be a factor in discouraging new housing construction in New York.

Rationing of canned foods in the United States begins March 1. Meat rationing (canned meat and fish are included) begins March 29, but the ration is 28 ounces per week, and meat production rises by 50 percent. Meat consumption actually rises to 128.9 pounds per capita on an annual basis as the wartime economic boom puts more money into working people's pockets and as meat prices are rolled back to September 1942 levels.

An estimated 20 percent of U.S. beef goes into black market channels, bacon virtually disappears from stores, western cattle rustlers kill and dress beef in mobile slaughterhouses and sell the meat to packinghouses, and wholesalers force butchers to buy hearts, kidneys, lungs, and tripe in order to get good cuts of meat.

Butchers upgrade meat, selling low grades at ceiling prices and at the ration-point levels of top grade.

Less than one-fourth of Americans have "good" diets, according to a nutrition study undertaken in 1941.

75 percent of U.S. white bread is enriched with iron and some B vitamins, up from 30 percent in 1941.

Sale of butter, lard, fats, and oils is halted for a week beginning March 21. Average annual butter consumption falls to 11 pounds per capita, down from 17 pounds in the 1930s, as Americans forgo some of their 4-ounces-per-week ration in order to save red stamps for meat. Butter is often unavailable, since most butterfat is employed to make cheese for Lend-Lease aid.

U.S. margarine is subject to a 10 percent federal tax if artificially colored (25¢ per pound if colored by the consumer or used uncolored). Millions of housewives use vegetable dye to color their white margarine yellow, but as more consumers turn to margarine, Eleanor Roosevelt campaigns for a repeal of the margarine tax.

Sale of sliced bread is banned by Agriculture Secretary Claude Wickard in a move to hold down prices.

Flour and fish join the list of rationed foods, but coffee is derationed in July. Americans eat far better than do citizens of the other belligerent nations (Britons enjoy only about two-thirds of what Americans are allowed under rationing programs).

U.S. chemist Russell E. Marker, 41, pioneers development of oral contraceptives with the discovery of diosgenin, a chemical whose molecular structure is almost a match for that of the female hormone progesterone (*see* 1934). Using an extract from the root of the barbasco plant, a member of the Dioscorea family that grows wild in Mexico, Marker works in a Mexico City pottery shop, produces 2,000 grams of synthetic progesterone worth $80 per gram in just 2 months, and will join with a small Mexican drug firm to form Syntex, S.A. Another group of chemists will buy him out, but Syntex will become a major supplier of raw materials for oral contraceptives (*see* Pincus, 1955; Enovid 10, 1960).

1944

Moscow and Helsinki end hostilities under terms of a treaty negotiated by Soviet diplomat Aleksandra Kollontai, now 72 (*see* 1917).

German occupation forces in Hungary capture patriot Hannah Senesh, 23, who has volunteered with five young men to parachute behind enemy lines on a suicidal rescue mission. A native Hungarian who emigrated to Palestine in 1939 to fulfill her Zionist dreams, she has kept a diary since age 13. She is executed along with her comrades.

Allied invasion forces land in Normandy June 6 (D-Day) and are soon pushing back German units. Tech. Sgt. Mabel Carney, 26, of the Women's Army Corps is the first U.S. woman in Normandy after the landing. French women who have consorted with enemy occupiers are shorn of their hair as the Germans retreat. By September, the U.S. 1st Army under Gen. Omar Bradley has breached the Siegfried Line and is fighting on German soil.

Remote-controlled German V-1 (Vengeance) rockets have hit London beginning June 12 and are succeeded September 8 by faster and deadlier V-2 rockets, which also hit Antwerp, killing hundreds of women as well as men.

More than 20,000 Japanese civilians on Saipan, including thousands of women and children, commit suicide with hand grenades and jump off 150-meter cliffs July 8 as U.S. troops complete their conquest of the Marianas island. To be captured would be a disgrace, they have been told, and only 1,000 surrender July 9. B-29s begin daylight raids on Tokyo from Saipan November 24, killing many more women and children.

Washington wit Alice Roosevelt Longworth says of New York Governor Thomas E. Dewey, a diminutive man with black hair, black moustache, and a faint smile, "How do you expect people to vote for a man who looks like a bridegroom on a wedding cake?" Republican Dewey loses his bid to defeat Longworth's cousin, Franklin D. Roosevelt, who wins an unprecedented fourth term in the November presidential election.

Helen Gahagan Douglas wins election to Congress from Los Angeles's 14th Congressional District and is appointed to the House Foreign Affairs Committee. She will be reelected in 1946 and 1948, both times by wide margins (*see* 1939; 1950).

The U.S. Senate rises to its feet December 19 to pay tribute to Sen. Hattie Carraway (R. Ark.), who has been defeated by Rep. William Fulbright, 39, for the seat she has held since 1932.

The Union of Italian Women (*Unione delle Donne Italiane*, or UDI) founded late in the year attracts anti-Fascists of all political stripes to continue the spirit of the Resistance (*see* 1943).

 Arabs riot at Damascus May 26 as Syria permits women to remove their veils in public.

Women and children are locked inside a church by Nazi SS troops at the French town of Oradour-sur-Glane June 10 while their men are shot in retaliation for the capture of an SS officer by the resistance. Fires are started on the church altar, and when the women try to escape they are shot by the Germans, who poke their guns through the windows to fire on those inside. Some 642 people are massacred.

Amsterdam Jew Otto Frank and his family are betrayed to the Gestapo August 4 after more than 2 years in hiding and deported with eight others in the last convoy of cattle trucks to the extermination camp at Auschwitz. Local housewife Miep Gies and her husband, Jan, have kept the Frank family in a camouflaged annex above Frank's small pectin trading company offices, where Mrs. Gies has been employed. Frank's daughter Anne, 15, has her head shaved at Auschwitz (the Reich uses women's hair for packing around U-boat pipe joints and for other purposes), but is not gassed. She will be shipped to the Bergen-Belsen concentration camp and die there in March of next year, probably of typhus, but three notebooks left behind at 263 Prinsengracht in Amsterdam will be found to contain her diary, chronicling the period in which she and her family hid from the Gestapo.

French women gain the right to vote on the same basis as men under terms of a new enfranchisement bill.

 The Japanese Girls' Volunteer Corps of high school girls, organized in January to create a new pool of factory workers, relieves Japanese men for active military service. The law is changed in March to recruit unmarried girls and women aged 12 to 40; any who refuse to work in industry are subject to 1 year's imprisonment and a fine of £1,000. Some 472,000 girls are employed 15 hours per day in the Volunteer Corps, many of them on night shifts, and women in the workforce total 2,256,000, a figure that will grow by next year to 3,130,000.

 The Harvard-IBM Mark I Automatic Sequence Controlled Calculator is the first automatic, general-purpose digital computer. It has 760,000 parts and 500 miles of wire, requires 4 seconds to perform a simple multiplication and 11 seconds for a simple division, and is subject to frequent breakdown, but the U.S. Navy assigns WAVES lieutenant Grace Brewster (Hopper), 38, to develop operating programs for the massive contraption, and she is the third person to program it (*see* 1952).

The Psychology of Women, Volume I: Girlhood by Austro-Hungarian-American Freudian analyst Helene Deutsch (*née* Rosenbach), 59, provides physicians with a theoretical basis for the long-standing belief that the center of a woman's mental and emotional life lies in her reproductive organs.

Childbirth Without Fear: The Principles and Practices of Natural Childbirth by Grantly Dick-Read is published in America and attracts new believers to the idea that giving birth without anesthesia can be only minimally painful and can actually be a spiritual experience (*see* 1942). Critics scoff that natural childbirth is a metaphysical idea, not a scientific one, and most U.S. women continue to be delivered under at least some anesthesia (*see* Lamaze, 1951).

Quadruplets are delivered by cesarean section for the first time November 1 at Philadelphia.

The first operation to save a "blue baby" is performed November 9 at Baltimore's Johns Hopkins Children's Hospital by surgeon Alfred Blalock, 45, who proceeds on the premise advanced by his colleague Helen Taussig, 46, that anoxemia can be cured by bypassing the pulmonary artery. Prevented by a congenital pulmonary artery defect from getting enough blood into their lungs, many infants have been born blue, grown progressively weaker, and either died or been doomed to chronic invalidism. The surgical technique developed by Blalock and Taussig will permit blue babies to live normal lives (and have normal color).

∞ Evangelist Aimee Semple McPherson dies of a sleeping powder overdose at Oakland September 27 at age 54 (*see* 1926). Despite accusations of adultery, alcoholism, fraud, hypocrisy, perjury, grand theft, and physical assault, she has never been convicted, and an estimated 45,000 weeping mourners file past her coffin between October 6 and 8. She is buried with great ceremony October 9.

Seventeen magazine begins publication in September. Publishing heir Walter H. Annenberg, 36, has started the periodical for young girls.

Nonfiction: *Anything Can Happen* by U.S. writer Helen Papashvily (*née* Waite), 38, is an account of her husband's immigration from Soviet Georgia in 1923 and his comic 20-year process of Americanization.

Fiction: *Winter Tales* by Isak Dinesen; *The Ballad and the Source* by Rosamond Lehmann; *For Love Alone* by Christina Stead; *Elders and Betters* by Ivy Compton-Burnett; *There Were No Windows* by Norah Hoult; *Love on the Supertax* by English novelist-critic Marghanita Laski, 29; *The Leaning Tower, and Other Stories* by Katherine Anne Porter; *Boston Adventure* by U.S. novelist–short story writer Jean Stafford, 29; *Green Dolphin Street* by English novelist Elizabeth Goudge, 44; *The Women on the Porch* by Caroline Gordon; *Lusty Wind for Carolina* by U.S. novelist Inglis Fletcher, 56; *Lebanon* by Caroline Miller; *Dragonwyck* by U.S. novelist Anya Seton, 28; *Alina* by journalist-novelist Martha Gellhorn; *While We Still Love* (in England, *The Unconquerable*) by Helen MacInnes; *Jassy* by Norah Lofts; *Strange Fruit* by U.S. novelist Lillian Smith, 46, is about a lynching in a racially segregated Georgia town in the years following World War I (its realistic language and ironic treatment of miscegenation, sexuality, and abortion cause an uproar, and the book is banned by Boston's Watch and Ward Society); *Conduct Yourself Accordingly* by Margaret Culkin Banning.

Poetry: *Teijo kushu* by Japanese *haiku* poet Teijo Nakamura (*née* Hamako), 44; *Beast in View* by Muriel Rukeyser.

Juvenile: *The Park Book* by U.S. author Charlotte Zolotow (*née* Shapiro), 29, with illustrations by H. A. Rey.

Painting: *Pelvis III* by Georgia O'Keeffe.

Sculpture: *Landscape Sculpture* (wood) by Barbara Hepworth; *Wendell L. Willkie* (bust) by Melvina Hoffman.

Theater: Georgia Burke in Edward Chodorov's *Decision* 2/2 at New York's Belasco Theater, a melodrama about fascism in America and U.S. race relations, 160 perfs.; *The Searching Wind* by Lillian Hellman 4/12 at New York's Fulton Theater, with Cornelia Otis Skinner, now 42, Dudley Digges, Montgomery Clift, 318 perfs.; Hilda Simons and Canada Lee in Philip Yordan's *Anna Lucasta* 8/30 at New York's Mansfield Theater (Ruby Dee, now 16, will join the cast in 1946), 957 perfs.; *I Remember Mama* by John Van Druten (who has adapted Kathryn Farber's book *Mama's Bank Account*) 10/19 at New York's Music Box Theater, with Mady Christians, Frances Heflin, Joan Tetzel, Marlon Brando, and Oscar Homolka, 714 perfs.; *Harvey* by U.S. playwright Mary Coyle Chase, 37, 11/1 at New York's 48th Street Theater, with Frank Fay, 1,775 perfs. (Pulitzer Prize); Alfred Lunt and Lynn Fontanne in Terence Rattigan's *O Mistress Mine* (*Love in Idleness*) 12/20 at London's Lyric Theatre (it will move to Broadway in January and run for 451 perfs., giving the Lunts their biggest success).

Films: Jean-Louis Barrault and Arletty (Léonie Barhiat), 46, in Marcel Carné's *Children of Paradise* (*Les Enfants du Paradis*); Barbara Stanwyck and Fred MacMurray in Billy Wilder's *Double Indemnity*; Eddie Bracken, Ella Raines (originally Raubes), and William Demarest in Preston Sturges's *Hail the Conquering Hero*; Clifton Webb, Gene Tierney, and Dana Andrews in Otto Preminger's *Laura*; Eddie Bracken and Betty Hutton in Preston Sturges's *The Miracle of Morgan's Creek*; Mickey Rooney and Elizabeth Taylor, 12, in Clarence Brown's *National Velvet*. Also: Cary Grant, Priscilla Lane (originally Mullican), 27, Josephine Hull, Raymond Massey, and Peter Lorre in Frank Capra's *Arsenic and Old Lace*; Tallulah Bankhead, William Bendix, and Walter Slezak in Alfred Hitchcock's *Lifeboat*; Claudette Colbert, Jennifer Jones, and Joseph Cotten in John Cromwell's *Since You Went Away*;

Charles Laughton and Ella Raines in Robert Siodmak's *The Suspect*; Robert Newton, Celia Johnson, 36, and John Mills in David Lean's *This Happy Breed*; Fredric March, Betty Field, Skippy Homeier, and Agnes Moorehead in Leslie Fenton's *Tomorrow the World*; Swedish actress Mai Zetterling, 19, and Stig Jarrel in Alf Sjöberg's *Torment*; Alexander Knox, Charles Coburn, and Irish-born actress Geraldine Fitzgerald, 29, in Henry King's *Wilson*; Joan Bennett and Edward G. Robinson in Fritz Lang's *The Woman in the Window*.

Hollywood musicals: Judy Garland in Vincente Minnelli's *Meet Me in St. Louis* with Hugh Martin–Ralph Blane songs that include "The Trolley Song," "The Boy Next Door," the title song, and "Have Yourself a Merry Little Christmas"; Rita Hayworth and Gene Kelly in Charles Vidor's *Cover Girl* with Jerome Kern–Ira Gershwin songs that include "Long Ago (and Far Away)"; Gene Kelly and Deanna Durbin in Robert Siodmak's *Christmas Holiday* with Frank Loesser songs that include "Spring Will Be a Little Late This Year."

Dale Evans (originally Frances Octavia Smith), 32, teams up with singing star Roy Rogers (who will marry her in 1948) in the film *The Cowboy and the Senorita*. She will become known as the queen of the westerns.

Ballet: Martha Graham in *Appalachian Spring* 10/30 at the Library of Congress in Washington, D.C., with music by Aaron Copland; Graham in *Herodiade* 10/30 at the Library of Congress, with music by Paul Hindemith.

Opera: Swedish soprano (Märta) Birgit Nilsson (Svensson), 26, makes her debut at Stockholm's Royal Opera, singing the role of Agathe in the 1821 von Weber opera *Der Freischutz* as did Jenny Lind in 1838; U.S. mezzo-soprano Blanche Thebom, 26, makes her Metropolitan Opera debut 12/14 as Wotan's wife, Fricka, in the 1870 Wagner opera *Die Walküre*.

Indian singer Madurai Shanmukhavadivu Subbulakshmi, 27, gains international fame with her appearance at the All-India Music and Dance Conference at Bombay.

"Bricktop," now 49, opens a Mexico City café with backing from tobacco heiress Doris Duke (*see* 1925; 1949).

Broadway musicals: Bobby Clark and June Havoc in *Mexican Hayride* 1/28 at the Winter Garden Theater, with a book by Herbert and Dorothy Fields, Cole Porter songs that include "Count Your Blessings," 481 perfs.; Celeste Holm as Evalina in *Bloomer Girl* 10/5 at the Shubert Theater, with Harold Arlen–Yip Harburg songs that include "Evalina" and "It Was Good Enough for Grandma," 653 perfs.; dancer Sono Osato, Betty Comden, 25, Adolph Green, and Nancy Walker in *On the Town* 12/28 at the Adelphi Theater, with music by Leonard Bernstein, dances derived from the ballet *Fancy Free*, 563 perfs.

Popular songs: U.S. vocalist Margaret Whiting, 20, records "Moonlight in Vermont" (her late father, songwriter Richard Whiting, died in February 1938, and Johnny Mercer, his last regular collaborator, has encouraged her to pursue her singing career); Billie Holiday records "Lover Man"; The Andrews Sisters record "Rum and Coca-Cola" by Jeri Sullivan and Paul Barron, lyrics by comedian Morey Amsterdam; Anita O'Day records "And Her Tears Flowed like Wine" with the Stan Kenton band, has an immediate hit, briefly rejoins the Gene Krupa band, and then goes on her own; "Jealous Heart" by Nashville country music singer Jenny Lou Carson; "Linda" by Ann Ronell; "Candy" by Mack Davis, Joan Whitney, and Alex Kramer; "You Always Hurt the One You Love" by Robert Allan and Doris Fisher; former Newark Baptist Church choir singer Sarah (Lois) Vaughan, 20, who won an amateur contest at Harlem's Apollo Theater 2 years ago, records "I'll Wait and Pray" 12/31 with Billy Eckstine's big band to begin a notable career.

Pauline Betz wins in women's singles at Forest Hills.

A New Jersey court rules May 10 that tobacco heiress Doris Duke's Nevada divorce is invalid and constitutes a fraud on the judicial system, but a New York judge upholds the Nevada divorce in November and charges James H. R. Cromwell with fraud, deception, and extortion. Duke, heiress Barbara Hutton, Gloria Vanderbilt, and Thelma, Lady Furness (twin sister of Gloria's mother, who had a long affair with the duke of Windsor before he married Wallis Simpson), are all dropped from the New York social register (*see* 1947).

A gunman connected with the French Resistance opens fire on screen star Danielle Darrieux as she rides in a car soon after the liberation of Paris August 25. Her husband, Porfirio Rubirosa, is hit in the kidney but recovers (*see* 1942; 1947).

President Roosevelt has his campaign train diverted to a stop in New Jersey, where he visits his old friend Lucy Mercer Rutherford, whose husband has recently died.

 A gang of white youths at Abbeville, Ala., abducts and rapes Recy Taylor, 24, a black wife and mother. One member of the gang confesses and names his accomplices, but prosecutors cannot find a grand jury that will hand down an indictment. A National Committee for Equal Justice distributes pamphlets written by a reporter and a prominent black writer suggesting that the youths believed they would not be punished and that white women are only slightly safer than black women from such attacks.

 U.S. meat rationing ends May 3.

 Moscow publishes edicts in the summer aimed at replacing the millions of war dead suffered by the nation. The edicts reward mothers with cash payments that increase according to the number of their children, confer decorations on those with especially large families, and erect obstacles to divorce.

1945

German test pilot Hanna Reitsch, 33, flies high-ranking officers into Berlin in April, eluding Allied forces that surround the city. Her exploits have won her the Iron Cross, but although Adolf Hitler approved her proposal to train women suicide pilots of rockets aimed at British targets, the plan was abandoned last year after D-Day. Her plan to organize a squadron of women fliers to fight on the same terms as the men of the Luftwaffe was rejected out of hand.

U.S. troops land on Okinawa in April. Some 143 Japanese high school girls and their 15 teachers have organized a nursing corps to treat wounded soldiers but have been pushed back to Miwa village at the southern end of the island, where they commit suicide with poison gas in a cave in order to avoid capture.

World War II ends in Europe May 7 as Germany agrees to unconditional surrender. Adolf Hitler has committed suicide at age 56 in his Berlin bunker April 30 along with his mistress, Eva Braun, 33, who has married him the night before. Japan sues for peace August 10 after U.S. nuclear devices are exploded over Hiroshima and Nagasaki. The war has killed an estimated 54.8 million people (most of them civilians in the Soviet Union, Germany, China, and Japan), and many millions more are left crippled, blind, mutilated, homeless, widowed, orphaned, and impoverished.

Anne O'Hare McCormick of the *New York Times* talks to a Frenchwoman who is clearing away bomb rubble that is smothering her kitchen garden: "Who's to save the cabbages and onions if I don't?" the woman tells her. "They're all that's left of all the work of all my life. And somebody has to begin clearing away this mess."

President Roosevelt has died of a cerebal hemorrhage April 12 at age 63, just hours after posing in his Warm Springs, Georgia, cottage for a portrait by painter Elizabeth Shumatoff that his longtime friend Lucy Mercer Rutherford has arranged. Eleanor Roosevelt is recalled from a meeting of the Thrift Club in Philadelphia and told in Washington of her husband's death.

A San Francisco meeting to discuss the formation of an international body to be called the United Nations has delegates that include Australian feminist Lady Jessie Mary Grey Street, 56.

Lady Astor, now 65, retires from Parliament after having been repeatedly returned since her first election in 1919.

Russian Orthodox nun Maria Skobtsova, 53, goes to the gas chamber at the the Ravensbrück concentration camp on the eve of Easter. Having fled the excesses of Bolshevism in her homeland, she became a nun in 1932 despite twice having been married and divorced, worked to house and feed French derelicts, gave succor to Jews in wartime Paris, and was arrested in 1943 and sent to Ravensbrück. It will be said that she went to her death voluntarily "in order to help her companions die."

Italian, Greek, Hungarian, Yugoslavian, Irish, Guatemalan, and Senegalese women gain the right to vote on the same basis as men.

Japanese feminist Iusae Ichikawa, now 52, organizes the Confederation of New Japanese Women with objectives that include clean elections and political education for women (*see* 1919).

Japanese women gain voting rights December 15 under terms of a new election law passed by the Diet under pressure from Allied occupation authorities (*see* 1946).

Nearly half of all U.S. women, including 1.47 million mothers of young children, have held a job at some time during the war, working in offices, factories, shipyards, and shops. Washington has told women that victory could not be achieved without their entry into the work force (but has also said, "Now, as in peacetime, a mother's primary duty is to her home and children"). Some 250,000 have worked in plants making electrical equipment, 100,000 on production lines producing ammunition, 300,000 in aircraft plants, 150,000 in shipyard jobs as riveters, welders, and crane operators. More than half of all female workers have for the first time in history been married women, and columnist Max Lerner has expressed fears that the war has created a "new Amazon" who will "outdrink, outswear, and outswagger the men."

U.S. women lose their jobs as men return from the war and reclaim positions they left when they joined the service, but the number of women in the work force has climbed from 14 million to 19 million and will never again fall to 14 million (although most women workers are from families with below-average incomes).

The nuclear devices exploded over Hiroshima and Nagasaki (above) have been developed in a U.S. crash program called the Manhattan Project. Chinese-American physicist Chien-shiung Wu, 33, at Columbia worked out a method last year for producing large quantities of fissionable uranium and perfected an improved Geiger counter. Physicist Leona Libby (*née* Marshall), 26, helped construct the first thermal column. She will design and build the first nuclear reactor and invent an advanced analytical machine—the rotating neutron spectrometer.

Britain's Royal Society agrees for the first time to elect women fellows. Crystallographer Kathleen Lonsdale, who served a month in prison during the war for refusing to pay a fine imposed on women who did not register for civil defense or other national service in 1939 (she was a convinced pacifist), becomes the first female fellow (*see* 1929).

The Psychology of Women, Volume II: Motherhood by Babette Deutsch expands on the theories expounded in last year's book. She presents the image of the masochistic, hysterical female who fantasizes about being raped to such a degree that "even the most experienced judges are misled in trials of innocent men accused of rape."

The American Cancer Society is created by a renaming of the American Society for the Control of Cancer, founded in 1913.

Hospital deliveries account for 79 percent of U.S. births, up from 37 percent in 1935. Cesarean deliveries have increased significantly.

Former British M.P. Ellen Cicely Wilkinson, 54, is appointed the nation's first woman minister of education in the new Labour government of Prime Minister Clement Atlee. A member of the Communist party from 1920 until her first election to Parliament in 1924, she has been an outspoken feminist.

Former *Woman's Home Companion* war correspondent Doris Fleeson, 44, becomes the first syndicated woman political columnist, wearing white gloves and a Sally Victor hat as she covers Washington, going to the White House every day, and covering politics like a police reporter. United Features Syndicate places her column in more than 100 papers around the country.

Nonfiction: *The Egg and I* by U.S. writer Betsy Bard McDonald, 37, has sales of 1 million copies its first year; the author quit her art studies at the University of Washington in 1927 to marry an insurance salesman, he took her to a chicken ranch on the Olympic Peninsula, and they split in 1931; *Home to India* by Madras-born U.S. writer Santha Rama Rau, 22, whose mother, now 52, is a leader of India's women's movement; *Mme. Pompadour* (biography) by English writer Nancy (Freeman) Mitford, 40.

Fiction: *La Douleur* by French novelist Marguerite Duras (Marguerite Donnadieu), 31, who has worked for the Resistance during the war; *The Axe Is Behind the Cupboard* (*Bak skapet star øksen*) (stories about life under German occupation and the girlfriends [*tysketøser*] of German soldiers) by Norwegian writer Torborg Nedreaas, 39; *Krane's Café* (*Kranes konditori*) by Cora Sandel; *At Mrs. Lippincote's* by English novelist Elizabeth Taylor (*née* Coles), 33, whose husband, John, a candy factory director, has been through the war with the RAF; *The Pursuit of Love* by Nancy Mitford (above); *The Ghostly Lover* by U.S. novelist Elizabeth Hardwick, 29; *The Demon Lover* by Elizabeth Bowen; *The House in Clewe Street* by Mary Lavin; *The Trojan Brothers* by Pamela Hansford Johnson; *The Little Company* by Eleanor Dark; *The Friendly Persuasion* by U.S. novelist Jessamyn West, 43; *The Forests of the South* by Caroline Gordon; *Mexican Village* by Mexican-American novelist Josefina Maria Niglia, 35; *Forever Amber* by U.S. novelist Kathleen Winsor, 29; *The Yellow Room* by Mary Roberts Rinehart, now 69; *Horizon* by Helen MacInnes; *Pearls Before Swine* by Margery Allingham; *The Innocent Flower* by Charlotte Armstrong.

Poetry: *A Street in Bronzeville* by Chicago poet Gwendolyn Brooks, 28.

German graphic artist Käthe Kollwitz dies outside Dresden at Moritzburg Castle April 22 at age 77.

Sculpture: *Portrait* by French sculptor Germaine Richier, 41, who has spent the war years at Zurich.

Theater: Laurette Taylor, Eddie Dowling, Julie Haydon, and Anthony Rose in Tennessee Williams's *The Glass Menagerie* 3/31 at New York's Plymouth Theater, 561 perfs. (Margo Jones, 31, has directed the play); Betty Field (Mrs. Elmer Rice) and Wendell Corey in Rice's *Dream Girl* 12/14 at New York's Coronet Theater, 348 perfs.

Films: Judith Anderson, British actress June Duprez, 27, Barry Fitzgerald, Walter Huston, and Louis Hayward in René Clair's *And Then There Were None*; Mervyn Johns, Roland Culver, Michael Redgrave, Sally Ann Howes, and British actress Googie (*née* Georgette) Withers, 28, in Cavalcanti, Basil Dearden, Robert Hamer, and Charles Crichton's *Dead of Night*; Ray Milland and Jane Wyman (originally Sarah Jane Fulks), 31, in Billy Wilder's *The Lost Weekend*; Zachary Scott and Betty Field in Jean

Renoir's *The Southerner*; Robert Montgomery and Donna Reed (originally Mullenger), 23, in John Ford's *They Were Expendable*; Dorothy McGuire, 25, and Joan Blondell, 35, in Elia Kazan's *A Tree Grows in Brooklyn*. Also: Gene Tierney, John Hodiak, and William Bendix in Henry King's *A Bell for Adano*; Margaret Rutherford (*née* Taylor), 52, Rex Harrison, and Constance Cummings (originally Halverstadt), 34, in David Lean's *Blithe Spirit*; Judy Garland and Robert Walker in Vincente Minnelli's *The Clock,* which celebrates the quick courtships of wartime couples; Bette Davis in Irving Rapper's *The Corn Is Green*; William Eythe, Lloyd Nolan, and Swedish actress Signe Hasso (originally Larsson), 35, in Henry Hathaway's *The House on 92nd Street*; Joan Crawford, Jack Carson, Zachary Scott, and Ann Blyth, now 17, in Michael Curtiz's *Mildred Pierce*; Gracie Fields and Monty Woolley in Lewis Seiler's *Molly and Me*; Edward G. Robinson and Margaret (originally Angela Maxine) O'Brien, 7, in Roy Rowland's *Our Vines Have Tender Grapes*; English actress Ann Todd, 36, and James Mason in Compton Bennett's *The Seventh Veil*; Ingrid Bergman and Gregory Peck in Alfred Hitchcock's *Spellbound*.

Hollywood musicals: Jeanne Crain, 19, and Dana Andrews in Walter Lang's *State Fair* with Rodgers and Hammerstein songs that include "It Might as Well Be Spring" and "It's a Grand Night for Singing."

Stage musicals: *Up in Central Park* 1/27 at New York's Century Theater, with music by Sigmund Romberg, book by Dorothy Fields, now 39, and her brother Herbert, lyrics by Dorothy Fields, 504 perfs.; Jan Clayton as Julie Jordan and John Raitt as Billy Bigelow (Liliom) in *Carousel* 4/19 at New York's Majestic Theater, with Rodgers and Hammerstein songs that include "If I Loved You," "June Is Bustin' Out All Over," "Soliloquy," and "You'll Never Walk Alone," 890 perfs.; Ivor Novello, Muriel Barron, and Margaret Rutherford in *Perchance to Dream* 4/21 at the London Hippodrome, with book, music, and lyrics by Novello, 1,022 perfs.; Joyce Grenfell, Madge Elliott, and Cyril Ritchard in *Sigh No More* (revue) 8/22 at London's Piccadilly Theatre, with music and lyrics by Noël Coward, 213 perfs.; Cicely Courtneidge in *Under the Counter* 11/22 at London's Phoenix Theatre, with songs by Manning Sherwin and Harold

Purcell; Joan McCracken, Mitzi Green, and Bill Talbert in *Billion-Dollar Baby* 12/21 at New York's Alvin Theater, with music by Morton Gould, lyrics by Betty Comden and Adolph Green, 219 perfs.

Ballet: Cuban ballerina Alicia Alonso (Alicia Ernestina de la Caridad del Cobre Martínez Hoya), 23, and Hugh Laing in *Undertow* 4/10 at New York's Metropolitan Opera House, with music by William Schuman, choreography by Antony Tudor.

Opera: Joan Cross, now 44, creates the role of Ellen Orford, Edith Coates is Auntie in the Benjamin Britten opera *Peter Grimes,* which has its premiere 6/7 at Sadler's Wells Theatre, London; U.S. soprano Maria Callas (originally Cecilia Sophia Anna Maria Kalogeropoulos), 21, makes her debut at the Athens Royal Opera singing the role of Martha in the 1903 d'Albert opera *Tiefland*; U.S. soprano Dorothy Kirsten, 28, makes her Metropolitan Opera debut singing the role of Mimi in the 1896 Puccini opera *La Bohème.*

Popular songs: Louisville-born jazz and blues singer Helen Humes, 32, records "Be-Ba-Ba-Le-Ba."

Sarah Cooke wins in women's singles at Forest Hills.

Woolworth heiress Barbara Hutton obtains a legal separation from actor Cary Grant February 15. Uunlike her previous husbands, he asks not a cent in settlement (*see* 1942; 1947).

Heiress Gloria Vanderbilt turns 21 February 20, inherits $4,748,000, obtains a legal divorce 2 months later from her husband Pat Di Cicco, now 35, and elopes the next day to Mexico, where she marries London-born conductor Leopold Stokowski, 63 (*see* 1941; 1955).

Teen-aged U.S. girls in many cities have flirted with soldiers at bus stations, engaged in prostitution, and formed gangs called "wolf packs" in the absence of fathers who are in military service and mothers who hold jobs.

Some 85 percent of U.S. bread is commercially baked, up from 66 percent in 1939.

Tupperware Corp. is founded by former E. I. DuPont chemist Earl W. Tupper, who has designed plastic refrigerator bowls and canisters with a patented seal that prevents leaking, as he will demonstrate at Tupperware Home Parties.

Le Cordon Bleu reopens at 24 rue du Champs de Mars near Les Invalides in Paris under the direction of Belgian entrepreneur Mme. Elizabeth Brassard after having been closed by the war (*see* 1934). Brassard will run the school for more than 30 years, and her students will include Audrey Hepburn and Julia Child (*see* 1961).

U.S. butter rationing ends November 23.

1946

Puerto Rican political activist Felisa Rincón de Gautier, 49, is elected mayor of San Juan after a 14-year career of urging other women to get involved in politics. She will develop a child care center and work to improve the city's housing, sanitation, health, and education.

Emily Greene Balch, now 79, is a co-winner of the Nobel Peace Prize, sharing it with U.S. religious leader and social worker John R. Mott, 81.

 Japanese women vote for the first time April 10 (*see* 1945); 83 women stand for election to the Diet, 39 win seats. A new Japanese Constitution, adopted November 3, expands women's rights (*see* Equal Rights Amendment, 1947).

Italian women vote on the same basis as men for the first time as the nation ends its monarchy and becomes a republic.

Women in Palestine, Kenya, Liberia, and Vietnam gain the right to vote on the same basis as men.

Mexican women gain the right to vote in municipal elections (*see* 1935; 1953).

France's "Loi Marthe Richard" closes Paris brothels following a campaign by Assemblywoman Richard, 58, who has deplored the enslavement of women in houses of prostitution. She became the sixth woman in the world to fly an airplane 34 years ago, served as a spy in World War I and stole the German plan for U-boat attacks on U.S. troopship convoys from the bedroom of naval attaché Hans von Krohn in Spain. Her legislation does not outlaw prostitution, but bordellos are no longer licensed, medical examinations are dropped, and demimondaines have to solicit in the streets.

The U.S. Office of Price Administration (OPA) expires June 29 when the president vetoes a Compromise Price Control act; Congress revives the OPA July 25 with a new Price Control act.

Canada institutes family allowances (*see* Britain, 1945). Sales of children's shoes jump from 762,000 pairs per month to 1,180,000 as parents receive financial aid.

High meat prices bring demands that President Truman resign, but prices soften when the government withdraws from the market in the summer, and prices break when the OPA (above) removes price ceilings in the fall.

Meat price controls end October 15, and President Truman issues an executive order November 9 lifting all wage and price controls except those on rents, sugar, and rice.

The U.S. inflation that will continue for decades begins December 14 as President Truman removes curbs on housing priorities and prices by executive order. President Roosevelt's inflation control order of April 1943 kept prices from climbing more than 29 percent from 1939 to 1945 as compared with a 63 percent jump in the 1914 to 1918 period, but Truman is more worried about a possible postwar depression than about inflation.

London's Brook Street Bureau has its beginnings in a Mayfair agency started by local entrepreneur Margery Hurst (*née* Berney), 33, to supply secretaries on a daily basis. She will establish schools for administrative and secretarial workers as her company grows to have 200 branches in the United Kingdom, Canada, the United States, Australia, and Hong Kong.

Japanese women form an organization to protect women from occupation-force authorities who pick up women in the street and subject them to examination for sexually transmitted diseases.

The Common Sense Book of Baby and Child Care by New York psychiatrist Benjamin Spock, 43, will be used to raise a generation of children along permissive lines of behavioral standards. It will be retitled *Baby and Child Care* and become an all-time best seller.

"Mother Cabrini" is canonized at Rome July 7 and becomes America's first saint (*see* 1889). She was naturalized in 1909 and died at Chicago in December 1917 at age 67.

Colleges and universities throughout the world struggle to cope with swollen enrollments after years in which many have gone bankrupt or come close. U.S. college enrollments reach an all-time high of more than 2 million as returning veterans crowd classrooms with help from the G.I. Bill of Rights.

The *New York Herald-Tribune* appoints reporter Marguerite Higgins, 25, bureau chief of its Berlin office.

Elle, a new fashion magazine that will challenge *Vogue* and *Harper's Bazaar*, begins publication at Paris under the direction of former film scriptwriter Françoise Giroud, 30, and Hélène Lazareff. Giroud has served time in prison for her Resistance activities during the Nazi occupation (*see L'Express*, 1953).

Family Circle magazine begins monthly publication in September after 14 years as a weekly supermarket giveaway. The cover price is 5¢, the September issue has 96 pages, some chains drop the magazine, others accept it as a profit-making item.

Nonfiction: *Woman as Force in History: A Study in the Traditions and Realities* by Mary R. Beard, now 70; *The Chrysanthemum and the Sword: Patterns of Japanese Culture* by Ruth Benedict, who has never been to Japan but whose book will nevertheless be a classic in its field.

Fiction: *Ladders to Fire* by Anaïs Nin; *Delta Wedding* by Eudora Welty; *The Member of the Wedding* by Carson McCullers; *Day with the King* by Gladys Schmitt; *That Lady* by Kate O'Brien; *The River* by Rumer Godden; *The King's General* by Daphne du Maurier; *The Reluctant Widow* by Georgette Heyer; *Palladian* by Elizabeth Taylor; *To See a Fine Lady* by Norah Lofts; *The Gypsy's Baby* (stories) by Rosamond Lehmann; *The Rise of Henry Morcar* by Phyllis Bentley; *The Train (Sputniki)* by Russian novelist Evira (Federovna) Panova, 41; *Medaliony* (stories about Nazi concentration camp atrocities) by Zofja Nalkowska; *Going Alone (Hitori yuku)* by Taiko Hirabayashi, now 41; *Letty Fox: Her Luck* by Christina Stead; *My Career Goes Bung* by Miles Franklin, now 67; *The River Road* by Frances Parkinson Keyes; *This Side of Innocence* by Taylor Caldwell; *Over at the Crowleys* by Kathleen Norris; *Green Grass of Wyoming* by Mary O'Hara; *Ride the Pink Horse* by Dorothy B. Hughes; *Miss Pym Disposes* by Josephine Tey.

Poetry: *The Double Image* by English poet Denise Levertov, 23; *Poems—North and South* by U.S. poet Elizabeth Bishop, 35, includes "Florida," "The Map," "The Fish," "The Man-Moth," "The Unbeliever," and "A Miracle for Breakfast" (Pulitzer Prize, 1956); *Family Circle* by U.S. poet Eve Merriam, 30; *The Moving Image* by Australian poet Judith Wright, 31.

Painting: *Faun Playing the Pipe* and *Françoise with a Yellow Necklace* by Pablo Picasso, whose mistress, Françoise Gilot, will give birth next year to his son Claude.

Sculpture: *Elegy II* and *Pelagos* (both wood) by Barbara Hepworth.

Photographer Alfred Stieglitz dies at New York July 13 at age 82, survived by Georgia O'Keeffe, now 58.

Theater: Judy Holliday (originally Judith Tuvim), 22, Paul Douglas, and Gary Merrill in Garson Kanin's *Born Yesterday* 2/4 at New York's Lyceum Theater, 1,642 perfs.; *Whitman Avenue* by U.S. playwright Maxine Wood, 36, 6/5 at New York's Cort Theater, with Canada Lee and Vivian Baber in a play about discriminatory housing practices (Margo Jones has directed); *The Respectful Prostitute (La Putain Respecteuse)* by Jean-Paul Sartre 11/8 at the Théâtre-Antoine, Paris; Ingrid Bergman in Maxwell Anderson's *Joan of Lorraine* 11/18 at New York's Alvin Theater, with Sam Wanamaker as the director of a star playing the role of Joan of Arc (Margo Jones is the real play's director), 201 perfs.; *Another Part of the Forest* by Lillian Hellman 11/20 at New York's Fulton Theater, with Patricia Neal, 20, and Mildred Dunnock, 40, 182 perfs.

The American Repertory Theater is founded by U.S. actress-director-producer Margaret Webster, 41, U.S. director-producer Cheryl Crawford, now 44, and English actress Eva Le Gallienne, 47, but will not survive for long.

Films: Fredric March, Myrna Loy, Teresa Wright, and Dana Andrews in William Wyler's *The Best Years of Our Lives*; Humphrey Bogart, Lauren Bacall (Betty Joan Perske), 21, and Martha Vickers (Martha MacVicar), 21, in Howard Hawks's *The Big Sleep*; Celia Johnson and Trevor Howard in David Lean's *Brief Encounter*; John Mills and English actress Valerie Hobson, 29, in David Lean's *Great Expectations*; James Stewart, Donna Reed, Lionel Barrymore, and Thomas Mitchell in Frank Capra's *It's a Wonderful Life*; Burt Lancaster and Ava Gardner (Lucy Johnson), 23, in Robert Siodmak's *The Killers*; Linda Darnell, Henry Fonda, and Victor Mature in John Ford's *My Darling Clementine*; Anna Magnani, 38, and Aldo Fabrizi in Roberto Rosselini's *Open City*; Lana Turner and John Garfield in Tay Garnett's *The Postman Always Rings Twice*; David Niven and Kim Hunter (Janet Cole), 23, in Michael Powell and Emeric Pressburger's *Stairway to Heaven*. Also: Irene Dunne and Rex Harrison in John Cromwell's *Anna and the King of Siam*; Jennifer Jones and Charles Boyer in Ernst Lubitsch's *Cluny Brown*; Bette Davis, Claude Rains, and Paul Henreid in Irving Rapper's *Deception*; Gérard Philipe and Micheline Presle (Micheline Chassagne), 24, in Claude Autant-Lara's *Devil in the Flesh*; Rita Hayworth (who sings "Put the Blame on Mame") and Glenn Ford in Charles Vidor's *Gilda*; Joan Crawford and John Garfield in Jean Negulesco's *Humoresque*; Gregory Peck and Joan Bennett in Zoltan Korda's *The Macomber Affair*; Ingrid Bergman, Cary Grant, and Claude Rains in Alfred Hitchcock's *Notorious*; Tyrone Power and Gene Tierney in Edmund Goulding's *The Razor's Edge*; Dorothy McGuire, 28, George Brent, and Ethel Barrymore, now 67, in Robert Siodmak's *The Spiral Staircase*; Pierre Blanchar and Michele Morgan in Jean Delannoy's *La Symphonie Pastorale*; Geraldine Fitzgerald, Sydney Greenstreet, and Peter Lorre in Jean Negulesco's *Three Strangers*; Gregory Peck, Jane Wyman, and Claude Jarman, Jr., in Clarence Brown's *The Yearling*.

Hollywood musicals: Bing Crosby, Fred Astaire, and Joan Caulfield in Stuart Heisler's *Blue Skies* with Irving Berlin songs that include "A Couple of

Song-and-Dance Men"; Judy Garland, William Powell, Fred Astaire, and Gene Kelly in Vincente Minnelli's *Ziegfeld Follies*; Judy Garland in George Sidney's *The Harvey Girls* with Harry Warren–Johnny Mercer songs that include "O the Atchison, Topeka and the Santa Fe" (*see* Fred Harvey restaurants, 1876); June Haver, Vivian Blaine, and Celeste Holm in H. Bruce Humberstone's *Three Little Girls in Blue* with songs that include "You Make Me Feel So Good" and "On the Boardwalk at Atlantic City" by Joseph Myron, lyrics by Mack Gordon.

Stage musicals: Mary Martin and Yul Brynner in *Lute Song* 2/6 at New York's Plymouth Theater, with songs that include "Mountain High, Valley Low," 142 perfs.; Pearl Bailey, 28, heads an all-black cast in *St. Louis Woman* 3/30 at New York's Martin Beck Theater with Harold Arlen–Johnny Mercer songs that include "Come Rain or Come Shine," 113 perfs.; Betty Garrett in *Call Me Mister* 4/18 at New York's National Theater, with songs that include "South America, Take It Away," 734 perfs.; Ethel Merman and Ray Middleton in *Annie Get Your Gun* 5/16 at New York's Imperial Theater, with a book based on the life of markswoman Phoebe "Annie Oakley" Mozee of Buffalo Bill's Wild West Show (*see* 1885), Irving Berlin songs that include "Anything You Can Do," "Doin' What Comes Naturally," "The Girl That I Marry," "You Can't Get a Man with a Gun," "I Got the Sun in the Morning" and "There's No Business Like Show Business," 1,147 perfs.; Mary Martin in *Pacific 1860* 12/19 at London's Theatre Royal in Drury Lane, with music and lyrics by Noël Coward, 129 perfs.

Opera: English contralto Kathleen (Mary) Ferrier, 34, makes her stage debut as Lucretia and Joan Cross creates the role of the Female Chorus in the Benjamin Britten opera *The Rape of Lucretia,* which has its first performance 7/13 at Glyndebourne (Ferrier has toured the provinces during the war and sung with the Bach Choir at London); Elisabeth Schwarzkopf, now 30, makes her debut with the Vienna Staatsoper; Italian soprano Renata Tebaldi, 24, makes her debut at Milan's La Scala.

Ballet: Martha Graham in *The Serpent Heart* 5/10 at Columbia University's McMillin Theater, with

music by Samuel Barber, choreography by Graham; Gisella Caccialanza, Tanaquil LeClerq, and Todd Bolender in *The Four Temperaments* 11/20 at New York's Central High School of the Needle Trades, with music by Paul Hindemith, choreography by George Balanchine.

Oklahoma-born ballerina Maria Tallchief, 19, quits the Ballets Russes and joins the new Grand Ballet de Monte Carlo started by Russian emigré George Balanchine, 42. Daughter of an Osage chief, Tallchief becomes Balanchine's second wife (*see* 1947).

Popular songs: "La Vie en Rose" by Italian-born Paris composer Louiguy (Louis Guglielmi), 30, lyrics by French chanteuse Edith Piaf (Edith Giovanna Gassion), 31; "Put the Blame on Mame" by Allan Robert and Doris Fischer (for the film *Gilda,* above); country singer Molly O'Day (LaVerne Lois Williams), 23, records "The Tramp on the Street" with her husband Lynn (*né* Leonard) Davis, 32, and their band, the Cumberland Mountain Folks.

Pauline Betz wins in women's singles at both Wimbledon (where tournament play resumes after a 6-year lapse) and Forest Hills.

U.S. golfer Patty Berg, 28, defeats Betty Jameson in the final round September 1 to win the first U.S. Women's Open. (She was named Female Athlete of the Year in 1938 and 1943 and will be given the same honor in 1955.)

The skimpy two-piece bikini swimsuit designed by French couturier Louis Réard is modeled (by a stripper) at a Paris fashion show July 5, 4 days after the first U.S. atomic bomb test and creates a sensation. Banned at Biarritz and other resorts, it will not be seen on U.S. beaches until the early 1960s.

French couturière Jeanne Lanvin dies July 6 at about 79 after a career in which she has joined with a few others in setting the style for world fashion (*see* perfume, 1925).

Estée Lauder, 38, makes her first sale to Saks Fifth Avenue. The New York beautician, born Josephine Esther Mentzer, has joined with her husband Joseph, also 38, to make and market cosmetics that will grow to outsell those of Elizabeth Arden, Helena Rubinstein, or Revlon.

New York fashion designer Ceil Chapman (*née* Mitchell), 32, wins the American Fashion Critics' Award. Her elaborate, feminine styles have attracted customers who include Greer Garson and Mary Martin.

Danish entrepreneur Lilly Braengaard, 26, begins a sewing business in a leaky old house at Vejle, Jutland, where she and two assistants must work under umbrellas during heavy rains. Her initial capital is 15 kroner ($2). In a few years, having moved to dryer quarters, she will begin specializing in wedding gowns, developing a business that within 20 years will have 10 Miss Lilly stores in Denmark plus one in Stockholm.

The repeal of U.S. order L85 October 19 permits dressmakers to lengthen skirts and ends wartime austerity.

British-made nylon hosiery goes on sale in December. The stockings are the first nylon consumer goods made in Britain (*see* 1940).

Tide, introduced by Procter & Gamble, is the first detergent strong enough for washing clothes as well as dishes (*see* Persil, 1907). By the end of 1949, one out of every four U.S. washing machines will be using Tide.

The new Westinghouse Laundromat is a front-loading machine that requires a low-sudsing soap or detergent.

 London police answer a summons June 21 and rush to a Notting Hill hotel where the mutilated nude corpse of a 32-year-old woman has been found in bed with its ankles tied to the bedposts. Margery Aimee Gardner has separated from her husband and was dancing the evening of June 20 at a London nightclub with Neville George Clevely Heath, 29, who has a history of passing himself off as a military officer. He signed the hotel register for the room in which Mrs. Gardner's body has been found. A woman walking her dog at Bournemouth soon afterward discovers the mutilated body of another young woman, Doreen Marshall. Police arrest Heath, a jury finds him guilty of both murders, and he is hanged October 26.

 The Office of Price Administration decontrols U.S. meat prices October 15 to ease an acute shortage and ends price controls on all foods and beverages except sugar and rice October 23.

 U.S. birthrates soar as returning servicemen begin families and add to existing ones. The nation has 3,411,000 births, up from 2,858,000 last year.

1947

 India gains independence August 15 from Britain, which sets up Pakistan as an independent Muslim state with Mohammed Ali Jinnah, 71, of the Muslim League as governor-general. His sister Fatima, 53, who serves as his hostess and is always at his side, has opposed Conservative Orthodox attitudes toward women and worked since 1934 for the social emancipation and welfare of women. Fatima Jinnah will become known as *Madar-i-Millat* ("Mother of the Country").

A "Hollywood Black List" of alleged Communist sympathizers compiled at a conference of studio executives meeting at New York's Waldorf-Astoria Hotel names an estimated 300 writers, directors, actors, and others known or suspected to have Communist party affiliations or of having invoked the Fifth Amendment against self-incrimination when questioned by the House Un-American Activities Committee. The film industry blacklists the "Hollywood Ten" November 25, and all draw short prison sentences for refusing to testify. Dalton Trumbo's screen credits include the 1943 film *Tender Comrade* with Ginger Rogers, whose mother has tearfully testified before the Dies Committee that her daughter had to utter the "Communist line" in the film "Share and share alike—that's democracy."

U.S. women mourn the death of suffragist pioneer Carrie Chapman Catt, who dies March 9 at age 88.

Women in Bulgaria, China, Nepal, Pakistan, and Venezuela gain the right to vote on the same basis as men (*see* Argentina, below)

A Japanese Equal Rights Amendment adopted May 5 gives women legal grounds when they bring lawsuits charging discrimination. Pushed through by U.S. occupation authorities, the amendment makes it illegal to discriminate by sex for political, social, or economic reasons. A Department of Women's and Children's Affairs is established, and a woman, Kikue Yamakawa, 57, is appointed the first director.

A Japanese labor law enacted September 1 establishes a minimum wage, and limits working hours for the first time. It requires that employers give days off (including 2 extra days per month for menstruating women), provide for 6 weeks' maternity leave, give mothers time to nurse their infants, and pay equal wages for equal work (a provision that will generally be ignored).

Argentina grants woman suffrage September 9 following efforts by First Lady Eva Perón (née María Eva Duarte Ibarguren), 28. "Evita," as she is called, met Col. Juan Domingo Perón when she was 15 and trying to be a singer and actress; when he was arrested 2 years ago, she went on the radio to plead with the people that they rally and free him, he married her that December, and he was elected president last year (see 1951).

Eva ("Evita") Perón worked for woman suffrage in Argentina and was popular despite her husband's excesses. AP/WIDE WORLD PHOTOS

A Japanese civil law enacted in December allows women over age 18 to marry without parental permission, permits women as well as men to be heads of families, denies husbands rights over their wives' property, and gives female offspring equal rights of inheritance.

Nonfiction: *The Meaning of Treason* by Rebecca West; *Gravity and Grace* (*La Pesanteur et la grâce*) by the late French philosopher Simone Weil, who died in 1943 at age 34 of voluntary starvation while working for the Resistance in England after refusing to eat more than her compatriots were receiving from Nazi occupation authorities.

Fiction: *Hetty Dorval* by Canadian novelist Ethel (Davis) Wilson (née Bryant), 57 (born in South Africa, she was removed to England after her parents died and from there taken to Canada); *The Harp in the South* by New Zealand–born Australian writer Ruth Park, 24; *I'll Survive* (*Watashi wa ikuru*) by Taiko Hirabayashi; *Banshu Plain* (*Banshu heiya*) by Yuriko Miyamoto; *Nothing Grows by Moonlight* (*Av måneskinn gror der ingenting*) by Torborg Nedreaas; *The Mountain Lion* by Jean Stafford; *Gentleman's Agreement* by U.S. novelist Laura Zametkin Hobson, 47, examines the covert anti-Semitic practices institutionalized in U.S. society; *The Clever Sister* by Margaret Culkin Banning; *East Side, West Side* by Marcia Davenport; *Came a Cavalier* by Frances Parkinson Keyes; *The Web of Days* by U.S. novelist Edna L. Lee, 57; *Alexandra* by Gladys Schmitt; *The Bishop's Mantle* by Agnes Turnbull; *Manservant and Maidservant* by Ivy Compton-Burnett; *The Museum of Cheats* (stories) by Sylvia Townsend Warner; *An Avenue of Stones* by Pamela Hansford Johnson; *Beyond the Blue Mountains* by English novelist Jean Plaidy (Eleanor Burford Hibbert), 41, whose many books, written under three different pen names (see 1960), will be translated into 20 languages; *Friends and Lovers* by Helen MacInnes; *Silver Nutmeg* by Norah Lofts; *In a Lonely Place* by Dorothy B. Hughes.

Painting: *Undulating Arrangement* (oil pigments on Masonite with lighter pigments on corrugated glass) by I. Rice Pereira; *Promenade* (oil on panel) by Lee Krasner, who 2 years ago married painter Jackson Pollock.

Sculpture: *The Blind Leading the Blind* (wood) and *Quarantania* (painted wood on wooden base) by French sculptor Louise Bourgeois, 36; *Pendour* (wood) by Barbara Hepworth.

Japan's Association of Women Artists gives its first annual exhibition July 2 to 13 at Tokyo. The association has been founded by 11 women to raise artistic standards and give opportunities for young women artists in the male-dominated art world.

Theater: Director Margo Jones, now 34, opens her Theater 1947 6/3 on the grounds of the State Fair Association at Dallas with a performance of William Inge's new play *Farther Off from Heaven* (the theater-in-the-round will change its name each New Year's Eve, and before her accidental death in 1955 Jones will produce 85 plays, 57 of them from new scripts); Judith Anderson, John Gielgud, and Florence Reed in Robinson Jeffers's *Medea* 10/20 at New York's National Theater, 214 perfs.; *Happy Birthday* by Anita Loos 11/2 at New York's Broadhurst Theater, with Helen Hayes as a drab Newark librarian who comes to life in a barroom, 564 perfs.; Jessica Tandy as Blanche DuBois, Marlon Brando, Kim Hunter as Stella Kowalski, and Karl Malden in Tennessee Williams's *A Streetcar Named Desire* 12/3 at New York's Ethel Barrymore Theater, 855 perfs.

The Tony Awards, established by the American Theatre Wing, honor outstanding Broadway plays, directors, performers, scenic designers, costumers, etc. The name *Tony* honors Antoinette Perry, who headed the Theatre Wing during World War II but died in June of last year at age 58; the awards rival the Oscars given since 1928 by the Motion Picture Academy of Arts and Sciences.

Films: Deborah Kerr, Flora Robson, Sabu, and Jean (Merilynn) Simmons, 18, in Michael Powell and Emeric Pressburger's *Black Narcissus*; John Garfield and German-born actress Lilli Palmer (Lilli Peiser), 33, in Robert Rossen's *Body and Soul*; Dana Andrews, Jane Wyatt, 35, and Lee J. Cobb in Elia Kazan's *Boomerang*; Wendy Hiller, Roger Livesey, and Finlay Currie in Michael Powell and Emeric Pressburger's *I Know Where I'm Going*; Irene Dunne and William Powell in Michael Curtiz's *Life with Father*; Edmund Gwenn, Irish-American actress Maureen O'Hara (Maureen Fitzsimmons), 25, John Payne, and Natalie Wood (Natasha Gurdin), 9, in George Seaton's *Miracle on 34th Street*. Also: Ronald Colman and Signe Hasso in George Cukor's *A Double Life*; Loretta Young and Joseph Cotten in H. C. Potter's *The Farmer's Daughter*; Gene Tierney and Rex Harrison in Joseph L. Mankiewicz's *The Ghost and Mrs.*

Muir; Martha Raye (Maggie Yvonne O'Reed), 31, and Charles Chaplin in Chaplin's *Monsieur Verdoux*; Tyrone Power and Joan Blondell in Edmund Goulding's *Nightmare Alley*; Robert Mitchum, Kirk Douglas, and Jane (originally Bettejane) Greer, 23, in Jacques Tourneur's *Out of the Past*; Harriet White in Roberto Rossellini's *Paisan*; George Sanders and London-born actress Angela Lansbury, 21, in Albert Lewis's *The Private Affairs of Bel Ami*; (Dixie) Wanda Hendrix, 19, and Robert Montgomery in Montgomery's *Ride the Pink Horse*; Susan Hayward and Robert Young in Irving Pichel's *They Won't Believe Me*; Eleanor Parker, 25, and Ronald Reagan in Irving Rapper's *The Voice of the Turtle*; Ann Blyth, Jessica Tandy, and Charles Boyer in Zoltan Korda's *A Woman's Vengeance*.

President Truman's daughter, Margaret, 23, makes her professional radio debut March 16, singing with the Detroit Symphony, and appears as a soprano soloist August 23 at the Hollywood Bowl.

Opera: *The Mother of Us All* 5/7 at Columbia University's Brander Matthews Hall with Dorothy Dow as Susan B. Anthony, music by Virgil Thomson, libretto by the late Gertrude Stein, who died at Paris last July at age 72; Joan Cross creates the role of Lady Billows in the Benjamin Britten opera *Albert Heering,* which has its premiere 6/20 at the Glyndebourne Opera Festival; Kathleen Ferrier creates a sensation at Glyndebourne with her acting in *Orfeo ed Euridice* (Lucretia and Euridice will be her only operatic roles). Edith Coates joins the newly formed Covent Garden company, where she will remain until 1967; Swedish soprano (Anna) Elisabeth Söderström, 20, makes her debut as Bastienne in the 1768 Mozart opera *Bastien und Bastienne* at Stockholm's Drottningholm Court Theater; soprano Grace Moore has died in a KLM DC-3 plane crash at Copenhagen January 31 at age 45; Elisabeth Lutyens's chamber opera *The Pit* is given its first performance.

Ballet: Martha Graham in *Night Journey* 5/3 at Cambridge, Mass., with music by William Schuman. George Balanchine takes his wife, Maria Tallchief, to Paris, where she becomes the first American since 1839 to dance at the Paris Opéra.

Broadway musicals: Ella Logan and David Wayne in *Finian's Rainbow* 1/10 at the 46th Street Theater, with Burton Lane–Yip Harburg songs that include "If This Isn't Love," "How Are Things in Glocca Morra?," "Old Devil Moon," "Look to the Rainbow," "When I'm Not Near the Girl I Love," and "That Great Come-and-Get-It-Day," 725 perfs.; Phil Silvers, Nanette Fabray, and Helen Gallagher in *High Button Shoes* 10/9 at the Century Theater, with Jule Styne–Sammy Cahn songs that include "Papa, Won't You Dance with Me," 727 perfs.; law school dropout Lisa Kirk, 22, sings "The Gentleman Is a Dope" in Rodgers and Hammerstein's *Allegro* 10/10 at the Majestic Theater, 315 perfs.; Paul and Grace Hartman and Elaine Stritch, 22, in *Angel in the Wings* 12/11 at the Coronet Theater, with Bob Hilliard–Carl Sigman songs that include "Civilization (Bongo, Bongo, Bongo)," 197 perfs.

Popular songs: "Mañana—Is Soon Enough for Me" by Peggy Lee and her husband, guitarist Dave Barbour; Ella Fitzgerald records "How High the Moon"; Nellie Lutcher, 31, records "Hurry On Down" and "He's a Real Gone Guy."

U.S. gospel singer Mahalia Jackson, 36, records "Move on Up a Little Higher" and scores a huge success. Seven other hymns recorded by Jackson will have sales of more than a million copies each, including "I Believe," "I Can Put My Trust in Jesus," and "He's Got the Whole World in His Hands."

Elizabeth Arden (Florence Nightingale Graham), now 62, wins the Kentucky Derby with her 3-year-old Jet Pilot.

Margaret Osborne, 29 (U.S.), wins in women's singles at Wimbledon, Althea Louise Brough, 24, at Forest Hills.

The "New Look" introduced by Paris couturier Christian Dior, 42, February 12 lowers skirt lengths to 12 inches from the floor, pads brassieres, unpads shoulders, adds hats, makes present wardrobes obsolete, and wins quick support from fashion magazines and the $3 billion U.S. garment industry, which has suffered from the fact that women during the war have found it comfortable to wear slacks, low-heeled shoes, and loose-fitting sweaters. Labor lawyer Anna Rosenberg declares, "Let the new look of today become the forgotten look of tomorrow," and more than 300,000 women join "Little Below the Knee" Clubs to protest the New Look, but most women resist the new fashion only briefly and then succumb, slavishly adopting not only long, full peg-top skirts (with corsets to take two or even three inches off their waistlines), V-necks, curving waists, sloping shoulders, and frothy blouses, but also clogs, espadrilles, spike-heeled "naked sandals," and fezzes.

Ajax cleanser, introduced by Colgate-Palmolive-Peet, is a silica-sand product that is more likely to scratch than feldspar cleansers such as Bon Ami and Dutch cleanser but requires less elbow grease and soon outsells its rivals (*see* Comet, 1956).

Woolworth heiress Barbara Hutton, now 34, marries the French amateur cycling champion Prince Igor Nikolaiewitsch Troubetzkoy, 35, March 1. The mayor of Chur, 60 miles from Zurich, performs the ceremony that makes Prince Troubetzkoy Hutton's fourth husband (*see* 1951).

Tobacco heiress Doris Duke, now 34, is married September 1 in the Dominican consulate at Paris to Porfirio Rubirosa, now 40, whom she met last year at Rome. Her lawyers have forced him to sign a prenuptial agreement renouncing any claim to her fortune, and she has bought him a 17th-century house at 46, rue de Bellechasse on the Left Bank as a wedding gift. Guests include *Harper's Bazaar* editor Carmel Snow, who has selected the bride's outfit (*see* 1949).

Britain's Princess Royal Elizabeth, 21, is married at London November 20 to her cousin Philip, Lieutenant Mountbatten, 26, who has been made Prince Philip, duke of Edinburgh.

The U.S. Army convicts 971 soldiers of having committed acts of rape in the European Theater of Operations between January 1942 and June 1947.

U.S. household sugar rationing ends June 11, but widespread food shortages continue in the wake of World War II and crop failures exacerbate the situation. President Truman urges meatless and eggless days October 5 to conserve grain for hungry Europe, and a Friendship Train leaves Los Angeles November 8 on a 10-day cross-country tour to collect food for European relief.

Riots sweep India's cities following the assassination January 30 of spiritual leader Mohandas K. Gandhi by a Hindu extremist at age 78.

The State of Israel is proclaimed May 14. Five Arab countries send troops to invade the onetime British protectorate of Palestine when the British mandate expires May 15, but the new state, which enlists women in its armed forces, repels the invaders and Jews in countries all over the world apply for immigration.

Wilhelmina of the Netherlands abdicates September 4 at age 68 after a 58-year reign. Her daughter, 39, will reign as Juliana until 1980.

"Axis Sally" is indicted for treason at Washington September 10. Maine-born emigrée Mildred Elizabeth Gillars, now 48, took a job as a German radio announcer in 1940 at the urging of her German lover and broadcast to U.S. troops from December 11, 1941, through May 8, 1945, becoming the highest-salaried broadcaster in the Reich. Persuading captured U.S. soldiers to record messages to their families and families, she doctored them to insert Nazi propaganda. She started her propaganda talks to Allied troops with appeals such as "Hello, gang. Throw down those little old guns and toddle off home. There's no getting the Germans down." Found cowering in the cellar of a bombed-out building in Frankfurt-am-Main, she has been returned by the army to stand trial (*see* 1949).

Mme. Chiang Kai-shek arrives at Washington December 1 to request U.S. help as the Communist forces of Mao Zedong engulf China, but revelations of corruption in her husband's Nationalist regime have cooled enthusiasm for Mme. Chiang's cause.

 Israel (above), Iraq, the Republic of Korea, and Suriname grant women the right to vote on the same basis as men (*see* Iran, 1980).

Former South African socialite Helen Beatrice May Joseph (*née* Fennell), 43, obtains a divorce from her dentist husband and helps found the Congress of Democrats, the white wing of the African National Congress, to fight racial discrimination. Born in England, Mrs. Joseph served as an information and welfare officer in the Women's Auxiliary Air Force during World War II and later became a social worker in Cape Town and Johannesburg, where she saw the realities of South Africa's racial policies (*see* 1956).

Women in Israel (above) work in the fields and factories on the same basis as men (but *see* 1972).

A Universal Declaration of Human Rights adopted by the United Nations General Assembly at Paris December 10 at 3 A.M. is based on the U.S. Bill of Rights, the Magna Carta, and the French Declaration of the Rights of Man. Eleanor Roosevelt has fought for the Declaration (authored primarily by René Cassin, 61) and wins a standing ovation.

Reformer Kamaldevi Chattopadhyay, 44, founds the Indian Cooperative Union to assist refugees uprooted by partition of the subcontinent into India and Pakistan. Her first cooperative is a farm at Chattarpur, near Delhi, and her Union joins in building the new city of Faridavad to rehabilitate 30,000 refugees, providing tools and directions. Chattopadhyay soon starts hand-loom cooperatives.

 English archaeologist Mary Douglas Leakey (*née* Nicol), 35, discovers the skeleton of a 1.7-million-year-old dryopithecine (primitive ape) at Rusinga on Lake Victoria. She met African-born archaeologist and anthropologist Louis S. B. Leakey, now 45, in 1934 when she prepared drawings for his book *Adam's Ancestors*, became his second wife in 1936, and gains international attention for his work with her discovery (*see* 1959).

British biochemist Dorothy (Mary) Hodgkin (*née* Crowfoot), 38, uses X-ray crystallography to analyze the complex structure of vitamin B12. The project will take 8 years, she will be the first researcher to solve a biological mystery with computer analysis, and she will go on to analyze the structures of other molecules, including penicillin and insulin (*see* 1964).

 Parliament enacts a British National Health Services law July 5 to offer taxpayer-financed "cradle-to-the-grave" medical care. The effect of the new measure, which makes medical service free, will be to lower dramatically Britain's infant mortality and maternal death rates to levels below those in the United States, and reduce death rates from bronchitis, influenza, pneumonia, tuberculosis, and some other diseases to levels below U.S. rates.

Dramamine is developed by Johns Hopkins physicians who discover accidentally that an antiallergy drug relieves motion sickness. A clinic patient being treated for hives (urticaria) with beta-diaminoethyl-bendohydryl-ether-8-chlorotheophyllinate reports that taking 50 milligrams by mouth before boarding a streetcar prevents the motion sickness she has usually experienced. Control groups on the U.S. troop transport *General Ballou* test the drug while en route to Bremerhaven for occupation duty.

Sexual Behavior in the Human Male by Indiana University zoologist Alfred Charles Kinsey, 54, indicates that many sex acts heretofore thought to be perversions are so common as to be considered almost normal. Kinsey has conducted interviews with some 18,500 men and women throughout America with funds provided by the National Research Council and the Rockefeller Foundation. The "Kinsey Report" arouses great controversy (*see* 1953).

Albanian missionary Agnes Gonxha Bojaxhiu, 38, who went to India at age 17, leaves her convent at Calcutta to found the Missionaries of Charity. As Mother Teresa, she will expand the organization to operate food centers, schools, and orphanages in more than 25 countries (*see* 1979).

Fiction: *City of Corpses* (*Kabane no machi*) by Yoko Ota, who was at Hiroshima when the atomic bomb exploded there 3 years ago; *Late Chrysanthemum* (*Bangiku*) by Fumiko Hayashi; *Falsehood* (*Kyogi*) and *Record of Babble* (*Houmatsu no kiroku*) by Ineko Sata; *Two Gardens* (*Futatsu no niwa*) by Yuriko Miyamoto; *The Sun Shines over the Sanggan River* by Ding Ling is about Chinese land reform; *House of Liars* (*Mentzogna e sortilegio*) by Italian novelist Elsa Morante, 30; *The Factory* (*Kruzhilika*) by Evira Panova; *Portrait of a Man Unknown* (*Portrait d'un inconnu*) by Nathalie Sarraute; *The Enchanted Drink* (*Der Zaubertrank*) (stories) by Helene Voigt-Diederichs; *A Little Tea, A Little Chat* by Christina Stead; *Storm of Time* by Eleanor Dark; *The Corner That Held Them* by Sylvia Townsend Warner; *The Black Laurel* by Storm Jameson; *I Capture the Castle* by English playwright Dodie Smith, now 51; *A Candle for St. Jude* by

Rumer Godden; "The Lottery" by U.S. writer Shirley Hardie Jackson, 29, in the June 26 *New Yorker* magazine; *The Wine of Astonishment* by Martha Gellhorn; *Dinner at Antoine's* by Frances Parkinson Keyes; *Annie Jordan: a Novel of Seattle* by U.S. novelist Mary Brinker Post, 42; *Fire in the Morning* by U.S. novelist Elizabeth Spencer, 27; *A Light in the Window* by Mary Roberts Rinehart.

Poetry: *Shadow of a Flower* (*Kaei*) by Taijo Nakamura.

Painting: *Christina's World* by U.S. painter Andrew Nelson Wyeth, 31, captures the youthful vigor and anguish of Cushing, Me., cripple Christina Olsen, 55, in a work that will be widely reproduced.

Sculpture: *Teilhard de Chardin* (bust) by Melvina Hoffman portrays the French Jesuit theologian, paleontologist, and philosopher Pierre Teilhard de Chardin, 67.

Theater: Anne Jackson, 22, and Margaret Phillips in Tennessee Williams's *Summer and Smoke* 10/6 at New York's Music Box Theater, 100 perfs.; Joyce Redman as Anne Boleyn, Rex Harrison as Henry VIII in Maxwell Anderson's *Anne of the Thousand Days* 12/8 at New York's Shubert Theater, 286 perfs.

The Margaret Webster Shakespeare Company founded by director-producer Webster will tour the United States for years, performing in high school auditoriums, university theaters, and public halls.

Films: Jeanne Crain, Linda Darnell, and Ann Sothern in Joseph Mankiewicz's *A Letter to Three Wives*; Scottish ballerina Moira Shearer (Moira Shearer King), 22, Anton Walbrook, and Marius Goering in Michael Powell and Emeric Pressburger's *The Red Shoes*; Linda Darnell and Rex Harrison in Preston Sturges's *Unfaithfully Yours*. Also: Silvana Mangano, 18, Vittorio Gassman, and Raf Vallone in Giuseppe De Santis's *Bitter Rice*; Jean Arthur and Marlene Dietrich in Billy Wilder's *A Foreign Affair*; Irene Dunne and Barbara Bel Geddes, 25, in George Stevens's *I Remember Mama*; Jane Wyman and Lew Ayres in Jean Negulesco's *Johnny Belinda*; Humphrey Bogart, Edward G. Robinson, and Lauren Bacall in John Huston's *Key Largo*; Stanley Holloway and Margaret Rutherford in Henry Cornelius's *Passport to Pimlico*; Maureen O'Hara and Robert Young in Walter Lang's *Sitting Pretty*; Olivia de Havilland in Anatole Litvak's *The Snake Pit*; Eleanor Parker and Alexis Smith in Peter Godfrey's *The Woman in White*.

Bette Davis earns $328,000 from Warner Bros.—more than any male star except Bogart and more than any other woman professional. Deanna Durbin earns $323,477, Betty Grable $299,333.

Hollywood musicals: Judy Garland and Gene Kelly in Vincente Minnelli's *The Pirate* with Cole Porter songs that include "Be a Clown"; Canadian-born actress Yvonne de Carlo (originally Peggy Middleton), 24, Tony Martin, and Peter Lorre in John Berry's *Casbah* with Harold Arlen–Leo Robin songs that include "For Every Man There's a Woman."

Broadway musicals: Nancy Walker and Harold Lang in *Look Ma I'm Dancing* 1/29 at the Adelphi Theater, with Hugh Martin songs that include "Shauny O'Shay," 188 perfs.; Bobby Clark and Irene Rich (Irene Luther), 51, in *As the Girls Go* 11/13 at the Winter Garden Theater, with Jimmy McHugh–Harold Adamson songs that include "It Takes a Woman to Make a Man," 420 perfs.; Alfred Drake, Patricia Morrison (Eileen Patricia Augusta Fraser Morrison), 29, Lisa Kirk, and Harold Lang in *Kiss Me, Kate* 12/30 at the New Century Theater, an adaptation of the 1596 Shakespeare comedy *The Taming of the Shrew* with Cole Porter songs that include "We Open in Venice," "I've Come to Wive It Wealthily," "I Hate Men," "Another Opening, Another Show," "Why Can't You Behave?," "Were Thine that Special Face," "Too Darn Hot," "Where Is the Life That Late I Led," "Always True to You in My Fashion," "So in Love," "Tom, Dick or Harry," "Wunderbar," "Brush Up Your Shakespeare," 1,077 perfs.

Ballet: Alicia Alonso and John Kriza in *Fall River Legend* 4/22 at New York's Metropolitan Opera House, with music by Morton Gould, choreography by Agnes de Mille; Maria Tallchief as Eurydice, Tanaquil LeClercq as the leader of the Bacchantes in *Orpheus* 4/28 at the New York City Center, with music by Igor Stravinsky, choreography by George Balanchine; Moira Shearer creates the title role in *Cinderella* 12/27 at London's Royal Opera House in Covent Garden, with music by Serge Prokofiev, choreography by Frederick Ashton.

Cantata: Eleanor Steber (who has commissioned the work) sings in Samuel Barber's *Knoxville—Summer of 1915* 4/19 at Boston's Symphony Hall.

Elizabeth Maconchy, now 41, wins the Edward Evans prize for her Fifth Quartet.

Popular songs: Patti Page (Clara Ann Fowler), 20, records "Confess" and has her first big success (she first sang under the name Patti Page for a Tulsa, Okla., radio show sponsored by Page Dairy Co.); Margaret Whiting records "A Tree in a Meadow" by British songwriter Billy Reid; Nellie Lutcher records "Fine Brown Frame."

Louise Brough wins in women's singles at Wimbledon, Margaret Osborne du Pont at Forest Hills.

Canadian figure skater Barbara Ann Scott wins her event in the winter Olympics at St. Moritz, Swiss skier Hedi Schlunegger wins the downhill ski event in 2 minutes, 28.3 seconds, U.S. skier Gretchen Fraser the slalom in 1 minute, 57.2 seconds. Dutch runner Fanny (Francina) Blankers-Koen, 30, wins the 100-meter in 11.9 seconds, the 200-meter in 24.4 seconds, and the 80-meter hurdles in 11.2 seconds at the summer games in London (reporters call her the "flying Dutch housewife;" U.S. athlete Alice Coachman, 26, wins the running high jump (5 feet, 6⅛ inches) and becomes the first black woman gold medalist, Hungarian athlete Olga Gyarmati the long jump (18 feet, 8½ inches), French athlete Micheline Ostermeyer the shot-put (45 feet, 1½ inches) and discus throw (137 feet, 6½ inches), Austrian athlete Herma Bauma the javelin throw (149 feet, 6 inches). Danish swimmer Greta Andersen wins the 100-meter freestyle in 1 minute, 6.3 seconds, U.S. swimmer Ann Curtis the 400-meter freestyle in 5 minutes, 17.8 seconds, Danish swimmer Karen Harup the 100-meter backstroke in 1 minute, 14.4 seconds, Dutch swimmer Nel van Vliet the 200-meter breaststroke in 2 minutes, 57.2 seconds, U.S. swimmer Victoria M. Draves the springboard dive and the platform dive.

Scrabble is copyrighted by Newtown, Conn., entrepreneur James Brunot, who has taken over the "crossword game" played with wooden tiles on a board from his friend Alfred M. Butts, 48, who invented the game in 1931 and called it Criss-Cross (his wife, Nina, was better at the game than he was). Brunot retires from his day job, renames the game, and begins manufacturing it at the rate of a few dozen sets per week (*see* 1952).

Christian Dior's "New Look" catches on worldwide with women eager to abandon the square, mannish, waistless shapes of past decades, but some women protest the profligate use of fabric in light of persistent world shortages (*see* 1947).

New York fashion designer Anne Klein (*née* Hannah Golofsky), 27 (or 43, or somewhere in between), joins with her husband, Ben, to form Junior Sophisticates, a new Seventh Avenue firm for which she creates a dress plus jacket. She began as a freelance design sketcher at age 15 and will go on to design the A-line dress and long, pleated, plaid skirts with blazers (*see* 1968).

New York fashion designer Hannah Troy (*née* Stern), 47, introduces the short-waisted "petite" size. She has noticed in a California May Company store that women were pulling at their shoulders and waistlines because the dresses they were trying on did not fit properly. After studying measurements of women volunteers for the WACS and WAVES in World War II, she has concluded from the statistics that women are typically short-waisted, whereas most fashions are designed for long-waisted women.

Tobacco heiress Doris Duke obtains a divorce in October from Porfirio Rubirosa, charging extreme cruelty, "entirely mental in character," which has injured her general health (*see* 1947). Reported to have prodigious sexual endowments, he is rumored to have slept with socialite Brenda Frazier, film stars Joan Crawford, Dolores Del Rio, and Susan Hayward, and the wives of some prominent industrialists, but he and Duke remain friends (*see* 1953).

Dial soap, introduced by Chicago's Armour and Co., is the world's first true deodorant soap. It employs the bacteria-killing chemical hexachlorophene discovered in World War II.

Birth control pioneer Margaret Sanger founds the International Planned Parenthood Federation (*see* 1927; Pincus, 1951).

A "eugenic protection" law enacted in occupied Japan authorizes abortion on demand. Japan's population is nearly 80 million, up from 64.5 million in 1930.

The Soviet authorities arrest U.S. journalist Anna Louise Strong, now 64, charge her with espionage, and deport her in late February. She has lived in the Soviet capital for 24 years and consistently expressed pro-Soviet views. An FBI agent hands her a subpoena when she arrives at New York's La Guardia Airport February 23, obliging her to testify before a federal grand jury investigating communism.

"Axis Sally" is found guilty of wartime treason March 10 and sentenced to 30 years in prison plus a fine of $10,000 (*see* 1948). She will serve 12 years in the Federal Reformatory for Women at Alderston, W. Va.

The People's Republic of China is proclaimed at Beijing October 1 with Mao Zedong as chairman of the Central People's Administrative Council. His wife, Jiang Qing, 35, is a onetime stage and film actress 20 years his junior and 2 years younger than revolutionary Qing Qeqing, who in 1929 married Gen. Zhu De (24 years her senior) and was one of the few women to make the Long March from 1934 to 1936, when the Red Army was forced to abandon its southern base and travel 800 miles to the northwest. She is one of the leaders of China's women's movement.

Minnesota politician (Helen) Eugenie Anderson, 40, is named ambassador to Denmark October 12 and becomes the first U.S. woman ambassador; Washington hostess Perle Mesta (*née* Skirvin), 59, whose father made a fortune in Texas oil and whose late husband did likewise with a Pittsburgh machine company, wins appointment as U.S. ambassador to Luxembourg, where she will serve until 1953. Active in Oklahoma politics and the women's rights movement in the 1930s, she switched from the GOP to the Democratic party and attached herself to an obscure U.S. senator from Missouri named Truman. Asked at her first staff meeting how she wants to be addressed, she replies, "You can call me Madame Minister" (*see* Broadway musical, 1950).

The Geneva Conventions adopted April 12 revise the conventions of 1864, 1907, and 1929. They provide for "free passage of all consignments of essential foodstuffs, clothing, and tonics intended for children under 15, expectant mothers, and maternity cases" in event of war but do not specifically outlaw sieges, blockades, or "resource denial" operations and do not address conflicts that are partly internal and partly international (*see* Vietnam, 1962).

"Tokyo Rose" goes on trial for treason in July at San Francisco. Los Angeles–born UCLA graduate Iva Toguri D'Aquino, 34, is one of at least a dozen Tokyo radio announcers who were called "Tokyo Rose" by English-speaking listeners in the Pacific during the war. She did the work under pressure from Japanese secret police after being caught in Tokyo at the outbreak of the war, refused to renounce her U.S. citizenship as did two other woman announcers (who thus could not be charged with treason), and married a Portuguese national in 1945. Government officials threaten and intimidate defense witnesses, the prosecution bribes a witness to give false testimony and tries to bribe an AP reporter to lie on the witness stand, the trial lasts 13 weeks and costs $750,000, the judge's instructions make it impossible for the jury to acquit, D'Aquino is found innocent of eight alleged overt acts of treason but guilty on one count of trying to undermine U.S. morale. Sentenced to 6 years in prison, she will serve 6½.

Japan begins training women for service in the nation's diplomatic corps.

Huk Liberation Army gunmen in Manila kill Aurora Quezon, widow of the first Filipino president, in an attack April 28.

China (above), Indonesia, and Costa Rica grant women the right to vote on the same basis as men. Chile grants woman suffrage after a long campaign, but women must vote separately from men.

A new minimum wage act passed by Congress October 26 amends the Fair Labor Standards Act of 1938 and raises the minimum hourly wage from 40¢ to 75¢ (*see* 1955).

Male and Female by Margaret Mead is published.

Eleanor Roosevelt expresses support in her newspaper column for pending legislation that would give $300 million in federal aid to public schools. New York's Cardinal Spellman opposes the mea-

sure because it would exclude parochial and other private schools, he calls Mrs. Roosevelt's position "unworthy of an American mother," but Mrs. Roosevelt immediately reiterates her belief in the principle of separating church and state.

Tokyo University admits women for the first time since its founding in 1877.

Harvard Law School announces October 9 that it will begin admitting women.

Hockaday Associates is founded by New York advertising veteran Margaret Hockaday, 42, who starts out in a converted barbershop and will continue for nearly 40 years.

Harlequin Enterprises, Ltd., is founded at Toronto. Owned largely by the *Toronto Star*, the new publishing house will turn out 12 new titles each month, and its romantic pulp novellas for women will outsell books of any other paperback publisher.

Nonfiction: *The Second Sex* (*Le Deuxième Sexe*) by French philosopher-novelist Simone de Beauvoir, 41, will be the Bible of feminists (*see* 1953); *The Need for Roots* (*L'Enracinement*) by the late Simone Weil; . . . *Au coeur des Himalayas; le Nepal* by Alexandra David-Neel; *This I Remember* by Eleanor Roosevelt.

Fiction: *The Heat of the Day* by Elizabeth Bowen; *Two Worlds and Their Ways* by Ivy Compton-Burnett; *The Holiday* by Stevie Smith; *Little Boy Lost* by Marghanita Laski; *A Wreath of Roses* by Elizabeth Taylor; *A Summer to Decide* by Pamela Hansford Johnson completes the trilogy she began in 1942; *The Golden Apple* (stories) by Eudora Welty; *The Oasis* by Mary McCarthy; *The House of Incest* by Anaïs Nin; *The Innocent Traveller* by Ethel Wilson; *Love in a Cold Climate* by Nancy Mitford; *Give Us Our Years* by Margaret Culkin Banning; *The Question of Gregory* by Elizabeth Janeway; *The Queen Bee* by Edna L. Lee; *A Calf for Venus* by Norah Lofts; *Poor Man's Orange* by Ruth Park; *Rest and Be Thankful* by Helen MacInnes; *More Work for the Undertaker* by Margery Allingham.

Poetry: *Woman to Man* by Judith Wright.

Sculpture: *Rhythmic Form* (wood) by Barbara Hepworth.

Films: Katharine Hepburn and Spencer Tracy in George Cukor's *Adam's Rib*; Broderick Crawford and Mercedes McCambridge in Robert Rossen's *All the King's Men*; Olivia de Havilland, Ralph Richardson, and Montgomery Clift in William Wyler's *The Heiress*; Orson Welles, Joseph Cotten, Trevor Howard, and Italian actress Alida Valli, 27, in Carol Reed's *The Third Man*; English actress Joan Greenwood, 28, and Basil Radford in Alexander Mackendrick's *Whisky Galore* (in America, *Tight Little Island*). Also: Michele Morgan, Ralph Richardson, and Bobby Henrey in Carol Reed's *The Fallen Idol*; Welsh-born actress Peggy Cummins, 23, and John Dall in Joseph H. Lewis's *Gun Crazy*; (Elizabeth) Jean Peters, 22, Ray Milland, and Paul Douglas in Lloyd Bacon's *It Happens Every Spring*; Jennifer Jones, James Mason, Van Heflin, and Louis Jourdan in Vincente Minnelli's *Madame Bovary*; Dame Edith Evans, now 61, plays her only film role in Thorold Dickinson's *Queen of Spades* with Anton Walbrook; James Stewart and June Allyson in Sam Wood's *The Stratton Story*; Farley Granger and Cathy O'Donnell (Ann Steely), 26, in Nicholas Ray's *They Live by Night*; James Cagney and Virginia Mayo (originally Jones), 29, in Raoul Walsh's *White Heat*; Maureen O'Hara, Gloria Graham, and Melvyn Douglas in Nicholas Ray's *A Woman's Secret*.

Ingrid Bergman shocks moviegoers August 5 by announcing that she is divorcing her husband, Dr. Peter Lindström, and abandoning her movie career; Bergman has been living with Italian director Robert Rosselini and in 6 months will bear his son Robertino out of wedlock, creating a furor.

Stage musicals: Mary Martin, Ezio Pinza, Myron McCormick, Juanita Hall, 47, as "Bloody Mary," Betta St. John, and William Tabbert in *South Pacific* 4/7 at the Majestic Theater, with Rodgers and Hammerstein songs that include "Some Enchanted Evening," "Younger than Springtime," "I'm in Love with a Wonderful Guy," "This Nearly Was Mine," "I'm Gonna Wash That Man Right Out of My Hair," "A Cockeyed Optimist," "Honey Bun," "You've Got to Be Carefully Taught," "Dites-moi Pourquoi," "There Is Nothing like a Dame," "Happy Talk," and "Bali Ha'i," 1,925 perfs.; Cicely Courtneidge as the British ambassador to a South American country in *Her Excellency* 6/22 at the

Simone de Beauvoir's book The Second Sex (Le Deuxième Sexe) *struck an international blow for feminism.* UPI/BETTMANN

Theater: Lee J. Cobb as salesman Willie Loman, Mildred Dunnock, Arthur Kennedy, and Cameron Mitchell in Arthur Miller's *Death of a Salesman* 2/10 at New York's Morosco Theater, 742 perfs.; Ralph Bellamy, Les Tremayne, Alexander Scourby, and Maureen Stapleton, 23, in Sidney Kingsley's *Detective Story* 3/23 at New York's Hudson Theater, 581 perfs.

The Stella Adler Conservatory of Acting founded at New York by actress-teacher Adler, now 48, will educate players (including Marlon Brando) in the (Stanislavski) Method system of acting.

Television drama: *The Goldbergs* 1/17 on CBS is the first TV situation comedy. Derived from the radio show first aired in 1929, it stars Molly Berg, now 50, will continue until late June 1951, and will be followed by dozens of "sitcoms."

London Hippodrome, with songs by Manning Sherwin and Harry Par-Davis; Carol Channing (Bennington '45) in *Gentlemen Prefer Blondes* 12/8 at the Ziegfeld Theater, with Jule Styne–Leo Robin songs that include "A Little Girl from Little Rock," "Diamonds Are a Girl's Best Friend," and "Bye Bye Baby," 740 perfs.

Opera: Elisabeth Schwarzkopf makes her Salzburg Festival debut as the Countess Almaviva in Mozart's 1786 opera *Le Nozze di Figaro*. She will continue performing at Salzburg nearly every year until 1964.

Popular songs: Ruth Brown (*née* Weston), 21, a former Portsmouth, Va., church choir singer, records "So Long"/"It's Raining" to begin a notable rhythm & blues career; "Scarlet Ribbons (for Her Hair)" by Evelyn Danzig, lyrics by Jack Segal; "Mona Lisa" by Jay Livingston and Ray Evans.

Mahalia Jackson records "Let the Power of the Holy Ghost Fall on Me."

"Bricktop" opens a club in Rome's Via Veneto with backing from Doris Duke (*see* 1944).

Wilson Sporting Goods agrees May 29 to sponsor formation of a Ladies Professional Golf Association (LPGA), which will become an officially chartered organization next year.

Louise Brough wins in women's singles at Wimbledon, Margaret Osborne du Pont at Forest Hills.

Bullfighter Conchita Cintrón, now 27, makes her farewell appearance in a Spanish ring, dismounts to show that she can fight on foot, executes a perfect series of passes but drops her sword, allowing the bull to live, and is promptly arrested for violating the law against women fighting on foot (it will not be repealed until 1973). She marries a Portuguese nobleman and retires to Lisbon.

U.S. bowler Marian Laddewig, 35, wins the first national All-Star games open to women December 8. She will win five consecutive titles and two subsequent titles.

Revlon introduces "Fire and Ice," a new lipstick and nail enamel that is advertised with a frankly sexual approach in advertisements featuring model Suzy Parker and copy created by agency vice president Kay Daly, 29, who will join Revlon in 1961.

Lever Brothers introduces Surf laundry detergent with advertising claims that no rinsing is needed after washing. Procter & Gamble responds by advertising that its 3-year-old Tide detergent washes clothes "so miracle clean no rinsing needed." Colgate's Fab echoes the claim.

Clothes rationing ends in Britain.

Congress passes a federal Housing Act July 15 to fund slum clearance and low-rent public housing projects. Sen. Robert Taft (R., Ohio) sponsored the legislation.

Title I of the new Housing Act (above) encourages municipalities to acquire and resell substandard areas at prices below cost for private redevelopment.

A two-bedroom U.S. house typically sells for $10,000 while a five-bedroom New York apartment rents for $110 per month. A four-bedroom duplex cooperative apartment in the East 60s near Park Avenue with two-story living room and wood-burning fireplace in its 16x21-foot library sells for $8,250 with annual maintenance of $2,970, an eight-room co-op on Fifth Avenue in the 70s with three bedrooms, 30x17-foot living room, and a view of Central Park sells for $7,434 with annual maintenance of $3,591.

Meat, dairy products, and sugar remain in short supply in Britain, and sales are restricted.

General Mills and Pillsbury introduce prepared cake mixes. Pillsbury inaugurates Bake-Offs to develop recipes using its flour (both men and women are eligible to compete in the contests, which will be held annually). Beginning in 1968, contestants will be permitted to use Pillsbury mixes or refrigerated products as well as Pillsbury flour.

Sara Lee Cheese Cake is introduced by Chicago baker Charles Lubin, 44, whose refrigerated product will make his Kitchens of Sara Lee (named after his daughter) one of the world's largest bakeries.

1950

The Republican Women's Club at Wheeling, W.Va., hears from Sen. Joseph McCarthy (R. Wisc.)

February 7 that Communists have infiltrated the U.S. State Department.

A Federal jury at New York finds March 7 that former U.S. Department of Justice analyst Judith Coplon, 28, and United Nations engineering staff employee Valentin A. Gubitchev, 33, were guilty of spying for Moscow. FBI agents arrested them a year ago as they were walking on Third Avenue near 16th Street; slips regarding FBI security reports were found in Coplon's handbag, her job involved the study of Soviet espionage, and the jury of six men and six women rejects her lawyer's arguments that she was collecting material for a book, and that she and Gubitchev acted furtively because they were in love and feared that their liaison would bring down the wrath of Gubitchev's wife or cost Coplon her job.

Dresden's Mozart Girls Choir seeks protection as political refugees at West Berlin April 4.

Communist North Korean forces invade South Korea June 25. President Truman joins with the United Nations 5 days later in authorizing use of U.S. ground forces to help repel the invasion. Chinese forces come into the conflict on North Korea's side in early November.

Hollywood actress Jean Muir is dropped from the cast of *The Aldrich Family* August 28 following allegations that she has had Communist associations.

Rep. Helen Gahagan Douglas, now 47, loses her bid for election to the U.S. Senate. Rep. Richard M. Nixon, 37, who won election in 1946 by charging that veteran congressman H. Jerry Voorhis had Communist support, uses the same smear tactics against Douglas to gain the Senate seat.

India grants women the right to vote on the same basis as men (*see* Pakistan, 1947).

Testament for Social Science by English social scientist Barbara Frances Wootton, 53, endeavors to assimilate the social and natural sciences.

The antibiotic mystatin announced by U.S. Department of Agriculture fungus authority Elizabeth Hazen, 65, and USDA chemist Rachel Brown, 52, is the first safe fungicide, effective for everything from curing athlete's foot, ringworm, life-threatening human diseases, and Dutch elm disease, to restoring moldy paintings and books. Scientists hail it as the first biomedical breakthrough since the 1928 discovery of penicillin. Hazen has found a soil sample on a friend's farm in Virginia, she showed it to Brown when they met 2 years ago, and within a year they had found and separated the antifungal substance, which will be marketed through a nonprofit research foundation. Sales will generate profits of $13 million in the next 30 years, and it will all go into grants, playing a key role in mycology research. Hazen and Brown refuse any share in the royalties and will live until their deaths on Civil Service salaries and pensions.

Hollywood: The Dream Factory by anthropologist Hortense Powdermaker expresses concern about the impact on society of a community that is dominated by crass values and projects those values in the films it makes.

Blue Cross programs cover 37 million Americans, up from 6 million in 1940, but most Americans have no health insurance (*see* 1969; Britain, 1948; Medicare, 1965).

The U.S. ranks tenth among all countries in terms of life expectancy for men, but its ranking will drop sharply in the next decade and a half.

Sales of Lydia Pinkham's Vegetable Compound fall below $2 million for the first time in a decade (*see* 1926; 1968).

Pope Pius XII proclaims the dogma of the bodily assumption of the Virgin Mary.

The National Council of the Churches of Christ in the United States is created by 25 Protestant and four Eastern Orthodox church groups with 32 million members.

U.S. Catholic schools report June 4 that they have enrolled a record 3.5 million pupils for fall classes. Roman Catholic bishops issue a statement at Washington, D.C., November 18 protesting sex education in public schools.

Educating Our Daughters: A Challenge to the Colleges by U.S. author Lynn White, Jr., 43, says that college-educated women have a special duty to ensure a stable population by counteracting the "sterility" that is overtaking better-educated and more affluent women and thus threatening democracy. Higher education, he says, must instill the idea that it is both an "incentive" and a "duty" to bear at least three children in order to counteract the "drift toward totalitarianism."

Only 2 percent of Japanese university students are women.

Haloid Co. of Rochester, N.Y., produces the first Xerox copying machine (*see* Carlson, 1938; Haloid, 1946; model 914, 1960).

Nonfiction: *Waiting for God* (*Attente de Dieu*) by the late Simone Weil; Agnes (Elizabeth) Meyer (*née* Ernst), 63, wife of *Washington Post* publisher Eugene Meyer, writes in the August *Atlantic Monthly* that the American woman, as a mother, has the primary responsibility of stopping the moral decay in U.S. society. Having herself borne five children, she says that "democratic civilization" depends upon the triumph of the truly feminine, maternal woman, and she extols the "vocation" of motherhood, saying that a woman can live in the fullest sense only by "conceiving, gestating, delivering, nursing, and rearing children of her own"; *A l'ouest barbare de la vaste Chine* and . . . *Au Pays deys brigands gentilshommes* by Alexandra David-Neel; *East of Home* by Santha Rama Rau.

Fiction: *The Sea Wall* by Marguerite Duras; *The Grass Is Singing* by Persian-born Rhodesian novelist Doris (May) Lessing (*née* Tayler), 31; *The Magic Prism* (*Trylleglasset*) (stories) by Torborg Nedreaas; *The Lost Traveller* by Antonia White; *Some Tame Gazelle* by English novelist Barbara Pym, 37; *Mary O'Grady* by Mary Lavin; *Cocktail Bar* by Norah Hoult; *A Breath of Air* by Rumer Godden; *The World My Wilderness* by Rose Macaulay; *The Beautiful Visit* by English novelist Elizabeth (Jane) Howard, 27; *The Writer's Situation* by Storm Jameson; *Joy Street* by Frances Parkinson Keyes; *Milestone* (or *Signpost*; *Dohyo*) by Yuriko Miyamoto; *The Crown of Glory* by Agnes Turnbull; *Strangers on a Train* by U.S. mystery novelist Patricia Highsmith, 29.

Poetry: *Annie Allen* by Gwendolyn Brooks wins a Pulitzer Prize, making Brooks the first black writer to win the award.

Theater: Ethel Waters, Julie (Julia) Harris, 24, and Brandon de Wilde in Carson McCullers's *The*

Member of the Wedding 1/5 at New York's Empire Theater, 501 perfs. (New York Drama Critics' Circle Award); Alec Guinness, English actress Cathleen Nesbit, 60, and Irene Worth, 33, in T. S. Eliot's *The Cocktail Party* 1/21 at New York's Henry Miller Theater, 409 perfs.; Shirley Booth, Sidney Blackmer, and Joan Loring in William Motte Inge's *Come Back, Little Sheba* 2/15 at New York's Booth Theater, 191 perfs.; Celeste Holm and Reginald Owen in Louis Verneuil's *Affairs of State* 9/25 at New York's Royale Theater, 610 perfs.; Uta Hagen and Paul Kelly in Clifford Odets's *The Country Girl* 11/10 at New York's Lyceum Theater, 235 perfs.; Lilli Palmer and Rex Harrison in John Van Druten's *Bell, Book, and Candle* 11/14 at New York's Ethel Barrymore Theater, 233 perfs.

Films: Bette Davis, Anne Baxter, 27, and Celeste Holm in Joseph L. Mankiewicz's *All about Eve*; Spencer Tracy, Elizabeth Taylor, and Joan Bennett in Vincente Minnelli's *Father of the Bride*; Barry Jones and Olive Sloane in John Boulting's *Seven Days to Noon*; Gloria Swanson, William Holden, and Erich von Stroheim in Billy Wilder's *Sunset Boulevard* (it is Swanson's 63rd feature, and she has agreed to play the role of silent-screen star Norma Desmond for $53,333 when once she earned up to $1 million per year). Also: Sterling Hayden, Louis Calhern, and Jean (Ver) Hagen, 26, in John Huston's *The Asphalt Jungle*; Judy Holliday, William Holden, and Broderick Crawford in George Cukor's *Born Yesterday*; Patricia (originally Patsy) Neal, 23, and John Garfield in Michael Curtiz's *The Breaking Point*; Ralph Richardson, Ann Todd, and Nigel Patrick in David Lean's *Breaking the Sound Barrier*; James Stewart and Josephine Hull in Henry Koster's *Harvey*; Anna Neagle (who married director Wilcox in 1943) in Herbert Wilcox's *Lady with the Lamp*; Richard Widmark, Paul Douglas, and Barbara Bel Geddes in Elia Kazan's *Panic in the Streets*; Valerie Hobson, John Howard Davies, and John Mills in Anthony Pelissier's *The Rocking Horse Winner*; Anton Walbrook, Simone Simon, German-born actress Simone Signoret (originally Simone-Henriette-Charlotte Kaminker), 29, Serge Reggiani, Danielle Darrieux, and Jean-Louis Barrault in Max Ophuls's *La Ronde*; Claudette Colbert and Sessue Hayakawa in Jean Negulesco's *Three Came Home*; James Stewart and Shelley Winters (originally Shirley Schrift), 28, in Anthony Mann's

Winchester 73; Robert Donat and Margaret Leighton, 28, in Anthony Asquith's *The Winslow Boy*; Rosalind Russell and Ray Milland in Edward Buzzell's *A Woman of Distinction*; Ann Sheridan in Norman Foster's *Woman on the Run*.

Television shows: *What's My Line?* 2/2 on CBS stations, with emcee John Charles Daley, Jr., 35, and panelists: actress Arlene Francis (Kazanjian), 41; columnist Dorothy Kilgallen, now 36; and anthologist Louis Untermeyer, 64, who try to guess the occupations of guests. Publisher Bennett A. Cerf, 51, will replace Untermeyer in 1952, and the show will continue until 9/3/67. *Your Show of Shows* debuts on NBC stations with comedians Sid Caesar, Imogene Coca, Carl Reiner, and Howard Morris. It will continue with 160 weekly programs until 1954.

Washington Post critic Paul Hume writes a disparaging review of a song recital by Margaret Truman and receives a vituperative letter in longhand from the president on White House stationery dated December 6.

Opera: Spanish soprano Victoria de Los Angeles (*née* Victoria Gómez Cima), 26, makes her London debut at Covent Garden singing the role of Mimi in the 1896 Puccini opera *La Bohème*, goes on to make her Milan debut at La Scala, and will make her Metropolitan Opera debut next year in the 1859 Gounod opera *Faust* (she will appear regularly at Covent Garden until 1961, singing such roles as Manon Lescaut and Cio-cio-san); U.S. soprano Roberta Peters, 20, makes her Metropolitan Opera debut 11/17, replacing her ailing colleague Nadine Conner in the role of Zerlina in the 1787 Mozart opera *Don Giovanni*.

Broadway musicals: Ethel Merman as U.S. Ambassador to Luxembourg Perle Mesta (*see* 1949) in *Call Me Madam* 10/12 at the Imperial Theater, with Irving Berlin songs that include "Hostess with the Mostes' on the Ball," "It's a Lovely Day Today," "The Ocarina," and "The Best Thing for You," 644 perfs.; Robert Alda, Vivian Blaine, Sam Levene, and Isabel Bigley in *Guys and Dolls* 11/24 at the 46th Street Theater, with Frank Loesser songs that include "Luck, Be a Lady," "Fugue for Tinhorns," "I've Never Been in Love Before," "A Bushel and a Peck," "Adelaide's Lament," "Sue Me," and "If I Were a Bell," 1,200 perfs.; Charlotte Greenwood, William Eythe, and Peggy Rea in *Out of This World*

12/21 at the New Century Theater, with Cole Porter songs that include "Use Your Imagination," 157 perfs.

Popular songs: Teresa Brewer, 19, records "Music, Music, Music" and has her first hit; "Teardrops from My Eyes" establishes Ruth Brown as the top rhythm & blues singer; Patti Page records "Tennessee Waltz" and has another big hit.

Gospel singer-songwriter Margaret Allison, 30, records her "Touch Me, Lord Jesus," which has sales of 500,000 copies in less than 6 months.

The mambo is introduced from Cuba to U.S. dance floors.

Louise Brough wins in women's singles at Wimbledon, Margaret Osborne du Pont at Forest Hills. Player Gussie Moran has shocked many in the stands at Wimbledon by wearing lace underwear that showed every time she swung her racquet.

Florence Chadwick, 31, swims the English Channel August 20 and beats the record set by Gertrude Ederle in 1926. The San Diego stenographer crosses from France to England in 13 hours, 20 minutes (*see* 1951).

Cotton's share of the U.S. textile market falls to 65 percent, down from 80 percent in 1940, and man-made fibers—mostly rayons and acetates—increase their share to more than 20 percent (*see* 1960).

Miss Clairol, introduced by Clairol Co., takes half the application time needed by other hair colorings (*see* 1931).

U.S. cosmetics maker Hazel Gladys Bishop, 44, introduces the first no-smear lipstick.

A Texas court acquits a black man of raping a black woman who rented a room from him (*Killingsworth* v. *State*). Her "feigned and passive resistance" does not constitute sufficient grounds for a case of rape, the court rules January 25.

Otis Elevator installs the first passenger elevators with self-opening doors in the Atlantic Refining building at Dallas. Self-service elevators will force thousands of operators—women as well as men—to seek other means of employment.

A federal tax of 10¢ per pound on U.S. margarine is removed, as are all federal restrictions on coloring margarine yellow. Butter is in such short supply that retail prices often top $1 per pound, and U.S. consumers turn increasingly to margarine, whose average retail price is 33¢ per pound versus an average of 73¢ for butter.

General Foods introduces Minute Rice.

Betty Crocker's Picture Cookbook is a U.S. best-seller.

1951

 A federal judge at New York finds Ethel Rosenberg (*née* Greenglass), 35, her husband, Julius, 34, and a male friend guilty March 30 of having sold atomic secrets to Soviet agents. Mrs. Rosenberg's brother worked at the Los Alamos nuclear research station in New Mexico; she and Julius are sentenced to death April 5 (*see* 1953).

Eva Perón announces her candidacy for vice president, the military objects, she disclaims any intentions of running August 22, an Argentine Army group stages a revolt against President Perón's repressive regime September 28, but he wins reelection November 11 with campaign help from the popular Evita.

 The United Nations drafts a convention on women's rights August 19.

Mongolia grants women the right to vote on the same basis as men.

Switzerland's Parliament votes September 20 to kill a woman suffrage bill.

United Nations delegates receive copies of a petition from the Communist Civil Rights Congress charging a "conspiracy whereby finance joins with the state and terrorist organizations to disenfranchise Americans for political power and private profit." Headed "We Charge Genocide," the petition argues that claims of rape, particularly by white women against black men, are genocidal.

Accused rapist Willie McGee is executed after being convicted of having raped a white woman in her own bed in 1945. The prosecution has produced little or no evidence, and there are suspicions

that the woman charged rape in order to keep her husband from discovering that she and McGee, a black man, had been having an affair.

 One of every four middle-class U.S. wives is in the work force, up from 7 percent in 1945. More than half of all female college graduates are employed.

State "fair trade" price-fixing laws are not binding on retailers, the U.S. Supreme Court rules May 21. Price wars begin immediately, and department stores are mobbed.

Lillian Vernon Corp. has its beginnings in a mail-order business started by Mount Vernon, N.Y., newlywed Lillian Hochberg, 22, who takes $500 in wedding-gift money, buys a 5-inch classified ad in *Seventeen* magazine, and offers a monogrammed belt in black, tan, or red for $7. Hochberg's husband makes only $75 per week from his small ladies' clothing store, her father agrees to make the belts for $3 each, she does the monogramming, and within 3 months she has $32,000 in orders. Vernon (she will adopt the name legally in 1990) will put out her first catalog (eight pages, black and white) in 1954, and by 1992 she will be mailing 142 catalogs and running a business with sales of $162 million and a net profit of nearly $10 million.

 U.S. geneticist Barbara McClintock, 49, announces her discovery that genes are in a constant state of transformation. She and her colleague Harriet Creighton were urged by geneticist Thomas Hunt Morgan in 1931 to publish the results of their work in the *Proceedings of the National Academy of Sciences*, she received a 1933 Guggenheim fellowship, has been a director of the Genetic Society of America since 1934, and while other geneticists dismiss her notion that "jumping" genes in the chromosomes of a plant will change future generations of the plants they produce, calling the idea "crazy," McClintock will be vindicated (*see* 1983).

 Dr. Noel Browne, British minister of health, resigns under pressure April 11; he has proposed the introduction of free ante- and postnatal care for mothers as well as free medical care for all children under age 16. Catholic bishops have objected to Catholic mothers being exposed to gynecological information from non-Catholic doctors.

Paris obstetricians Fernand Lamaze and Pierre Vellay introduce a "psychoprophylaxis" method of "painless" childbirth derived from experimental work developed from ancient folk practices by Soviet scientists in the 1920s and 1930s and introduced this year in the Soviet Union as the "official" method of pain relief (*see* Read, 1944). Lamaze and Vellay have traveled to the Soviet Union to study the new methods of relieving pain without drugs and Lamaze has simplified the Pavlovian techniques, adding rapid, shallow breathing, or "panting." The Lamaze method, which calls for counteracting pain signals by concentrating the mind on extraneous sensations, appears to be different from the Read method in that it emphasizes the active role of the woman, who should never "cease to be the force which directs, controls, regulates . . . labor," but its system of rapid, shallow breathing is in fact virtually identical to the Read method in theory, practice, and goals (*see* 1956).

Recording for the Blind has its beginnings in a two-room New York office opened by former American Red Cross Nurses' Aide Corps assistant director Anne MacDonald (*née* Thompson), 54, who next year will persuade friends to establish studios at Athens, Ga., Chicago, Denver, Los Angeles, Oak Ridge, Tenn., and Phoenix. While working for the Women's Auxiliary of the New York Public Library, MacDonald has observed a program that provided recordings for blind veterans attending college on the G.I. Bill of Rights. Her organization will grow in 40 years to have 32 studios in 16 states with some 4,000 volunteers recording fiction and non-fiction books on tape for students from fifth grade to graduate school. They will record 80,000 books to serve about 33,000 "readers" per year.

Nonfiction: *War in Korea: The Report of a Woman Combat Correspondent* by *New York Herald Tribune* reporter Marguerite Higgins (who is accused by her male rivals of having slept with generals to get information that scooped the competition); *The Origins of Totalitarianism* by German-American political theorist Hannah Arendt, 44, who fled Adolf Hitler's dictatorship; *The Secret Oral Teachings in Tibetan Buddhist Sects* (*Les enseignements secrets dans les sects bouddhista Tibétanites; la vue pénétrante*) and *L'Inde hier, aujourd'hui, demain* by Alexandra David-Neel, now 82; *A Man Called Peter*

by U.S. writer Katherine Marshall (*née* Wood), 36; *The Sea Around Us* by U.S. biologist Rachel Louise Carson, 44.

Fiction: *Hadrian's Memoirs* (*Les Memoires d'Hadrien*) by French novelist Marguerite Yourcenar, 48; *Tattered Humans* (*Ningenboro*) by Yoko Ota wins Japan's Women's Literature Award; *Floating Cloud* (*Ukigumo*) and *Rice* (*Meshi*) by Fumiko Hayashi; *The Amber Necklace* (*Die Bernsteinkette*) (stories) by Helene Voigt-Diederichs; *The Ballad of the Sad Café* (stories) by Carson McCullers; *The Smoking Mountain* (stories) by Kay Boyle; *In the Absence of Angels* (stories) by U.S. author Hortense Calisher, 39; *Fallen Away* by Margaret Culkin Banning deals with marriage between people of differing religions; *The Strange Children* by Caroline Gordon, who was received into the Catholic church and is preoccupied with grace and salvation; *Loving Without Tears* by Molly Keane; *My Cousin Rachel* by Daphne du Maurier; *The Quiet Gentleman* by Georgette Heyer; *A Game of Hide-and-Seek* by Elizabeth Taylor; *The Blessing* by Nancy Mitford; *The Witch Diggers* by Jessamyn West; *The Daughter of Time* by Josephine Tey; *Neither Five Nor Three* by Helen MacInnes.

Poetry: *Collected Poems* by Marianne Moore (1952 Pulitzer Prize); *A Change of World* by U.S. poet Adrienne Cecile Rich, 22; *Gull* (*Miyakodori*) by Teijo Nakamura; *Urania* by Ruth Pitter.

Sculpture: *Contrapuntal Forms, Vertical Forms,* and *Rock Form* (Penwith) (all wood) by Barbara Hepworth.

Theater: Clive Brook and German-born actress Betsy von Furstenberg, 18, in the late Philip Barry's *Second Threshold* 1/2 at New York's Morosco Theater, 126 perfs.; Maureen Stapleton and Don Murray in Tennessee Williams's *The Rose Tattoo* 2/3 at New York's Martin Beck Theater, 306 perfs.; *The Autumn Garden* by Lillian Hellman 3/7 at New York's Coronet Theater, with Florence Eldridge, Kent Smith, and Jane Wyatt, 101 perfs.; Jessica Tandy and Hume Cronyn in Jan de Hartog's *The Four Poster* 10/24 at New York's Ethel Barrymore Theater, 632 perfs.; Julie Harris as Sally Bowles and William Prince as Christopher Isherwood in John Van Druten's *I Am a Camera* 11/28 at New York's Empire Theater, 262 perfs.

Television: *Search for Tomorrow* 9/19 on CBS (daytime); *Love of Life* 9/9 on CBS (daytime); *I Love Lucy* 10/15 on CBS, with Lucille Ball as Lucy Ricardo and her husband, Desi Arnaz, as Ricky (to 5/6/1957); *Kukla, Fran & Ollie* becomes an NBC network show after having appeared on local Chicago television (Fran Allison will play opposite Burr Tillstrom's puppets for 6 years on NBC and ABC-TV).

Films: Katharine Hepburn, Humphrey Bogart, and Robert Morley in John Huston's *The African Queen*; Patricia Neal and Michael Rennie in Robert Wise's *The Day the Earth Stood Still*; Michele Morgan and Henry Vidal in Alessandro Blasetti's *Fabiola*; Robert Donat and Viennese actress Maria Schell, 25, in John Boulting's *The Magic Box*; Patricia Walters in Jean Renoir's *The River*; Vivien Leigh and Marlon Brando in Elia Kazan's *A Streetcar Named Desire*. Also: Robert Stack, Joy Page, Gilbert Roland, and Katy Jurado (Maria Jurado Garcia), 24, in Budd Boetticher's *The Bullfighter and the Lady*; Michael Redgrave, Jean Kent (Joan Summerfield), 30, and Nigel Patrick in Anthony Asquith's *The Browning Version*; Fredric March

Katharine Hepburn played a spinster, one of her most memorable roles, in The African Queen. CULVER PICTURES, INC.

and Mildred Dunnock in Laslo Benedick's *Death of a Salesman*; Brigitte Fossey in René Clement's *Forbidden Games* (*Jeux Interdits*); Alec Guinness and Joan Greenwood in Alexander Mackendrick's *The Man in the White Suit*; Gene Tierney, John Lund, and Thelma Ritter, 45, in Mitchell Leisen's *The Mating Season*; Anna Neagle in Herbert Wilcox's *Odette*; John Howard Davies, Robert Newton, and Hermione Baddeley, 44, in Gordon Parry's *Tom Brown's Schooldays*; Denise Darcel, Robert Taylor, Hope Emerson, and Lenore Lonergan in William Wellman's *Westward the Women*.

Hollywood musicals: French dancer-actress Leslie Caron, 20, Gene Kelly, and Oscar Levant in Vincente Minnelli's *An American in Paris* with music by the late George Gershwin.

Broadway musicals: Gertrude Lawrence and Yul Brynner in *The King and I* 3/29 at the St. James Theater, with a book based on Margaret London's novel *Anna and the King of Siam* based in turn on diaries kept by the late Anna Leonowens (*see* 1862), Rodgers and Hammerstein songs that include "Getting to Know You," "Hello, Young Lovers," "We Kiss in a Shadow," "Shall We Dance?," and "Whistle a Happy Tune," 1,246 perfs.; Shirley Booth and Johnny Johnston in *A Tree Grows in Brooklyn* 4/19 at the Alvin Theater, with Arthur Schwartz–Dorothy Fields songs that include "Make the Man Love Me," "Look Who's Dancing," and "I'll Buy You a Star," 267 perfs.; Peruvian soprano Yma Sumac (Emperatrice Chavarri), 23, who appeared at the Hollywood Bowl 2 years ago, puppeteers Bil and Cora Baird, and singer Barbara (Nell) Cook, 23, in *Flahooley* 5/14 at the Broadway Theater, with Sammy Fain–Yip Harburg songs that include "Here's to Your Illusions," 40 perfs.; Ann Crowley and Eddie Dowling in *Paint Your Wagon* 11/12 at the Shubert Theater, with Frederick Loewe–Alan Jay Lerner songs that include "They Call the Wind Maria," "I Talk to the Trees," and "I Still See Elisa," 289 perfs.

English-born U.S. jazz pianist-composer Marian Margaret McPartland (*née* Turner), 31, forms her own trio.

Opera: U.S. soprano Leontyne Price, 22, makes her stage debut in the 1934 Virgil Thomson opera *Four Saints in Three Acts*; Jennie Tourel, now 41, sings in the world premiere of the Stravinsky opera *The Rake's Progress* 9/11 at the Teatro la Fenice, Venice.

Ballet: New Orleans–born ballerina Janet Collins, 34, makes her debut with the Metropolitan Opera in the 1871 Verdi opera *Aïda*: she is the first black artist to perform on the stage at the Met and will be in the Met's corps de ballet until 1954; Canadian ballerina Melissa Hayden (Mildred Herman), 28, and Hugh Laing in *The Miraculous Mandarin* 9/6 at the New York City Center, with music by the late Béla Bartók; Tanaquil LeClerq and Jerome Robbins in *The Pied Piper* 12/4 at the New York City Center, with music by Aaron Copland.

Popular songs: Rosemary Clooney, 23, records "Come-On-A My House" by author-playwright William Saroyan and his cousin Ross Bagdasarian with a jangly harpsichord backup orchestrated by Mitch Miller; Jo Stafford, 30, records "Shrimp Boats" and has her first big success; Patti Page records "Mocking Bird Hill"; "Too Young" by Sid Lippman, lyrics by Sylvia Dee.

Doris Hart, 26 (U.S.), wins in women's singles at Wimbledon, Maureen Connolly ("Little Mo"), 16, at Forest Hills.

Florence Chadwick becomes the first woman to cross the English Channel from England to France (*see* 1950). She makes the crossing from Dover September 11 in 16 hours, 22 minutes.

Egyptian commoner Narriman Sadek, 17, marries King Farouk, 31, May 6 at Cairo.

Woolworth heiress Barbara Hutton, now 38, obtains a divorce from Prince Igor Troubetzkoy, who has demanded $3 million as a parting gift but does not get it. She has had two major operations, weighs only 86 pounds, and is persuaded by Doris Duke to recuperate at Duke's Honolulu home, Shangri-la (*see* 1954).

Japanese fashion designer Hanae Mori, 25, opens a studio in Tokyo's Shinjuku district to begin what will become a worldwide empire. She will soon be creating costumes for Japan's growing movie industry (*see* 1965).

New York designer Ann Fogarty (*née* Whitney), 32, wins the Fashion Critics' Award. She has perfected the New Look (*see* 1947) and will modify the Empire style with a "camise" look for young women sized 6 to 12.

The Roman Catholic Church at Madrid announces July 7 that scanty bathing attire will henceforth be forbidden.

Europe sees its first striptease show as the Crazy Horse Saloon opens in a former coal cellar on the Champs-Elysées in Paris. Ex-painter, ex-decorator, ex–antique dealer, ex-restaurateur Alain Bernardin, 32, has hired the Slim Briggs orchestra from Houston, offers striptease shows, and creates a sensation.

A Stockholm court fines an 18-year-old sailor September 22 for kissing his girl in public.

Australian sheep raisers introduce the virus disease myxomatosis in an effort to kill off rabbits, which are consuming enough grass to feed 40 million sheep. Virologist Dame Jean Macnamara, now 52, has helped obtain the controversial virus from South America, where the disease is endemic, and will be credited with saving the wool industry more than £30 million (*see* polio, 1925).

Gerber Products starts using MSG (monosodium glutamate) in its baby foods to make them taste better to mothers (*see* 1969).

Britain's first supermarket chain begins operations in September. Premier Supermarkets opens its first store in London's Earls Court (*see* 1948).

Margaret Sanger urges development of an oral contraceptive for humans. She visits with Gregory Goodman Pincus, scientific director of the Worcester Foundation for Experimental Biology, and promises him a grant to follow up on experiments he has conducted on fertility in animals (*see* 1948). Pincus has brought Min-chueh Chang, an expert in artificial insemination and sperm biology, from Cambridge University to work with his team at Worcester (*see* 1954).

1952

Britain's Queen Elizabeth II inherits the throne February 6 upon the death of her father, George VI, who has succumbed to lung cancer at age 56 after a reign of more than 15 years. His widow, now

51, will continue for more than 4 decades to make herself popular. His elder daughter, now 25, who drove a truck every day during World War II, flies home from a visit to East Africa and begins a long reign in which the Empire will decline from 40 nations to no more than 12 with the British monarch having an effective voice in only one.

Playwright Lillian Hellman defies the Dies Committee May 22, testifying that she is not a "Red" but will not say whether or not she was 3 or 4 years ago because such testimony "would hurt innocent people in order to save myself. . . . I cannot and will not cut my conscience to fit this year's fashions." But the Communist "witch-hunt" continues, ruining many careers (see 1950).

Argentina's First Lady Eva "Evita" Perón dies of cancer July 26 at 33, plunging the country into mourning. More popular than her husband, Juan, a champion of women who has won them the vote and persuaded the legislature to legalize divorce, she has also been quick to punish any who criticized her by having them tortured or simply "disappeared."

 Argentinian women vote for the first time on the same basis as men (see 1947).

Soprano Dorothy Maynor, 41, who sang at President Truman's inauguration in 1949, appears at Washington's Constitution Hall February 17, becoming the first black artist to perform commercially in the D.A.R. auditorium since before 1939.

Parliament passes legislation May 15 giving British women civil servants compensation equal to that of their male colleagues.

Greek women gain the right June 12 to vote on the same basis as men.

Chifuren, a Japanese women's organization for civil rights and consumer affairs, is founded by Shigeri Takayama, 53, who before the war helped found the League for the Defense of Women's Rights to take part in government. She has organized aid for the widows of men killed in battle and will served in the upper house of the Diet.

 Congress amends the Social Security Act of 1935 to increase benefits to the elderly by 12.5 percent and permit pension recipients to earn as much as $75 per month without loss of benefits.

Naval Reserve officer Grace Brewster Hopper, now 46, invents the first computer compiler, making it possible for the first time to program a computer automatically instead of writing instructions for each new software package (see Mark I, 1944). A Vassar graduate with a Yale PhD in mathematics, Hopper is employed as a senior programmer for Remington Rand and works on Univac, the first large-scale commercial computer. She will be credited with inventing COBOL, the first user-friendly English-language business-oriented languge for computers.

British biochemist Rosalind Pitt-Rivers and others isolate the thyroid hormone tri-iodothyronine.

A poliomyelitis epidemic affects more than 50,000 Americans; 3,300 die, thousands are left crippled.

U.S. microbiologist Jonas Edward Salk, 38, tests a vaccine against polio, administering a hypodermic solution based on killed viruses. He has studied the findings of Australian virologists Jean Macnamara and Macfarlane Burnet (see 1925; 1954).

Columbia-Presbyterian Medical Center anesthesiologist Virginia Apgar, 43, devises a scoring system for evaluating the heart rate, breathing, muscle tone, reflexes, and skin color of newborn infants to determine whether or not they need special help to stay alive. One of the few medical students at Columbia University in the early 1930s, Dr. Apgar is head of the Medical Center's anesthesiology department and its first female professor.

Former American G.I. Christine (originally George) Jorgenson, 26, returns to New York from Copenhagen December 15 wearing a fur coat and high heels after 2,000 hormone injections and six sex-change operations, one of which removed what she called her "malformation," meaning her penis. She sells her life story to *American Weekly* for $30,000 (her parents say the money will be used to help others "suffering in the no-man's-land of sex") and will do a nightclub act in which she will sing "I Enjoy Being a Girl" and do impersonations of Marlene Dietrich (see 1953).

 Nonfiction: *A House Is Not a Home* by former New York madam Polly Adler, whose best-seller contains revelations that make her internationally famous; *Amy Vanderbilt's Complete Book of Etiquette* by former International News Service columnist Amy Vanderbilt, 43, whose 700-page volume is a source of customs, mores, and manners by a relative of the late Commodore Vanderbilt (who had no manners at all); *Love Conquers Nothing: A Glandular History of Civilization* (in England, *Love Conquers Nothing: A New Look at Old Romances*) by Emily Hahn.

Fiction: *Wise Blood* by U.S. novelist Flannery O'Connor, 27; *The Groves of Academe* by Mary McCarthy; *The Catherine Wheel* by Jean Stafford; *Martha Quest* by Doris Lessing; *The Sugar House* (second volume of a trilogy) by Antonia White; *Excellent Women* by Barbara Pym; *A Many-Splendoured Thing* by Chinese-born English physician-novelist Han Suyin, 35, who completed her medical studies at London after the death of her husband, General Tang, in China's civil war and now marries an English police officer at Singapore, where she practices in an anti-tuberculosis clinic; *A Light for Fools* (or *Dead Yesterdays*, *Tutti in nostri*) by Natalia Ginzburg; *The People with the Dogs* by Christina Stead; *Catherine Carter* by Pamela Hansford Johnson, who in 1950 married physicist-author C. P. Snow, having divorced her first husband; *The Equations of Love: Tuesday and Wednesday* and *Lilly's Story* by Ethel Wilson; *Elf Fire* (*Onibi*) by Nobuko Yoshiya, who gains acceptance as a serious writer at age 56; *The Scale of Life* (*Waage des Lebens*) by Helene Voigt-Diedrichs, now 77; *Giant* by Edna Ferber; *Confessors of the Name* by Gladys Schmitt; *Steamboat Gothic* by Frances Parkinson Keyes; *Madam, Will You Talk?* by English novelist Mary (Florence Elinor) Stewart (*née* Rainbow), 39; *Naked to Mine Enemies* by U.S. novelist Susan Yorke, 37, who was born in a German prison camp to Dutch and Belgian parents; *The Swimming Pool* by Mary Roberts Rinehart, now 77, whose mystery has been rejected by the *Saturday Evening Post* but whose novella *The Frightened Wife* will be serialized in the *Post* next year; *The Tiger in the Smoke* by Margery Allingham; *Vanish in an Instant* by Canadian mystery novelist Margaret Millar (*née* Sturm), 37; *The Singing Sands* by the late Josephine Tey (Elizabeth MacKintosh), who has died February 13 at age 55.

Poetry: *The Ermine* by Ruth Pitter; *Houses by the Sea* by the late Robin Hyde, who died of benzedrine poisoning in England in 1939.

Juvenile: *The Borrowers* by English writer Mary Norton, 49; *The Storm Book*, *Indian Indian*, and *Do You Know the Magic Word?* by Charlotte Zolotow.

Painting: *Mountains and Sea* by U.S. painter Helen Frankenthaler, 25, who has studied under Mexican painter Rufino Tamayo at Bennington, been influenced by Jackson Pollock and Hans Hofmann, developed a technique of applying very thin paint to unprimed canvas, allowing it to soak in and create atmospheric blots, and begun a relationship with New York critic Clement Greenberg. New York painter Elaine Marie Katherine de Kooning (*née* Fried), 32, gives her first exhibition at the Stable Gallery. Married to the Dutch-American painter Willem de Kooning, 48, she will teach at Bard College, Cooper Union, Yale, Carnegie-Mellon, and other colleges.

Sculpture: *Group II (People Waiting)* (wood) by Barbara Hepworth; *The Devil with Claws* by Germaine Richier.

New York's Metropolitan Museum of Art gets its first women trustees March 17: Mrs. Vincent Astor, Mrs. Ogden Reid, and Mrs. Sheldon Whitehouse.

Theater: José Ferrer and Judith Evelyn in Joseph Kramm's *The Shrike* 1/15 at New York's Cort Theater, 161 perfs.; Edna Best and Basil Rathbone in S. N. Behrman's *Jane* 2/1 at New York's Coronet Theater, 100 perfs.; Joyce Carey and Alfred Lunt in Noël Coward's *Quadrille* 9/12 at London's Phoenix Theatre; Shirley Booth and Dino DiLuca in Arthur Laurents's *The Time of the Cuckoo* 10/15 at New York's Empire Theater, 263 perfs.; *The Mousetrap* by Agatha Christie 11/25 at London's 453-seat Ambassadors Theatre, with Richard Attenborough and Sheila Sim in a melodrama that will move March 25, 1974, to the larger St. Martin's Theatre, will still be playing when Dame Agatha dies early in 1976, and will continue for many years after; Neva Patterson and Tom Ewell in George Axelrod's *The Seven-Year Itch* 11/20 at New York's Fulton Theater, 1,141 perfs.

The U.S. television industry adopts a moral code March 1 raising the necklines of women who appear on TV.

Films: Gary Cooper and Grace Kelly, 22, in Fred Zinneman's *High Noon*; John Wayne, Maureen O'Hara, and Barry Fitzgerald in John Ford's *The*

Quiet Man. Also: Kirk Douglas, Lana Turner, and Dick Powell in Vincente Minnelli's *The Bad and the Beautiful*; Simone Signoret in Jacques Becker's *Casque d'Or*; Burt Lancaster and Shirley Booth in Daniel Mann's *Come Back, Little Sheba*; Lilli Palmer and Rex Harrison in Irving Reis's *The Four-Poster*; Anna Magnani in Jean Renoir's *The Golden Coach*; Betty Hutton, Charlton Heston, Cornell Wilde, and James Stewart in Cecil B. De Mille's *The Greatest Show on Earth*; Claire Bloom (Blume), 21, and Charles Chaplin in Chaplin's *Limelight*; Michael MacLiammoir, Suzanne Cloutier, and Orson Welles in Welles's *Othello*; Stewart Granger and Eleanor Parker in George Sidney's *Scaramouche*; Bette Davis, Sterling Hayden, and Natalie Wood in Stuart Heisler's *The Star*; Harriet Andersson, 20, and Lars Ekborg in Ingmar Bergman's *Summer with Monika*; Susan Hayward in Walter Lang's *With a Song in My Heart*, based loosely on the life of Broadway musical star Jane Froman (*see* 1943); Jean Kent, Susan Shaw (Patsy Sloots), 23, Hermione Baddeley, and Dirk Bogarde in Anthony Asquith's *The Woman in Question*.

Hollywood musicals: Debbie (*née* Mary Frances) Reynolds, 16, Donald O'Connor, Jean Hagen, Cyd Charisse (Tula Ellice Finklea), 29, and Gene Kelly in Kelly and Stanley Donen's *Singin' in the Rain*, a spoof on early talking pictures with songs that include "My Lucky Star," "Broadway Melody," "Good Morning," and the title song.

Broadway musicals: *New Faces* 5/16 at the Royale Theater, with singer-actress Eartha Kitt, 24, and Alice Ghostley, songs that include "Love Is a Simple Thing" by Jane Carroll, lyrics by Arthur Siegal, "Monotonous" by Arthur Siegal, lyrics by Jane Carroll and Nancy Graham, 365 perfs.; Sheila Bond and Jack Cassidy in *Wish You Were Here* 6/25 at the Imperial Theater, with Harold Rome songs that include "Where Did the Night Go?" and the title song, 598 perfs.

Popular songs: Teresa Brewer records "Till I Waltz Again with You"; Jo Stafford records "Jambalaya" and "You Belong to Me"; Rosemary Clooney records "Botch-A-Me," "Half As Much," and "Tenderly"; Atlanta-born choir singer Gladys Knight, 8, wins *Ted Mack's Amateur Hour* television talent show singing Nat King Cole's "Too Young"

and forms the Pips with her brother Merald "Bubba" Knight, 10, her sister Brenda, 9, her cousins Edward Patten, 13, William Guest, 11, and William's sister Elenor (*see* 1961).

Seattle skier Jeanette Burr, 23, wins the Swiss National Ski Championship at Grindelwald January 13.

Austrian skier Trude Jochum-Beiser wins the downhill event in 1 minute, 47.1 seconds in the winter Olympics at Oslo, Vermont skier Andrea Mead Lawrence, 20, the slalom in 2 minutes, 10.6 seconds and the giant slalom in 2 minutes, 6.8 seconds, British figure skater Jeanette Altwegg the gold medal in her event. Australian runner Marjorie Jackson, 21, beats Fanny Blankers-Koen to win the 100-meter dash in 11.5 seconds and the 200-meter dash in 23.7 seconds at the summer games in Helsinki, Australian runner Shirley S. de la Hunty wins the 80-meter hurdles in 10.9 seconds, South African athlete Ester Brand the running high jump (5 feet, 5 3/4 inches), New Zealand athlete Yvette Williams the long jump (20 feet, 5 3/4 inches), Soviet athlete Galina Zybina the shot put (50 feet, 1½ inches), Czech athlete Dana Zatopek the javelin throw (265 feet, 7 inches). Hungarian swimmer Katalin Szoke wins the 100-meter freestyle in 1 minute, 6.8 seconds, Hungarian swimmer Valerie Gyenge the 400-meter freestyle in 5 minutes, 12.1 seconds, South African swimmer Joan Harrison the 100-meter backstroke in 1 minute, 14.3 seconds, Hungarian swimmer Eva Szekely the 200-meter breaststroke in 2 minutes, 51.7 seconds, U.S. diver Patricia McCormick, 22, the springboard dive and platform dive.

Maureen Connolly wins in women's singles at both Wimbledon and Forest Hills.

Scrabble gains popularity after a vacationing Macy's executive sees it played at a resort and orders a few dozen sets for the store to sell (*see* 1948). Orders pour in, James Brunot (who pays inventor Alfred Butts about 3¢ per set) hires 35 workers to produce 6,000 sets per week, cannot keep up with demand, and finally turns over operations to the Bay Shore, Long Island, firm Selchow & Righter, which rejected the game years ago. Scrabble will appear in six languages.

An article in the *Yale Law Journal* suggests that rape victims bear a responsiblity for the actions of their attackers because of the "unusual inducement to malicious or psychopathic accusation inherent in the sexual nature of the crime." Model penal codes of the next two decades will incorporate this concept.

War-inflated food prices are so high that Gen. Dwight D. Eisenhower uses them as a campaign issue in his presidential campaign, but farm prices will fall 22 percent in the next 2 years and food prices will fall as a consequence.

No-Cal Ginger Ale, introduced by Kirsch Beverages of Brooklyn, N.Y., uses cyclamates in place of sugar, is the first palatable sugar-free soft drink, and begins a revolution in the beverage industry (*see* cyclamates, 1950). Russian-American Hyman Kirsch, now 75, started a soft-drink business in 1904 with a 14x30-foot store in Brooklyn's Williamsburg section. Physicians at the Kingsbrook Medical Center he founded asked Kirsch in 1949 to develop a sugar-free, salt-free soft drink for obese, diabetic, and hypertensive patients (*see* Diet-Rite Cola, 1962).

Pream powdered instant cream for coffee is introduced by M. and R. Dietetic Laboratories, Inc., of Columbus, Ohio (*see* Coffee-Mate, 1961).

New York State repeals its law against selling yellow-colored margarine; other dairy states continue to prohibit its sale (*see* 1943; 1967).

A contraceptive tablet developed by Chicago's G. D. Searle laboratories is made of phosphated hesperiden (*see* 1960; Pincus, Hoagland, 1954).

The first international organization for birth control is founded November 29 at Bombay.

1953

Publisher's wife and former playwright Clare Boothe Luce, now 49, takes office March 3 as U.S. ambassador to Italy (but *see* 1954).

Soviet dictator Josef Stalin dies at Moscow March 5 at age 73.

Britain's Elizabeth II is crowned June 2 at Westminster Abbey.

Elizabeth II was destined to witness a diminishing British Empire in a reign of more than 40 years.

Ethel Rosenberg and her husband, Julius, are executed June 19 for transmitting U.S. atomic secrets to Soviet agents (*see* 1951); President Eisenhower has rejected their clemency plea; a new series of U.S. atomic tests begins in the Nevada desert.

Hundreds of Cuban women fight police in midtown Havana December 5 as they attempt to march to a rally organized by the Society of Friends of the Republic. Members of the Women's Martí Centennial Civic Front, allied with the 26th of July movement headed by revolutionist Fidel Castro Ruiz (who lives in exile in Mexico), they sustain casualties: scores are beaten and many arrested (*see* 1959).

Mexico and Sudan grant women the right to vote on equal terms with men.

Federal tax reductions should be postponed until the budget is balanced, says President Eisenhower, who appoints tall, vivacious, Utah-born Republican party worker Ivy (Maude) Priest (*née* Baker), 47, Treasurer of the United States (the second woman to hold that position). Per capita state taxes have increased from $29.50 to $68.04 since 1943, the Census Bureau reveals.

Some 63.4 million Americans are gainfully employed by September; unemployment falls to its lowest point since the close of World War II.

Jacqueline Cochran, now 43, flies a Canadian-built F-86 Sabre jet fighter over Edwards Air Force Base May 18 and becomes the first woman to break the sound barrier, sending sonic booms across the desert as she pulls out of steep dives at speeds above 760 miles per hour. She also sets a new international speed record of 652 miles per hour for a 100-kilometer closed course. French flier Jacqueline Auriol breaks the sound barrier August 29, becoming the second woman to do it.

A book by German-American aeronautical engineer Irmgard Flugge-Lotz, 50, explains her theory of "discontinuous automatic control," which will lead to the development of automatic on-off aircraft control systems, thus permitting further development of jet aircraft. Flugge-Lotz, who married her colleague Wilhelm Flugge in 1938, established at age 28 what became known as the Lotz method for calculating the spanwise (fuselage-to-wingtip) distribution of a wing's lifting force. The late Hermann Goering overlooked the anti-Nazi views that she shared with her husband in order to use their technical abilities, and the couple emigrated to America after the war.

Polyethylene plastic becomes practical with help from German chemist Karl Ziegler, who invents a new catalytic process for producing it by using atmospheric pressure instead of the 30,000-pounds-per-square-inch pressure required by the I.C.I. process of 1935. Ziegler's process ushers in a new era of low-cost plastics.

A plastic valve mechanism for aerosol cans developed by U.S. inventor Robert H. Abplanalp, 30, sharply lowers production costs. The Abplanalp valve will lead to the marketing of countless consumer products propelled by freon gas from low-cost containers (*see* 1945).

A one-page article in the April 25 issue of the British scientific journal *Nature* announces the discovery of "a structure for the salt of deoxyribose nucleic acid (DNA)." U.S. genetic researcher James Dewey Watson, 25, and English geneticist Francis H. C. Crick, 37, of Cambridge University have seen X-ray diffraction studies of hydrated DNA material made by King's College, London, researcher Rosalind Elsie Franklin, 33, whose own paper is published in the April 25 *Nature*. Her colleague Maurice Wilkins has shown Watson and Crick her photographs without her permission, she quits King's College to pursue a new study on the structure of viruses, she will die of cancer in 1958 at age 37, and she will not share in the honors that the

men will receive for discovering the basic structure of a double helix showing how genetic chromosome material in animal and human cells can duplicate itself, thus creating the modern science of molecular biology.

A new U.S. Department of Health, Education and Welfare established by Congress April 11 incorporates most of the functions of the Federal Security Agency. Former WAC commander Oveta Culp Hobby is named first secretary of HEW.

Sexual Behavior in the Human Female by Alfred C. Kinsey makes the following observation: "The vagina walls are quite insensitive in the great majority of females. . . . There is no evidence that the vagina is ever the sole source of arousal, or even the primary source of erotic arousal, in any female." Half the women surveyed by Kinsey said they engaged in sexual intercourse before marriage, one-third with two or more men. One of every four admitted to having had extramarital intercourse.

Danish endocrinologist Christian Hamburger, who enabled George Jorgenson to become Christine Jorgenson, receives so many applications from Americans who want the same procedure that Denmark's minister of justice restricts sex-change operations to native Danes (*see* 1952; 1956).

Literacy House is established at Allahabad and at Lucknow by U.S. educator Welthy Honsiger Fisher, 73, who at age 44 married a Methodist Episcopal bishop, worked with him in India and America until his death in 1938, and became a close friend of Mohandas K. Gandhi and Bengali novelist Rabindranath Tagore. Using her innovative portable libraries and classroom kits (roll-up blackboards, crayons, slates, chalk, and lamps) that can be transported on bicycles, thousands of teachers will go out from Literacy House to give instruction in functional literacy.

L'Express begins publication at Paris under the direction of *Elle* editor Françoise Giroud, now 37, and her economist lover Jean-Jacques Servan-Schreiber, 30. In 10 years they will turn the journal of leftist opinion into a highly successful newsmagazine modeled on *Time* and *Newsweek*.

Playboy magazine begins publication in December with a nude calendar photograph of Hollywood comedienne Marilyn Monroe (originally Norma Jean Baker), 26, who, when asked what she had on when the picture was taken, replies, "The radio." Chicago publisher Hugh Hefner, 27, has started his frankly sexist magazine with an initial investment of $10,000. He features nude photography and ribald cartoons (*see Penthouse*, 1969).

Nonfiction: *The Second Sex* in an English translation of the 1949 book by Simone de Beauvoir. Topeka, Kan., psychiatrist Karl Augustus Menninger, 60, calls it "a pretentious and inflated tract on feminism," but Philip Wylie, whose 1942 book *Generation of Vipers* introduced the term "Momism," says it is "one of the few great books of our time." *More in Anger: Some Opinions Uncensored and Unteleprompted of Marya Mannes* (essays): "Let us by all means love men and marry them, bear children and love them, cook well and like it; but let that not be an end any more than a man's work is an end, but rather parts of an infinitely larger whole which is membership in the human race." *The Glitter and the Gold* (autobiography) by the former Consuelo Vanderbilt, who was divorced from the Duke of Marlborough in 1920, married French aviator Jacques Balsan in 1921, and fled France with him in 1940.

Fiction: *The Lying Days* and *The Voice of the Serpent* by South African novelist Nadine Gordimer, 29; *Martereau* by Nathalie Sarraute; *Span of the Year* (*Vremena goda*) by Evira Panova; *The Tar Still* (*Tjärdalen*) by Swedish novelist Sara Lidman, 30; *No Barrier* by Eleanor Dark; *Destination Chungking* by Han Suyin; *Kingfishers Catch Fire* by Rumer Godden; *Who Calls the Tune* (in America, *Eyes of Green*) by English novelist Nina (Mary) Bawden (*née* Mabey), 28; *The Crown Princess and Other Stories* and *Hackenfeller's Ape* by Irish novelist Brigid (Antonia) Brophy, 24; *The Echoing Grove* by Rosamond Lehmann; *The Victorian Chaiselongue* by Marghanita Laski; *Wildfire at Midnight* by Mary Stewart; *Children Are Bored on Sunday* by Jean Stafford; *Cress Delahanty* by Jessamyn West; *I and My True Love* by Helen MacInnes.

Poetry: *Poems* by English poet Elizabeth Jennings, 27; *The Gateway* by Judith Wright.

Juvenile: *Nisei Daughter* by Seattle-born author Monica Sone, 34, who was one of 110,000 Japanese

Americans, many of them native-born citizens, who were evacuated to "relocation camps" pursuant to Executive Order 9066, issued by President Roosevelt February 19, 1942.

Painting: *Open Wall* by Helen Frankenthaler; *City Vertical* (collage) and *The City* (collage) by Lee Krasner.

Theater: Jennie Egan, Arthur Kennedy, and Walter Hampden in Arthur Miller's *The Crucible* 1/22 at New York's Martin Beck Theater, an account of the 1692 Salem witch trials intended as a parallel to the persecution of alleged Communist sympathizers in the United States, 197 perfs.; Janice Rule, 21, Ralph Meeker, Paul Newman, Kim Stanley (Patricia Kimberly Reid), 28, and Eileen Heckart, 33, in William Inge's *Picnic* 2/19 at New York's Music Box Theater, 477 perfs.; Eli Wallach, Frank Silvera, Jo Van Fleet, 31, Martin Balsam, Barbara Baxley, Hurd Hatfield, and Michael Griggs in Tennessee Williams's *Camino Real* 3/19 at New York's Martin Beck Theater, 60 perfs.; Deborah Kerr and John Kerr in Robert Anderson's *Tea and Sympathy* 9/30 at New York's Ethel Barrymore Theater, 712 perfs.; Laurence Olivier and Vivien Leigh in Terence Rattigan's *The Sleeping Prince* 11/5 at London's Phoenix Theatre; Judith Anderson in *In the Summer House* by novelist Jane Bowles 12/29 at New York's Playhouse Theater (Bowles and her husband have lived in Tangier since 1952), 55 perfs.

Film: Richard Burton, Jean Simmons, and Victor Mature in Henry Koster's *The Robe*, first film to be produced in CinemaScope. Designed to counter the inroads that television is making on movie theater receipts, CinemaScope employs screens much wider than those used for conventional films and has a stereophonic soundtrack.

More notable films: Burt Lancaster, Montgomery Clift, Deborah Kerr, and Frank Sinatra in Fred Zinneman's *From Here to Eternity*; Leslie Caron and Mel Ferrer in Charles Walters's *Lili*; Machiko Kyo and Masayuki Mori in Kenji Mizoguchi's *Princess Yang Kwei Fei*; Harriet Andersson and Ake Grönberg in Ingmar Bergman's *Sawdust and Tinsel*; Alan Ladd, Jean Arthur, and Brandon De Wilde in George Stevens's *Shane*; Chieko Higashiyama and Chishu Ryu in Yasujiro Ozu's *Tokyo Story*. Also: Dorothy Dandridge, 30 (as a southern schoolteacher) and Harry Belafonte in Gerald Mayer's *Bright Road*; Ida Lupino's *The Hitch-Hiker*; Kinuyo Tanaka's *Love Letter* (*Koibumi*) (Tanaka, 44, is a former screen actress turned director); Ava Gardner and Clark Gable in John Ford's *Mogambo*; James Stewart, Janet Leigh (Jeanette Morrison), 26, Ralph Meeker, and Robert Ryan in Anthony Mann's *The Naked Spur*; Belgian-born actress Audrey Hepburn (Edda van Heemstra Hepburn-Ruston), 24, and Gregory Peck in William Wyler's *Roman Holiday*; Mexican actress Rosoura Revueltas in Herbert Biberman's *Salt of the Earth*, a profeminist drama about New Mexico mineworkers (Revueltas is blacklisted along with director Biberman, actor Will Geer, the producer, and the screenwriter as paranoia about "Reds" continues to fester); South African actress Glynis Johns, 29 (as Mary Tudor), and Richard Todd in Ken Annakin's *The Sword and the Rose*.

Hollywood musical: Fred Astaire, Cyd Charisse, Jack Buchanan, Nanette Fabray, and Oscar Levant in Vincente Minnelli's *The Band Wagon* with Arthur Schwartz–Howard Dietz songs that include "That's Entertainment," "Triplets," "By Myself," and "Shine on Your Shoes."

Broadway musicals: Helen Gallagher in *Hazel Flagg* 2/11 at the Mark Hellinger Theater, with Jule Styne–Bob Hilliard songs that include "Every Street's a Boulevard in Old New York," 190 perfs.; Rosalind Russell and Edie Adams (Edith Enke), 25, as Eileen in *Wonderful Town* 2/25 at the Winter Garden Theater, with a book based on the 1940 stage play *My Sister Eileen*, music by Leonard Bernstein, lyrics by Betty Comden and Adolph Green, songs that include "Ohio," "A Quiet Girl," and "Conga!," 559 perfs.; Gwen (originally Gwyneth Evelyn) Verdon, 28, in *Can-Can* 5/7 at the Shubert Theater, with Cole Porter songs that include "I Love Paris," "C'est Magnifique," and "It's All Right with Me," 892 perfs.; Isabel Bigley and Joan McCracken in *Me and Juliet* 5/28 at the Majestic Theater, with Rodgers and Hammerstein songs that include "No Other Love," 358 perfs.

Popular songs: Rhythm & blues singer Willie Mae "Big Mama" Thornton, 26, records "Hound Dog," written for her by Jerry Lieber and Mike Stoller; rhythm & blues singer LaVern (originally Delores LaVern) Baker, 24, records "Soul on Fire"/"How Can You Leave a Man Like This?" and launches herself on a notable career; Paris-born French-German guitarist-singer Caterina Valenti, 22, records "Malagueña" by Cuban composer Ernest Lecuona and has her first hit; Alabama-born folk singer-guitarist Odetta (Holmes Felious Gordon), 22, travels to San Francisco and makes her first recordings; Teresa Brewer records "Ricochet"; Oklahoma-born country singer–bass player Jean Shepard, 19, records "Dear John Letter" with singer Ferlin Husky and has her first hit (one of 10 children, the five-foot one-inch blonde started singing with her own band at age 14); "Hi-Lili, Hi-Lo" by Helen Deutsch, music by Bronislau Kapes (for the film *Lili*); Eartha Kitt records "C'est Si Bon" and "Santa Baby"; Patti Page records "How Much Is That Doggie in the Window?"; Rosemary Clooney sings Irving Berlin's 1942 song "White Christmas" with Bing Crosby (in the eponymous film).

Opera: Kathleen Ferrier makes her final public appearance in February, falls ill after singing in only two of the four scheduled performances of Gluck's *Orfeo ed Euridice*, and dies October 8 at age 41. U.S. soprano Phyllis Curtin, 30, makes her debut with the New York City Opera with which she will sing for the next 10 years in all the major Mozartian heroine roles, Violetta, Salome, and Cressida (in William Walton's 1954 opera *Troilus and Cressida*) while singing also at Frankfurt, Vienna, Milan, and Buenos Aires. Joan Cross creates the role of Elizabeth I in the new Britten opera *Gloriana* 6/8 at London's Covent Garden.

Ballet: Melissa Hayden begins 20 years as principal dancer of the New York City Ballet, with which she has danced since 1949.

First performance: *Proud Thames* overture by Elizabeth Maconchy.

Boston ice dancer Tenley Albright, 17, completes a 6-year comeback from poliomyelitis by winning the world figure-skating championship February 15 at Davos, Switzerland.

Maureen Connolly wins the "grand slam" in tennis, taking the Australian, French, English, and U.S. women's singles championships.

Swimmer Florence Chadwick sets a new English Channel speed record of 14 hours, 42 minutes September 4 and sets another record October 7 by swimming the Bosphorus from Europe to Asia and back again.

British designer Laura Ashley (*née* Mountney), 28, designs scarves on her kitchen table to begin what will become a worldwide business (*see* 1967).

Washington Times-Herald photographer Jacqueline Lee Bouvier, 24, is married at Newport, R.I., September 12 to U.S. Senator John Fitzgerald Kennedy, 36 (D., Mass.).

Woolworth heiress Barbara Hutton, now 41, meets Porfirio Rubirosa, now nearly 45, and marries him December 30 in her living room at New York's Pierre Hotel against the advice of her uncle E. F. Hutton and aunt Marjorie Merriweather Post (*see* 1949). Rubirosa has refused to sign anything that did not give him a guarantee of $3 million, payable in advance, but has been persuaded by Hutton's lawyers to accept $2.5 million (*see* 1954).

The Mississippi Court of Appeals reverses the conviction of a man found guilty of rape, saying that he should have been permitted to present testimony of a prior relationship with his victim "regardless of how false the testimony may have been."

Connecticut's Senate convenes April 18 to debate the state's law calling for a fine of not less than $50, or imprisonment of not less than 60 days, or both, for "any person who shall use any drug, medicinal article or instrument for the purpose of preventing conception."

Alfred Kinsey's survey of female sexual behavior (above) reports that 22 percent of his married respondents said that they had had at least one abortion.

1954

The Italian government objects January 29 that U.S. Ambassador Clare Boothe Luce is interfering in Italian domestic affairs, but she will continue in the post until 1957.

Japanese mothers begin collecting signatures for an anti–nuclear weapon petition, starting a movement that will attract delegates from dozens of countries in August of next year to the first international conference at Tokyo.

The Supreme Court rules 9 to 0 May 17 in *Brown v. Board of Education* that racial segregation in public schools is unconstitutional. Chief Justice Earl Warren orders the states to proceed "with all deliberate speed" to integrate educational facilities, but Topeka, Kan., requests time to formulate a plan for racial balance. It was at Topeka that Oliver Brown filed suit in 1951 action after his daughter, Linda Carol, then 8, had been denied admission to the all-white Sumner School, obliging her to travel an hour and 20 minutes each day and cross a hazardous railyard to reach her bus stop. Topeka will repeat its request for more time for the next 20 years. Novelist Zora Neale Hurston criticizes the landmark decision on the grounds that pressure to integrate will be harmful to thriving black institutions.

India outlaws bigamy September 17.

Racially segregated facilities were part of Southern life in America before the Supreme Court outlawed them.

Only 154 Americans have annual incomes of $1 million or more, down from 513 in 1929, when $1 million had far more purchasing power.

A U.S. taxpayer with a net income of $100,000 may now pay more than $67,000 in taxes, up from $16,000 or less in 1929, and the individual tax exemption is $600, down from $1,500 in 1929. Income taxes will be reduced slightly next year, but the average tax rate, including surtax, is just above 20 percent and taxpayers in top brackets pay 87 percent.

Wall Street's Dow Jones Industrial Average finally passes the 381.17 high of 1929 November 23 and closes the year above 404, up from 280.

Detroit's Northland, opened in March with 100 stores, is the world's largest shopping center and a monument to the American exodus from the inner city.

Aviatrix Jacqueline Cochran, piloting a Sabre jet, becomes the first woman to break the sound barrier (see 1942; 1964).

Italian neurobiologist Rita Levi-Montalcini, 45, helps discover nerve-growth factor, a previously unknown biological mechanism that stimulates the growth of hair cells. Her work will win her a 1987 Nobel Prize.

Pittsburgh schoolchildren receive the first mass poliomyelitis immunization shots February 23 (see 1955; Salk, 1952). Polish-American virologist Albert Bruce Sabin, 48, tests a live-virus vaccine that will prove more effective than Salk's killed-virus vaccine (see 1960).

President Eisenhower proposes a "reinsurance" plan that will encourage private initiative to strengthen U.S. health services. A survey of medical costs reveals that 16 percent of U.S. families go into debt each year to pay for treatment.

British women increasingly have their babies delivered in hospitals: 54 percent of infants are born in hospitals, up from 15 percent in 1927. In the United States the rate is even higher.

Nonfiction: *A History of Women* (*Josei saei no rekishi*) by Itsue Takamure (first volume); *The Edge of the Sea* by Rachel Carson.

Fiction: *The Mandarins* by Simone de Beauvoir; *Bonjour Tristesse* by French novelist Françoise Sagan, 19; *A Proper Marriage* by Doris Lessing; *Under the Net* by English novelist (Jean) Iris Murdoch, 35; *Beyond the Glass* (third volume of a trilogy) and *Strangers* (stories and poems) by Antonia White; *The Flint Anchor* by Sylvia Townsend Warner; *A Death Occurred* by Norah Hoult; *Bless This House* by Norah Lofts; *And the Rain My Drink* by Han Suyin; *An Impossible Marriage* by Pamela Hansford Johnson; *The Flower Girls* by Clemence Dane; *The Span of the Year* (*Vrema gota*) by Evira Panova; *A Visitor from Afar* (*Enrai no kyaku*) by Japanese novelist Ayako (*née* Chizuko) Sono, 23; *Half Human* (*Hanningen*) by Yoko Ota; *Hungry Months and Days* (*Himojii tsukihi*) by Fumiko Enji, who wins the Women's Literature Prize; *The Ponder Heart* by Eudora Welty; *The Bride of Innisfallen* (stories) by Welty; *The Birds' Nest* by Shirley Jackson; *A Spy in the House of Love* by Anaïs Nin; *Swamp Angel* by Ethel Wilson; *We Are for the Dark* (ghost stories) by Elizabeth Howard; *The Royal Box* by Frances Parkinson Keyes; *My Brother's Keeper* by Marcia Davenport; *The Blunderer* by Patrica Highsmith; *The King's Vixen* (in England, *Flaming Janet Cowan, a Lady of Galloway*) by British novelist Pamela Hill, 33.

Poetry: *Another Animal* by U.S. poet May Swenson, 35; *Animal, Vegetable, Mineral* by Babette Deutsch.

Painting: *Grand Street Brides* by New York abstract expressionist Grace Hartigan, 32; *Blue Spot, Shattered Light* (both collages), *Forest #1*, and *Forest #2* by Lee Krasner. Frida Kahlo dies of cancer at Coyoacán, Mexico, July 13 at age 44 (her coffin, draped in the Soviet flag, lies in state in the rotunda of the National Institute of Fine Arts, guarded by notables including former President Cárdenas).

Theater: *King of Hearts* by Jean Kerr and Eleanor Brooke 4/1 at New York's Lyceum Theater, with Cloris Leachman, 27, Donald Cook, and Jackie Cooper, 69 perfs.; *Ladies of the Corridor* by Dorothy Parker and Arnaud d'Usseau 10/21 at New York's Longacre Theater, with Betty Field, June Walker, Edna Best, Vera Allen, and Walter Matthau, 45 perfs.; Geraldine Page, 29, and Richard Coogan in N. Richard Nash's *The Rain-*

maker 10/28 at New York's Cort Theater, 125 perfs.; Patty McCormack, Nancy Kelly, and Eileen Heckart in Maxwell Anderson's *The Bad Seed* (from the novel by William March) 12/8 at New York's 46th Street Theater, 332 perfs.

Films: Marlon Brando, Eva Marie Saint, 30, Rod Steiger, and Karl Malden in Elia Kazan's *On the Waterfront*; James Stewart, Grace Kelly, and Wendell Corey in Alfred Hitchcock's *Rear Window*; Kinuyo Tanaka, Kisho Hanayagi, and Kyoko Kagawa in Kenji Mizoguchi's *Sansho the Bailiff*. Also: William Holden and Grace Kelly in Mark Robson's *The Bridges at Toko-Ri*; Spencer Tracy, Robert Wagner, and (Elizabeth) Jean Peters, 28, in Edward Dmytrik's *Broken Lance*; Kazuo Hasegawa and Kyoko Kagawa in Kenji Mizoguchi's *Chikamatsu Monogatori* (*The Crucified Lovers*); Simone Signoret and Henri-Georges Clouzot's wife, Vera, in Clouzot's *Diabolique*; Machiko Kyo and Kazuo Hasegawa in Teinosuke Kinugasa's *Gate of Hell*; Kay Kendall (Justine McCarthy), 28, and Kenneth More in Henry Cornelius's *Genevieve*; Claire Trevor, Laraine Day, John Wayne, and Robert Stack in William A. Wellman's *The High and the Mighty*; Kinyo Tanaka's *Moon Rising* (*Tsuki Wa Noborinu*); Audrey Hepburn and Humphrey Bogart in Billy Wilder's *Sabrina*; Fernandel and Françoise Arnoul (Françoise Glautch), 22, in Henri Verneuil's *The Sheep Has Five Legs*; June Allyson, Arlene Dahl, Lauren Bacall, and Clifton Webb in Jean Negulesco's *Woman's World*.

Hollywood musicals: Dorothy Dandridge (mouthing words sung by soprano Marilyn Horne), Pearl Bailey, and Harry Belafonte in Otto Preminger's *Carmen Jones*, with music from the 1875 Bizet opera *Carmen*.

Opera: *The Threepenny Opera* 3/10 at New York's off-Broadway Theatre de Lys, with Kurt Weill's widow, Lotte Lenya, now 55, who created the role of Jenny in the original 1928 Berlin production; Joan Cross, now 54, creates the role of Mrs. Grose in the new Britten opera *The Turn of the Screw* 9/14 at Venice's Teatro la Fenice; *Infidelio* by Elisabeth Lutyens is the story of a broken love affair that backtracks from a girl's suicide to her first meeting.

Italian soprano Renata Scotto, 21, makes her debut at La Scala in Milan.

Impressario Carol Fox, 28, launches the Lyric Opera of Chicago, whose 3-week season includes the U.S. debut of Maria Callas in the 1831 Bellini opera *Norma*. Fox will assume full control in 1956, rename her company the Lyric Opera of Chicago, and begin to make it a leading opera company with a 3-month season of eight productions.

Broadway musicals: Janis Paige and John Raitt in *The Pajama Game* 5/13 at the St. James Theater, with Richard Adler–Jerry Ross songs that include "Hey, There," "There Once Was a Man," "7½ Cents," "Hernando's Hideaway," and chorus girl-choreographer Carol Haney, now 31, knocking 'em dead with "Steam Heat," 1,063 perfs.; Mary Martin, Cyril Ritchard, and Margalo Gilmore in *Peter Pan* 10/20 at the Winter Garden Theater, with music by Mark Charlap and Jule Styne, lyrics by Carolyn Leigh, 27, additional lyrics by Betty Comden and Adolph Green, songs that include "I'm Flying," "Never-Never Land," "Tender Shepherd," "I Won't Grow Up," and "I've Gotta Crow," 152 perfs.; Pearl Bailey, Diahann Carroll (Carol Diahann Johnson), 19, and Juanita Hall in *House of Flowers* 12/30 at the Alvin Theater, with Harold Arlen–Truman Capote songs, 165 perfs.

Hollywood musicals: Jane Powell (Suzanne Bruce), 25, and Howard Keel in Stanley Donen's *Seven Brides for Seven Brothers* with Johnny Mercer–Gene Paul songs; Judy Garland and James Mason in George Cukor's *A Star Is Born* with Harold Arlen–Ira Gershwin songs.

Popular songs: "Little Things Mean a Lot" by U.S. songwriters Edith Lindeman and Carl Stutz; U.S. folk singer-songwriter Wanda Jackson, 17, records her duet "You Can't Have My Love" with Billy Grey; Jo Stafford records "Make Love to Me."

The cha-cha-cha based on the classic Cuban danzón is introduced to U.S. dance floors, where it will become a standard Latin dance step.

Maureen Connolly wins in women's singles at Wimbledon, Doris Hart at Forest Hills.

Marilyn Monroe is married at San Francisco January 14 to former New York Yankees baseball star Joe DiMiaggio. The marriage will be brief.

Woolworth heiress Barbara Hutton buys her husband, Porfirio Rubirosa, a 400-acre Dominican citrus plantation, a string of 15 polo ponies, a Lancia motorcar, and various pieces of jewelry for his 45th birthday, January 22, but leaves him February 20 after 53 days of marriage and obtains a legal separation a few weeks later (*see* 1953; 1955).

Suburban Cleveland housewife Marilyn Sheppard dies at home July 4 at age 31. Police accuse her osteopath-surgeon husband, Samuel Sheppard, 30, of having murdered her, and a jury will convict him after a much-publicized trial.

Let's Eat Right to Keep Fit by California nutrition evangelist (Daisy) Adelle Davis, 50, declares that fertile eggs are superior to infertile, opposes pasteurization of milk, and recommends dangerously high daily doses of vitamins A, D, and E. By no means a qualified nutritionist (her 1927 bachelor's degree from the University of California at Berkeley was in household science), Davis is the author of *Let's Cook It Right* (1947) and *Let's Have Healthy Children* (1951), and although her books are full of factual errors they will sell in the millions of copies (mostly in paperback), contributing to the phenomenal growth of the health food movement, which thrives on stories of pesticide residues and food additives, and the diet supplement industry, which thrives on the fallibility of physicians and the fact that so many Americans cannot afford proper medical advice, which makes them turn to self-help books of dubious merit. Davis will claim (falsely) that magnesium alone offers a useful treatment for epilepsy, that nephrosis patients should take potassium chloride, and that fluoridation of community drinking water poses a health risk.

Frozen "TV" Brand Dinners are introduced by C. A. Swanson & Sons of Omaha, which has been marketing frozen chicken, beef, and turkey pies.

Margaret Sanger addresses the Japanese Diet April 15 (she is the first woman to do so), urging birth control.

China's National People's Congress hears its first public call for birth control September 18. Shao Lizi, who was a birth control advocate before 1949, makes the plea. Mao Zedong's second in command, Liu Shaoqi, convenes a symposium at Beijing in December to discuss "the problem of birth control" (*see* 1956).

An oral contraceptive pill developed by Gregory G. Pincus, Hudson Hoagland, and Min-cheh Chang, 45, at the Worcester Foundation employs the synthetic progesterone hormone norethisterone (called norethindrone in the United States), developed by steroid chemist Carl Djerassi of Syntex, S.A. (*see* 1943; Sanger, 1951). Much cheaper than natural progesterone, which must be obtained from animals, Djerassi's norethisterone is also six to eight times more powerful.

Research at the Worcester Foundation (above) has been funded in large part by feminist Katherine McCormick (*née* Dexter), now 79, who last year gave it $150,000 and will continue giving this amount each year until her death in 1967 at age 92. She was M.I.T.'s second woman graduate in 1904 and that year married reaper inventor Cyrus McCormick's son Stanley, who soon afterwards was hospitalized with schizophrenia and in 1909 declared legally incompetent, making his wife enormously rich. Having no children, she became an early supporter of Margaret Sanger, helping to smuggle diaphragms into the United States when they were illegal (*see* 1955).

1955

Indonesia and Nicaragua grant women the the right to vote on the same basis as men. Peru grants voting rights to women September 7.

Black Mississippi teenager Emmet Till is murdered August 28 after allegedly having wolf-whistled at a white woman and asked her for a date. The woman's brothers, J. W. and Roy Bryant, are arrested, tried, and acquitted on grounds that the body of the murder victim may not have been Till's (despite a ring on his finger that had led to earlier identification). The incident intensifies racial tensions throughout the South.

The Interstate Commerce Commission acts November 25 to ban racial segregation on interstate buses and trains and in terminal waiting rooms. Montgomery, Ala., buses remain segregated by law, but local seamstress Rosa Parks, 42, refuses to give up her seat on a downtown bus to a white man December 1. The bus driver says, "If you don't stand up, I'm going to call the police and have you arrested." Given a summons, she decides with her mother and husband to make hers a test case challenging segregation, and her action precipitates a general boycott of Montgomery buses under the leadership of Rev. Martin Luther King, Jr., who 2 years ago married budding soprano Coretta Scott.

The Woman's Trade Union League of New York is dissolved as interest in organized labor wanes. The League has pioneered over the past half century in attacking sexual segregation in the workplace, trying to unionize not only industrial workers but also white-collar and domestic employees while calling for regulation of working conditions in factories, offices, and even homes. It has lobbied for comparable-worth laws, maternity insurance, government-funded child care, fair rents and food prices, better housing, and improved public education.

Explorer Louise Boyd, now 67, charters a plane and becomes the first woman ever to fly over and around the North Pole. She first visited the Arctic on a whim in 1924 and made half a dozen trips to the region thereafter (see 1933).

The U.S. federal minimum wage rises from 75¢ per hour to $1 August 12 by act of Congress.

Some 12 million U.S. workers are unionized, a number that will increase to 20 million in the next 20 years.

U.S. shopping centers increase in number to 1,800, proliferating rapidly as Americans move out of the central cities to live in the sprawling suburbs (see Northland, 1954).

More than 100 cases of poliomyelitis develop among Americans injected with certain lots of Salk vaccine produced by Cutter Laboratories, which has failed to inactivate the polio virus through a manufacturing error. The Salk vaccine is nevertheless judged highly effective (see 1954).

Mrs. Sheldon Robbins is named cantor of the Massapequa, Long Island, Reformed Jewish temple, becoming the first woman cantor.

"Ann Landers Says" is introduced in the Chicago Sun-Times by journalist Esther Pauline Friedman Lederer, 37, whose confidential column will be syndicated to hundreds of newspapers, as will that of

her twin sister, Pauline, who will write the "Dear Abby" column under the name Abigail Van Buren. Lederer has seen her husband, Jules, found Budget Rent-a-Car and prosper but will divorce him in 1975 after 36 years of marriage.

The $64,000 Question quiz show debuts on television in June. Most contestants, it will turn out in 1958, have been fed answers, but Columbia University experimental psychology student Joyce Bauer Brothers, 28, has memorized the Ring Encyclopedia and in December wins $64,000 with her command of facts about prizefighting. By the end of the 1950s she will have her degree and, as Dr. Joyce Brothers, will be dispensing advice in a newspaper column and on TV shows.

Nonfiction: Gift from the Sea (autobiographical essays) by Anne Morrow Lindbergh; Chiang Kaishek: An Unauthorized Biography by Emily Hahn, who has taught English and writing in China and Hong Kong; Teacher, Annie Sullivan Macy: A Tribute by the Foster Child of Her Mind by Helen Keller, now 75.

Fiction: To Whom She Will (in the United States, Amrita) by Cologne-born writer Ruth Jhabvala (née Prawer), 28, who became a British citizen in 1948 and has lived in India since 1951; Lolita by Russian-American novelist Vladimir Nabokov, 56, whose tale of a middle-aged European's love for a passionate 12-year-old American "nymphet" is a satire that reverses the usual contrast between American innocence and European worldliness; A Good Man Is Hard to Find (stories) by Flannery O'Connor includes "The Artificial Nigger" and "Parker's Back"; A Charmed Life by Mary McCarthy; The Simple Truth by Elizabeth Hardwick; The Dowry by Margaret Culkin Banning; The Persistent Image by Gladys Schmitt; An Episode of Sparrows by Rumer Godden; The Odd Flamingo by Nina Bawden; Winter Harvest by Norah Lofts; Cloudberry Land (Hjortonlandet) by Sara Lidman; The Hidden River by Storm Jameson; A Child in the House by Irish novelist Janet McNeill, 47; Time Walked (Seryozha) by Evira Panova; The Talented Mr. Ripley by Patricia Highsmith; Witness for the Prosecution by Agatha Christie; Pray for a Brave Heart by Helen MacInnes.

Poetry: The Diamond Cutters by Adrienne Rich; The Two Fires by Judith Wright.

Juvenile: *Eloise* by U.S. entertainer Kay Thompson, 43, whose heroine lives at the Plaza Hotel; *The Little Bookroom* (stories) by Eleanor Farjeon, now 74.

Painting: *Stretched Yellow*, *Milkweed*, *Desert Moon*, *Image on Green (Jungle)*, *Blue Level*, *Bald Eagle*, *Shooting Gull*, and *Porcelain* (all collages) by Lee Krasner.

Sculpture: *One and Others* (painted wood) by Louise Bourgeois; *Oval Sculpture (Delos)* (wood) by Barbara Hepworth.

Theater: Kim Stanley and Albert Salmi in William Inge's *Bus Stop* 3/2 at New York's Music Box Theater, 478 perfs.; Barbara Bel Geddes, Ben Gazzara, Mildred Dunnock, and folk singer Burl Ives as "Big Daddy" in Tennessee Williams's *Cat on a Hot Tin Roof* 3/24 at New York's Morosco Theater, 694 perfs.; J. Carrol Naish, Van Heflin, Eileen Heckart, and Jack Warden in Arthur Miller's *A View from the Bridge* 9/29 at New York's Coronet Theater, 149 perfs.; Susan Strasberg and Joseph Schildkraut in Frances Goodrich and Albert Hackett's *The Diary of Anne Frank* 10/5 at New York's Cort Theater, 717 perfs.; Ben Gazzara, Shelley Winters, Frank Silvera, and Anthony Franciosa in Michael Gazzo's *A Hatful of Rain*, about drug addiction, 11/9 at New York's Lyceum Theater, 398 perfs.

Films: Julie Harris, James Dean, Raymond Massey, and Burl Ives in Elia Kazan's *East of Eden*; Michael Redgrave, Sheila Sim, Alexander Knox, and Denholm Elliott in Leslie Norman's *The Night My Number Came Up*; Natalie Wood, Sal Mineo, and James Dean (who is killed September 30 in an automobile accident at age 24) in Nicholas Ray's *Rebel Without a Cause*; Ulla Jacobsson, Harriet Andersson, Eva Dahlbeck, and Jarl Kulle in Ingmar Bergman's *Smiles of a Summer Night*. Also: Alastair Sim, Joyce Grenfell, Hermione Baddeley, and Beryl Reid in Frank Launder's *The Belles of St. Trinians*; Glenn Ford and Ann Francis in Richard Brooks's *The Blackboard Jungle*; Susan Hayward and Richard Conte in Daniel Mann's *I'll Cry Tomorrow*; William Holden, Kim (*née* Marilyn) Novak, 22, and Rosalind Russell in Joshua Logan's *Picnic*; Anna Magnani and Burt Lancaster in Daniel Mann's *The Rose Tattoo*; Dirk Bogarde and British beauty Virginia McKenna, 24, in Brian Desmond Hurst's *Simba*; Katharine Hepburn and Rossano Brazzi in

David Lean's *Summertime*, a film version of the Arthur Laurents play *Time of the Cuckoo*.

Actress Debbie Reynolds, now 23, marries actor Eddie Fisher at Grossinger's in the Catskills September 26.

Hollywood musicals: Gordon MacRae, Shirley Jones, 21, and Charlotte Greenwood in Fred Zinneman's *Oklahoma!*; Betty Garrett, Janet Leigh, Jack Lemmon, and Bob Fosse in Richard Quine's *My Sister Eileen*.

Broadway musicals: German actress Hildegarde Neff, 29 (as Ninotchka), George Tobias, Julie Newmar, Don Ameche, and David Opatashu in *Silk Stockings* 2/24 at the Imperial Theater, with Cole Porter songs that include "All of You," 478 perfs.; Gwen Verdon in *Damn Yankees* 5/5 at the 46th Street Theater, with Richard Adler–Jerry Ross songs that include "Whatever Lola Wants," "You've Got to Have Heart," and "Two Lost Souls," 1,019 perfs.; Metropolitan Opera soprano Helen Traubel, now 56, in *Pipe Dream* 11/3 at the Shubert Theater, with Rodgers and Hammerstein songs that include "All at Once You Love Her."

The merengue, introduced to U.S. dance floors by New York teacher Albert Butler, 61, and his wife, Josephine, is an adaptation of a Dominican one-step combining the rumba and *paso doble*.

Popular songs: "Dance with Me, Henry" and "The Wallflower" by U.S. rhythm & blues singer Etta James (Etta Hawkins), 17; Teresa Brewer records "I Gotta Go Get My Baby" and "Let Me Go Lover"; Jean Shepard records "Beautiful Lies" and "Satisfied Mind" (she will join the cast of *Grand Ole Opry* next year).

Louise Brough wins in women's singles at Wimbledon, Doris Hart at Forest Hills.

Florence Chadwick breaks her 1951 Channel swim speed record October 12, crossing Le Manche in 13 hours, 33 minutes.

The stiletto heel comes into fashion for women and sweeps the world. Marilyn Monroe will be quoted as saying, "I don't know who invented the high heel but women owe him a lot," but while some women profess to find high heels more comfortable than flats, most say their feet are "killing" them after a

Marilyn Monroe had nothing but praise for stiletto-heeled shoes. Not every woman agreed. CULVER PICTURES, INC.

few hours in heels, and the new, sharp heels damage floors and carpets.

Heiress Gloria Vanderbilt Di Cicco Stokowski, now nearly 30, moves in January from the 12-room New York apartment that she shares with her husband, conductor Leopold Stokowski, now 73 (*see* 1955). She obtains a divorce and will be remarried next year to film director Sidney Lumet, who has been married to actress Rita Gam.

Woolworth heiress Barbara Hutton wins a divorce from Porfirio Rubirosa July 30. She marries former German tennis star Baron Gottfried von Cramm November 8 at Versailles.

Welsh-born English nightclub hostess Ruth Ellis (*née* Neilson), 28, shoots her former lover in a jeal-ous rage outside a Hampton pub April 10 (he has been trying to end their often violent relationship). She is hanged July 13 (no other woman will receive the death penalty in Britain for more than 40 years).

Long Island socialite Ann (Eden) Woodward (*née* Crowell), 33, shoots her husband, banker–horse breeder William Woodward, Jr., 35, just after 2 o'clock on the morning of October 30 and tells police she mistook him for a prowler. Awakened by a sound downstairs, she picks up a rifle and aims at a moving shape in the night. Police find her bent over her husband's naked body; she is not prosecuted.

The Soviet Union resumes legalized abortion on demand subject to certain safeguards but discour-ages abortion and birth control (*see* 1936).

The Fifth International Conference on Planned Parenthood convenes at Tokyo and hears Gregory Pincus speak about inhibition of ovulation in women who have taken progesterone or norethyn-odrel, acive ingredients in newly developed contra-ceptive pills that will soon be spoken of collectively as The Pill (*see* 1954). The new oral contraceptive has a failure rate of only one pregnancy per thou-sand women per year (*see* Puerto Rico study, 1957).

1956

Alabama graduate student Autherine Juanita Lucy, 26, enters the University of Alabama at Tuscaloosa February 3 but is allowed to attend classes for only a few days before riots erupt on campus and she is suspended by the board of trustees for "her own safety." The first black student to be admitted to the university, she has been pelted with rotten eggs February 7 by a racist mob screaming, "Let's kill her," and chanting, "Hey, hey, ho, where did Autherine go? Hey, hey, ho, where in hell did the nigger go?" "That girl sure has guts," says NAACP lawyer Thurgood Marshall. The U.S. District Court rules February 29 that the university must readmit her, but it expels her March 1, charging that she has made libelous statements (e.g. accusing university officials of cooperating with the white mob).

South Carolina schoolteacher Septima Poinsette Clark, 58, is dismissed from her job and loses her retirement benefits when she refuses to resign from

Autherine Lucy tried to enter the lily-white University of Alabama but was hounded out by racists. LIBRARY OF CONGRESS

the NAACP and stop protesting a state law, passed April 19, that forbids a city employee to affiliate with any civil rights organization. Clark, whose retirement pay will be restored in 1976 after 20 years of fighting the system, will travel throughout the South in the next 5 years teaching prospective voters how to write their names, write letters, balance their checkbooks, and vote in elections (*see* 1961).

South African civil rights worker Helen Joseph leads a march of 20,000 women on the Union Buildings in Pretoria to protest the extension of laws requiring blacks to carry passes (*see* 1948). She is arrested, charged with treason, and next year will be placed under a ban order (*see* 1961).

Egypt, Tunisia, Comoros, and Mauritius grant women the right to vote on the same basis as men.

A new Japanese law enacted May 21 outlaws brothels, ends licensed prostitution, but permits individual prostitutes to operate so long as they do not solicit in public (*see* 1958).

$ New York stockbroker Josephine Holt Bay (*née* Perfect), 56, becomes president of A. M. Kidder & Co., the first woman ever to head a member firm of the New York Stock Exchange.

French scientist Irène Joliot-Curie dies March 17 at age 58 from radiation-induced leukemia.

Harvard appoints Cecilia Payne-Gaposhkin, now 56, professor and chairman of its Department of Astronomy, a position that she will hold until her retirement in 1965 (*see* 1933).

The National Childbirth Trust is founded in Britain to expose more women to Grantly Dick-Read's natural childbirth ideas.

Painless Childbirth by Fernand Lamaze develops the theories advanced by Lamaze and Pierre Vellay in 1951 (*see* 1959).

La Leche League International, Inc., has its beginnings in the Chicago suburb of Franklin Park, Ill., where Marian (Mrs. Clement R.) Tompson and Mary (Mrs. Gregory) White have mastered the technique of breast-feeding. Mrs. Tompson, the wife of a research engineer, ran into problems trying to breast-feed her first three children and was told each time by a physician to put the baby on the bottle. Mrs. White's husband, a physician, was taught nothing about breast-feeding in medical school. The two women determined to learn everything they could about breast-feeding, which was once an almost universal practice but is now used by only about 22 percent of U.S. mothers, down from 38 percent 10 years ago, partly because more mothers are in the workforce and find it difficult to accommodate breast-feeding on demand in their schedules. When Tompson and White nurse their babies in public at a fashionable North Side picnic, other women gather around admiringly. Atmospheric testing of nuclear weapons has produced radioactive fallout which has fallen on the grass and been consumed by cows, whose milk contains six times as much strontium 90 as human milk, and mothers' milk has numerous other advantages over milk from cows, goats, ewes, and mares. Tompkins and White have organized a meeting to discuss ways and means to encourage other mothers to breast-feed and instruct them in that "womanly art." They have enlisted the support of pediatricians, obstetricians, allergists, and other medical specialists who share their belief in the value of breast-feeding. Since the Virgin Mary's Spanish title is *Nuestra Sonora de la Leche y Buen Parto* ("Our Lady of the Milk and Good Delivery") and Spanish wet nurses are called *madres de la leche*, the women call their information-dispensing organization La Leche League. By 1976 it will be La Leche League International, Inc., with 2,868 groups in 42 countries, but women in lower socioeconomic classes will continue to consider bottle-feeding more "modern" and convenient (the incidence of breast-feeding in the United States will decline to 18 percent in the next 10 years before recovering).

Romania's first woman physician announces September 5 at a symposium on aging at Karlsruhe that she has found an effective antidote to aging. Dr. Ana Aslan, 58, claims that her "GH3" (procaine hydrochloride, or Novocaine) can not only produce a 12 to 20 percent increase in longevity but can also eliminate depression, produce muscular vigor, and alleviate angina pectoris, arthritis, and high blood pressure. Her rationale: "GH3" is an antidote to MAO (monoamine oxidase), an enzyme that builds up in the brain beginning at age 45, according to some research, and ultimately displaces other vital substances in the brain, causing mental depression. Director of the Institute of Geriatrics at Bucharest since 1951, she says that she has learned to modify, or "buffer," procaine, has tested it for 5 years, and has seen it produce a regrowth of hair in some patients and a restoration of original hair color in a few others. She publishes her findings in a German medical journal, and although research clinicians cannot replicate her "results," her clinic at Bucharest begins to receive a stream of visitors in search of restored youth and vitality. Dr. Aslan obtains government support to establish 144 clinics in agricultural and industrial areas for a massive research effort on GH3, which she calls Gerovital GH3 and will market in more than 14 countries.

Prof. Cecilia Payne-Gaposhkin (above) is the first woman to become a tenured professor at Harvard.

Liquid Paper Co. has its beginnings at Dallas, where Texas Bank & Trust divorcée typist Bette Claire Nesmith (*née* McMurray), 32, applies for a patent and trademark on a product (she initially calls it "Mistake Out") designed to cover up typing errors (the carbon-film ribbons of the new IBM electric typewriters make erasures almost impossible). Having noticed that lettering artists always paint over their mistakes, she has put some tempera waterbase paint in a bottle and applied it with a watercolor brush. Co-workers have asked for bottles of their own, and Nesmith works nights and weekends improving the correction-fluid formula in her kitchen. She offers the idea to IBM, which rejects it, so she turns her garage into a bottling factory. By the end of next year she will be selling 100 bottles per month but will keep her job until she is fired for accidentally typing "The Liquid Paper Company" instead of her employer's name at the bottom of a letter (*see* 1968).

Nonfiction: *Women's Two Roles* by Swedish sociologist-politician Alva Myrdal (*née* Reimer), 54, and English psychoanalyst Viola Klein, who say, "The futility of existence in the upper middle class was the very mainspring which motivated the social revolution usually called the emancipation of women," it is the "need of society" that all "available labor resources, male and female," be utilized, and "Making husbands, and fathers, full partners in the affairs of their families, instead of mere '*visiteurs du soir*,' seems to us so much to be desired that, with a general shortening of working time in mind, we think the full-time employment of married women preferable to their doing part-time work"; "Woman's Four Seasons" ("*Onna no shiki*") (essay) by Japanese *haiku* poet Teijo Nakamura.

Fiction: *A Certain Smile* (*Un Certain Sourire*) by Françoise Sagan; *The Towers of Trebizond* by Rose Macaulay, who produces her most successful novel at age 75; *Mother and Son* by Ivy Compton-Burnett; *The Nature of Passion* by Ruth Prawer Jhabvala; *Six Feet of the Country* (stories) by Nadine Gordimer; *The Last of the Wine* by English-born South African novelist Mary Renault (Eileen Mary Challens), 51, who was trained as a nurse, has made only two brief trips to the Mediterranean, yet writes knowledgeably and compellingly of ancient Athenians; *The Solitary Child* by Nina Bawden; *The Last Resort* by Pamela Hansford Johnson; *Time Walked* (*Serezha*) by Evira Panova; *Ballad* (*Jiuta*) by Japanese novelist Sawako Ariyoshi, 25; *Elegy* (*Banka*) by Japanese novelist Yasuko Harada, 28; *Cotter's England* by Christina Stead; *The Black Prince* (stories) by New Orleans writer Shirley Ann

Grau, 27; *O Beulah Land* by West Virginia–born novelist Mary Lee Settle, 38; *Imperial Woman* by Pearl S. Buck, now 64; *The Malefactors* by Caroline Gordon; *Poule de Luxe* and *Freighter* by Susan Yorke; *Peyton Place* by U.S. novelist Grace Metalious (*née* Repentigny), 31; *Atlas Shrugged* by Ayn Rand; *The Long View* by Elizabeth Howard; *Afternoon of an Autocrat* and *The Deadly Gift* by Norah Lofts; *Tea at Four O'Clock* by Janet McNeill; *Death of a Fool* by Dame Ngaio Marsh (who in 1948 was made a dame of the Order of the British Empire); *A Dram of Poison* by Charlotte Armstrong.

Juvenile: *One Hundred and One Dalmatians* by Dodie (Dorothy Gladys) Smith, now 60.

Poetry: *Collected Poems* by English poet Kathleen Raine, 48; *The Unicorn and Other Poems* by Anne Morrow Lindbergh.

Painting: *Embrace* and *Birth* (both oil on canvas) by Lee Krasner, now 48, whose husband, Jackson Pollock, dies in an auto accident on Long Island August 17 at age 44. Marie Laurencin has died of a heart attack at Paris June 8 at age 70 and is buried in Père-Lachaise Cemetery wearing a white dress with a rose in her hand and Apollinaire's love letters close to her heart.

Sculpture: *Stringed Figure (Curlew)* (wood) by Barbara Hepworth.

Theater: *The Chalk Garden* by Enid Bagnold 4/4 at London's Theatre Royal, 658 perfs.; *Look Back in Anger* by English playwright John Osborne, 27, 5/8 at London's Royal Court Theatre, with Kenneth Haigh, Mary Ure, and Alan Bates, expresses the frustration of radical youth in a strident attack on the middle class; Fredric March, Florence Eldridge, Jason Robards, Jr., Bradford Dilman, and Katharine Ross, 12, in the late Eugene O'Neill's *Long Day's Journey into Night* 11/7 at New York's Helen Hayes Theater, an autobiographical play about alcoholism and drug addiction by the playwright, who died late in 1953 at age 65, 390 perfs.; Ruth Gordon and Arthur Hill in Thornton Wilder's *The Matchmaker* 12/5 at New York's Royale Theatre, 486 perfs. (it will be the basis of the 1964 musical *Hello, Dolly!*).

Television: *As the World Turns* 4/2 on CBS (Irna Phillips, now 54, has created the new soap opera); *Edge of Night* 4/2 on ABC (both daytime).

Films: Ingrid Bergman, Yul Brynner, Helen Hayes, and Akim Tamiroff in Anatole Litvak's *Anastasia*; Danny Kaye, Glynis Johns, and Basil Rathbone in Norman Panama and Melvin Frank's *The Court Jester*; Gary Cooper, Dorothy McGuire, and Marjorie Main in William Wyler's *Friendly Persuasion*; Rock Hudson, Elizabeth Taylor, and the late James Dean in George Stevens's *Giant*; Anthony Quinn, Giulietta Masina, and Richard Basehart in Federico Fellini's *La Strada*. Also: French actress Brigitte Bardot (Camille Javal), 22, in Roger Vadim's *And God Created Woman* (*Et Dieu Créa la Femme*); Marilyn Monroe, Eileen Heckart, and Don Murray in Joshua Logan's *Bus Stop*; Donald Sutherland and Brooke Adams, 8, in Don Siegel's *Invasion of the Body Snatchers*; Gregory Peck, Jennifer Jones, and Fredric March in Nunnally Johnson's *The Man in the Grey Flannel Suit*; John Gielgud, Ralph Richardson, Claire Bloom, and Laurence Olivier in Olivier's *Richard III*; Paul Newman and Italian actress Pier Angeli (Anna Maria Pierangeli), 24, in Robert Wise's *Somebody Up There Likes Me*; Machiko Kyo in Kenji Mizoguchi's *Street of Shame*; Marlon Brando, Glenn Ford, and Michiko Kyo in Daniel Mann's *The Teahouse of the August Moon*.

Stage musicals: English singer-actress Julie Andrews (Julia Elizabeth Wells), 20, as Eliza Doolittle, Rex Harrison as Professor Higgins in *My Fair Lady* 3/15 at New York's Mark Hellinger Theater, with a book based on the 1914 Bernard Shaw play *Pygmalion*, Frederick Loewe–Alan Jay Lerner songs that include "Why Can't the English Teach Their Children How to Speak?," "The Rain in Spain," "The Street Where You Live," "I'm Getting Married in the Morning," "I've Grown Accustomed to Her Face," and "I Could Have Danced All Night," 2,717 perfs.; Sammy Davis, Jr. and Sr. and Chita Rivera in *Mr. Wonderful* 3/22 at New York's Broadway Theater, with songs that include "Too Close for Comfort," 388 perfs.; Vivien Leigh, Alan Webb, and Joyce Carey in Noël Coward's *South Sea Bubble* 4/25 at London's Lyric Theatre, 276 perfs.; Robert Weede, Art Lund, and Jo Sullivan in *The Most Happy Fella* 5/3 at New York's Imperial Theater, with a book based on the 1924 Sidney Howard play *They Knew What They Wanted*, Frank Loesser songs that include "Big D" and "Standing on the Corner," 676 perfs.; Edie Adams as Daisy Mae and Peter Palmer as Abner

Yokum in *Li'l Abner* 11/10 at the St. James Theater, with Charlotte Rae as Mammy Yokum, Tina Louise (Tina Blacker), 22, as Appassionata von Climax, Stubby Kaye, and Julie Newmar, songs that include "Jubilation T. Cornpone," 693 perfs.; Judy Holliday and Jean Stapleton in *Bells Are Ringing* 11/29 at the Shubert Theater, with music by Jule Styne, lyrics by Betty Comden and Adolph Green, songs that include "Just in Time" and "The Party's Over," 924 perfs.

Opera: *The Ballad of Baby Doe* 7/7 at Colorado's Central City Opera House with music by U.S. composer Douglas Stuart Moore, 61, libretto based on the career of silver magnate Horace Tabor and his widow (*see* 1880); English mezzo-soprano Janet (Abbott) Baker, 23, makes her operatic debut at Glyndebourne singing the role of Roza in the 1878 Smetana opera *The Secret* (*Tagernstvi*); Maria Callas makes her Metropolitan Opera debut 10/2 in the lead role of the 1831 Bellini opera *Norma*.

Ballet: Ballerina Tanaquil LeClercq, now 26, is stricken with poliomyelitis while dancing at Copenhagen and paralyzed from the waist down.

Popular songs: "Love Me Tender" by rock 'n' roll guitarist-singer Elvis Presley, 21, and Vera Walson; "Heartbreak Hotel" by Elvis Presley, Mae Boren Axton, Tommy Durden; Teresa Brewer records "A Tear Fell"; Caterina Valenti records Ernest Lecuona's "The Breeze and I"; Patti Page records "Old Cape Cod" and "Allegheny Moon."

U.S. figure skater Tenley Albright wins her event at the winter Olympics in Cortina d'Ampezzo, Italy. Swiss skier Madeleine Berthod wins the downhill in 1 minute, 40.1 seconds, Swiss skier Renée Colliard the slalom, German skier Ossi Reichert the giant slalom in 1 minute, 39.9 seconds. Australian runner Betty Cuthbert wins the 100-meter dash in 11.5 seconds and the 200-meter in 23.4 seconds at the summer games in Melbourne. Shirley S. de la Hunty wins the 80-meter hurdles in 10.7 seconds, U.S. athlete Mildred McDaniel the running high jump (5 feet, 9¼ inches), Polish athlete Elzbieta Krzesinska the long jump (20 feet, 9¾ inches), Soviet athlete Tamara Tishkyevich the shot put (54.5 feet), Czech athlete Olga Fikotova the discus throw (176 feet, 1½ inches), Soviet athlete Inessa Janzeme the javelin throw (176 feet, 8 inches). Australian swimmer Dawn Fraser, 19, wins the 100-meter freestyle in 1

minute, 2 seconds, Australian swimmer Lorraine Crapp the 400-meter freestyle in 4 minutes, 54.6 seconds, British swimmer Judy Grinham the 100-meter backstroke in 1 minute, 12.9 seconds, German swimmer Ursala Happe the 200-meter breaststroke in 2 minutes, 53.1 seconds, U.S. swimmer Shelley Mann the 100-meter butterfly in 1 minute, 11 seconds, Patricia McCormick, now 26, the springboard and platform dive events (the only woman in Olympic history to score a "double-double"—two gold medals in each of two Olympiads).

Shirley Fry, 29 (U.S.), wins in women's singles at both Wimbledon and Forest Hills.

Grace Kelly, now 26, is married April 19 at Monaco to Prince Rainier II.

Marilyn Monroe, now 30, is married June 29 to playwright Arthur Miller (her third husband).

"Does she or doesn't she?" ask advertisements for "Miss Clairol" hair coloring that show children with mothers to convey the idea that hair coloring is not just for women of dubious virtue (*see* 1950). Written by New York copywriter Shirley Polykoff, the ads bid for beauty parlor acceptance by answering the question, "Only her hairdresser knows for sure." As of 1950, only 7 percent of U.S. women dyed their hair; within a dozen years the figure will be nearly 70 percent.

Comet, a silica-sand cleanser introduced by Procter & Gamble to compete with Colgate's Ajax (*see* 1947), will soon be the top seller.

Actress and health enthusiast Gloria Swanson, now 57, lectures congressmen's wives on the hazards of American foods. They persuade their husbands to support a Food Additives Amendment to the Food, Drug and Cosmetic Act of 1938, which Rep. James J. Delaney (D., N.Y.) has been pushing without success (*see* 1958).

China's Ministry of Public Health issues a directive in August requiring local health agencies to promote birth control actively (*see* 1954). A major propaganda campaign gets under way to encourage family size limitation, but authorities maintain that the campaign has been motivitated not by concern about runaway population growth but rather out of concern for the health and welfare of mothers and children. Abortion and sterilization do not play major roles in the effort and are available only under stringent limitations (*see* 1957).

Portland, Ore., housewife Ruth Alice Kistler (*née* Taylor), 57, gives birth October 18 at Glendale, Calif., to a daughter, Susan, and becomes the oldest woman to bear a child (claims of deliveries at older ages have been made over the years but never with convincing proof). Kistler's age is 57 years, 129 days.

1957

 Arkansas State Press publisher Daisy Lee Bates (*née* Gatson), 42, leads the Little Rock Nine in its fight to desegregate Central High School, defying racist threats that include burning crosses on her front lawn. She stops a man from throwing a Molotov cocktail one night by firing her .38 over his head.

Colombia, Honduras, and Malaysia grant women the right to vote on the same basis as men.

Britain's *Report of the Committee on Homosexual Offences and Prostitution* (Wolfenden Report), issued in September, calls for an end to the requirement that "annoyance" be established before a constable may book a prostitute for soliciting a customer above the age of 21, but the recommendation on homosexuality is what creates a controversy. It recommends an end to punitive laws against homosexuality "between consenting adults in private." Reading University chancellor Sir John Wolfenden, 51, heads the committee; its recommendations receive support from the Church of England (*see* Street Offences Act, 1959).

A Great Leap Forward launched by Mao Zedong in the People's Republic of China puts more than half a billion peasants into 24,000 "people's communes." The people are guaranteed food, clothing, shelter, and child care, but deprived of all private property.

$ A University of Wisconsin study shows that 20 percent of Americans still live below the "poverty line" (*see* 1959).

¥ Congress funds a National Cancer Institute to seek cures for the disease that is second only to heart disease as a cause of death in the United States.

 The *Woman's Home Companion* folds January 4 after 85 years of monthly publication.

Nonfiction: *The Natural Superiority of Women* by English-American anthropologist Ashley Montagu, 52, who says, "The old chestnut about women being more emotional than men has been forever destroyed by the evidence of two world wars. Women under blockade, bombardment, concentration-camp conditions survive them vastly more successfully than men. The psychiatric casualties of populations under such conditions are *mostly* masculine"; *Memoirs of a Catholic Girlhood* by Mary McCarthy; *Gypsy* (autobiography) by stripteaser Gypsy Rose Lee (*see* Stage musicals, 1959); *Voltaire in Love* by Nancy Mitford; *Please Don't Eat the Daisies* (essays) by playwright Jean Kerr.

Fiction: *The Comforters* by Scottish novelist Muriel Spark (*née* Camberg), 39, who at age 19 traveled to Southern Rhodesia to marry a 32-year-old schoolteacher whom she had met at a dance and with whom she spent 7 unhappy years, prevented by wartime travel restrictions from returning home; *Arturo's Island* (*L'Isola di Arturo*) by Elsa Morante, wife of Alberto Moravia; *Valentino* (stories) by Natalia Ginzburg; *Esmond in India* by Ruth Prawer Jhabvala; *Woman's Hill* (*Onnazaka*) by Fumiko Enji; *Ohan* (novella) by Chiyo Uno; *Noren* by Japanese novelist Toyoko Yamazaki, 33; *The Fountain Overflows* by Rebecca West; *Devil by the Sea* by Nina Bawden; *A Small Fire* by Gladys Schmitt; *Love and Salt Water* by Ethel Wilson; *Scent of Cloves* by Norah Lofts; *Thunder on the Right* by Mary Stewart; *A Cup of Tea for Mr. Thorgill* by Storm Jameson; *Angel* by Elizabeth Taylor; *The Other Side of the Wall* by Janet McNeill; *The Blue Camellia* by Frances Parkinson Keyes; *Deep Water* by Patricia Highsmith.

Poetry: *Hear It Now* by Denise Levertov; *Not Waving but Drowning* by Stevie Smith.

Juvenile: *Little Bear* by Danish-American author Else Holmelund Minarik will be translated into 17 foreign languages including Urdu and Bengali, will have U.S. sales of 1 million in the next 20 years, and begins a series of "I Can Read Books"; *A Friend Is Someone Who Likes You* by U.S. author Joan Walsh Anglund, 24.

Painting: *Billboard* by Grace Hartigan.

Theater: Sybil Thorndike, Leueen MacGrath, Carol Lynley, 14, and Frank Conroy in Graham Greene's *The Potting Shed* 1/29 at New York's Bijou Theater, 157 perfs.; Maureen Stapleton and Cliff Robertson in Tennessee Williams's *Orpheus Descending* 3/21 at New York's Martin Beck Theater, 68 perfs.; Wendy Hiller, Franchot Tone, and Cyril Cusack in the late Eugene O'Neill's *A Moon for the Misbegotten* 5/2 at New York's Bijou Theater, 68 perfs.; Irish actress Siobhan McKenna, 35, Art Carney, and Theodore Bikel in Morton Wishengrad's *The Rope Dancers* 11/20 at New York's Cort Theater, 189 perfs.; Jo Van Fleet, Anthony Perkins, and Arthur Hill in *Look Homeward, Angel* (based on the 1929 Thomas Wolfe novel), 11/28 at New York's Ethel Barrymore Theater, 564 perfs.; Pat Hingle, Teresa Wright, and Eileen Heckart in William Inge's *The Dark at the Top of the Stairs* 12/5 at New York's Music Box Theater, 468 perfs.

Films: Ruby Dee, John Cassavetes, Sidney Poitier, and Jack Warden in Martin Ritt's *Edge of the City*; Giulietta Masina in Federico Fellini's *Nights of Cabiria*; Ingrid Thulin, Bibi Andersson, 22, and Victor Sjöström in Ingmar Bergman's *Wild Strawberries*; Marlene Dietrich, Tyrone Power, Charles Laughton, and Elsa Lanchester in Billy Wilder's *Witness for the Prosecution*. Also: Katharine Hepburn and Spencer Tracy in Walter Lang's *Desk Set*; Patricia Neal, Lee Remick, 21, Andy Griffith, and Walter Matthau in Elia Kazan's *A Face in the Crowd*; Maria Schell in Helmut Kautner's *The Last Bridge*; James Cagney (as Lon Chaney, Jr.), Dorothy Malone, and Jane Greer in Joseph Pevney's *Man of a Thousand Faces*; Lana Turner, Betty Field, Hope Lange, 23, Diane Varsi, 19, Mildred Dunnock, Lloyd Nolan, and Arthur Kennedy in Mark Robson's *Peyton Place*; Marlon Brando, Ricardo Montalban, Miiko Taka, and Japanese-born actress Miyoshi Umeki (as Katsumi) in Joshua Logan's *Sayonara*; Joanne (Gignilliat) Woodward, 27, David Wayne, and Lee J. Cobb in Nunnally Johnson's *The Three Faces of Eve*; British actress Yvonne Mitchell (Yvonne Joseph), 32, Sylvia Syms, 23, and Anthony Quayle in J. Lee Thompson's *Woman in a Dressing Gown*.

Norma Talmadge dies in her sleep at Las Vegas December 24 at age 64 (or 60). She made at least 67 pictures before retiring in 1930, but arthritis has confined her to a wheelchair for several years.

Hollywood musicals: Audrey Hepburn, Gary Cooper, and Maurice Chevalier in Billy Wilder's *Love in the Afternoon* with songs that include "Fascination" and "C'est Si Bon"; Gene Kelly, dancer Mitzi Gaynor (Francesca Mitzi von Gerber), 25, Kay Kendall, and Taina Elg in George Cukor's *Les Girls*; Fred Astaire, Audrey Hepburn, Kay Thompson, and model Suzy Parker in Stanley Donen's *Funny Face*; Doris Day (von Kappelhoff), 33, John Raitt, and Carol Haney in George Abbott and Stanley Donen's *The Pajama Game*.

Broadway musicals: Beatrice Lillie, Billie de Wolfe, and Jane Morgan in *The Ziegfeld Follies* 3/11 at the Winter Garden Theater, the 24th and final edition of the *Follies* 50 years after its first opening, 123 perfs.; Gwen Verdon and Thelma Ritter in *New Girl in Town*, a musical version of the 1921 Eugene O'Neill play *Anna Christie*, 5/14 at the 46th Street Theater, with Bob Merrill songs that include "Sunshine Girl," 431 perfs.; veteran nightclub singer Lena Horne, now 40, Ricardo Montalban, and Ossie Davis in *Jamaica* 10/31 at the Imperial Theater, with Harold Arlen–Yip Harburg songs, 558 perfs.

Popular songs: U.S. country singer Patsy Cline (Virginia Patterson Hensley), 24, sings "Walkin' after Midnight" by Donn Hecht 1/28 for Arthur Godfrey's Talent Scouts to begin a career in which she will score hits with songs such as "Heartaches," "Cry Not For Me," and "Fingerprints"; Detroit cabaret singer Della Reese (Dellareese Taliaferro), 25, records "In the Still of the Night" and then has a hit with her recording of "And That Reminds Me"; U.S. jazz singer Abbey Lincoln (Anna Marie Wooldridge), 27, makes her recording debut with "Affair . . . The Story of a Girl In Love"; *In London* (album) by Teresa Brewer, who has a hit single with "You Send Me" by Sam Cooke; "Bye Bye, Love" by Felice and Boudleaux Bryant; "Young Love" by Carole Joyner and Ric Cartey; "Old Cape Cod" by Claire Hothrock, Milt Yakers, and Allan Jeffrey; "Jim Dandy" by LaVern Baker.

The Boston Opera Group, founded by local conductor-producer Sarah Caldwell, 28, will rename itself the Opera Company of Boston as it gains a reputation for innovative productions.

Elisabeth Söderström makes her Glyndebourne debut singing the role of the composer in the 1916 Strauss opera *Ariadne auf Naxos*.

Patricia McCormick enters the arena at Ciudad Juárez, Mexico, January 20 as the first U.S. woman bullfighter.

Althea Gibson, 29 (U.S.), wins in women's singles at Wimbledon (the first black American to be invited to play there). She receives a ticker tape parade up Broadway July 11, New York mayor Robert Wagner tells her, "If we had more women like you the world would be a better place," and she goes on to win the singles title at Forest Hills.

Parents Without Partners, founded in February by French-American journalist Jacqueline Bernard, 36, and Jim Egleson, is a group for divorced or widowed parents that will grow to become an international organization with 250,000 members in the United States alone.

Spandex is introduced by E. I. DuPont under the name Lycra for use, initially, in girdles and bras. A petroleum-based product based on World War II synthetic-rubber research, the durable elastic fiber will soon be used in bathing suits, support stockings, waistbands, and toreador pants—and eventually will be in body-hugging athletic wear.

Britain's Queen Elizabeth II announces November 14 that debutantes will no longer be presented at court.

English physician John Bodkin Adams, 58, goes on trial at Eastbourne in March for the murder of Edith Alice Morrell, a rich patient who, like some of his previous rich patients, most of them women, has died under mysterious circumstances after being treated with heroin and morphine prescribed by Dr. Adams. Morell added a codicil cutting Adams out of her will just before she died, but he has grown rich on bequests from other deceased patients. Adams wins acquittal but resigns from the National Health Service and is struck off the Medical Register. He will be reinstated by the General Medical Council in 1961, and his supporters will say that while he may have benefited as a benefi-

ciary of many of his patients, he simply practiced a form of euthanasia.

China's Great Leap Forward virtually eliminates rats, bedbugs, houseflies, and mosquitoes over wide areas in a prodigious outburst of human energy as women join with men in attacking the pests.

U.S. per capita margarine consumption overtakes butter consumption for the first time. The average American uses 8.6 pounds of margarine per year versus 8.3 pounds of butter (*see* 1960).

The United States has a record 4.3 million births.

Gregory Pincus and Boston gynecologist John Rock, 67, begin an intensive trial of birth control pills to prevent unwanted births in the Rio Piedras section of San Juan, Puerto Rico. Working with the Family Planning Association of Puerto Rico, a Planned Parenthood affiliate, they use pills containing 10 mg of G. D. Searle's synthetic progesterone norethynodrel and 0.15 mg of mestranol, a synthetic estrogen. Women who take The Pill for 20 days of the month in January and February experience normal menstrual flow at the end of the month, but nearly 20 percent report at least one side effect, including dizziness, headache, weight gain, stomach pain, or diarrhea (*see* 1955; Enovid-10, 1960).

China's Ministry of Public Health takes steps to relax limitations on sterilization and abortion (*see* 1956). Birth control clinics throughout the country are expected to set up "guidance committees" (*see* 1971).

1958

A Gallup Poll survey published January 15 shows that former First Lady Eleanor Roosevelt, now 73, is the most widely admired woman in America.

Veteran Harlem civil rights leader Ella Josephine Baker, 54, moves to Atlanta in January to coordinate the Crusade for Citizenship, a voter rights campaign started by the Southern Christian Leadership Conference and backed by the charisma of SCLC president Rev. Martin Luther King, Jr. Baker favors decision making at a local, grassroots level, saying that "strong people don't need strong leaders," and her egalitarian, nonclerical position will bring her into conflict with SCLC leadership (*see* 1960).

Venezuelan women protest government restrictions January 17 and are attacked by Caracas police wielding machetes, but the government of Gen. Marcos Pérez Jimínez is overthrown 6 days later.

Moroccan women gain the right to choose their own husbands. The government restricts polygamy.

Tokyo's Yoshiwara prostitute district is closed April 1 after 341 years of operation. U.S. occupation authorities, who left in 1953, were unable to close it, but feminist Fusaye Ichikawa, who was elected to the Diet in 1952, has waged a campaign to end legalized prostitution (*see* 1956).

South African social worker Winnie Nomzano, 24, of the Baragwanath General Hospital is arrested for taking part in a women's demonstration against the nation's apartheid pass laws. She marries lawyer Nelson Mandela, an executive in the African National Congress (*see* 1962).

U.S. unemployment reaches a postwar high of more than 5.1 million, and the Department of Labor reports that a record 3.1 million Americans are receiving unemployment insurance benefits. Economic recession grips the nation with nearly one-third of major industrial centers classified as having "substantial" unemployment.

The upper 1 percent of Americans enjoys nearly 9 percent of the nation's total disposable income, down from 19 percent of disposable income in 1929. 64 percent of households have incomes above $4,000 per year, up from 40 percent in 1929, but white families average twice as much as nonwhite families.

The median U.S. family income is $5,087, up from $3,187 in 1948 (half of all families have incomes below the median, half above), but prices have climbed along with incomes.

A house that cost $47,409 in 1948 sells for $59,558, a family-size Chevrolet that sold for $1,255 sells for $2,081, a gallon of gasoline has climbed from 25.9¢ to 30.4¢, a pair of blue jeans that sold for $3.45 sells

for $3.75, a pair of men's shoes that was $9.95 is now $11.95, a daily newspaper that cost 3¢ now costs 5¢, a year's tuition at Harvard that cost $455 costs $1,250, a hospital room that cost $13.09 per day costs $28.17, a pound of round steak that cost 90.5¢ costs $1.04, a Nathan's hot dog that cost 20¢ costs 25¢, a ticket to a Broadway musical that cost $6.00 costs $8.05.

Some prices have come down: a ranch mink coat that cost $4,200 in 1948 costs $4,000, a round-trip flight to London from New York that cost $630 costs $453.60, a phone call from New York to Topeka, Kan., that cost $1.90 costs $1.80 (day rate), a pound of chicken that cost 61.2¢ has come down to 46.5¢.

Nonfiction: *Memoirs of a Dutiful Daughter* (*Mémoires d'une jeune fille rangée*) by Simone de Beauvoir. *On My Own* by Eleanor Roosevelt (above); *Beloved Infidel: The Education of a Woman* by gossip columnist Sheila Graham, now 50 (*see* 1933), who met writer F. Scott Fitzgerald at a 1937 cocktail party, encouraged him to continue writing and begin his Hollywood novel *The Last Tycoon* (he died in her arms in 1940 with the book still unfinished), and by 1964 will have displaced Hedda Hopper and Louella Parsons as the leading Hollywood columnist in an era when a reporter's opinion can be crucial to the success or failure of a film or actor; *Alexander's Path* by Freya Stark, who was awarded a Cross of the British Empire in 1953.

Fiction: *Spinster* by New Zealand novelist Sylvia (Constance) Ashton-Warner, 53; *A World of Strangers* by Nadine Gordimer; *The Mask of a Woman* (*Nyomen*) by Fumiko Enji; *Gear Wheel* (*Haguruma*) by Ineko Sata; *Hananoren* by Toyoko Yamazaki; *Sentimental Story* (*Sentimentalny roman*) by Evira Panova tells of the difficult working conditions she experienced in the 1920s when she was employed by a small Rostov newspaper; *As Music and Splendour* by Kate O'Brien; *The Mountain Is Young* by Han Suyin; *The Greengage Summer* by Rumer Godden; *The Blackmailer* by English novelist Isabel Colegate, 26; *A Ripple from the Storm* by Doris Lessing; *Leech* (*Kjop ikke Dondi*) by Cora Sandel; *The Winthrop Woman* by Anya Seton; *The Sundial* by Shirley Jackson; *The Best of Everything* by U.S. novelist Rona Jaffe, 26; *Victorine* by Frances

Parkinson Keyes; *A Furnished Room* by Janet McNeill; *Nine Coaches Waiting* by Mary Stewart; *North from Rome* by Helen MacInnes.

Poetry: *The Double Bed from the Feminine Side* by Eve Merriam; *A Cage of Spines* by May Swenson.

Juvenile: *Do You Know What I'll Do?* by Charlotte Zolotow.

Painting: *White Study* (oil on canvas) and *The Garden* (paint, wood, found objects) by Canadian-born U.S. artist Agnes Martin, 46.

Sculpture: *Sea Form (Porthmeor)* (bronze) by Barbara Hepworth.

New York photographer Diane Arbus (*née* Nemerov), 35, begins 2 years of study with Austrian-American documentary photographer Lisette Model, now 51, who befriends her and will help Arbus get through her separation and divorce in the 1960s.

Theater: Anne Meacham in Tennessee Williams's *The Garden District* (*Suddenly Last Summer* and *Something Unspoken*) 1/7 at New York's York Theater; Anne Bancroft (Anna Maria Italiano), 26, as Gittel Mosca and Henry Fonda in William Gibson's *Two for the Seesaw* 1/16 at New York's Booth Theater, 750 perfs.; Ralph Bellamy as Franklin D. Roosevelt, Mary Fickett as Eleanor in Dore Schary's *Sunrise at Campobello* 1/30 at New York's Cort Theater, 556 perfs.; Beatrix Lehmann in Harold Pinter's *The Birthday Party* 5/19 at London's Lyric Theatre; Tom Clancy, Eric Portman, Helen Hayes, Kim Stanley, and Betty Field in the late Eugene O'Neill's *A Touch of the Poet* 10/2 at New York's Helen Hayes Theater, 284 perfs.; France Nuyen and William Shatner in Paul Osborn's *The World of Suzie Wong* 10/14 at New York's Broadhurst Theater, 508 perfs.; *The Pleasure of His Company* by Cornelia Otis Skinner and Samuel Taylor 10/22 at New York's Longacre Theater, with Skinner and Cyril Ritchard, 474 perfs.; Jason Robards, Jr. (and Sr.), English actress Rosemary Harris, 28, Salome Jens, and George Grizzard in Budd Schulberg and Harvey Breit's *The Disenchanted* (based on Schulberg's novel) 12/3 at New York's Coronet Theater, 189 perfs.; Eli Wallach, Maureen Stapleton, Vincent Gardenia, Morris Carnovsky, and Suzanne Pleshette, 21, in S. N.

Behrman's *The Cold Wind and the Warm* 12/8 at New York's Morosco Theater, 120 perfs.

Films: Laurence Harvey and Simone Signoret in Jack Clayton's *Room at the Top*; Rita Hayworth, Deborah Kerr, David Niven, Wendy Hiller, and Burt Lancaster in Delbert Mann's *Separate Tables*; Charlton Heston, Janet Leigh, and Welles in Orson Welles's *Touch of Evil*; James Stewart, Kim Novak, and Barbara Bel Geddes in Alfred Hitchcock's *Vertigo*. Also: Rosalind Russell in Morton DaCosta's *Auntie Mame*; Elizabeth Taylor, Paul Newman, and Burl Ives in Richard Brooks's *Cat on a Hot Tin Roof*; Susan Hayward in Robert Wise's *I Want to Live!*; Richard Burton, Claire Bloom, and Dame Edith Evans, now 70, in Tony Richardson's *Look Back in Anger*; Rock Hudson, Dorothy Malone, and Robert Stack in Douglas Sirk's *The Tarnished Angels*; Russ Tamblyn and June Thornton in George Pal's *tom thumb*; Marlon Brando, Montgomery Clift, Dean Martin, and Hope Lange in Edward Dmytryk's *The Young Lions*.

Hollywood musical: Leslie Caron, Maurice Chevalier, and Louis Jourdan in Vincente Minnelli's *Gigi* with Frederick Loewe–Alan Jay Lerner songs that include "Thank Heaven for Little Girls," "The Night They Invented Champagne," and the title song.

Stage musicals: Elizabeth Seal, Keith Mitchell, and Clive Revill in *Irma la Douce* 7/17 at London's Lyric Theatre, with music by French composer Marguerite Monmot, 1,512 perfs.; Pat (originally Chiyoko) Suzuki, 27, Juanita Hall, Myoshi Umeki (as the mail-order bride Mei Li), and Larry Blyden in *Flower Drum Song* 12/1 at New York's St. James Theater, with Rodgers and Hammerstein songs, 601 perfs.

Opera: Eleanor Steber creates the title role of Samuel Barber's new opera *Vanessa* 1/15 at New York's Metropolitan Opera; Spanish mezzo-soprano Teresa Berganza, 23, makes her first British appearance at Glyndebourne as Cherubino in the 1786 Mozart opera *Le Nozze di Figaro* and sings at Dallas as Isabella in the 1813 Rossini opera *L'Italiana in Algeri*.

Popular songs: Mahalia Jackson records Duke Ellington's "Black, Brown, and Beige" with the

Ellington orchestra; Anita O'Day sings the 1924 song "Tea for Two" and the 1925 song "Sweet Georgia Brown" at the Newport Jazz Festival; "Splish Splash" by Bobby Darin and Jean Murray.

Althea Gibson wins in women's singles at both Wimbledon and Forest Hills.

Romanian athlete Iolanda Balas clears six feet in the high jump October 18, becoming the first woman to do so (*see* 1925).

Japan breaks with tradition June 18 by permitting Crown Prince Akihito, 24, to choose his own bride.

Americans buy 100 million Hula Hoops, introduced by Wham-O Mfg., but the fad is short-lived.

A Los Angeles inquest finds April 11 that Lana Turner's daughter, Cheryl Crane, 14, and her father, restaurateur Stephen Crane, committed "justifiable homicide" in stabbing to death Lana's lover, Hollywood hoodlum Johnny Stompanato, 32, after he threatend her with serious injury or death if she left him.

A Lincoln, Nebraska, jury finds Caril Ann Fugate, 15, guilty of murder and she is sentenced to life imprisonment November 21. She and her boyfriend, Charles Starkweather, 20, who had just lost his job as a garbage truck helper, drove through Nebraska and Wyoming in late January after shooting Caril's mother, Velda, and her husband, and clubbing Caril's younger sister to death. They killed seven more people in the next three days before Wyoming police caught them January 30.

A food additives amendment to the Food, Drug and Cosmetic Act of 1938 passed by Congress permits no food additives other than those used widely for many years and "generally recognized as safe" (GRAS list) unless the FDA agrees after a thorough review of test data that the new additive is safe at the intended level of use.

The Delaney "cancer clause" inserted in the new amendment (above) by congressman James J. Delaney states that if *any* amount of any additive can be shown to produce cancer when ingested by humans or test animals, no amount of that additive may be used in foods for human consumption (*see* Swanson, 1956; cyclamates, 1969).

Sweet 'n Low sugarless sweetener, introduced by Cumberland Packing Co. of Brooklyn, N.Y., uses saccharin in place of sugar.

English Roman Catholic economist Colin Clark deplores birth control. He writes in the magazine *Nature*, "When we look at the British in the seventeenth and eighteenth centuries, at the Greeks in the sixth century B.C., the Dutch in the seventeenth century, and the Japanese in the nineteenth century, we must conclude that the pressure of population upon limited agricultural resources provides a painful but ultimately beneficial stimulus, provoking unenterprising agrarian communities into greater efforts in the fields of industry, commerce, political leadership colonization, science, and [sometimes . . .] the arts."

Abortion in the United States by Great Neck, Long Island, physician's wife Mary Steichen Calderone, 53, reports on conferences of the Planned Parenthood Federation but is almost totally ignored (*see* 1955; Colorado, 1967).

1959

Indian political leader Indira Gandhi, only daughter of the late Prime Minister Jawaharlal Nehru, is elected president of the Congress Party February 2 at age 41.

Cuban revolutionary leader Fidel Castro Ruiz, now 32, assumes office as premier February 16 after a 2-year rebellion (*see* 1953). His younger brother Raul's wife, Wilma Espin, 26, trained as a chemical engineer, is made head of the Cuban Women's Movement at Fidel's request and will promulgate a family code (*El Código*) giving the force of law to the division of household labor, but she is not a feminist and (perhaps reflecting her brother-in-law's views) will be a harsh critic of the U.S. feminist movement.

British ballerina Margot Fonteyn is arrested April 20 by Panamanian police on suspicions of fomenting a revolution. Her husband, Roberto Arias, the son of a former president of Panama, eluded capture by jumping from his yacht to a passing shrimp boat.

Former U.S. Ambassador to Italy Clare Boothe Luce is confirmed April 28 as ambassador to Brazil but resigns at her husband's request May 1 following criticism by Sen. Wayne Morse (D. Ore.), who says she has "poisoned" the atmosphere of goodwill that her mission requires.

Madagascar and Tanzania grant women the right to vote on the same basis as men.

The Street Offences Act passed by Britain's Parliament July 16 makes it an offense "for a common prostitute to loiter or solicit in a secret or public place for the purpose of prostitution," and says, "A constable may arrest without warrant anyone he finds in a street or public place and suspects, with reasonable cause, to be committing an offence under this section." English and Welsh prostitutes will circumvent the law by posting their telephone numbers at news kiosks or buying dogs and walking them as an excuse for being in the streets (*see* 1869; 1957).

Some 22.5 million U.S. women work away from home, mostly on factory assembly lines or as office workers, retail clerks, schoolteachers, nurses, laundresses, and domestic servants.

Russian archaeologist Tatiana Proskouriakov finds a pattern of dates indicating a list of important events in the lives of certain Mayan individuals in the Yucatán. The find enables scholars to decipher the periods in which certain rulers reigned and thus establish dynasties, but scholars will argue about whether the Mayan styphs represent ideas, words, or both.

Mary Leakey, now 55, captures public attention by finding the skull of an *Australopithicus boisei*—a 1.75-million-year-old hominid—while she is being filmed at Olduvai Gorge in Tanzania, where she has been working since 1951 (*see* 1948). Her find brings huge new funding for the excavations that she and her husband are making (*see* 1976).

West German clinics observe 12 cases of the birth defect phocomelia. Infants are born with flipper-like stubs in place of one or more normal limbs. Not one case has been seen in the past 5 years, and the large number sounds alarms (*see* 1960).

Thank You, Dr. Lamaze: A Mother's Experience in Painless Childbirth by U.S. writer Marjorie Karmel helps to popularize the Lamaze method, which has been championed in America by English psychotherapist Elisabeth Bing (*see* 1956). By next year, the Lamaze method will be the most popular psychophysical way to relieve the pain of childbirth in the United States, with expectant mothers in upper socio-economic levels attending Lamaze classes to train like athletes and educate themselves in techniques that fit into the new, sentimentally pleasing craze for naturalness. Anthropologist Margaret Mead, however, will suggest that natural childbirth is itself unnatural because it imposes "artifices" such as breathing routines on the laboring woman. Mead herself demanded and obtained delivery without anesthesia at a New York hospital in 1939, saying that she had never heard women in primitive societies describe the pains of childbirth (*see* 1991).

New York physicist in medicine Rosalyn S. Yalow (*née* Sussman), 38, begins with a colleague to develop a new method of radioimmunoassay that will permit the measurement of blood levels of hormones, enyzmes, and drugs. It shows that diabetics have high blood levels of insulin and will be used to detect hepatitis in potential blood donors (*see* 1977).

Pope John XXIII announces October 11 that Mother Elizabeth Anne Seton will be beatified and become the first American-born saint.

Saudi Arabia's King Faisal permits education for girls despite protests from some religious groups.

New York journalist Marie Torre, 35, serves 10 days in the Hudson County Jail at Jersey City, N.J., after being convicted on contempt charges for refusing to divulge the identity of a "CBS executive" she quoted in a January 1957 TV column that appeared in the *New York Herald Tribune* and 49 other newspapers. According to Torre, he had said that Judy Garland was "known for a highly developed inferiority complex," "couldn't make up her mind," and was "terribly fat." Garland sued CBS for breach of contract and libel, demanding nearly $1.4 million, Torre told the court last year that to reveal the executive's name would be a betrayal of her entire profession, the sentencing judge has called her the "Joan of Arc of her profession," but Anthony Lewis of the *New York Times* says that if a reporter "hides behind the cloak of press freedom," then every "irresponsible gossip columnist would be encouraged to make up nasty little items themselves and then attribute them to unnamed sources."

Nonfiction: *The Tiger House: The Last Days of the Maharajahs* by Emily Hahn; *My Russian Journey* by Santha Rama Rau.

A federal district court at New York July 21 lifts a U.S. Post Office ban on distributing the 1928 D. H. Lawrence novel *Lady Chatterley's Lover* despite protests that the book uses such words as "fuck" and "cunt" and is explicit in its descriptions of the sex act. Grove Press has distributed an unexpurgated version of the book, Postmaster General Arthur E. Summerfield has banned it from the mails, and Judge Frederick van Pelt Bryan, 55, rules in Grove's favor. His 30-page decision in *Roth* v. *the United States* says not only that the book is not obscene but also that the postmaster general is neither qualified nor authorized to judge the obscenity of material to be sent through the mails; he is empowered only to halt delivery of matter already judged obscene.

Fiction: *Memento Mori* by Muriel Spark; *The Little Disturbances of Man: Stories of Women and Men at Love* by U.S. writer Grace Paley, 36; *The Planetarium (Le Planetarium)* by Nathalie Sarraute; *Aimez-Vous Brahms?* by Françoise Sagan; *The Haunting of Hill House* by Shirley Jackson; *The Town House* by Norah Lofts; *The Humbler Creation* and *Skipton* (which some will consider her best novel) by Pamela Hansford Johnson; *Change Here for Babylon* by Nina Bawden; *Search Party* by Janet McNeill; *Lantana Lane* by Eleanor Dark; *Grey Afternoon (Haiiro no gogo)* by Ineko Sata; *The River Ki (Kinokawa)* by Sawako Ariyoshi; *Dear and Glorious Physician* by Taylor Caldwell; *The Sea Change* by Elizabeth Howard; *The Third Choice* by Elizabeth Janeway; *The John Wood Case* by Ruth Suckow, now 67; *False Scent* by Ngaio Marsh.

Poetry: *Valentines to the Wide World: Poems* by U.S. poet Mona (Jane) Van Duyn, 38; *With Eyes in the Back of Our Heads* by Denise Levertov.

Sculpture: *White on White* by U.S. sculptor Louise Nevelson, 59. Germaine Richier returns to Paris in April for a large exhibition of her work but dies of cancer at Montpellier July 31 at age 54.

New York's Guggenheim Museum opens on Fifth Avenue between 88th and 89th streets to house the collection of the late copper magnate Solomon R. Guggenheim, whose mentor, Hilla Rebay, induced him to buy dozens of canvases by the late abstractionist Wassily Kandinsky. Collector Peggy Guggenheim calls the new museum "My uncle's garage, that Frank Lloyd Wright thing on Fifth Avenue."

Theater: *A Taste of Honey* by English playwright Shelagh Delaney, 20, 2/10 at London's Wyndham Theatre, 617 perfs.: "Women never have young minds. They are born three thousand years old" (I, 2); Gertrude Berg and Cedric Hardwicke in Leonard Spigelgass's *A Majority of One* 2/16 at New York's Shubert Theater, 558 perfs.; Geraldine Page and Paul Newman in Tennessee Williams's *Sweet Bird of Youth* 3/10 at New York's Martin Beck Theater, 378 perfs.; *Raisin in the Sun* by U.S. playwright Lorraine Hansberry, 29, 3/11 at New York's Ethel Barrymore Theater, with Sidney Poitier, Ruby Dee, Diana Sands, 24, Claudia McNeil, 530 perfs. (Hansberry has taken her title from a Langston Hughes poem containing the line "What happens to a dream deferred?/ Does it dry up/ Like a raisin in the sun?"); Patty (*née* Anna Maria) Duke, 12, as Helen Keller and Anne Bancroft as Anne Sullivan in William Gibson's *The Miracle Worker* 10/19 at New York's Playhouse Theater, 702 perfs.

Films: James Stewart and Lee Remick in Otto Preminger's *Anatomy of a Murder*; Cary Grant, Eva Marie Saint, and James Mason in Alfred Hitchcock's *North by Northwest*; Gregory Peck, Ava Gardner, and Fred Astaire in Stanley Kramer's *On the Beach*; Jack Lemmon, Tony Curtis, and Marilyn Monroe in Billy Wilder's *Some Like It Hot*. Also: Marpessa Dawn and Breno Mello in Marcel Camus's *Black Orpheus*; U.S. actress Jean Seberg, 21, and Jean-Paul Belmondo in Jean-Luc Godard's *Breathless*; Bernadette O'Farrell and Bill Travers in Frank Launder's *The Bridal Path*; Orson Welles, Diane Varsi, Dean Stockwell, and Bradford Dilman in Richard Fleischer's *Compulsion*; Millie Perkins, 21, Joseph Schildkraut, and Shelley Winters in George Stevens's *The Diary of Anne Frank*; Machiko Kyo and Ganjiro Nakamura in Yasujiro Ozu's *Floating Weeds*; Jeanne Moreau, 30, in Louis Malle's *The Lovers*; Peter Sellers and Jean Seberg in

Jack Arnold's *The Mouse That Roared*; Audrey Hepburn, Peter Finch, and Dame Edith Evans in Fred Zinneman's *The Nun's Story*; Doris Day and Rock Hudson in Michael Gordon's *Pillow Talk*; Elizabeth Taylor, Katharine Hepburn, and Montgomery Clift in Joseph L. Mankiewicz's *Suddenly Last Summer*.

Stage musicals: Carol Burnett, 22, and Jack Gilford in *Once upon a Mattress* 5/11 at New York's Phoenix Theater, with music by Mary Rodgers, lyrics by Marshall Barer, 458 perfs.; Ethel Merman and Jack Klugman in *Gypsy* 5/21 at New York's Broadway Theater, with a book based on the 1957 autobiography by stripteaser Gypsy Rose Lee, Jule Styne–Stephen Sondheim songs that include "Small World," "Together Wherever We Go," and "Everything's Coming Up Roses," 702 perfs.; *Lock Up Your Daughters* 5/28 at London's new Mermaid Theatre, with music by Laurie Johnson, lyrics by Lionel Bart (Lionel Begleiter), 328 perfs.; Mary Martin, Theodore Bikel, and Kurt Kasznar in *The Sound of Music* 11/16 at New York's Lunt-Fontanne Theater, with Rodgers and Hammerstein songs that include "Climb Every Mountain," "Do-Re-Mi," "Edelweiss," "My Favorite Things," and the title song, 1,443 perfs.

Ballet: U.S. ballerina Patricia McBride, 18, makes her debut with the New York City Ballet; Alicia Alonso, now 37, becomes prima ballerina and director of the Ballet Nacional de Cuba.

Opera: U.S. soprano Anna Moffo, 26, makes her Metropolitan Opera debut singing the role of Violetta in the 1853 Verdi opera *La Traviata*; German soprano Christa Ludwig, 31, makes her Metropolitan Opera debut; Elisabeth Söderström makes her Metropolitan Opera debut as Susanna in the 1786 Mozart opera *Le Nozze di Figaro*; Birgit Nilsson, now 41, makes her Metropolitan Opera debut 12/18 singing the role of Isolde in the 1865 Wagner opera *Tristan und Isolde* (she will be the leading Wagnerian soprano in the 1960s and '70s).

U.S. folk singer Joan (Chandoz) Baez, 19, appears at the Newport Folk Festival and becomes an overnight sensation with what one critic calls her "achingly pure soprano" voice. In the next decade she will depart from her repertory of old English ballads to sing out against war, bigotry, and complacency.

Popular songs: North Carolina–born jazz pianist-singer Nina Simone (Eunice Waymon), 26, who has studied at New York's Juilliard School of Music, records "I Love You, Porgy" from the 1935 George Gershwin opera *Porgy and Bess* and "My Baby Just Cares for Me"; Sarah Vaughan, now 35, records "Broken-Hearted Melody" and has her biggest success (*see* 1944); Della Reese records "Don't You Know" (adapted from "Musetta's Waltz" in the 1896 Puccini opera *La Bohème*) and "Not One Minute More"; Eartha Kitt records "Somebody Bad Stole the Wedding Bell" and "Yellow Bird"; country singer Skeeter Davis (Mary Frances Penick), 27, records "Set Him Free" and has her first solo hit (she formed a duo 10 years ago with her friend Betty Jack Davis, then 16, and performed as the Davis Sisters at small clubs and on a Lexington, Ky., radio station, achieving success in the early 1950s with "I've Forgotten More Than You'll Ever Know," but Betty Jack was killed 8/2/53 and Davis was critically injured when another car struck theirs as they were returning from Cincinnati; Atlanta-born singer Brenda Lee (Brenda Mae Tarpley), 14, records "Sweet Nothin's"; Molly O'Day, now 36, records "Come Walk with Me"; "Waterloo" by John Loudermilk and Marijohn Wilkin.

Maria Bueno, 19 (Brazil), wins in women's singles at both Wimbledon and Forest Hills.

French swimsuit designer Claude Kogan, 40, and Belgian skier Claudine van der Strate-Ponhoz, 26, die with their Sherpa guide in an October blizzard that catches them 23,000 feet up on Nepal's Cho Oyu (the "Turquoise Goddess"), a 26,867-foot Himalayan peak, eighth highest in the world and one of the most dangerous. The four-foot ten-inch Kogan, whose husband, Georges, died in a mountaineering accident a few years ago, set out August 21 from Katmandu with an all-woman team of 11 climbers from five countries to prove that experienced women climbers could match the skill and endurance of men.

Lady Astor celebrates her 80th birthday May 19. Addressing Winston Churchill in her 50s, she said, "My dear Winston, if I were your wife I'd put poison in your tea." (Replied Churchill, "My dear Nancy, if I were your husband I'd drink it.") Today she says, "Years ago I thought old age would be dreadful because I should not be able to do the things I would want to do. Now I find there is nothing I want to do after all." She is well known for her remark "I married beneath me. All women do."

The Barbie doll introduced by California entrepreneur Ruth Handler, 42, and her artist husband, Eliot, is allegedly based on dolls handed out to patrons of a West Berlin brothel. The busty doll with her endless wardrobe enriches the Handlers' toy firm, Mattel, Inc.

Pantyhose—waist-high nylon hose requiring no garters, garter belts, or corsets—are introduced under the name Panti-Legs by Glen Raven Mills of Altamahaw, N.C., whose president, Allen Gant, has heard his wife, Ethel, complain about her problems with nylon stockings and garter belts, especially during pregnancy. Nylon sales have been flat of late while sales of stretch tights in opaque colors have been rising, so Gant has stitched a pair of seamed stockings to a big nylon crotch and put out the product in 10 sizes. Stripper Sally Rand begs Gant to make seamless Panti-Legs, and he improves the product by making them much more elastic, so they'll be easier to put on and remove, and in more sizes (see 1967).

Former Iranian shepherdess Farah Dibah, 20, is married December 21 to Shah Mohammed Riza Pahlevi, 40. It is his third marriage.

A housing bill passed by Congress September 23 authorizes expenditure of $1 billion over a 2-year period with $650 million earmarked for slum clearance.

Tang, introduced by General Foods, is an "aromatic, orangy-tasting powder" for use as a "breakfast beverage" in place of orange juice.

Supermarkets account for 69 percent of all U.S. food store sales even though they represent only 11 percent of food stores.

1960

Sinhalese parliamentarian Sirimavo Bandaranaike, 44, is sworn in July 21 as prime minister of Ceylon—the world's first elected female head of state.

She will serve until 1965 and then again from 1970 to 1977 (Ceylon will revert to its traditional name, Sri Lanka—resplendent island—in 1972).

Sen. John F. Kennedy, now 43, wins election to the presidency by defeating Vice President Nixon, capturing 303 electoral votes to Nixon's 219 (a minority candidate gets 45). Kennedy will be the first Roman Catholic U.S. president and his wife, Jacqueline, the first Catholic First Lady.

Four black North Carolina college students stage a sit-in February 1 at a whites-only F. W. Woolworth lunch counter in Greensboro, N.C. The sit-in spreads within 2 weeks to 11 cities in Alabama, Virginia, and three other states. The Congress of Racial Equality and the NAACP call for a nationwide boycott of F. W. Woolworth in March. Ella Baker quits the SCLC to work in a YWCA regional student office, using it to recruit backers and student members of a new organization (below). Support groups for the sit-in demonstrators are formed at 21 northern schools, including Harvard, Yale, Princeton, the University of Chicago, City College of New York, and the University of California, Berkeley. Bennett College student government president Gloria E. Brown, 21, participates in a sit-in at the Greensboro lunch counter. "I was scared," she will later say. "We knew what could happen to us. We knew it was a time when we were being watched very, very carefully." The demonstrations continue through April; Greensboro desegregates its lunch counters July 25.

Atlanta civil rights activist Ruby (née Rubye) Doris Smith, 18, is arrested with others after a student lunch-counter sit-in protesting Jim Crow laws. She and three others (the "Rockville Four") refuse to be released on bail, preferring to serve jail sentences that will draw attention to their cause (see 1965).

Switzerland's Parliament decides March 6 to grant women the right to vote in municipal elections.

Zaire and Gabon grant women the right to vote on the same basis as men.

Japan's divorce rate falls to 0.74 percent, down from 1.39 percent in 1906 because women can now choose their husbands instead of being forced into marriage.

A Canadian Bill of Rights becomes law, guaranteeing women and men equal treatment before the law when they are in an equal situation, but few such situations will be judged to exist in actual litigation.

The Student Non-Violent Coordinating Committee (SNCC) founded in October at the initiative of Ella Baker (above) and others is based on Baker's ideas of democratic, decentralized leadership (see 1958). It will use more aggressive action to challenge racism and vigilante violence in rural areas of the Deep South (see 1964).

The official Soviet newspaper *Izvestia* announces January 30 that women outnumber men among Russian professional specialists, even though they make up only 45 percent of the nation's labor force. The U.S.S.R. has 300,000 women physicians, 233,000 women engineers, and 110,000 women scientists, according to the report, and 1,283,000 of the nation's schoolteachers are women. So many men were lost in World War II that the country could not survive without encouraging women to prepare themselves for professional careers.

More than 34 percent of U.S. women over age 14 and 31 percent of all married women are in the labor force, up from 25 percent of women over age 14 in 1940. Only 10 percent of working women are farmhands or servants, down from 50 percent in 1900.

Canadian-born FDA researcher Frances Kelsey (*née* Oldham), 46, keeps thalidomide off the U.S. market by delaying approval of a Cincinnati firm's application to market the tranquilizer under the brand name Kevadon. Produced by a West German pharmaceutical house and widely used in Britain and West Germany for sleeplessness, nervous tension, asthma, and relief of nausea in early pregnancy, thalidomide is said to have no side effects, but Kelsey notes that it is not effective in making animals sleepy, observes that some British patients have complained of numbness in feet and fingers after using it, and points out that phocomelia is becoming endemic in West Germany, where 83 such birth defects appear at the clinics that saw 12 last year (see 1961).

The Association for the Improvement of Maternity Services (AIMS) has its beginnings in the Society for the Prevention of Cruelty to Pregnant Women, founded in Britain to campaign for the right to have a baby free from interference unless the mother wants it or there are clear medical indications that it is needed.

The Sabin live-virus polio vaccine is given to 180,000 Cincinnati schoolchildren in its first large-scale test (see 1954). Taken by mouth, it provides lifetime protection without booster shots, apparently "spreads" to safeguard people who have not even received the vaccine, and will eventually supplant the Salk vaccine.

Care of the Dying by English nurse Cicely Mary Strode Saunders, 42, will lead to the founding of the modern hospice movement (see 1967).

Television debates give Sen. Kennedy the edge that enables him to defeat Vice President Nixon (above) more by his appearance and manner than anything he says (radio listeners believe Nixon won the debates). TV debates will not be used in a presidential election again until 1976.

The Xerox 914 copier begins a revolution in office paperwork reproduction (see 1950). The first production line Xerox copier is called the 914 because it makes copies of up to 9 by 14 inches on ordinary paper.

Nonfiction: *Problems of Women's Liberation: A Marxist Approach* by U.S. writer Evelyn Reed, 54, who worked as an assistant in Leon Trotsky's Mexican household for nearly 2 years before his assassination in 1940; *In the Days of McKinley* by Margaret Leech, now 67; *Born Free: The Lioness of Two Worlds* by Czech-born author-painter Joy Adamson (*née* Joy Friedericke Victoria Gessner), 50, whose third husband is a Kenya game warden; *The Snake Has All the Lines* (essays) by Jean Kerr.

Fiction: *To Kill a Mockingbird* by Alabama novelist Harper Lee, 34 (Pulitzer Prize); *The Violent Bear It Away* by Flannery O'Connor; *The Constant Nymph* by Marcia Davenport; *Incense to Idols* by Sylvia Ashton Warner; *The Country Girls* by Irish novelist Edna O'Brien, 28; *The Great Fortune* by English novelist Olivia Manning, 45; *Just like a Lady* (in America, *Glass Slippers Always Pinch*) by Nina Bawden; *Don't Tell Alfred* by Nancy Mitford; *The Light in the Piazza* by Elizabeth Spencer; *Music from a Blue Well* (*Musikk fra en blå bronn*) by Torborg Nedreaas; *The Householder* by Ruth Prawer Jhabvala; *Prisoner* (*Shujin*) by Japanese novelist Yumiko Kurahashi, 24; *Know Nothing* by Mary Lee Settle; *Away from Home* (outside the United States, *Carnival in Rio*) by Rona Jaffe; *Echo Answers* by Margaret Culkin Banning; *Mistress of Mellyn* by English novelist Victoria Holt (Eleanor Burford Hibbert, now 54); *Naked in Babylon* by U.S. novelist Gwen Davis, 24; *Testament of Trust* by Faith Baldwin; *This Sweet Sickness* by Patricia Highsmith; *Decision at Delphi* by Helen MacInnes; *Death and the Joyful Woman* by English mystery novelist Ellis Peters (Edith Mary Pargeter), 46.

Poetry: *To Bedlam and Part Way Back* by U.S. poet Anne Sexton (*née* Harvey), 32; *The Colossus* by Sexton's close friend Sylvia Plath, 27; *Times Three: Selected Verse from Three Decades* by U.S. poet Phyllis McGinley, 55 (Pulitzer Prize), whose 1959 poem "The Honor of Being a Woman" included the line "We have not owned our freedom long enough to know exactly how to use it."

Juvenile: *Love Is a Special Way of Feeling* by Joan Walsh Anglund; *Mystery of the Haunted Pool* by U.S. author Phyllis A. (Ayame) Whitney, 57.

Painting: *Islands #1* (oil and pencil on canvas), *The Ages* (oil on canvas), *Mountain* (ink on paper), and *Ocean Water* (ink on paper) by Agnes Martin; *Polar Stampede, The Eye Is the First Circle*, and *Seated Nude* (charcoal on paper) by Lee Krasner.

Theater: *Toys in the Attic* by Lillian Hellman 2/25 at New York's Hudson Theater, with Maureen Stapleton and Jason Robards, Jr., 556 perfs.; Barbara Baxley and James Daley in Tennessee Williams's *Period of Adjustment* 11/10 at New York's Helen Hayes Theater, 132 perfs.; Canadian actress Colleen Dewhurst, 34, Arthur Hill, and Lillian Gish in Tad Mosel's *All the Way Home* 11/30 at New York's Belasco Theater, a play based on the late James Agee's only novel, 334 perfs.

Films: Jack Lemmon, Shirley MacLaine (Shirley Beatty), 26, and Fred MacMurray in Billy Wilder's *The Apartment*; Janet Leigh and Anthony Perkins in Alfred Hitchcock's *Psycho*; Deborah Kerr, Robert Mitchum, and Peter Ustinov in Fred Zinneman's *The Sundowners*. Also: Monica Vitti (Monica

Ceciarelli), 27, in Michelangelo Antonioni's *L'Avventura*; Marcello Mastroianni, Swedish actress Anita Ekberg, 29, and French actress Anouk Aimée (Françoise Sorya), 28, in Federico Fellini's *La Dolce Vita*; Burt Lancaster and Jean Simmons in Richard Brooks's *Elmer Gantry*; Emmanuelle Riva and Eiji Okada in Alain Resnais's *Hiroshima Mon Amour* (whose screenplay is by novelist Marguerite Duras); John and Faith Hubley's *Moonbird* (animated short); Greek actress Melina (*née* Maria Amalia) Mercouri, 34, in Jules Dassin's *Never on Sunday*; Alain Delon, Renato Salvatori, and Claudia Cardinale, 21, in Luchino Visconti's *Rocco and His Brothers*; Dean Stockwell, Trevor Howard, and Wendy Hiller in Jack Cardiff's *Sons and Lovers*; John Mills, Dorothy McGuire, and Sessue Hayakawa in Ken Annakin's *The Swiss Family Robinson*.

Television ventriloquist and puppeteer Shari Lewis (*née* Hurwitz), 26, wins a Peabody Award for entertaining children with her "Lambchop" and other characters.

Broadway musicals: Dick Van Dyke, Chita Rivera, and Kay Medford in *Bye Bye Birdie* 4/14 at the Martin Beck Theater, with Charles Strouse–Lee Adams songs that include "Put On a Happy Face," 607 perfs.; Tammy Grimes, 24, as the *Titanic* heroine (*see* 1912) in *The Unsinkable Molly Brown* 11/3 at the Winter Garden Theater, with music and lyrics by Meredith Willson, 532 perfs.; Richard Burton, Julie Andrews, and Robert Goulet in *Camelot* 12/3 at the Majestic Theater, with Frederick Loewe–Alan Jay Lerner songs that include "If Ever I Would Leave You" and the title song, 873 perfs.; Lucille Ball and Keith Andes in *Wildcat* 12/11 at the Alvin Theater, with Cy Coleman–Carolyn Leigh songs that include "Hey, Look Me Over," 171 perfs.; Phil Silvers and Nancy Walker in *Do Re Mi* 12/26 at the St. James Theater, with music by Jule Styne, lyrics by Betty Comden and Adolph Green, 400 perfs.

Popular songs: Della Reese records "Someday"; church choir singer Tina Turner (Annie Mae Bullock), 21, records "A Fool in Love" and has her first big rhythm-and-blues success; "My Sweet Home" by gospel singer-songwriter Margaret Allison; country music singer Loretta Lynn (*née* Webb [she married Oliver V. "Moody" Lynn at age 13 and moved from her native West Virginia to Bellingham, Wash.]), 25, records "Honky Tonk Girl," makes her first guest appearance on *Grand Ole Opry*, and soon becomes an *Opry* regular; Skeeter James records "I'm Falling Too"; Etta James records "All I Could Do Was Cry"; "The Faraway Part of Town" by Hollywood songwriter Dory Previn (*née* Langdon), 25, and her husband, André; "Itsy Bitsy Teenie Weenie Yellow Polka Dot Bikini" by Lee Pockriss and Paul J. Vance; Brenda Lee records "I'm Sorry" (which will sell more than 10 million copies), "I Want to Be Wanted," and "Rockin' Around the Christmas Tree."

Opera: Spanish soprano Montserrat Caballé, 27, makes her debut at La Scala as a flower girl in the 1882 Wagner opera *Parsifal*; Teresa Berganza makes her Covent Garden debut singing the role of Rosina in the 1816 Rossini opera *Il Barbiere di Siviglia*; U.S. contralto-soprano Grace Melzia Bumbry, 23, makes her debut in a guest appearance at the Paris Opéra in the role of Almirez in the 1871 Verdi opera *Aïda* (she was a joint winner with Martina Arroyo, now 24, at the Metropolitan Opera auditions 2 years ago); Canadian soprano Teresa Stratas, 22, makes her Metropolitan Opera debut after having won last year's Met auditions; Victoria de Los Angeles makes her Metropolitan Opera debut in the 1859 Gounod opera *Faust*; U.S. soprano Patricia Brooks, 22, makes her New York City Opera debut 10/12 as Marianne in the 1909 Strauss opera *Der Rosenkavalier* and soon graduates to the role of Sophie; U.S. soprano Eileen Farrell, 40, makes her Metropolitan Opera debut 12/6 singing the title role in Gluck's opera *Alcestis* (she has sung on radio and in films since 1940, made her operatic debut 4 years ago at Tampa, Fla., and has been singing with the Chicago and San Francisco opera companies).

First performances: *Piano e Forte* by Elisabeth Lutyens at London's Wigmore Hall.

Queens, N.Y., figure skater Carol Heiss, 20, wins her event in the winter Olympics at Squaw Valley, Calif. (and goes on to win her fifth straight world title March 4 at Vancouver, B.C.). German skier Heidi Biebl wins the downhill in 1 minute, 37.6 seconds, Canadian skier Anne Heggtveigt the slalom

in 1 minute, 49.6 seconds, Swiss skier Yvonne Ruegg the giant slalom in 1 minute, 39.9 seconds. U.S. sprinter Wilma Rudolph, 20, wins the 100-meter and 200-meter events at the summer Olympics in Rome, going on to run the anchor leg for the 4 x 100-meter relay team and becoming the first American woman to win three track-and-field gold medals in a single Olympiad (stricken with polio at age 4 and paralyzed in the left leg, Rudolph began physical therapy at age 6, traveling 50 miles by bus twice a week to Nashville with her mother, always sitting in the back because she was black, and in 5 years could walk without a leg brace. She is now called "the fastest woman on earth"). Soviet runner Ljudmila Shevcova wins the 800-meter run in 2 minutes, 4.3 seconds, Soviet runner Irina Press wins the 80-meter hurdles in 10.8 seconds, Romanian athlete Iolanda Balas the running high jump (6 feet, 2¾ inches), Soviet athlete Vera Krepkina the long jump (20 feet, 10¾ inches), Soviet athlete Tamara Press the shot-put (56 feet, 9⅞ inches), Soviet athlete Nina Ponomareva the discus throw (180 feet, 8¼ inches), Soviet athlete Elvira Ozolina the javelin throw (183 feet, 8 inches). Dawn Fraser wins the 100-meter freestyle in 1 minute, 1.2 seconds, U.S. swimmer Chris von Saltzka the 400-meter freestyle in 4 minutes, 50.6 seconds, U.S. swimmer Lynn Burke the 100-meter backstroke in 1 minute, 9.3 seconds, British swimmer Anita Lonsbrough the 200-meter breaststroke in 2 minutes, 49.5 seconds, U.S. swimmer Carolyn Schuler the 100-meter butterfly in 1 minute, 9.5 seconds, German swimmer Ingrid Kramer the springboard dive and platform dive events.

Maria Bueno wins in women's singles at Wimbledon, Darlene Hard, 24, at Forest Hills.

Cotton's share of the U.S. textile market falls to 65 percent, down from 68 percent in 1950, while manmade fabrics increase their share to 28 percent with polyesters commanding 11 percent of the market (*see* 1970).

Convicted kidnapper-rapist Caryl (*né* Carol) Whittier Chessman dies in the gas chamber at San Quentin May 2 at age 38 after nine stays of execution since he was sent to Death Row July 3, 1948. He was arrested that year and convicted on 17 counts of robbery, kidnapping, sexual abuse, and attempted rape after a 3-day crime spree in lover's-lane areas around Los Angeles.

It takes 8 to 10 weeks and just 7 pounds of feed to produce a meaty broiler chicken in the United States, down from 12 to 15 weeks and 12 pounds of feed for a scrawnier (but tastier) broiler in 1940.

Enovid-10, approved by the Food and Drug Administration May 9 and introduced in August by G. D. Searle, is the first commercially available oral contraceptive. Searle biochemist Byron Riegel, 53, has headed the group that developed The Pill, which contains 10 mg of norethynodrel (*see* Puerto Rican test, 1957). Fifty women at Birmingham, England, have cooperated with Searle to make the first British test of an oral contraceptive, but British authorities have ruled March 30 that while The Pill is effective in terms of preventing pregnancy it produces too many side effects for general use (*see* 1961).

The Pill (above) uses synthetic steroids, sells at 55¢ each, and costs a woman $11 per month. Condoms continue to account for $150 million of the $200 million U.S. contraceptive business, with diaphragms and spermicidal creams and gels accounting for most of the rest.

1961

Idealistic U.S. women with college degrees join with like-minded men in signing up for the Peace Corps of Young Americans for Overseas Service, created March 1 by President Kennedy, who has said in his inaugural address, "Ask not what your country can do for you—ask what you can do for your country." Peace Corps volunteers will work to improve education, agriculture, and living standards in Latin America, Asia, Africa, Oceania, and—eventually—Eastern Europe.

President Kennedy arrives at Paris May 31 for talks with President de Gaulle, who compliments First Lady Jacqueline Bouvier Kennedy. JFK quips that his real mission in Paris is to "escort Jacqueline Kennedy."

Algerian nationalist Djamila Boupacha, 19, is arrested on charges of having bombed a café near

Jacqueline Kennedy brought new style and glamour to the White House, but only for a few short years. AP/WIDE WORLD PHOTOS

the University of Algiers. She will be tortured in prison and sexually abused before her release through a general amnesty next year but will continue to fight for independence from France.

The Maharanee of Jaipur Tayatri Devi, 42, wins election to India's Parliament by one of the largest pluralities in the nation's history. Born in London, raised in the Himalayan foothills, and educated in England, at a Swiss finishing school, and at Shantiniketan University in Bolpur, she studied shorthand and typing before her marriage to the maharajah in 1940 and has started Jaipur's first public school for girls. She has fought against *purdah*—the traditional concealment of women.

Atlanta students Charlayne Hunter, 19, and Hamilton "Hamp" Holmes, 20, defy racist epithets as they enter the University of Georgia at Athens, ending segregation at the school pursuant to a January 6 federal court order. Daughter of a U.S. Army chaplain, Hunter has transferred from Wayne State University in Detroit. She hopes for a career in journalism and, she will later write, has "studied the comic-strip character Brenda Starr as I might have studied a journalism textbook" (*see* 1940; Nonfiction, 1992).

Septima Clark joins the Southern Christian Leadership Conference (SCLC) as director of education and teaching (*see* 1956). Now 63, the "grand lady of civil rights" will defy Ku Klux Klan and White Citizen's Council intimidation as she works to increase literacy and citizenship training.

South African apartheid foe Helen Joseph is acquitted of treason after a marathon trial but for the next 10 years, as a banned person, will not be permitted to receive visitors on weekends or at nights or to socialize with more than one person at a time (*see* 1956; 1978).

Rwanda grants women the right to vote on the same basis as men.

The U.S. Supreme Court rules unanimously November 20 to uphold a Florida law exempting women from jury duty unless they volunteer. The right to an impartially selected jury "does not entitle one accused of crime to a jury tailored to the circumstances of the particular case, whether relating to the sex or other condition of the defendant, or the nature of the charges to be tried," says the Court. Mrs. Gwendolyn Hoyt was convicted by an all-male jury in 1958 of murdering her husband with a baseball bat, and the Court upholds her conviction. Three states (Alabama, Mississippi, and South Carolina) do not permit women to serve on juries, and 18 allow women to be excused from jury duty (but *see* 1975).

A new Fair Labor Standards Act signed into law by President Kennedy May 5 takes effect in September, raising the minimum wage to $1.15 per hour.

A Louis Harris poll shows that 23 percent of U.S. working women work to support themselves, 18 percent to support their families, 49 percent for extra money, 9 percent for "something interesting to do."

The U.S. Gross National Product reaches $521 billion, up 60 percent since World War II as measured in constant dollars.

Acetaminophen tablets gain FDA approval in July as an alternative to aspirin. The analgesic, introduced under the brand name Tylenol by McNeill Laboratories division of Johnson & Johnson, is far less likely to cause gastric irritation, reduces fever, is effective against headaches and toothaches, but does not have aspirin's other properties (e.g., reducing muscular and arthritic pain).

Phocomelia deforms 302 newborn infants in West Germany, a Hamburg physician notes that mothers of several of the infants have taken the tranquilizer drug thalidomide, and the German Ministry of Health issues a warning to physicians (*see* 1960; 1962).

The IBM Selectric typewriter, introduced by International Business Machines, has a moving, interchangeable "golf ball" cluster of type, will be linked in 1964 to a magnetic tape recorder that permits automated, individually addressed original copies of any letter, and by 1975 will account for an estimated 70 to 80 percent of the electric typewriter market (*see* word processor, 1974).

Nonfiction: *The Useless Sex* (*Il sesso inutile: Viaggo intorno alla donna*) by Italian journalist Oriana Fallaci, 31; *Gifts of Passage* by Santha Rama Rau; *Elsa* by Joy Adamson.

Fiction: *The Prime of Miss Jean Brodie* by Muriel Spark; *Mrs. Golightly and Other Stories* by Ethel Wilson; *Seduction of the Minotaur* by Anaïs Nin; *Sunday Night to Monday Morning* (*Sunnudagskvöld til mánudags morguns*) (stories) by Icelandic writer Asta Sigurdardóttir, 31; *Voices in the Evening* (*Le voce de la serra*) by Natalia Ginzburg; *Tell Me a Riddle* (stories) by U.S. writer Tillie Olsen, 48; *False Entry* by Hortense Calisher; *God Without Humans* (*Ninjen no inai kami*) by Yumiko Kurahashi; *Rembrandt* by Gladys Schmitt; *Not a Word about Nightingales* by U.S. novelist Maureen Howard (*née* Kearns), 31; *Agency House, Malaya* by Susan Yorke; *The House at Old Vine* by Norah Lofts; *The Ivy Tree* by Mary Stewart; *Last Score* by Storm Jameson.

Poetry: *Halfway* by U.S. poet Maxine Kumin (*née* Winokur), 36; *Double Persephone* by Canadian poet Margaret (Eleanor) Atwood, 21; *Birds* by Judith Wright.

Painting: *Words* (ink on paper mounted on canvas) and *Galleries* (ink on paper) by Agnes Martin. Vanessa Bell dies at her country home April 7 at age 81; Grandma Moses dies at Hoosick Falls, N.Y., December 13 at age 101.

Sculpture: *Single Form (September)* (wood) by Barbara Hepworth; *Katharine Cornell* (bust) by Melvina Hoffman, now 66 (the actress is now 63).

Theater: *Mary, Mary* by Jean Kerr 3/8 at New York's Helen Hayes Theater, with Barbara Bel Geddes, Barry Nelson, 1,572 perfs.; Ruby Dee, Godfrey Cambridge, Bea Richards, Alan Alda, and Ossie Davis as Purlie Victorious Judson in Davis's *Purlie Victorious* 9/28 at New York's Cort Theater, 261 perfs.; Patrick O'Neal, Bette Davis, Margaret Leighton, and Alan Webb in Tennessee Williams's *The Night of the Iguana* 12/28 at New York's Royale Theater, 316 perfs.

Former Saks Fifth Avenue fashion designer Ellen Stewart, 41, rents a small basement in New York's Greenwich Village and opens Café La Mama, an experimental theater club.

Joan Rivers (Joan Alexandra Molinsky), 24, makes her debut as a stand-up comedian with the Chicago improvisational troupe Second City.

Films: Jeanne Moreau, 32, Oskar Werner, and Henri Serre in François Truffaut's *Jules and Jim*; James Cagney, Arlene Francis, and Horst Buchholz in Billy Wilder's *One, Two, Three*; Claudia McNeil, Sidney Poitier, Ruby Dee, Diana Sands, and Louis Gossett in Daniel Petrie's *Raisin in the Sun*; Sophia Loren (Sophia Scicoloni), 26, Eleanora Brown, and Jean-Paul Belmondo in Vittorio De Sica's *Two Women*. Also: Audrey Hepburn, George Peppard, Martin Balsam, Patricia Neal, and Mickey Rooney in Blake Edwards's *Breakfast at Tiffany's*; Shirley Clark's *The Connection* with William Redfield; Deborah Kerr, Michael Redgrave, Martin Stephens, and Pamela Franklin, 12, in Jack Clayton's *The Innocents*, a film version of the 1898 Henry James short story "The Turn of the Screw"; Rock Hudson, Doris Day, and Edie Adams in Delbert Mann's *Lover Come Back*; Marilyn Monroe, Montgomery Clift, and Clark Gable (who dies 11/16 at age 59) in John Huston's *The Misfits*; Natalie Wood, Warren Beatty, Sandy Dennis, Barbara Loden, Audrey Christie, and Phyllis Diller in Elia Kazan's *Splendor in the Grass*; Geraldine Fitzgerald and Laurence Harvey in Peter Glenville's *Summer and Smoke*; Rita Tushingham, 19, and Robert Stephens in Tony Richardson's *A Taste of Honey*; Dirk Bogarde and Sylvia Sims in Basil Dearden's *Victim*; Silvia Pinal and Fernando Rey in Luis Buñuel's *Viridiana*; Hayley Mills, 15, and Alan Bates in Bryan Forbes's *Whistle Down the Wind*.

Marion Davies dies of cancer at Los Angeles September 22 at age 64, leaving an estate worth upward of $20 million, most of it invested in real estate.

Hollywood musicals: Natalie Wood, Puerto Rican actress Rita Moreno, 29, and Richard Beymer in Robert Wise's *West Side Story*.

Broadway musicals: Italian-American singer Anna Maria Alberghetti, 24, Kaye Ballard, and Jerry Orbach in *Carnival* 4/13 at the Imperial Theater, with songs by Bob Merrill, 719 perfs.; Robert Weede, onetime Metropolitan Opera soprano Mimi Benzell, 40, and Yiddish Theater veteran Molly Picon, 64, in *Milk and Honey* 10/10 at the Martin Beck Theater, with songs by Jerry Herman, 543 perfs.; Sydney Chaplin, singer Carol Lawrence, 27, and Orson Bean in *Subways Are for Sleeping* 12/27 at the St. James Theater, with music by Jule Styne, lyrics by Betty Comden and Adolph Green, songs that include "Comes Once in a Lifetime," 205 perfs.

Ballet: U.S. ballerina Suzanne Farrell, 16, makes her debut with the New York City Ballet.

Opera: U.S. soprano (Mary) Leontyne Price, now 34, makes her Metropolitan Opera debut singing the role of Leonora in the 1853 Verdi opera *Il Trovatore* and receives a 45-minute ovation. The seventh black woman to debut at the Met, she will be the first to achieve worldwide status as "prima donna assoluta"; Phyllis Curtin, now 38, makes her Metropolitan Opera debut singing the role of Fiordiligi in the 1791 Mozart opera *Cosí Fan Tutte*; U.S. soprano Evelyn Lear (*née* Shulman), 35, creates the title role in Giselher Kleber's opera *Alkmene* at the Deutsches Oper; English soprano

Elizabeth (Jean) Harwood, 23, makes her operatic debut at Glyndebourne in the 1791 Mozart opera *Die Zauberflöte* and joins the Sadler's Wells company.

English cellist Jacqueline du Pré, 16, makes her professional debut in March at London's Wigmore Hall playing a 1672 Stradivarius cello that has been presented to her anonymously.

First performances: *Symphonies for Solo Piano with Harps and Percussion* by Elisabeth Lutyens 7/28 at the Proms (commissioned by the BBC, it has been written with the peculiar acoustics of the Albert Hall in mind).

Popular songs: *Aretha* (album) by soul singer Aretha Louise Franklin, 19; "Bye Bye Baby" by Motown songwriter-singer Mary Wells, 18; *A Maid of Constant Sorrow* (album) by U.S. guitarist-singer-songwriter Judy (Judith Marjorie) Collins, 22, includes "Wild Mountain Thyme" and "I Know Where I'm Going"; Nina Simone records the blues song "Trouble in Mind" and begins to make herself the poet of the civil rights movement; "Right or Wrong" by Wanda Jackson; "Will You Still Love Me Tomorrow?" and "Up on the Roof" by U.S. songwriter Carole King, 19, and her husband, lyricist Jerry Goffin, 22; Gladys Knight, now 18, and the Pips record "Every Beat of My Heart"; Anita O'Day records "All The Sad Young Men"; Molly O'Day records "Wreck on the Highway"; *Skeeter Davis* (album) and "Optimistic" by Davis; "Crazy" and "I Fall to Pieces" by Patsy Cline.

The Supremes sign a contract with Berry Gordy's 4-year-old Motown Corp. and cut their first records. Detroit singers Diana Ross, Mary Wilson, and Florence Ballard are still in their teens, but as the Supremes they will make eight gold records in less than 2 years and have seven top records.

Angela Mortimer, 29, wins in women's singles at Wimbledon, Darlene Hard at Forest Hills.

Wilma Rudolph sets a new women's record July 19 at Stuttgart, running the 100-meter dash in 11.2 seconds.

The Death and Life of Great American Cities by U.S. social critic Jane Jacobs, 45, observes that cities were safer and more pleasant when they consisted of neighborhood communities where people lived in relatively low-priced buildings, knew their neighbors, and lived in the streets and on their doorsteps rather than in the depersonalized environment characteristic of modern cities. Critic Lewis Mumford, 65, notes that congested 18th-century cities were hardly safer or healthier.

Coffee-Mate nondairy creamer is introduced by Carnation Co. (*see* Pream, 1952). The powder, which will find wide use in offices, is made of corn syrup solids, vegetable fat, sodium caseinate, and various additives.

Canned pet foods are among the three top-selling categories in U.S. grocery stores. Americans feed an estimated 25 million pet dogs, 20 million pet cats.

Cookbook: *Mastering the Art of French Cooking* by Cordon Bleu graduate Julia Child (*née* McWilliams), 49, of Boston with Louisette Bertholle and Simone Beck (Simone Suzanne Renée Madeleine [Simca] Beck-Fishbacher), 57.

Britain's National Health Service announces January 30 that contraceptive pills will be available beginning December 4. Conovid pills, made by G. D. Searle with 5 mg of hormone, are the first oral contraceptives sold in Britain.

Some 800,000 U.S. women have prescriptions filled for The Pill. Some complain of swollen breasts, weight gain, migraine headaches, nausea, or blurred vision but are assured that such side effects are temporary and will disappear with longer use (*see* 1962).

A birth control clinic opens at New Haven, Conn., but is forced to close after 9 days. The order will not be rescinded for nearly 4 years (*see* New York, 1929; Supreme Court, 1965).

The Lippes Loop intrauterine device for birth control, developed by Buffalo, N.Y., physician Jack Lippes, will be implanted within 8 years in an estimated 8 million women worldwide. Not strictly speaking a contraceptive, the IUD does not prevent the egg and sperm from coming together but rather makes the womb unreceptive to implantation of the fertilized egg, which is expelled as an early miscarriage in the monthly menses. Since it is not a drug, it has not been investigated for safety by the U.S.

Food and Drug Administration (FDA) and its sales are not regulated (*see* Dalkon Shield, 1971).

A *Ladies' Home Journal* poll of young women finds that "most" want four children and "many" want five, but U.S. birthrates have been dropping since 1957 and will continue to fall sharply as women's education and employment rise.

1962

 U.S. First Lady Jacqueline Kennedy arrives at New Delhi March 12 on a 2-week goodwill tour, accompanied by her sister, Lee (Princess Stanislaus) Radziwill. She has come from Rome, where she was received in a private audience by Pope John XXIII and conversed with him in fluent French.

Former First Lady and U.S. envoy to the United Nations Eleanor Roosevelt dies at New York November 7 at age 78.

Mississippi sharecropper Fannie Lou Hamer (*née* Townsend), 45, responds to a voter registration drive mounted by the Student Non-Violent Coordinating Committee (SNCC). She fails her registration test, as do virtually all other Mississippi blacks, and when news of her activity leaks out she is fired from her plantation job and forced to vacate the house in which she and her husband, Perry, have lived for 18 years. She makes a second visit to the courthouse and succeeds in having her name placed on the voter rolls by convincing the registrar that she will keep coming back until she is registered (*see* 1963).

The United Farm Workers (UFW) is founded by California labor organizer Cesar Chavez with support from New Mexican organizer Dolores Huerta (*née* Fernandez), 32, who will be arrested 18 times in the next dozen years as she devotes her life to signing up workers, leading boycotts, fighting the use of pesticides that damage workers' health, and lobbying in behalf of migrant workers in the state legislature at Sacramento and in Congress, obtaining disability insurance, unemployment insurance, old-age pensions, and other benefits that have been denied them. Huerta will be called "La Pasionaria" of the farmworkers.

Dolores Huerta worked with Cesar Chavez to get the United Farm Workers off the ground. CHIE NISHIO

South African authorities arrest African National Congress leader Nelson Mandela and sentence him to life imprisonment (the ANC was declared an illegal organization last year). Mandela's wife, Winnie, is banned and severely restricted, but she will defy the order and become a spokeswoman for the ANC in her husband's absence (*see* 1976).

Algeria grants women the right to vote on the same basis as men (*see* Tunisia, 1956; Morocco, 1963).

Britain gets her first woman high court judge October 8 as Elizabeth Lane takes her seat.

 Catalyst opens its first office to help women enter and reenter the workforce. Founder Felice N. Schwartz (*née* Nierenberg), 36, started the National Scholarship Service and Fund for Negro Students after graduation from Smith College and headed it for 6 years before taking a job as production v.p. for a heavy manufacturing company. Her New York–based national nonprofit organization will provide research information in the areas of leadership development and training, mentoring, flexible work arrangements, work and family supports, etc., to help women in business and professional life, and it will help corporations recruit qualified women to serve on boards of directors.

The face of small-town America begins to change as the first Wal-Mart store opens at Rogers, Arkansas. Retail merchant Sam Moore Walton, 44, has run a Ben Franklin store with his brother James at Bentonville; he proposed a chain of discount stores in small towns; Ben Franklin dismissed the idea, and Walton has gone into business for himself. His chain will grow to have more than 1,500 stores by 1990, putting many local Main Street stores out of business as shoppers drive to the outskirts of town for better prices. Sales will pass those of Sears, Roebuck by 1991.

Kmart discount stores are opened by the 63-year-old S. S. Kresge Co., whose five-and-ten-cent stores are losing money. By 1977 Kresge will have sales second only to those of Sears but Wal-Mart (above) will pass it in the 1980s.

Copper Town by anthropologist Hortense Powdermaker is a study of the media in Northern Rhodesia (later Zambia) and their effect on a troubled colonial society.

Britain and France remove thalidomide from the market (*see* 1960; 1961). The *Washington Post* credits FDA researcher Frances Kelsey with having prevented thalidomide birth defects in thousands of U.S. infants (July 15 editorial), she receives praise in the Senate for her "courage and devotion to the public interest," President Kennedy gives her a medal for distinguished service in a White House ceremony, but U.S. physicians have received thousands of sample packages of Kevadon and have given a few to expectant mothers.

The thalidomide affair (above) spurs Congress to pass the Kefauver legislation giving the FDA extensive new authority to regulate the introduction of new drugs. The new law also contains provisions to prevent drug firms from overcharging and from confusing buyers of prescription drugs.

President Kennedy has requested a law that will police the pharmaceutical industry in a message that asked also for a broad program of consumer protection, a "Consumer Bill of Rights" that would include a "Truth in Lending" law and a "Truth in Packaging" law (*see* 1968; 1966).

U.S. researcher John F. Enders, 65, produces the first successful measles vaccine, but it will not be introduced until 1966 (*see* Salk, 1952).

90 percent of U.S. households have at least one TV set; 13 percent have more than one.

First Lady Jacqueline Kennedy conducts television viewers through the White House February 14, presenting historical facts along with the human side of previous executive mansion occupants. Many antiques and paintings have been donated to the White House in response to her pleas. CBS and NBC carry the program simultaneously.

ABC begins color telecasts for 3.5 hours per week beginning in September, 68 percent of NBC prime evening time programming is in color, but CBS confines itself to black and white after having transmitted in color earlier. All three networks will be transmitting entirely in color by 1967.

Veteran *Harper's Bazaar* fashion editor Diana Vreeland, now 62, joins *Vogue* as editor in chief (*see* 1937). She will continue in the *Vogue* position until 1971, exercising great influence on what chic American women wear (*see* below).

Nonfiction: *To Light a Candle* (autobiography) by Welthy Honsiger Fisher, now 83 (*see* education, 1953); *The Rich Nations and the Poor Nations* by English economist Barbara Mary Ward, 48; *Forever Free* by Joy Adamson; *The Guns of August* by U.S. historian Barbara Tuchman (*née* Wertheim), 50, is about World War I; *Sex and the Single Girl* by U.S. writer Helen Gurley Brown, 40.

Fiction: *Ship of Fools* by Katherine Anne Porter; *We Have Always Lived in the Castle* by Shirley Jackson; *The Lonely Girl* by Edna O'Brien; *Flesh* by Brigid Brophy; *Penelope at War* (*Penelope al guerra*) by Oriana Fallaci; *Incense and Floral Tributes* (*Kouge*) by Sawako Ariyoshi; *End of Summer* (*Natsu no owari*) by Japanese novelist Harumi Setouchi, 40, who will become a Buddhist nun in 1973; *Get Ready for Battle* by Ruth Prawer Jhabvala; *A Spirit Rises* by Sylvia Townsend Warner; *The Spoiled City* by Olivia Manning; *The Golden Notebook* by Doris Lessing; *Dearly Beloved* by Anne Morrow Lindbergh; *Love and Friendship* by U.S. novelist Alison Lurie, 35; *Someone's in the Kitchen with Dinah* by Gwen Davis; *The Cry of the Owl* by Patricia Highsmith; *An Error of Judgment* by Pamela Hansford Johnson; *Early Harvest* by Janet McNeill; *Harvest of Hope* and *The West Wind* by Faith Baldwin; *The Moon-Spinners* by Mary Stewart; *The Pale Horse* by Agatha Christie; *Cover Her Face* by English mystery writer P. D. (Phyllis Dorothy) James, 42.

Poetry: *The Jacob's Ladder* by Denise Levertov; *All My Pretty Ones* by Ann Sexton; *Waterlily Fire* by Muriel Rukeyser.

Juvenile: *The Summer Birds* by English author Penelope (Jane) Farmer, 33; *Mr. Rabbit and the Lovely Present* by Charlotte Zolotow (illustrated by Maurice Sendak).

Painting: *Movements with Squares* by English artist Bridget (Louise) Riley, 31; *Blue Flower* (oil, glue, nails, and canvas on canvas), *Little Sister* (oil on canvas), and *Starlight* (oil on canvas) by Agnes Martin; Elaine de Kooning is commissioned to do a portrait of President Kennedy for the Truman Library at Independence and winds up with countless sketches and two dozen canvases in her efforts to capture the young chief executive's restless energy. Natalia Goncharova dies at Paris October 17 at age 81. A believer in free love, she married Mikhail Larimov 7 years ago only to be sure that whoever survived would inherit the other's works.

Sculpture: *Single Form (Memorial)* (stone) by Barbara Hepworth; *Mongolian Archer* by Melvina Hoffman.

Theater: *The Knack* by English playwright Ann Jellicoe, 34, 3/27 at London's Royal Court Theatre; Jason Robards, Jr. and Sandy Dennis, 24, in Herb Gardner's *A Thousand Clowns* 4/5 at New York's Eugene O'Neill Theater, 428 perfs.; Uta Hagen as Martha, Arthur Hill as George in Edward Albee's *Who's Afraid of Virginia Woolf?* 10/13 at New York's Billy Rose Theater, 664 perfs.; Charles Boyer, Agnes Moorehead, and Henry Daniell in S. N. Behrman's *Lord Pengo* 11/19 at New York's Royale Theater, 175 perfs.; Paul Ford, Maureen O'Sullivan, and Orson Bean in Sumner Arthur Long's *Never Too Late* 11/27 at New York's Playhouse, 1,007 perfs.

Films: Jolanta Umecka, Leon Niemczyk, and Zygmunt Malanowicz in Roman Polanski's *Knife in the Water*. Also: William Holden and Lilli Palmer in George Seaton's *The Counterfeit Traitor*; Jack Lemmon and Lee Remick in Blake Edwards's *Days of Wine and Roses*; Laurence Harvey, Frank Sinatra, Janet Leigh, Angela Lansbury in John Frankenheimer's *The Manchurian Candidate*; Ann Bancroft and Patty Duke, now 15, in Arthur Penn's *The Miracle Worker*; Paul Newman and Geraldine Page in Richard Brooks's *Sweet Bird of Youth*; Bette Davis and Joan Crawford in Robert Aldrich's *Whatever Happened to Baby Jane?*; Ingrid Thulin, Gunnar Björnstrand, and Max von Sydow in Ingmar Bergman's *Winter Light*.

Marilyn Monroe takes an overdose of sleeping pills and dies at her Hollywood home August 5 at age 36.

Hollywood musical: Morton Da Costa's *The Music Man* with Robert Preston, Shirley Jones, music and lyrics by Meredith Willson, songs that include "Trouble."

Broadway musicals: Diahann Carroll and Richard Kiley in *No Strings* 3/15 at the 54th Street Theater, with Richard Rodgers songs that include "The Sweetest Sounds," 580 perfs.; Sid Caesar, Joey Faye, and Virginia Martin in *Little Me* 11/17 at the Lunt-Fontanne Theater, with Cy Coleman–Carolyn Leigh songs that include "Real Live Girl," 257 perfs.

Opera: Italian soprano Adriana Maliponte, 19, makes her Paris Opéra debut in March singing the role of Micaela in the 1875 Bizet opera *Carmen*; U.S. mezzo-soprano Shirley Verrett, 31, appears in *Carmen* at the Spoleto Festival and makes a sensation; she will debut at the New York City Opera in 1964, at La Scala in 1966, and at the Met in 1968.

U.S. pianist Ruth Laredo (neé Mechler), 24, makes her orchestral debut at New York's Carnegie Hall playing with Leopold Stokowski and the American Symphony Orchestra.

First performances: *Quincunx* by Elisabeth Lutyens 7/12 at the Cheltenham Festival (scored for a very large orchestra, the work is is based on a geometrical astrological pattern and employs the 12-tone scale, whose use Lutyens has pioneered in Britain).

"We Shall Overcome" is copyrighted by Nashville, Tenn., schoolteacher Guy Carawan, who has added rhythmic punch to a song that will be the hymn of the U.S. civil rights movement and sung in protest demonstrations throughout the world. The late Zilphia Horton, co-director of the Highlander Folk Center at Monteagle, Tenn., learned it from striking black tobacco workers at Charleston, S.C., in the mid-1940s and taught it to folk singer Pete Seeger in 1947 and to Frank Hamilton (who added a verse).

Popular songs: *Peter, Paul and Mary* (album) by a trio that includes Mary (Ellin) Travers, 25, Peter Yarrow, 24, and Paul Stukey, 23; *Golden Apples of the Sun* by Judy Collins includes "Minstrel Boy" and "The Silkie"; "The One Who Really Loves You," "You Beat Me to the Punch," and "Two Lovers" by Mary Wells; Esther Philipps records "Release Me"; Etta James records "Something Has Got a Hold On Me;" Gladys Knight and the Pips record "Letter Full of Tears"; Texas-born rhythm & blues singer-songwriter Barbara Lynn (Barbara Lynn Ozen), 20, records "You'll Lose a Good Thing"; Patsy Cline records her songs "She's Got You" and "When I Get Through with Me You'll Love Me Too"; Skeeter Davis records "Where I Ought to Be."

Mrs. Karen Hantze Susman, 19 (U.S.), wins in women's singles at Wimbledon, Margaret Smith, 19 (Australia), at Forest Hills.

Tobacco heiress Doris Duke's mother dies in April at age 90; the "richest girl in the world," now 49, inherits more millions.

Diana Vreeland of *Vogue* (above) will become famous for pronouncing corduroy "cor du roi" and for such aphorisms as "Pink is the navy blue of India" and "The bikini is the most important thing since the atomic bomb." Of Coco Chanel she says, "Her first customers were princesses and duchesses, and she dressed them like secretaries and stenographers" (*see* 1913; 1971).

Philip Morris introduces "Marlboro Country" to advertise its top filter-tip cigarette against R. J. Reynolds's Winston brand. The cowboy theme will make Marlboro, originally a "woman's" brand that came with a choice of ivory or red ("beauty") tips, the leading brand worldwide for women smokers as well as men.

Silent Spring by Rachel Carson warns of dangers to wildlife in the indiscriminate use of persistent pesticides such as DDT. Her book will lead to a federal ban on the use of DDT, despite testimony by reputable scientists that the pesticide poses no hazard to humans nor even to birds.

Britain has a cold spell that freezes outdoor house pipes, interferes with plumbing, and creates general misery.

Diet-Rite Cola, introduced by Royal Crown Cola, is the first sugar-free soft drink to be sold nationwide to the general public. The cyclamate-sweetened cola will soon have powerful competitors (*see* No-Cal, 1952; Tab, 1963).

Frozen, dehydrated, and canned potatoes account for 25 percent of U.S. potato consumption.

The U.S. Food and Drug Commission releases a report August 4 to the effect that since September 1961 28 American women developed blood clots that are believed to have resulted from taking oral contraceptives, and that six have died. G. D. Searle disputes any causal relationship but, under pressure from U.S. Food and Drug Commissioner George A. Larrick, issues a warning to physicians August 7 that taking Searle's Enovid oral contraceptive may raise a woman's risk of blood clots. The American Medical Association issues a statement 2 days later, saying that it has made a "careful scien-

The Pill, it was called—an oral contraceptive that really worked but had unwanted side-effects at first. MALAYSIAN POSTER, WORLD HEALTH ORGANIZATION, NATIONAL LIBRARY OF MEDICINE

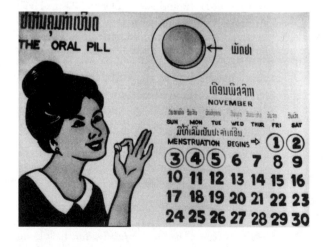

tific review of oral contraceptives" and "found absolutely no evidence that [their] use . . . [causes] thrombophlebitis [blood clots in a vein]."

China resumes the birth control campaign suspended in her Great Leap Forward Program of 1958, but a proposal by the World Health Organization that it offer family-planning advice brings rebukes by 30 nations (but *see* 1965).

About 96 percent of British women now marry by age 45, up from 83 percent in 1921. Average age at marriage worldwide is now about 24, up from about 17 at the turn of the century, and this has had a greater effect in reducing fertility in much of the world than the introduction of oral contraceptives.

Pope John XXIII convenes Vatican II October 11—less than a century after Vatican I was convened in 1869. The world's population has tripled since 1869 to 3.1 billion.

1963

Jacqueline Kennedy, now 34, impresses the world with her stoicism after the assassination of her husband at Dallas November 22. She required 2 pints of blood after giving birth by Caesarean section in August to a third child, who was premature and died after 1½ days. The First Lady, who has planned and conducted the restoration of the White House during John F. Kennedy's brief 1,000 days in office, stands beside Lyndon B. Johnson as he takes the oath of office aboard Air Force One and plans the state funeral for her late husband, whose body she cradled after he was shot while driving in an open touring car.

Britain's Profumo–Christine Keeler scandal makes world headlines. The war minister Lord John Dennis Profumo is charged with having been intimate with call girl Christine Keeler, 21, to whom he was introduced naked in a swimming pool by Viscount Astor's osteopath and artist friend Stephen Ward, who has his own cottage at Astor's Cliveden estate and whose mistress, model Marilyn "Mandy" Rice-Davies, 18, is Keeler's flatmate (she has previously been mistress to the notorious London slumlord Peter Rachman, and when told in court that Lord Astor has denied knowing her, she replies, "He

would, wouldn't he?"). Ward, who faces charges of living off immoral earnings, claims that Profumo has used his flat to meet Keeler. Profumo is married to actress Valerie Hobson, but the real scandal arises from the fact that Keeler is sleeping with Soviet naval attaché Evgeny "Honeybear" Ivanov, a known spy attached to the Russian embassy who has asked Keeler to find out from Profumo when nuclear warheads will be delivered to West Germany. Profumo confesses to the affair and resigns in early June, Keeler draws a 9-month sentence in December for perjury and conspiracy to obstruct justice.

U.S. civil rights worker Coretta Scott King places a call Easter Sunday, April 14, to President Kennedy asking for the release of her husband, Rev. Martin Luther King, Jr., who led a march of 50 volunteers 2 days earlier despite concerns that his arrest would seriously hinder vital fund-raising efforts. He and Ralph Abernathy were placed in solitary confinement.

Congress votes June 10 to guarantee women equal pay for equal work, but the Equal Pay Act will prove difficult to enforce. By 1991, U.S. women will still be earning 70 cents for every dollar earned by men, up from 60 cents now; the figures for black and Hispanic women will be 62 cents and 54 cents, respectively, and a woman earning an hourly wage will be more likely to receive close to equal pay than a white-collar worker, who may receive only half what a man earns doing the same work.

Mississippi activist Fannie Lou Hamer is arrested while returning home from a civil rights meeting at Winona and beaten severely by her jailers (*see* 1962). Some of the injuries she sustains will prove permanent (*see* 1964).

Students Vivian Malone and James A. Hood enter the University of Alabama despite vows by Gov. George Wallace that no blacks will be admitted. Malone will defy harrassment and in 1965 will become the university's first black graduate.

Four black Alabama schoolgirls are killed and 19 people injured September 15 when a bomb explodes at Birmingham's 16th Street Baptist Church while 200 are attending Sunday services. The deaths of Denise McNair, 11, Carole Robertson, 14, Addie Mae Collins, 14, and Cynthia Wesley, 14, provoke racial riots, police dogs are used to attack civil rights demonstrators, and two black schoolboys are killed later the same day.

Morocco and Congo grant women the right to vote on the same basis as men. Iran grants voting rights to women.

Soviet cosmonaut Lieut. Valentina Vladimirovna Tereshkova, 26, returns to earth June 19 aboard the spaceship *Vostok VI* after making 48 revolutions of the globe in less than 3 days; she volunteered for the mission, proved that her physical endurance and stamina were equal to those of a man, went through arduous technical and physical training, and is the first woman to circle the globe in outer space. Premier Khrushchev notes that she was in space longer than all four U.S. astronauts combined, and scoffs at the West's "bourgeois" notion that woman is the weaker sex.

U.S. factory workers average more than $100 per week for the first time in history, but unemployment reaches 6.1 percent by February.

More than 50 million U.S. taxpayers support the Treasury, up from 4 million in 1939. Most income taxes are paid by payroll withholdings.

New Hampshire conducts the first state lottery—a sweepstakes ostensibly to raise money for state education. The state ranks last in terms of state aid to education, the lottery will not raise this ranking nor will it contribute more than 3 percent of state education aid in any year, but other states will follow New Hampshire's example as politicians seek substitutes for income taxes, postponing fundamental tax reforms and adequate funding for social services.

U.S. federal employees number 2.5 million, up from 1.13 million in 1940.

Two-thirds of the world's automobiles are in the United States (which has 6 percent of the world's population).

A 52-year-old woman comes into the office of Brooklyn, N.Y., obstetrician-gynecologist Robert A. Wilson for a checkup February 13; her skin is unwrinkled, her breasts firm, her stature erect, and she tells him that she is still menstruating regularly. It turns out that she has used oral contraceptives

since age 49, and Wilson begins a study of 82 patients to see if birth control pills may "prevent menopause" (*see* book, 1966).

Mother Seton is beatified at Rome March 17 (*see* 1959).

Reading the Lord's Prayer or verses from the Bible in U.S. public schools is unconstitutional, the Supreme Court rules June 17 in *School District of Abington Township* v. *Schempp*. The decision caps a campaign by atheist Madalyn Murray O'Hair (*née* Mays), 44.

Pope Paul VI breaks with tradition November 2 and admits five women as delegates to Vatican II.

AT&T introduces transistorized electronic Touch-Tone telephones November 18 in two Pennsylvania communities on an optional basis at extra cost. They have far more capabilities than the electromechanical dial phones introduced in 1919.

Nonfiction: *The Feminine Mystique* by U.S. feminist Betty Naomi Friedan (*née* Goldstein), 42, argues that women as a class suffer various forms of discrimination but are victimized especially by a system of delusions and false values that encourages them to find personal fulfillment through their husbands and children: "It can be less painful for a woman not to hear the strange, dissatisfied voice stirring within her"; "Over and over women heard in voices of tradition and Freudian sophistication that they could desire no greater destiny than to glory in their own femininity . . . to pity the neurotic, unfeminine, unhappy women who want to be poets or physicians or presidents"; "How did Chinese women, after having their feet bound for many generations, finally discover they could run?"; "It is easier to live through someone else than to become complete yourself" (*see* NOW, 1966); *The Force of Circumstances* (*La Force des choses*) by Simone de Beauvoir; *Teacher* by novelist Sylvia Ashton-Warner, who has taught grammar school to white and Maori children in her native New Zealand (this book was actually written before her novels but could not find a publisher); *Eichmann in Jerusalem* by Hannah Arendt; *The American Way of Death* by English-American writer Jessica (Lucy) Mitford, 45, deplores U.S. traditions of burial and the methods of undertakers.

Betty Friedan, who helped start NOW, argued in The Feminine Mystique *against finding fulfillment in marriage.* CHIE NISHIO

Fiction: "Divided Heaven" by East German writer Christa Wolf, 34, tells of a young woman who prefers the security of an East German working community to the perils of West Berlin; *Cliffs of Fall, and Other Stories* by Australian-American author Shirley Hazzard, 32; *The Girls of Slender Means* by Muriel Spark; *The Andalusian Shawl* (*Lo scialle andaluso*) (stories) by Elsa Morante; *Family Sayings* (*Lessico famigliare*) by Natalia Ginzburg; *The Mountain Stream* (*Keiryu*) by Ineko Sata; *The River Arita* (*Aritagawa*) by Sawako Ariyoshi; *Sentimental Journey* by Japanese novelist Seiko Tanabe, 35; *The Great White Tower* (*Shiroi Kyotō*) by Toyoko Yamazaki begins serialization September 15 in the weekly *Sunday Mainichi*; *Like Birds, Like Fishes and Other Stories* by Ruth Prawer Jhabvala; *The Golden Fruits* (*Les Fruits d'or*) by Nathalie Sarraute; *A Summer Bird-Cage* by English novelist

Margaret Drabble, 24; *Four Faces* by Han Suyin; *The Bell Jar* by the late U.S. poet Sylvia Plath, who has taken her own life February 11 at age 31 (her autobiographical novel is an account of manic depression); *A Man and Two Women* (stories) by Doris Lessing; *The Benefactor* by U.S. novelist-critic Susan Sontag, 30; *The Group* by Mary McCarthy; *If Morning Ever Comes* by U.S. novelist Anne Tyler, 22; *Textures of Life* by Hortense Calisher; *The Quality of Mercy* by Margaret Culkin Banning; *The King's Orchard* by Agnes Turnbull; *Old Red and Other Stories* by Caroline Gordon; *The Birds* by Daphne du Maurier; *The Battle of Villa Fiorito* by Rumer Godden; *The Concubine: A Novel Based upon the Life of Anne Boleyn, Henry VIII's Second Wife* by Norah Lofts; *Night of Silence, Who Is Here?* by Pamela Hansford Johnson; *The Finishing Touch* by Brigid Brophy; *The Colour of Rain* by English novelist Catherine Ady (Emma Tennant), 26; *The China Governess* by Margery Allingham; *Dead Water* by Dame Ngaio Marsh; *The One-Faced Girl, The Mark of the Hand, A Little Less Than Kind*, and *The Witch's House* by Charlotte Armstrong; *The Venetian Affair* by Helen MacInnes.

Poetry: *Requiem* by Anna Akhmatova, now 75, whose book was banned in the U.S.S.R. but is published at Munich (it is a cycle of poems on the Stalin purges, during which her only son was arrested); *Snapshots of a Daughter-in-Law* by Adrienne Rich; *Collected Poems, 1919–1962* by Babette Deutsch; *Selected Poems* by Australian poet Rosemary Dobson, 43.

Juvenile: *The Wolves of Willoughby Chase* by English writer Joan (Delano) Aiken, 38, daughter of poet-novelist Conrad Aiken; *Amelia Bedelia* by U.S. author Peggy (*née* Margaret Cecile) Parish, 36; *Mystery of the Hidden Hand* by Phyllis A. Whitney.

Painting: *Whispering* (watercolor on paper) by Agnes Martin.

Sculpture: *The Wave* (Plexiglas, wood, and beads) by Agnes Martin; *Two Forms with White* (*Greek*) (wood and stone) by Barbara Hepworth.

Eastman Kodak introduces Instamatic cameras that can be loaded with film cartridges. Eastman also introduces Kodachrome-X, Ektachrome-X, and

Kodacolor-X films with twice the speed of their predecessors.

Theater: Hermione Baddeley and Mildred Dunnock in Tennessee Williams's *The Milk Train Doesn't Stop Here Anymore* 1/16 at New York's Morosco Theater, 69 perfs.; Elizabeth Ashley (*née* Cole), 22, Robert Redford, Mildred Natwick, and Kurt Kasznar in Neil Simon's *Barefoot in the Park* 10/23 at New York's Biltmore Theater, 1,502 perfs.

Films: Patricia Neal, Paul Newman, Melvyn Douglas, and Brandon de Wilde in Martin Ritt's *Hud*; Burt Lancaster, Claudia Cardinale, and Alain Delon in Luchino Visconti's *The Leopard*. Also: Jessica Tandy, Tippi (*née* Nathalie) Hedren, 28, Rod Taylor, and Suzanne Pleshette in Alfred Hitchcock's *The Birds*; Audrey Hepburn, Cary Grant, and Walter Matthau in Stanley Donen's *Charade*; Julie Harris and Claire Bloom in Robert Wise's *The Haunting*; Margaret Rutherford (as Miss Marple), Robert Morley, and Flora Robson in George Pollock's *Murder at the Gallop*; Ingrid Thulin and Gunnel Lindblom in Ingmar Bergman's *The Silence*; John and Faith Hubley's *The Hole* (animated short).

First performances: *The Country of the Stars* by Elisabeth Lutyens (based on a text by Boethius) 3/20 at London's Holy Trinity Church (commissioned by the *Musical Times*); *Motet* Opus 27 by Lutyens (set to a text by the Austrian philosopher Ludwig Wittgenstein) 12/5 at London.

Opera: Janet Baker sings the role of Polly in a revival of the 1728 Pepusch-Gay work *The Beggar's Opera* at London. She appeared last year as Dido with the English Opera at the Aldeburgh Festival in the 1689 Purcell opera *Dido and Aeneas*.

Broadway musical: Barbara Cook and Jack Cassidy in *She Loves Me* 4/23 at the Eugene O'Neill Theater, with Jerry Bock–Sheldon Harnick songs that include "Days Gone By," 301 perfs.

Popular songs: "Blame It on the Bossa Nova" by U.S. songwriters Cynthia Weil and Barry Mann; English pop singer Dusty Springfield (Mary Isabel Catherine Bernadette O'Brien), 24, scores her first hit with "Silver Threads and Golden Needles"; *Judy Collins #3* (album) includes Bob Dylan's "Masters of War" and Tim Rose's antiwar song "Come Away Melinda"; U.S. singer Lesley Gore, 17, has beginner's luck with her recording of "It's My Party," will have other hits through 1967, but will make little money from her career until 1988; Brenda Lee, now 18, records "As Usual," has another hit, and by 1969 will have had 48 of her singles and 15 of her albums on the pop music charts; "Come and Get These Memories" by Motown (Detroit) singers Martha and the Vandellas (Martha Reeves, 22; Rosalind Ashford, 20; and Annette Sterling; Motown secretary Reeves has nagged her boss Berry Gordy to let her cut a record, she has recruited two fellow secretaries, and their record is a hit); *End of the World* (album) and *Cloudy* (album) by Skeeter Davis, who hits the charts with two hot singles, "I'm Saving My Love" and "(It's Not) The End of the World."

Country singer Patsy Cline records "Faded Love," "Leavin' on Your Mind," and "Sweet Dreams (Of You)" and dies 3/5 in the crash of a twin-engine Comanche in Tennessee while en route home from a Kansas City benefit (Cowboy Copas, Hawkshaw Hawkins, and pilot Randy Hughes are also killed). Dead at age 31, Cline has been a star for 5 years. Hawkins's widow, Jean Shepard, now 29, is left with two small boys to raise.

Singer Madurai Shanmukhavadivu Subbulakshmi, now 47, appears at the Edinburgh Festival to great acclaim. She will sing at the United Nations in New York in 1966.

Margaret Smith wins in women's singles at Wimbledon, Maria Bueno at Forest Hills.

New York Governor Nelson A. Rockefeller, 54, divorces his wife of 31 years and on May 4 marries the former Mrs. Margaretta Fitler Murphy, whose nickname is "Happy." Many believe the divorce and remarriage will ruin any chance Rockefeller may have for winning the presidency.

Mary Kay Cosmetics, Inc., is founded by Texas-born entrepreneur Mary Kay Wagner, 44 (approximate), who worked for a division of Stanley Home Products from 1938 to 1952. Her door-to-door sales company has first-year revenues of $200,000 and will grow in the next 15 years to gross $35 million.

The miniskirt appears in December in "swinging" London. Designed by Welsh fashion pioneer Mary Quant, 29, the provocative new skirt comes to 6 inches above the knee. (Paris designer André Courrèges introduces the skirt almost simultaneously but will be better known for his boots.) Quant and her husband, Alexander Plunket-Greene, opened a shop, the Bazaar, with a partner 8 years ago on the King's Road, Chelsea, and attracted a following among the district's writers, artists, photographers, models, and their friends who dropped in to drink brandy and buy her boots, patterned stockings, and other "mod" creations. Their enterprise (Mary Quant Limited) will become an international conglomerate of fashion, cosmetics, fabrics, bed linens, children's books, dolls, and wine, and Quant's skirt eventually will dwindle to micro-mini lengths.

Newsweek copy girl Janice Wylie, 21, and her roommate Emily Hoffert, 23, a grade school teacher, are clubbed and stabbed to death August 28 during an attempted burglary of their apartment at 57 East 88th Street.

Weight Watchers is founded by Queens, N.Y., housewife Jean Nidetch (*née* Slutsky), 39, a one-time compulsive eater who has reduced her own weight from 214 pounds (size 44) to 142 with help from a high-protein diet developed by Norman Jolliffe, 62, of the New York City Department of Health's Obesity Clinic. Using a form of group therapy, completely proscribing some foods while permitting others without restriction, Weight Watchers will grow into a worldwide operation with average weekly attendance of half a million.

Julia Child prepares Boeuf Bourguignonne on television in February as she begins a series of cooking demonstrations on Boston's educational TV station WGBH.

Average annual U.S. per capita meat consumption reaches 170.6 pounds, but veal consumption drops to 5 pounds, down from 9.7 in 1949. Chicken consumption is 37.8 pounds, up from 23.5 in 1945, when chicken was more costly than beef.

Average annual U.S. per capita butter consumption falls to 6.7 pounds, down from 18.3 in 1934 and 7.5 in 1960; margarine 9.3 pounds, up from 8.6 in 1957; cheese 9.4 pounds, up from 7 in 1949.

Tab, introduced by Coca-Cola, is a cyclamate-sweetened cola drink that competes with Royal Crown's Diet-Rite (*see* 1962; Diet Pepsi, 1965).

1964

Britain's Labour party wins the general elections in October. Harold Wilson, 48, begins a ministry that will continue until 1970 with former Labour party chairwoman Barbara Anne Castle (*née* Betts), 53, as minister of overseas development. An M.P. since 1945, Castle will become minister of transport next year and in 1968 will become the first secretary of state for employment and productivity.

U.S. Senator Margaret Chase Smith, 66 (R., Me.), makes a bid for the Republican presidential nomination, which goes instead to Sen. Barry Goldwater of Arizona, who is crushed by Lyndon Johnson in the November election. Smith has served in the Senate since 1948 and will continue until 1972.

Hawaiian voters elect Patsy Mink (*née* Takemoto), 36, to Congress; she is the first congresswoman of Japanese descent.

The legal status of Québecois women improves with passage of an Equal Rights Bill after campaigning by Liberal legislator Claire Kirkland Casgrain (*see* voting rights, 1940). Women in Quebec gain the right to be legal guardians of their children, a reform that the other provinces adopted before 1923; women may sign leases and enter into business transactions without their husbands' consent.

The Civil Rights Act signed by President Johnson July 2 not only prohibits racial discrimination in employment, places of public accommodation, publicly owned facilities, union membership, and federally funded programs but also, in Title VII, forbids sex discrimination in the workplace (*see* 1971).

Mississippi civil rights worker Fannie Lou Hamer enlists northern college students in a summer project to boost voter registration. She attends the Democratic Convention at Atlantic City in August, and when the Convention's credentials committee holds televised hearings on whether to seat the integrated Mississippi Freedom Democratic Party launched by Ella Baker and other SNCC leaders or the all-white delegation of party regulars, she delivers a speech describing her beating last year. The MCDP is not seated, but Hamer's speech is heard by President Johnson, who tries to divert attention from her by calling a sudden press conference. By 1972, 62.2 percent of Mississippi's eligible black voters will be registered, up from about 6 percent this year, and much of the credit will be given to Ella Baker and Fannie Lou Hamer.

Fannie Lou Hamer spearheaded the drive to enroll African-American voters in Southern election districts. SCHOMBURG CENTER, NYPL

President Johnson calls for "total victory" in a "national war on poverty" March 16. He signs an Economic Opportunity Act August 20 and appoints R. Sargent Shriver, 48, to head the new Office of Economic Opportunity (OEO). Brother-in-law of the late President Kennedy, Shriver will coordinate such agencies as the Job Corps, the Neighborhood Youth Corps, Volunteers in Service to America (VISTA), community action programs, and a Head Start program designed to help preschool children achieve higher levels of health, nutrition, and preparedness for school.

German aviatrix Geraldine Mock completes a solo round-the-world flight April 16, becoming the first woman to accomplish the feat. She took off March 19, made 21 stops, and has flown a total of 22,858.8 miles in a single-engine plane.

Jacqueline Cochran logs a speed of 1,429 miles per hour—the fastest ever flown by a woman.

Dorothy Hodgkin, now 54, is awarded the Nobel Prize for Chemistry (*see* 1948). When she is awarded the British Order of Merit next year, it will be the first time a woman has received the honor since Florence Nightingale.

The Surgeon General's Report issued January 11 by Dr. Luther L. Terry, 52, links cigarette smoking to lung cancer and other diseases (*see* 1954). The lung cancer rate among U.S. men will increase in the next decade from 30 per 100,000 to 50 and will more than double among women to 10 per 100,000 as young people increase cigarette smoking despite warnings (*see* FTC, 1968).

The Medicare Act signed by President Johnson July 30 at Independence, Mo., sets up the first government-operated health insurance program for Americans age 65 and over. Harry Truman, now 84, urged such coverage in 1949, the American Medical Association has opposed the amendment to the Social Security Act of 1935. Funded by payroll deductions, federal subsidies, and (initially) $3 per month in individual premiums, Medicare covers 20 million seniors (mostly women, since they outlive men).

The Roman Catholic liturgy in the United States changes November 29 to include use of English in some prayers; the entire mass will be in English by Easter 1970, but some priests will defy the Vatican and stick to Latin.

U.S. parochial school enrollment reaches an all-time high of 5.6 million pupils. The figure will fall to below 3.5 million within 10 years.

The Head Start program (above) is based on a concept that will be credited to Vanderbilt University psychologist Susan W. Gray, 51, who worked with poor children in Murfreesboro, Tenn., to develop an Early Training Project.

Former First Lady Jacqueline Kennedy goes on national television January 14 to thank Americans for their expressions of sympathy over the loss of her husband last November.

Nonfiction: *A Choice, Not an Echo* by U.S. political activist Phyllis Schlafly, 40, maintains that the Republican party is run by an elite group; *After Nora Slammed the Door: American Women in the 1960s—The Unfinished Revolution* by poet Eve Merriam; *Claremont Essays* by The *Nation* magazine literary critic Diana Trilling (*née* Rubin), 59; *The Oysters of Locmariaquer* by U.S. writer Eleanor Clark, 51; *The New Meaning of Treason* by Rebecca West; *A Very Easy Death* (*Une Mort tres douce*) by Simone de Beauvoir describes her mother's death from cancer.

Fiction: *The Garrick Year* by Margaret Drabble; *The Snow Ball* by Brigid Brophy; *Girls in Their Married Bliss* by Edna O'Brien; *The Keepers of the House* by Shirley Ann Grau (Pulitzer Prize); *With Shuddering Fall* by U.S. novelist Joyce Carol Oates, 26; *Collages* by Anaïs Nin; *African Stories* by Doris Lessing; *Extreme Magic* (novella and stories) by Hortense Calisher; *The Single Eye* by English novelist-poet Maureen Duffy, 31; *This Rough Magic* by Mary Stewart; *The Aristide Case* by Storm Jameson; *The Maiden Dinosaur* (in America, *The Belfast Friends*) by Janet McNeill; *Statues in the Garden* by Isabel Colegate; *Up the Down Staircase* by Russian-born New York schoolteacher-humorist Bel Kaufman, 53; *The Vine and the Olive* by Margaret Culkin Banning touches on the still-touchy subject of birth control; *The Lovely Man* by Faith Baldwin; *I Never Promised You a Rose Garden* by U.S. novelist Hannah Green (Joanne Greenberg [*née* Goldenberg]), 32, whose story of a young girl's battle against schizophrenia is partly autobiographical; *The Two Faces of January* by Patricia Highsmith; *The Expendable Man* by Dorothy B. Hughes; *From Dune to Death* by English mystery novelist Ruth (Barbara) Rendell (*née* Kruse), 34.

Poetry: *The Circle Game* by Margaret Atwood; *Rediscoveries* by Elizabeth Jennings; *City Sunrise* by Judith Wright.

Juvenile: *Harriet the Spy* by U.S. author Louise Fitzhugh, 35; *I Know a Lady* by Charlotte Zolotow.

Sculpture: *Homage to the 6,000,000* by Louise Nevelson; *Three Monoliths* (marble) by Barbara Hepworth.

Theater: Jason Robards, Jr., Barbara Loden, David Wayne, Hal Holbrook, Salome Jens, Ruth Attaway, (Dorothy) Faye Dunaway, 23, Zohra Lampert, and Ralph Meeker in Arthur Miller's *After the Fall* 1/23 at New York's ANTA Theater–Washington Square, 208 perfs.; *Any Wednesday* by U.S. playwright Muriel Resnik 2/18 at New York's Music Box Theater, with Sandy Dennis, Gene Hackman, and Rosemary Murphy, 982 perfs.; Salome Jens, Jason Robards, Jr., Barbara Loden, Ralph Meeker, and David Wayne in S. N. Behrman's *But for Whom Charlie* 3/12 at New York's ANTA Theater–Washington Square, 39 perfs.; Pat Hingle, Rip Torn, and Diana Sands in James Baldwin's *Blues for Mr. Charlie* 4/23 at New York's ANTA Theater, 148 perfs.; Martin Sheen, Jack Albertson, and Irene Dailey in Frank D. Gilroy's *The Subject Was Roses* 5/25 at New York's Royale Theater, 832 perfs.; *The Sign in Sidney Brustein's Window* by Lorraine Hansberry 10/15 at New York's Longacre Theater, 101 perfs. (Hansberry will die of cancer early next year at age 36); Alan Arkin, Eli Wallach, and Anne Jackson, 28, in Murray Schisgal's *Luv* 11/11 at New York's Booth Theater, 901 perfs.; *Poor Richard* by Jean Kerr 12/2 at New York's Helen Hayes Theater, with Alan Bates and Gene Hackman, 118 perfs.; Irene Worth and John Gielgud in Edward Albee's *Tiny Alice* 12/30 at New York's Billy Rose Theater, 167 perfs.

Films: Julie Andrews and Dick Van Dyke in Robert Stevenson's *Mary Poppins;* Kim Stanley and Richard Attenborough in Bryan Forbes's *Seance on a Wet Afternoon*; Peter Sellers and German-born actress Elke Sommer (originally Schletz), 22, in Blake Edwards's *A Shot in the Dark*; Melina Mercouri, Robert Morley, and Peter Ustinov in Jules Dassin's *Topkapi*; Sophia Loren and Marcello Mastroianni in Vittorio De Sica's *Yesterday, Today, and Tomorrow*. Also: Julie Andrews and James Garner in Arthur Hiller's *The Americanization of Emily*; Jean-Paul Belmondo and Claudia Cardinale in Philippe de Broca's *Cartouche*; "sex kitten" Brigitte Bardot, Fritz Lang, and Michel Piccoli in Jean-Luc Godard's *Contempt*; Sophia Loren, Stephen Boyd, and James Mason in Anthony Mann's *The Fall of the Roman Empire*; Barbara Barrie and Bernie Hamilton in Larry Peerce's *One Potato, Two Potato*; Stefania Sandrelli and Saro Urzi in Pietro

Germi's *Seduced and Abandoned*; Shirley MacLaine in J. Lee Thompson's *What a Way to Go* with a script by Betty Comden and Adolph Green from a story by Gwen Davis; Kyoko Kishida and Eiji Okada in Hiroshi Teshigahara's *Woman in the Dunes*; Peter Sellers, Tippy Walker, and Angela Lansbury in George Roy Hill's *The World of Henry Orient*.

Television: *Crossroads* on British television with veteran actress Noele Gordon, 44, as the owner of a motel (to 1981).

Screen musicals: French beauty Catherine Deneuve (Catherine Dorléac), 21, in Jacques Demy's *The Umbrellas of Cherbourg* (*Les Parapluies de Cherbourg*); Audrey Hepburn and Rex Harrison in George Cukor's *My Fair Lady*; Debbie Reynolds in Charles Walters's *The Unsinkable Molly Brown*.

Broadway musicals: Carol Channing in *Hello, Dolly!* 1/16 at the St. James Theater, with songs by Jerry Herman, 2,844 perfs.; Barbra (*née* Barbara Joan) Streisand, 21, as the late Fanny Brice in *Funny Girl* 3/26 at the Winter Garden Theater, with Jule Styne–Bob Merrill songs that include "People" and "Don't Rain on My Parade," 1,348 perfs.

Opera: Janet Baker sings the title role in Benjamin Britten's 1946 opera *The Rape of Lucretia*.

Popular songs: "It's My Way" by Canadian Amerind folk singer–songwriter Buffy Sainte Marie, 23; *In Concert* (album) by Judy Collins includes Tom Paxton's song "The Last Thing on My Mind"; Martha and the Vandellas record "Heatwave," "Quicksand," "Live Wire," and "Dancing in the Street"; "Pass Me By" by Carolyn Leigh, music by Cy Coleman (for the film *Father Goose*); Dusty Springfield records "I Only Want to Be with You" and scores again; the Supremes record "Where Did Our Love Go?"; Mary Wells records "My Guy" by Smokey Robinson plus "Once Upon a Time" and "What's the Matter with You Baby?" both written with Marvin Gaye, and tours England with the Beatles in the fall; British singer Marianne Faithfull, 18, records Mick Jagger and Keith Richards's "As Tears Go By"; Lesley Gore records "You Don't Own Me," written with John Maera and Dave White; *I Forget More* (album) and *Let Me Get Close* (album) by Skeeter Davis, who has a hot single with "Gonna

Get Along Without You Now" and co-writes "Home Breaker" and "He Says the Same Things To Me"; "Second Fiddle (To an Old Guitar)" by Jean Shepard, whom a French critic has called "the Edith Piaf of country America."

Dutch figure skater Sjoukje Dijkstra wins her event in the winter Olympics at Innsbruck, Austrian skier Christi Haas wins the downhill in 1 minute, 55.39 seconds, French skiers Christine Goitschel the slalom in 1 minute, 29.86 seconds and Marielle Goitschel the giant slalom in 1 minute, 52.24 seconds. U.S. runner Wyomia Tyus, 18, wins the 100-meter dash in 11.4 seconds at the summer Olympics in Tokyo, U.S. runner Edith McGuire the 200-meter in 23 seconds, Betty Cuthbert the 400-meter in 52 seconds, British runner Ann Packer the 800-meter in 2 minutes, 1.1 seconds, German runner Karin Balzer the 80-meter hurdles in 10.5 seconds (with help from the wind), Iolanda Balas the running high jump (6 feet, 2¾ inches), British athlete Mary Rand the long jump (22 feet, 2 inches), Tamara Press the shot put (59 feet, 6 inches) and the discus throw (187 feet, 10¾ inches), Romanian athlete Mihaela Penes the discus throw (198 feet, 7½ inches), Soviet athlete Irena Press the pentathlon. Dawn Fraser wins the 100-meter freestyle in 59.5 seconds, U.S. swimmer Ginny Duenkel the 400-meter in 4 minutes, 43.3 seconds, U.S. swimmer Cathy Ferguson the 100-meter backstroke in 1 minute, 7.7 seconds, Soviet swimmer Galina Prozumenschikova the 200-meter breaststroke in 2 minutes, 46.4 seconds, U.S. swimmer Sharon Stouder the 100-meter butterfly in 1 minute, 4.7 seconds, U.S. swimmer Donna de Varona the 400-meter individual medley in 5 minutes, 18.7 seconds, Ingrid Kramer Engel the springboard dive event, U.S. swimmer Lesley Bush the platform dive.

Maria Bueno wins in women's singles at both Wimbledon and Forest Hills.

Vogue magazine gives the miniskirt its imprimatur by showing it in its March issue (*see* 1963).

The topless bathing suit introduced by California designer Rudi Gernreich will lead to a general abandonment of brassieres by young women.

San Francisco's Condor Night Club introduces topless dancers June 19; Carol Doda, the star attraction, has had 20 weeks of silicone injections to inflate her breast size to 44 inches. Doda and her fellow entertainers will be arrested next year for "lewd conduct," they will be acquitted, and she will continue at the Condor until 1985. The dancers will be bottomless beginning September 3, 1969, California will enact a law that year permitting local communities to ban topless dancing and establishments that permit such dancing. The Condor Club will halt both topless and bottomless shows in 1988.

A British court finds three women guilty of indecent exposure August 21 for wearing topless dresses.

Dynel is introduced by Union Carbide, whose new synthetic fiber will be used in textiles, fake furs, and hairpieces.

U.S. annual cigarette consumption reaches 524 billion—more than 4,300 smokes for every American over age 18.

The tobacco industry halts advertising in college newspapers, magazines, sports programs, and on college radio stations, in response to public pressure.

Carlton cigarettes are introduced by the American Tobacco but low-tar cigarettes will not begin to gain popularity until 1970.

"The Boston Strangler" makes his final attack in January. He has broken into a dozen apartments since mid-1962 to rob, violate, and kill women (not always by strangling them). Cambridge police take Albert Henry DeSalvo, 32, into custody November 4 but do not say he is the "strangler." DeSalvo was sentenced to prison on robbery counts in 1961, was paroled after 11 months, claims to have raped at least 1,000 women, and will boast to inmates at Bridgewater State Hospital that he has killed 13 women.

The Kitty Genovese case raises alarms about America's growing isolation, callousness, and inhumanity (*see* Jacobs book on cities, 1961). An attacker stalks Queens, N.Y., bar manager Catherine Genovese early in the morning of March 13; 38 of her Kew Gardens neighbors hear her wild calls for help; nobody interferes for fear of "getting involved"; the neighbors watch from windows while Genovese is stabbed to death; nobody phones the police until half an hour later.

The U.S. food stamp program conducted at Rochester, N.Y., from 1939 to 1943 is reactivated on a broad scale by the U.S. Department of Agriculture to help feed needy Americans (*see* 1959; 1967).

U.S. October food prices: round steak $1.07 lb., up from 92¢ in 1954; sugar 59¢ for a 5-lb. bag, up from 52¢; coffee 82¢ lb., down from $1.10; bread 21¢ lb. loaf, up from 17¢; eggs 57¢ doz., down from 60¢; milk 48¢ ½-gal., up from 45¢; butter 76¢ lb., up from 72¢; lettuce 25¢ per head, up from 19¢.

Pop-Tarts toaster pastries are introduced by Kellogg's.

The Time Has Come by Boston Catholic physician John Rock, now 74, rejects the Church's position against artificial contraceptive methods. Rock helped develop the progesterone contraceptive pill, and Catholic women are as likely to use it as Jewish, Muslim, or Protestant women.

A dozen U.S. states have tax-supported birth control programs, most of them in the South, where Catholic influence is weak and where whites try to hold down black birthrates. There are 450 public birth control clinics in the nation (*see* 1965).

1965

Former Howard University Law School dean Patricia Roberts Harris, 40, goes to Luxembourg as U.S. ambassador. She is the first black woman to attain ambassadorial rank.

Texas voters elect lawyer Barbara Charline Jordan, 30, to the State Senate; she becomes that body's first black senator since 1883 (*see* 1972).

Civil rights leader Viola Liuzzo (*née* Gregg), 38, is overtaken after a high-speed chase and shot dead March 25 by four Ku Klux Klansmen outside Montgomery while driving a car with a black passenger as marchers from Selma arrive after a 4-day walk. 25,000 attend the rally at Montgomery, Ala., that day. Selma has been the focus of civil rights demonstrations throughout February and March; President Johnson has sent in 3,000 federalized National Guardsmen and military police.

North Carolina judge James B. McMillan orders busing of schoolchildren to achieve racial desegregation as required by the 1954 Supreme Court decision. His order for crosstown busing in the Charlotte–Mecklenburg County school system starts a pattern that will be followed in much of the country, but the use of busing creates a storm of controversy (*see* 1971).

Ruby Doris Smith Robinson (her married name) dies of lymphoma at Atlanta at age 25 (*see* 1960). She has been a leader in the Student Non-Violent Coordinating Committee (SNCC), registering voters, being arrested for trying to use whites-only toilets, and participating with Freedom Riders in challenging segregation of buses in interstate travel.

An all-white federal jury at Montgomery, Ala., returns a verdict of guilty December 3 against the three Ku Klux Klan members who murdered Viola Liuzzo (above), and they receive 10-year prison sentences.

President Johnson outlines programs for a "Great Society" that will eliminate poverty in America January 4 in his State of the Union message; he signs a $1.4 billion program of federal-state economic aid to Appalachia into law March 9, but U.S. military involvement in Southeast Asia escalates, draining the U.S. economy.

New York City's welfare roll grows to 480,000. The number of welfare recipients, most of them women with dependent children, will be 1.2 million by 1975, and the city's welfare agency will account for more than a quarter of the city's $12 billion budget with half the welfare aid reimbursed by the federal government.

Britain freezes wages, salaries, and prices in an effort to check inflation and improve the nation's worsening trade deficit (*see* 1961; 1967).

The U.S. death rate falls to 943.2 per 100,000, down from 1,719 in 1900.

Congress votes $1.3 billion in federal aid to elementary and secondary schools.

40 percent of U.S. women receive bachelors' and masters' degrees, up from 24 percent in 1950.

Cosmopolitan magazine names Helen Gurley Brown editor, she says its circulation has flagged because it has emphasized fiction, and beginning with the May issue she turns it into what some critics call an antifeminist equivalent of *Playboy*, with a monthly "*Cosmopolitan* Girl" photographed, usually, by Francesco Scavullo.

Nonfiction: *Elsa and Her Cubs* by Joy Adamson, who will be murdered in 1980 by tribesmen who enter her home.

Fiction: *Everything That Rises Must Converge* by the late Flannery O'Connor, who died last year at age 39 of a rare disease; *Landlocked* by Doris Lessing; *Not for Publication* (stories) by Nadine Gordimer; *A Backward Place* by Ruth Prawer Jhabvala; *The River Hidaka* (*Hidakagawa*) by Sawako Ariyoshi; *One by One* by English-American journalist-novelist Penelope Gilliatt (*née* Conner), 33, who will develop her screenplay for *Sunday, Bloody Sunday* from the book; *The Nowhere City* by Alison Lurie is about Los Angeles; *After Julius* by Elizabeth Howard; *The Millstone* by Margaret Drabble; *August Is a Wicked Month* by Edna O'Brien; *The Flight of the Falcon* by Daphne du Maurier; *Friends and Heroes* (third novel in the Balkan Trilogy) by Olivia Manning; *Cork Street, Next to the Hatters: A Novel in Bad Taste* by Pamela Hansford Johnson (Lady Snow, since her husband, C. P. Snow, was given a life peerage last year); *Knights and Dragons* by Elizabeth Spencer; *How Far Is Bethlehem?* by Norah Lofts; *Talk to Me* by Janet McNeill; *The Mind Readers* by Margery Allingham.

Poetry: *Questions of Travel* by Elizabeth Bishop; *The Privilege* by Maxine Kumin; *Ariel* by the late Sylvia Plath; *Cock Crow* by Rosemary Dobson.

Juvenile: *Shadow of a Bull* by Polish-American author Maia Wojciechowska, 38, whose family escaped from Poland at the start of the German invasion in 1939 and who worked with her brother in France to commit acts of sabotage against the occupation forces; *When I Have a Little Girl* by Charlotte Zolotow.

Painting: *Orange Grove* and *Leaf* (both acrylic and pencil on canvas) by Agnes Martin.

The Federal Aid to the Arts Act signed by President Johnson September 30 establishes a National Endowment for the Arts and Humanities funded by an initial 3-year appropriation of $63 million.

Documentary photographer Dorothea Lange dies October 11 at age 70.

Theater: Bea Richards, Juanita Hall, and Frank Silvera in James Baldwin's *The Amen Corner* 4/15 at New York's Ethel Barrymore Theater, 84 perfs.; Vivien Merchant, Paul Rogers, Ian Holm, and Harold Pinter in Pinter's *The Homecoming* 6/3 at London's Aldwych Theatre; Beryl Reid and Eileen Atkins in *The Killing of Sister George* by English playwright Frank Marcus 6/8 at the Duke of York's Theatre, London ("Sister George" is the kindly district nurse played in the long-running BBC soap opera *Applehurst* by a sadistic, cigar-smoking, hard-drinking lesbian who bullies her 34-year-old blond flatmate "Childene" McNaughton and whose role has just been eliminated); Ralph Waite, Cliff Gorman, and Faye Dunaway in William Alfred's *Hogan's Goat* 11/11 at New York's American Place Theater in St. Clements Church, 607 perfs.; Lauren Bacall, Barry Nelson, and Brenda Vaccaro, 25, in Abe Burrows's *Cactus Flower* 12/8 at New York's Royale Theater, 1,234 perfs.

New York's Vivian Beaumont Theater opens in Lincoln Center October 21. Designed by Eero Saarinen in travertine and glass, the $9.6 million, 1,140-seat theater is named for the late philanthropist Mrs. Vivian Beaumont Allen.

Films: Laurence Olivier, Frank Finlay, Maggie Smith, 30, and Joyce Redman in Stuart Burge's *Othello*; Catherine Deneuve in Roman Polanski's *Repulsion*; Ida Kaminska, Elmar Klos, and Josef Kroner in Jan Kadar's *The Shop on Main Street*. Also: Indian-born British actress Julie Christie, 24, Dirk Bogarde, and Laurence Harvey in John Schlesinger's *Darling*; Jeanne Moreau in Luis Buñuel's *Diary of a Chambermaid*; Hanna Brejchova and Josef Sebanek in Milos Forman's *Loves of a Blonde*; Jason Robards, Jr., Barbara Harris (originally Markowitz), 28, Barry Gordon, Martin Balsam, and Gene Saks in Fred Coe's *A Thousand Clowns*.

Linda Darnell dies April 10 at age 43 in a Chicago hospital where she has been treated for burns; Constance Bennett dies of a cerebral hemorrhage at a Fort Dix, N.J., hospital July 24 at age 61.

Stage musicals: *Baker Street* 2/16 at New York's Broadway Theater, with Fritz Weaver as Sherlock Holmes, music and lyrics by Marian Grudeff and Raymond Jessel, 313 perfs.; Barbara Harris in *On a Clear Day You Can See Forever* 10/17 at New York's Mark Hellinger Theater, with Burton Lane–Alan Jay Lerner songs that include the title song, 272 perfs.; Christine Holmes and Anna Neagle in *Charlie Girl* 12/15 at London's Adelphi Theatre, with music and lyrics by David Heneker and John Taylor, 2,202 perfs.

Houston arts patron Ima Hogg, now 83, establishes a scholarship for piano studies at the University of Texas.

Cellist Jacqueline du Pré, now 20, tours the United States. She will marry pianist-conductor Daniel Barenboim in 1967 and appear with him in duo recitals, but multiple sclerosis will cut short her career in 1973.

Ballet: dancer-choreographer Twyla Tharp, 24, breaks with the Paul Taylor Dance Company after 3 years and becomes a freelance choreographer with her own modern-dance troupe.

Opera: Montserrat Caballé, now 32, replaces U.S. mezzo-soprano Marilyn (Bernice) Horne, 31, 4/20 in a concert performance of the 1833 Donizetti opera *Lucrezia Borgia* and creates a sensation (she will be the leading Verdi and Donizetti soprano of her day); Italian soprano Mirella Freni (Fregni), 30, makes her Metropolitan Opera debut singing the role of Mimi in the 1896 Puccini opera *La Bohème*; Janet Baker sings the role of Dido in the 1689 Purcell opera *Dido and Aeneas* at Glyndebourne.

Big Brother and the Holding Company is founded by four male San Francisco rock musicians who will soon add singer Janis Lyn Joplin, 22, to their group.

Popular songs: "Leave a Little Love" by Scottish singer Lulu (Marie McDonald McLaughlin Lawrie), 16; "I Got You Babe" by U.S. singer-songwriter Sonny Bono, 30, who has married singer Cher Sarkisian, 21; *Tunes For Two* (album) (with Bobby Bare), *Written by Stars* (album), *Blueberry Hill* (album), and *Best of Skeeter Davis* (album) by Davis, whose top singles are "Sunglasses" and "Somebody Loves You."

Margaret Smith wins in women's singles at both Wimbledon and Forest Hills.

Hanae Mori presents her first overseas collection, "East Meets West," at New York (*see* 1951); buyers from stores such as Bergdorf Goodman and Neiman-Marcus order her dresses (*see* 1977).

British police arrest Manchester typist Myra Hindley, 23, and her Scottish lover Ian Brady, 28, on charges of murder. They will be found guilty of having tortured and killed Lesley Ann Downey, 10, and John Kilbride, 12, whose agonies they photographed and taped, and Edward Evans, 17, whose body is found in their house (the remains of the children will be found buried on Saddleworth Moor in the Pennine Hills). Hindley will confess to two other murders in 1986, and the body of Pauline Read will be found in August 1987.

Alice Crimmins tells New York police that she gave her daughter Alice (Missy), 7, and her son Edmund, Jr., 4, a supper of manicotti and green beans at 7:30 on the evening of July 13, put them to bed and 9, found them well when she checked at midnight, but found them missing when she went to wake them in the morning. The 26-year-old cocktail waitress, whose estranged husband is a mechanic at Kennedy International Airport, occupies a garden apartment at 150-22 72nd Drive in Kew Gardens Hills, Queens. Her little boy's body, strangled by a pajama top, is discovered July 15 in Flushing. The decomposed body of her little girl is found July 19 on an embankment overlooking the Van Wyck Expressway. New York City Medical Examiner Milton Helpern, 63, finds on autopsy that Missy died 2 hours after eating her manicotti and beans, his evidence raises doubts about the mother's testimony, and a court will eventually convict her of murder.

Congress appropriates funds to remove U.S. highway billboards at the urging of Claudia Alta "Lady Bird" Johnson (*née* Taylor), 53, wife of the president. All billboards on sections of interstate and primary highways not zoned "commercial or industrial" are to be razed by July 1, 1970, and states are to pass conforming laws and prepare laws. The "Lady Bird Bill" will not begin to take effect until 1970, when the Senate will vote unanimously to apply $100 million of the $5.5-billion-per-year Highway Trust Fund to compensate billboard companies for removal of their signs.

A major drought in the northeastern United States forces New York City to turn off air-conditioning in sealed skyscrapers in order to conserve water. City fountains are turned off, lawn watering is forbidden, and signs appear reading "Save water: shower with a friend."

Half of all Americans enjoy "good" diets, up from less than one-quarter in 1943, according to a new study.

Greenwich Village, New York, food faddist Beth Ann Simon dies at age 24 after having dwindled away to 70 pounds on a "macrobiotic" diet consisting chiefly of brown rice sprinkled with Gomashio (four parts sesame seeds to one part sea salt) eaten slowly with green tea. Zen Buddhists have disclaimed the diet, but cultists in the youth underground extoll it and open "macrobiotic" restaurants.

Diet Pepsi is introduced by Pepsi-Cola Co. (*see* Tab, 1963).

Home-delivered milk accounts for 25 percent of U.S. milk sales, down from more than 50 percent before World War II. The figure will be 15 percent by 1975.

The World Health Organization finds that family-planning advice is welcome where such advice was protested in 1962.

Oxfam decides to support family-planning projects as well as the programs for famine relief and food production it has backed since its founding in 1942.

Connecticut's 1879 law prohibiting sale of birth control devices is unconstitutional, the Supreme Court rules 7 to 2 June 7 in *Griswold* v. *Connecticut*. The case involved a New Haven clinic run by leaders of the state's Planned Parenthood League. Justice William O. Douglas, who writes the majority opinion, interprets several constitutional amendments to mean that a "zone of [personal] privacy" exists in which state and federal governments may not interfere.

The United States has 700 public birth control clinics with 33 states giving, or about to give, tax support to birth control (*see* 1964).

U.S. live births total some 300,000 less than in the peak year of 1957 and in some months are at a rate lower than in 1939.

1966

✗ India's prime minister Lal Bahadur Shastri dies of a heart attack January 11 at age 61. Mrs. Indira Nehru Gandhi, now 48, is elected to succeed Shastri January 19.

President Johnson appoints New York State Senator and former NAACP Legal Defense Fund lawyer Constance Baker Motley, 44, to the United States District Court January 25. A protégée of Supreme Court justice Thurgood Marshall, she has been proposed for appointment by Sen. Robert F. Kennedy (D., N.Y.), and she becomes the first black woman to hold a federal judgeship.

Mao Zedong's wife, Jiang Qing, gets her first political job December 5. Now 52, she is made cultural consultant to the General Political Department of the Chinese Army as Mao acts to end the insolence of Red Guard youths, but Mme. Mao will become increasingly sympathetic toward the youths.

✊ The U.S. Army's First Cavalry Division at An Khe in Vietnam's central highlands establishes an official military brothel within the perimeter of its base camp. So does the First Infantry Division at Lai Khei, near Saigon, and the Fourth Infantry Division at Pleiku. Most of the women inside the barbed-wire enclosures are Vietnamese refugees. The Committee for the Defense of Vietnamese Woman's Human Dignity and Rights is founded to protest the brothels and the rape of women by U.S. troops.

Algerian women walk out of a meeting with the Revolutionary Council March 8 after being told that they already have all the rights they seek and have no further need to fight for them.

The National Organization for Women (NOW) announces its founding in late June to help U.S. women gain equal rights. Founder and president of the new civil rights organization is Betty Friedan (*see* 1967; Smeal, 1977).

Women workers at a Levi Strauss factory in Georgia walk off the job August 10; some 450 employees participate in the strike.

Folk singer Joan Baez escorts a small group of black children to the door of an all-white elementary school at Grenada, Miss., September 19, but state patrol officers bar their entry (*see* 1967).

⚡ New York makes Fifth Avenue one-way southbound and Madison Avenue one-way northbound beginning January 14 to ease congestion caused by a transit strike (Third and Lexington avenues have been one-way since 1960); Tiffany & Co. president Walter Hoving, 68, has led opposition to the one-way traffic scheme and says Fifth Avenue is now a "superhighway."

☿ *Feminine Forever* by Brooklyn, N.Y., obstetrician-gynecologist Robert A. Wilson recommends estrogen-replacement therapy for women of almost every age to avoid everything from recurring acne and dull hair in young adulthood to menopausal discomfort and osteoporosis in later years (*see* 1963). The book has sales of more than 100,000 copies in its first 7 months, and millions read about estrogen-replacement therapy in magazine articles by or about Wilson.

The U.S. infant mortality rate falls to 24.3 per thousand live births, down from 29 in 1951, but the British rate falls to 20, down from 30, and the Swedish rate to 15. Inadequate health care delivery systems and poor nutrition among expectant mothers in low-income groups are held responsible for the relatively poor U.S. showing.

Baltimore's Johns Hopkins Hospital opens a Gender Identity Clinic and begins performing sex change operations (*see* Jorgenson, 1952). In the next six years it will do about 500 such operations, mostly on men wanting to be women. The United States has an estimated 7,500 would-be transsexuals who are often suicidal until the sex change procedure, which often raises their self-esteem. Hopkins requires that candidates for the procedure live as members of the opposite sex for several months before surgery.

The Supreme Court rules that material with redeeming social value is not censorable. The court modifies its antiobscenity stand of 1957, but still defines obscene material as any matter in which "to the average person applying contemporary standards, the dominant theme taken as a whole appeals to a prurient interest" (*see* 1967).

New York advertising copywriter Mary Georgene Wells (*née* Berg), 37, co-founds Wells, Rich, Greene, an agency that will gain fame initially by having sculptor Alexander Calder redesign the paint scheme of Braniff Airlines (whose CEO, Harding Lawrence, will divorce his wife next year to marry Wells) and dressing the flight attendants in uniforms designed by Emilio Pucci. WRG will drop Braniff to take the larger TWA account, and Mrs. Lawrence will become the highest-paid woman executive in America, deriving much of her income from the promotion of extra-long cigarettes to women smokers.

Nonfiction: *The Marquis de Sade* (*Faut-il brûler Sade?*) (*essays*) by Simone de Beauvoir; *Women: The Longest Revolution* by New Zealand–born British feminist Juliet Mitchel, 26; *A Mother in History* by novelist Jean Stafford examines the mother of JFK's assassin, Lee Harvey Oswald; *Spaceship Earth* by Barbara Ward; *Stranger and Friend: The Way of an Anthropologist* (autobiography) by Hortense Powdermaker, now 70; *Against Interpretation* by Susan Sontag; *The Proud Tower* by Barbara Tuchman.

Fiction: *Le Vice-consul* by Marguerite Duras; *Les Belles Images* by Simone de Beauvoir; *Wide Sargasso Sea* by Jean Rhys; *The Birds Fall Down* by Rebecca West; *Stranger with a Bag* (stories) by Sylvia Townsend Warner; *Cotters' England* by Christina Stead; *Collected Short Stories* by Katherine Anne Porter; *Jubilee* by poet Margaret Walker; *The Mask of Apollo* by Mary Renault; *The Late Bourgeois World* by Nadine Gordimer; *To Sting* by Chiyo Uno; *Seishu Hanaoka's Wife* (*Hanaoka seishu no tsuma*) by Sawako Ariyoshi; *The Evening of the Holiday* by Shirley Hazzard; *Trust* by U.S. novelist Cynthia Ozick, 38, who has spent 6½ years writing her Jewish novel; *To the Precipice* by U.S. novelist Judith Rossner (*née* Perelman), 31; *The Cherry in the Martini* by Rona Jaffe; *Bridgeport Bus* by Mau-

reen Howard; *I Took My Love to the Country* by Margaret Culkin Banning; *A Matter of Time* by Jessamyn West; *The Wedding Bargain* by Agnes Turnbull; *Rocannon's World* and *Plant of Exile* by U.S. fantasy and science fiction writer Ursula Le Guin (*née* Kroeber), 36; *There Is a Season* and *Evening Star* by Faith Baldwin; *The Double Image* by Helen MacInnes; *Death Shall Overcome* by U.S. mystery writer Emma Lathen (Mary J. Latis and Martha Hennisart); *Valley of the Dolls* by U.S. novelist Jacqueline Susann, 45, a former actress whose book comes under criticism for its profanity and its explicit description of breast cancer.

Poetry: *Live or Die* by Ann Sexton (Pulitzer Prize); *Still by Choice* by Ruth Pitter; *The Other Half* by Judith Wright.

Painting: *Desert* (ink on paper) and *Play II* (acrylic and pencil on canvas) by Agnes Martin.

Sculpture: *Four-Square* (*Walk Through*) (bronze) by Barbara Hepworth. Melvina Hoffman dies at her New York studio July 11 at age 81.

Theater: Rosemary Harris as Eleanor of Aquitaine and Robert Preston as Henry II in James Goldman's *The Lion in Winter* 3/3 at New York's Ambassador Theater, 92 perfs.; Albert Finney, Maggie Smith, and Derek Jacobi in Peter Shaffer's *Black Comedy* 3/8 at London's Old Vic Theatre; Jessica Tandy and Hume Cronyn in Edward Albee's *A Delicate Balance* 9/22 at New York's Martin Beck Theater, 132 perfs.

Films: Michael Caine and Shelley Winters in Lewis Gilbert's *Alfie*; Vanessa Redgrave, 29, and David Hemmings in Michelangelo Antonioni's *Blow-Up*; Virginia McKenna and Bill Travers in James Hill's *Born Free*; Stephen Boyd and Chicago-born actress Raquel Welch (Raquel Tejad), 26, in Richard Fleischer's *Fantastic Voyage*; Lynn Redgrave, 23, James Mason, Alan Bates, and Charlotte Rampling, 21, in Silvio Narizzano's *Georgy Girl*; Yves Montand and Ingrid Thulin in Alain Resnais's *La Guerre Est Finie*; Anouk Aimée and Jean-Louis Trintignant in Claude Lelouch's *A Man and a Woman*; Vanessa Redgrave in Karel Reisz's *Morgan!*; George Maharis, Richard Basehart, and Anne Francis in John Sturges's *The Satan Bug*; Rock Hudson and Salome Jens in John Frankenheimer's *Seconds*; Elizabeth Taylor and Richard Burton in Mike Nichols's *Who's Afraid of Virginia Woolf?*; Peter Kastner and Elizabeth Hartman in Francis Ford Coppola's *You're a Big Boy Now*.

Opera: Janet Baker sings the role of Hermia in the 1960 Benjamin Britten opera *A Midsummer Night's Dream* at Covent Garden and appears 12/2 in a song recital at New York's Town Hall.

First performances: *Catena* for Soprano, Tenor and 22 Instruments by Elisabeth Lutyens 6/7 in a BBC Invitation Concert (part of her cycle *The Changing Seasons*, the work is set to texts ranging from Japanese Nō plays to Dylan Thomas poems); Six Works by Lutyens 7/8 (her 60th birthday) set to poems from *The Valley of Hatsu-Se* in the original Japanese since Japanese versification is based on syllables.

Broadway musicals: Gwen Verdon in *Sweet Charity* 1/29 at the Palace Theater, with Cy Coleman–Dorothy Fields songs that include "Big Spender" and "If My Friends Could See Me Now," 608 perfs.; Angela Lansbury in *Mame* 5/24 at the Winter Garden Theater, with Jerry Herman songs that include "If He Walks into My Life," "Open a New Window," and "We Need a Little Christmas," 1,508 perfs.; Barbara Harris, Larry Blyden, and Alan Alda in *The Apple Tree* 10/18 at the Shubert Theater, with Jerry Bock–Sheldon Harnick songs, 463 perfs.; Jill Haworth as Sally Bowles, Jack Gilford, Lotte Lenya, and Joel Grey in *Cabaret* 11/20 at the Broadhurst Theater, with John Kander–Fred Ebb songs that include "Willkommen," "Money, Money," and the title song, 1,165 perfs.; Mary Martin and Robert Preston in *I Do! I Do!* 12/5 at the 46th Street Theater, with Harvey Schmidt–Tom Jones songs that include "My Cup Runneth Over," 584 perfs.

Popular songs: The Mamas and the Papas (Cass Elliott, 22, John E. A. Phillips, 30, Dennis Doherty, 24, Holly Michelle Gilham, 22) record "Monday, Monday" and "California Dreamin' " by Phillips; "Society's Child" by New York songwriter-singer Janis Ian (Janis Eddy Fink), 15, is about a white girl and a black boy; *Jefferson Airplane Takes Off* (album) by the Jefferson Airplane, a rock group whose lead singer is Grace Slick (*née* Wing), 22 (it has been playing at San Francisco's Fillmore Audi-

torium); *More Than a New Discovery* (album) by New York singer-songwriter Laura Nyro (originally Nigro), 19, includes "Wedding Bell Blues," "When I Die," and "Stoney End," which will be hits for the Fifth Dimension and Blood, Sweat and Tears (both rock groups) and for Barbra Streisand; *In My Life* (album) by Judy Collins; "Don't Come Home a-Drinkin' " by Loretta Lynn; "Little Wheel Spin and Spin" by Buffy Sainte-Marie; *Skeeter Sings Standards* (album) by Skeeter Davis; "If Teardrops Were Silver" by Jean Shepard; North Dakota country singer Lynn Anderson, 18, records "Ride, Ride, Ride" by her mother, Liz, 36, and joins Lawrence Welk's weekly TV show, with which she will sing until 1968.

Roberta Gibb Bingay runs in the Boston Marathon April 19—the first woman to compete in the 69-year-old event (since the marathon is for men only, Bingay wears a hooded sweatshirt to disguise her sex)—and finishes ahead of more than half the 415 men in the race (*see* 1967).

Mrs. Billie Jean King (*née* Moffitt), 22 (U.S.), wins in women's singles at Wimbledon, Maria Bueno at Forest Hills.

Pampers disposable diaper pads are successfully test marketed in Sacramento by Procter & Gamble, whose 6¢ pad begins a revolution in baby diapering.

English fashion designer Mary Quant is named an officer of the Order of the British Empire, the first woman designer to be so honored. But Tunisia's President Bourguiba outlaws miniskirts August 13.

Sophia Loren is married outside Paris April 9 to film director Carlo Ponti. Their 1957 marriage in Mexico brought charges of bigamy against Ponti, Italian authorities insisting that he was still married to his first wife; they have had the Mexican marriage annulled and were naturalized as French citizens so that Ponti could obtain a divorce in France. Italy has not recognized the divorce, and Loren's pictures have been banned in Arab countries since January of last year.

U.S. soap opera star Mia Farrow, 21, is married at Las Vegas July 19 to entertainer Frank Sinatra, 50. She is the daughter of film actress Maureen O'Sullivan and director John Farrow.

Washington, D.C., law clerk John Banzhaf III, 26, of the U.S. District Court writes a letter to WCBS-TV, New York, citing commercials that present smoking as "socially acceptable and desirable, manly, and a necessary part of a rich full life." He requests free time roughly equal to the time spent promoting "the virtues and values of smoking" to "present contrasting views on the issue of the benefits and advisability of smoking" (*see* 1967).

Some 13 million Americans will give up smoking in the next 4 years. The percentage of male smokers will drop from 52 percent to 42, of female smokers from 34 percent to 31.

Eight student nurses in a Chicago dormitory, all women, die July 13 at the hands of Richard F. Speck, 24, who has served time in Texas for theft, forgery, and parole violations that included threatening a woman with a knife. A Peoria jury will find Speck guilty on all eight counts of murder next year and recommend execution. A psychiatrist who examined Speck for 100 hours will tell newsmen that brain damage in conjunction with drugs and alcohol had left Speck not responsible for his acts. The Supreme Court will overrule the death sentence in 1971, and in 1972 a judge will impose eight sentences of 50 to 150 years each.

An article about rape in the *Stanford Law Review* says, "Although a woman may desire sexual intercourse, it is customary for her to say, 'no, no, no' (although meaning 'yes, yes, yes') and to expect the male to be the aggressor . . . The problem of determining whether the female really meant yes or no is compounded when, in fact, the female had no clearly determined attitude—that is, her attitude was one of ambivalence." The standard of resistance, the article concludes, must be high enough "to assure that the resistance is unfeigned and to indicate with some degree of certainty that the woman's attitude was not one of ambivalence or unconscious compliance and that her complaints do not result from moralistic afterthoughts," but it must also be low enough "to make death or serious bodily injury an unlikely outcome of the event."

Congress passes a Fair Packaging and Labeling Act (*see* Kennedy, 1962). The new "Truth in Packaging" law calls for clear labeling of the net weight of every package, bans phony "cents off" labels and phony "economy size" packages, and imposes controls over the confusing proliferation of package sizes, but food will continue to be sold in packages that make it hard for supermarket customers to know how much they are paying per pound.

The Vatican rescinds the rule forbidding U.S. Catholics to eat meat on Friday, but fish sales drop only briefly.

Cola drink bottlers and canners receive FDA dispensation not to list caffeine as an ingredient. Cola drinks generally have 4 milligrams of caffeine per fluid ounce, coffee 12 to 16.

Food prices are higher in poor neighborhoods of U.S. cities than in better neighborhoods according to a study. Ghetto food merchants charge more to compensate for "shrinkage."

Consumers boycott supermarkets at Denver and other cities, protesting high prices. The National Commission of Food Marketing concludes that food store profits are generally higher than for comparable industries and that in 20 years the grocery chains' returns on investment have averaged 12.5 percent and have never been lower than for other industries.

U.S. per capita consumption of processed potatoes reaches 44.2 pounds per year, up from 6.3 pounds in 1950.

New York assemblymen introduce a bill calling for reform of New York State's 19th-century abortion law, responding to an appeal by Manhattan Borough President Percy Sutton, who has seen the costs of illegal abortions in lives and maimings in the New York ghettos (*see* 1970; Colorado, 1967).

The Food and Drug Administration studies The Pill and reports "no adequate scientific data at this time proving these compounds unsafe for human use" (*see* 1962). But most U.S. women are reluctant to use oral contraceptives because of their reported side effects (*see* 1969). Coitus interruptus remains the most widely employed form of birth control in France, Czechoslovakia, and some other countries.

Romania outlaws abortion following the release of statistics showing that the nation has four times as many abortions as live births, but women will find ways to circumvent the law.

Japan's birthrate drops to 14 per thousand in the Year of the Fiery Horse. It is said that girls born this year will destroy their husbands; many woman have abortions or otherwise avoid giving birth this year lest they have daughters who may be unmarriagable. The birthrate will climb back up to 19.3 per thousand next year (but *see* 1980).

1967

✗ Lurleen Wallace, 40, wife of former Alabama Governor George Wallace, is sworn in as governor January 16 (state law has prevented his reelection) and announces that she will continue his fight against racial integration and "federal bureaucracy" while he seeks the presidency. A float sponsored by the Daughters of the Confederacy bears the legend "Lest We Forget," and Mrs. Wallace, mother of four, takes the oath of office, symbolically, on the same spot where Jefferson Davis was sworn in as president of the Confederate States of America in 1861. Gov. Wallace is the third woman to become a state governor.

A Women's Strike for Peace demonstrates outside the Pentagon February 15 as U.S. popular sentiment turns increasingly against the war in Vietnam while more troops are shipped overseas and casualties mount. About 2,500 women storm the Pentagon, demanding to see "the generals who send our sons to die." Martin Luther King, Jr., speaks out against the war in February, University of Wisconsin students push Dow Chemical recruiters off the campus to protest Dow's production of napalm, and Sen. Robert F. Kennedy (D., N.Y.) proposes that bombing of North Vietnam be halted so that troop withdrawal may be negotiated. Antidraft rallies bring out demonstrators in many cities.

Svetlana Alliluyeva, 40, daughter of the late Josef Stalin, walks into the U.S. embassy at New Delhi March 9 and defects to the West. Forced by her father to divorce her first husband in 1947 because he was Jewish, she has divorced the man her father arranged for her to marry, a man to whom she was engaged has died, and she has left two children behind. She arrives at New York April 21, saying that she seeks "self-expression," and in the early

1970s will marry William Wesley Peters, a U.S. architect (*see* 1984).

"I've never regretted being in the government," British Cabinet member Barbara Castle tells the *Sunday Times* in an interview published July 2. "I love responsibility and I don't mind unpopularity" (*see* 1964; 1969).

Folk singer Joan Baez is arrested October 14 for singing antiwar songs outside an Oakland, Calif., selective service center and serves 45 days in jail for disturbing the peace.

Folk singer Joan Baez lent her voice and prestige to the fight for social justice and civil rights. CHIE NISHIO

Former child film star Shirley Temple (Mrs. Charles A. Black), now 40, loses a bid for election November 13 to California's 11th Congressional District. Some of her 10 male rivals for the seat have labeled her a "hawk" on Vietnam, and another Republican, Korean war veteran Paul N. McCloskey, who is a "dove" on Vietnam, wins the special election.

Kentucky voters elect political campaign worker Georgia Montgomery Davis Powers, 44, to the state senate—the first woman (and first black person) ever elected. She will serve five 4-year terms, pressing for legislation on public accommodations, fair employment, open housing, and other issues important to women, children, and the poor.

The U.S. Supreme Court overturns Virginia's anti-miscegenation laws (and similar laws on the books of 15 other states) in a unanimous decision handed down June 12 in the case of *Loving* v. *Virginia*. Mildred Loving (*née* Jeter), 25, who is of black and Native American ancestry, and her white husband, Richard, were indicted in October 1958, pleaded guilty, were sentenced to 1 year's imprisonment, received suspended sentences on condition that they leave Virginia, moved to the District of Columbia, but returned to challenge their convictions and fight to have the statutes repealed.

The National Organization for Women (NOW) holds its first national conference at Washington and adopts a bill of rights calling for 1) an Equal Rights Constitutional Amendment, 2) enforcement of a law banning sex discrimination in employment, 3) maternity leave rights in employment and in Social Security benefits, 4) tax deduction for home and child care expenses for working parents, 5) child day care centers, 6) equal and unsegregated education, 7) equal job-training opportunities and allowances for women in poverty, and 8) the right of women to control their reproductive lives.

Australia grants women the right to vote on the same basis as men (*see* New Zealand, 1898).

New York stockbroker Muriel Siebert, 35, pays a reported $445,000 to buy a seat on the New York Stock Exchange—the first time a woman has had her own seat. She began her career as a Wall Street research trainee in 1954, became a top airline stock analyst, and has earned an annual salary reportedly above $500,000.

A Census Bureau report in December shows that 41 percent of nonwhite families in the United States make less than $3,300 per year versus 12 percent of white families, that 7.3 percent of nonwhites are unemployed versus 3.4 percent of whites, and that 29 percent of blacks live in substandard housing versus 8 percent of whites.

U.S. wage rates will rise by 92 percent in the next 10 years, buying power by only 8 percent.

U.S. mass transit rides fall to 8 billion, down from 23 billion in 1945, as prosperous Americans rely at an ever-growing rate on private cars to reach suburban homes and shopping centers.

A new Chevrolet sells for less than $2,500 in the United States.

A pulsar (pulsating star) is discovered by Cambridge University astronomical research student (Susan) Jocelyn Bell, 24, working with Anthony Hewish, 43, and using a giant 4.5-acre radarlike dish to detect electromagnetic waves from outside the earth's atmosphere. The radio dish produces weekly data amounting to some 400 feet of recorder chart paper. Bell is looking for "interstellar scintillation"—pulsating celestial radio sources that have previously been observed—when she begins in August to notice odd signals coming in during the small hours of the morning, when scintillation is usually the weakest. The signals disappear and reappear until November, when Bell learns from a high-speed recorder that the signals are pulsating at a regular interval of just over a second. Celestial radio signals previously recorded have been emitted on a constant basis. Bell's finding will be published next year.

Cicely Saunders founds St. Christopher's Hospice, Sydenham, for terminally ill patients and promotes the ideas she first expressed in her 1960 book *Care of the Dying*: e.g., that dying is a natural part of living rather than a failure of medicine, that people should be allowed to die with dignity, and that effective pain control and sensitive nursing can enhance the quality of death (*see* 1969).

Smoking-withdrawal clinics proliferate across the United States, but Americans buy 572.6 billion cigarettes—210 packs per adult (*see* 1966; Smokenders, 1969).

Britain's first color TV broadcasting begins July 1 as BBC2 transmits 7 hours of programming, most of it coverage of lawn tennis from Wimbledon.

The Public Broadcasting Act signed into law by President Johnson November 7 creates a Corporation for Public Broadcasting to broaden the scope of noncommercial radio and TV beyond its educational role. Federal grants (plus funds from foundations and business and private contributions) will within 3 years rival NBC, CBS, and ABC with National Public Radio and Public Broadcasting Service (TV) networks.

The Federal Communications Commission notifies CBS that its programs dealing with the effects of smoking on health are not sufficient to offset the influence of the 5 to 10 minutes of cigarette commercials the network's New York television station is broadcasting each day. The FCC acts in response to a formal complaint against WCBS-TV filed by John Banzhaf (*see* 1966).

Congress creates a Commission on Obscenity and Pornography. The commission will conclude that pornography does not contribute to crime or sexual deviation and will recommend repeal of all federal, state, and local laws that "interfere with the right of adults who wish to do so to read, obtain, or view explicit sexual materials" (*see* 1969).

Nonfiction: *At Wit's End* by U.S. housewife–newspaper columnist Erma Bombeck, 40; *The Company She Kept* by Albany, N.Y., English professor Doris Grumbach (*née* Isaac), 49, is a literary biography of Mary McCarthy that creates a controversy by charging that McCarthy's novels were actually autobiography; *The Beautiful People* by U.S. journalist Marilyn Bender, 42, is about the fashion world.

Fiction: *The Woman Destroyed* (*La Femme rompue*) by Simone de Beauvoir; *A Puzzleheaded Girl* by Christina Stead; *A Woman of My Age* by Nina Bawden; *Jerusalem the Golden* by Margaret Drabble; *The Paradox Players* by Maureen Duffy; *A Weekend with Claud* by English actress-novelist Beryl Bainbridge, 33; *The Fat Woman's Joke* by English novelist Fay Weldon, 34; *Okuni of Izumo* (*Izumo no Okuni*) by Sawako Ariyoshi is about a woman who planted the seeds of Kubuki theater; *Digging Out* by U.S. novelist Anne Richardson (*née* Roth), 31, who has married psychoanalyst Henry Roiphe in January; *The Magic Toy Shop* by English novelist Angela Carter, 27; *Those Who Walk Away* by Patricia Highsmith; *Imaginary Friends* by Alison Lurie; *The Diary of a Mad Housewife* by New York novelist Sue Kaufman, 40; *The Small Window* by Janet McNeill; *Roseanna* by Swedish police novelist Maj Sjöwall, 32, and her husband, Per Wahlöo; *The Gabriel Hounds* by Mary Stewart.

Poetry: *Black Feeling, Black Talk* by U.S. poet Nikki (*née* Yolande Cornelia) Giovanni, 24, whose poem "The True Import of Present Dialogue, Black vs. Negro" begins, "nigger/ Can you kill/ Can you kill/ Can a nigger kill/ Can a nigger kill a honkie?"; *Outer Banks* by Muriel Rukeyser; *Half Sun, Half Sleep* by May Swenson.

Painting: *The Human Edge* by Helen Frankenthaler; *Hill* and *Adventure* (both acrylic and pencil on canvas) by Agnes Martin.

Sculpture: *Homage to Bernini* by Louise Bourgeois.

Theater: *MacBird* by U.S. playwright Barbara Garson, 25, 2/22 at New York's off-Broadway Village Gate Theater, with Stacy Keach, 386 perfs.; George Grizzard, Eileen Heckart, and Martin Balsam in Robert Anderson's *You Know I Can't Hear You When the Water's Running* 3/13 at New York's Ambassador Theater, 755 perfs.; Barbara Cook, Elliott Gould, and Heywood Hale Broun in Jules Feiffer's *Little Murders* 4/25 at New York's Broadhurst Theater.

Television drama: *The Forsyte Saga* with Eric Porter as Soames Forsyte, Kenneth More as his cousin, Susan Hampshire, 25, as his daughter Fleur in a serialized dramatization of the John Galsworthy novels on BBC and U.S. Public Broadcasting stations.

Films: Catherine Deneuve in Luis Buñuel's *Belle de Jour*; Faye Dunaway and Warren Beatty in Arthur Penn's *Bonnie and Clyde*; Dustin Hoffman, Ann Bancroft, and Katharine Ross, now 25, in Mike Nichols's *The Graduate*; Ludmila Savelyeva and Vyacheslav Tihonov in Sergei Bondarchuk's *War and Peace*. Also: Cliff Robertson and Claire Bloom in Ralph Nelson's *Charly*; Paul Newman, Jo Van Fleet, and George Kennedy in Stuart Rosenberg's *Cool Hand Luke*; folk singer and political activist Joan Baez, now 26, Bob Dylan, and others in D. A. Pennebaker's documentary *Don't Look Back*; Julie Christie, Peter Finch, Alan Bates, and Terence Stamp in John Schlesinger's *Far from the Madding Crowd*; Walter Matthau and Swedish-born actress Inger Stevens, 33, in Gene Kelly's *A Guide for the Married Man*; Bibi (originally Berit) Andersson, 31, and Liv (Johann) Ullmann, 27, in Ingmar Bergman's *Persona*; Lee Marvin and Angie Dickinson (Angeline Brown), 35, in John Boorman's *Point Blank*; Elizabeth Taylor and Richard Burton in Franco Zeffirelli's *The Taming of the Shrew*; Sidney Poitier and Judy Geeson in James Clavell's *To Sir with Love*; Shirley MacLaine, Elsa Martinelli, 35, Adrienne Cori, Anita Ekberg, Philippe Noiret, Peter Sellers, Vittorio Gassman, and Rossano Brazzi in Vittorio De Sica's *Woman Times Seven*.

Ann Sheridan dies of undisclosed causes at her San Fernando valley home January 21 at age 51; Vivien Leigh dies of tuberculosis at London July 8 at age 53.

U.S. cellist (Madeline) Charlotte Moorman, 33, of the American Symphony Orchestra plays topless 2/9 in a performance of Korean-American composer Nam June Peik's avant-garde *Opera Sextronique*, which calls for her to be unclothed above the waist. She is arrested by New York police and convicted on charges of indecent exposure after a 3-month trial.

Opera: Evelyn Lear, now 39, makes her Metropolitan Opera debut 3/17 in the title role of Martin David Levy's opera *Mourning Becomes Electra*.

The Opera Orchestra of New York is founded as a training group/workshop for apprentice orchestra musicians by local conductor Eve Queler (*née* Rabin), 31, who made her operatic conducting debut last year with an outdoor performance of the 1890 Mascagni opera *Cavalleria Rusticana* at Fairlawn, N.J. (*see* 1969).

Popular songs: "Somebody to Love" by the Jefferson Airplane makes that San Francisco rock group the first to gain wide acclaim; *Surrealistic Pillow* (album) by the Jefferson Airplane; "The Great Mandela" by Peter, Paul, and Mary is an antiwar song; Arizona-born singer Linda Ronstadt, 21, records "Different Drum" and begins her climb to the heights; Lulu, now 18, records "Let's Pretend" and Neil Diamond's "The Boat That I Row," appears in James Clavell's film *To Sir with Love*, and he records its title song; Martha and the Vandellas record "Jimmy Mack"; *Wildflowers* (album) by Judy Collins; "Ode to Billy Joe" by country singer-songwriter Bobbie Gentry (Roberta Streeter), 23;

country singer Dolly Parton, 21, records "Dumb Blonde"; *Tammy Wynette* (album) by Mississippi-born country singer Wynette Pugh, 25, who has hits with "Your Good Girl's Going to Go Bad," "I Don't Want to Play House," and "Elusive Dreams" (a duet with David Houston); "Yours Forever" by Jean Shepard; *Janis Ian* (album) by Ian; Dionne Warwick, 25, records "Valley of the Dolls" (theme song for film) by Dory Previn (whose marriage broke up 2 years ago); Gladys Knight and the Pips record "Everybody Needs Love," "Take Me in Your Arms and Love Me," and "I Heard It Through the Grapevine"; *Skeeter Davis Sings Buddy Holly* (album) by Davis, who has another hit single with "What Does It Take (To Keep a Man like You Satisfied?)"; *I Never Loved a Man (The Way I Love You)* (album) by Aretha Franklin, who also records Otis Redding's single "Respect."

The Boston Marathon April 19 includes a runner who has registered under the name K. Switzer and turns out to be Katherine Switzer (*see* 1966). Race officials try to remove her number, creating an uproar. The American Athletic Union issues a ruling that forbids women to compete in the same events with men on pain of losing their rights to compete anywhere. Switzer will fight the ruling and, beginning in 1972, the marathon will be open to women.

Billie Jean King wins in women's singles at both Wimbledon and Forest Hills.

U.S. and British panty hose sales climb as women adopt the miniskirt (*see* 1959, 1969; Quant, 1965)

Laura Ashley's husband sets her up in her own London shop (*see* 1953). Now 42, she has designed elegant dresses, combining Victorian-style prints with comfortable natural fabrics that find wide acceptance. By the time of her death in 1985 she will have factories in the Netherlands and stores on several continents selling not only clothing but also bed and table linens.

The water bed has its beginnings in a water-filled vinyl chair designed by San Francisco graduate student Charles P. Hall, who has earlier filled the chair with starch, then with Jell-O. Finding water a more comfortable filler, he creates a water-filled vinyl mattress.

President Johnson's daughter Lynda is married December 9 at the White House to marine corps Captain Charles Robb.

The Department of Agriculture returns $200 million of unused food aid funds to the Treasury.

Some 2.7 million Americans receive food stamp assistance as of Thanksgiving (*see* 1964; 1969).

Wisconsin permits sale of yellow margarine, becoming the last state to repeal laws against it, but like some other states it continues to impose special taxes on margarine at the behest of dairy interests (*see* New York, 1952).

U.S. bread sells at 22 to 25¢ per 1-lb. loaf.

The first compact microwave oven for U.S. home use is introduced by Amana Refrigeration, a subsidiary of Raytheon with facilities at Amana, Iowa, which applies its consumer marketing experience to Raytheon's microwave technology. Engineer Keishi Ogura of Japan Radio developed an improved electron tube 3 years ago, making possible a compact microwave oven that retails at $495.

Japanese microwave oven production reaches 50,000, up from 15,000 last year. Many Japanese households move directly from hibachi grills to microwave ovens.

Japan's birthrate climbs to 19.3 per 1,000 after its fall to 14 last year in the Year of the Fiery Horse.

France legalizes birth control, but diaphragms, intrauterine devices, and spermicidal creams and jellies remain generally unavailable.

Colorado leads the United States in liberalizing its 100-year-old abortion law. A new law signed by Gov. John A. Love April 25 permits therapeutic abortions in cases where three physicians at hospitals accredited by the state health board agree unanimously that the pregnancy would result in the death or permanent injury of the woman's physical or mental health, the child is "likely" to be born with "grave physical deformity or mental retardation," the pregnancy has resulted from rape or incest and no more than 16 weeks of gestation have passed, the mother was under age 16 when she became pregnant as a result of statutory rape or incest. Roman Catholics, who represent 6 percent of the state's 2 million people, have led opposition to the bill, which has passed the State Senate 20 to 13 and the lower house 40 to 21 with support from the Colorado Council of Churches. The new law has no Colorado residency requirement, and physicians in the state begin receiving inquiries from women all over the country.

The Abortion Bill passed by Parliament October 25 permits a woman to have an abortion under limited circumstances (*see* 1968).

The National Health Service Family Planning Act passed by Parliament permits dissemination of contraceptive advice.

The U.S. population passes 200 million November 20, having doubled in just 50 years. Demographers predict a population of 300 million by the year 2000 if present growth rates continue.

1968

Entertainer Eartha Kitt speaks out against the Vietnam War January 18 at a White House luncheon given by Mrs. Johnson for about 50 white and black women to discuss urban crime. Kitt links the crime rate to the escalation of the war. "You send the best of this country off to be shot and maimed," she says. "They rebel in the street."

German-born French fascism fighter Beate Klarsfeld (*née* Kunzel), 29, confronts West German Chancellor Kurt-George Kiesinger during the Christian Democratic party convention at West Berlin and slaps him in the face, drawing attention to his Nazi past. She is arrested and will serve a 1-year prison sentence, but Kiesinger will not be reelected. Not herself Jewish, Kunzel first heard about the Holocaust in 1960 from fellow student Serge Klarsfeld, a Jew whose father was one of some 70,000 French Jews killed at Auschwitz. She later married Klarsfeld, now a lawyer, and together they will work for the next 20 years to track down and expose former Nazis, including Kurt Lischka (who headed the Gestapo in France), the infamous "Butcher of Lyon," Klaus Barbie, and Auschwitz death camp doctor Joseph Mengele, despite beatings, car bombings, and death threats from neo-Nazis (*see* 1984).

Opposition to the Vietnam War, much of it by women, enables Sen. Eugene McCarthy, 52, (D. Minn.) to make a strong showing in the New Hampshire primary; his success persuades President Johnson to announce March 31 that he will not be a candidate for reelection. The assassinations of Martin Luther King, Jr., and Sen. Robert F. Kennedy traumatize the nation, the Democratic party convention at Chicago nominates Vice President Hubert Humphrey while police outside the convention hall brutalize demonstrators, former Vice President Richard Nixon squeaks out a victory in the November elections, and the war goes on.

Brooklyn's 12th Congressional District elects local activist Shirley Anita St. Hill Chisholm, 43, to the House of Representatives, where she will be the first elected black woman. She will serve for seven terms.

Los Angeles County superior court judge Shirley Mount Hufstedler, 43, is appointed to the U.S. Court of Appeals, becoming the first woman appellate justice (see education, 1979).

U.S. troops at My Lai village in Vietnam go on a rampage in March, systematically raping and abusing women, who are then killed. Three or more members of Charlie Company are charged with rape in the My Lai massacre, but all charges are quietly dropped. Soldiers will admit to reporters that rape is standard operating procedure (see 1970).

Coretta Scott King, now 40, bears up after her husband's murder April 5 and takes an active role in the civil rights movement (see religion, 1969).

Half of all U.S. mothers of school-age children are in the workforce as of March, and seven out of 10 work full time (80 percent of these have no husbands). All but 10 percent say they need the money, either to support themselves and their families or to pay for medical care, save for a child's education, or buy a house.

Congress enacts a Consumer Credit Protection Law. The "Truth in Lending" Act requires banks and other lending institutions to disclose clearly the true annual rate of interest and other financing costs on most types of loans.

Aerobics by U.S. air force Major Kenneth H. Cooper, M.D., launches Americans on a fitness

Coretta Scott King gained prominence in her own right after the shooting of her civil-rights pioneer husband. SCHOMBURG CENTER, NYPL

exercise kick that will lead to a craze for jogging, swimming, bicycling, and aerobic dancing to stimulate heart and lung functions by forcing the body to consume up to 50 milliliters of oxygen in 12 minutes (see 1971).

Lydia Pinkham Co. is acquired by Cooper Laboratories, which will continue to manufacture and market the patent medicine "Vegetable Compound" well into the next decade.

U.S. universities shut down as students demonstrate against the Vietnam War. French universities also have turbulent disorders.

New York magazine carries an interview by writer Gloria Steinem, 34, with the wife of former Vice President Richard Nixon (above) conducted aboard a plane on the campaign trail. Pat Nixon (*née* Thelma Catherine Ryan), 56, tells Steinem, "I haven't just sat back and thought of myself or my ideas or what I wanted to do. Oh, no, I've stayed interested in people. I've kept working. . . . I don't have time to worry about who I admire or who I identify with. I've never had it easy. I'm not like all you—all those people who had it easy." "Pat doesn't have a mink coat," her husband told television audiences 16 years ago in his famous "Checkers" speech, and she tells Steinem that a "good Republican cloth coat" is still good enough.

Journalist Gloria Steinem won notice for her interview with soon-to-be First Lady Pat Nixon on a 1968 campaign plane.
CHIE NISHIO

The 911 emergency telephone number instituted in New York to summon emergency police, fire, or ambulance assistance is the first such system in the United States (*see* Britain, 1937). By 1977 some 600 U.S. localities with a total population of 38 million will have 911 systems.

Action for Children's Television is founded by Newton, Mass., mother Peggy Charren and three other women who are concerned about the vapid violence and huckstering of unwholesome products on commercial programming directed at youngsters.

President-elect Nixon calls the congressional Commission on Obscenity and Pornography created last year "morally bankrupt" and says that "so long as I am in the White House, there will be no relaxation of the national effort to control and eliminate smut from our national life."

Liquid Paper Co. has sales of more than 10,000 bottles per day and grosses more than $1 million (*see* 1956; 1975).

Nonfiction: *Man and Woman: The Human Condition* by Eve Merriam; *The Church and the Second Sex* by U.S. feminist Mary Daly, 40, analyzes the effects of male bias; *Slouching Towards Bethlehem* (essays) by U.S. journalist-novelist Joan Didion, 33; *Trip to Hanoi* by Susan Sontag.

Fiction: *The Quest for Christa T.* by Christa Wolf argues for the self-realization of women in a socialist society; *The Abyss* by Marguerite Yourcenar is set in northern Europe in the 16th century; *Expensive People* by Joyce Carol Oates; *A State of Change* by Penelope Gilliatt, who joins the staff of the *New Yorker* magazine, where she will remain until 1979; *Long Journey in a Dream* (*Nagai yumeji*) by Yumiko Kurahashi; *Dark Sea* (*Umikura*) by Sawako Ariyoshi; *Dance of the Happy Shades* (stories) by Canadian writer Alice Munro (*née* Laidlaw), 37; *Tigers Are Better-Looking* (stories) by Jean Rhys; *A Stronger Climate: Nine Stories* by Ruth Prawer Jhabvala; *The Wedding Group* by Elizabeth Taylor; *Another Part of the Wood* by Beryl Bainbridge; *And the Wife Ran Away* by Fay Weldon; *The White Crow* by Storm Jameson, now 77; *Many a Green Isle* by Agnes Turnbull; *A Wizard of Earthsea* by Ursula Le Guin; *The Salzburg Connection* by Helen MacInnes.

Poetry: *The Speed of Darkness* by Muriel Rukeyser; *Black Judgement* by Nikki Giovanni includes her poem "Nikki Rosa."

Sculpture: *Accession III* (fiberglass and plastic tubing) by German sculptor Eva Hesse, 32.

New York art dealer Paula Cooper, 30, opens her own gallery in Soho (south of Houston Street), where she will show works by Elizabeth Murray, Lynda Benglis, Jennifer Bartlett, and other women as well as those by male artists.

Theater: Australian actress Zoë Caldwell, 34, in Jay Allen's *The Prime of Miss Jean Brodie* (adapted from the Muriel Spark novel) 1/16 at New York's Helen Hayes Theater, 378 perfs.; Hal Holbrook,

Lillian Gish, Matt Crowley, and Teresa Wright in Robert Anderson's *I Never Sang for My Father* 1/25 at New York's Longacre Theater, 124 perfs.; Pat Hingle, Kate Reid, and Arthur Kennedy in Arthur Miller's *The Price* 2/7 at New York's Morosco Theater, 429 perfs.; James Earl Jones and Jane Alexander (*née* Quigley), 28, in Howard Sackler's *The Great White Hope* 10/3 at New York's Alvin Theater, 276 perfs.; Julie Harris and Glenda Farrell in Jay Allen's *Forty Carats* 12/26 at New York's Morosco Theater, 780 perfs.

Britain's Theatres Act effectively abolishes the Lord Chamberlain's powers of censorship (*see* 1737).

Films: Katharine Hepburn and Peter O'Toole in Anthony Harvey's *The Lion in Winter*; Julie Christie, George C. Scott, and Richard Chamberlain in Richard Lester's *Petulia*; Mia Farrow, now 23, and John Cassavetes in Roman Polanski's *Rosemary's Baby*; Liv Ullmann and Max von Sydow in Ingmar Bergman's *Shame*. Also: Jeanne Moreau, Claude Rich, and Jean-Claude Brialy in François Truffaut's *The Bride Wore Black*; Steve McQueen, Robert Vaughn, and English-born actress Jacqueline Bisset, 21, in Peter Yates's *Bullitt*; Gena Rowlands, 32, and John Marley in John Cassavetes's *Faces*; Rod Steiger, George Segal, and Lee Remick in Jack Smight's *No Way to Treat a Lady*; Charlton Heston, Roddy McDowall, and Kim Hunter in Franklin J. Shaffner's *Planet of the Apes*; Joanne Woodward in Paul Newman's *Rachel, Rachel*; Leonard Whiting and Argentine-born British ingénue Olivia Hussey, 17, in Franco Zeffirelli's *Romeo and Juliet*; Elizabeth Taylor, Mia Farrow, and Robert Mitchum in Joseph Losey's *Secret Ceremony*; Burt Lancaster, Janice Rule, and Kim Hunter in Frank and Eleanor Perry's *The Swimmer*; Mireille Darc in Jean-Luc Godard's *Weekend*.

Film critic Pauline Kael, 49, goes to work for the *New Yorker*, where her sometimes scathing reviews will appear for more than 20 years.

Kay Francis dies of cancer at her New York apartment August 26 at age 63; Tallulah Bankhead dies of pneumonia and emphysema at New York December 12 at age 66.

Film musical: Barbra Streisand as Fanny Brice in William Wyler's *Funny Girl*.

Stage musicals: Jerry Orbach and Jill O'Hara in *Promises, Promises* 12/1 at New York's Shubert Theater, with Burt Bacharach–Hal David songs that include "Wherever You Are" and "I'll Never Fall in Love Again," 1,281 perfs.

Opera: Elizabeth Harwood makes her Covent Garden debut singing the role of Fiakermilli in the 1933 Strauss opera *Arabella*, going on to make her New York debut in an October Town Hall recital.

Popular songs: "Both Sides Now" by Canadian-born U.S. singer-guitarist-songwriter Joni Mitchell (originally Roberta Joan Anderson), 25; *Eli and the Third Confession* (album) by Laura Nyro includes "Stoned Soul Picnic," "Sweet Blindness," and "Eli's Coming"; *Papas and the Mamas—Mamas and the Papas* (album) with singer Cass Elliott; Gladys Knight and the Pips record "The End of Our Road"; Loretta Lynn records her song "This City"; *Here Is Barbara Lynn* (album) includes the hit single "This Is the Thanks I Get"; Tammy Wynette records "D-I-V-O-R-C-E" and "Take Me to Your World"; Dolly Parton records "Just Because I'm a Woman"; Etta James records "Tell Mama"; "The Windmills of Your Mind" by Alan and Marilyn Bergman, music by Michel Legrand (for the film *The Thomas Crown Affair*).

 U.S. figure skater Peggy Fleming, 19, wins the gold medal in the winter Olympics at Grenoble, France (and goes on to win the world title March 2 at Geneva), Austrian skier Olga Pall wins the downhill in 1 minute, 40.87 seconds, Marielle Goitschel wins the slalom in 1 minute, 25.86 seconds, Canadian skier Nancy Greene wins the giant slalom in 1 minute, 51.97 seconds. Wyomia Tyus wins the 100-meter dash in 11 seconds at the summer Olympics in Mexico City, Polish runner Irena Szewinska, 24, the 200-meter in 22.5 seconds (she won her first gold medal in the sprint relay at Tokyo), French runner Colette Besson the 400-meter in 52 seconds, U.S. runner Madeline Manning the 800-meter run in 2 minutes, 0.9 seconds, Australian runner Maureen Caird the 80-meter hurdles in 10.3 seconds, Czech athlete Miloslava Rezkova the running high jump (5 feet, 11¼ inches), Romanian athlete Viorica Ciscopoleanu the long jump (22 feet, 4½ inches), East German athlete Margitta Gummel the shot put (64 feet, 4 inches), Romanian athlete Lia Manoliu the discus throw (191 feet, 2½ inches), Hungarian athlete Angela Nemeth the javelin throw (198 feet), West German athlete Ingrid Becker the pentathlon. U.S. swimmer Marge Jan Henne wins the 100-meter freestyle in 1 minute, U.S. swimmer Debbie Meyer, 16, the 200-meter in 2 minutes, 10.5 seconds, the 400-meter in 4 minutes, 31.8 seconds, and the 800-meter in 9 minutes, 24 seconds (she is the first woman ever to win three gold medals in one Olympiad), U.S. swimmer Kaye Hall the 100-meter backstroke in 1 minute, 6.2 seconds, U.S. swimmer Pokey Watson the 200-meter backstroke in 2 minutes, 24.8 seconds, Yugoslav swimmer Djurdjica Bjedov the 100-meter breaststroke in 1 minute, 15.8 seconds, U.S. swimmer Sharon Wichman the 200-meter breaststroke in 2 minutes, 44.4 seconds, Australian swimmer Lynn McClements the 100-meter butterfly in 1 minute, 5.5 seconds, Dutch swimmer Ada Kok the 200-meter butterfly in 2 minutes, 24.7 seconds, U.S. swimmer Claudia Kolb the 200-meter individual medley in 2 minutes, 24.7 seconds and the 400-meter in 5 minutes, 8.5 seconds, U.S. swimmer Sue Gossick the springboard dive event, Czech swimmer Milena Duchkova the platform dive.

Billie Jean King wins in women's singles at Wimbledon, Margaret Smith Court at Forest Hills. (Sarah) Virginia Wade, 22 (Brit), wins the first U.S. Open women's singles.

Cathy Kusner becomes the first licensed woman jockey in U.S. racing.

Congress enacts a Uniform Monday Holiday Law to give Americans 3-day holidays. Scheduled to take effect beginning in 1971, the new law follows centuries-old European laws and orders that Washington's Birthday, Memorial Day, Columbus Day, and Veterans Day be observed on Mondays regardless of what day of the week February 22, May 30, October 30, or November 11 may be.

The Jacuzzi Whirlpool bath introduced in June at California's Orange County Fair by the 53-year-old farm-pump maker Jacuzzi Bros. begins a fad only slightly related to hydrotherapy. Originally invented by Italian-American engineer Candido Jacuzzi, 65, to relive his infant son's arthritis with hydrotherapy, the $700 Jacuzzi "Roman Bath" will spawn a host of imitators.

Enzyme detergents introduced by Procter & Gamble, Lever Brothers, and Colgate-Palmolive create problems in U.S. water and sewage systems.

Anne Klein & Co. is founded by New York fashion designer Klein, now 47 (or 63, or somewhere in between), and her second husband (*see* 1948); she will continue to design until her death in 1974.

Former First Lady Jacqueline Kennedy, now 39, is remarried on the Greek island of Skorpios October 20 to shipping magnate Aristotle Onassis, 68. Washington wit Alice Roosevelt Longworth, now 86, says, "Hasn't anyone ever warned Jacqueline Kennedy about Greeks bearing gifts?"

Sicilian rape victim Franca Viola, 20, is married December 4 to an accountant who defies the custom that says a raped woman is dishonored and cannot marry anyone except her rapist (in this case an admirer whom she has spurned).

President Nixon's younger daughter, Julie, 20, is married at New York December 22 to former President Eisenhower's son, David, also 20.

Virginia Slims cigarettes are introduced by Philip Morris, Inc., with the slogan "You've come a long way, baby." The brand is targeted at women, with the word "slims" in the name intended to remind women that cigarettes are not fattening (*see* Lucky Strike, 1928; tennis, 1970).

U.S. cigarette sales decline slightly to 571.1 billion as adults smoke an average of 205 packs, down from 210 last year. FTC studies show that while filter-tips dominate the market, most cigarettes yield more tars and nicotine in their smoke because tobacco companies are using tobacco leaf higher in tars and nicotine.

The Citizens Board of Inquiry into Hunger and Malnutrition in the United States observes that federal food aid programs reach only 18 percent of the nation's poor.

The Department of Agriculture liberalizes its food stamp program (*see* 1967). It expands from two to 42 the number of counties where federal authorities will handle the program, which in some areas is resisted by local authorities (*see* 1969).

One cigarette brand tried cynically to co-opt the women's liberation movement. Baby? A long way?

The average American eats 11 pounds of fish per year, the highest since the mid-1950s.

Pope Paul VI condemns artificial measures for birth control in his encyclical *Humanae Vitae*. Laypersons and even some priests attack the condemnation.

Britain legalizes abortion April 27 as the Abortion Act, which received royal assent late last year, overturns an 1861 law that made abortion a crime under all circumstances. The new law makes all abortion legal if two registered physicians find that "continuance of pregnancy would involve risks to the life or injury to the physical or mental health of the pregnant woman or the future well-being of herself or of the child or her children." Parliament will come under growing pressure to let women, not doctors, make the decision to abort a pregnancy.

Opponents of the new law predict that 400,000 abortions will be performed each year (but *see* 1969).

1969

Russian-born, Milwaukee-raised Palestine pioneer Golda Meir (*née* Mabovitch), 70, is sworn in as Israel's fourth premier February 17 and will hold office for 5 embattled years. Foreign minister from 1956 to 1966 and before that the minister of labor, she has been opposed by Agudat Israel, a religious party whose members adhere to the Orthodox rule that Jewish men do not look at "strange women."

Queen's University, Belfast, undergraduate Bernadette Josephine Devlin, 21, is one of 12 Northern Irish members seated in Britain's House of Commons, becoming the youngest M.P. since the election of William Pitt the younger in 1781. She views the situation in Ulster as a class struggle, not a religious war, since Protestants on the lower economic scale are as much exploited as the predominantly working-class Roman Catholics who constitute one-third of Northern Ireland's population (*see* 1971).

British Cabinet member Judith Constance Mary Hart, 45, is named minister of overseas development, a position that she will hold off and on for the next decade as she works to help solve the problems of Third World nations.

North Vietnamese Foreign Minister Mme. Nguyen Thi Binh at Paris announces a 10-point peace program May 8. Chief negotiator for the National Liberation Front and foreign minister of the Provisional Revolutionary government, she submits a plan for the unification of Vietnam, but it is rejected by the other peace conference delegates.

The body of a former campaign worker for the late Robert Kennedy is retrieved on the morning of July 19 from a 1967 Oldsmobile sedan that plunged into Poucha Pond on Chappaquiddick Island off Martha's Vineyard some hours earlier and is upside down in 8 feet of water. Mary Jo Kopechne, 28, left a party some hours earlier with Sen. Edward M. Kennedy, 36 (D., Mass), who drove off Dike Bridge, allegedly tried to save the young woman, but has unaccountably failed to report the accident to police for 10 hours. Kennedy defied tradition January 4 by challenging Russell Long of Louisiana after only 6 years' tenure and defeating the 20-year veteran to become assistant majority leader, but the July incident raises questions as to his judgment and blights his credibility as a statesman.

"I have never consciously exploited the fact that I am a woman," British Cabinet member Barbara Castle tells the *Observer* in an interview published October 5. " I wouldn't dare try that, even if I knew how to. I have too much respect for my male colleagues to think they would be particularly impressed."

A bomb explodes at Manhattan's Criminal Court building November 12—the eighth government or corporate building to be bombed since July 26. Police and FBI agents arrest four militant radicals, including Jane Hale Alpert, 24, hours later. They also seek Pat Swinton in connection with the bombings, but she will evade apprehension and Alpert will jump bail (*see* 1974).

International Women's Day is rescued from desuetude March 8 at Berkeley, Calif., by St. Louis-born feminist Laura X (originally Laura Rand Orthwein), 29, who last year called for a revival of the day in a film review for the student newspaper *Daily Californian*. She and her friends started the Women's History Research Center Library (by 1974 it will have a collection of nearly 1 million documents about women's issues from all over the world) and set up an emergency shelter for battered women and their children. They now put out a pamphlet, "Women in World History," and stage a parade to mark International Woman's Day. Laura X adopts that name (she has used others) in protest against woman's legal position as chattel slaves of their fathers and husbands (*see* crime, 1978).

A booming U.S. economy employs a record number of workers, unemployment falls to its lowest level in 15 years, the prime interest rate is 7 percent, the dollar is strong in world money markets, and Wall Street's Dow Jones Industrial Average rises above 1,000 for the first time in history.

43 percent of U.S. women over age 16 and 41 percent of all married women are in the labor force, up from 34 percent of women over age 14 and 31 per-

cent of married women in 1960; only 4 percent are farmhands or domestic servants.

The average U.S. automobile wholesales at $2,280, up from $1,880 in 1959.

Blue Cross health insurance programs cover some 68 million Americans, up from 37 million in 1950, and Blue Shield surgical insurance covers roughly 60 million. Hospital insurance policies issued by private, for-profit companies (often as part of a package that includes life insurance) cover another 100 million, and some 7 million are covered by nonprofit programs other than Blue Cross; third-party groups pay more than 90 percent of most U.S. city hospital bills.

A crisis in U.S. health care delivery looms as the cost of medical care escalates, in large part because patients can in many cases receive insurance benefits only if hospitalized, because they often are hospitalized unnecessarily by sympathetic physicians, because Blue Cross and other insurers pay hospitals on a cost-plus basis without scrutinizing costs too carefully, because physicians order countless tests to protect themselves from malpractice suits, because hospital administrators install costly equipment and facilities that are underutilized, and because hospital workers receive higher wages.

On Death and Dying by Swiss-American physician Elisabeth Kübler-Ross, 43, encourages humane treatment and counseling of terminally ill patients. Her work will spur development of hospices for the dying.

Harlem's Hale House has its beginnings when Lorraine Hale sees a young heroin addict nodding off in the street with a 2-month-old infant falling out of her arms. She suggests that the woman take her baby to "my mother," Clara Hale (*née* McBride), 64, who accepts the child and within 2 months has turned her three-bedroom apartment into a nursery with 20 drug-addicted infants in cribs. Given help by Manhattan Borough President Percy Sutton, she obtains a Harlem brownstone where she will care for about 1,000 babies, many of them addicted since birth, in the next 23 years.

Coretta Scott King speaks from the pulpit of St. Paul's Cathedral in London March 16, the first woman to do so.

A caucus at the convention of the National Council of Churches in November presents an angry statement accusing the Church of maintaining "anachronistic attitudes toward women." Mrs. Betty Schiess, 46, a mother of six who wants to be a minister, receives support from the Diocese of Central New York, which presents a resolution to the convention urging the admission of women to the ministry. "All that is required to do so is the addition of the feminine pronoun to the canon on ordination," it says.

Barnard College women in New York stage a sleep-in March 9, moving into dormitory rooms vacated by male Columbia students in a bid to integrate the dorms. "When you isolate people you only accentuate the differences," one student says. "Psychologically and educationally, it's a more natural way to live," adds another.

The Supreme Court rules unanimously April 7 that a Georgia antipornography law is unconstitutional. "If the First Amendment means anything," writes Justice Thurgood Marshall, "it means that a state has no business telling a man, sitting alone in his own house, what books he may read or what films he may watch." The decision reverses the conviction of an Atlanta man whose house was involved in a gambling raid and found to contain three reels of "dirty" films.

Penthouse magazine begins publication at New York in September. U.S. publisher Robert Guccione, 38, started the magazine at London in March 1965. He does not use an airbrush to eliminate pubic hair from nude photographs, and he challenges Hugh Hefner's *Playboy*, whose newsstand sales he will overtake by 1975 (see 1953).

The National Association of Broadcasters has announced a plan July 8 to phase out cigarette advertising on radio and television over a 3-year period beginning January 1, 1970 (see 1967).

Sesame Street debuts in November on U.S. Public Service television stations and starts to revolutionize children's attitudes toward learning and adults' attitudes about what children are capable of learning. Designed by the Children's Television Workshop and funded by the Ford Foundation, Carnegie Corp., and U.S. Office of Education,

Sesame Street teaches preschool children letters and numbers with the same techniques used in commercial television programs such as the 14-year-old *Captain Kangaroo* show. *Sesame Street* introduces characters such as Oscar the Grouch, Big Bird, the Cookie Monster, Ernie, and Grover.

Nonfiction: *Unlearning the Lie: Sexism in School* by U.S. feminist Barbara Grizzuti Harrison, 35; *Styles of Radical Will* by Susan Sontag; *Toward a Radical Middle: Fourteen Pieces of Reporting and Criticism* by Italian-American journalist Renata Adler, 30, who has been a *New Yorker* magazine writer-reporter since 1962; *An Unfinished Woman* (autobiography) by Lillian Hellman, who writes, "By the time I grew up, the fight for the emancipation of woman, their rights under the law, in the office, in bed, was stale stuff"; *Mary, Queen of Scots* by English biographer Antonia Fraser (*née* Pakenham), 37.

Fiction: *The Bluest Eye* by U.S. novelist Toni Morrison (*née* Chloe Anthony Wofford), 38; *Collected Stories* by Jean Stafford (Pulitzer Prize); "Unter den Linden" (story) by Christa Wolf; *Destroy, She Said* by Marguerite Duras; *Between Life and Death* (*Entre la vie et la mort*) by Nathalie Sarraute; *The Four-Gated City* by Doris Lessing; *In This House of Brede* by Rumer Godden; *The Waterfall* by Margaret Drabble; *The House on the Strand* by Daphne du Maurier; *Come Back if It Doesn't Get Better* (stories) by Penelope Gilliatt; *them* by Joyce Carol Oates (National Book Award); *Real People* by Alison Lurie; *The Fame Game* by Rona Jaffe; *The Lost Queen* (in England, *The Lost Ones*), *The King's Pleasure*, and *Madeslin* by Norah Lofts, now 65; *Monument to the Unknown* (*Mumeihi*) by Ayaka Sono; *The Adventures of Sumiya-Kisutor* (*Sumiyakiuto Q. no boken*) by Yumiko Kurahashi; *The Sound of the Wind* (*Kaze no oto*) by Chiyo Uno, now 71; *Something in Disguise* by Elizabeth Howard; *Masabi* by Margaret Culkin Banning, now 78, whose second husband is president of Oliver Iron Mining Co.; *The Velvet Hammer* by Faith Baldwin, now 76; *The Bayou Road* by Mignon G. Eberhart, now 80; *Murder to Go* by Emma Lathen; *The Winter People* by Phyllis Whitney; *The Left Hand of Darkness* by Ursula Le Guin.

Poetry: *The Animal's Arrival* by Elizabeth Jennings is about mental illness and hospital treatment;

Good Times by U.S. poet (Thelma) Lucille Clifton (*née* Sayles), 34.

Juvenile: *The One in the Middle Is the Green Kangaroo* by U.S. author Judy Blume (*née* Sussman), 30; *A Girl Called Al* by U.S. author Constance C. (Clarke) Green, 45; *Charlotte, Sometimes* by Penelope Farmer; *Goodbye, Dove Square* by Janet McNeill.

Painting: *Night Empire* (acrylic on canvas) by U.S. painter Elizabeth Murray, 29.

Sculpture: *Cumul I* (marble) by Louise Bourgeois.

Look magazine editor Patricia Carbine accepts a suggestion from Philadelphia-born photographer Mary Ellen Mark, 29, that she do a picture story on Italian film director Federico Fellini making *Fellini Satyricon*. Mark, who has been shooting stills for United Artists in Hollywood, goes on to shoot another story in France on filmmaker François Truffaut, and takes pictures in London for a piece on English efforts to control the use of heroin.

Theater: *To Be Young, Gifted and Black* by the late Lorraine Hansberry (adapted by Robert Nemiroff) 1/2 at New York's off-Broadway Cherry Lane Theater, with Barbara Baxley, Cicely Tyson, 380 perfs.; Keir Dullea, Blythe Danner, and Eileen Heckart in Leonard Gersh's *Butterflies Are Free* 10/21 at New York's Booth Theater, 1,128 perfs.; James Coco and Linda Lavin, 32, in Neil Simon's *Last of the Red Hot Lovers* 12/28 at New York's Eugene O'Neill Theater, 706 perfs.

Films: Paul Newman, Robert Redford, Katharine Ross, and Cloris Leachman, 43, in George Roy Hill's *Butch Cassidy and the Sundance Kid*. Also: Barbara Hershey (originally Herzstein), 22, Richard Thomas, and Cathy Burns in Frank Perry's *Last Summer*; Vanessa Redgrave as Isadora Duncan in Karel Reisz's *The Loves of Isadora*; Claudia Cardinale, Charles Bronson, and Henry Fonda in Sergio Leone's *Once Upon a Time in the West*; George Lazenby and (Enid) Diana (Elizabeth) Rigg, 31, in Peter R. Hunt's *On Her Majesty's Secret Service*; Liv Ullmann, Bibi Andersson, and Max von Sydow in Ingmar Bergman's *The Passion of Anna*; Maggie Smith, 35, in Ronald Neame's *The Prime of Miss Jean Brodie*; James Garner and Joan Hackett, 35, in Burt Kennedy's *Support Your Local Sheriff*; Jane

(Seymour) Fonda, 31, Michael Sarrazin, and English actress Susannah York, 27, in Sidney Pollack's *They Shoot Horses, Don't They?*; Yves Montand and Greek actress Irene Papas, 43, in Constantin Costa-Gavras's *Z*.

Film musical: Shirley MacLaine in Bob Fosse's *Sweet Charity*.

Broadway and off-Broadway musicals: Angela Lansbury and Milo O'Shea in *Dear World* 2/6 at the Mark Hellinger Theater, an adaptation of the 1945 Jean Giraudoux play *The Madwoman of Chaillot* with songs by Jerry Herman, 132 perfs.; Katharine Hepburn as the late Coco Chanel in *Coco* 12/18 at the Mark Hellinger Theater, with André Previn–Alan Jay Lerner songs, 332 perfs.

Judy Garland is found dead of a drug overdose in a locked bathroom of her London apartment June 22 at age 47. She has been married five times, had three children, and tried suicide at least 20 times as she swallowed amphetamine pills in an effort to maintain her weight.

The Woodstock Music and Art Fair in the Catskill Mountains at Bethel, N.Y., draws 300,000 youths from all over America for 4 days in August to hear Joan Baez, Jimi Hendrix, Ritchie Havens, the Jefferson Airplane, the Who, the Grateful Dead, Carlos Santana, and other rock stars. Despite traffic jams, thunderstorms, and shortages of food, water, and medical facilities the gathering is orderly with a sense of loving and sharing, but thousands in the audience are stoned or tripping on marijuana ("grass," "pot," "maryjane"), hashish ("hash"), lysergic acid diethylamide (LSD), barbiturates ("downs"), amphetamines ("uppers"), mescaline, cocaine, and other drugs.

Opera: U.S. soprano Jessye Norman, 24, makes her operatic debut singing the role of Elisabeth in the 1845 Wagner opera *Tannhäuser* at Berlin's Deutsch Oper and goes on to sing the role of Countess Almaviva in the 1786 Mozart opera *Le Nozze di Figaro*; New York soprano Beverly Sills (*née* Belle Silverman), 40, makes her debut at La Scala in Milan.

Eve Queler conducts her Opera Orchestra of New York in a concert performance of the 1900 Puccini opera *Tosca* at Alice Tully Hall 12/1 (*see* 1967).

Popular songs: Japanese artist Yoko Ono, 35, marries John Lennon of the Beatles in March and the two hold a "Bed-In for Peace" in the honeymoon suite at the Amsterdam Hilton and later release their first single, "Give Peace a Chance;" "Make Love to Me" by Dusty Springfield; *New York Tendaberry* by Laura Nyro includes "Tom Cat Goodbye" and "Captain Saint Lucifer"; *Young, Gifted and Black* (album) by Nina Simone, whose eloquent songs will cause the U.S. show business establishment to blackball her; *Who Knows Where the Time Goes?* (album) by Judy Collins includes "My Father" (her father, Chuck, is a Denver bandleader and disk jockey); *Gliding Bird* (album) by country singer Emmy Lou Harris, 22; *Greatest Hits Vol. 1* (album) by Tammy Wynette, whose single "Stand by Your Man" (written with recording executive Billy Sherrill) wins her a spot in the cast of *Grand Ole Opry*.

Hialeah Race track exercise rider Diane Crump, 20, rides a 48-to-1 shot to a tenth place finish in a 12-horse field February 7, becoming the first U.S. woman jockey to compete against men at a parimutuel track. Barbara Jo Rubin, 19, rides Cohesion to victory at Charles Town, W.Va., February 22 to become the first woman jockey to win a race at a U.S. Thoroughbred track.

Mrs. Adrianne Shirley "Anne" Jones (*née* Hardon), 30, wins in women's singles at Wimbledon, Margaret Smith Court at Forest Hills.

The National Women's Hall of Fame is founded at Seneca Falls, N.Y.

U.S. panty hose production reaches 624 million pair, up from 200 million last year, as American women switch from nylon hosiery.

Smokenders is founded February 18 by U.S. entrepreneur Jacqueline (Mrs. Jon) Rogers, 45, who has rented a hotel meeting room, placed advertisements in newspapers, and attracted a crowd of 23 who pay $3 each. Rogers tells them they will stop smoking in 6 weeks (most of them do) and launches an enterprise that will draw more than 100,000 smokers in the next decade. Smokenders uses techniques similar to those of Alcoholics Anonymous and Weight Watchers.

Heroin sales to New York schoolchildren have jumped as a result of the federal government's Operation Intercept program to restrict the flow of marijuana from Mexico, says an expert testifying before a joint legislative committee at Washington, D.C. The price of marijuana, he says, has climbed so high that heroin sells at a competitive price.

The Tate-LaBianca murders make headlines in August. Screen actress Sharon Tate Polanski, 26, is murdered at her Bel-Air home in Benedict Canyon early in the morning of August 10 along with coffee heiress Abigail Folger, 25, her common-law husband, Wojiciech "Voytek" Frykowski, 32, Hollywood hair stylist Jay Sebring, 35, and delivery boy Steven Earl Parent. Supermarket chain president Leno LaBianca, 44, and his wife, Rosemary, 38, are murdered later in the day at Los Angeles. Police say the murders are unrelated, but a jury late next year will find ex-convict Charles M. Manson, 32, and his hippie cult family guilty of all seven murders. (Manson has allegedly mesmerized his followers with drugs, sex, and religion.)

21 million U.S. children participate in the National School Lunch Program. About 3.8 million receive lunch free or at substantially reduced prices, and the figure soon will rise to 8 million.

Japanese lathe operator Takako Nakamura, 28, throws herself off a speeding train after discovering that she has been poisoned by inhaling cadmium fumes while working for the Toho Zinc Co. Prime Minister Eisaku Sato announces tearfully that he is determined to secure passage of strong antipollution laws.

Arizona orders a 1-year moratorium on use of DDT after milk in the state proves to have high levels of the pesticide.

Mother's milk contains four times the amount of DDT permitted in cows' milk, says Sierra Club executive vice president David Brower in testimony before the House Merchant Marine and Fisheries Committee. "Some wit suggested that if [mother's milk] were packaged in some other container we wouldn't allow it across state lines," says Brower.

Major U.S. baby food makers halt use of monosodium glutamate (MSG) after tests show that mice fed large amounts of the flavor enhancer suffer brain damage.

Britain has 28,859 abortions in the 10 months ending February 25 and exceeds 1,000 per week in England and Wales by late July. The National Health Service pays for 60 percent of the abortions (*see* 1968).

Canada legalizes abortion and homosexuality May 14 in a sweeping new criminal code law.

California's supreme court rules in September that the state's antiabortion law of 1850 is unconstitutional. The law infringes on a woman's right to decide whether to risk childbirth and bear children, says the court in *People* v. *Dr. Leon P. Belous*. Washington, D.C., district court judge Gerhard A. Gesell rules in November that the district's antiabortion laws are unconstitutional and not valid.

A "Second Report on Oral Contraceptives" released in September by an FDA Advisory Committee on Obstetrics and Gynecology concludes that side effects will produce fatalities in about 255 of the 8.5 million U.S. women now on The Pill, but that the benefits of oral contraceptives nevertheless outweigh their risks (*see* 1970).

1970

 Capt. Ernest L. Medina and five other soldiers are charged with premeditated murder and rape of civilian women at the South Vietnamese village of My Lai (Songmy) in mid-March 1968. West Point's superintendent resigns following accusations that he and 13 other officers suppressed information: Gen. Samuel W. Koster commanded the Americal Division, whose First Battalion C Company was involved in the massacre of 47 civilians. A secret army investigation has reportedly found that the number of victims dwindled as information moved up the chain of command but that U.S. troops did indeed commit acts of murder, rape, sodomy, and maiming against "noncombatants."

An explosion in New York's Greenwich Village March 6 completely wrecks a town house at 18 West 11th Street allegedly used by members of the Weather Underground to produce bombs. One member, Diane Oughton, is killed. Police arrest Weather Underground activist Bernardine Dohrn, 27 (she will jump bail), and call in the FBI to help look for Kathy Boudin, 26, and Catherine Platt

Wilkerson, 25, one of whom was reportedly naked and both of whom were bruised and lacerated. They borrowed clothing from a neighbor and fled the scene. Wilkerson, whose father owned the antebellum house, was a member of the SDS (Students for a Democratic Society) delegation to Hanoi in 1967 and has allegedly joined the ultramilitary Weathermen faction of SDS.

13 women guerrillas escape from a Uruguayan jail March 8, a date chosen because it is International Women's Day.

College campus radicals who oppose his policies in Vietnam are "bums," says President Nixon May 1.

Kent State University students in Ohio rally at noon May 4 to protest the widening of the war in Southeast Asia. National Guardsmen open fire on the 1,000 students and four fall dead, including Sandra Lee (*née* Gittel) Scheuer, 20, of Youngstown and Allison Krause, 19, of Pittsburgh. Eight others are wounded.

An antiwar rally May 9 brings 75,000 to 100,000 peaceful demonstrators to Washington, D.C. President Nixon is unable to sleep and drives to the Lincoln Memorial before dawn to talk for an hour with students protesting the war.

Police in Mississippi open fire May 15 on a women's dorm at Jackson State College, killing two, wounding a dozen others.

The U.S. Army commissions its first women generals in 196 years June 11. Col. Elizabeth P. Hoisington, 52, director of the 12,000-member Women's Army Corps, and Col. Anna Mae Hays, 50, Army Nurse Corps director, were nominated by President Nixon May 15 for brigadier generals.

Secretary of the Interior Walter J. Hickel sends a letter to President Nixon warning that the administration is contributing to anarchy and revolt by turning its back on American youth and that further attacks on the motives of young people by Vice President Agnew will solidify hostility and make communication impossible.

Black Panther Party leader Kathleen Cleaver (*née* Neal), 25, who joined her husband, Eldridge, in exile in Algeria last year and gave birth there to a son, gives birth in North Korea to a daughter, returns to Algiers, and at year's end tells an interviewer who asks her about the role of women in a revolution, "I won't answer that. No one ever asks what men's role in the revolution is. Everything women do is viewed as secondary in a capitalist society. Even having a baby is viewed as secondary because men can't do it. But in a socialist society the labor force needs everybody, and women are not looked on as secondary."

 The Italian Senate votes October 9 to legalize divorce for the first time.

The U.S. Department of Justice files a suit of sex discrimination against Libbey-Owens and the United Glass and Ceramic Workers of North America (Ohio).

Philadelphia activist Margaret "Maggie" Kuhn, 65, founds the Gray Panthers and begins fighting for the rights of retired Americans. Forced to retire from her job with the Presbyterian Church mission because of a mandatory retirement age policy, Kuhn feels "wounded and angry at having been sent out to pasture to get lost."

Feminists demonstrate to "liberate" the men's bar at New York's Biltmore Hotel. McSorley's, a 116-year-old New York bar, admits its first woman patron August 10 after Mayor John Lindsay signs a bill prohibiting sexual discrimination in public places (with a few exceptions such as Turkish baths), making New York the first major city to have such a law.

A nationwide U.S. Women's Strike for Equality celebrates the 50th anniversary of suffrage; more than 10,000 people march down New York's Fifth Avenue August 26 carrying placards with demands for "emancipation," and many hear speeches by Betty Friedan, Gloria Steinem, Rep. Bella Abzug (*née* Savitzky), 50 (the first Jewish woman elected to Congress), and Kate Millett (below), who call for more day care centers, nonsexist advertising, and a revision of some Social Security laws. "Man is not the enemy," says Friedan; "man is a fellow victim."

$ Some 25.5 million Americans live below the poverty line—$3,908 per year for a family of four—and another 10.2 million live only slightly above the line. Nearly half the 35.7 million total are in the South.

Women marched down New York's Fifth Avenue to assert their rights and protest discrimination. CHIE NISHIO

The Women's Bureau of the U.S. Department of Labor reports that median earnings for women ($5,323 per year) are 59.4 percent of the median for men ($8,966), down from 63.9 percent in 1955.

 An armed man and woman commandeer an Israeli El Al flight September 6 en route from Tel Aviv to London, but security guards on the plane mortally wound the man and passengers subdue the woman. Jailed at London, she turns out to be Leila Khaled, 24, a former student at Beirut's American University who took part in a hijacking last year.

Palestinian militants hijack a TWA 707 and a Swissair DC-8 September 6 and force them to land outside Amman, Jordan. Militants hijack a BOAC VC-10 a few days later and force it to land on the same strip; they blow up all three planes after removing the passengers, who are held hostage for several weeks until British, West German, Swiss, and Israeli authorities release Leila Khaled (above) and other Arabs.

Twelve U.S. flight attendants file a multimillion-dollar sex discrimination suit against TWA.

Human Sexual Inadequacy by U.S. psychoanalysts William Howell Masters, 54, and Virginia E. Johnson (*née* Hershel), 45, will lead to a proliferation of sex therapy clinics at which couples will be encouraged to put less emphasis on intercourse, more on nonsexual physical contact, as a way of reducing tensions and promoting natural, loving sex. Masters and Johnson, whose book *Human Sexual Response* appeared in 1966, refute the Freudian notion that there are two kinds of female orgasm and that vaginal orgasm can be achieved only through vaginal penetration by the penis (*see* 1905): anatomically, they say, all female orgasms are centered in the clitoris, whether they result from direct manual stimulation of the clitoris, from the thrusting of the penis in the vagina, or from stimulation of other erogenous areas, such as the breasts, and the orgasm resulting from masturbation is more intense than that resulting from sexual intercourse. Once a woman experiences orgasm, she is likely to have several orgasms in rapid succession, they have found.

The Lutheran Church ordains its first woman pastor.

U.S. public schools are for the most part "grim," "joyless," and "oppressive," and they fail to educate children adequately, says a study commissioned by the Carnegie Corporation.

A House subcommittee holds the first hearings ever on sex discrimination in education.

U.S. colleges close down in antiwar demonstrations and some will remain closed for the balance of the spring term as students coordinate plans for strikes and demonstrations. Ivy League schools go coed (but Barnard, Bryn Mawr, Mount Holyoke, Smith, and Wellesley will remain strictly for women, while Radcliffe will be virtually swallowed up by Harvard). Women receive degrees along with men at

Harvard for the first time June 11, and Harvard elects its first women overseer (Helen Homans Gilbert of Washington, D.C., chairs Radcliffe's board of trustees).

Time and *Newsweek* run cover stories on the women's movement. *Newsweek* pays a settlement to 46 editorial workers to resolve a sex discrimination suit. The August issue of the *Ladies' Home Journal* carries a special supplement in response to a sit-in by 100 women in the magazine's office to protest its portrayal of women.

Nonfiction: *Sexual Politics* by U.S. feminist Kate (Katherine Murray) Millett, 35, who says, "Our society, like all other historical societies, is a patriarchy. The fact is evident at once if one recalls that the military, industry, technology, universities, science, political office, and finance—in short, every

Kate Millett's book Sexual Politics *articulated a philosophy for what was coming to be called "women's lib."* CHIE NISHIO

avenue of power within the society, including the coercive force of the police, is entirely in male hands"; *The Female Eunuch* by Australian feminist Germaine Greer (*née* Reginal), 31, who says, among other things, "I'm sick of pretending that some fatuous male's self-important pronouncements are the objects of my undivided attention," "I refuse to be a female impersonator. I am a woman, not a castrate," "Women fail to understand how much men hate them," and "Freud is the father of psychoanalysis. It has no mother"; *Slam the Door Softly* by Clare Boothe Luce, now 67, who writes "NORA. When a man can't explain a woman's actions, the first thing he thinks about is the condition of her uterus"; *In Defense of the Women's Movement* by Evelyn Reed; *I Know Why the Caged Bird Sings* (autobiography) by St. Louis–born writer-singer-entertainer-black activist Maya Angelou, 42, who was raped by her mother's boyfriend at age 8, was mute for the next 5 years, gave birth to a son at age 16, but fills her book with humor, optimism, and homespun philosophy; *Interview with History* (*Intervista con la storia*) by Oriana Fallaci; *Divine Disobedience: Profiles on Catholic Radicalism* by Polish-born U.S. writer Francine du Plessix Gray (*née* Jochaud), 39; *Please Touch: A Guided Tour of the Human Potential Movement* by *Life* magazine staff writer Jane (Temple) Howard, 35; *How to Make It in a Man's World* by New York publishing executive Letty Cottin Pogrebin, 31; *Unbought and Unbossed* (autobiography) by Shirley Chisholm; *Goodness Had Nothing to Do with It* (autobiography) by Mae West, now 77; *The New Latins: Fateful Change in South and Central America* by U.S. journalist Georgie Anne Geyer, 35; *Wallflower at the Orgy* (articles) by New York writer Nora Ephron, 39.

Fiction: *A Guest of Honor* by Nadine Gordimer; *Weep Dear Man* (*Grat elskede mann*) by Norwegian novelist Bjorg Vik, 35; *An Island of Sacrifice* (*Ikinie no shima*) by Ayako Sono; *Shadow of a Tree* (*Jugi*) by Ineko Sata; *Anti-Tragedy* (*Hanhigeki*) by Yumiko Kurahashi; *A Pagan Place* by Edna O'Brien; *The Bay of Noon* by Shirley Hazzard; *Losing Battles* by Eudora Welty; *Play It as It Lays* by Joan Didion; *The Edible Woman* by Margaret Atwood; *Up the Sandbox!* by Anne Richardson Roiphe is about the conflict between being a young

mother and the dream of a liberated woman that part of her wants to be; *The Perfectionist* by U.S. novelist Gail Godwin, 33; *Lovesounds* by U.S. novelist-journalist Gail Sheehy (*née* Henion), 32; *The Wheel of Love* (stories) by Joyce Carol Oates includes "Where Are You Going? Where Have You Been?" and "The Region of Ice"; *A Slipping Down Life* by Anne Tyler; *The Honours Board* by Pamela Hansford Johnson (Lady Snow); *A Sea-Grape Tree* by Rosamond Lehmann; *Not One of Us* by English novelist June (Valerie) Thompson, 40; *Whistle and I'll Come to You* by Agnes Turnbull; *Take What You Want* by Faith Baldwin; *The Crystal Cave* by Mary Stewart.

Poetry: *Relearning the Alphabet* by Denise Levertov; *To See, To Take* by Mona Van Duyn; *We Are BaddDD People* by U.S. poet Sonia Sanchez (*née* Driver), 35; *Re-Creation* by Nikki Giovanni includes her poem "Revolutionary Dreams"; *The Nightmare Factory* by Maxine Kumin; *Iconographs* by May Swenson; *Lucidities* by Elizabeth Jennings.

Juvenile: *Are You There, God? It's Me, Margaret* and *Iggie's House* by Judy Blume; *The Summer of the Swan* by U.S. writer Betsy Cromer Byars, 42; *Some of the Days of Everett Anderson* by Lucille Clifton; *Prefects of the Chalet School* by the late Elinor Brent-Dyer, who died last year at age 75.

Painting: *Andy Warhol* by Alice Neel.

Sculpture: *Untitled* (rope piece) by Eva Hesse, who dies of a brain tumor at New York May 29 at age 34.

Theater: Maureen Stapleton in Neil Simon's *The Gingerbread Lady* 12/13 at New York's Plymouth Theater, 193 perfs.

Former stripteaser Gypsy Rose Lee dies of lung cancer April 26 at age 56.

Television: *The Mary Tyler Moore Show* 9/19 on NBC with Moore, 32, Ed Asner, Ted Knight (to 9/3/1977).

Films: Jack Nicholson, Karen Black (Karen Blanche Ziegler), 28, and Susan Anspach in Bob Rafelson's *Five Easy Pieces*; French actress Dominique Sanda (Dominique Varaine), 19, in Bernardo Bertolucci's *The Garden of the Finzi-Continis*; Dustin Hoffman and Faye Dunaway in Arthur Penn's *Little Big Man*;

Elliott Gould, Donald Sutherland, and Sally Keller-man, 33 (as "Hot Lips" Hoolihan), in Robert Alt-man's *M*A*S*H*; John Sichel, Joan Plowright, 40, Alan Bates, and Laurence Olivier in Olivier's *Three Sisters*. Also: Pearl Bailey and Beau Bridges in Hal Ashby's *The Landlord*; Ali (*née* Elizabeth Alice) MacGraw, 32, and Ryan O'Neal in Arthur Hiller's *Love Story*; Liza Minnelli, 24 (daughter of the late Judy Garland), Ken Howard, and Robert Moore in Otto Preminger's *Tell Me That You Love Me, Junie Moon*; Jean Yanne, Michael Duchaussoy, and Caroline Cellier in Claude Chabrol's *This Man Must Die*; Catherine Deneuve and Fernando Rey in Luis Buñuel's *Tristana*; Ellen Burstyn (Edna Rae Gillooly), 37, Rip Torn, and James Callahan in Joseph Strick's *Tropic of Cancer*; Glenda Jackson, 34, Eleanor Brown, Alan Bates, and Oliver Reed in Ken Russell's *Women in Love*.

Film musicals: Joan Baez, the Jefferson Airplane, Joe Cocker, the Who, and others in Michael Wadleigh's *Woodstock* (a documentary account of last year's gathering at Bethel, N.Y.); David Maysles, Albert Maysles, and Charlotte Swerin's *Gimme Shelter* with the Rolling Stones (a documentary account of last year's Altamont rock concert); Barbra Streisand in Gene Kelly's *Hello, Dolly*.

Broadway and off-Broadway musicals: *The Last Sweet Days of Isaac* 1/26 at the Eastside Playhouse, with Austin Pendleton, music by Nancy Ford, lyrics by Gretchen Cryer, 465 perfs.; Melba Moore in *Purlie* 3/15 at the Broadway Theater, with Gary Geld–Peter Udell songs that include "I Got Love," 688 perfs.; Lauren Bacall in *Applause* 3/30 at the Palace Theater, with Charles Strouse–Lee Adams songs, book by Betty Comden and Adolph Green, 896 perfs.; Elaine Stritch in *Company* 4/26 at the Alvin Theater, with Stephen Sondheim songs, 706 perfs.

Popular songs: *Yoko Ono/Plastic Ono Band* and *John Lennon/Plastic Ono Band* (albums); "I'll Never Fail in Love Again" by Bobbie Gentry; "Coal Miner's Daughter" by Loretta Lynn; *Whales and Nightingales* (album) by Judy Collins; *Silk Purse* (album) by Linda Ronstadt includes "Long Long Time"; U.S. singer (and onetime drummer) Karen Carpenter, 20, records the Burt Bacharach–Hal David number "(They Long to Be) Close to You" with her brother Richard on keyboards and has her first big hit; Diana Ross records "Ain't No Mountain High Enough" and "Reach Out and Touch Somebody's Hand"; *First Take* (album) by soul singer Roberta Flack, 31; *Anita O'Day at the Berlin Festival* (album) by O'Day; *First Songs of the First Lady* (album), *Ways to Love a Man* (album), *The World of Tammy Wynette* (album), *Tammy's Touch* (album), *Greatest Hits* (album), and "The Wonders You Perform" by Tammy Wynette; "Another Lonely Night" by Jean Shepard; *What About Me* (album) and "Snowbird" by Nova Scotia–born country singer–ukelele player Anne Murray, 25; *Christmas and the Beads of Sweat* (album) by Laura Nyro; Lynn Anderson records "Rose Garden." Janis Joplin dies of a drug overdose at Hollywood, Calif., October 3 at age 27.

Opera: U.S. soprano Judith Blegen, 28, makes her Metropolitan Opera debut in January as Papagena in Mozart's 1791 opera *The Magic Flute* (*Die Zauberflöte*); U.S. mezzo-soprano Frederica Von Stade, 14, makes her Metropolitan Opera debut in January as the Third Boy in *Die Zauberflöte*; Marilyn Horne makes her Metropolitan Opera debut 3/3 in the role of Adalgisa in the 1871 Verdi opera *Aïda* (Sutherland sings the title role); Beverly Sills makes her London debut at Covent Garden singing the title role in the 1835 Donizetti opera *Lucia di Lammermoor*; Adriana Maliponte appears at La Scala in the title role of the 1884 Massenet opera *Manon*; a *New York Sunday News* critic writes 11/22 that conductor Eve Queler "has the edge on all other music conductors because she's shapelier than Leopold Stokowski, prettier than Leonard Bernstein, and has better legs than William Steinberg," but Queler shrugs off the sexist comment and continues to conduct great music.

Ballet: Kirov Ballet Company star Natalia Makarova, 29, defects to the West while on tour in London and will join the American Ballet Theater in New York, making frequent guest appearances with the Royal Ballet, Covent Garden, and other companies.

Diane Crump rides in the Kentucky Derby, the first woman jockey to enter the Run for the Roses (*see* 1969).

Margaret Smith Court wins in women's singles at both Wimbledon and Forest Hills.

The first Virginia Slims tennis tournament opens September 23 at Houston (*see* tobacco, 1968). Sponsored by cigarette maker Philip Morris, it is the first tournament for women professionals held separately from male players. Billie Jean King is among the organizers.

The first New York Marathon September 23 attracts 126 starters who run around Central Park 4 times. A Far Rockaway fireman wins the event, which will grow to attract more than 25,000 male and female runners who will start on Staten Island and finish in Central Park.

U.S. women balk at a new midiskirt decreed by fashion arbiters. Unsold garments are returned to manufacturers, women wear their skirts as long or short as they like, and slaves to fashion fade from the scene.

Man-made fabrics raise their share of the U.S. textile market to 56 percent, up from 28 percent in 1960, with polyesters enjoying a 41 percent share of the market and cotton only 40 percent, down from 65 percent in 1960. E. I. du Pont's patent on polyester has run out, other companies have entered the market, and some big chemical companies have helped mills that use polyester-cotton blends with massive consumer advertising to proclaim the virtues of durable-press fabrics.

Adult Americans give up cigarettes in growing numbers, but smoking among teenagers increases: 36.3 percent of Americans aged 21 and over smoke cigarettes, down from 42.5 percent in 1964, 42.3 percent of adult males smoke cigarettes, down from 52.5 percent in 1964, 30.5 percent of adult females smoke cigarettes, down from 31.5 percent.

A California Superior Court judge and three others are killed in an August shootout at a San Rafael courtroom. Former UCLA teaching assistant Angela Yvonne Davis, 26, who has been fired on grounds that she is a Communist, is charged with having bought the 12-gauge shotgun used by the Soledad Brothers in their escape, she is arrested October 16 at New York on charges of flight to avoid prosecution for her alleged role in the courtroom shootout, extradited to California, and

booked December 22 for murder, kidnapping, and criminal conspiracy (*see* 1972).

Antiwar activist Jane Fonda is arrested at Cleveland November 3 and charged with having smuggled drugs and kicking a police officer.

Earth Day April 21 sees the first mass demonstrations against pollution and other desecrations of the planet's ecology. Environmentalists block off streets and employ other means to raise U.S. awareness of threats to the environment of Spaceship Earth (in the phrase of the late Adlai Stevenson).

The National Research Council warns expectant mothers in the United States not to restrict weight gain too severely. A Committee on Maternal Nutrition of the NRC says that at least half of infant mortalities are preventable through use of prenatal care, adequately trained personnel at delivery, correction of dietary deficiencies, proper hygiene, and health education, and it says that a weight gain of 20 to 25 pounds in pregnancy is permissible.

U.S. breakfast foods come under fire July 23 from former Nixon administration hunger consultant Robert Burnett Choate, Jr., 46, who testifies before a Senate subcommittee that 40 of the top 60 dry cereals have little nutritional content. "The worst cereals are huckstered to children" on television, says Choate.

A U.S. Occupational Safety and Health Act signed by President Nixon December 29 compromises differences between labor and management and establishes an office that will work to minimize hazards in industry.

The Poison Prevention Packaging Act passed by Congress December 30 requires that manufacturers of drugs, sulfuric acid, turpentine, and other potentially dangerous products put safety tops on their containers so that children will not be able to open them. The act will take effect in 1972, and fatalities from aspirin and other potential poisons will drop.

Santa Ana, Calif., municipal judge Paul G. Mast dismisses abortion charges against physician R. C. Robb in January, ruling that a woman has the constitutional right not to bear children. The Therepeutic Abortion Act of 1967 is unconstitutional, Judge Mast rules.

The most liberal abortion law in the United States goes into effect July 1 in New York State. At least 147 women undergo abortions, more than 200 register at municipal hospitals for the procedure, bringing the application total to more than 1,200, and "Right to Life" groups continue to protest the new law as they do also new, liberalized abortion laws in Colorado, Alaska, and Hawaii.

The chemical synthesizing of prostaglandin gives medicine a new way to terminate pregnancies in hospitals.

Birth control pills may produce blood clots, warns the Food and Drug Administration (*see* 1969). The FDA sends letters to more than 300,000 physicians urging them to pay close attention to the risks involved in taking The Pill and to inform their patients. Activists disrupt Senate subcommittee hearings on The Pill, protesting that the witnesses are mostly male doctors and that women are being used as "guinea pigs" in testing The Pill's safety and efficacy.

1971

 Pakistani forces invade East Pakistan March 25, Bengali separatists blow up major bridges, railroads, and communications lines before being subdued, but guerrillas resist the Pakistani army of occupation (*see* below).

Member of Parliament Bernadette Devlin gives birth to a baby out of wedlock and loses Catholic support but continues the aggressive political tactics in behalf of Irish independence for which she has been sentenced to 9 months' imprisonment (*see* 1969). She will marry in 1973 and not stand for reelection in 1974 (*see* 1981).

The Principality of Liechtenstein's male electorate votes February 28 to deny suffrage to women, but most Swiss cantons finally grant women the right to vote on the same basis as men.

A women's rights demonstration at London March 6 brings out 4,000 marchers.

Pakistani troops (above) methodically rape hundreds of thousands of Bengali women, many of whom commit suicide because their violation has made them unmarriagable.

Mothers of U.S. schoolchildren cheer or groan, depending on their sympathies, following a unanimous decision by the Supreme Court April 20 that upholds busing to achieve racial balance where segregation has official sanction and where school authorities have offered no acceptable alternative to busing. The court rules in the case of *Swann* v. *Charlotte-Mecklenburg Board of Education* that the 1954 *Brown* v. *Board of Education* decision does not require that a district's racial composition be reflected in every one of the district's schools, but the district must show that if it has all-black or all-white schools this is not the result of deliberate segregation policies, and since school systems have traditionally employed bus transportation, busing may be used to correct racial imbalance (*see* 1965). Federal authorities impose a strict busing plan on the Austin, Tex., school system in May, a federal judge rejects the plan in late July, Alabama's Gov. Wallace says the Nixon administration has done more than any preceding administration to desegregate public schools, and President Nixon publicly repudiates the Austin plan August 3; he orders that busing be limited "to the minimum required

Busing black children to white schools and vice versa helped achieve racial balance but raised cries of protest. MICHAEL LLOYD CARLEBACH/NANCY PALMER

by law" (the busing ordered in Charlotte, N.C., is actually less than that used to preserve segregation).

A strike involving 500 women workers begins May 5 at Elba, Ala., and continues for 8 months. A strike by 300 women at the Alliance Manufacturing Co. begins June 2 at Shenandoah, Va.

The Twenty-sixth Amendment, ratified July 1, lowers the U.S. voting age from 21 to 18 for both women and men.

The National Women's Political Caucus is founded by a nonpartisan group of U.S. women in July to seek more political power for women. Founders include Mississippi civil rights activist Fannie Lou Hamer, now 54, who takes issue with some of the middle-class feminists, saying, "I got a black husband, six feet three, 240 pounds, with a 14 shoe, that I don't *want* to be liberated from. We are here to work side by side with this black man in trying to bring liberation to all people."

"I am not elevating women to sainthood, nor am I suggesting that all women share the same views, or that all women are good and all men bad," says Rep. Bella Abzug (D., N.Y.) July 10 in a speech to the National Women's Political Caucus (above) at Washington, D.C. "Women have screamed for war. Women, like men, have stoned black children going to integrated schools. Women have been and are prejudiced, narrow-minded, reactionary, even violent. *Some* women. They, of course, have a right to vote and a right to run for office. I will defend that right, but I will not support them or vote for them."

The Supreme Court rules unanimously January 25 in *Phillips* v. *Martin Marietta* that Title VII of the 1964 Civil Rights Act prohibits "not only overt discrimination but also practices that are fair in form, but discriminatory in operation." A company may not deny employment to women with children of preschool age unless the same criterion applies to men, the Court rules. A law that permits one hiring policy for women and another for men is unconstitutional.

A NOW conference announces formation of a task force on the "masculine mystique"—the male-held conviction that it is appropriate to use violence to resolve problems.

Bella Abzug went to Washington as the first Jewish congresswoman—and made her presence felt. CHIE NISHIO

The Center for Non-Violent Social Change is founded at Atlanta by Coretta Scott King, widow of slain civil rights leader Rev. Martin Luther King, who herself led a protest at Charleston 2 years ago.

Some 6,000 U.S. feminists stage a March for Equality up New York's Fifth Avenue from 44th Street to Central Park's 72nd Street Mall August 26 carrying banners with slogans such as "Crush Phallic Imperialism," "Pills for Men," "Woman Power," and "Sisterhood Is Powerful." Mayor John Lindsay proclaims Women's Rights Day, greets the city's first woman police captain, meets for an hour and a half with feminist leaders, some of them in the city government, and reportedly agrees to a "substantial increase" in the number of women in top city jobs.

Two Catholic Belfast women are tarred and feathered November 10 for dating British soldiers.

 U.S. imports top exports by $2.05 billion—the first trade deficit since 1888. President Nixon kills the 10 percent surcharge on imports December 20 and raises the official gold price, thus devaluing the dollar by 8.57 percent.

The average U.S. taxpayer gives the government $400 for defense, $125 to fight the war in Indochina, $40 to build highways, $30 to explore outer space, $315 for health activities ($7 for medical research).

 Cleveland surgeon George Crile tells a Los Angeles conference on breast cancer that his studies have shown no difference in the 5-year survival rate between breast cancer patients who have had radical mastectomies and those who have had "simple" mastectomies in which chest muscles were left intact (70 percent of the women in both groups were alive after 5 years; *see* 1974; Halsted, 1889).

The American College of Obstetricians and Gynecologists gives official approval to nurse-midwives, who deliver fewer than 20,000 babies per year (*see* 1990).

Researchers at the Anderson Tumor Institute in Texas isolate the cold-sore herpesvirus from the lymph cell cancer known as Burkitt's lymphoma. One form of herpesvirus has been associated with the earliest stage of cervical cancer in women (*see* 1960).

Soft contact lenses win FDA approval March 18. Invented in 1962 by Czech technician Otto Wichterle, the $300 lenses are more comfortable than hard lenses, introduced in 1939, but are intended to last only a year.

Malibu, Calif., dancer Jacki Sorensen conducts the first aerobic dance class (*see* Cooper book, 1968). Six women follow Sorensen's instructions in a church basement, dancing aerobically to the sound of rock music, and making fitness a social event rather than a solitary pursuit (*see* 1972).

Cigarette smoking has become a cause of death comparable to the great epidemic diseases typhoid and cholera in the 19th century, says Britain's Royal College of Physicians in a sharply worded report.

U.S. physicians receive an FDA warning in November against prescribing DES (diethylstilbestrol) or related hormones for pregnant women (*see* 1941). Massachusetts General Hospital researchers have concluded that daughters of women who took the synthetic hormone to prevent miscarriage have an increased risk 20 years later of developing clear-cell adenocarcinoma, a rare but tragic form of vaginal cancer (*see* below).

The National Cancer Act signed into law by President Nixon December 24 authorizes appropriations of $1.5 billion per year by the National Cancer Institute to combat America's second leading cause of death; the massive effort will yield few practical results in the next two decades.

Washington journalist Connie (Constance Yu-Hwa) Chung, 24, joins CBS-TV's Washington Bureau, which is recruiting women reporters to make up for past discrimination. Daughter of a Nationalist Chinese diplomat, she will cover Sen. George McGovern's presidential campaign next year as second-string correspondent, broadcasting chiefly on radio, and will later report extensively on the Watergate scandal (*see* 1989).

WNBC-TV in New York makes reporter Norma R. Quarles, 34, co-anchor of its 6 o'clock evening newscast.

The Electric Company debuts in October on U.S. Public Broadcasting Service TV stations. Like *Sesame Street*, it is the product of Joan Ganz Cooney's Children's Television Workshop.

New York City's Consumer Affairs Commissioner Bess Myerson starts a TV program December 6 under the name *What Every Woman Wants to Know*.

Diana Vreeland, now over 70, resigns as editor in chief of *Vogue* (*see* 1962). She will become fashion consultant to the Metropolitan Museum of Art in 1973, beginning with a retrospective show of clothes by Balanciaga from his first collection in 1938 to the wedding dress he will make next year for the granddaughter of Spanish dictator Gen. Francisco Franco.

Nonfiction: *Sex in the Marketplace: American Women at Work* by U.S. economist Juanita Kreps (*née* Morris), 51; *Man's World, Woman's Place: A Study in Social Mythology* by U.S. writer Elizabeth Janeway (*née* Hall) 57; *The Young Woman's Guide to Liberation* by U.S. feminist Karen DeCrow (*née* Meyer), 33; *The Liberated Woman and Other Americans* (essays) by New York writer Midge Decter (*née* Rosenthal), 44; *Just Wait Till You Have Children of Your Own* by Erma Bombeck; *Stillwell and the American Experience in China* by Barbara Tuchman (Pulitzer Prize); *In the Shadow of Man* by English primatologist Jane Van Lawick-Goodall, 38, who was picked by Louis S. B. Leakey in 1957 to study great apes because he believed that women were more patient and perceptive observers than men; *Gateways and Caravans: A Portrait of Turkey* by Freya Stark, now 78, who will be made a dame of the British Empire next year; *Diet for a Small Planet* by U.S. writer Frances Lappé (*née* Moore), 27, who says the Western world is eating too high on the food chain and must eat less meat if the rest of the world is to survive.

Fiction: *Birds of America* by Mary McCarthy; *Lives of Girls and Women* by Alice Munro; *An Experience of India* (stories) by Ruth Prawer Jhabvala; *The Pagan Rabbi, and Other Stories* by Cynthia Ozick; *Queenie* by Hortense Calisher; *By the Next Blue Moon* (*Ved neste nymåne*) by Torborg Nedreaas; *Mrs. Palfrey at the Claremont* by Elizabeth Taylor; *Wandering Soul* (*Yukon*) by Fumiko Enji, now 66, wins Japan's Literature Award; *Any Village* by Faith Baldwin; *The Lathe of Heaven* and *The Tombs of Atuan* by Ursula Le Guin; *Message from Malaga* by Helen MacInnes; *A Rose for Virtue: The Very Private Life of Hortense, Stepdaughter of Napoleon I, Mother of Napoleon III* by Norah Lofts.

Poetry: *The Motorcycle Betrayal Poems* by U.S. poet Diane Wakoski, 34; *A Perfect Circle* by U.S. poet Linda Pastan (*née* Olenik), 39; *It's a New Day: Poems for Young Brothas and Sistuhs* by Sonia Sanchez.

Juvenile: *Then Again, Maybe I Won't* and *Freckle Juice* by Judy Blume.

Painting: *Beer Glass* (oil on canvas) by Elizabeth Murray. Irene Rice Pereira dies of emphysema at Marbella, Spain, January 11 at age 68.

The body of photographer Diane Arbus, now 48, is found in her Westbeth, New York City, apartment July 28; she has taken her own life after a career of photographing other people's traumatic experiences. Margaret Bourke-White dies of Parkinson's disease at her Connecticut home August 27 at age 65.

Theater: Estelle Parsons, Nancy Marchand, and Julie Harris in Paul Zindel's *And Miss Reardon Drinks a Little* 2/25 at New York's Morosco Theater, 108 perfs.; Peter Falk, Lee Grant (originally Lyova Haskell Rosenthal), 39, and Vincent Gardenia in Neil Simon's *The Prisoner of Second Avenue* 11/11 at New York's Eugene O'Neill Theater, 780 perfs.

Television: *All in the Family* 1/12 on CBS with Carroll O'Connor as Archie Bunker in a series devised by Norman Lear, 48. Co-starring Jean Stapleton as Bunker's wife, Edith (he calls her "The Dingbat" but she shows a certain intuitive wisdom and—in a sharp departure from the usual sitcom formulas—will go through menopause), Sally Struthers as his daughter Gloria (who will be the victim of an attempted rape in one episode and will have a miscarriage), and Rob Reiner, the show violates sacrosanct taboos against ethnic and bathroom humor and will break new ground.

Films: Louise Lasser, 30, and Woody Allen in Allen's *Bananas*; Timothy Bottoms, Jeff Bridges, Ben Johnson, Cloris Leachman, Ellen Burstyn, Cybill Shepherd, 21, and Eileen Brennan, 34, in Peter Bogdanovich's *The Last Picture Show*. Also: Aurora Cornu and Jean-Claude Brialy in Eric Rohmer's *Claire's Knee*; Jean-Louis Trintignant, Stefanià Sandrelli, and Dominique Sanda in Bernardo Bertolucci's *The Conformist*; George C. Scott and Diana Rigg in Arthur Hiller's *The Hospital*; Paul Scofield and Irene Worth in Peter Brook's *King Lear*; Jane Fonda as a call girl and Donald Sutherland in Alan J. Pakula's *Klute*; Warren Beatty, Julie Christie, and Shelley Duvall, 22, in Robert Altman's *McCabe and Mrs. Miller*; Lynn Carlin, Buck Henry, and Linnea Heacock in Milos Forman's *Taking Off*; Barbara Loden's *Wanda* with

Loden and Michael Higgins; William Holden, Ryan O'Neal, Karl Malden, and Lynn Carlin in Blake Edwards's *Wild Rovers*.

Opera: Eve Queler conducts her Opera Orchestra in a concert performance of the 1643 Monteverdi opera *L'Incoronazione di Poppea* 2/2 at New York's Alice Tully Hall; Adriana Maliponte makes her Metropolitan Opera debut 3/22 singing the role of Mimi in the 1896 Puccini opera *La Bohème*.

The Society of Women Musicians gives a Diamond Jubilee concert at London's Queen Elizabeth Hall; the group has attained its objectives and will disband next year, using its assets to award prizes to women composers and performers.

Broadway musicals: Yvonne De Carlo, Gene Nelson, Alexis Smith, and Dorothy Collins in *Follies* 4/14 at the Winter Garden Theater, with Stephen Sondheim songs that include "Broadway Baby," 521 perfs.; Raul Julia, Clifton Davis, and Diana Davila in *Two Gentlemen of Verona* 12/1 at the St. James Theater (after 14 performances at the off-Broadway Public Theater), with Galt MacDermot–John Guare songs, 627 perfs.

Popular songs: *Tapestry* (album) by Carole King, now 29, includes her songs "I Feel the Earth Move," "Beautiful," "It's Too Late" and "You've Got a Friend" (it will have sales of more than 13 million copies by 1983); *Blue* (album) by Joni Mitchell; "I Don't Know How to Love Him" by Australian singer-songwriter Helen Reddy, 29; English vocalist Olivia Newton-John, 21, records Bob Dylan's song "If Not for You"; *Gonna Take a Miracle* (album) by Laura Nyro; *Living* (album) by Judy Collins; *Bonnie Raitt* (album) by U.S. singer-guitarist Raitt, 22; "You're Looking at Country" by Loretta Lynn; Dolly Parton records "Coat of Many Colors" and has her biggest hit to date; *We Sure Can Love Each Other* (album), *Greatest Hits Vol. II* (album), and *We Go Together* (album, with husband George Jones, 40) by Tammy Wynette; Barbara Lynn records her song "(Until Then) I'll Suffer"; *Skeeter* (album) and *It's Hard to be a Woman* (album) by Skeeter Davis; Lynn Anderson records "How Can I Unlove You?"; Diana Ross records "Remember Me"; *Fly* (album) by Yoko Ono, whose reggae-style song "Sisters O Sisters" is her first explicitly feminist creation.

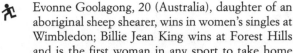

 Evonne Goolagong, 20 (Australia), daughter of an aboriginal sheep shearer, wins in women's singles at Wimbledon; Billie Jean King wins at Forest Hills and is the first woman in any sport to take home more than $100,000 in a single season.

Canada's Prime Minister Pierre Elliott Trudeau, 51, is married March 4 at North Vancouver, B.C., to Margaret Sinclair, 22. Trudeau has dated many women, including actress-singer Barbra Streisand.

President Nixon's elder daughter, Trish (Patricia), 25, is married in the White House Rose Garden (despite a light rain) June 12 to Edward Finch Cox, 24, who was known at Harvard as "Fast Eddie." It is the first outdoor wedding in the 171-year history of the executive mansion.

Belgian-American dress designer Diane Simone Michelle von Furstenberg, 24, opens a one-woman business based on her simple, body-hugging shirt-dress which she will build into a worldwide business marketing not only ready-to-wear clothing but also cosmetics, handbags, scarves, shoes, and sunglasses.

 New York's 400-bed Women's Detention Center is closed June 13 for reasons of overcrowding. Arrests of women for major crimes have increased steeply all over America.

Berkeley, Calif., women organize the Bay Area Women Against Rape in response to discriminatory treatment of rape victims by police departments, hospitals, and courts. Similar groups will spring up across the country in the 1970s.

Food shortages in Chile impel many women to support right-wing military commander Augusto Pinochet's revolt against the socialist Allende regime. The women launch a "March of the Empty Pots" demonstration, Chile's Communist newspaper says the CIA has organized the revolt, and President Salvador Allende announces December 28 that the government will take over food distribution.

 Annual U.S. beef consumption reaches 113 pounds per capita, up from 85.1 pounds in 1960. Consumption will peak at 128.5 pounds in 1976 as Americans eat more than 50 billion hamburgers, paying more than $25 billion for beef in various forms.

The hormone LHRH, isolated by Polish-American biochemist Andrew Schally, 44, is shown to be essential to human ovulation.

Nearly 350 French women declare that they have had abortions and demand that the procedure be legalized. The women include writer Simone de Beauvoir and actresses Catherine Déneuve and Jeanne Moreau (*see* 1972).

The Dalkon Shield, an intrauterine device made by A. H. Robbins, Inc., is introduced for contraception. More than 4 million of the IUDs will be sold by 1975, producing an international outbreak of pelvic infections, miscarriages, congenital birth defects, and maternal deaths (*see* 1974).

An official Chinese document calls in July for a limitation of two children per family. The limit heretofore has been three.

U.S. sales of DES continue to climb, despite the FDA warning against its use by pregnant women (above), as marketers promote use of the steroid as a "morning-after" pill that can prevent implantation of a fertilized egg in the womb.

1972

✗ Denmark's Frederick IX dies January 14 at age 72 after a 25-year reign. He is succeeded by his daughter, 31, who will reign as Margrethe II.

Rep. Shirley Chisholm announces her candidacy for president of the United States January 25, becoming the first black to run for the nation's highest office.

Seven nuns are arrested in an antiwar protest at New York's St. Patrick's Cathedral April 30.

Congresswoman Bella Abzug (D., N.Y.) introduces a resolution May 9 calling for the impeachment of President Nixon following his decision to mine North Vietnamese harbors.

Colorado voters elect Denver lawyer and teacher Patricia Schroeder (*née* Scott), 42, to the U.S. House of Representatives, where she will serve for more than 20 years.

Barbara Jordan wins election to the U.S. House of Representatives, where she will serve her Texas

Shirley Chisholm was the first black woman elected to Congress. She even had presidential ambitions. CHIE NISHIO

congressional district for three terms. She is the first black woman ever to be elected to Congress from a southern state.

California voters elect East Los Angeles lawyer Yvonne Braithwaite Burke, 40, to the House of Representatives, where she will serve three terms. She is the first woman sent to Congress by California in 20 years and the first black woman ever.

 The Equal Opportunity Commission (EOC) receives enforcement powers in March and begins taking noncomplying companies to court. An EOC report says that America's largest employer of women—American Telephone & Telegraph, its subsidiaries, and 24 operating companies nationwide—is also "without doubt the largest oppressor of women workers in the United States." It will compel AT&T to give $38 million in back pay to women and minorities.

The U.S. Senate votes 84 to 8 March 22 to submit an Equal Rights Amendment to the states for ratification: "Equality of rights under the law shall not be denied or abridged by the United States or by any State on account of sex." Rep. Martha Griffiths (*née* Wright), 60 (D., Mich.), is credited with having devised the strategy that got the proposed amendment out of committee. Hawaii is the first state to ratify; getting enough other states to join will prove difficult.

Capital punishment is unconstitutional, the U.S. Supreme Court rules in a 5-to-4 decision handed down June 29 in *Furman* v. *Georgia*, a case involving a convicted black rapist sentenced to death. The ruling that the death penalty represents "cruel and unusual punishment" spares 600 men and women on Death Row, and brings the United States into line with 37 other countries (in Europe, only France and Spain still have legal execution). The record will show that capital punishment does not deter violent crime, but later Court decisions will permit executions under some circumstances.

The National Welfare Rights Organization founded by former U.S. "welfare mother" Johnnie Tillmon, 46, mobilizes people and resources to focus attention on the multi-layered inequities of the nation's welfare system, which is encouraging the real and fraudulent breakup of marriages when men cannot support their wives and children.

The Pink Panthers movement, founded by Japanese pharmacist Misako Enoki, 33, will hold sit-ins and protest rallies, focus on women's rights to abortion, equal hiring, equal pay, equitable property settlements and alimony, and easier access to contraceptive pills, which in Japan can be dispensed only as medicine, not as birth control aids, and only by doctors, most of whom are men. Members of the radical feminist group wear white military uniforms with pink helmets and will grow to number 4,000 (but *see* 1977).

Israeli women reject "women's lib," according to a poll conducted by Hebrew University sociologists, who interview hundreds of women in Jerusalem and Tel Aviv. Nearly two-thirds favor a large family, 75 percent think being "a good mother and a good homemaker" is woman's most noble goal, only 8 percent favor married women holding jobs outside the home "as a means of self-expression," and fewer than 5 percent consider sexual attraction sufficient reason for going to bed with a man. "Women's lib is just a lot of foolishness," Prime Minister Golda Meir tells a group of visiting U.S. women. "It's the men who are discriminated against. They can't bear children. And no one's likely to do anything about it." But thousands of Israeli women whose marriages have failed are unable to obtain legal divorces because a wife may not be granted a divorce without her husband's consent, and ultra-Orthodox parties block any change in the law.

Golda Meir was effective as Israel's prime minister for 5 years but had no use for "women's liberation." LIBRARY OF CONGRESS

Women's Aid is founded at London by Erin Pizzey to protect battered women. The support group will outgrow its tiny house in the residential suburb of Chiswick and move in 1974 into a rambling Victorian mansion where abused women can receive shelter, legal help, and time to sort out their problems.

Australia orders equal pay for women December 15.

English astronomer (Eleanor) Margaret Burbidge (*née* Beachey), 45, is named director of the Royal Greenwich Observatory, the first woman to hold the position. Burbidge went to America in 1955 and, together with her husband, Geoffrey, and two other men, showed in 1956 how heavier elements could be built up from lighter elements in the interiors of stars.

A new Surgeon General's Report on smoking issued January 10 warns that nonsmokers exposed to cigarette smoke may suffer health hazards (*see* 1964). Later evidence will show that carbon monoxide and other toxins in "sidestream" smoke actually present greater perils to nonsmokers than to smokers, bringing new pressure to protect airline passengers (and flight attendants), office workers, and others from the minority whose cigarette smoke threatens their health and comfort.

Aerobics for Women by aerobics pioneer Dr. Kenneth Cooper and his wife, Millie, begins with Millie's statement "I sit here now thinking about what aerobics has done for me in terms of my figure (dress size down to size 8 from size 12), my weight (down 10 to 12 pounds), my energy and sense of well-being, the luxury of being able to eat what I please without worrying about calories, and my freedom from tension and insomnia, and I feel rather smug" (*see* 1968).

The U.S. Navy appoints its first woman admiral June 1. She is Navy Nurse Corps director Alene B. Duerck, who was commissioned an ensign in 1943, remained on active duty until 1946, and was recalled during the Korean war. She directs nursing at 39 naval hospitals and a number of dispensaries.

Work by Edinburgh researchers on alpha-feto protein (AFP) provides a means of testing amniotic fluid from pregnant women for the presence of anencephaly defects, in which the fetal brain fails to develop, or spina bifida (divided spine). If AFP results indicate a high level of risk, the woman can be referred for amniocentesis or further testing.

Boston hospital pharmacist Jane Hirsh (*née* Iorio), 32, founds Copley Pharmaceutical, Inc., with her brother Theodore. Wanting to raise a family and needing a job where she can have a crib in her office, she starts a company that she will move into generic drugs beginning in 1984 and in 1993 sell a 51 percent interest to a German company for $546 million in cash.

Sally J. Priesand, 26, is ordained as full-time rabbi at the Monmouth Reform Temple in Tinton Falls, N.J., becoming the first American woman rabbi. By the end of 1981 there will be 35 women rabbis (out of 1,325), and roughly one-third of all Reform rabbinical students will be women, but Orthodox and Conservative Jewry will resist women's ordination.

The Anglican church ordains its first two women priests November 28.

Five Oxford colleges agree April 28 to break 750 years of tradition and admit women. Other Oxford colleges have had women students since the 1920s, and there have been women's colleges at Oxford since the founding of Somerville in 1879.

Title IX of the Higher Education Act signed into law by President Nixon June 23 bans sex bias in athletics and other activities at all educational institutions receiving federal aid.

Jacqueline Onassis asks a federal court March 6 for an injunction against freelance photographer Ronald E. Galella, who has sued her for $1.3 million, saying that she is interfering with his livelihood. A judge in Washington issues an order July 5 barring Galella from going near Mrs. Onassis, whom he has allegedly called "Jackie" and "Baby," while "lunging" at her to get shots of her outside her Fifth Avenue, New York, apartment building, in a theater, seeing friends, shopping, or riding a bicycle with her son, John F. Kennedy, Jr.

Ms. magazine begins publication in July with former *Look* editor Patricia Carbine as publisher, feminist writer Gloria Steinem, now 38, as editor. A Spring preview issue has carried a column headed "What's a Ms.?" and answered it: "For more than 20 years, 'Ms.' has appeared in secretarial handbooks as the suggested form of address when a woman's marital status is unknown, a sort of neutral combination of 'Miss' and 'Mrs.' Now 'Ms.' is being adopted as a standard form of address by women who want to be recognized as individuals, rather than being identified by their relationship with a man. After all, if 'Mr.' is enough to identify 'male,' then 'Ms.' should be enough to identify 'female'! . . . The use of 'Ms.' isn't meant to protect either the married or the unmarried woman from social pressure—only to signify a female human being. It's symbolic and important. There's a lot in a name" (see *New York Times*, 1974).

Spare Rib magazine begins publication at London to give British feminists a new voice.

Washington Post reporter Carl Bernstein phones Attorney General John Mitchell September 28 to say that his paper is about to publish a story on the June 17 break-in at the Watergate apartment complex and is told, "All that crap, you're putting it in the paper? It's all been denied. Katie Graham [*Post* publisher Katharine Meyer Graham, 54] is gonna get her tit caught in a big fat wringer if that's published."

Nonfiction: *The Descent of Woman* by Welsh feminist Elaine (Neville) Morgan (*née* Floyd), 51: "The rumblings of women's liberation are only one pointer to the fact that you already have a discontented work force. And if conditions continue to lag so far behind the industrial norm and the discomfort increases, you will find . . . that you will end up with an inferior product"; *Born Female: The High Cost of Keeping Women Down* by New York writer Caroline Bird (*née* Mahoney), 57; *Women and Madness* and *Wonder Woman* by New York psychiatrist Phyllis Chesler, 31; "Witches, Midwives and Nurses: A History of Women Healers" (pamphlet) by U.S. writers Barbara Ehrenreich (*née* Alexander), 31, and Deirdre English; *Women's Estate* by Juliet Mitchel; *Bella! Ms. Abzug Goes to Washington* (autobiography) by Congresswoman Abzug (above); *Herself: An Autobiographical Work* by novelist Hortense Calisher. *The New Portuguese Letters* by Maria Isabel Barreno, Maria Teresa Horta, and Maria Velho da Costa, all of whom are arrested by authorities on charges of "abuse of the freedom of the press" and outraging public decency. The book is banned and all copies confiscated. Court proceedings begin in October under provisions of a new law making writers, publishers, printers, and distributors legally responsible for the morality of works they put before the public (*see* 1974). *The New 100 Years War* by Georgie Anne Geyer; *Hawaii: The Sugar-coated Fortress* by Francine du Plessix Gray; *Only One Earth—The Care and Maintenance of a Small Planet* by Barbara Ward, now 68, who will be made a life peer in 1976.

Fiction: *The Persian Boy* by Mary Renault; *The Needle's Eye* by Margaret Drabble, who divorces the father of her three children; *An Accidental Man* by Iris Murdoch; *In the Ditch* by Nigerian-born British novelist (Florence Onye) Buchi Emecheta, 28, who explores man's cruelty to woman; *A Memory and*

Other Stories by Mary Lavin; *Harriet Said* by Beryl Bainbridge; *The Optimist's Daughter* by Eudora Welty (Pulitzer Prize); *Long Division* by Anne Richardson Roiphe is about a wife and mother who has been deserted by her husband; *Do You Hear Them?* (*Vous les entendez?*) by Nathalie Sarraute; *The Castaways* by English novelist Sheila Fugard (*née* Meiring), 40, who married South African playwright Athol Fugard in 1956; *The Story of a Non-Marrying Man* by Doris Lessing; *The Human Trap* (*Ningen no wana*) by Ayako Sono; *How She Died* by U.S. novelist Helen Yglesias (*née* Bassine), 57; *Nobody's Business* (stories) by Penelope Gilliatt; *Cat-o-Nine-Deaths* by Argentine novelist Luisa Valenzuela, 33; *The Other Woman* by Rona Jaffe; *Standard Dreaming* by Hortense Calisher; *Glass People* by Gail Godwin; *Odd Girl Out* by Elizabeth Howard; *The Glory of Hera* by Caroline Gordon, now 76; *The Farthest Shore* by Ursula Le Guin; *All Visitors Must Be Announced* by New York advertising copywriter turned novelist Helen Van Slyke, 53; *Sheila Levine Is Dead and Living in New York* by U.S. novelist Gail Parent (*née* Kostner), 32; *The Flowering* by Agnes Turnbull; *One More Time* by Faith Baldwin; *The Flame and the Flower* by U.S. novelist Kathleen (Erin) Woodiwiss (*née* Wingrove), 33, pioneers the bodice-ripping erotic historical novel; *Memoirs of an Ex–Prom Queen* by U.S. novelist Alix Kates Shulman, 40.

Poetry: *Monster: Poems* by U.S. poet Robin Morgan, 31; *Up Country: Poems of New England* by Maxine Kumin (Pulitzer Prize); *Footprints* by Denise Levertov; *My House* and *The Women and the Men* by Nikki Giovanni.

Juvenile: *Tales of a Fourth-Grade Nothing*, *It's Not the End of the World*, and *Otherwise Known as Sheila the Great* by Judy Blume; *Till the Break of Day* (autobiography) by Maia Wojciechowska; *Freaky Friday* by composer-author Mary Rodgers; *William's Doll* by Charlotte Zolotow.

Painting: *Madame Cézanne in Rocking Chair* by Eizabeth Murray.

Theater: Diana Rigg and Michael Hordern in Tom Stoppard's *Jumpers* 2/2 at London's National Theatre (Old Vic); Elizabeth Wilson and Tom Aldridge in David Rabe's *Sticks and Bones* 3/1 at New York's John Golden Theater (after 121 perfs. at the off-

1972

Broadway Public Theater), 366 perfs. (total); Jane Alexander and Jerry Orbach in Bob Randall's *6 Rooms Riv Vu* 10/17 at New York's Helen Hayes Theater, 247 perfs.

Television: *The Waltons* 9/13 on CBS with Richard Thomas, actress Michael Learned, 33, Ralph Waite, Will Geer, and Ellen Corby (*née* Hansen), 59 (to 8/13/1981).

Films: Fernando Rey, Delphine Seyrig, Stéphane Audran (Colette Stéphane Jeanmaire Dacheville), 39, and Bulle Ogier in Luis Buñuel's *The Discreet Charm of the Bourgeoisie*; Cicely Tyson, Paul Winfield, and Kevin Hooks in Martin Ritt's *Sounder*. Also: Harriet Andersson, Liv Ullmann, and Ingrid Thulin in Ingmar Bergman's *Cries and Whispers*; Alan Bates and Janet Suzman in Peter Medak's *A Day in the Death of Joe Egg*; Linda Lovelace (Linda Boreman) in Gerard Damiano's pornographic *Deep Throat*; Marlon Brando, Al Pacino, James Caan, and Diane Keaton, 23, in Francis Ford Coppola's *The Godfather*; Geraldine Page and Cliff Robertson in Robertson's *J. W. Coop*; Jack Nicholson, Bruce Dern, and Ellen Burstyn in Bob Rafelson's *The King of Marvin Gardens*; Diane Keaton and Woody Allen in Herbert Ross's *Play It Again, Sam*; Robert Duvall and Olga Bellin in Joseph Anthony's *Tomorrow*.

Hollywood musicals: Liza Minnelli, Michael York, and Joel Grey in Bob Fosse's *Cabaret*; Diana Ross in Sidney J. Furie's *Lady Sings the Blues* (a distorted biography of the late jazz-blues singer Billie Holiday, who died in July 1959 at age 44).

Broadway musical: Micki Grant (*née* Minnie Perkins McCutcheon), 30, in *Don't Bother Me, I Can't Cope* 4/19 at the Playhouse, with music and lyrics based on ballads, calypso songs, and gospel music, 1,065 perfs.

Popular songs: "I Am Woman" by Helen Reddy; *Some Time in New York City* (album) by Yoko Ono and John Lennon includes their song "Woman Is the Nigger of the World"; *Anticipation* (album) by U.S. rock singer-composer Carly Simon, 27; *The Divine Miss M* (album) by U.S. singer-comedienne Bette Midler, 26; Gladys Knight and the Pips record "Help Me Make It Through the Night"; Skeeter Davis records "One Tin Soldier"; "Neither One of Us (Wants to Be the First to Say Goodbye)"

by Gladys Knight and the Pips; *Lady Sings the Blues* (album) by U.S. singer Linda Ronstadt; *Linda Ronstadt* (album) has a backup group that will evolve into the Eagles; Olivia Newton-John records George Harrison's song "What Is Life?"; *Tammy's Bedtime Story* (album), "My Man," *Me and the First Lady* (album, with husband George Jones), and "This Cere-Money" (with Jones) by Tammy Wynette; U.S. soul singer-songwriter Milly Jackson records "A Child of God" and "Ask Me What You Want"; Roberta Flack scores a hit with "The First Time Ever I Saw Your Face"; *It Is Finished* (album) by Nina Simone.

Opera: *Time Off? Not a Ghost of a Chance!* 3/1 at the Sadler's Wells Theatre, London, with music and libretto by Elisabeth Lutyens.

Long Island City, N.Y., runner Nina Kuscsik wins the first women's competition in the 76th annual Boston Marathon April 17 in 3 hours, 8 minutes, 58 seconds.

Austrian figure skater Beatrix Schuba wins her event at the winter Olympics at Sapporo, Japan; Swiss skier Marie-Thérèse Nadig wins the downhill in 1 minute, 36.68 seconds, U.S. skier Barbara Cochran wins the slalom in 1 minute, 31.24 seconds, Nadig the giant slalom in 1 minute, 29.90 seconds. East German runner Renate Stecher wins the 100-meter dash 11.07 seconds and the 200-meter in 22.4 seconds at the summer Olympics in Munich, East German runner Monika Zehrt the 400-meter in 51.08 seconds, West German runner Hildegarde Falck the 800-meter run in 1 minute, 58.6 seconds, Soviet runner Ludmila Bragina the 1,500-meter in 4 minutes, 1.4 seconds, West German athlete Ulrike Meyfarth the running high jump (6 feet, 3⅜ inches), West German athlete Heidemarie Rosendahl the long jump (22 feet, 3 inches), Soviet athlete Nadezhda Chizhova the shot put (69 feet), Soviet athlete Faina Melnik the discus throw (218 feet, 7 inches), East German athlete Ruth Fuchs the javelin throw (209 feet, 7 inches), British athlete Mary Peters the pentathlon. Soviet gymnast Olga Korbut, 17, wins three gold medals, Soviet gymnast Ludmila Turischeva, 20, wins two gold medals. U.S. swimmer Sandra Neilson wins the 100-meter freestyle in 58.59 seconds, Australian swimmer Shane Gould the 200-meter in 2 minutes, 3.56 seconds and the 400-meter in 4 minutes, 19.04 seconds, U.S. swimmer Keena Rothhammer the 800-meter in 8 minutes, 53.68 seconds, U.S. swimmer Melissa Belote the 100-meter backstroke in 1 minute, 5.78 seconds and the 200-meter in 2 minutes, 19.19 seconds, U.S. swimmer Catherine Carr the 100-meter breaststroke in 13.58 seconds, Australian swimmer Beverly Whitfield the 200-meter in 2 minutes, 41.71 seconds, Japanese swimmer Mayumi Aoki the 100-meter butterfly in 1 minute, 3.34 seconds, U.S. swimmer Karen Moe the 200-meter in 2 minutes 15.57 seconds, Shane Gould the 200-meter individual medley in 2 minutes, 23.07 seconds, Australian swimmer Gail Neall the 400-meter in 5 minutes, 2.97 seconds, U.S. swimmer Micki King the springboard dive event, Swedish swimmer Ulrika Knape the platform dive.

British rower Sylvia Cook, 21, and her companion, John Fairfax, 33, arrive at Hayman Island off Australia April 22 with blistered hands after having rowed 8,000 miles across the Pacific from San Francisco in a $5,000 rowboat.

Billie Jean King wins in women's singles at both Wimbledon and Forest Hills.

The Dallas Cowboys football team introduces the first professional cheerleaders—seven scantily clad women with full figures who attract far more attention than the high school girls who previously cavorted at Cowboys games. Texas writer Molly Ivins, now 28, will write in the *Progressive*, "There's no denying that what those girls do is dress up in costumes that would do credit to a strip-tease artiste and then prance about in front of hundreds of people shaking their bums and jiggling their tits."

Angela Davis is tried on charges of having helped the Soledad Brothers shoot their way out of a San Rafael, Calif., courtroom in 1970, but an all-white jury at San Jose acquits her June 4.

The first rape crisis centers open at Ann Arbor, Mich., Los Angeles, and Washington, D.C., under the aegis of the National Institute of Justice Law Enforcement Assistance Administration.

An amendment to the School Lunch Act signed into law by President Nixon September 26 (PL 92433) establishes a Women, Infants and Children (WIC) program to improve diets in the nation's most nutritionally vulnerable population group.

A Massachusetts law prohibiting sale or dispensing of contraceptives to single persons is unconstitutional, the Supreme Court rules March 22.

A Los Angeles woman who fits diaphragms is charged with practicing without a license.

The National Center for Health Statistics reports May 23 that the U.S. birthrate has fallen to 15.8 per 1,000—the lowest since the survey began in 1917.

Ms. magazine (above) carries an advertisement headlined "We have had abortions." It is signed by women who include Eve Auchincloss, Lorraine Beebe, Patricia Bosworth, Kay Boyle, Susan Brownmiller, Hortense Calisher, Lucinda Cisler, Shirley Clarke, Judy Collins, Mary Cunningham, Karen DeCrow, Barbralee D. Diamonstein, Susan Edmiston, Nora Ephron, Lee Grant, Gail Greene, Lillian Hellman, Elizabeth Janeway, Lucy Jarvis, Billie Jean King, Maxine Kumin, Viveca Lindfors, Marya Mannes, Anaïs Nin, Grace Paley, Eleanor Perry, Letty Pogrebin, Mary Rodgers, Nora Sayre, Ann Sexton, Susan Sontag, Gloria Steinem, and Barbara W. Tuchman.

French teenager Marie-Claire Chevalier, who became pregnant at 16, goes on trial in October on charges of having had an illegal abortion (*see* 1971). Giselle Halami, a lawyer who has founded the abortion rights journal *Choisir*, argues that the law against abortions is enforced mainly against women of the lower classes, and the girl is acquitted. Her mother, Michèle, 38, has supported her decision to seek an abortion and is tried as an accomplice. Prominent actresses and writers who include Simone de Beauvoir testify that they, too, have had abortions but have never been bothered by the police. Michèle Chevalier pays a small fine, and within weeks doctors are performing free abortions in major cities.

1973

A cease-fire in Vietnam January 28 ends direct involvement of U.S. ground forces in Indochinese hostilities. America's combat death toll has reached 45,958.

Last year's Watergate break-in creates a national scandal. Martha Mitchell, wife of the attorney general, tells reporters April 16 that President Nixon's claim that he did not meet with Attorney General Mitchell was a "god-blessed lie." Katharine Graham's *Washington Post* wins a Pulitzer Prize for public service May 7 in recognition of its Watergate stories. Nixon's secretary, Rose Mary Woods, testifies November 26 that she had, through a "terrible mistake," pressed the wrong button on her tape recorder October 1, 1972, and caused an 18-minute gap in a conversation between Nixon and his aide H. R. Haldeman 3 days after the break-in.

Chile's President Salvador Allende Gossens is ousted in a military coup September 11. Police say he has committed suicide; his wife insists he has been murdered. "We often heard the [U.S.] State Department did not want Allende in power," she says. "Financial interests always predominate."

The newspaper *Asahi Shimbun* honors feminist Fusae Ichikawa, now 78, in January for her contributions to the progress of women in Japan (*see* 1945). She has refused a medal that Emperor Hirohito wanted to confer upon her (*see* 1980).

Jordan grants women the right to vote on the same basis as men.

U.S. lawyer Marion Wright Edelman, 34, founds the Children's Defense Fund, an advocacy group to which she can bring experience gained as director of the NAACP Legal Defense and Education Fund.

COYOTE (an acronym for Call Off Your Old Tired Ethics) is founded at San Francisco by prostitutes, ex-prostitutes, lawyers, and service organizations to seek legalization of prostitution, protect prostitutes against arrest, and give those who are arrested proper legal representation. President of the new organization is Margot St. James.

Anita Loos, now 82, is quoted in the *Observer* December 30 as having said, "I'm furious about the Women's Liberationists. They keep getting up on soapboxes and proclaiming that women are brighter than men. That's true, but it should be kept very quiet or it ruins the whole racket."

Washington State politician Dixy Lee Ray, 58, is named head of the Atomic Energy Commission in February following the resignation of James Schlesinger, who becomes head of the CIA. Ray has urged expansion of nuclear power, consumer activist Ralph Nader calls her "Ms. Plutonium," and many environmentalists oppose her.

The U.S. Public Health Service announces January 17 that studies have linked smoking to increased risk of fetal and infant abnormalities.

The FDA announces April 1 that it will recall diet drugs containing amphetamines.

Nonfiction: *Our Bodies, Our Selves: A Course by and for Women* by the Boston Women's Health Collective; "Complaints and Disorders: The Sexual Politics of Sickness" (pamphlet) by Barbara Ehrenreich and Deirdre English; *Beyond God the Father* by Mary Daly, who has given up trying to reform Roman Catholic attitudes and become a radical feminist; *A Different Woman* by Jane Howard; *Hustling: Prostitution in Our Wide-Open Society* by Gail Sheehy; *The New Chastity and Other Arguments Against Women's Liberation* by Midge Decter; *The Female Woman* by Greek-born London journalist Arianna Huffington (*née* Stassinopoulos), 23, who draws fire from Germaine Greer by saying that the women's movement denies or ignores the longings of millions of women for intimacy, children, and a family (Huffington wrote her book soon after graduation from Cambridge, where she was only the third woman to head the university debating society, the Cambridge Union); *Fire in the Lake: The Vietnamese and Americans in Vietnam* by U.S. journalist Frances FitzGerald, 33 (Pulitzer Prize); *Pentimento* (autobiography) by Lillian Hellman; *Kind and Usual Punishment: The Prison Business* by Jessica Mitford; *Food in History* by English writer Reay Tannahill, 43; *Small Talk* (memoir) by Naomi Mitchison, now 76, who has lived since 1937 in Carradale on the Mull of Kintyre, Scotland; *I Lost Everything in the Post-Natal Depression* by Erma Bombeck.

Fiction: *Fear of Flying* by U.S. novelist Erica Jong, 31; *Caro Michele* (*Dear Michael*, or *No Way*) by Natalia Ginzburg; *The Black Prince* by Iris Murdoch; *The Dressmaker* (in America, *The Secret Glass*) by Beryl Bainbridge; *Do with Me What You Will* by Joyce Carol Oates; *Sula* by Toni Morrison; *Rubyfruit Jungle* by U.S. writer Rita Mae Brown, 28; *Eagle Eye* by Hortense Calisher; *Once Is Not*

Enough by Jacqueline Susann, who will die of cancer next September at age 53; *No Bed of Roses* by Faith Baldwin; *The Hollow Hills* by Mary Stewart; *Going Home* by San Francisco advertising copywriter-turned-novelist Danielle Fernande Steel, 26, who will churn out best-selling romances at a dazzling rate; *The Time of the Crack* by Emma Tennant; *Death Camp* by June Thompson.

Poetry: *Diving into the Wreck: Poems, 1971–1972* by Adrienne Rich; *To Be of Use* by U.S. poet-novelist Marge Piercy, 37; *Half Lives* by Erica Jong (above); *Alive* by Judith Wright, now 58; *Ego-Tripping and Other Poems for Young People* by Nikki Giovanni.

Juvenile: *The Ghost of Thomas Kempe* by English novelist Penelope (Margaret) Lively (*née* Low), 40; *The Summer of My German Soldier* by U .S. author Bette Greene, 39; *Deenie* by Judy Blume; *The Eighteenth Emergency* by Betsy Cromer Byars.

Painting: *Wave Painting* by Elizabeth Murray.

Theater: *Finishing Touches* by Jean Kerr 2/8 at New York's Plymouth Theater, with Barbara Bel Geddes and Robert Lansing, 164 perfs.; Richard Biers and Sheila Hancock in Alan Ayckbourn's *Absurd Person Singular* 7/4 at London's Criterion Theatre; Christopher Plummer and Marsha Mason, 31, in Neil Simon's *The Good Doctor* 11/27 at New York's Eugene O'Neill Theater, 208 perfs.

Films: Malcolm McDowell and Welsh actress Rachel Roberts, 40, in Lindsay Anderson's *O Lucky Man!*; Ryan O'Neal, Tatum O'Neal, 9, and Madeline Kahn, 30, in Peter Bogdanovich's *Paper Moon*; Liv Ullmann, Erland Josephson, and Bibi Andersson in Ingmar Bergman's *Scenes from a Marriage*. Also: Richard Dreyfuss and Candy Clark in George Lucas's *American Graffiti*; Jacqueline Bisset, Jean-Pierre Aumont, and François Truffaut in Truffaut's *Day for Night*; Ellen Burstyn, Max von Sydow, and Linda Blair, 14, in William Friedkin's *The Exorcist*; Keith Mitchell, Donald Pleasence, and Charlotte Rampling in Waris Hussein's *Henry VIII and His Six Wives*; Robert Shaw and English actress Sarah Miles, 29, in Alan Bridges' *The Hireling*; Marlon Brando and Maria Schneider in Bernardo Bertolucci's *Last Tango in Paris*; Max von Sydow and Liv Ullmann in Jan Troell's *The New Land*; Tim-

othy Bottoms, Lindsay Wagner, 24, and John Houseman in James Bridges' *The Paper Chase*; Fernando Fernán Gómez and Teresa Gimpera in Victor Erice's *Spirit of the Beehive*; Edward Woodward, Christopher Lee, and Swedish actress Britt Ekland (Britt-Marie Eklund), 31, in Robin Hardy's *The Wicker Man*; Janet Margolin, Beau Bridges, and Ron Leibman in Douglas N. Schwarz's *Your Three Minutes Are Up*.

Veronica Lake dies of acute hepatitis July 7 at age 53 in a Burlington, Vt., hospital. She appeared in 26 pictures before alcoholism ended her career and obliged her to take work as a New York hotel barmaid.

Ballet: Choreographer Dame Marie Rambert (she was made a dame of the British Empire in 1962), now 84, is quoted in the February issue of *Dancemagazine* as saying, "I don't do cartwheels any more, but I still do a *barre* to keep supple" (*see* 1913).

Broadway and off-Broadway musicals: Len Cariou, Hermione Gingold, and Glynis Johns in *A Little Night Music* 2/25 at the Shubert Theater, with Stephen Sondheim songs that include "Send in the Clowns," 600 perfs.; Michele Lee in *Seesaw* 3/18 at the Uris Theater, with Cy Coleman–Dorothy Fields songs, 296 perfs.; Ernestine Jackson and Joe Morton in *Raisin* 10/18 at the 46th Street Theater, with a book from the 1959 Lorraine Hansberry play *Raisin in the Sun*, Judd Woldon–Robert Britten songs, 847 perfs.

Popular songs: *Approximately Infinite Universe* (album) by Yoko Ono includes "What a Bastard the World Is" (about the inequality of female/male relationships) and "I Have a Woman Inside My Soul" about the repression of feelings for the sake of appearance; Olivia Newton-John records John Denver's song "Take Me Home, Country Roads"; *True Stories and Other Dreams* (album) by Judy Collins includes songs of her own composition; *No Secrets* (album) by Carly Simon; "Leave Me Alone" by Helen Reddy; "Touch Me in the Morning" by Diana Ross; *Don't Cry Now* (album) by Linda Ronstadt; *Imagination* (album) by Gladys Knight and the Pips includes "Midnight Train to Georgia," "I've Got to Use My Imagination," and "Neither One of Us (Wants to Be the First to Say Goodbye)"; *It Don't Mean a Thing If It Ain't Got That Swing* (album) by Teresa Brewer (with Duke Ellington and His Orchestra); Skeeter Davis records "Don't Forget to Remember"; Dolly Parton records "Jolene"; Anne Murray records "Denny's Song" and "Send a Little Love My Way"; Milly Jackson records "Hurts So Good"; Roberta Flack records "Killing Me Softly with His Song" and Janis Ian's "Jesse."

Jockey Robin Smith rides Alfred Gwynn Vanderbilt's 4-year-old colt North Sea to victory in a 6-horse field March 1 in the $27,450 Paumanok Handicap at New York's Aqueduct Raceway, becoming the first woman jockey to win a U.S. stakes race.

Swimmer Lynne Cox swims the English Channel in 9 hours, 36 minutes—a new world record for both women and men.

Billie Jean King wins in women's singles at Wimbledon, Margaret Court at Forest Hills. The United States Tennis Association has announced July 19 that the U.S. Open will award equal prize money to women and men.

A tennis match promoted as the "battle of the sexes" ends in defeat for former Wimbledon champion Bobby Riggs, now 55, who loses 6-4, 6-3, 6-3 to Billie Jean King September 20 at the Houston Astrodome.

U.S. textile mills produce 482 million square yards of cotton denim, up from 437 million in 1971. The figure will soar to 820 million by 1976 as demand booms for blue jeans and denim jackets.

The U.S. median sales price of an existing single-family house reaches $28,900, up from $20,000 in 1968. By 1976 the price will be $38,100.

Nutrition labeling regulations promulgated by the Food and Drug Administration standardize the type of information to be presented on U.S. food packages.

A committee formed in 1970 by U.S. grocers and manufacturers to improve productivity issue a recommendation in April for a Universal Product Code (UPC) design for all supermarket items. The package code is designed to permit electronic scanners at check-out counters to "read" the price of

The Universal Product Code and electronic scanners began to shorten check-out lines at U.S. supermarkets.

each item and trigger a computer that will record the price automatically, thus eliminating checker error and facilitating inventory control. Retailers balk at installing the costly equipment needed, consumers will protest elimination of individually marked prices, but use of the scanners will grow rapidly in the 1980s.

Food prices soar in the United States, Japan, and Europe in the wake of last year's Soviet wheat and soybean purchases, which have forced up the price of feed grains and consequently of meat, poultry, eggs, and dairy products as well as of baked goods. U.S. consumer groups organize boycotts to protest rising prices, but prices will continue to rise.

President Nixon orders a freeze on all retail food prices June 13, saying he will "not let foreign sales price meat and eggs off the American table."

The Supreme Court rules 7 to 2 January 22 in *Roe* v. *Wade* that abortion should be a decision between a woman and her physician. A married pregnant woman was allowed to bring her case under the name "Jane Roe" against a Florida district attorney. Justice Harry A. Blackmun, who writes the majority opinion, notes that the Constitution does not explicitly mention any right of privacy, and he rejects the argument that a woman has an absolute right "to terminate her pregnancy at whatever time, in whatever way, and for whatever reason she alone chooses," but he says that in the first 3 months of pregnancy the decision to have an abortion lies with the woman and her doctor, and the state's interest in her welfare is not "compelling" enough to warrant any interference. For the next 3 months of pregnancy a state may "regulate the abortion procedure in ways that are reasonably related to maternal health," such as licensing and regulating the facilities involved. For the last 10 weeks of pregnancy, a period during which the fetus is judged to be capable of surviving if born, any state may prohibit abortion if it wishes. Justices Rehnquist and White dissent. Cardinal Cook of New York calls the Court's action "shocking" and "horrifying." Cardinal Krol of Philadelphia calls it an "unspeakable tragedy for this nation." Alan F. Gutmacher, president of the Planned Parenthood Federation of America, calls the decision "a wise and courageous stroke for the right to privacy and for the protection of a woman's physical and emotional health." Most states are obliged to rewrite their antiabortion statutes to reflect the ruling. "Right-to-life" groups work to undermine the ruling.

"Abortion is a woman's choice" vs. "Abortion is murder": It was an argument neither side could win. CHIE NISHIO

A French physician is arrested on charges of having performed an illegal abortion (*see* 1972); 10,000 people take part in a march to urge repeal of the abortion law, and legislation to legalize abortion is introduced in the Parlement (*see* 1974).

IUD insertions in China increase to 14 million, up from 6 million 2 years ago, as birth control efforts increase, but population growth continues at a rapid rate (*see* 1976).

1974

 Vietnamese women at Saigon observe International Women's Day March 8 by demonstrating against the government.

Golda Meir wins reelection as Israel's prime minister March 10 but resigns a month later, citing schisms within her own Labor party with regard to military planning errors.

Argentine dictator Juan Perón dies July 1 at age 78. His vice president and third wife, María Estela (Isabel) Martínez Perón, 43, becomes the hemisphere's first woman chief of state (*see* 1976).

Black Panther co-founder Huey Newton flees to Cuba after being accused of killing a 17-year-old Oakland prostitute (he will ultimately be acquitted). He names his lover, Elaine Brown, 31, as the new leader of the party; she joined the Panthers in 1968 and will head it until 1977.

President Nixon admits August 5 that he ordered a cover-up of the Watergate break-in for political reasons as well as those of national security. He resigns 3 days later to avoid impeachment, the first president ever to quit office. Vice President Gerald R. Ford is sworn in as president, and he grants Nixon a pardon.

Connecticut voters elect former Secretary of State Mrs. Ella Grasso (*née* Tambussi), 55, to the governorship. The first woman to gain a state governorship in her own right (*see* "Ma" Ferguson, 1917; 1924), she will chair the Governors' Commission on the Status of Women.

Greek parliamentary elections in November see 34 women candidates vying for seats in the 300-member body. Two women won seats in the last election, in 1964, but although Greek women have an activist tradition that dates to ancient times, a network of laws continues to keep the institution of male supremacy intact: a woman still needs a dowry to get married because she is considered a burden on her husband, and a woman must obey the man who heads the household.

Militant radical Jane Alpert, now 29, gives herself up November 14, 4 years after jumping bail in connection with 1969 bombings in New York. An article by Alpert in *Ms.* magazine last year urged women to renounce left-wing policies, break from such "male supremacist" groups as the Weathermen, and "work for ourselves."

Federal judge W. Arthur Gerrity rules June 21 that the Boston School Committee has deliberately segregated schools by race; he adopts a plan calling for exchange of students in black Roxbury and white South Boston, but buses carrying blacks to South Boston September 12 encounter white mobs shouting, "Nigger, go home!" Violence ensues, and in October Governor Francis W. Sargent calls out the National Guard to prevent a race war.

French publisher Françoise Giroud, now 58, is named in July to the newly created Cabinet post of Secretary of State for the Condition of Women in France. She works to amend antidiscrimination laws to prohibit sex discrimination, permit working women to sign tax returns with their husbands, police the stereotyping of women as sex objects in advertising, secure better retirement and social security benefits for women, and increase child care services and maternity leave.

J. P. Stevens textile workers in seven mills at Roanoke Rapids, N.C., vote August 28 for representation by the Textile Workers Union of America. The TWUA lost an election at Roanoke Rapids in 1958 but 1,685 of the 3,133 employees now endorse the union, thanks in part to organizing efforts by millhand Crystal Lee Sutton (*née* Jordan), 34. Textiles have accounted for 30 to 50 percent more sales than southern agricultural products, and provide one out of four jobs in five southern states (40 percent of North Carolina's labor force is employed in the mills), yet this has been the only major U.S. industry not organized. Charges of unfair labor practices will continue to be filed against J. P. Stevens, which continues to harass and dismiss union supporters in its 83 U.S. plants. The 140,000-member TWUA will merge with the 360,000-member Amalgamated Clothing Workers of America in

Crystal Lee Sutton's fight for unionization of North Carolina textile workers was the basis of a Hollywood movie. CHIE NISHIO

1976 to form the ACTWU and launch the most intensive boycott ever undertaken by organized labor and begin a massive organizing drive at Stevens plants, 79 of them in the South.

Economic recession deepens throughout the world following last year's hike in oil prices by major petroleum producers. Inflation, meanwhile, raises prices in most of the free world.

The U.S. Consumer Price Index rises by 12.2 percent following last year's 8.8 percent increase. Increases averaged less than 2.4 percent in the 25 years from 1948 to 1972, and the CPI actually declined in 1949 and 1954, but it will go up another

7 percent next year, 4.8 percent in 1976, and 6.8 percent in 1977.

Japanese women workers average 53.9 percent as much pay as men, as compared with 86.7 percent for French women, 80.1 percent for Australian, 77 percent for Danish, 69.9 percent for West German, 63.3 percent for Swiss, 60.7 percent for British. The Japanese average is lowered considerably by the fact that so many women quit after marriage or when they have their first child.

Nuclear fuel facility laboratory technician Karen Gay Silkwood, 28, dies in an automobile crash near Oklahoma City November 13 on her way to meet with a *New York Times* reporter and a union official. She has planned to document her allegations that Kerr-McGee Nuclear Corp. has falsified quality control reports on fuel rods and that 40 pounds of highly dangerous plutonium are missing from the Kerr-McGee plant near Crescent, Okla. Investigators find high levels of radiation in Silkwood's apartment.

The computerized axial tomography (CAT) scanner developed in England by EMI, Ltd. (formerly Electrical Musical Instruments, Ltd.) with money from sales of Beatles records gains wide use not only for diagnosing brain damage but also for whole-body scanning. The device assembles thousands of X-ray images into a single, remarkably detailed picture of the body's interior. It revolutionizes diagnostic medicine but costs upwards of $500,000 (*see* MRI, 1982).

U.S. insurance companies raise rates on malpractice policies, forcing up physicians' fees and hospital rates. More companies will hike rates next year, and some will stop writing malpractice policies as the unique U.S. tort system boosts health care costs, obliging obstetricians in some areas to pay such high insurance rates that they must give up their practices.

New York Governor Nelson A. Rockefeller's second wife, Happy, has a double mastectomy at Memorial Sloan-Kettering Hospital, which performs 40 mastectomies per day.

First Lady Betty Ford undergoes a radical mastectomy for breast cancer September 28. A preliminary report on a nationwide study released a few weeks later confirms the 1971 findings of Dr. George Crile equating recurrence rates in women who have had radical versus those who have had "simple" mastectomies: the incidence of breast cancer will increase in the next 20 years, but use of the the Halsted radical procedure will virtually disappear and "lumpectomies" will increase in popularity.

Eleven women deacons are named to the Episcopal priesthood July 29 at Philadelphia's Church of the Advocate. A banner displayed in front of the church reads "In Christ there is neither male nor female."

South Carolina evangelist Jim Bakker, 34, and his wife, Tammy Fay, found the PTL (Praise the Lord) television ministry, which will become a multi-million-dollar religious empire (*see* 1987).

The Great School Boards, New York City: 1805– 1973 by local activist Diane Ravitch (*née* Silvers), 36, says that city schools have always had trouble educating the children of poor immigrants, and that schools cannot solve all the problems of society. While good schools can provide a pathway "from the gutter to the university" for the talented few, they can do little to assure that no Americans will live under conditions that can be called "the gutter."

The *New York Times* is picketed March 4 by 50 women's groups from the tri-state area protesting the paper's refusal to use the designation "Ms." when so requested, employ terms such as "spokesperson" and "chairperson," or give more than sporadic coverage to women's news except on the Family/Style page or in the back pages. The *Times* will not begin using "Ms." until the mid-1980s—long after other major papers have begun to do so.

Word processors with cathode-ray tube displays and speedy printers begin to replace typewriters as the economic recession (above) encourages business managers to automate offices. The IBM Selectric typewriter introduced in 1961 was given a magnetic tape and turned into a primitive word processor in 1964, but IBM's machine has cost $10,000, vs. $600 for a regular office typewriter, and has actually cut productivity because secretaries sat back and watched it type. Vydek is first to introduce a text-editing computer with a CRT

The battle to gain acceptance for the term "Ms." pitted feminists against some formidable foes. CHIE NISHIO

screen and printer. By 1976 impact printers with bidirectional "daisy wheels" will be printing documents at 30 to 55 characters per second, vs. 15 for the typing ball on a power typewriter, while secretaries key in material for other documents.

Nonfiction: *God with Running Nose* (*Hanatarashigami*) (autobiography) by Japanese writer Sei Yoshino (*née* Wakamatsu), 74, whose book about the hardships of farming on reclaimed land wins a prize established by a famous critic; a Portuguese judge drops all charges against the authors of *The New Portuguese Letters* and proclaims it a work of literary merit following an April 25 coup d'état that has ended more than 40 years of Fascist dictatorship (*see* 1972); *Conundrum* by British writer Jan (born James Humphrey) Morris, 47, who writes, "I was three or perhaps four when I realized that I had been born into the wrong body, and should really

be a girl" (Morris has had a sex-change operation); "Some Are Born Great" by Adela Rogers St. John, now 80, in the *Los Angeles Herald-Examiner* October 13: "The modern woman is the curse of the universe. A disaster, that's what. She thinks that before her arrival on the scene no woman ever did anything worthwhile before, no woman was ever liberated until her time, no woman really ever amounted to anything"; *Sexual Honesty: By Women for Women* by U.S. cultural historian Shere D. Hite, 31; *And Jill Came Tumbling After: Sexism in American Education*, edited by U.S. writers Judith Stacey, Susan Bereaud, and Joan Daniels; *From Reverence to Rape: The Treatment of Women in the Movies* by U.S. journalist Molly Haskell, 34, whose husband is film critic Andrew Sarris; *Sexist Justice* by Karen DeCrow; *Women Hating* by U.S. radical feminist Andrea Dworkin, 37; *Psychoanalysis and Feminism* by Juliet Mitchell; *Pilgrim at Tinker's Creek* by U.S. poet Annie Dillard (*née* Doak), 29 (Pulitzer Prize); *Flying* by Kate Millett.

Fiction: *Celestial Navigation* by Anne Tyler; *The War Between the Tates* by Alison Lurie; *The Sacred and Profane Love Machine* by Iris Murdoch; *The Conservationist* by Nadine Gordimer; *Second-Class Citizen* by Buchi Emecheta; *The Bottle Factory Outing* by Beryl Bainbridge; *Enormous Changes at the Last Minute* (stories) by Grace Paley; *Something I've Been Meaning to Tell You* (stories) by Alice Munro; *Yonnondaio: From the Thirties* by Tillie Olsen, now 61, who has been working on the novel since the 1930s; *The Odd Woman* by Gail Godwin; *Family Secrets* by Rona Jaffe; *The Devil's Hand* by the late Edith Summers Kelley (*see* 1923), who died in 1956 at age 72; *The Dispossessed* by Ursula Le Guin; *Time and the Hour* by Faith Baldwin; *The Wolf and the Wind* by Kathleen Woodiwiss; *The Snare of the Hunter* by Helen MacInnes; *Sweet and Low* by Emma Lathen; *The Long Revenge* by June Thompson.

Poetry: *The Death Notebooks* by Anne Sexton, who has terminal cancer and dies at Weston, Mass., October 4 at age 45 in an apparent suicide. *Laguna Woman: Poems* by University of Arizona, Tucson, English instructor Leslie Marmon Silko, 26.

Juvenile: *Blubber* by Judy Blume; *Everett Anderson's Year* by Lucille Clifton; *A Billion for Boris* by Mary Rodgers; *My Grandson Lew* by Charlotte

Zolotow; *A Child in Prison Camp* by Canadian-born Japanese author-illustrator Shizuye Takashima, 46, who as a teenager in 1942 was interned for 4 years with her family in a "relocation facility."

Sculpture: *The Destruction of the Father* (mixed media) by Louise Bourgeois.

Theater: Kate Nelligan and Edward Fox in David Hare's *Knuckle* 3/4 at London's Comedy Theatre; Marlo Thomas, Dick Van Patten, and Irwin Corey in Herb Gardner's *Thieves* 4/7 at New York's Broadhurst Theater, 312 perfs.; Cynthia Harris, Doris Rafelo, Emory Bass, and J. Frank Luca in Terrence McNally's *Bad Habits* 5/5 at New York's Booth Theater (after 96 perfs. at the Astor Place Theater), 273 perfs.

Films: Alan Bates and Jessica Tandy in Harold Pinter's *Butley*; Jack Nicholson, Faye Dunaway, and John Huston in Roman Polanski's *Chinatown*. Also: Ellen Burstyn and Kris Kristofferson in Martin Scorsese's *Alice Doesn't Live Here Anymore*; Gene Wilder, Cleavon Little, Madeline Kahn, and Mel Brooks in Brooks's *Blazing Saddles*; Warren Beatty and Paula Prentiss (Paula Ragusa), 35, in Alan J. Pakula's *The Parallax View*; Jean-Claude Brialy and Monica Vitti in Luis Buñuel's *The Phantom of Liberty*; Goldie Hawn, 28, and William Atherton in Steven Spielberg's *Sugarland Express*; Shelley Duvall, 25, and Keith Carradine in Robert Altman's *Thieves like Us*.

Broadway musical: Carol Channing in *Lorelei* 1/27 at the Palace Theater, a revised version of the 1949 musical *Gentlemen Prefer Blondes*, Jule Styne–Betty Comden–Adolph Green songs, 321 perfs.

Opera: Tatiana Troyanos, now 35, makes her Metropolitan Opera debut in March singing the role of Octavian in the 1911 Strauss opera *Der Rosenkavalier*.

Popular songs: "Hey Joe (Version)/Piss Factory" by rock singer-songwriter-poet Patti Smith, 28, et al. features a monologue written by Smith for Patty Hearst (her "Piss Factory" is a spoken reminiscence of her experiences on a New Jersey production line); *Heart like a Wheel* (album) by Linda Ronstadt includes "You're No Good," "When Will I Be Loved?," Buddy Holly's "It Doesn't Matter Anymore," and the title song by Anna McGarrigle;

Gladys Knight and the Pips record "Best Thing That Ever Happened to Me"; *Kogen* (album) by Japanese composer-pianist Toshiko Akiyoshi, 44, and her husband, Lew Tabakin, a tenor saxophonist and flutist with whom she started a large Los Angelese rehearsal band last year (it will be the leading big band in jazz by 1980); Olivia Newton-John records "Let Me Be There" and "I Honestly Love You"; Lulu records David Bowie's song "The Man Who Sold the World" and has a hit single; "The Way We Were" by Marilyn and Alan Bergman, music by Marvin Hamlisch (title song for Sydney Pollack's film); *Band on the Run* (album) and "Jet" by former Beatles singer-composer Paul McCartney for his backup group Wings (McCartney, his wife, Linda Eastman, 32, and Denny Laine, 30); *Hot Cakes* (album) by Carly Simon; *Caught Up* (album) by Milly Jackson; *Another Lonely Song* (album, co-written with Billy Sherrill and N. Wilson), *We're Gonna Hold On* (album, with George Jones), and *Woman to Woman* (album) by Tammy Wynette; *Highly Prized Possession* (album), *Love Song* (album), and "He Thinks I Don't Care" by Anne Murray; Lynn Anderson records "Sing About Love."

Little League Baseball announces June 12 that its teams will be open to girls.

Christine Marie "Chris" Evert, 19 (U.S.), wins in women's singles at Wimbledon, Billie Jean King at Forest Hills. *A Long Way, Baby: Behind the Scenes in Women's Pro Tennis* by New York journalist Grace Lichtenstein (*née* Rosenthal), 32, is an exposé (*see* Virginia Slims tournament, 1970).

"Streaking" becomes a popular U.S. fad as male and female college students dash naked between dormitories.

New York fashion designer Anne Klein dies March 20 at age 52 (or 68) (*see* 1968). Her protégée, Donna Karan (*née* Faske), 26, who has worked for Klein since 1967, steps in and works with her co-designer, Louis dell'Olio, to keep the Anne Klein name alive (*see* 1984).

San Francisco black militants calling themselves the Symbionese Liberation Army (members include Nancy Ling Perry, 27, Emily Harris [*née* Schwartz], 27, and Harris's husband, William, 29) kidnap publishing heiress Patricia Hearst, 19, February 5 and demand $2 million in ransom. They then demand $230 million in free food for the poor of California. A San Francisco bank robbery April 15 nets $10,960, and an automatic camera at the bank records Hearst holding a submachine gun for the robbers (*see* 1975).

Soledad, Calif., housewife Inez Garcia, 30, is brutally raped by one man March 19 while another blocks her escape. She receives a phone call afterward from the men, who threaten to kill her if she does not leave town (her husband is an inmate of Soledad Prison); hysterical and in shock, she loads her .22-caliber rifle, finds her attackers, and shoots Miguel Jiminez to death after he throws a knife a her. She goes on trial for murder at Salinas August 19, the prosecution alleges that she was not raped, she is convicted of second-degree murder, Judge Stanley Lawson sentences her to a prison term of 5 years to life, but she will appeal the verdict on grounds of justified self-defense (*see* 1977).

Michigan adopts a revised sexual-assault code and becomes the first state to shift in rape cases from an emphasis on the victim's actions to those of her attacker.

Average U.S. food prices: white bread 34.5¢ per one lb. loaf (up from 27.6¢ last year); sugar 32.3¢ lb., up from 15.1¢; rice 44¢ lb., up from 26¢; potatoes 24.9¢ lb., up from 20.5¢; coffee $1.28 lb., up from $1.04.

Dalkon Shield maker A. H. Robins Co. agrees May 15 to remove its intrauterine device from the market in response to FDA pressure (*see* 1971). The pregnancy rate among women using the device is 10 percent, as compared with 3 percent for most other IUDs, and seven women have died from uterine infections related to using the Dalkon Shield. Of the 3 to 5 million women using IUDs, 2 million have been using the Dalkon Shield (*see* 1985).

French Minister of Health Simone Veil, 47, sponsors a liberalized abortion law (*see* 1973).

New Delhi has massive demonstrations against the Indira Gandhi government March 6 as at least 100,000 people march through the city. India's high

court rules June 11 that Gandhi used corrupt practices to gain election to Parliament in 1971, that her election was invalid, and that she must resign. Gandhi vows to remain in office and has more than 750 political opponents arrested. Antigovernment violence breaks out at New Delhi June 30, Gandhi announces steps to reduce prices, reduce peasants' debts, and achieve fairer distribution of land in an appeal for political support, but she suppresses dissent and imposes strict press censorship.

The U.S. Army reports May 2 that women are joining its ranks in record numbers, but although the number has tripled in 4 years to 35,000 they still account for only 4.5 percent of the total 780,000. Maj. Gen. Jeanne M. Holm predicts that women will soon fly air force fighter planes, serve aboard navy warships, and even participate in combat (*see* 1993).

President Ford is threatened by a pistol-pointing woman September 5 as he approaches the California State Capitol at Sacramento; agents pull the gun from the hand of Lynette Alice "Squeaky" Fromme, 26, who turns out to be a follower of cult leader and murderer Charles Manson. Ford actually comes under fire September 22 as he steps out of the St. Francis Hotel at San Francisco; activist Sara Jane Moore, 45, has fired the shot, which misses the president.

 Cambodia's new Khmer Rouge government begins a wholesale slaughter of intellectuals, political enemies, dissidents, and peasants guilty of "mistakes." Evacuees are settled in rural "communes," families are separated, marriage is abolished, and everyone over age 10 is put to work in the fields.

The United Nations proclaims the start of Woman's Year January 1. The World Congress for International Woman's Year opens at Berlin October 20 with 1,952 delegates, observers, and guests from 141 countries, including 29 in Europe, 33 in Asia, 44 in Africa, 33 in the Western Hemisphere, Australia, and New Zealand.

Uganda sends Bernadette Olowo to Rome January 10, and she becomes the first woman envoy to the Vatican.

Angola gains independence from Portugal and grants women the right to vote on the same basis as men (*see* Portugal, 1976).

The Supreme Court reverses its 1961 decision with regard to all-male juries, ruling 8 to 1 January 21 in *Taylor* v. *Louisiana* that "it is untenable to suggest these days that it would be a special hardship for each and every woman to perform jury service or that society cannot spare *any* women from their present duties . . . . If it ever was the case that women were unqualified to sit on juries, or were so situated that none of them should be required to perform jury service, that time is long past." The Sixth Amendment stipulates that a defendant has the right to a jury drawn from a fair cross section of the community, and a Louisiana law allowing women automatic exemption from jury duty violates that amendment, the Court declares. (The ruling has little practical effect since all states, including Louisiana, have repealed statutes exempting women from jury duty, although in some states women are treated differently from men.)

French prostitutes occupy a church at Lyons June 2 and organize strikes to protest police harassment.

The English Collective of Prostitutes is founded by Brooklyn-born prostitute Selma James. Its Women's Center will serve as a clearinghouse for such organizations as Women Against Rape, Wages for Housework, and the like (*see* 1982).

Parliament enacts a Sex Discrimination Act which goes into effect simultaneously with an Equal Pay Act, requiring that women receive equal compensation to that of men performing similar work. Employers are given 5 years to upgrade women's wages and salaries, but many will reclassify jobs to keep women's pay lower. A high percentage of women are in traditional "women's jobs" that offer no prospect for promotion or pay increase.

Hourly wages for production workers average $6.22 in the United States, up from $3.15 in 1965; $7.12 in Sweden, up from $1.86; $6.46 in Belgium, up from $1.32; $6.19 in West Germany, up from $1.41; $4.57 in France, up from $1.19; $4.52 in Italy, up from $1.10; $3.20 in Britain, up from $1.13; $3.10 in Japan, up from 48¢.

Baruch College business school professor Donna Shalala, 34, serves as director and treasurer of New York City's Municipal Assistance Corporation (MAC) as the city attempts to deal with a fiscal crisis.

Argentine President Isabel Perón agrees July 8 to raise wages in order to stop a general strike.

Mary Leakey announces October 30 at Washington, D.C., that she has uncovered jaws and teeth of 11 skeletons 25 miles south of Tanzania's Olduvai Gorge that date back 3.75 million years and have human characteristics. Her husband, Louis, died in 1972 (*see* 1959; 1976).

The first monoclonal antibodies—laboratory-made versions of the antibodies produced by the body to fend off viruses and other "foreign" substances—open a new era in diagnostic and therapeutic medicine.

Karen Ann Quinlan goes into a coma April 15 after drinking alcohol mixed with small doses of Librium and Valium. The 21-year-old Landing, N.J., woman will be kept alive in a respirator for more than 8 years, even after her respirator is turned off June 10, 1976, following a court battle. She will be fed by a nasal tube and given antibiotics to ward off infections despite the fact that there is no hope of recovery, and her much-publicized case will raise continuing arguments about the right to die.

Lyme disease is identified in Lyme, Conn. Transmitted primarily by the bite of a tick found on white-tailed deer, white-footed field mice, and other animals, the bacterial infection can lead to serious neurological, cardiac, or arthritic complications. It will spread quickly throughout most of the northeast and middle Atlantic states, Wisconsin, Minnesota, and the West Coast.

The United States has 725,000 hysterectomies, only 20 percent of which can be justified as treatment for cancer and other life-threatening disorders. More wombs are removed than tonsils, and the U.S. rate, which has increased 25 percent since 1970, is two and a half times that in Britain, four times that in Sweden. Most of the procedures are performed on women who have excessive fears of pregnancy or are worried lest they get uterine or ovarian cancer.

The World Council of Churches elects two women at Nairobi December 6.

The U.S. Supreme Court rules 5 to 4 January 22 in *Goss* v. *Lopez* that unless their presence poses a physical threat, students may not be temporarily suspended from school for misconduct without some attention to due process. But the Court rules October 20 that spanking and paddling do not violate the 14th Amendment provided that teachers first give children fair warning.

The U.S. Department of Health, Education and Welfare Administration releases new regulations June 3 designed to equalize opportunities for women in schools and colleges.

Chicago schoolteacher Marva Nettles Collins receives pension money after 14 years of teaching in public schools and founds Westside Preparatory School, building a schoolroom in her house and using it to help 18 young children from the city's ghetto, a number that will rise to more than 250 as the school grows to occupy two buildings.

Boston schools reopen September 8 with heavy police protection against demonstrators who oppose busing to achieve integration.

Liquid Paper Co. employs more than 200 people to produce 25 million bottles of its product and sell them in 31 countries (*see* 1968). Divorcée Nesmith, who married Robert Graham 4 years ago, resigns as chairman of the board to devote herself to charitable, religious, and artistic pursuits. The product, which is not without imitators, has become a staple in offices worldwide. Gillette Corp. will buy Liquid Paper in 1979 for $47.5 million, plus a royalty to Mrs. Graham on every bottle sold until the year 2000 (she will be worth $50 million when she dies in May 1980 at age 56), but increased use of word processors in place of office typewriters will wither the demand for Liquid Paper.

Nonfiction: *Against Our Will: Men, Women and Rape* by U.S. feminist Susan Brownmiller, 40; *Sisters in Crime* by U.S. educator Freda Adler, 41, who writes, "It is little wonder that rape is one of the least-reported crimes. Perhaps it is the only crime in which the victim becomes the accused and, in reality, it is she who must prove her good reputation, her mental soundness, and her impeccable propriety"; *Women: A Feminist Perspective* by U.S. writer-educator Susan Griffin, 32, who writes, "Rape is a form of mass terrorism. . . . The fear of rape keeps women off the streets at night. Keeps women at home. Keeps women passive and modest for fear that they be thought provocative"; *Women's Evolution from Matriarchal Clan to Patriarchal Family* by Evelyn Reed, now 69; *Crazy Salad: Some Things about Women* (articles) by Nora Ephron; *Letter to a Child Never Born (Lettera a un bambino mai nato)* by Oriana Fallaci; *Getting Yours: How to Make the System Work for the Working Woman* by Letty Cottin Pogrebin; *The Morning Breaks: The Trial of Angela Davis* by Bettina Aptheker, 31, who was a leader in the Free Speech Movement at the University of California, Berkeley, in the 1960s; *Liberal Parents, Radical Children* by Midge Decter; *Shana Alexander's State-by-State Guide to Women's Legal Rights* by New York journalist Shana Alexander (*née* Ager), 49; *The Young Russians* by Georgie Anne Geyer; *Age and Work: The Changing Composition of the Labor Force* by Juanita Kreps; *Everybody Who Was Anybody: A Biography of Gertrude Stein* by English scholar-novelist Janet Hobhouse, 27; *All Change Here* (memoir) by Naomi Mitchison; *On Photography* by Susan Sontag.

Fiction: *Looking for Mr. Goodbar* by Judith Rossner is based on the story of Roseann Quinn, a 27-year-old schoolteacher who was killed by a man she took home from a singles bar; *Heat and Dust* by Ruth Prawer Jhabvala; *Burger's Daughter* by Nadine Gordimer; *The Little Hotel* by Christina Stead; *The Realms of Gold* by Margaret Drabble; *The Peacock Spring* by Rumer Godden; *Female Friends* and *Down among the Women* by Fay Weldon, who has written the first episodes of the BBC series *Upstairs, Downstairs*; *The Story of Eli (Historien om Eli)* by Norwegian novelist Liv Kølltzow, 30, is about the conditions that hinder women's liberation; *Where Are the Children?* by U.S. novelist Mary Higgins Clark, 43, who was widowed 11 years ago and obliged to support her five children; *Families and Survivors* by U.S. novelist Alice Adams, 49; *Before My Time* by Maureen Howard; *The Mixed Blessing* by Helen Van Slyke; *New Girl in Town* by Faith Baldwin; *The Female Man* by U.S. science fiction novelist Johanna Russ, 38; *Superwoman* by English novelist Shirley Conran (*née* Pearce), 43; *Sweet William* by Beryl Bainbridge; *The Last of the Country House Murders* by Emma Tennant; *By Hook or by Crook* by Emma Lathen.

Poetry: *House, Bridge, Fountain, Gate* by Maxine Kumin; *Aspects of Eve* by Linda Pastan; *Growing Points* by Elizabeth Jennings; *Threshold* by Sheila Fugard; *End of Drought* by Ruth Pitter, now 78.

Sculptor Dame Barbara Hepworth dies in a fire at her Cornwall studio in St. Ives May 20 at age 72. She has been ill with throat cancer.

Theater: Rita Moreno and Jerry Stoller in Terrence McNally's *The Ritz* 1/20 at New York's Longacre Theater, 406 perfs.; Deborah Kerr, Barry Nelson, and Frank Langella in Edward Albee's *Seascape* 1/26 at New York's Shubert Theater, 63 perfs.; Ellen Burstyn and Charles Grodin in Bernard Slade's *Same Time, Next Year* 3/13 at New York's Brooks Atkinson Theater, 1,444 perfs.; Hilary Jean Beane and Diane Oyama Dixon in Ed Bullins's *The Taking of Miss Janie* 5/4 at New York's Mitzi E. Newhouse Theater, 42 perfs.; Alan Bates, Jacqueline Pearce, and Julian Glover in Simon Gray's *Otherwise Engaged* 7/30 at the Queen's Theatre, London.

Films: Candice Bergen, 29, Gene Hackman, and James Coburn in Richard Brooks's *Bite the Bullet*; Lily Tomlin, 36, Shelley Duvall, and Keith Carradine in Robert Altman's *Nashville*; Jack Nicholson and Louise Fletcher in Milos Forman's *One Flew over the Cuckoo's Nest*; Lina Wertmuller's *Swept Away . . .* with Giancarlo Giannini and Mariangela Melato. Also: Swiss-born actress Marthe (*née* Marte) Keller, 30, and André Dussolier in Claude Lelouch's *And Now My Love*; Ryan O'Neal and Marisa Berenson in Stanley Kubrick's *Barry Lyndon*; Michele Morgan and Serge Reggiani in Claude Lelouch's *Cat and Mouse*; Donald Sutherland, Karen Black, Burgess Meredith, and William Atherton in John Schlesinger's *The Day of the Locust*; Joan Micklin Silver's *Hester Street* with Steven Keats and Carol Kane; Margarethe von Trotta in Volker Schlöndorff's *The Lost Honor of Katharina Blum*; Gene Hackman and Jennifer Warren in Arthur Penn's *Night Moves*; Jack Lemmon and Anne Bancroft in Melvin Frank's *The Prisoner of Second Avenue*; Jeff Bridges, Sam Waterston, and Elizabeth Ashley in Frank Perry's *Rancho Deluxe*; Bruce Dern, Barbara Feldon, and Michael Kidd in Michael Richie's *Smile*.

Susan Hayward dies at Beverly Hills March 14 at age 53 after suffering a seizure related to a brain tumor.

Opera: Beverly Sills makes her Metropolitan Opera debut in a new production of the 1826 Rossini opera *Le Siège de Corinth*; Canadian soprano Lois McDonall, 36, makes her London debut at Covent Garden as a solo voice in the 1919 Strauss opera *Die Frau ohne Schatten*; U.S. soprano Leona Mitchell, 26, makes her Metropolitan Opera debut in December singing the role of Micaëla in the 1875 Bizet opera *Carmen*; Filipina soprano Evelyn Mandac, 30, makes her Metropolitan Opera debut 12/19 singing the role of Loretta in the 1918 Puccini opera *Gianni Schicchi*.

Broadway musicals: Geoffrey Holder and Stephanie Mills in *The Wiz* 1/5 at the Majestic Theater, with Charlie Smalls songs that include "Ease on Down the Road," 1,666 perfs.; Chita Rivera, Gwen Verdon, and Jerry Orbach in *Chicago* 6/3 at the Forty-sixth Street Theater, with John Kander–Fred Ebb songs, 922 perfs.; *A Chorus Line* 10/19 at the Shubert Theater (after 101 perfs. at the off-Broadway Public Theater plus previews), with Marvin Hamlisch–Edward Kleban songs, 6,137 perfs.

Josephine Baker dies April 12 at age 68 leaving 12 adopted children whom she has called her "rainbow tribe."

Discotheques enjoy a resurgence unequaled since the early 1960s in major U.S. and European cities. Highly formula-conforming disco records by Van McCoy, Donna Summer, the Bee Gees, and others will dominate popular music until 1979.

Popular songs: *Between the Lines* (album) by Janis Ian, now 24, includes "At Seventeen"; *Judith* (album) by Judy Collins includes Stephen Sondheim's song "Send in the Clowns"; *This Is Me* (album) by Caterina Valenti, now 44; The Captain and Tenille (U.S. musician Tony Tenille, 32, and her husband, Daryl Dragon, 33) score a hit singing "Love Will Keep Us Together"; *Horses* (album) by Patti Smith mixes rock music and poetry; *Playing Possum* (album) by Carly Simon; Olivia Newton-John records "Please Mr. Please"; *Prisoner in Disguise* (album) by Linda Ronstadt; *Smile* (album) by

Laura Nyro; *Still Caught Up* (album) by Milly Jackson; "I Still Believe in Fairy Tales" by Tammy Wynette.

 Japanese mountaineer Junko Tabei, 35, arrives at the summit of Everest May 16 and becomes the first woman ever to scale the world's highest peak.

Billie Jean King wins in women's singles at Wimbledon, Chris Evert at Forest Hills.

U.S. tennis racquet sales peak at 9.2 million units; they will fall to 5 million by 1978.

Beaufort County, N.C., jail inmate Joan (pronounced JoAnn) Little, 21, is acquitted August 15 of murder charges in connection with the August 27, 1974, killing of Clarence Alligood, a 62-year-old, 200-pound white prison guard. While she was being held on a breaking-and-entering charge, Alligood entered her cell and forced her to perform fellatio on him; she then jabbed him 11 times with the ice pick he had been holding. Little has been supported by NOW and other women's organizations. "I owe my victory to the people and not to the judicial system," she tells the press after the 5-week trial. "If my sisters are ever faced with the similar situation, and I hope they never do, maybe now there is a law that says a black woman has the right to defend herself." She will escape from the North Carolina Correctional Facility for Women in October 1977, flee to New York, be apprehended, and be returned to North Carolina in June 1978 to finish serving her original 7- to 10-year sentence for stealing $200 worth of goods from a trailer at Washington, N.C., in 1973.

FBI agents at San Francisco apprehend Patricia Hearst September 18 along with remnants of the Symbionese Liberation Army (*see* 1974). She is held on bank robbery charges.

The body of English prostitute Wilma McCann is discovered October 30, and newspapers run headlines about the "Yorkshire Ripper" that recall memories of the 1888 murders committed by "Jack the Ripper" (*see* 1981).

New York's City Council enacts a "Pooper Scooper" law following a campaign waged largely by activist Fran Lee (Mrs. Samuel Weiss), 65, a former actress and onetime kindergarten teacher. Dog owners are required by the law to clean up the mess left when they walk their animals, and peer pressure makes most owners cooperate.

The Toxic Substances Control Act signed by President Ford October 12 requires phasing out all production and sale of PCBs (polychlorinated biphenyls) within 3 years. The measure imposes strict technology requirements on the chemical industry and will oblige smaller firms to quit production. PCBs have been linked to cancer and birth defects, and Congress has voted 319 to 45 August 23 to adopt the tough new environmental law.

The Indoor Air Act passed by the Minnesota state legislature requires all public places to have smoke-free areas, but enforcement will prove difficult. Arizona banned smoking in public places in May 1973, declaring smoking a public nuisance and a health hazard. It extended the ban last year, but tobacco industry lobbyists work to prevent passage of such laws and to defeat popular referenda on smoking in public places, warning voters against "Big Brother."

U.S. soft drinks edge past coffee in popularity and will pass milk next year.

Britain's birthrate falls to 12.2 per 1,000, lower even than the nadir of 1933, but while average family size has decreased the number of women bearing children has actually increased.

1976

 Chairman Mao Zedong dies of Parkinson's disease September 10 at age 82. His widow, Jiang Qing, is imprisoned early in October along with other "radicals" in her "Gang of Four" for having undermined the party, government, and economy. Shanghai crowds attack effigies of Jiang Qing.

Pro-Palestinian terrorists hijack a Paris-bound Air France Airbus over Greece June 27 and force its pilot to land at Bengazi, Libya, and then at Uganda's Entebbe Airport outside Kampala, demanding the release of 53 prisoners being held in Israel, Kenya, and Europe. They release 47 women, children, and sick people June 29, release another 100 July 1, but hold 98 passengers and 12 crew members hostage. Airborne Israeli commandos fly

2,500 miles to Kampala, storm the plane at Entebbe early on the morning of July 4, rescue almost all the hostages, kill the 10 hijackers along with perhaps 20 Ugandan soldiers, and escape with only two casualties, including Soviet emigrée Ida Borowlcz, 56, who was shot dead by an Arab gunman while lying on the floor in the airport.

Argentina has a bloodless coup March 24 after months of terrorist attacks, robberies, and murders. Public officials and legislators have left office, scoffing openly at Juan Perón's widow and her ministers. A military junta arrests Isabelita Perón and declares martial law. She will be imprisoned for 5 years on charges of having abused public property and will settle in Madrid after her release.

German leftist terrorist Ulrike Meinhof hangs herself in her cell at Stuttgart's Stammheim Prison May 9 at age 42 after nearly 44 months in prison as West Germany's Baader-Meinhof gang trial continues. Meinhof's burial in West Berlin a week later attracts a crowd of 4,000, many of them sympathizers wearing masks or with their faces painted white.

A British soldier in Belfast shoots an Irish Republican Army getaway car driver in the head August 10, the car jumps a curb and crushes three small children to death, critically injuring their mother. The woman's sister, Mairead Corrigan, 32, a secretary, goes on TV a few hours later to denounce the IRA, becoming the first Catholic woman in Ulster who has dared challenge the gunmen. She meets Betty Williams, mother of two, who lives a few blocks from the scene of the tragedy, and the two begin organizing the People's Peace Movement. Within 2 weeks they have some 30,000 Protestant and Catholic women behind them demanding the end to the violence in Northern Ireland. Corrigan and Williams will receive a Nobel Peace Prize next year.

Georgia governor James Earl "Jimmy" Carter, Jr., 52, defeats Gerald Ford's bid for reelection. Carter's wife, Rosalynn (née Smith), 46, takes an active role in the campaign and will be a participant in the new administration.

Congresswoman Bella Abzug (D., N.Y.) has given up her seat to seek her party's nomination for the U.S. Senate but has narrowly lost to onetime Harvard professor Daniel Patrick Moynihan.

California voters elect Los Angeles political activist Maxine Waters, 38, to the State Assembly, where she will work on such issues as sex abuse prevention, rising to become majority whip and the most influential woman in California politics.

President-elect Carter (above) names former U.S. Ambassador to Luxembourg Patricia Harris, now 53, Secretary of Housing and Urban Development (HUD) December 21. She will be the first black woman to serve in any presidential Cabinet.

Portugal grants women the right to vote on the same basis as men (*see* Spain, 1931; Angola, 1975).

An International Tribunal on Crimes Against Women opens March 8 at the Palais des Congrès, Brussels. Delegates include Egyptian physician-novelist Nawal el-Saadawi, 45, whose writings have addressed the social and political factors that oppress women (she has taken a radical view of sexual taboos in Arab society; *see* 1981).

The Soweto township 10 miles southwest of Johannesburg explodes in racial violence June 16 as 10,000 students protest the teaching of the Afrikaans language and go on a rampage. Riot squads restore order in 11 townships but only after 176 people (including two whites) have been killed, 1,139 (including 22 police officers) injured. Winnie Mandela, who has been arrested and rearrested many times since 1969 for breaking her banning order, is relocated to the outskirts of the Orange Free State town of Brandford and forced to live under primitive conditions. She will be back in court within 2 years for breaking her ban but will be given a suspended sentence (*see* 1978; 1986).

President-elect Carter (above) appoints New York City's Human Rights Commission head Eleanor Holmes Norton, 39, to head the U.S. Equal Employment Opportunity Commission, its first woman chair.

Half of all British mothers are now in the nation's workforce, up from 10 percent in 1900.

Mary Leakey finds three trails of fossilized hominid footprints at Laetoli, 30 miles south of Olduvai Gorge, and says that they prove without a doubt that human ancestors walked upright 3.6 million years ago (*see* 1975).

∞ Bavarian epileptic student Anneliese Michel, 23, dies of starvation July 1 after months of ritual by "exorcists" Arnold Renz, 65, Ernst Alt, 38, and the woman's parents, Josef Michel, 59, and Anna, 45. Bishop Josef Stangl approved the exorcism to rid Anneliese of "demons" at the recommendation of Jesuit priest Adolf Rodewiyk of Frankfurt and appointed Renz and Alt to carry out the ritual.

A general convention of the Episcopal church, the House of Bishops, and the House of Lords announces September 16 that it has approved the ordination of women as priests.

Chinese universities reopen following the death of Mao Zedong (above). Most closed at the start of the Cultural Revolution in 1966. Those that remained open admitted students on political rather than academic grounds, scholars were sent to work in the countryside, and library acquisitions were halted. Academic degrees, abolished as an invidious status distinction, will not be reintroduced until 1980, and only 1 percent of college-age men and women will be able to attend college as compared to nearly 50 percent in America.

The U.S. Military Academy at West Point and U.S. Air Force Academy at Colorado Springs admit their first women cadets. West Point accepts 119 women cadets July 7 after 174 years of male-only enrollment.

New York's multicollege City University of New York (CUNY) levies tuitions for the first time since its founding in 1849. Under pressure from blacks, Hispanics, and community groups, CUNY adopted an open-admissions policy in 1970, and its enrollment has swelled from 174,000 to 268,000, mostly blacks and Hispanics. Its faculty has grown from 7,800 to 12,800. Budget cuts will reduce enrollment to 172,000 by 1980, and the faculty will be cut by some 3,000.

The *Harvard Law Review*, founded in 1887, names Law School student Susan Estrich, 24, its first woman president.

Word processors made by Wang Laboratories begin to revolutionize offices with workstations that share central computers.

Fax (facsimile transmission) machines gain ground as second-generation technology cuts transmission time from 6 minutes per page to 3. The devices translate a printed page or graphics into electronic signals, transmit them over telephone lines, and print out signals received from other fax machines thousands of miles (or one block) away. Government offices, law enforcement agencies, news agencies, publishers, and banks are the major users. Prices fall for machines, but quality remains poor (*see* 1982).

New York television journalist Barbara Walters, 44, accepts a 5-year contract from American Broadcasting Company to co-host the network's nightly news program for $1 million per year. Despite the remark of a former NBC News president in 1971 that "audiences are less prepared to accept news from a woman's voice than from a man's," she has successfully been co-anchoring NBC's morning *Today* Show. Indianapolis-born WMAQ-TV Chicago television news co-anchor Jane Pauley, 26, succeeds Walters as news co-anchor of the *Today* show, a position that she will hold until 1990.

Nonfiction: *Of Woman Born: Motherhood as Experience and Institution* by poet Adrienne Rich, who writes, "Probably there is nothing in human nature more resonant with charges than the flow of energy between two biologically alike bodies, one of which has lain in amniotic bliss inside the other, one of which has labored to give birth to the other. The materials are here for the deepest mutuality and the most painful estrangement"; *The Woman Warrior: Memoirs of a Girlhood among Ghosts* by Los Angeles–born writer Maxine Hong Kingston, 35; *Passages: Predictable Crises of Adult Life* by Gail Sheehy; *The Welfare Mother* by Austrian-American journalist Susan Sheehan (*née* Sachsel), 39; *The Hite Report: A Nationwide Study of Female Sexuality* by Shere D. Hite; *Scoundrel Time* (autobiography) by Lillian Hellman, now 71, who sues Mary McCarthy for libel after McCarthy says that "every word she writes is a lie, including 'and' and 'the' "; Hellman will die in 1984 before the case comes to trial; *First You Cry* by NBC Network News correspondent Betty Rollin, 40, who found a lump in her breast 3 years ago, heard her physician dismiss it as a harmless cyst, did a report on First Lady Betty Ford's mastectomy in 1974, read the statistics on breast cancer, sought a second diagnosis, learned that she had a malignancy, and had her breast removed; *The Curse: A Cultural History of Menstruation* by University of North Dakota English professor Emily Toth (*née* Fitzgibbons), 32 (with Janice Delaney and Mary Jane Lupton); *Spirit-controlled Woman* by Christian fundamentalist Beverly LaHaye, 38, who calls the clitoral orgasm a myth, says, "All married women are capable of orgasmic ecstasy. No Christian woman should settle for less," but "The woman who is truly Spirit-filled will want to be totally submissive to her husband. . . . This is a truly liberated woman. Submission is God's design for women"; *The Grass is Always Greener Over the Septic Tank* by Erma Bombeck; *Lyndon Johnson and the American Dream* by Harvard professor Doris Helen Kearns, 33, who last year married Washington insider Richard Goodwin.

Fiction: *Meridian* by U.S. novelist Alice Walker, 32; *Lady Oracle* by Margaret Atwood; *Bloodshed and Three Novellas* by Cynthia Ozick; *Woman on the Edge of Time* by Marge Piercy; *Chilly Scenes of Winter* by U.S. novelist Ann Beattie, 29, whose book *Distortions* (stories) is also published; *Searching for Caleb* by Anne Tyler; *Family Feeling* by Helen Yglesias; *Ordinary People* by U.S. novelist Judith (Ann) Guest, 45; *Rite of Passage* by Sheila Fugard; *The Bride Price* by Buchi Emecheta; *How I Became Holy Mother and Other Stories* by Ruth Prawer Jhabvala; *Lovers and Tyrants* by Francine du Plessix Gray; *Kinflicks* by U.S. novelist Lisa Alther (*née* Reed), 32; *The Last Chance* by Rona Jaffe; *Speedboat* by journalist Renata Adler; *A Sea-Change* by U.S. novelist Lois Gould, 38; *The Autobiography of My Mother* by U.S. novelist Rosellen Brown, 37; *Dream Children* (stories) by Gail Godwin; *Miss Herbert (The Suburban Wife)* by Christina Stead, now 74; *Blaming* by the late Elizabeth Taylor, who died last year at age 63; *The Stepdaughter* by British novelist Caroline (*née* Lady Caroline Hamilton-Temple) Blackwood, 45; *A Quiet Life* by Beryl Bainbridge; *Remember Me* by Fay Weldon; *Henry and Cato* by Iris Murdoch; *Thursday's Child* by Faith Baldwin; *Afternoon of a Good Woman* by Nina Bawden; *The Takeover* by Muriel Spark; *David Meyer Is a Mother* by Gail Parent; *Interview With the Vampire* by U.S. novelist Anne Rice (*née* O'Brien); *Where Late the Sweet Birds Sang* by U.S. science fiction novelist Kate Wilhelm (*née* Katie Gertrude Meredith), 48, is about cloning and its consequences for humanity; *No Quarter Asked* by U.S. pulp novelist Janet (Ann)

Dailey (*née* Haradon), 32, is the first of more than 80 Harlequin paperback romances that she will write (she follows it this year alone with *Boss Man from Oklahoma*, *Savage Land*, *Land of Enchantment*, *Fire and Ice*, *The Homeplace*, and *After the Storm*; her books will outsell those of any other woman author except Barbara Cartland); *A Demon in My View* by Ruth Rendell; *Agent in Place* by Helen MacInnes.

Poetry: *Gathering the Tribes* by U.S. poet Carolyn (Louise) Forche, 26; *A Husband's Notes about Her* by Eve Merriam, now 60; *The Gates* by Muriel Rukeyser, now 63; *Instructions to the Double* by U.S. poet Tess Gallagher (*née* Bond), 33; *Lady of the Beasts* by Robin Morgan.

Juvenile: *Roll of Thunder, Hear My Cry* by U.S. author Mildred (Delois) Taylor, 33; *A Stitch in Time* by Penelope Lively; *Forever* by Judy Blume.

Painting: *Falcon Avenue, Seaside Walk, Dwight Street, Jarvis Street, Greene Street* (baked enamel on silk screen grid, enamel on 80 steel plates) by California-born artist Jennifer Bartlett (*née* Losch), 35; *Beginner* by Elizabeth Murray, who was Bartlett's best friend at Mills College in the early 1960s; *Imperfect Indicative* (collage of charcoal and paper on linen) and *Imperative* (collage of oil and paper on panel) by Lee Krasner.

Photographer Imogen Cunningham dies June 24 at San Francisco at age 93, having taught at the Art Institute of San Francisco almost to the end.

Theater: Lynn Redgrave and John Heffernan in Jules Feiffer's *Knock Knock* 2/24 at New York's Biltmore Theater, 38 perfs.; Tammy Grimes and George Grizzard in Neil Simon's *California Suite* 6/10 at New York's Eugene O'Neill Theater, 445 perfs.; *For Colored Girls Who Have Considered Suicide/When the Rainbow is Enuf* by U.S. playwright Ntozake Shange (Paulette Williams), 27, 9/15 at New York's Booth Theater (after 120 perfs. at the Public Theater) with Trazana Beverly, Laurie Carlos, Rise Collins, Aku Kadogo, June League, Paul Moss, and Shange, 867 perfs. (total); Fred Gwynne, Henderson Forsythe, and Diane Ladd in Preston Jones's *A Texas Trilogy* (*Lu Ann Hampton Laverty Oberlander*, *The Oldest Living Graduate*, and *The Last Meeting of the Knights of the White Magnolia*) 9/22 at New York's Broadhurst Theater, 22 perfs. in repertory.

Television series: Linda Carter plays the role of "Wonder Woman" in a new U.S. series based on a 1940s comic strip character.

Films: Faye Dunaway, Peter Finch, William Holden, and Robert Duvall in Sidney Lumet's *Network*; Lina Wertmuller's *Seven Beauties* with Giancarlo Giannini; Geory Desmouceaux and Philippe Goldman in François Truffaut's *Small Change*. Also: Myriam Boyer and Jean-Luc Bideau in Alain Tanner's *Jonah Who Will Be 25 in the Year 2000*; Jeanne Moreau's *Lumière*, with Moreau, Francine Racette, Lucia Bose, and Caroline Cartier; John Wayne and Lauren Bacall in Don Siegel's *The Shootist*; Robert De Niro, Cybill Shepherd, and Harvey Keitel in Martin Scorsese's *Taxi Driver*; Isabelle Adjani and Roman Polanski in Polanski's *The Tenant*.

Opera: Adriana Maliponte makes her London debut at Covent Garden in February singing the role of Nedda in the 1892 Leoncavallo opera *I Pagliacci*.

Broadway musicals: *Bubblin' Brown Sugar* 3/2 at the ANTA Theater, with music and lyrics by Danny Holgate, Enice Kemp, and Lillian Lopez plus old songs by Duke Ellington, Noble Sissle, Eubie Blake, Andy Razaf, Fats Waller, and others, 766 perfs.; Vinette Carol in *Your Arms Too Short to Box with God* 12/22 at the Lyceum Theater, with Alex Bradford–Micki Grant songs, 427 perfs.

Popular songs: *Bread and Roses* (album) by Judy Collins includes the feminist title song; *Hasten Down the Wind* (album) by Linda Ronstadt; "Love Hangover" by U.S. songwriters Pam Sawyer, 38, and Marilyn McLeod, 34; "Down So Low" by U.S. songwriter Tracy Nelson, 32, is recorded by Linda Ronstadt; "Ruby" by Helen Reddy; "Disco Lady" by H. Scales, L. Vance, and Don Davis; "Love to Love You Baby" by U.S. singer-songwriter Donna Summer (Donna Gaines), 27, who first gained fame as a disco singer in Munich; " 'Til I Can Make It on My Own," "Golden Ring," and "You and Me" by Tammy Wynette, whose marriage to George Jones has ended in divorce.

Punk rock gains favor among Britain's working-class youth with its highly amplified, politically rebellious style. U.S. bands performing at New York's CBGB's and Max's Kansas City rock clubs will develop this new wave rock with its back-to-basics approach.

U.S. figure skater Dorothy Hamill wins her event in the winter Olympics at Innsbruck, West German skier Rosi Mittermeier wins the downhill in 1 minute, 46.16 seconds and the slalom in 1 minute, 30.54 seconds, Canadian skier Kathy Kreiner wins the giant slalom in 1 minute, 29.13 seconds. West German runner Annegret Richter wins the 100-meter dash in 11.08 seconds in the summer Olympics at Montreal, West German runner Baerbel Eckert the 200-meter in 22.37 seconds, Poland's Irene Szewinska, now 30, the 400-meter in a record-breaking 49.29 seconds, Soviet runner Tatiana Kazankina the 800-meter run in 1 minute, 54.94 seconds and the 1,500-meter in 4 minutes, 5.48 seconds, East German runner Johanna Schaller the 100-meter hurdles in 12.77 seconds, East German athlete Rosemarie Ackerman the running high jump (6.4 inches), East German athlete Angela Voigt the long jump (22 feet, ½ inch), Bulgarian athlete Ivanka Christova the shot put (69 feet, 5 inches), East German athlete Evelin Schlaak the discus throw (226 feet, 4 inches), Ruth Fuchs the javelin throw (216 feet, 4 inches), East German athlete Siegrun Siegl the pentathlon. Romanian gymnast Nadia Comaneci, 14, achieves seven perfect scores and wins three gold medals. East German swimmer Kornelia Ender wins the 100-meter freestyle in 55.65 seconds and the 200-meter in 1 minute, 59.26 seconds, East German swimmer Petra Thumer the 400-meter in 4 minutes, 09.89 seconds and the 800-meter in 8 minutes, 37.14 seconds, East German swimmer Ulrike Richter the 100-meter backstroke in 1 minute, 1.83 seconds and the 200-meter in 2 minutes, 13.43 seconds, East German swimmer Hannelore Anke the 100-meter breaststroke in 1 minute, 11.6 seconds, Soviet swimmer Marina Koshevaia the 200-meter in 2 minutes, 33.35 seconds, Kornelia Ender the 100-meter butterfly in 1 minute, 0.13 seconds, East German swimmer Andrea Pollack the 200-meter in 2 minutes, 11.41 seconds, East German swimmer Ulrike Tauber the 400-meter individual medley in 4 minutes, 42.77 seconds, U.S. swimmer Jennifer Chandler the springboard dive event, Soviet swimmer Elena Vaytsekhovskaia the platform dive.

Chris Evert wins in women's singles at both Wimbledon and Forest Hills.

Liz Claiborne fashions are introduced January 19 by New York fashion designer Elisabeth Claiborne,

46, and her husband, Arthur Ortenberg (they have two other partners), whose affordable, casual, mix-and-match sportswear separates for working women will break new ground. Born and raised in Brussels (her father was a banker from New Orleans), she returned with her family to the United States before the Nazis invaded Belgium in 1940, studied art in Europe after the war, worked on Seventh Avenue for designer Tina Lesser beginning in 1950, had a series of other bosses, and has been a top dress designer since the 1960s, but has waited until her son and two stepchildren finished college before introducing her own label. The Ortenbergs will build a company with 3,400 employees before they retire from active management in June 1989 with stock valued at nearly $100 million.

Canadian rapist Henry Williams, 26, requests at his trial January 15 that he be castrated to prevent further offenses. A mental patient, he is being sentenced to his third life term, having raped and murdered a 19-year old student in 1976. A defense psychiatrist cites a Danish study showing that 900 castrations produced "desired results" 90 percent of the time.

New York's .44-caliber killer claims his first victim early in the morning of July 29. A man who will prove to be David Berkowitz, 24, of Yonkers approaches an Oldsmobile double-parked in front of a Bronx apartment house and opens fire with a .44-caliber Bulldog revolver on medical technician Donna Lauria, 18, who has just returned from a Manhattan discothèque with her friend Jody Valenti, 19, a nurse; Berkowitz begins a 12-month career in which he will terrorize the city, killing five women and one man, leaving seven wounded (*see* 1977).

Perrier water is introduced in U.S. markets after 113 years in Europe. Although consumers prefer cheaper brands like Canada Dry in blind taste tests, Perrier sales will reach $177 million in a decade as fitness-minded Americans switch from alcoholic beverages.

India announces a plan February 25 to penalize parents who have more than two children.

Mead Johnson, Ortho Pharmaceuticals (a Johnson & Johnson subsidiary), and Syntex Laboratories—

the three largest U.S. marketers of sequential birth control pills (Ortho is the leading marketer of *all* oral contraceptives), announce February 25 that they are withdrawing their products as a result of "new evidence" linking the pills to endometrial cancer. Sold under names such as Oracon, Ortho-Novum SQ, and Norquen, they account for about 10 percent of all oral contraceptives sold in America.

Bejing announces that China's birthrate has fallen to 12.6 per 1,000, down from 26 per 1,000 in 1970, but few people believe the figures (*see* 1978).

The U.S. Supreme Court rules 6 to 3 July 1 that a 1974 Missouri law requiring a husband's consent for a first-trimester abortion is unconstitutional (*Planned Parenthood of Central Missouri* v. *Danforth*). Writes Justice Blackmun, "The obvious fact is that when the wife or the husband disagree . . . only one of the two marriage partners can prevail. Since it is the woman who physically bears the child and who is the more directly and immediately affected by the pregnancy . . . , the balance weighs in her favor." The court rules November 8 that a law blocking use of Medicaid funds for abortions is unconstitutional (but *see* 1977).

The Hyde Amendment to the Health, Education and Welfare appropriations bill clears Congress by a 256-114 vote September 16 and bars use of federal funds for abortions "except where the life of the mother would be endangered if the fetus were brought to term." From 250,000 to 300,000 U.S. women received Medicaid-funded abortions in 1975, critics call the new legislation discriminatory and unconstitutional, supporters—including Rep. Henry Hyde, 52 (R., Ill.)—contend that the government should not use tax revenues to fund operations which a substantial percentage of Americans consider immoral (*see* 1980).

1977

Economist Juanita Kreps, now 56, is sworn in as Secretary of Commerce in President Carter's Cabinet: she is the first woman to hold that position.

California's Governor Edmund G. "Jerry" Brown, Jr., appoints his Secretary of Agriculture and Services Rose Elizabeth Bird, 40, as the state's chief justice February 12. A former Stanford law teacher, she is the first woman on the Supreme Court, has had no judicial experience for the $66,896 position, but has drafted the state's historic Agricultural Relations Act.

Prime Minister Indira Gandhi frees most of India's political prisoners, but voters repudiate her repressive 18-month "emergency" rule, which has tried to stifle political opposition in the world's largest democracy; former Prime Minister Morarji R. Desai, 81, returns to power and promises to restore morality to government.

West German terrorists murder the attorney general in charge of the Baader-Meinhof gang prosecu-

Indira Gandhi, daughter of Pandit Nehru, served as India's prime minister on and off for 15 years. AP/WIDE WORLD PHOTOS

tion April 7 along with his driver and bodyguard (*see* 1976). Andreas Baader and two accomplices are convicted 3 weeks later and sentenced to life terms for murder, complicity in 34 attempted murders, and forming a criminal association. "So-called political motives" are no excuse for terrorism, says the judge, and no reason for clemency. The head of the Dresdner Bank, Jürgen Ponto, is murdered at Frankfurt July 30 by his granddaughter, 26, an RAF member (*see* 1974). Further outrages ensue, and Baader is found shot dead in his cell October 18 at Stuttgart's Stammheim Prison; his girlfriend, Gudrun Ensslin, 37, is found hanging from a bar in her cell window. West Germany mobilizes 30,000 police officers and restricts civil liberties.

The Argentine women's group Las Madres de los Desparecidos keeps a silent vigil, parading through the streets of Buenos Aires with pictures of "disappeared" daughters, sons, husbands, and fathers who have been secretly seized and in most cases murdered as "subversives" by the military government that is trying to eliminate Peronist and other elements opposed to its repressive regime. Founded in April by patriot Azunclena De Vincenti, the group carries placards that may say, "Donde está Pedro?" or "Donde está Rosa?" They demand explanations.

Spanish heroine Dolores Iburruri "La Pasionaria," now 81, returns May 13 after 38 years in exile, most of them spent at Moscow. Having protested the Soviet invasion of Czechoslovakia in 1968, she stands for election on the Communist ticket in the June parliamentary elections—Spain's first free elections since 1936—but loses at the polls.

Actress Melina Mercouri, now 52, wins a landslide election to the Greek Parliament. She denounced the takeover of her country's government by a right-wing military junta 10 years ago, spent most of 7 years in exile at Paris, and returned in 1974— 2 days after the collapse of the junta.

The New Japan Women's party wins only .4 percent of the popular vote in Japan's parliamentary elections. Misako Enoki terminates her radical feminist Pink Panthers movement (*see* 1972) but says it has established an awareness of the liberation issue and shown that a woman can be an "assertive fighter" yet remain beautiful and feminine.

Rape victim Inez Garcia is acquitted of all charges March 5 after having spent 22 months behind bars (*see* 1974).

The National Organization for Women (NOW) makes Ohio housewife Eleanor Cutri Smeal, 38, its first salaried president. She succeeds Karen DeCrow.

Militant suffragist Alice Paul dies July 9 at age 92.

A sex discrimination class action suit against the *Reader's Digest* ends November 4 with a verdict in favor of eight named plaintiffs. The magazine is ordered to pay $1.375 million in back pay and salary increases to 5,635 present and former female employees (an average of only $244 each) (*see New York Times*, 1978).

The National Women's Conference at Houston November 18 to 21 assembles 20,000 women, men, and children from all parts of the political spectrum in the first federally sponsored gathering to discuss and act upon issues of concern to women. Included are mothers, daughters, grandmothers, homemakers, working women, students, the First Lady, two former First Ladies, members of Congress, etc.

 Zambia's Village Industry Service is founded by entrepreneur Joyce Mapoma to develop cottage industries and business skills.

The first MRI (magnetic resonance imaging) scanner is tested July 2 by Brooklyn, N.Y., medical researcher Raymond V. Damadian, 39, whose diagnostic tool will be widely used to detect cancer and other abnormalities without exposing patients to X-ray radiation. The scanner is based on the phenomenon that nuclei of some atoms line up in the presence of an electromagnetic field. The FDA will approve commercial sale of MRI scanners in 1984 (*see* 1982).

Mammography for breast cancer detection increases with the growing use of new film/screen techniques using very low X-ray radiation doses and a Xerox process that produces breast images on charged selenium-contact aluminum plates which are then transferred to special paper. Radiation risk is considered negligible, and the survival rate when the cancer is detected in the localized stage with negative lymph nodes is 90 percent or more (the rate drops to 60 percent if the cancer has spread). Women are encouraged to self-examine their breasts, consult a physician if any suspicious lumps are felt, and have biopsies if their mammograms indicate any abnormality.

Lung cancer deaths among U.S. women (14.9 per 100,000, up from 1.5 per 100,000 in 1930) pass colorectal cancer deaths (14.3 per 100,000) and begin to approach breast cancer deaths (*see* Virginia Slims Tournament, below).

Dr. Rosalyn S. Yalow and two male scientists share the Nobel Prize for medicine (*see* 1959). Previous winners have virtually all been men, and in her acceptance speech at Oslo Yalow speaks out against

Mammography helped to make breast cancer less of a threat to women's lives than lung cancer. MEDICAL TRIBUNE

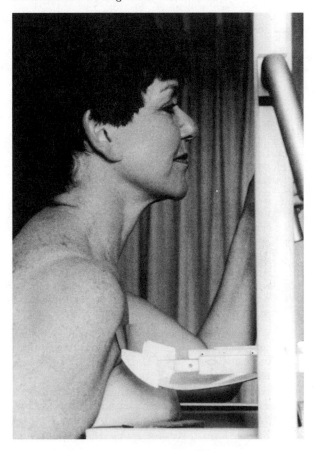

discrimination, saying, "The world cannot afford the loss of the talents of half its people if we are to solve the many problems which beset us."

West Point officials change their criteria for recruiting, testing, and training women cadets after 1 year of experience (*see* 1976). Of the 119 women appointed in the summer of 1976, 30 have dropped out or been dismissed. Women from the Deep South and those with some college have proved less likely to stay the course than other cadets.

Brown University agrees September 18 to give tenure to professors Louise Lanphere, Claude Carey, and Helen Cseer to settle a sex discrimination suit. The out-of-court settlement includes a cash award totaling $48,500. A federal judge sets affirmative action goals and timetables for the university. By 1991, Brown will have 67 tenured female faculty members, up from 12, with a total of 128 female faculty members, up from 52.

Television reporter Judy (Caroline) Woodruff, 30, becomes White House correspondent for the National Broadcasting Company (NBC). She will spend much of her career working for Public Television before moving to Cable News Network (CNN) in 1993.

Nonfiction: *The Power of the Positive Woman* by Phyllis Schlafly, now 53, says that women as a class are essentially different from men and should therefore not compete, so while she expresses approval for existing equal rights legislation and federal sex discrimination suits that have paved the way for "a future in which [the American woman's] educational and employment options are unlimited," she opposes the Equal Rights Amendment on grounds that it is redundant, since "The Positive Woman in America today has a near-infinite opportunity to control her own destiny, to reach new heights of achievement, and to motivate and influence others" (Schlafly, who opposes abortion, divorce, and extra-marital sex, will mount a Stop-ERA lobbying campaign that will effectively block the amendment in many states); *We Must March, My Darlings* (essays) by Diana Trilling, now 72, who has returned to her alma mater, Radcliffe, for nearly 9 weeks with her husband, Lionel; *Going Too Far: The Personal Chronicles of a Feminist* by poet Robin Morgan; *My Mother/My Self* by U.S. writer

Nancy Friday, 40, whose interviews with more than 300 women, including some psychologists and sociologists, have told her that mothers and daughters both feel an inappropriate sense of guilt about what they think they could have done when they actually feel a suffocating dependency and fear of loss because women have been taught to suppress their feelings; *Pink Collar Workers: Inside the World of Women's Work* by U.S. writer Louise Kapp Howe, 42; *The Managerial Woman* by U.S. writers Margaret Hennig and Anne Jardim; *I Am the Fire of Time: The Voices of Native American Women*, edited by Jane B. Katz.

Phyllis Schlafly campaigned against virtually everything that U.S. feminists were struggling for. LIBRARY OF CONGRESS

Fiction: *The Women's Room* by U.S. novelist Marilyn French (*née* Edwards), 47; *The Ice Age* by Margaret Drabble; *The Slave Girl* by Buchi Emecheta; *The Shrine and Other Stories* by Mary Lavin; *The Road to Lichfield* by Penelope Lively; *The Danger Tree* by Olivia Manning; *Injury Time* by Beryl Bainbridge; *Words of Advice* by Fay Weldon; *Thy Servant Heareth* (*Din tjänare hör*) by Sara Lidman; *The Thorn Birds* by Australian novelist Colleen McCullogh, 39; *Song of Solomon* by Toni Morrison (National Book Award); *A Book of Common Prayer* by Joan Didion; *Earthly Possessions* by Anne Tyler; *Ceremony* by Leslie Marmon Silko; *Property Of* by New York novelist Alice Hoffman, 25; *Wifey* by Judy Blume; *Great Granny Webster* by Caroline Blackwood, whose husband, poet Robert Lowell, dies of a heart attack at New York September 12;

Sita by Kate Millett; *Blood Tie* by Mary Lee Settle (National Book Award); *How to Save Your Life* by Erica Jong; *On Keeping Women* by Hortense Calisher; *Torch Song* by Anne Richardson Roiphe is about a failed marriage; *Adam's Eve* by Faith Baldwin, now 83; *Winds of Love* by Agnes Turnbull, now 88; *Captive Bride* by U.S. historical romance novelist (Helen) Johanna Lindsey (*née* Howard), 25; *Passion's Promise* by Danielle Steel; *A Question of Identity* by June Thompson.

Juvenile: *Starring Sally J. Freedman as Herself* by Judy Blume.

Painting: *Untitled Film Stills* (black-and-white photographs) by U.S. artist Cindy Sherman, 23; *Searchin'*, *New York Dawn*, and *Spring Point* by Elizabeth Murray; *392 Broadway* (baked enamel on silk-screen grid, enamel on steel plates), *17 White Street* (baked enamel on silk screen, enamel on steel plates, 80 plates), and *Graceland Mansion* (baked enamel on silk-screen grid, enamel on steel plates, 80 plates) by Jennifer Bartlett, who idolized the late Elvis Presley when she was a child and was upset by his death at Memphis August 16 at age 42 (her work, begun before he died, shows the same symbolic house from five different angles in horizontal sequence at five different times of day in five different painting styles).

New York art dealer Mary Boone, 26, opens her own gallery at 420 West Broadway in Soho.

Theater: Jessica Tandy and Hume Cronyn in D. L. Coburn's *The Gin Game* 10/6 at New York's John Golden Theater, 518 perfs.; Max von Sydow as August von Strindberg, Bibi Andersson, Eileen Atkins, and Werner Kemperer in Per Olov Enquist's *The Night of the Tribades* (*Tribadernes natt, or Lesbian's Night*) 10/12 at New York's Helen Hayes Theater, 12 perfs.; Cliff Gorman, Anita Gillette, Judd Hirsch, and Ann Wedgeworth in Neil Simon's *Chapter Two* 12/4 at New York's Imperial Theater, 857 perfs.

Television: *Roots* 1/27–30 on ABC with LeVar Burton, Cicely Tyson, Maya Angelou, Ben Vereen.

Films: Diane Keaton, Shelley Duvall, and Woody Allen in Allen's *Annie Hall*; Jane Fonda, Vanessa Redgrave, and Jason Robards in Fred Zinnemann's *Julia*; Krystyna Janda in Andrzej Wajda's *Man of*

Marble. Also: Joan Micklin Silver's *Between the Lines* with John Heard and Lindsay Crouse; Julie Christie and Fritz Weaver in Donald Cammell's *Demon Seed*; Michiyo Kogure in Kenji Mizoguchi's *A Geisha*; Richard Dreyfuss and Marsha Mason, 37, in Herbert Ross's *The Goodbye Girl*; Barbara Kopple's documentary *Harlan County, U.S.A.*; Lily Tomlin and Art Carney in Robert Benton's *The Late Show*; Robert De Niro, Gérard Dépardieu, Donald Sutherland, Burt Lancaster, Dominique Sanda, Stefanià Sandrelli, and Sterling Hayden in Bernardo Bertolucci's *1900*; Dolores Santamaria and Kidlat Tahimik in Tahimik's *The Perfumed Nightmare*; Sissy (*née* Mary Elizabeth) Spacek, 26, Shelley Duvall, and Janice Rule in Robert Altman's *Three Women*; Vittorio Gassman, Nino Manfredi, and Stefanià Sandrelli in Ettore Scola's *We All Loved Each Other So Much*.

Bette Davis, now 68, receives the American Film Institute's Lifetime Achievement Award in ceremonies at Beverly Hills March 2. She is the first woman to be so honored. Joan Crawford dies May 10 at age 73.

Hollywood musicals: John Travolta and Karen Lynn Gorley in John Badham's *Saturday Night Fever*, music and lyrics by the Bee Gees, songs that include "Stayin' Alive," "How Deep Is Your Love?," and the title song.

Broadway musicals: Andrea McArdle as the cartoon character "Little Orphan Annie" in *Annie* 4/21 at the Alvin Theater with Charles Strouse–Martin Charnin songs, 2,377 perfs.

German violin protégée Anne-Sophie Mutter, 13, makes her professional debut playing the Mozart Violin Concerto in G major with the Berlin Philharmonic under Herbert von Karajan at the Easter Salzburg Festival, goes on to play at the Salzburg Summer Festival, and makes her London debut with Daniel Barenboim and the English Chamber Orchestra.

Opera singer Maria Callas dies of a heart attack at her Paris home September 16 at age 53.

Popular songs: *Blondie* (album) and *Plastic Letters* (album) by the New York new wave rock group Blondie (Miami-born singer-songwriter Debbie [Deborah] Harry, 32, guitarist Chris Stein, 28, and others); *You Light Up My Life* (album) by U.S. recording artist Debbie (Deborah Ann) Boone, 21, includes "End of the World" and "He's a Rebel"; Olivia Newton-John records "Sam" and "Hopelessly Devoted to You"; *Simple Dreams* (album) by Linda Ronstadt; "Let's Get Together," "Southern California" (with ex-husband George Jones), and "One of a Kind" by Tammy Wynette; *Reba McEntire* (album) by Oklahoma country singer-songwriter McEntire, 23, who last year married a member of the Professional Rodeo Cowboy Association and helps him run a ranch when not on tour or appearing on *Grand Ole Opry*.

U.S. auto racer Janet Guthrie, 39, becomes the first woman to qualify for and race in the Indianapolis 500. Driving with a broken wrist, she comes in eighth.

Chris Evert wins the $50,000 Virginia Slims Tournament March 27 at New York.

Virginia Wade wins in women's singles at Wimbledon, Chris Evert at Forest Hills.

U.S. golfer Judy Rankin (*née* Torluemke), 24, is the top money winner on the LPGA circuit for the second year in a row.

Hanae Mori opens her Haute Couture Maison at Paris (*see* 1965).

U.S. blue jean sales top 500 million pairs, up from 150 million in 1957 and just over 200 million in 1967. Levi Strauss & Co. remains the largest producer, but higher-priced designer jeans increase their share of the market and counterfeit labels proliferate.

The Boy Scouts of America, founded in 1910, changes its name February 22 to Scouting/USA.

Canadian Prime Minister Pierre Trudeau and his wife, Margaret, announce at Ottawa May 27 that they they are separating after 6 years of marriage. He retains custody of their children.

Jacqueline Onassis negotiates a settlement with the estate of her late husband, Ari, who died in mid-May 1975 at age 75. She is to receive $20 million—more than twice the $250,000 per year provided for in his will and nearly seven times the $3 million set-

tlement that rumors say he would have paid if there had been a divorce.

Surveys show that the number of U.S. adults under age 35 living alone has more than doubled since 1970. Analysts ascribe the growing trend toward leaving home early and marrying late to such factors as easier credit, an increased wariness about marriage, and greater career opportunities for young women. More and more married couples now live apart, usually to pursue independent careers, and often see each other only on weekends.

 Philip Morris sponsors the Virginia Slims tennis tournament (above) to promote its Virginia Slims cigarette brand, whose advertising targets women (*see* 1968; medicine, above).

 New York's .44-caliber killer continues his murders (*see* 1976). He kills Wall Street clerk Christine Freund, 25, January 29 as she sits with her boyfriend in his car in Ridgewood, Queens. He shoots Virginia Voskerichain, 19, in the face at point-blank range March 8 less than 100 yards from the Freund shooting. He shoots Bronx student Valentine Suriani, 18, and her boyfriend Alexander Esau, 20, of Manhattan in a parked car April 17 a few blocks from last year's Lauria murder. He shoots Bronx student Judy Placido, 17, and her boyfriend Sal Lupo, 20, of Brooklyn June 26 in a parked car outside a Bayside, Queens, discotheque, but both survive. Flatbush, Brooklyn, woman Stacy Moscowitz, 20, and her Bensonhurst boyfriend Robert Violante, 20, are shot July 31; she dies after extensive brain surgery, he is blinded. Psychotic Yonkers postal worker David Berkowitz, 24, is arrested August 10 and claims that he has acted on orders from the dog of his neighbor Sam Carr, 64, who says he does not know him.

Canada stops granting licenses to carry handguns for protection of property and requires licenses for rifles and shotguns as well as for handguns.

 Kenya's Green Belt Movement, founded by Nairobi University biologist Wangari Maathai, 37, will be responsible for planting nearly 5 million trees in the next 10 years. Daughter of a farmworker, Maathai is the first Kenyan woman to earn a PhD and the first to head a department at the university. She is a pioneer not only in the environmental movement but also in the struggle for women's rights.

 Physician James Sammons testifies for the American Medical Association before the Congressional Commerce Oversight Committee that many Catholic women have hysterectomies because they are conflicted about using contraceptive measures forbidden by the Church and come to their doctors with "symptoms." If they are "sick" and "need" a hysterectomy, Sammons says, then they are off the hook, and they have little trouble finding compliant surgeons.

Nothing in the Constitution requires that states use Medicaid money to fund elective abortions, nor does any federal law, says the Supreme Court in a 6-to-3 ruling handed down June 20 (*Beal* v. *Doe* and *Maher* v. *Roe*). The Senate votes 56 to 42 June 29 to bar the funding of elective abortions except in cases of rape, incest, or medical necessity. The House votes 238 to 162 August 2 to bar such funding except where childbirth would endanger the life of the mother. Right-to-life groups have mobilized to defeat politicians supporting legalized abortion; critics object that abortion, while legal, is becoming a privilege for the rich. President Carter concedes that discriminating against the poor in abortion matters is unfair but echoes the late President Kennedy in saying, "There are many things in life that are not fair." Rosaura Jiminez, 27, dies in pain October 3 at the hands of an illegal McAllen, Texas, abortionist, leaving a 5-year-old daughter. The cutback in federal Medicaid funds for abortion drove her to seek out the local woman, and hers is the first recorded death by illegal abortion since the cutback.

India's birth control efforts will collapse in the wake of Indira Gandhi's defeat (above) when it is revealed that 500 unmarried women were forcibly sterilized during Gandhi's "emergency" and that 1,500 men died as a result of improper vasectomies. The scandal will make the very words "family planning" taboo, the Ministry of Health and Family Planning will become the Ministry of Health and Family Welfare, and while surgical sterilization will remain the surest and most prevalent form of birth control, voluntary sterilization will decline to 1.8 million per year, down from more than a million

per month in 1975. Millions of women will become pregnant who would not have done so had government programs not been cut back.

1978

The Pentagon promotes the commander of the Army military police school at Fort McClellan, Ala., June 30. A former WAC commander, Brig. Gen. Mary Clarke, 57, becomes the army's first two-star major general.

Kansas voters elect Republican Nancy Kassebaum (*née* Landon), 46, to the U.S. Senate. Daughter of onetime governor and 1936 presidential candidate Alfred M. Landon, the former Senate staff worker becomes the only woman senator.

South African apartheid foe Helen Joseph is jailed for contempt after refusing to testify against Winnie Mandela, whose husband, Nelson, has been imprisoned since 1962 (*see* 1961). Joseph, now 72, has visited Mrs. Mandela at Brandford along with Jackie Bosman, Ilona Kleinschmidt, 28, and Barbara Waite, 42. Bridget Oppenheimer, wife of the diamond- and gold-mining magnate, has been moved by the Soweto riots and inspired by the example of women in Northern Ireland to form the liberal group Women for Peace.

Qing Qeqing, now 66, becomes president of the All-China Women's Federation.

Nearly 100,000 demonstrators assemble on the Mall at Washington, D.C., July 9 to support an extension of the 7-year deadline for ratification of the Equal Rights Amendment beyond March 22, 1979. Held in humid 90° weather, the largest women's gathering in the world marks the start of renewed efforts to obtain ratification, which is only three states short of being achieved (*see* Schlafly book, 1977). Many participants are dressed in white, like early suffragists (a few elderly women who marched in 1919 turn out), they carry purple, yellow, and white banners, and Rep. Barbara Mikulski (D., Md.) says, "Mrs. Schlafly, wherever you are, eat your heart out." The House votes 233 to 189 August 15 to extend the deadline by 39 months, and the Senate follows suit 60 to 36 October 6 (but *see* 1982).

1978

The fight for an Equal Rights Amendment produced a giant, but ultimately fruitless, march in Washington. CHIE NISHIO

Participants in the Washington demonstration (above) include Mormon feminist Sonia Johnson (*née* Harris), 42, of Virginia, whose position puts her into conflict with Church teachings (*see* 1979).

The *New York Times* settles a class action sex discrimination suit October 6 during an 88-day newspaper strike that has shut down all three of the city's dailies. The *Times* agrees to pay $350,000, including an average of $454.54 each in back pay (the *Times* calls the payments "annuities") for 550 women and to institute an affirmative action program.

Nearly 80 percent of women in the U.S. workforce in March hold clerical, sales, service, plant, or factory jobs. More than half of all husband-wife families have two or more wage earners. Only 140,000 women working in the private sector earn $25,000 per year or more as compared with 4,173,000 men.

The U.S. Department of Labor issues regulations designed to increase the number of women in blue-collar construction jobs. Appalachian women's and citizens' groups organize the Coal Employment Project to encourage hiring of women and minorities in the coal pits.

British women mark the 50th anniversary of suffrage July 2 but note that while women represent 40 percent of the workforce they still earn on average only 65 percent as much as men, women seldom appear on company boards or in top executive ranks, and the mandatory retirement age for women is 60, whereas for men it is 65. Under the income tax law, a husband is responsible for filling out his wife's tax return, making it impossible for her to hide any of her income from him, and a survey has revealed that seven out of ten British wives do not know how much their husbands earn.

Legislation signed by President Carter October 10 authorizes the minting of silver dollars bearing the portrait of Susan B. Anthony, but the small coins will be confused with quarters and enjoy little popularity.

Five women in a West Virginia plant submit to sterilization in order to keep their jobs following an announcement by American Cyanamid Co. that it will bar women of reproductive capability from jobs that expose them to lead compounds.

The Women and Health Roundtable reports that 23.7 percent of students enrolled at medical schools in the past year were women, an increase of 87 percent over 1973.

The National Cancer Institute reports that lung cancer in women increased 30 percent from 1973 to 1976.

About one-quarter of British physicians are women, but the higher-paid specialties, such as surgery, continue for the most part to be closed to women.

More women than men enter U.S. colleges for the first time in history, but a report by the National Association of Secondary School Principals declares that the percentage of women high school principals has declined from 10 percent in 1965 to 7 percent this year.

The Revisionists Revised: A Critique of the Radical Attack on Schools (essays) by Diane Ravitch is a polemic refuting recent suggestions that teaching in public schools reflects a conspiracy against the proletariat or an assault upon human spontaneity. Education has meant different things to different people over the years, she says, but the poorest Americans have consistently placed their hopes for their children in formal education, and with good reason.

Self magazine begins publication at New York in January as Condé Nast expands.

Working Woman magazine begins publication at New York in March.

The French feminist magazine *F.* begins publication at Paris.

Nonfiction: *The Reproduction of Mothering: Psychoanalysis and the Sociology of Gender* by University of California (Santa Cruz) sociologist Nancy (Julia) Chodrow, 34, challenges the traditional view that females are biologically predisposed toward nurturing infants (she argues that mothering fulfills a psychological need for a reciprocal infancy that begins in her own infancy, when she and her mother perceive each other as extensions of themselves); *Gyn/Ecology: The Metaethics of Radical Feminism* by Mary Daly; *For Her Own Good: 150 Years of the Experts' Advice to Women* by Barbara Ehrenreich and Deirde English; *The Life of the Mind* by the late Hannah Arendt, who died in 1975 at age 69; *Nuclear Madness: What You Can Do!* by New Zealand physician Helen (Mary) Caldicott (*née* Brionowski), 40 (with Nancy Herington and Nahum Stiskin) (Caldicott, who fought to stop France from testing nuclear bombs in the South Pacific, moved to the United States last year, and is active in seeking a freeze on nuclear weapon construction); *Lying: Moral Choice in Public and Private Life* by Swedish-American writer Sisela Bok (*née* Myrdal, daughter of social scientists Alva and Gunnar Myrdal), 43, whose husband, Derek, is president of Harvard; *Metropolitan Life* (essays) by New York writer Fran (Frances Ann) Lebowitz, 27; *Families* by Jane Howard; *Silences* by Tillie Olsen; *A Distant Mirror* by Barbara Tuchman; *Visions of Glory: A History and a Memory of Jehovah's Witnesses* by Barbara Grizzuti Harrison; *A Prison and a Prisoner* by Susan Sheehan; *If Life Is a Bowl of Cherries, What Am I Doing in the Pits?* by Erma Bombeck.

Fiction: *Final Payments* by U.S. novelist Mary Gordon, 28; *Six of One* by Rita Mae Brown; *The Sea, The Sea* by Iris Murdoch; *The Battle Lost and Won* by Olivia Manning; *Palace Without Chairs: A Baroque Novel* by Brigid Brophy; *Splendid Lives* (stories) by Penelope Gilliatt; *Listening to Billie* by Alice Adams; *Violet Clay* by Gail Godwin; *A Stranger Is Watching* by Mary Higgins Clark; *A Woman of Independent Means* by U.S. novelist Elizabeth Forsythe Hailey, 40; *A Pirate's Love* by Johanna Lindsey; *Sisters and Strangers* by Helen Van Slyke; *The Wind from Hastings* by U.S. novelist Morgan Llewelyn (*née* Snyder; she will change her name to Llewelyn in August 1981); *Now and Forever* by Danielle Steel; *Scruples* by Beverly Hills novelist Judith Krantz (*née* Tarcher), 50; *Compromising Positions* by U.S. novelist Susan Isaacs, 35; *Prelude to Terror* by Helen MacInnes, now 70.

Poetry: *The Retrieval System* by Maxine Kumin; *The Five Stages of Grief* by Linda Pastan; *On Your Own* by Tess Gallagher; *Cotton Candy on a Rainy Day* by Nikki Giovanni.

Painting: *Children Meeting* by Elizabeth Murray; *Diptych* (collage of charcoal and paper on canvas) by Lee Krasner.

Theater: John Wood, Marian Seldes, and Victor Garber in Ira Levin's *Deathtrap* 2/26 at New York's Music Box Theater, 1,793 perfs.; Diana Rigg, Peter Machin, William Marlowe, Ohu Jacobs, and David Langton in Tom Stoppard's *Night and Day* 11/8 at London's Phoenix Theatre; Michael Gambon, Daniel Massey, and Penelope Wilton in Harold Pinter's *Betrayal* 11/15 at London's National Theatre (Lyttleton); Richard Hamilton, Mary McDonnell, Tom Noonan, and Jacqueline Brooks in Sam Shepard's *Buried Child* 12/5 at New York's off-Broadway Theater de Lys, 152 perfs.

Television: *Dallas* 4/2 on CBS with Larry Hagman (as J. R. Ewing), Barbara Bel Geddes, Victoria Principal (to 5/3/91).

Films: Robert De Niro, Meryl (originally Mary Louise) Streep, 29, Christopher Walken, and John Savage in Michael Cimino's *The Deer Hunter*; Jill Clayburgh, 33, and Alan Bates in Paul Mazursky's *An Unmarried Woman*. Also: Nino Manfredi and Danish-born actress Anna Karina (Hanne Karin Bayer), 38, in Franco Brusati's *Bread and Chocolate*; Jane Fonda and Jon Voight in Hal Ashby's *Coming Home*; Richard Gere, Brooke Adams, and Linda Manz in Terrence Malick's *Days of Heaven*; Gérard Dépardieu, Carol Laure, Riton, and Patrick Deware in Bertrand Blier's *Get Out Your Handkerchiefs*; Claudia Weill's *Girlfriends* with Melanie Mayron; Walter Matthau, Glenda Jackson, and Art Carney in Howard Zieff's *House Calls*; Kristin Griffith, Mary Beth Hurt, Diane Keaton, and Richard Jordan in Woody Allen's *Interiors*.

Hollywood musical: Sonia Braga and Jose Wilkes in Bruno Barreto's *Dona Flor and Her Two Husbands*.

Stage musicals: Imogene Coca, Kevin Kline, John Cullum, and Madeline Kahn in *On the 20th Century* 2/19 at New York's St. James Theater, with Cy Coleman–Betty Comden–Adolph Green songs, 453 perfs.; Ken Page, Amelia McQueen, André De Shields, and Charlotte Woodward in *Ain't Misbehavin'* 5/9 at New York's Longacre Theater, with music and lyrics mostly by the late Thomas Wright "Fats" Waller, who died in 1943, songs that include "Honeysuckle Rose," "Mean to Me," "The Joint Is Jumpin'," and the title song, 1,604 perfs.; Elizabeth Swados, 27, in *Runaways* 5/13 at New York's Plymouth Theater (after 76 perfs. at the Public/Cabaret Theater), with songs by Swados, 274 perfs.; Carlin Glynn, Henderson Forsythe, and Delores Hall in *The Best Little Whorehouse in Texas* 6/19 at New York's 46th Street Theater, with songs by Carol Hall, 1,584 perfs.; Elaine Paige as Eva Perón in *Evita* 6/21 at London's Prince Edward Theatre, with Andrew Lloyd Webber–Tim Rice songs that include "Don't Cry For Me, Argentina"; Liza Minnelli in *The Act* 10/9 at New York's Majestic Theater, with John Kander–Fred Ebb songs, 233 perfs.; Dorothy Loudon and Vincent Gardenia in *Ballroom* 12/14 at New York's Majestic Theater, with music by Gilly Goldenburg, lyrics by Alan and Marilyn Bergman, 116 perfs.

Popular songs: *Easter* (album) by Patti Smith; "Because the Night" by Smith and Bruce Springsteen; *Parallel Lines* (album) by the rock group Blondie includes the single "Heart of Glass"; Olivia Newton-John records "A Little More Love" and emerges as a film star with John Travolta in *Grease*; *Vested* (album) by Laura Nyro includes "My Innocence" and "American Dreamer"; *Blue Light in the Basement* (album) by Roberta Flack; "Here You Come Again" by Cynthia Weil and Barry Mann; Nina Simone records "Baltimore"; Lynn Anderson records "Last Love of My Life"; Tammy Wynette records "Womanhood"; Reba McEntire records "Last Night, Ev'ry Night."

Martina Navratilova, 21 (Czech), wins in women's singles at Wimbledon, Chris Evert in women's singles at the new USTA stadium in Flushing Meadow, Queens, New York.

Santa Clara, Calif., swimmer Penny Dean sets a new English Channel speed record July 29, swimming the 20-mile distance from England to France in 7 hours, 42 minutes.

U.S. golfer Nancy Lopez, 21, wins an unprecedented five consecutive LPGA tournaments, pocketing $161,235—the most any first-year professional, man or woman, has ever won.

Female reporters cannot be barred from locker rooms at New York's Yankee Stadium under a ruling handed down in September by federal judge Constance Baker Motley in a case filed last year by *Sports Illustrated* reporter Melissa Lincoln (*née* Ludtke).

Elizabeth (Lisa) Hallaby, 26, daughter of U.S. aviation executive Najeeb Hallaby, is married at Amman July 15 to Jordan's King Hussein, 42, whose first wife died and who has divorced his second, Princess Muna. He gives Elizabeth the name Noor al-Hussein and makes her queen of Jordan.

Shipping heiress Christina Onassis, 27, is married August 1 at a Moscow "wedding palace" to former Soviet merchant marine official Sergei Kausov, 37. She says that she has been brought up with every luxury and now wants to live a normal life, wash dishes, and take care of her husband.

Americans buy 13 million pairs of running shoes and 42 million pairs of "look-alike" jogger-type sneakers.

Huggies disposable diapers, introduced by Kimberly-Clark, have an hourglass shape and elastic fit that challenge Procter & Gamble's Pampers (*see* 1966; 1980).

A New Jersey man is convicted May 26 of kidnaping and raping his estranged wife, despite a state law saying that a man who forces his wife to have sex is not committing rape. The U.S. Supreme Court rules June 5 that a New Hampshire statutory rape law is unconstitutional because it punishes men and not women.

Oregon restaurant worker John Rideout, 20, is acquitted December 27 of having beaten his wife,

Greta, and raped her in the presence of their 2½-year-old daughter, Jenny, October 10. Oregon last year became the third state to permit prosecution of a husband for raping his wife, but this is the first case in which a woman was allegedly raped while still living with her husband. A jury of eight women and four men decides in the husband's favor. "I don't think justice was done," Mrs. Rideout tells reporters.

The National Clearinghouse on Marital & Date Rape, started by Laura X at Berkeley, Calif., works to enact marital rape laws in every state of the union (see 1969; 1993).

British and European feminists hold "Reclaim the Night" demonstrations in dangerous city districts, writing and speaking out against judges who treat rape lightly and give lenient sentences for it. Britain has about 100 refuge houses for battered women, and there is pressure on Parliament to provide public housing for victims of wife beating, which is widespread.

Love Canal east of Niagara Falls, N.Y., makes headlines in August as scores of residents are evacuated from houses built over an abandoned excavation site used from 1947 to 1953 to dump toxic chemical waste. A high incidence of birth defects and illnesses has been reported in the neighborhood, and there will be further evacuations in the next few years.

Michigan and Maine voters approve a ban on no-deposit, no-return bottles—a victory for environmentalists. The Glass Packaging Institute and other lobby groups work to prevent passage of "bottle bills" against nonreturnables. Oregon, Vermont, Iowa, and Connecticut have banned such bottles. Industry groups claim that litter recycling laws are more effective than outright bans.

Hua Guofeng tells the Fifth International People's Congress in February that China's birthrate must be lowered to less than 10 per 1,000 within 3 years (see 1979).

Italy votes May 18 to legalize abortion in the first 90 days of pregnancy, although girls under 18 must have parental approval and some will still patronize back-alley abortionists, fearing that state-run facilities may compromise their privacy. The Vatican continues to call abortion homicide.

Officials at a National Right to Life Committee convention June 2 urge 2,000 delegates to step up political efforts to adopt an antiabortion amendment to the Constitution.

The world's first "test tube baby," Louise Brown, is born July 25 at London's Oldham Hospital, where consultant gynecologist Patric Steptoe and physiologist Robert Edwards have fertilized an egg from Mrs. Lesley Brown's womb with sperm from her husband and have reimplanted the fertilized egg in the mother's womb. Surgeons had been unable to remove a blockage in the fallopian tubes leading to her uterus.

A New York woman sues a local hospital for having destroyed her test tube embroyo and is awarded $50,000 August 19.

A woman tried for murder in Kentucky in connection with a self-induced abortion is found not guilty August 31 by reason of insanity.

Planned Parenthood Federation of America names Faye Wattleton, 35, as its president. She becomes the first woman to head the agency as prolife activists in several states harass and vandalize abortion clinics.

1979

Iran's Mohammed Reza Shah Pahlevi flees to Egypt January 16 after nearly 38 years in power during which women have gained some rights. The Shiite fundamentalist Muslim leader Ayatollah Ruhollah Khomeini, 78, flies into Teheran February 1 after 15 years in exile, his supporters rout the elite Imperial Guard February 11, and turmoil continues throughout the year, with thousands killed in rioting and mass executions (see 1978; Shiites, 680).

Chicago votes April 3 to make former consumer sales commissioner Jane (Margaret) Byrne (née Burke), 45, the city's first woman mayor. She wins election with 82 percent of the vote.

British Conservative leader Margaret Hilda Roberts Thatcher, 53, becomes the nation's first woman prime minister when her party regains power May 3, winning the general election by the largest majority any party has received since 1966. Prime Minis-

Margaret Thatcher served as Britain's prime minister for 12 years—longer than any man in the century. AP/WIDE WORLD PHOTOS

ter Callaghan has lost a vote of confidence by one vote in Britain's House of Commons March 28, the first time such a vote has defeated a government since 1924. Mrs. Thatcher has promised to cut income taxes, scale down social services, and reduce the role of the state in daily life.

French Minister of Health Simone Veil becomes president of the European Community's first democratically elected parliament.

U.S.-educated German political leader Petra (Karin) Kelly, 32, quits the Social Democratic party in protest against its policies toward nuclear defense, health, and women. Stepdaughter of a U.S.

Army colonel, Kelly and some friends found the Green party, whose antinuclear environmental views will attract many followers (*see* 1983).

A new Greek law that takes effect February 2 allows a spouse who has been separated for more than 6 years to obtain a divorce even if her/his partner is unwilling to grant the divorce.

Some 15,000 Iranian women march on Teheran's Palace of Justice March 10 to protest the Ayatollah Khomeini's revocation of the 1975 Family Protection Law, his abolition of coeducational schools, and government pressure to wear the *chador*, a heavy veil that obscures the face. The new theocratic government (above) is not moved and will continue to require that all women, even non-Muslims visiting from abroad, wear the *chador* when they appear in public.

First Lady Rosalynn Carter delivers an address at New York April 26 urging women in state legislatures to join in forcing male support for the Equal Rights Amendment and women in her audience of women communicators to "put the heat on your senators" to nominate women for federal judgeships.

A federal law that takes effect April 29 forbids U.S. employers to discriminate against pregnant employees or any other disabled workers.

Navajo elderwoman Katherine Smith, 60, fires her rifle September 1 at a government crew building a barbed-wire fence that will come within 14 feet of a ceremonial hogan on her land in Arizona. Arrested, she is tried but acquitted, becoming a symbol of Navajo determination to protect the people's cultural integrity and prevent the intrusion of commercial interests into sacred land that includes Big Mountain.

Double- and even triple-digit inflation plagues much of the world. U.S. prices increase 13.3 percent for the year, the largest jump in 33 years, and the Federal Reserve Board's move in October to tighten the money supply sparks a jump in loan rates that will continue for 6 months. Banks raise their prime loan rate to 14.5 percent October 9, Wall Street's Dow Jones Industrial Average falls 26.48 points that day, and the New York Stock

Exchange has a record 81.6-million-share day October 10 as small investors panic. The U.S. gross national product has risen by more than a third in constant dollars since 1969, and unemployment has averaged less than 6 percent (it topped 9 percent in only one calendar year, versus a peak of 25 percent in the 1930s, when the GNP rose by only 4 percent and stock prices declined by only 31 percent as compared to 42 percent in the 1970s).

Iran's new government announces February 17 that exports of oil will resume March 5 at a price about 30 percent higher than that set by the OPEC nations in December 1978. Iranian oil production averages only 3.4 million barrels per day for the year, down from 5.4 million last year. Since the 900,000 barrels of Iranian crude imported daily by the United States last year supplied 6 percent of U.S. consumption, the drop in Iranian imports creates genuine fuel shortages in many states.

U.S. motorists line up at filling stations from spring through summer and are often unable to obtain more than a few gallons at a time.

An accident at Unit II of the Three Mile Island nuclear generating station near Harrisburg, Pa., March 28 raises alarms that the year-old reactor may explode and release radioactive cesium. The overheated reactor shuts down automatically, but Metropolitan Edison Company operators, misled by ambiguous indicators, think water pressure is building and shut down pumps still operating; the reactor heats up further, and tons of water that have poured out through the stuck-open valve overflow into an auxiliary building through a valve that should have been shut. The reactor core does not melt down despite exposure and damage. Some 144,000 people, mostly pregnant women and small children, are evacuated from the Middletown area. Little radiation is released.

Nine new U.S. nuclear reactors begin commercial production; France, Japan, the Soviet Union, and other nations continue to expand nuclear energy capabilities and reduce dependence on petroleum, but the malfunction at Three Mile Island (above) discourages new atomic energy facilities. U.S. utility companies cancel 11 reactor orders and will cancel more next year, installation of other reactors is indefinitely delayed. Inflation, high interest rates,

and declining demand for electricity limit construction of new reactors as much as does public opinion.

A federal jury at Oklahoma City decides May 18 that Kerr-McGee must pay $10.5 million to the estate of the late Karen Silkwood (*see* 1974).

First Lady Rosalynn Carter testifies before a congressional committee February 7 in behalf of the mentally ill. No president's wife has testified on Capitol Hill since Eleanor Roosevelt did it in the 1940s.

Former Secretary of Housing and Urban Development Patricia Harris, now 55, is sworn in as Secretary of Health and Human Services August 3, succeeding Joseph Califano.

The Jane Fonda Workout Studio opens at Beverly Hills with strenuous calisthenics and Hollywood glamour. "Go for the burn," Fonda exhorts her patrons (*see* 1982).

Medicare-funded kidney dialysis treatment costs $851 million for 46,000 U.S. patients, nearly 20 percent of them bedridden more or less permanently and about half unable to work. The escalating costs of hemodialysis raise questions about how much the nation can afford without slighting other health needs.

The Moral Majority is founded by Lynchburg, Va., evangelist Jerry Falwell, 46, of the Thomas Road Baptist Church, whose weekly *Old Time Gospel Hour* airs on more than 300 U.S. television stations and 64 foreign stations. The new political action group will register millions of new voters by November 1980 in an effort to block the Equal Rights Amendment, impede reform of the criminal code, disrupt the White House Conference on the Family, and fight abortion liberalization. It will continue until 1989.

Concerned Women of America is founded by members of the so-called religious right to oppose the growing feminist movement.

The Mormon Church excommunicates feminist Sonia Johnson in December on charges of "serious defection from the Church and its doctrines" in working for the Equal Rights Amendment (*see* 1978). Her husband will soon divorce her (*see* 1982).

Mother Teresa, now 69, is awarded the Nobel Peace Prize for her work with the poor of Calcutta and elsewhere (*see* 1948).

Federal judge Shirley Hufstedler is named by President Carter as the nation's first secretary of education.

U.S. spending on education reaches $151.5 billion, up from $8.3 billion in 1950, with $126.5 billion coming from government sources. But student proficiency scores will drop sharply in the next decade as the nation falls behind countries that spend much less.

Nonfiction: *On Lies, Secrets and Silence* by poet Adrienne Rich, who writes, "I am a feminist because I feel endangered, psychically and physically, by this society and because I believe that the women's movement is saying that we have come to an edge of history when men—insofar as they are embodiments of the patriarchal idea—have become dangerous to children and other living things, themselves included"; *Sexual Harassment of Working Women: A Case of Sex Discrimination* by feminist Connecticut lawyer Catherine A. MacKinnon, 43; *Women of a Certain Age: A Midlife Search for Self* by U.S. author Lillian Rubin (*née* Breslow), 55; *With Child: A Diary of Motherhood* by Phyllis Chesler; *The Gnostic Gospels* by Barnard College religious historian Elaine Pagels (*née* Hiesey), 36, who has studied more than 50 scrolls, written in Coptic by a heretical sect of Christians in the 1st or 2nd century and found by an Egyptian farmer in 1945; *I'm Dancing As Fast As I Can* by U.S. author Barbara Gordon, 44, who took muscle-relaxant anticonvulsant drug Valium for back pain and blames it for her chronic insomnia, convulsions, and hallucinations; *Scribble, Scribble: Notes on the Media* by Nora Ephron; *You May Well Ask* (memoir) by Naomi Mitchison, now 82.

Fiction: *Territorial Rights* by Muriel Spark; *Life Before Man* by Margaret Atwood; *Young Adolf* by Beryl Bainbridge; *Five for Sorrow, Ten for Joy* by Rumer Godden; *Familiar Passions* by Nina Bawden; *The Joys of Motherhood* by Buchi Emecheta, who came to London with her student husband and five children in 1962 but has long been a single mother; *Sleepless Nights* by Elizabeth Hardwick, now 63; *Sally Hemings* by U.S. novelist Barbara

Chase-Riboud (*née* West), 44, deals with an alleged 38-year liaison between Thomas Jefferson and his slave-mistress; *The Cutting Edge* by Penelope Gilliatt; *The Stained Hand of God* (*Kame no yogoretta te*) by Ayako Sono; *Only Children* by Alison Lurie; *A Woman of Substance* by English-American journalist-novelist Barbara Taylor Bradford, 46; *Secrets and Surprises* (stories) by Ann Beattie; *Beautiful Girl* (stories) by Alice Adams; *Black Tickets* (stories) by U.S. writer Jayne Anne Phillips, 27; *Vanishing Animals and Other Stories* by U.S. writer Mary Morris, 32; *Vida* by Marge Piercy; *The White Album* by Joan Didion; *Class Reunion: A Novel* by Rona Jaffe; *A Necessary Woman* by Helen Van Slyke; *Season of Passion* and *Summer's End* by Danielle Steel; *Ashes in the Wind* by Kathleen Woodiwiss; *The Habit of Loving* (in England, *Deadly Relations*) by June Thompson.

Juvenile: *Goodbye, Chicken Little* by Betsy Cromer Byars.

Painting: *At the Lake, Morning* (baked enamel on silk-screen grid, enamel on steel plates; oil on canvas, 45 plates, two canvases) and *Swimmers Atlanta: Flare* (oil on canvas; baked enamel on silk-screen grid, enamel on steel plates, 72 plates, two canvases) by Jennifer Bartlett; *The Dinner Party* (table with embroidered runners and surrounding place settings symbolizing 39 guests representing different aspects of women's history from primordial goddesses to contemporary writers and artists), a group effort by women organized under the direction of U.S. artist Judy Chicago (originally Cohen), 40. Inscribed on the floor are the names of 999 women of achievement. Sonia Delaunay dies at Paris December 4 at age 94; the last survivor of the pre-1914 Paris art world, she broke a femur nearly 2 years ago, has been confined to a wheelchair ever since, but is in good spirits at her death because she has just received a big check from Tokyo for a Robert-Sonia Delaunay retrospective exhibition.

Theater: Constance Cummings in Arthur Kopit's *Wings* 1/28 at New York's Lyceum Theater, 113 perfs.; Frances Sternhagen and Tom Aldredge in Ernest Thompson's *On Golden Pond* 2/28 at New York's New Apollo Theater, 126 perfs; *Cloud Nine* by English playwright Caryl Churchill, 40, 3/29 at London's Royal Court Theatre, with Anthony Sher,

Jim Hooper, and Carol Hayman; Tom Conti and Jean (Lyndsey Tarren) Marsh, 44, in Brian Clark's *Whose Life Is It Anyway?* 4/17 at London's Trafalgar Theatre; Kevin Kline and Roxanne Hart in Michael Weller's *Loose Ends* 6/7 at New York's Circle in the Square Theater, 270 perfs.; Mia Farrow, Anthony Perkins, and Carole Cook in Bernard Slade's *Romantic Comedy* 11/8 at New York's Ethel Barrymore Theater, 396 perfs.

Television series: *Knots Landing* 12/27 on CBS with Donna Mills, Ted Shackelford (to 5/12/93).

Films: Jane Fonda and Jack Lemmon in James Bridge's *The China Syndrome*; Giancarlo Giannini, Laura Antonelli, and Brazilian-born actress Jennifer O'Neill, 32, in Luchino Visconti's *The Innocent*; Meryl Streep and Dustin Hoffman in Robert Benton's *Kramer v. Kramer*. Also: Jeanne Moreau's *L'Adolescente*, with Laetitia Chauveau and Simone Signoret; Jerome Krabbé and Renée Soutendijk in Paul Verhoeven's *The Fourth Man*; Conchata Ferrell and Rip Torn in Richard Pearce's *Heartland*; Mariel Hemingway, 18, Diane Keaton, Marshall Brickman, and Woody Allen in Allen's *Manhattan*; Polish-born German actress Hanna Schygulla, 36, in Rainer Werner Fassbinder's *The Marriage of Maria Braun*; Gillian Armstrong's *My Brilliant Career* with Judy Davis; Sally Field, 33, in Martin Ritt's *Norma Rae*, based on North Carolina labor organizer Crystal Lee Sutton (see human rights, 1974); German-born Polish actress Nastassja Kinski (Nakszynski), 18, Peter Firth, and Leigh Lawson in Roman Polanski's *Tess*; Eddie Constantine and Hanna Schygulla in Rainer Werner Fassbinder's *Third Generation*; Brad Dourif, Ned Beatty, Amy Wright, and Daniel Shor in John Huston's *Wise Blood*.

Mary Pickford dies May 29 at age 86; actress Jean Seberg, now 40, disappears from her Paris apartment in late August wearing only a blanket and carrying barbiturates; her body is found in the backseat of her car September 8 in an exclusive section of the city.

Film musical: Roy Scheider, Jessica Lange, 20, and Ben Vereen in Bob Fosse's *All That Jazz*.

Stage musicals: Lucie Arnaz, 19, and Robert Klein in *They're Playing Our Song* 2/11 at New York's Imperial Theater, with Marvin Hamlisch–Carole Bayer Sager songs, 1,082 perfs; Angela Lansbury and Len Cariou (as the "demon barber of Fleet Street") in *Sweeney Todd* 3/1 at New York's Uris Theater, with Stephen Sondheim songs that include "Pretty Women," 558 perfs.; Ann Miller and Mickey Rooney in *Sugar Babies* 10/8 at New York's Mark Hellinger Theater, with Jimmy McHugh–Arthur Malvin songs, 1,208 perfs.

Popular songs: *Hard Times for Lovers* (album) by Judy Collins; "Bad Girls" by Donna Summer; *Don't Take Love for Granted* (album) by Lulu; *Wave* (album) by the Patti Smith Group, which gives its last performance in September at Florence, Italy, for a crowd of 70,000; *Just Tammy* (album) by Tammy Wynette; *New Kind of Feeling* (album) by Anne Murray, who also has hits with the singles "I Just Fall in Love Again," "Shadows in the Moonlight," and "Broken-Hearted Me"; *Out of a Dream* (album) by Reba McEntire includes the duet (with Jackie Ward) "That Makes Two of Us"; McEntire's singles "Runaway Heart" and "Sweet Dreams" are also hits.

Eleven concertgoers are crushed to death December 3 in a stampede for seats to a concert by the Who at Cincinnati's Riverfront Coliseum, casting a pall over the $2-billion-per-year rock concert business.

Opera: The New York City Opera appoints a new director—veteran soprano Beverly Sills, now 50, who has sung with the Opera since 1955.

Australian coloratura soprano Joan Sutherland, 52, is named a dame of the British Empire.

The Walkman cassette player introduced by Sony Corp: is a $200 pocket stereo with two pairs of earphones, making it possible to hear high-fidelity sound in any location without disturbing one's neighbors. It is the brainchild of Sony chairman Akio Morita, now 58, and will soon have an FM radio version.

Maine-born runner Joan Benoit, 21 (Bowdoin '79), enters her first Boston Marathon and beats all other women contestants. She took up running 6 years ago to strengthen muscles weakened in a skiing accident (*see* 1983).

U.S. sprinter Evelyn Ashford, 22, overtakes her 1976 Olympic teammate Brenda Morehead to break the 11-second barrier in the women's 100-meter dash June 16 at the Amateur Athletic Union outdoor track and field championships at Mount San Antonio College in Walnut, California.

Martina Navratilova wins in women's singles at Wimbledon, Tracy Ann Austin, 16, in U.S. women's singles.

Former Vice President Nelson A. Rockefeller suffers a heart attack and dies January 26 at age 70, reportedly while making love to a young woman friend in a midtown hideaway.

Michelle Triola Marvin, 46, who has taken actor Lee Marvin's last name but never married him, sues March 10 for "palimony." She contends that she gave up a promising singing career in 1964 to serve him as cook, companion, and confidante, lived with him until 1970, and is entitled to half the $3.6 million he earned during that period. Marvin, 55, agrees April 18 to pay her $104,000.

Maryland's Court of Appeals reverses the conviction of a rapist. The victim may have said no, the court rules, but she did not resist physically to the full extent of her capabilities (*Goldberg* v. *State*).

The U.S. Supreme Court rules 6 to 3 January 9 that a 1974 Pennsylvania statute requiring that a physician try to save the life of a fetus is unconstitutional (*Colautti* v. *Franklin*). The Court rules 8 to 1 July 2 that a Massachusetts law requiring unmarried, underage girls to get permission from their parents or a court judge before they can have abortions is unconstitutional (*Bellotti* v. *Baird*).

Chinese Deputy Premier Deng Xiaoping issues orders early in the year for a vigorous strengthening of family-planning policies, with Han couples limited to one child (96 percent of Chinese are Hans). The state calls on all couples to have "only one child if possible, two at the most, with a period of 3 or 4 years between them." The option of having two is dropped within a few months as provincial authorities pass laws requiring that all couples practice family planning and impose severe financial penalties on couples who have two or more children. A Chinese girl who marries is by custom taken into her husband's family and is no longer responsible for her own parents, so for rural families the new state policy raises fears that if their first and only child is

a daughter there will be no one to care for them in their old age. Female infanticide has been largely eradicated since 1949, but the new one-child rule revives the practice in some parts of China. Chinese manufacturers produce their first ultrasound machines; within a decade they will be turning out 10,000 per year, another 2,000 will be imported, ultrasound will be used to determine fetal gender, and many females will be aborted (*see* 1982).

1980

India's former Prime Minister Indira Gandhi regains power January 6 in an election victory engineered by her son Sanjay, 33, only 33 months after a humiliating defeat. Called ruthless and autocratic for pushing slum clearance projects that left thousands homeless and family-planning programs that included forced sterilizations, Sanjay has been convicted on one of more than a dozen criminal charges that he reaped huge profits from a state project to produce small, cheap automobiles, none of which ever came off the assembly line. Sanjay and a flight instructor die June 23 in a plane crash while doing illegal aerial acrobatics.

Canadian government minister Jeanne Sauvé (*née* Benoit), 57, is elected Speaker of Parliament April 14 and, as the first woman Speaker, draws sharp criticism from Conservatives on grounds that she is unfamiliar with the often baroque procedures of the almost all-male House and lacks established ties to its membership. A onetime television journalist and freelance columnist, Mrs. Sauvé has served in Prime Minister Trudeau's Cabinet, most recently overseeing the environment and communications. In the next 4 years she will win over the opposition, gaining a reputation for firmness and fairness (*see* 1984).

Juliana of the Netherlands abdicates on her 71st birthday April 30 and is succeeded after a 32-year reign by her daughter Beatrix, 42. The new queen, more pretentious than her mother, is married to a former officer in Hitler's SS. Demonstrations rock Amsterdam, Rotterdam, and Utrecht.

Iceland elects Reykjavík City Theater director Vigdis Finnbogadottir, 50, "President Vigdis."

Divorced in 1963, she adopted a baby daughter as a single parent in 1972, and she is the first woman anywhere in world history to be elected head of state. She will be reelected in 1984 and again in 1988.

A draft registration measure signed by President Carter June 27 requires that some 4 million U.S. men aged 19 and 20 register. Congress has excluded women, despite a request by Carter that they be included.

U.S. voters turn Carter out of office and elect former California governor Ronald Wilson Reagan, 69, an ex–Hollywood actor who campaigns with slick television commercials and wins 489 electoral votes to Carter's 149. Leading liberal Democrats lose as the Republicans gain control of the Senate for the first time since the 1950s.

English-American hostess Pamela Churchill Harriman (*née* Digby), 60, founds Democrats for the '90s to provide encouragement and financial support for politicians who will oppose Reagan's policies. Widow of former New York Governor/diplomat W. Averell Harriman and, before that, of Hollywood producer Leland Hayward, she divorced her first husband, Randolph Churchill, by whom she had a son, Winston Spencer. Her political action committee, PAMPAC, will raise millions of dollars in political contributions for Democratic party candidates (*see* 1993).

Weather Underground activist Bernardine Dohrn, now 38, turns herself in to Chicago police December 3; she has been a fugitive since 1970 and is blamed for several acts of terrorism by her left-wing group, including some bombings. "I regret not at all my efforts to side with the forces of revolution," she tells reporters. "The nature of the system has not changed. . . . The system of violence and degradation against women is openly encouraged."

Three U.S. nuns and a lay missionary are killed in December as violence continues in El Salvador between government security forces and leftist guerrillas.

Iran grants women the right to vote on the same basis as men (*see* Iraq, 1948), but Iranian women demonstrate at the president's office July 8 to protest the Islamic dress code (*see* 1979).

Japanese feminist Fusae Ichikawa, now 86, wins reelection to the Sanlin, upper house of the Diet, with more votes nationwide than any other candidate (*see* 1973). Universally known and widely respected, she organizes a conference of 48 women's organizations ranging from radical to conservative, and it is generally conceded that no one else could have done it.

"Listen, America!" by Moral Majority leader Rev. Jerry Falwell concludes, "The Equal Rights Amendment strikes at the foundation of our entire social structure."

Double-digit inflation continues in the United States with prices rising 12.4 percent by year's end as compared to 13.3 percent last year, fueling opposition to President Carter. Some countries have triple-digit inflation. A U.S. recession in the second quarter cuts real output by 9.9 percent; the economy is on the rise again by fall.

President-elect Reagan (above) has campaigned on what his running mate George Bush called "voodoo economics" (based on supply-side ideology) during the primary elections, but Bush drops his opposition at the convention.

British unemployment rises above 2 million for the first time since 1935 (when the workforce was one-third smaller) as recession depresses the economies of many countries. By year's end, unemployment reaches nearly 2.5 million, up from 800,000 early in 1975, and industrial production falls 5 percent as the government's monetarist policies try to stem a new burst of inflation, which again climbs above 20 percent, double the rate when Thatcher took office.

More than 52 percent of women aged 15 to 64 in Western countries are in the workforce, up from 45 percent in 1960. In Japan, 54.9 percent are in the workforce, down from 60.1 percent in 1960 when more women were employed in agriculture.

U.S. personal bankruptcies jump to 367,000, up from 209,500 last year. A new federal bankruptcy law that went into effect October 1, 1979, enables individuals to protect much more of their property against seizure by creditors.

Some 36 million Americans receive monthly Social Security checks, 26 million Medicare benefits, 22 million Medicaid benefits, 18 million food stamps, 15 million veterans' benefits, 11 million Aid to Families with Dependent Children funds; millions of students receive federal scholarship aid (*see* education, below); 27 million children benefit from school lunch programs, and most of these categories overlap. Ronald Reagan (above) promises to reduce the size of government.

U.S. gasoline prices average $1.20 to $1.23 per gallon for most of the year, up from 66.1¢ in 1978 but still less than half the price in most countries.

A task force appointed by the National Institutes of Health issues a 500-page report blaming the rising rate of cesarean deliveries on advances in medical technology (such as electronic fetal monitoring and epidural anaesthesia), legal aggressiveness in bringing malpractice suits, and changing attitudes on the part of mothers and fathers, who are having babies at older ages (*see* 1894). Courts have held that in order to provide the "accepted standard of care" in a problem birth the physician should perform a cesarean section, so obstetricians now operate at the first sign of trouble. Most mental retardation originates during pregnancy, not at delivery, but doctors opt for C-sections to be on the safe side. Being older, many women are having just one baby, and they want it to be perfect. While a woman who delivers vaginally is rarely indisposed for more than a week, recovery from a cesarean involves 6 or more weeks of soreness, which may make nursing more uncomfortable. A cesarean is now usually performed with a low transverse incision, which involves less blood loss, lowered risk of infection, and less risk of subsequent uterine rupture than a vertical incision, and obstetricians try to make the incision close to or beneath the pubic hairline (*see* 1916; 1988).

The U.S. Centers for Disease Control at Atlanta reports 299 cases of Toxic Shock Syndrome, 25 of them fatal. The FDA asks for mandatory labeling of tampon packages to warn women of TSS. Procter & Gamble announces September 22 that it is withdrawing its tampon Rely, which is suspected of harboring the bacterium *Staphyloccus aureus* and acting as a breeding agent, but the company notes that TSS has been reported in some areas where Rely is not sold, and that it has also stricken some men.

A new U.S. Department of Education begins operations May 4. Health, Education and Welfare becomes Health and Human Services pursuant to a law enacted last year in fulfillment of a Carter campaign pledge to teachers. Critics say the new department, with 17,000 full-time employees and a $17 billion annual budget, will curtail local control of schools.

The Académie Française elects novelist Marguerite Yourcenar, now 76, to its membership March 6; she is the first woman member since the Académie's founding in 1635.

Only 29,019 U.S. high school students score above 650 on the verbal part of the Scholastic Aptitude Test (SAT; *see* 1900), down from 53,794 in 1972. Only 73,386 score above 650 on the mathematics part, down from 93,868. Educators suggest that young people are reading less because of TV and changing social values, that students are taking fewer difficult courses, that college admissions standards and course requirements have fallen. A general decline in SAT scores began in 1964.

More than a third of 11 million U.S. college students receive some federal financial aid, up from 14 percent in 1970, as tuition and other costs rise to average $3,500 per year at state universities, more than $7,500 at private ones (tuition, room, and board at Harvard come to $9,170, at Yale $9,110). Federal aid to college students reaches $4.5 billion, up from $600 million in 1970, and the higher education bill signed by President Carter October 3 lets parents borrow up to $3,000 per year per student at 9 percent interest in addition to the $2,500 per year that a student can borrow on his/her own (*see* 1978; 1990).

Nonfiction: *China Men* by Maxine Hong Kingston; *Sex in History* by Reay Tannahill.

Fiction: *The Transit of Venus* by Shirley Hazzard; *Nuns and Soldiers* by Iris Murdoch; *The Shooting Party* by Isabel Colegate; *A Soldier's Embrace* (stories) by Nadine Gordimer; *The Castle Within a Castle* (*Shiro no naka no shiro*) by Yumiko Kurahashi; *The Middle Ground* by Margaret Drabble; *Judgment Day* by Penelope Lively; *The Sum of Things* (third novel in the Balkan trilogy) by Olivia Manning, now 65; *Winter Garden* by Beryl Bainbridge;

The Clan of the Cave Bear by Oregon novelist Jean (Marie) Auel, 44; *Falling in Place* by Ann Beattie; *Morgan's Passing* by Anne Tyler; *Fanny* by Erica Jong; *Rich Rewards* by Alice Adams; *Bellefleur* by Joyce Carol Oates; *The Cradle Will Fall* by Mary Higgins Clark; *Close Relations* by Susan Isaacs; *The Best Laid Plans* by Gail Parent; *The Feast of All Saints* by Anne Rice; *Barn Blind* by U.S. novelist Jane Smiley, 31; *To Love Again* by Danielle Steel; *Photo Finish* by Dame Ngaio Marsh, now 81; *Murder in the White House* by Margaret Truman; *The Lake of Darkness* by Ruth Rendell; *Alibi in Time* by June Thompson.

Poetry: *Satan Says* by U.S. poet Sharon Olds, 37; *Setting the Table* by Linda Pastan.

Painting: *Joined* and *Breaking* (both oil on two canvases) by Elizabeth Murray; *At Sea, Japan* (watercolor, gouache on six sheets of paper) by Jennifer Bartlett; *Crisis Moment* (collage of oil and paper) and *Vernal Yellow* (collage of oil and paper on canvas) by Lee Krasner.

Japan's Sogetsu school of flower arrangement (*ikebana*) is taken over by film director Hiroshi Teshigahara, 53, upon the death of his sister, Kasumi, at age 47 (their father, who founded the school in 1927, died last year at age 79). The new *iemoto* (hereditary head) is well known for his 1964 film *Woman in the Dunes* and will continue to direct and produce motion pictures and operas.

Theater: *Piaf!* by English playwright Pam Gems 1/15 at Wyndham's Theatre, London, with Jane Lapotaire as France's legendary "little sparrow" Edith Piaf (*see* 1946), who died 10/11/63 at age 47; Judd Hirsch and Trish Hawkins in Lanford Wilson's *Talley's Folly* 2/10 at New York's Brooks Atkinson Theater, 279 perfs.; John Rubinstein as the speech therapist for hearing-impaired students and Phyllis Freilich (totally deaf since birth) as the student he marries in Mark Medoff's *Children of a Lesser God* 3/30 at New York's Longacre Theater, 854 perfs.; Charles Brown, L. Scott Caldwell, and Michelle Shay in Samm-Art Williams's *Home* 5/7 at New York's Cort Theater, 279 perfs.; Mark Kingston and Julie Walters in Willy Russell's *Educating Rita* 8/19 at London's Piccadilly Theatre (after a run at the Warehouse Theatre); Swoosie Kurtz, 26, and Christopher Reeve in Lanford Wilson's *The Fifth of July* 11/3 at New York's New Apollo Theater, 511 perfs.

Films: Susan Sarandon (*née* Tomalin), 33, and Burt Lancaster in Louis Malle's *Atlantic City*; Mark Hamill, Harrison Ford, and Carrie Fisher, 23, in Irvin Kershner's *The Empire Strikes Back*; Mary Tyler Moore, Donald Sutherland, and Timothy Hutton in Robert Redford's *Ordinary People*. Also: Theresa Russell and Art Garfunkel in Nicolas Roeg's *Bad Timing: A Sensual Obsession*; Sissy Spacek as country singer Loretta Lynn in Michael Apted's *Coal Miner's Daughter*; Leslie Caron and Maja Komorowska in Krzysztof Zanussi's *The Contract*; Angie Dickinson and Michael Caine in Brian De Palma's *Dressed to Kill*; Christine Buchegger, Robert Atzorn, and Martin Benath in Ingmar Bergman's *From the Life of the Marionettes*; Jocelyn Berube in Micheline Lanctot's *The Handyman*; Isabelle (Anne) Huppert, 25, and Gérard Dépardieu in Maurice Pialat's *Loulou*; Diane Sommerfield and James H. Jacobs in Robert Sickinger's *Love in a Taxi*; Gérard Dépardieu and Nicole Garcia in Alain Resnais's *Mon Oncle d'Amerique*; Jane Fonda, Lily Tomlin, and Dolly Parton as secretaries with a sexist boss in Colin Higgins's *9 to 5*; Goldie Hawn as a U.S. Army volunteer in Howard Zieff's *Private Benjamin*; English actress Eva Le Gallienne, now 81, Ellen Burstyn, and Sam Shepard in Daniel Petrie's *Resurrection*.

Mae West dies of a stroke at Hollywood November 22 at age 87. Her witticisms survive her: "When women go wrong, men go right after them"; "It's not the men in my life that count; it's the life in my men"; "I was Snow White . . . but I drifted."

Broadway musical: Wanda Richert, Tammy Grimes, and Jerry Orbach in *42nd Street* 8/25 at the Winter Garden Theater, with music and lyrics from the 1933 Hollywood musical, 3,486 perfs.

Jane Frohman dies at her home in Columbia, Mo., April 22 at age 72.

Violinist Anne-Sophie Mutter makes her North American concert debut 1/3 playing Mendelssohn's Violin Concerto in E minor with the New York Philharmonic under Zubin Mehta at Avery Fisher Hall.

San Francisco's Louise M. Davis Symphony Hall opens September 16 with 3,000 seats across the street from the 48-year-old War Memorial Opera House.

Popular songs: *Double Fantasy* (album) by John Lennon and Yoko Ono (who sees her husband shot to death; *see* crime, below); Olivia Newton-John appears in the film *Xanadu* and records its theme song; *Diana* (album) by Diana Ross, who also records the singles "Upside Down" and "Coming Out"; *Living in the USA* (album) by Linda Ronstadt includes her version of Elvis Costello's "Alison"; *Mad Love* (album) by Ronstadt includes "How Do I Make You"; *Love Has No Reason* (album), *With My Song* (album) and *Savin' It Up* (album) by Debbie Boone; *Running from My Life* (album) by Judy Collins; *I'll Always Love You* (album), *A Country Collection* (album), *Anne Murray's Greatest Hits* (album), "Lucky Me," "I'm Happy Just to Dance With You," and "Could I Have This Dance" by Anne Murray; "Two-Story House" (with ex-husband George Jones) and "He Was There (When I Needed You)" by Tammy Wynette; "I Still Long to Hold You (Now and Then)," "(You Lift Me) Up to Heaven," and "I Can See Forever in Your Eyes" by Reba McEntire.

East German figure skater Anett Poetzsch wins her event in the winter Olympics at Lake Placid, Austrian skier Annemarie Proell Moeser wins the downhill in 1 minute, 37.52 seconds, Liechtensteiner skier Hanni Wenzel wins the slalom in 1 minute, 25.09 seconds and the giant slalom in 2 minutes, 41.66 seconds. Soviet runner Lyudmila Kondratyeva wins the 100-meter dash in 11.06 seconds at the summer Olympics in Moscow (which are banned by the United States and 57 other nations to punish the U.S.S.R. for invading Afghanistan), East German runner Barbara Wockel wins the 200-meter in 22.03 seconds, East German runner Marita Koch the 400-meter in 48.88 seconds, Soviet runner Nadezhda Olizarenko the 800-meter run in 1 minute, 53.5 seconds, Tatiana Kazankina the 1,500-meter in 3 minutes, 56.6 seconds, Soviet runner Vera Komisova the 100-meter hurdles in 12.56 seconds, Italian athlete Sara Simeoni the high jump (6 feet, 5½ inches), Soviet athlete Tatiana Kolpakova the long jump (23 feet, 2 inches), East German athlete Ilona Sluplanek the shot put (73 feet, 6 inches), East German athlete Evelin Jahl the discus throw (229 feet, 6½ inches),

Cuban athlete Maria Colon the javelin throw (224 feet, 5 inches), Soviet athlete Nadyeszhda Tkachenko the pentathlon. East German swimmer Barbara Krause wins the 100-meter freestyle in 54.79 seconds and the 200-meter in 1 minute, 58.33 seconds, East German swimmer Ines Diers the 400-meter in 4 minutes, 8.76 seconds, Australian swimmer Michelle Ford the 800-meter in 8 minutes, 28.90 seconds, East German swimmer Rica Reinisch the 100-meter backstroke in 1 minute, 0.86 seconds and the 200-meter in 2 minutes, 11.77 seconds, East German swimmer Ute Geweniger the 100-meter breaststroke in 1 minute, 10.22 seconds, Soviet swimmer Lina Kachushite the 200-meter in 2 minutes, 29.54 seconds, East German swimmer Caren Metschuck the 100-meter butterfly in 1 minute, 0.42 seconds, East German swimmer Ines Geissler the 200-meter in 2 minutes, 10.44 seconds, East German swimmer Petra Schneider the 400-meter individual medley in 4 minutes, 36.29 seconds, Soviet swimmer Irina Kalinina the springboard dive event, East German swimmer Martina Jaschke the platform dive.

Cuban-American Boston Marathon winner Rosie Ruiz, 26, of New York crosses the finish line April 21 in a near-record 2:31:56, but turns out to have cheated. Montreal runner Jacqueline Gareau is the true winner, and officials soon recognize her as such.

Evonne Goolagong Cawley, now 28 (Australia), wins in women's singles at Wimbledon, Chris Evert-Lloyd wins in U.S. women's singles.

Luvs disposable diapers, introduced by Procter & Gamble, are "super-absorbent" and have elastic gathers. Huggies, introduced by Kimberly-Clark 2 years ago, have cut into sales of P&G's Pampers.

The U.S. Supreme Court rules 6 to 3 in October against hearing an appeal from an Illinois Supreme Court decision that a woman with a sleep-in boyfriend has violated the state's antifornication statute and thus forfeited her right to custody of her three children. An estimated 1.1 million Americans live together out of wedlock (*see* 1977), and an estimated 25 percent or more of these households include children, but close to 95 percent of U.S. women marry at least once in their lives, up from 75 to 80 percent at the turn of the century.

A *Cosmopolitan* magazine sex survey of 106,000 women finds that 41 percent of married women have had extramarital affairs, up from 8 percent in 1948.

The Official Preppy Handbook edited by New York writer Lisa Birnbach tells its readers, tongue-in-cheek, "In a true democracy everyone can be upper class and live in Connecticut. It's only fair. . . . It is the inalienable right of every man, woman, and child to wear khaki. Looking, acting, and ultimately being Prep is not restricted to an elite minority."

Rollerblade, Inc., is founded near Minneapolis by Canadian hockey player Scott Olsen, 20, who has bought a Chicago company's patent for an in-line roller skate and perfected the design with his brother Brennan, 16, using a blade of polyurethane wheels and a molded ski-type boot.

U.S. cigarette sales rise slightly to 614.5 billion with low-tar brands accounting for nearly 49 percent, up from 16.7 percent in 1976, despite growing evidence that the "safer" cigarettes offer only limited health benefits and may even pose new hazards because of flavor-boosting additives. Smoking has dropped 28 percent since 1970 among men 20 and older, 13 percent among adult women, 20 percent among teenage boys. Smoking among teenage girls has increased by 51 percent since 1968.

"Scarsdale Diet" creator Dr. Herman Tarnower, 69, is shot fatally March 10 in his Harrison, N.Y., house by Madeira School headmistress Jean Struven Harris, 56, who claims it was an accident. She will be convicted of murder and imprisoned until early 1993, when she will be pardoned after sustaining a heart attack.

John Lennon of Beatles fame is shot fatally December 8 outside the Dakota apartment building in New York while his wife, Yoko Ono, looks on in horror. Lennon's death at age 40 increases demands for gun control laws, but President-elect Reagan says more effective laws would not have prevented Lennon's shooting by a deranged fan. U.S. handgun killings average 29 per day, and 55 million "Saturday night specials" and other handguns are believed to be in circulation, easily obtainable through 175,000 federally licensed dealers (often just by showing a driver's license, which need not be checked for authenticity in many states) or through illicit channels.

The California Supreme Court strikes down the state's 1872 rape law requiring the victim to assert her level of resistance.

U.S. housing starts fall below 1.3 million, down 33 percent from last year, as prices rise and high interest rates put mortgages out of reach for many prospective buyers. Government programs assist 44.1 percent of the housing starts, but more than 15 percent of builders are forced to quit the industry.

The U.S. Supreme Court upholds the Hyde Amendment of 1976 in a 5-to-4 ruling handed down June 30 to the delight of antiabortion groups. Abortions paid for by Medicaid funds fell from 295,000 to only 2,100 for fiscal 1978, 3,900 for fiscal 1979, but some states continue to pay for abortions (average cost: $200) entirely out of their own funds and without federal reimbursement (*see* 1989).

Beijing announces in September that the nation's goal is to limit China's population to 1.2 billion by the year 2000 (but *see* 1988).

Japan's birthrate falls to an all-time low of 13.66 per thousand—lower even than in 1966 (the Year of the Fiery Horse). In a survey conducted last year by the newspaper *Mainichi Shimbun*, most people gave the high cost of education as their reason for not having more children, although others cited the fact that they could not depend on their children for support in their old age. Well over half of those interviewed said they practiced birth control, but only 78.4 percent of respondents had ever heard of The Pill, which is available only by prescription, and only 3.1 percent said they would use it. Condoms remain Japan's leading form of contraception.

Australian government agencies inject aboriginal girls with the synthetic hormone Depo-Provera (depomedroxy-progesterone acetate, or DMPA) for contraception without their knowledge to restrict the black birthrate. Developed by Upjohn in 1957, the hormone inhibits ovulation by releasing hormones into the bloodstream over a period of 3 months or more, but once injected it remains in the system until it works itself out, so unpleasant side effects can be irremediable (*see* 1992).

1981

 Northern Ireland's former parliamentary speaker Sir Norman Stronge and his son are assassinated by terrorists January 21—4 days after an attempt at Belfast on northern Irish nationalist Bernadette Devlin McAliskey, now 33, and her husband, who have supported IRA hunger strikers. Devlin has been shot and seriously wounded but makes a defiant appearance in Spain.

Mao Zedong's widow, Jiang Qing, is sentenced to death January 25 and dragged from the courthouse shouting, "It is right to rebel! Making revolution is no crime!" Her sentence is later suspended.

Former Norwegian environmental minister Gro Harlem Brundtland, 42, becomes prime minister. A Harvard-trained physician with four children, she is Norway's first woman prime minister and will become prime minister again in 1986.

President Reagan names former Georgetown University political science professor Jeane Duane Kirkpatrick (*née* Jordan), 54, as permanent U.S. representative to the United Nations.

Houston City Controller and dedicated feminist Kathryn Jean "Kathy" Whitmire (*née* Niederhofer), 35, beats the city's political establishment in a runoff with the local sheriff, who has called her "that little lady." Only five feet tall, she wins election as mayor of a city long regarded as a masculine bastion of Big Oil, country-western music, and good-ol'-boy attitudes.

Former British Minister of Education Shirley Williams, 51, who entered Parliament in 1964 as a Labour party member, quits the party to help found the Social Democratic party (SDP) and becomes its first member to win election to Parliament.

Dame Rebecca West, now 88, is interviewed on U.S. Public Television in July by journalist Bill Moyers, 47, and says about Prime Minister Thatcher, "Men would rather be ruined by one of their own sex than saved by a woman." Men, she says, may be duller than women because they have less challenge in entering the everyday world of jobs and careers.

Spanish antiterrorist police open a major operation against the Basque separatist organization ETA October 22, arresting Jimina Alonso Matthias and Carmen Santos, two well-known radical feminists, along with a male college professor. Two teenage daughters of Mrs. Alonso Matthias are also detained. A group of 100 feminists immediately protests the arrests, drawing up a petition stating that the women have a well-known public record "in the struggle for the defense of public rights and the rights of women in particular." Police claim that Mrs. Alonso Matthias has led them to an arms cache that ETA guerillas placed in the woods near her house in suburban Torrelodones.

 Spain legalizes civil divorce for the first time since 1939 under a law enacted June 1, but the Church forbids Catholics to seek divorces under the new law.

President Reagan appoints Arizona Judge Sandra O'Connor (*née* Day), 51, to the Supreme Court July 7. Although she has had only 18 months' experience on the state appeals court, she was graduated third in her Stanford University Law School class (Justice William Rehnquist was first), championed women's rights in her 6 years as a state legislator and sided against antiabortion zealots, favors the proposed Equal Rights Amendment, is opposed by right-to-life activists, is confirmed by the Senate September 21, and becomes the first woman justice on the high court.

Cairo police break into the home of Egyptian feminist physician-writer Nawal el-Saadawi, now 50, September 5, seize some of her papers, and imprison her along with 1,535 others on charges of "stirring up sectarian strife." She is held for more than 80 days and interrogated twice for publishing "articles critical of President [Anwar] Sadat's policies," and although she is released after Sadat's assassination October 6 her books continue to be banned. Some have called her "the Simone de Beauvoir of the Arab world" for attacking her culture's obsession with virginity and its acceptance of clitoridectomy. "Society looks at the woman as a tool of love," she wrote in 1977, "and deprives her of the one organ which will make her be good at it."

Wyoming voters elect Harriet Elizabeth "Liz" Byrd, 55, to the state House of Representatives, where she becomes the first black legislator elected since statehood in 1890.

U.S. lawyer Arnette R. Hubbard is installed July 31 as the first woman president of the National Bar Association, an organization of black lawyers.

$ The U.S. prime interest rate reaches 21.5 percent, highest since the Civil War, as double-digit inflation and high unemployment plague the economy.

President Reagan signs a bill August 13 mandating the deepest tax and budget cuts in U.S. history. It follows "supply-side" economic theories that reject Keynesian ideas popular since the 1930s. Supply-siders, led by California economist Arthur Laffer, 40, claim that reducing taxes will encourage business and the rich to invest in taxable activities rather than parking income in nonproductive tax shelters and will thus help the overall economy. While "Reagonomics" will be credited with producing the longest peacetime boom in history, it will also lead to neglect of cities, deterioriation of infrastructure, and massive deficits financed by foreign borrowing.

President Reagan addresses the nation on television September 29 appealing for fiscal austerity and asking for an additional $13 billion in spending cuts for fiscal 1982. He astonishes supply-siders by requesting $3 billion in tax increases.

IBM introduces its first personal computer August 12 and soon has 75 percent of the market. Its PC uses a Microsoft disk operating system (MS-DOS) and competitors quickly introduce lower-priced "clones."

AIDS (Acquired Immune Deficiency Syndrome) begins taking a worldwide toll that will be compared to that of the Black Death in the 14th century. San Francisco and New York physicians report that a few dozen previously healthy homosexual men have died of Kaposi's sarcoma, a form of cancer endemic in Africa but rare in the rest of the world. The men have suffered abnormalities of the immune system. New York doctors realize they have seen a number of similar cases in the past few years, all unexplained. More cases appear each month. Drug addicts, mostly black and Hispanic, in New York, Newark, and other northeastern cities begin dying of a previously rare pneumonia and other diseases brought on by a collapse of the body's disease-fighting ability. Invariably fatal,

AIDS will be diagnosed in more than 32,000 Americans by early 1987, and nearly 60 percent will have died. Spread by exchange of bodily fluids containing a retrovirus, AIDS finds its victims almost exclusively among homosexual males, drug addicts using contaminated needles, and people given prophylactic medical shots with such needles. AIDS will be epidemic in parts of Africa, with as many female victims as male, and within a decade will be killing women as well as men throughout Asia, Europe, and the Americas. The specter of AIDS will lead to an increased use of condoms, which provide some protection against transmission of the retrovirus.

Human immunodeficiency virus did not seem at first to affect women, but they, too, soon began to die of AIDS.

Nearly 120 nations vote in May to approve a voluntary international code, drawn up under the auspices of the World Health Organization, that restricts marketing of infant formula to women, many of them illiterate, who have been encouraged to use infant formula, often made from contaminated water or diluted to the point that infants are malnourished, rather than breast-feeding their babies. The only dissenting vote has been that of the United States, which has rejected the code as antagonistic to free trade and contrary to American antitrust laws and rights of free speech (*see* Nestlé, 1982).

California State University at Fullerton names a new president: former cancer researcher and Connecticut College Dean Jewel Plummer Cobb, M.D., 57, will increase enrollment to 22,000.

India's female literacy rate is 24.88 percent as compared with 46.74 percent for males; while nearly 84 percent of boys aged 6 to 14 are enrolled in schools, only 54 percent of girls of those ages are in school.

Nonfiction: *The Second Stage* by Betty Friedan says about the women's movement, "Our failure was our blind spot about the family." She writes about women's need "to give and get love and nurture." The "confrontational" political tactics which she formerly espoused she now finds too "masculine" (Phyllis Schlafly says Friedan has "just put another nail in the coffin of feminism"). *Pornography: Men Possessing Women* by Andrea Dworkin; *From Housewife to Heretic* by Mormon feminist Sonia Johnson (*see* 1979); *Mrs. Harris: The Death of the Scarsdale Diet Doctor* by Diana Trilling; *Social Studies* by Fran Lebowitz; *Miss Manners' Guide to Excruciatingly Correct Behavior* by *Washington Post* columnist Judith (Sylvia) Martin (*née* Perlman), 43.

Fiction: *July's People* by Nadine Gordimer; *The House with the Glass Veranda* (*Huset med den blinde glassveranda*) by Norwegian novelist Herbjorg Wassmo, 39; *Shiloh and Other Stories* by U.S. writer Bobbie Ann Mason, 42; *Tar Baby* by Toni Morrison; *Sweetsir* by Helen Yglesias; *Real Life* (stories) by Gail Godwin; *Good Behavior* by Molly Keane, now 77, whose success leads to the republishing of her earlier novels; *The Collected Stories of Caroline Gordon* by the late Gordon, who has died in April at age 85; *Funeral Games* by Mary Renault; *The Fate of Mary Rose* by Caroline Blackwood; *At Paradise Gate* by Jane Smiley; *World Without End* by Francine du Plessix Gray; *Mazes and Monsters* by Rona Jaffe; *Woman's Work* by New York advertising copywriter–turned–novelist Anne Tolstoi Wallach, 52; *The Company of Women* by Mary Gordon; *Original Sins* by Lisa Alther; *How Mickey Made It* (stories) by Jayne Anne Phillips; *Love, Remembrance*, and *Palomino* by Danielle Steel; *Walking Naked* by Nina Bawden; *The Night She Died* by Welsh-born English mystery novelist Dorothy Simpson (*née* Preece), 48, introduces

Inspector Luke Thanet; *Shadow of a Doubt* by June Thompson.

Poetry: *Waiting for My Life* by Linda Pastan; *Mythic Things* by Sheila Fugard; *Love Poems* by Danielle Steel.

Painting: *Brush's Shadow, Heart and Mind*, and *Just in Time* (all oil on two canvases), *Painter's Progress* (oil on 19 canvases), and *Walk* (pastel drawing on paper) by Elizabeth Murray; *Self-Portrait* by Alice Neel, now 81, who shows herself in her armchair wearing only her eyeglasses; *Twelve Hour Crossing, March Twenty-First* and *Between Two Appearances* (both collages of oil and paper on canvas) by Lee Krasner.

Theater: *Steaming* by English playwright Nell Dunn, 45, 7/1 at London's Theatre Royal, Stratford East; Brooke Adams, Mark Blum, and Ben Masters in Kevin Wade's *Key Exchange* 7/14 at New York's off-Broadway Orpheum Theater; Claudette Colbert and Jean-Pierre Aumont in Jerome Chodorov and Norman Panama's *A Talent for Murder* 10/1 at New York's Biltmore Theater, 77 perfs.; Polly Draper and Elizabeth Franz in Christopher Durang's *Sister Mary Ignatius Explains It All for You* 10/16 at New York's Playwrights Horizons Theater, 947 perfs.; *Crimes of the Heart* by U.S. playwright Beth Henley, 29, 11/4 at New York's John Golden Theater, with Mia Dillon, Holly Hunter, 23, Lizbeth Mackay, and Peter MacNicol, 535 perfs. (Pulitzer Prize, New York Drama Critics' Circle Award); Katharine Hepburn and Dorothy Loudon in Ernest Thompson's *The West Side Waltz* 11/10 at New York's Ethel Barrymore Theater, 126 perfs.; Frances Steegmuller, Harold Gould, and Bob Dishy in Jules Feiffer's *Grownups* 12/10 at New York's Lyceum Theater, 13 perfs.

Films: Hanna Schygulla and Bruno Ganz in Volker Schlöndorff's *Circle of Deceit*; Fernando Ramos da Silva and Marilia Pera in Hector Babenco's *Pixote*. Also: Gene Hackman and Barbra Streisand in Jean-Claude Tramont's *All Night Long*; John Gielgud, Dudley Moore, and Liza Minnelli in Steve Gordon's *Arthur*; Isabelle Huppert, 26, and Philippe Noiret in Bertrand Tavernier's *Coup de Torchon*; Jill Clayburgh as the first woman Supreme Court justice and Walter Matthau in Ronald Neame's *First Monday in October*; Meryl Streep and Jeremy Irons in Karel Reisz's *The French Lieutenant's Woman*; Simone Signoret and Jean Rochefort in Moshe Mizrahi's *I Sent a Letter to My Love*; Diane Keaton as Louise Bryant, Maureen Stapleton as Emma Goldman, and Warren Beatty as John Reed in Beatty's *Reds*.

Film actress Natalie Wood disappears off the family yacht *Splendour* and drowns November 28 at age 43.

Television series: *Dynasty* 1/12 on ABC with English film actress Joan (Henrietta) Collins, 47, John Forsythe and Linda Evans; *Cagney and Lacey* 10/8 on ABC with Sharon Gless and Tyne Daley.

Broadway musicals: Phyllis Hyman and P. J. Benjamin in *Sophisticated Ladies* 2/1 at the Lunt-Fontanne Theater, with music by the late Duke Ellington, 767 perfs.; Lauren Bacall and Harry Guardino in *Woman of the Year* 3/29 at the Palace Theater, with John Kander–Fred Ebb songs, 770 perfs.; Jennifer Holliday in *Dreamgirls* 12/21 at the Imperial Theater, with Henry Krieger–Tom Eyen songs, 1,522 perfs.

Popular songs: Olivia Newton-John's video "Physical" capitalizes on the new interest in aerobics (*see* Reebok, 1982); "O Superman" by Chicago-born artist-musician Laurie Anderson, 34; "Bette Davis Eyes" by U.S. songwriters Donna Weiss and Jackie De Shannon; Reba McEntire records her songs "I Don't Think Love Ought to Be That Way" and "Today All Over Again"; *You Brought Me Back* (album) by Tammy Wynette includes the single "Cowboys Don't Shoot Straight (Like They Used To)."

MTV (Music Television) goes out to cable TV subscribers beginning August 1 with visual presentations of pop hits.

Oxford student Sue Brown is coxswain for the shell that beats Cambridge by eight lengths April 4 in the 152nd Oxford-Cambridge boat race. She is the first woman to cox a male crew.

Chris Evert-Lloyd wins in women's singles at Wimbledon, Tracy Austin at Flushing Meadow.

Tonia Schlegel, 13, of Hamilton, Ohio, wins the annual All-American Soap-Box Derby in August, becoming the first girl to capture the event.

Lady Diana Spencer, 20, is married to Britain's Prince Charles, 32, at St. Paul's Cathedral, London, July 29 (*see* 1992).

British police capture a suspect in the "Yorkshire Ripper" murders that have been committed since 1975 in the Midlands and the north of England. Truck driver Peter Sutcliffe, 34, whose wife drives a school bus, is charged in January with having killed 13 women, some of them prostitutes, mostly by beating them in the head with a hammer and stabbing them with a screwdriver. He is found guilty May 22 of 13 murders plus seven attempted murders and given a life sentence on each count.

The U.S. Department of Agriculture responds to cuts in the school lunch program by announcing in September that ketchup can be counted as a vegetable. The public outcry forces President Reagan to restore funds for school lunches.

Jane Brody's Nutrition Book by *New York Times* columnist Jane Brody, 40 (her "Personal Health" column began appearing in 1976), is an antidote to the nutrition quackery offered by less responsible writers.

Aspartame gains FDA approval for tabletop use October 22. U.S. chemist James M. Schlatter discovered in 1955 while trying to develop an anti-ulcer drug that a mixture of the amino acids aspartic acid and phenylalanine had a sweet taste. Two teaspoons of sugar contain 32 calories; aspartame provides the same sweetening with 4 calories. Marketed by G. D. Searle under the brand name NutraSweet, the artificial sweetener is far costlier than saccharin but does not have saccharin's bitter aftertaste. Other countries have permitted the sale of aspartame, which is also made by Ajinomoto in Japan (*see* 1983).

Increased use of condoms because of the AIDS epidemic (above) will reduce reliance on IUDs, The Pill, and other forms of contraception that do not provide any protection against transmission of the AIDS retrovirus. About 90 percent of married couples in most Western countries now employ some form of contraception, but use of the condom lags far behind sterilization, oral contraceptives, and IUDs.

The world's population reaches 4.5 billion, up from 2.5 billion in 1950, with at least 957 million in the People's Republic of China, where female infanticide increases despite its illegality. The legal age for marriage is 25 for women, 26 for men; every Chinese factory, office, village, and collective farm is given an annual quota of permissible live births; the head of that unit, the party secretary, then decides which of the young couples in the unit will receive a certificate permitting conception; when a woman is delivered, there is often a bucket of water under the bed, and if the child is a girl it may be drowned.

India has a sex ratio of 935 females to 1,000 males, down from 972 to 1,000 in 1901, despite the fact that female infants are biologically stronger at birth. UNICEF studies indicate that girl babies are breast-fed less frequently and for a shorter duration than boy babies, who are also given better health care.

1982

 Rep. Shirley Chisholm announces February 10 that she will not seek another term.

U.S.-Soviet relations grow chillier as the arms-rattling Reagan administration pushes to build up U.S. military strength. Former KGB director Yuri V. Andropov, who came to power in November of last year upon the death of Leonid I. Brezhnev, receives a letter from Manchester, Me., fifth-grader Samantha Smith, 11, who asks him why he wants to "conquer the whole world, or at least our country." The Kremlin makes public his reply April 25: he reminds Samantha of the losses suffered by his country in World War II, when the United States and the U.S.S.R. were allies, and says his people want very much to live in peace and "cooperate and trade with all our neighbors on the globe, no matter how close or far away they are, certainly, with such a great country as the United States of America." He calls her "a courageous and honest girl, resembling in some ways Becky, Tom Sawyer's friend from the well-known book by Mark Twain. All kids in our country, boys and girls alike, know and love this book. Yes, Samantha, we in the Soviet Union are endeavoring and doing everything so there will be no war between our two countries, so that there will be no war at all on earth." She travels to Moscow with her parents at his invitation in July and receives a warm welcome everywhere she visits but does not meet with Andropov, who is too ill (he will die early next year) (*see* Smith, 1985).

A Vietnam War memorial dedicated at Washington November 13 displays the names of all 57,692 killed or missing U.S. soldiers, sailors, marines, and airmen etched into black granite. The monument was designed last year by Yale architecture student Maya Ying Lin, now 22.

President Reagan's budget address February 6 has called for much higher military appropriations and less spending on social programs. Congress votes 346 to 68 to increase military spending by 6 percent after inflation (Reagan had asked for a 13 percent boost) over fiscal 1982. But the Boland Amendment to the defense appropriations bill, approved unanimously by Congress December 8, bans use of defense funds to support CIA efforts to overthrow Nicaragua's Sandinista government. Congressmen Edward P. Boland (D., Mass.) and Tom Hakins (D., Iowa) have introduced the measure.

A rally against the nuclear arms race brings 800,000 demonstrators into New York's Central Park June 12.

 An Equal Rights Amendment to the U.S. Constitution comes within three states of being ratified but the deadline for ratification passes June 30. Mormon feminist Sonia Johnson has joined with seven other women in May to stage a 37-day Women's Fast for Justice at the Illinois state capitol in Springfield and been hospitalized several times during the fast. ERA opponent Phyllis Schlafly, whose 7-year-old Eagle Forum has joined with the Moral Majority, the American Conservative Union, and Catholic, Baptist, Orthodox Jewish, and Mormon church groups to reach state legislators on an individual basis, will turn her organization's attention to helping Nicaragua's contra rebels, working for parental rights in U.S. public schools, and revising public school curricula.

New York City's Fire Academy graduates 11 women and 103 men in ceremonies June 10 on Randall's Island. The Uniformed Firefighters Association has tried to block the graduation on grounds that standards were lowered for the probationary training program, but the Fire Department has denied the charges and welcomes the first women firefighters in its 117-year history.

Members of the English Collective of Prostitutes stage a sit-in at a church in central London's King's Cross red light district in November to protest police harassment following complaints from residents. A local official investigates their grievances and recommends changes in the 1959 Street Offenses Act with regard to soliciting. The law is amended to remove prison sentences for soliciting and loitering for prostitution, but the prostitutes charge that police are making more arrests and that magistrates are imposing heavier fines.

$ Recession continues throughout most of the world, international trade declines, unemployment in the United States reaches 10.8 percent in November (the highest since 1940), and the number of Americans living below the poverty line is the highest in 17 years.

The National Organization for Native American Women (NONAW) is founded at Albuquerque, N.M., to support and develop the competency of Indian women and provide employment opportunities for them through networking, education, self-help programs, and the like.

Federal Reserve Board Chairman Paul Volcker announces October 2 that the war against inflation has gone too far and that he is abandoning his experiment with monetarism. An 18-month recession ends in November.

❋ German-American astronomy student Martine Kempf, 23, uses a home-rental PC to design a computer program that responds to spoken commands. Her father, a polio victim, designed a hand-controlled motorcar and has made a business designing cars for the handicapped. She has seen German children whose mothers took thalidomide and who were born without hands to maneuver their wheelchairs. Kempf will start a company in California's "Silicon Valley" to manufacture and market her invention, and within 4 years her Katalivox will be used to operate voice-activated microscopes and wheelchairs.

 Nestlé S.A. issues guidelines March 16 for complying with the voluntary international code that discourages unnecessary use of infant formula and encourages breast-feeding (*see* 1981). A 5-year boycott of Nestlé products has persuaded the world's largest supplier of infant formula (Nestlé distributes its formula in 140 countries) to change its marketing practices, which have been blamed for contributing to countless infant deaths in developing countries. Nestlé, which has been distributing free samples directly to mothers and promoting formula as a modern and superior alternative to mothers' milk, agrees to curtail distribution of samples at hospitals and health care centers and says that it will provide samples only if they are requested by a physician or qualified medical professional (*see* 1984).

Martine Kempf's Katalivox (above) will find its biggest market in microsurgery, where it will enable physicians to operate magnifying equipment without using their hands.

MRI (magnetic resonance imaging) machines, introduced in Britain, cost 50 percent more than CAT-scanning devices (*see* 1974) but give physicians a superior new diagnostic tool, permitting them to monitor blood flowing through an artery, to see the reaction of a malignant tumor to medication, etc. (*see* 1977).

U.S. medical school graduates flock to enter the field of cosmetic surgery, which has become the fastest-growing specialty, and newspapers in some cities are full of advertisements for breast enlargements. The FDA declares breast implants "a potentially unreasonable risk of injury" but does not pursue further research (*see* 1985; 1988).

U.S. plastic surgeons begin using liposuction, or suction lipectomy, a fat-scraping and -vacuuming technique introduced from Europe, to enlarge women's breasts; the vanity procedure will result in at least 11 deaths—and probably more than twice that many—in the next five years, usually from the release of fat emboli into the heart, lungs, and brain. Most women who want breast augmentation opt for silicone gel implants.

A new Surgeon General's Report issued in March by U.S. Surgeon General C. Everett Koop, 65, calls cigarette smoking the chief preventable cause of death. Lung cancer kills about 111,000 Americans, up from 18,313 in 1950. More than 30 million Americans have quit smoking since 1964, but smoking-related health care costs the nation $13 billion, while lost production and wages cost another $25 billion. More U.S. women than men smoke for the second year in a row.

The National Council on Women's Health has its beginnings in the National Council on Women in Medicine founded by Polish-American physician Lila A. Wallis, 61.

A Chicago assassin laces bottles of Tylenol capsules with cyanide, seven die in late September, and Tylenol maker Johnson & Johnson promptly recalls the product October 5, destroying 31 million Tylenol capsules on store shelves and in home medicine chests. Reintroduced in triple-sealed safety packages, Tylenol will regain 95 percent of its top market share in 3 months.

The Jane Fonda Workout videotape becomes the best-selling video yet. *The Jane Fonda Workout Book* is also a best-seller.

Mississippi State College for Women changes its name to Mississippi University for Women and accepts its first male student following a five-to-four U.S. Supreme Court decision (*Mississippi University for Women v. Hogan*). The school's "policy of excluding males from admission to the School of Nursing," the Court says, "tends to perpetuate the stereotyped view of nursing as an exclusively woman's job."

"Electronic mail" via fax machines gains popularity as third-generation Japanese technology cuts transmission time to 20 seconds per page, down from the 6 minutes of first-generation machines, and thus reduces telephone charges from $4 per page to less than $1 (*see* 1976). The new machines are cheaper than and compatible with earlier models. By year's end, there are 350,000 U.S. fax installations, up from 69,000 in 1975, and the first directory of users will be out next year.

Nonfiction: *In a Different Voice: Psychological Theory in Women's Development* by U.S. author Carol Gilligan, 46; *Is There No Place on Earth for Me?* by Susan Sheehan (Pulitzer Prize); *Woman and the*

Demon: The Life of a Victorian Myth by U.S. feminist Nina Auerbach, 39; *Having It All* by Helen Gurley Brown.

Fiction: *The Color Purple* by Alice Walker (Pulitzer Prize); *Dinner at the Homesick Restaurant* by Anne Tyler; *The Burning House* by Ann Beattie; *The Women of Brewster Place* by U.S. novelist Gloria Naylor, 32; *Levitation: Five Fictions* by Cynthia Ozick; *The House of the Spirits* (*La casa de los espiritos*) by Chilean novelist Isabel Allende, 40, whose uncle Salvador Allende Gossens, the nation's president, was murdered in a right-wing coup 9 years ago; *Summer Marker* (*Natsu no shiori*) by Ineko Sata, now 78; *Nellie Without Hugo* by Janet Hobhouse; *Quotations from Other Lives* (stories) by Penelope Gilliatt; *A Bloodsmoor Romance* by Joyce Carol Oates; *A Mother and Two Daughters* by Gail Godwin; *The Valley of Horses* by Jean Auel; *White Horses* by Alice Hoffman; *A Cry in the Night* by Mary Higgins Clark; *Defects of the Heart* by Barbara Gordon; *Grace Abounding* by Maureen Howard; *Getting It Right* by Elizabeth Howard, who also writes scripts for the BBC television series *Upstairs, Downstairs; Lace* by Shirley Conran; *The Horse Goddess* by Morgan Llewelyn; *Crossings, Once in a Lifetime,* and *A Perfect Stranger* by Danielle Steel; *A Rose in Winter* by Kathleen Woodiwiss; *"A" Is for Alibi* by California mystery novelist Sue (Taylor) Grafton, 42, introduces the female cop–turned–private detective Kinsey Millhone; *Indemnity Only* by Chicago mystery novelist Sara Paretsky, 35, introduces the feminist private investigator V. I. Warshawsky; *Murder in the Supreme Court* by Margaret Truman; *Six Feet Under* by Dorothy Simpson; *To Make a Killing* (in America, *Portrait of Lilith*) by June Thompson.

Poetry: *Letters from a Father and Other Poems* by Mona Van Duyn; *Our Ground Time Here Will Be Brief: New and Selected Poems* by Maxine Kumin; *The Country Between Us* by Carolyn Forche.

Juvenile: *The Secret Diary of Adrian Mole, Aged 13¾* by English writer Sue Townsend, 36, whose story aired as a BBC radio series (*The Secret Diary of A. Mole*) in January; *Summer Switch* by Mary Rodgers; *The Animal, the Vegetable, and John D. Jones* by Betsy Cromer Byars.

Painting: *Keyhole, Beam* (oil on three canvases), *Yikes* (oil on two canvases), *Popeye* (pastel and charcoal on eight sheets of cut and pasted paper), *Hear* (pastel on two sheets of paper), and *Last Night* (pastel on eight sheets of paper) by Elizabeth Murray; *In the Garden* by Jennifer Bartlett.

Theater: Patricia Routledge and Paul Eddington in Michael Frayn's *Noises Off* 2/23 at London's Lyric Theatre, Hammersmith; Elizabeth Ashley, Geraldine Page, and Amanda Plummer, 25, in John Pielmeier's *Agnes of God* 3/30 at New York's Music Box Theater, 599 perfs.; *Top Girls* by Caryl Churchill 9/1 at London's Royal Court Theatre, with Gwen Taylor, Deborah Findlay and Carol Hayman; *Foxfire* by U.S. playwrights Susan Cooper and Hume Cronyn 11/10 at New York's Ethel Barrymore Theater, with Cronyn, Jessica Tandy, 213 perfs.; Felicity Kendal and Roger Rees in Tom Stoppard's *The Real Thing* 11/16 at London's Strand Theatre; Susan Sarandon and James Russo in William Mastrosimone's *Extremities* 12/22 at New York's West Side Arts Theater, 317 perfs.; George Hearn and Barbara Baxley in Anthony Shaffer's *Whodunnit* 12/30 at New York's Biltmore Theater, 157 perfs.

Films: Dee Wallace and Henry Thomas in Steven Spielberg's *E.T.: The Extra-Terrestrial*; Klaus Kinski and Claudia Cardinale in Werner Herzog's *Fitzcarraldo*; Dustin Hoffman, Jessica Lange, 33, and Geena (*née* Virginia) Davis, 33, in Sydney Pollack's *Tootsie*; Robin Williams, Mary Beth Hurt, and Glenn Close, 35, in George Roy Hill's *The World According to Garp*. Also: Beatrice Romand in Eric Rohmer's *Le Beau Mariage*; Wilhelmina Wiggins Fernandez and Frederic Andrei in Jean-Jacques Beineix's *Diva*; Mary Woronov and Bartel in Paul Bartel's *Eating Raoul*; Barbara Sukowa and Armin Mueller-Stahl in Rainer Maria Fassbinder's *Lola*; Margarethe von Trotta's *Marianne and Juliane* with Jutta Lampe and Barbara Sukowa; Jack Lemmon and Sissy Spacek in Constantin Costa-Gavras's *Missing*; Anne Claire Poirier's *Over Forty* with Roger Blay and Monique Mercure; Mariel Hemingway, Scott Glenn, and Patrice Donnelly in Robert Towne's *Personal Best*; Jessica Nelson, Teresanne Joseph, and Lyn Traverse in Ed Stabile's *Plainsong*; Craig T. Nelson and JoBeth Williams, 31, in Tobe Hooper's *Poltergeist*; Susan Seidelman's *Smithereens*

with Susan Berman; Paul Newman and Charlotte Rampling in Sidney Lumet's *The Verdict*.

Screen star Romy Schneider is found dead May 29 at age 43; Ingrid Bergman dies of cancer at Stockholm August 29 at age 67; Princess Grace of Monaco (*née* Grace Kelly) dies of a brain hemorrhage September 14 at age 52 following an automobile accident.

Television series: *Cheers* 9/29 on NBC with Ted Danson, Shelley Long and Rhea Perlman (to 5/12/93).

Opera: Jessye Norman, now 37, makes her U.S. stage debut 11/22 with the Opera Company of Philadelphia.

Film opera: Teresa Stratas, Placido Domingo, and Cornell MacNeil in Franco Zeffirelli's *La Traviata*.

Film musicals: Willie Mae Ford Smith, 78, and other gospel singers in George T. Nierenberg's documentary *Say Amen, Somebody*; the Southern California Community Choir, Mighty Clouds of Joy, Shirley Caesar, and Twinkie Clark and the Clark Sisters in David Leivick, Frederick A. Ritzenberg, and James Cleveland's concert film *Gospel*; Julie Andrews, James Garner, and Robert Preston in Blake Edwards's *Victor/Victoria*.

Stage musical: Ellen Green in *Little Shop of Horrors* 7/27 at New York's off-Broadway Orpheum Theater, with Alan Menken–Howard Ashman songs, 2,209 perfs.

Popular songs: *Times of Our Lives* (album) by Judy Collins; *Big Science* (album) by Laurie Anderson; "Up Where We Belong" by Jack Nitzsche and Buffy Sainte-Marie, lyrics by Will Hennings (for the film *An Officer and a Gentleman*); *Take Me to Your Heart Again* (album) by Lulu; "That's What Friends Are For" by Carol Bayer Sager and Burt Bacharach.

Kate Smith, now 73, receives the Medal of Freedom from President Reagan October 26 for inspiring the nation with her renditions of Irving Berlin's "God Bless America," which she has been singing since 1938.

Martina Navratilova wins in women's singles at Wimbledon, Chris Evert-Lloyd at Flushing Meadow.

Reebok aerobic shoes gain prominence for the first time. Boston camping-equipment distributor Paul B. Fireman, now 38, obtained the U.S. license 3 years ago for British Reebok running shoes, started Reebok International with British financing, and introduces the $45 Freestyle glove-leather aerobic dance shoe in fashion colors.

Cookbook: *Entertaining* by U.S. promoter Martha Stewart (*née* Kostyra), 33, with Elizabeth Hawes contains recipes that are mostly either derivative, overdifficult, or just plain don't work, but the seductive illustrations (deep-dish pies inside woven baskets, vodka bottles encased with long-stemmed roses in slabs of ice, poached pears with candied violets in a crystal bowl filled with wine, Martha creating her "signature basket" filled with "plump, radiant, perfectly ripe" strawberries) begin a multi-million-dollar empire of magazines (*Martha Stewart Living*), books, videotapes, and the like.

TV and film comic John Belushi is found dead of an apparent drug overdose at age 33 March 5 in a rented bungalow at Hollywood's Château Marmont. His girlfriend, Cathy Smith, will be indicted on murder charges next year.

Danish-born New York financial consultant Claus von Bülow, 55, is found guilty March 16 of having tried to murder his wife, Pittsburgh heiress Martha "Sunny" von Bülow (*née* Sharp), 50, who married him in 1966 and since December 1980 has been in an irreversible coma induced by a double injection of insulin administered at their Newport, R.I., mansion. He has contended that his wife was suicidal and gave herself the overdose, but a housemaid has found a black bag containing hypodermic needles in his closet and has testified that she once observed him just watch while his wife went into shock. Von Bülow, who had stood to inherit $14 million tax free, is sentenced May 7 to 30 years in prison (but *see* 1985).

A Michigan appeals court upholds the conviction of a man found guilty of third-degree assault on a woman who resisted verbally but not physically. Her verbal pleas were enough to prove nonconsent, the court rules (*People* v. *Jansson*).

Preliminary Chinese census results released July 1 show that children born in the baby boom after the famine of 1959–61 will soon reach marriage and childbearing age, threatening the goal of holding population size to 1.2 billion by the year 2000. The Chinese Constitution is amended to state that family planning is a citizen's duty; it orders the adoption of provincial or local laws to make compliance with the one-child rule mandatory, even at the risk of disregarding minority rights and even if coercion is required. A woman pregnant without permission must attend study classes where she is threatened until she consents to an abortion (some abortions are performed in the third trimester). Any woman who refuses IUD insertion, sterilization, or abortion receives repeated visits at home from the cadres until her family breaks under the strain.

A Chinese newspaper notes that if female infanticide is not stopped immediately there will be a serious imbalance between the sexes 20 years hence, but Qian Xin Zhong, the woman in charge of state family planning, says that female infanticide cannot be blamed on the one-child policy since it existed long before (she ignores the fact that such infanticide had almost disappeared before the law was imposed).

1983

Europeans turn out by the thousands April 1 in a "Green" movement to protest the presence of U.S. nuclear weapons on the Continent. Green party leader Petra Kelly, now 36, is among 17 Green members elected to the West German Parliament (Bundestag).

Margaret Thatcher wins a landslide victory at the polls June 9, assuring herself of at least 5 more years as Britain's prime minister. The election, says Labour leader Denis Healey, "put the people at the mercy of the most reactionary, right-wing, extremist government in British history."

Former Philippine senator Benigno S. Aquino, Jr., 50, returns from exile to Manila August 21 and is shot dead upon arrival by an unknown gunman who is himself immediately shot dead. The last national leader still held in detention in 1980, Aquino was permitted to leave the country that year for open-heart surgery in the United States. He formed an anti-Marcos coalition in January 1982 and worked from abroad to restore democracy to the Philippines. Despite warnings that ailing President Ferdinand Marcos, his wife, Imelda, or their political allies (or opponents) would kill him, Aquino had decided it was time to organize opposition to Marcos at home (*see* 1986).

 The Vatican issues a new Catholic code expanding women's rights January 19.

The Greek Parliament votes unanimously January 29 to adopt a law intending to give wives an equal voice to their husbands in all matters of family life, but Greece continues to have a male-dominated society in which wives cannot work outside the home without their husbands' permission and daughters cannot obtain passports without their fathers' permission.

Women in Need has its beginnings in a shelter for homeless women opened February 14 at New York's Church of St. Mary the Virgin in West 46th Street by former alcoholism counselor Rita Zimmer, 39, whose nonprofit organization, started with $15,000, will grow to administer four shelters, a day care center, an 8-week summer camp, a clinic for alcoholics, AIDS prevention workshops, and a midtown drop-in center that serves more than 1,000 meals per week to homeless families.

The U.S. Civil Rights Commission criticizes the Reagan administration June 15 for failing to appoint more women and members of minorities to high-level positions in the federal government. Members of the commission serve at the president's pleasure, and President Reagan fires all four members, including Prof. Mary Frances Berry, 45, who was appointed by President Carter in 1980 and strongly supports an active federal government role in civil rights enforcement. (Jill Ruckelshouse, Glendina Cardenas Ramirez, and a rabbi are also fired.) Berry sues in Federal District Court, wins her case, and is reinstated after a law signed by Reagan November 30 reconstitutes the Commission as an independent agency jointly administered by the president and Congress. Its eight members need not be confirmed by the Senate and may be removed only for neglect of duty or malfeasance.

The National Women's Political Caucus opens a meeting at San Antonio July 10 with 400 delegates. Many wear buttons bearing such messages as, "Jane Wyman was right" (a reference to President Reagan's first wife, who divorced him), "I'm a Republican woman and I want my party back," and "We haven't come that far, and don't call me baby."

Former Kansas City KMBC-TV co-anchor Christine Craft, 45ish, sues Metromedia, Inc., for sex and age discrimination after being demoted on account of her appearance; she is awarded $500,000 August 8, cheering such TV personalities as Barbara Walters of ABC, now 51, CBS White House correspondent Lesley Stahl, 41, and Judy Woodruff of PBS, now 36, but a federal judge overturns the award October 31, ruling that since viewers had found her too informal in dress, too opinionated, and lacking in "warmth and comfort," the station was justified in firing her.

Congress votes November 15 to defeat a bill that would revive the Equal Rights Amendment.

 U.S. physicist Sally Kristin Ride, 32, lands in the space shuttle *Challenger* at Edwards Air Force Base, Calif., June 24 after a 6-day mission—the first American woman to go into space.

 Social Security legislation signed by President Reagan April 20 delays the 1983 cost-of-living increase for 6 months, boosts payroll deductions beginning in 1984, gradually raises the minimum retirement age to 67 by 2027, requires that new federal employees join the system, and mandates that some benefits of higher-income retirees be subject to federal income taxes. The reforms are designed to ensure the system's solvency for the next 75 years.

Geneticist Barbara McClintock, now 81, is awarded the Nobel Prize for physiology/medicine (*see* 1951).

 Ibuprofen receives nonprescription drug status in Britain; over-the-counter products containing the drug begin gaining on aspirin and acetaminophen products even though they are far more likely to produce ulcers. British researcher Stewart S. Adams of Boots Co. developed the nonsteroidal anti-inflammatory drug, used heretofore only in high-dose prescription drugs.

Crack—crystallized cocaine that can be smoked to produce a short but intense high—is developed by drug traffickers, probably Dominicans, in the Bahamas and soon appears in West Coast U.S. cities. The low-priced, highly addictive drug (cocaine hydrochloride + baking soda + a "comeback" filler boiled with water) opens a mass market for cocaine among adolescents and young adults, increasing crime rates, devastating families and communities, and multiplying health emergencies and the incidence of syphilis and AIDS as users engage in indiscriminate sex.

"Just Say No" is the slogan for a new program to combat drug use unveiled by First Lady Nancy Reagan in October. Critics say she has picked up the issue to counter her negative image as a woman of wealth.

A new Bible released by the National Council of Churches October 14 omits or blurs gender references to God. God is called either Father and Mother or the One, *man* is replaced by *humanity* or *humankind*. The Lutheran and Greek Orthodox churches, calling the new language irreverent and inaccurate, flatly refuse to use it, and it will prove short-lived.

Nonfiction: *The Hearts of Men: American Dreams and the Flight from Commitment* by Barbara Ehrenreich; *Buying the Night Flight: The Autobiography of a Woman Foreign Correspondent* by Georgie Anne Geyer; *Gorillas in the Mist: A Remarkable Woman's Thirteen-Year Adventure in the African Rain Forest with the Greatest of the Great Apes* by U.S. zoologist Dian Fossey, 51, who serves as scientific director of the Karisoke Research Centre at Ruhengeri, Rwanda (Fossey will be murdered at Ruhengeri in December 1985); *Motherhood: The Second Oldest Profession* by Erma Bombeck.

Fiction: *At the Bottom of the River* by Antigua-born U.S. novelist Jamaica Kincaid (originally Elaine Potter Richardson), 34; *The Bone People* by New Zealand novelist Keri Hulme, 36, whose central character, Kerewin Holmes, is, like the author, one-eighth Maori; *Heartburn* by Nora Ephron; *Mr. Bedford of the Muses* (novella and stories) by Gail Godwin; *Voice of the Heart* by Barbara Taylor Bradford; *Crossroads* by Mary Morris; *The Ice House* by Nina Bawden; *The Lizard's Tail* by Luisa Valen-

zuela, who came to the United States 4 years ago; *The Cannibal Galaxy* by Cynthia Ozick; *August* by Judith Rossner; *Dancing in the Dark* by Janet Hobhouse; *Changes* and *Thurston House* by Danielle Steel; *So Speaks the Heart* by Johanna Lindsey; *Puppet for a Corpse* by Dorothy Simpson.

Poetry: *American Primitive* by U.S. poet Mary Oliver, 47 (Pulitzer Prize); *PM/AM: New and Selected Poems* by Linda Pastan; *Those Who Ride the Night Winds* by Nikki Giovanni.

Juvenile: *Everett Anderson's Goodbye* by Lucille Clifton.

Painting: *26 Rue Vavin*, *87 Boulevard Raspail*, and *Dog and Cat* (all oil on two canvases), *Wind* (oil on five canvases), *Pool and Boy* (both oil on three canvases) by Jennifer Bartlett, who divorced her first husband a dozen years ago and marries French film actor Mathieu Carrière (about 10 years her junior); *Table Turning* and *Deeper than D.* (both oil on two canvases), *Sail Baby* (oil on three canvases), *More Than You Know* (oil on nine canvases), and *Sophie Last Summer* (charcoal and pastel on five sheets of paper) by Elizabeth Murray; Lee Krasner, now 75, has a retrospective exhibition of her work at the Houston Museum of Fine Arts and New York's Museum of Modern Art.

Theater: *Painting: Churches* by U.S. playwright Tina Howe, 45, 2/8 at New York's off-Broadway South Street Theater, with Marian Seldes, Donald Moffatt, and Frances Conroy, 206 perfs.; *Fen* by Caryl Churchill 3/9 at London's Almeida Theatre, with Jenny Stoller and Bernard Strother; *'night, Mother* by U.S. playwright Marsha Norman, 35, 3/31 at New York's Golden Theater, with Kathy Bates and Anne Pitoniak, 380 perfs.; Mary Miller and Frank Windsor in Hugh Williams's *Pack of Lies* 10/26 at London's Lyric Theatre; *Isn't It Romantic* by U.S. playwright Wendy Wasserstein, 33, 12/15 at New York's Playwrights Horizons Theater, with Lisa Banes, Betty Comden, and Chip Zuin, 233 perfs.

Lynn Fontanne dies of pneumonia at Genesse Depot, Wis., July 30 at age 95. Her late husband, Alfred Lunt, to whom she was married for 55 years, died in August 1977 at age 84.

Films: Shirley MacLaine, Debra Winger, 28, and Jack Nicholson in James L. Brooks's *Terms of*

Endearment. Also: Christian Patey and Sylvie van den Essen in Robert Bresson's *L'Argent*; Mary Dore, Sam Sills, and Noel Buckner's Spanish Civil War documentary *The Good Fight*; Bruno Ganz and Teresa Madruga in Alain Tanner's *In the White City*; Vittorio Gassman, Ruggero Raimondi, and Geraldine Chaplin, 39, in Alain Resnais's *Life Is a Bed of Roses*; Mark Hamill, Harrison Ford, and Carrie Fisher in Richard Marquand's *Return of the Jedi*; Lynne Litman's *Testament* with Jane Alexander; Gene Hackman, Nick Nolte, and Joanna Cassidy in Roger Spottiswoode's *Under Fire*.

Gloria Swanson dies of a heart ailment at New York Hospital April 4 at age 84; Norma Shearer dies of bronchial pneumonia at the Motion Picture Country Hospital in Los Angeles June 12 at age 80 (she has been blind for years and mentally deranged for decades).

Hollywood musicals: Jennifer Beals in Adrian Lyne's *Flashdance* with music by Irene Cara; Barbra Streisand's *Yentl* with Streisand, Mandy Patinkin, and Amy Irving, 29, music by Michel Legrand, lyrics by Alan and Marilyn Bergman.

Broadway and off-Broadway musicals: Doug Henning and Chita Rivera in *Merlin* 2/13 at the Mark Hellinger Theater, with Elmer Bernstein–Michael Levinson–William Link songs, 199 perfs.; Tisha Campbell, 14, in *Mama, I Want to Sing* 3/25 at the 667-seat off-Broadway Hecksher Theater, with gospel music by Rudolph V. Hawkins, book and lyrics by Vy Higginsen and Ken Wydro, 2,213 perfs.; Twiggy (Leslie Hornby), dancer Tommy Tune, and dancer Charles "Honi" Coles in *My One and Only* 5/1 at the St. James Theater, with music from old Gershwin musicals, 762 perfs.

Popular songs: *She's So Unusual* (album) by Queens, N.Y.–born rock singer Cyndi Lauper, 30, includes "Girls Just Want to Have Fun"; *Madonna* (album) by Michigan-born rock singer Madonna (*née* Madonna Louise Veronica Ciccone), 25, includes "Borderline" and "Lucky Star" (she goes on, later in the year, to record "Holiday"); *Sweet Dreams (Are Made of This)* (album) by English guitarist-songwriter David Stewart and Scottish singer Annie Lennox, 29; Olivia Newton-John appears in the film *Two of a Kind* with John Travolta and records its theme "Twist of Fate"; *The*

Songs of Bessie Smith (album) by Teresa Brewer, now 52 (with Count Basie and his orchestra). Karen Carpenter dies February 4 at age 32 of heart failure induced by anorexia nervosa.

Opera: Jessye Norman makes her Metropolitan Opera debut 9/26 singing the role of Cassandra in the 1689 Purcell opera *Dido and Aeneas*, going on later to sing the title role.

Japanese violin prodigy Midori (Goto), 11, makes her debut with the New York Philharmonic.

Anne-Sophie Mutter acquires a 1710 Stradivarius reportedly worth $300,000 to replace the problematical 1703 Stradivarius given her by the West German government.

Joan Benoit wins her second Boston Marathon April 19, setting a women's record of 2:22:42.

Martina Navratilova wins in women's singles at both Wimbledon and Flushing Meadow.

Cabbage Patch dolls marketed by Coleco Industries become black market items as stores sell out to eager parents and grandparents. The craze will reach its peak in 1985, with buyers paying nearly $600 million at retail.

Syracuse University undergraduate Vanessa Williams, 20, wins the Miss America Pageant title at Atlantic City September 17, becoming the first black Miss America (but *see* 1984).

An Arizona court finds polygamist Giovanni Vigliotto, 53, guilty of fraud and bigamy February 8. He married an Arizona woman in 1981 and allegedly abandoned her in a San Diego motel, skipping with $36,000 of her money and property. He claims to have married more than 105 women in 33 years.

Big Dan's Tavern at New Bedford, Mass., is the scene of a gang rape March 6 when a young woman, mother of two, walks in, has a few drinks, talks to her friend the waitress, and is forcibly raped on a pool table while several patrons cheer. Four men are arrested and released on $1,000 bail.

Environmental Protection Agency scandals make headlines. Rita M. Lavelle, who heads the EPA's Superfund program to clean up toxic waste, is fired by President Reagan February 7 (she will serve 4 months in prison for lying to Congress); EPA Administrator Anne McGill Burford resigns under fire March 9; and Secretary of the Interior James G. Watt resigns October 9 after fighting to open federal lands to private exploitation, including oil drilling. Watt has offended with a lighthearted comment that his coal advisory commission was a well-balanced mix: "I have a black, a woman, two Jews, and a cripple."

U.S. soft drink makers begin using NutraSweet, initially in combination with saccharin, to sweeten diet beverages (*see* 1981).

The Supreme Court rules 6 to 3 June 15 that many local abortion restrictions are unconstitutional. In *City of Akron v. Akron Center for Reproductive Health*, it strikes down "informed consent" provisions requiring a physician to tell a patient that the fetus is a human being from the moment of conception, describe the fetus's development, and list all possible physical and emotional consequences of an abortion. In *Planned Parenthood of Kansas City, Mo., v. Ashcroft* it strikes down a requirement that any abortion after the first trimester must be performed in a hospital. (Justices White, Rehnquist, and Sandra Day O'Connor dissent in both cases.)

Chinese family-planning head Qian Xin Zhoe announces in December that any woman with one child must be fitted with an IUD. Many women believe that they cannot conceive while they are nursing an infant, and this false notion is responsible in part for the increased incidence of second and third pregnancies.

1984

Jeanne Sauvé, Canada's Speaker of Parliament, is named governor-general and becomes the first woman to hold that post, which is largely ceremonial but highly respected (*see* 1980). She will hold it until 1990.

"Women rule the world," singer Bob Dylan tells *Rolling Stone* magazine in an interview published June 21. "No man has ever done anything that a woman either hasn't allowed him to do or encouraged him to do."

India's Prime Minister Indira Gandhi is assassinated by two Sikh members of her personal guard October 31 at age 66. Sikh extremists have occupied the Golden Temple at Amritsar, Mrs. Gandhi has sent in troops June 5 to 6, and 600 to 1,200 have been killed in a bloody takeover of the temple. The Sikhs, who control prosperous Punjab state, have pressed for independence, as have some other Indian states, and Mrs. Gandhi has been determined to keep the nation united by whatever means. She has said the night before, "I don't mind if my life goes in the service of the nation. If I die today every drop of my blood will invigorate the nation."

The French government awards Beate Klarsfeld, now 46, and her husband, Serge, the chevalier of the Legion d'Honneur in recognition of their efforts to expose former Nazi war criminals (*see* 1968). She was nominated by Israel in 1977 for the Nobel Peace Prize.

Svetlana Alliluyeva Peters, now 58, returns to Moscow in November and regains her Soviet citizenship (*see* 1967). Disillusioned with the United States and never happy, she divorced her U.S. architect husband and moved to England in August 1982 with her daughter Olga, now 13.

Queens, N.Y., congresswoman Geraldine Ferraro, 48, runs with former Vice President Walter Mondale, 56, in a bid to defeat President Reagan, but Reagan, now 73, wins 59 percent of the popular vote and is reelected with 525 electoral votes to 13 for the Mondale-Ferraro team, which carries only the District of Columbia and Mondale's home state of Minnesota. Ferraro has been the first woman candidate for vice president on a major party ticket.

Prime Minister Thatcher forbids union membership at Britain's General Communications Headquarters and offers £1,000 for each union card turned in. All but 150 GCHQ employees accept the offer.

New York's City Council enacts legislation (Local Law 63) banning discrimination in clubs that have more than 400 members, provide regular meal service, and regularly receive "payment for dues, fees, use of space, facilities, services, meals or beverages directly from or on behalf of non-members for the

Congresswoman Geraldine Ferraro was the first major-party woman candidate for U.S. vice president. CHIE NISHIO

furtherance of trade or business." The law is designed in part to protect professional and business women, who have been excluded from clubs such as the Union League, University, Athletic, and Century Association, at which men often conduct business. Dues payments by employers make a club subject to the law (*see* 1988).

Soviet cosmonaut Svetlana Savitskaya, 35, walks in space July 25 and is the first woman to do so. Biologist Dr. Kathryn Sullivan, 33, follows suit October 11 as a member of the seven-member *Challenger* crew, largest ever, and is the first U.S. woman to perform an extravehicular activity in space.

U.S. economic growth rises at a 6.8 percent rate, highest since 1951, while the Soviet economy, with grain harvests below target, grows by only 2.6 percent, lowest since World War II. The inflation rate, 3.7 percent, is the lowest since 1967. But U.S. budget and trade deficits rise to record levels, and the Department of Housing and Urban Development reports May 1 that 250,000 to 350,000 Americans are homeless.

British cosmetics chain entrepreneur Anita Roddick (*née* Anita Lucia Perella), 40, offers shares in her Body Shop company to public investors and quickly has a net worth of $2 million. She went into business with her husband, Thomas Gordon, in 1976 selling cosmetics made from natural ingredients and "stripped of hype," will be named Britain's Business Woman of the Year next year, and within a decade the diminutive Roddick and her husband will have nearly 900 shops worldwide and be worth close to $350 million as Roddick agitates for condom use, Amnesty International, and other causes.

The Macintosh, introduced by Apple January 24, is a "user-friendly" personal computer with superior graphics capabilities.

More than 20,000 pregnant U.S. women choose amniocentesis, a procedure first used in the late 1960s to detect chromosomal abnormalities or recombinant DNA markers for disease—most commonly Down syndrome (trisomy 21)—in unborn infants. Between the 16th and 20th weeks of pregnancy, a tiny amount (less than 1/8 cup) of amniotic fluid, containing cells sloughed off by the fetus, is taken from the uterus; the cells are grown in a culture and then examined for genetic defects, a procedure that takes 2 to 4 weeks of complex laboratory work that costs $400 to $1,000 (even states that fund abortion often do not fund amniocentesis, so accessibility is a problem). Many genetic defects—e.g. Tay-Sachs disease, Cooley's anemia, sickle-cell anemia, and spina bifida—can be detected by prenatal diagnosis, but amniocentesis is surer. Chances of giving birth to an infant with Down syndrome are about 1 in 2,000 at age 22, 1 in 885 at age 30, 1 in 365 at age 35, and 1 in 109 at age 40. Named for British physician J. Langdon Down (1828–1896), Down syndrome, or mongolism, means mental retardation, and where once scarcely any Down syndrome children survived beyond age 20, many can now live to age 50 or more. About 95% of Down syndrome pregnancies are terminated (second-trimester abortions are done with saline or urea injections into the uterus to kill the fetus, although drugs are sometimes used to induce early labor; dilation and evacuation procedures are also performed by vacuuming out the amniotic fluid and then removing the fetus). Chorionic villus sampling (CVS), a newer technique that employs a plastic cannula inserted into the vagina at 8 to 12 weeks, samples fetal cells from the chorionic membrane surrounding the fetus and will be used as an alternative to amniocentesis because results are available within a few days instead of 2 to 4 weeks. CVS poses a 3 percent risk to the fetus, as compared with .5 percent for amniocentesis, but it permits a relatively safe first-trimester abortion if an abnormality is detected.

Ultrasound diagnostic procedures, which cost only a fraction of the price of amniocentesis or CVS (above), are employed in China, India, and other developing countries to determine the sex of a fetus before the 16th week of pregnancy. Female fetuses are aborted at an alarming rate in China and India, where male births consequently outnumber female by a wide margin (*see* population, 1981).

The Infant Formula Action Coalition announces January 29 that it is ending a 7-year boycott of Nestlé products pending ratification of an agreement to be ratified at Mexico City February 2 (*see* 1982). The 70 members of the Coalition include the National Organization for Women.

Nonfiction: *Sex and Destiny: The Politics of Human Fertility* by onetime feminist Germaine Greer champions chastity, arranged marriages, and the Muslim *chador* (she describes her book as an "attack upon the ideology of sexual freedom"); *The Restless Woman* by Beverly LaHaye, who has founded the rightist Concerned Women of America group; *Pure Lust: Elemental Feminist Philosophy* by Mary Daly; *Myths of Coeducation: Selected Essays* by U.S. teacher-lecturer Florence Howe (*née* Rosenfeld), 55, who founded the Feminist Press in 1970 to publish works by women authors and advocates including women's studies in college curricula, whose "implicit message to women students" at present, she writes, "is this simple: men work, write, and make history, psychology, theology; women get married, have babies, and rear them"; *First Lady from Plains* by former First Lady Rosalynn Carter, now 54; *Missile Envy: The Arms Race and Nuclear War* by Helen Caldicott; *Kate Quinton's Days* by Susan Sheehan; *Unplanned Souls: The Indian Summer of the English Aristocrats, 1880–1918* by English writer Angela Maria Lambert (*née* Helps), 44; *D.V.* (memoirs) by fashion oracle Diana Vreeland, now 84; *The Weaker Vessel* by Lady Antonia Fraser is about 17th-century Englishwomen.

Fiction: *Hôtel du Lac* by English novelist and art historian Anita Brookner, 56; *The Lover* (*L'Amant*) by Marguerite Duras, now 70; *House on Moon Lake* by Italian novelist Francesca Duranti, 49; *Watson's Apology* by Beryl Bainbridge; *Foreign Affairs* by Alison Lurie (Pulitzer Prize); *Foreign Bodies* by Barbara Grizzuti Harrison; *Stones for Ibarra* by U.S. novelist Harriet Doerr, 74 (American Book Award); *Democracy* by Joan Didion; *Parachutes and Kisses* by Erica Jong; *Love Medicine* by U.S. novelist Louise Erdreich, 30; *Separate Checks* by U.S. novelist Marianne Wiggins, 37; *Dreams of Sleep* by Charleston novelist Josephine Humphreys, 39; *Of Love and Shadows* (*De amor y de sombra*) by Isabel Allende; *A Brutal Nursery Story for Grownups* (*Otona no tame no zankokudōwa*) by Yumiko Kurahashi; *Stillwatch* by Mary Higgins Clark; *Almost Paradise* by Susan Isaacs; *Smart Women* by Judy Blume; *A Revolutionary Woman* by Sheila Fugard; *Corrigan* by Lady Caroline Blackwood; *Bard: The Odyssey of the Irish* by Morgan Llewelyn; *Full Circle* by Danielle Steel; *Come Well the Stranger* by Kathleen Woodiwiss; *Silver Wings, Santiago Blue* by Janet Dailey (her first hardcover book); *Close Her Eyes* by Dorothy Simpson; *Sound Evidence* by June Thompson; *Deadlock* by Sara Paretsky.

Poetry: *The Dead and the Living* by Sharon Olds.

Juvenile: *The Growing Pains of Adrian Mole* by Sue Townsend follows its hero past his 16th birthday.

Painting: *Creek* by Jennifer Bartlett; *Can You Hear Me?* (oil on four canvases), *Her Story* (oil on three canvases), *Both Hands* (charcoal and pastel with clay on two sheets of paper), and *Sleep* (oil on canvas) by Elizabeth Murray. Alice Neel dies of cancer at New York October 13 at age 84.

Theater: Polly Adams and Clive Francis in Michael Frayn's *Benefactors* 4/4 at London's Vaudeville Theatre; *The Miss Firecracker Contest* by Beth Henley 5/27 at New York's off-Broadway Manhattan Theater Club, with Holly Hunter and Mark Linn-Baker; David Threlfell and Frances Sternhagen in James Duff's *The War at Home* 6/13 at London's Hampstead Theatre; William Hurt, Harvey Keitel, Christopher Walken, Jerry Stiller, and Sigourney Weaver, 34, in David Rabe's *Hurlyburly* 8/7 at New York's Ethel Barrymore Theater, 343 perfs.; Steven

Bauer, Glenn Headley, and Laurie Metcalf in Lanford Wilson's *Balm in Gilead* 9/6 at New York's off-Broadway Minetta Lane Theater, 143 perfs.; Theresa Merritt and Charles S. Dutton in August Wilson's *Ma Rainey's Black Bottom* 10/11 at New York's Cort Theater, 225 perfs.

Films: Canadian-born actress Geneviève Bujold, 42, Keith Carradine, and Lesley Ann Warren, 37, in Alan Rudolph's *Choose Me*; Robin Williams and Maria Conchita Alonso in Paul Mazursky's *Moscow on the Hudson*; Albert Finney and Jacqueline Bisset in John Huston's *Under the Volcano*; Lisa Eichhorn in John Hanson's *Wildrose*.

Stage musicals: Liza Minnelli and Chita Rivera in *The Rink* 2/9 at New York's Martin Beck Theater, with John Kander–Fred Ebb songs, 204 perfs.; *The Secret Diary of Adrian Mole, Aged 13 3/4* 12/12 at Wyndham's Theatre, London, with book by Sue Townsend, songs by Ken Howard and Olive Blakeley.

Ethel Merman is found dead in her New York apartment February 15 at age 76, 10 months after undergoing surgery for a brain tumor.

Popular songs: *Like a Virgin* (album) by Madonna includes the title song and "Material Girl"; *Home Again* (album) by Judy Collins; *A Mother's Spiritual* (album) by Laura Nyro; *Private Dancer* (album) by Tina Turner makes her an international pop diva with hits that include "I Might Have Been Queen," "What's Love Got to Do with It?," "Show Some Respect," and "Better Be Good to Me" (co-written with Holly Knight); "Do They Know It's Christmas?" by British songwriters Bob Geldof and Midge Ure. Blues singer Willie Mae "Big Mama" Thornton dies of heart and liver complications at Los Angeles July 25 at age 57 (drug and alcohol abuse has shrunk her weight from 350 pounds down to 95).

East German figure skater Katarina Witt wins her event in the winter Olympics at Sarajevo, Yugoslavia, Swiss skier Michela Figini wins the downhill in 1 minute, 13.36 seconds, Italian skier Paoletta Magoni the slalom in 1 minute, 36.47 seconds, U.S. skier Debbie Armstrong the giant slalom in 2 minutes, 20.98 seconds. U.S. runner Evelyn Ashford wins the 100-meter dash in 10.97 seconds at the summer Olympics in Los Angeles, U.S. runner Valerie Brisco-Hooks the 200-meter in 21.81 seconds and the 400-meter in 48.83 seconds, Romanian runner Doina Melinte the 800-meter run in 1 minute, 57.60 seconds, Italian runner Gabriella Dorio the 1,500-meter run in 4 minutes, 3.25 seconds, Romanian runner Maricica Puica the 3,000-meter run in 8 minutes, 35.96 seconds. South African athletes have been banned, but South African runner Zola Budd, 18, who has run 5,000 meters in a record 15:01.83, has been accorded British citizenship in April because of her parental background, she has refused to condemn apartheid, and her career comes to an end after an accidental collision with U.S. runner Mary Dekker. U.S. runner Benita Fitzgerald-Brown wins the 100-meter hurdles in 12.84 seconds, Moroccan runner Nawai el-Moutawakel the 400-meter hurdles in 54.61 seconds, Ulrike Meyfarth the running high jump (6 feet, 7½ inches), Romanian athlete Anisoara Stanciu the long jump (22 feet, 10 inches), Dutch athlete Ria Stalman the discus throw (214 feet, 5 inches), British athlete Tessa Sanderson the javelin throw (228 feet, 2 inches), Italian athlete Daniele Masala the pentathlon. Joan Benoit, now 27, wins the first women's Olympic marathon in 2 hours, 24 minutes, 52 seconds, U.S. gymnast Mary Lou Retton, 16, the gold medal in all-round gymnastics (she has scored a perfect 10 in the vault at a Madison Square Garden meet March 18 and is the most decorated U.S. athlete at the Olympics). U.S. swimmer Carrie Steinseifer wins the 100-meter freestyle in 55.92 seconds, U.S. swimmer Mary Wayle the 200-meter in 1 minute, 59.23 seconds, U.S. swimmer Tiffany Cohen the 400-meter in 4 minutes, 7.10 seconds, U.S. swimmer Theresa Andrews the 100-meter backstroke in 1 minute, 2.55 seconds, Dutch swimmer Jolanda DeRover the 200-meter in 2 minutes, 12.38 seconds, Dutch swimmer Petra Van Staveren the 100-meter breaststroke in 1 minute, 09.88 seconds, Canadian swimmer Anne Ottenbrite the 200-meter in 2 minutes, 30.38 seconds, U.S. swimmer Mary Meagher the 100-meter butterfly in 59.26 seconds and the 200-meter in 2 minutes, 6.90 seconds, U.S. swimmer Tracy Caulkins the 200-meter individual medley in 2 minutes, 12.64 seconds and the 400-meter in 4 minutes, 39.21 seconds, Canadian swimmer Sylvie Bernier the springboard dive event, Chinese swimmer Zhou Jihong the platform dive.

Cincinnati General Motors dealer Marge Schott, 56, who has inherited her late husband's business, buys the local National League baseball franchise for an estimated $11 million. The Reds lost $4 million last year, but Schott (and player-manager Pete Rose) will increase attendance by 85 percent to 2.4 million by 1990 (see 1993).

Martina Navratilova wins both the British and U.S. women's singles titles.

Trivial Pursuit revives the board-game industry. Developed by a Canadian entrepreneur, the game is introduced in U.S. stores and has sales of $777 million.

Vanessa Williams, now 21, gives up her Miss America title under pressure July 23 when it is learned that the September issue of *Penthouse* magazine will contain nude photographs of her taken several years ago (she had sworn that she had never committed any acts of "moral turpitude"). Contestant Suzette Charles, who was first runner-up in last year's contest, becomes the second black Miss America.

Donna Karan mounts her first show as an independent designer (see 1974). She and her partner launched Anne Klein II last year and gained quick success, but the Japanese conglomerate that owns a majority stake in Anne Klein has urged Karan to start her own label. She has resisted, Takiyho has sacked her while agreeing at the same time to back her new company, and she breaks all records at a special sale for customers of Bergdorf Goodman, the top U.S. fashion retailer.

Free Hold, introduced by the French cosmetic giant L'Oreal, is the first hair mousse—an aerosol foam containing negatively charged polymers (to create fullness) that promises to leave hair shiny, smooth, soft, and manageable, with good "body." By year's end more than two dozen competing brands are on the market, driving out sprays, which leave hair stiff and sticky.

New York's "Mayflower Madam" makes headlines following an October 11 raid by officers of the Manhattan North Public Morals District on a small, first-story apartment at 307 West 74th Street and, 1 hour later, the arrest of a young woman in a $300-per-night room at the Parker Meridien Hotel, where she has been entertaining a "John" (actually an undercover cop). Three young women at the West 74th Street apartment have been shredding documents, but police find records linking them to a $1-million-per-year ring of 20 or 30 call girls working for one "Sheila Devlin." She turns out to be Sidney Biddle Barrows, 32, who surrenders October 16 to the Manhattan district attorney. The landlord of her West 80th Street apartment has been trying to evict her for alleged "business use" offenses and excessive "traffic," but Barrows is listed in the social register and is a descendant (on the Barrows side) of two Pilgrims who landed at Plymouth in 1620 (she attended the annual party of the Mayflower Society in March). Barrows has trained her "girls" to behave as if they, like she, attended finishing school; she has forbidden them to use condoms, instructed them to kiss clients on the lips, discouraged them from using drugs or alcohol, urged them to be "romantic" and "loving," used the yellow pages and the *Village Voice* to advertise for recruits, and advertised "escort services" under the names Cachet, Elan, and Finesse, each with a different address, in the classified telephone directory. After plea bargaining, Barrows is let off with a $5,000 fine; she is permitted to keep more than $150,000 in profits, and her list of 3,000 clients (said to include company presidents, lawyers, physicians, and Arab sheiks who paid $200 to $400 per hour or $1,150 for the night) is not made public. Women Against Pornography estimates that the city has some 25,000 prostitutes.

Florida killer Christopher Wilder, 39, a suspect in the abduction of 11 young women in several different states and the murder of some, is traced to northern New Hampshire where he dies in a struggle with police April 13.

The bodies of three women, a teenage girl, and six children are discovered April 15 in a Brooklyn apartment. The perpetrator of the mass murder is unknown.

A North Carolina appeals court reverses the conviction of a man found guilty of having raped his three daughters. The father was known to carry a gun, had frequently beaten the young girls' mother and threatened to kill them all, but the court finds October 16 that the girls had no reason to suspect that he would use force and did not put up enough resistance (*State* v. *Lester*).

The North Carolina Supreme Court acquits the defendant in a rape case on grounds that the accused was not shown to have used excessive force. It is clear that the woman had sex without her consent, the court reasons, and past experience with the defendant made her afraid to refuse, but the fact that he has been violent in the past is irrelevant since in this instance he demonstrated no force immediately before the alleged rape (*State* v. *Alston*).

North Carolina murderer Mrs. Margie Velma Barfield, 52, is executed by fatal injection November 2 outside Raleigh. She has been convicted of killing her fiancé and has confessed to killing three others by arsenic poisoning, Gov. James P. Hunt has denied clemency, and she is the first U.S. woman to be executed since 1962.

Pennsylvania's Superior Court rewrites the state's rape law to make the threat or act of forcible compulsion the determining factor in such cases, but a man who coerced a 14-year-old girl into having sex with him on threat of returning her to a detention home (she has been living with him and his wife) is found not guilty, since psychological duress may be construed as seduction, not rape (*Commonwealth* v. *Mlinarich*).

New York State's chief justice rules at Albany December 20 that a man is not exempted from prosecution for rape just because the victim is his wife; defendant Mario Liberta is convicted of having raped the woman to whom he is legally married (*see* 1978).

The average price of a new U.S. single-family house tops $101,000 in May, crossing the six-figure mark for the first time.

U.S. funding of international birth control programs is halted by order of the Reagan administration.

The Chinese government changes its family-planning program slightly to allow a small increase in exceptions to the one-child rule: 5 to 10 percent of families will be permitted to have two children, and this will be increased to 20 percent.

 Emily's List, a political action committee whose purpose is to support worthy U.S. women Democratic party candidates, is founded by IBM heiress and longtime political activist Emily Ellen Malcolm, 38, who sets out to raise money from men as well as women donors (she herself has anonymously been donating $500,000 per year to various causes).

Samantha Smith, who wrote to Soviet party secretary Yuri Andropov in 1982, dies in a plane crash August 26 at age 13 with her father when their Beechcraft goes down half a mile from the Auburn-Lewiston (Maine) airport and explodes, killing also the pilot, first officer, and four other passengers. They were en route home from London, where Samantha was filming a new TV series.

Swiss-born Vermont Democrat Madeleine Kunin (*née* May), 52, is elected governor of the state that she served as lieutenant governor from 1978 to 1982.

Chilean women demonstrate at Santiago September 5 against the repressive military regime of Gen. Augusto Pinochet that has ruled since 1973. Beaten back by troops with water cannon, the women shout that they have "clean hands" as opposed to those of their adversaries. Ten people are killed in 3 days of rioting (*see* 1988).

 The U.S. Supreme Court rules June 27 that a labor union cannot penalize workers who quit during a strike.

 Karen Ann Quinlan, comatose since 1975, dies of pneumonia June 11 at age 31 after a court permits removal of her respirator.

The U.S. Food and Drug Administration requires makers of silicone gel implants to broaden their warnings of the possible risks involved in having implant procedures (*see* 1982; 1988).

A nationwide study by University of Pittsburgh breast cancer researcher Bernard Fisher finds that lumpectomy plus radiation prevents recurrence of early breast tumors with the same effectiveness as mastectomy, but many women will still opt for mastectomies.

China permits marketing of tampons for the first time July 8.

Movie actor Rock Hudson (*née* Roy Scherer, Jr.) collapses at the Paris Ritz July 21 and dies of AIDS at Beverly Hills October 2 at age 59, shocking Americans into heightened awareness of the disease that is killing tens of thousands of men each year and is beginning to infect women.

The U.S. Supreme Court rules 5 to 4 July 1 that public school teachers may not teach in parochial schools.

Murdoch Magazines and Hachette Publications bring out a U.S. version of the 44-year-old French fashion magazine *Elle*, making *Vogue* look a little dowdy. *Elle*'s circulation will quickly reach 825,000, knocking *Harper's Bazaar* to third place among U.S. fashion magazines.

Nonfiction: *Strangers and Sisters: Women, Race, and Immigration* by U.S.-born British feminist Selma James, 55, who writes,"Political women [in Iran] are tortured and raped before execution. They rape nine-year-old women in prison because it is against God if they execute a virgin woman. Women are attacked in various horrific ways, such as acid being thrown in their faces, their hair being burnt if it is not covered. It means that just to be a woman in Iran is a political crime"; *Romantic Imprisonment: Women and Other Glorified Outcasts* by Nina Auerbach; *Darlinghissima: Letters to a Friend* by the late Janet Flanner with commentary by former Rizzoli bookstore head Natalia Murray (*née* Danesi), now 82, who met Flanner, 10 years her senior, at a New York party in January 1940 and became her lover the following summer; *Last Wish* by Betty Rollin tells how her mother, Ida, had terminal cancer in October 1983 and was able to commit suicide with the author's help.

Fiction: *The Good Apprentice* by Iris Murdoch; *The Handmaid's Tale* by Margaret Atwood; *Annie John* by Jamaica Kincaid; *The Accidental Tourist* by Anne Tyler; *They Sleep Without Dreaming* (stories) by Penelope Gilliatt; *The Finishing School* by Gail Godwin; *The Mammoth Hunters* by Jean Auel; *Birth of a Lake* (*Kosui tanjō*) by Ayako Sono; *The Good Terrorist* by Doris Lessing; *In Country* by Bobbie Ann Mason; *Fortune's Daughter* by Alice

Hoffman; *After the Reunion: A Novel* by Rona Jaffe; *Eve: Her Story* by Penelope Farmer; *A Family Likeness* (stories) by Mary Lavin, now 73; *The Bus of Dreams and Other Stories* by Mary Morris; *Mum and Mr. Armitage* (stories) by Beryl Bainbridge; Steel; *The Glory Game* by Janet Dailey; *Last Seen Alive* by Dorothy Simpson; *A Dying Fall* by June Thompson; *"B" Is for Burglar* by Sue Grafton; *Killing Orders* by Sara Paretsky.

Poetry: *The Long Approach* by Maxine Kumin; *A Fraction of Darkness: Poems* by Linda Pastan.

Painting: *Interior Perspective* (*Discordant Harmony*) by Canadian-American painter Dorothea Rockburne; *Kitchen Painting* (oil on two canvases) and *Open Book* (oil on five canvases) by Elizabeth Murray; *Elands and Bull* (acrylic on canvas), *Purple Wall* (oil on canvas), and *Green-gold Wall* (acrylic on canvas) by Elaine de Kooning, who has been inspired by the paleolithic cave paintings at Lescaux in France and Altamira in Spain, which she finds close in spirit to 20th-century art; *Grotesques* (photographic series) by Cindy Sherman.

Films: Jane Fonda and Anne Bancroft in Norman Jewison's *Agnes of God*; Don Ameche, Hume Cronyn, Jack Gilford, Gwen Verdon, Maureen Stapleton, Jessica Tandy, and Steve Guttenberg in Ron Howard's *Cocoon*; Darcy Glover, Whoopi Goldberg (Caryn Johnson), 35, Chicago TV talk show hostess Oprah Winfrey, 31, and Adolph Caesar in Steven Spielberg's *The Color Purple*; Miranda Richardson in Mike Newell's *Dance with a Stranger*; Gabriel Byrne, Greta Scacchi, and Denholm Elliott in David Drury's *Defense of the Realm*; Susan Seidelman's *Desperately Seeking Susan* with Madonna; Jane Birkin and Trevor Howard in Marion Hansel's *Dust*; Masako Natsume and Shima Iwashata in Masahiro Shinoda's *MacArthur's Children*; Saeed Jaffray, Gordon Warnecke, and Daniel Day-Lewis in Stephen Frears's *My Beautiful Laundrette*; Meryl Streep and Robert Redford in Sidney Pollack's *Out of Africa*; Jack Nicholson, Kathleen Turner, 29, and Anjelica Huston, 32, in John Huston's *Prizzi's Honor*; Mia Farrow and Woody Allen in Allen's *Purple Rose of Cairo*; Robert Duvall and Glenn Close in Christopher Cain's *The Stone Boy*; Agnes Varda's *Vagabond* with Sandrine Bonnaire.

Ruth Gordon dies at Edgartown, Mass., August 28 at age 88; Simone Signoret dies of cancer at her Normandy country house September 30 at age 64; Anne Baxter suffers a stroke and dies at New York's Lenox Hill Hospital December 12 at age 62.

Stage musicals: Ruth Brown, Linda Hopkins, and a cast of 41 perform 21 vaudeville songs from the 1920s, '30s, and '40s in *Black and Blue* 11/25 at Paris's Châtelet Théâtre; George Rose, Karen Morrow, and Howard McGillin in *The Mystery of Edwin Drood* 12/2 at New York's Imperial Theater, with Rupert Holmes songs that include "Perfect Strangers," "Don't Quit While You're Ahead," and "Moonfall," 608 perfs.

Live Aid, a marathon rock concert at Philadelphia July 13, raises $70 million for starving Africans. Organized by Irish singer Bob Geldof, the concert features such stars as Joan Baez, Phil Collins, Bob Dylan, Mick Jagger, Madonna, Paul McCartney, Sting, Tina Turner, and U2.

Popular music: *Who's Zoomin' Who?* (album) by Aretha Franklin; *Soul Kiss* (album) by Olivia Newton-John.

Compact discs and CD players are introduced with superior sound qualities. Music lovers hail the improvement and begin to shift to the new technology.

Libby Riddles, 28, leaves Anchorage March 3 and drives her 13-dog team 1,135 miles in 17 days, arriving at Nome March 20 to become the first woman winner of Alaska's grueling Iditarod Trail Dog Sled Race. She finishes 3 hours ahead of the runner-up. Susan Butcher, 30, was in the lead when a moose killed two of her dogs and injured 13 others (*see* 1986).

Martina Navratilova wins in women's singles at Wimbledon, Hana Mandlikova, 23 (Czech), at Flushing Meadow.

Boston-born Los Angeles merchant Robert Y. Greenberg, 45, sees that less than 20 percent of athletic shoes are bought for athletic use, closes his L.A. Gear apparel store and concentrates on importing Korean-made L.A. Gear fashion sneakers for teenage girls. His sales for the year are $11 million, will more than triple that to $36 million next year as he designs fashion hightops for girls, will hit $224 by 1988, and by 1989 will be third in the business behind Nike and Reebok (*see* 1982).

Cook County, Ill., housewife Cathleen Webb (*née* Crowell), a born-again Christian, retracts charges May 12 that she was raped in 1977 by Gary Dotson, who was sent to prison on her evidence in 1979 and has served 8 years. She changes her story to say that she had sex that night with her boyfriend (who denies it) and, because she feared pregnancy, blamed Dotson. Her case reinforces the notion that women frequently invent charges of rape.

Claus von Bülow is acquitted June 10 of the charges that he twice tried to kill his wife, Sunny, who remains in a coma from an insulin overdose (*see* 1982).

Coca-Cola announces in April that it is replacing its famous 99-year-old formula with a sweeter Coca-Cola designed for younger tastes. Protests from longtime Coke drinkers force the company to reintroduce its traditional beverage under the name Coke Classic.

U.S. drug maker A. H. Robins announces April 2 that it has set aside $615 million to settle claims brought by users of its contraceptive device the Dalkon Shield (*see* 1974). The company has been forced into bankruptcy to protect itself from lawsuits brought by women who claimed the Dalkon Shield had caused infertility or infections.

1986

Sugar heiress Corazón C. Aquino, 53, assumes the presidency of the Philippines February 26 after winning election amid charges of ballot tampering by Ferdinand Marcos. Widow of opposition leader Benigno Aquino, who was killed at age 59 upon his arrival at Manila in 1983, "Cory" receives support from key military leaders and Marcos is flown to Guam after U.S. pressure has been applied to make him leave Manila. He is given sanctuary in Hawaii after a 20-year rule with his wife, Imelda (*née* Romualdez), that has bled the country of perhaps $10 billion. (He has offered to repay $5 billion, but the Aquino government has rejected the offer.)

Corazón Aquino won election to the presidency of the Philippines, ending years of Marcos oppression. AP/WIDE WORLD PHOTOS

Terrorist incidents continue to take their toll. Guards at London's Heathrow Airport avert a tragedy April 17 when they arrest a British woman with explosives in her luggage, planted there by her Jordanian fiancé in an effort to blow up a Tel Aviv–bound El Al flight.

Pakistani opposition leader Benazir Bhutto, 33, whose father, Zulfikar Ali, was executed in 1979 at Rawalpindi, is arrested August 14 and locked up after addressing an Independence Day protest rally at Karachi. She has demanded the resignation of President Mohammad Zia ul-Haq, who overthrew her father in 1977. The Reagan administration has supported the repressive Zia regime, which does not free Ms. Bhutto until September 8 (*see* 1988).

Congresswoman Barbara Ann Mikulski, now 50, wins election to the U.S. Senate with help from $150,000 contributed by women on Emily's List (*see* 1985). The Maryland politician is the first woman Democrat to win a Senate seat.

Corazón Aquino restores civil rights in the Philippines March 2 in her first public declaration.

Winnie Mandela returns to Soweto (*see* 1976). Her home and clinic were burned down last year, and she has broken her ban to continue the struggle against apartheid. She receives a visit from Coretta Scott King, who pointedly refuses to meet with South Africa's President Botha.

Chinese university students demand democratic freedoms guaranteed by the nation's constitution but denied by her leaders. Tens of thousands engage in demonstrations that jeopardize their future careers, but traditional values preclude the rooting of democratic principles in the People's Republic (*see* 1989).

The Pentagon issues an order calling for the exposure and dismissal of homosexuals. The action will lead to the discharge of many of the army and navy's most productive female personnel, including some top-ranking women officers.

U.S. women professionals outnumber men for the first time but average substantially less in pay than their male counterparts.

All seven astronauts aboard the U.S. space shuttle *Challenger* perish January 28 as their craft explodes 73 seconds after liftoff from Florida's Cape Canaveral. Included are NASA biomedical engineer Judith A. Resnik, 36, and Concord, N.H., schoolteacher (Sharon) Christa McAuliffe, 37, who was chosen from 11,000 applicants to be the first ordinary citizen in space.

The U.S. national debt tops $2 trillion, up from $1 trillion in 1981.

The nation's trade deficit worsens despite a weakening dollar, setting a record of over $170 billion. The budget deficit also worsens.

Singer stops making sewing machines. It announces plans to spin off its sewing operations to a separate firm and concentrate on aerospace.

Nuclear energy receives a setback April 26 when the Soviet Union's Chernobyl power plant near Kiev in the Ukraine explodes, sending clouds of radioactive fallout across much of Europe. More than 30 fire-fighters and plant workers die in the first weeks after the accident; predictions of future cancer deaths due to radioactive exposure range from 6,500 to 45,000. Vast tracts of Soviet land will remain uninhabitable and unarable for thousands of years.

World oil prices collapse, bottoming out at $7.20 per barrel in July.

A U.S. law effective in August makes it illegal for hospitals to discharge patients because they can no longer afford to pay, but nearly one-third of Americans have inadequate health insurance or none at all, and Medicaid payments are so low that many physicians avoid taking Medicaid patients.

Harvard's Faculty of Arts and Sciences votes November 18 to establish a concentration in women's studies.

Nonfiction: *Re-Making Love: The Feminization of Sex* by Barbara Ehrenreich, Elizabeth Hess, and Gloria Jacobs; *A Lesser Life: The Myth of Women's Liberation in America* by scholar Sylvia Ann Hewlett, 40, who follows the line of ERA critic Phyllis Schlafly; *Cities and the Wealth of Nations* by Jane Jacobs.

Fiction: *Dessa Rose* by University of California at San Diego Afro-American literature professor Sherley Anne Williams, 42; *Marya: A Life* by Joyce Carol Oates; *Expensive Habits* by Maureen Howard; *The Love of Horses and Other Stories* by Tess Gallagher; *Belinda* by Anne Rampling (Anne Rice); *Te Kaihan = The Windeater* by Keri Hulme; *Missus* by Ruth Park completes the trilogy she began with *The Harp in the South* in 1947; *Regrets Only* by Washington, D.C., journalist-novelist Sally Quinn, 45; *Act of Will* by Barbara Taylor Bradford; *Private Scores* by Anne Tolstoi Wallach; *Filthy Lucre, or The Tragedy of Andrew Ledwhistle and Richard Soleway* by Beryl Bainbridge; *Wanderlust* by Danielle Steel, whose books in 2 years have sold more than 13 million mass-market paperbacks; *"C" Is for Corpse* by Sue Grafton; *Last Seen Alive* by Dorothy Simpson; *The Dark Stream* by June Thompson.

Poetry: *Thomas and Beulah* by U.S. poet Rita (Frances) Dove, 34 (Pulitzer Prize). Adrienne Rich wins the first Ruth Lilly Poetry Prize, established by Indianapolis philanthropist Lilly (the $25,000 award will be tripled in 1993).

Painting: *Chain Gang* (oil on four canvases) by Elizabeth Murray; *Rose Bison* (oil on canvas), *Gold Grotto* (oil on canvas), *Blue Bison* (acrylic on canvas), *Morning Wall* (acrylic on canvas tryptich), and *Red Bison Blue Horse* (oil on canvas) by Elaine de Kooning. Georgia O'Keeffe dies at Santa Fe, New Mexico, March 6 at age 98.

Sculpture: *Nature Study* (bronze) by Louise Bourgeois.

Theater: Julia McKenzie and Martha Jarvis in Alan Ayckbourn's *A Woman in Mind* 9/3 at London's Vaudeville Theatre; *Coastal Disturbances* by Tina Howe 11/19 at New York's off-Broadway Second Stage Theater, with Annette Bening, Timothy Daly, Rosemary Murphy, and Addison Powell, 350 perfs.; Jonathan Silverman, Linda Lavin, Phyllis Newman, Jason Alexander, John Randolph, and Philip Sterling in Neil Simon's *Broadway Bound* 12/4 at New York's Broadhurst Theater, 756 perfs.

Television: *L.A. Law* 9/15 on NBC with Harry Hamlin, Jill Eikenberry, and Richard Dysart.

Films: Sigourney Weaver in James Cameron's *Aliens*; Jon Voight, JoBeth Williams, and Annabeth Gish in Eugene Corr's *Desert Bloom*; Michael Caine, Mia Farrow, Carrie Fisher, and Woody Allen in Allen's *Hannah and Her Sisters*; Margarethe von Trotta's *Rosa Luxemburg* with Barbara Sukowa; Marie Riviere in Erich Rohmer's *Summer*; Tsutomu Yamazaki and Ken Watanabe in Juzo Itami's *Tampopo*; Lizzie Borden's *Working Girls* with Louise Smith, Ellen McElduff, and Amanda Goodwin.

Film musical: Rick Moranis, Ellen Greene, and Vincent Gardenia in Frank Oz's *Little Shop of Horrors.*

Stage musical: Michael Crawford and Sarah Brightman in *Phantom of the Opera* 10/9 at Her Majesty's Theatre, London, with Andrew Lloyd Weber–Charles Hart songs.

Popular songs: *Whitney Houston* (album) by onetime New Hope (Pa.) Baptist Church choir singer Whitney Houston, 23, includes "You Give Good

Love" and "Saving All My Love for You"; *True Blue* (album) by Madonna; *Rapture* (album) by Anita Baker; *Control* (album) by U.S. vocalist Janet Jackson, 20, whose brother Michael is an entertainment superstar.

Susan Butcher wins the Iditarod Trail Dog Sled Race (now 1,157 miles; *see* 1985). She will win it again next year, in 1988, and in 1990.

Martina Navratilova wins in women's singles at both Wimbledon and Flushing Meadow.

Nintendo video games debut in America and wow the youngsters with sophisticated graphics and entries like "The Legend of Zelda," in which the hero, Link, must rescue Zelda. Founded in 1898 to manufacture playing cards, Nintendo has U.S. sales of $300 million as kids demand the $100 players and $35-to-$40 cartridges. Sales will hit $830 million next year and top $3.4 billion by 1990.

Grossinger's resort in the Catskills is demolished after 72 years of serving a New York–area social group that has become increasingly assimilated into the American mainstream.

Schenectady, N.Y., mother Mary Beth Tinning, 43, is arrested February 7; nine of her children, none older than 2, have died in the past 14 years.

Pasadena County, Calif., Supreme Court Justice Gilbert C. Alston dismisses rape and sodomy charges brought by Hispanic prostitute Rhonda DaCosta, 30, against a 20-year-old white male, saying that a "whore is a whore is a whore." A prostitute cannot, by definition, be raped, the judge insinuates.

The U.S. Supreme Court rules 5 to 4 June 11 that a Pennsylvania statute is unconstitutional because it requires, among other things, that a physician use the abortion method that provides the best opportunity for the fetus to be born alive (*Thornburgh* v. *American College of Obstetricians and Gynecologists*).

The steroid abortifacient drug RU486 (mifepristone) developed in 1980 by French endocrinologist Etienne-Emile Baulieu, 60, wins approval in September for testing in France and the People's Republic of China. Roussel-Uclaf withdraws the drug in October but promptly resumes sale on orders from the French government after women put pressure on their representatives (*see* 1988).

1987

Gov. Kay A. Orr (*née* Stark), 48, is inaugurated at Lincoln, Neb., January 8, becoming the nation's first Republican woman governor.

Fawn Hall, secretary to marine corps Col. Oliver North at the National Security Council, admits to a congressional committee February 25 that she helped North revise and shred documents that might have implicated him in deals that involved using money from sales of arms to Iran for supplying contra forces in Nicaragua. She testifies June 9 that she smuggled documents out of the office by concealing them under her clothing. "Sometimes you just have to go above the law," she says.

Model Donna Rice, 27, is seen by newspaper reporters going into the Washington, D.C., town house of Sen. Gary Hart (D., Colo.) one night and not coming out until the next morning. Presidential hopeful Hart, a married man, has been photographed with Rice on a trip to Bimini aboard his friend's yacht *Monkey Business*. He bows out of the presidential race May 8, and although he reenters December 16 with support from his wife, Lee, his chances are blighted by the Donna Rice affair.

British voters reelect Prime Minister Margaret Thatcher's Conservative government to a third term June 11, but former Westminster City Council member Diane Julie Abbott, 34, is elected as a Labour candidate for Hackney North and Stoke Newington and becomes the first black woman M.P.

Italian voters elect porn star Cicciolina (Ilona Staller), 34, to the nation's Parliament.

Hartford voters elect Connecticut Assemblywoman Carrie Saxon Perry, 56, mayor; she becomes the first black woman mayor of a major U.S. city.

Oklahoma Cherokee Wilma Mankiller, 41, is elected chief of the 108,000-member Cherokee Nation—the first female chief of the second largest tribe (only the Navajos are more numerous). The Cherokee operate industries, health clinics, and cultural programs that employ about 1,700 with an annual budget of $52 million, and Mankiller aims to see that her people solve their own economic and social problems.

A U.S. Supreme Court ruling January 13 upholds the right to require leaves for pregnant women. The Court rules 6 to 3 March 25 that giving women and minorities job preference over better-qualified white males is not unconstitutional. The Court rules May 4 that Rotary Clubs must admit women.

NOW (the National Organization for Women) elects feminist Molly Yard president at Philadelphia July 18. Yard, who will not give her age, is in her 60s or 70s.

Battery accounts for the death of at least 10 U.S. women per day, according to studies of police and hospital reports. By 1991, battery will be the leading cause of injury in adult U.S. women.

U.S. Surgeon General C. Everett Koop tells a House subcommittee February 10 that condom commercials should be permitted on TV to help stop the AIDS epidemic.

U.S. spending on health care rises to $500 billion, up 9.8 percent over 1986 (the 1987 inflation rate is 4.4 percent).

First Lady Nancy Reagan is operated on for a breast tumor in October and elects to have a mastectomy rather than a lumpectomy, because "given my nature, I'd be worried to death. There were people, including doctors, who thought I had taken too drastic a step in choosing the mastectomy," she will later say. "The director of the Breast Cancer Advisory Center was quoted in the *New York Times* as saying that my decision had 'set us back ten years.' I resented these statements, and I still do."

PTL minister Jim Bakker resigns March 19 after revelations that he cheated on his wife, Tammy Faye, in 1980 with church secretary Jessica Hahn and used ministry money to buy Hahn's silence (*see* 1974). The Rev. Jerry Falwell takes over the PTL Ministry (*see* 1989).

Spelman College at Atlanta announces April 5 that it has appointed a new president: Hunter College anthropology professor Johnnetta Cole (*née* Betsch), 50, is the first black women to head Spelman since its founding in 1881.

Nonfiction: *Feminism Unmodified: Discourses on Life and Law* by Catherine A. MacKinnon; *The Closing of the American Mind* by University of Chicago Plato scholar Allan Bloom, 52, who deplores what he calls the feminist transformation of society, which has filled women with demands and desires and depleted men of vigor. "Feminism has triumphed over the family," has "led to the suppression of modesty," and enabled women to bear children "on the female's terms with or without fathers," he writes; *The Fitzgeralds and the Kennedys: An American Saga* by Doris Kearns Goodwin; *Adam and Eve in the City: Selected Nonfiction* by Francine du Plessix Gray.

Fiction: *Beloved* by Toni Morrison (Pulitzer Prize); *A Sport of Nature* by Nadine Gordimer; *The Radiant Way* by Margaret Drabble; *Her Mother's Daughter* by Marilyn French; *Bluebeard's Egg* (stories) by Margaret Atwood; *The Age of Grief* (stories) by Jane Smiley; *The Messiah of Stockholm* by Cynthia Ozick; *Mama* by U.S. novelist Terry McMillan, 35; *Postcards from the Edge* by Hollywood actress-novelist Carrie (Frances) Fisher, 30 (daughter of Debbie Reynolds and Eddie Fisher); *Eva Luna* by Isabel Allende; *Moon Tiger* by Penelope Lively; *Rich in Love* by Josephine Humphreys; *Herself in Love* (stories) by Marianne Wiggins; *Circles of Deceit* by Nina Bawden; *Fine Things* and *Kaleidoscope* by Danielle Steel; *"D" Is for Deadbeat* by Sue Grafton; *Bitter Medicine* by Sara Paretsky; *Element of a Doubt* by Dorothy Simpson; *No Flowers by Request* by June Thompson.

The National Museum of Women in the Arts opens in April two blocks from the White House at Washington, D.C., under the direction of Wilhelmina Cole Holladay, 64, who has toured U.S. and European galleries and found that women artists since at least the 17th century have generally gone unrecognized by the art establishment. The new museum, which has 67,000 members, owns 500 works of art, and its inaugural exhibition is entitled *American Women Artists, 1830–1930.*

Painting: *The Hunger Artist* by Elizabeth Murray.

Theater: Mary Alice and James Earl Jones in August Wilson's *Fences* 3/26 at New York's 46th Street Theater, 526 perfs.; Dana Ivey, Morgan Freeman, and Ray Gill in Alfred Uhry's *Driving Miss*

Daisy 4/15 at New York's Playwrights Horizons Theater, 80 perfs.; Maggie Smith and Margaret Tyzack in Peter Shaffer's *Lettice and Lovage* 10/27 at London's Globe Theatre.

Geraldine Page dies of a heart attack at New York June 13 at age 62.

Films: Stéphane Audran in Gabriel Axe's *Babette's Feast*; Gillian Armstrong's *High Tide* with Judy Davis; Cher, Nicolas Cage, Olympia Dukakis, 56, and Danny Aiello in Norman Jewison's *Moonstruck*. Also: Anjelica Huston in John Huston's *The Dead*; Joan Plowright and Bernard Hill in Peter Greenaway's *Drowning by Numbers*; Anne Bancroft and Anthony Hopkins in David Jones's *84, Charing Cross Road*; Sarah Miles, now 46, and David Hayman in John Boorman's *Hope and Glory*; Nicolas Cage and Holly Hunter, 28, in Joel Coen's *Raising Arizona*.

Rita Hayworth dies of Alzheimer's disease at New York May 14 at age 68; Pola Negri dies at San Antonio, Texas, August 1 at age 87.

Broadway musical: Bernadette Peters and Joanna Gleason in *Into the Woods* 11/5 at the Martin Beck Theater, with Stephen Sondheim–James Lapine songs, 764 perfs.

Popular songs: *Hometown Girl* (album) by U.S. country singer-guitarist-songwriter Mary-Chapin Carpenter, 29; *Trio* (album) by Emmy Lou Harris, Dolly Parton, and Linda Ronstadt; *Canciones de Mi Padre* (album) by Ronstadt; *Trust Your Heart* (album) by Judy Collins, now 48; "Somewhere Out There" by James Horner, Barry Mann, and Cynthia Weil; *Whitney* (album) by Whitney Houston.

Martina Navratilova wins in women's singles at both Wimbledon and Flushing Meadow.

Rykä Inc. is founded in February at Weymouth, Massachusetts, by entrepreneur Sheri Poe and her husband, Martin Birrittella, to import and market athletic shoes made specifically for women. The Birrittellas have had a New Hampshire–based business selling gift items, including back rollers and other fitness-related merchandise, and although Martin holds a patent on an exercise sandal they are only on the periphery of the footwear industry. Their gift business has taken them to South Korea and Taiwan, where visits to shoe factories have made them suspect that the major shoemakers were neglecting women. Because each of their shoes comes with four extra eyelets and the eyelets are farther from the vamp than on most shoes, Rykä shoes can be laced tighter for what the company calls custom-like fit (few athletic shoes are width sized). Women's lines at larger companies are designed simply by shrinking the last used for men's shoes to smaller dimensions. This ignores the fact that women's feet—because women have different hips and pelvises—hit the ground differently. The Birrittellas have contracted with the Asian factories to produce shoes that are gender specific. Like their competitors, they provide proprietary designs and materials and then have shoes manufactured to their own specifications. Rykä (the Birrittellas made up the name; like Häagen Dazs for ice cream, it means nothing) have some patented technology, including nitrogen moldings that fit into the shoe's foundation and resemble clear rubber bouncing balls (*see* 1988).

Japan's highest court makes marital rape a crime in a ruling handed down in July.

Wappingers Falls, N.Y., schoolgirl Tawana Brawley, 15, is found November 28 half naked with "KKK" and "Nigger" smeared with dog feces on her body. She claims six white men, one of them wearing a police badge, kidnapped her November 24 and repeatedly raped her. Self-serving lawyers take up her case, which inflames the black media, but a grand jury investigation will show that she left home for 4 days and staged her condition to avoid violent punishment from her stepfather.

U.S. microwave oven sales reach a record 12.6 million (*see* 1967). Sears, Roebuck's Kenmore is the largest-selling brand, followed by Sharp's and General Electric's. Food companies rush to develop microwavable food products.

A New Jersey judge rules March 31 that surrogate mother Mary Beth Whitehead (*née* Messer), 20, has no parental rights to "Baby M," the daughter she bore March 27, 1986, for William Stern, whose wife, Elizabeth, 41, a pediatrician with a mild case of multiple sclerosis, was afraid that pregnancy would be injurious to her health. The Sterns, who have named the baby Melissa, offered Mrs. Whitehead $10,000 to be artificially inseminated and carry their child, but Mrs. Whitehead has named the girl Sara and refused to give her up. The judge, who has called her "manipulative, impulsive, and exploitive" in insisting on keeping the baby, rules that in the absence of any law governing the situation it is in the best interests of the child that she be raised by the Sterns, who are ordered to pay Mrs. Whitehead the $10,000 surrogacy fee which she has rejected.

Johannesburg mother Pat (Mrs. Raymond) Anthony, 48, becomes a grandmother October 1 when she gives surrogate birth by cesarean section to her own daughter's triplets. Karen Ferreira-Jorge (*née* Raymond) had her uterus removed 3 years ago after giving birth to a son, her mother has been artificially inseminated with the sperm of Karen's gym-instructor husband, Alcino, and the triplets are delivered prematurely. South Africa's medical profession is generally opposed to surrogate births, but some ministers of the Dutch Reformed Church have been supportive; legal experts are divided as to who is the legal guardian of a surrogate child.

1988

 Onetime Mafia courtesan Judith Exner Campbell, 54, admits in a February 29 *People* magazine interview that she acted as a courier between President John F. Kennedy and mob boss Sam Giancana from 1960 until after JFK's inauguration in 1961, crisscrossing the country carrying sealed manila envelopes. Exner has previously written about her 2½-year affair with Kennedy (they were introduced at a Las Vegas hotel February 7, 1960, by singer Frank Sinatra, who later introduced her to Giancana) but did not disclose her role as his go-between with the mob; now, terminally ill with lung cancer, she acknowledges that she lied to a Senate committee in 1975 when she said that Kennedy was unaware of her friendship with mobsters.

Former Philippine President Ferdinand Marcos and his wife, Imelda, are indicted October 21 on fraud and racketeering charges and ordered to New York. They face 50 years' imprisonment and fines totalling $1 million. Marcos, now 71, is called too ill to travel; tobacco heiress Doris Duke sends her plane to pick up Imelda in Honolulu and bring her east for arraignment. The former beauty queen and First Lady arrives at the New York courthouse wearing a floor-length turquoise silk *terno*—the Philippine national dress; the judge imposes a bail of $5 million, she declares herself indigent, but she goes back to her Waldorf-Astoria suite and phones Duke, who posts bail of $5.3 million in municipal bonds and reportedly pays for her friend's stay in the $1,800-per-night suite at the Waldorf; Imelda, who receives a congratulatory phone call from President Reagan and his wife, Nancy, says, "Doris Duke has saved my faith in America."

Vice President George Herbert Walker Bush accepts the Republican party's nomination in August with an address written largely by White House speechwriter Peggy Noonan (Rahn), 36, who calls for "a thousand points of light" (private charity) in lieu of government spending and makes promises—"Read my lips—no new taxes." Noonan, a protégée of Reagan communications director Pat Buchanan, is a onetime Democrat who wrote the line in a Reagan speech calling Nicaragua's contras "the moral equal to our Founding Fathers." Bush wins the November elections, defeating Massachusetts governor Michael Dukakis (whose campaign was directed by Harvard Law School professor Susan Estrich, now 36), and will continue President Reagan's policies with few modifications.

Benazir Bhutto, whose father, Prime Minister Zulfikar Ali Bhutto, was executed by Gen. Mohammed Zia ul-Haq in 1979, is elected prime minister of Pakistan in December and becomes the first woman to head a modern Muslim state (*see* 1236; 1986).

 "Women are entitled to dress attractively, even provocatively if you like, to be friendly with casual acquaintances and still say no at the end of the evening without being brutally assaulted," says London judge Richard Rougier, 55, March 4 in imposing sentence on a rapist at the Old Bailey. "This sort of brutal violence, particularly to women, has got to be dealt with severely. You broke her jaw just because she wasn't prepared to go to bed with you."

Iraqi forces use poison gas March 16 against Kurdish civilians in the town of Halabja, killing at least

Benazir Bhutto was elected prime minister of Pakistan, becoming the first woman to head a modern Muslim state. AP/WIDE WORLD PHOTOS

4,000 men, women, and children (some estimates say 12,000).

Rangoon police club a student to death in March and let 41 suffocate in a crammed van. Aung Sang Suu Kyi, 44, daughter of a Burmese hero who was assassinated in 1947, returns from exile in England in April. A political protest in front of Convocation Hall on the Rangoon University campus June 21 leads to a march by 1,000 students in downtown Rangoon. Police crack down, and thousands are killed in the ensuing weeks.

The U.S. Supreme Court rules unanimously June 20 in *New York State Club Association, Inc.,* v. *The City of New York* that the city's 1984 law banning discrimination against women and minorities in private clubs with more than 400 members does not violate First Amendment rights. The ruling supports the city's human rights law and will affect clubs in every other U.S. city.

U.S. unemployment falls in April to 5.4 percent, lowest since 1974.

Median weekly U.S. earnings: lawyer $914, pharmacist $718, engineer $717, physician $716, college teacher $676, computer programmer $588, high school teacher $521, registered nurse $516, accountant $501, editor, reporter $494, actor, director $488, writer, artist, entertainer, athlete $483, mechanic $424, truck driver (heavy) $387, carpenter $365, bus driver $335, laborer $308, secretary $299, truck driver (light) $298, machine operator $284, janitor $258, hotel clerk $214, cashier $192 (source: Bureau of Labor Statistics).

The poverty rate of U.S. families headed by women has declined sharply as a result of women obtaining better-paying jobs. Families headed by women are still 4.5 times as likely to be poor as families headed by men. Such families constitute 15 percent of the population but more than 50 percent of the poor. Welfare policies give the poor incentives to avoid marriage, but nearly three out of four young black women who bear children out of wedlock marry by the time they are 24 and thus emerge from poverty.

A gaping hole opens in the fuselage of a 19-year-old Aloha Airlines Boeing 737 April 28, flight attendant C. B. Lansing is swept to her death, but the plane lands safely at Maui Airport and the airline industry institutes new maintenance procedures; a Pan Am 747 explodes in midair over Lockerbie, Scotland, December 21, killing all 259 aboard plus 11 on the ground (a bomb planted by a Mideastern terrorist in Frankfurt is blamed).

Prozac, introduced in January by Eli Lilly, is an antidepressant drug that will be used in the next few years by millions of women and men not just for clinical depression but simply to feel better.

U.S. health care spending reaches $51,926 per capita as costs run out of control, accounting for 11.1 percent of gross national product. Sweden spends 9.1 percent, Canada and France 8.5, the Netherlands 8.3, West Germany 8.1, Austria and Switzerland 8, Ireland 7.9, Finland and Iceland 7.5, Belgium 7.1, Luxembourg and New Zealand 6.9, Australia and Norway 6.8, Italy and Japan 6.7, Britain 6.2, Denmark 6.1, Spain 6, Portugal 5.6, Greece 3.9, Turkey 3.6. Every industrial nation except the United States and South Africa has a national health care program.

A congressional investigation raises alarms about cosmetic breast surgery, FDA product surveillance investigators find that the failure rate of breast implants is among the highest of any surgery-related procedure they have studied, and a Dow Corning study finds that silicone gel implants cause cancer in more than 23 percent of test rats (*see* 1985). FDA Commissioner Dr. Frank Young dismisses the Dow Corning study, saying, "The risk to humans, if it exists at all, would be low" (*see* 1991).

One out of four U.S. babies is born by cesarean section—up from one out of 20 in 1970 (only Brazil has a higher rate) (*see* 1980). Cesarean section is the most frequently performed operation in U.S. hospitals: an estimated 934,000 such procedures are performed this year, and the cost tops $3 billion. The Health Insurance Association of America reports that in northeastern metropolitan areas 2 years ago doctors charged $230 more for a C-section than for a vaginal delivery—$1,210 as opposed to $980. A cesarean requires 4 more days in hospital, making it twice as long, and twice as expensive, as a vaginal birth, and hospital charges for a cesarean are about $1,050 higher.

Baton Rouge, La., television evangelist Jimmy Swaggart, 52, confesses sin February 21 and is removed from his pulpit by the Assemblies of God after revelations that he has had sex with a prostitute. Swaggart has lost 69 percent of his viewers and 72 percent of the enrollment at his Bible college. He is defrocked April 8 and ordered to stay off TV for a year but returns in 3 months.

The U.S. Census Bureau reports that 87 percent of U.S. women aged 25 to 29 have high school diplomas versus 84.7 percent of men in that age group; 21.9 percent of the women have had 4 years of college, versus 23.4 percent of the men.

National Public Radio news analyst and Congressional correspondent Cokie Roberts (*née* Boggs), 46, joins American Broadcasting Company in a similar capacity. She continues her work for NPR.

Nonfiction: *Pornography and Civil Rights: A New Day for Women's Equality* by Catherine A. MacKinnon and Andrea Dworkin; *The Bride Stripped Bare:*

The Artist and the Nude in 20th Century America by Janet Hobhouse; *Nothing to Declare: Memoirs of a Woman Traveling Alone* by Mary Morris.

Fiction: *Breathing Lessons* by Anne Tyler (Pulitzer Prize); *The Fifth Child* by Doris Lessing; *Second Chances* by Alice Adams; *Greenlanders* by Jane Smiley; *Loving and Giving* by Molly Keane, now 84; *. . . And Members of the Club* by Ohio novelist Helen Hooven Santmyer (*née* Wright), 88; *The Bean Trees* by Arizona novelist Barbara Kingsolver, 33; *To Be the Best* by Barbara Taylor Bradford; *Spence + Lila* by Bobbie Ann Mason; *Kitchen* by Japanese novelist Banana Yoshimoto, 24; *Zoya* by Danielle Steel; *Blood Shot* (in England, *Toxic Shock*) by Sara Paretsky; *"E" Is for Evidence* by Sue Grafton; *Suspicious Death* by Dorothy Simpson.

Poetry: *A Guide to Forgetting* by Tess Gallagher, who 9 years ago married writer Raymond Carver (her third marriage).

Sculpture: *Diva* and *Lazarus* by U.S. sculptor Alison Saar, 32. Louise Nevelson dies at New York April 17 at age 88.

Theater: *The Heidi Chronicles* by Wendy Wasserstein 4/15 at New York's off-Broadway Playwrights Horizons Theater, with John Allen, Peter Friedman, and Boyd Gaines (Pulitzer Prize, New York Drama Critics' Circle Award); David Rasche, Bob Balaban, and Felicity Huffman in David Mamet's *Speed-the-Plow* 5/2 at New York's Royale Theater, 278 perfs.; *Our Country's Good* by U.S.-British playwright Timberlake (*née* Lael Louisiana) Wertenbaker (based on *The Playmaker* by Thomas Keneally) 9/1 at London's Royal Court Theatre, with Nick Dunning, Ron Cook, Linda Bassett, and Lesley Sharp; Joyce Van Patten, 54, André Gregory, and Ken Howard in Neil Simon's *Rumors* 11/17 at New York's Broadhurst Theater, 531 perfs.

Films: Jodie (*née* Alicia Christina) Foster, 26, as a gang-rape victim and Kelly McGillis, 31, as her lawyer in Jonathan Kaplan's *The Accused*; Gena Rowlands in Woody Allen's *Another Woman*; Penny Marshall's *Big* with Tom Hanks; Meryl Streep and Sam Neill in Fred Schepisi's *A Cry in the Dark*; Glenn Close, John Malkovich, and Michelle Pfeiffer, 30, in Stephen Frears's *Dangerous Liaisons*; James Wilbym and Kristin Scott Thomas in Charles Sturridge's *A Handful of Dust*; Philip Davis and

Ruth Sheen in Mike Leigh's *High Hopes*; Christine Lahti, 38, and Judd Hirsch in Sidney Lumet's *Running on Empty*; Marina Goldovskaya's documentary *Solovki Power*, about a Soviet gulag (prison camp) in the White Sea's Solovetsky archipelago; Nobuko Miyamoto and Tsutomou Yamazaki in Juzo Itami's *A Taxing Woman*; Daniel Day-Lewis, Lena Olin, and Juliette Binoche in Philip Kaufman's *The Unbearable Lightness of Being*; Carmen Marua in Pedro Almodóvar's *Women on the Verge of a Nervous Breakdown*; Melanie Griffith, Sigourney Weaver, and Harrison Ford in Mike Nichols's *Working Girl*.

Television series: *Roseanne* debuts 10/18 on ABC with former Denver stand-up comic Roseanne Barr, 36, as a rotund, salty-tongued, male-baiting blue-collar mother of three. The show will soon have a larger audience than any other; *Murphy Brown* debuts November 17 on CBS with Candice Bergen, now 42, in the title role (written by creator-producer Diane English, 40) of a TV network reporter.

Candice Bergen gained more acclaim in the TV series Murphy Brown *than she ever had in films.* CHIE NISHIO

Popular songs: *The Rumour* (album) by Olivia Newton-John; "So Emotional" by Whitney Houston.

Anne-Sophie Mutter plays with eight major orchestras in the United States and Canada, performs in Europe, returns to the United States to make her Carnegie Hall debut 12/14 (she has been limiting her public appearances to 80) and launch her first North American recital tour.

Katarina Witt wins her second figure-skating gold medal in the winter Olympics at Calgary, Alberta, West German skier Marina Kiehl wins the downhill in 1 minute, 25.86 seconds, Swiss skier Vreni Schneider the slalom in 1 minute, 36.69 seconds and the giant slalom in 2 minutes, 6.49 seconds. U.S. runner (Delorez) Florence Griffith-Joyner, 28, wins the 100-meter dash in 10.54 seconds and the 200-meter in 21.34 seconds at the summer Olympics in Seoul, South Korea; Soviet runner Olga Bryzguina wins the 400-meter in 48.65 seconds, East German runner Sigrun Wodars the 800-meter run in 1 minute, 56.10 seconds, Romanian runner Paula Ivan the 1,500-meter in 3 minutes, 53.96 seconds, Soviet runner Tatiana Samolenko the 3,000-meter in 8 minutes, 26.53 seconds, Bulgarian runner Jordanka Donkova the 100-meter hurdles in 12.38 seconds, Australian runner Debra Flintoff-King the 200-meter in 53.17 seconds, Portuguese runner Rosa Mota the marathon in 2 hours, 25 minutes, 40 seconds, U.S. athlete Louise Ritter the running high jump (6 feet, 8 inches), U.S. athlete Jackie Joyner-Kersee, 26, the long jump (24 feet, 3½ inches), Soviet athlete Natalya Lisovskaya the shot put (72 feet, 11½ inches), East German athlete Martina Hellmann the discus throw (237 feet, 2½ inches), East German athlete Petra Felke the javelin throw (245 feet), Jackie Joyner-Kersee the pentathlon. Soviet gymnast Elena Shoushounova wins the gold medal for best all-round performance, Romanian gymnast Daniela Silvas wins three golds. East German swimmer Kristin Otto wins the 100-meter freestyle in 54.93 seconds, East German swimmer Heike Friedrich the 200-meter in 1 minute, 57.65 seconds, U.S. swimmer Janet Evans the 400-meter in 4 minutes, 3.85 seconds and the 800 meter in 8 minutes, 20.20 seconds, Kristin Otto the 100-meter backstroke in 1 minute, 0.89 seconds, Hungarian swimmer Krisztina Egerszwegi the 200-meter in 2 minutes, 9.29 seconds, Bulgarian swimmer Tainia Dangalakova the 100-meter breaststroke in 1 minute, 7.95 seconds, East German swimmer Silke Hoerner the 200-meter in 2 minutes, 26.71 seconds, Kristin Otto the 100-meter butterfly in 59 seconds, East German swimmer Kathleen Nord the 200-meter in 2 minutes, 9.51 seconds, East German swimmer Daniela Hunger the 200-meter individual medley in 2 minutes, 12.59 seconds, Janet Evans the 400-meter in 4 minutes, 37.76 seconds, Chinese swimmer Gao Min the springboard dive event, Chinese swimmer Xu Yanmei the platform dive.

Steffi Graf, 19 (W. Ger), wins tennis's first "grand slam" since Margaret Court of England did it in 1970.

Rykä runs into quality control problems with its athletic shoes for women (*see* 1987). There are complaints about stitching. One chain of athletic shoe stores sends back nearly its entire shipment for fall 1988. The problems will be corrected, but in the meantime companies like Nike are preparing to market their own technically specialized shoes for women. Undeterred, the company finds podiatrists to back up its claim: because they are made on a last specially developed for women, Rykä shoes are the only ones specifically designed for the fairer sex. Many store buyers and customers agree that Rykä is indeed contoured to the feminine foot. The company focuses its efforts on southern California, where L.A. Gear first prospered; it advertises on local radio stations and in three California magazines, offers discounts to aerobics instructors, gets itself named official shoe of the Miss Teen USA pageant, and gives some Rykä stock (plus a small stipend) to Jake Steinfeld, a Hollywood body trainer whose syndicated TV show "Body by Jake" has a certain following. Steinfeld gets some of his celebrity clients, including Bette Midler, to wear Rykäs. But major companies such as United States Shoe and Brown Shoe are also making athletic footwear for women, the first with its Easy Spirit Line, the second with NaturalSport shoes. U.S. Shoe quotes podiatrists who say that women's feet are not just smaller than men's but also differ anatomically. A woman's heel is much narrower relative to the overall length of her foot. Her Achilles tendon and even the general width of her foot are often narrower relative to her foot's overall length. Her arch is appreciably higher than that of a man, considering the size of her foot. Her Achilles ten-

don is much shorter than a man's. Her calf muscles start lower on her leg and come into her Achilles tendon lower on her leg. In most cases she has less lateral (side-to-side) strength in her feet than a man, which tends to make her feet and ankles wobble when she walks and often wears down the inside or outside of her heels. But while U.S. Shoe and Brown will promote their shoes as having "sneaker-like" comfort combined with high fashion, most women will find them too dowdy to wear on fancy occasions or for business and less comfortable than sneakers for everyday use.

"Preppy" murder suspect Robert E. Chambers, Jr., pleads guilty March 25 to first-degree manslaughter in the 1986 killing of Jennifer Levin after a 13-week trial in which his lawyers have tried to depict his victim as a tramp. He admits in plea-bargaining arrangement on the 9th day of jury deliberations that he intended to injure Levin seriously and "thereby caused her death." Chambers says August 10 that he will not contest a $25 million wrongful death suit filed against him by Levin's parents.

Nestlé S.A. of Switzerland (through its Carnation subsidiary, acquired 3 years ago) introduces Good Start H.A. (hypoallergenic) infant formula in a bid to seize part of the $1.6 billion U.S. infant formula market from Abbot Laboratories (Similac) and Bristol-Myers (Enfamil). Pediatricians are quick to recommend Good Start for colicky babies, but mothers of milk-allergic infants begin to report serious reactions: some babies vomit violently after ingesting Good Start and then go limp. Despite efforts to encourage breast-feeding, some 80 percent of U.S. infants are still given formula at least some of the time.

Canada's Supreme Court rules January 28 that a law restricting abortion is unconstitutional.

The Reagan Administration acts January 29 to bar most family-planning clinics from providing abortion assistance if they receive federal funds.

Operation Rescue is founded by upstate New York abortion foe Randall Terry, 26, a used-car salesman who sets out to padlock doors of family-planning clinics. A 26-year-old upstate New York sailor files suit to stop his fiancée from having an abortion.

Right-to-lifers mounted Operation Rescue in an effort to close down legal U.S. abortion clinics. AP/WIDEWORLD PHOTOS

The FDA gives approval May 23 to cervical cap contraceptives, long available in Europe. The agency issues a formal ruling that no oral contraceptive may contain more than 50 micrograms (0.05 milligrams) of estrogen, a limit recommended by the British Committee on Safety in Drugs in 1969.

A federal jury finds G. D. Searle guilty in a case that involves testing and marketing the company's Copper-7 intrauterine contraceptive device. The jury awards plaintiffs $8.7 million.

France and China act September 24 to authorize use under medical supervision of the steroid drug RU486 (mifepristone), which induces abortion in the first months of pregnancy by stopping the circulation of progesterone in the system, thus making the uterus incapable of sustaining the developing fetus (*see* 1986). News of France's action produces public demonstrations. Hoechst-Roussel, U.S. subsidiary of the West German maker Roussel-Uclaf, does not apply for FDA approval lest prolife groups boycott the company's other products (*see* 1990).

China's central authorities give up hope that the nation's population can be held to 1.2 billion by the year 2000 (*see* 1980). Peng Peiyun, who takes over as fourth head of the State Family-Planning Commission, acknowledges that the figure was probably unrealistic; the population is already over 1 billion, and she says that by 2000 it will likely be 1.27 billion.

1989

European women join with men to overthrow Communist regimes in Russia, East Germany, Czechoslovakia, and Romania. Chinese women are killed along with men as the Beijing government cracks down on prodemocracy demonstrators in Tiananmen Square.

Former Philippine president Ferdinand Marcos dies of cardiac arrest September 28 at age 72, leaving his wife, Imelda, a rich widow.

A *New York Times* poll of 1,025 women conducted in late June shows that 67 percent agree that the nation "continues to need a strong women's movement to push for benefits that benefit women"; 27 percent disagree. A second survey, taken a month later, finds that 23 percent of women believe that the most important problems facing women are those encountered on the job.

More than 56 million U.S. women are in the civilian workforce and represent 45 percent of that workforce, up from 38 percent in 1970. Nearly half of all accountants and bus drivers are women, up from 23.3 percent and 29.7 percent, respectively, in 1970. One out of five doctors and lawyers is a woman (in 1970, only 7 percent of doctors and 3 percent of lawyers were women). The *New York Times* poll (above) shows that 83 percent of working mothers and 72 percent of working fathers are torn by the conflicting demands of job and family; 48 percent of women interviewed say they have had to sacrifice too much for their gains; both sexes say that their children and family life have been the chief casualties; and 27 percent of women say the most important goal of the women's movement should be to help women balance work and family, including child care.

Physicians from the Ochsner Medical Institutions at New Orleans report in June that mammograms of six women who have received breast implants failed to reveal incipient breast cancers. The implants made the small tumors look benign when they should have appeared suspicious. Radiologists from the Emory Clinic at Atlanta say they now take three X rays rather than two of a breast containing an implant, pushing the implant aside manually as much as possible before taking the third X ray, and that this technique permits detection of cancers in 10 of 11 women with augmented breasts (*see* 1988; 1991).

New Mexico physicians report three cases in women aged 37 to 43 of an unusual blood disorder—eosinophilia myalgia syndrome—marked by high white-cell count, body rash, muscle and joint pain, extreme weakness, and trouble chewing. It is thought to be caused by a mystery virus. A journalist discovers that the women diagnosed with having the disorder all took L-tryptophan for insomnia and premenstrual syndrome. L-tryptophan is an amino acid commonly used as a food supplement; it has not required Food and Drug Administration approval, and manufacturers scoff at suggestions that their product may be linked to the blood disorder. When the *Albuquerque Journal* runs a front-page story suggesting that such a link does exist, physicians all over the state begin to report cases of eosinophilia. State environmental epidemiologist Dr. Millicent Eidson asks for a voluntary sales ban on L-tryptophan and urges that anybody using the product stop immediately pending an investigation by health officials. Reports of eosinophilia begin coming from physicians in Missouri, Arizona, Oregon, Mississippi, Texas, California, Virginia, Minnesota. By November 12 there are 55 such reports; the story hits front pages across the country November 18. The FDA issues a recall of all products containing L-tryptophan as a major component. Eosinophilia cases soon total 287 in 37 states and the District of Columbia, and one woman, in Oregon, has died. Within 5 months the cases will total 1,500, and 63 will prove fatal; most victims are women who have taken the dietary supplement.

Mirabella magazine begins publication in June. Grace Mirabella, who edited *Vogue* for 16 years, raising circulation from 400,000 to 1.2 million before she was sacked a year ago, has started the new fashion magazine with backing from Australian publisher Rupert Murdoch.

Albuquerque Journal Santa Fe bureau reporter Tamar Stieber, 34, wins a Pulitzer Prize for her investigative work on the L-tryptophan story (above). Afraid of losing the story to a more experienced reporter, she has worked on the story for 16 days straight with no more than 4 hours' sleep per night.

CBS-TV news correspondent Diane Sawyer, 43, joins American Broadcasting Company in February at a multimillion-dollar salary and is co-anchor of *PrimeTime Live* when it premieres in August.

NBC-TV national news anchor Connie Chung, who moved to New York 6 years ago and now earns close to $1 million per year, returns to CBS News for a reported salary of $6 million over 3 years (*see* 1971). Now 42, she anchors the Sunday evening shows, often substitutes for Dan Rather on weekdays, and beginning in September hosts her own newsmagazine, *Saturday Night with Connie Chung*, persuading actor Marlon Brando to grant his first television interview in 16 years.

Nonfiction: *The Second Shift* by University of California, Berkeley, sociologist Armalie Hochschild, who argues that the majority of women shoulder the two burdens of work at home plus a paid job outside, a situation that can undermine not only their own family lives and well-being but also those of their loved ones; *Justifiable Homicide: Battered Women, Self-Defense and the Law* by Seattle lawyer Cynthia K. Gillespie, 48, who argues that English law, on which U.S. law is based, was designed for men and lacked protections for women against abusive partners; *Toward a Feminist Theory of the State* by Catherine A. MacKinnon; *Fear of Falling: The Inner Life of the Middle Class* by Barbara Ehrenreich; *Holding the Line: Women and the Great Arizona Mine Strike of 1983* by novelist Barbara Kingsolver; *Nineteen Thirty-nine: The Last Season of Peace* by Angela Lambert.

Fiction: *The Joy Luck Club* by U.S. novelist Amy Tan, 37; *Cat's Eye* by Margaret Atwood; *You Must Remember This* by Joyce Carol Oates; *After You've Gone* (stories) by Alice Adams; *The Waiting Room* by Mary Morris; *Disappearing Acts* by Terry McMillan; *The Mummy, or, Ramses the Damned* by Anne Rice; *Homeland and Other Stories* by Barbara Kingsolver (above); *A Natural Curiosity* by Margaret Drabble; *John Dollar* by Marianne Wiggins, who last year married Bombay-born British writer Salman Rushdie (Iran's Ayatollah Khomeini has offered a $3 million reward to anyone who kills her husband, whom he has accused of "blaspheming" Islam in his 1988 book *The Satanic Verses*); *Love among the Single Classes* by Angela Lambert; *The Bridesmaid* by Ruth Rendell; *Dead by Morning* by

Dorothy Simpson; *"F" Is for Fugitive* by Sue Grafton.

Historical Portraits by Cindy Sherman is a photographic series. Elaine de Kooning dies of lung cancer at Southampton (N.Y.) Hospital February 1 at age 68.

Washington's Corcoran Gallery announces June 12 that it has canceled an exhibition of work by the late U.S. photographer Robert Mapplethorpe, who died last year of AIDS. A few homoerotic pictures are included in the show, and Sen. Jesse Helms (R., N.C.) introduces legislation that would bar the National Endowment for the Arts from funding "obscene" work. Congress votes in September to establish a panel that will evaluate standards for judging if art is obscene (*see* 1993).

Theater: Colleen Dewhurst, Jason Robards, Swoosie Kurtz, and Richard Thomas (a rotating cast) in A. R. Gurney's *Love Letters* 10/31 at New York's Edison Theater; Jane Lapotaire, 44, as U.S. poet Joy Davidman Gresham, Nigel Hawthorne as C. S. Lewis in William Nicholson's *Shadowlands* 10/23 at the Queen's Theatre, London; Tom Hulce and Roxanne Hart in Aaron Sorkin's *A Few Good Men* 11/15 at New York's Music Box Theater; John Kani, Lisa Fugard, and Courtney B. Vance in Athol Fugard's *My Children, My Africa* 12/18 at New York's off-off-Broadway Perry Street Theater.

Films: Kathleen Turner and William Hurt in Lawrence Kasdan's *The Accidental Tourist*; Mia Farrow, Anjelica Huston, Martin Landau, and Woody Allen in Allen's *Crimes and Misdemeanors*; Jessica Tandy and Morgan Freeman in Bruce Beresford's *Driving Miss Daisy*; Anjelica Huston, Sophie Stein, Lena Olin, and Ron Silver in Paul Mazursky's *Enemies, A Love Story*; Michel Blanc and Sandrine Bonnaire in Patrice Leconte's *Monsieur Hire*; Steve Martin and Mary Steenburgen, 37, in Ron Howard's *Parenthood*; Anita Zagaria and Joseph Long in Jon Amiel's *Queen of Hearts*; Al Pacino and Ellen Barkin, 33, in Harold Becker's *Sea of Love*; Miriam Makeba in Nigel Noble's *Voices of Sarafina!*

Lucille Ball undergoes heart surgery at a Los Angeles hospital and dies a week later (April 26) at age 77; Bette Davis dies at Neuilly-sur-Seine outside Paris October 7 at age 81.

Stage musicals: Jonathan Pryce and Filipina beauty Lea Salonga, 18, in *Miss Saigon* 9/20 at London's Theatre Royal Drury Lane, with Alain Boubil and Claude-Michel Schönberg music, lyrics by Richard Maltby, Jr.; Karen Akers, Gerrit de Beer, and David Carroll in *Grand Hotel* 11/12 at New York's Martin Beck Theater, with Robert Wright–George Forest songs.

Popular songs: *Forever Your Girl* (album) by former Los Angeles Lakers cheerleader Paula Abdul, 26, whose well-choreographed music video singles "Straight Up" and "Fool Hearted" help her debut album sell more than 11 million copies worldwide (her 1990 income, mostly from endorsements for Reebok and Diet Coke, will be $23 million); Tina Turner records "Steamy Windows"; *Rhythm Nation 1814* (album) by Janet Jackson; *Nick of Time* (album) by Bonnie Raitt includes her own song "The Road's My Middle Name" as well as John Hiatt's "Thing Called Love" and Bonnie Hayes's "Have a Heart" (Raitt has quit drinking and calls it her "first sober album"); *State of the Heart* (album) by Mary-Chapin Carpenter includes "How Do," "Never Had It So Good," "Something of a Dream," and the video favorite "This Shirt"; *Life at the Bottom Line* by Laura Nyro, now 42, includes "The Wild World" and "Japanese Restaurant."

Steffi Graf wins both the British and U.S. Open singles titles.

A 29-year-old investment banker jogging in New York's Central Park is raped and left for dead April 19 by a "wolf pack" of black and Hispanic youths. Her identity is protected, and her attackers are caught and indicted.

A Fort Lauderdale, Fla., jury finds a rape-case defendant not guilty October 4 on grounds that the victim—a 22-year-old Coconut Creek woman—was wearing a tank top, a sheer mini-skirt, and no underpants (*Florida* v. *Lloyd*). "She asked for it," says the jury foreman.

A Rockford, Ill., prosecutor tries to have a woman indicted on grounds that her use of cocaine in pregnancy caused the death of her newborn infant.

New York hotel operator Leona Helmsley, 69, is convicted August 30 on 33 counts of income tax evasion and massive tax fraud; she is sentenced to 4 years in prison and fined $7.1 million. A former housekeeper has testified that Mrs. Helmsley told her, "Only the little people pay taxes."

University of Montreal engineering student Marc Lepine, 25, walks into a Polytechnique classroom and cafeteria with a hunting rifle December 6 and goes on a shooting rampage, killing 14 women (he calls them "a bunch of fucking feminists") and wounding 12, including two men. He then shoots himself to death, leaving a suicide note that blames women—feminists in particular—for ruining his life. One of his victims is the mayor's baby-sitter. Police describe him as a "loner" repeatedly frustrated in his relationships with women. News of the killing sends shock waves across Canada and among women everywhere.

The U.S. Supreme Court returns the issue of abortion to the political arena, ruling July 3 in *Webster* v. *Reproductive Health Services* that states can limit access to abortion. Right-to-life groups hail the 5-to-4 decision, prochoice groups anticipate further erosion of the 1973 *Roe* v. *Wade* decision, the Florida legislature votes October 12 to reject measures proposed by the governor to restrict abortion, but Pennsylvania adopts strict new laws on abortion. Congress votes in October to weaken the Hyde Amendment of 1976 by authorizing Medicaid payment for abortions in victims of rape and incest; President Bush vetoes the measure, and Congress fails to override.

Political candidates supported by right-to-life advocates all lose in the November elections.

Romania permits abortion for the first time in 24 years following the death of dictator Nicolae Ceauşescu.

1990

Nicaraguan voters elect coalition leader Violetta Barrios de Chamorro, 60, to the presidency February 25. Widow of *La Prensa* editor Antonio de Chamorro, who opposed the Samoza regime and was shot to death in 1978, the president-elect has had no political experience and has gained election with U.S. help.

Iraqi forces invade Kuwait August 2 after Kuwait refuses demands by President Saddam Hussein, who has interpreted remarks by U.S. ambassador to Iraq April Gillespie that Washington will not oppose him. President Bush says Iraq's aggression "will not stand," and Gillespie is recalled.

Washington, D.C., voters elect their first woman mayor: former Democratic National Committee treasurer Sharon Pratt Dixon, 46, has campaigned on a promise to clean up corruption of her male predecessor, who has been convicted on drug charges.

Ireland elects leftist lawyer-parliamentarian Mary Robinson, 46, president November 9. The nation's first woman president and the first chief executive since 1945 with no affiliation to the dominant Fianna Fail political grouping, she has campaigned vigorously, accusing the "patriarchal, male-dominated presence of the Catholic church" (she is herself a Roman Catholic, married to a Protestant) of holding back women's rights in Ireland, and speaking out in favor of reforming laws that prohibit divorce, legalizing homosexuality, giving wide access to contraceptives, and ending the constitutional ban on abortion. Robinson is sworn in for a 7-year term December 3 but has limited power beyond calling for new elections after a government loses support.

British Prime Minister Margaret Thatcher resigns November 22—forced out after 11½ years in office, the longest ministry of the century.

Kuwaiti women lead public demonstrations against Saddam Hussein (above) and play active roles in the underground resistance against the Iraqi occupation.

German Green party leader Petra Kelly delivers the keynote address to the National Organization for Women June 30 (*see* 1983): "Male-led revolutions have often been so tragically . . . mere power exchanges in a basically unaltered structure. . . . The women were always suddenly pushed in[to] the background. These revolutions were often based on the concept of dying for a cause. I think feminists conceive [of] transformation [as] . . . daring to live for a cause. . . . The most pernicious of all patriarchal tactics is to keep women a divided world caste."

"Women in Africa work like beasts of burden, fetching firewood, carrying water, looking after the children, and growing food," reports the June issue of *New Internationalist* magazine. "They are Africa's main food producers but have little time to devote to the task. Often they are not legally regarded as adults; they frequently have no land rights; and a husband can keep his wife's earnings."

Some 50 heavily veiled Saudi women gather in front of a Riyadh supermarket November 6, dismiss their chauffeurs, take the wheels of their own cars, and drive in a convoy in defiance of the strict Islamic law that forbids them to drive automobiles in public. Police soon stop and detain them, six are suspended from their teaching jobs at King Saud University, and the government announces that it remains impermissible for women to drive cars on pain of punishment.

Kuwaiti women, by contrast to the Saudis (above), do not wear veils in public and drive high-priced cars on the nation's freeways while chatting on cellular telephones, but they are not allowed to vote, and although a Kuwaiti labor code, adopted in 1964, provides that "a female laborer shall be granted a wage similar to that of a man if she carries out the same work," the law exempts domestic servants. Women in Kuwait employ maids, often from the Philippines or Sri Lanka, who receive 30 to 45 dinars per month (the minimum wage is 170 dinars), commonly work 18 hours per day 7 days per week, and are frequently abused, beaten, even raped.

The Americans with Disabilities Act signed by President Bush July 26 bans discrimination in employment, public accommodations, transportation, and telecommunications against the nation's 43 million disabled persons. The law provides new protection for workers with AIDS.

The Soviet Parliament approves a property law March 6, voting 350 to 3 to give private citizens the right to own the means of production—or at least small factories and other business enterprises—for the first time since the early 1920s. President Gorbachev comes under increasing attack as Soviet citizens try to cope with shortages. The Parliament gives him virtually free rein September 25 to decontrol the economy, but Gorbachev moves cautiously and prices escalate.

A new British taxation law, effective in April, provides for married women to be taxed separately from their husbands (*see* Stopes, 1925).

President Bush concedes June 26 that "tax revenue increases" are needed along with spending cuts to reduce a projected $160 billion budget deficit—19 months after winning election on a pledge of "no new taxes." Congress rejects a budget reconciliation measure October 5, federal employees are furloughed briefly for lack of money, and a compromise tax bill is not signed until November. Some Republican losses in the polls are blamed on Bush's flip-flop, and he then repeats his "no new taxes" pledge despite growing evidence that the "supply-side" economic experiment of the 1980s has served only to pile up a massive national debt.

U.S. women earn on average 67 cents for every dollar earned by a man doing comparable work, and while this is up from 57 cents in 1970 it remains a source of grievance for working women.

America's record 8-year economic boom ends in July as the country goes into recession. Britain and France also slump, Germany and Japan remain economically robust.

Nurse-midwives attend the deliveries of nearly 142,000 infants in U.S. hospitals, up from fewer than 20,000 in 1975 (*see* 1971). While this is still only 3 to 4 percent of hospital births, nurse-midwives attend roughly one-third of deliveries at free-standing birth centers.

The U.S. Supreme Court rules 5 to 4 June 25 that a state may sustain the life of a comatose patient in the absence of "clear and convincing evidence" that the patient would have wanted treatment stopped (*see* Quinlan, 1985).

The Clinical Laboratory Improvement Amendments (CLIA) enacted by Congress in September dictate how laboratories must read specimens, including Pap smears (*see* 1943).

The incidence of breast cancer in the United States is 105 per 100,000, up from 59 in 1940, when life expectancy was lower. If a woman lives to age 85, she has a one in nine chance of contracting breast cancer, up from a lifetime risk of one in 20 half a century ago, but her chances of having osteoporosis or a fatal heart attack are far higher.

U.S. surgeons perform about 590,000 hysterectomies, down from a peak of about 750,000 in 1980, but critics say the number is still far too high, given the fact that cheaper and less hazardous remedies are available for uterine fibroids (leiomyomas), which commonly shrink after menopause; abnormal uterine bleeding; endometriosis; genital prolapse; and chronic pelvic pain.

∞ The Supreme Soviet ends decades of religious repression September 26, forbidding government interference in religious activities and giving citizens the right to study religion in homes and private schools.

🎓 Tuition at Harvard, Vassar, Wellesley, and other top U.S. colleges tops $14,000 per year, total expenses exceed $20,000, but 80 percent of undergraduates attend public universities, where tuition averages less than $2,000 per year, another 16 percent go to private colleges where tuition is below $10,000, scarcely 4 percent pay more, and up to two-thirds of these receive scholarships, subsidized loans, or both.

🖋 Nonfiction: *Sexual Personae: Art and Decadence from Nefertiti to Emily Dickinson* by U.S. literary scholar Camille Paglia, 43, who stirs up passions with attacks on "whining" feminists whose scholars "can't think their way out of a wet paper bag" and says that "if civilization had been left in female hands we would still be living in grass huts." She gives lectures in which she blasts Gloria Steinem and others; *You Just Don't Understand* by U.S. linguistics professor Deborah Tannen, who writes, "In this era of opening opportunities women are beginning to move into positions of authority. At first we assumed they could simply talk the way they always had, but this often doesn't work. Another logical step is that they could change their styles and talk like men. Apart from the repugnance of women's having to do all the changing, this doesn't work either, because women who talk like men are judged differently—and harshly. . . . For most women, the language of conversation is primarily a language of rapport: a way of establishing connections and negotiating relationships. . . . For most men, talk is primarily a means to preserve independence and

negotiate and maintain status in a hierarchical social order. . . . It seems that having information, expertise, or skill at manipulating objects is not the primary measure of power for most women. Rather, they feel their power enhanced if they can be of help." *The Worst Years of Our Lives: Irreverent Notes from a Decade of Greed* by Barbara Ehrenreich; *What I Saw at the Revolution* by presidential speechwriter Peggy Noonan (*see* politics, 1988); *Soviet Women: Walking the Tightrope* by Francine du Plessix Gray; *My Life as a Woman* by TV comedienne Roseanne Barr (*see* sports, below).

Fiction: *Inshallah* by Oriana Fallaci; *My Son's Story* by Nadine Gordimer; *Symposium* by Muriel Spark; *Lucy* by Jamaica Kincaid; *Caroline's Daughters* by Alice Adams; *Friend of My Youth* (stories) by Alice Munro; *Learning Urdu* (stories) by Marianne Wiggins; *Mother Earth, Father Sky* by U.S. novelist Sue Harrison (*née* McHaney), 40, is about an Aleutian girl during the Ice Age; *The Women in His Life* by Barbara Taylor Bradford; *Message from Nam* by Danielle Steel; *Surrender the Pink* by Carrie Fisher; *Animal Dreams* by Barbara Kingsolver; *No Talking after Lights* by Angela Lambert; *"G" Is for Gumshoe* by Sue Grafton.

Poetry: *Near Changes* by Mona Van Duyn (Pulitzer Prize; Ruth Lilly Poetry Prize).

Juvenile: *Mississippi Bridge* and *The Road to Memphis* by Mildred Taylor.

🎭 Theater: Gerard McSorley, Frances Tomelty, Paul Herzberg, Catherine Byrne, and Barry McGovern in Brian Friel's *Dancing at Lughnasa* 4/24 at Dublin's Abbey Theatre; Barnard Hughes, Mary-Lou Parker, and Timothy Hutton in Craig Lucas's *Prelude to a Kiss* (about AIDS) 5/1 at New York's Helen Hayes Theater, 440 perfs.; James McDaniel, Stockard Channing, and John Cunningham in John Guare's *Six Degrees of Separation* 6/14 at New York's Mitzi E. Newhouse Theater.

Films: Anjelica Huston, John Cusack, and Annette Bening in Stephen Frears's *The Grifters*; Sean Connery and Michelle Pfeiffer in Fred Schepisi's *The Russia House*. Also: Barbara Kopple's documentary *American Dream* about meatpackers; Patrick Swayze, Demi Moore, 27, and Whoopi Goldberg in Jerry Zucker's *Ghost*; Mel Gibson, Glenn Close,

Alan Bates, and Paul Scofield in Franco Zeffirelli's *Hamlet;* Fred Ward and Maria de Medeiros in Philip Kaufman's *Henry & June*; Edward Clements and Carolyn Farina in Whit Stillman's *Metropolitan*; Paul Newman and Joanne Woodward in James Ivory's *Mr. and Mrs. Bridge*; Lena Tolze in Michael Verhoeven's *The Nasty Girl*; Meryl Streep and Shirley MacLaine in Mike Nichols's *Postcards from the Edge*; Jeremy Irons, Glenn Close, and Ron Silver in Barbet Schroeder's *Reversal of Fortune*.

Barbara Stanwyck dies of congestive heart failure at a Santa Monica, Calif., hospital January 20 at age 82 after a career in which she made made than 80 films; Greta Garbo dies at New York Hospital April 15 at age 84 (she has not made a film since 1941); Irene Dunne dies of heart failure at Holmby Hills, Calif., September 4 at age 92.

Broadway musical: La Chanze and Jerry Dixon in *Once on This Island* 10/18 at the Booth Theater, with Stephen Flaherty–Lynn Ahrens songs, choreography by Graciela Daniele.

Popular songs: *I Do Not Want What I Haven't Got* (album) by Irish vocalist Sinead O'Connor, 34, includes the single "Nothing Compares 2U" by Prince; *I'm Your Baby Tonight* (album) by Whitney Houston includes "All the Man That I Need"; *Shooting Straight in the Dark* (album) by Mary-Chapin Carpenter includes "You Win Again," "Going Out Tonight," "Right Now," and the Cajun stomp "Down at the Twist and Shout."

TV comedienne Roseanne Barr sings the national anthem in July at the All-Star Game in San Diego, is booed for her poor performance, grabs her crotch, and spits on the field. Her Neilson rating drops from 14.6 to 13 and her audience share falls from 26 to 22 (*see* 1988). ABC blames competition in her new time slot, not any backlash reaction to her San Diego appearance.

Martina Navratilova wins her ninth women's singles title at Wimbledon (a record), Gabriela Sabatini, 20 (Arg), wins the U.S. Open singles title.

An illegal social club in the Bronx is set afire March 25, killing 87 in the worst New York conflagration since the Triangle Shirtwaist Factory fire of March 25, 1911. A Cuban immigrant has been rejected by the club's hatcheck girl and set the fire in retaliation; he is charged with 87 counts of murder.

Six white fraternity members at St. John's University in Brooklyn, N.Y., are arrested on charges of having sexually abused a foreign-born black woman. All are released on bail but not permitted to return to college, three will be acquitted, two will plead guilty to lesser charges, and one will accept a plea bargain, accepting responsibility for forcing the woman to perform oral sex against her will.

The University of Florida introduces FARE (Fraternity Acquaintance Education)—a program designed to educate men in fraternities or on athletic teams about date rape.

The Supreme Court rules 5 to 4 June 25 in *Hodgson* v. *Minnesota* that a state may require a pregnant girl to inform both her parents before having an abortion.

Ortho Pharmaceuticals reports that 15 percent of U.S. girls aged 15 to 17 are on The Pill, 49 percent of women aged 18 to 24, 38 percent of those between 25 and 29, 28 percent between 30 and 34, 10 percent between 35 and 39, 4 percent between 40 and 44.

Roussel-Uclaf expands marketing of its abortifacient drug RU486 to Britain, but political opposition blocks moves to market it in China, the U.S.S.R., Scandinavia, and the United States (*see* 1988; 1993).

The Norplant contraceptive system (levonorgestrel implants) approved by the FDA December 10 is the first really new birth control measure since The Pill of the mid-1960s. Devised by Rockefeller Foundation researcher Sheldon J. Segal, 64, and already used in 14 other countries, it is surgically implanted in six thin capsules under the skin of a woman's upper arm and slowly releases a synthetic version of the female hormone progestin over a 5-year period. By the end of 1992 more than 500,000 American women, many of them on Medicaid, will have been implanted, but while reversible and more effective than most other contraceptive measures, Norplant is also more expensive.

The U.S. Census reveals that America's 11.5 million widows range in age mostly from 30 to 70 with a median age of 56. Fifty percent of all U.S. women over age 65 are widows.

1991

 U.S. and allied missiles and planes bomb targets in Iraq and Kuwait beginning January 17, ground troops invade Iraq February 24, and Operation Desert Storm continues for 100 hours, driving Iraqi forces out of Kuwait and restoring the emirate.

Somalia's president Mohammed Siad Barre flees his capital, Mogadishu, January 26 as rebels of the United Somali Congress end a 21-year dictatorship in which women have received the right to vote, to divorce, and to gain custody of their children.

Jiang Qing, widow of the late Mao Zedong, reportedly takes her own life in early June at age 77. Other members of her "Gang of Four" remain in detention.

Former Philippine First Lady Imelda Marcos returns to Manila November 4 after nearly 6 years' exile to face tax fraud and other charges. She stays in a $2,000-per-day suite at the Westin-Philippine Plaza but is evicted after 4 weeks and obliged to move into a modest two-story concrete house.

Burmese opposition leader and human rights activist Aung San Suu Kyi, now 46, is awarded the Nobel Peace Prize but remains under house arrest and is unable to travel to Stockholm to accept. Czechoslovakia's President Vaclav Havel has nominated her for the prize, calling her "an outstanding example of the power of the powerless" who has "refused to be bribed into silence."

 "Female circumcision is a physiological chastity belt," writes South African journalist Sue Armstrong in the February 2 issue of *New Scientist*. "[A] traditional practice that affects an estimated 80 million people in the world today, [it] entails different things in different cultures. The mildest form—known to Muslims as 'sunna' and the least common—involves the removal of the prepuce or hood of the clitoris. It is the only operation analogous to male circumcision. Excision involves the removal of the clitoris and the labia minora; while infibulation involves the removal of all the external genitalia and the stitching up of the two sides of the vulva to leave only a tiny opening for the passage of urine and menstrual blood."

Somalia's Mohammed Siad Barre (above) has sponsored a health campaign to end genital mutilation, but while Somali women wear no veils, often sport sleeveless dresses, and do not behave submissively toward men, nearly all still undergo ritual clitoridectomy at a young age to discourage sexual intercourse outside marriage. (The procedure is common, if not universal, in about 20 African countries, several Middle Eastern nations, and in parts of Indonesia, Malaysia, India, and Pakistan, mostly among Muslims and animists but also among some Christians.) Removing her clitoris reduces a woman's sexual pleasure and is sometimes combined with infibulation—stitching up the vulva to prevent penetration before marriage (girls who are not virgins will not find suitable husbands). Female operators using unsterilized knives carry out the mutilations, removing the labia as well as the clitoris. Girls are tied down and given no anesthesia for the procedures, which often lead to infection. As a woman is repeatedly unstitched and restitched during her childbearing years, she may suffer massive scar formations that obstruct walking, intercourse and menstruation may be extremely painful, and she may develop fistulas, vulval abscesses, or incontinence, to say nothing of increased susceptibility to AIDS.

The annual Tailhook convention of U.S. Navy aviators at the Las Vegas Hilton September 5 to 7 attracts 4,000 people, some of whom wear T-shirts reading "Women Are Property." Earlier conventions were mostly stag affairs except for prostitutes and "groupies." This time, scantily clad women tend bar while strippers generally end up nude and participate in simulated sex acts with drunken members of the audience (which includes active and retired admirals as well as lower-ranking officers), pornographic films are shown, women are encouraged to expose their breasts in exchange for squadron T-shirts, and at least 25 women passing down a certain hallway are made to run the "gauntlet," meaning that they are encircled by as many as 70 groping male officers and sexually molested to varying degrees, a practice begun in 1986. Navy helicopter pilot Lt. Paula Coughlin, 30, files the first formal complaint, and a rear admiral is relieved of duty November 4 for not having reported the incident quickly enough (*see* 1992).

Sexual harassment in the U.S. workplace is the focus of public attention in mid-October as University of Oklahoma Law School professor Anita Hill, 35, charges that Supreme Court nominee Clarence Thomas, 45, made indecent remarks to her while head of the Equal Opportunity Commission 8 years ago and, earlier, in the Department of Education. Both are black, but Thomas claims he is being "lynched" as an "uppity" black; the Senate votes 52 to 48 to confirm his appointment to succeed Thurgood Marshall.

Ohio Governor Richard F. Celeste grants clemency to 26 women serving prison sentences for killing their abusive husbands or companions.

Anita Hill challenged nominee Clarence Thomas's moral qualifications to sit on the Supreme Court. AP/WIDE WORLD PHOTOS

A November 24 *Observer* magazine story by British journalist Peter Hillmore says, "In buses all over Kenya you will see women sitting together. They do this to try and avoid being molested by male passengers. Even educated middle-class women obediently stay at home at night while their husbands go out and spend money on their girlfriends. Occasionally they will write to newspaper agony columns; they are told to close their eyes and think of Kenya. They cannot be advised to leave their husbands, because under African customary law, which operates in most parts of the country, women are not allowed to own property and will get nothing from a divorce."

Three Korean women go to Tokyo in December and tell journalists about having been kidnapped and forced to work in Japanese Army brothels during World War II. The government insists that such brothels were run by independent entrepreneurs and never by the Army (but *see* 1992).

$ Soviet citizens panic January 29 when the evening news reports that savings accounts have been frozen and 50- and 100-ruble banknotes will be withdrawn from circulation. Many have their savings in such notes, but the government decrees that large bills may be exchanged for their equivalent only up to a maximum of 1,000 rubles (about one month's salary), or 200 in the case of pensioners. The move is designed to halt inflation and quash black-market currency traders.

Inflation moderates in the United States, but rents are 35 percent above the 1982–84 average, electricity 28 percent higher, medical care 56 percent higher, food 34 percent higher, entertainment 28 percent higher, footwear 24 percent higher, apparel nearly 9 percent higher. Public transit is virtually unchanged on average, gasoline slightly lower, fuel oil nearly 7 percent lower.

℞ Federally funded research links foam-coated breast implants to cancer, a Federal District Court jury at New York in March awards $4.5 million to a woman whose implant ruptured as a surgeon tried to remove it (she later developed breast, ovarian, and uterine cancer, but the judge later set aside $3 million of the jury award), a congressional subcommittee puts pressure on the FDA, and in April the agency gives implant manufacturers 90 days in which either to demonstrate that their devices are safe or to take them off the market. (More than 2 million U.S. women have undergone implant surgery in the past 30 years; of the 150,000 who have the surgery each year at a cost of $2,500 to $4,000, about 80 percent do so for cosmetic reasons, only 20 percent for reconstruction after mastectomy. Silicone gel breast implants had been on the market for about 15 years when Congress authorized the FDA to regulate them in 1976, and they have never been approved by the FDA.) Bristol-Myers Squibb immediately withdraws its two breast-implant brands and announces September 23 that it is quitting the business. The FDA tells implant makers September 25 that they must give physicians warning information that patients can understand. An FDA advisory panel votes 9 to 1 November 13 that a Dow Corning subsidiary has failed to prove the safety of its silicone gel implants, many women contend that the government has no business depriving them of their option to have breast implants, they link implant surgery to self-esteem and support cosmetic surgeons who oppose any ban, but critics warn that the implants can rupture, releasing silicone into the body and causing autoimmune disease disorders. A member of the FDA panel charges December 20 that the Dow Corning subsidiary withheld documents that raised safety concerns about its implants (*see* 1992).

A Swedish study reported in a September issue of the *Journal of the National Cancer Institute* suggests that the synthetic hormone tamoxifen may reduce by 40 percent the risk of a woman who has had cancer in one breast developing cancer in her other breast. Breast cancer affects one out of nine U.S. women (180,000 are diagnosed this year with having the disease, 46,000 will die of it).

The National Breast Cancer Coalition is founded by U.S. activists who demand more research on the causes of breast cancer. Made up mostly of volunteers, the coalition secures a $43 million increase in national funding for breast cancer research in its first year (*see* 1992).

Parents of half the 4 million babies born in the United States go through some form of Lamaze-type education prior to delivery, up from about 25 percent in 1986, and above a certain income level nearly every expectant couple attends Lamaze-type classes (*see* 1959). Instructors certified by the non-profit American Society of Psychoprophylaxis in Obstetrics/Lamaze, based in Washington, conduct about half the classes, which typically cost $150 per couple.

∞ The Episcopal Bishop of Washington, D.C., ordains Elizabeth L. Carl, 44, as a priest of the church June 5, acknowledging that she "has for number of years openly lived in a loving and intimate relationship with another woman" to whom she has made a lifelong and monogamous commitment, and while that troubles him he points to the "strength, leadership, spirituality, intellect, moral understanding, and commitment to Christ" that she has displayed.

The *New York Times* publishes a story April 17 profiling a woman who has accused William Kennedy Smith, a nephew of Sen. Edward F. Kennedy (D., Mass.), of having raped her on the grounds of the Kennedy estate in Palm Beach, Fla. The story, which gives the woman's name (Patrica Bowman) and quotes unidentified sources in characterizing her history, draws fire from *Times* columnist Anna Quindlen, 38, whose April 21 column recalls the discretion shown by the paper in the case of the 1988 Central Park jogger story and concludes that any woman who accuses a "well-connected man" of rape "had better be prepared to see not only her name but her drinking habits in print . . ." The *Times* publishes an apology April 26 after receiving a lot of criticism, Smith is indicted May 11 (he will be acquitted after a sensational trial in which questions are raised about his accuser's sexual history and mental state), and the *Times* runs a story sympathetic to his accuser May 12.

The Supreme Court rules June 21 that states and localities may prohibit nude dancing without violating First Amendment rights. Laws may require that dancers wear at least G-strings and pasties, the Court rules in a 5-to-4 decision. Critics fear that the ruling may lead to further censorship.

Nonfiction: *Backlash: The Undeclared War Against American Women* by *Wall Street Journal* reporter Susan Faludi, 31: "If establishing masculinity depends most of all on succeeding as the prime breadwinner, then it is hard to imagine a force more directly threatening to fragile American manhood than the feminist drive for economic equality"; *The Beauty Myth* by U.S. writer Naomi Wolf, 29: "We are in the midst of a violent backlash against feminism that uses images of female beauty as a political weapon against women's advancement: the beauty myth"; *When the Bough Breaks: The Cost of Neglecting Our Children* by Sylvia Ann Hewlett; *Molly Ivins Can't Say That, Can She?* by *Dallas Times-Herald* columnist (since 1980) Ivins, now 47.

Fiction: *A Thousand Acres* by Jane Smiley (Pulitzer Prize); *Object Lessons* by *New York Times* syndicated columnist Anna Quindlen (above); *The Gates of Ivory* (third novel in a trilogy) by Margaret Drabble; *St. Maybe* by Anne Tyler; *Remember* by Barbara Taylor Bradford; *Damage* by Irish novelist Josephine Hart, who is married to advertising agency director Maurice Saatchi; *Heartbeat* and *No Greater Love* by Danielle Steel; *"H" Is for Homicide* by Sue Grafton.

Sculpture: *Cleavage* (marble) by Louise Bourgeois; *Terra Firma* (a homeless man, supine on the ground) by Alison Saar.

Theater: Irene Worth, Mercedes Ruehl, and Kevin Spacey in Neil Simon's *Lost in Yonkers* 2/21 at New York's Richard Rodgers Theater, 780 perfs.; Patrick Barlow, Victoria Carling, and Kevin Allen in Ben Elton's *Silly Cow* 2/27 at London's Haymarket Theatre; Sarah Jessica Parker, Patrick Breen, and Ron Rifkin in Jon Robin Baitz's *The Substance of Fire* 3/17 at New York's Playwrights Horizon Theater; John Quayle, Simon Cadell, and Su Pollard in Marc Camoletti's *Don't Dress for Dinner* 3/26 at London's Apollo Theatre; Jason Robards and Judith Ivey in Israel Horovitz's *Park Your Car in Harvard Yard* 11/7 at New York's Music Box Theater.

Eva Le Gallienne dies of heart failure at her Weston, Conn., home June 3 at age 92; Colleen Dewhurst dies of cancer at her South Salem, N.Y., home August 21 at age 67.

Films: Warren Beatty and Annette Bening in Barry Levinson's *Bugsy*; River Phoenix and Keanu Reeves in Gus Van Sant's *My Own Private Idaho*; Jennie Livingston's documentary *Paris Is Burning* about homosexual black and Latino men; Martha

Coolidge's *Rambling Rose* with Robert Duvall, Diane Ladd, and Ladd's daughter Laura Dern, 25; Jodie Foster and Anthony Hopkins in Jonathan Demme's *The Silence of the Lambs*; Geena Davis and Susan Sarandon in Ridley Scott's *Thelma and Louise*.

Dame Margot Fonteyn dies of cancer at a Panama City, Panama, hospital February 21 at age 71; Martha Graham dies of cardiac arrest at her New York home April 1 at age 96.

Stage musicals: *The Will Rogers Follies* 3/31 at New York's Palace Theater, with Cy Coleman–Betty Comden and Adolph Green songs, Tommy Tune choreography; Daisy Eagan and Mandy Patinkin in *The Secret Garden* 4/25 at New York's St. James Theater, with music by Lucy Simon, book and lyrics by Marsha Norman based on the 1903 Burnett story.

Popular songs: *Spellbound* (album) by Paula Abdul (written by V. Jeffrey Smith and Peter Lord of the Family Stand); "Baby Baby" by Amy Grant; *Walking on Thin Ice* (CD single) by Yoko Ono; *Luck of the Draw* (album) by Bonnie Raitt.

Steffi Graf wins in women's singles at Wimbledon, Monica Seles, 17 (Yugo), in U.S. women's singles.

The first women's World Cup soccer final is held at Guangzhou (Canton). The U.S. team beats Norway November 30 to win the Cup 2 games to 1.

Jane Fonda is married on her 54th birthday December 21 to Atlanta media tycoon Robert Edward "Ted" Turner, 53, at his ranch outside Tallahassee, Fla.

Channelview, Texas, housewife Wanda Webb Holloway, 37, is convicted September 3 on a charge of murder for hire. Her eighth-grade daughter, Shanna Harper, 13, tried out for the school cheerleading squad and was rejected; another girl, Amber Heath, made the squad 2 years in a row, and Mrs. Holloway wanted Amber and her mother, Verna, eliminated before the two girls went to high school. Police caught Mrs. Holloway before her hit man could carry out the killing, Amber Heath makes the cheerleading squad again, Shanna is rejected again; Mrs. Holloway is sentenced to 15 years in prison.

Miss Black America contestant Desirée Washington, 18, files rape charges against world heavyweight champion Mike Tyson, accusing him of having lured her into his hotel room at Indianapolis July 10 and violating her (*see* 1992).

The Law Lords of Britain's House of Lords (equivalent to the U.S. Supreme Court) decide October 24 to reject a 250-year-old legal principle that there is no such crime as rape inside marriage.

California has its fifth straight year of drought. Farmers control 83 percent of the water delivered by vast federal, state, and City of Los Angeles dams, aqueducts, and reservoirs; they pay as little as $2.50 per acre-foot to irrigate their crops while cutbacks are imposed on angry residents of the booming cities, who resent use of precious Sierra Nevada and Colorado river water to grow crops such as rice.

Average U.S. food prices in January: white bread 70.5¢ 1 lb. loaf, French bread $1.28, eggs (grade A, large) $1.10 doz., milk $1.38 ½-gal., chicken 89¢ lb., ground beef $1.65 lb. (all figures higher in the Northeast, lower in the South).

The U.S. Supreme Court rules 5 to 4 May 23 in *Rust* v. *Sullivan* that Congress did not violate the Constitution in 1970 when it barred employees of federally financed family-planning clinics from providing information about abortion. President Bush vetoes legislation allowing abortion to be discussed.

Poland's state-financed hospitals perform 29,989 abortions, down from 105,332 in 1988, when Communists ran the government and the Church had less influence. Pope John Paul II visits his native land, where abortion is the leading form of birth control, and appeals in June for a legislative ban on the practice (*see* 1991; 1993).

1992

Britain's House of Commons gets its first woman speaker in April. Betty Boothroyd, 62, a onetime dancer and a Labour member of Parliament since 1973, has a record of support for women's rights, but only 60 of Parliament's 651 members are women.

German Green party leader Petra Kelly is found dead of a gunshot wound at age 44 October 19 in the apartment at Bonn that she has shared with Gert Bastian, 69, who has either murdered his partner and then killed himself or died with her in a mutual suicide pact (no note is found) (*see* 1990). Kelly served in the Bundestag until 1990, when the pragmatic western wing of the Green party was ousted in the first election after unification of Germany. She and Bastian, a former major general who was forcibly retired from the German Army in 1980 for opposing deployment of U.S. cruise missiles in West Germany, have been speaking out against the increasing incidence of antiforeigner violence in Germany.

Philippine voters elect Gen. Fidel V. Ramos, 64, to succeed Corazón Aquino as president; he takes office June 30 in the first peaceful change of Filipino government since November 1965.

U.S. voters elect Arkansas governor William Jefferson Blythe "Bill" Clinton, 46, to the presidency, rejecting George Bush's reelection bid as the economic recession shows few signs of abating. Bush wins 18 states with 168 electoral votes to Clinton's 370 while taking 38 million popular votes to Clinton's 44 million (Dallas billionaire H. Ross Perot, who entered the race October 1, gets 19 million).

Clinton (above) has been smeared during the primary campaign in New Hampshire by allegations by Little Rock cabaret singer Gennifer Flowers in a supermarket tabloid that he had had a 12-year extramarital affair with her beginning when she was a TV reporter. Clinton has denied the allegations while admitting to having had troubles in his marriage over the years. He has objected to being penalized for keeping his marriage together "in the way that divorced people once were for having had marriages that failed." His wife, Hillary (*née* Rodham), 45, has stood by him and faced down his attackers, campaigning with him and, after a gaff in which she has seemed to disparage homemakers, helping to bring in women voters chilled by the Reagan-Bush stand on abortion rights (47 percent of women vote for Clinton, 41 percent of men).

California elects two women to the U.S. Senate; former San Francisco mayor Dianne Feinstein (*née* Goldman), 59, and Congresswoman Barbara Boxer (*née* Levy), 52, are both Democrats. Washington State elects Democrat Patty Murray, 42, and Illinois elects Democrat Carol Braun (*née* Moseley), 45, who becomes the first black woman U.S. senator. All four candidates have benefited from contributions by Emily's List, whose membership has swelled to 24,000 by year's end—up from 3,500 in 1990 and 12,000 in the spring—in large part because of outrage over the treatment of Anita Hill in last year's Senate confirmation hearings of Justice Clarence Thomas.

President-elect Clinton (above) names more women to his Cabinet than any previous president. Among them are economist Alice Rivlin (*née* Mitchell), 61, as deputy director of the Office of Management and Budget; University of Wisconsin at Madison chancellor Donna Shalala, now 51, as secretary of Health and Human Services; and Connecticut corporate lawyer Zoë Baird, 40, as attorney general (*see* 1993).

Guatemalan Quiché political and human rights activist Rigoberta Menchu, 32, is awarded the Nobel Peace Prize. Says the prize committee, "She stands out as a vivid symbol of peace and reconciliation across ethnic, cultural, and social dividing lines" in her own country and abroad.

Japanese history professor Yoshiaki Yoshimi, 40, reveals in January that beginning in the mid-1930s the Imperial Army recruited young women and girls, mostly children and teenagers from Korea and China but some from Japan, as "comfort women" to provide sex for the military and thus keep soldiers from raping civilians in Japanese-controlled areas of China (*see* 1991). Between 100,000 and 200,000 such women were eventually lured or forcibly sent to battlefronts across East Asia, obliged to live in filthy shanties, and sometimes required to have sex with soldiers at 15-minute intervals day and night. Sexually transmitted disease was rampant, and thousands of women died, including many who were apparently killed by soldiers. Survivors were generally unmarriagable because nonvirgins in Korea found it almost impossible to find husbands. Prime Minister Kiichi Miyazawa is forced by Yoshimi's evidence (an official document entitled "Regarding the Recruitment of Women for Military Brothels" and bearing the *hankos* [personal stamps] of high-ranking officers)

to concede that the government has covered up the situation for more than 40 years and offers an apology to the Korean people, saying that Tokyo will have to find a way to redress the women's grievances but not promising any financial reparations. The new emperor Akihito is burned in effigy.

Sexual harassment in the Japanese workplace draws censure April 16 as a district court rules in favor of an unmarried woman in Fukuoka who has claimed that a male employee at the small publishing company for which she worked had spread rumors that she was promiscuous. It is the first such case ever filed in Japan.

Revelations about last September's Tailhook sex scandal lead the U.S. Senate to hold up the promotions and transfers of roughly 9,000 navy and marine officers until they can prove that they were not involved. Lt. Coughlin has persuaded a sympathetic admiral to launch an investigation, President Bush has met with her at the White House June 26, she has gone public with her accusations, the secretary of the navy resigns, and the Pentagon's inspector general takes over the investigation. Two admirals are fired and one reassigned in late September as the investigation into the incident continues (*see* 1993).

Former Reagan speechwriter Patrick J. Buchanan helps turn women against President Bush (above) with his keynote speech at the Republican Convention August 17: "Elect me, and you get two for the price of one, Mr. Clinton says of his lawyer-spouse. And what does Hillary believe? Well, Hillary believes that 12-year-olds should have the right to sue their parents, and Hillary has compared marriage and the family as institutions to slavery and life on Indian reservations. Well, speak for yourself, Hillary. Friends, this is radical feminism . . ."

Vice President Dan Quayle assails the *Murphy Brown* TV series for glamorizing unwed motherhood. He was quoted 3 years ago as saying about his wife, Marilyn, that she "has a very major cause and a very major interest that is a very complex and consuming issue with her. And that's me." Feminists say that Quayle has an agenda hostile to women and exaggerates the problem, but the U.S. Census Bureau next July will report a sharp increase in the number of women who become mothers without marrying, especially among educated professionals. Nearly one-fourth of the nation's unmarried women become mothers, an increase of 60 percent over 1982. Among white women who have attended college, the number has nearly doubled; among women with professional or managerial jobs, it has nearly tripled. Overall, about one-quarter of all U.S. children are born out of wedlock, and among single women aged 18 to 44 who have never married, 24 percent have become mothers, up from 15 percent in 1982; the rate among those who have had at least one year of college has risen to 11.3 percent, up from 5.5 percent; among managerial and professional women it has risen from 3.1 percent to 8.3 percent, and although it has risen from 49 percent to 56 percent among black women (two-thirds of black children are born out of wedlock) and from 23 percent to 33 percent among Hispanic women, the increase in those groups has been much slower than among white women, where the rate has risen from 7 percent to 15 percent. Many of these women, although unmarried, are living with partners when they give birth. Critics of Quayle argue that marriage can sometimes make matters worse, as in a case where a woman is married to an abusive man.

A November 22 *Washington Post* story contains allegations by 10 women that they have been the objects of improper sexual advances by Sen. Robert Packwood (R., Ore.), who was relected November 5 after having denied such allegations. A staunch campaigner for women's rights, Packwood now apologizes for his behavior, without specifying what that behavior was, and does not dispute the women's charges. Demands for his resignation will continue, and more women will report having received uninvited sexual advances from the senator (*see* 1993).

Serbian forces in Bosnia open concentration camps and impose "ethnic cleansing" measures to rid the country of Muslims and other opponents. Serbians rape and impregnate thousands of Muslim women as a matter of policy, and many Muslim men kill their sisters rather than allow them to bear Serbian-fathered children.

Russia and other former Soviet nations struggle with inflation and unemployment as they try to follow Poland's more successful example of moving from a state economy to a market economy.

Japanese companies lay off workers and cut salaries as recession begins to affect them even as U.S. economic conditions begin to improve.

Mall of America opens in August at Bloomington, Minn., after 7 years of construction. The $500 million shopping mall, largest in the world, will soon have 400 stores (including Bloomingdale's, Macy's, Nordstrom, Sears, The Limited, Victoria's Secret, and Benetton) encircling an amusement park, attracting shoppers from all over the world (many come from Japan on package tours), and taking in $2 million per day.

Queen Elizabeth agrees in late November to start paying taxes on her private income and to pay $1.3 million of the royal family's expenses, breaking with tradition, but British taxpayers will bear the estimated $90 million cost of repairs to Windsor Castle, which has been damaged by fire.

The U.S. Census Department reports that 47 percent of families headed by single mothers live in poverty as compared to 8.3 percent of families headed by two parents.

A study reported in the British medical journal *Lancet* January 4 shows that hormones and drugs used to treat breast cancer remain effective for at least 10 years—long after the treatment has ceased. Benefits of the synthetic hormone tamoxifen, or a combination of chemotherapeutic drugs, are even more striking in the second 5-year period than in the first.

The U.S. Food and Drug Administration orders a moratorium in January on silicone breast implants (*see* 1991). FDA Commissioner David Kessler has been shown internal Dow Corning memos and documents revealing that the company's subsidiary rushed a new silicone gel implant to market in 1975, delayed doing certain safety tests for years, and misled plastic surgeons about the risk that silicone could ooze out and spread to other parts of the body. The documents were produced in a Michigan trial and in a December trial involving Mariann Hopkins, 48, a Sonoma County, California, woman whose implants burst and who allegedly developed mixed connective-tissue disease as a result. ("I am not a piece of machinery for which they manufactured a new part. I am real. I am somebody's mother and somebody's wife," the plaintiff said. Dow Corning said she had had the painful disorder before receiving the implants, but a federal jury at San Francisco awarded her $7.5 million, most of it in punitive damages.) Other women have blamed ruptured (and even intact) implants for carpal tunnel syndrome (a connective-tissue disease), lupus, arthritis, swollen joints, chronic hepatitis, scleroderma, facial rash, hair loss, night sweats, chronic fatigue, and breast, ovarian, liver, and uterine cancer. FDA issues an order in April that silicone gel breast implants be removed from the market. A Houston woman wins a $25 million verdict against Bristol Myers Squibb December 23 over silicone gel implants.

The National Breast Cancer Coalition wins $300 million more in federal funding after financing a seminar and gaining support from U.S. Senator Tom Harkin (D., Iowa), who proposes that the $25 million budgeted by the army for screening and diagnosis be increased to $210 million for breast cancer research (*see* 1991). The Coalition sets out to obtain 175,000 signatures—one for each U.S. woman who will be diagnosed as having breast cancer this year (46,000 will die of the disease)—and winds up delivering 600,000 signatures to Washington in October, which is "Breast Cancer Awareness Month." Congress votes 87 to 4 to transfer $210 million from the defense budget to the domestic budget for breast cancer research.

France bans smoking in public places beginning November 1, but French smokers generally defy the ban.

Women still make up only 7 to 13 percent of professors at U.S. Ivy League universities (excluding medical schools), despite sharp gains since 1972, and while male professors at Harvard average $93,600 per year, women of equal rank average $79,900. At colleges nationwide, more than half of all students are female, but only 27.6 percent of faculty members are women.

Antioch College institutes rules requiring students to obtain explicit verbal consent before exchanging so much as a kiss. The rules will be changed next year to make it the man's responsibility to dispel any ambiguity.

British-born magazine editor Tina Brown, 39, who took over the ailing *Vanity Fair* early in 1984 and made it thrive, is installed as editor of the 68-year-old *New Yorker*; beginning with the October 5 issue, she puts bylines at the tops of articles and stories, increases the use of color, and makes controversial design changes calculated to stem the magazine's losses. Newsstand sales will soon double and advertising revenues increase.

Nonfiction: *The Measure of Our Success: A Letter to My Children and Yours* by Marian Wright Edelman; *The Girls in the Balcony: Women, Men, and The New York Times* by *Times* veteran Nan Robertson, 66, whose title refers to the discriminatory 1955 rule of Washington's National Press Club (changed in 1971, when women were admitted to membership) that permitted women correspondents to cover speeches given at the club's luncheons but only if they squeezed themselves into a hot balcony where they could barely hear and could not ask questions; *Revolution from Within* by Gloria Steinem; *The Silent Passage* by Gail Sheehy explores the psychological and social significance of female menopause; *Women Who Run with the Wolves* by U.S. Jungian analyst Clarissa Pinkola Estés, 49, reinterprets myths and folk tales in terms of women's psyches; *In My Place* by Public Television reporter Charlayne Hunter-Gault, who in 1961 helped desegregate the University of Georgia; *The Wives of Henry VIII* by Lady Antonia Fraser.

Fiction: *Postcards* by Vermont novelist E. (Edna) Annie Proulx, 57; *The Queen and I* by Sue Townsend; *Personal Effects* by Francesca Duranti; *Turtle Moon* by Alice Hoffman; *Jazz* by Toni Morrison; *Bailey's Cafe* by Gloria Naylor; *Natural History* by Maureen Howard; *The Volcano Lover* by Susan Sontag; *Black Water* by Joyce Carol Oates is based on Mary Jo Kopechne's drowning in 1969; *The Tale of the Body Thief: The Vampire Chronicles* by Anne Rice; *Bastard out of Carolina* by U.S. novelist Dorothy Allison, 43; *Waiting to Exhale* by Terry McMillan; *My Sister the Moon* by Sue Harrison; *Family Money* by Nina Bawden; *A Rather English Marriage* by Angela Lambert; *Time and Tide* by Edna O'Brien; *Ripley under Water* by Patricia Highsmith; *Jewels* by Danielle Steel; *"I" Is for Innocent* by Sue Grafton.

Poetry: *Looking for Luck* by Maxine Kumin; *Noon Crossing Bridge* and *Portable Kisses* by Tess Gallagher; *Strands* by Keri Hulme.

Theater: *The Sisters Rosensweig* by Wendy Wasserstein 10/22 at New York's Mitzi E. Newhouse Theater, with Jane Alexander, Madeline Kahn, and Frances McDormand.

Judith Anderson dies at Santa Barbara, Calif., January 3 at age 93; Nancy Walker at Studio City, Calif., March 25 at age 69; Molly Picon at Lancaster, Pa., April 5 at age 93; Sandy Dennis at Westport, Conn., March 2 at age 54; Shirley Booth at Chatham, Mass., October 16 at age 94.

Films: Josie Lawrence, Miranda Richardson, Joan Plowright, and Polly Walker in Mike Newell's *Enchanted April*; Dustin Hoffman and Geena Davis in Stephen Frears's *Hero*; Emma Thompson, Vanessa Redgrave, and Anthony Hopkins in James Ivory's *Howards End*; Blythe Danner, Judy Davis, Mia Farrow (with whom Woody Allen has a nasty and highly publicized legal battle over his relations with their adopted daughter and custody of their son Satchel), and Allen in Allen's *Husbands and Wives*; Catherine Deneuve and Linh Dan Pham in Régis Wargnier's *Indochine*; Penny Marshall's *A League of Their Own* with Geena Davis and Lori Petty as catcher and pitcher, respectively, of the Rockford Peaches in the All-American Girls Professional Baseball League; Nora Ephron's *This Is My Life* with Julie Kavner, script by Ephron and her sister Delia.

Mae Clark dies at Woodland Hills, Calif., April 29 at age 84; Marlene Dietrich at Paris May 6 at age 90; Gene Tierney at Houston November 6 at age 70.

Broadway musicals: Jodi Benson and Harry Groener in *Crazy for You* 2/19 at the Shubert Theater, with old Gershwin songs; Tonya Pinkins, 29, Savion Glover, and Gregory Hines (as the late "Jelly Roll" Morton) in *Jelly's Last Jam* 4/26 at the Virginia Theater, with music by Morton, lyrics by Susan Birkenhead.

Popular songs: *Ingénue* (album) by Canadian vocalist k. d. lang (Katherine Dawn Lang), 30, includes the single "Constant Craving"; *The Bodyguard* (album) by Whitney Houston for her eponymous film includes her reading of Dolly Parton's "I Will Always Love You"; *Wynonna* (album) by country-western singer Wynonna Judd, 27, includes the singles "She Is His Only Need," "What It Takes," and "All of This Love from Here" (her family group the Judds, with which she has appeared since the early 1980s, broke up last year when her mother, Naomi, retired with chronic hepatitis); *Come On, Come On* (album) by Mary-Chapin Carpenter, now 34, includes "He Thinks He'll Keep Her," a sarcastic song about a perfect wife who walks out on her husband but finds frustration in a menial job.

 U.S. figure skater Kristi Yamaguchi wins her event in the winter Olympics at Albertville, France, Canadian skier Kerrin Lee-Gartner wins the downhill in 1 minute, 52.55 seconds, Austrian skier Petra Kronberger wins the slalom in 1 minute, 32.68 seconds, Swedish skier Pernilla Wiberg wins the giant slalom in 2 minutes, 12.74 seconds. U.S. runner Gail Devers wins the 100-meter dash in 10.82 seconds at the summer Olympics in Barcelona, U.S. runner Gwen Torrence the 200-meter in 21.81 seconds, French runner Marie-Jose Perec the 400-meter run in 48.83 seconds, Dutch runner Ellen van Lengen the 800-meter in 1 minute, 55.54 seconds, Algerian runner Hassiba Boulmerka the 1,500-meter in 3 minutes, 55.30 seconds, Unified Team (former Soviet) runner Elena Romanova the 3,000-meter in 8 minutes, 46.04 seconds, Ethiopian runner Deratru Tulu the 10,000-meter in 31 minutes, 6.02 seconds, Unified Team runner Valentina Yegorova the marathon in 2 hours, 32 minutes, 41 seconds, Greek runner Paraskevi Patoulidou the 100-meter hurdles in 12.64 seconds, British runner Sally Gunnell the 400-meter in 53.23 seconds, German athlete Heike Henkel the high jump (6 feet, 7½ inches), German athlete Heike Drechsler the long jump (23 feet, 5¼ inches), Unified Team athlete Svetlana Kriveleva the shot put (69 feet, 1½ inches), Cuban athlete Maritza Marten Garcia the discus throw (222 feet, 10 inches), German athlete Silke Renke the javelin throw (224 feet, 2½ inches), Jackie Joyner-Kersee the heptathlon. Unified Team gymnast Tatiana Gutsu wins the gold medal for all-round best. Chinese swimmer Yang Wenyi wins the 50-meter freestyle in 24.76 seconds, Chinese swimmer Zhuang Yong the 100-meter in 54.64 seconds, U.S. swimmer Nicole Haislett the 200-meter in 1 minute, 57.90 seconds, German swimmer Dagmar Hase the 400-meter in 4 minutes, 7.18 seconds, Janet Evans (now 20) her second 800-meter in 8 minutes, 25.52 seconds, Hungarian swimmer Krisztina Egerszegi the 100-meter backstroke in 1 minute, 00.68 seconds and the 200-meter in 2 minutes, 7.06 seconds, Unified Team swimmer Elena Roudkovskaia the 100-meter breaststroke in 1 minute, 8 seconds, Japanese swimmer Kyoko Iwasaki the 200-meter in 2 minutes, 26.65 seconds, Chinese swimmer Qian Hong the 100-meter breaststroke in 58.62 seconds, U.S. swimmer Summer Sanders the 200-meter in 2 minutes, 8.67 seconds, Chinese swimmer Lin Li the 200-meter individual medley in 2 minutes, 11.65 seconds, Krisztina Egerszegi the 200-meter in 4 minutes, 36.54 seconds, Gao Min her second springboard diving gold medal, Chinese swimmer Fu Mingxia the platform dive.

Steffi Graf wins in women's singles at Wimbledon, Monica Seles at Flushing Meadow.

British Prime Minister John Major announces December 9 that Prince Charles and Princess Diana have separated after 11 years of marriage but will not divorce. Charles's sister Anne, 42, the princess royal, who has won an uncontested divorce in April from her husband, Capt. Mark Phillips, marries Timothy Laurence, 37, a Royal Navy commander, in mid-December, becoming the first high-ranking member of the modern-day British royal family to divorce and remarry. Elizabeth II calls the year "annus horribilis."

Japan moves in March to crack down on the *yakuza*—gangsters who have for decades engaged more or less openly in extortion, prostitution, gambling, and drug dealing.

Former world heavyweight boxing champion Mike Tyson is convicted February 10 on charges of having raped Desirée Washington and is sentenced March 26 to 6 years' imprisonment (*see* 1991).

Swarthmore College outside Philadelphia initiates a date-rape prevention program, becoming the first school to do so.

Hurricane Andrew strikes the Bahamas August 22, killing 4, and hits south of Miami August 24, killing 15, leaving 250,000 homeless, and causing $20 billion in damage before blowing into Louisiana; Hurricane Iniki flattens the Hawaiian island of Kauai September 11, killing two, injuring 98.

Famine kills more than 300,000—mostly women and children—in Somalia as the nation falls into anarchy (*see* 1991) and armed thugs prevent world food aid from relieving starvation. Scenes of starving people appear on world TV screens, the UN Security Council moves December 3 to approve U.S.-led military intervention, and the first of some 28,000 troops arrive in Somalia December 9.

Civil war in Sudan starves hundreds of thousands, similar conditions prevail in Mozambique, but television does not show them.

Ireland's attorney general obtains an injunction February 7 to prevent a 14-year-old girl from traveling to England for an abortion, although no efforts have been made in the past to prevent thousands of Irish women from getting legal abortions in England and Wales. The girl was raped in December by a friend's father in a middle-class Dublin suburb, and her family has approached police to inquire if genetic material should be obtained from the aborted fetus for possible use as criminal evidence. Irish law permits abortion only in cases where the mother's life is in danger, a judge upholds the injunction February 17, President Mary Robinson tells a meeting of women's groups at Waterford February 20, "We must move on to a more compassionate society," pop singer Sinead O'Connor joins demonstrations at Dublin that day and tells the media about her two abortions in Britain, the Catholic Bishops' Conference says it opposes restrictions on travel and that the Church cannot coerce people to obey its teachings, and Ireland's Supreme Court rules February 26 that the girl is free to leave the country for her abortion.

A prochoice demonstration sponsored by NOW at Washington, D.C., April 5 brings out a crowd of 750,000 activists—the largest march ever held at the capital—to hear speeches by NOW president Patricia Ireland and others against opponents of legalized abortion.

The U.S. Supreme Court reaffirms its 1973 *Roe* v. *Wade* decision on abortion, but its 5-to-4 ruling June 29 in *Planned Parenthood* v. *Casey* supports a Pennsylvania law limiting a woman's right to abortion, which in any case is unavailable in 83 percent of America. The Court December 7 lets stand a Mississippi law requiring a 24-hour waiting period, which effectively bars many poorer women from obtaining legal abortions.

The injectable synthetic hormone Depo-Provera (depo-medroxy-progesterone acetate, or DMPA), approved by the FDA for contraception November 4, has been available for years in many other countries (*see* 1980).

Poland's state-financed hospitals stop performing abortions in May (*see* 1991); private abortionists flourish, but the cost is so prohibitively high that many women travel to Ukraine or Czechoslovakia, where the procedure is much cheaper. Deaths from bungled attempts at self-administered abortion increase (*see* 1993).

California grandmother Mary Shearing, 53, gives birth at Anaheim November 10 to twins, one delivered vaginally and the other by cesarean section. She has become pregnant through test tube fertilization, using embryos obtained from donated eggs and sperm from her 32-year-old husband, Don. Hormones were used in the first trimester to sustain pregnancy.

Orchard Park, N.Y., mother Geraldine Wesolowski, 53, gives birth December 28 to her grandson, Matthew Mark. She has agreed to be a surrogate mother for her daughter-in-law, whose egg, fertilized in a laboratory dish with her son Mark's sperm, has been implanted in Mrs. Wesolowski's uterus. Labor has been induced, and the boy is delivered vaginally.

1993

✗ President Clinton withdraws his nomination of Zoë Baird for attorney general January 22 following her admission that she broke the law by hiring undocumented Peruvian immigrants for domestic help and not paying their Social Security taxes. New York judge Kimba M. Wood, 49, withdraws February 5 for similar reasons, even though she violated no laws. Thousands of U.S. women employ illegal immigrants for child care positions, and filing the required tax returns for such help is so complex that many simply ignore the law. Florida state prosecutor Janet Reno, 54, is nominated February 11 and confirmed March 13, comes under fire April 19

for authorizing an attack on a religious cult outside Waco, Texas, in which 86 people are killed, nearly 20 of them children, but wins admiration for being straightforward about accepting responsibility for the FBI's action.

Czech-born presidential adviser Madeleine K. Albright, 55, is appointed U.S. ambassador to the United Nations.

Pamela Harriman, now 73, is appointed U.S. ambassador to France.

Texas state treasurer Kathryn Ann "Kay" Bailey Hutchison, 49, wins election June 6 to the U.S. Senate seat vacated by Secretary of the Treasury Lloyd Bentsen. The Republican, who has tried to straddle the prolife/prochoice issue on abortion, swamps her Democratic opponent 2 to 1.

Canada's ruling Progressive Conservative party votes June 13 to elect Defense Minister Kim Campbell, 46, to succeed Brian Mulroney, who announced his resignation as prime minister in February. A Vancouver lawyer, Campbell is the nation's first woman prime minister, but her party is swept from power in October elections and she loses not only her office but her seat in Parliament.

Turkey's center-right True Path party votes June 13 to choose Economic Minister Tansu Ciller, 47, as the successor to Prime Minister Suleyman Demirel, who resigned in May to succeed the late President Turgut Ozal, who died in office. A Yale-educated economist, Ciller promises victory in the March 1994 elections and is considered a certainty to become the nation's first woman prime minister, but a crowd of 200,000 Islamic militants demonstrates against her at Ankara and she draws criticism for waffling on Turkey's treatment of Kurds.

Washington, D.C., circuit judge Ruth Ginsburg (*née* Bader), 60, is confirmed August 3 as the second woman U.S. Supreme Court justice, succeeding Byron White, who has resigned. Her appointment by President Clinton June 14 cheers many women, who note that Ginsburg argued six women's rights cases before the Court from 1973 to 1976 and won five of them. She was obliged to work as a legal secretary after getting her degree from Columbia Law School because law firms were not hiring women associates.

Former Japanese Socialist party head Takako Doi, 64, wins election August 6 as Speaker of Parliament. She is the first woman to hold the prestigious position.

 The facts that Attorney General Janet Reno (above) is unmarried and has no children stir up resentments that married women with children are at a disadvantage in the professional and business worlds. Women's groups are mostly silent on the issue, but Authors Guild president Erica Jong writes in the *New York Times* February 10 that the "nanny" issue is based on a 1986 law that is based, in turn, on "a system intended to exclude mothers who are also achievers. Is it any wonder that for most of history only childless women became leaders? . . . The solution is [government-subsidized] child care."

A family and medical leave bill signed by President Clinton February 5 requires employers to permit unpaid leave and not discharge workers who must take time off for such reasons as attending sick family members, but the law applies only to companies with 50 employees or more (most larger companies already have such plans), and it falls far short of legislation in Europe (even Greece, a poor country, provides 15 weeks' paid maternity leave, and a mother is guaranteed her job for a year after giving birth). Critics of the new U.S. law say that while it is well intentioned its effect actually hurts women, thousands of whom are laid off in the weeks before the measure takes effect August 5 as employers rely on part-time or contract workers to keep their full-time staffs below the threshold level of 50.

A report by the Pentagon's inspector general, released April 23, finds that 49 civilian women, 22 servicewomen, six female government employees, six wives, and six servicemen were victims of sexual abuse at the navy's 1991 Tailhook convention and recommends that at least 140 officers be referred to the services for possible disciplinary action on charges of indecent assault, exposure, conduct unbecoming an officer, or lying to investigators. It also recommends civilian review of cases involving 30 navy officers above the rank of captain, or flag officers; two marine corps general officers; and three navy reserve flag officers who attended the convention. The Pentagon announces

April 27 that Defense Secretary Les Aspin will order the military to drop most of its restrictions on women in aerial and naval combat, permitting them to fly as fighter and bomber pilots and to serve on many warships.

A fire at a Bangkok doll factory May 10 kills more than 200 Thai workers, most of them young women, whose bodies are found piled up against locked doors or beneath stairways that collapsed as they tried to escape. More than 400 are injured, many seriously, by leaping from high windows. Guards say they were ordered to lock the doors to prevent thefts and keep workers from sneaking out. Although the tragedy is compared to New York's Triangle Shirtwaist Factory fire of 1911, most factories in Third World countries are no safer than the Bangkok doll factory and working conditions for many female employees are horrendous.

President Clinton comes under attack from blacks and feminists June 5 after withdrawing his nomination of University of Pennsylvania law professor Lani Guinier, 43, to be Assistant Attorney General for Human Rights. Janet Reno (above) has favored the appointment, but leading Senate Democrats have opposed it, citing articles Guinier has written on the Voting Rights Act, and Clinton says he fears that committee hearings would be divisive.

California Fulbright scholar Amy Elizabeth Biehl, 26, is killed at the black township of Guguletu outside Johannesburg August 25 by a mob of young men who mistake her for a white settler (she has actually been working to help South Africans complete their transition from apartheid to democracy). Racial and tribal animosities remain intense.

The Senate Ethics Committee investigates allegations of sexual harassment against Sen. Packwood (*see* 1992). It winds up deciding not to take any action, enraging many Washington State voters.

The U.S. Supreme Court rules unanimously November 9 in *Harris* v. *Forklift Systems Inc.* that plaintiffs in sexual harassment cases need not show that they have sustained severe psychological damage or job impairment. Justice O'Connor says that federal law against harassment applies when "the [workplace] environment would reasonably be perceived, and is perceived, as hostile or abusive."

The Pentagon issues rules December 22 that permit lesbians and gay men to serve in the military so long as they remain mum about their sexual orientation and do not engage in homosexual acts.

 President Clinton's choice of University of California economics professor and trade expert Laura D'Andrea Tyson, 45, as the first woman to head the President's Council of Economic Advisers draws criticism of reverse sexism, but Tyson works hard to sell the president's economic plan to Congress and the public.

Take Our Daughters to Work Day, sponsored by the Ms. Foundation for Women, is observed by some U.S. companies April 28 "to make girls visible, valued, and heard," 150 girls crowd into the cattle pit at Chicago's Mercantile Exchange to trade mock pizza-future contracts, but Beverly LaHaye, president of Concerned Women for America, says, "Noticeably missing from the Ms. Foundation's definition of the workplace is the home, where mothers do their most important work. . . . This is another example of feminists denigrating motherhood and the choice of many women to remain in the home."

Tobacco heiress Doris Duke dies of cardiac arrest at age 80 October 28 at her house in Beverly Hills, Calif., leaving most of her $1.2 billion fortune to charity.

The FDA begins January 5 to evaluate the safety of breast implants containing saline. Author Betty Rollin has dismissed alarms about such implants ("If they break, it's only water") and said that plastic surgeons resist using them only because they are more difficult to insert, but others have questioned their safety.

First Lady Hillary Rodham Clinton is given an office in the West Wing of the White House and named January 25 to head a commission charged with creating a health plan for the nation. It is the most influential position a president's wife has ever had. She bans smoking in the White House February 1.

The presidential commission to create a national health plan (above) includes Donna E. Shalala, the new secretary of Health and Human Services.

A U.S. health-cost study released in May finds that more than 16 percent of hysterectomies performed at health maintenance organizations are inappropriate and an additional 25 percent are of questionable benefit. This challenges the view that HMOs contain costs by limiting unnecessary care.

The American Psychiatric Association votes at its annual meeting in May at San Francisco to list a severe form of premenstrual syndrome (PMS) as a "depressive disorder" in its new manual of mental illness, calling it "Premenstrual Dysphoric Disorder," or PDD. Recognizing the syndrome will improve treatment and provide better standards for research, the society contends. The National Organization for Women (NOW) decries the decision, saying that it invites discrimination against women in employment, custody hearings, and insurance, but Chicago psychiatrist Nada Stotland replies that PDD, unlike PMS, is a disabling depression.

President Clinton appoints as U.S. Surgeon General the head of the Arkansas Health Department.

First Lady Hillary Rodham Clinton worked to create a national health plan for the United States. CHIE NISHIO

Dr. Joycelyn Elders, 58, who has crusaded for the reduction of teenage pregnancy, saying that a poor adolescent with a baby is "captive to a slavery the 13th Amendment did not anticipate." Abortion opponents and religious fundamentalists have attacked her, saying that her school-based sex education clinics promoted abortion.

∞ Roman Catholic religious orders decline in number worldwide as fewer young women opt for chastity, celibacy, and devotion. U.S. convents dwindle in size, and some close down as the number of American nuns in all orders combined falls to 94,000, down from 178,000 in 1968.

A History of God by former English nun Karen Armstrong, 48, is based on the idea that the deity is a product of creative human imagination. An honorary member of the Association of Muslim Social Scientists, Armstrong teaches at London's Leo Baeck College for the Study of Judaism.

The Chicago Board of Education announces June 25 that it has selected New York's deputy school chancellor Argie K. Johnson, 54, as general superintendent of its school system, the sixth person to have that job in 13 years. The decentralized Chicago district has been called the worst in the nation, but Johnson says she believes in the reforms that are under way and wants to be a part of them.

The University of Pennsylvania chooses Yale provost Judith Rodin, 49, as the first female president of an Ivy League school.

Enrollment in U.S. women's colleges reaches a 14-year high, partly out of concern that women at coeducational schools may be treated differently from men, partly because women fear sexual harassment.

Nonfiction: *Fire with Fire: The New Female Power and How It Will Change the 21st Century* by Naomi Wolf; *The Morning After: Sex, Fear, and Feminism on Campus* by Princeton graduate student Katie Roiphe, 25, who says mass hysteria has exaggerated and even invented male sexual assault, concludes that this has set back the cause of women's liberation ("Again and again, the rape-crisis movement peddles images of gender relations that deny female desire and infantilize women"), and takes issue with Catherine MacKinnon's crusade against pornography; *Sexual Violence: Our War Against Rape* by New York prosecutor Linda A. Fairstein, 46, who writes, "Rape remains the only crime in which the victims . . . are stigmatized by others for their victimization and blamed for their participation in an act committed by forcible compulsion" but disputes the radical feminist view that rape has nothing to do with sexuality; *In No Uncertain Terms* by former South African member of Parliament Helen Suzman, now 76, who fought against apartheid; *A Woman's Worth* by U.S. writer Marianne Williamson, 40, who writes, "Womanhood is a mass pain of unspoken depth," "Most of us want a masculine man, but there's no way to have one unless we become feminine women"; *The Fountain of Age* by Betty Friedan, now 72, who criticizes menopausal hormone therapy, nursing-home operators, and nursing-home insurance vendors; *The Late Show: A Sentimental but Practical Survival Plan for Women over 50* by Helen Gurley Brown, now 71.

Fiction: *The Shipping News* by E. Annie Proulx (National Book Award); *Feather Crowns* by Bobbie Ann Mason; *The Jade Cabinet* by U.S. novelist Rikki Ducornet (*née* Erica DeGre), 50; *The Robber Bride* by Margaret Atwood; *The Green Knight* by Iris Murdoch; *Cleopatra's Sister* by Penelope Lively; *The Infinite Plan* by Isabel Allende; *The Furies* by the late Janet Hobhouse, who died of ovarian cancer in 1991 at age 42; *Almost Perfect* by Alice Adams; *Consider This, Señora* by Harriet Doerr; *The Rest of Life* (three novellas) by Mary Gordon; *Foxfire: Confessions of a Girl Gang* by Joyce Carol Oates; *If You Knew Me* by Anne Roiphe; *Sweet Water* by U.S. novelist Christina Baker Klein, 29; *Pigs in Heaven* by Barbara Kingsolver; *Angel* by Barbara Taylor Bradford; *Lasher* by Anne Rice; *Vanished* by Danielle Steel; *"J" Is for Judgment* by Sue Grafton.

Poetry: *Firefall* by Mona Van Duyn.

A 2-month Whitney Museum exhibit entitled "The Subject of Rape" opens at New York June 23 with text and graphic displays by artists who include Lutz Bacher, Eva Rivera Castro, Peggy Diggs, Laura Fields, Ashley King, Suzanne Lacy, Ana Mendieta, Jennifer Montgomery, Maryanne Murray, Deborah Orloff, Kym Ragusa, Sahri Rothfarb,

Collier Schorr, Lorna Simpson, Clarissa T. Sligh, Soo Jin Kim, Nancy Spero, Annie West, Sue Williams, and David Wojnarowicz.

President Clinton names actress Jane Alexander, now 53, to chair the National Endowment for the Arts. Announcing the appointment in August, Clinton says, "The endowment's mission of fostering and preserving our nation's cultural heritage is too important to remain mired in the problems of the past. [Alexander] will be a tireless and articulate spokesperson for the value of bringing art into the lives of all Americans."

 Joyce Carey dies at London February 28 at age 94; Helen Hayes at Nyack, N.Y., March 17 at age 92; Eugenia Leontovich at New York April 2 at age 93.

Films: Michelle Pfeiffer, Daniel Day-Lewis, and Winona Ryder in Martin Scorsese's *The Age of Innocence*; Maggie Greenwald's *The Ballad of Little Jo* with Suzy Amis as Josephine Monaghan; Helena Bergstrom in Colin Nutley's *House of Angels*; Gillian Armstrong's *The Last Days of Chez Nous* with Lisa Harrow, Bruno Ganz, and Kerry Fox; Regina Torne and Lumi Cavazos in Alfonso Arau's *Like Water for Chocolate*; Jane Campion's *The Piano* with Holly Hunter, Sam Neil, and Harvey Keitel; Emma Thompson and Anthony Hopkins in James Ivory's *The Remains of the Day*; Debra Winger and Anthony Hopkins in Richard Attenborough's *Shadowlands*; Stockard Channing, Donald Sutherland, and Will Smith in Fred Schepisi's *Six Degrees of Separation*; Nora Ephron's *Sleepless in Seattle* with Meg Ryan and Tom Hanks; Angela Basset as singer Tina Turner in Brian Gibson's *What's Love Got to Do with It?*

Audrey Hepburn dies of colon cancer at Tolocherraz, Switzerland, January 20 at age 63; Lillian Gish at Nyack, N.Y., February 28 at age 99; Ruby Keeler of cancer at Palm Springs, Calif., February 28 at age 82; Ann Todd at London May 6 at age 82. Choreographer Agnes de Mille dies of a stroke in her Greenwich Village, New York, apartment October 7 at age 88.

 Hollywood musical: Agnieszka Holland's *The Secret Garden* with Kate Maberly, Heydon Prowse, and Maggie Smith, music by Zbigniew Preisner.

Broadway musical: Chita Rivera, now 60, sings and dances (despite a recent auto accident in which one leg was smashed) in *Kiss of the Spider Woman* 5/3 at the Broadhurst Theater, with Brent Carver, songs by John Kander and Fred Ebb.

Popular music: *Mi Tierra* (album) by Cuban-born singer Gloria Estefan, 35, who has been a star of the Miami Sound Machine; *Slow Dancing with the Moon* (album) by Dolly Parton, now 47, includes performances by guest stars Mary-Chapin Carpenter and Emmylou Harris.

 Hungarian chess grandmaster Judit Polgar, 16, defeats veteran Boris Spassky, 56, in a 10-game exhibition match at Budapest in February. She wins $110,000 of the $200,000 purse.

Cincinnati Reds owner Marge Schott is suspended for the season following complaints that she has made bigoted remarks about players (*see* 1984).

Jockey Julie Krone, 29, rides Colonial Affair to victory in the Belmont Stakes June 5, becoming the first woman to win any horserace in America's Triple Crown of turf classics. Three other women jockeys—Patti Cooksey, Diane Crump, and Andrea Seefeldt—have failed in three Kentucky Derby races and one Preakness, and no woman has ever before ridden in the grueling 1½-mile Belmont. It is Krone's third Belmont attempt (she has also ridden in a Kentucky Derby).

The Women's Tennis Council announces that it will not renew its sponsorship with Philip Morris after the expiration of its agreement next year and will seek a different sponsor for what has been called the Virginia Slims championships. Health groups announce that they will continue to demonstrate at every Virginia Slims event until the contracts expire.

Steffi Graf wins in singles at Wimbledon and in the U.S. Open at Flushing Meadow.

 Japan's Crown Prince Naruhito, 33, is married at Tokyo June 9 to Harvard- and Oxford-educated commoner Masako Owada, 29, a former Foreign Ministry star who until January was involved in shuttle diplomacy with Washington on such issues as semiconductor trade talks and Japan's refusal to accept foreign lawyers. The couple arrives by train at Ise June 25 and makes a ceremonial report of their marriage the following day to the sun goddess Amaterasu.

Austin leatherwork artist Elizabeth Xan Wilson, 26, identifies herself in court May 14 as the accuser of convicted rapist Joel Rene Valdez, 28, who is sentenced to 40 years' imprisonment for a September 16, 1992, sexual assault on Wilson, whose insistence that he wear a condom to protect her from AIDS raised questions about her possible complicity (one grand jury refused to indict him, but a second grand jury did). The lawyer for Valdez has told the court that his client has the I.Q. of a 7-year-old and was drunk. Wilson, who has testified that she acted to save her life from AIDS and that self-defense does not equal consent, tells the court, "I'm not the same person at all since Mr. Valdez chose to take a part of my life, my soul, and my body, and that I will never be able to reclaim. I no longer trust my neighbors or strangers. I have many sleepless nights. After being raped, I have felt tainted, violated, filthy, and abused. I fear that I will never have a healthy relationship with a man if he knows that I was raped. It's almost as if you feel that it's tattooed on your forehead. Anyone can be raped. It doesn't just happen to people you read about in the newspapers. It happens to people you know. Rape has a unique status in the justice system. Rape is the only felony that places the onus on the survivor."

Ecuadorian-born Virginia manicurist Lorena L. Bobbitt, 24, cuts off two-thirds of the penis of her sleeping husband, John Wayne Bobbitt, 26, after an alleged sexual assault June 23; the organ is reattached in 9 hours of microsurgery; a jury of nine women and three men acquit the husband of marital sexual assault November 10; and Mrs. Bobbitt will be acquitted early next year of malicious assault.

Long Island, N.Y., police notice a pickup truck without a license plate on the Southern State Parkway at 3:28 in the morning of June 28, chase the driver for 20 minutes until he crashes into a light pole on Old Country Road at Mineola, and discover a woman's body in the back of the truck. Unemployed landscape gardener Joel Rifkin, 34, takes police to the bodies of other women and claims to have had sex with 17 prostitutes before murdering them.

North Carolina becomes the 50th state in which marital rape is a felony under legislation enacted July 1, although some states have exceptions to their laws. Laura X in Berkeley has canvassed state legislators to persuade them to pass the laws.

Los Angeles police arrest Hollywood madam Heidi Fleiss, 27, in August, shutting down a 3-year-old prostitution ring that has attracted some of the biggest names in the film colony (at $1,500 a night) and made Fleiss rich.

President Clinton marks the 20th anniversary of the landmark Supreme Court decision in *Roe* v. *Wade* January 22 by signing memoranda that reverse abortion restrictions imposed by the Reagan and Bush administrations. Federally financed clinics are free to provide abortion counseling, military hospitals may perform abortions, federally financed research may use fetal tissue, foreign aid may be given to international family-planning programs that include abortion-related activities, and the policy against importing the injectable abortifacient drug RU486 for personal use should be reviewed.

President Lech Walesa signs legislation in February that makes Poland one of Europe's most restrictive nations with regard to abortion (*see* 1992). Abortions may be performed only in cases of rape or incest, when the mother's health is seriously endangered, or where tests have revealed serious fetal defects.

Pope John Paul II issues a statement imploring the 50,000 Bosnian rape victims not to abort the fetuses conceived in the Serbian program of "ethnic cleansing" against Muslims (and in some cases by Muslims against Serbian women) (*see* 1992).

Pensacola, Fla., physician David Gunn, 47, is shot three times in the back during a demonstration outside his Women's Medical Services Clinic March 10 and dies 2 hours later while in surgery at a local hospital. Other abortion clinics in Florida and Texas have been burned by arsonists or sprayed with noxious chemicals, but Gunn's murder is the first of its kind.

Germany's Constitutional Court rules May 28 that abortion violates a constitutional provision requiring the state to protect human life. While abortions are therefore illegal, the high court says that women who undergo abortions in their first trimesters should not be prosecuted, nor should their doctors. But since they are illegal, health insurance plans will not pay for abortions, and state-supported hospitals will stop performing them. Bishops hail the judicial ruling, but Brandenburg's Minister for Social Affairs Regine Hildebrandt calls it "a return to the Middle Ages." Parliament senior member Heidemarie Wieczorek-Zeul says it effectively legalizes abortion for women who can pay $200 to $650 but puts abortion beyond the reach of poorer women; protesters at Cologne, Potsdam, and other cities take to the streets to demonstrate against the ruling.

Endocrinologist Etienne-Emile Baulieu, inventor of the abortifacient RU486 (above), and his French colleagues describe successful tests of an RU486 pill in the *New England Journal of Medicine* in May, and a *Journal* editorial calls efforts to block use of the drug in America a "disgrace."

The first female condom, approved by the U.S. Food and Drug Adminstration May 10, is less effective than latex male condoms in protecting women against pregnancy and sexually transmitted diseases but has the advantage of putting women in control of contraception.

Supreme Court nominee Ruth Bader Ginsburg (above) says in her Senate committee hearings July 21, "It is essential to a woman's equality with man that she be the decision maker, that her choice be controlling. If you impose restraints, you are disadvantaging her because of her sex. The state controlling a woman would mean denying her full autonomy and full equality."

Index

Index

vows, 240, 254, 393
Wright, Fanny, on, 228
Zwingli, Huldreich, on, 108
Married Women's Property Act,
Massachusetts, 263
married women's property laws,
Britain, 293
Mississippi, 239
New York State, 235, 251
Marsh, Jean, English actress,
663
Marsh, Mae, U.S. film star, 399,
406, 409
Marsh, Ngaio, New Zealand-
born mystery novelist, 478,
497, 500, 562, 571, 587,
667
Marshall, Katherine, U.S. writer,
543
Marshall, Penny, Hollywood
film director, 697, 715
Marston Moor, Battle of, 144
Martel, Charles, Frankish leader,
51
Martha and the Vandellas,
Motown (Detroit) singing
group, 588, 592, 604
Martin, Agnes, U.S. artist, 568,
575, 579, 583, 587, 594,
598, 603
Martin, Judith, "Miss Manners"
columnist-author, 672
Martin, Maria, U.S. artist who
assisted Audubon, 240
Martin, Mary, Broadway musical
star, 498, 516, 527, 537,
555, 572, 599
Martin, Mrs. Bradley, U.S. steel
heiress, 352
Martin, Virginia, Broadway musical star, 583
Martineau, Harriet, English
writer-critic, 238, 240
Martinelli, Elsa, Italian film star,
604
Martínez, Marianne von, Austrian singer-pianist-com-
poser, 188
Marua, Carmen, Spanish film
actress, 698
Marvell, Andrew, English poet,
157
Marvin, Lee, Hollywood film
star, 664
Marx, Eleanor, English socialist,
340
Marx, Karl, German socialist,
251, 287, 288, 300, 312
Mary II, English queen, 156,
161, 164

Mary Kay Cosmetics, 588
Mary Magdalene, 110
Mary of Burgundy, 97, 98
Mary of Guelders, Scottish
queen, 96
Mary of Modena, wife of Eng-
land's James II, 155, 161
Mary of Nazareth, mother of
Jesus, 22, 25, 41, 539
Mary Poppins, fictional English
governess, 479
Mary Tudor, English queen,
105, 114, 117–119
Mary, English queen, 156
Mary, Queen of Scots, 114, 116,
119–122, 126, 132
Mary, wife of Britain's George V,
339, 342, 386
Mascagni, Pietro, Italian com-
poser, 337
Masham, Abigail, Lady, British
court favorite, 170
Mason jar, 269
Mason, Bobbie Ann, U.S. novel-
ist, 672, 688, 697, 720
Mason, Eva, U.S. soprano, 406
Mason, Marsha, U.S. actress,
633, 653
Massachusetts colony,
Quakers and, 150
witches in, 145, 163
Massachusetts Institute of Technology, women and, 294
Massachusetts,
contraception in, 631
cotton mills in, 219
divorce law in, 264
education in, 319, 353
labor in, 271, 303
minimum wage law in, 394
women's rights in, 199, 263
Massina, Giulietta, Italian film
star, 562, 565
Massinger, Philip, English playwright, 136
Masters and Johnson, U.S. sex
therapists, 617
Masters, Sybilla Righton, New
Jersey colony inventor,
172
Mata Hari, Dutch-born German
"spy," 411
Maternity Center Association of
New York, 416
maternity leave, Japan, 529
mathematics, Germain and, 219
Mather, Cotton, Boston clergyman, 164
Matilda, duchess of Normandy,
60

Matilda, English queen, 62–64
Matilda, marchioness of Tus-
cany, 61, 62
Matilda, wife of William the
Conqueror, 60, 61
Matrimonial Causes Act, Britain,
266, 435
Matsui, Sumako, Japanese ac-
tress, 393
Matthews, Jessie, English ac-
tress, 456, 463
Matzeliger, Jan, U.S. lasting
machine inventor, 322
Maubray, John, English physi-
cian, 174
Maud (*see* Matilda, English
queen)
Maudsley, Henry, British physi-
cian, 294
Maupassant, Guy de, French
writer, 318
Mauritius, suffrage in, 560
Maxikova, Mariya, Soviet mezzo
soprano, 433
Maximilian, Mexican emperor,
284
May Company, U.S. retailer,
314
May, Edna, Broadway musical
star, 352
Mayans, 47, 49
calendar of, 47
Mayer, Constance, French
painter, 212, 222
Mayer, Maria Goeppert, German-American physicist,
504
Mayflower, 136
Mayflower Madam, New York,
686
Maynor, Dorothy, U.S. soprano,
546
Mayo, Katherine, U.S. journalist, 442, 450
Mayo, Virginia, Hollywood
screen player, 537
Mayreder, Rosa, Austrian feminist, 373
Mayron, Melanie, Hollywood
screen player, 657
Maywood, Augusta, U.S. ballerina, 240
Mazarin, Cardinal, French statesman, 143, 145, 147, 150
Mazarin, Hortense Mancini,
duchesse de, English court-
iere, 158
Mazepa-Koledinsky, Ivan Stepanovich, Ukrainian cos-
sack, 160

McAfee, Mildred H., Wellesley
president-WAVES comman-
der, 510
McAliskey, Bernadette Devlin
(*see* Devlin, Bernadette) 670
McAllister, Ward, New York
social arbiter, 302, 323,
332
McArdle, Andrea, Broadway
musical star, 653
McAteer, Myrtle, U.S. tennis
player, 358
McAuliffe, Christa, U.S. school-
teacher and astronaut, 690
McAvoy, May, Hollywood film
star, 443
McBride, Mary Margaret, New
York radio personality,
478
McBride, Mrs. John (*see* Gonne,
Maud)
McBride, Patricia, U.S. balle-
rina, 572
McCall's magazine, 309
McCambridge, Mercedes, Hol-
lywood screen player, 537
McCardell, Claire, U.S. fashion
designer, 465, 498, 509, 513
McCarthy, Mary, U.S. novelist,
511, 536, 547, 557, 564,
587, 603, 624, 646
McCarthy, Sen. Eugene, 606
McCarthy, Sen. Joseph, 538
McClellan, Gen. George B.,
Union Army, 274
McClendon, Rose, U.S. actress,
466, 474
McClintock, Barbara, U.S.
geneticist, 542, 679
McCloy, Helen, U.S. mystery
novelist, 497
McClung, Nellie, Canadian fem-
inist, 427
McComas, Carroll, U.S. actress,
425
McCormack, Patty, U.S. child
actress, 555
McCormick, Anne O'Hare, U.S.
journalist, 428, 454, 487,
492, 521
McCormick, Cyrus H., U.S.
reaper inventor, 325
McCormick, Katherine, U.S.
feminist, 556
McCormick, Nettie Fowler, Chi-
cago businesswoman, 325
McCormick, Patricia, U.S. bull-
fighter, 566
McCormick, Patricia, U.S.
Olympic diver, 548, 563

Index

New York (cont'd)
Grand Central in, 398
hospitals in, 264, 302, 310
labor in, 266, 391, 457
law against sexual discrimination in, 616
merchants in, 275, 278, 284
midwifery in, 482
Pooper Scooper law in, 644
population of (1822), 224
private clubs in, 367, 379, 682, 696
prostitution in, 313, 441, 485, 516, 686
Radio City Music Hall in, 470
retail merchants in, 301, 304, 327
slums of, 366
Statue of Liberty in, 329
tenements in, 321, 362
traffic in, 597
welfare in, 594
Women's Detention Center in, 625
women's rights in, 198
New Yorker magazine, 442, 500, 533, 608, 714
New Zealand,
health care in, 696
suffrage in, 342, 352
Newman, Phyllis, U.S. actress, 691
Newmar, Julie, Broadway musical star, 558, 563
Newnham College, Cambridge, 297, 317, 334
Newport, Capt. Christopher, 132
Newport, R.I., "cottages" at, 365
Newsday, Long Island newspaper, 504
newspaper, first English daily, 167
Newton, Isaac, English mathematician, 188
Newton-John, Olivia, British pop singer, 625, 630, 633, 639, 643, 654, 658, 668, 673, 681, 689, 698
Nguyen Thi Binh, Mme., North Vietnamese foreign minister, 610
Niagara Falls, 309, 362
Nicaragua, 703
suffrage in, 556
Nichols, Anne, U.S. playwright, 433
Nichols, Mary, Massachusetts educator, 237

Nicholson, Jack, Hollywood film star, 618, 630, 639, 643, 680, 688
Nidetch, Jean, founder of Weight Watchers, 589
Nieuw Amsterdam, 151
Nightingale, Florence, English nurse, 263, 267, 270, 271, 273, 304, 377
Nightingale-Bamford School, New York, 375, 424
Niglia, Josefina Maria, Mexican-American novelist, 523
Nihell, Elizabeth, English midwife, 187
Nijinska, Bronislava, Russian ballerina-choreographer, 437
Nijinsky, Waslaw, Russian ballet dancer, 397, 399
Nijō, Japanese Buddhist nun, 78
Nilsson, Brigit, Swedish soprano, 520, 572
Nin, Anaïs, U.S. writer, 500, 525, 536, 554, 578, 591, 631
Nintendo video games, 692
Nixon, Julie, president's daughter, 609
Nixon, Pat, U.S. First Lady, 606
Nixon, Richard M., 539, 573, 574, 606, 609, 615, 620, 623, 625, 626, 628, 631, 632, 634, 635
Nixon, Trish, daughter of president, 625
No-Cal Ginger Ale, 549
Noailles, Anna, comtesse de, French poet, 361, 364, 366, 370, 373, 378, 388, 436, 450, 478
Nobunaga, Oda, Japanese strongman, 122, 123, 125
Noddak, Ida, German physicist, 442
Noether, Emmy, German mathematician, 420
Nogami, Yaeko, Japanese novelist, 378, 409, 439
Noonan, Peggy, U.S. presidential speech writer, 695, 705
Nora, heroine of Ibsen play *A Doll's House,* 316
Nordenflycht, Hedvig C., Swedish feminist poet, 181
Nordenflycht, Hedvig, Swedish feminist poet, 189
Nordica, Lilian, U.S. soprano, 316, 339
Norman, Dorothy, U.S. photographer, 451

Norman, Jessye, U.S. soprano, 613, 677, 681
Norman, Marsha, U.S. actress-playwright, 680, 710, 721
Normand, Mabel, U.S. film star, 399, 402, 417
Normandy, Robert II, duke of, 59
Norris, Kathleen, U.S. novelist, 392, 428, 429, 469, 526
North Carolina,
divorce in, 333
education in, 303
marital rape law in, 722
rape ruling in, 686, 687
North London Collegiate School, 256
North, Col. Oliver, U.S. Marine Corps, 692
Northwestern University, women and, 297, 364
Norton, Caroline, Irish poet and feminist, 229, 235–237, 239, 241, 243, 266, 276, 286
Norton, Eleanor Holmes, U.S. public servant, 645
Norton, Mary, English author, 547
Norway, 670
health care in, 696
suffrage in, 377, 398
Nova Scotia, suffrage in, 415
Novak, Kim, Hollywood screen player, 558, 568
Nováková, Tereza, Czech novelist, 370, 385, 402
Novarro, Ramon, Hollywood film star, 437, 443, 451, 470
Noyes, John Humphrey, U.S. clergyman, 248, 252, 258, 315
nuclear fission, 499
nude dancing, U.S. Supreme Court decision on, 709
Nugent, Maude, New York songwriter, 349
Nugent, Moya, English actress, 425
Nurse Corps, U.S. Army, 353, 615
Nurse, Rebecca, alleged Salem "witch," 163
nursing, 270, 271, 360, 442
Bellevue Hospital, New York, and, 302
Civil War and, 273
Crimean War and, 263
Japan, 424
Japanese Army and, 346

Mississippi University for Women and, 676
U.S. Navy and, 628
Wald, Lillian, and, 343, 344
Nuthall, Betty, English tennis player, 463
NutraSweet (aspartame), artificial sweetener, 673
Nuyen, France (France Nguyen Vannga), U.S. actress, 568
nylon, 482, 494
stockings, 506, 528, 573
Nyro, Laura, U.S. pop singer, 599, 608, 614, 619, 625, 644, 658, 685, 702
Nzinga, African queen, 137, 142, 143, 145, 146, 151

O'Brien, Edna, Irish novelist, 574, 582, 591, 594, 618, 714
O'Brien, Kate, Irish novelist, 465, 488, 497, 507, 515, 525, 567
O'Brien, Margaret, Hollywood child film star, 523
O'Connor, Flannery, U.S. novelist, 547, 557, 574, 594
O'Connor, Sandra Day, U.S. Supreme Court justice, 670, 682, 718
O'Connor, Sinead, Irish rock singer, 706, 716
O'Day, Anita, U.S. pop singer, 509, 520, 569, 580, 619
O'Day, Hannah, Irish-American labor leader, 368
O'Day, Molly, U.S. country singer, 527, 572, 580
O'Donnell, Cathy, Hollywood screen player, 537
O'Farrell, Bernadette, Irish film actress, 571
O'Hair, Madalyn Murray, U.S. atheist, 586
O'Hanlon, Virginia, New York Santa Claus doubter, 351
O'Hara, Jill, Broadway musical star, 608
O'Hara, Mary, U.S. author, 507, 515, 526
O'Hara, Maureen, Hollywood film star, 530, 534, 537, 547
O'Keeffe, Georgia, U.S. painter, 438, 450, 455, 458, 505, 519, 526, 691
O'Leary, Mrs. Patrick, Chicago housewife, 299
O'Neal, Tatum, Hollywood screen player, 633

Index

Sparta, ancient, girls' education in, 9

Spartacus League, Germany, 401, 418

Speck, Richard, Chicago murderer, 600

speculum, vaginal, 255, 262

Spee, Friederich von, German Jesuit poet, 139

Speght, Rachel, English author-poet, 136

Spelman College, 693

Spelterina, Maria, U.S. daredevil, 309

Spence School, New York, 340

Spence, Catherine Helen, Australian writer, 263

Spencer, Anna, U.S. feminist college professor, 396

Spencer, Elizabeth, U.S. novelist, 533, 574, 594

Spewack, Bella, U.S. playwright, 483

Speyer, Diet of, 110

Speyer, Leonora, U.S. poet, 447

spinning frame, 192

spinning wheel,
    invention of, 77
    New England, 165

Spitalny, Phil, and His All-Girl Orchestra, 480

Spock, Benjamin, U.S. pediatric authority, 525

Spottiswoode, Alicia Ann, Scottish composer, 239

Spreckels, Claus, California sugar magnate, 338

Sprenger, Jacob, German inquisitor, 99

Springfield, Dusty (Mary), English pop singer, 588, 592, 614

Sri Lanka, 573

Staël, Mme. (Germaine) de, French libertine, 202, 206, 208, 211, 213, 215, 217, 221

Stafford, Jean, U.S. novelist-story writer, 519, 529, 547, 551, 598, 612

Stafford, Jo, U.S. pop singer, 509, 545, 548, 555

Stahl, Lesley, U.S. TV journalist, 679

Stalin, Josef, Soviet dictator, 549, 601

Standard, Battle of the, 63

Standard Oil Company, 363, 370

Stanhope, Lady Hester, British Orientalist, 214

Stanislas Leszczynksi, Polish king, 175

Stanley, Kim, U.S. actress, 551, 558, 568, 591

Stanton, Elizabeth Cady, U.S. feminist, 240, 251, 259, 260, 269, 271, 275, 278, 284–286, 288, 289, 290, 293, 296, 299, 307, 317, 340, 351, 363, 377

Stanwyck, Barbara, Hollywood film star, 502, 508, 519, 706

Stapleton, Jean, U.S. actress, 563, 624

Stapleton, Maureen, U.S. actress, 537, 543, 565, 568, 575, 618, 673, 688

Star Chamber, English, 142

Stark, Freya, British travel writer, 474, 478, 488, 504, 511, 567, 624

Starr, Belle, Texas outlaw, 335

Starr, Ellen Gates, Chicago social worker, 333, 366

Statue of Liberty, New York, 329

Stavers, Susan, Boston creator of Minute Tapioca, 347

Stead, Christina, Australian novelist, 478, 488, 504, 519, 526, 533, 547, 561, 598, 603, 642, 647

Stearns, John, upstate New York physician, 223

Steber, Eleanor, U.S. soprano, 506, 534, 568

Steegmuller, Frances, U.S. actress, 672

Steel, Danielle, U.S. novelist, 633, 653, 657, 662, 667, 672, 676, 680, 684, 688, 691, 693, 697, 710, 714, 720

Steele, Sir Richard, London essayist, 170

Steen, Marguerite, English novelist, 469, 478, 507

Steenburgen, Mary, Hollywood film actress, 702

Steiff, Margrete, German seamstress-doll maker, 368

Stein, Gertrude, U.S. writer, 375, 379, 385, 396, 401, 442, 446, 474, 480, 492, 530

Stein, Sophie, Hollywood screen player, 702

Steinem, Gloria, U.S. journalist-author, 606, 616, 628, 631, 714

stenography, 316

stenotypy, 309

Stephen of Blois, English king, 62, 63, 65

Stephens College, South Carolina, 234

Stephens, Alice Barber, U.S. painter, 316, 351

Stephens, Ann S. Winterbotham, U.S. novelist, 272

Stern, Daniel, French writer, 254, 256

Sternhagen, Frances, U.S. actress, 662, 684

Sterry, Charlotte Cooper, English tennis player, 362

stethoscope, 221

Stetson, Charlotte Perkins (*see* Gilman, Charlotte Perkins) 357

Stettheimer, Florine, U.S. painter, 421, 425, 440

Stevens, Inger, Swedish-born Hollywood screen player, 603

Stevens, Nettie, U.S. geneticist, 372

Stevens, Risë, U.S. contralto, 502

Stevenson, Robert Louis, Scottish novelist-poet, 322

Stewart, A. T., Irish-American retail merchant, 275, 313

Stewart, Ellen, New York theater-club owner, 579

Stewart, Frances Teresa, mistress to England's Charles II, 150, 152

Stewart, James, Hollywood film star, 489, 498, 501, 505, 526, 537, 540, 548, 552, 555, 568, 571

Stewart, Maria W., Boston orator, 231

Stewart, Martha, U.S. promoter, 678

Stewart, Mary, English novelist, 547, 551, 564, 568, 578, 583, 591, 603, 618, 633

Stickney, Dorothy, U.S. actress, 455, 470, 497, 501

Stieber, Tamar, New Mexican journalist, 701

Stieglitz, Alfred, New York photographer–gallery owner, 396, 451, 526

Stilicho, Roman soldier, 38, 39

Stoffels, Henrickje, Rembrand's common-law wife and model, 152

Stokes, Edward S., New York financier, 300

Stokowski, Leopold, English-American orchestra conductor, 524, 559, 583

Stoller, Jenny, English actress, 680

Stone, Hannah, U.S. feminist, 286, 491

Stone, Helen, U.S. songwriter, 437

Stone, Lucy, U.S. feminist, 249, 255, 264, 268, 290

Stopes, Marie, English birth-control pioneer, 408, 417, 426, 430, 438, 441, 456

Storni, Alfonsina, Argentinian poet, 409, 417, 443, 497

Storyville, New Orleans red-light district, 356, 412

stove, White House and, 258

Stowe, Harriet Beecher, U.S. novelist, 245, 254, 255, 258–260, 265, 292, 295, 296, 307, 341

Strabo, Greek geographer, 8

Strachey, Lytton, English biographer, 378

Strange, Michael (Blanche Oelrichs), U.S. poet, 420

Straponi, Giosapina, Italian soprano, 240, 244

Strasberg, Susan, U.S. actress, 558

Strata del Po, Anna Maria, Italian soprano, 177–179

Stratas, Teresa, Canadian soprano, 576, 677

Stratemeyer, Edward, U.S. author and syndicate head, 462

Stratton-Porter, Gene, U.S. novelist, 370

Straus, Ida, Titanic casualty, 395

Straus, Isidor, R. H. Macy head and Titanic casualty, 395

Strauss, Richard, German composer, 373, 386, 393, 409, 421

Stravinsky, Igor, Russian composer, 388, 437, 545

streaking, 639

Streep, Meryl, Hollywood film star, 657, 663, 672, 688, 697, 706

Street, Lady Jessie, Australian feminist, 521

Streisand, Barbra, U.S. singer-actress, 592, 599, 608, 619, 672, 681

Van Buren, Abigail (Pauline Friedman), "Dear Abby" columnist, 557
Van Buren, Martin, 230
Van de Velde, Th. H., Dutch gynecologist, 449
van den Essen, Sylvie, Swiss film actress, 681
van der Strate-Ponhoz, Claudine, Belgian skier-mountaineer, 572
Van Doren, Irita, New York Herald-Tribune Book Review editor, 447
Van Duyn, Mona, U.S. poet, 571, 618, 676, 705, 720
van Dyck, Anthony, Dutch painter, 140
Van Fleet, Jo, U.S. actress, 551, 565, 603
Van Hoosen, Bertha, Chicago physician, 405
Van Lawick-Goodall, Jane, English primatologist, 624
Van Lew, Elizabeth, Union Civil War spy, 274, 282
Van Patten, Joyce, U.S. actress, 697
Van Slyke, Helen, U.S. novelist, 629, 642, 657, 662
Van Vorst, Marie, U.S. reformer, 366, 373
Vanbrugh, Irene, English actress, 332
Vanbrugh, John, English playwright, 165
Vanbrugh, Violet, English actress, 332
Vandals, 42
Vanderbilt, Alva (Mrs. William K.), 307, 323, 348, 384
Vanderbilt, Amy, U.S. etiquette arbiter, 547
Vanderbilt, Consuelo, U.S. heiress, 348, 551
Vanderbilt, Cornelius, New York railroad magnate, 292, 294, 313
Vanderbilt, Gloria, U.S. heiress, 481, 509, 520, 524, 559
Vanity Fair magazine, 399, 714
Varsi, Diane, Hollywood screen player, 565, 571
Vashti, queen to Persia's Ahasuerus, 16
Vassar College, 273, 283
baseball at, 285
Vaughan, Hester, alleged New York child killer, 288, 289
Vaughan, Sarah, U.S. jazz singer, 520, 572

Veblen, Thorstein, Chicago social scientist, 354, 355
Veil, Simone, French health minister, 640, 660
Velez, Lupe, Broadway musical star, 475
Vellay, Pierre, French obstetrician, 543
venereal disease, 81
Venezuela, 567
suffrage in, 528
Venice,
bubonic plague in, 139
dogaressas in, 80, 89
Genoa and, 76
Milan and, 102
Ottoman Turks and, 123
slave trade in, 51
women's rights in, 73
Venuta, Benay, U.S. actress, 498
Vera-Ellen (Vera Ellen Rohe), U.S. actress, 493, 503, 505, 512
Verdi, Giuseppe, Italian composer, 240, 244, 247, 248, 262, 267, 309, 311
Verdon, Gwen, Broadway musical star, 552, 558, 565, 599, 643, 688
Vermont,
bottle bill in, 659
education in, 469
Vernese, Giulia, mistress to Pope Alexander VI, 103
Verrett, Shirley, U.S. mezzo soprano, 583
"Very lights," 278
Vestal Virgins, 29
Vestris, Mme., English soprano-theater manager, 219, 220, 222, 226, 230, 231, 238, 239
Vesuvius, eruption of, 29
Vetsera, Marie, mistress to Austrian crown prince Rudolph, 333
Vickers, Martha, Hollywood screen player, 526
Victor, Sally, New York hat designer, 481
Victoria, British queen, 236, 240, 242, 244, 268, 269, 293, 310, 346, 350, 360
Victory Gardens, U.S., in World War II, 513
Viebig, Clara, German novelist, 347, 351, 357, 364, 370, 381
Vienna,
Ottoman siege of, 159
sweating sickness in, 110

Vietnam War, 597, 601, 605, 606, 610, 615, 626, 631
memorial to at Washington, D.C., 674
Vietnam,
China and, 25, 26
suffrage in, 524
Vigée-Lebrun, Elisabeth, French painter, 196, 199, 200, 202, 203, 209, 214, 215
Vik, Bjorg, Norwegian novelist, 618
Villiers, Barbara, mistress to England's Charles II, 149, 150, 154, 155
Viola, Franca, Sicilian rape victim, 609
Vionnet, Evelyn, Paris couturiere, 421, 503
Virgin, cult of the, 41
Virginia colony, 132, 191, 193
slavery and, 136
slavery in, 173
tobacco and, 134
women's rights in, 198
Virginia Slims tennis tournament, 721
Virginia,
education in, 374, 375, 401
miscegenation laws in, 602
rape laws in, 272
Visconti, Bianca Maria, wife to Francesco Sforza, 94
Visconti, Filippo Maria, duke of Milan, 92
Visigoths, 39, 40, 51
Vitti, Monica, Italian film star, 575, 639
Vivanti, Annie, Italian novelist, 388
Vivonne de Savelli, Catherine de (*see* Rambouillet) 132
Vogue magazine, 340, 385, 592, 623, 688, 701
Voigt-Diederichs, Helene, German novelist, 361, 373, 378, 428, 443, 458, 478, 511, 533, 543, 547
Voltaire, French philosopher-novelist, 172, 176, 180, 189
Voluntary Parenthood League, 422
von Bulow, Martha "Sunny," U.S. heiress, 678, 689
von Furstenberg, Betsy, German-born U.S. actress, 543
von Furstenberg, Diane, Belgian-American fashion designer, 625
Von Stade, Frederica, U.S. mezzo soprano, 619

von Stroheim, Erich, Hollywood film director, 440, 443, 451, 459, 540
von Trotta, Margarethe, German actress-film director, 643, 677, 691
Vorse, Mary Heaton, New York reformer, 381
Vreeland, Diana, U.S. fashion-magazine editor, 492, 582, 584, 623, 684

Wac-Chanil-Ahau, Lady, Mayan ruler, 49
Wade, Virginia, English tennis player, 609, 654
Wägner, Elin, Swedish novelist, 381, 388, 409, 413, 432, 439, 450, 492, 497, 507
Wagner, Lindsay, Hollywood screen actress, 633
Wagner, Richard, German composer, 257, 295
Waite, Barbara, South African apartheid opponent, 655
Wakefield, Sarah, Sioux captive, 278
Wakoski, Diane, U.S. poet, 624
Wal-Mart stores, 582
Wald, Lillian D., New York social worker, 343, 344, 366
Waldemar IV, Danish king, 82
Wales,
Black Death in, 82
education in, 337
England and, 71, 112
Wales, Julia Grace, University of Wisconsin professor, 404
Walesa, Lech, Polish president, 722
Walker, Alice, U.S. novelist, 647, 676
Walker, June, U.S. actress, 443, 466, 554
Walker, Margaret, English poet-novelist, 511, 598
Walker, Mary Edward, Civil War surgeon, 407
Walker, Mary, U.S. physician, 264, 283
Walker, Nancy, U.S. actress, 508, 520, 534, 575, 715
Walker, Polly, English actress, 715
Walker, Sarah Breedlove, U.S. hair-straightener inventor, 389
Walker, Tippy, Hollywood screen player, 592